P9-DBT-752

BY WILL DURANT

The Story of Philosophy
Transition
The Pleasures of Philosophy
Adventures in Genius

BY WILL AND ARIEL DURANT

THE STORY OF CIVILIZATION:

The Lessons of History
Interpretations of Life

THE STORY OF CIVILIZATION: PART XI

THE
OF
NAPOLEON

A History of European Civilization
from 1789 to 1815

by

Will and Ariel Durant

SIMON AND SCHUSTER

NEW YORK · 1975

LIBRARY OF CONGRESS CATALOGING IN PUBLICATION DATA

DURANT, WILLIAM JAMES, 1885–
    THE AGE OF NAPOLEON.

    (HIS THE STORY OF CIVILIZATION; PT. 11)
    BIBLIOGRAPHY: P. 781
    INCLUDES INDEX.
        1. EUROPE—CIVILIZATION.   2. EUROPE—HISTORY—
    1789–1815.   3. NAPOLÉON I, EMPEROR OF THE FRENCH,
    1769–1821.   I. DURANT, ARIEL, JOINT AUTHOR.
    II. TITLE.
    CB53.D85 PT. 11   [CB411]   909S [940.2'7]   75–6888
    ISBN 0–671–21988–X (PT. 11)

TO ETHEL

Preface

"By the middle of the twentieth century," says the *Encyclopaedia Britannica* (XVI, 10a), "the literature on Napoleon already numbered more than 100,000 volumes." Why add to the heap? We offer no better reason than to say that the Reaper repeatedly overlooked us, and left us to passive living and passive reading after 1968. We grew weary of this insipid and unaccustomed leisure. To give our days some purpose and program we decided to apply to the age of Napoleon (1789–1815) our favorite method of integral history—weaving into one narrative all memorable aspects of European civilization in those twenty-seven years: statesmanship, war, economics, morals, manners, religion, science, medicine, philosophy, literature, drama, music, and art; to see them all as elements in one moving picture, and as interacting parts of a united whole. We would see Prime Minister William Pitt ordering the arrest of author Tom Paine; chemist Lavoisier and mystic Charlotte Corday mounting the guillotine; Admiral Nelson taking Lady Hamilton as his mistress; Goethe foreseeing a century of events from the battle of Valmy; Wordsworth enthusing over the French Revolution, Byron over the Greek; Shelley teaching atheism to Oxford bishops and dons; Napoleon fighting kings and imprisoning a pope, teasing physicians and philosophers, taking half a hundred scholars and scientists to conquer or reveal Egypt, losing Beethoven's dedication to the *Eroica* for an empire, talking drama with Talma, painting with David, sculpture with Canova, history with Wieland, literature with Goethe, and fighting a fifteen-year war with the pregnable but indomitable Mme. de Staël. This vision roused us from our septua-octo-genarian lassitude to a reckless resolve to turn our amateur scholarship to picturing that exciting and eventful age as a living whole. And shall we confess it?—we had nurtured from our adolescence a sly, fond interest in Napoleon as no mere warmonger and despot, but as also a philosopher seldom deceived by pretense, and as a psychologist who had ceaselessly studied human nature in the mass and in individual men. One of us was rash enough to give ten lectures on Napoleon in 1921. For sixty years we have been gathering material about him, so that some of our references will be to books once helpful and now dead.

So here it is, a labor of five years, needing a lifetime; a book too long in total, too short and inadequate in every part; only the fear of that lurking Reaper made us call a halt. We pass it on, not to specialist scholars, who will learn nothing from it, but our friends, wherever they are, who have been patient with us through many years, and who may find in it some moment's illumination or brightening fantasy.

WILL AND ARIEL DURANT

ACKNOWLEDGMENTS

First of all, to our daughter, Ethel Durant Kay, who not only typed the manuscript immaculately, but often improved it with corrections and suggestions. She has been a patient and helpful companion to us at every stage of our enterprise.

To our dear friends Arthur Young and Gala Kourlaeff, who lent us precious books from their private collections.

To the Los Angeles Public Library, and more directly to its Hollywood Branch and the ladies at its reference desk, and especially to Mrs. Edith Cruikshank and Mrs. Elizabeth Fenton.

To J. Christopher Herold, whose books on Napoleon and Mme. de Staël have been a light and a treasure to us; and to Leslie A. Marchand, whose masterly three-volume *Byron* has moderated, with its wealth of information, a Byronic addiction already passionate in 1905, when WD prayed God to release the crippled poet from hell.

To Vera Schneider, who brought to the months-long task of copy editing all the scope and precision of her scholarship. Our book has profited immensely from her work.

And to our dear friend Fernand, Comte de Saint-Simon, who gave so much of his time to guiding us to Napoleoniana in Paris, Versailles, and Malmaison.

All in all, in life and history, we have found so many good men and women that we have quite lost faith in the wickedness of mankind.

NOTE

In excerpts, italics for emphasis are never ours unless so stated.

Certain especially dull passages, not essential to the story, are indicated by reduced type.

No consistent formulation is possible: coins bearing the same names now as then usually bought, two hundred years ago, much more than now, but sometimes less. History is inflationary, if only through repeated debasements of the currency as an old way of paying governmental debts; but the notion that goods cost less in the past than now is probably the enchantment of distance; in terms of labor required to earn the money to buy them they generally cost more. By and large, allowing for many exceptions and national variations, we may equate some European currencies of 1789 with United States currencies of 1970 as follows.

crown, $6.25	lira, $1.25
ducat, $12.50	livre, $1.25
florin, $2.50	louis d'or, $25.00
franc, $1.25	mark, $1.25
groschen, ¼ cent	pound, $25.00
guilder, $5.25	shilling, $1.25
guinea, $26.25	sou, 5 cents
gulden, $5.00	thaler, $5.25
kreuzer, ½ cent	

Table of Contents

BOOK III: BRITAIN: 1789–1812

BOOK IV: THE CHALLENGED KINGS: 1789–1812

List of Illustrations

THE page numbers following the captions refer to discussions in the text of the subject or the artist, or sometimes both.

BOOK I

THE FRENCH REVOLUTION

1789–99

CHAPTER I

The Background of Revolution

1774–89

I. THE FRENCH PEOPLE

FRANCE was the most populous and prosperous nation in Europe. Russia in 1780 had 24 million inhabitants, Italy 17 million, Spain 10 million, Great Britain 9 million, Prussia 8.6 million, Austria 7.9 million, Ireland 4 million, Belgium 2.2 million, Portugal 2.1 million, Sweden 2 million, Holland 1.9 million, Switzerland 1.4 million, Denmark 800,000, Norway 700,000, France 25 million.[1] Paris was the largest city in Europe, with some 650,000 inhabitants, the best-educated and most excitable in Europe.

The people of France were divided into three orders, or classes (états— states or estates): the clergy, some 130,000[2] souls; the nobility, some 400,000; and the Tiers État, which included everybody else; the Revolution was the attempt of this economically rising but politically disadvantaged Third Estate to achieve political power and social acceptance commensurate with its growing wealth. Each of the classes was divided into subgroups or layers, so that nearly everyone could enjoy the sight of persons below him.

The richest class was the ecclesiastical hierarchy—cardinals, archbishops, bishops, and abbots; among the poorest were the pastors and curates of the countryside; here the economic factor crossed the lines of doctrine, and in the Revolution the lower clergy joined with the commonalty against their own superiors. Monastic life had lost its lure; the Benedictines, numbering 6,434 in the France of 1770, had been reduced to 4,300 in 1790; nine orders of "religious" had been disbanded by 1780, and in 1773 the Society of Jesus (the Jesuits) had been dissolved. Religion in general had declined in the French cities; in many towns the churches were half empty; and among the peasantry pagan customs and old superstitions competed actively with the doctrines and ceremonies of the Church.[3] The nuns, however, were still actively devoted to teaching and nursing, and were honored by rich and poor alike. Even in that skeptical and practical age there were thousands of women, children, and men who eased the buffets of life with piety, fed their imaginations with tales of the saints, interrupted the succession of toilsome days with holyday ritual and rest, and found in religious hopes an anodyne to defeat and a refuge from bewilderment and despair.

The state supported the Church because statesmen generally agreed that the clergy gave them indispensable aid in preserving social order. In their view the natural inequality of human endowment made inevitable an un-

3

equal distribution of wealth; it seemed important, for the safety of the possessing classes, that a corps of clerics should be maintained to provide the poor with counsels of peaceful humility and expectation of a compensating Paradise. It meant much to France that the family, buttressed with religion, remained as the basis of national stability through all vicissitudes of the state. Moreover, obedience was encouraged by belief in the divine right of kings—the divine origin of their appointment and power; the clergy inculcated this belief, and the kings felt that this myth was a precious aid to their personal security and orderly rule. So they left to the Catholic clergy almost all forms of public education; and when the growth of Protestantism in France threatened to weaken the authority and usefulness of the national Church, the Huguenots were ruthlessly expelled.

Grateful for these services, the state allowed the Church to collect tithes and other income from each parish, and to manage the making of wills—which encouraged moribund sinners to buy promissory notes, collectible in heaven, in exchange for earthly property bequeathed to the Church. The government exempted the clergy from taxation, and contented itself with receiving, now and then, a substantial *don gratuit*, or free grant, from the Church. So variously privileged, the Church in France accumulated large domains, reckoned by some as a fifth of the soil;[4] and these it ruled as feudal properties, collecting feudal dues. It turned the contributions of the faithful into gold and silver ornaments which, like the jewels of the crown, were consecrated and inviolable hedges against the inflation that seemed ingrained in history.

Many parish priests, mulcted of parish income by the tithe, labored in pious poverty, while many bishops lived in stately elegance, and lordly archbishops, far from their sees, fluttered about the court of the king. As the French government neared bankruptcy, while the French Church (according to Talleyrand's estimate) enjoyed an annual income of 150 million livres,* the tax-burdened Third Estate wondered why the Church should not be compelled to share its wealth with the state. When the literature of unbelief spread, thousands of middle-class citizens and hundreds of aristocrats shed the Christian faith, and were ready to view with philosophic calm the raids of the Revolution upon the sacred, guarded hoard.

The nobility was vaguely conscious that it had outlived many of the functions that had been its reasons for being. Its proudest element, the nobility of the sword (*noblesse d'épée*), had served as the military guard, economic director, and judiciary head of the agricultural communities; but much of these services had been superseded by the centralization of power and administration under Richelieu and Louis XIV; many of the seigneurs now lived at the court and neglected their domains; and their rich raiment, fine manners, and general amiability[5] seemed, in 1789, insufficient reason for owning a fourth of the soil and exacting feudal dues.

The more ancient families among them called themselves *la noblesse de*

* A livre or a franc in the France of 1789 was the approximate equivalent of $1.25 in the United States of 1970.

race, tracing their origin to the Germanic Franks who had conquered and renamed Gaul in the fifth century; in 1789 Camille Desmoulins would turn this boast against them as alien invaders when he called for revolution as a long-delayed racial revenge. Actually some ninety-five percent of the French nobility were increasingly bourgeois and Celtic, having mated their lands and titles to the new wealth and agile brains of the middle class.

A rising portion of the aristocracy—the *noblesse de robe*, or nobility of the gown—consisted of some four thousand families whose heads had been appointed to judicial or administrative posts that automatically endowed their holders with nobility. As most such posts had been sold by the king or his ministers to raise revenue for the state, many of the purchasers felt warranted in regaining their outlay by a genial susceptibility to bribes;[6] "venality in office" was "unusually widespread in France,"[7] and was one of a hundred complaints against the dying regime. Some of these titles to office and rank were hereditary, and as their holders multiplied, especially in the *parlements*, or law courts, of the various districts, their pride and power grew to the point where in 1787 the Parlement of Paris claimed the right to veto the decrees of the king. In terms of time the Revolution began near the top.

In *Qu'est-ce que le Tiers état?*—a pamphlet published in January, 1789— the Abbé Emmanuel-Joseph Sieyès asked and answered three questions: What is the Third Estate? Everything. What has it been till now? Nothing. What does it want to be? Something,[8] or, in Chamfort's emendation, *tout*— everything. It was nearly everything. It included the bourgeoisie, or middle class, with its 100,000 families[9] and its many layers—bankers, brokers, manufacturers, merchants, managers, lawyers, physicians, scientists, teachers, artists, authors, journalists, the press (the fourth "estate," or power); and the *menu peuple*, "little people" (sometimes called "the people"), consisting of the proletariat and tradesmen of the towns, the transport workers on land or sea, and the peasantry.

The upper middle classes held and managed a rising and spreading force: the power of mobile money and other capital in aggressive, expansive competition with the power of static land or a declining creed. They speculated on the stock exchanges of Paris, London, and Amsterdam, and, in Necker's estimate, controlled half the money of Europe.[10] They financed the French government with loans, and threatened to overthrow it if their loans and charges were not met. They owned or managed the rapidly developing mining and metallurgical industry of northern France, the textile industry of Lyons, Troyes, Abbeville, Lille, and Rouen, the iron and salt works of Lorraine, the soap factories of Marseilles, the tanneries of Paris. They managed the capitalist industry that was replacing the craft shops and guilds of the past; they welcomed the doctrine of the Physiocrats[11] that free enterprise would be more stimulating and productive than the traditional regulation of industry and trade by the state. They financed and organized the transformation of raw materials into finished goods, and transported these from pro-

ducer to consumer, making a profit at both ends. They benefited from
thirty thousand miles of the best roads in Europe, but they denounced the
obstructive tolls that were charged on the roads and canals of France, and
the different weights and measures jealously maintained by individual provinces. They controlled the commerce that was enriching Bordeaux, Marseilles, and Nantes; they formed great stock companies like the Compagnie
des Indes and the Compagnie des Eaux; they widened the market from the
town to the world; and through such trade they developed for France an
overseas empire second only to England's. They felt that they, not the
nobility, were the creators of France's growing wealth, and they determined
to share equally with nobles and clergy in governmental favors and appointments, in status before the law and at the royal courts, in access to all the
privileges and graces of French society. When Manon Roland, refined and
accomplished but bourgeoise, was invited to visit a titled lady, and was asked
to eat with the servants there instead of sitting at table with the noble guests,
she raised a cry of protest that went to the hearts of the middle class.[12] Such
resentments and aspirations were in their thoughts when they joined in the
revolutionary motto, "Liberty, equality, and fraternity"; they did not mean
it downward as well as upward, but it served its purpose until it could be
revised. Meanwhile the bourgeoisie became the most powerful of the forces
that were making for revolution.

It was they who filled the theaters and applauded Beaumarchais' satires of
the aristocracy. It was they, even more than the nobility, who joined the
Freemason lodges to work for freedom of life and thought; they who read
Voltaire and relished his erosive wit, and agreed with Gibbon that all religions are equally false for the philosopher and equally useful for the statesman. They secretly admired the materialism of d'Holbach and Helvétius; it
might not be quite just to the mysteries of life and mind, but it was a handy
weapon against a Church that controlled most of the minds, and half the
wealth, of France. They agreed with Diderot that nearly everything in the
existing regime was absurd—though they smiled at his longing for Tahiti.
They did not take to Rousseau, who smelled of socialism and reeked with
certainty; but they, more than any other section of French society, felt and
spread the influence of literature and philosophy.

Generally the *philosophes* were moderate in their politics. They accepted
monarchy, and did not resent royal gifts; they looked to "enlightened despots" like Frederick II of Prussia, Joseph II of Austria, even Catherine II of
Russia, rather than to the illiterate and emotional masses, as engineers of reform. They put their trust in reason, though they knew its limits and malle-
ability. They broke down the censorship of thought by Church and state,
and opened and broadened a million minds; they prepared for the triumphs
of science in the nineteenth century, even—with Lavoisier, Laplace, and
Lamarck—amid the turmoil of revolution and war.

Rousseau disassociated himself from the *philosophes*. He respected reason, but gave high place to sentiment and an inspiring, comforting faith;
his "Savoyard Vicar's Profession of Faith" provided a religious stance to

Robespierre, and his insistence upon a uniform national creed allowed the Committee of Public Safety to make political heresy—at least in wartime—a capital crime. The Jacobins of the Revolution accepted the doctrine of *The Social Contract:* that man is by nature good, and becomes bad by being subjected to corrupt institutions and unjust laws; that men are born free and become slaves in an artificial civilization. When in power the Revolutionary leaders adopted Rousseau's idea that the citizen, by receiving the protection of the state, implicitly pledges obedience to it. Wrote Mallet du Pan: "I heard Marat in 1788 read and comment on *The Social Contract* in the public streets, to the applause of an enthusiastic auditory."[13] Rousseau's sovereignty of the people became, in the Revolution, the sovereignty of the state, then of the Committee of Public Safety, then of one man.

The "people," in the terminology of the Revolution, meant the peasants and the town workers. Even in the towns the factory employees were a minority of the population; the picture there was not a succession of factories but rather a humming medley of butchers, bakers, brewers, grocers, cooks, peddlers, barbers, shopkeepers, innkeepers, vintners, carpenters, masons, house painters, glass workers, plasterers, tilers, shoemakers, dressmakers, dyers, cleaners, tailors, blacksmiths, servants, cabinetmakers, saddlers, wheelwrights, goldsmiths, cutlers, weavers, tanners, printers, booksellers, prostitutes, and thieves. These workers wore ankle-length pantaloons rather than the knee breeches (*culottes*) and stockings of the upper classes; so they were named "sansculottes," and as such they played a dramatic part in the Revolution. The influx of gold and silver from the New World, and the repeated issuance of paper money, raised prices everywhere in Europe; in France, between 1741 and 1789, they rose 65 percent, while wages rose 22 percent.[14] In Lyons 30,000 persons were on relief in 1787; in Paris 100,000 families were listed as indigent in 1791. Labor unions for economic action were forbidden; so were strikes, but they were frequent. As the Revolution neared, the workers were in an increasingly despondent and rebellious mood. Give them guns and a leader, and they would take the Bastille, invade the Tuileries, and depose the King.

The peasants of France, in 1789, were presumably better off than a century before, when La Bruyère, exaggerating to point a theme, had mistaken them for beasts.[15] They were better off than the other peasants of Continental Europe, possibly excepting those of northern Italy. About a third of the tilled land was held by peasant proprietors; a third was farmed out by noble, ecclesiastical, or bourgeois owners to tenants or sharecroppers; the rest was worked by hired hands under supervision by the owner or his steward. More and more of the owners—themselves harassed by rising costs and keener competition—were enclosing, for tillage or pasturage, "common lands" on which the peasants had formerly been free to graze their cattle or gather wood.

All but a few "allodial" (obligation-free) peasant holders were subject to feudal dues. They were bound by contract charter to give the seigneur—the lord of the manor—several days of unpaid labor every year (the *corvée*) to aid him in farming his land and repairing his roads; and they paid him a toll whenever they used those roads. They owed him a moderate quitrent annually in produce or cash. If they sold their holding he was entitled to 10 or 15 percent of the purchase price.[16] They paid him if they fished in his waters or pastured their animals on his field. They owed him a fee every time they used his mill, his bake-house, his wine- or oil-press. As these fees were fixed by the charters, and lost value through inflation, the owner felt warranted in extracting them with increasing rigor as prices rose.[17]

To support the Church that blessed his crops, formed his children to obedience and belief, and dignified his life with sacraments, the peasant contributed to it annually a tithe—usually less than a tenth—of his produce. Heavier than tithe or feudal dues were the taxes laid upon him by the state: a poll or head tax (*capitation*), the *vingtième* or twentieth of his yearly income, a sales tax (*aide*) on his every purchase of gold or silver ware, metal products, alcohol, paper, starch . . . , and the *gabelle*, which required him to buy in each year a prescribed amount of salt from the government at a price fixed by the government. As the nobility and the clergy found legal or illegal ways of avoiding many of these taxes—and as, in wartime levies, well-to-do youths could buy substitutes to die in their place—the main burden of support for state and Church, in war and peace, fell upon the peasantry.

These taxes, tithes, and feudal dues could be borne when harvests were good, but they brought misery when, through war damages or the weather's whims, the harvest turned bad, and a year's exhausting toil seemed spent in vain. Then many peasant owners sold their land or their labor, or both, to luckier gamblers with the soil.

The year 1788 was marked by merciless "acts of God." A severe drought stunted crops; a hailstorm, raging from Normandy to Champagne, devastated 180 miles of usually fertile terrain; the winter (1788–89) was the severest in eighty years; fruit trees perished by the thousands. The spring of 1789 loosed disastrous floods; the summer brought famine to almost every province. State, church, and private charity strove to get food to the starving; only a few individuals died of hunger, but millions came close to the end of their resources. Caen, Rouen, Orléans, Nancy, Lyons, saw rival groups fighting like animals for corn; Marseilles saw 8,000 famished people at its gates threatening to invade and pillage the city; in Paris the working-class district of St.-Antoine had 30,000 paupers to be cared for.[18] Meanwhile a trade-easing treaty with Great Britain (1786) had deluged France with industrial products down-pricing native goods and throwing thousands of French laborers out of work—25,000 in Lyons, 46,000 in Amiens, 80,000 in Paris.[19] In March, 1789, peasants refused to pay taxes, adding to fears of national bankruptcy.

Arthur Young, traveling in the French provinces in July, 1789, met a peasant woman who complained of the taxes and feudal dues that kept her always at the edge of destitution. But, she added, she had learned that "something was to be done by some great folks for such poor ones, . . . for the taxes and the dues are crushing us."[20] They had heard that Louis XVI was a good man, eager to reform abuses and protect the poor. They looked hope-fully to Versailles, and prayed for the long life of the King.

II. THE GOVERNMENT

He was a good man, but hardly a good king. He had not expected to rule, but the early death of his father (1765) made him dauphin, and the tardy death of his grandfather Louis XV (1774) made him, at the age of twenty, master of France. He had no desire to govern men; he had a knack with tools, and was an excellent locksmith. He preferred hunting to ruling; he counted that day lost in which he had not shot a stag; between 1774 and 1789 he ran down 1,274 of them, and killed 189,251 game; yet he was al-ways unwilling to order the death of a man; and perhaps he lost his throne because he bade his Swiss Guards to hold their fire on August 10, 1792. Returning from his hunts he ate to the steadily increasing capacity of his stomach. He became fat but strong, with the gentle strength of a giant who fears to crush with his embrace. Marie Antoinette judged her husband well: "The King is not a coward; he possesses abundance of passive courage, but he is overwhelmed by an awkward shyness and mistrust of himself. . . . He is afraid to command. . . . He lived like a child, and always ill at ease, under the eyes of Louis XV, until the age of twenty-one. This constraint con-firmed his timidity."[21]

His love for his Queen was part of his undoing. She was beautiful and stately, she graced his court with her charm and gaiety, and she forgave his tardiness in consummating their marriage. The tightness of his foreskin made coitus unbearably painful to him; he tried again and again, for seven years, shunning the simple operation that would have solved his problem; then, in 1777, the Queen's brother Joseph II of Austria persuaded him to submit to the knife, and soon all was well. Perhaps it was a sense of guilt at so often arousing and then failing his mate that made him too tolerant of her gambling at cards, her extravagant wardrobe, her frequent trips to Paris for opera that bored him, her Platonic or Sapphic friendship with Count von Fersen or the Princesse de Lamballe. He amused his courtiers, and shamed his ancestors, by being visibly devoted to his wife. He gave her costly jewels, but she and France wanted a child. When children came she proved to be a good mother, suffering with their ailments and moderating nearly all her faults except her pride (she had never been less than part of royalty) and her repeated intervention in affairs of state. Here she had some excuses, for Louis could seldom choose or keep a course, and often waited for the Queen to make up his mind; some courtiers wished he had her quick judgment and readiness to command.

The King did all he could to meet the crises laid upon him by the weather, the famine, the bread riots, the revolt against taxes, the demands of the nobility and the Parlement, the expenses of the court and the ad-ministration, and the growing deficit in the Treasury. For two years

(1774–76) he allowed Turgot to apply the Physiocratic theory that freedom of enterprise and competition, and the unhindered dictatorship of the market—of supply and demand—over the wages of labor and the prices of goods, would enliven the French economy and bring added revenue to the state. The people of Paris, accustomed to think of the government as their sole protection against greedy manipulators of the market, opposed Turgot's measures, rioted, and rejoiced at his fall.

After some months of hesitation and chaos, the King called Jacques Necker, a Swiss Protestant financier domiciled in Paris, to be director of the Treasury (1777–81). Under this alien and heretical leadership Louis undertook a brave program of minor reforms. He allowed the formation of elected local and provincial assemblies to serve as the voice of their constituents in bridging the gap between the people and the government. He shocked the nobles by denouncing the *corvée*, and by declaring, in a public statement (1780), "The taxes of the poorest part of our subjects [have] increased, in proportion, much more than all the rest"; and he expressed his "hopes that rich people will not think themselves wronged when they will have to meet the charges which long since they should have shared with others."[22] He freed the last of the serfs on his own lands, but resisted Necker's urging to require a like measure from the nobility and the clergy. He established pawnshops to lend money to the poor at three percent. He forbade the use of torture in the examination of witnesses or criminals. He proposed to abolish the dungeons at Vincennes and to raze the Bastille as items in a program of prison reform. Despite his piety and orthodoxy he allowed a considerable degree of religious liberty to Protestants and Jews. He refused to punish free thought, and allowed the ruthless pamphleteers of Paris to lampoon him as a cuckold, his wife as a harlot, and his children as bastards. He forbade his government to spy into the private correspondence of the citizens.

With the enthusiastic support of Beaumarchais and the *philosophes*, and over the objections of Necker (who predicted that such a venture would complete the bankruptcy of France), Louis sent material and financial aid, amounting to $240,000,000, to the American colonies in their struggle for independence; it was a French fleet, and the battalions of Lafayette and Rochambeau, that helped Washington to bottle up Cornwallis in Yorktown, compelling him to surrender and so bring the war to a close. But democratic ideas swept across the Atlantic into France, the Treasury stumbled under its new debts, Necker was dismissed (1781), and the bourgeois bondholders clamored for financial control of the government.

Meanwhile the Parlement of Paris pressed its claim to check the monarchy through a veto power over the decrees of the King; and Louis-Philippe-Joseph, Duc d'Orléans—his cousin through direct descent from a younger brother of Louis XIV—almost openly schemed to capture the throne. Through Choderlos de Laclos and other agents he scattered money and promises among politicians, pamphleteers, orators, and prostitutes. He threw open to his followers the facilities, court, and gardens of his Palais-Royal; cafés, wineshops, bookstores and gambling clubs sprang up to accommodate the crowd that gathered there day and night; the news from Versailles was brought there speedily by special couriers; pamphlets were born there every hour; speeches resounded from platforms, tables, and chairs; plots were laid for the deposition of the King.

Harassed to desperation, Louis recalled Necker to the Ministry of Finance (1788). On Necker's urging, and as a last and perilous resort that might save or overthrow his throne, he issued, on August 8, 1788, a call to the communities of France to elect and send to Versailles their leading nobles, clerics, and commoners to form (as had last been done in 1614) a States- or Estates-General that would give him advice and support in meeting the problems of the realm.

There were some remarkable features about this historic call to the country by a government that for almost two centuries had apparently thought of the commonalty as merely food providers, taxpayers, and a periodic tribute to Mars. First the King, again at Necker's urging, and over nobiliar protests, announced that the Third Estate should have as many deputies and votes, in the coming assembly, as the two other estates combined. Second, the election was to be by the nearest approach yet made in France to universal adult suffrage: any male aged twenty-seven or more, who had paid in the past year any state tax however small, was eligible to vote for the local assemblies that would choose the deputies to represent the region in Paris. Third, the King added to his call a request to all electoral assemblies to submit to him *cahiers*, or reports, that would specify the problems and needs of each class in each district, with recommendations for remedies and reforms. Never before, in the memory of Frenchmen, had any of their kings asked advice of his people.

Of the 615 *cahiers* taken to the King by the delegates, 545 survive. Nearly all of them express their loyalty to him, and even their affection for him as clearly a man of goodwill; but nearly all propose that he share his problems and powers with an elected assembly that would make up with him a constitutional monarchy. None mentioned the divine right of kings. All demanded trial by jury, privacy of the mails, moderation of taxes, and reform of the law. The *cahiers* of the nobility stipulated that in the coming States-General each of the orders should sit and vote separately, and no measure should become law unless approved by all three estates. The *cahiers* of the clergy called for an end to religious toleration, and for full and exclusive control of education by the Church. The *cahiers* of the Third Estate reflected, with diverse emphasis, the demands of the peasants for a reduction of taxes, abolition of serfdom and feudal dues, universalization of free education, the protection of farms from injury by the hunts and animals of the seigneurs; and the hopes of the middle class for careers open to talent regardless of birth, for an end to transport tolls, for the extension of taxes to the nobility and the clergy; some proposed that the King should wipe out the fiscal deficit by confiscating and selling ecclesiastical property. The first stages of the Revolution were already outlined in these *cahiers*.

In this humble call of a king to his citizens there was a noticeable deviation from impartiality. Whereas outside Paris any man who had paid a tax was eligible to vote, in Paris only those could vote who had paid a poll tax of six livres or more. Perhaps the King and his advisers hesitated to leave to the 500,000 sansculottes the selection of men to represent in the States-General the best intelligence of the capital; the democratic problem of quality versus quantity, of getting brains by counting noses, appeared here on the eve of the Revolution that was, in 1793, to declare for democracy. So the sansculottes were left out of the legitimate drama, and were led to feel that only through the violent force of their number could they express their aliquot part of the general will. They would be heard from, they would be avenged. In 1789 they would take the Bastille; in 1792 they would dethrone the King; in 1793 they would be the government of France.

CHAPTER II

The National Assembly

May 4, 1789–September 30, 1791

I. THE STATES-GENERAL

ON May 4 the 621 deputies of the Third Estate, dressed in bourgeois black, followed by 285 nobles under plumed hats and in cloth of lace and gold, then by 308 of the clergy—their prelates distinguished by velvet robes—then by the King's ministers, and his family, then by Louis XVI and Marie Antoinette, all accompanied by troops and inspired by banners and bands, marched to their designated meeting place, the Hôtel des Menus Plaisirs (Hall of Minor Diversions), a short distance from the royal palace at Versailles. A proud and happy crowd flanked the procession; some wept with joy and hope,[1] seeing in that apparent union of the rival orders a promise of concord and justice under a benevolent king.

Louis addressed the united delegates with a confession of near-bankruptcy, which he attributed to a "costly but honorable war"; he asked them to devise and sanction new means of raising revenue. Necker followed with three hours of statistics, which made even revolution dull. On the next day the unity faded; the clergy met in an adjoining smaller hall, the nobles in another; each order, they felt, should deliberate and vote apart, as in that last States-General, 175 years ago; and no proposal should become law without receiving the consent of each order and the King. To let the individual votes of the congregated deputies decide the issues would be to surrender everything to the Third Estate; it was already evident that many of the poorer clergy would side with the commoners, and some nobles—Lafayette, Philippe d'Orléans, and the Duc de La Rochefoucauld-Liancourt—entertained dangerously liberal sentiments.

A long war of nerves ensued. The Third Estate could wait, for new taxes required their approval to get public acceptance, and the King was waiting anxiously for those taxes. Youth, vitality, eloquence, and determination were with the commoners. Honoré-Gabriel-Victor Riqueti, Comte de Mirabeau, brought them his experience and courage, the power of his mind and his voice; Pierre-Samuel du Pont de Nemours offered his knowledge of Physiocrat economics; Jean-Joseph Mounier and Antoine Barnave brought them legal knowledge and strategy; Jean Bailly, already famous as an astronomer, cooled with his calm judgment their excited deliberations; and Maximilien de Robespierre spoke with the persistent passion of a man who would not be silent until he had his way.

Born in Arras in 1758, Robespierre had now only five years to live, but in most of these he would move near or at the center of events. His mother died when he was seven; his father disappeared into Germany; the four orphans were brought up by relatives. An earnest and avid student, Maximilien won a scholarship at the Collège Louis-le-Grand in Paris, took his degree in law, practiced at Arras, and acquired such repute for his advocacy of reforms that he was among those sent from the province of Artois to the States-General.

He had no advantages of appearance to reinforce his oratory. He was only five feet three inches tall—his sole concession to brevity. His face was broad and flat, and pitted with smallpox; his eyes, weak and spectacled, were of a greenish blue that gave Carlyle some excuses for calling him "the sea-green Robespierre." He spoke for democracy, and defended adult male suffrage, despite warnings that this might make the lowest common denominator the rule and standard of all. He lived as simply as a proletaire, but he did not imitate the trousered sansculottes; he dressed neatly in dark-blue tailcoat, knee breeches, and silk stockings; and he rarely left home before dressing and powdering his hair. He roomed with the carpenter Maurice Duplay in the Rue St.-Honoré; he dined at the family table, and managed on his deputy's pay of eighteen francs a day. From that foot of earth he was soon to move most of Paris, later most of France. He talked too frequently of virtue, but he practiced it; stern and obdurate in public, in his private relations "he was generous, compassionate, and ever willing to serve"; so said Filippo Buonarroti, who knew him well.[2] He seemed quite immune to the charms of women; he spent his affection upon his younger brother Augustin and Saint-Just; but no one ever impugned his sexual morality. No gift of money could bribe him. When, in the Salon of 1791, an artist exhibited a portrait of him simply inscribed "The Incorruptible,"[3] no one seems to have challenged the term. He thought of virtue in Montesquieu's sense, as the indispensable basis of a successful republic; without unpurchasable voters and officials democracy would be a sham. He believed, with Rousseau, that all men are by nature good, that the "general will" should be the law of the state, and that any persistent opponent of the general will might without qualm be condemned to death. He agreed with Rousseau that some form of religious belief was indispensable to peace of mind, to social order, and to the security and survival of the state.

Not till near his end did he seem to doubt the full identity of his judgment with the popular will. His mind was weaker than his will; most of his ideas were borrowed from his reading, or from the catchwords that filled the revolutionary air; he died too young to have acquired sufficient experience of life, or knowledge of history, to check his abstract or popular conceptions with patient perception or impartial perspective. He suffered severely from our common failing—he could not get his ego out of the way of his eyes. The passion of his utterance convinced himself; he became dangerously certain and ludicrously vain. "That man," said Mirabeau, "will go far; he believes all that he says."[4] He went to the guillotine.

In the National Assembly, in its two and a half years, Robespierre made some five hundred speeches,[5] usually too long to be convincing, and too argumentative to be eloquent; but the masses of Paris, learning of their tenor, loved him for them. He opposed racial or religious discrimination, proposed emancipation of the blacks,[6] and became, till his final months, the tribune and defender of the people. He accepted the institution of private property, but wished to universalize small-scale ownership as an economic basis for a sturdy democracy. He called inequality of wealth "a necessary and incurable evil,"[7] rooted in the natural inequality of human ability. In this period he supported the retention of the monarchy, properly limited; an attempt to overthrow Louis XVI, he thought, would lead to such chaos and bloodshed as would end in a dictatorship more tyrannical than a king.[8]

Nearly every deputy heard the young orator impatiently except Mirabeau, who respected the careful preparation and exposition of Robespierre's arguments. Elsewhere[9] we have watched Mirabeau growing up painfully under a brilliant but brutal father, avidly absorbing every available influence of life in travel, adventure, and sin; seeing human frailty, injustice, poverty, and suffering in a dozen cities; imprisoned by the King at his father's request, pillorying his enemies in vituperative pamphlets or passionate appeals; and at last, in a lusty and double triumph, elected to the States-General by the Third Estate of both Marseilles and Aix-en-Provence, and coming to Paris as already one of the most famous, colorful, and suspected men in a country where crisis was evoking genius as rarely in history before. All literate Paris welcomed him; heads appeared at windows to watch his carriage pass; women were excited by rumors of his amours, and were fascinated as well as repelled by the scars and distortions of his face. The deputies listened in thrall to his oratory, though they were suspicious of his class, his morals, his aims. They had heard that he lived beyond his means, drank beyond reason, and was not above selling his eloquence to mitigate his debts; but they knew that he berated his class in defense of commoners, they admired his courage, and doubted they would ever see such a volcano of energy again.

There was more oratory in those hectic days, and more political maneuvering than the Hôtel des Menus Plaisirs could house, and they overflowed in journals, pamphlets, placards, and clubs. Some delegates from Brittany formed the Club Breton; soon it opened its membership to other deputies, and to other wielders of tongue or pen; Sieyès, Robespierre, and Mirabeau made it a sounding board and testing place for their ideas and schemes; here was the first form of that powerful organization that would later be called the Jacobins. Freemason lodges were active, too, usually on the side of constitutional monarchy; but there is no evidence of a secret Freemason conspiracy.[10]

Perhaps it was in the Club Breton that Sieyès and others planned the strategy by which the nobles and the clergy were to be drawn into united action with the Third Estate. Sieyès reminded the commonalty that it comprised 24 million out of the 25 million souls in France; why should it longer hesitate to speak for France? On June 16 he proposed to the deputies in the Menus Plaisirs that they should send a final invitation to the other orders to join them, and that, if they refused, the delegates of the Third Estate should declare themselves the representatives of the French nation, and proceed to legislate. Mirabeau objected that the States-General had been summoned by the King, was legally subject to him, and could legally be dismissed at his will; for the first time he was shouted down. After a night of argument and physical combat the question was put to the vote: "Shall this meeting declare itself the National Assembly?" The count was 490 for, 90 against. The delegates had pledged themselves to a constitutional government. Politically the Revolution had begun, June 17, 1789.

Two days later the clerical order, separately assembled, voted 149 to 137 to merge with the Third Estate; the lower clergy was casting its lot with the commonalty that it knew and served. Shocked by this desertion, the hierarchy joined the nobility in an appeal to the King to prevent the union of the orders, if necessary by dismissing the Estates. Louis responded, on the evening of June 19, by ordering the Hôtel des Menus Plaisirs to be closed at once to permit its preparation for seating the three orders at a "royal session" to be held on June 22. When the deputies of the Third Estate appeared on the twentieth they found the doors locked. Believing that the King intended to dismiss them, they gathered in a nearby tennis court (Salle du Jeu de Paume); Mounier proposed to the 577 deputies gathered there that each should sign an oath "never to separate, and to meet wherever circumstances might require, until a constitution should be firmly established." All but one of the delegates took this oath, in an historic scene that Jacques-Louis David would soon depict in one of the major paintings of that age. From that time the National Assembly was also the Constituent Assembly.

Postponed for a day, the royal session opened on June 23. To the united gathering the King had an aide read, in his presence, a statement reflecting his conviction that without the protection of the nobility and the Church he would be reduced to political impotence. He rejected as illegal the claim of the Third Estate to be the nation. He agreed to end the corvée, lettres de cachet, internal traffic tolls, and all vestiges of serfdom in France; but he would veto any proposal that impaired "the ancient and constitutional rights . . . of property, or the honorific privileges of the first two orders." He promised equality of taxation if the higher orders consented. Matters concerning religion or the Church must receive the approval of the clergy. And he ended with a reassertion of absolute monarchy:

> If, by a fatality which I am far from anticipating, you were to abandon me in this great enterprise, I alone would provide for the welfare of my people. I alone should regard myself as their true representative. . . . Consider, gentlemen, that none of your projects can have the force of law without my special approbation. . . . I order you, gentlemen, to disperse at once, and to appear tomorrow morning each in the room set apart for his own order.[11]

The King, most of the nobles, and a minority of the clergy left the hall. The Marquis de Brézé, grandmaster, announced the King's will that the room should be cleared. Bailly, president of the Assembly, replied that the assembled nation could not accept such an order, and Mirabeau thundered to Brézé, "Go and tell those who sent you that we are here by the will of the people, and will leave our places only if compelled by armed force."[12] It was not strictly true, since they had come by invitation of the King, but the delegates expressed their sense of the matter by crying out, "That is the will of the Assembly." When troops of the Versailles Garde du Corps tried to enter the hall a group of liberal nobles, including Lafayette, barred the entrance with their drawn swords. The King, asked what should be done, said wearily, "Let them stay."

On June 25 the Duc d'Orléans led forty-seven nobles to join the Assembly; they were greeted with a delirium of joy, which was enthusiastically echoed in and around the Palais-Royal. Soldiers of the Garde Française fraternized there with the revolutionary throng. On that same day the capital had its own peaceful revolution: the 407 men who had been chosen by the Paris sections to select the deputies for Paris met at the Hôtel de Ville and appointed a new municipal council; the royal council, lacking military support, peaceably abdicated. On June 27 the King, yielding to Necker and circumstance, bade the upper orders to unite with the triumphant Assembly. The nobles went, but refused to take part in the voting, and soon many of them retired to their estates.

On July 1 Louis summoned ten regiments, mostly German or Swiss, to come to his aid. By July 10 six thousand troops under Maréchal de Broglie had occupied Versailles, and ten thousand under Baron de Besenval had taken up positions around Paris. Amid turmoil and terror, the Assembly proceeded to consider the report that had been submitted on July 9 for a new constitution. Mirabeau begged the deputies to retain the King as a bulwark against social disorder and mob rule. He pictured Louis XVI as a man of good heart and generous intentions, occasionally confused by shortsighted counselors; and he asked, prophetically:

> Have these men studied, in the history of any people, how revolutions commence and how they are carried out? Have they observed by what a fatal chain of circumstances the wisest men are driven far beyond the limits of moderation, and by what terrible impulses an enraged people is precipitated into excesses at the very thought of which they would have shuddered?[13]

The delegates followed his advice, for they too felt groundswells emanating from the sidewalks of Paris. But instead of meeting a measured loyalty with substantial concessions to the Third Estate, Louis outraged radicals and liberals alike by dismissing Necker a second time (July 11), replacing him with the Queen's uncompromising friend Baron de Breteuil, and (July 12) making the warrior de Broglie minister for war. The chips were down.

II. THE BASTILLE

On July 12 Camille Desmoulins, a Jesuit graduate, leaped upon a table outside the Café de Foy near the Palais-Royal, and denounced the dismissal of

Necker and the summons of alien troops. "The Germans will enter Paris to-night to butcher the inhabitants," he cried, and called upon his hearers to arm themselves. They did, for the new municipal council made little resistance when they broke in and commandeered the weapons housed in the Hôtel de Ville. The armed rebels now paraded the streets, upholding busts of Necker and the Duc d'Orléans, and pluming their hats with cockades of green; when it became known that this was also the color of the uniforms worn by the servants and guard of the hated Comte d'Artois (younger brother of the King), the green cockade was displaced by one of red, white, and blue—the national colors.

Fearing indiscriminate violence, destruction of property, and financial panic, the bankers closed the Bourse, and the middle classes formed their own militia, which became the nucleus of the Garde Nationale under Lafay-ette. Nevertheless some agents of the bourgeoisie, to protect the now se-curely middle-class Assembly, contributed to finance the popular resistance to an absolute monarchy, and the winning of the Garde Française from royal to democratic sentiments.[14] On July 13 the crowd re-formed; enlarged by recruits from the underworld and the slums, it invaded the Hôtel des Invalides (Veterans' Hospital), and seized 28,000 muskets and some cannon. Besenval, doubting that his troops would fire upon the people, kept them idle in the suburbs. The armed populace now controlled the capital.

What should it do with its power? Many suggested an attempt upon the Bastille. That old fortress, on the east side of Paris, had been built, year by year since 1370, to incarcerate important victims of royal or noble ire, usually committed by *lettres de cachet*—secret orders of the king. Under Louis XVI very few prisoners were held there; only seven now remained; Louis himself had rarely issued a *lettre de cachet*, and in 1784 he had asked an architect to submit plans for the demolition of the gloomy bastion.[15] But the people did not know this; they thought of it as a dungeon holding the victims of a brutal despotism.

Yet the rebels had apparently no intention of destroying it when, after a night's rest, they converged upon it on that July 14 which was to become the national holiday of France. Their aim was to ask the governor of the prison to let them enter and appropriate the gunpowder and firearms re-portedly accumulated behind those walls. They had till now found a little gunpowder, but without more their many muskets and few cannon would give them no protection if Besenval should bring in his troops against them. However, those walls—thirty feet thick, one hundred feet high, protected by towers concealing artillery, and surrounded by a moat eighty feet wide—counseled caution. Members of the new municipal council, joining the crowd, offered to seek a peaceable arrangement with the governor of the fort.

He was Bernard-René Jordan, Marquis de Launay, a man, we are as-sured, of genteel education and amiable character.[16] He received the depu-tation courteously. They proposed to guarantee the pacific behavior of the rebels if he would remove the cannon from their firing stations and order his 114 soldiers to hold their fire. He agreed, and entertained his visitors for lunch. Another committee received a similar pledge, but the besiegers cried out that they wanted ammunition, not words.

While the two sides parleyed, some clever workmen climbed to the controls and lowered two drawbridges. The eager attackers rushed over these into the courtyard; de Launay ordered them to return; they refused; his soldiers fired upon them. The invaders were getting the worst of it when the Garde Française brought up five cannon and began to demolish the walls. Under this cover the crowd poured into the prison, and fought a hand-to-hand battle with the soldiers; ninety-eight of the attackers were killed, and one of the defenders, but the crowd increased in number and fury. De Launay offered to surrender if his men were allowed to march out safely with their arms. The crowd leaders refused. He yielded. The victors killed six more soldiers, freed the seven prisoners, seized ammunition and weapons, took de Launay captive, and marched in triumph to the Hôtel de Ville. On the way some of the crowd, infuriated by the casualties it had suffered, beat the bewildered aristocrat to death, cut off his head, and raised it on a pike. Jacques de Flesselles, a merchant provost who had misled the electors as to the whereabouts of arms, was cut down on the Place de Grève, and his severed head was added to the parade.

On July 15 the electors of the section assemblies made Bailly mayor of Paris, and chose Lafayette to head a new National Guard, and the happy sansculottes began to demolish the Bastille stone by stone. The King, shocked and frightened, went to the Assembly and announced that he had dismissed the troops that had invested Versailles and Paris. On July 16 a conference of nobles advised him to leave under the protection of the departing regiments, and to seek asylum in some provincial capital or foreign court. Marie Antoinette warmly supported this proposal, and collected her jewels and other portable treasures for the journey.[17] Instead, on the seventeenth, Louis recalled Necker, to the delight of both the financial community and the populace. On the eighteenth the King traveled to Paris, visited the Hôtel de Ville, and signified his acceptance of the new council and regime by affixing to his hat the red-white-and-blue cockade of the Revolution. Returning to Versailles, he embraced his wife, his sister, and his children, and told them, "Happily no [more] blood has been shed, and I swear that never shall a drop of French blood be spilled by my order."[18] His younger brother the Comte d'Artois, taking his wife and mistress with him,[19] led the first group of *émigrés* out of France.

III. ENTER MARAT: 1789

The capture of the Bastille was not merely a symbolic act and a blow against absolutism; it saved the Assembly from subordination to the King's

army at Versailles, and it saved the new government of Paris from domination by the environing troops. Quite unintentionally it preserved the
bourgeois Revolution; but it gave the people of the capital arms and ammunition, permitting further developments of proletarian power.

It gave fresh courage and more readers to the journals that further excited
the Parisians. The *Gazette de France*, the *Mercure de France*, and the *Journal de Paris* were old established newspapers, and kept an even keel; now
appeared Loustalot's *Les Révolutions de Paris* (July 17, 1789), Brissot's *Le
Patriote français* (July 28), Marat's *L'Ami du peuple* (September 12), Desmoulins' *Révolutions de France* (November 28) . . . Add to these a dozen
pamphlets born each day, rioting in the freedom of the press, raising new
idols, shattering old reputations. We can imagine their contents by noting
the descent of the word *libel* from their name *libelles*—little books.

Jean-Paul Marat was the most radical, reckless, ruthless, and powerful of
the new scribes. Born in Neuchâtel, Switzerland, May 24, 1743, of a Swiss
mother and a Sardinian father, he never ceased to worship another native
expatriate—Rousseau. He studied medicine in Bordeaux and Paris, and practiced it with moderate success in London (1765–77). The stories that were
later told of the crimes and absurdities he committed there were probably
concoctions by his enemies in the journalistic license of the times.[20] He received an honorary degree from the University of St. Andrews—which,
however, as Johnson put it, was "growing richer by degrees."[21] Marat wrote
in English and published in London (1774) *The Chains of Slavery*, a fiery
denunciation of European governments as conspiracies of kings, lords, and
clergy to hoodwink the people and keep them in subjection. He returned to
France in 1777, served as veterinarian in the stables of the Comte d'Artois,
and rose to be physician to the Count's Garde du Corps. He earned some
reputation as a lung and eye specialist. He published treatises on electricity,
light, optics, and fire; some of these were translated into German; Marat
thought they entitled him to membership in the Académie des Sciences, but
his attack on Newton made him suspect to the Academicians.

He was a man of intense pride, hampered by a succession of ailments that
made him irritable to the point of violent passion. His skin erupted with an
unmanageable dermatitis, from which he found temporary relief by sitting
and writing in a warm bath.[22] His head was too massive for his five feet of
height, and one eye was higher than the other; understandably he courted
solitude. Doctors bled him frequently to ease his pains; in quieter intervals
he bled others. He worked with the intensity of a consuming ambition. "I
allot only two of the twenty-four hours to sleep. . . . I have not had fifteen
minutes' play in over three years."[23] In 1793, perhaps from too much indoor life, his lungs became affected, and he felt, unknown to Charlotte
Corday, that he had not long to live.

His character suffered from his ailments. His compensatory vanity, his fits
of temper, his delusions of grandeur, his furious denunciations of Necker,
Lafayette, and Lavoisier, his mad calls for mob violence, overlaid a fund of

courage, industry, and dedication. The success of his journal was due not merely to the exciting exaggerations of his style but still more to his fervent, unremitting, unbribable support of the voteless proletaires.

Nevertheless he did not overrate the intelligence of the people. He saw chaos rising, and added to it; but, at least for the time being, he counseled not democracy but a dictatorship subject to recall, revolt, or assassination, as in Rome's republican days. He suggested that he himself would make a good dictator.[24] At times he thought that the government should be managed by men of property, as having the largest stake in the public weal.[25] He viewed the concentration of wealth as natural, but he proposed to offset it by preaching the immorality of luxury and the divine right of hunger and need. "Nothing superfluous can belong to us legitimately as long as others lack necessities. . . . Most ecclesiastical wealth should be distributed among the poor, and free public schools should be established everywhere."[26] "Society owes to those among its members who have no property, and whose labor scarcely suffices for their support, an assured subsistence, the wherewithal to feed, lodge, and clothe themselves suitably, provision for attendance in sickness and old age, and for bringing up children. Those who wallow in wealth must supply the wants of those who lack the necessaries of life"; otherwise the poor have the right to take by force whatever they need.[27]

Most members of the successive assemblies distrusted and feared Marat, but the sansculottes among whom he lived forgave his faults for his philosophy, and risked themselves to hide him when he was sought by the police. He must have had some lovable qualities, for his common-law wife stayed with him devotedly to his end.

IV. RENUNCIATION: AUGUST 4–5, 1789

"This country," wrote Gouverneur Morris from France on July 31, 1789, "is at present as near to anarchy as society can approach without dissolution."[28] Merchants controlling the market turned shortages of grain to their profit by raising the price; barges carrying food to the towns were attacked and pillaged en route; disorder and insecurity disrupted transportation. Paris was running riot with criminals. The countryside was so subject to marauding robbers that in several provinces the peasants armed themselves in their "Great Fear" of these lawless hordes; in six months 400,000 guns were acquired by the alarmed citizens. When the Great Fear subsided, the peasants decided to use their weapons against tax collectors, monopolists, and feudal lords. Armed with muskets, pitchforks, and scythes, they attacked the châteaux, demanded to be shown the charters or title deeds that allegedly sanctioned the seignorial rights and dues; if shown them, they burned them; if resisted, they burned the château; in several instances the owner was killed on the spot. This procedure, beginning in July, 1789, spread till it reached every part of France. In some places the insurgents carried placards claiming that the King had delegated to them full powers in their districts.[29] Often the destruction was indiscriminate in its fury; so the peasants on the lands of the Abbey of Murbach burned its library, carried off its plate and linen, uncorked its wine casks, drank what they could, and let the remainder flow down the drain. In eight communes the inhabitants invaded the monasteries, carried off the title deeds, and explained to the monks that the clergy were now subject to the people. "In Franche-Comté," said a report to the National Assembly, "nearly forty châteaux and seignorial mansions have been pillaged or burned; in Langres three out of five; in the Dauphiné twenty-seven; in the Viennois district all the monasteries; . . . countless assassinations of lords or rich bourgeois."[30] Town officials who tried to stop these "Jacqueries" were deposed; some were beheaded. Aristocrats abandoned their homes and sought safety elsewhere, but almost everywhere they encountered the same "spontaneous anarchy." A second wave of emigration began.

On the night of August 4, 1789, a deputy reported to the Assembly at Versailles: "Letters from all the provinces indicate that property of all kinds is a prey to the most criminal violence; on all sides châteaux are being burned, convents destroyed, and farms abandoned to pillage. The taxes, the feudal dues are extinct, the laws are without force, and the magistrates without authority."[31] The remaining nobles perceived that the revolution, which they had hoped to confine to Paris and to quiet with minor concessions, was now national, and that feudal dues could no longer be maintained. The Vicomte de Noailles proposed that "all feudal dues shall be redeemable . . . for a money payment or commuted at a fair valuation. . . . Seignorial *corvées*, serfdom, and other forms of personal servitude shall be abolished without compensation"; and, ending class exemptions, "taxes shall be paid by every individual in the kingdom in proportion to his income."

Noailles was poor, and would suffer quite tolerably by these measures, but the Duc d'Aiguillon, among the richest of the barons, seconded the proposal, and made a startling admission: "The people are at last trying to cast off a yoke which has weighed upon them for many centuries past; and we must confess that—though this insurrection must be condemned . . . an excuse can be found for it in the vexations of which the people have been the victims."[32] This avowal moved the liberal nobles to enthusiastic support; they crowded one another in coming forward to relinquish their questioned privileges; and after hours of enthusiastic surrender, at two o'clock on the morning of August 5, the Assembly proclaimed the emancipation of the peasantry. Some cautious clauses were later added, requiring the peasants to pay, in periodic installments, a fee in redemption of certain dues; but resistance to these payments made their collection impracticable, and effected the real end of the feudal system. The signature of the King to the "great renunciation" was invited by Article XVI, which proclaimed him, thereby, the "Restorer of French Liberty."[33]

The wave of humanitarian sentiment lasted long enough to produce another historic document—a Declaration of the Rights of Man and of the Citizen (August 27, 1789). It was proposed by Lafayette, who was still warm with the impressions left upon him by the Declaration of Independence and the bills of rights proclaimed by several of the American states. The younger nobles in the Assembly could support the notion of equality because they had suffered from the hereditary privileges of the oldest son, and some, like Mirabeau, had borne arbitrary imprisonment. The bourgeois delegates resented aristocratic exclusiveness in society, and the noble monopoly of the higher posts in civil or military service. Almost all the delegates had read Rousseau on the general will, and accepted the doctrine of the philosopher that basic rights belonged to every human being by natural law. So there was little resistance to prefacing the new constitution with a declaration that seemed to complete the revolution. Some articles can bear repetition:

> Article 1. Men are born and remain free and equal in rights. . . .
> Article 2. The aim of all political association is the natural and imprescriptible rights of man. These rights are liberty, property, security, and resistance to oppression. . . .
> Article 4. Liberty consists in the freedom to do everything which injures no one else; hence the exercise of the natural rights of each man has no limits except those which assure to the other members of society the enjoyment of the same rights. These limits can be determined only by law. . . .
> Article 6. Law is the expression of the general will. Every citizen has a right to participate personally, or through his representative, in its formation. . . . All citizens, being equal in the eyes of the law, are equally eligible to all dignities and to all public positions and occupations, according to their abilities. . . .
> Article 7. No person shall be accused, arrested, or imprisoned except in the cases, and according to the forms, prescribed by law. . . .
> Article 9. As all persons are held innocent until they have been declared guilty, if arrest shall be deemed indispensable, all harshness not essential to the securing of the prisoner's person shall be severely repressed by law.
> Article 10. No one shall be disquieted on account of his opinions, including his religious views, provided their manifestation does not disturb the public order established by law.
> Article 11. The free communication of ideas and opinions is one of the most precious of the rights of man. Every citizen may, accordingly, speak, write, and print with freedom, but shall be responsible for such abuses of this freedom as shall be defined by law. . . .
> Article 17. Since property is an inviolable and sacred right, no one shall be deprived thereof except where public necessity, legally determined, shall clearly demand it, and then only on condition that the owner shall have been previously and equitably indemnified.[34]

Even in this affirmation of democratic ideals some imperfections remained. Slavery was allowed to continue in the French Caribbean colonies until the Convention abolished it in 1794. The new constitution restricted the ballot, and eligibility to public office, to payers of a specified minimum of taxes. Civil rights were still withheld from actors, Protestants, and Jews. Louis XVI withheld his agreement to the declaration on the ground that it

would stir up further unrest and disorder. It remained for the Parisian populace to force his consent.

V. TO VERSAILLES: OCTOBER 5, 1789

All through August and September there were riots in Paris. Bread was
running short again; housewives fought for it at the bakeries. In one of these
riots a baker and a municipal officer were slain by the angry populace. Marat
called for a march upon the Assembly and the royal palace at Versailles:

> When public safety is in peril the people must take power out of the hands
> of those to whom it is entrusted. . . . Put that Austrian woman [the Queen]
> and her brother-in-law [Artois] in prison. . . . Seize the ministers and their
> clerks and put them in irons. . . . Make sure of the mayor [poor, amiable, star-
> gazing Bailly] and his lieutenants; keep the general [Lafayette] in sight, and
> arrest his staff. . . . The heir to the throne has no right to a dinner while you
> want bread. Organize bodies of armed men. March to the National Assembly
> and demand food at once. . . . Demand that the nation's poor have a future
> secured to them out of the national contribution. If you are refused join the
> army, take the land, as well as the gold, which the rascals who want to force
> you to come to terms by hunger have buried, and share it among you. Off with
> the heads of the ministers and their underlings. Now is the time![35]

Frightened by the journals and disorder in Paris, and by mass demonstrations in Versailles, Louis reverted to the advice of his ministers—that soldiers
yet untouched by revolutionary ideas should be brought in to protect him,
his family, and the court. Late in September he sent to Douai for the Flanders Regiment. It came, and on October 1 the King's Garde du Corps welcomed it with a banquet in the opera house of the palace. When Louis and
Marie Antoinette appeared, the troops, half drunk with wine and visible
majesty, burst into wild applause. Soon they replaced the national tricolor
emblems on their uniforms with cockades of the Queen's colors—white and
black; one report said that the discarded colors, now dear to the Revolution,
were later trodden under dancing feet.[36] (Mme. Campan, first lady of the
chamber to the Queen, and an eyewitness, denied this detail.[37])

The story was enlarged as it traveled to Paris, and was accentuated by a
report that an army was gathering near Metz with intent to march to Versailles and disperse the Assembly. Mirabeau and other deputies denounced
this new military threat. Marat, Loustalot, and other journalists demanded
that the people should compel both the royal family and the Assembly to
move to Paris, where they could be under the watchful eye of the populace.
On October 5 the market women of the city, who knew the food shortage
at first hand, took the lead in forming a brigade to march on Versailles, ten
miles away. As they proceeded they called upon men and women to join
them; thousands did. It was not a tragic or somber procession; a lusty French
humor seasoned it; "We will bring back the baker and the baker's wife,"
they cried, "and we shall have the pleasure of hearing Mirabeau."[38]

Arrived at Versailles under a heavy rain, they gathered in haphazard array, eight thousand strong, before the high gates and iron paling of the royal palace, and demanded access to the King. A delegation went to the Assembly and insisted that the deputies should find bread for the crowd. Mounier, then presiding, went with one of the delegation, pretty Louison Chabry, to see Louis. She was so choked with emotion on seeing him that she could only cry, "*Pain*," and fell in a swoon. When she recovered Louis promised her to find bread for the wet and hungry multitude. On departing, she sought to kiss his hand, but he embraced her like a father. Meanwhile many attractive Parisiennes mingled with Flemish troops, and convinced them that gentlemen do not fire upon unarmed women; several soldiers took the famished sirens into their barracks and gave them food and warmth. At eleven o'clock that night Lafayette arrived with fifteen thousand of the National Guard. He was received by the King, and pledged him protection, but he joined Necker in advising him to accept the people's demand that he and the Queen should come to live in Paris. Then, exhausted, he retired to the Hôtel de Noailles.

Early on the morning of October 6 the weary, angry crowd poured through a chance opening of the gate into the courtyard of the palace, and some armed men forced their way up the stairs to the apartment where the Queen was asleep. In her petticoat, and with the Dauphin in her arms, she fled to the King's room. Palace guards resisted the invasion, and three of them were killed. Lafayette, tardy but helpful, quieted the tumult with assurances of accord. The King went out on the balcony, and promised to move to Paris. The crowd cried, "*Vive le Roi!*," but demanded that the Queen show herself. She did, and stood her ground when a man in the gathering aimed his musket at her; his weapon was beaten down by those near him. Lafayette joined Marie Antoinette and kissed her hand in sign of loyalty; the softened rebels vowed to love the Queen if she would come and live in the capital.

As noon approached, a procession formed without precedent in history: in front the National Guard and the royal Garde du Corps; then a coach bearing the King, his sister Madame Élisabeth, the Queen, and her two children; then a long line of carts carrying sacks of flour; then the triumphant Parisians, some women perched on cannon, some men holding aloft on spikes the heads of slain palace guards; at Sèvres they stopped to have these heads powdered and curled.[39] The Queen doubted she would reach Paris alive, but that night she and the rest of the royal family slept in hastily prepared beds in the Tuileries, where French kings had slept before the Fronde rebellion had made the capital hateful to Louis XIV. A few days later the Assembly followed, and was housed in the theater of the same palace.

Once again the populace of Paris had taken charge of the Revolution by forcing the King's hand. Now, subject to his subjects, he accepted the Declaration of the Rights of Man as a *fait accompli*. A third wave of emigration began.

VI. THE REVOLUTIONARY CONSTITUTION: 1790

Freed from royal resistance, but uncomfortably aware of the surveillant city, the Assembly proceeded to write the constitution that would specify and legalize the achievements of the Revolution.

First, should it retain the kingship? It did, and allowed it to be hereditary, for it feared that until the sentiments of legitimacy and loyalty could be transferred from the monarch to the nation, the mesmerizing aura of royalty would be necessary to social order; and the right of transmission would be a guard against wars of succession and such schemes as were then brewing in the Palais-Royal. But the powers of the king were to be strictly limited. The Assembly would vote him annually a "civil list" for his expenses; any further outlay would require application to the legislature. If he left the kingdom without the Assembly's permission he could be deposed, as he would shortly see. He could choose and dismiss his ministers, but each minister would be required to submit a monthly statement of his disposal of the funds allotted to him, and he could at any time be arraigned before a high court. The king was to command the Army and the Navy, but he could not declare war, or sign a treaty, without the legislature's prior consent. He should have the right to veto any legislation submitted to him; but if three successive legislatures passed the vetoed bill it was to become law.

Should the legislature, so supreme, have two chambers, as in England and America? An upper chamber could be a check to hasty action, but it could also become a bastion of aristocracy or old age. The Assembly rejected it, and, as a further guard, declared an end to all hereditary privileges and titles except the king's. The legislature was to be elected by "active citizens" only —male adult property holders paying in direct taxes an amount equal to the value of three days' work; this included prosperous peasants but excluded hired labor, actors, and proletaires; these were classed as "passive citizens," for they could easily be manipulated by their masters or their journalists to become tools of reaction or violence. On this arrangement 4,298,360 men (in a population of 25 million souls) enjoyed the franchise in the France of 1791; 3 million adult males were voteless. The bourgeois Assembly, fearful of the city populace, was certifying the bourgeois Revolution.

For electoral and administrative purposes the constitution divided France into eighty-three *départements*, each of these into communes (43,360). For the first time France was to become a unified nation, without privileged provinces or internal tolls, and all with one system of measurements and laws. Penalties were fixed by law, and were no longer at the discretion of a judge. Torture, the pillory, and branding were abolished, but the death penalty was retained, to Robespierre's present discontent and future convenience. Persons accused of crime could choose to be tried by a jury of "active citizens" chosen by lot; a minority of three votes out of twelve would suffice for acquittal. Civil cases were decided by judges. The old *parlements*, which had begotten a second aristocracy, were replaced by a new judiciary appointed by the electoral assemblies. A high court was chosen by lot from lower-court justices, two to a *département*.

Two immense and related problems remained: how to avoid bankruptcy, and how to regulate the relations between Church and state. Taxes were failing to finance the government, and the Church held enviable wealth untaxed. It took the recently appointed bishop of Autun, Charles-Maurice de Talleyrand-Périgord, to propose (October 11, 1789) the solution: let the property of the Church be used for the payment of the national debt.

Talleyrand is one of the doubly *intriguing* characters in history. He came of an old family distinguished for its military services, and he would probably have followed a similar career had he not permanently dislocated his foot by a fall at the age of four; he had to limp his way through life, but managed to surmount every obstacle. His parents resigned him to the Church. In the seminary he read Voltaire and Montesquieu, and maintained a mistress nearby. Apparently he was expelled (1775), but in that year (his twenty-first) he received from Louis XVI the Abbey of St.-Denis in Reims. He was ordained a priest in 1779, and on the next day became vicar general to his uncle the Archbishop of Reims. He continued to please highborn ladies; by one of them he had a son, who became an officer under Napoleon. In 1788 Talleyrand was appointed bishop of Autun over the protests of his pious mother, who knew that he was a man of little faith. Nevertheless he drew up for presentation to the States-General a program of reforms which so impressed his clergy that they made him their deputy.[40]

Despite desperate opposition by its clerical members, the Assembly (November 2, 1789) voted, 508 to 346, to nationalize ecclesiastical property, then valued at three billion francs.[41] It pledged the government to "provide in a fitting manner for the expenses of public worship, the maintenance of the ministers, and the relief of the poor." On December 19 it empowered a Caisse de l'Extraordinaire to sell 400 million francs' worth of "assignats"— notes assigning to the holder a right to a stated amount of ecclesiastical property, and bearing interest at five percent until a sale could be effected. With proceeds from these assignats the government paid off its more urgent debts, so assuring the support of the financial community for the new regime. But the buyers of the assignats found it difficult to make satisfactory purchases; they used them as currency; and as the state issued more and more of them, and inflation continued, they lost value except in the payment of taxes, where the Treasury was compelled to receive them at their face worth. So the Treasury again found itself with losses exceeding its income year after year.

Having crossed the Rubicon, the Assembly (February 13, 1790) suppressed monasteries, allowing pensions to the dispossessed monks;[42] nuns were left untouched, as performing valued services in education and charity. On July 12 a "Civil Constitution of the Clergy" was promulgated, regulating the priests as paid employees of the state, and recognizing Catholicism as the national religion. Protestants and Jews might worship freely in their private conventicles, but without support from the government. Catholic bishops were to be chosen by the electoral assemblies of the departments; and in this voting non-Catholic electors—Protestant, Jew, or agnostic—were free to participate.[43] All priests, before receiving any stipend from the state, were required to pledge full obedience to the new constitution. Of the 134 bishops in France, 130 refused to take this oath; of the 70,000 parish priests, 46,000 refused.[44] The great majority of the population sided with the non-jurors, and boycotted the services of the jurant priests. The rising conflict between the conservative Church, supported by the people, and the pre-dominantly agnostic assemblies, supported by the upper middle class, became a main factor in the waning of the Revolution. Chiefly because of this unpopular legislation the King long refused to sign the new constitution.

Others had reasons for rejecting it. Robespierre led a strong minority in protesting that the restriction of the franchise to property owners violated the Declaration of the Rights of Man, and was a provocative insult to the Parisian proletaires who had repeatedly saved the Assembly from the armies of the King. The peasantry agreed with townspeople in resenting the abandonment of the governmental regulations that had in some measure protected producers and consumers from a "free market" manipulated by distributors.

Nevertheless the Assembly felt, with some justice, that the constitution was a remarkable document, giving legal and definitive form to the triumphant Revolution. The middle-class deputies, now supreme, considered that the commonalty—of whom the majority were still illiterate—was not ready to share, in proportion to its numbers, in the deliberations and decisions of the government. Besides, now that the nobility had fled, was it not the turn of the bourgeoisie to direct a state increasingly dependent upon a wisely managed and energetically advancing economy? So the Assembly, regardless of the King's hesitations, declared France a constitutional monarchy; and, on June 5, 1790, it invited the eighty-three departments to send their federated National Guards to join the people of Paris and the government of France on the Champ-de-Mars in celebrating—on the first anniversary of the taking of the Bastille—the fulfillment of the Revolution. As the invitation and the enthusiasm spread, thirty foreigners, led by a rich Dutchman known to history as "Anacharsis Cloots,"* entered the Assembly on June 19, and asked for the honor of French citizenship, and for admission to the Feast of the Federation as an "embassy of the human race." It was so ordered.

But the hilly Field of Mars had to be sculptured for the occasion: an area three thousand by one thousand feet had to be leveled and terraced to hold 300,000 men, women, and children; and a central mound was to be raised for an altar at which King, princes, prelates, deputies, and commoners would mount and pledge their loyalty to the nation now legally reborn. And yet only fifteen days were left for the sculpturing. Who now can rival the four-

---

* Baron Jean-Baptiste du Val-de-Grâce received his nickname from a character in a then popular romance by the Abbé Barthélemy.

teen pages[45] in which Carlyle told how the people of Paris, male and female, young and old, came with picks and spades and wheelbarrows and song— "Ça ira!" (It Will Go!)—reshaped that vast terrain, and reared those terraces and that Autel de la Patrie? Which of us today would dare write with such brave blowing of rhetorical trumpets and prophetic ecstasy—especially if nearly half our manuscript had been burned by a hasty maid, and we had to gather and polish our scattered gems again? What a fire must have smoldered in that dour Scot to survive such a holocaust!

So, in the week before the new holyday, soldiers from all of France traveled to Paris, and sometimes the Parisian National Guard marched out many miles to meet and escort them. On July 14, 1790, they all entered the Field of Mars in proud procession, fifty thousand strong,[46] their banners waving, their bands playing, their throats hoarse with their lusty songs, and 300,000 exalted Parisians joining in. Bishop Talleyrand-Périgord, not yet excommunicate, said Mass; two hundred prelates and priests mounted the altar and took the oath; the King pledged himself to obey the new laws to the best of his ability, and all the assemblage cried out, "*Vive le Roi!*" When the cannon sounded a salute, thousands of Parisians who had not been able to attend raised a hand toward the Champ-de-Mars, and made their pledge. In nearly every town similar festivities were held, with wine and food shared in common, and Catholic and Protestant pastors embracing as if they were Christians. How could any Frenchman doubt that a glorious new age had dawned?

VII. MIRABEAU PAYS HIS DEBTS: APRIL 2, 1791

One man, at least, could doubt, and one woman. To Louis and his Queen the Tuileries seemed a glass house in which their every move was subject to silent approval or prolonged condemnation by the populace. On August 31, 1790, a Swiss regiment in the King's service at Nancy mutinied over delayed pay and official tyranny. Some of the rebels were shot down by the National Guard; some were sent to the galleys; some were hanged. Hearing of this, a crowd of forty thousand Parisians converged threateningly upon the royal palace, denouncing Lafayette, blaming the King for the "Nancy massacre," and demanding the resignation of his ministers. Necker quietly departed (September 18, 1790) to live with his family at Coppet on Lake Geneva. Lafayette advised the King to pacify Paris by accepting the constitution.[47] The Queen, however, suspected the general of planning to replace her as the power behind the throne, and so clearly expressed her antipathy that he left the court and resigned to Mirabeau the task of salvaging the monarchy.[48]

Mirabeau was willing. He had need of money to support his lavish way of life; he felt that a coalition of King and Assembly was the only alternative to rule by leaders of the mob; and he saw no contradiction in pursuing this policy and replenishing his funds. As far back as September 28, 1789, he had written to his friend La Marck*: "All is lost. The King and Queen will be swept away, and you will see the populace triumphing over their helpless bodies."[49] And to the same friend, on October 7: "If you have any influence with the King or the Queen, persuade them that they and France are lost if the royal family does not leave Paris. I am busy with a plan for getting them away."[50] Louis rejected the plan, but he consented to finance Mirabeau's defense of the monarchy. Early in May, 1790, he agreed to pay the great adventurer's debts, to allow him $1,000 a month, and to reward him with $192,000 if he succeeded in reconciling the Assembly with the King.[51] In August the Queen gave him a private interview in her gardens at St.-Cloud. So great was the aura of majesty that the dragon of rebellion trembled with devotion when he kissed her hand. To his intimates he spoke of her ecstatically: "You know not the Queen. Her force of mind is prodigious. She is a man for courage."[52]

He considered himself "paid but not bought"; according to La Marck "he accepted payment for keeping his own opinions."[53] He had no intention of defending absolutism; on the contrary, the statement which he submitted to the King's ministers on December 23, 1790, was a program for reconciling public liberty with the royal authority: "To attack the Revolution would be to overshoot the mark, for the movement that makes a great people give itself better laws deserves support. . . . Both the spirit of the Revolution and many elements in its constitution must be accepted. . . . I regard all the effects of the Revolution . . . as conquests so irrevocable that no upheaval, short of dismembering the realm, could destroy them."[54]

He labored with devotion and bribes to save the remnants of royal authority. The Assembly suspected his venality but respected his genius. On January 4, 1791, it chose him its president for the usual term of two weeks. He astonished all by the order of his management and the impartiality of his decisions. He worked all day, ate and drank all evening, and wore himself out with women. On March 25 he entertained two dancers from the Opéra. The next morning he was seized with violent intestinal cramps. He attended the Assembly on the twenty-seventh, but returned to his rooms exhausted and trembling. The news of his illness spread through Paris; theaters were closed out of respect for him; his house was besieged by people asking about his condition; one youth came offering his blood for transfusion.[55] Talleyrand told him: "It is not easy to reach you; half of Paris is permanently outside your door."[56] Mirabeau died after much suffering, April 2, 1791.

On April 3 a delegation from the electors of Paris asked the Assembly to convert the Church of St.-Geneviève into a shrine and tomb for French heroes, and that this Panthéon ("of all the gods"), as it was soon to be called, should bear on its front the inscription *"Aux grands hommes la Patrie reconnaissante"* (To its great men a grateful Fatherland). It was done, and Mirabeau was buried there on April 4 after what Michelet thought "the most

---

*Comte Auguste de La Marck (1753–1833), not the biologist Jean-Baptiste de Monet, Chevalier de Lamarck (1744–1829).

extensive and popular funeral procession that had ever been in the world";[57] the historian estimated the crowd at between three and four hundred thousand—in the streets and the trees, at windows or on roofs; all of the Assembly except Pétion (who had secret evidence of Mirabeau's receiving money from the King); all the Jacobin Club; twenty thousand National Guards; "One would have thought they were transferring the ashes of Voltaire—of one of those men who never die."[58] On August 10, 1792, proofs were found among the fallen King's papers of payments to Mirabeau, and on September 22, 1794, the Convention ordered the tarnished hero's remains removed from the Panthéon.

VIII. TO VARENNES: JUNE 20, 1791

The King, reluctant to surrender the nobility, the clergy, and the monarchy to total denudation of their ancient authority, and convinced that a people so individualistic and impetuous as the French would obey no rule, permit no restraints, not sanctioned and ingrained by time, clung hopefully to the vestigial powers still left him, and resisted the daily urging of nobles and the Queen that he should escape from Paris, perhaps from France, and return with an army, native or foreign, strong enough to reestablish him upon a reinvigorated throne. He signed (January 21, 1791) the Civil Constitution of the Clergy, but he felt that he was betraying the faith that had been his precious refuge against the disappointments of his life. He was profoundly shocked by the Assembly's decision (May 30, 1791) to have the remains of Voltaire transferred to the Panthéon; it seemed intolerable to him that the arch-infidel of the century should be carried in triumph to lie with honors in what, only yesterday, had been a consecrated church. He gave his long-withheld consent to the Queen to prepare for a flight across the frontier. Her devoted friend, Count Axel von Fersen, raised money for the escape, and arranged the details; the King, certainly a gentleman, probably not a cuckold, thanked him fervently.[59]

All the world knows that story: how the King and Queen disguised as M. and Mme. Korff, with their children and attendants, left the Tuileries furtively at midnight of June 20–21, 1791, and rode all next day, in joy and fear, 150 miles, to Varennes, near the frontier of what is now Belgium (then the Austrian Netherlands); how they were stopped there and arrested by peasants armed with pitchforks and clubs and led by Jean-Baptiste Drouet, postmaster of Ste.-Menehould. He sent to the Assembly for instructions; soon Barnave and Pétion came with the answer: Bring your captives, unharmed, back to Paris. Now it was a three days' drive, leisurely led by sixty thousand of the National Guard. On the way Barnave sat in the royal coach opposite the Queen; he had been trained in the surviving chivalry of the Old Regime; he felt the glamour of royal beauty in distress. He wondered what would be her fate, and that of the children she guarded. By the time they reached Paris he was her slave.

Through his efforts and other cautious considerations, the Assembly rejected the cry of the sansculottes for immediate deposition. Who could tell what anarchy would ensue? Would the bourgeois Assembly, and all property, be at the mercy of the unfranchised Parisian populace? So the word went out that the King had not fled but had been abducted; he must be allowed to keep his head, at least for a while, and as much of his crown as the new laws had left him. The radical leaders protested; the clubs and the journals called for the people to assemble on the Field of Mars; on July 17, 1791, fifty thousand came, and six thousand signed a demand for the King's abdication.[60] The Assembly ordered Lafayette and the National Guard to disperse the rebels; these refused, and some of them stoned the Guard; the angry soldiers fired, killing fifty men and women; so ended the universal brotherhood that had been pledged there a year before. Marat, proscribed and hunted by the police, lived in dank cellars, and called for a new revolution. Lafayette, his popularity ended, returned to the front, and waited impatiently for a chance to escape from the mounting chaos of France.

The King, grateful for a reprieve, went in subdued state to the Assembly on September 13, 1791, and formally signed his assent to the new constitution. Returning to his desolate palace and Queen, he broke down and wept, and begged her to forgive him for having brought her from her happiness in Vienna to the shame of this defeat, and the mounting terror of this imprisonment.

As that month neared its end, the Assembly prepared to conclude its labors. Perhaps the deputies were tired, and felt that they had done enough for a lifetime. And indeed, from their standpoint, they had accomplished much. They had presided at the collapse of the feudal system; they had abolished hereditary privileges; they had rescued the people from monarchical absolutism and an idle, arrogant aristocracy; they had established equality before the law, and had ended imprisonment without trial. They had reorganized local and provincial administration. They had chastened the once independent and censorious Church by confiscating its wealth and declaring freedom of worship and thought; they had revenged Jean Calas and Voltaire. They had seen with pleasure the emigration of reactionary nobles, and had put the upper middle class in control of the state. And they had embodied these changes in a constitution to which they had won the consent of the King, and of the great majority of the population, as a promise of national unity and peace.

The National and Constituent Assembly completed its record by arranging for the election of a Legislative Assembly to transform the constitution into specific laws, and to meet with deliberation the problems of the future. Robespierre, hoping that a fresh poll would bring a more representative personnel to power, persuaded his fellow deputies to disbar themselves from election to the new legislature. Then, on September 30, 1791, "the most memorable of all political assemblies"[61] declared itself dissolved.

CHAPTER III

The Legislative Assembly

October 1, 1791–September 20, 1792

I. PERSONS OF THE DRAMA

THE elections for the second revolutionary congress were zealously monitored by the journalists and powerfully supervised by the clubs. Since censorship of the press had almost disappeared, the journalists had acquired new influence on public policy. Brissot, Loustalot, Marat, Desmoulins, Fréron, Laclos—each had a periodical for his tribune. Paris alone had 133 journals in 1790, and there were hundreds in the provinces. Nearly all of them followed a radical line. Mirabeau had told the King that if he wished to keep his throne or his head he must buy some popular journalists. "The old nobility," said Napoleon, "would have survived if it had known enough to become master of printing materials. . . . The advent of cannon killed the feudal system; ink will kill the modern system."[1]

The clubs were almost as effective as the journals. The Breton Club, having followed King and Assembly to Paris, renamed itself Society of the Friends of the Constitution, and leased as a meeting place the refectory of a former Jacobin monastery near the Tuileries; later it expanded into the library, and even the chapel.[2] The Jacobins, as history came to call them, were at first all deputies, but they soon enriched their membership by admitting persons prominent in science, literature, politics, or business; here former deputies like Robespierre, self-debarred from the new Assembly, found another fulcrum of power. Dues were high, and until 1793 most of the members came from the middle class.[3]

The Jacobin influence was multiplied by the organization of affiliated clubs in many of the communes of France, and their general acceptance of the parent club's lead in doctrine and strategy. There were some 6,800 Jacobin clubs in 1794, totaling half a million members.[4] They formed an organized minority in a disorganized mass. When their policies were supported by the journals their influence was second only to that of the communes—which, through their municipal councils and constituent sections, controlled the local regiments of the National Guard. When all these forces were in harmony the Assembly had to do their bidding or face an unruly gallery, if not armed insurrection.

An Englishman in Paris in 1791 reported that "clubs abound in every street."[5] There were literary societies, sporting associations, Freemason lodges, workmen's gatherings. Finding the Jacobins too expensive and bourgeois, some radical leaders formed in 1790 the "Society of the Friends of Man and the Citizen," which the Parisians soon called the Cordeliers Club, because it met in the former monastery of the Cordelier (Franciscan) friars; this gave a platform to Marat, Hébert, Desmoulins, and Danton. Finding the Jacobins too radical, Lafayette, Bailly, Talleyrand, Lavoisier, André and Marie-Joseph de Chénier, and Du Pont de Nemours formed the "Society of 1789," which began, in 1790, regular meetings in the Palais-Royal, to support the tottering monarchy. Another monarchical group, led by Antoine Barnave and Alexandre de Lameth, formed a club briefly known to history as the Feuillants, from their meeting in the convent of Cistercian monks so named. It was a sign of the rapid secularization of Parisian life that several abandoned monasteries were now centers of political agitation.

The rival tempers of the clubs showed during the elections which slowly harvested, from June to September, 1791, the ballots for the new Assembly. The loyalists, softened to tolerance by education and comfort, relied on persuasion and bribery to garner votes; the Jacobins and the Cordeliers, hardened by the marketplace and the streets, seasoned bribery with force. Interpreting the law to the letter, they kept from the polls anyone who refused to take an oath of allegiance to the new constitution; so the great majority of practicing Catholics were automatically excluded. Crowds were organized to raid and disperse meetings of loyalists, as in Grenoble; in some cities, like Bordeaux, the municipal authorities forbade all club meetings except of the Jacobins; in one town the Jacobins and their followers burned a ballot box suspected of harboring a conservative majority.[6]

Despite such democratic trimmings, the election sent to the Legislative Assembly a substantial minority dedicated to preserving the monarchy. These 264 "Feuillants" occupied the right section of the hall, and thereby gave a name to conservatives everywhere. The 136 deputies who acknowledged themselves Jacobins or Cordeliers sat at the left on an elevated section called the Mountain; soon they were named Montagnards. In the center sat 355 delegates who refused to be labeled; they came to be called the Plain. Of the 755 total 400 were lawyers, as befitted a lawmaking body; now the lawyers succeeded the clergy in control of the nation. Nearly all the deputies were of the middle class; the Revolution was still a bourgeois feast.

Until June 20, 1792, the most vigorous group in the legislature was that which later received the name of the department of the Gironde. They were not an organized party (nor were the Montagnards), but they were nearly all from regions of industrial or commercial activity—Caen, Nantes, Lyons, Limoges, Marseilles, Bordeaux. The inhabitants of these thriving centers were accustomed to considerable self-rule; they controlled much of the money, the commerce, the foreign trade of the realm; and Bordeaux, capital of the Gironde, proudly remembered having nurtured Montaigne and Montesquieu. Nearly all the leading Girondins were members of the Jacobin Club, and they agreed with most other Jacobins in opposing the monarchy and the Church; but they resented the rule of all France by Paris and its populace, and proposed instead a federal republic of largely self-governed provinces.

Condorcet was their theorist, philosopher, specialist in education, finance, and utopia; we have long since paid our debt to him.* Their great orator was Pierre Vergniaud: born at Limoges of a businessman father; left a seminary, studied law, practiced at Bordeaux, and was sent thence to the Legislative Assembly, which repeatedly made him its president. Still more influential was Jacques-Pierre Brissot, native of Chartres, something of an adventurer, sampling occupations, climates, and moral codes in Europe and America, briefly imprisoned in the Bastille (1784), founder (1788) of the Société des Noirs Amis, and sturdy worker for the emancipation of slaves. Sent to the Assembly as a deputy from Paris, he took charge of foreign policy, and led the way into war. Condorcet introduced him and Vergniaud to Mme. de Staël; they became devoted attendants at her salon, and helped her lover, the Comte de Narbonne-Lara, to appointment as minister of war by Louis XVI.[7] For a long time the Girondins were called Brissotins.

History remembers better Jean-Marie Roland de La Platière, chiefly because he married a brilliant woman who provided him with ideas and style, deceived him, celebrated his memory, and dignified her ascent to the guillotine with a famous and possibly legendary sentence. When Jeanne-Manon Phlipon, aged twenty-five, met Jean-Marie at Rouen in 1779, he was forty-five years old, incipiently bald, and somewhat worn out by business cares and philosophical rumination. He had a pleasant paternal smile, and preached a noble stoicism that enchanted Manon. She was already familiar with the ancient classics and heroes; she had read Plutarch at the age of eight, sometimes substituting him for the prayerbook when in church; "Plutarch prepared me to be a republican."[8]

She was a high-spirited child. "On two or three occasions when my father whipped me I bit the thigh across which he placed me,"[9] and she never lost her bite. But also she read the lives of the saints, and prophetically longed for martyrdom; she felt the beauty and moving solemnity of Catholic ritual, and retained her respect for religion, and some vestiges of the Christian creed, even after relishing Voltaire, Diderot, d'Holbach, and d'Alembert. She did not take much to Rousseau; she was too tough for his sentiment. Instead she lost her heart to Brutus (either one), to both the Catos, and both the Gracchi; it was from them that she and the Girondins took political ideals. She read, too, the letters of Mme. de Sévigné, for she aspired to write perfect prose.

She had suitors, but she was too conscious of her accomplishments to tolerate any ordinary lover. Perhaps, at twenty-five, she thought it best to compromise. She found in Roland "a strong mind, incorruptible honesty, knowledge, and taste. . . . His gravity made me consider him, as it were, without sex."[10] After their marriage (1780) they lived in Lyons, which she described as "a city superbly built and situated, flourishing in commerce and

* *Rousseau and Revolution,* 894–97.

manufactures, . . . famed for riches of which even the Emperor Joseph was envious."[11] In February, 1791, Roland was sent to Paris to defend the business interests of Lyons before the committees of the Constituent Assembly. He attended meetings of the Jacobin Club, and developed a close friendship with Brissot. In 1791 he persuaded his wife to move with him to Paris.

There she graduated from his secretary to his adviser; not only did she draw up his reports with an elegance that revealed her mind and hand, but she seems to have guided his political policy. On March 10, 1792, through the influence of Brissot, he was made minister of the interior to the King. Meanwhile Manon established a salon where Brissot, Pétion, Condorcet, Buzot and other Girondins regularly met to formulate their plans.[12] She gave them food and counsel, and to Buzot her secret love; and she followed or preceded them bravely to death.

II. WAR: 1792

It was a critical period for the Revolution. The *émigrés*, by 1791, had assembled twenty thousand troops at Coblenz, and were making headway with their appeals for help. Frederick William II of Prussia listened, for he thought he might use this opportunity to enlarge his realm along the Rhine. The Emperor Joseph II of the Holy Roman Empire might have gone to his sister's aid, but his people too were in revolt, he was something of a revolutionist himself, and he was dying. His brother Leopold II, who succeeded him in 1790, was not inclined to war, but he issued with the King of Prussia a cautious "Declaration of Pillnitz" (August 27, 1791), inviting other rulers to join them in efforts to restore in France "a monarchical form of government which shall at once be in harmony with the rights of sovereigns, and promote the welfare of the French nation."

Strange to say, both the monarchists and the republicans favored war. The Queen had repeatedly urged her imperial brothers to come to her rescue; and the King had explicitly asked the rulers of Prussia, Russia, Spain, Sweden, and Austria-Hungary to collect an armed force to restore the royal power in France.[13] On February 7, 1792, Austria and Prussia signed a military alliance against France; Austria was hungry for Flanders, Prussia for Alsace. On March 1 Leopold II died, and was succeeded by his son Francis II, who itched for battle by proxy and for glory in person. In France Lafayette favored war in the hope that he would be commander in chief, and so be in a position to dictate to both the Assembly and the King. General Dumouriez, minister for foreign affairs, favored war in expectation that the Netherlands would welcome him as their liberation from Austria, and might reward him with a minor crown. Since there was as yet no talk of conscription, the peasantry and the proletariat accepted war as now a necessary evil because the unhindered return of the *émigrés* would restore and perhaps vengefully intensify the injustices of the Old Regime. The Girondins favored war because they expected Austria and Prussia to attack France, and counterattack was the best defense. Robespierre opposed the war on the ground that the proletariat would shed their blood for it, and the middle class would pocket any gains. Brissot outtalked him; "the time has come," he cried, "for a new crusade, a crusade for universal freedom."[14] On April 20, 1792, the Legislative Assembly, with only seven dissenting votes, declared war upon Austria only, hoping to divide the allies. So began the twenty-three years of the Revolutionary and Napoleonic Wars. On April 26 Rouget de Lisle, at Strasbourg, composed "The Marseillaise."

But the Girondins had not calculated on the condition of the French Army. On the eastern front it numbered 100,000 men, opposing only 45,000 Austrian troops; but they were officered by men nurtured in the Old Regime. When General Dumouriez ordered these officers to lead their soldiers into action, they replied that their raw volunteers were not prepared, with either weapons or discipline, to face trained soldiery. When, nevertheless, the order to advance was repeated, several officers resigned, and three cavalry regiments went over to the enemy. Lafayette sent to the Austrian governor at Brussels an offer to lead his National Guard to Paris and restore the authority of the King if Austria would agree not to enter French territory. Nothing came of the proposal except Lafayette's later impeachment (August 20, 1792), and his flight to the enemy.

Matters reached a crisis when the Legislative Assembly sent to the predominantly Girondist ministry measures seeking the King's signature for the establishment of a protective armed camp around Paris, and for the discontinuance of state stipends for nonjuring priests and nuns. The King, in a flurry of decision, not only refused to sign, but dismissed all the ministers except Dumouriez, who soon resigned to take command on the Belgian front. When the news of these vetoes circulated through Paris it was interpreted as a sign that Louis was expecting an army, French or alien, to reach Paris soon and put an end to the Revolution. Wild plans were made to evacuate the capital, and to form a new revolutionary army on the farther side of the Loire. The Girondist leaders spread among the sections a call for a mass demonstration before the Tuileries.

So on June 20, 1792, an excited crowd of men and women—patriots, ruffians, adventurers, fervent followers of Robespierre, Brissot, or Marat—forced their way into the courtyard of the Tuileries, shouting demands and taunts, and insisting on seeing *"Monsieur et Madame Véto."* The King ordered his guards to let a number of them in. Half a hundred came, brandishing their varied weapons. Louis took his stand behind a table, and heard their petition—to withdraw his vetoes. He answered that these were hardly the fit place and circumstances for considering such complex matters. For three hours he listened to arguments, pleas, and threats. One rebel shouted, "I demand the sanction of the decree against the priests; . . . either the sanction or you shall die!" Another pointed his sword at Louis, who remained apparently unmoved. Someone offered him a red cap; he put it gaily on his head; the invaders shouted, *"Vive la nation! Vive la liberté!"* and finally *"Vive le Roi!"* The petitioners left, and reported that they had given the

King a good scare; the crowd, dissatisfied but tired, melted back into the city. The decree against the nonjuring clergy was enforced despite the veto; but the Assembly, anxious to dissociate itself from the populace, gave the King an enthusiastic reception when, at its invitation, he came to accept its pledge of continued loyalty.[15]

The radicals did not relish this ceremonious reconciliation of the bourgeoisie with the monarchy; they suspected the sincerity of the King, and resented the readiness of the Assembly to stop the Revolution now that the middle class had consolidated its economic and political gains. Robespierre and Marat were gradually turning the Jacobin Club from its bourgeois sentiments to wider popular sympathies. The proletariat in the industrial cities was moving toward cooperation with the workers of Paris. When the Assembly asked each of the departments to send a detachment of the Federation of National Guards to join in celebrating the third anniversary of the fall of the Bastille, these "Fédérés" were mostly chosen by the city communes, and favored radical policies. One particularly rebel regiment, 516 strong, set out from Marseilles on July 5, vowing to depose the King. On their march through France they sang the new song that Rouget de Lisle had composed, and from them it took the name that he had not intended— "The Marseillaise."*

The Marseillese and several other delegations of Fédérés reached Paris after July 14, but were asked by the Commune of Paris to delay their return home; it might have need of them. The Commune—the central bureau of delegates from the forty-eight "sections" of the city—was now dominated by radical leaders, and was day by day, from its offices in the Hôtel de Ville, replacing the municipal officials as the government of the capital.

On July 28 the city was again shocked into fear and rage by learning of the manifesto issued by the Duke of Brunswick from Coblenz:

> Their Majesties the Emperor and the King of Prussia having intrusted to me the command of the united armies which they had collected on the frontiers of France, I desire to announce, to the inhabitants of that kingdom, the motives which have determined the policy of the two sovereigns, and the purposes which they have in view.
>
> After arbitrarily violating the rights of the German princes in Alsace Lorraine, disturbing and overthrowing good order and legitimate government in the interior of the realm, . . . those who have usurped the reins of government have at last completed their work by declaring an unjust war on his Majesty the Emperor, and attacking his provinces in the Low Countries. . . .
>
> To those important interests should be added another matter of solicitude, . . . namely, to put an end to the anarchy in the interior of France, to check the attacks upon the throne and the altar, to . . . restore to the King the security and the liberty of which he is now deprived, and to place him in a position to exercise once more the legitimate authority which properly belongs to him.
>
> Convinced that the sane portion of the French nation abhors the excesses of

---

* "The Marseillaise" was accepted by the Convention as the national anthem on July 14, 1795. It was rejected by Napoleon and Louis XVIII, was restored in 1830, banned by Napoleon III, and finally adopted in 1879.

the faction which dominates it, and that the majority of the people look forward with impatience to the time when they may declare themselves openly against the odious enterprises of their oppressors, his Majesty the Emperor and his Majesty the King of Prussia call upon them and invite them to return without delay to the path of reason, justice, and peace. In accordance with these views I . . . declare:

　　1. That . . . the two allied courts entertain no other object than the welfare of France, and have no intention of enriching themselves by conquests. . . .

　　7. The inhabitants of the towns and villages who may dare to defend themselves against the troops of their Imperial and Royal Majesties and fire upon them . . . shall be punished immediately according to the most stringent laws of war, and their houses shall be . . . destroyed. . . .

　　8. The city of Paris and all its inhabitants shall be required to submit at once and without delay to the King. . . . Their Majesties declare . . . that if the Château of the Tuileries is entered by force or attacked, if the least violence be offered to . . . the King, the Queen, and the royal family, and if their safety and liberty be not immediately assured, they will inflict an ever memorable vengeance by delivering over the city of Paris to military execution and complete destruction. . . .

　　It is for these reasons that I call upon and exhort, in the most urgent manner, all the inhabitants of the kingdom not to oppose the movements and operations of the troops which I command, but rather, on the contrary, to grant them everywhere a free passage, and to assist . . . them with all good will. . . .

　　Given at the headquarters at Coblenz, July 25, 1792.

CHARLES WILLIAM FERDINAND,
DUKE OF BRUNSWICK-LÜNEBURG[16]

　　That somber eighth paragraph (perhaps offered to the amiable Duke by vengeful *émigrés*[17]) was a challenge to the Assembly, the Commune, and the people of Paris to abandon the Revolution or to resist the invaders by whatever means and at whatever cost. On July 29 Robespierre, addressing the Jacobin Club, demanded, as a defiance to Brunswick, the immediate overthrow of the monarchy, and the establishment of a republic with manhood suffrage for all. On July 30 the Marseillese Fédérés, still in Paris, joined other provincial detachments in pledging aid in deposing the King. On August 4 and the following days section after section of the city sent notice to the Assembly that it no longer acknowledged a king; and on August 6 a petition was presented to the deputies that Louis should be deposed. The Assembly took no action. On August 9 Marat published an appeal to the people to invade the Tuileries, arrest the King and his family, and all promonarchical officials, as "traitors whom the nation . . . ought first to sacrifice to the public welfare."[18] That night the Commune and the sections rang the tocsin calling for a massing of the people around the Tuileries the next morning.

　　Some came as early as 3 A.M.; by seven o'clock twenty-five sections had sent their quotas of men armed with muskets, pikes, and swords; some came with cannon; eight hundred Fédérés joined in; soon the crowd numbered nine thousand. The palace was defended by nine hundred Swiss and two hundred other guards. Hoping to discourage violence, Louis led his family from the royal chambers into the palace theater, where the Assembly was in chaotic session; "I come here," he said, "to prevent a great crime."[19] The insurgents were allowed to enter the courtyard. At the foot of the stairs leading to the King's bedroom the Swiss forbade further advance; the crowd pressed against them; the Swiss fired, killing a hundred or more men and women. The King sent orders to the Swiss to cease fire and withdraw; they did, but the crowd, led by the Marseillese, overwhelmed them; most of the Swiss were slain; many were arrested; fifty were taken to the Hôtel de Ville, where they were put to death.[20] The servants, including the kitchen staff, were slaughtered in a mad festival of blood. The Marseillese sang "The Marseillaise" to the accompaniment of the Queen's harpsichord; a tired prostitute rested on the Queen's bed. The furniture was burned, the wine cellars were sacked and drained. In the nearby courts of the Carrousel the happy crowd set fire to nine hundred buildings, and shot at firemen who came to put out the flames.[21] Some of the victors paraded with banners made from the red uniforms of the dead Swiss Guards—the first known instance of a red flag used as the symbol of revolution.[22]

The Assembly tried to save the royal family, but the murder of several deputies by the invading crowd persuaded the remainder to surrender the royal refugees to the disposition of the Commune. It locked them under strict guard in the Temple, an old fortified monastery of the Knights Templar. Louis yielded without resistance, grieving over his now white-haired wife and his ailing son, and waiting patiently for the end.

III. DANTON

During these convulsive weeks the deputies of the Right had almost all ceased attendance at the Assembly; after August 10 only 285 remained of the original 745 members. This rump legislature now voted to replace the King and his advisers with a provisional Executive Council; an overwhelming vote chose Georges Danton to head the Council as minister of justice, Roland to be minister of the interior, Joseph Servan to be minister of war. The choice of Danton was in part an attempt to quiet the Parisians, with whom he was very popular; besides, he was at that time the ablest and strongest character in the revolutionary movement.

He was thirty-three years old, and would die at thirty-five; revolution is a prerogative of youth. Born at Arcis-sur-Aube, in Champagne, he followed his father into law; he prospered as an attorney in Paris, but he chose to live in the same building with his friend Camille Desmoulins, in the Cordeliers working-class district; soon they became prominent in the Cordeliers Club. His lips and nose had been disfigured by a childhood accident, and his skin was potted with smallpox; but few remembered this when they confronted his tall figure and massive head, or felt the force of his perceptive and decisive thought, or heard his violent—often profane—speech rolling like thunder over a revolutionary assembly, a Jacobin club, or a proletarian crowd.

His character was not as brutal or domineering as his face or his voice. He could be rude and apparently unfeeling in his judgment—as in approving the September Massacres—but he had some tenderness latent in him, and no venom; he was ready to give and quick to forgive. Oftentimes his aides were surprised to find him countermanding his own Draconian orders, or protecting victims of his severe instructions; soon he was to lose his life because he dared to suggest that the Terror had gone too far, and that a time for mercy had come. Unlike the sober Robespierre, he relished Rabelaisian humor, worldly pleasures, gambling, beautiful women. He made and borrowed money; bought a fine home in Arcis, and large parcels of church property. People wondered how he had come upon the necessary sums; many suspected him of having taken bribes to protect the King. The evidence against him is overwhelming;[23] yet he committed himself to the most advanced measures of the Revolution, and seems never to have betrayed any of its vital interests. He took the King's money and worked for the proletariat. Even so, he knew that a proletarian dictatorship is a contradiction in terms, and can be only a moment in political time.

He had too much education to be a utopian. His library (to which he hoped soon to retire) included 571 volumes in French, seventy-two in English, fifty-two in Italian; he could read English and Italian well. He had ninety-one volumes of Voltaire, sixteen of Rousseau, all of Diderot's *Encyclopédie*.[24] He was an atheist, but he had some sympathy for the considerations that religion offered to the poor. Hear him in 1790, sounding like Musset a generation later:[25]

> For my part I admit I have known but one God—the God of all the world and of justice. . . . The man in the fields adds to this conception . . . because his youth, his manhood, and his old age owe to the priest their little moments of happiness. . . . Leave him his illusions. Teach him if you will, . . . but do not let the poor fear that they may lose the one thing that binds them to life.[26]

As a leader he sacrificed everything to the end of preserving the Revolution from foreign attack and internal chaos. For these purposes he was willing to cooperate with anyone—with Robespierre, Marat, the King, the Girondins; but Robespierre envied him, Marat denounced him, the King distrusted him, the Girondins were alarmed by his face and his voice, and shivered under his scorn. None of them could make him out: he organized war and negotiated for peace; he roared like a lion and talked of mercy; he fought for the Revolution and helped some royalists to escape from France.[27]

As minister of justice he labored to unite all revolutionary ranks in throwing back the invaders. He took responsibility for the uprising of the populace on August 10; the war needed the support of those wild spirits; they would make ardent soldiers. But he discouraged the premature attempts to support revolutions against foreign kings; this would unite all monarchs in hostility to France. He fought against the proposal of the Girondins to withdraw the government and the Assembly behind the Loire; such a retreat would shatter the morale of the people. The time had gone for discussion;

it had come for action, for building new armies and fortifying them with spirit and confidence. On September 2, 1792, in a passionate speech, he uttered a phrase that roused France and rang through a tumultuous century. The Prussian-Austrian forces had entered France and were winning victory after victory. Paris hovered between resolute response and a demoralizing fear. Danton, speaking for the Executive Council, went before the Assembly to rouse them and the nation to courage and action:

> It is a satisfaction for the minister of a free state to announce to them that their country is saved. All are stirred, all are enthusiastic, all burn to enter the contest. . . . One part of our people will guard our frontiers, another will dig and arm the entrenchments, the third, with pikes, will defend the interior of our cities. . . . We ask that anyone refusing to give personal service, or to furnish arms, shall meet the punishment of death. . . .
>
> The tocsin we shall sound is not the alarm signal of danger; it orders the charge on the enemies of France. To conquer we have to dare, to dare again, always to dare—and France is saved! [De l'audace, encore de l'audace, toujours l'audace—et la France est sauvée!]

It was a powerful historic speech, but on that same day the most tragic episode of the Revolution began.

IV. THE MASSACRE: SEPTEMBER 2–6, 1792

The emotional fever that came to its peak on September 2 took some remote sources of its heat from the swelling conflict between religion and the state, and the effort to make worship of the state a substitute for religion. The Constituent Assembly had accepted Catholicism as the official religion, and had undertaken to pay the priests as salaried employees of the state. But the dominant radicals in the Paris Commune saw no reason why the government should finance the propagation of what it looked upon as an Oriental myth so long allied with feudalism and monarchy. These views found acceptance in the clubs, and finally in the Legislative Assembly. The result was a series of measures that made the enmity of Church and state a recurrent threat to the Revolution.

A few hours after the dethronement of the King the Commune sent to the sections a list of priests suspected of antirevolutionary sentiments and aims; as many of these as could be apprehended were sent to various prisons, where they soon played a leading part in the massacres. On August 11 the Assembly ended all control of education by the Church. On August 12 the Commune forbade the public wearing of religious vestments. On August 18 the Assembly renewed a nationwide decree to the same effect, and suppressed all surviving religious orders. On August 28 it called for the deportation of all priests who had not sworn allegiance to the Civil Constitution of the Clergy; they were given a fortnight in which to leave France; some 25,000 priests fled to other lands, and reinforced there the propaganda of the émigrés. Since the clergy had heretofore kept parish registers of births, marriages, and deaths, the Assembly had to transfer this function to lay authorities. As most of the population insisted on solemnizing these events with sacraments, the attempt to discard the ancient ceremonies widened the breach between the piety of the people and the secularism of the state.[28] The Commune, the Jacobins, the Girondins, and the Montagnards all concurred in hoping that devotion to the young republic would become the religion of the people; that Liberty, Equality, and Fraternity would replace God, the Son, and the Holy Ghost, and that the furtherance of the new Trinity could be made the overriding aim of social order and the final test of morality.

The official opening of the new republic was deferred to September 22, first day of the new year. Meanwhile some eager futurists petitioned the Assembly that, as a gesture toward the universal democracy of their dreams, "the title of French citizen should be granted to all foreign philosophers who have with courage upheld the cause of liberty and have deserved well of humanity." On August 26 the Assembly responded by conferring French citizenship upon Joseph Priestley, Jeremy Bentham, William Wilberforce, Anacharsis Cloots, Johann Pestalozzi, Thaddeus Kosciusko, Friedrich Schiller, George Washington, Thomas Paine, James Madison, and Alexander Hamilton.[29] Alexander von Humboldt came to France, he said, "to breathe the air of liberty, and to assist at the obloquies of despotism."[30] The new religion seemed to be spreading its branches so soon after taking root.

On September 2 it put on its Sunday clothes, and expressed its devotion in diverse ways. Young and middle-aged men gathered at recruiting points to volunteer for service in the Army. Women lovingly sewed warm garments for them, and grimly prepared bandages for prospective wounds. Men, women, and children came to their section centers to offer weapons, jewelry, money for the war. Mothers adopted children dependent upon soldiers or nurses who were leaving for the front. Some men went to the prisons to kill priests and other enemies of the new faith.

Ever since the Duke of Brunswick's manifesto (July 25, 1792) the revolutionary leaders had acted as men tend to act when their lives are threatened. On August 11 the public commissioners at the Hôtel de Ville sent a strange note to Antoine Santerre, then in military command of the sections: "We are informed that a plan is being formed for going round the prisons of Paris and carrying off all the prisoners, in order to execute prompt justice upon them. We beg you to extend your supervision to those of the Châtelet, the Conciergerie, and La Force"—three main centers of detention in Paris.[31] We do not know how Santerre interpreted this message. On August 14 the Assembly appointed an "extraordinary tribunal" to try all enemies of the Revolution; but the sentences there decreed fell far short of satisfying Marat. In his *Ami du Peuple* of August 19 he told his readers: "The wisest and best course to pursue is to go armed to the Abbaye [another prison], drag out the traitors, especially the Swiss officers [of the royal guard] and their accomplices, and put them to the sword. What folly it is to give them a trial!"[32] Moved with this enthusiasm, the Commune made

Marat its official editor, assigned him a place in its assembly room, and added him to its Comité de Surveillance.[33]

If the populace heard Marat, and obeyed him to the best of their ability, it was because they too were in a fury and tremor of hate and fear. On August 19 the Prussians had crossed the frontiers, led by King Frederick William II and the Duke of Brunswick, and accompanied by a small force of *émigrés* vowing vengeance upon all revolutionists. On August 23 the invaders captured the Fortress of Longwy, allegedly through connivance by its aristocratic officers; by September 2 they had reached Verdun, and a premature report reached Paris that morning that this supposedly impregnable bastion had fallen (it fell that afternoon); now the road to Paris was open to the enemy, for no French army was on that route to stop them. The capital seemed at their mercy; the Duke of Brunswick expected soon to dine in Paris.[34]

Meanwhile revolution against the Revolution had broken out in far separate regions of France—the Vendée and Dauphiné; and Paris itself harbored thousands of people who sympathized with the fallen King. Since September 1 a pamphlet had been circulating which warned that a plot existed to free the prisoners and lead them in a massacre of all revolutionists.[35] The Assembly and the Commune were calling upon all able-bodied men to join the army that would march out to meet the advancing enemy; how could these men leave their women and children to the mercy of such an outpouring of royalists, priests, and habitual criminals from the prisons of Paris? Some sections voted a resolution that all priests and suspected persons should be put to death before the departure of the volunteers.[36]

About 2 P.M. Sunday, September 2, six carriages bearing nonjuring priests approached the Abbaye jail. A crowd hooted them; a man leaped upon the step of one carriage; a priest struck him with a cane; the crowd, cursing and multiplying, attacked the prisoners as they alighted at the gate; their guards joined in the attack upon them; all thirty were slain. Exalted by the sight of blood and the safe ecstasy of anonymous killing, the crowd rushed over to the Carmelite Convent and killed the priests who had been incarcerated there. In the evening, after a rest, the crowd, now enlarged by criminals and ruffians, and by lusty Fédérés troops from Marseilles, Avignon, and Brittany, returned to the Abbaye, forced all its prisoners to march out, sat in a rapid informal judgment upon them, and delivered the great majority of them— any Swiss or priest, or monarchist, or ex-servant of the King or Queen— to a gauntlet of men who dispatched them with swords, knives, pikes, and clubs.

At first the executioners were exemplary; there was no thievery—the valuables taken from the victims were transmitted to the Communal authorities; later the tired laborers kept such trophies as their due. Each received, for a day's work, six francs, three meals, and all the wine he wanted. Some showed signs of tenderness; they congratulated those exonerated, and escorted the distinguished among them to their homes.[37] Some were especially ferocious; they prolonged the sufferings of the condemned for the keener amusement of spectators; and one enthusiast, after withdrawing his sword from General Laleu's breast, inserted his hand into the wound, tore out the heart, and put it to his mouth as if to eat it[38]—a custom once popular in savage days. Each killer, when tired, took a rest, drank, and soon resumed his labors, until all the prisoners in the Abbaye had passed through the street-side court to liberty or death.

On September 3 the judges and the executioners moved toward other prisons—La Force and the Conciergerie; there, with fresh workers and new victims, the holocaust went on. Here was a famous lady, the Princesse de Lamballe, once very rich and very beautiful, beloved of Marie Antoinette; she had shared in plots to save the royal family; now, forty-three years old, she was beheaded and mutilated; her heart was snatched out of her body, and was eaten by a fervent republican;[39] her head was borne on a pike and paraded beneath a window of the Queen's cell at the Temple.[40]

On September 4 the slaughter moved to the prisons of Tour St.-Bernard, St.-Firmin, the Châtelet, the Salpêtrière; there, in the case of young women, rape replaced murder. Among the inmates at Bicêtre, an insane asylum, were forty-three youths, from seventeen to nineteen years of age, most of them placed there by their parents for treatment; all were slain.[41]

For two days more the massacre continued in Paris, until its victims totaled between 1,247[42] and 1,368.[43] The people were divided in judgment on the event: Catholics and royalists were horrified, but revolutionists argued that the violent response was warranted by the threats of Brunswick and the exigencies of war. Pétion, the new mayor of Paris, received the executioners as hard-working patriots, and refreshed them with drink.[44] The Legislative Assembly sent some members to the Abbaye scene to recommend due process of law; they returned to report that the massacre could not be stopped; finally the Assembly leaders—Girondins as well as Montagnards—agreed that the safest attitude was one of approval.[45] The Commune sent representatives to share in the task of the extempore judges. Billaud-Varenne, deputy attorney for the Commune, joined the scene at the Abbaye, and congratulated the killers: "Fellow citizens, you are immolating your enemies; you are performing your duty."[46] Marat proudly took credit for the entire operation. At her trial a year later Charlotte Corday, asked why she had killed Marat, answered, "Because it was he who caused the massacres of September." Challenged for proof, she replied, "I can give you no proof; it is the opinion of all France."[47]

When Danton was asked to stop the slaughter he shrugged his shoulders; "it would be impossible," he argued; and "why," he asked, "should I disturb myself about those royalists and priests, who were only waiting the approach of foreigners to massacre us? . . . We must put our enemies in fear."[48] Secretly he withdrew from the prisons more than one of his friends, and even some of his personal enemies.[49] When a fellow member of the Executive Council protested against the killings Danton told him, "Sit down. It was necessary."[50] And to a youth who had asked, "How can you help calling it horrible?" he answered, "You are too young to understand these

matters. . . . A river of blood had to flow between the Parisians and the
émigrés."[51] The Parisians, he thought, were now pledged to the Revolution.
And those volunteers who were leaving to meet the invaders knew now
that they could expect no mercy if they surrendered. They would in every
sense be fighting for their lives.

September 2 was also the day on which the Legislative Assembly, feeling
that the turn of events had made a ruin of the constitution which it had been
chosen to implement, voted to call a national election for a Convention that
would draw up a fresh constitution suited to the new condition of France
and the rising demands of the war. And since peasants, proletaires, and bourgeois alike were being called to defend a country called theirs, it seemed intolerable that any of these, taxpayers or not, should be kept from the ballot
box. So Robespierre won his first major victory: the Convention in which
he was to be a major figure was chosen by manhood suffrage.

On September 20 the Legislative Assembly ended its last session, not
knowing that on that day, at a village called Valmy, between Verdun and
Paris, a French army under Dumouriez and François-Christophe Kellermann
had met the professional troops of Prussia and Austria under the Duke of
Brunswick, and had fought them to a draw—in effect a victory, since after
the battle the King of Prussia ordered his battered regiments to retreat—
abandoning Verdun and Longwy—from French territory. Frederick William II could not afford to be bothered with distant France now that he was
competing with his neighbors Russia and Austria to see which would take
the biggest bite in partitioning Poland; moreover, his soldiers were suffering
disgracefully from diarrhea inflicted by the grapes of Champagne.[52]

It was at that battle that Goethe, present on the staff of the Duke of
Saxe-Weimar, made (we are told) a famous remark: "From today and
from this place begins a new epoch in the history of the world."[53]

CHAPTER IV

The Convention

September 21, 1792–October 26, 1795

I. THE NEW REPUBLIC

THE election to this third assembly, which was to see both the culmination and the decline of the Revolution, was even more subtly
managed by the Jacobins than that of 1791. The process was carefully indirect: the voters chose electors, who met in electoral committee and chose
the deputies to represent their district in the Convention. Both elections
were by voice vote and in public; at each stage the voter risked injury if he
offended the local leaders.[1] In the cities conservatives refused to vote; "the
number of abstentions was enormous";[2] of 7 million persons qualified to
vote, 6.3 million stayed away.[3] In Paris the voting began on September 2,
and continued for several days while, at the prison gates, massacres sent out
hints how to vote and survive. In many districts pious Catholics refrained
from voting; hence the strongly royalist Vendée elected nine deputies of
whom six would vote for the execution of the King.[4] In Paris the electoral
assembly met in the Jacobin Club, with the result that all twenty-four of
the deputies chosen to represent the capital were convinced republicans and
supporters of the Commune: Danton, Robespierre, Marat, Desmoulins,
Billaud-Varenne, Collot d'Herbois, Fréron, David (the painter). . . . In the
provinces the Girondins did some rigging of their own; so Brissot, Roland,
Condorcet, Pétion, Gaudet, Barbaroux, and Buzot earned the right to serve
and die. Among the foreigners elected were Priestley, Cloots, and Paine.
The Duc d'Orléans, renamed Citizen Philippe Égalité, was chosen to represent a radical section of Paris.

When the Convention convened in the Tuileries on September 21, 1792,
it had 750 members. All but two were of the middle class; two were workingmen; nearly all were lawyers. The 180 Girondins, organized, educated,
and eloquent, took the lead in legislation. On the ground that there was no
present danger of invasion, they secured a relaxation of the laws against
suspects, *émigrés*, and priests, and of wartime control over the economy;
free enterprise was restored; soon there were complaints of profiteering and
price manipulation. To squelch a movement among radicals for the confiscation of large estates and their division among the people, the Gironde, on the
first day of the Convention, carried a measure proclaiming the sanctity of
private property. So appeased, the Gironde agreed with the Mountain and
the Plain in declaring, on September 22, 1792, the First French Republic.

On the same day the Convention decreed that, after a year of readjustment, the Christian calendar should be replaced, in France and its possessions, by a Revolutionary Calendar, in which the years would be named I (from September 22, 1792, to September 21, 1793), II, III . . . , and the months would be named by their typical weather: Vendémiaire (vintage), Brumaire (mist), and Frimaire (frost), for autumn; Nivôse (snow), Pluviôse (rain), and Ventôse (wind), for winter; Germinal (budding), Floréal (flowering), and Prairial (meadows), for spring; and Messidor (harvest), Thermidor (warmth), and Fructidor (fruit), for summer. Each month was to be divided into three *décades* of ten days each; each *décade* was to end in a *décadi*, replacing Sunday as a day of rest. The five remaining days, called *sans-culottides*, were to be national festivals. The Convention hoped that this calendar would remind Frenchmen not of religious saints and seasons but of the earth and the tasks that made it fruitful; Nature would replace God. The new calendar came into use on November 24, 1793, and died at the end of Anno Domini 1805.

The Gironde and the Mountain agreed on private property, the republic, and the war upon Christianity; but on several other issues they differed to the point of death. The Girondins resented the geographically disproportionate influence of Paris—its deputies and its populace—on measures affecting all France; the Montagnards resented the influence of merchants and millionaires in determining the votes of the Girondins. Danton (whose section had given him 638 electoral votes out of a possible 700) resigned his place as minister of justice to undertake the task of uniting the Gironde and the Mountain in a policy of seeking peace with Prussia and Austria. But the Girondins distrusted him as the idol of radical Paris, and called for a record of his expenditures as minister; he could not account to their satisfaction for the sums he had laid out (he was a great believer in bribes), nor could he explain where he had found the money to buy three houses in or near Paris, and a large estate in the department of Aube; undeniably he had been living in a grand style. Calling his questioners ingrates, he gave up his labors for internal and external conciliation, and joined forces with Robespierre.

Though second only to Danton in popularity with the sections, Robespierre was as yet a secondary figure among the deputies. In their balloting for the presidency of the Convention he received six votes, Roland 235. To most of the deputies he was a dogmatist fertile in generalities and moral platitudes, a cautious opportunist who waited patiently for every opening to added power. An underlying consistency in his proposals had given him a slowly rising influence. He had kept from direct involvement in the attack upon the Tuileries or in the September Massacres, but he had accepted them as putting the fear of the people into the policies of the bourgeoisie. From the beginning he had advocated adult male suffrage—though in practice he had winked at keeping royalists and Catholics from the polls. He had defended the institution of private property, and had discouraged the appeal of a few impoverished souls for the confiscation and redistribution of possessions; however, he had proposed inheritance and other taxes that would "reduce by gentle but efficacious measures the extreme inequalities of wealth."[5] Meanwhile he bided his time, and allowed his rivals to wear themselves out with passion and extremes. He seemed convinced that some-day he would rule—and predicted that someday he would be killed.[6] "He knew, as all these men knew, that almost from hour to hour he carried his life in his hand."[7]

It was neither Robespierre nor Danton but Marat who completely cham-pioned the proletariat. On September 25, to celebrate the new republic, he changed the name of his periodical to *Journal de la République française*. He was now forty-nine years old (Robespierre was thirty-four, Danton thirty-three); he had less than a year of life remaining to him, but he filled it with an uncompromising campaign against the Girondins as enemies of the people, agents of that rising commercial bourgeoisie which seemed re-solved to make the Revolution the political aim of a "free enterprise" econ-omy. His violent diatribes reverberated through Paris, stirring the sections to insurgency, and generating in the Convention an almost universal hos-tility. The Girondins denounced what they called the "triumvirate" of Dan-ton, Robespierre, and Marat, but Danton disowned him and Robespierre avoided him; he sat with the Mountain, but usually friendless and alone. On September 25, 1792, Vergniaud and others read to the Convention docu-ments indicating that Marat had called for a dictatorship and had evoked the massacres. When the ailing "tribune of the people" rose to defend himself he was assailed with cries of "Sit down!" "It seems," he said, "that I have a great number of personal enemies in this assembly." "All of us!" cried out the Girondins. Marat proceeded to repeat his demand for a dictatorship on the limited Roman style, and acknowledged his incitations to violence, but he exonerated Danton and Robespierre from any association with his plans. A deputy proposed that he be arrested and tried for treason; the motion was defeated. Marat took a pistol from his pocket, held it to his head, and an-nounced, "If my indictment had been decreed, I would have blown my brains out at the foot of the tribune."[8]

The Girondins—who had led France into war—were strengthened in these months by the victories of French troops and the extension of French power and revolutionary ideas. On September 21, 1792, General Anne-Pierre de Montesquiou-Fezensac led his forces to the easy conquest of Savoy (then part of the kingdom of Sardinia); "the progress of my army," he reported to the Convention, "is a triumph; in both country and town the people come out to meet us; the tricolor cockade is worn on all sides."[9] On September 27 another French division entered Nice unopposed; on September 29 it took Villefranche. On November 27, at the request of local political leaders, Savoy was incorporated into France.

The conquest of the Rhineland was more difficult. On September 25 General Adam-Philippe de Custine led his volunteers to the capture of Speyer, taking three thousand prisoners; on October 5 he entered Worms; on October 19, Mainz; on October 21, Frankfurt-am-Main. To win Belgium (a dependency of Austria) to the Revolution, Dumouriez had to fight at

Jemappes (November 6) one of the major battles of the war; the Austrians, after long resistance, retreated, leaving four thousand dead on the field. Brussels fell on November 14, Liège on the twenty-fourth, Antwerp on the thirtieth; in these cities the French were welcomed as liberators. Instead of obeying the Convention's orders to move south and join his forces with Custine's, Dumouriez dallied in Belgium and enriched himself in dealings with speculators in army supplies. Reprimanded, he threatened to resign. Danton was sent to appease him; he succeeded, but suffered guilt by association when (April 5, 1793) Dumouriez defected to the enemy.

Intoxicated with these victories, the Convention leaders adopted two complementary policies: to extend France to her "natural boundaries"—the Rhine, the Alps, the Pyrenees, and the seas—and to win the frontier populations by pledging them military aid in achieving economic and political freedom. Hence the bold decree of December 15, 1792:

> From this moment the French nation proclaims the sovereignty of the people [in all cooperating regions], the suppression of all civil and military authorities which have hitherto governed you, and of all the taxes which you bear, under whatever form; the abolition of the tithe, of feudalism, . . . of serfdom . . . ; it also proclaims the abolition among you of all noble and ecclesiastical corporations, and of all prerogatives and privileges as opposed to equality. You are, from this moment, brothers and friends, all are citizens, equal in rights, and all alike are called to govern, to serve, and to defend your country.[10]

This "Edict of Fraternity" brought a mess of problems upon the young republic. When the conquered ("liberated") territories were taxed to support the French occupation, they complained that one master and his tax had been replaced by another. When the church hierarchy in Belgium, Liège, and the Rhineland, long accustomed to hold or share the ruling authority, saw itself challenged in both theology and power, it joined hands across frontiers and creeds, to repel, and if possible to destroy, the French Revolution. When, on November 16, 1792, to win the merchants of Antwerp to the French cause, the Convention decreed the opening of the River Scheldt to all navigation—whereas the Peace of Westphalia (1648) had closed it to all but the Dutch—Holland prepared to resist. The monarchs of Europe interpreted the Convention's pledge as a declaration of war against all kings and feudal lords. The First Coalition against France began to take form.

The Convention decided to burn all bridges behind it by bringing Louis XVI to trial for treason. Since August 10 the Temple had given a semi-humane imprisonment to most of the royal family: the King, thirty-eight; the Queen, thirty-seven; his sister, "Madame Élisabeth," twenty-eight; his daughter, Marie-Thérèse ("Madame Royale"), fourteen; and his son, the Dauphin Louis-Charles, seven. The Girondins did all they could to delay the trial, for they knew that the evidence would compel conviction and execution, and that would intensify the attack of the Powers upon France. Danton agreed with them, but a new figure on the scene, Louis-Antoine

Saint-Just, aged twenty-five, caught the attention of the Convention by his impassioned call for regicide: "Louis has combated the people and has been defeated. He is a barbarian, a foreign prisoner of war; you have seen his perfidious designs. . . . He is the murderer of the Bastille, of Nancy, of the Champ-de-Mars, . . . of the Tuileries. What enemy, what foreigner has done you more harm?"[11] This attack might have made the judicious pause, but on November 20 an iron box discovered in a wall of the royal chambers in the Tuileries, and brought to the Convention by Roland, powerfully supported the charge of treason. It contained 625 secret documents, which revealed the King's dealings with Lafayette, Mirabeau, Talleyrand, Barnave, various *émigrés* and conservative journalists; clearly Louis, despite his affirmation of loyalty to the constitution, had plotted the defeat of the Revolution. The Convention ordered a veil to be thrown over the bust of Mirabeau; the Jacobins smashed a statue that had commemorated Mirabeau in their club. Barnave was arrested in Grenoble; Lafayette fled to his army; Talleyrand, as always, escaped. On December 2 some delegates from the sections appeared before the Convention and demanded immediate trial of the King; soon the Paris Commune sent strong recommendations to the same effect. On December 3 Robespierre joined in the cry. Marat carried a motion that all voting in the trial should be by voice and in public—which placed the hesitant Girondins at the mercy of the sansculottes in the galleries and in the streets.

The trial began on December 11, 1792, before the full Convention. According to Sébastien Mercier, one of the deputies, "the back of the hall was converted into boxes, as in a theater, in which ladies wearing the most charming attire ate ices and oranges and drank liqueurs. . . . One could see ushers . . . escorting the mistresses of the Duke of Orléans."[12] The King was shown some of the documents found in the box; he denied his signature and all knowledge of the box. He met questions by pleading lapses of memory or putting the responsibility upon his ministers. He asked for a four-day deferral to let him employ his attorneys. Chrétien de Malesherbes, who had protected the *philosophes* and the *Encyclopédie* under Louis XV, offered to defend the King; Louis sadly accepted, saying, "Your sacrifice is the greater because you are exposing your own life, though you cannot save mine."[13] (Malesherbes was guillotined in April, 1794.) Meanwhile agents of the foreign Powers proposed to buy some votes for the King; Danton agreed to serve as purchasing agent; but the sum required proved to be more than their Majesties were willing to invest.[14]

On December 26 Romain de Sèze presented the case for the defense. The Constitution, he argued, gave no authority to the deputies to try the King; he had been within his human rights in fighting for his life. He was one of the kindest and most humane men, and one of the most liberal rulers, who had ever sat on the throne of France. Had the deputies forgotten his many reforms? Had he not inaugurated the Revolution by summoning the States-General, and inviting all Frenchmen to tell him of their wrongs and their desires? The prosecutors replied that the King had negotiated with foreign powers for the defeat of the Revolution. Why should an exception be made because the man guilty of treason had inherited the throne? As long as he remained alive, plots would be laid to restore him to his pre-Revolution powers. It would be well to make an example which all monarchs might contemplate before betraying the hopes of their people.

Voting on the King's guilt began on January 15, 1793. Out of 749 members 683, including his cousin Philippe d'Orléans, declared for conviction.[15] A motion to submit this verdict to ratification or repeal by the people of France through the primary assemblies was opposed by Robespierre, Marat, and Saint-Just, and was defeated by 424 votes to 287. "An appeal to the people—" said Saint-Just, "would not that be the recall of the monarchy?" Robespierre had long advocated democracy and universal male suffrage, but now he hesitated to trust it; "virtue," he said (meaning republican fervor), "has always been in a minority on the earth."[16]

When, on January 16, the final question was put—"What sentence has Louis, King of the French, incurred?"—both factions broke out into violence in the streets. There and in the galleries the crowd cried out for the death sentence, and threatened the life of anyone who should vote for anything less. Deputies who, the evening before, had vowed never to ask for the King's execution, now fearing for their lives, voted for his death. Danton yielded. Paine held firm; Philippe d'Orléans, ready to succeed his cousin, voted for his elimination. Marat voted for "death within twenty-four hours"; Robespierre, who had always opposed capital punishment, now argued that a live king would be a danger to the republic;[17] Condorcet appealed for the abolition of capital punishment now and forever. Brissot warned that a verdict of death would bring all the monarchs of Europe into war against France. Some deputies added a comment to their votes: Paganel said, "Death!—a king is made useful only by death"; Millaud said, "Today, if death did not exist, it would have to be invented"—echoing Voltaire on God. Duchâtel, dying, had himself borne to the tribunal, voted against Louis' death, and then died.[18] The final tally was 361 for death, 334 for a reprieve.

On January 20 a former member of the King's Garde du Corps killed Louis-Michel Lepeletier de Saint-Fargeau, who had voted for death. On January 21 a coach, surrounded by an armed escort, and passing along streets lined by the National Guard, carried Louis XVI to the Place de la Révolution (now the Place de la Concorde). Before the guillotine he tried to speak to the multitude: "Frenchmen, I die innocent; it is from the scaffold and near to appearing before God that I tell you so. I pardon my enemies. I desire that France—" but at that point Santerre, head of the Paris National Guard, called, "*Tambours!*" and the drums drowned out the rest. The populace looked in somber silence as the heavy blade fell, tearing through flesh and bone. "On that day," a spectator later recalled, "everyone walked slowly, and we hardly dared look at one another."[19]

II. THE SECOND REVOLUTION: 1793

The execution of the King was a victory for the "Mountain," for the Commune, and for the policy of war. It united the "regicides" in fatal dedication to the Revolution, since they would be the chosen victims of a Bourbon restoration. It left the Girondins divided and desperate; they had split on the vote; they now moved in Paris in fear of their lives, and longed for the relative peace and order of the provinces. Roland, sick and disillusioned, resigned from the Executive Council the day after the execution of the King. Peace, which had been made possible by the absorption of Austria and Prussia in the partition of Poland, was now made impossible by the fury of European monarchs at the beheading of one of their fraternity.

In England William Pitt, prime minister, who had thought of making war against France, found nearly all resistance to that policy gone from a Parliament and a public shocked by the news that royalty itself had been laid under the guillotine—as if they themselves, through their ancestors, had never laid the axe upon Charles I. Pitt's real reason, of course, was that French mastery of Antwerp would give to Britain's ancient foe the key to the Rhine—the principal avenue of British trade with Central Europe. That danger took sharper form when, on December 15, 1792, the Convention decreed the annexation of Belgium to France. Now the road was open to French control of Holland and the Rhineland; all that rich and well-populated valley could then be closed to a Britain that lived by exporting the products of an expanding industry. On January 24, 1793, Pitt dismissed the French ambassador; on February 1 the Convention declared war upon both England and Holland. On March 7 Spain joined them, and the First Coalition—Prussia, Austria, Sardinia, England, Holland, Spain—began the second stage in the effort to check the Revolution.

A succession of disasters brought the Convention to a tardy realization of the difficulties it faced. The Revolutionary armies relaxed after their initial victories; thousands of volunteers quit after serving the term for which they had enlisted; the total of troops on the eastern front had fallen from 400,000 to 225,000; and these, through the incompetence and venality of the contractors whom Dumouriez protected and milked, were poorly clothed and fed. The generals repeatedly ignored the instructions sent them by the government. On February 24 the Convention resorted to conscription to raise new armies, but it favored the rich by allowing them to buy substitutes. Revolts against conscription broke out in several provinces. In the Vendée, dissatisfaction with conscription and the cost and scarcity of food joined with anger at the anti-Catholic legislation to generate so widespread a rebellion that an army had to be diverted from the front to control it. On February 16 Dumouriez led twenty thousand troops in an invasion of Holland; the regiments that he left as a garrison in Belgium were surprised and annihilated by an Austrian force under the Prince of Saxe-Coburg; Dumouriez

himself was defeated at Neerwinden (March 18); and on April 5 he defected to the Austrians with a thousand men. In that month the representatives of England, Prussia, and Austria met and laid plans for the subjugation
of France.

Internal difficulties, added to these external setbacks, threatened the collapse of the French government. Despite expropriation of ecclesiastical and
émigré property, the new assignats were losing value almost overnight;
valued at forty-seven percent of their face value in April, 1793, they fell to
thirty-three percent three months later.[20] New taxes were so widely resisted
that the cost of their collection almost equaled their returns. Forced loans
(as of May 20–25, 1793) despoiled the rising bourgeoisie; when this class
used the Girondins to protect its interests in the government, it deepened
the conflict between Gironde and Mountain in the Convention. Danton,
Robespierre, and Marat won the Jacobin Club from its original bourgeois
policies to more radical ideas. The Commune, led now by Pierre Chaumette
and Jacques Hébert, used the latter's fiery journal, *Père Duchesne*, to rouse
the city and besiege the Convention with demands for the conscription of
wealth. Day after day Marat waged war against the Girondins as protectors
of the rich. In February, 1793, Jacques Roux and Jean Varlet led a group of
proletarian "Enragés" in assailing the high cost of bread and insisting that
the Convention should set maximum prices for the necessaries of life.
Harassed by a storm of problems, the Convention surrendered the tasks of
the year 1793 to committees whose decisions it came to accept with a minimum of debate.

Most of these committees were assigned to particular areas of activity
and rule: agriculture, industry and commerce, accounting, finance, education, welfare, or colonial affairs. Usually manned by specialists, they did
much good work, even amid the mounting crises; they prepared a new constitution, and left a heritage of constructive legislation that Bonaparte found
helpful in forming the Code Napoléon.

To guard against foreign agents, internal subversion, and political offenses,
the Convention (March 10, 1793) appointed a Committee of General Security as a national department of police, with practically absolute authority
to make domiciliary visits without warning and to arrest anyone on suspicion of disloyalty or crime. Additional committees of surveillance were
organized for the communes and sections of the cities.

Also on March 10 the Convention set up a Revolutionary Tribunal to try
suspects sent to it; these were allowed defenders, but the judgment of the
jurors was not subject to appeal or review. On April 5 the Convention appointed, as principal prosecutor before the Tribunal, Antoine-Quentin
Fouquier-Tinville, a lawyer famous for searching and merciless examinations,
but capable, now and then, of humane sentiments;[21] however, he has come
down to us in an engraving that shows him with a face like an eagle and a
nose like a sword. The Tribunal began its sittings on April 6 in the Palais de
Justice. As the war proceeded, and the number of persons sent up for trial
became unmanageably large, the Tribunal more and more syncopated its

legal procedure, and tended to pronounce an early verdict of guilty in nearly all cases sent to it by the Committee of Public Safety.

This Comité de Salut Public, established on April 6, 1793, replaced the Executive Council, and became the principal arm of the state. It was a war cabinet; it must be viewed not as a civil government acknowledging constitutional restraints, but as a body legally authorized to lead and command a nation fighting for its life. Its powers were limited only by its responsibility to the Convention; its decisions had to be submitted to the Convention, which in nearly all cases turned them into decrees. It controlled foreign policy, the armies and their generals, the civil functionaries, the committees on religion and the arts, the secret service of the state. It could open private and public correspondence; it disposed of secret funds; and through its own "representatives on mission" it controlled life and death in the provinces. It met in the rooms of the Pavillon de Flore, between the Tuileries and the Seine, and gathered for conference around a "green [cloth-covered] table" which for a year became the seat of the French government.

At its head, till July 10, sat Danton, now for the second time chosen to be leader of the nation in peril. He began at once by persuading his colleagues, and then the Convention, that the government should publicly renounce any intention to meddle in the internal affairs of any other nation.[22] At his urging, and over the objections of Robespierre, the Convention sent out tentatives for peace to each member of the Coalition. He persuaded the Duke of Brunswick to halt his advance, and he succeeded in arranging an alliance with Sweden.[23] He tried again to make peace between the Mountain and the Gironde, but their differences were too deep.

Marat intensified his attacks upon the Girondins, and with such mounting violence that they secured (April 14, 1793) a decree of the Convention that he should be tried by the Revolutionary Tribunal for advocating murder and dictatorship. At his trial a multitude of sansculottes gathered in the Palais de Justice and the adjacent streets, vowing to "avenge any outrage perpetrated on their favorite defender." When the frightened jurors freed him his followers carried him in triumph on their shoulders to the Convention. There he threatened vengeance on his accusers. Thence he was carried through a cheering crowd to the Jacobin Club, where he was enthroned in the presidential chair.[24] He resumed his campaign, demanding that the Girondins be excluded from the Convention as bourgeois betrayers of the Revolution.

He won a precarious victory when the Convention, over the protests and warnings of the Gironde, decreed a maximum price for grains at every stage of their passage from producer to consumer, and ordered governmental agents to requisition from the growers all produce needed to meet the public need.[25] On September 29 these measures were extended into a "general maximum" fixing the price of all basic commodities.[26] The eternal war between producer and consumer was now accentuated; peasants revolted against conscription of their crops;[27] production fell as the profit motive felt blocked by the new laws; a "black market" developed, supplying at high prices those who could afford to pay. Markets that obeyed the maximum ran out of grain and bread; hunger riots again ran through city streets.

The Girondins, bitterly resentful of the pressure placed upon the Convention by the lower orders of Paris, appealed to their middle-class electors in the provinces to rescue them from the tyranny of the mob. Vergniaud wrote to his electors in Bordeaux, May 4, 1793: "I summon you to the tribune to defend us, if there is still time, to avenge liberty by exterminating tyrants";[28] and Barbaroux wrote likewise to his supporters in Marseilles. There and at Lyons the bourgeois minority allied themselves with former nobles to expel their radical mayors.

On May 18 the Girondin deputies persuaded the Convention to appoint a committee to examine the operations of the Paris Commune and its sections in attempting to influence legislation. All of the members of the committee were Girondins. On May 24 the Convention ordered the arrest of Hébert and Varlet as agitators; the Commune, with sixteen sections concurring, demanded their release; the Convention refused. Robespierre, at the Jacobin Club on May 26, urged the citizens to revolt: "When the people is oppressed, when it has no resource left but itself, he would be a coward indeed who should not call upon it to rise. It is when all laws are violated, it is when despotism is at its height, it is when good faith and decency are being trampled under foot, that the people ought to rise in insurrection. That moment has arrived."[29] In the Convention on May 27 Marat demanded the suppression of the committee "as hostile to liberty, and as tending to provoke that insurrection of the people which is only too imminent, owing to the negligence with which you have allowed commodities to rise to an excessive price." That night the Mountain secured passage of a measure abolishing the committee; the prisoners were freed; but on May 28 the Girondins reestablished the committee by a vote of 279 to 238. On May 30 Danton joined Robespierre and Marat in calling for "revolutionary vigor."

On May 31 the sections sounded the tocsin for a rising of the citizens. Gathering at the Hôtel de Ville, these formed an insurrectionary council, and secured the support of the Paris National Guard under the radical leader Hanriot. Protected by these and a swelling crowd, the new council entered the Convention hall and demanded that the Girondins be indicted before the Revolutionary Tribunal; that the price of bread be fixed at three sous a pound throughout France; that any resulting deficit be met by a levy on the rich; and that the right to vote be provisionally reserved to sansculottes.[30] The Convention conceded only the second suppression of the hated committee. The warring parties retired for the night.

Returning to the Convention on June 1, the council called for the arrest of Roland, whom the sansculottes identified with the bourgeois interests. He escaped to southern hospitality. Mme. Roland tarried behind, planning to plead for him before the Convention; she was arrested and was lodged in the Abbaye jail; she never saw her husband again. On June 2 a crowd of eighty thousand men and women, many armed, surrounded the Convention hall, and the Guard aimed its cannon at the building. The council informed the deputies that none of them would be permitted to leave until all its demands had been met. Marat, dominating the rostrum, called out the names of those Girondins whom he recommended for arrest. Some managed to elude the Guard and the crowd, and fled to the provinces; twenty-two were put under house arrest in Paris. From that day till July 26, 1794, the Convention was to be the obedient servant of the Mountain, the Committee of Public Safety, and the people of Paris. The Second Revolution had defeated the bourgeoisie, and had established, *pro tem*, the dictatorship of the proletariat.

The victors gave form to the new order by commissioning Hérault de Séchelles and Saint-Just to formulate the new constitution that had been ordered on October 11, 1792. It restored adult male suffrage, and added the right of every citizen to subsistence, education, and insurrection. It limited the rights of property by considerations of public interest. It proclaimed freedom of religious worship, graciously recognized a Supreme Being, and declared morality to be the indispensable faith of society. Carlyle, who could not stomach democracy, called this "the most democratic constitution ever committed to paper."[31] It was accepted by the Convention's (June 4, 1793), and was ratified by a vote of one fourth of the electorate, 1,801,918 to 11,610. This Constitution of 1793 remained on paper only, for on July 10 the Convention renewed the Committee of Public Safety as a ruling power, superior to all constitutions, till peace should return.

III. EXIT MARAT: JULY 13, 1793

Three of the Girondin refugees—Pétion, Barbaroux, and Buzot—found protection in Caen, a northern stronghold of the "federalist" reaction against Parisian domination of the national government. They made speeches, denounced the sansculottes and especially Marat, organized parades of protest, and planned an army to march upon the capital.

Charlotte Corday was among their most ardent auditors. Descendant of the dramatist Pierre Corneille, born of a titled, impoverished, strongly royalist family, she was educated in a convent and served two years as a nun. Somehow she found opportunity to read Plutarch, Rousseau, even Voltaire; she lost her faith and thrilled to the heroes of ancient Rome. She was shocked on hearing that the King had been guillotined, and she was roused to indignation by the fulminations of Marat against the Girondins. On June 20, 1793, she visited Barbaroux, then twenty-six and so handsome that Mme. Roland had likened him to the Emperor Hadrian's *inamorato* Antinous. Charlotte was nearing her twenty-fifth birthday, but she had other things than love on her mind. All she asked was a letter of introduction to a deputy who might arrange her admission to a meeting of the Convention. Barbaroux gave her a note to Lauze Duperret. On July 9 she left by stagecoach for Paris. Arriving on July 11, she bought a kitchen knife with a six-inch blade. She planned to enter the Convention chamber and slay Marat in his seat, but she was informed that Marat was sick at home. She found his address, went there, but was refused admittance; Monsieur was in his bath. She returned to her room.

The bath was now Marat's favorite desk. His disease, apparently a form of scrofula, had worsened; he found relief from it by sitting immersed to the waist in warm water to which minerals and medicines had been added; a moist towel was thrown over his shoulders, and a bandana soaked in vinegar bound his head. On a board spanning the tub he kept paper, pen, and ink, and there, day after day, he wrote the material for his journal.[32] He was cared for by his sister Albertine and, since 1790, by Simonne Évrard, who began as his servant and, in 1792, became his common-law wife. He married her without benefit of clergy, "before the Supreme Being, . . . in the vast temple of Nature."[33]

From her room Charlotte sent a note to Marat appealing for an audience. "I come from Caen. Your love for the nation ought to make you anxious to know the plots that are being laid there. I await your reply."[34] She could not wait. On the evening of July 13 she knocked again at his entrance door. Again she was denied entry, but Marat, hearing her voice, called to let her in. He received her courteously, and bade her be seated; she brought her chair up close to him. "What is going on at Caen?" he asked (or so she later reported their strange conversation). "Eighteen deputies from the Convention," she answered, "rule there in collusion with the *département*" officials. "What are their names?" She gave them; he wrote them down, and passed sentence on them: "They will soon be guillotined." At that point she drew her knife and drove it into his chest with such force that it penetrated the aorta; blood poured from the wound. He cried out to Simonne, "*À moi, ma chère amie, à moi!*—To me, my dear friend, to me!" Simonne came, and he died in her arms. Charlotte, rushing from the room, was intercepted by a man who beat down her resistance with a chair. Police were called, came, and took her away. "I have done my duty," she said; "let them do theirs."[35]

Marat must have had some good qualities to have won the united love of two rival women. His sister dedicated her remaining years to sanctifying his memory. Once a prosperous physician, he left at his death nothing more than some scientific manuscripts and twenty-five sous.[36] He had been a fanatic, but a man fanatically devoted to the masses whom nature and history had forgotten. The Cordeliers Club preserved his heart as a sacred relic, and thousands came to view it with "breathless adoration."[37] On July 16 all the remaining deputies, and many men and women from the revolutionary sections, followed his corpse to its burial in the gardens of the Cordeliers. His statue, carved by David, was set up in the hall of the Convention; and on September 21, 1794, his remains were transferred to the Panthéon.

Charlotte's trial was short. She acknowledged her deed, but no guilt; she said she had merely avenged the victims of the September Massacres, and other objects of Marat's wrath; "I killed one man to save a hundred thousand."[38] In a letter to Barbaroux she frankly claimed that "the end justifies the means."[39] Within a few hours after her conviction she was executed on the Place de la Révolution. She received proudly the curses of the attending crowd, and rejected the offer of a priest to give her a religious end.[40] She died before she could realize how fatal her deed would be to the Girondins whom she had thought to serve. Vergniaud, speaking for them, realized this, and forgave her: "She has killed us, but she has taught us how to die."[41]

IV. THE "GREAT COMMITTEE": 1793

The Convention had reserved the right to revise, monthly, the membership of the Committee of Public Safety. On July 10—his peace policy, foreign and domestic, having failed—it removed Danton; then on July 25, as if to show its continuing regard, it elected him its president for the customary fortnightly term. His first wife had died in February, leaving him with two young children; on June 17 he had married a girl of sixteen; by July 10 he was redomesticated.

On July 27 Robespierre was appointed to the Committee. Danton had never cared for him; "that man," he said, "has not wits enough to cook an egg."[42] Yet, on August 1, he urged the Convention to give the Committee absolute power. Perhaps in a reaction of regret for this advice he remarked to Desmoulins, as they saw a sunset inflaming the Seine, "the river is running blood." On September 6 the Convention proposed to restore him to the Committee; he refused.[43] Weary and ill, he left Paris on October 12, and sought rest in the home that he had bought in his native Arcis-sur-Aube, in the valley of the Marne. When he returned, on November 21, the Seine was running blood.

During that summer the "Great Committee," as it came to be called, took its historic form. Now it consisted of twelve men: all of the middle class, all with good education and incomes, all acquainted with the *philosophes* and Rousseau; eight of them lawyers, two engineers; only one of them, Collot d'Herbois, had ever worked with his hands; a proletarian dictatorship is never proletarian. We call the roll:

1. Bertrand Barère, thirty-eight, added to divers duties the task of presenting and defending before the Convention the decisions reached by the Committee, and having them confirmed by decrees; amiable and persuasive, he turned death sentences into eloquence, and statistics into poetry. He made few surviving enemies, changed with the political tide, and lived to the age of eighty-six, long enough to learn the mortality of governments and ideas.

2. Jean-Nicolas Billaud-Varenne, thirty-seven, argued that the Catholic Church was the most dangerous enemy of the Revolution, and had to be destroyed. He kept in touch and tune with the sections and the Commune, and followed his uncompromising policies with a pertinacity that made even his fellow committeemen fear him. He took charge of correspondence and relations with the provinces, headed the new administrative machinery, and became for a time "the most powerful member of the Committee."[44]

3. Lazare Carnot, forty, already distinguished as a mathematician and

military engineer, took charge of the French armies, mapped campaigns, instructed and disciplined generals, won universal respect for his ability and integrity. He alone of the Committee is honored throughout France today.

4. Jean-Marie Collot d'Herbois, forty-three; formerly an actor, he had suffered the disabilities that oppressed the theatrical profession before the Revolution; he never forgave the bourgeoisie for closing its doors to him, or the Church for holding him, by his profession, excommunicate. He became the most severe of the Twelve in dealing with the "aristocracy of merchants," and once proposed, as a measure of economy, that the Paris prisons —crowded with suspects, hoarders, and profiteers—should be blown up with mines.[45]

5. Georges Couthon, thirty-eight, was so crippled by meningitis that he had to be carried in a chair wherever he went; he attributed the ailment to sexual excesses in his youth, but he was adored by his wife. He was a man of kind heart and iron will who distinguished himself by his humane administration of pivotal provinces during the Terror.

6. Marie-Jean Hérault de Séchelles, thirty-four, seemed out of place and step among the Duodecemvirs; he was a noble of the robe, a wealthy lawyer, noted for his elegant manners and Voltairean wit. When he felt the revolutionary tide swelling under him he joined in the attack upon the Bastille, wrote most of the Constitution of 1793, and served as a rigorous executor of the Committee's policies in Alsace. He lived comfortably, and kept a noble mistress, until the guillotine fell upon him on April 5, 1794.

7. Robert Lindet, forty-seven, had charge of food production and distribution in the increasingly managed economy, and accomplished logistic wonders in feeding and clothing the armies.

8. Claude-Antoine Prieur-Duvernois, called "Prieur of the Côte d'Or," aged thirty, accomplished similar miracles in supplying the armies with munitions and matériel.

9. Pierre-Louis "Prieur of the Marne," thirty-seven, spent his rough energy trying to win Catholic and royalist Brittany to the Revolution.

10. André-Jeanbon Saint-André, forty-four, of Protestant lineage and Jesuit education, became captain of a merchant vessel, then a Protestant minister; he took charge of the French Navy at Brest, and led it into battle with a British fleet.

11. Louis-Antoine Saint-Just, twenty-six, was the youngest and strangest of the Twelve, the most dogmatic, indomitable, and intense, the *enfant terrible* of the Terror. Brought up in Picardy by his widowed mother, admired and indulged, he fell passionately in love with Saint-Just, rejected all rules, fled to Paris with his mother's silver, spent it on prostitutes,[46] was caught and briefly jailed, studied law, and wrote an erotic poem in twenty cantos, celebrating rape, especially of nuns, and extolling pleasure as a divine right.[47] In the Revolution he found at first an apparent legitimation of his hedonism, but its ideals inspired him to exalt his individualism into a Roman *virtus* that would sacrifice everything to make those ideals come true.[48] He transformed himself from an epicurean into a stoic, but remained a romantic to the end.

"When the day comes," he wrote, "which satisfies me that I cannot endow the French people with mild, vigorous, and rational ways, inflexible against tyranny and injustice, on that day I will stab myself."[49] In *Republican Institutions* (1791) he argued that the concentration of wealth made a mockery of political and legal equality and liberty. Private riches must be limited and spread; the government should be based upon peasant proprietors and independent artisans; universal education and relief must be provided by the state. Laws should be few, intelligible, and short; "long laws are public calamities."[50] After the age of five all boys should be brought up by the state in spartan simplicity, living on vegetables and trained for war. Democracy is good, but in wartime it should yield to dictatorship.[51] Elected to the Committee on May 10, 1793, Saint-Just gave himself resolutely to hard work; he rebutted rumors of his having a mistress by claiming that he was too busy for such amusements. The willful and excitable youth became a stern disciplinarian, a capable organizer, a fearless and victorious general. Returning in triumph to Paris, he was chosen president of the Convention (February 19, 1794). Proud and confident, overbearing to others, he humbly accepted the leadership of Robespierre, defended him in his defeat, and—aged twenty-six years and eleven months—accompanied him to death.

12. Robespierre did not quite replace Danton as the master mind or will of the Twelve; Carnot, Billaud, Collot were too tough to be ruled; Robespierre never became dictator. He worked by patient study and devious strategy rather than by open command. He maintained popularity with the sansculottes by living simply with plain folk, extolling the masses and defending their interests. On April 4, 1793, he had offered the Convention "A Proposed Declaration of the Rights of Man and the Citizen":

> Society is obliged to provide for the subsistence of all its members, either by procuring work for them or by assuring the means of existence to those who are unable to work. . . . The aid indispensable to whoever lacks necessaries is a debt of whoever possesses a surplus. . . . To make resistance to oppression subject to legal forms is the last refinement of tyranny. . . . Every institution that does not assume that the people are good, and that the magistrates are corruptible, is vicious. . . . The men of all countries are brothers.[52]

All in all these twelve men were not mere murderers, as superficial acquaintance might describe them. It is true that they followed too readily the tradition of violence that had come down to them from the wars of religion and the Massacre of St. Bartholomew's Eve (1572); most of them learned to execute their enemies without qualm, sometimes with virtuous satisfaction; but they claimed the needs and customs of war. They themselves were subject to these mishaps; any one of them could be challenged, deposed, and sent to the guillotine; several ended so. At any moment they were subject to insurrection by the Paris populace, or the National Guard, or an ambitious general; any major defeat on the front or in a rebellious province might topple them. Meanwhile they labored night and day on their various tasks: from eight in the morning till noon in their offices or subcommittees; from one to four in the afternoon in attending the Convention; from eight till late in the evening in consultation or debate around the green table in their conference room. When they took charge France was torn with civil war by emergent capitalism in Lyons, by Girondin uprisings in the south, by Catholic and royalist revolts in the west; it was threatened by foreign armies in the northeast, the east, and the southwest; it was suffering defeat on land and sea, and was blockaded in every port. When the Great Committee fell, France had been hammered into political unity by dictatorship and terror; a new breed of young generals, trained, and sometimes led into battle, by Carnot and Saint-Just, had thrown back the enemy in decisive victories; and France, alone against nearly all of Europe, had emerged triumphant against everything but herself.

V. THE REIGN OF TERROR: SEPTEMBER 17, 1793–JULY 28, 1794

1. The Gods Are Athirst

The Terror was a recurrent mood as well as a specific time. Strictly it should be dated from the Law of Suspects, September 17, 1793, to the execution of Robespierre, July 28, 1794. But there had been the September Terror of 1792; there was to be a "White Terror" in May, 1795; another terror would follow the fall of Napoleon.

The causes of the famous Terror were external danger and internal disorder, leading to public fear and tumult, and begetting martial law. The First Coalition had retaken Mainz (July 23), had invaded Alsace, and had entered Valenciennes, a hundred miles from Paris; Spanish troops had captured Perpignan and Bayonne. French armies were in disarray, French generals were ignoring the orders of their government. On August 29 French royalists surrendered to the British a French fleet, and a precious naval base and arsenal at Toulon. Britannia ruled the waves, and could at leisure appropriate French colonies on three continents. The victorious Allies debated the dismemberment of France, and restored feudal rights as they advanced.[53]

Internally the Revolution seemed to be breaking apart. The Vendée was aflame with counterrevolutionary ardor; Catholic rebels had defeated the forces of the state at Vihiers (July 18). Aristocrats, at home or as *émigrés*, were confidently planning restoration. Lyons, Bourges, Nîmes, Marseilles, Bordeaux, Nantes, Brest fell to the revolting Gironde. Class war was rising between rich and poor.

The economy was itself a battlefield. The price controls established on May 4 and September 29 were being defeated by the ingenuity of greed. The urban poor approved the maxima; the peasants and the merchants opposed them, and increasingly refused to grow or distribute the price-limited foods; the city stores, receiving less and less produce from market or field, could satisfy only the foremost few in the queues that daily formed at their doors. Fear of famine ran through Paris and the towns. In Paris, Senlis, Amiens, Rouen the populace came near to overthrowing the government in protest against the shortage of food. On June 25 Jacques Roux led his band of Enragés to the Convention and demanded that all profiteers—among whom he included some deputies—be arrested and made to disgorge their new wealth.

> Yours is no democracy, for you permit riches. It is the rich who have reaped, in the last four years, the fruits of the Revolution; it is the merchant aristocracy, more terrible than the nobility, that oppresses us. We see no limit to their extortions, for the price of goods is growing alarmingly. It is time that the death struggle between the profiteers and the workers should come to an end. . . . Are the possessions of knaves to be more sacred than human life? The necessities of life should be available for distribution by administrative bodies, just as the armed forces are at their disposition. [Nor would it suffice to take a capital levy from the rich, so long as the system is unchanged, for] the capitalist and the merchant will the next day raise an equal sum from the sansculottes . . . if the monopolies and the power of extortion are not destroyed.[54]

In slightly less communistic terms Jacques Hébert denounced the bourgeoisie as traitors to the Revolution, and urged the workers to seize power from a negligent or cowardly government. On August 30 a deputy pronounced the magic word: Let Terror be the order of the day.[55] On September 5 a crowd from the sections, calling for "war on tyrants, hoarders, and aristocrats," marched to the headquarters of the Commune in the Hôtel de Ville. The mayor, Jean-Guillaume Pache, and the city procurator, Pierre Chaumette, went with their delegation to the Convention and voiced their demand for a revolutionary army to tour France with a portable guillotine, arrest every Girondin, and compel every peasant to surrender his hoarded produce or be executed on the spot.[56]

It was in this atmosphere of foreign invasion, and of a revolution within the Revolution, that the Committee of Public Safety built and guided the armies that led France to victory, and the machinery of terror that forged a distraught nation into unity.

On August 23, on bold plans presented by Carnot and Barère, the Convention ordered a levy en masse unparalleled in French history:

> From now until such time as its enemies have been driven out of the territory of the Republic, all Frenchmen are permanently requisitioned for the service of the armies. The young shall go and fight, the married men shall forge weapons and transport food, the women shall make tents and clothes and serve in the hospitals, the old men shall have themselves carried into public places to rouse the courage of the warriors and preach hatred of kings and the unity of the nation.

All unmarried men from eighteen to twenty-five years of age were to be drafted into battalions under banners reading: *"Le peuple français debout contre les tyrants!"* (The French people standing up against the tyrants!).

Soon Paris was transformed into a throbbing arsenal. The gardens of the Tuileries and the Luxembourg were covered with shops producing, among other matériel, some 650 muskets a day. Unemployment vanished. Privately owned weapons, metal, surplus clothing, were requisitioned; thousands of mills were taken over. Capital as well as labor was conscripted; a loan of a billion livres was squeezed from the well-to-do. Contractors were told what to produce; prices were fixed by the government. Overnight, France became a totalitarian state. Copper, iron, saltpeter, potash, soda, sulfur, formerly dependent in part on imports, had now to be found in, taken from, the soil of a France blockaded on every frontier and at every port. Luckily the great chemist Lavoisier (soon to be guillotined) had in 1775 improved the quality, and increased the production, of gunpowder; the French armies had better gunpowder than their enemies. Scientists like Monge, Berthollet, and Fourcroy were called upon to find supplies of needed materials, or to invent substitutes; they were at the head of their fields at the time, and served their country well.

By the end of September France had 500,000 men under arms. Their equipment was still inadequate, their discipline poor, their spirit hesitant; only saints can be enthusiastic about death. Now for the first time propaganda became a state industry, almost a monopoly; Jean-Baptiste Bourchotte, minister of war, paid newspapers to present the nation's case, and saw to it that copies of these journals were circulated in the army camps, where there was little else to read. Members or representatives of the Committee went to the front to harangue the troops and keep an eye upon the generals. In the first important engagement of the new campaign—at Hondschoote September 6–8, against a force of British and Austrians—it was Debrel, a Committtee commissioner, who turned defeat into victory after General Houchard had proposed retreat. For this and other errors the old soldier was sent to the guillotine on November 14, 1793. Twenty-two other generals, nearly all of the Ancien Régime, were imprisoned for blunders, or apathy, or neglect of the Committee's instructions. Younger men, brought up in revolution, took their places—men like Hoche, Pichegru, Jourdan, Moreau, who had the viscera to apply Carnot's policy of persistent attack. At Wattignies, on October 16, when 50,000 French recruits faced 65,000 Austrians, the forty-year-old Carnot shouldered a musket and marched with Jourdan's men into battle. The victory was not decisive, but it raised the morale of the Revolutionary armies and strengthened the authority of the Committee.

On September 17 the obedient Convention passed the Law of Suspects, empowering the Committee or its agents to arrest, without warning, any returned émigré, any relative of an émigré, any public official suspended and not reinstated, anyone who had given any sign of opposition to the Revolution or the war. It was a harsh law, which forced all but avowed revolutionists—therefore nearly all Catholics and bourgeois—to live in constant fear of arrest, even of death; the Committee justified it as needed to maintain at least an outward unity in a war for national survival. Some émigrés agreed with the Twelve that fear and terror were legitimate instruments of rule in critical situations. The Comte de Montmorin, former foreign minister under Louis XVI, wrote in 1792: "I believe it necessary to punish the Parisians by terrorism." The Comte de Flachslander argued that

French resistance to the Allies would "continue until the Convention has been massacred." A secretary to the King of Prussia commented on the *émigrés:* "Their language is horrible. If we are prepared to abandon their fellow citizens to their vengeance, France would soon be no more than one monstrous cemetery."[57]

The Convention faced a choice between terror and mercy in the case of the Queen. Putting aside her early extravagance, her intrusion into affairs of state, her known distaste for the populace of Paris (offenses that hardly deserved decapitation), there was no doubt that she had communicated with *émigrés* and foreign governments in an effort to halt the Revolution and restore the traditional powers of the French monarchy. In these operations she felt that she was using the human right of self-defense; her accusers considered that she had violated laws passed by the elected delegates of the nation, and had committed treason. Apparently she had revealed to the enemies of France the intimate deliberations of the royal Council, even the campaign plans of the Revolutionary armies.

She had borne four children to Louis XVI: a daughter, Marie-Thérèse, now fifteen; a son who had died in infancy; a second son, who had died in 1789; a third son, Louis-Charles, now eight, whom she considered to be Louis XVII. Helped by her daughter and her sister-in-law Élisabeth, she watched in anxiety and then despair as continued confinement broke the health and spirit of the boy. In March, 1793, she was offered a plan for her escape; she refused it because it required her to leave her children behind.[58] When the government learned of the abandoned plot it removed the Dauphin from his mother despite her struggles, and kept him in isolation from his relatives. On August 2, 1793, after a year of imprisonment in the Temple, the Queen, her daughter, and her sister-in-law were removed to a room in the Conciergerie—that part of the Palais de Justice which had formerly been occupied by the superintendent of the building. There the "Widow Capet," as she was called, was treated more kindly than before, even to having a priest come and say Mass in her cell. Later that month she consented to another attempt to escape; it failed; now she was transferred to another room and put under stricter guard.

On September 2 the Committee met to decide her fate. Some members were in favor of keeping her alive as a pawn to be surrendered to Austria in return for an acceptable peace. Barère and Saint-André called for her execution as a means of uniting the signers of the sentence with a bond of blood. Hébert, from the Commune, told the Twelve, "I have in your name promised the head of Antoinette to the sansculottes, who are clamoring for it, and without whose support you yourselves would cease to exist. . . . I will go and cut it off myself if I have to wait much longer for it."[59]

On October 12 the Queen submitted to a long preliminary examination; and on October 14 and 15 she was tried before the Revolutionary Tribunal, with Fouquier-Tinville as chief prosecutor. She was questioned from 8 A.M. to 4 P.M. and from 5 to 11 P.M. on the first day, and from 9 A.M. to 3 P.M. on the next. She was accused of transferring millions of francs from the

French Treasury to her brother Joseph II of Austria, and with inviting alien forces to invade France; and it was suggested, for good measure, that she had tried to "corrupt" her son sexually. Only the last accusation unnerved her; she replied, "Nature refuses to answer such a charge brought against a mother. I appeal to all mothers here." The audience was moved by the sight of this woman, whose youthful beauty and gaiety had been the talk of Europe, now white-haired at thirty-eight, clad in mourning for her husband, fighting for her life with courage and dignity against men who were apparently resolved to break her spirit with a protracted ordeal merciless to both body and mind. When it was over she was blind with fatigue, and had to be helped to her cell. There she learned that the verdict was death.

Now in solitary confinement, she wrote a letter of farewell to Madame Élisabeth, asking her to transmit to her son and daughter the directions the King had left for them. "My son," she wrote, "must never forget his father's last words, which I expressly repeat to him: 'Never seek to avenge my death.' "[60] The letter was not delivered to Madame Élisabeth; it was intercepted by Fouquier-Tinville, who gave it to Robespierre, among whose secret papers it was found after his death.

On the morning of October 16, 1793, the executioner, Henri Sanson, came to her cell, bound her hands behind her back, and cut off her hair at the neck. She was taken in a cart along a street lined with soldiers, past hostile, taunting crowds, to the Place de la Révolution. At noon Sanson held up her severed head to the multitude.

Having struck its stride, the Revolutionary Tribunal now issued death sentences at the rate of seven per day.[61] All available aristocrats were seized, and many were executed. The twenty-one Girondins who had been under guard since June 2 were put on trial on October 24; the eloquence of Vergniaud and Brissot availed them not; all were granted a quick and early death. One of them, Valazé, stabbed himself as he left the court; his dead body was placed among the condemned and carted to the scaffold, where it took its turn under the indifferent blade. "The Revolution," said Vergniaud, "is like Saturn, it is devouring its own children."[62]

Consider the wrath and fear that these events must have brought to Manon Roland, now awaiting her fate in the Conciergerie, which had become a steppingstone to the guillotine. Her imprisonment had had some amenities; friends brought her books and flowers; she collected in her cell a little library centered around Plutarch and Tacitus. As a stronger anodyne she immersed herself in writing her recollections, terming them an *Appel à l'impartiale postérité*—as if posterity too would not be divided. As she described her youth the remembrance of *tempi felici* made bitterer her contemplation of present days. So she wrote, on August 28, 1793:

> I feel my resolution to pursue these memories deserting me. The miseries of my country torment me; an involuntary gloom penetrates my soul, chilling my imagination. France has become a vast Golgotha of carnage, an arena of horrors, where her children tear and destroy one another. . . . Never can history

paint these dreadful times, or the monsters that fill them with their barbarities.
... What Rome or Babylon ever equaled Paris?[63]

Foreseeing that her turn would come soon, she wrote into her manuscript a word of farewell to her husband and to her lover, who had as yet escaped the snares prepared for them:

> O my friends, may propitious fate conduct you to the United States, the sole asylum of freedom.* . . . And you, my spouse and companion, enfeebled by premature old age, eluding with difficulty the assassins, shall I be permitted to see you again? . . . How long must I remain a witness to the desolation of my native land, the degradation of my countrymen?[64]

Not long. On November 8, 1793, before the Revolutionary Tribunal, she was charged with complicity in Roland's alleged misuse of public funds, and with having sent from her cell letters of encouragement to Barbaroux and Buzot, who were then inciting revolt against the Jacobin control over the Convention. When she spoke in her own defense the carefully selected spectators denounced her as a traitress. She was declared guilty and was guillotined on the same day in the Place de la Révolution. An uncertain tradition tells how, looking at the statue of Liberty that David had set up in the majestic square, she cried out, "O Liberty, what crimes are committed in your name!"[65]

A procession of revolutionaries followed her. On November 10 came the mayor-astronomer Bailly, who had given the red cockade to the King, and had ordered the National Guard to fire upon the untimely petitioners on the Champ-de-Mars. On November 12 the guillotine caught up with Philippe Égalité; he could not make out why the Montagnards wished to dispatch so faithful an ally; but he had the blood of kings in his veins, and had itched for a throne; who could tell when that itch would frenzy him again? Then, on November 29, Antoine Barnave, who had tried to protect and guide the Queen. Then Generals Custine, Houchard, Biron . . .

Roland, having thanked the friends who had risked their lives to protect him, set out alone on a walk, November 16, sat down against a tree, and wrote a note of farewell: "Not fear but indignation made me quit my retreat, on learning that my wife had been murdered. I did not wish to remain longer on an earth polluted with crimes."[66] Then he forced his sword into his body. Condorcet, after writing a paean to progress, took poison (March 28, 1794). Barbaroux shot himself, survived, and was guillotined (June 15). Pétion and Buzot, pursued by agents of the government, killed themselves in a field near Bordeaux. Their bodies were found on June 18, half devoured by wolves.

2. The Terror in the Provinces

There were other Girondins, still wearing heads. In some towns, like Bordeaux and Lyons, they had gained the upper hand; they had to be

---

* Five years later Congress passed the Alien and Sedition Acts, sharply restricting public criticism of the government.

wiped out, the Jacobins felt, if their moves toward provincial autonomy were to be overcome and France made one and Jacobin. For this and other purposes the Committee of Public Safety sent out over France its "representatives on mission," and gave them, subject to itself, almost absolute authority in their allotted terrain. They might depose elected officials, appoint others, arrest suspects, draft men for the Army, levy taxes, enforce price controls, exact loans, requisition produce, clothing, or materials, and set up or confirm local committees of public safety to serve as agencies of the Great Committee in Paris. The representatives accomplished miracles of revolutionary and military organization, often amid a hostile or apathetic environment. They put down opposition without mercy, sometimes with enthusiastic excess.

The most successful of them was Saint-Just. On October 17, 1793, he and Joseph Lebas (who gladly let him take the lead) were dispatched to save Alsace from an Austrian invasion that was making rapid conquests in a territory congenitally German by language, literature, and ways. The French Army of the Rhine had been thrown back upon Strasbourg, and was in a mood of defeatism and mutiny. Saint-Just learned that the troops had been tyrannically treated, badly led, and perhaps betrayed, by officers inadequately enamored of the Revolution; he had seven of them executed before the assembled force. He listened to grievances, and remedied them with characteristic decisiveness. He requisitioned from the prosperous classes all surplus shoes, coats, overcoats, and hats, and from the 193 richest citizens he extracted nine million livres. Incompetent or apathetic officials were dismissed; convicted grafters were shot. When the French army met the Austrians again the invaders were driven out of Alsace, and the province was restored to French control. Saint-Just returned to Paris, eager for other tasks, and almost forgetting that he was engaged to the sister of Lebas.

Joseph Le Bon did not live up to his name as Committee representative. Warned by his employers to beware of "false and mistaken humanity," the blue-eyed ex-curé thought to please them by "shortening" 150 Cambrai notables in six weeks, and 392 in Arras; his secretary reported that Le Bon killed "in a sort of fever" and, on reaching home, mimicked the facial contortions of the dying to amuse his wife.[67] He himself was cut short in 1795.

In July, 1793, Jean-Baptiste Carrier was commissioned to suppress the Catholic revolt in the Vendée, and to make Nantes secure against further rebellion. Hérault de Séchelles, of the Committee, explained to him, "We can become humane when we are certain of victory."[68] Carrier was inspired. In a moment of ecological enthusiasm he declared that France could not feed its rapidly growing population, and that it would be desirable to cure the excess by cutting down all nobles, priests, merchants, and magistrates. At Nantes he objected to trial as a waste of time; all these suspects (he commanded the judge) "must be eliminated in a couple of hours, or I will have you and your colleagues shot."[69] Since the prisons at Nantes were crowded almost to asphyxiation by those arrested and condemned, and there was a shortage of food, he ordered his aides to fill barges, rafts, and other craft with fifteen hundred men, women and children—giving priority to priests—and to have these vessels scuttled in the Loire. By this and other means he disposed of four thousand undesirables in four months.[70] He justified himself by what seemed to him the laws of war; the Vendéans were in revolt, and every one of them would remain an enemy of the Revolution till death. "We will make France a graveyard," he vowed, "rather than not regenerate it in our own way."[71] The Committee had to restrain his fervor by threatening to arrest him. He was not frightened; in any case, he said, "we shall all be guillotined, one after another." In November, 1794, he was summoned before the Revolutionary Tribunal, and on December 16 he illustrated his prophecy.

Stanislas Fréron (son of Voltaire's favorite enemy) and other agents of the Committee rouged the Rhone and the Var with the blood of the unconverted: 120 at Marseilles, 282 at Toulon, 332 at Orange.[72] By contrast Georges Couthon was the quality of mercy on his mission to gather recruits for the Army in the department of Puy-de-Dôme. At Clermont-Ferrand he reorganized the industries into concentration on the production of matériel for the new regiments. When the citizens saw that he wielded his authority with justice and humanity they became so fond of him that they took turns in carrying him in his chair. During his mission not one person was executed by "revolutionary justice."[73]

Joseph Fouché, once a professor of Latin and physics, was now thirty-four years old, not yet Balzac's "ablest man I've ever met."[74] He seemed made for intrigue: lean, angular, tight-lipped, sharp of eye and nose, sober, secret, silent, tough; he was to rival Talleyrand in rapid transformations and devious survivals. To outward observances he was a dutiful family man, as modest in his habits as he was bold in his ideas. In 1792 he was elected to the Convention from Nantes. At first he sat and voted with the Gironde; then, foreseeing its fall and the supremacy of Paris, he moved up to the Mountain and issued a pamphlet calling upon the Revolution to pass from its bourgeois to a proletarian phase. To advance the war, he argued, the government should "take everything beyond what a citizen needs; for superfluity is an obvious and gratuitous violation of the rights of the people." All gold and silver should be confiscated until the war ended. "We shall be harsh in the fullness of the authority delegated to us. The time for half-measures . . . is over. . . . Help us to strike hard blows."[75] As representative on mission in the department of Loire Inférieure, and especially in Nevers and Moulins, Fouché opened war on private property. By requisitioning money, precious metal, weapons, clothing, and food, he was able to equip the ten thousand recruits whom he had enlisted. He ransacked the churches of their gold and silver monstrances, vessels, candelabra, and sent these to the Convention. The Committee found it unprofitable to check his ardor, and judged him just the man to help Collot d'Herbois in restoring Lyons to the revolutionary faith.

Lyons was almost the capital of French capitalism. Among its 130,000 souls were financiers with connections all over France, merchants having outlets all over Europe, captains of industry controlling a hundred factories, and a large body of proletaires who heard with envy how their own class in Paris had almost captured the government. At the beginning of 1793, under the leadership of the ex-priest Marie-Joseph Chalier, they achieved a similar victory. But religion proved stronger than class. At least half the workers were still Catholic, and resented the anti-Christian turn of Jacobin policy; when the bourgeoisie mobilized its diverse forces against the proletarian dictatorship, the workers divided, and a coalition of businessmen, royalists, and Girondins expelled the radical government and put to death Chalier and two hundred of his followers (July 16, 1793). Thousands of workingmen left the city, settled in the environs, and waited for the next turn of the Revolutionary screw.

The Committee of Public Safety sent an army to overthrow the victorious capitalists. Couthon, legless, came from Clermont to lead it; on October 9 it forced its way in, and reestablished Jacobin rule. Couthon thought a policy of mercy advisable in a city whose population so largely depended upon continued operation of the factories and the shops, but the Paris Committee thought otherwise. On October 12 it put through the Convention, and sent to Couthon, a directive composed by Robespierre in a fury of revenge for Chalier and the two hundred executed radicals. It read in part: "The city of Lyons shall be destroyed. Every habitation of the rich shall be demolished. . . . The name of Lyons shall be effaced from the list of the Republic's cities. The collection of houses left standing shall henceforth bear the name of Ville Affranchisée [the Liberated City]. On the ruins of Lyons shall be raised a column attesting to posterity the crimes and the punishment of the royalists."[76]

Couthon did not relish the operation here assigned him. He condemned one of the more expensive dwellings to demolition, and then was borne off to more congenial labors at Clermont-Ferrand. He was replaced at Lyons (November 4) by Collot d'Herbois, who was soon joined by Fouché. They began with a mock-religious ceremony in commemoration of Chalier as the "savior-god who had died for the people"; leading the procession was a donkey garbed as a bishop bearing a miter on his head and dragging a crucifix and a Bible on his tail; in a public square the martyr was honored by eulogies, and a bonfire was made of the Bible, a missal, sacramental wafers, and wooden images of sundry saints.[77] For the revolutionary purification of Lyons Collot and Fouché created a "Temporary Commission" of twenty members, and a tribunal of seven to try suspects. The commission issued a declaration of principles which has been called "the first communist manifesto" of modern times.[78] It proposed to ally the Revolution with the "immense class of the poor"; it denounced nobility and bourgeoisie, and told the workers: "You have been oppressed; you must crush your oppressors!" All products of French soil belonged to France; all private wealth must be put at the service of the Republic; and as a first step toward social justice a tax of thirty thousand livres must be taken from anyone having an income of ten thousand per year. Large sums were raised by jailing nobles, priests, and others, and confiscating their property.

This declaration was not well received by the people of Lyons, a considerable minority of whom had risen into the middle class. On November 10 a petition signed by ten thousand women recommended mercy for the thousands of men and women who had been crowded into the jails. The commissioners replied sternly, "Shut yourselves up in the privacy of your household tasks. . . . Let us see no more of the tears that dishonor you."[79] On December 4, perhaps to make matters clear, sixty prisoners, condemned by the new tribunal, were marched out to an open space across the Rhone, were stationed between two trenches, and were buried by successive *mitraillades*—showers of slugs or grapeshot from a row of cannon. On the next day, at the same spot, 209 prisoners, tied together, were mowed down by a similar *mitraillade;* and on December 7 two hundred more. Thereafter the slaughter proceeded more leisurely by guillotine, yet so rapidly that the stench of the dead began to poison the city air. By March, 1794, the executions in Lyons had reached 1,667—two thirds of them of the middle or upper class.[80] Hundreds of expensive homes were laboriously destroyed.[81]

On December 20, 1793, a deputation of citizens from Lyons appeared before the Convention to ask for an end to the vengeance; but Collot had beaten them to Paris, and successfully defended his policy. Fouché, left in charge of Lyons, continued the Terror. Learning that Toulon had been recaptured, he wrote to Collot: "We have only one way of celebrating victory. This evening we send 213 rebels under the fire of the lightning bolt."[82] On April 3, 1794, Fouché was recalled to give an account of himself before the Convention. He escaped punishment, but never forgave Robespierre for accusing him of barbarity; someday he would take his revenge.

The Committee of Public Safety slowly recognized that the provincial Terror had been carried to a costly excess. In this matter Robespierre was a moderating influence; he took the lead in recalling Carrier, Fréron, Tallien, and requiring an accounting of their operations. The provincial Terror ended in May, 1794, while it was being intensified in Paris. By the time Robespierre himself had become its victim (July 27–28, 1794) it had taken 2,700 lives in Paris, 18,000 in France;[83] other guessers raise the total to 40,000.[84] Those jailed as suspects amounted to some 300,000. As the property of the executed reverted to the state, it was a profitable Terror.

3. The War Against Religion

Now the deepest division was between those who treasured religious faith as their final support in a world otherwise unintelligible, meaningless, and tragic and those who had come to think of religion as a managed and costly superstition blocking the road to reason and liberty. This division was deepest in the Vendée—coastal France between the Loire and La Rochelle— where the dour weather, the rocky, arid soil, the repetitious trajectory of births and deaths, left the population almost immune to the wit of Voltaire and the winds of the Enlightenment. Townsmen and peasants accepted the Revolution; but when the Constituent Assembly promulgated the Civil Constitution of the Clergy—confiscating the property of the Church, making all priests the employees of the state, and requiring them to swear fidelity to the regime that had shorn them—the peasants supported their priests in refusing assent. The call to their youth to volunteer, or be conscripted, for the Army set fire to the revolt; why should these boys gives their lives to protect an infidel government rather than their priests and altars and household gods?

So, on March 4, 1793, rioting broke out in the Vendée; nine days later it had spread throughout the region; by May 1 there were thirty thousand rebels under arms. Several royalist nobles joined the rural leaders in turning these recruits into disciplined troops; before the Convention realized their strength they had taken Thouars, Fontenay, Saumur, Angers. In August the Committee of Public Safety sent into the Vendée an army under General Kléber, with instructions to destroy the peasant forces and devastate all regions supporting them. Kléber defeated the Catholic army at Cholet on October 17, and crushed it at Savenay on December 23. Military commissions from Paris were set up in Angers, Nantes, Rennes, and Tours, with orders to put to death any Vendéan bearing arms; at or near Angers 463 men were shot in twenty days. Before the Vendéans were subdued by Marshal Hoche (July, 1796), half a million lives had been lost in this new religious war.

In Paris much of the population had become indifferent to religion. In this regard there had been a frail accord between the Mountain and the Gironde; they had joined in reducing the power of the clergy, and in establishing a pagan calendar. They had encouraged the marriage of priests, even to decreeing deportation for any bishop who had tried to prevent it. Under protection of the Revolution some two thousand priests and five hundred nuns took mates.[85]

The Committee's representatives on mission usually made de-Christianization a special element in their procedure. One ordered a priest imprisoned until he married. At Nevers, Fouché issued rigorous rules for the clergy: they must marry, must live simply like the Apostles, must not wear clerical dress, or perform religious ceremonies, outside their churches; Christian funeral services were abolished, and cemeteries must display an inscription telling the public that "death is an eternal sleep." He prevailed upon an archbishop and thirty priests to throw away their cowls and don the red cap of revolution. In Moulins he rode at the head of a procession in which he smashed all crosses, crucifixes, and religious images en route.[86] In Clermont-Ferrand Couthon proclaimed that the religion of Christ had been turned into a financial imposture. By hiring a physician to make tests before the public, he showed that the "blood of Christ" in a miracle-producing phial was merely colored turpentine. He ended the state payment of priests, confiscated the gold and silver vessels of the churches, and announced that churches that could not be transformed into schools might with his approval be torn down to build houses for the poor. He proclaimed a new theology in which Nature would be God, and heaven would be an earthly utopia in which all men would be good.[87]

The leaders of the campaign against Christianity were Hébert of the Paris City Council and Chaumette of the Paris Commune. Warmed by Chaumette's oratory and Hébert's journalism, a crowd of sansculottes invaded the Abbey of St.-Denis on October 16, 1793, emptied the coffins of French royalty there entombed, and melted the metal for use in the war. On November 6 the Convention accorded the communes of France the right to officially renounce the Christian Church. On November 10 men and women from the working-class quarters and the ideological haunts of Paris paraded through the streets in mock religious dress and procession; they entered the hall of the Convention and prevailed upon the deputies to pledge attendance at that evening's fete in the Cathedral of Notre-Dame—renamed the Temple of Reason. There a new sanctuary had been arranged, in which Mlle. Candeille of the Opéra, robed in a tricolor flag and crowned with a red cap, stood as the Goddess of Liberty, attended by persuasive ladies who sang a "Hymn to Liberty" composed for the occasion by Marie-Joseph de Chénier. The worshipers danced and sang in the naves, while in the side chapels, said hostile reporters, profiteers of freedom celebrated the rites of love.[88] On November 17 Jean-Baptiste Gobel, bishop of Paris, yielding to popular demand, appeared before the Convention, abjured his office, handed over to the president his episcopal crozier and ring, and donned the red cap of freedom.[89] On November 23 the Commune ordered all Christian churches in Paris closed.[90]

The Convention, on second thought, wondered had it not overplayed its anti-Christian hand. The deputies were nearly all agnostics, pantheists, or atheists, but several of them questioned the wisdom of infuriating sincere Catholics, who were still in the majority, and many of them ready to take up arms against the Revolution. Some, like Robespierre and Carnot, felt that religion was the only force that could prevent repeated social upheavals against inequalities too deeply rooted in nature to be removed by legislation. Robespierre believed that Catholicism was an organized exploitation of superstition,[91] but he rejected atheism as an immodest assumption of impossible knowledge. On May 8, 1793, he had condemned the *philosophes* as hypocrites who scorned the commonalty and angled for pensions from kings. On November 21, at the height of the de-Christianizing festivities, he told the Convention:

> Every philosopher and every individual may adopt whatever opinion he pleases about atheism. Anyone who wishes to make such an opinion a crime is absurd, but the public man or the legislator who should adopt such a system would be a hundred times more foolish still. . . .
> Atheism is aristocratic. The idea of a great Being who watches over oppressed innocence and punishes triumphant crime is essentially the idea of the people. This is the sentiment of Europe and the world; it is the sentiment of

the French people. That notion is attached neither to priests nor to superstition nor to ceremonies; it is attached only to the idea of an incomprehensible
Power, the terror of wrongdoers, the stay and comfort of virtue.[92]

Danton here agreed with Robespierre: "We never intended to annihilate
the reign of superstition in order to set up the reign of atheism. . . . I demand
that there be an end of those antireligious masquerades in the Convention."[93]

On December 6, 1793, the Convention reaffirmed freedom of worship,
and guaranteed the protection of religious ceremonies conducted by loyal
priests. Hébert protested that he too rejected atheism, but he joined the
forces that aimed to reduce Robespierre's popularity. Robespierre saw him
now as a major enemy, and waited for a chance to destroy him.*

4. The Revolution Eats Its Children

Hébert's strength lay in the sansculottes, who might be marshaled through
the sections and the radical press to invade the Convention and restore the
rule of Paris over France. Robespierre's strength, formerly based in the
Parisian populace, now lay in the Committee of Public Safety, which dominated the Convention through superior facilities for information, decision,
and action.

In November, 1793, the Committee was at the peak of its repute, partly
because of the successful levy en masse, but especially because of military
triumphs on several fronts. The new generals—Jourdan, Kellermann, Kléber,
Hoche, Pichegru—were sons of the Revolution, untrammeled by old rules
and tactics or faded loyalties; they had under their command a million
men still inadequately armed and trained but roused to valor by the thought
of what might happen to them and their families if the enemy should break
through the French lines. They were checked at Kaiserslautern, but they
recovered and took Landau and Speyer. They drove the Spaniards back
over the Pyrenees. And, with the help of the young Napoleon, they recaptured Toulon.

Since August 26 a motley force of English, Spanish, and Neapolitan
troops, protected by an Anglo-Spanish fleet and abetted by local conservatives, had held that port and arsenal, strategically located on the Mediterranean. For three months a revolutionary army had laid siege to it, to no
avail. A promontory, Cap l'Aiguillette, divided the harbor and overlooked
the arsenal; to gain that point would be to command the situation; but the
British had blocked the land approach to the cape with a fort so strongly
armed that they called it Little Gibraltar. Bonaparte, aged twenty-four, saw
at once that if the hostile squadron could be forced to leave the harbor, the

---

* Cf. John Morley, writing *c.* 1880: "The struggle between Hébert, Chaumette, and the
Common Council of Paris on the one part, and the Committee of Public Safety and Robespierre on the other, was the concrete form of the deepest controversy that lies before modern society: can the social union subsist without a belief in a Supreme Being? Chaumette
answered Yes, and Robespierre answered No . . . Robespierre followed Rousseau, . . . Chaumette followed Diderot."[94]

occupying garrison, losing supplies from the sea, would have to abandon the town. By resolute and risky reconnoitering he found, in the jungle, a place from which his artillery could with some safety bombard the bastion. When his cannon had demolished its walls a battalion of French troops stormed the fort, slew its defenders, captured or replaced its guns. These were brought into action upon the enemy fleet; Lord Hood ordered the garrison to abandon the city, and his ships to depart; and on December 19, 1793, the French Army restored Toulon to France. Augustin Robespierre, the local representative of the Committee, wrote to his brother praising the "transcendent merit" of the young artillery captain. A new epic began.

These victories, and those of Kléber in the Vendée, freed the Committee to deal with internal problems. There was an allegedly "foreign plot" to assassinate the revolutionary leaders, but no convincing evidence was found. Corruption was spreading in the production and delivery of army supplies; "in the Army of the South there are thirty thousand pairs of breeches wanting—a most scandalous want."[95] Speculation was helping market manipulation to run up the prices of goods. A governmental maximum had been set for the prices of important products, but producers complained that they could not keep to these prices if wages were not similarly controlled. Inflation was checked for a time, but peasants, manufacturers, and merchants cut down production, and unemployment increased while prices rose. As supplies ran low, housewives had to stand in one line after another for bread, milk, meat, butter, oil, soap, candles, and wood. Queues formed as early as midnight; men and women lay in doorways or on the pavement while waiting for the shop to open and the procession to move. Here and there hungry prostitutes offered their wares along the line.[96] In many cases strong-arm groups invaded the stores and marched away with the goods. Municipal services broke down; crime flourished; police were scarce; uncollected refuse strewed and fouled the streets. Like conditions harassed Rouen, Lyons, Marseilles, Bordeaux . . .

Arguing that the Committee had mismanaged the economy, and that profiteers had seized the ship of state, the sansculottes of Paris, who had been the mainstay of Robespierre, transferred their support to Hébert and Chaumette, and listened avidly to proposals for the nationalization of all property, all wealth, or at least all land. One section leader proposed to cure economic distress by putting all rich people to death.[97] By 1794 it was a common complaint, among workingmen, that the bourgeoisie had walked off with the Revolution.

Toward the end of '93 new challenges to the Committee came from a powerful revolutionary leader and a brilliant journalist. Despite the pretended ferocity of Danton there was in him an amiable streak that winced at the execution of the Queen and the violence of the Terror. On his return from Arcis he judged that the expulsion of invaders from the soil of France and the execution of the most active enemies of the Revolution left little reason for continued terror or war. When Britain offered peace he advised acceptance. Robespierre refused, and intensified the Terror on the ground that the government was still beset by disloyalty, conspiracy, and corruption. Camille Desmoulins, once secretary to Danton, long his admiring friend, and, like him, enjoying a happy marriage, made his journal, *Le Vieux Cordelier*, the mouthpiece of the "Indulgents," or pacifiers, and called for an end to the Terror.

> Liberty is no nymph of the opera, nor a red cap, nor a dirty shirt and rags. Liberty is happiness, reason, equality, justice, the Declaration of Rights, your sublime Constitution [still hibernating].
>
> Would you have me recognize this liberty, have me fall at her feet, and shed all my blood for her? Then open the prison doors to the 200,000 citizens whom you call suspects. . . . Do not think that such a measure would be fatal to the public. It would, on the contrary, be the most revolutionary that you could adopt. You would exterminate all your enemies by the guillotine? But was there ever greater madness? Can you destroy one enemy on the scaffold without making two others among his family and friends?
>
> I am of a very different opinion from those who claim that it is necessary to leave the Terror the order of the day. I am confident that liberty will be assured, and Europe conquered, as soon as you have a Committee of Clemency.[98]

Robespierre, heretofore friendly to Desmoulins, was alarmed by this appeal to open the prisons. Those aristocrats, priests, speculators, and swelling bourgeois—would they not, if released, resume all the more confidently their schemes to exploit or destroy the Republic? He was convinced that the fear of arrest, speedy condemnation, and a ghastly death was the only force that would keep the enemies of the Revolution from plotting its fall. He suspected that Danton's sudden quality of mercy was a ruse to save from the guillotine some associates lately arrested for malfeasance, and to protect Danton himself from exposure of his relations with these men. Some of them—Fabre d'Églantine and François Chabot—were tried on January 17, 1794, and were found guilty. Robespierre concluded that Danton and Desmoulins were bent on unseating and putting an end to the Committee. He concluded that he would never be safe as long as these old friends of his were alive.

He kept his foes disunited, and played their opposed factions against each other; he encouraged the attacks of Danton and Desmoulins upon Hébert, and welcomed their aid in opposing the war against religion. Hébert countered by supporting the riots of townspeople against the cost and scarcity of food; he condemned both the government and the Indulgents; on March 4, 1794, he denounced Robespierre by name, and on March 11 his followers at the Cordeliers Club openly threatened insurrection. A majority of the Committee agreed with Robespierre that the time had come to act. Hébert, Cloots, and several others were arrested, and were tried on a charge of malfeasance in the distribution of provisions to the people. It was a subtle accusation, for it left the sansculottes doubtful of their new leaders; and before they could decide upon revolt the men were condemned, and were quickly led to the guillotine (March 24). Hébert broke down and wept; Cloots, Teutonically calm as he waited for his turn to die, called to the crowd, "My friends, don't confuse me with these rascals."[99]

Danton must have realized that he had been used as a tool against Hébert, and was now of little value to the Committee. Even so he continued to alienate the Committee by advocating mercy and peace—policies requiring the members to repudiate the Terror that had preserved them and the war that had excused their dictatorship. He urged an end to the killing; "Let us," he said, "leave something to the guillotine of opinion." He still planned educational projects and judiciary reforms. And he remained defiant. Someone told him that Robespierre was planning his arrest; "If I thought he had even the idea of it," he answered, "I would eat his heart out."[100] In the almost "state of nature" to which the Terror had reduced France many men felt that they had to eat or be eaten. His friends urged him to take the initiative and attack the Committee before the Convention. But he was too tired in nerve and will to follow his own historic summons to audacity; he was exhausted by breasting, through four years, the waves of the Revolution, and now he let the undertow carry him away unresisting. "I would rather be guillotined than guillotine others," he said (it had not always been so); "and, besides, I am sick of the human race."[101]

It was apparently Billaud-Varenne who took the initiative in recommending death for Danton. Many members of the Committee agreed with him that to allow the campaign of the Indulgents to go on was to surrender the Revolution to its enemies at home and abroad. Robespierre was for a time reluctant to conclude that the life of Danton should be summarily shortened. He shared with the other members of the Committee the belief that Danton had allowed some moneys of the state to stick to his fingers, but he recognized the services that Danton had rendered to the Revolution, and he feared that a sentence of death for one of its greatest figures would lead to insurrection in the sections and the National Guard.

During this period of Robespierre's hesitation Danton visited him two or three times, not only to defend his financial record but to convert the somber patriot to the policy of ending the Terror and seeking peace. Robespierre remained unconvinced, and grew more hostile. He helped Saint-Just (whom Danton had often ridiculed) to prepare the case against his greatest rival. On March 30 he joined the Committee of Public Safety and the Committee of General Security in their united resolve to secure from the Revolutionary Tribunal a sentence of death for Danton, Desmoulins, and twelve men lately convicted of embezzlement. A friend of "the Titan" rushed the news to him and urged him to leave Paris and hide himself in the provinces. He refused. The next morning the police arrested him and Desmoulins, who lived on the floor above him. Imprisoned in the Conciergerie, he remarked, "On a day like this I organized the Revolutionary Tribunal. . . . I ask pardon for it of God and man. . . . In revolutions authority remains with the greatest scoundrels."[102]

On April 1, Louis Legendre, recently a representative on mission, proposed to the deputies that Danton be sent for from prison and allowed to defend himself before the Convention. Robespierre stopped him with an ominous glare. "Danton," he cried, "is not privileged. . . . We shall see this day whether the Convention will be able to destroy a pretended idol long since rotted away."[103] Then Saint-Just read the bill of charges that he had prepared. The deputies, each mindful of his own safety, ordered that Danton and Desmoulins be brought immediately to trial.

On April 2 they were led before the Tribunal. Perhaps to confuse the issues, they were made part of a batch of men including Fabre d'Églantine, other "conspirators" or embezzlers, and—to the general surprise as well as his own—Hérault de Séchelles, suave member of the Committee, now accused of association with the Hébertists and the foreign plot. Danton defended himself with force and satirical wit, which made such an impression on the jury and spectators[104] that Fouquier-Tinville dispatched an appeal to the Committee for a decree that would silence the defense. The Committee obliged by sending to the Convention a charge that the followers of Danton and Desmoulins were, with their knowledge, plotting to rescue them by force; on this basis the Convention declared the two men to be outlaws—which meant that, being "outside the (protection of the) law," they might now be killed without due process of law. On receiving this decree the jurymen announced that they had received sufficient testimony, and were ready to render a verdict. The prisoners were returned to their cells; the spectators were dismissed. On April 5 the unanimous verdict was announced: death for all the accused. Hearing it, Danton predicted, "Before these months are out the people will tear my enemies to pieces."[105] And again: "Vile Robespierre! The scaffold claims you too. You will follow me."[106] From his cell Desmoulins wrote to his wife: "My beloved Lucile! I was born to make verses and to defend the unfortunate. . . . My darling, care for your little one; live for my Horace; speak to him of me. . . . My bound hands embrace you."[107]

On the afternoon of April 5 the condemned men were carted to the Place de la Révolution. En route Danton prophesied again: "I leave it all in a frightful welter. Not a man of them has an idea of government. Robespierre will follow me; he is dragged down by me. Ah, better be a poor fisherman than meddle with the governing of men."[108] On the scaffold Desmoulins, near the breaking point of his nerves, was third in the line to death, Danton was the last. He too thought of his young wife, and murmured some words for her, then caught himself: "Come, Danton, no weakness." As he approached the knife he told the executioner, "Show my head to the people; it is worth it."[109] He was thirty-four years old, Desmoulins too; but they had lived many lives since that July day when Camille called upon the Parisians to take the Bastille. Eight days after their death Lucile Desmoulins, along with Hébert's widow and Chaumette, followed them to the guillotine.

The slate seemed clear; all the groups that had challenged the Committee of Public Safety had been eliminated or suppressed. The Girondins were dead or dispersed; the sansculottes had been divided and silenced; the clubs —excepting the Jacobin—had been closed; the press and the theater were under strict censorship; the Convention, cowed, left all major decisions to the Committee. Under that tutelage, and instructed by its other committees, the Convention passed laws against hoarders and speculators, proclaimed free, universal primary education, abolished slavery in the French colonies, and established a welfare state with social security, unemployment benefits, medical aid for the poor, and relief for the old. These measures were in large part frustrated by war and chaos, but they remained as ideas to inspire succeeding generations.

Robespierre, his hands incarnadined but free, now attended to restoring God to France. The attempt to replace Christianity with rationalism was turning the country against the Revolution. In Paris the Catholics were rebelling against the closing of the churches and the harassment of priests; more and more of the lower and middle classes were going to Sunday Mass. In one of his eloquent addresses (May 7, 1794) Robespierre argued that the time had come to reunite the Revolution with its spiritual progenitor Rousseau (whose remains had been transferred to the Panthéon on April 14); the state should support a pure and simple religion—essentially that of the Savoyard Vicar in *Émile*—based upon belief in God and an afterlife, and preaching civic and social virtue as the necessary foundation of a republic. The Convention agreed, hoping that this move would appease the pious and mitigate the Terror; and on June 4 it made Robespierre its president.

In this official capacity, on June 8, 1794, he presided over a "Feast of the Supreme Being," before 100,000 men, women, and children assembled in the Champ-de-Mars. At the head of a long procession of skeptical deputies the Incorruptible walked with flowers and wheat ears in his hand, to the accompaniment of music and choral song. A great car drawn by milk-white oxen carried sheaves of golden corn; behind it came shepherds and shepherdesses representing Nature (in her fairer moods) as one form and voice of God. On one of the basins that adorned the Field of Mars, David, the leading French artist of the age, had carved in wood a statue of Atheism supported by sculptured vices and crowned with Madness; over against these he had raised a figure of Wisdom triumphant over all. Robespierre, embodiment of virtue, applied a torch to Atheism, but an ill wind diverted the blaze to Wisdom. A magnanimous overall inscription announced: "The French people recognizes the Supreme Being, and the immortality of the soul."[110] Similar ceremonies were held throughout France. Robespierre was happy, but Billaud-Varenne told him, "You begin to bore me with your Supreme Being."

Two days later Robespierre induced the Convention to decree an astonishing reinforcement of the Terror; it was as if he was answering and defying Danton as, with the Feast, he had rebuked Hébert. The Law of 22 Prairial (June 10, 1794) established the death penalty for advocating monarchy or calumniating the republic; for outraging morality; for giving out false news; for stealing public property; for profiteering or embezzling; for impeding the transport of food; for interfering in any way with the prosecution of the war. Furthermore the decree empowered the courts to decide whether the accused should be allowed counsel, what witnesses should be heard, when the taking of evidence should end.[111] "As for myself," said one juryman, "I am always convinced. In a revolution all who appear before this Tribunal ought to be condemned."[112]

Some excuses were given for this intensification of the Terror. On May 22 an attempt had been made on the life of Collot d'Herbois; on May 23 a young man was intercepted in an apparent attempt to assassinate Robespierre. Belief in a foreign plot to kill the leaders of the Revolution led the Convention to decree that no quarter should be given to British or Hanoverian prisoners of war. The prisons of Paris held some eight thousand suspects who might revolt and escape; they had to be immobilized by fear.

So began the especially "Great Terror," lasting from June 10 to July 27, 1794. In not quite seven weeks 1,376 men and women were guillotined—155 more than in the sixty-one weeks between March, 1793, and June 10, 1794.[113] Fouquier-Tinville remarked that heads were falling "like slates from a roof."[114] The people no longer went to executions, these had become so common; rather they stayed home, and watched every word they spoke. Social life nearly ceased; the taverns and brothels were almost empty. The Convention itself was reduced to a skeleton; out of its original 750 deputies only 117 now attended, and many of these abstained from voting lest they compromise themselves. Even Committee members lived in fear that they would fall under the axe of the new triumvirate—Robespierre, Couthon, and Saint-Just.

Probably it was the war that led powerful individuals to submit to so irritating a concentration of authority. In April, 1794, the Prince of Saxe-Coburg had led another army into France, and any defeat of the French defenders could lead to a chaos of fear in Paris. The British blockade was trying to keep American provisions from France, and only the defeat of a British fleet by a French convoy (June 1) enabled precious cargoes to reach Brest. Then a French army threw back the invaders near Charleroi (June 25), and a day later Saint-Just led a French force to a decisive victory at Fleurus. Coburg withdrew from France, and on July 27 Jourdan and Pichegru crossed the frontier to establish French authority in Antwerp and Liège.

This triumphant repulse of the princely incursion may have shared in destroying Robespierre; his multiplying enemies could feel that the country and the Army would survive the shock of an open conflict to the death at the heart of the government. The Committee of General Security was at odds with that of Public Safety over the policing power, and within the latter body Billaud-Varenne, Collot d'Herbois, and Carnot were in rising revolt against Robespierre and Saint-Just. Feeling their hostility, Robespierre avoided Committee meetings between July 1 and 23, hoping that this would cool their resentment of his leadership; but it gave them more opportunity to plan his fall. Moreover, his strategy faltered: on July 23 he made enemies of former supporters by yielding to the plaints of businessmen and signing a decree establishing maximum wages for labor; in effect, because of depreciated currency, the decree lowered some wages to half of what they had been before.[115]

It was the terrorists returned from the provinces—Fouché, Fréron, Tal-

lien, Carrier—who decided that their lives depended on the elimination of
Robespierre. It was he who had recalled them to Paris and had demanded of
them an account of their missions. "Come, tell us, Fouché," he asked, "who
deputed you to tell the people that there is no God?"[116] At the Jacobin
Club he proposed that Fouché submit to interrogation about his operations
in Toulon and Lyons, or be struck from membership. Fouché refused to
submit to such an examination, and retaliated by circulating a list of men
who, he claimed, were among Robespierre's new candidates for the guillotine. As for Tallien, he needed no such instigation; his charming mistress,
Thérésa Cabarrus, had been arrested on May 22, allegedly on Robespierre's
orders; rumor said she had sent Tallien a dagger. Tallien swore to free her
at whatever cost.

On July 26 Robespierre made his last speech before the Convention. The
deputies were hostile, for many of them had reacted against the hasty execution of Danton, and many more blamed Robespierre for having reduced the
Convention to impotence. He tried to answer these charges:

> Citizens: . . . I need to open my heart, and you need to hear the truth. . . .
> I have come here to dispel cruel errors. I have come to stifle the horrible oaths
> of discord with which certain men want to fill this temple of liberty. . . .
> What foundation is there for this odious system of terror and slander? To
> whom must we show ourselves terrible? . . . Is it tyrants and rascals who fear
> us, or men of good will and patriots? . . . Do we strike terror into the National
> Convention? But what are we without the National Convention?—we who
> have defended the Convention at the peril of our lives, who have devoted our-
> selves to its preservation while detestable factions plot its ruin for all men to
> see? . . . For whom were the first blows of the conspirators intended? . . . It
> is we whom they seek to assassinate, it is we whom they call the scourge of
> France. . . . Some time ago they declared war on certain members of the Com-
> mittee of Public Safety. Finally they seemed to aim at destroying one man. . . .
> They call me tyrant. . . . They were particularly anxious to prove that the
> Revolutionary Tribunal was a tribunal of blood, created by me alone, and
> which I dominate absolutely for the purpose of beheading all men of good
> will. . . .
> I dare not name [these accusers] here and now. I cannot bring myself to
> tear away completely the veil that covers this profound mystery of crimes.
> But this I affirm positively: that among the authors of this plot are the agents
> of that system of venality intended by foreigners to destroy the Republic. . . .
> The traitors, hidden here under false exteriors, will accuse their accusers, and
> will multiply all stratagems . . . to stifle the truth. Such is part of the con-
> spiracy.
> I will conclude that . . . tyranny reigns among us; but not that I must keep
> silence. How can one reproach a man who has truth on his side, and who
> knows how to die for his country?[117]

There were some blunders in this historic speech—surprisingly many for
one who had heretofore picked his way with caution amid the pitfalls of
politics; power dements even more than it corrupts, lowering the guard of
foresight and raising the haste of action. The tone of the speech—the proud
presumption not only of innocence but of "a man who has the truth on his
side"—could be judicious only in a Socrates already half inclined to death.

It was hardly wise to incite and infuriate his enemies by threatening them with exposure—that is, with death. It was unwise to affirm that the Convention was free from fear of the Terror, when it knew that it was not. Worst of all, by refusing to name the men he proposed to indict, he multiplied those deputies who might consider themselves future victims of his wrath. The Convention received his appeal coldly, and defeated a motion to print it. Robespierre repeated the speech that evening at the Jacobin Club, to great applause; and there he added an open attack upon Billaud-Varenne and Collot d'Herbois, who were present. They went from the club to the rooms of the Committee, where they found Saint-Just writing what he too boldly told them was to be their indictment.[118]

The next morning, July 27 (the 9th of Thermidor), Saint-Just rose to present that indictment to a Convention dark with hostility and tense with fear. Robespierre sat directly before the rostrum. His devoted host, Duplay, had warned him to expect trouble, but Robespierre had confidently reassured the soothsayer, "The Convention is in the main honest; all large masses of men are honest."[119] Unluckily the presiding officer on that day was one of his sworn foes—Collot d'Herbois. When Saint-Just began to read his bill of accusation, Tallien, expecting to be included, sprang to the platform, pushed the young orator aside, and cried out, "I ask that the curtain be torn away!" Joseph Lebas, loyal to Saint-Just, tried to come to his aid, but his words were drowned out by a hundred voices. Robespierre demanded a chance to be heard, but he too was shouted down. Tallien raised aloft the weapon that had been sent him, and declared, "I have armed myself with a dagger, which shall pierce his breast if the Convention has not the courage to decree his accusation."[120]

Collot yielded the chair to Thuriot, who had been an ally of Danton. Robespierre approached the podium shouting; Thuriot's bell outrang most of Robespierre's words, but some of them surmounted the tumult: "For the last time, President of Assassins, will you give me leave to speak?" The Convention roared its disapproval of this form of address, and one deputy uttered the fatal words: "I demand the arrest of Robespierre." Augustin Robespierre spoke up like a Roman: "I am as guilty as my brother; I share his virtues; I ask that my arrest be decreed with his." Lebas begged and received the same privilege. The decree was voted. Police took the two Robespierres, Saint-Just, Lebas, and Couthon, and hurried them to the Luxembourg jail.

Fleuriot-Lescot, then mayor of Paris, ordered the prisoners transferred to the Hôtel de Ville, where he received them as honored guests, and offered them his protection. The heads of the Commune bade Hanriot, head of the National Guard in the capital, to take soldiers and guns to the Tuileries, and hold the Convention captive until it revoked its decree of arrest; but Hanriot was too drunk to carry out his mission. The deputies appointed Paul Barras to raise a force of gendarmes, go to the Hôtel de Ville, and rearrest the prisoners. The mayor again appealed to Hanriot, who, unable to reassemble the Paris National Guard, gathered an impromptu collection of sansculottes instead; but they had now little love for the man who had lowered their wages and killed Hébert and Chaumette, Danton and Desmoulins; besides, rain began to fall, and they melted away to their work or their homes. Barras and his gendarmes easily seized control in the Hôtel de Ville. Seeing them, Robespierre tried suicide, but the shot triggered by his unsteady hand passed through his cheek and only shattered his jaw.[121] Lebas, steadier, blew his own brains out. Augustin Robespierre broke a leg in a useless leap from a window. Couthon, with lifeless legs, was thrown downstairs, and lay there helpless till the gendarmes carried him to jail with the two Robespierres and Saint-Just.

The following afternoon (July 28, 1794) four tumbrils conveyed these four, with Fleuriot, Hanriot (still drunk), and sixteen others to the guillotine in what we now admire as (*pro tempore*) the Place de la Concorde. En route they heard from the onlookers divers cries, among them "Down with the maximum!"[122] They found a fashionable audience awaiting them: windows overlooking the square had been rented at fancy prices; ladies came arrayed as for a festival. When Robespierre's head was held up to the crowd a shout of satisfaction rose. One more death might mean little, but this one, Paris felt, meant that the Terror had come to an end.

VI. THE THERMIDOREANS: JULY 29, 1794 – OCTOBER 26, 1795

On July 29 the victors of the 9th Thermidor sent seventy members of the Paris Commune to death; thereafter the Commune was subject to the Convention. The tyrannical Law of 22 Prairial was revoked (August 1); imprisoned opponents of Robespierre were released; some of his followers took their places.[123] The Revolutionary Tribunal was reformed to allow fair trials; Fouquier-Tinville was called upon to defend his record, but his ingenuity preserved his head till May 7, 1795. The Committees of Public Safety and General Security survived, but their claws were clipped. Conservative periodicals bloomed; radical journals died through lack of public support. Tallien, Fouché, and Fréron found that they could share in the new leadership only by getting the Convention to ignore their roles in the Terror. The Jacobin clubs were closed throughout France (November 12). The long-intimidated deputies of the "Plain" moved to the right; the "Mountain" fell from power; and on December 8 seventy-three surviving Girondin delegates were restored to their seats. The bourgeoisie recaptured the Revolution.

The relaxation of government allowed the revival of religion. Aside from that small minority which had received a college education, and that upper middle class which had been touched by the Enlightenment, most Frenchmen, and nearly all Frenchwomen, preferred the saints and ceremonies of the Catholic calendar to the rootless festivals and formless Supreme Being of Robespierre. On February 15, 1795, a treaty of peace was signed with the

Vendée rebels, guaranteeing them freedom of worship; a week later this was extended to all France; and the government pledged the separation of Church and state.

More difficult was the problem of simultaneously satisfying those perennial enemies: producers and consumers. The producers clamored for repeal of the maximum on prices; consumers demanded an end to the maximum on wages. The Convention, now controlled by enthusiastic believers in freedom of enterprise, competition, and trade, heard the conflicting appeals, and abolished the maxima (December 24, 1794); now the workers were free to seek higher wages, the peasants and merchants were free to charge all that the traffic would bear. Prices rose on the wings of greed. The government issued new assignats as paper money, but their value fell even more rapidly than before: a bushel of flour that had cost the Parisians two assignats in 1790 cost them 225 in 1795; a pair of shoes rose from five to two hundred, a dozen eggs from sixty-seven to 2,500.[124]

On April 1, 1795, several localities in Paris broke out once more in riots over the price of bread. An unarmed crowd invaded the Convention, demanding food and an end to the persecution of radicals; several deputies from the melting Mountain supported them. The Convention promised immediate relief, but it summoned the National Guard to disperse the rioters. That night it decreed the deportation of radical leaders—Billaud-Varenne, Collot d'Herbois, Barère, Vadier—to Guiana. Barère and Vadier evaded arrest; Billaud and Collot were carried off to a hard life in the South American colony. There the two anticlericals fell sick, and were cared for by nuns. Collot succumbed. Billaud survived, took a mulatto slave as a wife, became a contented farmer, and died in Haiti in 1819.[125]

Public protest became violent. Placards appeared calling for insurrection. On May 20 a throng of women and armed men invaded the Convention, crying out for bread, for the liberation of arrested radicals, and finally for the abdication of the government. One deputy was killed by a pistol shot; his severed head, raised on a pike, was presented before the Convention president, Boissy d'Anglas, who gave it a formal salute; then troops and rain drove the petitioners to their homes. On May 22 soldiers under General Pichegru surrounded the working-class Faubourg St.-Antoine and forced the remaining armed rebels to surrender. Eleven Montagnard deputies were arrested, charged with complicity in the uprising; two escaped, four killed themselves, five, dying of self-inflicted wounds, were hurried to the guillotine. A royalist deputy urged the arrest of Carnot; a voice protested, "He organized our victories," and Carnot survived.

Now—May and June, 1795—a "White Terror" raged in which Jacobins were victims and the judges were bourgeois "Moderates" allied with religious bands: "Companies of Jesus," "Companies of Jehu," "Companies of the Sun." At Lyons (May 5) ninety-seven former Terrorists were massacred in prison; at Aix-en-Provence (May 17) thirty more were butchered "with refinements of barbarity"; similar ceremonies took place at Arles, Avignon, and Marseilles. At Tarascon (May 25) two hundred masked men seized the fortress, bound the prisoners, and flung them into the Rhone. At Toulon the workers rose against the new Terror; Isnard, one of the restored Girondins, led troops against them and exterminated them (May 31).[126] The Terror had not ended; it had changed hands.

The victorious bourgeoisie no longer needed proletarian allies, for it had won the support of the generals, and these were winning victories that raised their prestige even with the sansculottes. On January 19, 1795, Pichegru took Amsterdam; Stadtholder William IV fled to England; Holland, for a decade, became the "Batavian Republic" under French tutelage. Other French armies recaptured and held the left bank of the Rhine. The Allies, defeated and quarreling, left France for easier prey in Poland. Prussia, absorbed in preventing Russia from taking everything in the Third Partition (1795), sent emissaries to Paris, then to Basel, to negotiate a separate peace with France. The Convention could afford to be demanding, for it looked with trepidation toward a peace that would bring to Paris or elsewhere thousands of half-brutalized troops who had been living at the expense of conquered lands but would now add to crime, disease, and tumult in cities already crying for work and bread. And the restless generals, swollen with victory—Pichegru, Jourdan, Hoche, Moreau—would they resist the temptation to seize the government through a military *coup d'état?* So the Convention sent to Basel Marquis François de Barthélemy, with instructions to hold out for French possession of the left bank of the Rhine. Prussia protested and yielded; Saxony, Hanover, and Hesse-Cassel followed suit; and on June 22 Spain ceded to France the eastern part (Santo Domingo) of the island of Hispaniola. War with Austria and England continued—just enough to keep French soldiers at the fronts.

On June 27, thirty-six hundred *émigrés,* brought over from Portsmouth in British ships, landed on the promontory of Quiberon in Brittany, and joined up with royalist "Chouan" bands in an effort to revive the Vendée revolt. Hoche in a brilliant campaign defeated them (July 21), and on a motion by Tallien the Convention had 748 captured *émigrés* put to death.

On June 8, 1795, the ten-year-old Dauphin died in prison, not demonstrably the result of ill usage, but probably from scrofula and despondency. The royalists thereupon acknowledged the older of Louis XVI's two surviving brothers, the *émigré* Comte de Provence, as Louis XVIII, and swore to place him on the throne of France. This unreformed Bourbon announced (July 1, 1795) that if restored he would re-establish the Ancien Régime intact, with absolute monarchy and feudal rights. Hence the united support that the French bourgeoisie, peasantry, and sansculottes gave to Napoleon through a dozen wars.

Nevertheless France was weary of revolution, and began to tolerate monarchist sentiments that were appearing in some journals, salons, and prosperous homes: only a king legitimized by heredity and tradition could bring order and security back to a people fearful and unhappy after three years of political and economic disruption, religious division, constant war, and uncertainty of work, food, and life. Half or more of southern France was deeply alienated from Paris and its politicians. In Paris the section assemblies, once dominated by sansculottes, were now increasingly controlled by businessmen, and some of them had been captured by royalists. At the theaters those lines that spoke of the "good old days" before 1789 were openly applauded. Youngsters, constitutionally rebellious, were now rebelling against revolution; they organized themselves in bands called Jeunesse Dorée (Gilded Youth), Merveilleux (Freaks), or Muscadins (Fruits); proud of their rich or bizarre dress, their long or curly hair, they walked the streets wielding dangerous clubs and boldly proclaiming royalist sentiments. It had become so unfashionable to support the revolutionary government that when a premature report went the rounds that the Convention was breaking up, the news was greeted with joy, and some Parisians danced in the streets.

But the Convention took its time dying. In June, 1795, it began to draw up another constitution, far different from the democratic and never practiced Constitution of 1793. Now it adopted a bicameral legislature, in which the consent of an upper chamber of older and experienced deputies would be required for the enactment of any measure adopted by a lower chamber more directly open to popular movements and new ideas. The people, said Boissy d'Anglas, are not wise or stable enough to determine the policy of a state.[127] So this "Constitution of the Year III" (i.e., the year beginning September 22, 1794) revised the Declaration of the Rights of Man (1789) to check popular delusions of virtue and power; it omitted the proposition that "men are born, and remain, free and equal in rights," and explained that equality meant merely that "the law is the same for all men." Election was to be indirect: the voters would choose delegates to the "electoral college" of their department, and these electors would choose the members of the national legislature, the judiciary, and the administrative agencies. Eligibility to the electoral colleges was so limited to owners of property that only thirty thousand Frenchmen chose the national government. Woman suffrage was proposed to the Convention by one deputy, but was disposed of by another deputy's question "Where is the good wife who dares maintain that the wish of her husband is not her own?"[128] State control of the economy was rejected as impractical, as stifling invention and enterprise, and as slowing the growth of national wealth.

This constitution contained some liberal elements: it affirmed religious liberty and, within "safe limits," the freedom of the press (then largely controlled by the middle class).* Furthermore, the ratification of the constitution was to be left to adult male suffrage, with a surprising proviso: two thirds of the deputies to the new assemblies must be members of the existing Convention, and if that number should not be chosen the re-elected members were to fill the two thirds by cooptation of additional present deputies; this, argued the endangered delegates, was necessary for the continuity of experience and policy. The voters were docile: of 958,226 ballots cast, 941,853

---

* The word *liberal*, as applied to economics and politics, meant a free economy under a minimal government.

accepted the constitution; and of 263,131 votes on the two-thirds require-
ment, 167,758 approved.[129] On September 23, 1795, the Convention made
the new constitution the law of France, and prepared to retire in good order.

It could claim some achievements despite its months of disorder and Terror, of subservience to its committees, of frightened purging of its membership at the command of the sansculottes. It had maintained some rule of law
in a city where law had lost its aura and its roots. It had consolidated the
empowerment of the bourgeoisie, but it had tried to control the greed of
merchants sufficiently to keep a turbulent populace just above starvation. It
had organized and trained armies, had raised able and devoted generals, had
repelled a powerful coalition, and had won a peace that left France protected by natural frontiers of the Rhine, the Alps and Pyrenees, and the
seas. Amid all these consuming efforts it had established the metric system, it
had founded or restored the Museum of Natural History, the École Polytechnique, and the School of Medicine; it had inaugurated the Institute of
France. It felt that now, after three years of miraculous survival, it deserved
a peaceful death and two thirds of a resurrection.

But it was to be a bloody death, in the manner of the time. The plutocrats and royalists, who had captured the Lepeletière section of Paris around
the stock exchange, rose in revolt against that legislated rebirth. Other sections, for their own diverse reasons, joined them. Together they improvised
a force of 25,000 men, who advanced to positions that commanded the
Tuileries and therefore the Convention (13 Vendémiaire, October 5, 1795).
The frightened deputies appointed Barras to extemporize a defense. He commissioned the twenty-six-year-old Bonaparte, then idle in Paris, to gather
men, supplies, and, above all, artillery. The hero of Toulon knew where the
cannon were housed, sent Murat and a force to secure them; they were
brought to him, and were placed at points overlooking the advancing insurgents. A command to disperse was broadcast; it was disdained. Napoleon
ordered his artillery to fire; between two and three hundred of the besiegers
fell; the rest fled. The Convention had survived its last ordeal, and Napoleon,
decisive and ruthless, entered upon the most spectacular career in modern
history.

On October 26 the Convention declared itself dissolved, and on November 2, 1795, the final phase of the Revolution began.

CHAPTER V

The Directory

November 2, 1795 – November 9, 1799

I. THE NEW GOVERNMENT

IT was composed of five bodies. First, a Council of Five Hundred (Les Cinq Cents), empowered to propose and discuss measures, but not to make them into laws. Second, a Council of (250) Ancients, or elders (Les Anciens), who had to be married and forty or more years old; they were authorized not to initiate legislation but to reject, or ratify into law, the "resolutions" sent to them by the Five Hundred. These two assemblies, constituting the Legislature (Corps Législatif) were subject to annual replacement of a third of their membership by the vote of the electoral colleges. The executive part of the government was the Directory (Directoire), composed of five members, at least forty years of age, chosen for a five-year term by the Ancients from fifty names submitted by the Five Hundred. Each year one of the directors was to be replaced by the choice of a new member. Independent of these three bodies and of each other were the judiciary and the Treasury, chosen by the electoral colleges of the departments. It was a government of checks and balances, designed for the protection of the victorious bourgeoisie from an unruly populace.

The Directory, lodged in the Luxembourg Palace, soon became the dominant branch of the government. It controlled the Army and Navy and determined foreign policy; it supervised the ministers of the interior, of foreign affairs, of marine and colonies, of war and finance. By the natural centripetal tendency by which power flows to leadership, the Directory became a dictatorship almost as independent as the Committee of Public Safety.

The five men first chosen as directors were Paul Barras, Louis-Marie de Larevellière-Lépaux, Jean-François Rewbell, Charles Letourneur, and Lazare Carnot. All of these had been regicides, four had been Jacobins, one— Barras—had been a viscount; now they adjusted themselves to a bourgeois regime. All were men of ability, but, excepting Carnot, they were not distinguished by scrupulous integrity. If survival is the test of worth, Barras was the most able, serving first Louis XVI, then Robespierre, and helping both of them to their deaths; maneuvering safely through crisis after crisis, through mistress after mistress, gathering wealth and power at every turn, giving Napoleon an army and a wife, outliving them, and dying in easy circumstances in re-Bourbonized Paris at the age of seventy-four (1829);[1] he had nine lives and sold them all.

The problems faced by the Directory in 1795 might by their diverse multitude excuse some failures of their government. The populace of Paris was always facing destitution; the British blockade joined conflicts within the economy to impede the movement of food and goods. Inflation deflated the currency; in 1795 five thousand assignats were needed to buy what a hundred had bought in 1790. As the Treasury paid interest on its bonds in assignats at their face value, the rentiers who had invested in government "securities" as a protection in old age found themselves joining the rebellious poor.[2] Thousands of Frenchmen bought stocks in a wild race to cheat inflation; when values had been swollen to their peak, speculators unloaded their holdings; a wild race to sell collapsed stock prices; the innocent found that their savings had been harvested by the clever few. The Treasury, having forfeited public confidence, repeatedly faced bankruptcy, and declared it in 1795. A loan exacted from the rich resulted in price rises by merchants and the ruin of luxury trades; unemployment rose; war and inflation went on.

Amid the chaos and poverty the communistic dream that had inspired Mably in 1748, Morelly in 1755, Linguet in 1777* continued to warm the hearts of the desperate poor; it had found voice in Jacques Roux in 1793. On April 11, 1796, the working-class quarters of Paris were placarded with posters offering an "Analysis of the Doctrine of Babeuf." Some of its articles:

> 1. Nature has bestowed on every man an equal right to the enjoyment of all goods. . . .
> 3. Nature has imposed on every man the obligation of labor; no one, without crime, can abstain from work. . . .
> 7. In a free society there should be neither rich nor poor.
> 8. The rich who will not part with their superfluity in favor of the indigent are the enemies of the people. . . .
> 10. The purpose of the Revolution is to destroy inequality and to establish the common happiness.
> 11. The Revolution is not at an end, for the rich absorb all goods of every kind, and are in exclusive domination, while the poor labor as actual slaves, . . . and are nothing in the eyes of the state.
> 12. The Constitution of 1793 is the true law of the French. . . . The Convention has shot down the people who demanded its enforcement. . . . The Constitution of 1793 ratified the inalienable right of each citizen to exercise political rights, to assemble, to demand what he believes useful, to educate himself, and not to die of hunger—rights which the counterrevolutionary act [Constitution] of 1795 has completely and openly violated.[3]

François-Émile "Gracchus" Babeuf, born in 1760, first entered recorded history in 1785 as an agent employed by landlords to enforce their feudal rights over the peasantry. In 1789 he changed sides, and drew up for distribution a *cahier* demanding the abolition of feudal dues. In 1794 he settled in Paris, defended and then attacked the Thermidoreans, was arrested, and emerged in 1795 as a fervent communist. Soon he organized the Société des Égaux (Band of Equals). He followed up his "Analysis" with a proclama-

---

* Cf. *Rousseau and Revolution*, 80–84.

tion entitled "Act of Insurrection," signed by the "Insurrectionary Committee of Public Safety." A few articles:

> 10. The Council and the Directory, usurpers of popular authority, will be dissolved. All their members will be immediately judged by the people. . . .
> 18. Public and private property are placed in the custody of the people.
> 19. The duty of terminating the Revolution, and of bestowing upon the Republic liberty, equality, and the Constitution of 1793, will be confided to a national assembly, composed of a democrat from each department, appointed by the insurgent people upon the nomination of the Insurrectionary Committee.
> The Insurrectionary Committee of Public Safety will remain in permanence until the total accomplishment of the Insurrection.[4]

This sounds ominously like a call for another dictatorship, a change of masters from one Robespierre to another. In his journal *Tribune du Peuple*, Babeuf amplified his dream:

> All that is possessed by those who have more than their proportional part in the goods of society is held by theft and usurpation; it is therefore just to take it from them. The man who proves that by his own strength he can earn or do as much as four others is none the less in conspiracy against society, because he destroys the equilibrium and . . . precious equality. Social instruction must progress to the point where they deprive everyone of the hope of ever becoming richer, or more powerful, or more distinguished by his enlightenment and his talents. Discord is better than a horrid concord in which hunger strangles one. Let us go back to chaos, and from chaos let a new regenerated earth emerge.[5]

An *agent provocateur* informed the Directory that an increasing number of Parisian proletaires were reading the placards and journals of Babeuf, and that an armed uprising had been planned for May 11, 1796. On May 10 an order was issued for his arrest and that of his leading associates: Filippo Buonarrotti, A. Darthé, M.-G. Vadier, and J.-B. Drouet. After a year's imprisonment, during which several attempts to free them failed, they were tried at Vendôme on May 27, 1797. Buonarrotti served a prison sentence, Drouet escaped. Babeuf and Darthé, condemned to death, tried suicide, but were hurried to the guillotine before they could die. Their plan, of course, was so impracticable, so innocent of the nature of man, that even the proletariat of Paris had not taken it seriously. Besides, by 1797, poor and rich alike, in France, had found a new hero, the most fascinating dreamer and doer in the political history of mankind.

II. THE YOUNG NAPOLEON: 1769–95

"No intellectual exercise," said Lord Acton, "can be more invigorating than to watch the working of the mind of Napoleon, the most entirely known as well as the ablest of historic men."[6] But who today can feel that he has truly and wholly known a man—though some 200,000 books and booklets have been written about him—who is presented by a hundred learned historians as the hero who struggled to give unity and law to Europe, and by a hundred learned historians as the ogre who drained the blood of France, and ravaged Europe, to feed an insatiable will to power and war? "The French Revolution," said Nietzsche, "made Napoleon possible; that is its justification."[7] Napoleon, musing before the tomb of Rousseau, murmured, "Perhaps it would have been better if neither of us had ever been born."[8]

He was born at Ajaccio August 15, 1769. Fifteen months earlier Genoa had sold Corsica to France; only two months earlier a French army had validated the sale by suppressing Paoli's revolt; on such trivia history has turned. Twenty years later Napoleon wrote to Paoli: "I was born when my country was dying. Thirty thousand Frenchmen disgorged upon our shores, drowning the throne of liberty in a sea of blood; such was the hateful spectacle that offended my infant eyes."[9]

Corsica, said Livy, "is a rugged, mountainous, almost uninhabitable island. The people resemble their country, being as ungovernable as wild beasts."[10] Contact with Italy had softened some part of this wildness, but the rough terrain, the hard and almost primitive life, the mortal family feuds, the fierce defense against invaders, had left the Corsicans of Paoli's time fit for guerrilla warfare or a *condottiere*'s enterprise rather than for the concessions that violent instincts must make to prosaic order if civilization is to form. Civility was growing in the capital, but during most of the time that Letizia Ramolino Buonaparte was carrying Napoleon she followed her husband from camp to camp with Paoli, lived in tents or mountain shacks, and breathed the air of battle. Her child seemed to remember all this with his blood, for he was never so happy as in war. He remained to the end a Corsican, and, in everything but date and education, an Italian, bequeathed to Corsica by the Renaissance. When he conquered Italy for France the Italians received him readily; he was the Italian who was conquering France.

His father, Carlo Buonaparte, could trace his lineage far back in the history of Italy, through a lusty breed living mostly in Tuscany, then in Genoa, then, in the sixteenth century, migrating to Corsica. The family treasured a noble pedigree, which was recognized by the French government; the *de*, however, was shed when, in the Revolution, a title to nobility was a step toward the guillotine. Carlo was a man of adaptable talent; he fought under Paoli for Corsican freedom; when that movement failed he made his peace with the French, served in the Franco-Corsican administration, secured the admission of two of his sons to academies in France, and was among the deputies sent to the States-General by the Corsican nobility. Napoleon took from his father his gray eyes, and perhaps his fatal gastric cancer.[11]

He took more from his mother. "It is to my mother and her excellent principles that I owe all my success, and any good that I have done. I do not hesitate to affirm that the future of the child depends upon its mother."[12] He resembled her in energy, courage, and mad resolution, even in fidelity to the proliferating Bonapartes. Born in 1750, Letizia Ramolino was fourteen when she married, thirty-five when widowed; she bore thirteen children between

1764 and 1784, saw five of them die in childhood, raised the rest with stern authority, glowed with their pride, and suffered with their fall.

Napoleon was her fourth, the second to survive infancy. Oldest was Joseph Bonaparte (1768–1844), amiable and cultured epicurean; made king of Naples and then of Spain, he hoped to be the second emperor of France. After Napoleon came Lucien (1775–1840), who helped him seize the French government in 1799, became his passionate enemy, and stood by his side in the heroic futility of the "Hundred Days." Then Maria Anna Elisa (1777–1820), proud and able grand duchess of Tuscany, who opposed her brother in 1813, and preceded him to death. Then Louis (1778–1846), who married the kindly Hortense de Beauharnais, became king of Holland, and begat Napoleon III. Then Pauline (1780–1825), beautiful and scandalously gay, who married Prince Camillo Borghese, and still holds court, in Canova's softly contoured marble in the Galleria Borghese, as one of the lasting delights of Rome. "Pauline and I," Napoleon recalled, "were Mother's favorites: Pauline because she was the prettiest and daintiest of my sisters, and I because a natural instinct told her that I would be the founder of the family's greatness."[13] Then Maria Carolina (1782–1839), who married Joachim Murat and became queen of Naples. Lastly, Jérôme (1784–1860), who founded the Bonapartes of Baltimore, and rose to be king of Westphalia.

In 1779 Carlo Buonaparte secured from the French government the privilege of sending Napoleon to a military academy at Brienne, some ninety miles southeast of Paris. It was a cardinal event in the boy's life, for it destined him to a martial career, and—almost to the end—to think of life and destiny in terms of war. Brienne became a formative ordeal for a lad of ten, so far from home in a strange and strict environment. The other students could not forgive his pride and temper, which seemed so disproportionate to his obscure nobility. "I suffered infinitely from the ridicule of my schoolmates, who jeered at me as a foreigner." The young maverick withdrew into himself, into studies, books, and dreams. His inclination to taciturnity was deepened; he spoke little, trusted no one, and kept himself from a world that seemed organized to torment him. There was one exception: he made friends with Louis-Antoine Fauvelet de Bourrienne, also a product of 1769; they defended each other, fought each other; after long separations Bourrienne became his secretary (1797), and remained close to him until 1805.

Isolation enabled the young Corsican to excel in studies that fed his hunger for eminence. He fled from Latin as from something dead; he had no uses for its Virgilian graces or its Taciturnian terseness. He received little instruction in literature or art, for the teachers were mostly innocent of these lures. But he took eagerly to mathematics; here was a discipline congenial to his demand for exactitude and clarity, something beyond prejudice and argument, and of constant use to a military engineer; in this field he led his class. Also he relished geography; those varied lands were terrain to be studied, people to be ruled; and they were food for dreams. History was for him, as for Carlyle, a worship and rosary of heroes, especially those who guided nations or molded empires. He loved Plutarch even more than

Euclid; he breathed the passion of those ancient patriots, he drank the blood of those historic battles; "There is nothing modern in you," Paoli told him; "you belong wholly to Plutarch."[14] He would have understood Heine, who said that when he read Plutarch he longed to mount a horse and ride forth to conquer Paris. Napoleon reached that goal through Italy and Egypt, but flank attacks were his forte.

After five years at Brienne, Bonaparte, now fifteen, was among the students selected from the twelve military schools of France to receive advanced instruction at the École Militaire in Paris. In October, 1785, he was assigned as second lieutenant of artillery to the La Fère Regiment stationed at Valence on the Rhone. His total pay there was 1,120 livres per year;[15] out of this, apparently, he sent something to help his mother care for her growing brood. As his father had died in February, and Joseph was as yet without means, Napoleon had become acting head of the clan. On his furloughs he made several visits to Corsica, lonesome, he said, for "the smell of its earth," for its "precipices, high mountains, and deep ravines."[16]

At Valence, and in 1788 at Auxonne, he earned the respect of his fellow officers by his rapid progress in military sciences and arts, his quickness to learn, his fertility in practical suggestions, and his readiness to share in the hard physical work of managing artillery. He carefully studied the *Essai de tactique générale* (1772) and other martial texts by Julie de Lespinasse's negligent lover, Jacques-Antoine-Hippolyte de Guibert. Napoleon was no longer an outcast; he made friends, attended theaters, heard concerts, took lessons in dancing, and discovered the charms of women. On a furlough in Paris (January 22, 1787) he laboriously talked himself into an unpremeditated adventure with a streetwalker; "that night," he assures us, "I knew a woman for the first time."[17] Nevertheless some somber moods remained. At times, alone in his simple room, he asked himself why, in pure logic, he should continue to live. "As I must die sometime, it would perhaps be better if I killed myself."[18] But he could not think of any pleasant way.

He found time, in his free hours, to extend his self-education in literature and history. Mme. de Rémusat, later lady-in-waiting to Josephine, thought that he was "ignorant, reading but little, and that hurriedly";[19] and yet we find that at Valence and Auxonne he read dramas by Corneille, Molière, Racine, and Voltaire,[20] memorized some passages, reread Amyot's translation of Plutarch, and studied Machiavelli's *Prince*, Montesquieu's *Esprit des lois*, Raynal's *Histoire philosophique des deux Indes*, Marigny's *Histoire des arabes*, Houssaye's *Histoire du gouvernement de Vénise*, Barrow's *Histoire d'Angleterre*, and many more. He took notes as he read, and made summaries of the major works; 368 pages of these notes survive from his youth.[21] He was of the Italian Renaissance in character, and of the French Enlightenment in mind. But also the romantic streak in him responded to the passionate prose of Rousseau and the poems ascribed to "Ossian," which he relished "for the same reason that made me delight in the murmur of the winds and waves."[22]

When the Revolution came he welcomed it, and spent another furlough,

in 1790, working for full acceptance of the new regime. In 1791 he submitted to the Academy of Lyons—in competition for a prize offered by
Raynal—an essay on "What truths or sentiments should be imputed to men
to further their happiness?" Perhaps under the spell of Rousseau's *Julie, ou
La Nouvelle Héloïse*, which had "turned his head,"[23] the young army officer
replied: Teach them that the best life is a simple one, parents and children
tilling the soil, enjoying its fruits, far from the exciting and corrupting influence of the city. All a man needs for happiness is food and clothing, a hut
and a wife; let him work, eat, beget, and sleep, and he will be happier than
a prince. The life and philosophy of the Spartans was the best. "Virtue consists in courage and strength; . . . energy is the life of the soul. . . . The
strong man is good; only the weak man is bad."[24] Here the young Napoleon
echoed Thrasymachus[25] and foreshadowed Nietzsche, who returned the
compliment by making Napoleon a hero of the will to power.[26] Amid the
argument he went out of his way to condemn absolute monarchy, class
privileges, and ecclesiastical trumpery. The Lyons Academy rejected the
essay as immature.

In September, 1791, Napoleon again visited his native land. He rejoiced in
the decree by which the Constituent Assembly had made Corsica a *département* of France, and had dowered its people with all the privileges of French
citizens. Withdrawing his vows of vengeance upon the nation that had so
violently made him a Frenchman, he felt that the Revolution was creating a
brilliant new France. In an imaginary conversation—*Le Souper de Beau-
caire*—published at his own expense in the fall of 1793, he defended the
Revolution as "a combat to the death between the patriots and the despots
of Europe,"[27] and urged all the oppressed to join in the struggle for the
rights of man. His old hero Paoli, however, felt that membership of Corsica
in the French nation would be acceptable to him only if he were given full
authority in the island, with finances to be supplied by France, but with the
rigorous exclusion of French soldiers from Corsican soil. Napoleon thought
this proposal extreme; he broke with his idol, and opposed Paoli's candidates
in the Ajaccio municipal election of April 1, 1792. Paoli won, and Napoleon
returned to France.

In Paris, on June 20, he saw the populace invade the Tuileries; he marveled that the King did not disperse the "cannibals" with a fusillade from his
Swiss Guards. On August 10 he saw the sansculottes and the Fédérés drive
the royal family from the palace; he described the crowd as "the lowest
scum; . . . they do not belong to the working classes at all."[28] With rising
reservations he continued to support the Revolution, being now an officer
in its Army. In December, 1793, as already related, he distinguished himself
in the capture of Toulon. The commendation sent to Robespierre resulted in
the appointment of Napoleon as brigadier general at the age of twenty-four;
but it shared in his being arrested as a *Robespierriste* (August 6, 1794) after
Robespierre's fall. He was imprisoned at Antibes, and was scheduled for trial
and possible execution; he was released after a fortnight, but was placed on
inactive service at reduced pay. In the spring of 1795 (he tells us) he was

wandering along the Seine, meditating suicide, when a friend, encountering him, revived him with a gift of thirty thousand francs;[29] Napoleon later returned the sum manifold. In June Boissy d'Anglas described him as "a little Italian, pale, slender, and puny, but singularly audacious in his views."[30] He thought for a time of going to Turkey, reorganizing the Sultan's army, and carving out for himself some Oriental realm. In a more practical mood he drew up for the War Ministry a plan of campaign for driving the Austrians out of Italy.

Then, in one of those whims of history that open a door to the inevitable, the Convention, besieged (October 5, 1795) by royalists and others, assigned Barras to organize its defense. He decided that a blast of artillery would do it, but no artillery was at hand. He had noted Napoleon's enterprise at Toulon; he sent for him, commissioned him to secure and use artillery; it was done, and Napoleon became at once famous and infamous. When the War Ministry needed a bold and enterprising commander to lead the Army of Italy, Carnot (or Barras[31]) secured the appointment for Bonaparte (March 2, 1796). Seven days later the happy general married the still beautiful Josephine.

III. JOSEPHINE DE BEAUHARNAIS

She was a Creole—i.e., a person of French or Spanish descent born and raised in tropical colonies. The island of Martinique, in the Caribbean, had been French for 128 years when Marie-Josèphe-Rose Tascher de la Pagerie was born there in 1763 of an old Orléans family. Her uncle, Baron de Tascher, was then governor of the port; her father had been a page in the household of the Dauphine Marie-Josèphe, mother of Louis XVI. She was educated at the Convent of the Ladies of Providence in Fort-Royal (now Fort-de-France), seat of the colonial government. The curriculum then consisted of catechism, deportment, penmanship, drawing, embroidery, dancing, and music; the nuns believed that these would get a woman much further than Latin, Greek, history, and philosophy; and Josephine proved them right. She became, as had been said of Mme. de Pompadour, "a morsel for a king."

At sixteen she was taken to France and was married to Vicomte Alexandre de Beauharnais, then only nineteen, but already experienced in the philandering ways of the French aristocracy. Soon his long and frequent absences betrayed his adulteries, and left in the impressionable Josephine the conviction that the Sixth Commandment was not intended for the upper classes. She gave herself devotedly to her two children—Eugène (1781–1824) and Hortense (1783–1837), who rewarded her with their lifelong loyalty.

When the Revolution came, the Vicomte adjusted his politics to the new regime, and for five years he kept his head. But as the Terror proceeded, any title to nobility could be a warrant for arrest. In 1794 both Alexandre and

Josephine were apprehended, and separately imprisoned; and on July 24 he was guillotined. While awaiting a similar fate Josephine accepted the amorous advances of General Lazare Hoche.[32] She was among the many nobles released after the fall of Robespierre.

Made almost destitute by the confiscation of her husband's wealth, and anxious to provide care and education for her children, Josephine used the lure of her dark-blue eyes and languorous beauty to make a friend of Tallien and a lover of the rising Barras.[33] Much of Beauharnais' confiscated wealth was restored to her, including an elegant carriage and a team of black horses;[34] presently she was next only to Mme. Tallien as a leader of Directory society. Napoleon described her salon as "the most distinguished in Paris."[35]

He attended some of her soirees, and was fascinated by her mature charms, her easy grace, and what her indulgent father called her "exceedingly sweet disposition."[36] She was not impressed by Bonaparte, who appeared to her as a sallow youth with a "lean and hungry look," and a corresponding income. She sent her son, now fourteen, to solicit his aid in recovering the confiscated sword of her husband. Eugène was so comely and modest that Napoleon at once agreed to attend to the matter. It was done; Josephine called on him to thank him; and invited him to lunch for October 29. He came, and was conquered. As early as December, 1795, she admitted him to her bed,[37] but they were reluctant to marry. He reminisced at St. Helena: "Barras did me a service by advising me to marry Josephine. He assured me that she belonged to both the old and the new society, and that this fact would bring me more support; that her house was the best in Paris, and would rid me of my Corsican name; finally that through this marriage I should become quite French."[38] Barras gave her similar advice, for reasons still debated;[39] here, he told her, is a man who gives every sign of forging a high place for himself in the world. Napoleon was not deterred by her former amours; "Everything about you pleased me," he would soon write to her, "even to the memory of the error of your ways . . . Virtue, for me, consisted of what you made it."[40]

They were married on March 9, 1796, by a purely civil ceremony; Tallien and Barras served as witnesses; no relatives were invited. To mitigate the disparity of their ages—he twenty-seven, she thirty-three—Napoleon registered himself as twenty-eight, Josephine wrote her age as twenty-nine.[41] They spent their wedding night at her home. He encountered virile opposition from her pet dog, Fortuné. "That gentleman," he tells us, "was in possession of Madame's bed. . . . I wanted to have him leave, but to no avail; I was told to share the bed with him or sleep elsewhere; I had to take it or leave it. The favorite was less accommodating than I was"; at the worst possible moment the dog bit his leg, so severely that he long kept the scar.[42]

On March 11, torn between his new delight and his ruling passion for power and glory, Napoleon left to lead the Army of Italy, in one of the most brilliant campaigns in history.

IV. ITALIAN WHIRLWIND: MARCH 27, 1796 – DECEMBER 5, 1797

The military situation had been simplified by treaties with Prussia and Spain, but Austria refused peace so long as France clung to her conquests in the Netherlands and along the Rhine. England continued the war at sea, and granted a subsidy of £600,000 to Austria to finance the war on land. Austria had ruled Lombardy since 1713. She was now allied with Charles Emmanuel IV, king of Sardinia and Piedmont, who hoped to regain Savoy and Nice, taken by the French in 1792.

The Directory, led in this matter by Carnot, planned its military operations for 1796 as a three-pronged assault upon Austria. One French army, under Jourdan, was to attack the Austrians on the northeast front along the Sambre and the Meuse; another, under Moreau, was to proceed against the Austrians along the Moselle and the Rhine; a third, under Bonaparte, was to attempt the expulsion of the Austrians and the Sardinians from Italy. Jourdan, after some victories, encountered the superior forces of the Archduke Karl Ludwig, suffered defeats at Amberg and Würzburg, and retreated to the west bank of the Rhine. Moreau advanced into Bavaria almost to Munich, then, learning that the victorious Archduke could cut his line of communications or attack him in the rear, he withdrew into Alsace. The Directory, as a final hope, turned to Napoleon.

Reaching Nice on March 27, he found the "Army of Italy" in no condition to face the Austrian and Sardinian forces that blocked the narrow entrance into Italy between the Mediterranean and the towering Alps. His troops numbered some 43,000, brave men accustomed to mountain war, but ill-clothed, ill-shod, and so poorly fed that they had to steal in order to live;[43] hardly thirty thousand of them could be called upon for arduous campaigns. They had scant cavalry and almost no artillery. The generals over whom the twenty-seven-year-old commander had been placed—Augereau, Masséna, Laharpe, and Sésurier—were all older than Napoleon in service; they resented his appointment, and were resolved to make him feel their superior experience; but at their first meeting with him they were awed into quick obedience by the confident clarity with which he explained his plans and gave his orders.

He could overawe his generals, but he could not free himself from the spell that Josephine laid upon him. Four days after reaching Nice he put his maps and orderlies aside and wrote to her a letter hot with the ardor of a youth who had just discovered depths of passion under his dreams of power:

Nice, 31 March, 1796
Not a day passes without my loving you, not a night but I hold you in my arms. I cannot drink a cup of tea without cursing the martial ambition that separates me from the soul of my life. Whether I am buried in business, or

leading my troops, or inspecting the camps, my adorable Josephine fills my mind. . . .

My soul is sad, my heart is in chains, and I imagine things that terrify me. You do not love me as you did; you will console yourself elsewhere. . . .

Goodbye, my wife, my tormentor, my happiness, . . . whom I love, whom I fear, the source of feelings that make me as gentle as Nature herself, and of impulses under which I am as catastrophic as a thunderbolt. I do not ask you to love me forever, or to be faithful to me, but simply . . . to tell me the truth. . . . Nature has made my soul resolute and strong, while yours she has constructed of lace and gauze. . . . My mind is intent on vast plans, my heart utterly engrossed with you. . . .

Goodbye! Ah, if you love me less it must be that you never loved me at all. Then were I indeed to be pitied.

BONAPARTE[44]

He wrote to her again on April 3 and 7, amid the rising tempo of the war. He studied all the information he could get about the enemy forces that he must defeat: an Austrian army under Beaulieu at Voltri near Genoa; another under Argentau at Montenotte, farther west; and a Sardinian army under Colli at Ceva, farther north. Beaulieu assumed that his lines of communications would serve to inform him should any of his armies need urgent help. On that basis he could reasonably expect to repel the French attack, for his combined forces outnumbered the French about two to one. Napoleon's strategy was to move as many of his troops, as secretly and rapidly as possible, to confront one of the defending armies, and overwhelm it before either of the other two could come to its aid. The plan involved rapid marches by the French over rough and mountainous routes; it required hardy and resolute warriors. Napoleon sought to arouse them with the first of those famous proclamations that were no small part of his armament:

> SOLDIERS, you are hungry and naked. The Republic owes you much, but she has not the means to pay her debts. I am come to lead you into the most fertile plains that the sun beholds. Rich provinces, opulent towns; all shall be at your disposal. Soldiers! with such a prospect before you, can you fail in courage and constancy?[45]

It was an open invitation to plunder, but how else could he get these unpaid men to bear long marches and then face death? Napoleon, like most rulers and revolutionists, never allowed morality to hinder victory, and he trusted to success to whitewash his sins. Should not Italy contribute to the cost of her liberation?

The first goal of his strategy was to smash the Sardinian army and induce the King of Sardinia to retire to Turin, his Piedmont capital. A series of crucial and successful engagements—Montenotte (April 11), Millesimo (April 13), Dego (April 15), and Mondovi (April 22)—shattered the Sardinian forces and compelled Charles Emmanuel to sign at Cherasco (April 28) an armistice ceding Savoy and Nice to France, and, in effect, withdrawing from the war. In those battles the young commander impressed his subordinates with his keen and quick perception of developments, needs, and opportunities, his clear and decisive orders, the logic and success of tactics completing the foresight of strategy that often caught the enemy on flank or rear. The older generals learned to obey him with confidence in his vision and judgment; the younger officers—Junot, Lannes, Murat, Marmont, Berthier—developed for him a devotion that repeatedly faced death in his cause. When, after these victories, the exhausted survivors reached the heights of Monte Zemoto—from which they could view the sunlit plains of Lombardy—many of them broke out in a spontaneous salute to the youth who had led them so brilliantly.

Now they did not have to plunder in order to live; wherever he established French rule Napoleon taxed the rich and the ecclesiastical hierarchy, and persuaded or ordered the towns to contribute to the upkeep and orderly behavior of his troops. On April 26, at Cherasco, he addressed his army in a clever eulogy that cautioned them against pillage:

> SOLDIERS:
>
> You have in a fortnight won six victories, taken twenty-one standards, fifty-five pieces of artillery, and conquered the richest part of Piedmont. . . . Without any resources you have supplied all that was necessary. You have won battles without cannon, passed rivers without bridges, made forced marches without shoes, camped without brandy and often without bread. . . . Your grateful country will owe its prosperity to you. . . .
>
> But, soldiers, you have done nothing as yet compared with what there still remains to do. Neither Turin nor Milan remains to you. . . . Is there anyone among you whose courage is lacking? Is there anyone who would prefer to return across the summits of the Apennines and the Alps and bear patiently the disgrace of a slavish soldier? No, there is none such among the conquerors of Montenotte, of Dego, of Mondovi. All of you are burning to extend the glory of the French people. . . .
>
> Friends, I am promising you this conquest, but there is one condition which you must swear to fulfill. That is to respect the peoples whom you deliver, and repress the horrible pillage which certain scoundrels, incited by our enemies, commit. Otherwise you will not be the deliverers of the people but their scourges. . . . Your victories, your bravery, your success, the blood of your brothers who have died in battle—all will be lost, even honor and glory. As for me and the generals who have your confidence, we should blush to command an army without discipline and restraint. . . . Anyone who engages in pillage will be shot without mercy.
>
> Peoples of Italy, the French army comes to break your chains; the French people is the friend of all peoples. You may receive them with confidence. Your property, your religion, and your customs will be respected. . . . We have no grudge except against the tyrants who oppress you.
>
> BONAPARTE

There had been much pillage in that first campaign; there would still be some despite this plea and threat. Napoleon had some looters shot, and pardoned others. "These wretches," he said, "are excusable; they have sighed for three years after the promised land, . . . and now that they have entered it they wish to enjoy it."[46] He appeased them by letting them share in the contributions and provisions that he exacted from the "liberated" towns.

Amid all this turmoil of marches, battles, and diplomacy he thought almost hourly of the wife he had left so soon after their wedding night. Now that she might safely pass over the Cévennes he begged her, in a letter of April 17, to come to him. "Come quickly," he wrote on April 24, 1796; "I warn you, if you delay longer, you will find me ill. These fatigues and your absence—the two together are more than I can bear. . . . Take wings, and fly. . . . A kiss upon your heart, another a little lower, another lower still, far lower!"[47]

Was she faithful? Could she, so accustomed to her pleasures, content herself for months with epistolary adulation? That same April a handsome officer, Hippolyte Charles, aged twenty-four, found his way to her. In May she invited Talleyrand to meet him. "You will be wild about him. Mesdames Récamier, Tallien, and Hamelin have all lost their heads over him."[48] She became so enamored of him that when Murat came to her from Bonaparte with money and instructions for joining him in Italy, she delayed on the ground of illness, and allowed Murat to send word to his chief that she gave signs of pregnancy. Napoleon wrote to her on May 13: "It is true, then, that you are pregnant! Murat . . . says that you are not feeling well and that thus he does not deem it prudent for you to undertake so long a journey. So I am to be still longer deprived of the joy of clasping you in my arms! . . . Is it possible that I shall be denied the joy of seeing you with your little pregnant belly?"[49] He rejoiced prematurely; she was never to give him a child.

Meanwhile he led his men through a dozen battles to the prize of Lombardy—the rich and cultured city of Milan. At Lodi, on the west bank of the Adda, his main force caught up with the main Austrian army under Beaulieu. Beaulieu retreated, crossed the river on a 200-meter-long wooden bridge, and then placed his artillery in a position to prevent a similar crossing by the French. Napoleon bade his cavalry to ride north till they could find a place to ford the stream, and then to pass south and attack the Austrian rear. Keeping his infantry sheltered behind the walls and houses of the town, he shared actively in directing the fire of his artillery against the Austrian guns that covered the bridge. When his cavalry suddenly appeared on the east bank and charged into the Austrians, he ordered his grenadiers to lead the way across the bridge. They tried, but the Austrian artillery halted them. Napoleon rushed forward and joined Lannes and Berthier in leading them. The Austrians were routed (May 10, 1796), losing two thousand prisoners. Beaulieu withdrew to Mantua, and the French army, after a day's rest, marched on to Milan. It was from this action that the French troops, moved by Bonaparte's reckless but inspiring exposure of himself to enemy fire, conferred upon him the affectionate title "Le Petit Caporal"—the Little Corporal.

Shortly after this victory he received from the Directory a proposal so insulting that he risked his career on his reply. Those five men, who had been enjoying the celebrations with which Paris received the news of Napoleon's achievements, informed him (May 7) that his army was now to be divided into two parts; one was to be put under the command of General François-Étienne Kellermann (son of the victor of Valmy), and charged with protecting the French in north Italy from Austrian attacks; the other, under Bonaparte, was to march south and bring the Papal States and the kingdom of Naples under French control. Napoleon saw in this not only a personal injury but, even more, a cardinal error in strategy: not only would an attack upon the Papacy enflame all the Catholics of Europe, including France, against the Revolution, but Catholic Austria was already preparing to send a powerful force, under the experienced Field Marshal Count Dago-bert von Wurmser, to drive him back into France. He answered that the Army of Italy would need its united and replenished strength to preserve its gains; that it could be successfully led only by an undivided command; that he would therefore yield his place to General Kellermann, and would offer his resignation.

The Directory received this message along with reports of Napoleon's latest military and diplomatic successes. For the young general—proud with victory, and feeling that those distant politicians were not as well placed as he to negotiate treaties according with the resources of the enemy and the condition of the French army—had assumed the right to make peace as well as war, and to determine the price that each Italian city or state should pay to enjoy the protection, rather than suffer the avidity, of his troops. So, after entering Milan in triumph (May 15, 1796), he arranged truces with the Duke of Parma, the Duke of Modena, and the King of Naples, by which he guaranteed them peace with France and protection from Austria, and speci-fied what donations each of these principalities was to pay for this benevo-lent amity. They paid painful sums, and bore in grim impotence the theft of art masterpieces from their galleries, palaces, and public squares.

Milan made him welcome. For nearly a century it had longed for freedom from Austrian rule, and this young warlord was unusually gracious for a conqueror. He was congenial to Italian speech and ways, appreciative of Italian women, music, and art; they did not realize at once how fondly he appreciated Italian art. In any case, was he not, except for a month or so, an Italian? Visibly he gathered about him Italian artists, poets, historians, phi-losophers, scientists, and talked familiarly with them; for a time he seemed to be Lodovico Sforza and Leonardo da Vinci reborn and merged. What could be more charming than his letter to the astronomer Barnaba Oriani?—

> Learned men in Milan used not to enjoy the consideration they deserved. Hidden in their laboratories, they thought themselves happy if kings and priests did them no harm. It is not so now. In Italy thought has become free. There is no more Inquisition, no more intolerance, no more tyranny. I invite all learned men to meet together, and to tell me what methods should be adopted, or what needs supplied, in order to give the sciences and the fine arts a new life. . . . Pray express these sentiments for me to the distinguished men of learning dwelling in Milan.[50]

Napoleon incorporated Milan and other cities in a Republic of Lombardy, whose citizens were to share with the French in liberty, equality, fraternity, and taxes. In a proclamation to the new citizens (May 19, 1796) he ex-plained that since the liberating army had paid a high price for freeing Lom-bardy, the liberated should contribute some twenty million francs to the upkeep of his troops; this, surely, was a small contribution for so fertile a country; moreover, the tax should "be levied on the rich . . . and on church corporations," so as to spare the poor.[51] Not so much publicity had accompanied the previous day's order that "an agent should follow the French army in Italy, to seek out and transfer to the Republic all the objects of art, science, and so forth, that are in the conquered towns."[52] The Italians could only revenge themselves with a pun: "*Non tutti Francesi sono ladroni, ma buona parte*" (Not all Frenchmen are robbers, but a good part are). Napoleon, however, was following the example set by the Convention and the Directory.

This artistic spoliation of conquered or liberated lands had scant precedent; it aroused indignation everywhere except in France, and set a model for later warriors. Most of the spoils were sent to the Directory, were received there with pleasure, and found their way into the Louvre, where the *Mona Lisa*, though raped, never lost her smile. Napoleon kept little of the Italian revenues for himself;[53] some of them were invested in judicious bribes; much went to pay the troops and so moderate their zeal to steal.

Having feathered a nest for his bride, he importuned her (May 18) to come and join him. "Milan . . . cannot but please you, for this is a very beautiful land. As for me, I shall be wild with joy. . . . I am dying of curiosity to see how you carry your child. . . . *Addio, mio dolce amor.* . . . Come quickly to hear the fine music and to see beautiful Italy."[54] While his letter traveled he returned to the business of driving the Austrians from Italy. On May 20 he was again with his troops; and knowing that they would soon have to face many obstacles and armies, he addressed them in another eloquent proclamation:

> SOLDIERS!
> You have rushed like a torrent from the heights of the Apennines; you have overthrown and scattered every force that opposed your march. . . . The Po, the Ticino, the Adda could not stop your progress by a day. . . . Yes, soldiers, you have done much, but is there nothing left for you to do? . . . No! I see you already flying to arms; a slothful repose wearies you; every day lost for your glory is lost, too, for your happiness. Let us move on! We still have forced marches to make, enemies to overcome, laurels to win, wrongs to avenge. . . .
> Let not the people be disturbed by our advance; we are the friends of all peoples! . . . You will have the immortal glory of changing the face of the most beautiful part of Europe. The free French nation . . . will give to Europe a glorious peace. . . . Then you will return to your homes, and your fellow citizens, singling you out, will say, "He was with the Army of Italy."[55]

On May 27 they resumed their advance through Lombardy. Ignoring the fact that Brescia was Venetian territory, Napoleon occupied it, and made it the first center of the new campaign. When Venice sent envoys to protest, Bonaparte, in one of his feigned rages, frightened them by demanding why Venice had already allowed the Austrians to use Venetian towns and roads; the envoys offered an apology, and agreed to his similar use of Venetian terrain.[56] A swift march brought the French army to Peschiera; the Austrian detachment that had been left there fled; Napoleon had the strategic fortress strengthened to protect his communications, and pushed on to Mantua, where the remnants of Beaulieu's three armies had taken refuge behind apparently inexpugnable defenses. Napoleon left part of his forces to besiege the citadel. Another part he sent south to drive the British from Leghorn; it was done, and a popular revolt soon forced them to leave Corsica. Murat found it simple to evict the Austrian envoy from Genoa, and to incorporate that Mediterranean bastion in a Republic of Liguria under French control. Seldom had Italy seen so many changes of power in so short a time.

Napoleon returned to Milan and awaited Josephine. She came, on July 13, and the victor embraced his conqueror. The next day the city honored her with a special performance at La Scala, followed by a ball at which all the local notables were presented to her. After three days of ecstasy the general had to return to his troops at Marmirolo, from which he sent her a paean of youthful adoration:

> I have been sad every moment since our parting. I know no happiness save when I am with you. . . . The charms of my incomparable Josephine kindle a flame that burns incessantly in my heart, through my senses. When shall I ever be free of anxiety and responsibility, free to spend all my time with you, with nothing to do but love you . . . ?
> A few days ago I thought I loved you, but now that I have seen you again I love you a thousand times more. . . .
> Ah, I implore you, let me see that you have faults. Be less beautiful, less gracious, less kind, less tender. Above all, never be jealous, never weep. Your tears rob me of my reason, set my blood aflame. . . .
> . . . Come quickly to join me, so that at least before we die we can say: "We have had many joyous hours together." . . .[57]

She obeyed despite the danger of enemy snipers en route, caught up to him at Brescia, and accompanied him to Verona. There a courier brought him word that a fresh Austrian army was entering Italy under the command of Count von Wurmser, who had recently driven the French from Mannheim. It was calculated that this host would outnumber three to one the forces under Napoleon. Anticipating possible disaster, he sent Josephine back to Peschiera, and arranged to have her taken thence to Florence. Meanwhile he ordered the French detachments that he had left before Mantua to abandon the siege and to come by a safe roundabout route to join his main army. They arrived in time to take part in the battle of Castiglione (August 5, 1796). Wurmser, not expecting so early an attack, was leading his divisions southward in too thin a line. Napoleon pounced upon the unprepared Austrians, confused them into flight, and took fifteen thousand prisoners. Wurmser retreated to Rovereto; the French pursued and defeated him there, and again at Bassano; the disheartened old general fled with the remnants of his army to seek refuge behind the battlements of Mantua. Napoleon left some regiments to hold him there.

But now 60,000 additional Austrians, under Baron Alvinczy, poured down over the Alps to meet the 45,000 men left to Bonaparte. He met them at Arcole, but they were on the other side of the River Adige, and could be reached only by crossing a bridge under fire. Again, as at Lodi on the Adda, Napoleon was among the first to cross.* "When I was in the raging turmoil of the fight," he later recalled, "my adjutant, Colonel Muiron, threw himself toward me, covered me with his body, and received the bullet which was intended for me. He sank at my feet."[58] In the three-day battle that followed (November 15–17, 1796), the Austrians, after a brave fight, fell back in an orderly retreat. Alvinczy reorganized them at Rivoli, but there they were defeated again, and Alvinczy, having lost thirty thousand men, led the survivors back to Austria. Wurmser, losing hope of rescue, and taking pity on his starving men, surrendered (February 2, 1797), and the French conquest of Lombardy was complete.

Insatiate, Napoleon turned his face and forces south toward the Papal States and politely asked Pius VI to give him Bologna, Ferrara, Ravenna, Ancona, and their subject lands. By the Treaty of Tolentino (February 19, 1797) the Pope surrendered these city-states, and paid an "indemnity" of fifteen million francs toward the French army's expense account. Then, master of all north Italy except Piedmont and Venice, Napoleon reorganized his army, added to them some regiments formed in Italy and a fresh division from France under General Bernadotte, led 75,000 men across the Alps through three feet of snow, and proposed to strike at Vienna itself, the imperial center of the attack upon the French Revolution.

The Emperor Francis II sent against him forty thousand men under the Archduke Karl Ludwig, fresh from victories along the Rhine. Surprised by the reported number of the advancing French, and respectful of Napoleon's reputation, Karl adopted a strategy of retreat. Bonaparte followed until he was within sixty miles of the Austrian capital. With or without a battle he might have taken the city, then humming with old Haydn and young Beethoven. But in that case the government would fall back toward Hungary, the war could lengthen in time and space, and, with winter setting in, the French army would find itself in hostile and unfamiliar territory, subject at any moment to a flank attack. In a rare moment of modesty, and with a caution that might have served him well in his later years, Napoleon sent the Archduke an invitation to negotiate a truce. The Archduke refused; Napoleon inflicted severe defeats upon his forces at Neumarkt and Umzmarkt; Karl agreed to talk. At Leoben, April 18, 1797, the young commanders signed a preliminary peace, subject to ratification by their governments.

The road to ratification was blocked by Austria's refusal to surrender— and Napoleon's resolve to keep—his conquests in Lombardy. An apparently minor event gave him a gambler's chance to escape this impasse. He had occupied several cities belonging to Venice; in some of these towns insurrections had broken out against the French garrisons. Charging the Venetian Senate with having instigated these uprisings, Napoleon deposed it and set up in its place a municipal structure subject to French control and shorn of

---

* Gros's famous painting of the young commander—eyes flashing, hair blown by the wind, standard in one hand, sword in the other—crossing the bridge at Arcole was painted shortly afterward in Milan, and became the *pièce de résistance* at the Paris Salon of 1801.

its mainland possessions. When the time came to transform the preliminaries of Leoben into the Treaty of Campoformio (October 17, 1797), Napoleon offered Austria a free hand in absorbing Venice into her empire in return for the cession of Lombardy and Belgium, and recognition of French rights to the left bank of the Rhine. Nearly all Europe, forgetting a thousand treaties, reacted with horror to this diplomatic philanthropy with other people's property.

The new Machiavelli insisted, however, on keeping for France the Venetian islands in the Adriatic—Corfu, Zante, Cephalonia. "These," Napoleon wrote to the Directory on August 16, 1797, "matter more to us than all the rest of Italy put together. They are vital to the wealth and prosperity of our commerce. If we are effectively to destroy England we must get hold of Egypt. The huge Ottoman Empire, perishing day by day, forces us to anticipate events, and to take early steps for the preservation of our commerce in the Levant."[59] The graybeards of the chancelleries had little to teach this youth of twenty-eight.

With serene assumption of diplomatic authority, he reorganized his conquests into a Cisalpine Republic centering on Milan and a Ligurian Republic around Genoa, both governed by native democracies under French protection and power. Then, having revenged and reversed Caesar's Roman conquest of Gaul, the Little Corporal, big with honors and spoils, returned to Paris to have his treaties ratified by the transformed Directory which he had helped to install.

V. THE *COUP D'ÉTAT* OF THE 18TH FRUCTIDOR: SEPTEMBER 4, 1797

It was not the same Paris that he had known in the crowd-ruled days of '92 and '93. Ever since the fall of Robespierre in '94 the capital had followed the countryside in an intensifying reaction—religious and political— against the Revolution. Catholicism, led by nonjuring priests, was regaining its hold upon a people that had lost belief in an earthly substitute for supernatural hopes and consolations, for sacraments, ceremonies, and processional holydays. The *décadi*, or decimal day of rest, was increasingly ignored; the Christian Sunday was flagrantly respected and enjoyed. France was voting for God.

And for a king. In homes and salons, in the press and on the streets, even in section assemblies once ruled by sansculottes, men and women aired regrets for *bonhomme* Louis XVI, found excuses for Bourbon faults, and asked could any other government than an authoritative monarchy bring order, safety, prosperity, and peace out of the chaos, crime, corruption, and war that were desolating France? Returned *émigrés* congregated in such number that a wit called their favorite Parisian purlieu *le petit Coblenz* (from the haven of titled exiles in Germany); and there one could hear the monarchical philosophies that were being preached abroad by Bonald and de Maistre. The electoral assemblies, overwhelmingly bourgeois, were sending to the

Council of Ancients and the Council of Five Hundred more and more deputies ready to flirt with royalty if it offered a property guarantee. By 1797
the monarchists in the Councils were strong enough to elect to the Directory the Marquis de Barthélemy. Lazare Carnot, a director since 1795, had
turned to the right in reaction against the propaganda of Babeuf, and looked
with complacent eye upon religion as a vaccination against communism.

The firmly republican Directors—Barras, Larevellière-Lépaux, and Rewbell
—felt endangered in their tenure and their lives by the movement toward
monarchism, and decided to risk all on a *coup d'état* that would eliminate
its leaders from both the Councils and the Directory. They sought popular
support from the radical Jacobins, who had been hiding in bitter obscurity
during the conservative revival. They sought military support by appealing
to Napoleon to send them from Italy a general capable of organizing Parisian
soldiery for the defense of the republic. He was willing to accommodate
them; a Bourbon revival would frustrate his plans; the road must be kept
open for his own rise to political power, and the time was not ripe for that
plunge. He sent them tough Pierre Augereau, veteran of many campaigns.
Augereau enlisted a part of Hoche's troops; with these, on the 18th Fructidor, he invaded the legislative chambers, arrested fifty-three deputies, many
royalist agents, and Directors Barthélemy and Carnot. Carnot escaped to
Switzerland; most of the others were deported to sweat and wither in South
American Guiana. In the elections of 1797 the radicals won control of the
Councils; they added Merlin of Douai and Jean-Baptiste Treilhard to the
victorious "triumvirs," and gave this revised Directory almost absolute
power.[60]

When Napoleon reached Paris, December 5, 1797, he found a new Terror
operating, aimed at all conservatives, and substituting Guiana for the guillotine. Nevertheless all classes seemed to unite in feting the invincible young
general who had added half of Italy to France. He put aside for the present
his look of stern command. He dressed modestly, and pleased variously: the
conservatives by lauding order; the Jacobins by appearing to have raised
Italy from vassalage to liberty; the intelligentsia by writing that "the true
conquests, the only ones that leave no regrets, are those that are made over
ignorance."[61] On December 10 the dignitaries of the national government
honored him with an official welcome. Mme. de Staël was there, and her
Memoirs preserve the scene:

> The Directory gave General Bonaparte a solemn reception which in some
> respects marked an epoch in the history of the Revolution. They chose for
> this ceremony the court of the Luxembourg Palace; no hall would have been
> vast enough to contain the crowd that was attracted; there were spectators in
> every window and on the roof. The five Directors, in Roman costume, were
> placed on a stage in the court; near them were the deputies of the Council of
> the Ancients, the Council of Five Hundred, and the Institute. . . .
> Bonaparte arrived very simply dressed, followed by his aides-de-camp or
> assistant officers; all of them taller than he, but bent with the respect they
> showed him. The elite of France, gathered there, covered the victorious gen-

eral with applause. He was the hope of every man, republican or royalist; all saw the present and the future as held in his strong hands.[62]

On that occasion he handed the Directors the completed Treaty of Campo-formio. It was officially ratified, and Napoleon could for a time rest on his victories in diplomacy as well as war.

After attending a sumptuous party given in his honor by the indestructible Talleyrand (then minister for foreign affairs), he retired to his home in the Rue Chantereine. There he relaxed with Josephine and her children, and for some time kept himself so out of the public eye that his admirers commented on his modesty and his detractors rejoiced over his decline. However, he made a point of visiting the Institute; he talked mathematics with Lagrange, astronomy with Laplace, government with Sieyès, literature with Marie Joseph de Chénier, and art with David. Probably he was already meditating a sally into Egypt, and thought of taking with him a garnishment of scholars and scientists.

The Directory saw something to be suspected in such uncharacteristic modesty; this youth, who in Italy and Austria had behaved as if he were the government—might he not decide to behave likewise in Paris? Hoping to keep him busy at a distance, they offered him command of the fifty thousand soldiers and sailors that were assembling at Brest for an invasion of England. Napoleon studied the project, rejected it, and warned the Directory, in a letter of February 23, 1798:

> We should give up any real attempt to invade England, and content ourselves with the appearance of it, while devoting all our attention and resources to the Rhine. . . . We must not keep a large army at a distance from Germany. . . . Or we might make an expedition into the Levant, and threaten the commerce of [England with] India.[63]

There was his dream. Even amid the Italian campaigns, he had pondered the possibilities of a foray into the Orient: in the soft decay of the Ottoman realm a bold spirit, with brave and hungry men, might forge a career, might carve an empire. England ruled the oceans, but her hold on the Mediterranean could be loosed by taking Malta; her hold on India could be weakened by taking Egypt. In that land, where labor was cheap, genius and francs might build a fleet, courage and imagination might sail over that distant sea to India, and take from the British colonial system its richest possession. In 1803 Napoleon confessed to Mme. de Rémusat:

> I do not know what would have happened to me had I not conceived the happy thought of going to Egypt. When I embarked I did not know but that I might be bidding an eternal farewell to France; but I had little doubt that she would recall me. The charm of Oriental conquest drew my thoughts away from Europe more than I should have believed possible.[64]

The Directory fell in with his proposals, partly because it thought it would be safer if he were at a distance. Talleyrand concurred for reasons still disputed; his mistress Mme. Grand alleged that he did it to "favor his

English friends"—presumably by diverting to Egypt the army that was threatening to invade England.[65] The Directory delayed consent because the expedition would be costly, would consume men and matériel needed for protection against England and Austria, and might bring Turkey (the indolent sovereign of Egypt) into a new coalition against France. But the rapid advance of the French army in Italy—the subjection of the Papal States and the kingdom of Naples—brought succulent spoils to the Directory; and in April, 1798, with Napoleon's approval, another French army invaded Switzerland, set up the Helvetic Republic, exacted "indemnities," and sent money to Paris. Now the Egyptian dream could be financed.

Napoleon began at once to issue detailed orders for a new armada. Thirteen ships of the line, seven frigates, thirty-five other warships, 130 transports, 16,000 seamen, 38,000 troops (many from the Army of Italy), with necessary equipment and matériel, and a library of 287 volumes, were to assemble at Toulon, Genoa, Ajaccio, or Civitavecchia; and scientists, scholars, and artists were happy to accept invitations to what promised to be an exciting and historic union of adventure and research. Among them were Monge the mathematician, Fourier the physicist, Berthollet the chemist, Geoffroy Saint-Hilaire the biologist; and Tallien, having surrendered his wife to Barras, found passage among the savants. They noted with pride that Napoleon now signed his letters "Bonaparte, Member of the Institute and General-in-chief."[66] Bourrienne, who had joined Napoleon as secretary at Campoformio in 1797, accompanied him on this voyage, and gave a detailed account of its fate. Josephine too wanted to come along; Napoleon allowed her to accompany him to Toulon, but he forbade her to board ship. However, he took with him her son Eugène de Beauharnais, who had endeared himself to Napoleon by his modesty and competence, and by a loyalty that became an undiscourageable devotion. Josephine mourned this double departure, wondering whether she would ever see her son or her husband again. From Toulon she went to Plombières to take the "fertility waters," for now she, as well as Napoleon, wanted a child.

On May 19, 1798, the main fleet sailed from Toulon to bring medieval romance into modern history.

VI. ORIENTAL FANTASY: MAY 19, 1798–OCTOBER 8, 1799

The purpose of the armada had been so well concealed that nearly all the 54,000 men set out with no knowledge of their destination. In a characteristic proclamation to the new "Army of the Orient" Napoleon merely called it a "wing of the Army of England," and asked his sailors and warriors to trust him though he could not yet define their task. The secrecy served some purpose: the British government was apparently misled into thinking that the flotilla was preparing to fight its way past Gibraltar and join in the invasion of England. Nelson's ships were lax in their watch on the Mediterranean, and the French argosy evaded them.

On June 9 it sighted Malta. The Directory had bribed the grandmaster and other dignitaries of the Knights of Malta* to make only a token resistance;[67] as a result the French took the supposedly impregnable fortress with the loss of only three men. Napoleon dallied there a week to reorganize the administration of the island Gaulward. There Alfred de Vigny, poet-to-be but then a child of two years, was introduced to the conqueror, who raised him and kissed him; "when he lowered me carefully to the deck he had won one more slave."[68] The godlike man, however, was seasick nearly all the way to Alexandria. Meanwhile he studied the Koran.

The fleet reached Alexandria July 1, 1798. The port was guarded by a garrison, and a landing there would be costly; yet an early and orderly disembarkation was imperative if the squadron was not to be surprised by Nelson's fleet. The neighboring surf was threateningly rough, but Napoleon in person led a landing party of five thousand men upon an unprotected beach. These, without cavalry or artillery, advanced at night upon the garrison, overcame it at the cost of two hundred French casualties, took possession of the city, and provided the protection under which the ships deposited the soldiers and their armament upon Egyptian soil.

Armed with this victory and a few words of Arabic, Napoleon persuaded the local leaders to sit down with him in conference. He amused and then impressed them by his knowledge of the Koran and his clever use of its phrases and ideas. He pledged himself and his army to respect their religion, laws, and possessions. He promised—if they would help him with laborers and supplies—to win back for them the lands seized by the Mameluke mercenaries who had made themselves masters of Egypt under indolent dynasties. The Arabs half agreed, and on July 7 Napoleon bade his wondering army follow him across 150 miles of desert to Cairo.

They had never experienced such heat, such thirst, such blinding sand, such indefatigable insects, or such disabling dysentery. Bonaparte partly quieted their complaints by sharing their hardships silently. On July 10 they reached the Nile, drank their fill, and refreshed their flesh. After five more days of marching, their vanguard sighted, near the village of Kobrakit, an army of three thousand Mamelukes: "a splendid body of mounted men" (Napoleon recalled them), "all gleaming with gold and silver, armed with the best London carbines and pistols, and the best sabers of the East, riding perhaps the best horses on the Continent."[69] Soon the Mameluke cavalry fell upon the French line, front and flank, only to be felled by the musketry and artillery of the French. Wounded in flesh and pride, the Mamelukes turned and fled.

On July 20, still eighteen miles from Cairo, the victors caught sight of the Pyramids. That evening Napoleon learned that an army of six thousand

* So the medieval order of the Hospital of St. John of Jerusalem had come to be known from their long occupancy of Malta (1530 ff.).

mounted Mamelukes, under twenty-three district beys, had assembled at Embaba, ready to challenge the infidel invaders. The next afternoon they fell in full force upon the French in the crucial battle of the Pyramids. There, if we may trust Napoleon's memory, he told his soldiers, "Forty centuries have their eyes upon you."[70] Again the French met the onslaught with cannon, musket fire, and fixed bayonets; seventy of them died there, and fifteen hundred Mamelukes; many of the defeated, in heedless flight, leaped into the Nile and were drowned. On July 22 the Turkish authorities in Cairo sent Napoleon the keys of the city in token of surrender. On July 23 he entered the picturesque capital without any offensive display.

From that center he issued orders for the administration of Egypt by Arab divans (committees) subject to his control. He prevented pillage by his troops, and protected existing property rights, but he continued and appropriated, for the support of his army, the taxes customarily levied by the Mameluke conquerors. He sat down with native leaders, professed respect for Islamic rites and art, recognized Allah as the one and only god, and asked for Moslem aid in bringing a new prosperity to Egypt. He summoned his scientists to design methods of eliminating plagues, introducing new industries, improving Egyptian education and jurisprudence, establishing postal and transport services, repairing canals, controlling irrigation, and joining the Nile with the Red Sea. In July, 1799, he organized local and French savants into the Institute of Egypt, and set up spacious quarters for it in Cairo. It was these scholars who prepared the twenty-four massive volumes financed and published by the French government as *Description de l'Égypte* (1809–28). One of these men, known to us only as Bouchard, found in 1799, in a town thirty miles from Alexandria, the Rosetta Stone, whose inscription, in two languages and three scripts (hieroglyphic, demotic, and Greek) enabled Thomas Young to begin (1814), and Jean-François Champollion to establish (1821), a method of translating hieroglyphic texts, thereby opening up to "modern" Europe the astonishingly complex and mature civilization of ancient Egypt. This was the chief—and the only significant—result of Napoleon's expedition.

For a while he was allowed to enjoy the pride of conquest and the zest of administration. In later retrospect he told Mme. de Rémusat:

> The time which I passed in Egypt was the most delightful of my life. . . . In Egypt I found myself free from the wearisome restraints of civilization. I dreamed all sorts of things, and I saw how all that I dreamed might be realized. I created a religion. I pictured myself on the road to Asia, mounted on an elephant, with a turban on my head, and in my hand a new Koran, which I should compose according to my own ideas. . . . I was to have attacked the English power in India, and renewed my relations with old Europe by my conquest. . . . Fate decided against my dream.[71]

Fate's first blow was the information conveyed to him by an aide-de-camp, Andoche Junot, that Josephine had taken a lover in Paris. The great dreamer, with all his intellectual brilliance, had neglected to consider how hard it would be for so tropical a plant as Josephine to go for many months without some tangible appreciation of her charms. For some days he mourned and raged. Then, on July 26, 1798, he sent a despondent letter to his brother Joseph:

> I may be in France again in two months. . . . There is plenty to worry me at home. . . . Your friendship means a lot to me; were I to lose it, and see you betraying me, I should be a complete misanthrope. . . .
> I want you to arrange to have a country place ready for me when I return, either in Burgundy or near Paris. I am counting on spending the winter there, and seeing no one. I am sick of society. I need solitude, isolation. My feelings are dried up, and I am bored with public display. I am tired of glory at twenty-nine; it has lost its charm; and there is nothing left for me but complete egotism. . . .
> Goodbye, my one and only friend. . . . My love to your wife and Jérôme.

He found some distraction by taking as a mistress a young Frenchwoman who had followed her officer husband to Egypt. Pauline Fourès could not resist the interest that Napoleon took in her gay beauty; she returned his smiles, and made no insuperable protest when he cleared his path by sending M. Fourès on a mission to Paris. When the husband learned the reason for his distinction he returned to Cairo and divorced Pauline. Napoleon too thought of divorce, and played with the idea of marrying Pauline and begetting an heir; but he reckoned without Josephine's tears. Pauline was solaced with a substantial gift, and survived the mishap by sixty-nine years.

A week after Junot's revelation, a major disaster imprisoned the Army of the Orient in its victory. On leaving his fleet at Alexandria, Napoleon (according to Napoleon) had ordered Vice-Admiral François-Paul Brueys to unload all matériel useful to the troops, and then to sail as soon as possible to French-held Corfu; every measure must be taken to avoid interception by the British. Bad weather delayed Brueys' departure; meanwhile he anchored the squadron in the neighboring Bay of Abukir. There, on July 31, 1798, Nelson found him and soon attacked. The opposed forces seemed evenly matched: the English with fourteen ships of the line and one brig, the French with thirteen ships of the line and four frigates. But the French crews were rebelliously homesick and inadequately trained; the British sailors had made the sea their second home; now their superior discipline, seamanship, and courage won the day—and night, for the bloody conflict lasted till dawn of August 1. At 10 P.M. on July 31, Brueys' 120-gun flagship blew up, killing nearly all men aboard, including the Vice-Admiral himself, aged forty-five. Only two French vessels escaped capture. Altogether the French lost over 1,750 dead, 1,500 wounded; the British lost 218 dead, 672 (including Nelson) wounded. This and Trafalgar (1805) were the last attempts of Napoleonic France to question England's domination of the seas.

When the news of this overwhelming reverse reached him at Cairo, Bonaparte realized that his conquest of Egypt had been made meaningless. His tired adventurers were now shut off, by both land and sea, from French aid, and must soon be at the mercy of a hostile population and an uncongenial environment. It is to their young commander's credit that in his own grief he found time to console the widow of his vice-admiral:

Cairo, August 19, 1798

Your husband was killed by a cannon ball whilst fighting on board his ship. He died honorably, and without suffering, as every soldier would wish to die.

Your sorrow touches me to the quick. It is a dread moment when we are parted from one we love. . . . If there were no reason for living it would be better to die. But when second thoughts come, and you press your children to your heart, your nature is revived by tears and tenderness, and you live for the sake of your offspring. Yes, Madame, you will weep with them, you will nurture them in infancy, you will educate their youth; you will speak to them of their father and your grief, of their love and the Republic's. And when you have linked your soul to the world again through the mutual affection of mother and child, I want you to count as of some value my friendship, and the lively interest that I shall always take in the wife of my friend. Be assured that there *are* men . . . who can turn grief into hope because they feel so intimately the troubles of the heart.[72]

Adversities multiplied. Almost every day there were attacks upon the French settlements by Arabs, Turks, or Mamelukes unreconciled to their new masters. On October 16 the populace of Cairo itself erupted in revolt; the French suppressed it at some cost to their morale; and Napoleon, abandoning for a time the role of an amiable conqueror, ordered the decapitation of every armed rebel.[73]

Hearing that Turkey was preparing an army to reach and reclaim Egypt, he determined to meet the challenge by leading thirteen thousand of his men into Syria. They set out on February 10, 1799, captured El 'Arish, and crossed the Sinai Desert. Napoleon's letter of February 27 described some aspects of that ordeal: heat, thirst, "brackish water, often none at all; we ate dogs, monkeys, and camels." Happily they found at Gaza, after a hard battle, a flourishing agriculture and orchards of incomparable fruit.

At Jaffa (March 3) they were stopped by a walled city, a hostile populace, and a citadel defended by 2,700 virile Turks. Napoleon sent them an emissary to offer terms; these were rejected. On March 7, French sappers made a breach in the wall; French troops rushed in, killed the resisting population, and pillaged the town. Napoleon sent Eugène de Beauharnais to restore order; he offered a safe exit to all who would surrender; the citadel troops, to save the town from further desolation, gave up their arms, and were brought as prisoners to Napoleon. He threw up his hands in dismay. "What can I do with them?" he asked. He could not take 2,700 prisoners along on the march; his men had all they could do to find food and drink for themselves. He could not spare a guard numerous enough to take the Turks to imprisonment in Cairo. If he set them free there was nothing to prevent them from fighting the French again. Napoleon called a council of his officers and asked them for their judgment. They decided that the best course was to kill the prisoners. Some three hundred were spared; 2,441 (including civilians of all ages and both sexes) were shot, or were bayoneted to save ammunition.[74]

The invaders marched, and on March 18 they reached the heavily fortified town of Acre. The Turkish resistance was led by Djezzar Pasha, aided by Antoine de Phélippeaux—who had been Napoleon's fellow student at Brienne. The French laid siege, without the siege artillery that had been sent them by sea from Alexandria; an English squadron under Sir William Sidney Smith captured those weapons, delivered them to the fort, and then kept the garrison supplied with food and matériel during the siege. On May 20, after two months' effort and heavy losses, Napoleon ordered a retreat to Egypt. "Phélippeaux," he mourned, "held me back before Acre. If it had not been for him I would have been master of the key to the Orient. I would have gone on to Constantinople, and would have restored the Eastern Empire."[75] In 1803, not foreseeing 1812, he said to Mme. de Rémusat, "my imagination died at Acre. I shall never allow it to interfere with me again."[76]

The return along the coast was a succession of tragic days, with marches sometimes of eleven hours between wells, to find almost undrinkable water that poisoned the body and hardly quenched thirst. A heavy burden of wounded or plague-stricken men slowed the procession. Napoleon asked the physicians to administer fatal doses of opium to the incurably diseased; they refused, and Napoleon withdrew his suggestion.[77] He ordered all horses to be turned over to the task of carrying the sick, and gave to his officers the example of marching on foot.[78] On June 14, after a march of three hundred miles from Acre in twenty-six days, the exhausted army made a triumphal entry into Cairo, displaying seventeen enemy flags and sixteen Turkish officers captured, as proof that the expedition had been a proud success.

On July 11 a hundred vessels deposited at Abukir an army of Turks commissioned to drive the French from Egypt. Napoleon marched north with his best troops, and inflicted upon the Turks so overwhelming a defeat (July 25) that many of them rushed to death in the sea rather than face the onrushing French cavalry.

From English newspapers sent to him by Sidney Smith, Napoleon was astonished to learn that a Second Coalition of the Powers had driven the French out of Germany and had recaptured nearly all of Italy from the Alps to Calabria.[79] The whole edifice of his victories had collapsed in a series of disasters from the Rhine and the Po to Abukir and Acre; and now, in a humiliating checkmate, he found himself and his decimated legions bottled up in a hostile blind alley where only a little time would be needed for their annihilation.

About the middle of July he received from the Directory an order, sent him on May 26, to return to Paris at once.[80] He resolved to get back to France somehow, despite the encompassing British; to forge a path to power; and to displace the fumbling leaders who had allowed all his gains in Italy to be so quickly annulled. Back in Cairo he arranged affairs military and administrative, and appointed the reluctant Kléber to command the battered remains of the Egyptian dream. The treasury of the army was empty, and was six million francs in debt; the pay of the soldiers was four million in arrears; their number, their morale, were falling with every day, while their reluctant hosts were increasing in strength, and waiting with silent patience for another opportunity to revolt. At any time the governments of Turkey and Great Britain might send to Egypt a force that, with native aid, could sooner or later bring the French to a helpless surrender. Napoleon knew all this, and could only excuse his departure by claiming that he was needed in Paris and had been ordered to return. When he bade goodbye to the troops (to each of whom he had promised six hectares of land after a triumphant homecoming) he vowed, "If I have the good fortune to reach France the rule of those babblers [*bavards*] will be finished,"[81] and aid would come to these immured conquerors. It never came.

Two frigates—the *Muiron* and the *Carrère*—had survived the holocaust at Abukir. Napoleon sent word to have them prepared for an attempt to reach France. On August 23, 1799, he, with Bourrienne, Berthollet, and Monge, boarded the *Muiron;* Generals Lannes, Murat, Denon, and others followed on the *Carrère*.[82] By permission of fog and the great god Chance they escaped all the eyes and scouts of Nelson's fleet. They could not stop at Malta, for the victorious British had seized that stronghold on February 9. On October 9 the ships anchored off Fréjus, and Napoleon and his aides were rowed to shore at St.-Raphaël. Now it was to be *aut Caesar aut nullus*— either Caesar or nobody.

VII. THE DECLINE OF THE DIRECTORY: SEPTEMBER 4, 1797– NOVEMBER 9, 1799

The successes of the French armies—culminating in the submission of Prussia at Basel in 1795, of Austria at Campoformio in 1797, and of Naples and Switzerland in 1798—softened the French government into an almost Oriental lassitude. The two chambers of the Corps Législatif submitted to the Directory, and the five Directors acknowledged the leadership of Barras, Rewbell, and Larevellière. These men seem to have adopted the motto that legend ascribed to Pope Leo X: "Since God has given us this office, let us enjoy it." Blessed with apparent security by a period of relative peace, and taught by experience that governmental positions are especially insecure in revolutions, they feathered their nests for their fall. When isolated England offered peace in July, 1797, it was told that this could be arranged by the payment of £500,000 to Rewbell and Barras; and apparently a bribe of £400,000 was exacted from Portugal for the peace granted it in August of that year.[83] Rewbell was rapacious, and Barras needed an elastic income to keep Mme. Tallien and his associates in good humor, and to maintain his luxurious apartment in the Luxembourg Palace.[84] Talleyrand, as minister of foreign affairs, seldom lost an opportunity to make the Revolution finance his aristocratic tastes; Barras calculated that Talleyrand's tips often exceeded 100,000 livres in a year.[85] In October, 1797, three American commissioners came to Paris to settle a dispute about American vessels captured by French privateers; according to President John Adams, they were told that agreement could be reached by a loan of 32 million florins to the Directors, and by a private *douceur* of £50,000 to Talleyrand.[86]

The ruling triumvirate faced so many problems that most of their faults might be forgiven them—at least an evening's refreshment in the smiles of fair women. They averted another fiscal collapse by collecting traditional taxes more insistently, restoring defunct taxes like transport tolls, and levying new taxes—as on licenses and stamps, windows and doors. They presided over a nation torn in body and soul, in province and class, by conflicting aims: nobles and plutocrats, Vendéan Catholics, Jacobin atheists, Babeuvian socialists, merchants demanding liberty, a populace dreaming of equality and living on the edge of starvation; luckily the good harvests of 1796 and 1798 shortened the bread lines.

The victory of the "liberal" over the monarchical Directors in 1797 had been achieved by enlisting the support of the radicals. In partial payment therefor the triumphant trio censored the bourgeois-leaning press and theater, rigged elections, made arrests without warning, and renewed the Hébertist campaign against religion. Education of the young was taken from nuns and entrusted to lay instructors who were ordered to keep all super-natural ideas out of their teaching.[87] In twelve months of 1797–98, a total of 1,448 priests were deported from France, 8,235 from Belgium. Of 193 ec-clesiastics deported on the ship *Décade* only thirty-nine were alive two years later.[88]

While internal conflict flourished, external danger rose. In Belgium, Hol-land, and the Rhineland the rapacity of the Directory made new enemies of new friends; taxes were high, youths resisted conscription, forced loans in-furiated the influential, seizure of gold and silver and art from the churches alienated clergy and people alike. In three years the Directory took in from these lands and Italy two billion livres.[89] After the departure of Bonaparte for Egypt "the Directory continued a policy of conquest, or rather of rapine, occupying territories for money's sake, pillaging the population, exacting 'indemnities' from local governments, making France an object of execration."[90] "The French Republic," said the monarchist Mallet du Pan, "is eating Europe leaf by leaf, like the head of an artichoke. It revolutionizes nations that it may despoil them, and it despoils them that it may subsist."[91] War had become profitable, peace would be ruinous. Suspecting that the ship of state was sailing into a storm, Talleyrand resigned his ministry (July 20, 1798), and retired to spend his spoils.[92]

Napoleon had given a stimulating example of how war could be made to pay, and his reckless operations were in part responsible for the military woes that befell France in the decline of the Directory. He had too quickly and superficially subjected Italy to a French protectorate, and had left his conquests in the hands of subordinates who lacked his soothing subtlety and diplomatic skill. He had reckoned too optimistically on the willingness of the new Italian republics to pay France for their freedom from Austria. He had underestimated the vigor with which England would resist the French occupation of Malta and Egypt. How long would flouted Turkey resist the invitations of its ancient enemies, Russia and Austria, to join them in disciplining these *nouveaux-riches* revolutionaries? How long would the partitioning of Poland keep Russia, Prussia, and Austria too busy in the east to restore the divine right of kings in the west?

Nearly all the monarchs of Europe watched for an opportunity to renew the attack upon France. They saw it when Napoleon took himself and 35,000 of France's best troops to Egypt; they seized it when that army seemed safely imprisoned by Nelson's victory at Abukir. Czar Paul I accepted election as grandmaster of the Knights of Malta, and pledged himself to drive the French from that pivotal isle. He offered his aid to Ferdinand IV in recapturing Naples. He dreamed of finding friendly ports for Russian ships in Naples, Malta, and Alexandria, and thereby making Russia a Mediterranean power. On December 29, 1798, he signed an alliance with England. When Emperor Francis II gave free passage through Austrian territory for a Russian army moving toward the Rhine, France declared war upon Austria (March 12, 1799). Austria thereupon joined Russia, Turkey, Naples, Portugal, and England in the Second Coalition against France.

The weakness of the Directory was exposed in this conflict, which it had provoked and could have foreseen. It was tardy in preparation, unsuccessful in war finance, and clumsy in conscription. It called up 200,000 men, and found only 143,000 of them fit for service; of them only 97,000 obeyed the summons; thousands of these deserted on the way, so that only 74,000 reached their allotted regiments. There they found a chaotic inadequacy of clothing, equipment, and arms. The spirit that had once animated the armies of the republic was gone from these men who had experienced the years of national disorder and disillusionment. The ruthless determination and discipline with which the Committee of Public Safety had planned and waged war in 1793 were missing in the Directory that led France in 1798.

There were some initial and deceiving successes. Piedmont and Tuscany were conquered, occupied, and taxed. The victory of King Ferdinand IV in driving the French out of Rome was annulled by the French under Jean-Étienne Championnet, who entered Rome on December 15. Ferdinand and his court, with Lady Hamilton and twenty million ducats, retreated to Palermo under the protection of Nelson's fleet. Championnet captured Naples, and set up the Parthenopean Republic under the protectorate of France. As the war proceeded, and fresh contingents joined the Russian-Austrian-English troops, the French forces found themselves outnumbered 320,000 to 170,000. The French generals, despite the brilliance of Masséna's operations in Switzerland, lacked the ability of Bonaparte to overcome superior numbers with superior strategy, tactics, and discipline. Jourdan was defeated at Stockach (March 25, 1799), retreated to Strasbourg, and resigned. Schérer was defeated at Magnano (April 5), retreated in disorder, lost nearly all his army, and turned his command over to Moreau. Then a veritable "devil of a man," Aleksandr Suvorov, arrived with eighteen thousand Russians, and led them and some Austrian divisions in a ferocious campaign that wrested from the French one after another of the regions that

Napoleon had won in 1796–97; he entered Milan victorious on April 27; Moreau fell back to Genoa; Napoleon's Cisalpine Republic came to an early end. Left perilously alone with his small army in Switzerland, Masséna abandoned his conquests there, and withdrew to the Rhine.

Having so easily restored Lombardy to Austria, Suvorov marched out from Milan to meet a French force coming up from Naples and Rome; at the Trebbia (June 17–19, 1799) he so overwhelmed it that only a shattered remnant reached Genoa. The Parthenopean Republic came to an early end; Ferdinand resumed his Neapolitan throne, and established a reign of terror in which hundreds of democrats were put to death. Joubert, placed in command of all surviving French forces in Italy, led them against Suvorov at Novi (August 15); he exposed himself recklessly, and was killed at the outset of the battle; the French fought bravely but in vain; twelve thousand of them fell on that field; and France, learning of this culminating catastrophe, realized that its hard-won frontiers were crumbling, and that Suvorov's Russians might soon be on French soil. The imagination of the populace in Alsace and Provence pictured him and his men as "giant barbarians," as a tidal wave of savage Slavs pouring into the towns and hamlets of France.

The country, so recently proud of its strength and its victories, was now in a state of confusion and fear rivaling that which in 1792 had led to the September Massacres. The Vendée was again in revolt; Belgium was rising against its French overlords; forty-five of the eighty-six departments of France were nearing a complete breakdown of government and morale. Armed youths were fighting the officials sent to conscript them; municipal officers and tax collectors were murdered; hundreds of brigands were terrorizing merchants and travelers on city streets and country roads; criminals overpowered the gendarmes, opened the jails, released the prisoners, and added them to their ranks; every estate, abbey, and home was subject to pillage; the "Great Terror" of 1794 had returned. The nation looked hopefully for protection by the men it had sent to Paris; but the Councils had surrendered to the Directory, and the Directory seemed but another usurping oligarchy, ruling by bribery, chicanery, and force.

In May, 1799, the once-abbé Sieyès—who, ten long years ago, had sparked the Revolution by asking "What is the Third Estate?" and had answered that it was, and should call itself, the nation—was drawn out of his cautious obscurity, and was elected to the Directory; for, as a maker of constitutions, he had become identified with law and order. He agreed to serve, on condition that Rewbell would resign; Rewbell resigned with a consolatory severance pay of 100,000 francs.[93] On June 18 a strong minority of Jacobins in the two legislative chambers forced Directors Larevellière, Treilhard, and Merlin to yield their places to Louis-Jérôme Gohier, Jean-François Moulin, and Roger Ducos. Fouché was made minister of police, and Robert Lindet became head of the Treasury; both were resurrections from the Committee of Public Safety. The Jacobin Club in Paris was reopened, and heard praises of Robespierre and Babeuf.[94]

On June 28 the Legislature, under Jacobin influence, levied a forced loan of a hundred million livres in the form of a tax ranging from thirty to seventy-five percent upon incomes above a moderate level. Prosperous citizens hired lawyers to find loopholes in the law, and listened amiably to plots for the overthrow of the government. On July 12 the Jacobins secured passage of a Law of Hostages: every commune in France was ordered to compile a roster of local citizens related to the outlawed nobility, and to keep them under surveillance; for every robbery committed these hostages were to be fined; for every murder of a "patriot" (one loyal to the existing regime) four hostages were to be deported. This decree was met with a cry of horror from the upper classes, and with no compensating welcome from the commonalty.

After a decade of excitement, class strife, foreign wars, political upsets, lawless tribunals, tyrannical spoliations, executions, and massacres, nearly all of France was sick of the Revolution. Those who looked back sadly to the "good old days" of Louis XVI felt that only a king could bring France back to order and sanity. Those who cherished Catholic Christianity prayed for the time when they would be freed from rule by atheists. Even some graduate skeptics who had shed all supernatural belief had come to doubt that a moral code unsupported by a religious faith could resist unfettered passions and antisocial impulses rooted in centuries of insecurity, hunting, and savagery; many creedless parents were sending their children to church, prayer, confession, and First Communion as hopeful sources of modesty, family discipline, and mental peace. Peasants and bourgeois proprietors who owed their lands to the Revolution, and wanted to keep them, had come to hate the government that so often came to tax their crops or conscript their sons. Town workers were clamoring for bread even more desperately than before the fall of the Bastille; they saw merchants, manufacturers, speculators, politicians, Directors, living in luxury; they had come to look upon the Revolution as merely the replacement of the nobility by the bourgeoisie as the masters and profiteers of the state. But their bourgeois masters too were discontent. The unsafe and neglected roads made travel and commerce toilsome and hazardous; the forced loans and high taxes discouraged investment and enterprise; in Lyons thirteen thousand of fifteen thousand shops had been abandoned as profitless, adding thousands of men and women to the unemployed. Le Havre, Bordeaux, and Marseilles had been ruined by the war and the consequent British blockade. The diminishing minority that still talked of liberty could hardly associate it with the Revolution, which had destroyed so many liberties, had passed so many terrifying laws, and had sent so many men and women to prison or the guillotine. Women, except the wives, mistresses, and daughters of the old and the new rich, moved anxiously from one shopping line to another, wondering would the stock of goods run out, would their sons, brothers, or husbands ever return from the war, would the war ever end. Soldiers accustomed to violence, theft, and hatred, suffering not only from defeat but from the shortage and shoddiness of supplies, were soured by repeated revelations of corruption in the men who led or fed or clothed them; when they came home or to Paris they found similar dishonesty in society, commerce, industry, finance, and government; why should they let themselves be killed for so tarnished a dream? The mirage of a bright new world receded and vanished as the Revolution marched on.

Some spirits were raised for a while by news that the Allies had quarreled and parted, and had been beaten back in Switzerland and the Netherlands; that Masséna had recovered the initiative and had cut a Russian army in two at Zurich (August 26, 1799), that the terrible Slavs were in retreat, and Russia had left the Coalition. Frenchmen began to wonder what if some able general like Masséna, Moreau, Bernadotte, or, best of all, Bonaparte, safely back from Egypt, should lead a battalion into Paris, throw out the politicians, and give France order and security, even at the cost of liberty? Most Frenchmen had come to the conclusion that only a centralized government under one authoritative leader could end the chaos of revolution, and give the country the order and security of civilized life.

VIII. NAPOLEON TAKES CHARGE: THE 18TH BRUMAIRE (NOVEMBER 9), 1799

Sieyès agreed. Studying his fellow Directors, he saw that none of them —not even the crafty Barras—had in him the combination of intellect, vision, and will needed to bring France to sanity and unity. He was pregnant with a constitution, but he wanted a general to aid him in its birth and serve him as his arm. He had thought of Joubert, but now Joubert was dead. He sent for Moreau, and almost persuaded him to be the "man on horseback"; but when they learned that Napoleon was returning from Egypt, Moreau told Sieyès: "There is your man; he will make your *coup d'état* much better than I could."[95] Sieyès pondered; Napoleon could be the man, but would he accept Sieyès and the new constitution as his guides?

On October 13 the Directors notified the Councils that Bonaparte had landed near Fréjus; the members rose in acclamation. For three days and nights the people of Paris celebrated the news with drinking in the taverns and singing in the streets. At every town on the route from the coast to the capital the populace and its masters turned out to greet the man who seemed to them the symbol and assurance of victory; they had not yet heard of the debacle in Egypt. In several centers, reported the *Moniteur*, "the crowd was such that traffic could hardly advance."[96] In Lyons a play was staged in his honor, and an orator told him, "Go and fight the enemy, defeat him, and we will make you king."[97] But the little general, silent and somber, was thinking how he should deal with Josephine.

When he reached Paris (October 16), he went directly to the house which he had bought in the street which had been renamed, in his honor, the Rue de la Victoire. He had hoped to find his errant wife there, and to dismiss her from his life. She was not there, and for two reasons. First, on April 21, 1799, while he was besieging Acre, she had bought a 300-acre estate, Malmaison, some ten miles down the Seine from Paris; Barras had advanced her the 50,000 francs as the initial payment on the 300,000-francs cost; and Captain Hippolyte Charles was her first guest in the roomy châ-teau.[98] Second, she and her daughter had left Paris four days before to drive toward Lyons in the hope of meeting Bonaparte on the way. When Jose-phine and Hortense discovered that Napoleon had chosen an alternative route, they turned back, though literally sick of travel, and retraced two hundred miles to the capital. In the interim her aged father-in-law, the Mar-quis de Beauharnais, came to Napoleon to plead her cause: "Whatever her faults, forget them; do not cast dishonor upon my white head, and upon a family that holds you in honor."[99] Bonaparte's brothers urged him to di-vorce his wife, for his family resented her power over him; but Barras warned him that a public scandal would hurt his political career.

When the exhausted mother and daughter arrived at 3 Rue de la Victoire (October 18), Eugène met them on the landing, and warned them to ex-pect a storm. Letting him attend to his sister, Josephine climbed the stairs and knocked at the door of Napoleon's room. He answered that he was resolved never to see her again. She sank down upon the stairs and wept until Eugène and Hortense raised her and led her back to make a united appeal. Napoleon later reported: "I was profoundly stirred. I could not bear the sobs of those two children. I asked myself, should they be made the victims of their mother's failing? I reached out, caught hold of Eugène's arm and drew him back to me. Then Hortense came . . . with her mother. . . . What was there to say? One cannot be human without being heir to human weaknesses."[100]

In those brooding days he kept out of the public eye; he knew that a public man must not be too public. At home and abroad he wore civilian dress, to discourage rumors that the Army was planning to seize the gov-ernment. He made two visits: one to pay his respects to the eighty-year-old Mme. Helvétius at Auteuil; the other to the Institute. There he talked of the Egyptian expedition as having been undertaken in large part in the inter-ests of science; Berthollet and Monge supported him; Laplace, Lagrange, Cabanis, and many others listened to him as to a scientist and a philoso-pher.[101] At this meeting he encountered Sieyès, and won him with one re-mark: "We have no government because we have no constitution, or at least not the one we need; your genius must give us one."[102]

Soon his home became a center of secret negotiations. He received visitors from Left and Right. He promised the Jacobins to preserve the republic and defend the interests of the masses; but also, he later frankly declared, "I received the agents of the Bourbons."[103] However, he kept himself apart from any faction, especially the Army. General Bernadotte, who had some notion of heading the government himself, advised him to stay out of poli-tics and be content with another military command. Napoleon listened with more satisfaction to civilians like Sieyès, who advised him to take over the government and inaugurate a new constitution. This might require stretch-ing or breaking a law or two; but the Council of Ancients, alarmed by a

Jacobin revival, would wink at a little illegality; and the Council of Five Hundred, despite its strong Jacobin minority, had recently elected Lucien Bonaparte its president. Of the five Directors, Sieyès and Ducos pledged themselves to Napoleon; Talleyrand undertook to persuade Barras to retire on his laurels and loot; Gohier, president of the Directory, was half in love with Josephine, and could be immobilized by her smiles.[104] Some bankers probably sent assurance of friendly francs.[105]

In the first week of November a rumor spread through Paris that the Jacobins were preparing an uprising of the populace. Mme. de Staël took the report seriously enough to prepare for a quick exit if violence should break out.[106] On November 9 (the henceforth famous eighteenth day of the month Brumaire) the Council of Ancients, using its constitutional powers, ordered both itself and the Council of Five Hundred to transfer their assemblies, on the morrow, to the royal palace in suburban St.-Cloud. Stretching its constitutional powers, it appointed Bonaparte commander of the Paris garrison, and bade him come at once to the Ancients in the Tuileries and take the oath of service. He came, escorted by sixty officers, and pledged himself in terms sufficiently general to allow some latitude of later interpretation: "We want a republic based on liberty, equality, and the sacred principles of national representation. We will have it, I swear!"[107]

Emerging from the hall, he told the assembled troops, "The Army is reunited with me, and I am reunited with the Corps Législatif." At this juncture one Bottot, secretary to Barras, brought to Napoleon a message from the once powerful Director, asking for a safe-conduct for exit from Paris. In a voice which he hoped the soldiers and civilians would hear, Napoleon overwhelmed poor Bottot with an apostrophe that was almost a sentence of death upon the Directory: "What have you done with this France which I left you in its full splendor? I left you peace, and I find war; I left you victories, and I find defeats! I left you millions from Italy; I find everywhere spoliation and misery. What have you done with the hundred thousand Frenchmen whom I knew, my companions in glory? They are dead."

Napoleon's auditors did not know that he was borrowing some of these lines from a Grenoble Jacobin; they felt their force, and long treasured them in memory as a justification of the coup that was to follow. Then, fearing that his words would arouse Barras to antagonism, he took Bottot aside and assured him that his personal sentiments about the Director remained unchanged.[108] He mounted his horse, reviewed the troops, and returned to Josephine all atremble with his success as an orator.

On November 10 General Lefebvre led five hundred men of the Paris garrison to St.-Cloud, and stationed them near the royal palace. Napoleon and some of his favorite officers followed; and after them came Sieyès, Ducos, Talleyrand, Bourrienne. They watched the Council of Ancients assemble in the Gallery of Mars, and the Council of Five Hundred in the adjoining Orangerie. As soon as Lucien Bonaparte called the Five Hundred to order he was met with protests against the presence of soldiers around the palace; cries arose of "No dictatorship! Down with the dictators! We are free men here; the bayonets do not frighten us!" A motion was presented that every deputy should proceed to the rostrum and audibly renew his oath to protect the constitution. It was so ordered, and this balloting proceeded leisurely till four in the afternoon.

The Ancients also took their time, on the ground that it had to wait for the Five Hundred to submit proposals. Napoleon, fretting in a nearby room, feared that unless some decisive action were soon taken his cause would be lost. Between Berthier and Bourrienne he made his way to the rostrum of the Ancients, and attempted to stir these old men into action. But he, who was so eloquent in proclamations, and so decisive in conversation, was too pent up with emotions and ideas to extemporize an orderly address to a legislative body. He spoke abruptly, vehemently, almost incoherently:

> You are on a volcano! . . . Allow me to speak with the freedom of a soldier. . . . I was at peace in Paris when you called upon me to execute your commands. . . . I gather my comrades; we have flown to your rescue. . . . People cover me with calumnies; they talk of Caesar, of Cromwell, of military government. . . . Time presses; it is essential that you take prompt measures. The Republic has no government; only the Council of Ancients remains. Let it take measures, let it speak; I will be your agent in action. Let us save liberty! Let us save equality![109]

A deputy interrupted him: "And the constitution?" Napoleon replied with angry passion, "The constitution? You yourselves have destroyed it; you violated it on the eighteenth Fructidor; you violated it on the twenty-second Floréal; you violated it on the thirtieth Prairial. It no longer holds any man's respect." When challenged to name the men behind the alleged Jacobin plot, he named Barras and Moulin; asked for evidence, he faltered, and could think of nothing more convincing than an appeal to the soldiers who stood at the entrance: "You, my brave comrades, who accompany me, brave grenadiers, . . . if any orator, brought by a foreigner, dares pronounce the words *Hors la loi*, let the lightning of war crush him instantly."[110] Questions and objections overwhelmed the speaker; his words became more confused; his aides came to his rescue and escorted him from the chamber.[111] He appeared to have ruined his enterprise.

He resolved to try again, and this time to face the enemy directly—the Jacobin-colored Five Hundred. Escorted by four grenadiers, he made his way into the Orangerie. The deputies were angered by the military display; the hall resounded with cries of "*À bas le dictateur! À bas le tyran! Hors la loi!* [Outlaw him!]"; this was the cry that had precipitated the fall and death of Robespierre. A motion to declare Napoleon an outlaw was made; Lucien Bonaparte, chairman, refused to put it to a vote; resigning the presidency of the Five Hundred to a friend, he mounted the tribune, and spoke in defense of his brother. Excited deputies surrounded Napoleon. "Is it for this that you won your victories?" one asked; others pressed upon him so closely that he was near to fainting; the grenadiers forced their way to him and led him out of the hall. Revived by the open air, he mounted a horse and appealed to the troops, who stood amazed by his torn clothing and disheveled hair. "Soldiers, may I count upon you?" he asked. "Yes," many said, but others hesitated. Napoleon was again confused; his grand design again seemed shattered.

He was saved by his brother. Lucien, hurrying from the Orangerie, jumped upon the nearest horse, rode up beside Napoleon, and spoke to the disorganized guardsmen with authority, eloquence, and considerable bending of the truth:

> As president of the Council of Five Hundred I declare to you that the immense majority of the Council is at this moment terrorized by some stiletto-armed representatives who besiege the tribune and threaten death to their colleagues. . . . I declare that these audacious brigands, doubtless paid by England, have rebelled against the Council of the Ancients, and have dared to speak of outlawing the general charged with executing the Ancients' decree. . . . I entrust to warriors the responsibility of delivering the majority of their representatives. Generals, soldiers, citizens, you must recognize as legislators for France only those who rally to me. As for those who persist in remaining in the Orangerie, let force expel them.[112]

Lucien grasped a sword, pointed it at Napoleon's breast, and swore that if his brother should ever attack the liberty of the French people he would kill him with his own hand.

Thereupon Napoleon gave orders for the drums to sound, and for the troops to invade the Orangerie and disperse the disobedient deputies. Murat and Lefebvre led the way, shouting; the grenadiers followed, crying, *"Bravo! À bas les Jacobins! À bas les '93! C'est le passage du Rubicon!"* When the deputies saw the bayonets advancing upon them, most of them fled, some by jumping from windows; a minority gathered around Lucien. That triumphant master of ceremonies proceeded to the Ancients and explained to them that the Five Hundred had experienced a healing purge. The Ancients, glad to survive, passed a decree replacing the Directory with three "Provisional Consuls"—Bonaparte, Sieyès, and Ducos. About a hundred of the Five Hundred were organized into a second chamber. Both chambers then adjourned till February 20, 1800, leaving the Consuls to write a new constitution and to govern France. "Tomorrow," Napoleon said to Bourrienne, "we shall sleep at the Luxembourg."[113]

CHAPTER VI

Life under the Revolution

1789–99

I. THE NEW CLASSES

HERE we stop time in its flight, and look at a people suffering concentrated history. Like the twenty years between Caesar's crossing of the Rubicon and the accession of Augustus (49–29 B.C.), the twenty-six years between the taking of the Bastille and the final abdication of Napoleon (1789–1815) were as rich in memorable events as centuries had been in less convulsive and remolding periods. Nevertheless, under the tremors of government, the flux of institutions, and the exaltations of genius, the elements and graces of civilization carried on: the production and distribution of food and goods, the quest and transmission of knowledge, the discipline of instinct and character, the exchanges of affection, the mitigations of toil and strife with art, letters, charity, games, and song; the transmutations of imagination, faith, and hope. And indeed were not these the reality and continuum of history, beside which the surface agitations of governments and heroes were the incidental and evanescent contours of a dream?

1. *The peasantry*. Many of them, in 1789, were still day laborers or sharecroppers, working other men's land; but by 1793 half the soil of France was owned by peasants, most of whom had bought their acres at bargain prices from the confiscated properties of the Church; and all but a few peasants had freed themselves from feudal dues. The stimulus of ownership turned labor from drudgery into devotion, daily adding to the surplus that built homes and comforts, churches and schools—if only the taxgatherer could be propitiated or deceived. And taxes could be paid with assignats—government paper money—at their face value, while products could be sold for assignats multiplied a hundred times to equal their nominal worth. Never had the French earth been so zealously and fruitfully tilled.

This liberation of the largest class in a now casteless society was the most visible and lasting effect of the Revolution. These sturdy providers became the strongest defenders of the Revolution, for it had given them the land, which a Bourbon restoration might take away. For the same reason they supported Napoleon, and for fifteen years gave him half of their sons. As proud property owners they allied themselves politically with the bourgeoisie, and served, throughout the nineteenth century, as conservative ballast amid the repeated paroxysms of the state.

Pledged to equality of rights, the Convention (1793) abolished primo-geniture, and ruled that property must be willed in equal shares to all the testator's children, including those born out of wedlock but acknowledged by the father. This legislation had important results, moral and economic: reluctant to condemn their heirs to poverty by periodic divisions of the patrimony among many children, the French cultivated the old arts of family limitation. The peasants remained prosperous, but the population of France grew slowly during the nineteenth century—from 28 million in 1800 to 39 million in 1914, while that of Germany rose from 21 million to 67 million.[1] Prospering on the land, French peasants were slow to move into towns and factories; so France remained predominantly agricultural, while England and Germany developed industry and technology, excelled in war, and dominated Europe.

2. *The proletariat*. Poverty remained, and was most severe, among the landless peasants, the miners, and the workers and tradesmen in the towns. Men delved into the earth to find the metals and minerals for industry and war; saltpeter was necessary to gunpowder, and coal increasingly replaced wood as a generator of motive power. Towns were bright and lively by day, dark and subdued at night, till 1793, when the communes installed street lighting in Paris. Craftsmen worked in their candle-lit shops; trades-men displayed, and peddlers hawked, their goods; at the center an open market; near the summit a castle and a church; on the outskirts a factory or two. Guilds were abolished in 1791, and the National Assembly declared that henceforth every person was to be "free to do such business, exercise such profession, art, or trade, as he may choose."[2] The "Law of Le Chapel" (in 1791) forbade workers to combine for united economic action; this pro-hibition remained in effect till 1884. Strikes were forbidden but frequent and sporadic.[3] The workers struggled to keep their wages from being diluted by inflation of the currency; generally, however, they kept their wages abreast of rising prices.[4] After the fall of Robespierre the employers tightened their control, and the condition of the proletariat worsened. By 1795 the sans-culottes were as poor and harassed as before the Revolution. By 1799 they had lost faith in the Revolution, and in 1800 they submitted hopefully to the dictatorship of Napoleon.

3. *The bourgeoisie* triumphed in the Revolution because it had more money and brains than either the aristocracy or the plebs. It purchased from the state the most lucrative portions of the property that had been confis-cated from the Church. Bourgeois wealth was not tied up in immobile land; it could be transferred from place to place, from purpose to purpose, from person to person, and from anywhere to any legislator. The bourgeoisie could pay for troops and governments and insurrectionary crowds. It had acquired experience in the administration of the state; it knew how to col-lect taxes, and it influenced the Treasury through its loans. It was more practically educated than the nobility or the clergy, and was better equipped

to rule a society in which money was the circulating blood. It looked upon poverty as the punishment for stupidity, and upon its own riches as the just reward of application and intelligence. It took no stock in government by sansculottes; it denounced the interruption of government by proletarian uprisings as an intolerable impertinence. It was resolved that when the sound and fury of revolution subsided, the bourgeoisie would be master of the state.

It was in France a commercial rather than an industrial bourgeoisie. There was no such replacement of farms by pasturage as was then driving English peasants from their fields to the towns to form a cheap labor force for factories; and the British blockade prevented in France the export trade that could sustain expanding industries. So the factory system developed more slowly in France than in England. There were some substantial capitalistic organizations in Paris, Lyons, Lille, Toulouse . . . , but most French industry was still in the craft and shop stage, and even the capitalists delegated much handwork to rural or other homes. Except for wartime authoritarian flurries, and some Jacobin flirtations with socialism, the Revolutionary government accepted the Physiocratic theory of free enterprise as the most stimulating and productive economic system. The peace treaties with Prussia in 1795 and Austria in 1797 released the restrictions upon the economy, and French capitalism, like the English and the American, entered the nineteenth century with the blessings of a government that governed least.

4. *The aristocracy* had lost all power in the direction of the economy or the government. Most of its members were still *émigrés*, living abroad in humiliating occupations; their properties had been confiscated, their incomes had stopped. Of those nobles who had remained or had returned, many were guillotined, some joined the Revolution, the rest, till 1794, hid in precarious obscurity and repeated harassment on their estates. Under the Directory these disabilities were lessened; many *émigrés* came back; some recovered part of their property; and by 1797 many voices whispered that only a monarchy, supported and checked by a functioning aristocracy, could restore order and security to French life. Napoleon agreed with them, but after his own fashion, and in his own time.

5. *Religion* in France, as the Revolution neared its end, was learning to get along without the help of the state. Protestants, then five percent of the population, were freed from all civil disabilities; the limited freedom of worship granted them by Louis XVI in 1787 was made complete by the Constitution of 1791. A decree of September 28, 1791, extended all civil rights to the Jews of France, and set them on a legal equality with all other citizens.

The Catholic clergy, formerly the First Estate, now suffered from the hostility of a Voltairean anticlerical government. The upper classes had lost belief in the doctrines of the Church; the middle classes had acquired most of its landed wealth; by 1793 the property of the Church, once valued at

two and a half billion livres,[5] had been sold to its enemies. In Italy the Papacy
had been deprived of its states and their revenues, and Pius VI had been
made a prisoner. Thousands of French priests had fled to other countries,
and many of them were living on Protestant alms.[6] Hundreds of churches
had been closed, or had had their treasures confiscated. Church bells had
been silenced or melted down. Voltaire and Diderot, Helvétius and d'Holbach had apparently won their war against the Church.

The victory was not clear. The Church had lost its wealth and political
power, but its vital roots remained in the loyalty of the clergy and the
needs and hopes of the people. Many males in the large cities had strayed
from the faith; yet nearly all became churchgoers for a day on Christmas
and Easter; and at the height of the Revolution (May, 1793), when a priest
carried the consecrated Host along a Paris street, all onlookers (an eyewitness reported)—"men, women, and children—fell on their knees in adoration."[7] Even skeptics must have felt the mesmerism of the ceremony, the
never-fading beauty of the tale; and they may have pondered Pascal's
"wager"—that one would be wise to believe, since in the end the believer
would lose nothing, unbelievers everything, if proved wrong.

Under the Directory the French nation was divided between a people
slowly returning to its traditional faith and a government resolved to establish, by law and education, a purely secular civilization. On October 8,
1798, the purged and newly radical Directory sent to all teachers in the departmental schools the following instructions:

> You must exclude from your teaching all that relates to the dogmas or rites
> of any religion or sect whatever. The Constitution certainly tolerates them,
> but the teaching of them is not part of public instruction, nor can it ever be.
> The Constitution is founded on the basis of universal morality; and it is this
> morality of all times, all places, all religions—this law engraven on the tablets
> of the human family—it is this that must be the soul of your teaching, the ob-
> ject of your precepts, and the connecting link of your studies, as it is the bind-
> ing knot of society.[8]

Here, clearly put, was one of the most difficult enterprises of the Revolution, as it is one of the difficult problems of our time: to build a social order
upon a system of morality independent of religious belief. Napoleon was to
judge the proposal impracticable; America was to cleave to it till our time.

6. *Education.* So the state took control of the schools from the Church,
and strove to make them the nursery of intelligence, morality, and patriotism. On April 21, 1792, Condorcet, as chairman of public instruction,
presented to the Legislative Assembly an historic report pleading for the
reorganization of education, so that the "ever-increasing progress of enlightenment may open an inexhaustible source of aid to our needs, of remedies for our ills, of means to individual happiness and common prosperity."[9]
War delayed the implementation of this ideal, but on May 4, 1793, Condorcet renewed the appeal, though on a narrower basis. "The country," he

said, "has a right to bring up its own children; it cannot confide this trust to family pride nor to the prejudices of individuals. . . . Education [should be] common and equal for all French people. . . . We stamp upon it a great character, analogous to the nature of our government and the sublime doctrines of our republic."[10] This formulation seemed to substitute one form of indoctrination for another—nationalist instead of Catholic; nationalism was to be the official religion. On October 28, 1793, the Convention ordained that no ecclesiastic could be appointed as teacher in state schools. On December 19 it proclaimed that all primary schools were to be free, and attendance at them was made compulsory on all boys. Girls were expected to get education from their mothers, or from convents or tutors.

The reorganization of secondary schools had to wait for peace; even so, on February 25, 1794, the Convention began to establish those "Écoles Centrales" which were to be the departmental lycées, or high schools, of the future. Special schools were opened for mines, public works, astronomy, music, arts and crafts; and on September 28, 1794, the École Polytechnique began its prestigious career. The French Academy was suppressed on August 8, 1793, as an asylum of old reactionaries, but on October 25, 1795, the Convention inaugurated the Institut National de France, which was to include various academies for the encouragement and regulation of all sciences and arts. Here gathered the scientists and scholars who carried on the intellectual traditions of the Enlightenment, and gave lasting significance to Napoleon's foray into Egypt.

7. The "Fourth Estate"—the journalists and the press—may have been more influential than the schools in forming the mind and the mood of France in these effervescent years. The people of Paris—and, somewhat less so, of France—swallowed newsprint greedily every day. Satirical sheets prospered, goring politicians and pundits to the delight of the commonalty. The Revolution, in the Declaration of the Rights of Man, had pledged itself to maintain the freedom of the press; it did so throughout the rule of the National and Constituent Assemblies (1789–91); but as the heat of party strife rose, each side signalized its victories by limiting the publications of its enemies; in effect the liberty of the press died with the execution of the King (January 21, 1793). On March 18 the Convention decreed death for "whosoever should propose an agrarian law, or any law subversive of territorial, commercial, or industrial property"; and on March 29 the triumphant regicides persuaded the Convention to decree death for "whosoever should be convicted of having composed or printed works or writings which might provoke the . . . reestablishment of royalty, or any other power injurious to the sovereignty of the people."[11] Robespierre had long defended the freedom of the press, but after sending Hébert, Danton, and Desmoulins to the guillotine he put an end to the journals that had supported them. During the Terror all liberty of speech disappeared, even in the Convention. The Directory restored freedom of the press in 1796, but revoked it a year later

after the *coup d'état* of the 18th Fructidor, and deported the editors of forty-two journals.[12] Liberty of speech and press was not destroyed by Napoleon; it was dead when he came to power.[13]

II. THE NEW MORALITY

1. *Morality and Law*

Having discarded the religious basis of morals—love and fear of a watchful, recording, rewarding, and punishing God, and obedience to laws and commandments ascribed to him—the liberated spirits of France found themselves with no defense, except through the ethical echoes of their abandoned creeds, against their oldest, strongest, most individualistic instincts, ingrained in them by primitive centuries of hunger, greed, insecurity, and strife. Leaving the Christian ethic to their wives and daughters, they cast about for a new conception that might serve as a moral anchor in a sea of turbulent individuals who feared nothing but force. They hoped to find this in *civisme*—citizenship in the sense of accepting the duties as well as the privileges of belonging to an organized and protective society; in every moral choice the individual, in return for that protection and many communal services, must recognize the good of the community to be the overriding law—*salus populi suprema lex*. It was a noble attempt to establish a natural ethic. Going back across Christian centuries, the philosopher deputies—Mirabeau, Condorcet, Vergniaud, Roland, Saint-Just, Robespierre—discovered in classical history or legend the models they sought: Leonidas, Epaminondas, Aristides, the Brutuses, Catos, and Scipios; these were men to whom patriotism was the sovereign obligation, so that a man might righteously kill his children or his parents if he thought it necessary for the good of the state.

The first round of revolutionaries fared reasonably well with the new morality. The second round began on August 10, 1792: the Paris populace deposed Louis XVI, and assumed the irresponsible absolutism of power. Under the Old Regime some graces of the aristocracy, some touches of the humanitarianism preached by philosophers and saints, had mitigated the natural tendencies of men to despoil and attack one another; but now there followed, in macabre procession, the September Massacres, the execution of the King and the Queen, and the spread of the Terror and the guillotine in what one victim, Mme. Roland, described as "a vast Golgotha of carnage."[14] The Revolutionary leaders became profiteers of war, making the liberated regions pay liberally for the Rights of Man; the French armies were told to live on the conquered regions; the art treasures of the liberated or the defeated belonged to victorious France. Meanwhile legislators and army officers connived with suppliers to cheat the government and the troops. In the *laissez-faire* economy, producers, distributors, and consumers labored to mulct one another, or to evade the maximum allowable price or wage. These or analogous deviltries had of course existed for some millenniums before the Revolution; but in the attempt to control them the new morality of *civisme* seemed as helpless as the fear of the gods.

As the Revolution increased the insecurity of life and the instability of laws, the rising tensions in the people expressed themselves in crime, and sought distraction in gambling. Duels continued, but less frequently than before. Gambling was forbidden by edicts of 1791 and 1792, but secret *maisons de jeu* multiplied, and by 1794 there were three thousand gambling houses in Paris.[15] During the upper-class affluence of the Directory years men wagered large sums, and many families were ruined by the turn of the wheel. In 1796 the Directory entered the game by restoring the Loterie Nationale. In a petition to the Convention the Tuileries section of the Paris Commune asked for a law suppressing all gambling houses and brothels. "Without morals," it argued, "there can be no law and order; without personal safety, no liberty."[16]

The Revolutionary governments labored to give a new system of laws to a people excitable, violent, and left morally and legally unmoored by the decline of faith and the death of the King. Voltaire had called for a total revision of French law, and a unifying reconciliation of the 360 provincial or district codes into one coherent digest for all of France. That call was not heard amid the uproar of revolution; it had to wait for Napoleon. In 1780 the Academy of Châlons-sur-Marne offered a prize for the best essay on "The Best Way of Mitigating the Harshness of French Penal Law Without Endangering Public Safety."[17] Louis XVI responded by abolishing torture (1780), and in 1788 he announced his intention to have all French criminal law revised into a consistent national code; moreover, "we shall seek all means of mitigating the severity of punishments without compromising good order." The conservative lawyers then dominating the *parlements* of Paris, Metz, and Besançon opposed the plan, and the King, fighting for his life, laid it aside.

The *cahiers* presented to the States-General of 1789 appealed for several legal reforms: trials should be public, the accused should be allowed the help of counsel, *lettres de cachet* should be banned, trial by jury should be established. In June the King announced an end to *lettres de cachet,* and the other reforms were soon made law by the Constituent Assembly. The jury system, which had existed in medieval France, was restored. The legislators were now sufficiently immune to ecclesiastical influence, and alert to business needs, to proclaim, October 3, 1789 (centuries after the fact), that the charging of interest was not a crime. Two laws of 1794 freed all slaves in France and her colonies, and gave Negroes the rights of French citizens. On the ground that "an absolutely free state cannot allow any corporation within its bosom," diverse laws of 1792–94 forbade all fraternities, academies, literary societies, religious organizations, and business associations. Strangely enough, the Jacobin clubs were spared, but labor unions were forbidden. The Revolution was rapidly replacing the absolute monarch with the omnipotent state.

The diversity of old legislation, the enactment of new laws, and the growing complexity of business relations fostered the multiplication of lawyers, who now replaced the clergy as the first estate. Since the dissolution of the *parlements* they were not formally organized, but their knowledge of the law in all its loopholes, and of legal procedure in all its devices and delays, gave them a power which the state—itself a conglomerate of lawyers—found it hard to control. Citizens began to protest against the law's delays, the subtleties of attorneys, and the expensive legislation that made exasperatingly unreal the equality of all citizens before the courts.[18] The successive assemblies tried various measures to reduce the number and the power of the attorneys. In a fury of antilawyer laws they suppressed notaries (September 23, 1791), closed all schools of law (September 15, 1793), and decreed (October 24, 1793): "The office of attorney-at-law is abolished, but litigants may empower mere mandatories to represent them."[19] These regulations, often evaded, remained on the books until Napoleon reinstated the attorneys on March 18, 1800.

The Revolution made better headway in reforming the criminal code. Procedure was made more public; there was to be an end (for a while) to secrecy of examinations and anonymity of witnesses. Prisons ceased to be prime instruments of torture; in many prisons the inmates were allowed to bring in books and furniture, and to pay for imported meals; persons jailed as suspects, but not yet convicted, might visit one another, play games,[20] and at least play at love; we hear of some warm affairs, like that of prisoner Josephine de Beauharnais with prisoner General Hoche. The Convention, which had sanctioned hundreds of executions, announced at its final session (October 26, 1795): "The penalty of death will be abolished throughout the French Republic from the day of the proclamation of peace."

Meanwhile the Revolution could claim that it had improved the method of capital punishment. In 1789 Dr. Joseph-Ignace Guillotin, member of the States-General, proposed to replace the hangman and the axe man with a massive mechanical blade whose fall would separate a man from his head before he had any time to feel physical pain. The idea was not new; it had been used in Italy and Germany since the thirteenth century.[21] After some experimental use of the doctor's knife on dead bodies, the "guillotine" was erected (April 25, 1792) in the Place de Grève (now the Place de la Hôtel de Ville) and then elsewhere, and executions were accelerated. For a time they attracted large crowds, some of them merry, and including women and children;[22] but soon they were so frequent that they became a negligible commonplace; "people," reported a contemporary, "just went on working in their shops when the tumbrils passed, not even bothering to raise their heads."[23] Lowered heads lasted longest.

2. Sexual Morality

Between the tumbrils, among the ruins, love and venery survived. The Revolution had neglected the hospitals, but there, and on battlefields and in

the slums, charity eased pain and grief, goodness countered evil, and parental affection survived filial independence. Many sons wondered at parental
inability to understand their revolutionary ardor and new ways; some of
them threw off the old moral restraints, and became careless epicureans.
Promiscuity flourished, venereal disease spread, foundlings multiplied, per-
versions floundered on.

Comte Donatien-Alphonse-François de Sade (1740–1814) came of a high-
placed Provençal family, rose to be governor general of the districts Bresse
and Bugey, and seemed destined for the life of a provincial administrator.
But he seethed and fermented with sexual imagery and desires, and sought
for a philosophy that might justify them. After an affair involving four girls,
he was sentenced to death at Aix-en-Provence (1772) for "crimes of poison-
ing and sodomy."[24] He escaped, was captured, escaped, committed further
enormities, fled to Italy, returned to France, was arrested in Paris, was imprisoned in Vincennes (1778–84), in the Bastille, and at Charenton (1789).
Released in 1790, he supported the Revolution; in 1792 he was secretary of
the Section des Piques. During the Terror he was arrested on the false assumption that he was a returned émigré. He was released after a year, but in
1801, under Napoleon, he was imprisoned for having published *Justine*
(1791) and *Juliette* (1792). These were novels of sexual experience, normal
and abnormal; the author preferred the abnormal, and spent his considerable
literary skill in defending it; all sexual desires, he argued, are natural, and
should be indulged with a clear conscience, even to deriving erotic pleasure
from the infliction of pain; in this last sense he became immortal with a word.
He spent the last years of his life in various prisons, wrote clever plays, and
died in the insane asylum at Charenton.

We hear of homosexuality among college students during the Revolution,[25] and may presume its popularity in jails. Prostitutes and brothels were
especially numerous near the Palais-Royal, in the Gardens of the Tuileries,
in the Rue St.-Hilaire and the Rue des Petits Champs; they could be found
also at theaters and the opera, and even in the galleries of the Legislative Assembly and the Convention. Pamphlets were circulated giving the addresses
and fees of houses and women. On April 24, 1793, the Temple section issued
an order: "The General Assembly, . . . desiring to put a stop to the incalculable misfortune caused by the dissoluteness of public morals, and by the
lubricity and immodesty of the female sex, hereby nominates commissioners," etc.[26] Other sections took up the campaign; private patrols were
formed, and some careless offenders were arrested. Robespierre supported
the effort, but after his death the assiduity of the guardians relaxed, the *filles*
reappeared, and prospered under the Directory, when women of wide sexual
experience became leaders of fashion and society.

The evil may have been mitigated by the increasing facility of early marriage. No priest was necessary; after September 20, 1792, only civil marriage was legal; and this required merely a mutual pledge signed before a
civil authority. In the lower classes there were many cases of a couple living

together unwed and unmolested. Bastards were plentiful; in 1796 France re-corded 44,000 foundlings.[27] Between 1789 and 1839, twenty-four percent of all brides in the typical town of Meulan were pregnant when they came to the altar.[28] As in the Ancien Régime, adultery in the husband was often con-doned; men of means were likely to have mistresses, and under the Direc-tory these were displayed as openly as wives. Divorce was legalized by a decree of September 20, 1792; thereafter it could be obtained through mu-tual agreement before a municipal officer.

Paternal authority was lessened by the moderate growth of women's legal rights, and still more by the self-assertion of emancipated youth. Anne Plumptre, who traveled in France in 1802, reported a gardener as telling her:

> "During the Revolution we dared not scold our children for their faults. Those who called themselves patriots regarded it as against the fundamental principles of liberty to correct children. This made these so unruly that very often, when a parent presumed to scold his child, the latter would tell him to mind his own business, adding, 'We are free and equal; the Republic is our only father, and no other.' . . . It will take a good many years to bring them back to minding."[29]

Pornographic literature abounded, and (according to a contemporary news-paper) was the favorite reading of the young.[30] Some previously radical parents began by 1795 (as in 1871) to send their sons to schools directed by priests, in the hope of saving them from the general loosening of manners and morals.[31] For a time it seemed that the family must be a casualty of the French Revolution, but the restoration of discipline under Napoleon re-prieved it until the Industrial Revolution fell upon it with more gradual but more sustained and fundamental force.

Women had held a high place in the Old Regime through the grace and refining influence of their manners, and by the cultivation of their minds; but these developments were mostly confined to the aristocracy and the upper middle class. By 1789, however, the women of the commonalty visi-bly emerged into politics; they almost made the Revolution by marching to Versailles and bringing King and Queen back to Paris as the captives of a commune bursting with its newly discovered power.* In July, 1790, Con-dorcet published an article "On the Admission of Women to the Rights of the State." In December an attempt was made by a Mme. Aëlders to estab-lish clubs devoted to woman's liberation.[32] Women made themselves heard in the galleries of the Assemblies, but attempts to organize them for the ad-vancement of their political rights were lost in the excitement of war, the fury of the Terror, and the conservative reaction after Thermidor. Some gains were made: the wife, like the husband, could sue for divorce, and the mother's consent, as well as the father's, was required for the marriage of her children under age.[33] Under the Directory, women, though voteless, be-

* Legend has probably exaggerated the role played in these events by the exuberant cour-tesan Thérèse de Méricourt (1762-1817).

came an open power in politics, promoting ministers and generals, and proudly displaying their new freedom in manners, morals, and dress. Napoleon, aged twenty-six, described them in 1795:

> The women are everywhere—at plays, on public walks, in libraries. You see very pretty women in the scholar's study room. Only here [in Paris], of all the places on earth, do women deserve such influence, and indeed the men are mad about them, think of nothing else, and live only through and for them. A woman, in order to know what is due her, and what power she has, must live in Paris for six months.[34]

III. MANNERS

Like almost everything else, manners felt the swing of the pendulum to revolt and return. As the aristocracy fled before the leveling storm they took with them their lordly titles, courteous address, perfumed language, flowery signatures, confident ease, and leisurely grace. Soon the suavity of the salon, the decorum of the dance, and the diction of the Academy became stigmata of the nobility, which might incur, for their practitioners, detention as suspect antediluvians who had escaped the flood.[35] By the end of 1792 all Frenchmen in France had become *citoyens*, all Frenchwomen *citoyennes*, in careful equality; no one was *Monsieur*ed or *Madame*d; and the courtly *vous* of singular address was replaced by the *tu* and *toi* of the home and the street. Nevertheless, as early as 1795, this *tutoiement* was passing out of style, *vous* was back in fashion, *Monsieur* and *Madame* were displacing *Citoyen* and *Citoyenne*.[36] Under Napoleon, titles reappeared; by 1810 there were more of them than ever before.

Dress changed more slowly. The well-to-do male had long since adopted, and now refused to discard, the once noble accouterment of the three-cornered high-crowned hat, silk shirt, flowing bow tie, colored and embroidered waistcoat, full-dress coat reaching to the knee, breeches ending at various levels below the knees, silk stockings, and square-toed buckled shoes. In 1793 the Committee of Public Safety tried to "modify the present national costume, so as to render it appropriate to republican habits and the character of the Revolution";[37] but only the lower middle class adopted the long trousers of the workingmen and tradesmen. Robespierre himself continued to dress like a lord, and nothing surpassed in splendor the official costumes of the Directors, paced by Barras. Not till 1830 did pantaloons win the battle against knee breeches (*culottes*). Only the sansculottes wore the red bonnet of revolution, and the carmagnole.*

The dress of women was affected by the Revolution's belief that it was following in the footsteps of republican Rome and Periclean Greece. Jacques-Louis David, who dominated French art from 1789 to 1815, took

---

* The carmagnole led a double life: it was the song and jig made popular by the workers of southern France, and also the short woolen jacket worn by immigrant laborers from Italy. Carmagnola is a town in Piedmont.

classic heroes for his early subjects, and dressed them in classic styles. So the fashionable women of Paris, after the fall of the puritan Robespierre, discarded petticoats and chemises, and adopted as their principal garment a simple flowing gown transparent enough to reveal most of the soft contours that charmed the never satiated male. The waistline was unusually high, supporting the breasts; the neckline was low enough to offer an ample sample; and the sleeves were short enough to display enticing arms. Caps were replaced by bandeaux, and high-heeled shoes by heelless slippers. Doctors reported the deaths of gaily dressed women who had been exposed, at the theater or on promenade, to the quickly falling temperature of Paris evenings.[38] Meanwhile the Incroyables and the Merveilleuses—Unbelievable male and Marvelous female dandies—labored to win attention by extravagant garb. One group of women, appearing in male attire before the Council of the Paris Communes in 1792, received a gentle reprimand from Chaumette, its *procureur général:* "You rash women, who want to be men, aren't you content with your lot as it is? What more do you want? You dominate our senses; the legislator and the magistrate are at your feet, your despotism is the only one our strength cannot combat, because it is the despotism of love, and consequently a work of nature. In the name of that very nature, remain as nature intended you."[39]

Women, however, were sure they could improve upon nature. In an advertisement in the *Moniteur* for August 15, 1792, Mme. Broquin announced that she had not yet run out of her "famous powder for dyeing red or white hair chestnut or black, on a single application."[40] If necessary, unsatisfactory hair was covered with a wig—made, in many cases, from the cut tresses of guillotined young women.[41] In 1796 it was quite ordinary for men of the upper and middle strata to wear their hair long and in a braid.[42]

During the first two years of the Revolution the 800,000 population of Paris carried on its usual life, with only incidental attention to what was going on in the Assembly or the jails. Life was pleasant enough then for the upper classes: families continued to exchange visits and dinners, to attend dances, parties, concerts, and plays. Even during the violent period between the September Massacres of 1792 and the fall of Robespierre in July 1794, when there were 2,800 executions in Paris, life for nearly all the survivors went its customary round of work and play, of sexual pursuit and parental love. Sébastien Mercier reported in 1794:

> Foreigners reading our newspapers imagine us all covered with blood, in rags, and living wretched lives. Judge of their surprise when they reach that magnificent avenue in the Champs Élysées, on either side of which are elegant phaetons and charming, lovely women; and then . . . that magical perspective opening out over the Tuileries and . . . those splendid gardens, now more luxuriant and better tended than ever![43]

There were games—ball games, tennis, riding, horse races, athletic contests . . . There were amusement parks like the Tivoli Gardens, where—like twelve thousand others on a pleasant day—you could get your fortune told, buy dispensables in the boutiques, watch fireworks, tight-rope walkers, or balloon ascensions, hear concerts, or put your youngsters on the merry-go-round to play the *jeu de bagues* (catching the rings). You might sit in an open-air café, or under the pavilion of the Café de Foy, or in a high-class café like Tortoni's or Frascati's, or follow the tourists into night spots like the Caveau (Cellar), or the Sauvage, or Les Aveugles (where blind musicians entertained). You could go to a club to read or chat or hear political debate. You could attend one of the complex and colorful festivals organized by the state and decorated by famous artists like David. If you wished to try the new dance—the waltz—just imported from Germany, you could find a partner in some one of the three hundred public ballrooms in the Paris of the Directory.[44]

Now (1795), in the subsiding years of the Revolution, some *émigrés* were allowed to return; hidden nobles ventured from their protective lairs, and the bourgeoisie displayed its wealth in expensive homes and furniture, in jeweled women and lavish entertainments. The people of Paris emerged from their apartments and tenements to sample the sun or the evening air in the gardens of the Tuileries or the Luxembourg, or along the Champs-Élysées. Women blossomed out in their recklessly charming costumes, their pictured fans that said more than words, their gracefully shaped shoes that made concealed feet alluring. "Society" revived.

But the hundred or so families that now constituted it were not the pedigreed gentry and world-famous *philosophes* who had sparkled in the salons of pre-Revolution nights; they were mostly the *nouveaux-riches* who had garnered livres from ecclesiastical realty, army contracts, mercantile monopolies, financial finesse, or political friends. Some scattered survivors from Bourbon days came to the homes of Mme. de Genlis or the widows Condorcet and Helvétius; but most of the salons that opened after the death of Robespierre (Mme. de Staël's circle excepted) had no talent for brilliant conversation, and lacked the ease that in older times had come from long security in landed wealth. The top salon now was the one that met in the comfortable rooms of Director Barras in the Luxembourg Palace, or at his Château de Grosbois; and its allure was not in the lore of philosophers but in the beauty and smiles of Mmes. Tallien and Josephine de Beauharnais.

Josephine was not yet Bonaparte, and Mme. Tallien was no longer Tallien's wife. Married to him on December 26, 1794, and acclaimed for a while as "Notre Dame de Thermidor," she had left the fading Terrorist soon afterward, and had become the mistress of Barras. Some journalists gibed at her morals, but most of them returned her smiles, for there was nothing haughty in her beauty, and she was known for many kindnesses to women as well as to men. The Duchesse d'Abrantès described her later as "the Capitoline Venus, but even more lovely than the work of Pheidias; for you perceived in her the same perfection of features, the same symmetry in arms, hands, and feet, the whole animated by a benevolent expression."[45]* It was one virtue of Barras that he was generous to her and to Josephine, appreciated

---

* She married, in 1805, the Comte de Caraman (the future Prince de Chimay), and died in 1835.

their beauty in no merely sexual way, shared it, in his receptions, with hundreds of potential rivals, and put his blessing upon Napoleon's capture of Josephine.

IV. MUSIC AND DRAMA

Every grade of music flourished. You could get encores from a street singer for a coin, or you could join a crowd and frighten the bourgeois with "The Carmagnole" or "Ça ira," or you could shake the frontiers with "The Marseillaise," of which Rouget de Lisle had written all but the title. In the Concert-Feydeau you could marvel at Dominique Garat, the Caruso of his time, whose voice could evoke tremors in hearts and rafters, and was famous throughout Europe for its range. Amid the Terror of 1793 the Convention inaugurated the Institut National de Musique, and two years later it expanded this into the Conservatoire de Musique, granting it 240,000 livres per year for the free tuition of six hundred students. On the night when Robespierre was shot a Parisian could have heard *Armide* at the Opéra, or *Paul et Virginie* at the Opéra-Comique.[46]

Opera flourished during the Revolution. Besides putting Bernardin de Saint-Pierre's idyl to music in 1794, Jean-François Lesueur (1760–1837) scored another success, in the same year, with Fénelon's *Télémaque;* he aroused all France with the noise and terror of *La Caverne*, which received seven hundred performances; he continued to produce during Napoleon's ascendancy, and lived long enough to teach Berlioz and Gounod. In a much shorter life Étienne Méhul (1763–1817) wrote over forty operas for the Opéra-Comique, while his massive chorales—*Hymne à la raison* (1793) and *Chant du départ* (1794)—made him the musical idol of the Revolution.*

The greatest music-maker in the France of the Revolution was Maria Luigi Carlo Salvatore Cherubini. Born in Florence in 1760, "I began to learn music at six, and composition at nine."[48] By the age of sixteen he had composed three Masses, a Magnificat, a Te Deum, an oratorio, and three cantatas. In 1777 Leopold, the benevolent grand duke of Tuscany, granted him an allowance to study with Giuseppe Sarti at Bologna; in four years Cherubini became a master of contrapuntal composition. In 1784 he was invited to London, but he did not do well, and in 1786 he moved to Paris, which, except for short intervals, remained his home till his death in 1842. In his first opera there, *Démophon* (1788), he abandoned the lighthearted Neapolitan style of subordinating the story and the orchestra to arias, and followed Gluck into "grand opera," in which the arias were kept secondary to the development of the theme, and to choral and orchestral music. His greatest successes in the Paris of the Revolution were *Lodoïska* (1791) and *Médée* (1797). With his still more famous *Les Deux Journées* (1800) he began a troubled career under Napoleon. We may rejoin him under that shooting star.

There were over thirty theaters in Revolutionary Paris, and nearly all were crowded night after night, even during the Terror. Actors had been freed by the Revolution from the disabilities long since laid upon them by the Church; they could smile at excommunications, and at the exclu-

---

* During the Revolution the term *opéra-comique* ceased to mean a musical comedy, and was applied to any opera, tragic or comic, that contained spoken dialogue.[47] The Théâtre de l'Opéra-Comique was henceforth allowed to compete with the Académie de Musique in producing "serious" opera. About this time, too, some composers, like Méhul in *Ariodant* (1799), arranged to associate certain recurring orchestral passages with corresponding personages or situations; so began the leitmotif.

sion of their cadavers from Christian cemeteries. But they were subjected (1790–95) to a more alert censorship: the Convention required that no comedy should contain any aristocratic hero or sentiments; the theater was made an instrument of government propaganda. Comedy sank to a low level, and new tragedies followed the revolutionary line as well as the classic unities.

As usual the leading actors were more famous than the statesmen, and some, like François-Joseph Talma, were much more loved. His father was a valet who became a dentist, went to London, prospered, and sent his son to France for an education. After graduation François returned to serve as assistant to his father. He learned English, read Shakespeare, saw him performed, and joined a troupe of French actors playing in England. Back in France, he was admitted to the Comédie-Française, and made his debut in 1787 as Séïde in Voltaire's *Mahomet*. His well-proportioned figure, his classically chiseled features, his thick black hair and brilliant black eyes, helped him to advance, but his support of the Revolution alienated most of the company, which owed its existence to the favor of the King.

In 1785 Talma saw David's picture *The Oath of the Horatii;* he was struck not only by its dramatic power but by its careful fidelity to ancient dress. He resolved to introduce the same veracity into the costumes for his stage appearances. He astonished his confreres when he appeared in tunic and sandals, and with bare arms and legs, to play Proculus in Voltaire's *Brutus*.

He became friends with David, and absorbed some of his revolutionary ardor. When he played Marie-Joseph de Chénier's *Charles IX* (November 4, 1789) he put such passion into the antimonarchical passages—which pictured the young King as ordering the Massacre of St. Bartholomew's Eve—that he shocked most of his audience, and many of his companions, who still felt some loyalty to Louis XVI. As the Revolution warmed, the conflict between the "Reds" and the "Blacks" in the company and in the audience became so violent—leading to duels—that Talma, Mme. Vestris (the leading tragedienne), and other actors broke away from the royally privileged Comédie-Française, and set up their own company in the Théâtre de la République Française near the Palais-Royal. There Talma improved his art by studying the history, character, and dress of each person and period in his repertoire. He practiced control of his features to accompany every change of feeling or thought; he reduced the declamatory tone of his speeches and the theatrical expression of emotion; eventually he became the acknowledged master of his art.

In 1793 the older company, renamed the Théâtre de la Nation, produced *L'Ami des lois*, a play salted with satire and ridicule of the Revolutionary leaders. On the night of September 3–4 the whole troupe was arrested. Talma's company accepted a rigid censorship: the plays of Racine were banned; the comedies of Molière were subjected to cuts and alterations; aristocratic titles—even *Monsieur* and *Madame*—were expunged from permitted plays; and a similar purification was demanded in all the theaters of France.[49]

After the fall of Robespierre the arrested actors were released. On May 31, 1799, as the Revolution neared its end, the old company and the new were united in the Comédie-Française, and made their home in the Théâtre-Français of the Palais-Royal, where it lives and prospers today.

V. THE ARTISTS

Art in Revolutionary France was affected by three external events: the deposition and emigration of the aristocracy; the excavations of ancient remains at Herculaneum and Pompeii (1738 ff.); and the rape of Italian art by Napoleon. The emigration removed from France most of the class with enough money and taste to buy works of art; and sometimes the artist, like Mme. Vigée-Lebrun, followed the *émigrés*. Fragonard, though completely dependent on the purses of the leisure class, supported the Revolution, and nearly starved. Other artists supported it because they remembered how the nobility had treated them as servants and hirelings, and how the Académie des Beaux-Arts had permitted only its own members to exhibit in its Salons. In 1791 the Legislative Assembly had opened the Académie to any qualified artist, French or foreign, to compete. The Convention abolished the Académie altogether as an essentially aristocratic institution; in 1795 the Directory replaced it with a new Académie des Beaux-Arts, and gave it headquarters in the Louvre. This had been made a public museum (1792); there the French artists were allowed to study and copy the works of Raphael, Giorgione, Correggio, Leonardo, Veronese, . . . even the horses of St. Mark's; never had stolen goods been so commendably used. In 1793 the Convention renewed the government's support of the Prix de Rome, and of the French Academy in Rome. Slowly the rising middle class replaced the nobility as buyers of art; the Salon of 1795 was crowded with spectators, overwhelmed by 535 paintings. Art prices rose.

Strange to say, the Revolution did not bring any radical movement in the arts. On the contrary, the inspiration given to neoclassicism by the exhuming of ancient sculpture and architecture near Naples, and by the writings of Winckelmann (1755 ff.) and Lessing (1766), had stimulated a revival of the classic style, with all its aristocratic connotations, and this reaction proved strong enough to withstand the Romantic and democratic influences of the Revolution. The artists of this leveling age (Prud'hon dissenting) accepted in theory and practice all the classic and nobiliary norms of order, discipline, form, intellect, reason, and logic as guards against emotion, passion, enthusiasm, license, disorder, and sentiment. French art under Louis XIV had observed these old rules of Quintilian and Vitruvius, of Corneille and Boileau; but under Louis XV and Louis XVI it had relaxed in baroque and frolicked in rococo. With Rousseau defending feeling, and Diderot upholding sentiment, it seemed that the age of Romanticism was at hand. It was in politics and literature, but not in art.

In 1774 Joseph-Marie Vien, excited by reports of the excavations at Herculaneum and Pompeii, started out for Italy, taking with him his pupil Jacques-Louis David. The youngster, all set for revolution, vowed that he would never be seduced by the conservative, aristocratic art of classical antiquity.[50] But there was something masterful in him that responded to the majesty of form, the logic of construction, the strength and purity of line, in the art of Greece and Rome. He resisted its masculine message for a time, gradually yielded to it, and brought it back with him to Paris. It harmonized with the Revolution's rejection of Christianity and the idealization of the Roman Republic, of the Catos and Scipios; it even accorded with Mme. Tallien's Greek gowns. Now it seemed due time to put aside the celestial aspirations of Gothic, the juvenile surprises of baroque, the gay frills of rococo, the rosy nudes of Boucher, the leaping petticoats of Fragonard. Now classic line and logic, cold reason, aristocratic restraint, and stoic form must be the art goals and principles of colorful, emotional, democratic, romantic, revolutionary France.

David, who was to dominate French art during the Revolution and the Empire, was born in Paris in 1748 of a prosperous bourgeois family which always kept him from want. He entered, at sixteen, the Académie des Beaux-Arts, studied under Vien, tried twice for the Prix de Rome, failed twice, locked himself up, and tried to starve himself to death. A neighboring poet missed him, sought him, found him, and wooed him back to food. David competed again in 1774, and won with a rococo painting, *Antiochus Dying for the Love of Stratonice*. In Rome he became enamored of Raphael, then put him aside as too femininely soft in mood and line; he found stronger nourishment in Leonardo, and a stately control of thought and form in Poussin. From Renaissance Madonnas he passed to ancient heroes of philosophy, myth, and war; and in the capital of Christianity he shed his Christian faith.

He returned to Paris in 1780, took a rich wife, and submitted in the Académie Salons a succession of classic subjects—*Belisarius, Andromache*, and some portraits. In 1784 he went to Rome to paint, against a Roman background, a picture commissioned by Louis XVI—*The Oath of the Horatii*. When he exhibited this in Rome an old Italian painter, Pompeo Batoni, told him, *"Tu ed io soli, siamo pittori; pel rimanente si puo gettarlo nel fiume"* (You and I alone are painters; as for the rest, they can jump into the river).[51] Back in Paris, he submitted his work, as *Le Serment des Horaces*, to the Salon of 1785. Here, in Livy's legendary history,[52] David found the spirit of the patriotism that had been the real religion of ancient Rome: three brothers of the Horatii family take an oath to settle the war between Rome and Alba Longa (seventh century B.C.) by a fight to the death with three brothers of the Curiatii clan. David pictured the Horatii swearing, and receiving swords from their father, while their sisters mourn; one of them was betrothed to one of the Curiatii. Frenchmen, who knew the story from Corneille's *Horace*, caught the picture's mood of intense patriotism, which counted the nation above the individual, even above the family.

A King sincerely dedicated to reform, and a city already stirring with revolution, united in applauding the artist, and his rivals acknowledged the skill with which he had revealed heroic courage, paternal sacrifice, and womanly grief. The success of *The Oath of the Horatii* was one of the most complete and significant in the annals of art, for it meant the triumph of the classic style.

Encouraged in his method and his choice of subjects, David turned to Greece and offered (1787) *The Death of Socrates.* Sir Joshua Reynolds, viewing the picture in Paris, pronounced it "the greatest endeavor in art since Michelangelo and Raphael; it would have been a credit to Athens in the time of Pericles."[53] Two years later David returned to Roman legend with *The Lictors Bringing Home to Brutus the Bodies of His Sons;* this was Livy's tale of the Roman Consul (509 B.C.) who sentenced his two sons to death for conspiring to restore the monarchy. The painting had been commissioned before the fall of the Bastille, apparently with no thought of the impending revolt. The King's Minister of Art forbade its exhibition, but public clamor secured its admission to the Salon of 1789. The crowds who came to see it hailed it as part of the Revolution, and David found himself the artistic mouthpiece of his time.

Thereafter he gave himself to the Revolution in a rare marriage of politics and art. He accepted its principles, illustrated its incidents, organized and adorned its fetes, and commemorated its martyrs. When the radical deputy Lepeletier de Saint-Fargeau was assassinated by a royalist (January 20, 1793), David set himself to commemorate the scene; within two months he presented the picture to the Convention, which hung it on the walls of its chamber. When Marat was slain (July 13, 1793) a crowd of mourners entered the Convention gallery; soon a voice from among them cried out, "Where are you, David? You have transmitted to posterity the likeness of Lepeletier dying for his country; there remains for you another picture to paint." David rose and said, "I will do it." He presented the completed painting to the Convention on October 11. It showed Marat half submerged in his bath, his head fallen back lifeless, one hand clasping a manuscript, an arm dropping limp to the floor. A block of wood beside the tub bore the proud inscription "To Marat David." It was a departure from David's characteristic style; revolutionary fervor had replaced neoclassicism with realism. Furthermore, this and the *Lepeletier* broke classic precedent by taking recent events as subjects; they made art a participant in the Revolution.

By 1794 David had become so prominent politically that he was elected to the Committee of General Security. He followed Robespierre's leadership, and arranged the procession and artistic decorations for the Feast of the Supreme Being. After Robespierre's fall David was arrested as one of his followers; after serving three months in prison he was released on the pleas of his pupils. He retired in 1795 to the privacy of his studio, but he returned to prominence in 1799 with a masterly panorama, *The Rape of the Sabines.* On November 10 Napoleon seized power, and David, fifty-one years old, began a new and triumphant career.

VI. SCIENCE AND PHILOSOPHY

Revolutions do not favor pure science, but they stimulate applied science to meet the needs of a society fighting for its liberty. So Lavoisier, the chemist-financier, helped the American and French Revolutions by improving the quality and production of gunpowder; Berthollet and other chemists, spurred by the English blockade, found substitutes for imported sugar, soda, and indigo. Lavoisier was guillotined as a profiteer (1794),[54] but, a year later, the Revolutionary government repudiated this act, and honored his memory. The Convention protected the scientists on its committees, and accepted their plans for a metric system; the Directory gave scientists high status in the new Institut de France; Lagrange, Laplace, Adrien-Marie Legendre, Delambre, Berthollet, Lamarck, Cuvier—names still shining in the history of science—were among its earliest members. Science for a time replaced religion as the staple of French education; the return of the Bourbons interrupted this movement, but their fall (1830) was accompanied by the exaltation of science in the "positive philosophy" of Auguste Comte.

Lagrange and Legendre left their lasting marks on mathematics. Lagrange formulated the "calculus of variations," whose equations are still part of the science of mechanics. Legendre worked on elliptic integrals from 1786 to 1827, when he published his results in a *Traité des fonctions*. Gaspard Monge, son of a peddler, invented descriptive geometry—a method of representing three-dimensional objects on a two-dimensional plane; he organized the national reclamation of copper and tin, wrote a famous text on the gentle art of manufacturing cannon, and served the Revolutionary government and Napoleon through a long career as mathematician and administrator. Laplace aroused the intelligentsia of Europe with his *Exposition du système du monde* (1796), which formulated a nebular hypothesis and tried to explain the universe as pure mechanism; when Napoleon asked him "Who made all this" machinery, Laplace replied, "I had no need of that hypothesis." Lavoisier, founder of modern chemistry, served as chairman of the commission that formulated the metric system (1790). Berthollet advanced both theoretical and practical chemistry, helped Lavoisier establish a new chemical nomenclature, and helped his embattled country by his method of converting ore into iron and iron into steel. Xavier Bichat pioneered in histology by his microscopic studies of tissues. In 1797 he began a famous series of lectures on physiology and surgery; he summarized his findings in *Anatomie générale* (1801). In 1799, aged twenty-eight, he was appointed physician at the Hôtel-Dieu. He was embarking upon a study of organic changes produced by disease when a fall put an end to his life (1802) at the age of thirty-one.

Pierre Cabanis may serve as a transition to philosophy, for though his time knew him chiefly as a physician, posterity came to think of him as a philosopher. In 1791 he attended the last illness of the dying Mirabeau. He lectured at the École de Médecine on hygiene, legal medicine, and the history of medicine; for a time he was head of all the hospitals of Paris. He was one of the many distinguished men who discreetly loved the ever lovable widow of the *philosophe* Helvétius. At her gatherings he met Diderot, d'Alembert, d'Holbach, Condorcet, Condillac, Franklin, and Jefferson. As a student of medicine he was especially attracted to Condillac, who was then dominating the French philosophical scene with his doctrine that all knowledge comes from sensations. The materialistic implications of this sensationism appealed to Cabanis; they accorded well with the correlations that he had found between mental and bodily operations. He shocked even the advanced thinkers of his time by saying: "To form a correct idea of the operations whose result is thought, it is necessary to regard the brain as a special organ whose particular function is to produce thought, just as the stomach and the intestines have the special function of carrying on the work of digestion, the liver that of filtering the bile, etc."[55]

Nevertheless Cabanis modified Condillac's analysis by maintaining (as Kant had recently done in his *Critique of Pure Reason*) that a sensation enters an organism which is already half formed at birth, is molded thereafter by every experience, and carries its past in its cells and memories to form part of a changing personality, including internal sensations, reflexes, instincts, feelings, and desires. The psychophysical totality so produced molds to its structure and purpose every sensation that it receives. In this sense Cabanis agreed with Kant that the mind is not a helpless *tabula rasa* upon which sensations are impressed; it is an organization for transforming sensations into perceptions, thoughts, and actions. However (Cabanis insisted), the mind that Kant so revered is not an entity separable from the physiological apparatus of tissues and nerves.

This apparently materialistic system was expounded in the first (1796) of twelve *mémoires* which Cabanis published together in 1802 as *Rapports du physique et du moral de l'homme*. They reveal a powerful mind (or brain) eagerly active over a widening area of curiosity and speculation. The first essay is almost a survey of physiological psychology, studying the neural correlates of mental states. The third analyzes the "unconscious": our accumulated memories (or neural inscriptions) may combine with external and internal sensations to generate dreams, or may unconsciously affect our ideas even in the most alert of waking states. The fourth holds that the mind ages with the body, so that the same person's ideas and character may be quite different in his seventies than in his twenties. The fifth is a suggestive discussion of how glandular secretions—especially the sexual—may affect our feelings and thoughts. The tenth essay contends that man has evolved through chance variations or mutations which became hereditary.

In a book purporting to be Cabanis' *Lettres sur les causes premières* (1824), published sixteen years after his death, he appears to retract his materialism, and to admit a First Cause endowed with intelligence and will.[56] The materialist may remind us that the great surgeon had warned us against the effect of an aging body upon its associated mind. The skeptic may suppose that the mystery of consciousness had led Cabanis to suspect materialism of simplifying a very complex and immediate reality. In any event it is good that a philosopher should remind himself, now and then, that he is a particle pontificating on infinity.

Two men survived from the age of the *philosophes* to meet in person the Revolution that had been so fervently desired. When the Abbé Raynal, who had made his name in 1770 with *Histoire philosophique . . . des deux Indes,* saw the *lumières* of the Enlightenment darkened by the excesses of the populace, he sent to the Constituent Assembly, on May 31, 1791, a letter of protest and prophecy. "I have long dared to tell kings of their duties; let me today tell the people of their errors." He warned that the tyranny of the crowd could be as cruel and unjust as the despotism of monarchs. He defended the right of the clergy to preach religion, so long as the opponents of religion or priestcraft were left free to speak their minds. He condemned alike the governmental financing of any religion (the state was then paying the salaries of priests) and the attacks upon priests by anticlerical mobs. Robespierre persuaded the irate Assembly to let the seventy-eight-year-old philosopher escape arrest, but Raynal's property was confiscated, and he died in destitution and disillusionment (1796).

Constantin Chasseboeuf de Volney lived through the Revolution, and knew every notable in Paris from d'Holbach to Napoleon. After years of travel in Egypt and Syria he was elected to the States-General, and he served in the Constituent Assembly till its dissolution in 1791. In that year he published the philosophical echoes of his wanderings in *Les Ruines, ou Méditations sur les révolutions des empires.* What had caused the collapse of so many ancient civilizations? Volney answered that they had declined because of the ignorance induced in their people by supernatural religions allied with despotic governments, and by difficulties in the transmission of knowledge from generation to generation. Now that mythological creeds were losing their hold, and printing had facilitated the preservation of knowledge and the transference of civilization, men might hope to build lasting cultures upon a moral code in which knowledge, growing and spreading, would extend man's control over his unsocial tendencies, and promote cooperation and unity. He was arrested in 1793 as a Girondin, and remained in prison for nine months. Released, he sailed to America, was welcomed by George Washington, was denounced as a French spy by President Adams (1798), and hurried back to France. He served as a senator under Napoleon, opposed the change from Consulate to Empire, and retired to a scholarly seclusion until Louis XVIII made him a peer in 1814. He died in 1820, having shared in deposing and restoring the Bourbons.

VII. BOOKS AND AUTHORS

Despite the guillotine, publishers embalmed the evanescent, poets rhymed and scanned, orators declaimed, dramatists mingled history and love, historians revised the past, philosophers chastised the present, and two women authors rivaled the men in depth of feeling, political courage, and intellectual power. One of these, Mme. Roland, we have met in prison and at the guillotine.

The Didot family, most famous of French publishers, continued to improve the casting of type and the bindings of books. François Didot had established the firm as printers and booksellers in Paris in 1713; his sons François-Ambroise and Pierre-François carried on experiments in typography, and issued a collection of French classics on commission from Louis XVI; François-Ambroise's son Pierre published editions of Virgil (1798), Horace (1799), and Racine (1801), so exquisite that the rich purchasers could enjoy them without reading them; Firmin Didot (1764-1836), another son of François-Ambroise, earned fame by founding a new type, and was credited with inventing stereotyping; and the company of Firmin Didot published in 1884 the magnificent edition of Paul Lacroix's *Directoire, Consulat, et Empire*, from which many items herein related have been filched; therein, for example, we learn that all through the Revolutionary period the sale of the works of Voltaire and Rousseau ran in the hundred thousands. A decree of the Convention (July 19, 1793) guaranteed an author's ownership of his copyrighted publications until ten years after his death.[57]

The two most famous poets of the Revolutionary decade began far apart in decoration and style, and ended under the same knife in 1794. Philippe-François Fabre d'Églantine composed pretty verses and successful plays; he became president of the Cordeliers Club, secretary to Danton, and deputy in the Convention, where he voted for the expulsion of the Girondins and the beheading of the King. Appointed to the committee for devising a new calendar, he invented many of the picturesquely seasonal names for its months. On January 12, 1794, he was arrested on charges of malversation, forgery, and dealings with foreign agents and mercantile profiteers. At his trial he sang his charming ballad *"Il pleut, il pleut, bergère; rentre tes blancs moutons"* ("It is raining, it is raining, shepherd; bring in your white sheep"); but the jurors had no ear for pastorals. On his way to the guillotine (April 5, 1794) he distributed copies of his poems to the people.

André-Marie de Chénier was a better poet with better morals, but no better fate. Born at Constantinople (1762) of a French father and a Greek mother, he divided his literary love between Greek poetry and French philosophy. He was educated in Navarre, came to Paris in 1784, made friends with David and Lavoisier, and accepted the Revolution with reservations. He opposed the Civil Constitution of the Clergy, which bound the state with the Catholic Church; he recommended to the National Assembly the complete separation of Church and state, and full freedom of worship for every faith; he condemned the September Massacres, praised Charlotte Corday for killing Marat, and wrote for Louis XVI a letter to the Convention asking for the right to appeal to the people from the sentence of death; this service made him suspect to the ruling Jacobins. Imprisoned as a Girondin, he fell in love with a pretty prisoner, Mlle. de Coigny, and addressed to her "La Jeune Captive," which Lamartine pronounced "the most melodious sigh that ever issued from the apertures of a dungeon."[58] Brought to trial, he refused to defend himself, and went to his death as a relief from an age of barbarism and tyranny. He had published only two poems in his lifetime, but his friends issued, twenty-five years after his execution, an edition of his collected verse, which established him as the Keats of French literature. It must have been his plaint, as well as hers, that he expressed in the final stanza of "The Young Captive":

> O mort, tu peux attendre, éloigne, éloigne-toi;
> Va consoler les coeurs que la honte, l'effroi,
>   Le pâle désespoir dévore.
> Pour moi Pâles encore a des asiles verts,
> Les amours des baisers, les Muses des concerts;
>   Je ne veux pas mourir encore.

> O Death, you need not haste!—begone! begone!
> Go solace hearts that shame and fear have known,
>   And hopeless woes beset.
> For me Pales [goddess of the flocks] still has her grassy ways,
> Love has its kisses, and the Muse her lays;
>   I would not die as yet.[59]

André's younger brother, Joseph de Chénier (1764–1811), was a successful drama-tist; recall the turmoil caused when Talma played *Charles IX*. He wrote the words for the martial "Chant du départ," and the "Hymne à la liberté" sung at the Feast of Reason; with a skillful translation he introduced to France Gray's *Elegy Written in a Country Churchyard*. Elected to the Convention, he became in a sense the official poet of the Revolution. In his later years he was commissioned by the Institut to compose a *Tableau historique de l'état et du progrès de la littérature française depuis 1789*. He died before completing it; even so it is an extensive record of writers once famous and now mostly forgotten even by educated Frenchmen. Immortals die soon after death.

Commanded and engulfed by politics during the Convention, literature recovered under the Directory. Hundreds of literary societies were formed, reading clubs multi-plied, the reading public grew. Most of it was content with novels; romantic fiction and poetry began to displace classic tragic drama. Macpherson's "Ossian," translated into French, became a favorite with a wide variety of readers, from chambermaids to Napoleon.

VIII. MME. DE STAËL AND THE REVOLUTION

Standing out from the word weavers by force of voice and character was a woman who, amid successful novels and a succession of lovers, accepted the Revolution, denounced the mob and the Terror, fought Napoleon at every step, and survived to victory while he languished in a living death. Germaine Necker had the advantage of being born to prominence and for-tune: her father, soon a millionaire, became France's minister of finance; her mother, once pursued by Edward Gibbon, gathered in her salon the cele-brated geniuses of Paris and beyond, to serve unwittingly or unwillingly in the education of her child.

She was born in Paris on April 22, 1766. Mme. Necker, insisting on being her chief tutor, filled her with an explosive mixture of history, literature, philosophy, Racine, Richardson, Calvin, and Rousseau. Germaine trembled with fashionable sensibility over Clarissa Harlowe's approach to a fate worse than death, and with youthful enthusiasm over Rousseau's call to freedom, but she proved painfully allergic to Calvinism, and resisted the insistent the-ology and discipline with which it was daily administered to her. More and more she shied away from her ailing, dominating mother, and fell in love with her virtuous but indulgent and providing father. This was the only liaison that she maintained with lasting fidelity; it made other attachments tangential and insecure. "Our destinies," she wrote, "would have united us forever if fate had made us contemporaries."[60] Meanwhile, to confuse her emotions with intellect, she was allowed, from puberty onward, to attend her mother's periodical meetings of the minds; there she pleased the pundits by her quickness of understanding and repartee. By the time she was seventeen she had become the star of the salon.

Now the problem arose of finding for her a husband who could match her mind and her prospective fortune. Her parents proposed William Pitt, the rising light of English politics; Germaine rejected the idea for the same reason that had led her mother to resist Gibbon—there was not enough sun in England, and the women there were beautiful but unheard. Baron Eric Magnus Staël von Holstein, being bankrupt, offered his hand; the Neckers held him at bay until he had become Swedish ambassador to France. This happened, and Germaine agreed to marry him because she expected to be more independent as a wife than as a daughter. On January 14, 1786, she became Baronne de Staël-Holstein; she was twenty, the Baron thirty-seven. We are assured that "she knew nothing of sexual love until her marriage";[61] but she was a quick learner in everything. The Comtesse de Boufflers, who presided at the wedding, described the bride as "so spoiled by admiration for her wit that it will be hard to make her realize her shortcomings. She is imperious and strong-willed to excess, and she has a self-assurance that I have never seen matched by any person of her age."[62] She was not beautiful, being masculine in build as well as mind; but her black eyes sparkled with vivacity, and in conversation she had no equal.

She went to live at the Swedish Embassy in the Rue du Bac, where she soon established her own salon; but also—since her mother was ailing—she took charge of the salon in the apartments over her father's bank. Necker had been dismissed from the Ministry of Finance in 1781, but he was recalled to office in 1788 to help turn aside the threat of revolution. He was now, despite his millions, the ideal of Paris, and Germaine, passionately supporting him with tongue and pen, had some reason to be proud. Politics, next to unlicensed love, became her meat and drink.

On Necker's advice Louis summoned the States-General; over Necker's resistance he bade the three estates sit separately, maintaining class distinction; On July 12, 1789, he dismissed Necker a second time, and ordered him to leave France at once. He and Mme. Necker drove to Brussels; Germaine, wild with wrath, followed them; Staël, forgetting his official duties, accompanied her and her fortune. On July 14 the Parisian populace stormed the Bastille and threatened the monarchy. The frightened King sent a courier to overtake Necker and call him back to Paris and office; Necker came; the people acclaimed him. Germaine rushed to Paris, and thereafter, till the September Massacres, felt every day the hot winds of revolution.

Associating its early stages with her father, and her politics with her income, she supported the States-General, but pleaded for a bicameral legislature under a constitutional monarchy assuring representative government, civil liberties, and the protection of property. As the Revolution proceeded she used all her influence to moderate the Jacobins and encourage the Girondins.

However, she outdistanced the Jacobins in her moral philosophy. Nearly all the men she met thought it reasonable that their marriages, having been unions of property and not of hearts, should allow for a mistress or two to give them excitement and romance; but they held that similar privileges could not be extended to the wife, since her infidelity would cause disruptive uncertainties in the inheritance of property. Germaine did not feel this argument, since in her case—an only child—the property in question and in prospect was almost wholly her own. She concluded that she should feel free to seek romance, even to sampling other beds.

She had soon lost respect for her husband, who was too obedient to be interesting, and too incompetent to be solvent. She did not object to his taking Mlle. Clairon as a mistress, but he was spending his official income on the seventy-year-old actress, was neglecting his duties as ambassador, was gambling and losing, and repeatedly accumulating debts which his wife and father-in-law reluctantly paid. So she made her way through a procession of lovers, for, as she was to say in *Delphine*, "Between God and love I recognize no mediator but my conscience"; and conscience could be managed. One of her first collaborators was Talleyrand, ex-bishop of Autun, who agreed with her on the flexibility of vows. After him came Comte Jacques-Antoine de Guibert, lately the *beau idéal* of Julie de Lespinasse; however, he died in 1790, aged forty-seven. A year earlier Germaine had formed a deeper and more lasting attachment with Louis de Narbonne-Lara. He was the son of an illegal union, and was himself, at thirty-three, the father of several bastards; but he was remarkably handsome, and had that ease and grace of manner which unpedigreed youth can seldom learn. By social heredity he was all for the aristocracy against an "upstart" bourgeoisie, but Germaine persuaded him to her ideas of a constitutional monarchy in which the propertied class would share in power with the nobility and the king. If we may believe her, Narbonne "changed his destiny for my sake. He broke his attachments and consecrated his life to me. In a word, he convinced me that ... he would consider himself happy to possess my heart, but that if he lost it irremediably he could not survive."[63]

On September 4, 1790, Necker, his liberal policy frustrated by the nobles around the King, resigned, and retired with his wife to a temporarily quiet life in his château at Coppet. Germaine joined them in October, but she soon tired of Swiss peace, and hurried back to what she called, by comparison, the delectable "gutter of the Rue du Bac."[64] There her salon hummed with the voices of Lafayette, Condorcet, Brissot, Barnave, Talleyrand, Narbonne, and her own. She was not content to set the pace for brilliant conversation; she longed to play a part in politics. She indulged the dream of leading France from Catholicism to Protestantism, but she hoped, through her nest of notables, to bring the Revolution to a peaceful rest in constitutional monarchy. With help from Lafayette and Barnave, she secured the appointment of Narbonne as minister of war (December 6, 1791). Marie Antoinette reluctantly supported the appointment. "What glory for Mme. de Staël," she commented; "what joy for her to have the whole army at her disposal!"[65]

Narbonne went too fast. On February 24, 1792, he presented to Louis XVI a memorandum advising the King to break with the aristocracy and give his trust and support to a propertied bourgeoisie pledged to maintain law and order and a limited monarchy. The other ministers angrily protested; Louis yielded to them, and dismissed Narbonne. Germaine's house of cards fell; and to put salt in her wounds her rival, Mme. Roland, secured, through Brissot, the appointment of her husband as minister of the interior.

Germaine lived in Paris through most of the terrible year 1792. On June 20, 1792, she witnessed (if only across the Seine) the storming of the Tuileries by a crowd whose unvarnished manners frightened her. "Their frightful oaths and shouts, their threatening gestures, their murderous weapons, offered a horrifying spectacle which could forever destroy the respect which the human race should inspire."[66] But that *journée* (as the French came to call an uprising of the populace) was an amiable rehearsal, crowned and appeased by the red cap of the Revolution on the King's head. On August 10, however, she witnessed, from her coign of safety, the bloody capture of the Tuileries by a mob that did not rest until the King and the Queen fled to a momentary protection by the Legislative Assembly. The triumphant rebels began to arrest every available aristocrat; Germaine spent her fortune liberally in protecting her titled friends. She hid Narbonne in the recesses of the Swedish Embassy; she stoutly resisted, and finally deflected, a search patrol; and by August 20 Narbonne was safe in England.

Still worse came on September 2, when the fear-maddened sansculottes led the arrested nobles and their supporters out of their jails and murdered them as they emerged. Mme. de Staël barely escaped that fate. After helping many of her friends to get out of Paris and France, she herself set forth, on that bright September 2, in a stately carriage with six horses and liveried servants, toward the city gates; she deliberately put on the style and insignia of the ambassadress in the hope of receiving diplomatic courtesies. Almost at the start the carriage was stopped by "a swarm of old women, issued from hell." Burly workingmen ordered the postilions to drive to the headquarters of the section; thence a gendarme conducted the party through hostile crowds to the Hôtel de Ville. There "I stepped out of the carriage, surrounded by an armed mob, and made my way through a hedge of pikes. As I mounted the stairway, which also was bristling with lances, a man pointed his pike at my heart. My policeman fended it off with his saber. If I had stumbled at that moment it would have been the end of me."[67] In the headquarters of the Commune she found a friend who secured her release; he escorted her to the embassy, and gave her a passport that enabled her, the next morning, to pass safely out of Paris on the long ride to Coppet. That was the day on which the head of the Princesse de Lamballe, parading on a pike, passed below the imprisoned Queen.

Germaine reached the arms of her parents on September 7. In October, hearing of revolution in Geneva, they moved eastward to Rolle, nearer to Lausanne. On November 20, 1792, the twenty-six-year-old mother gave birth to a son, Albert, whom she had been carrying with her through her adventures with death. Probably he had been sired by Narbonne, but her husband was led to believe, or pretend, that he was the father. At Rolle, and then at Coppet, she gave passing refuge to a number of men and women, titled or not, who were in flight before the coming Terror. "Neither she nor her father cared for opinion in the presence of misfortune."[68]

When she heard that Narbonne had offered to leave his refuge in England to come and testify in defense of Louis XVI, Germaine could not bear the thought that he would so endanger himself; she must go to England and dissuade him. She made her way through France and across the Channel, and joined Narbonne in Juniper Hall, at Mickelham near London, on January 21, 1793—the day that Louis was guillotined. Her former lover was too depressed by the news to give her much welcome; his aristocratic lineage reasserted itself, and his love for his mistress lost its ardor in his grief for the King. Talleyrand came from nearby London for frequent visits, and cheered them with his humor. Fanny Burney joined them, and reported (in Macaulay's summary) "that she had never heard such conversation before. The most animated eloquence, the keenest observation, the most sparkling wit, the most courtly grace, were united to charm her." She refused to believe the gossip that Narbonne and Germaine were living in adultery. She wrote to her father, the famous historian of music:

> This intimation was . . . wholly new to me, and I do firmly believe it a gross calumny. She loves him even tenderly, but so openly, so simply, so unaffectedly, and with such utter freedom from all coquetry. . . . She is very plain, he is very handsome; her intellectual endowments must be with him her sole attraction. . . . I think you could not spend a day with them and not see that their commerce is that of a pure but exalted . . . friendship.[69]

When Fanny became assured that this brilliant couple were living in shameless sin, she sorrowfully gave up her visits to Juniper Hall.

The little group was shunned, too, by earlier *émigrés*, who accused them of having too long defended the Revolution. On May 25, 1793, Germaine crossed to Ostend; then, as still the wife of the Swedish ambassador, she made her way safely to Bern, where she was met by her occasional husband, and went with him to Coppet. Thence she issued *Reflections on the Trial of the Queen, by a Woman*, a fervent appeal for mercy toward Marie Antoinette. But the Queen was guillotined on October 16, 1793.

Mme. Necker died on May 15, 1794. Her husband mourned her with a depth of affection that only long unity can bring. Germaine, not overwhelmed, moved to the Château of Mézerey, near Lausanne, to form a new salon, and to forget everything else in the arms of Count Ribbing. Narbonne, arriving tardily, found himself displaced, and returned to a former mistress. Sometime in the fall of 1794 a tall, freckle-faced, red-haired Swiss, Benjamin Constant, almost twenty-seven, met Germaine at Nyon, and began with her a long embattled union of literature and love.

Meanwhile Robespierre had fallen; the moderates came to power; now she might return to Paris. She did in May, 1795, made peace with her husband, and revived her salon at the Swedish Embassy. There she brought together the new leaders of the dying Convention—Barras, Tallien, Boissy d'Anglas, and literary lions like Marie-Joseph de Chénier. She plunged so avidly into politics that a deputy denounced her on the floor of the Convention as conducting a monarchist conspiracy while cuckolding her husband. The new Committee of Public Safety ordered her to leave France; by January 1, 1796, she was back in Coppet. There, between Constant and her books, she wrote a somber study, *De l'influence des passions*, dripping with Rousseau and feeling, echoing *The Sorrows of Werther*, and praising suicide. Her friends in Paris arranged ecstatic reviews. The Directory notified her that she might come to France, but not closer than twenty miles to the capital. She and Constant settled in a former abbey at Hérivaux. In the spring of 1797 she was allowed to join her husband in Paris. There, on June 8, she gave birth to a daughter, Albertine, of uncertain paternity. Amid these complications she secured, through Barras, the recall of Talleyrand from exile, and his appointment (July 18, 1797) as minister of foreign affairs. In 1798 Baron de Staël lost his post as ambassador. He gave Germaine an amicable separation in return for an allowance, and retired to an apartment in what is now the Place de la Concorde, where we shall find him dying in 1802.

On December 6, 1796, at a reception given by Talleyrand to the homecoming conqueror of Italy, she first met Napoleon. He spoke to her some words in praise of her father. For the first time in her life she was not ready with a response; "I was a bit troubled, first with admiration, then with fear."[70] She asked him a foolish question: "Who is the greatest woman, alive or dead?" He gave her an impish answer: "The one who has made the most children."[71] Four days later she saw him again when he received the acclaim of the Directors in the court of the Luxembourg Palace. She was puzzled by his mixture of modesty and pride; here, she felt, was a man who carried with him the destiny of France. She longed to be taken into his confidence, to share with him in great enterprises, perhaps to number him among her victories. She rejoiced like a secret lover when, on November 10, 1799, Lucien Bonaparte told her that Napoleon had emerged triumphant at St.-Cloud, and had been named First Consul—therefore, in effect, the ruler of France. She felt that an age of chaos and tarnished ideals had ended, and that another age of heroes and glory had dawned.

IX. AFTERTHOUGHTS

Having told the story of the French Revolution as impartially as old age allowed, it remains to face, within the same limitations, the questions that philosophy would ask: Was the Revolution justified by its causes or results? Did it leave any significant gains for the French people or humanity? Could its gains have been achieved without their cost in chaos and suffering? Does its record suggest any conclusions about revolutions in general? Does it shed any light upon the nature of man? We speak here only of political revolutions—rapid and violent changes of government in personnel and policy. A development without violence we should call an evolution; a quick and violent or illegal change of personnel without a change in the form of government would be a *coup d'état;* any open resistance to an existing authority is a rebellion.

The causes of the French Revolution were, in summary: (1) the rebellion of the *parlements*, weakening the authority of the King and the loyalty of the nobility of the robe; (2) the ambition of Philippe d'Orléans to replace Louis XVI on the throne; (3) the rebellion of the bourgeoisie against the financial irresponsibility of the state, the interference of the government with the economy, the uncooperative wealth of the Church in the face of national bankruptcy, and the fiscal, social, and appointive privileges of the aristocracy; (4) the rebellion of the peasantry against feudal dues and charters, state taxes, and church tithes; (5) the rebellion of the Paris populace against class oppression, legal disabilities, economic shortages, high prices, and military threats. The bourgeoisie and Philippe d'Orléans supplied the money that paid for the propaganda of journals and orators, the management of crowds, the reorganization of the Third Estate into a National Assembly which dictated a revolutionary constitution. The commonalty provided the courage, muscle, blood, and violence that frightened the King into accepting the Assembly and the constitution, and the aristocracy and the Church into surrendering their dues and tithes. Perhaps we should add as a minor cause the humanity and vacillation of a King averse to shedding blood.

The results of the French Revolution were so many, so complex, various, and lasting, that one would have to write a history of the nineteenth century to do them justice.

1. *The political results* were obvious: the replacement of feudalism by a free and partially propertied peasantry; of feudal by civil courts; of absolute monarchy by a property-limited democracy; of a titled aristocracy by a business bourgeoisie as the dominant and administrative class. Along with democracy came—at least in phrase and hope—equality before the law and in opportunity, and freedom of speech, worship, and press. These liberties were soon lessened by the natural inequality of men in ability, and their environmental inequality in homes, schools, and wealth. Almost as remarkable as these political, economic, and legal emancipations was their extension to north Italy, the Rhineland, Belgium, and Holland by the armies of the Revolution; in those regions too the feudal system was swept away, and it did not return when Napoleon fell. In this sense the conquerors were liberators, who tarnished their gifts with the exactions of their rule.

The Revolution completed that unification of semi-independent provinces —with their feudal baronies and tolls, their diverse origins, traditions, moneys, and laws—into a centrally governed France with a national army and a national law. This change, as Tocqueville pointed out, had been going on under the Bourbons; it would probably have been achieved, without the Revolution, by the unifying influence of a nationwide commerce which increasingly ignored provincial boundaries—very much as a national economy in the United States compelled the erosion of "states' rights" by a federal government compelled to be strong.

In like manner the emancipation of the peasantry, and the rise of the bourgeoisie to economic ascendancy and political power, would probably have come without the Revolution, though more slowly. The Revolution under the National Assembly (1789-91) was amply justified by its lasting results, but the Revolution under the governments of 1792-95 was a barbaric interlude of murder, terror, and moral collapse, inadequately excused by foreign conspiracies and attacks. When, in 1830, another revolution ended in the establishment of a constitutional monarchy, the result was approximately what had been achieved in 1791.

The gain made by the Revolution in unifying France as a nation was offset by the growth of nationalism as a new source of group animosity. The eighteenth century had tended, in the educated classes, to a cosmopolitan weakening of national differences in culture, dress, and language; armies themselves were largely international in their leaders and men. The Revolution replaced these polyglot warriors with national conscripts, and the nation replaced the dynasty as the object of loyalty and the font of war. A military brotherhood of generals succeeded to an aristocratic caste of officers; the power of patriotic troops overcame the spiritless employees of old regimes. When the French Army developed its own discipline and pride it became the only source of order in a chaotic state, the sole refuge from a babel of governmental incompetence and popular insurgency.

The Revolution unquestionably promoted liberty in France and beyond; for a while it extended the new freedom to the French colonies, and emancipated their slaves. But individual freedom contains its own nemesis; it tends to increase until it overruns the restraints necessary for social order and group survival; freedom unlimited is chaos complete. Moreover, the kind of ability needed for a revolution is quite different from the kind required for building a new order: the one task is furthered by resentment, passion, courage, and disregard for law; the other calls for patience, reason, practical judgment, and respect for law. Since new laws are not buttressed by tradition and habit, they usually depend upon force as their sanction and support; the apostles of freedom become, or yield to, wielders of power; and these are no longer the leaders of destructive mobs but the commanders of disciplined builders protected and supervised by a martial state. Fortunate is the revolution that can evade or shorten dictatorship and preserve its gains of liberty for posterity.

2. *The economic results* of the Revolution were peasant proprietorship and capitalism, each begetting endless effects of its own. Wedded to property, the peasants became a powerful conservative force, nullifying the socialistic drive of the propertyless proletariat, and serving as an anchor of underlying stability in a state—and through a century—turbulent with aftershocks of the Revolution. So protected in the countryside, capitalism devel-

oped in the towns; mobile money replaced landed wealth as an economic and political power; free enterprise escaped from governmental control. The Physiocrats won their battle for the determination of prices, wages, products, successes, and failures by competition in the "market"—the play of economic forces unimpeded by law. Goods moved from province to province without being harassed or delayed by internal tolls. Industrial wealth grew, and was increasingly concentrated at the top.

Revolution—or legislation—repeatedly redistributes concentrated wealth, and the inequality of ability or privilege concentrates it again. The diverse capabilities of individuals demand and necessitate unequal rewards. Every natural superiority begets advantages of environment or opportunity. The Revolution tried to reduce these artificial inequalities, but they were soon renewed, and soonest under regimes of liberty. Liberty and equality are enemies: the more freedom men enjoy, the freer they are to reap the results of their natural or environmental superiorities; hence inequality multiplies under governments favoring freedom of enterprise and support of property rights. Equality is an unstable equilibrium, which any difference in heredity, health, intelligence, or character will soon end. Most revolutions find that they can check inequality only by limiting liberty, as in authoritarian lands. In democratic France inequality was free to grow. As for fraternity, it was knifed by the guillotine, and became, in time, an agreement to wear pantaloons.

3. *The cultural results* of the Revolution are still influencing our lives. It proclaimed freedom of speech, press, and assembly; it severely reduced this, and Napoleon ended it, under stress of war, but the principle survived and fought repeated battles through the nineteenth century, to become an accepted practice or pretense in twentieth-century democracies. The Revolution planned and began a national system of schools. It encouraged science as a world view alternative to theology. In 1791 the Revolutionary government appointed a commission, headed by Lagrange, to devise, for a newly unified France, a new system of weights and measures; the resultant metric system was officially adopted in 1792, and was made law in 1799; it had to fight its way through the provinces, and its victory was not complete till 1840; it is painfully displacing the duodecimal system in Great Britain today.

The Revolution began the separation of Church and state, but this proved difficult in a France overwhelmingly Catholic and traditionally dependent upon the Church for the moral instruction of its people. The separation was not completed till 1905, and today it is weakening again under the pressure of a life-sustaining myth. Having attempted the divorce, the Revolution struggled to spread a natural ethic; we have seen that this failed. In one aspect the history of France in the nineteenth century was a long and periodically convulsive attempt to recover from the ethical collapse of the Revolution. The twentieth century approaches its end without having yet found a natural substitute for religion in persuading the human animal to morality.

The Revolution left some lessons for political philosophy. It led a widening minority to realize that the nature of man is the same in all classes; that revolutionists, raised to power, behave like their predecessors, and in some cases more ruthlessly; compare Robespierre with Louis XVI. Feeling in themselves the strong roots of savagery perpetually pressing against the controls of civilization, men became skeptical of revolutionary claims, ceased to expect incorruptible policemen and saintly senators, and learned that a revolution can achieve only so much as evolution has prepared and as human nature will permit.

Despite its shortcomings—and perhaps because of its excesses—the Revolution left a powerful impression upon the memory, emotions, aspirations, literature, and art of France, and of other nations from Russia to Brazil. Even to 1848 old men would be telling children of the heroes and terrors of that exciting time, that reckless, merciless questioning of all traditional values. Was it any wonder that imaginations and passions were stirred as seldom before, and that recurring visions of happier states spurred men and women to repeated attempts to realize the noble dreams of that historic decade? Tales of its brutalities led souls to pessimism and loss of every faith; there were to be Schopenhauers and Leopardis, Byrons and Mussets, a Schubert and a Keats, in the next generation. But there would be hopeful and invigorating spirits too—Hugo, Balzac, Gautier, Delacroix, Berlioz, Blake, Shelley, Schiller, Beethoven—who would share intensely in the Romantic uprising of feeling, imagination, and desire against caution, tradition, prohibition, and restraint. For twenty-six years France would wonder and waver under the spell of the Revolution and Napoleon—the greatest romance and greatest romantic of all; and half the world would be frightened or inspired by that event-full quarter century in which an exalted and suffering nation touched such heights and depths as history had rarely known before, and has never known since.

FIG. 1—JACQUES-LOUIS DAVID: *Unfinished portrait of Bonaparte*. Louvre, Paris. (Cliché des Musées Nationaux)   PAGES 90 ff.

FIG. 2—ENGRAVING AFTER A DAGUERREOTYPE: *The Palace of Versailles*. (The Bettmann Archive)

FIG. 3—ENGRAVING: *The Destruction of the Bastille, July 14, 1789.* (The Bettmann Archive)

Fig. 6—Miniature on ivory by Avy: *Vicomte Paul de Barras* (dated Year XII—1804). Muséum Calvet, Avignon.
PAGE 88

Fig. 7—Sketch: *Georges Jacques Danton, April 5, 1789.* (The New York Society Library)
PAGE 40

Fig. 8—Jean-Antoine Houdon: *Mirabeau.* Musée de Versailles. (Cliché des Musées Nationaux)
PAGE 15

FIG. 9—ENGRAVING BY HENRY COLBURN AFTER AN 1808 PAINTING BY FRANÇOIS GÉRARD: *Charles-Maurice de Talleyrand-Périgord* (1845). (The Bettmann Archive)

PAGE 27

FIG. 10—BOZE: *Jean-Paul Marat.* (The Bettmann Archive) PAGE 20

FIG. 11—ANTOINE-JEAN GROS: *Napoleon on the Bridge at Arcole*, DETAIL. Louvre, Paris.
(Cliché des Musées Nationaux)   PAGES 104, 237

Fig. 12—Studio of François Gérard: *The Empress Josephine*. Musée de Malmaison, Paris. (Cliché des Musées Nationaux)

FIG. 13—*Napoleon's study at Malmaison.* (Cliché des Musées Nationaux)

FIG. 14—JACQUES-LOUIS DAVID: *Bonaparte Crossing the Alps* (1801). Musée de Malmaison, Paris. (Cliché des Musées Nationaux)   PAGES 172, 281

FIG. 15—FRANÇOIS GÉRARD: *Emperor Napoleon I in His Coronation
Robes* (1805). The Dresden Museum. (The Bettmann Archive)

PAGES 198, 282

Fig. 16—Jacques-Louis David: *The Coronation of Napoleon*. Louvre, Paris. (Cliché des Musées Nationaux)

PAGES 198, 281

Fig. 17—Mme. Vigée-Lebrun: *Madame de Staël as Corinne*. Collection Musée d'Art et d'Histoire, Geneva. (Gift of Mme. Necker of Saussure) PAGE 288

FIG. 18—GIRODET: *François-René de Chateaubriand* (1809). Musée de S. Malo.
(Photo J. C. Philippot)   PAGE 308

FIG. 19—FRANÇOIS GÉRARD: *Madame Récamier*. Musée Carnavalet, Paris. (Photo Giraudon)

PAGES 272—73

FIG. 20—JACQUES-LOUIS DAVID: *Self-Portrait* (July, 1794). Louvre, Paris. (The Bettmann Archive) PAGES 140, 281

FIG. 21—ENGRAVING: *François-Joseph Talma*. (The New York Society Library) PAGES 138, 284

FIG. 22—SÈVRES PLAQUE: *Baron Georges-Léopold Cuvier*. Muséum National d'Histoire Naturelle, Paris. (Cliché Bibl. Mus. Paris)   PAGE 325

FIG. 23—ENGRAVING: *Jean-Baptiste de Lamarck*. (The Bettmann Archive)
          PAGE 327

Fig. 24—Engraving by B. Metzeroth: *Arc de Triomphe de l'Étoile, Paris.* (The Bettmann Archive)

PAGE 280

FIG. 25—ENGRAVING: *Napoleon I* (1807).

PAGE 237

FIG. 26—FRANÇOIS GÉRARD: *Empress Marie Louise*. Louvre, Paris. Cliché des Musées
Nationaux)

EDMUND KEAN.

FIG. 27—WOODCUT: *Edmund Kean as Hamlet.* (The Bettmann Archive)   PAGE 372

Fig. 28—Sketch by C. Martin: *J. M. W. Turner*. The National Portrait Gallery, London. PAGE 382

FIG. 29—JOHN CONSTABLE: *The Hay Wain* (1824). The National Gallery, London.

FIG. 30— J. M. W. TURNER: *Calais Pier*. The National Gallery, London.

FIG. 33—*Portrait of Erasmus Darwin.* (The New York Society Library)   PAGE 391

FIG. 34—ENGRAVING: *Sir Humphry Davy.* (The Bettmann Archive)   PAGE 390

FIG. 37—ENGRAVING BY JOHN LINNELL:
Thomas Malthus (1830). (The Bettmann Archive)   PAGES 345, 400

FIG. 38—J. WATTS: *Jeremy
Bentham*. Collection of Millard
Cox. (The Bettmann Archive)
          PAGE 403

FIG. 39—ENGRAVING: *Jane Austen*. (The Bettmann Archive)   PAGE 410

FIG. 40—WILLIAM ALLAN: *Sir Walter Scott* (1832). The National Portrait Gallery, London.   PAGE 505

FIG. 41—P. VANDYKE: *Samuel Taylor Coleridge* (1795). The National Portrait Gallery, London. PAGE 425

FIG. 42—F. L. CHANTREY: *Robert Southey* (1832). The National Portrait Gallery, London. PAGE 424

FIG. 43—R. WESTALL: *Lord Byron* (1813).
The National Portrait Gallery, London.
PAGE 455

FIG. 44—ENGRAVING BY THOMAS LANDSEER
AFTER AN 1818 DRAWING BY BENJAMIN R.
HAYDON: *William Wordsworth*. (The Bett-
mann Archive)   PAGE 418

FIG. 45—WILLIAM BLAKE: *Percy Bysshe Shelley*, WATERCOLOR. (The Bettmann Archive) PAGES 413, 467

FIG. 46—WILLIAM BLAKE: *The Flight into Egypt* (1806), WATERCOLOR. The Metropolitan Museum of Art, New York. (The Bettmann Archive)

NAPOLEON ASCENDANT

1799–1811

CHAPTER VII

The Consulate

November 11, 1799 – May 18, 1804

I. THE NEW CONSTITUTION

1. The Consuls

ON November 12, 1799, the Provisional Consuls—Napoleon, Sieyès, and Roger Ducos—aided by two committees from the old Councils, met in the Luxembourg Palace to rebuild France. Sieyès and Ducos, as members of the late Directory, already had apartments there; Napoleon, Josephine, Eugène, Hortense, and their staffs had moved in on November 11.

The victors in the *coup d'état* faced a nation in economic, political, religious, and moral disarray. Peasants worried lest some returning Bourbon should revoke their title deeds. Merchants and manufacturers saw their prosperity threatened by blockaded ports, neglected roads, and highway robbery. Financiers hesitated to invest in the securities of a government that had been so often overturned; now, when the situation cried out for law enforcement, public works, and poor relief, the Treasury had only twelve hundred francs at its disposal. Religion was in constant opposition: out of eight thousand Catholic priests in France, six thousand had refused to sign the Civil Constitution of the Clergy, and labored in quiet or open hostility to the state. Public education, withdrawn from the Church, was in ruins despite magnificent pronouncements and plans. The family, chief prop of social order, had been shaken by the freedom and prevalence of divorce, extempore marriages, and filial revolt. Public spirit, which in 1789 had risen to rare heights of patriotism and courage, was dying in a people weary of revolution and war, skeptical of every leader, and cynical of its own hopes. Here was a situation that called not for politics but for statesmanship, and not for leisurely democratic debate in spacious assemblies, but (as Marat had foreseen and urged) for dictatorship—for a combination of large perspectives, objective thought, tireless labor, discerning tact, and commanding will. The condition prescribed Napoleon.

At their first sitting Ducos proposed that the thirty-year-old general should take the chair. Bonaparte soothed Sieyès by arranging that each of the three should preside in turn, and suggesting that Sieyès should take the lead in formulating a new constitution. The aging theorist retired to his study and left Napoleon (Ducos complaisant) to issue decrees calculated to secure order in the administration, solvency in the Treasury, patience among factions, and a term of trust from a people disturbed by the forcible usurpation of power.

One of the ruling Consul's first acts was to put away his military uniform, and to adopt a modest civilian dress; he was to be a master of theater. He announced his intention, as soon as the new government should be established, to propose terms of pacification to England and Austria. His apparent ambition in those early days was not to drive England to surrender, but to quiet and strengthen France. He was at this time what Pitt was to call him, the Son of the Revolution—its product and protector, the consolidator of its economic gains; but he made it clear, too, that he wished to be the end of the Revolution—the healer of its internal strife, the organizer of its prosperity and peace.

He pleased the bourgeoisie—whose economic support was to be indispensable to his power—by condemning to deportation (November 17, 1799) thirty-eight individuals considered dangerous to the public peace; this was dictatorship with a vengeance, which aroused more murmurs than applause; soon he modified the decree to banishment in the provinces.[1] He rescinded the confiscatory tax, of twenty to thirty percent, which the Directory had levied upon all incomes above a moderate level. He revoked the law by which prominent citizens were kept under watch as hostages to be fined or deported for any antigovernment crimes committed in their localities. He pacified the Catholics of the Vendée by inviting their leaders to a conference, offering them assurances of goodwill, and signing with them (December 24) a truce that for a time put an end to the religious wars. He ordered all Catholic churches that had been consecrated before 1793 to be restored to Catholic worship on all days except the *décadi*.[2] On, or soon after, December 26 he recalled from banishment the victims of triumphant Revolutionary factions: former liberals of the National Assembly, including Lafayette; defused members of the Committee of Public Safety, like Barère; conservatives proscribed by the *coup d'état* of the 18th Fructidor, like Lazare Carnot, who returned to his labors in the Ministry of War. Bonaparte restored civic rights to well-behaved nobles, and to the peaceful relatives of *émigrés*. He put an end to the hate-feeding festivals like those that celebrated the execution of Louis XVI, the proscription of the Girondins, and the fall of Robespierre. He announced that he proposed to govern in the interest not of any one part—Jacobin, bourgeois, or royalist—but as a representative of the entire nation. "To govern in the interest of a party," he declared, "is sooner or later to be dependent upon it. They will never get me to do it. I am national."[3]

And so the people of France came to view him—nearly all but jealous generals and immovable Jacobins. As early as November 13 public opinion had turned decisively in his favor. "Every previous revolution," wrote the Prussian ambassador to his government on that day, "had inspired much distrust and fear. This one, on the contrary, as I myself can testify, has cheered the spirits of everyone, and has wakened the liveliest hopes."[4] On November 17 the Bourse had fallen to eleven francs; on the 20th it rose to fourteen; on the 21st, to twenty.[5]

When Sieyès brought to the other Consuls his plan for a "Constitution of the Year VIII" (1799) they soon saw that the former midwife of the Revolution had lost much of that admiration for the Third Estate which had inspired his challenging pamphlet of a decade back. He was now quite certain that no constitution could long uphold a state if the roots of both lay in the fluent will of an uninformed and emotional multitude. France had then almost no secondary schools, and its press was an agent of passionate partisanship that deformed, rather than informed, the public mind. His new constitution aimed to protect the state from popular ignorance at one end and despotic rule at the other. He half succeeded.

Napoleon revised Sieyès' proposals, but accepted most of them, for he too was in no mood for democracy. He did not conceal his opinion that the people were not equipped to decide wisely about candidates or policies; they were too amenable to personal charm, declamatory eloquence, bought periodicals, or Rome-oriented priests. The people themselves, he thought, would recognize their unfitness to meet the problems of government; they would be content if the new constitution as a whole should be submitted to them for acceptance or rejection in a general referendum. Sieyès now reformulated his political philosophy in a basic maxim: "Confidence ought to come from below; power ought to come from above."[6]

He began with a brief bow to democracy. All Frenchmen aged twenty-one or more were to vote for one tenth of their number to be communal notables; these were to vote for one tenth of their number to be departmental notables; these to vote for one tenth of their number to be national notables. There democracy ended: local officials were to be appointed from —not elected by—communal notables; departmental officials were to be appointed from departmental notables; national officials, from national notables. All appointments were to be made by the central government.

This was to consist of (1) a Conseil d'État, or Council of State, usually twenty-five men appointed by the chief of state, and authorized to propose new laws to (2) a Tribunat of one hundred tribunes authorized to discuss the measures so proposed, and to present its recommendations to (3) a Corps Législatif, or Legislature, of three hundred men authorized to reject, or to enact into law—but not to discuss—the measures so submitted; (4) a Sénat, usually of eighty men of mature mind, authorized to annul laws judged by it to be unconstitutional, to appoint the members of the Tribunate and the Legislature, to recruit new members for itself from the national notables, and to accept new members appointed to it by (5) the "grand elector."

This was the term that Sieyès had proposed for the head of the state, but Napoleon rejected the term and its description. He saw in the office, as Sieyès proceeded to describe it, a mere executive agent of laws passed without his participation or consent, and a starched figurehead to receive delegations and diplomats, and preside at official ceremonies. He felt no talent for such rituals; on the contrary, his head was swelling with proposals that he was resolved to transform into laws as soon as possible for a nation crying out for order, direction, and continuity. "Your Grand Elector," he told Sieyès, "is a do-nothing king, and the time of such *rois fainéants* is gone. What man of head and heart would submit to such a sluggish life at the price of six million francs and an apartment in the Tuileries? What?—nominate persons who act, and not act oneself? It is inadmissible."[7] He demanded the right to initiate legislation, to issue ordinances, to appoint to office in the central government not only from national notables, but wherever he found willing competence. His program of political, economic, and social reconstruction required a guaranteed tenure of ten years. And he wished to be called not "grand elector," which savored of Prussia, but "first consul," which carried the aroma of ancient Rome. Sieyès saw his constitution falling into monarchy, but was mollified by the presidency of the Senate and lucrative estates. He and Ducos resigned as consuls, and were replaced, at Napoleon's request (December 12, 1799), by Jean-Jacques Cambacérès as second consul, and Charles-François Lebrun as third.

It would be a mistake to class these two men as mere obedient functionaries. Each was a man of tried ability. Cambacérès, who had been minister of justice under the Directory, served now as legal counselor to Napoleon. He presided over the Senate, and (in the absence of the First Consul) over the Council of State. He played a leading role in formulating the Code Napoléon. He was a bit vain, and proud of the Lucullan dinners that he served; but his calm and thoughtful temper often saved the First Consul from impetuous mistakes. He warned Napoleon not to antagonize Spain, and to avoid Russia as a mattress grave. — Lebrun had been secretary to René de Maupeou in the effort to avert the bankruptcy of Bourbon France; he had shared in the financial legislation of the National Assembly and the Directory; now starting with an empty Treasury, he helped to organize the finances of the new government. Napoleon appreciated the quality of these men; when he became emperor he made Lebrun archtreasurer and Cambacérès archchancellor, and they remained faithful to him to the end.

Despite his conviction that the condition of France required early decisions and quick implementation of policies, Napoleon, in this freshman year of his course, submitted his proposals to the Council of State, heard them attacked and defended, and took an active part in the discussion. This was a new role for him; he was accustomed to command rather than to debate, and his thoughts now often outran his words: but he learned quickly and worked arduously, in and out of Council, to analyze problems and find solutions. He was as yet only "Citoyen-Consul," and allowed himself to be overruled.[8] The leaders of the Council—like Portalis, Roederer, Thibaudeau— were men of high caliber, not to be dictated to; and their memoirs abound in tributes to the Consul's willingness to work. Hear Roederer:

> Punctual at every sitting, prolonging the session five or six hours, . . . always returning to the question, "Is that just? Is that useful?" . . . subjecting each question to exact and elaborate analysis, obtaining information about bygone jurisprudence, the laws of Louis XIV and Frederick the Great. . . . Never did

the Council adjourn without its members knowing more than the day before—
if not through knowledge derived from him, at least through the researches
he obliged them to make. . . . What characterizes him above them all . . . [is]
the force, flexibility, and constancy of his attention. I never saw him tired. I
never found his mind lacking in inspiration, even when weary in body. . . .
Never did man more wholly devote himself to the work in hand, nor better
devote his time to what he had to do.[9]

In those days one could have loved Napoleon.

2. The Ministers

Besides arranging for legislation to govern France, he attended to the still
more difficult task of administration. He divided the work among eight ministries, and chose as their heads the ablest men he could find, regardless of
their party or their past; some had been Jacobins, some Girondins, some
royalists. In one or two cases he allowed personal fondness to overrule practical judgment; so he made Laplace minister of the interior, but soon found
the great mathematician-astronomer bringing "the spirit of infinitesimals into
administration";[10] he transferred him to the Senate, and gave the ministry to
brother Lucien.

The basic and almost desperate task of the Ministry of the Interior was to
restore the solvency and vitality of the communes or municipalities as the
foundation cells of the body politic. Napoleon expressed himself on their
condition in a letter to Lucien on December 25, 1799:

> Since 1790 the 36,000 local bodies have been like 36,000 orphan girls. Heir-
> esses of the old feudal rights, they [the communes] have been neglected or
> defrauded . . . by the municipal trustees of the Convention or the Directory.
> A new set of mayors, assessors, or municipal councilors has generally meant
> nothing more than a fresh form of robbery: they have stolen the byroad,
> stolen the footpath, stolen the timber, robbed the church, and filched the
> property of the commune. . . . If this system were to last another ten years,
> what would become of local bodies? They would inherit nothing but debts,
> and be so bankrupt that they would be asking charity of the inhabitants.[11]

This was Napoleon in a literary mood, and so a bit exaggerated. If true
it might have suggested that the communes should be allowed to choose their
own officials, as in Paris. But Napoleon had no liking for what the result had
been in Paris. As for lesser communes, "the Revolution," in the judgment of
its latest historian, "had unearthed but few villagers well enough educated
and cultivated to possess a sense of integrity and public interest";[12] and too
often such locally chosen rulers, like those sent from Paris, had proved to be
incompetent or corrupt or both. So Napoleon remained deaf to appeals for
communal self-rule. Going back to the Roman consular system, or to the
intendants of the late Bourbons, he preferred to appoint—or to have the
Interior Ministry appoint—to each *département* a ruling prefect, to each
arrondissement a subprefect, and to each commune a mayor; each appointee
to be responsible to his superior, and ultimately to the central government.
"All of the prefects" so appointed "were men of wide experience, and most

were very capable."[13] In any case they gave Napoleon far-reaching reins of power.

The civil service—the total administrative body—in Napoleonic France was the least democratic and the most efficient known to history, with the possible exception of ancient Rome. The people resisted the system, but it proved to be a defensible corrective of their acquisitive individualism; the restored Bourbons and the successive French republics retained it; and it gave the country a hidden and basic continuity through a century of political and cultural turmoil. "France lives today," wrote Vandal in 1903, "in the administrative frame and under the civil laws which Napoleon bequeathed to her."

A more immediate problem was the rehabilitation of the Treasury. On the recommendation of Consul Lebrun, Napoleon offered the Ministry of Finance to Martin-Michel Gaudin, who had refused that post under the Directory and had acquired a reputation for ability and honesty. His accession to the ministry guaranteed the support of the financial community for the new government. Substantial loans now came to the rescue of the state: one banker advanced 500,000 francs in gold, and asked no interest. Soon the Treasury had twelve million francs with which to pay its operating expenses and (always a first care with Napoleon) to feed and content the Army, poorly clothed and long unpaid. Gaudin at once transferred from local officials to the central government the power to assess and collect taxes; local corruption in these processes had been notorious. On February 13, 1800, Gaudin united various financial agencies into one Bank of France, financed by selling shares, and empowered to issue paper currency; soon the careful management of the bank made its notes as popular and trustworthy as cash. This in itself was a revolution. The bank was not a state institution; it remained in private hands; but it was buttressed, and partly controlled, by governmental revenues deposited there; and a Minister of the Treasury, Barbé-Marbois, was added to the Ministry of Finance to guard and manage state funds in the bank.

The most disagreeable part of administration was the prevention, detection, and punishment of crime, and the protection of governmental officials from assassination. Joseph Fouché was just the man for this work; he had had much experience with many forms of skulduggery; and, as a regicide marked out for vengeance by the royalists, he could be relied upon to protect Napoleon as the strongest barrier against a Bourbon restoration. While Gaudin coddled the bankers, Fouché kept the Jacobins in line with hopes that the First Consul would be a true son of the Revolution—protecting the commonalty against aristocracy and clergy, and France against reactionary powers. Napoleon distrusted and feared Fouché, and maintained a separate force of spies whose duties included spying upon the Minister of Police; but he was long at a loss to replace him. He did this gingerly in 1802, restored him in 1804, kept him till 1810. He appreciated Fouché's moderation in asking for funds, and winked at the sly Minister's partial financing of his force by confiscations from gambling casinos and contributions from brothels.[14]

A separate gendarmerie kept watch over streets, stores, offices, and homes, and presumably shared in the income of its wards.

The defense of the individual—even of the criminal—against the police, the law, and the state did not get as much attention in France as in the England of that time, but some of it was provided by a judiciary efficient and relatively free from the correlation of judgments with gifts. In assigning this branch of administration to the jurist André-Joseph Abrimal, Napoleon said: "Citizen, I do not know you, but I am told you are the honestest man in the magistracy, and that is why I name you Minister of Justice."[15] Soon France was covered with an abundance and diversity of courts, with grand and petty juries, justices of the peace, bailiffs, prosecutors, plaintiffs, notaries, advocates . . .

The protection of the state from other states was assigned to a Ministry of War under General Louis-Alexander Berthier, a Ministry of Marine under Denis Decrès, and a Ministry of Foreign Affairs (Ministère des Relations Extérieures) under the indestructible Talleyrand. He was now forty-five years old, with an established reputation for polished manners, intellectual penetration, and moral depravity. We last saw him (July 14, 1790) celebrating Holy Mass at the Champ-de-Mars festival; shortly afterward he wrote to his latest acquisition, Adélaïde de Filleul, Comtesse de Flahaut: "I hope you feel to what divinity I yesterday addressed my prayers and my oath of fidelity. You alone are the Supreme Being whom I adore, and will always adore."[16] He had a son by the Countess, but he quietly attended her wedding as the unseen giver of the bride.[17] His passion for feminine beauty was naturally accompanied by an appetite for francs, on which beauty lived. Since he rejected the Christian ethic as well as the Catholic theology, he adjusted his eloquence to lucrative causes, and earned a pretty bouquet from Carnot:

> Talleyrand brings with him all the vices of the old regime, without having been able to acquire any of the virtues of the new one. He has no fixed principles; he changes them as he does his linen, and takes them according to the wind of the day—a philosopher when philosophy is the mode; a republican now because that is necessary in order to become anything; tomorrow he will declare for an absolute monarchy if he can make anything out of it. I don't want him at any price.

Mirabeau agreed: "For money Talleyrand would sell his soul—and he would be right, for he would be trading muck for gold."[18]

There was, however, a limit to Talleyrand's gyrations. When the mob ejected the King and Queen from the Tuileries and set up a proletarian dictatorship, he made no curtsies to the new masters, but took a boat to England (September 17, 1792). He received a mixed reception there: warm from Joseph Priestley and Jeremy Bentham, George Canning and Charles James Fox;[19] cool from aristocrats remembering his share in the Revolution. In March, 1794, English tolerance ran out, and Talleyrand was ordered to leave the country within twenty-four hours. He sailed to the United States, lived comfortably there on the income from his property and investments, returned to France (August, 1796), and became foreign minister (July, 1797) under the Directory. In that capacity he added to his fortune by diverse means, so that he was able to deposit three million francs in British and German banks. Foreseeing the fall of the Directory, he resigned (July 20, 1799), and waited in comfort for Napoleon to call him back to office. The Consul did not wait long; on November 22, 1799, Talleyrand was again *ministre des relations extérieures.*

Bonaparte found him valuable as an intermediary between an upstart ruler and decaying kings. Through all his revolutions Talleyrand had preserved the dress, manners, speech, and mind of the old aristocracy: the easy grace (despite the twisted foot), the imperturbable composure, the subtle wit of a man who knew that at need he could kill with an epigram. He was a hard worker, a shrewd diplomat, who could rephrase in courteous elegance the impetuous bluntness of his unvarnished master. He made a principle "never to hurry" in reaching a decision[20]—a good motto for a lame man; in several instances his delays in forwarding a dispatch allowed Napoleon to recede from dangerous absolutes.

He wanted, under whatever banner, to live lavishly, seduce leisurely, and gather plums from any tree. When the Consul asked him how he had amassed so great a fortune, he answered disarmingly, "I bought stocks on the seventeenth Brumaire, and sold them three days later."[21] That was but a beginning; within fourteen months of resuming office he added fifteen million francs more. He played the market from "inside" knowledge, and he gathered "tidbits" from foreign powers who exaggerated his influence upon Napoleon's policies. By the end of the Consulate his fortune was estimated at forty million francs.[22] Napoleon found him revolting and irreplaceable. Echoing Mirabeau, he called the graceful cripple *"merde* in a silk stocking,"[23] using a term that carries less odor in French than in its Anglo-Saxon equivalent. Napoleon himself was above bribery, having acquired the French Treasury, and France.

3. The Reception of the Constitution

The new constitution met with much criticism when it was published (December 15, 1799) with the ingratiating claim, "It is founded on the true principles of representative government, on the sacred rights of property, equality, and liberty. The powers which it institutes will be strong and stable, as they must be in order to guarantee the rights of the citizens and the interests of the state. Citizens! the Revolution is made fast to the principles which began it; *it is finished.*"[24] These were spacious words, but Napoleon seems to have considered them justified because the constitution allowed for universal adult male suffrage in the first stages of election; it required more appointments to be made from "notables" directly or indirectly chosen by the voters; it confirmed the peasantry and the bourgeoisie in their possession of property purchased as the result of the Revolution; it confirmed the abolition of feudal dues and ecclesiastical tithes; theoretically, and subject to nature, it established the equality of all citizens before the law and in eligibility to any career—political, economic, or cultural; it set up a strong central government to control crime, end anarchy, corruption, and incompetent administration, and defend France against foreign powers; and it ended the Revolution by making it a *fait accompli,* a purpose realized within natural limits, a new form of social organization rooted in stable government, efficient administration, national liberty, and lasting law.

Nevertheless there were complaints. The Jacobins felt that they had been ignored in the "Constitution of the Year VIII"—that the "representative government" which it offered was a hypocritical surrender of the Revolution to the bourgeoisie. Several generals wondered why fate had not chosen one of them, instead of that puny Corsican, for political supremacy; "there was not one of the generals who did not conspire against me."[25] The Catholics mourned that the constitution confirmed the Revolution's confiscation of church property; rebellion rose again in the Vendée (1800). Royalists fretted because Napoleon was consolidating his position instead of calling Louis XVIII to restore Bourbon rule. As the royalists controlled most of the newspapers,[26] they launched a campaign against acceptance of the new regime; Napoleon replied (January 17, 1800) by suppressing sixty out of the seventy-three existing journals of France, on the ground that they were financed by foreign gold. The radical press was also reduced, and the *Moniteur* became the official organ of the government. Journalists, authors, and philosophers condemned this attack upon the freedom of the press; and now Mme. de Staël, having given up hope of playing Egeria, began a powerful and lifelong attack upon Napoleon as a dictator who was crucifying French liberty.

Napoleon defended himself by proxy in the *Moniteur.* He had not destroyed liberty; this had already been shattered by the need for centralized government in war, by the rigged elections of the Jacobins, by the dictatorship of rioting mobs, and by the repeated *coups d'état* of the Directory years; and what remained of it had been dragged in the mire of political bribery and moral decay. The liberty he was crucifying was the freedom of the crowd to be lawless, of the criminal to steal and kill, of the propagandist to lie, of the judge to take bribes, of the financier to embezzle, of the businessman to play monopoly. Had not Marat advocated—had not the Committee of Public Safety practiced—dictatorship as the only cure for the chaos of a society suddenly released from religious tutelage, class domination, and royal autocracy, and left to the urgency of instincts and the tyranny of crowds? Some discipline must now be found to reestablish that order which is the precondition of freedom.[27]

The peasantry did not need such arguments to decide their support of the constitution; they had the land, and secretly applauded any government that would squelch the Jacobins. Here, despite opposite economic interests, the city proletariat agreed with the tillers of the soil. The people of the tenements—workers in the factories, clerks in the shops, peddlers in the streets—

those who as sansculottes had fought for bread and power, had lost faith in a Revolution that had lifted them up, thrown them down, and left them shorn of hope; one magic still stirred them—the hero of war; and the conqueror of Italy could be no worse than the politicians of the Directory. And as for the bourgeoisie—bankers, merchants, businessmen—how could they reject the man who had so completely accepted the sanctity of property and freedom of enterprise? With him they had won the Revolution and inherited France. He was, till 1810, their man.

Confident that the great majority would support him, Napoleon submitted the new constitution to a plebiscite (December 24, 1799). We do not know if this referendum was managed and manacled like so many similar polls before or since. The official count reported 3,011,107 in favor of the constitution, 1,562 against it.[28]

Having those ayes behind him, Napoleon, with his family and aides, moved from the crowded Luxembourg to the royal and commodious Tuileries (February 19, 1800). He made the transit in a pompous procession with three thousand troops, generals on horseback, ministers in carriages, the Council of State in hackney coaches, and the First Consul in a coach drawn by six white horses. It was the first example of the many public displays with which Napoleon hoped to impress the public of Paris. He explained to his secretary:

> "Bourrienne, tonight at last we shall sleep in the Tuileries. You are better off than I: you are not obliged to make a spectacle of yourself, but may go your own way there. I must, however, go in procession; that disgusts me, but it is necessary to speak to the eyes. . . . In the Army simplicity is in the proper place; but in a great city, in a palace, the Chief of the Government must attract attention in every possible way, yet still with prudence."[29]

The ritual was triumphantly completed with but one disturbing note: on one of the guardhouses through which Napoleon passed into the courtyard of the palace he could have seen a large inscription reading "Tenth of August, 1792—Royalty in France is abolished, and shall never be restored."[30] As they walked through the rooms that had once displayed the wealth of the Bourbons, State Councilor Roederer remarked to the First Consul, *"Général, cela est triste"* (General, this is sad); to which Napoleon replied, *"Oui, comme la gloire"* (Yes, like glory).[31] For his work with Bourrienne he chose a spacious chamber adorned only with books. When he was shown the royal bedroom and bed, he refused to use them, preferring to sleep regularly with Josephine. However, that evening, not without pride, he said to his wife, "Come along, my little Creole, go lie down in the bed of your masters."[32]

II. THE CAMPAIGNS OF THE CONSULATE

Napoleon had established internal order, and conditions that promised an economic resurgence; but it still remained that France was surrounded by enemies in a war that France had begun on April 20, 1792. The French people longed for peace, but refused to abandon the territories that had been annexed during the Revolution: Avignon, Belgium, the left bank of the Rhine, Basel, Geneva, Savoy, and Nice. Nearly all of these were comprised in what the French called the "natural boundaries" of their country; and Napoleon, in the oath that he had taken on coming to power, had pledged himself to protect these borders—the Rhine, the Alps, the Pyrenees, and the seas—as essentially a return to the boundaries of ancient Gaul. Moreover, France had taken Holland, Italy, Malta, and Egypt; was she willing to give up these conquests as the price of peace, or would she soon reject any leader who negotiated the surrender of these profitable gains? The character of the French united with the character of Napoleon in a policy proud with nationalism and pregnant with war.

An escape from this destiny was suggested to Napoleon in a letter of February 20, 1800, from the man whom nearly all *émigrés* and royalists recognized as the legitimate ruler of France—Louis XVIII:

> SIR:
> Whatever may be their apparent conduct, men like you never inspire alarm. You have accepted an eminent station, and I thank you for having done so. You know better than anyone how much strength and power are requisite to secure the happiness of a great nation. Save France from her violence, and you will fulfill the first wish of my heart. Restore her King to her, and future generations will bless your memory. You will always be too necessary to the state for me ever to be able to discharge, by important appointments, the debt of my family and myself.
>
> LOUIS[33]

Napoleon let this appeal remain unanswered. How could he return the throne to a man who had promised his faithful followers to follow his own restoration with that of the *status quo ante* the Revolution? What would happen to the enfranchised peasants, or to the buyers of church property? What would happen to Napoleon? Already the royalists, who were daily plotting to remove him, were announcing what they would do to this upstart who dared to play king without ointment or pedigree.[34]

On Christmas Day, 1799, the day after the plebiscite had sanctioned his rule, Napoleon wrote to King George III of England:

> Called by the will of the French people to hold the highest office in the Republic, I think it proper, on assuming my functions, to inform Your Majesty of the fact by my own hand.
> Is there to be no end to the war which, for the past eight years, has dislocated every quarter of the globe? Is there no means by which we can come to an understanding? How is it that the two most enlightened nations in Europe, both stronger and more powerful than their safety and independence require, consent to sacrifice their commercial success, their internal prosperity, and the happiness of their homes, to dreams of imaginary greatness? How is it that they do not envisage peace as their greatest glory as well as their greatest need?
> Such sentiments cannot be strange to Your Majesty's heart, for you rule a free nation for the sole end of making it happy.
> I beg Your Majesty to believe that in broaching this subject, it is my sincere

desire to make a practical contribution . . . toward a generous peace. . . . The fate of every civilized nation depends upon the ending of a war which is embroiling the whole world.[35]

George III did not think it fitting that a king should answer a commoner; he delegated the task to Lord Grenville, who sent to Talleyrand (January 3, 1800) a sharp note denouncing the aggressions of France and declaring that England could not enter into negotiations except through the Bourbons, who must be restored as a precondition to any peace. A letter of Napoleon to Emperor Francis II received a similar reply from the Austrian Chancellor, Baron Franz von Thugut. Probably these literary reverses had been discounted; Napoleon did not have to be told that statesmen weigh words by counting guns. The reality remained that an Austrian army had recaptured north Italy and reached Nice, and that a French army, imprisoned in Egypt by the British and Turks, was nearing surrender or destruction.

Kléber, brave and brilliant general, unsuccessful diplomat, expected no relief, and openly shared in the despondency of his men. By his orders General Desaix signed at El 'Arish (January 24, 1800), with the Turks and the local English commander, a convention for the safe and orderly departure of the French, with their arms and baggage and the "honors of war," on ships to be supplied by the Turks to convey them to France; meanwhile the French were to deliver to the Turks the forts that had protected the Europeans from Egyptian revolts. These forts had been surrendered when word came from the British government refusing to accept the terms of evacuation, and insisting that the French lay down their arms and yield themselves up as prisoners of war. Kléber refused to do this, and demanded the return of the forts; the Turks would not agree to this, and advanced upon Cairo. Kléber led his ten thousand men to meet the Turks, twenty thousand strong, on the plains of Heliopolis. He revived the ardor of his troops with a simple message: "You possess in Egypt no more than the ground under your feet. If you recoil but one step you are undone."[36] After two days (March 20–21, 1800) of battle the wild courage of the Turks yielded to the disciplined tactics of the French, and the surviving victors returned to Cairo to wait again for help from France.

Napoleon could send them no rescue while Britain ruled the Mediterranean. But he had to do something about the fact that the seventy-one-year-old General Baron von Melas had led 100,000 of Austria's best soldiers in a victorious advance through north Italy to Milan. Napoleon sent Masséna to stop him; Masséna was defeated, and found refuge for his troops in the citadel of Genoa. Melas left a force to besiege him there, assigned additional detachments to guard the Alpine passes against attacks from France, and proceeded along the Italian Riviera until his vanguard reached Nice (April, 1800). The tables had been turned upon Napoleon: the city from which he had begun his conquest of Lombardy in 1796 was now in the hands of the nation he had defeated—while the better part of his famous Army of Italy, too sanguinely divided, was wasting away, helpless and desperate, in Egypt. It was the most direct challenge that Napoleon had yet received.

He put administration aside, and became again the commander in chief, raising money, troops, matériel, and morale, organizing supplies, studying maps, dispatching directives to his generals. To Moreau—the most outspoken of his martial foes—he entrusted the Army of the Rhine, with merciless instructions: cross the Rhine, cut your way through the Austrian divisions under Marshal Krug; then send 25,000 of your men over the St. Gotthard Pass into Italy to reinforce the Army of Reserve that Napoleon promised to have waiting for them near Milan. Moreau did most of this heroically, but felt, perhaps justly, that in his hazardous position he could spare to his chief only fifteen thousand men.

Of all the campaigns of history's greatest general, this of 1800 was the most subtly planned, and the most poorly executed. Under his direct command he had only forty thousand men, mostly conscripts unhardened to war. Stationed near Dijon, they might have moved south over the Maritime Alps to Nice for a frontal attack upon Melas; but they were too few and raw; and even if Melas were defeated in such an engagement he would have a protected line of retreat through north Italy to well-fortified Mantua. Instead, Napoleon proposed to lead his troops and their equipment over the St. Bernard Pass into Lombardy, unite with the men expected from Moreau, cut Melas' lines of communication, overcome the Austrian detachments guarding that line, and catch the old hero's army in disarray as it hurried back from the Riviera and Genoa toward Milan. Then he would destroy it or be destroyed; best of all, he would surround it, prevent its retreat, and compel its general—all courtesies observed—to surrender all north Italy. The Cisalpine Republic, pride of Napoleon's first campaigns, would be restored to its French allegiance.

One day (March 17, 1800), Napoleon bade Bourrienne unfold upon the floor a large map of Italy. "He lay down upon it, and desired me to do likewise." Upon certain points he inserted pins with red heads, upon other points pins tinged black. After moving the pins around into various combinations, he asked his secretary, "Where do you think I shall beat Melas? . . . Here in the plains of the [River] Scrivia," and he pointed to San Giuliano.[37] He knew that he was staking everything—all his victories military and political—upon one battle; but his pride sustained him. "Four years ago," he reminded Bourrienne, "did I not with a feeble army drive before me hordes of Sardinians and Austrians and scour the face of Italy? We shall do so again. The sun which now shines upon us is the same that shone at Arcole and Lodi. I rely on Masséna. I hope he will hold out in Genoa. But should famine compel him to surrender, I will retake Genoa and the plains of the Scrivia. With what pleasure shall I then return to my dear France, *ma belle France!*"[38]

He added preparation to foresight, and did not disdain attention to trivial details. He planned the route and the conveyances: Dijon to Geneva; by boat over the lake to Villeneuve; by horse, mule, carriage, charabanc, or on foot to Martigny; thence to St.-Pierre at the base of the pass; then over the mountain on thirty miles of road sometimes only three feet wide, often along precipices usually covered with snow, and subject at any moment to avalanches of snow, earth, or rock; then into the Valle d'Aosta. At every stage of this route Napoleon arranged to have food, clothing, and transport waiting for the men; at several points carpenters, saddlers, and other workmen were to be made available for repair work; and twice en route every soldier was examined to see if he was properly equipped. To the monks who lived in the hospice at the summit he sent money for bread, cheese, and wine with which to revive the soldiers. Despite all these preparations many shortages turned up; but those young conscripts seem to have borne them with a patience inspired by the silent courage of the veterans.

Napoleon left Paris on May 6, 1800. He had hardly disappeared when royalists, Jacobins, and Bonapartes began to replace him in case he should not return triumphant. Sieyès and others discussed the qualifications of Carnot, Lafayette, and Moreau as a new First Consul; and Napoleon's brothers Joseph and Lucien offered themselves as heirs apparent to the throne. Georges Cadoudal returned from England (June 3) to stir revolt among the Chouans.

The actual encounter with the St. Bernard Pass began on May 14. "We all proceeded along the goat paths, man and horse one by one," Bourrienne recalled. "The artillery was dismounted, and the guns, put into excavated tree trunks, were drawn by ropes. . . . When we reached the summit . . . we seated ourselves on the snow and slid down."[39] Cavalrymen dismounted, for a slip of their inexperienced horses might have carried man and beast to death. On each day another division completed the passage; by May 20 the transit was accomplished, and the Army of the Reserve was safe in Italy.

Napoleon remained at Martigny—a pleasant halfway station between Lake Geneva and the pass—till he saw the last parcel of supplies dispatched. Then he rode to the base and the top; there he stopped to thank the monks for refreshing his troops; then he slid down the slope on his greatcoat, and joined his army at Aosta on May 21. Lannes had already overcome the Austrian detachments met on the road. On June 2 Napoleon entered Milan a second time as victor over its Austrian garrison; the Italian population welcomed him as before; the Cisalpine Republic was joyously restored. Having been converted from the Mohammedan religion, the conqueror called a convocation of the Milanese hierarchy, assured them of his fidelity to the Church, and told them that on his return to Paris he would make peace between France and the Church. Having so protected his rear, he was free to form in detail the strategy of his campaign.

Both commanders violated a prime principle of strategy—not to divide their available forces beyond possibility of quick reunion. Baron von Melas, stationed with his main army at Alessandria (between Milan and Genoa), left garrisons at Genoa, Savona, Gavi, Acqui, Turin, Tortona, and other points of possible French attack. His rear guard, moving back from Nice to join him, was harassed by 20,000 Frenchmen under Suchet and Masséna—who had escaped from Genoa. Of the 70,000 Austrians who had crossed the Apennines from Lombardy into Liguria, only 40,000 were now available to

Melas for meeting Napoleon. Part of these he sent to recapture Piacenza as an indispensable avenue of escape to Mantua if his main army should be defeated. Napoleon also divided his forces perilously: 32,000 he left at Stradella to guard Piacenza; 9,000 at Tessino, 3,000 at Milan, 10,000 along the course of the Po and the Adda. He sacrificed the union of his army to the desire to close all roads of escape for Melas' men.

His generals cooperated in saving this policy of impasse from leaving Napoleon unprepared for the main battle. On June 9 Lannes led 8,000 men out from Stradella, and encountered 18,000 Austrians making for Piacenza. In a costly engagement at Casteggio the French were beaten back, though Lannes, covered with blood, still fought in the van; but a fresh force of 6,000 French arrived in time to turn the defeat into a victory near Montebello. Two days later Napoleon was gladdened by the arrival, from Egypt, of one of his most beloved generals, Louis Desaix, "who perhaps equaled Moreau, Masséna, Kléber, and Lannes in military talents, but surpassed them all in the rare perfection of his character."[40] On June 13 Napoleon sent him south to Novi with 5,000 men, to check on a rumor that Melas and his men were escaping to Genoa, where a British fleet could have given them escape, or reinforcement with food and matériel. So Napoleon's main army was still further diminished when, on June 14, the crucial battle came.

It was Melas who chose the spot. Near Marengo, a village on the Alessandria–Piacenza road, he observed an immense plain on which he could bring into united action the 35,000 men still available to him, and their two hundred pieces of artillery. However, when Napoleon reached this plain (June 13), he found no evidence that Melas was planning to venture out of Alessandria. He left at Marengo two divisions under General Victor, and one under Lannes, with Murat's cavalry and only twenty-four cannon. He himself turned with his Consular Guard toward Voghera, where he had arranged to meet his staff officers from his scattered armies. When he came to the Scrivia he found it so swollen by spring floods that he postponed his passage, and slept at Torre di Garofolo. It was a lucky delay; if he had gone on to Voghera he might never have reached Marengo in time to give the order that saved the day.

Early on June 14 Melas ordered his army to advance upon Marengo plain, and to fight its way through to Piacenza. Thirty thousand men surprised the 20,000 of Victor, Lannes, and Moreau; the French, despite their usual heroism, fell back before a decimating artillery barrage. Napoleon, awakened at Garofolo by the sound of distant cannon, sent a courier to call Desaix back from Novi; he himself rushed to Marengo. There the 800 grenadiers of his Guard plunged into the battle, but could not stop the Austrians; the French continued their retreat to San Giuliano. Melas, anxious to reassure the Emperor, sent a message to Vienna announcing victory. The same report was spread about Paris, to the consternation of the populace and the joy of the royalists.

They reckoned without Desaix. He too, on the road to Novi, heard the rumble of cannon. He turned back his 5,000 men at once, followed the sound, marched rapidly, reached San Giuliano by 3 P.M., and found his brother generals advising Napoleon to further retreat. Desaix protested; they told him, "The battle is lost"; he replied: "Yes, the battle is lost, but it is only three o'clock; there is time to win another."[41] They yielded; Napoleon organized a new line of attack, and rode among the troops to restore their spirit. Desaix led the action, exposed himself, was shot and fell from his horse; dying, he bade his next in command, "Conceal my death; it might dishearten the troops";[42] on the contrary, having learned of it, they rushed ahead, shouting that they would avenge their leader. Even so, they encountered almost immovable resistance. Seeing this, Napoleon sent word to Kellermann to go to the rescue with the full force of his cavalry. Kellermann and his men fell upon the flank of the Austrians with a wild fury that cut it in two; 2,000 of them surrendered; General von Zach, commanding in place of the absent Melas, was taken prisoner, and delivered his sword to Napoleon. Melas, summoned from Alessandria, came too late to affect the result; he returned to his headquarters brokenhearted.

Napoleon could not quite rejoice. He bore as a deep personal loss the death of the devoted Desaix; and many other officers were among the 6,000 Frenchmen who lay dead on Marengo plain. It was no comfort that 8,000 Austrians had died there on that day; these were a smaller percentage of the Austrians engaged than were the dead among the French.*

On June 15 Baron von Melas, seeing that the remnants of his armies were in no condition to renew the battle, asked Napoleon for truce terms. These were severe: the Austrians were to evacuate all Liguria and Piedmont, and all Lombardy west of the Mincio and Mantua; they were to turn over to the French all the fortresses in the surrendered regions; the Austrian troops were to be allowed to leave with all the honors of war, but only in proportion as the fortresses were placed in French hands. Melas bowed to these conditions, which saw all his joyous conquests annulled in one day, and sent to the Austrian Emperor a petition to confirm the agreement. On June 16 Napoleon sent his own message to Francis II, asking for a peace on all fronts. Some paragraphs of that letter could have come from a pacifist:

> There has been war between us. Thousands of Austrians and Frenchmen are no more. . . . Thousands of bereaved families are praying that fathers, husbands, and sons may return! . . . The evil is irremediable; may it at least teach us to avoid anything that might prolong hostilities! The prospect so affects my heart that I refuse to accept the failures of my previous advances, and take it upon myself to write again to Your Majesy, to entreat you to put an end to the misfortunes of Europe.
> On the battlefield of Marengo, surrounded by sufferers, and in the midst of 15,000 dead bodies, I implore Your Majesty to hear the cry of humanity, and not to allow the offspring of two brave and powerful nations to slaughter one another for the sake of interests of which they know nothing. . . .

---

* Only the difficulty of communication kept Napoleon from learning that on the same day that Desaix concluded his career his former commander, Kléber, was assassinated in Cairo. After another year of resistance to Turkish-British-Mameluke attacks, the French won the right to leave their prison (August, 1801) and return to France.

The recent campaign is sufficient proof that it is not France which threatens the balance of power. Every day shows that it is England—England, who has so monopolized world commerce and the empire of the seas that she can withstand singlehanded the united fleets of Russia, Sweden, Denmark, France, Spain, and Holland. . . .

The proposals that I think it right to make to Your Majesty are these:

(1) That the armistice be extended to all armies.

(2) That negotiators be sent by both sides, either secretly or publicly, as Your Majesty prefers, to some place between the Mincio and the Chiese, to agree upon means of guaranteeing the lesser powers, and to elucidate those articles of the Treaty of Campoformio which experience has shown to be ambiguous. . . .[43]

The Emperor was not visibly impressed. Obviously the young conqueror wished to consolidate his gains, but there was no indication that respect for human life had ever interfered with his campaigns. Probably neither the Consul nor the Emperor stopped to ask what either the French or the Austrians were doing in Italy. Baron von Thugut settled the matter by signing (June 20, 1800) a treaty by which England granted Austria a new subsidy on her pledge to sign no separate peace.[44]

Meanwhile Napoleon, playing all his cards, attended (July 18) a solemn Te Deum Mass at which the Milanese hierarchy expressed thanks to God for the expulsion of the Austrians. The laity celebrated the victory with parades in honor of the victor. "Bourrienne," he asked his secretary, "do you hear the acclamations still resounding? That noise is as sweet to me as the sound of Josephine's voice. How happy and proud I am to be loved by such a people!"[45] He was still an Italian, loving the language, the passion and beauty, the garlanded orchards, the indulgent religion, the melodious ritual and transcendent arias. But he was moved, too, by the plaudits of the crowds that gathered before the Tuileries on July 3, the morning after his nocturnal return to Paris. The people of France began to think of him as God's favorite; they drank eagerly from their cup of glory.

And Louis XVIII, heir to centuries of strife between Bourbon France and Hapsburg Austria, could hardly be indifferent to this new victory over old foes. Perhaps the young conqueror could still be persuaded to be a kingmaker, not a king. So, at an unknown date in the summer of 1800, he addressed Napoleon again:

You must have long since been convinced, General, that you possess my esteem. If you doubt my gratitude, fix your reward, and mark out the fortune of your friends. As to my principles, I am a Frenchman, merciful by character, and also by the dictates of reason.

No, the victor of Lodi, Castiglione, and Arcole, the conqueror of Italy and Egypt, cannot prefer vain celebrity to real glory. But you are losing precious time. We may ensure the glory of France. I say we, because I require the aid of Bonaparte, and he can do nothing without me.

General, Europe observes you. Glory awaits you, and I am impatient to restore peace to my people.

LOUIS[46]

To this, after much delay, Napoleon replied, on September 7:

> SIR:
>   I have received your letter. I thank you for your kind remarks about my-
> self. You must give up any hope of returning to France; you would have to
> return over a hundred thousand dead bodies. Sacrifice your private interests to
> the peace and happiness of France. . . . History will not forget. I am not un-
> touched by the misfortunes of your family. . . . I will gladly do what I can to
> render your retirement pleasant and undisturbed.[47]

Louis' letter had come from his temporary refuge in Russia; perhaps he
was there when Czar Paul I, in July, 1800, received from Napoleon a present
that almost turned the course of history. During the war of 1799 some
six thousand Russians had been captured by the French. Napoleon offered
them to England and Austria (who had been Russia's ally) in exchange for
French prisoners; the offer was refused.[48] Since France could make no legitimate use of these men, and found it expensive to maintain them, Napoleon
ordered them all to be armed, clothed in new uniforms, and sent to the Czar
without asking anything in return.[49] Paul responded with professions of
friendship with France, and by forming (December 18, 1800) the Second
League of Armed Neutrality against England. On March 23, 1801, Paul was
assassinated, and the Powers returned to the *status quo ante donum.*

Meanwhile the Austrian Emperor rejected the Alessandria armistice, and
sent 80,000 men under General von Bellegarde to hold the line along the
Mincio. The French replied by driving the Austrians from Tuscany, and by
attacking the Austrians in Bavaria. On December 3, 1800, Moreau's 60,000
men fought 65,000 Austrians at Hohenlinden (near Munich), and defeated
them so decisively—taking 25,000 prisoners—that the Austrian government,
seeing Vienna at Moreau's mercy, signed a general armistice (December 25,
1800), and agreed to negotiate with the French government a separate peace.
On his return to Paris Moreau received an acclaim that may have stirred
some conflicting emotions in Napoleon, for Moreau was the favorite candidate of both the royalists and the Jacobins to replace Napoleon as head of
the state.

Plots against Bonaparte's life continued undiscourageably. Early in 1800
a snuffbox, closely resembling the one that the First Consul habitually used,
was found on his desk at Malmaison; it contained poison amid the snuff.[50] On
September 14 and October 10 several Jacobins were arrested, charged with
conspiring to kill Napoleon. On December 24 three Chouans, sent from
Brittany by Georges Cadoudal, directed an "infernal machine," loaded with
explosives, against a group carrying the Consul and his family to the opera.
Twenty-two persons were killed, fifty-six were wounded—none of Napoleon's entourage. He went on to the opera with apparent calm; but on returning to the Tuileries he ordered a thorough investigation, the execution of the
imprisoned Jacobins, and the internment or deportation of 130 more who
were arrested on suspicion. Fouché, who believed that royalists, not Jacobins, were the criminals, apprehended a hundred of them, and had two of
these guillotined (April 1, 1801). Napoleon had overreacted and had over-

ridden the law, but he felt that he was fighting a war, and that he had to put some terror into the hearts of men who themselves scorned law. He was increasingly hostile to the Jacobins and lenient with royalists.

On October 20, 1800, he proposed to his aides to erase from the list of *émigrés* the names of those who would be allowed to return to France, and would receive such of their confiscated goods as had not been sold by the state or appropriated for governmental use. There were now approximately 100,000 *émigrés*, and many of them had asked for permission to come back. Over the protests of worried purchasers of confiscated property, Napoleon had 49,000 names "erased"; i.e., 49,000 of the *émigrés* were permitted to return. Further "erasures" were to be made from time to time, in the hope that this would reduce external hostility to France, and promote the general pacification of Europe. The royalists cheered; the Jacobins mourned.

The principal step in this program of peace was the meeting of the French and Austrian negotiators at Lunéville (near Nancy). Napoleon sent not Talleyrand but his own brother Joseph to argue the French case there; and Joseph accomplished his mission well. He was supported at each step by the inexorable Consul, who expanded his demands with every Austrian delay. Finally, seeing that the armies of France were absorbing nearly all Italy, and were knocking at the gates of Vienna, the Austrians yielded, and signed what they understandably called the "terrible" Peace of Lunéville (February 9, 1801). Austria recognized as French territory Belgium, Luxembourg, and the terrain along the left bank of the Rhine from the North Sea to Basel; she confirmed the Treaty of Campoformio; she accepted the suzerainty of France over Italy between the Alps and Naples and between the Adige and Nice, and the protectorate of France over the Batavian Republic (Holland) and the Helvetic Republic (Switzerland). "Austria is done for," wrote the Prussian minister Haugwitz; "it now rests with France alone to establish peace in Europe."[51] The Paris Bourse rose twenty points in a day, and Paris workers, preferring victories to votes, celebrated with cries of *"Vive Bonaparte!"* the achievements of Napoleon in diplomacy as well as war. Perhaps, however, Lunéville was war rather than diplomacy; it was the triumph of pride over prudence, for in it lay the seeds of many wars, ending in Waterloo.

Other negotiations brought more power. A pact with Spain (October 1, 1800) brought Louisiana to France. The Treaty of Florence (March 18, 1801) with the King of Naples gave France the isle of Elba and the possessions of Naples in central Italy, and closed Neapolitan ports to British and Turkish trade. The old French claim to St.-Domingue—the western section of Hispaniola—brought Napoleon into conflict with a man who almost rivaled him in force of character. François-Dominique Toussaint—self-named L'Ouverture—had been born a Negro slave in 1743. At the supposedly cautious age of forty-eight he led the slaves of St.-Domingue in a successful revolt, and took control first of the French, then of the Spanish, section of the island. He governed ably, but found it difficult to restore productive order among the liberated Negroes, who preferred the leisurely ways that seemed dictated by the heat. Toussaint allowed many former owners to return to their plantations and establish a work discipline verging on slavery. In theory he acknowledged French sovereignty over St.-Domingue; actually, however, he assumed the title of governor general for life, with the right to name his successor—very much as Napoleon was soon to do in France. In 1801 the First Consul sent twenty thousand troops under General Charles Leclerc to reclaim French authority in St.-Domingue. Toussaint fought valiantly, was overcome, and died in jail in France (1803). In 1803 the entire island fell to the British.

The British fleet, supported by the staying power of British commerce, industry, and character, remained, through all but two years of Napoleon's rule, the prime obstacle to his success. Protected by the Channel from the direct ravages of war, enriched by her unrivaled maritime trade, her colonial acquisitions and revenues, and her priority in the Industrial Revolution, England could afford to finance the armies of her Continental allies in repeated attempts to overthrow Napoleon. The merchants and manufacturers agreed with George III, the Tories, the *émigrés*, and Edmund Burke that the restoration of the Bourbons to the throne of France was the best means of recapturing the comfortable stability of the Old Regime. Nevertheless a strong minority in England, led by Charles James Fox, liberal Whigs, radical workingmen, and eloquent men of letters, objected that continued war would spread poverty and incite revolution, that Napoleon was now a *fait accompli*, and that the time had come for finding a *modus vivendi* with that invincible *condottiere*.

Moreover, they argued, Britain's behavior as mistress of the seas was making enemies for her and friends for France. British admirals claimed that their blockade of France required that British crews should have the right to board and search neutral vessels and confiscate goods bound for France. Resenting this practice as an infringement of their sovereignty, Russia, Sweden, Denmark, and Prussia formed (December, 1800) the Second League of Armed Neutrality, and proposed to resist any further British intrusion upon their ships. As the warmth of friction rose, the Danes seized Hamburg (which had become Britain's chief door to the markets of Central Europe), and the Prussians took George III's Hanover. Half the Continent, lately united against France, was now hostile to England. As France already controlled the mouths and left bank of the Rhine, English goods were largely kept from the markets of France, Belgium, Holland, Germany, Denmark, the Baltic States, and Russia. Italy was closing its ports to British trade; Spain was clamoring for Gibraltar, Napoleon was building an army and fleet for the invasion of England.

England fought back, and profited from some turns of fortune's wheel. A British fleet destroyed a Danish fleet in the harbor of Copenhagen (April 2, 1801). Czar Paul I was succeeded, and his French policy revoked, by Alexander I, who denounced Napoleon's invasion of Egypt, recognized the British capture of Malta from France, and signed a treaty with England (June 17, 1801); the Second League of Armed Neutrality faded away.

Nevertheless economic setbacks in Britain, the swelling French army at Boulogne, and the collapse of Austria despite costly subsidies, inclined England to thoughts of peace. On October 1, 1801, her negotiators signed a preliminary agreement which pledged France to yield Egypt to Turkey, and Britain to turn over Malta, within three months, to the Knights of St. John; France, Holland, and Spain were to recover most of the colonies that had been taken from them; France would remove all her troops from central and southern Italy. After seven weeks of further debate Great Britain and France signed the long-awaited Peace of Amiens (March 27, 1802). When Napoleon's representative reached London with the ratified documents, a happy crowd harnessed his horses and drew the carriage to the Foreign Office amid shouts of *"Vive la République française! Vive Napoléon!"*[52]

The French people were stirred with gratitude to the young man—still only thirty-two—who had so brilliantly brought ten years of war to an end. All Europe had acknowledged his ability as a general; now it saw that same clear mind and steady will shine in diplomacy too. And Amiens was but a beginning; on May 23, 1802, he signed a treaty with Prussia; on the next day, with Bavaria; on October 9, with Turkey; on October 11, with Russia. When November 9 approached—anniversary of the 18th Brumaire—he arranged that it should be celebrated as a Festival of Peace. On that day he proclaimed happily the goal of his labors: "Faithful to its aspirations and its promise, the government has not yielded to lust for hazardous and extraordinary enterprises. Its duty was to restore tranquillity to humanity, and, by means of strong and lasting ties, to draw together that great European family whose mission it is to mold the destinies of the world."[53] Perhaps this was the finest moment in his history.

III. REMAKING FRANCE: 1802–03

"At Amiens," said Napoleon at St. Helena, "I believed in all good faith that my own fate, and that of France, were settled. I was going to devote myself entirely to the administration of the country; and I believe that I should have done wonders."[54] This sounds like an attempt to remove the stains of a dozen campaigns; but the day after the Peace of Amiens was signed, Girolamo Lucchesini, Prussian ambassador at Paris, reported to his King that Napoleon was resolved "to turn to the benefit of agriculture, industry, commerce, and the arts all those pecuniary resources which war at once absorbs and besmirches." Napoleon, Lucchesini continued, talked with ardor about "canals to be completed and opened, roads to be made or repaired, harbors to be dredged, towns to be embellished, places of worship and religious establishments to be endowed, public instruction . . . to be provided for."[55] Actually a great deal of progress was made along these lines before war again seized priority over construction (May 16, 1803). Taxes were reasonable, were collected with a minimum of chicanery and cruelty, and were poured out in government contracts that helped to keep industry flourishing and labor employed. Commerce expanded rapidly after England lifted the blockade. Religion rejoiced over Napoleon's Concordat with the Papacy; the Institute began to establish a nationwide system of education; the law was codified and enforced; administration reached an excellence that verged on honesty.

Paris again, as under Louis XIV, became the tourist capital of Europe. Hundreds of Englishmen, forgetting the riotous cartoons that had lampooned Napoleon in the British press, braved rough roads and the rough Channel to get a glimpse of the miniature colossus who had defied and pacified the established Powers. Several members of Parliament were introduced to him; not least—in August, 1802—the past and future Prime Minister, Charles James Fox, who had long labored for peace between the English and the French. Foreigners were astonished at the prosperity that had come so quickly after Napoleon's rise to rule. The Duc de Broglie described the years 1800–03 as "the best and noblest pages in the annals of France."[56]

1. The Code Napoléon: 1801–04

"My real glory," Napoleon reminisced, "is not the forty battles I won—for my defeat at Waterloo will destroy the memory of those victories . . . What nothing will destroy, what will live forever, is my Civil Code."[57] "Forever" is an unphilosophical word; but the Code was his greatest achievement.

The inexhaustible ingenuity of deviltry periodically compels a society to improve and reformulate its ways of protecting itself from violence, robbery, and deceit. Justinian had tried this in A.D. 528; but the Corpus Iuris Civilis drawn up by his jurists was a coordinated collection of existing laws rather than a new structure of law for a changing and uprooted society. The problem was multiplied for France by the legal individuality of its provinces, so that a law in one region could not be assumed to hold sway in the next. Merlin of Douai and Cambacérès had presented the outlines of a new and unified code to the Convention in 1795, but the Revolution had no time to do this work; faced with a bewildering chaos, it added to it with a thousand hasty decrees, which it left for some lucid interval to mold into consistency.

Napoleon's peace settlements with Austria and Britain gave him this opportunity, however brief. On August 12, 1800, the three Consuls had commissioned François Tronchet, Jean Portalis, Félix Bigot de Préameneu and Jacques de Maleville to draw up a fresh plan for a concordant national code of civil law. The preliminary draft which they offered on January 1, 1801, was sent by Bonaparte to the leaders of the law courts for their criticisms and comments; these were submitted to Napoleon three months later, and were then reviewed by the legislative committee of the Council of State, led by Portalis and Antoine Thibaudeau. Having run all these gauntlets, the Code was taken up, title by title, by the whole Council through eighty-seven sittings.

Napoleon presided at thirty-five of these. He disclaimed any knowledge

of law, but he profited from the acumen and legal learning of his fellow
Consul Cambacérès. He joined in the discussions with a modesty that endeared him to the Council, and that would have surprised his later years.
They were inspired by his ardor and determination, and readily accorded
with his prolongation of their sessions from 9 A.M. to 5 P.M. They were not
enthusiastic when he convened them again in the evening. Once, at such a
nocturnal meeting, some members drowsed with fatigue. Napoleon called
them to consciousness with an amiable behest: "Come, gentlemen, we have
not yet earned our stipends."[58] In the judgment of Vandal the Code could
never have been completed had it not been for Napoleon's persistent urging
and friendly encouragement.[59]

The labors of the jurists and the Council were almost aborted when the
Code was subjected to debate in the Tribunate. This assembly, still warm
with the Revolution, condemned the Code as a betrayal of that explosion—
as a return to the tyrannical rule of the husband over his wife and of the
father over his children, and as the enthronement of the bourgeoisie over the
French economy. These charges were largely justified. The Code accepted
and applied the basic principles of the Revolution: freedom of speech, worship, and enterprise, and equality of all before the law; the right of all to
public trial by jury; the end of feudal dues and ecclesiastical tithes; and the
validity of purchases made, from the state, of confiscated church or seignorial property. But—following Roman law—the Code accepted the family as
the unit and bastion of moral discipline and social order, and gave it a basis
in power by reviving the *patria potestas* of ancient regimes: the father was
awarded full control over his wife's property, and full authority over his
children until they came of age; he could have them imprisoned on his word
alone; he could prevent the marriage of a son under twenty-six or a daughter under twenty-one. The Code violated the principle of equality before
the law by ruling that in disputes about wages the word of the employer,
other things equal, should be taken as against that of the employee. The
Revolution's ban on workingmen's associations (except for purely social purposes) was renewed on April 12, 1803; and after December 1 of that year
every laborer was required to carry a workbook recording his past career.
The Code—Napoleon agreeing—restored slavery in the French colonies.[60]

The Code represented the usual historical reaction from a permissive society toward tightened authority and control in the family and the state. The
leading authors of the legislation were men of years, alarmed by the excesses
of the Revolution—its reckless rejection of tradition, its easing of divorce, its
loosening of family bonds, its allowance of moral laxity and political riot
among women, its communal encouragement of proletarian dictatorships,
its connivance at September Massacres and Tribunal terrors; they were resolved to halt what seemed to them the disruption of society and government; and in these matters Napoleon, anxious for a steady France under his
hand, gave these feelings his resolute support. The Council of State agreed
with him that there should be a limit and early cloture on public debate over

the 2,281 articles of the Civil Code; the Tribunate and the Legislature fell in line; and on March 21, 1804, the Code—officially the Code Civil des Français, popularly the Code Napoléon—became the law of France.

2. The Concordat of 1801

Even so, the young Lycurgus was not satisfied. He knew from his own intense nature how little the soul of man is prone to law; he had seen in Italy and Egypt how close man remains, in his desires, to his animal and hunting past, violent and free; it was one of the marvels of history that these living explosives had been kept from shattering the social frame. Was it the policemen who had tamed them? It could not be, for policemen were few and far between, and a potential anarchist was hidden in every second citizen. What, then, had restrained them?

Napoleon, himself a skeptic, concluded that social order rested ultimately on the human animal's natural and carefully cultivated fear of supernatural powers. He came to look upon the Catholic Church as the most effective instrument ever devised for the control of men and women, for their grumbling or silent habituation to economic, social, and sexual inequality, and for their public obedience to divine commandments uncongenial to human flesh. If there could not be a policeman at every corner, there could be gods, all the more awesome because unseen, and multipliable at will and need into mystic beings, hortatory or minatory, ranged through grades of divinity and power from the desert anchorite to the ultimate commander, preserver and destroyer of stars and men. What a sublime conception!—what an incomparable organization for its dissemination and operation!—what a priceless support for teachers, husbands, parents, hierarchs, and kings! Napoleon concluded that the chaos and violence of the Revolution had been due, above all, to its repudiation of the Church. He resolved to restore the association of Church and state as soon as he could take the fangs out of horrified Jacobins and mortified philosophers.

Religion in the France of 1800 was in a confused flux not unrelated to the moral chaos left by the Revolution. A large minority of the people in the provinces—probably a majority in Paris—had become indifferent to the appeals of priests.[61] Thousands of Frenchmen, from peasants to millionaires, had bought from the state the property confiscated from the Church; these purchasers were excommunicated, and looked with no friendly eye upon those who denounced them as receivers of stolen goods. There were then eight thousand active priests in France; two thousand of these were *constitutionels*, who had sworn fealty to the confiscatory Constitution of 1791; the other six thousand were nonjurors who rejected the Revolution, and labored devoutly to annul it; and they were making progress. The nonemigrant nobles, and many of the bourgeoisie, were working to have religion restored as a bulwark to property and social order; many of these—some of them scions of the Revolution—were sending their children to schools managed or taught by priests and nuns who (they believed) knew better than ungowned laic teachers how to make respectful sons and modest daughters.[62] Religion was becoming fashionable in "society" and literature; soon (1802) Chateaubriand's massive eulogy, *Le Génie du christianisme*, was to become the talk of the time.

Seeking every aid to his rootless rule, Napoleon decided to win the spiritual and structural support of the Catholic Church. Such a move would at last quiet the rebellious Vendée, please the provinces, add six thousand priests to his spiritual gendarmerie; it would enlist the moral and spiritual influence of the Pope; it would take from Louis XVIII a major argument for a Bourbon restoration; and it would reduce the hostility—to France and Napoleon —of Catholic Belgium, Bavaria, Austria, Italy, and Spain. "So, as soon as I had power, I . . . reestablished religion. I made it the groundwork and foundation upon which I built. I considered it as the support of sound principles and good morality."[63]

This *apertura a destra* was resisted by the agnostics in Paris and the cardinals in Rome. Many ecclesiastics were reluctant to sanction any agreement that would tolerate divorce, or would abandon the claims of the French Church to its confiscated property. Many Jacobins protested that to recognize Catholicism as the national religion, protected and paid by the government, would be to surrender what they considered one of the major achievements of the late Revolution—the separation of state and Church. Napoleon frightened the cardinals by implying that if they rejected his proposals he might take a leaf from Henry VIII of England and completely divorce the French Church from Rome. He tried to quiet the skeptics by explaining that he would make the Church an instrument of the government in maintaining internal peace; but they feared that his proposal would become another step in the retreat from revolution to monarchy. He never forgave Lalande (the astronomer) "for having wished" (Bourrienne reports) "to include him in a dictionary of atheists precisely at the moment when he was opening negotiations with the court of Rome."[64]

These began at Paris November 6, 1800, and continued through eight months of maneuvering. The cardinals were experienced diplomats, but Napoleon had learned of the Pope's eagerness for an agreement, and held out for every condition favorable to his own power over the reconciled Church. Pius VII made one concession after another because the plan offered to end a decade of disaster for the Church in France; it would let him depose many bishops who had flouted the papal authority; it would enable him, with the help of French intervention, to get rid of the Neapolitan troops that had occupied his capital; and it would restore to the Papacy the "Legations" (Ferrara, Bologna, and Ravenna—usually ruled by papal legates) which had been ceded to France in 1797. — Finally, after a session that lasted till 2 A.M., the representatives of the Roman Church and the French state signed (July 16, 1801) the Concordat that was to govern their relations for a century. Napoleon ratified it in September, Pius VII in December. Napoleon, however, signed with the proviso that he might later make some "regulations providing against the more serious inconveniences that might arise from a literal execution of the Concordat."[65]

The historic document pledged the French government to recognize—and finance—Catholicism as the religion of the Consuls and the majority of the French people, but it did not make Catholicism the state religion, and it affirmed full freedom of worship for all the French, including Protestants and Jews. The Church withdrew its claims to confiscated ecclesiastical property, but the state agreed in recompense to pay the bishops an annual salary of fifteen thousand francs, and to pay lesser stipends to parish priests. The bishops, as under Louis XIV, were to be nominated by the government, and they were to swear fealty to the state; but they were not to function until approved by the pope. All "constitutional" bishops were to resign their sees; all orthodox bishops were restored, and the churches were officially (as they had been in fact) opened to orthodox worship. After much debate Napoleon yielded a precious point to the Church—the right to accept bequests.

To appease the more amiable of his skeptical critics, Napoleon unilaterally added to the Concordat 121 "Articles Organiques," to protect the preeminence of the state over the Church in France. No papal bull, brief, or legate, no decree of a general council or national synod, was to enter France without explicit permission from the government. Civil marriage was to be a legal prerequisite to a religious marriage. All students for the Catholic priesthood were to be taught Bossuet's "Gallican Articles" of 1682, which affirmed the legal independence of the French Catholic Church from "ultramontane" (over-the-mountains) rule.

So modified, the Concordat was presented to the Council of State, the Tribunate, and the Legislature on April 8, 1802. Not yet in terror of Napoleon, they openly and vigorously opposed it as a betrayal of the Enlightenment and the Revolution (it was essentially consistent with the Constitution of 1791). In the Tribunate the *philosophe* Count Volney engaged in spirited debate with the First Consul on the Concordat; and the Legislature elected to its presidency Charles-François Dupuis, author of a strongly anticlerical treatise, *L'Origine de tous les cultes* (1794). Napoleon withdrew the Concordat from discussion by the assemblies, and bided his time.

At the next nomination of members to the Tribunate and the Legislature many of the critics failed of reappointment by the Senate. Meanwhile Napoleon spread among the public the story and contents of the Concordat; as he had expected, the people cried out for its ratification. On March 25, 1802, Napoleon rose to overwhelming popularity by signing peace with England. So fortified, he again submitted the Concordat to the assemblies. The Tribunate passed it with only seven dissentient votes; the Legislature voted 228 for it, 21 against. On April 18 it became law; and on Easter Sunday, in a solemn ceremony in Notre-Dame, both the Peace of Amiens and the Concordat were proclaimed amid the groans of the revolutionists, the laughter of the military, and the joy of the people. A caricature ran the rounds of the barracks showing Napoleon drowning in a font of holy water; and an epigram said: "To be King of Egypt he believes in the Koran; to be King of France he believes the Gospel."

Napoleon consoled himself with the conviction that he had expressed the will of the great majority of Frenchmen, and that he had strengthened his power at the base, though he had weakened it at the top. He had restored the clergy, but since he appointed the bishops, and salaried them and some three thousand priests, he calculated that he could hold them with an economic leash; the Church, he thought, would be one of his instruments, singing his glory and supporting his policies. A little later he saw to it that a new catechism should teach French children that "to honor the Emperor is to honor God Himself," and that "if they should fail in their duties to the Emperor . . . they would be resisting the order established by God, . . . and would make themselves deserving of eternal damnation."[66] He expressed his gratitude to the clergy by attending Mass dutifully, but as briefly as possible.

He had, in these victorious moments, the conviction that he had won the whole Catholic world to his side. Actually the French clergy, never forgetting the loss of their lands, and resenting their salaried bondage to the state, looked more and more to the Pope for support against the ruler whom they secretly considered to be an infidel. "Gallican" by law, they became ultramontane in feeling; when the Emperor dispossessed Pius VII of lands that the Papacy had held for a thousand years—still more when the Pope was evicted from Rome and imprisoned in Savona and Fontainebleau—the clergy and the populace of France rose in defense of their Pontiff and their creed; and Napoleon found, too late, that the power of the myth and the word was greater than the might of the law and the sword.

IV. THE PATHS OF GLORY

Amid his projects and triumphs he had always to guard against challenges to his power and his life. The royalists in France were relatively quiet, for they hoped to persuade Napoleon that his safest course was to restore the Bourbons and accept some sinecure in return. They encouraged writers like Mme. de Genlis, whose historical romance *Mademoiselle de La Vallière* painted a pleasant picture of France under Louis XIV. They played on the secret royalism of Napoleon's secretary Bourrienne, and through him they sought to win Josephine. The pleasure-loving Creole had had a surfeit of political excitement; she feared that Napoleon, unless he changed his course, would seek monarchical power, and would divorce her to marry a woman more likely to give him an heir. Napoleon tried to quiet her fears with some amorous moments, and forbade her to meddle in politics.

He thought that the chief threat to his power lay not from royalists or Jacobins, but from the jealousy of the generals who led the Army on which his power ultimately had to rest. Moreau, Pichegru, Bernadotte, Murat, Masséna, had given open expression to their discontent. At a dinner hosted by Moreau some officers denounced Napoleon as a usurper; General Delmas called him "a criminal and a monster." Moreau, Masséna, and Bernadotte drew up a demand upon Napoleon to content himself with the government of Paris and its vicinity, and to divide the rest of France into regions to be allotted to them with almost absolute powers;[67] none of them, however, would undertake to deliver this proposal to the First Consul. Bernadotte, who controlled the Army of the West at Rennes, was repeatedly on the verge of rebellion, but lost his nerve.[68] "If I should suffer a serious defeat," said Bonaparte, "the generals would be the first to abandon me."[69]

It is against the background of this military plotting that we must interpret the antimilitaristic speech of Napoleon before the Council of State on May 4, 1802:

> In all countries force yields to civil qualities: the bayonet is lowered before the priest, . . . and before the man who becomes master by his knowledge. . . . Never will military government take hold in France unless the nation has been brutalized by fifty years of ignorance. . . . If we abstract from other relationships, we perceive that the military man knows no other law than force, reduces everything to force, sees nothing else. . . . The civil man, on the contrary, sees only the general good. The character of the military man is to will everything despotically; that of the civil man is to submit everything to discussion, reason, and truth; these are often deceptive, but meanwhile they bring light. . . . I do not hesitate to conclude that eminence belongs incontestably to the civil. . . . The soldiers are the children of the citizens, and the [true] army is the nation.[70]

Irked by a sense of insecurity, and always reaching for power, Napoleon suggested to his intimates that his plans for the further improvement and embellishment of France would require a longer tenure than the decade already granted him. On August 4, 1802, the Senate announced a new "Constitution of the Year X" (1801); this enlarged the Senate from forty to eighty members—all the new members to be named by the First Consul; and it made him consul for life. When his admirers proposed that he be given also the authority to choose his successor, he demurred with exceptional modesty; "hereditary succession," he said, "is irreconcilable with the principle of the sovereignty of the people, and impossible in France."[71] But when the Senate, after debating the proposal, approved it by a vote of twenty-seven to seven, the misguided seven covered their error by making the decision unanimous; and Napoleon graciously accepted the honor on condition that the public approve. On August 17 all adult males who were registered as French citizens were asked to vote on two questions: Should Napoleon Bonaparte be made consul for life? Should he be allowed to choose his successor? The reply was 3,508,885 yes, 8,374 no.[72] Presumably, as in other plebiscites, the government had means of encouraging an affirmative reply. The sentiment of the propertied classes was revealed when the Bourse reacted to the vote: the value index of traded shares, which had been seven on the day before Napoleon's coming to power, now rapidly rose to fifty-two.[73]

So fortified, he made some changes in his entourage. He chose a small group of men to be his Privy Council, through which, as his authority became indisputable, he could issue decrees in addition to the *senatus consulta* which were open to his use. He reduced the Tribunate from one hundred members to fifty, and required that its debates henceforth be secret. He dismissed the clever but incalculable Fouché as minister of police, and merged that ministry into a Department of Justice under Claude Régnier. Having discovered that Bourrienne was using his position to make a fortune, he dismissed him (October 20, 1802), and relied henceforth on the devoted service of Claude Méneval. Thereafter Bourrienne's *Memoirs* became unreliably hostile to Napoleon, and Méneval's *Memoirs* were unreliably favorable; however, taken in their algebraic sum, they still constitute the most intimate account of the miniature colossus who was to bestride Europe for the next ten years.

Perhaps it was the Plebiscite of 1802, added to the diverse triumphs at Marengo and Amiens, that ruined, in Napoleon, the moderation and perspective without which genius skirts the edge of madness. For each of the steps that raised him to vertiginous powers he found persuasive or forceful arguments. When the leaders of the Cisalpine Republic, centered in Milan, asked his help in drawing up a constitution, he offered one in which three electoral colleges—manned respectively by landowners, businessmen, and the professions—would choose a commission empowered to appoint the members of a legislature, a senate, and a council of state; these would choose a president. Meeting at Lyons in January, 1802, the delegates ratified this constitution, and invited Napoleon—whom they considered to be an Italian stranded in France—to be the first president of the new state. He came from Paris to address them—in Italian—and on January 26, by acclamation, the First Consul of France became the head of the Republica Italiana. All Europe wondered what would come next out of this new *stupor mundi*, this hypnotic marvel of the world.[74]

The alarm grew when he annexed Piedmont to France. That "Foot of the Mountain" had been occupied by the French in 1798; it lay beyond the "natural boundaries" that Napoleon had promised to protect; however, if restored to the King of Sardinia, it might become a hostile barrier between France and her Italian protectorates in Liguria and Lombardy. On September 4, 1802, Napoleon declared Piedmont a part of France.

In Switzerland, where he had found so many avenues to Italy, he could not proceed so confidently; those sturdy cantons, where men through centuries had counted liberty more precious than life, would have made any enemy pay heavily for conquest. However, they had for the most part welcomed the ideals of 1789, and in 1798 they had formed the Helvetic Republic under the protection of France. This met strong opposition from the owners of large estates, who, using peasants as soldiers, established a separate government at Bern, and challenged the pro-French Republic centered at Lausanne. Both parties sent agents to Napoleon to seek his support; he refused to receive the Bernese agent, who then appealed to England; England sent money and arms to the oligarchs. Napoleon sent troops to the

Republicans (November, 1802); so aided, these suppressed the Bernese revolt. Napoleon pacified both parties with an Act of Mediation (February 19, 1803) which established the Swiss Confederation as nineteen independent cantons, each with its own constitution, all under the protectorate of France, all obligated to send a quota of troops to the French Army. Despite this clause, the Act of Mediation, by English testimony, "received approval from many quarters, and was undoubtedly popular among the cantons."[75]

Nevertheless the English government looked upon these successive moves —in Lombardy, Piedmont, and Switzerland—as dangerous expansions of French influence, seriously disturbing that balance of Continental Powers which had become the keystone of British policy in Europe. Further resentment was aroused by the publication, in the *Moniteur* for January 30, 1803, of the official report submitted to the French government by Comte Horace Sébastiani, whom Napoleon had sent to examine the defenses of Cairo, Jaffa, Jerusalem, and Acre; the Count estimated that "6,000 men would suffice . . . to conquer Egypt."[76] The document aroused suspicion, in England, that Napoleon was contemplating another expedition to Egypt. The British government felt that it could no longer think of evacuating Malta and Alexandria; these now seemed indispensable to the defense of British power in the Mediterranean.

Still another expansion of Napoleon's influence agitated the British. The Treaty of Lunéville stipulated that the German rulers of principalities west of the Rhine, who had lost 4,375 square miles of taxable territory by the recognition of French sovereignty over that area, should be compensated with principalities east of the stream. Twenty German nobles sent representatives to Paris to urge their claims; Prussia and Russia joined in the hunt; Talleyrand collected another fortune in *pourboires*. Finally the distribution was made, mostly by "secularizing" city-states that had been governed by Catholic bishops for centuries. Napoleon's aim in this process had been to promote a Confederation of the Rhine as a buffer state between France and Austria-Prussia. Austria protested that the reshuffling of statelets would prove to be another step in the dissolution of the Holy Roman Empire. It did.

Angered by the widening grasp of Napoleon's arms, the ruling classes in England asked themselves might not war be less costly than such peace. The manufacturers protested that French control of the Rhine made France the arbiter of British trade with the most lucrative of European markets. Merchants complained that while the Peace of Amiens ended the British blockade of France, the French were laying prohibitive import dues on British products competitive with French industry.[77] The aristocracy denounced the peace as a disgraceful surrender to the French Revolution. Nearly all parties agreed that Malta must be held. Meanwhile the British press reviled Napoleon in stories, editorials, and cartoons; he protested to the British government, which told him that the British press was free; he bade the French press to retaliate in kind.[78]

Communications between the governments became increasingly bellicose.

Lord Whitworth, British ambassador, brusquely informed Napoleon that Britain would not leave Malta until the French government had given a satisfactory explanation of the expansionist moves it had made since the Peace of Amiens. On March 13, 1803, amid a large gathering of French and foreign dignitaries, Napoleon, confronting Whitworth as if for battle, charged the British with violating the peace treaty and arming for war; Whitworth, furious at such a transgression of diplomatic rules, thereafter preferred to deal with Talleyrand, who knew how to dress facts with courtesy. On April 25 Whitworth was instructed by his government to present an ultimatum: France must agree to English retention of Malta for at least ten years; she must withdraw from Holland, Switzerland, and Italy, and must recompense the King of Sardinia for the loss of Piedmont in the recent war. Napoleon ridiculed the proposals; Whitworth asked for, and received, his passport, and both sides prepared for war.

Realizing that England, controlling the seas, could at will take any French colony, Napoleon sold the territory of Louisiana to the United States for eighty million francs (May 3, 1803). England, still technically at peace, instructed its naval force to capture any French vessel they might encounter. War was officially declared on May 16, 1803, and continued for twelve years.

From that bitter moment Napoleon the administrator receded in history, and Napoleon the general, aged thirty-four, turned his soul to war. He ordered the arrest of all Britons still found on French soil. He bade General Mortier take Hanover at once, before it could be turned into a military base by the Hanoverian George III. What infuriated him was the thought that throughout a decade of conflict England had financed Continental armies against France, had blockaded French ports and seized French shipping and French colonies, and that through all these military activities she herself had remained immune from attack. So now he resigned himself to what in calmer moments he had rejected as an impracticable dream: he would try to cross that damnable ditch and make those merchants and bankers feel the touch of war upon their soil and flesh.

He ordered his generals to assemble 150,000 men and 10,000 horses along the coast at Boulogne, Dunkirk, and Ostend; he ordered his admirals to gather and equip, at Brest, Rochefort, and Toulon, powerful fleets which, when ready to sail and fight, were to find their way through a mesh of British vessels to harbors that a million workers would have prepared for them around Boulogne; and in those harbors men were to build hundreds of transport ships of all kinds. He himself repeatedly left Paris to tour the camps and docks, to mark the progress of the enterprise, and to inspire the soldiers, sailors, and laborers with an active presence that would seem to them a pledge of purpose and victory.

In the Channel, British men-of-war kept watch; and along the English coast—at Dover, Deal, and elsewhere—a hundred thousand patriots kept watch, night and day, resolved to resist to the death any attempt to invade their inviolable shores.

V. THE GREAT CONSPIRACY: 1803–04

On the night of August 21, 1803, an English frigate, commanded by Captain Wright, brought across the Channel from England eight Frenchmen under the lead of Georges Cadoudal, a fervent leader of the irreconcilable Chouans. They landed on a rocky cliff near Biville in Normandy, where natives in league with them drew them up by ropes. On December 10 Captain Wright brought from England to Biville a second group of conspirators, including the *émigré* noble Armand de Polignac. On a third crossing, January 16, 1804, the captain brought Jules de Polignac, and the French *émigré* generals Pichegru and Lajolais. Pichegru, after well-led victories with the Revolutionary armies, had plotted to restore the Bourbons, had been detected, and had escaped to England (1801). All three groups made their way to Paris, where they were concealed in the homes of royalists. Cadoudal later confessed that he had planned to kidnap Napoleon, and, if Napoleon resisted, to kill him.[79] We may believe that "Cadoudal was furnished by the British Government with drafts for a million francs to enable him to organize the insurrection in the capital";[80] but there is no evidence that the British government consented to assassination.

The plotters delayed action in the expectation that the Comte d'Artois, younger brother of Louis XVI, would join them in Paris,[81] ready to replace Napoleon; but he did not come. Meanwhile (January 28, 1804) Pichegru visited General Moreau and asked his cooperation; Moreau refused to join in any attempt to restore the Bourbons, but offered himself as ruler of France if Napoleon should be removed.[82] About this time Bernadotte gave Juliette Récamier the names of twenty generals who, he declared, were devoted to him and were eager to restore "the true Republic."[83] "I may fairly say," Napoleon recalled at St. Helena, "that during the months from September, 1803, to January, 1804, I was sitting on a volcano."[84]

On January 26 a Chouan named Querelle, who had been arrested three months before and was soon to be executed, revealed the details of the conspiracy in return for the commutation of his sentence. Guided by his confession, the slow-moving police of Claude Régnier found and arrested Moreau on February 15, Pichegru on February 26, the Polignac brothers on February 27, and Cadoudal on March 29. Cadoudal proudly admitted that he had planned to remove Napoleon from power, and that he had expected a French prince to meet him in Paris; but he refused to name any of his associates in the plot.[85]

Meanwhile an English agent named Drake had been collecting another group of conspirators in or near Munich, with a plan to raise an insurrection against Napoleon in the newly French regions on the west bank of the Rhine. If we may believe Méneval, "an order of the [British] King's Privy Council enjoined on the French exiles to betake themselves to the banks of the Rhine, under penalty of forfeiting their pensions; and a regulation fixed the amount of pay allotted to each officer, and each soldier."[86] When Napoleon's spies notified him of these developments he concluded that the Bourbon prince whom the London conspirators had awaited was among these *émigrés*. The Comte d'Artois could not be located among them; but in the little town of Ettenheim, some six miles east of the Rhine in the electorate of Baden, Napoleon's agents discovered—living in apparent quiet except for occasional but suspicious visits to Strasbourg[87]—Louis-Antoine-Henri de Bourbon-Condé, Duc d'Enghien, son of the Duc de Bourbon, and grandson of the Prince de Condé.

When this was reported to Napoleon he concluded that the thirty-two-year-old Duke was a leader of the conspiracy to depose him. The revelations of Querelle, and the arrests recently made in Paris, had thrown the once intrepid general into a state of excitement—perhaps of fear and wrath—that hurried him into decisions that he would always defend but (despite his protestations[88]) perhaps secretly regretted. He sent instructions to General Ordener to lead an armed force to Ettenheim, arrest the Duke, and bring him to Paris. The Duke was taken on the night of March 14–15, 1804, and on March 18 he was imprisoned in the Fortress of Vincennes, five miles east of Paris.

On March 20 Napoleon ordered a military court of five colonels and one major to go to Vincennes and try the Duke on charges of having, while in the pay of England, taken up arms against his own country. About the same time he sent General Savary, head of his special police, to watch over the prisoner and the trial. Enghien admitted that he had received money from English authorities, and that he had hoped to lead a force into Alsace.[89] The court pronounced him guilty of treason, and condemned him to death. He asked permission to see Napoleon; the court refused this, but proposed to send a message to Napoleon, recommending mercy. Savary overruled this proposal, and ordered the sentence of death to be carried out.[90]

Meanwhile Napoleon and his immediate circle, at Josephine's Malmaison, debated the fate of the Duke. They assumed that he would be found guilty—but should he be pardoned as an olive branch to the royalists? Talleyrand, who in 1814 was to chaperone the restoration of the Bourbons, advised execution as a quick way of ending the hopes and plots of the royalists; remembering his record in the Revolution, he feared for his property, perhaps his life, should the Bourbons return to power; he "wished," wrote Barras, "to put a river of blood between Napoleon and the Bourbons."[91] Cambacérès, coolest and most legal of the consular trio, favored delay. Josephine fell at Napoleon's feet and pleaded for Enghien's life, and her entreaties were seconded by her daughter Hortense and Napoleon's sister Caroline.

At some time that night, from Malmaison, Napoleon sent Hugues Maret to Paris with a message to Councilor of State Pierre Réal, bidding him to go to Vincennes, personally examine the Duke, and report the results to Malmaison. Réal received the message, but, exhausted by the day's labor, fell asleep in his room, and did not reach Vincennes till 5 A.M., March 21. Enghien had died before a firing squad at 3 A.M. in the prison yard. Savary, apparently thinking that he had served his master well, rode to Malmaison to give Napoleon the news. Napoleon retired to his private apartment, locked himself in, and refused all appeals from his wife to let her enter.

Bitter denunciation came from royalists and royalty. They were appalled at the idea of a commoner killing a Bourbon. The cabinets of Russia and Sweden sent protests to the Diet of the Holy Roman Empire at Ratisbon, and proposed that the invasion of Baden by the armed forces of France be made the subject of an international inquiry. The Diet made no answer, and the Elector of Baden refused to offend France. Czar Alexander I instructed his ambassador in Paris to demand an explanation of the execution; Talleyrand replied with an *argumentum ad hominem:* "If, when England was planning the assassination of Paul I, the authors of the plot had been known to be lurking at a stone's throw from the frontier, would they not have been seized with all possible speed?"[92] William Pitt was much comforted by the news of the execution; "Bonaparte," he said, "has now done himself more mischief than we have done him since the last declaration of war."[93]

The reaction in France itself was milder than many had expected. Chateaubriand resigned a minor appointment in the Ministry of Foreign Affairs; but when the head of that ministry, the imperturbable Talleyrand, gave a ball on March 24—three days after the death of Enghien—twenty members of the old French nobility, and representatives of all the European courts, attended.[94] Three months after the affair it had apparently disappeared from the public mind. Fouché, however, usually a keen observer, remarked of the execution, "*C'est plus qu'un crime, c'est une faute*" (It is more than a crime, it is a blunder).[95]

Napoleon may have felt some remorse, but he never admitted it. "These people," he said, "wanted to throw France into confusion, and to destroy the Revolution by destroying me; it was my duty both to defend and to avenge the Revolution. . . . The Duc d'Enghien was a conspirator like any other, and he had to be treated as such. . . . I had to choose between continuous persecution and one decisive blow, and my decision was not doubtful. I have forever silenced both royalists and Jacobins."[96] He would let them know that he was "not to be trifled with,"[97] that neither was his "blood ditch-water."[98] He thought, with some reason, that he had put the fear of death into the hearts of royalist plotters, who could now see that Bourbon blood would not save them. Actually, there were no further royalist plots to take Napoleon's life.

In the case of the conspirators who had been arrested in Paris he conducted himself with more caution and publicity. The trials were to be open, and the press was allowed to report them in detail. Though Bourrienne had opposed the execution of Enghien, Napoleon asked him to attend the trials and to give him an account of the proceedings. Pichegru did not wait to be tried; on April 4 he was found dead in his cell, strangled by his own cravat. In other cases the guilt was admitted or evident; but of Moreau no more was proved than that he had been openly hostile to Napoleon, and had concealed from the authorities his knowledge that Pichegru and others were proposing to unseat him by force. On June 10, 1804, the court pronounced sentence: nineteen conspirators were condemned to death, Moreau to two years' imprisonment. Cadoudal died impenitent on June 28. Of the remaining eighteen Napoleon pardoned twelve, including the two Polignacs. Moreau asked if his sentence might be changed to exile; Napoleon agreed, though he predicted that Moreau would continue to plot against him.[99] Moreau took ship to America, stayed there till 1812, returned to take service with the Russian Army, fought against Napoleon at Dresden (August 29, 1813), died of his wounds (September 2), and was buried in Russia.

VI. THE ROAD TO EMPIRE: 1804

Brooding over the conspiracy, Napoleon wondered why he had to do his work under constant threat of assassination, while the rulers who were repeatedly leagued against France—George III of England, Francis II of Austria and the Holy Roman Empire, Frederick William III of Prussia, and Alexander I of Russia—could expect to maintain their supremacy till their normal death, and could rely on the orderly transference of their sovereignty to their natural or designated heirs. It could not be because they had submitted their policies and appointments to democratic controls; they had not. Apparently the secret of their security lay in their "legitimacy"—the sanction of heritable rule by a public opinion formed to habit through generations and centuries.

Privately—ever less privately—Napoleon dreamed of absolute, consecrated, transmissible authority, even of a dynasty that might acquire the seal and aura of time. He felt that the tasks he longed to accomplish required the stability and continuity of absolute rule. Consider Caesar—how he had brought Roman laws and civilization to Gaul, had driven the Germans beyond the Rhine, and had won the title of *imperator*, the commander in chief; well, had not he, Napoleon, done these? What might Caesar have accomplished had he been spared assassination? Think of how much Augustus achieved in his forty-one years of imperial power, freed from the plebeian chaos that Caesar had ended, and supported by a Senate wise enough to subordinate palaver to genius. Napoleon, the son of Italy, the admirer of the ancient Romans, longed for such untrammeled continuity, and for the privilege, enjoyed by the second-century emperors, of choosing and training a successor.

But he also thought, and often spoke, of Charlemagne, who, in a reign of forty-six years (768–814), had brought order and prosperity to Gaul, had spread the laws of the Franks, as a civilizing force, into Germany and Italy, and had won—or commanded—consecration by a Pope; had not he, Napoleon, done all these things? Had he not restored in France the religion that was checking the pagan riot let loose by the Revolution? Did he not, like Charlemagne, deserve the crown for life?

Augustus and Charlemagne, those great restorers, had no faith in democracy; they could not subject their trained and considered judgments, their far-reaching plans and policies, to carping criticism and inconclusive debate by the corruptible delegates of popular simplicity. Caesar and Augustus had known Roman democracy in the vote-buying days of Milo and Clodius; they could not have governed at the behest of mindless mobs. Napoleon had seen Parisian democracy in 1792; he felt that he could not decide and act at the behest of impassioned crowds. It was time to call the Revolution closed, to consolidate its basic gains, and end the chaos and anxiety and class war.

Now, after chastening the royalists with an execution, he was ready to accept their basic claim—that France was not prepared, emotionally or mentally, for self-government; and that some form of authoritarian rule was indispensable. In 1804, according to Mme. de Rémusat, "certain persons, somewhat closely connected with politics, were beginning to assert that France felt the necessity of absolute right in the governing power. Political courtiers, and sincere supporters of the Revolution, seeing that the tranquillity of the country depended upon one life, were discussing the instability of the Consulate. By degrees the thoughts of all were once more turned to monarchy."[100] Napoleon agreed with them. "The French," he remarked to Mme. de Rémusat, "love monarchy and all its trappings."[101]

So, to begin with, he gave them the trappings. He ordered official costumes for the Consuls, the ministers, and the other personnel of the government; velvet was made prominent in these garments, partly to encourage its Lyons manufacturers. Napoleon gathered to his personal service four generals, eight aides-de-camp, four prefects, and two secretaries (Méneval had begged for assistance). The consular court took on a complexity of etiquette and protocol rivaling that of established royalty. Comte Auguste de Rémusat was put in charge of this ritual, while his wife Claire headed the four ladies who attended Josephine. Liveried servants and ornate carriages added to the ordained complexity of official life. Napoleon observed all these forms in public, but soon took refuge in the simplicity of his private ways. However, he smiled consent upon court festivities, fancy-dress or masked balls, and formal visits to the opera, where his wife might display gowns reminiscent of another extravagant queen, lately pitifully dead. Paris indulged him, as he indulged Josephine; after all, might not some flourishes and frippery be allowed to this young ruler, who was adding the statesmanship of Augustus to the victories of Caesar? It seemed so natural that *imperator* should become *empereur*.

Strange to say, many groups in France heard without resentment the rumors of an impending crown. Some 1,200,000 Frenchmen had bought, from the state, property confiscated from the Church or from *émigrés*; they saw no security for their title deeds except in preventing a return of the Bourbons; and they saw in the permanence of Napoleon's power the best protection against such a calamity. The peasants reasoned likewise. The proletariat was divided; it was still fond of the Revolution as having been so largely its work, but with a fondness fading as it enjoyed the steady employment and good wages that the Consulate had brought; and it was not immune to the rising cult of glory, or to the glamour of an empire that might surpass in splendor any of those that contended with France. The bourgeoisie was suspicious of emperors, but this would-be emperor had been faithfully and effectively their man. The lawyers, brought up on Roman law, were almost all in favor of transforming France into an *imperium* that would resume the work of Augustus and the philosopher-emperors from Nerva to Marcus Aurelius. Even the royalists, if they could not have a pedigreed Bourbon, would think it a step forward if monarchy should be restored in France. The clergy, though they knew that Napoleon's piety was political, were grateful for the restoration of the Church. Almost all classes, outside of Paris, believed that only a stable monarchical government could control the individualistic passions and class divisions that rumbled under the crust of civilization.

But there were negative voices. Paris, which had made the Revolution and had suffered for it in body and soul, could not without some audible or secret regrets lay it to rest with all its more or less democratic constitutions. The surviving Jacobin leaders saw in the contemplated change an end to their role in the guidance of France; and perhaps to their lives. The men who had voted for the execution of Louis XVI knew that Napoleon despised them as regicides; they had to rely on Fouché to protect them, but Fouché could be dismissed again. The generals who had hoped to divide and share Napoleon's power cursed the movement that was preparing to clothe in royal purple that "whippersnapper" from Corsica.[102] The philosophers and the savants of the Institute mourned that one of its members was planning to drown democracy in an imperial plebiscite.

Even in the nearly royal family there was a division of sentiment. Josephine was fearfully opposed to any move toward empire. Napoleon, made emperor, would even more powerfully itch for an heir, and therefore for a divorce, since he could expect none from her; so her whole dazzling world of dresses and diamonds could fall in ruins at any moment. Napoleon's brothers and sisters had long since urged him to get divorced; they hated the Creole as a wanton seducer, an obstacle to their own dreams of power; now they supported the drive toward empire as a step toward displacing Josephine. Brother Joseph formulated the argument that

> the conspiracy of Cadoudal and Moreau decided the declaration of an hereditary title. With Napoleon as consul for a period, a *coup-de-main* might overthrow him; as consul for life the blow of a murderer would have been required. He assumed hereditary rank as a shield; it would thus no longer suffice to kill him; the whole state would have to be overthrown. The truth is that the nature of things tended toward the hereditary principle; it was a matter of necessity.[103]

Councilors, senators, tribunes, and others in the government moved to complaisance with Napoleon's wishes, and for simple reasons: consent would merely lessen their freedom of debate—which was already vestigial; opposition might cost them their political lives; early complaisance might earn a rich reward. On May 2, 1804, the legislative bodies passed a triple motion: "1. That Napoleon Bonaparte . . . shall be appointed Emperor of the French Republic; 2. That the title of Emperor, and the Imperial power, shall be hereditary in his family. . . . 3. That care shall be taken to safeguard Equality, Liberty, and the rights of the people in their entirety." On May 18 the Senate proclaimed Napoleon emperor. On May 22 the registered voters of France, by ballots individually signed, approved this *fait accompli* by 3,572,329 yeas to 2,569 nays. Georges Cadoudal, hearing the news in his prison cell, remarked, "We came here to give France a king; we have given her an emperor."[104]

CHAPTER VIII

The New Empire

1804–07

I. THE CORONATION: DECEMBER 2, 1804

NAPOLEON slipped contentedly into imperial ways. Even before the plebiscite, he had begun (May, 1804) to sign his letters and documents with only his first name; soon, except in formal documents, he reduced this to a simple *N;* and in time that proud initial appeared on monuments, buildings, garments, carriages . . . He began to speak of the French people no longer as "citizens" but as "my subjects."[1] He expected more deference from his courtiers, readier assent from his ministers; however, he bore in grim silence Talleyrand's aristocratic ways, and accepted with some relish Fouché's irreverent wit. Appreciating the help Fouché had given in ferreting out conspirators, he restored him (July 11, 1804) to his former post as minister of police. When Napoleon thought to subdue Fouché's independence of thought and speech by reminding him of his having voted for the death of Louis XVI, Fouché replied, "Quite true. It was the first service I had the occasion to perform for Your Majesty."[2]

One thing was still lacking to this majesty: it had not been recognized and sanctified, as with other crowns, by the highest representative of the nation's religious faith. There was something, after all, in that medieval theory of divine right: to a people predominantly Catholic the anointment of its ruler by a pope who claimed to be the viceregent of God signified that this ruler had in effect been chosen by God, and therefore spoke with an almost divine authority. What idea could be more helpful in facilitating rule? And would not such anointment put Napoleon on a level with all European sovereigns, however rooted in the past? So he set his diplomats the task of persuading Pius VII that an unprecedented trip to Paris to crown the Son of the Revolution and the Enlightenment would symbolize the triumph of the Catholic Church over the Revolution and the Enlightenment. And would it not be useful to His Holiness to have, as a new *defensor fidei,* the most brilliant warrior in Europe? Some Austrian cardinals opposed the notion as a veritable sacrilege, but some canny Italians thought it would be quite a victory, not only for religion but also for Italy; "we should be placing an Italian family on the throne of France to govern those barbarians; we should be avenging ourselves on the Gauls."[3] The Pope was probably more practical: he would consent in the hope of bringing a repentant nation back

197

to papal obedience, and regaining several papal territories that had been taken by the armies of France.

Napoleon made as careful preparations for this mutual triumph as for a major war. The coronation rituals of the Old Regime were studied, adapted, and amplified. Processions were planned as by a choreographer, and each movement was timed. New dresses were designed for the ladies of the court; the best milliners gathered around Josephine, and Napoleon bade her wear the jewels of the Treasury as well as her own; despite the protests of his mother, brothers, and sisters, he was resolved to crown her as well as himself. Jacques-Louis David, who was to commemorate the event in the greatest painting of the age, rehearsed her and her attendants in every move and pose. Poets were paid to celebrate the event. The Opéra was instructed to prepare ballets that might stir a papal breast. Arrangements were made to protect the major streets with troops, and to line the nave of Notre-Dame with the Consular Guard in a veritable marriage of Caesar and Christ. Princes and dignitaries from other states were invited, and came. Multitudes arrived from the city, the suburbs, the provinces, and abroad, and bargained for places of vantage in the cathedral or on the routes. Shopkeepers hoped to reap fortunes, and did. Jobs and spectacles kept the people contented as perhaps never since the *panem et circenses* of Imperial Rome.

The affable Pius VII made his way leisurely, November 2–25, through cities and ceremonies in Italy and France, and was met by Napoleon at Fontainebleau. From that moment till the coronation the Emperor gave the Pope every courtesy except deference; the Emperor was not to be awed into admitting any superior power. The people of Paris—the most skeptical on earth at that time—welcomed the Pontiff as a spectacle; an escort of soldiers and priests led him to the Tuileries, where he was guided to a special apartment in the Pavillon de Flore. Josephine welcomed him, and seized the occasion to tell him that she had not been united with Napoleon in a religious marriage; Pius promised to remedy that defect before the coronation. On the night of November 29–30 he remarried them, and Josephine felt that a blessed obstacle had been raised against a divorce.[4]

Early on a cold December 2 a dozen processions left from different points to converge on Notre-Dame: deputations from the cities of France, from the Army and Navy, the legislative assemblies, the judiciary, and the administrative corps, the Legion of Honor, the Institute, the chambers of commerce . . . They found the cathedral nearly filled with invited civilians, but soldiers made way for them to their appointed places. At 9 A.M., from the Pavillon de Flore, the papal procession set forth: Pius VII and his servitors, the cardinals and the grand officers of the Curia, in gaily decorated coaches drawn by horses chosen for their spirit and beauty, all led by a bishop on a mule and bearing aloft the papal crucifix. At the cathedral they descended and walked in formal array up the steps, into the nave, and through lanes of stiff soldiers to their assigned stations—the Pope to his throne at the altar's left. Meanwhile, from another point of the Tuileries, the imperial cavalcade proceeded: first, Marshal Murat, governor of Paris, and his staff; then some specially distinguished regiments of the Army; then, in six-horse carriages, the leading officers of the government; then a carriage for the Bonaparte brothers and sisters; then a royal coach marked with a blazoned *N*, drawn by eight horses, and bearing the Emperor in purple velvet embroidered with gems and gold, and the Empress, at the peak of her precarious splendor, robed in silk and sparkling with jewelry, "her face so well made up that," though forty-one, "she looked like four-and-twenty."[5] Then eight more carriages, bearing the ladies and officers of the court. It took an hour for all these carriages to reach the cathedral. There Napoleon and Josephine changed to coronation robes, and took their places at the right of the altar; he on a throne, she on a smaller throne five steps below him.

The Pope ascended the altar; Napoleon, then Josephine, mounted to kneel before him; each of the two was anointed and blessed. Emperor and Empress stepped down to where General Kellermann stood with a crown on a tray. Napoleon took the crown and placed it on his head. Then, as Josephine knelt in piety and modesty before him, he—"with a kind of noticeable tenderness"[6]—placed a crown of diamonds upon her jeweled hair. All this was no surprise to the Pope, for it had been so arranged in advance.* The patient Pontiff then kissed Napoleon on the cheek, and pronounced the official formula, "*Vivat Imperator in aeternum.*" The Pope sang Mass. His assistants brought a book of the Gospels to him, and Napoleon, placing his hand on the book, recited the oath that still affirmed him to be the Son of the Revolution:

> I swear to maintain the territory of the Republic in its integrity; to respect and enforce the laws of the Concordat and the Freedom of Worship; to respect and enforce Equality before the Law, political and civil liberty, and the irreversibility of the sales of national property; to lay on no duty, to impose no tax, except according to law; to maintain the institution of the Legion of Honor; and to govern only in accordance with the interests, the happiness, and the glory of the French people.[8]

By three o'clock the ceremony was complete. Through an acclaiming crowd, under falling snow, the various groups proceeded back to their points of origin. The genial Pontiff, fascinated by the glamour of Paris and the hope of fruitful negotiations, remained in or near the capital for four months, frequently appearing on a balcony to bless a kneeling crowd. He found Napoleon politely immovable, and bore patiently the secular entertainments offered him by his host. On April 15, 1805, he left for Rome. Napoleon resumed his imperial projects and ways, confident that now, being as holy as any ruler, he could face unbendingly the powers that would soon unite to destroy him.

---

* Napoleon to Las Cases at St. Helena, August 15, 1816: "The Pope, sometime before my coronation, . . . consented not to place the crown on my head himself. He [also] dispensed with the ceremony of the public Communion. . . . 'Napoleon,' he observed [to the bishops who wanted Pius to insist on this], 'is not, perhaps, a believer; the time will no doubt come in which his faith will be restored.' "[7]

II. THE THIRD COALITION: 1805

By the end of 1804 all the European governments except England, Sweden, and Russia had recognized Napoleon as "emperor of the French," and some kings had addressed him as "brother."[9] On January 2, 1805, he again proposed peace to George III, and now addressed him as

> SIR AND BROTHER:
> Having been called by Providence, and by the voice of the Senate, the people, and the army, to the throne of France, my first feeling is a desire for peace.
> France and England are wasting their prosperity. They may contend for centuries, but are their Governments rightfully fulfilling their most sacred duty, and does not their conscience reproach them with so much blood shed in vain, for no definite end? I am not ashamed to take the initiative. I have, I think, sufficiently proved . . . that I do not fear the chances of war. . . . Peace is my heartfelt wish, but war has never been adverse to my renown. I implore Your Majesty not to deprive yourself of the happiness of bestowing peace on the world. . . . Never was there a better occasion . . . for imposing silence on passion, and for listening to the voice of humanity and reason. If this opportunity be lost, what term can be assigned to a war which all my endeavors might fail to terminate? . . .
> What do you hope to attain by war? The coalition of some Continental Powers? . . . To snatch her colonies from France? Colonies are objects of but secondary importance to France; and does not Your Majesty already possess more than you can keep? . . .
> The world is large enough for our two nations to live in it, and the power of reason is sufficient to enable us to overcome all difficulties if on both sides there is the will to do so. In any case I have fulfilled a duty which I hold to be righteous, and which is dear to my heart. I trust Your Majesty will believe in the sincerity of the sentiments I have expressed, and in my earnest desire to give you proof of them.
>
> NAPOLEON[10]

We do not know what private assurances of pacifist intent may have accompanied this proposal; in any case it did not swerve England from basing her security upon a balance of Continental Powers, and preserving this by encouraging the weak against the strong. George III, not yet a "brother," did not answer Napoleon, but on January 14, 1805, his Foreign Secretary, Lord Mulgrave, sent Talleyrand a letter that frankly stated England's terms for peace:

> His Majesty has no dearer wish than to embrace the first opportunity of once more procuring for his subjects the advantages of a peace which shall be founded on bases not incompatible with the permanent security and the essential interests of his States. His Majesty is convinced that this end can only be attained by an arrangement which will provide alike for the future security and tranquillity of Europe, and prevent a renewal of the dangers and misfortunes which have beset the Continent.
> His Majesty, therefore, feels it to be impossible to reply more decisively to

the question which has been put to him, until he has had time to communicate with those Continental Powers with whom he is allied, and particularly with the Emperor of Russia, who has given the strongest proofs of his wisdom and good feeling, and of the deep interest which he takes in the security and independence of Europe.[11]

William Pitt the Younger was currently prime minister of England (May, 1804–January, 1806). He represented, as the new financial bastion of Britain, the commercial interests that were almost the only British gainers from the war. They had borne substantial losses from French control of the mouths and course of the Rhine; but they were profiting from British control of the seas. This not only stifled most French maritime competition, it enabled Britain to seize French and Dutch colonies at will, and French vessels wherever found. On October 5, 1804, English ships seized several Spanish galleons bound for Spain with silver that would have enabled her to pay much of her debt to France. In December, 1804, England declared war upon Spain, and Spain placed her fleet at the disposal of France. With this exception, Britain, with superior diplomats and judicious subsidies, slowly won to her side Continental Powers richer in men than in gold.

Alexander I could not make up his mind whether he was a liberal reformer and benevolent despot or a martial conqueror called by destiny to dominate Europe. However, he was clear on several points: he wanted to round out his western boundaries by absorbing Wallachia and Moldavia, which belonged to Turkey; consequently he aspired, like the absorbing Catherine, to overcome Turkey, bestride the Bosporus and the Dardanelles, and, in due time, control the Mediterranean; already he held the Ionian Isles. But Napoleon had once captured those islands, and now longed for them; he still hungered for Egypt, and thirsted for the Mediterranean; he had talked of swallowing Turkey and half of the Orient. Here was a rival gourmand; one or the other must yield. For these and other reasons Alexander had no wish to see England make peace with France. In January, 1805, he signed an alliance with Sweden, which was already allied with England. On July 11 he completed with England a treaty which stipulated that Britain would pay Russia an annual subsidy of £1,250,000 for every 100,000 men contributed to the campaigns against France.[12]

Frederick William III of Prussia parleyed with Napoleon for a year in the hope of adding to his realm the province of Hanover, which the French had taken in 1803. Napoleon offered it on condition of an alliance which would pledge Prussia to support France in maintaining the new status; Frederick did not relish the thought of angry British warships along his coast. On May 24, 1804, he signed an alliance with Russia for united action against any French advance east of the Weser.

Austria too hesitated. If she joined the new coalition she would bear the first brunt of French attack. But Austria, even more closely than England, had felt the successive pushes of Napoleon's expanding power: the presidency of the Italian Republic, January, 1802; the French annexation of Piedmont, September, 1802; the Swiss submission to a French protectorate,

February, 1803; the assumption of the imperial title, May, 1804. And the pushes continued: on May 26, 1805, Napoleon received at Milan the Iron Crown of Lombardy; and on June 6 he accepted the request of the Doge of Genoa that the Ligurian Republic be incorporated into France. When, asked the Austrians, would this new Charlemagne stop? Could he not—unless most of Europe should unite to stop him—easily absorb first the Papal States and then the kingdom of Naples? What then would keep him from appropriating Venice and all of that luscious Venezia which was contributing so indispensably to Austrian revenues? Such was the mood of Austria when Britain offered her fresh subsidies, and Russia promised her 100,000 hardy troops in case France should attack. On June 17, 1805, Austria allied herself with England, Russia, Sweden, and Prussia, and the Third Coalition was complete.

III. AUSTERLITZ: DECEMBER 2, 1805

Against this quintuple alliance France had the hesitant support of Hesse, Nassau, Baden, Bavaria, and Württemberg, and the cooperation of the Dutch and Spanish fleets. From all quarters of his realm Napoleon drew money and conscripts, and organized three armies: (1) the Army of the Rhine, under Davout, Murat, Soult, and Ney, to challenge the main Austrian force under General Mack; (2) the Army of Italy, under Masséna, to meet the westward thrust of an Austrian army under the Archduke Karl Ludwig; and (3) the Grande Armée of Napoleon, presently gathered about Boulogne, but capable of being suddenly turned upon Austria. His hope was that a quick capture of Vienna would compel Austria to sign a separate peace, immobilizing her Continental allies, and leaving England unaided and besieged.

The young Emperor had come to hate England as the bane of his life and the chief obstacle to his dreams; he called her *"perfide Albion,"* and denounced British gold as the main source of France's woes. Night and day, amid a hundred other projects, he planned the building of a navy that would end Britannia's lordship of the seas. He poured funds and workers into naval arsenals like Toulon and Brest, and he tested a dozen captains to find an admiral who could lead the growing French Navy to victory. He thought he had found such a man in Louis de La Touche-Tréville, and strove to inspire him with the vision of a Britain invaded and overcome. "If we can be masters of the Channel for six hours we shall be masters of the world."[13] But La Touche-Tréville died in 1804, and Napoleon made the mistake of giving command of the French Navy to Pierre de Villeneuve.

Villeneuve had bungled his share in the Egyptian fiasco, and had given signs of both insubordination and timidity. He had no faith in the possibility of capturing control of the Channel for six hours, and he lingered in Paris until Napoleon ordered him to his post at Toulon. His instructions were subtle and complex: to lead his fleet out to sea, let Nelson pursue him with the main British flotilla, draw him on across the Atlantic to the West Indies, elude him among those islands, and return as swiftly as possible to the English Channel, where French, Dutch, and Spanish squadrons would join him in engaging the British vessels there long enough to let the French army, in its thousand boats, cross to England before Nelson could come back from the Caribbean. Villeneuve accomplished the first part of his task well: he lured Nelson to America, escaped him, and hurried back to Europe. But on reaching Spain he judged his ships and men to be in no condition to overcome the British guardians of the Channel; instead he sought the protection of a friendly harbor at Cádiz. Napoleon, frustrated in his plan, sent orders to Villeneuve to seek out Nelson's fleet and risk everything in a desperate challenge to British control of the seas.

Then, in a flurry of decision, the Emperor turned away from the Channel, and wheeled a hundred thousand men around to march south and east to the Rhine and beyond. All France followed in anxious hope the course of this Grande Armée, now so named by Napoleon, and every town on its itinerary bade it Godspeed on its enterprise. In nearly every church the clergy called upon the youth of the nation to obey the call to the colors; they proved from Scripture that Napoleon was now under the direct guidance and protection of God;[14] so soon had the Concordat come to fruit. Napoleon cooperated by arranging that twenty thousand carriages should be provided along the route to hurry and relieve the soldiers on their passage through France.[15] He himself rode to Strasbourg with Josephine, who was now all anxiety and devotion; her fortunes too hung on every throw of the dice. He promised that within a few weeks he would be master of Vienna.[16] At Strasbourg he left her in the care of Rémusat, and hurried on to the front.

His strategy, as usual, was to divide and conquer: to keep the Austrian armies from uniting; to destroy or immobilize the armed forces of Austria before the Russian horde whose aid they were expecting could arrive; and then to overwhelm the Russians in a victory that would compel his Continental enemies to at least a temporary peace. Despite gloomy days and dark nights of rain, mud, and snow, the Army of the Rhine carried out its share of the campaign with a thoroughness and dispatch that may serve as an illustration of how much Napoleon owed to his marshals. After a week of maneuvers General Mack's 50,000 men found themselves, at Ulm, hemmed in on three sides by the artillery, cavalry, and infantry of Davout, Soult, Murat, and Ney, and denied retreat by the width of the Danube behind them. Starved for food, and short of ammunition, the besieged Austrians threatened mutiny unless they were allowed to surrender. Mack did so at last (October 17, 1805); 30,000 of his troops were taken prisoner and sent to France. It was one of the least costly and most thorough and effective victories in the history of war. Emperor Francis II, and some Austrian survivors from Ulm, fled north to join the oncoming Russians, while Napoleon entered Vienna (November 12) without resistance and without display.

His triumph was soon soured by news that Villeneuve, pursuant to instructions, had gone out to meet Nelson in what proved for both of them a duel to the death. Nelson won at Trafalgar (October 21, 1805), but was mortally wounded; Villeneuve lost, and killed himself. Napoleon somberly put aside all hope of contesting British control of the seas; no course to victory seemed open but to win so many battles on land that the Continental Powers would be forced to follow France in closing their markets to British goods until the merchants of England should compel their government to sue for peace.

Leaving General Mortier and fifteen thousand men to hold Vienna, he set out on November 17 to join his troops and prepare them to meet two Russian armies marching south, one under the resolute Kutuzov, the other under Czar Alexander himself. The Russian Bear met the French Eagle at Austerlitz, a village in Moravia, on December 2, 1805. Before the battle Napoleon issued a proclamation to his legions:

> SOLDIERS:
> The Russian army appears before you to avenge the Austrian army of Ulm. . . . The positions which we occupy are formidable; while they are marching to turn my right, they will present their flank to me. . . .
> I shall myself direct your battalions. I shall keep out of the fire if, with your usual bravery, you throw disorder and confusion into the enemy's ranks. But if the victory should be for a moment uncertain, you will see your emperor the foremost to expose himself to danger. For victory must not hang doubtful on this day most particularly, when the honor of the French infantry, which so deeply concerns the honor of the whole nation, is at stake. . . . It behooves us to conquer these hirelings of England, who are animated with such bitter hatred of our nation. . . .
> This victory will put an end to the campaign, and we shall then be able to turn to our winter quarters, where we shall be joined by the new armies which are forming in France; and then the peace which I shall make will be worthy of my people, of you, and of myself.[17]

His first tactic was to capture a hill that would allow his artillery to rake the Russian infantry moving to flank his right. That hill was held by some of Kutuzov's bravest men; they gave way, re-formed, fought again, and were finally overcome by Napoleon's reserves. Soon the French artillery was decimating the Russians as they marched on the plain below; their center broke in terror and flight, dividing their army into disorganized halves faced at the one end by the infantry of Davout and Soult, at the other by the battalions of Lannes, Murat, and Bernadotte; and into the shattered center Napoleon sent his reserves to complete the rout. The 87,000 Russians and Austrians surrendered 20,000 prisoners and nearly all their artillery, and left 15,000 dead. Alexander and Francis fled with the remnants into Hungary, while their frightened ally, Frederick William III, humbly sued for peace.

In that holocaust the 73,000 French and their allies lost 8,000 dead or wounded. The exhausted survivors, long hardened to the sight of death, cheered their leader with wild enthusiasm. In a bulletin of December 3 he answered them with a promise that he would soon keep: "When all that is necessary for securing the happiness and prosperity of our country has been accomplished, I will lead you back to France. There you will be the object of my most tender solicitude. My people will welcome you with joy, and you will only have to say 'I was at the battle of Austerlitz' for people to exclaim, 'Behold a hero.' "[18]

IV. THE MAPMAKER: 1806–07

When William Pitt received the news of Austerlitz, he was nearing death. Seeing a map of Europe on a wall, he asked that it be removed. "Roll up that map," he said; "it will not be wanted these ten years."[19] Napoleon agreed, and remade the map.

He began by remaking Prussia and Austria. Talleyrand, whom he summoned to Vienna to phrase the imperial will in diplomatic language, advised him to give Austria moderate terms on condition of signing with France an alliance that might end the connection of English subsidies with Austrian policies, and might give France some support, even if only geographical, in conflict with Prussia and Russia. Napoleon, suspecting the fragility of alliances, thought rather to weaken Austria beyond possibility of challenging France again, and to win Prussia from Russia by an easy peace. Meanwhile he allowed Alexander to lead his surviving Russians back to Russia unpursued.

By a treaty signed in Maria Theresa's cabinet in the Austrian royal palace of Schönbrunn (December 5, 1805), Napoleon required Prussia to disband its Army, cede the margravate of Ansbach to Bavaria, and the principality of Neuchâtel to France, and to accept a binding alliance with its conqueror. Frederick William III expected to get in return the province of Hanover, which Napoleon was glad to promise him as a deterrent to any pro-English sentiment in Prussia.

The Treaty of Pressburg with Austria (completed in Napoleon's absence, December 26, 1805) was merciless. She had begun hostilities by invading Bavaria; she was now required to give up to Bavaria, Baden, and Württemberg all her lands in the Tirol, Vorarlberg, and south Germany. So enlarged, Bavaria and Württemberg became kingdoms, and Baden became a grand duchy allied with France. To recompense France for her outlay of men, money, and matériel in the war, Austria transferred to a French protectorate all her possessions in Italy, including Venice and its hinterlands; and she agreed to pay France an indemnity of forty million francs—part of which, Napoleon was happy to learn, had recently arrived from England.[20] In addition he ordered his art connoisseurs to send to Paris some choice pictures and statues from Austrian palaces and galleries. All this tribute of land and money and art the victor, in his Roman way, considered to be rightful spoils of war. Finally he ordered that a triumphal column be erected in the Place Vendôme in Paris, and be coated with metal taken from enemy cannon captured at Austerlitz.

Talleyrand signed these treaties, but, disappointed by the rejection of his advice, he began to use his influence—not always this side of treason—

against the further extension of Napoleon's power. He later excused himself as having served France by his disservices to his employer, but he made both of them pay.

On December 15, 1805, Napoleon left Vienna to join Josephine in Munich. There they assisted at the marriage of Eugène (who had been made viceroy of Italy) to the Princess Augusta, eldest daughter of Bavaria's King. Before the wedding Napoleon formally adopted Eugène as his son, and promised him the crown of Italy as his inheritance. It was a marriage of political convenience, to cement the alliance of Bavaria with France; but Augusta learned to love her husband, and helped to save him after his adoptive father's fall.

Emperor and Empress went on to Paris, where he was met with such official celebrations and public acclaim that Mme. de Rémusat wondered "if it be possible that a human head should not be turned by such excess of praise."[21] Facts helped to sober him. He found that during his absence mismanagement had brought the Treasury near to bankruptcy; the Austrian indemnity came to its rescue. He still had to contend with attempts upon his life, for on February 20, 1806, he received word from Charles James Fox, then prime minister of England, that he should be on his guard, since a would-be assassin had offered to kill Napoleon for a reasonable sum.[22] Fox had had the man kept under detention, but there were probably other such patriots for a price. As England was then at war with France, the Prime Minister's act lived up to both the Christian and the chivalric code. Amid homicide individual and collective, France, on January 1, 1806, returned to the Christian Gregorian calendar.

On May 2, after four months of administrative recuperation, the Emperor read to the Corps Législatif his "Report on the Condition of the Empire in 1806." It recounted briefly the victories of the Army, and the acquisition of allies and terrain; it described the flourishing condition of French agriculture and industry; it announced the Industrial Exhibition—something new in French history—that was to open at the Louvre in the fall; it noted the building or repair of harbors, canals, bridges, and 33,500 miles of roads—several of these across the Alps; it told of great structures in progress—the Temple de la Victoire (now La Madeleine), the Bourse or Stock Exchange, which lifted money into art, and the Arc de Triomphe de l'Étoile that was beginning to crown the Champs-Élysées; and it ended with the assurance which France was beginning to seek: "It is not conquests that the Emperor has in mind; he has exhausted the sphere of military glory. . . . To perfect the administration, and make it a source of lasting happiness and ever-increasing prosperity for his people, . . . such is the glory at which he aims."[23]

The mapmaking continued. On July 12, 1806, the incredible Emperor accepted, as a gift, another empire, composed of the kingdoms of Bavaria, Saxony, Württemberg, and Westphalia, the grand duchies of Baden, Berg, Frankfurt, Hesse-Darmstadt, and Würzburg, the duchies of Anhalt, Arenberg, Mecklenburg-Schwerin, Nassau, Oldenburg, Saxe-Coburg, Saxe-Gotha, Saxe-Weimar, and half a dozen petty principalities. The initiative in this remarkable marriage of friend and foe had been taken (according to Méneval)[24] by the "Prince Primate" Karl Theodor von Dalberg, formerly archbishop of Mainz. Under his lead the heads of the various states asked Napoleon to take them under his protection, pledged him contingents (totaling 63,000 men) for his armies, announced their separation from the Holy Roman Empire (which Charlemagne had established in A.D. 800), and formed the Confederation of the Rhine. Probably this new orientation of Teutonic regions was eased by the spread, among them, of the French language and literature. The intellectual community was almost international. Prussia naturally protested against the immense strengthening of France, but Austria, helpless in defeat, accepted the change. Since the withdrawal of sixteen princes and their states reduced the Holy Roman Empire to an inconsiderable fraction of its original extent, Francis II (August 6, 1806) renounced his title and prerogatives as head of the once spacious structure that Voltaire had called "not holy, not Roman, and not an empire," and henceforth he contented himself with the title of Francis I, Emperor of Austria.

Now the French Empire, and soon the Code Napoléon, extended in effect from the Atlantic to the Elbe. It included France, Belgium, Holland, the border states west of the Rhine, Geneva, and nearly all of Italy north of the Papal States. The man who had envied Charlemagne had apparently repeated Charlemagne's achievement of "giving laws to the West"—i.e., Western Europe. But from the Atlantic to the Elbe thoughtful souls wondered: How long can this brotherhood of Gaul and Teuton last?

V. JENA, EYLAU, FRIEDLAND: 1806–07

On August 15, 1806, France celebrated St. Napoleon's Day and Napoleon's thirty-seventh birthday. The country, wrote Mme. de Rémusat (usually critical), "was in a state of profound tranquillity. Day by day the Emperor met with less opposition. A firm, equable, and strict administration —which was just inasmuch as it was equal for all—regulated both the exercises of authority and the mode of supporting it. Conscription was rigorously enforced, but as yet the murmurs of the people were faint; the French had not then exhausted the sentiment of glory."[25] Best of all, Prime Minister Fox for England, and Count Peter Oubril for Russia, had opened negotiations for peace.

Prussia, however, was reeling toward war. Her shotgun union with France had proved costly: England and Sweden had declared war upon her; the British Navy had blockaded her ports and seized her ships on the seas; her economy was suffering; her people wondered why their King had made so damaging an alliance. Her elder statesmen, contemplating the splendor of an army still stiff with proud memories of Frederick the Great, and counting the manpower that Czar Alexander was preparing for another round with France, told the hesitant Frederick William III that a lasting alliance with Russia was Prussia's only alternative to being swallowed in Napoleon's gaping appetite. Queen Louise, beautiful and passionate, doted upon the handsome and courtly Alexander, called Napoleon a "monster," and scorned her husband's fear of that "scum from hell";[26] the regiment that bore her name wildly cheered her as, shapely in her colonel's uniform, she rode before them on the parade ground. Prince Louis Ferdinand, the King's cousin, itched for war as a path of glory to a throne.

On June 30, 1806, Frederick William sent Alexander an assurance that Prussia's treaty with France would never interfere with the treaty it had made with Russia in 1800. In July he was shocked to learn that Napoleon had received under his protectorate a Confederation of the Rhine which included several regions formerly held by Prussia and supposedly still within her sphere of influence. Furthermore the Prussian ambassador to France notified his master that Bonaparte was secretly proposing the return of Hanover to England as part of the price of peace; Hanover had been promised to Prussia; the King felt betrayed. On August 9 he ordered the mobilization of the Prussian Army. On August 26 Napoleon aroused Prussia still further by ordering—or allowing—the execution of Palm, a Nuremberg bookseller, for issuing a brochure urging resistance to France. On September 6, in a letter to the Czar, Frederick William pledged himself to join in an attack upon "the disturber of the universe."[27] On September 13 the gallant Fox died; this, Napoleon would later say, "was one of the fatalities of my career. If he had lived, peace would have been made."[28] The British ministry returned to a policy of a struggle to the death, and Alexander repudiated the tentative agreement that Oubril had signed with France. On September 19 Prussia sent to France an ultimatum that unless all French troops were within a fortnight removed to west of the Rhine, Prussia would declare war. Godoy, the wily minister then ruling Spain, offered its friendship to Prussia, and called the Spaniards to arms. Napoleon never forgot that move, and resolved that when opportunity offered he would set up a friendlier government in Spain. Reluctantly he left Paris and rode off with Josephine and Talleyrand to Mainz to face again the chances of war.

He must have lost his taste for battle, for when he had to part from Josephine at Mainz he suffered a nervous collapse. Possibly he had come to realize that no matter how often he risked his throne and life in war, no victory would ever win him an acceptable peace. Mme. de Rémusat described the scene as reported to her by her husband:

> The Emperor sent my husband to summon the Empress; he returned with her in a few moments. She was weeping. Agitated by her tears, the Emperor held her for a long time in his arms, and seemed almost unable to bid her farewell. He was strongly moved, and M. de Talleyrand was also much affected. The Emperor, still holding his wife to his heart, approached M. de Talleyrand with outstretched hand; then, throwing his arms around both at once, he said to M. de Rémusat, "It is very hard to leave the two persons one loves best." As he uttered these words he was overcome by a sort of nervous emotion, which increased to such a degree that he wept uncontrollably; and almost immediately an attack of convulsions ensued, which brought on vomiting. He was

placed in a chair, and drank some orange-flower water, but continued to weep for fully a quarter of an hour. At length he mastered himself, and rising suddenly, shook M. de Talleyrand's hand, gave a last embrace to his wife, and said to M. de Rémusat: "Are the carriages ready? Call the suite, and let us go."[29]

He had to hurry, for his strategy depended upon bringing his best forces against the Prussians before the Russians could reach the front. The Prussians were not yet united: in the fore were 50,000 men under Prince Friedrich Ludwig of Hohenlohe; farther back were 60,000 men under Frederick William and that same gentlemanly Duke of Brunswick who, fifteen years before, had vowed to destroy Paris; add some 30,000 Hanoverians, who had come without ecstasy to the aid of their new King; in all, 140,000 men. Napoleon had 130,000 soldiers, hastily assembled but skilled in maneuvers, strangers to defeat, and confidently led by Lannes, Davout, Augereau, Soult, Murat, and Ney. Lannes and Augereau caught one Prussian division at Saalfeld, a plain between the Saale and the Ilm, tributaries of the Elbe; the Prussians, unused to the quick maneuvers of the French, were routed, and there Prince Louis Ferdinand was killed (October 10, 1806).

The French rushed on, 56,000 of them, and came upon Hohenlohe's army near Jena, home of the famous university where Schiller had recently taught, and where Hegel, a year later, was to puzzle the world with a new philosophy. Napoleon deployed his forces in a complex web that enabled the divisions of Lannes and Soult to charge the enemy's center and left flank while Augereau's division attacked the right, and Murat's cavalry rode furiously into the disordered Prussians, who abandoned all formation and fled from the field. In their flight they ran into the broken battalions of the Duke of Brunswick, which had been routed at Auerstedt by a French army brilliantly led by Davout; there the Duke of Brunswick was mortally wounded. On that day, October 14, 1806, the Prussians lost 27,000 dead or wounded, 18,000 prisoners, and nearly all their artillery. Napoleon, that evening, sent a hurried report to Josephine: "We have met the Prussian army and it no longer exists. I am well, and press you to my heart."[30] In the following days Ney, Soult, and Murat, pursuing the fugitives, captured 20,000 more men. Davout and Augereau drove straight on to Berlin; it quickly surrendered; and on October 27 Napoleon entered the Prussian capital.

One of his first acts was to levy from Prussia and her allies a contribution of 160 million francs to pay the expenses of the French army.[31] In addition Berlin was required to supply the occupying forces with food, clothing, and medicines. Art scouts were ordered to dispatch to Paris the best pictures and statues in Berlin and Potsdam; Napoleon himself, in a tour of Potsdam, appropriated the sword of Frederick the Great.

From Berlin, November 21, 1806, he issued an historic decree: henceforth no vessel coming from Great Britain or her colonies should be allowed to enter any port in the French Empire, which now included the Hanseatic towns; no goods from Great Britain or her possessions were to be allowed entry into any territory governed by, or allied with, France; no Briton was to enter those lands. Finding all his military victories of no avail in persuading England to peace, and knowing that she would apply her blockade to any regions controlled by France, as she had (in May, 1806) extended it to all the coast from Brest to the Elbe,[32] Napoleon sought to turn that weapon around: Britain was to be shut out from the Continent, as the British fleet had shut out France and her allies from all maritime trade. Perhaps in this way, he hoped, the merchants and manufacturers of Britain might be moved to peace.

There were many weak points in the plan. Continental manufacturers, freed from British competition, would raise the prices of their products, and consumers would mourn the absence of British products to which they had become accustomed. There would be much smuggling and bribery. (Already Bourrienne, whom Napoleon had made minister at Hamburg, was amassing a fortune by selling exemptions from the blockade; Napoleon had to dismiss him again.) Russia was still allied with England, and British goods could cross the Russian frontiers into Prussia and Austria. British goods were daily pouring into the port of Danzig, which was still held by Prussian troops.

Though the Prussian Army had been shattered, and Napoleon was dictator in Berlin, his military situation was more immediately worrisome than his economic affairs. Most of Poland was held by Russia and Prussia, and Polish patriots were sending appeals to Napoleon to come and free their once proud country from these humiliating yokes; however, a well-equipped army of eighty thousand Russians, stationed west of the Vistula under Count Levin Bennigsen, was preparing to challenge any French intrusion into Polish affairs. The French army, slowly recovering from Jena, was not eager to offer such a challenge; unused to the damp Baltic cold, it looked with tremors at the approaching winter, and longed for home. Meanwhile a deputation came from Paris to Berlin, ostensibly to congratulate Napoleon on his brilliant victories, but really to beg him to make peace and return to a France that had begun to see in every Napoleonic victory the necessity for many more, each risking all. He told the delegates that he could not stop now; that the Russian challenge had to be met, and that the blockade of England would fail unless Russia were coaxed or forced to join in the plan. He bade his army advance into Prussian Poland; it met with no immediate resistance, and on December 19, 1806, Napoleon entered Warsaw unhindered and acclaimed.

All classes, from nobles still longing for the *liberum veto* to the peasants still suffering the disabilities of serfdom, united in seeing him as the miracle-worker who would annul the three partitions of their country by Russia, Prussia, and Austria, and would make Poland again a sovereign state. He returned plaudits with lauds, praised their nation, their heroes, and their women (who spoke French as readily as their own seductively sibilant tongue), and took one of these, Countess Marie Laczyńska Walewska, to his bed and heart. His appeals to her, before and after, were as humble and passionate as his early letters to his Josephine. Walewska refused him (we are told) until a group of Polish nobles, "in a document signed with all the first names in Poland," called upon her to sacrifice herself in the hope that Napoleon would thereby be moved to restore the integrity and independence of their thrice-partitioned country. It reminded her that Esther had given herself to Ahasuerus not out of love for him, but to save her people. "If but we could say the same, to your glory and our good fortune!"[33] When Josephine begged to be allowed to come up from Mainz, Napoleon used the bad roads of Poland as reason for bidding his wife, "Go back to Paris; . . . be bright and gay; perhaps I shall be there soon."[34]

Hibernating with Walewska, he hoped that the Russians would await the spring before troubling him. But when he sent a force under Marshal François-Joseph Lefebvre to capture Danzig, Bennigsen led nearly all his 80,000 men across the Vistula in a massive attack upon Lefebvre's columns as they neared Thorn. Couriers rushed back to notify Napoleon; he hurried north, and with 65,000 men, on February 8, 1807, he fought at Eylau (south of Königsberg) one of the costliest battles in his wars. The Russian artillery proved superior to the French; Augereau, old, wounded, and dazed, asked to be relieved of his command, alleging that he could no longer think clearly; Murat's cavalry broke the enemy's lines, but these re-formed, and stood their ground till evening. Then Bennigsen ordered a retreat, leaving 30,000 men killed or disabled on the field; however, he reported to the Czar that he had won a glorious victory. The Czar celebrated it with a Te Deum Mass at St. Petersburg.[35]

The French had won, but they had lost 10,000 wounded or dead, and the survivors wondered how they could resist another assault from those tough and innumerable Slavs. Napoleon too now had unwonted moods of gloom; that diseased stomach which was to kill him was already humbling him with pain. He never forgot the devoted care that Marie Walewska gave him through that trying winter in the army camp at Finkenstein. Nevertheless he labored daily, ordering food, clothing, and medicine for his troops, supervising military practice, summoning conscripts from his weary people and his reluctant allies, and issuing decrees for the government of France. In the meantime Czar Alexander I and King Frederick William III met at Bartenstein on April 26, 1807, and signed an agreement for dividing non-French Europe between them after the next battle, in which they expected the French army to be destroyed.

When that mutilated army had been reinforced, and cheered by the sprouting spring, Napoleon sent another detachment to take Danzig; it was done. Bennigsen, who had also rebuilt his battalions, received orders from Alexander to march to Königsberg, where he would be fortified by a Prussian garrison 24,000 strong. Bennigsen proceeded, but on the way he allowed his 46,000 men to rest at Friedland. There, at three o'clock in the morning of June 14, 1807 (anniversary of Marengo), they were awakened by an artillery barrage from 12,000 Frenchmen led by the reckless but undefeated Lannes. The Russians soon returned his fire, and his venture might have ended in disaster had not reinforcements come. Napoleon rushed up with his entire force, and hemmed in the Russians on every side except the River Alle, which denied them retreat. By 5 P.M. the French prevailed; the Russians took to boats or the water in desperate flight; 25,000 of them were left on the field. The French had lost 8,000, but they had won a decisive victory over the only Russian army then available to meet invasion. Russians and Prussians fled to Tilsit, losing so many hundreds to their French pursuers that their generals, Alexander permitting, asked for a truce. Napoleon granted it; then, leaving General Savary to hold and govern Königsberg, he himself proceeded to Tilsit to make peace with a broken King and a chastened Czar.

VI. TILSIT: JUNE 25 – JULY 9, 1807

At Tilsit, some sixty miles southeast of Königsberg, the rival armies peacefully faced each other on opposite sides of the River Niemen, and "a friendly understanding grew up between them";[36] the rival Emperors, however, at Alexander's suggestion, met cautiously in a tent on a raft moored in the middle of the stream. Each ruler was rowed to the raft; Napoleon reached it first (as every French soldier had expected), and had time to walk through the tent and welcome Alexander on the other side. They embraced, and the opposed armies joined in a lusty cheer; "it was a beautiful sight," said eyewitness Méneval.

Each ruler had reasons for being amiable: Napoleon's army was in no condition (in number or equipment, or in the security of its rear, or in the support it might expect from a France crying out for peace) to invade an unknown land almost limitless in space and men; and Alexander—disgusted with the weakness of his allies and his troops, fearful of insurrection in his Polish or Lithuanian provinces, and hotly embroiled with Turkey and his troops—was glad to get a breathing spell before undertaking to defeat a man who (excepting Acre) had never yet been overcome. Besides, this Frenchman who had been playing chess with the map of Europe was not the "monster" and "barbarian" described by the Czarina and the Königin, but an engagingly courteous fellow whose hospitality was unobtrusive but complete. After that first meeting, Alexander readily agreed that their further conferences should be held in Tilsit town, in commodious quarters arranged by Napoleon and near his own. Often they dined at his table, sometimes with Prussia's King, later with its Queen. For a time the Czar made himself a pupil, asking the Corsican to instruct him in the art of government, and agreeing with him that Louis XVIII (then living in Courland) lacked all the qualities needed in a sovereign, and "was the most insignificant nullity in Europe."[37]

Each of the Emperors thought the other charming and deceivable. After apparently amiable negotiations, they signed not only a treaty but an alliance. Russia was to keep her present possessions intact, but she would end her cooperation with England, and would join France in maintaining peace on the Continent. By a secret agreement Russia was to be free to take Finland from Sweden (which had been hostile to France since 1792), and France was to be free to conquer Portugal, which had become an outpost of England in the war. Alexander pledged himself to mediate a satisfactory peace between England and France, and, if this failed, to join France in opposing England with blockade and war. This pledge delighted Napoleon, for he valued the cooperation of Russia in the blockade far above any acquisition of terrain.

Unprepared to sacrifice these agreements, and to undertake a war *à outrance* with Russia, Prussia, and Austria, Napoleon put aside as impracticable the idea of restoring Poland to her pre-partition boundaries, and contented himself with establishing, out of Prussia's part of Poland, a grand duchy of Warsaw under a French protectorate. For this new state of two million persons he drew up (July 22, 1807) a constitution which abolished serfdom, made all citizens equal before the law, required public trials before juries, and prescribed the Napoleonic Code as the basis of legislation and justice. The *liberum veto*, the feudal dues, and the *fainéant* diet were abolished; the legislative power was to be vested in a senate of notables and a house of a hundred deputies; the executive, for the time being, was to be the King of Saxony, who was descended from former rulers of Poland. It was an enlightened constitution in terms of its place and time.

Generous to the Czar, Napoleon was merciless to the Prussian King who had broken his alliance with France to join her enemies. Frederick William III was required to surrender all Prussian territory west of the Elbe; most of this was reconstituted as the grand duchy of Berg and the kingdom of Westphalia. Nearly all of Prussian Poland went to the grand duchy of Warsaw, except that Danzig was made a free city under a French garrison. The surviving half of Prussia was to close its doors to British trade, was to join in war upon England if called upon, and was to be occupied by French forces until a heavy indemnity had been fully paid. Frederick William, who had not wanted the war, was emotionally stunned by these terms. Queen Louise, who had almost begotten the war, rushed up from Berlin (July 6), and appealed to Napoleon, with arguments, perfumes, smiles, and tears to soften his demands. He cooled her eloquence by offering her a chair (from which it is hard to be eloquent), and explained that someone had to pay for the war; and why not the government which, to wage it, had broken its treaty—at her behest? He sent her away with polite refusals, and on the next day ordered Talleyrand to conclude the treaties as previously formulated. The Queen went back to Berlin brokenhearted, and died within three years, at the age of thirty-four.

On July 9 the Emperors parted, each feeling that he had made a good bargain: Alexander had Russia, security on the west, and a free hand in Finland and Turkey; Napoleon had Berg, Westphalia, and a precarious truce. Years later he defined a "congress of the Powers" as "deceit agreed upon between diplomats; it is the pen of Machiavelli combined with the sword of Mahomet."[38] The next day he left for Paris, where he was received with hosannas of public gratitude not so much for his victories as for bringing peace. His report to the Corps Législatif on the state of the nation in 1807 was one of his proudest: Austria chastened, Prussia punished, Russia brought from enmity to alliance, new lands added to the Empire, 123,000 captives— and all expenses paid for by the defeated aggressors, without any rise of taxes in France.[39]

He announced, among many promotions, the elevation of Talleyrand to prince of Benevento. This brought the esurient abbé an added income of 120,000 francs, but it required his resignation as minister of foreign affairs, since protocol held that a ministry was beneath the dignity of a prince. In this way a difficult situation was eased, for Napoleon had come to distrust his brilliant but stealthy diplomat, and yet hesitated to antagonize him by a dismissal; indeed, he continued to use him in several major negotiations. After instructing his successor, Jean-Baptiste de Champagny, in the ways and wiles of his new office, Talleyrand was free to enjoy life at the luxurious château that he had bought at Valençay, partly with Napoleon's money.

On August 15 the court celebrated Napoleon's triumph with a fete recalling the splendor of the Grand Monarque: a concert, a ballet, an opera, and a reception attended by kings and ministers in formal costumes, and by women bearing fortunes in gowns and gems. Four days later he signalized his augmented royalty by abolishing the Tribunate, where a minority had for years dared to oppose his views and decrees. He softened the blow by appointing several harmless tribunes to administrative posts, and by merging most of the others with the Corps Législatif, which now acquired the right to discuss measures as well as to vote. The surviving and returned émigrés, in the reanimated palaces of the Faubourg St.-Germain, applauded Napoleon as almost worthy of noble birth. "Why isn't he legitimate?" they asked one another; then France would be perfect. Rarely again would he be so popular, powerful, and content.

CHAPTER IX

The Mortal Realm

1807–11

I. THE BONAPARTES

NAPOLEON had increased his burdens by multiplying his possessions, for the many regions that he had added to his empire differed in "race," language, religion, customs, and character; they could not be expected to give unquestioning obedience to a foreign rule that sent their taxes to Paris and their sons to wars. Whom could he choose to govern these principalities wisely and faithfully while he attended to unmanageable France? He could trust a few of his generals to administer some minor regions; so he made Berthier prince of Neuchâtel, and Murat grand duke of Berg and Cleves; but most of his generals were commanding spirits untrained in the devious subtleties of government; and several of them, like the ambitious Bernadotte, were jealous of his supremacy, and would not be content without a throne.

So he turned to his own brothers as offering a blood bond of loyalty, and as having some measure of that native force which had shared in winning the consulate and the empire. He probably exaggerated their abilities and potentialities, for he had a strong sense of family, and did his best to meet their rising expectations of a share in his fortune and power. He would reward them well, but would expect their cooperation with his policies—especially in the enforcement of that Continental Blockade through which he hoped to move England to peace. Perhaps, too, their collaboration might be a step toward the union of all Europe under one law and head (both of them his own), and so promote a general prosperity and an end to dynastic or nationalistic wars.

He began with his older brother, Joseph, who had served him reasonably well in negotiations with Austria and England. Cornwallis, after dealing with Joseph at Amiens, described him as "a well-meaning, although not a very able man, . . . sensible, modest, gentlemanlike, . . . fair and open, . . . whose near connection with the First Consul might perhaps be in some degree a check on the spirit of chicanery and intrigue which the Minister of the Interior [Talleyrand] so eminently possesses."[1] Joseph loved money as Napoleon loved power; as early as 1798 he had been able to buy, at Mortefontaine, near Paris, a sumptuous estate where he entertained friends, authors, artists, and visiting dignitaries with seignorial munificence. He itched to have his brother name him heir apparent to the imperial power, and he was not effusively satisfied when (March 30, 1806) Napoleon made him king of Naples—i.e., of southern Italy. The dethroned Bourbon, Ferdinand IV, clung to Sicily with the help of the British fleet, and his Queen Maria Carolina led an insurrection to restore him to his mainland throne. Napoleon sent forty thousand men, under Masséna and Régnier, to suppress the revolt at whatever cost; they did so, with a ferocity that left bitter memories for generations. Joseph tried to win the loyalty of his subjects by a mild and genial government, but Napoleon warned him that "a ruler, to establish himself, must make himself rather feared than loved." The final judgment was favorable:

> Joseph rendered me no assistance, but he is a very good man. . . . He loves me very sincerely, and I doubt not that he would do everything in the world to serve me. But his qualities are only suited to private life. He is of a gentle and kind disposition, possesses talent and information, and is altogether a very amiable man. In the discharge of the high duties which I confided to him he did the best he could. His intentions were good; and therefore the principal fault rests with me, who raised him above his proper sphere.[2]

Brother Lucien, born in 1775, had in him all the volatile elements that in Napoleon were controlled by a dominant ambition. In one sense Napoleon owed him the Consulate, for it was the refusal of Lucien, as president of the Five Hundred, to put to the vote the demand for outlawing the usurper, and his appeal to the soldiery to disperse the Council, that saved the day for Napoleon. Later he was a bit premature in proposing royal power for his brother, who removed him from the scene by sending him as ambassador to Spain. There he used all available means of swelling his private purse; soon, for a time, he was richer than Napoleon.[3] Returning to Paris, he refused the political marriage that Napoleon recommended to him, married his own choice, and went to live in Italy. He came back to Paris to stand by his brother through all the dangers of the Hundred Days. He was made for poetry and wrote a long epic on Charlemagne.

Brother Louis too had a mind and temper of his own—combined with a degree of ability and conviction that made him restless under his brother's dictation. Napoleon paid for his education, and took him to Egypt as an aide-de-camp. There Louis used a soldier's privilege to contract gonorrhea and then proved too impatient to let himself be completely cured.[4] In 1802, at Josephine's urging, Napoleon induced the reluctant Louis to marry the reluctant Hortense de Beauharnais. Louis was a boorish husband, Hortense an unhappy and unfaithful wife,[5] somewhat spoiled by the affection she received from her adoptive father. When she gave birth (December 15, 1802) to a boy, Napoléon-Charles, gossip named the First Consul as the father; and this unjust suspicion followed both Napoleon and Hortense to the end of their days. Napoleon gave some warrant for it by proposing to adopt the child, and by fondly calling him "our Dauphin," or heir apparent to the throne;[6] but the boy died at the age of five. Hortense went temporarily insane. In 1804 she gave birth to a second son, Napoléon-Louis, and in 1808 to Charles-Louis-Napoléon Bonaparte, who became Napoleon III.

On June 5, 1806, the Emperor made his difficult brother king of Holland. Louis fell in love with the Dutch people more readily than with his wife. He knew how much of Holland's prosperity depended upon its trade with England and her colonies; and when the Dutch found ways of violating the Continental Blockade against British goods, Louis refused to prosecute them. Napoleon insisted, Louis persisted. French troops marched into Holland; Louis abdicated (July 1, 1810); Napoleon annexed Holland to France, bringing it under his direct rule. Louis retired to Graz, became an author in prose and verse, and died at Livorno in 1846.*

Hortense separated from Louis in 1810, and received from Napoleon an endowment of two million francs per year for the care of her sons. To these she added another in 1811 as the result of a liaison with Comte Charles de Flahaut; however, Mme. de Rémusat tells us, Hortense was of an "angelic disposition, . . . so true, so purehearted, so perfectly ignorant of evil."[8] After Napoleon's first abdication she joined her mother at Malmaison, where she received marked attention from Czar Alexander. She dined with Louis XVIII, to the dismay of Bonapartists. When Napoleon returned from Elba she acted as hostess for him. When he abdicated again she secretly gave him a diamond necklace for which she had paid 800,000 francs; it was found under his pillow when he died at St. Helena, and was restored by General de Montholon to Hortense, who was thereby saved from poverty. She died in 1837, and was buried beside the remains of her mother in Rueil.[9] There were many lives in each life in those crucial days.

Jérôme Bonaparte, youngest of the brothers, divided his lives and wives between two hemispheres. Born in 1784, called at sixteen to serve in the Consular Guard, he fought a duel, was wounded, was banished to the Navy, sowed wild oats, and paid for them by borrowing from Bourrienne, who billed Napoleon for the unredeemed loans. When Jérôme, at Brest, asked for 17,000 francs, Napoleon wrote to him:

> I have received your letter, Sir Ensign; and I am waiting to hear that you are studying, on board your corvette, a profession which you ought to consider your road to glory. Die young, and I shall have some consolatory reflections; but if you live to sixty without having served your country, and without leaving behind you any honorable memories, you had better not have lived at all.[10]

Jérôme left the Navy in the West Indies, traveled to Baltimore, and there in

---

* Napoleon, at St. Helena, gave his version to Las Cases: "No sooner had Louis arrived in Holland than, fancying that nothing could be finer than to have it said that henceforth he was a Dutchman, he attached himself entirely to the party favorable to the English, promoted smuggling, and thus connived with our enemies. . . . What remained for me to do? Was I to abandon Holland to our enemies? Ought I to have given it another king? But in that case could I have expected more from him than from my own brother? Did not all the kings that I created act in nearly the same manner? I therefore united Holland to the Empire; and this act produced a most unfavorable impression in Europe, and contributed not a little to . . . our misfortunes."[7]

1803, age nineteen, he married Elizabeth Patterson, daughter of a local merchant. When he brought her to Europe a French court refused to recognize the marriage, on the ground that both husband and wife were minors, and Napoleon denied the wife entry into France. She went to England, and there gave birth to a son, Jerome Napoleon Bonaparte. She returned to America, received an allowance from Napoleon, ar.d became the grandmother of Charles Joseph Bonaparte, who served as Secretary of the United States Navy under Theodore Roosevelt.

Jérôme was given a command in the French Army, and distinguished himself in the campaigns of 1806–07, capturing several Prussian fortresses. Napoleon rewarded him by making him king of Westphalia—a composite of areas taken from Prussia, Hanover, and Hesse-Cassel. To give him a scent of royalty he secured for him in marriage Princess Catherine, daughter of the King of Württemberg. On November 15, 1807, Napoleon sent to Jérôme a letter in the best spirit of a still constitutional ruler:

> I enclose a constitution for your kingdom. It embodies the conditions on which I renounce all my rights of conquest, and all the claims I have acquired over your state. You must faithfully observe it. . . . Don't listen to those who say that your subjects are so accustomed to slavery that they will feel no gratitude for the benefits you give them. There is more intelligence in the kingdom of Westphalia than they would have you believe; and your throne will never be firmly established except upon the trust and affection of the common people. What German opinion impatiently demands is that men without hereditary rank, but of marked ability, shall have an equal claim upon your favor and employment, and that every trace of serfdom, or of a feudal hierarchy between the sovereign and the lowest class of your subjects, shall be done away with. The benefits of the Code Napoléon, public trial, and the introduction of juries, will be the leading features of your government. . . . For the extension and consolidation of your reign I count more upon the effects of these measures than upon the most resounding victories. I want your subjects to enjoy a degree of liberty, equality, and prosperity hitherto unknown to the German people. . . . Such a method of government will be a stronger barrier between you and Prussia than the Elbe, the fortresses, and the protection of France.[11]

Jérôme was still too young, at twenty-three, to appreciate this advice. Lacking the self-control and sober judgment needed in government, he indulged himself in every pomp and luxury, treated his ministers as underlings, and adopted a foreign policy of his own, irking a brother who had to think in terms of a continent. When Napoleon lost the pivotal battle of Leipzig (1813) Jérôme could not keep his "subjects" loyal to the imperial cause; his kingdom collapsed, and Jérôme fled to France. He supported his brother bravely at Waterloo, and then fled to his father-in-law's protection in Württemberg. He lived long enough to become a president of the Senate under his nephew Napoleon III, and had the luck to die (1860) at the peak of another mortal realm.

Eugène de Beauharnais was a better pupil. He was a lovable lad of fifteen when his mother married Napoleon; he at first resented the brusque young general as an intruder, but soon warmed to Napoleon's growing affection and solicitude. He was flattered to be taken to Italy and Egypt as aide-de-camp to the whirlwind conqueror; his sympathies were divided between husband and wife when he learned of his mother's infidelity; his tears restored their union, and thereafter the bond of loyalty between stepfather and stepson was never to be broken. On June 7, 1805, Napoleon made Eugène viceroy of Italy; but, seeing what a responsibility he was placing upon a youth of twenty-four, he left him a ream of advice.

> By entrusting you with the government of Our Kingdom of Italy, we have given you proof of the respect your conduct has inspired in us. But you are still at an age when one does not realize the perversity of men's hearts; I cannot therefore too strongly recommend to you prudence and circumspection. Our Italian subjects are more deceitful by nature than the citizens of France. The only way in which you can keep their respect and serve their happiness is by letting no one have your complete confidence, and by never telling anyone what you really think of the ministers and high officials of your court. Dissimulation, which comes naturally at a maturer age, has to be emphasized and calculated at yours. . . .
>
> In any position but that of Viceroy of Italy you may boast of being a Frenchman; but here you must forget it, and count yourself a failure unless the Italians believe that you love them. They know that there is no love without respect. Learn their language; frequent their society; single them out for special attention at public functions. . . .
>
> The less you talk, the better; you aren't well educated enough, and you haven't enough knowledge, to take part in formal debates. Learn to listen, and remember that silence is often as effective as a display of knowledge. Don't imitate me in every respect; you need more reserve. Don't preside often over the State Council; you have too little experience to do so successfully. . . . Anyhow, never make a speech there; . . . they would see at once that you aren't competent to discuss business. So long as a prince holds his tongue his power is incalculable; he should never talk unless he knows he is the ablest man in the room. . . .
>
> One last word: punish dishonesty ruthlessly. . . .[12]

Eugène fulfilled the Emperor's expectations. With the help of his ministers he reorganized finances, improved the civil service, built roads, introduced the Code Napoléon, and led the Italian Army with his usual courage and a growing skill. The pleased Emperor visited him in 1807, and took the occasion, by the "Milan Decree," to respond, with stringent regulations, to a British Order in Council requiring neutral vessels to touch at an English port before proceeding to the Continent. Eugène did his best to carry out the irritating Continental Blockade. He remained loyal to Napoleon through all wars and abdications, and died (1824) only three years after the death of his adoptive father. Stendhal's *Chartreuse de Parme* repeatedly testifies to Italy's loving memory of his enlightened rule.[13]

Having more lands than brothers, Napoleon endowed his sisters too with terrain. Elisa (Maria Anna), with her complaisant husband Felice Bacciocchi, was given the principalities of Piombino and Lucca; these she governed so well—financing public works, patronizing literature and art, encouraging Paganini—that in 1809 Napoleon made her grand duchess of Tuscany, where she continued her dictatorial beneficence.

Pauline Bonaparte, whom Napoleon considered the most beautiful woman of her time, found it unbearable to confine her charms to one bed. At seventeen (1797) she married General Charles Leclerc; four years later—probably to distance her frivolity—Napoleon bade her accompany her husband to St.-Domingue in the campaign against Toussaint L'Ouverture; Leclerc died there of yellow fever; Pauline returned to Europe with his corpse, and with her fabled beauty weakened by disease. In 1803 she married Prince Camillo Borghese, but she soon slipped into adultery, and Camillo sought solace with a mistress. Napoleon asked his and her uncle, Cardinal Fesch, to reprove her. "Tell her, from me, that she is no longer as pretty as she was, and that in a few years' time she will be much less so, whereas she can be good and be respected all her life."[14] Unchastened, Pauline separated from the Prince, and opened her lavish home to the gayest society. Napoleon made her duchess of Guastalla (in the province of Reggio Emilia in Italy), but she preferred to hold court in Paris. Charmed by her looks and ways and good nature, he tolerated her transgressions until, in a mirror, he saw her mocking his new Empress, Marie Louise. He banished her to Italy; soon she ruled a salon in Rome. Later on (as we shall see) she came to his aid in his misfortunes. In 1825 she was reunited with her husband, and died in his arms. "After all," he had said, "she was the kindest creature in the world."[15]

Caroline was almost as beautiful, and, in the final days, much more damaging. We are told that her skin was like pink satin; "her arms, hands, and feet were perfect, like those of all the Bonapartes." At seventeen (1799) she married Joachim Murat, who had already made his mark in the Italian and Egyptian campaigns. For these services, and his vital performance at Marengo, he was made grand duke of Berg and Cleves. While he was busy in his capital, Düsseldorf, Caroline remained in Paris, and allowed such intimacies to General Junot that Napoleon sent him to Bordeaux. Murat returned to Paris to reclaim his wife, but battle was his passion and danger was his hobby. In his frequent absences at the front Caroline took over the administration of their duchy, and managed so well that Murat was not missed except for his gorgeous costumes.

Above all this lusty band of brothers and sisters sat their mother, Letizia, firm, undeluded, and indestructible. She shared with fierce pride and grim grief their triumphs and disasters. In 1806 Napoleon made her, then fifty-six, the empress dowager, with an allowance of 500,000 francs per year. He provided her with a handsome home in Paris and many servitors, but she lived with her wonted frugality, saying that she was saving against a crash in his fortunes.[16] She was addressed as Madame Mère, but had and sought no political influence. She accompanied her son to Elba, and on his return; she watched with anxiety and prayer the drama of the Hundred Days. In 1818 she appealed to the Powers to release him from St. Helena as a man now too ill to be dangerous to them; she received no reply. She bore with her customary stoicism the death of Napoleon, Elisa, and Pauline, and of several grand-children. She died in 1836, aged eighty-six. *Voilà une femme!*

The family plan did not work, partly because it was not founded on the needs of the peoples ruled, and partly because every one of the rulers (except Eugène) was an individualist, with his own ideas and desires—Napoleon most so. He thought of his own power first, and laid down laws excellent as compared with a feudalism that had become functionless; but he hedged and diluted them by financial and military exactions. Though he was destroying feudalism, he was establishing another of his own—thinking of his brothers and sisters as holding fiefs of his giving, and therefore requiring them to be obedient vassals, to raise conscripts for his needs in time of war, and taxes in time of peace. He defended his conception of the situation by explaining that nearly all the territories so governed had been conquered in wars forced upon him by the Powers; therefore they were subject to the "laws" of war, and they were lucky to get the up-to-date laws of France and the paternal rule of an enlightened despot. As to his family, he summed up the matter sadly in St. Helena:

> It is very certain that I was poorly seconded by my family. . . . Much has been said of the strength of my character, but I was reprehensibly weak for my family, and they were well aware of it. After the first storm of [my] resistance was over, their perseverance and stubbornness always carried the day, and they did with me what they liked. I made great mistakes in this. If each one of them had given a common impulse to the masses I had entrusted to their rule, we could have marched together to the Poles; everything would have fallen before us; we should have changed the face of the globe. I did not have the good fortune of Genghis Khan, with his four sons, who knew no other rivalry than that of serving him faithfully. If I made a brother of mine a king, he at once thought himself king "by the grace of God," so contagious had this phrase become. He was no longer a lieutenant in whom I could repose confidence; he was one enemy more to beware of. His efforts did not tend to second mine, but to make himself independent. . . . They actually came to regard me as an obstacle. . . . Poor things! When I succumbed, their dethronement was not exacted or even mentioned by the enemy [it was automatic]; and not one of them is capable now of exciting a popular movement. Sheltered by my labor, they enjoyed the sweets of royalty; I alone bore the burden.[17]

Having conquered more principalities than he had princes and princesses of his blood, Napoleon conferred strategic minor dependencies upon his generals or other servitors. So Marshal Berthier received the province of Neuchâtel; Cambacérès became prince of Parma; Lebrun, duke of Piacenza. From other regions of Italy a dozen minor duchies were cut; Fouché became duke of Otranto, Savary of Rovigo. Ultimately, Napoleon hoped he would join the *disjecta membra* of Italy into one state, and make this a unit in a European Federation under the leadership of France and his dynasty. If only all those units, so proud of their differences and so jealous of their place, could sink these sustaining delusions in some sense of the whole—and in some readiness to let a distant and alien power write their laws and regulate their trade!

II. THE PENINSULAR WAR: I (OCTOBER 18, 1807 – AUGUST 21, 1808)

By 1807 almost all of mainland Europe was obeying the Berlin Decree. Austria joined the Continental Blockade in October 18, 1807; the Papacy protested but signed on December 12. Turkey was reluctant, but she might be brought to obedience by the continued cooperation of Russia and France. Portugal was allied with England, but she was bordered on the west by a Spain historically bound to France by her Bourbon dynasty, pledged to the blockade, and (it seemed) militarily at the mercy of Napoleon. Perhaps, the Emperor mused, something could be done—if only by marching through Spain—to bring Portugal to obedience despite British warships controlling her ports and British agents controlling her trade.

On July 19, 1807, Napoleon informed the Portuguese government that it must close its ports to British goods. It refused. On October 18 a French army of twenty thousand men, mostly unseasoned conscripts, under Andoche Junot, crossed the Bidassoa into Spain. It was welcomed by the people and the state, for the people were hoping that Napoleon would free their King from a treacherous minister, and that minister was hoping that Napoleon would reward his cooperation by letting him share in the dismemberment of Portugal.

The brilliant epoch of the Spanish Enlightenment had ended with the death of Charles III (1788). His now sixty-year-old son, Charles IV, though rich in good intentions, was poor in vitality and intellect; in Goya's famous picture *Charles IV and His Family* the King is visibly fonder of eating than of thinking, and Queen María Luisa is obviously the man. But she was also a woman; and, not satisfied with her obedient husband, she opened her arms to Manuel de Godoy, whom she raised from officer of the Royal Guard to be chief minister. The Spanish people, sexually the most moral in Europe, were scandalized by this liaison, but Godoy, unchastened, dreamed of conquering Portugal and of carving out for himself, if not a kingdom, at least a duchy of his own. He angled for Napoleon's aid, and tried to forget that in 1806 he had offered his active friendship to a Prussia planning war against France. Napoleon encouraged Godoy's hopes, and signed at Fontainebleau (October 27, 1807) an agreement for "the conquest and occupation of Portugal." The northwest, with Oporto, was to be an appanage of the Spanish Queen; the provinces of Algarve and Alentejo, in the south, were to be Godoy's; the central residue, with Lisbon, was to be under French control until further notice. Article XIII of the treaty added: "It is understood that the high contracting parties shall divide equally between themselves the islands, colonies, and other maritime possessions of Portugal."[18] Secret clauses stipulated that 8,000 Spanish infantry and 3,000 Spanish cavalry were to join Junot's army as it marched through Spain.

Unable to resist this combined force, the Portuguese royal family took ship to Brazil. On November 30, Junot entered Lisbon, and the conquest of

Portugal seemed complete. To pay for his operations he imposed upon his new subjects an indemnity of 100 million francs. Partly to go to Junot's help in case of a British expedition to Portugal, and probably with larger aims, Napoleon sent three additional armies into Spain, put them under the united command of Murat, and bade him occupy some strategic points near Madrid.

Discord in the Spanish government played into Napoleon's hands. The twenty-three-year-old Infante, or heir apparent, Ferdinand, fearing that Godoy would bar his way to the throne, lent himself to a plot to overthrow the favorite. Godoy discovered the scheme, had Ferdinand and his chief supporters arrested (October 27), and proposed to have them tried for treason. Two months later, having learned that the approaching Murat might seek to release the prisoners, Godoy freed them, and prepared to escape to America with the King and the Queen. Thereupon the city populace rose in revolt (March 17, 1808), captured Godoy, and threw him into a dungeon. The bewildered King resigned in favor of his son. On orders from Napoleon, Murat led French troops into Madrid (March 23), liberated Godoy, and refused to recognize Ferdinand as king. Charles rescinded his abdication, and confusion reigned. Talleyrand urged Napoleon to take the throne of Spain.[19]

Napoleon seized—perhaps had created—this opportunity. He invited both Charles IV and Ferdinand VII to meet him at Bayonne (some twenty miles north of the Spanish–French frontier), with a view to restoring order and stability to the government. The Emperor arrived on April 14, Ferdinand on April 20. Napoleon entertained the youth and his adviser, Canon Juan Escóiquiz, for dinner, and judged the youth too immature, emotionally and intellectually, to hold popular passions in leash and keep Spain in helpful league with France. He revealed this conclusion to Escóiquiz, who reluctantly conveyed it to Ferdinand. The Infante protested that he held the crown by his father's abdication. He sent couriers to Madrid to tell his supporters that he was helpless before the power of Napoleon. These couriers were intercepted, and their dispatches were brought to the Emperor; nevertheless the news of Ferdinand's situation reached the capital. Popular suspicion that Napoleon intended to end the Bourbon dynasty in Spain was heightened when news spread that Charles IV, the Queen, and Godoy had reached Bayonne on April 30, and that Murat, now ruling Madrid, had received orders to send the King's brother, younger son, and daughter to Bayonne. On May 2, 1808—a date long celebrated in Spanish history as the Dos de Mayo—an angry crowd gathered before the royal palace, tried to prevent the princes and princess from leaving, and stoned the French soldiers who were guarding the royal coach; some of these soldiers, we are told, were torn to pieces. Murat bade his troops fire upon the mob till it dispersed. It was so done, in a scene powerfully commemorated by Goya. The insurrection subsided in Madrid, and spread through Spain.

When the report of this outbreak reached Napoleon at Bayonne (May 5), he summoned both Charles and Ferdinand to his presence, and, in one of his calculated rages, condemned them for allowing Spain, by their incompetence, to fall into a disorder that made it dangerously unreliable as an ally of France. Father and mother heaped reproaches and abuse upon their son, accusing him of having contemplated parricide. Napoleon gave the frightened youth till eleven o'clock that evening to abdicate; if he refused, he would be turned over to his parents for imprisonment and trial for treason. Ferdinand yielded, and restored the crown to his father. Charles, longing for security and peace rather than for power, offered the scepter to Napoleon, who offered it to his brother Louis, who refused it, then to Jérôme, who felt not quite up to so dangerous a post, and finally to Joseph, who was in effect commanded to accept it. Charles, María Luisa, and Godoy were sent to live in guarded ease at Marseilles. Ferdinand and his brother were soothed with ample revenue, and Talleyrand was commissioned to house them comfortably and securely in his château at Valençay. Then, feeling that he had made a good bargain, Napoleon rode leisurely back to Paris, acclaimed at every step as the invincible master of Europe.

Murat, who had hoped to be king of Spain, went resentfully to replace Joseph as king of Naples. Joseph, after a stop at Bayonne, entered Madrid on June 10, 1808. He had become habituated to Naples, and soon missed, in stern and pious Spain, the joy of life that in Italy moderated the general flammability of the south Italian soul. He brought to Spain a semiliberal constitution hastily contrived by Napoleon, offering much of the Code Napoléon, but (as Charles IV had insisted) accepting Catholicism as the only legal religion in Spain. Joseph tried hard to be a popular ruler, and many Spanish liberals supported him; but the nobility held aloof, the clergy condemned him as a secret freethinker, and the populace was shocked to find that Napoleon had replaced their Church-blessed dynasty with a man who knew hardly a word of Spanish, and utterly lacked the charisma of time.

Slowly, then rapidly, the resentment grew from scowls to imprecations to revolt. Peasant bands arose in a hundred localities; armed themselves with the old weapons and sharp knives that had made every home an arsenal and every cloak a snare; and took as target any Frenchman who strayed from his barracks or squad. Against French carbines the Spanish clergy raised the cross; they denounced Joseph as "a Lutheran, a Freemason, a heretic," and summoned their flocks to insurrection "in the name of God, His Immaculate Mother, and Saint Joseph."[20] Popular enthusiasm boiled over, leading to such amputations, castrations, crucifixions, beheadings, hangings, and impalings as Goya pictured in *Los Desastres de la Guerra*. Spanish armies re-formed and joined the uprising; their united battalions overcame scattered and undermanned French garrisons; their leaders sometimes outgeneraled French officers handicapped by unfamiliarity with the terrain and the inadequate number, equipment, and training of their troops. At Bailén (northeast of Córdoba), on July 20, 1808, two French divisions, mistakenly supposing themselves surrounded by greatly superior forces, surrendered in one of the most ignominious defeats in history: 22,800 men were made prisoners and were interned on the little island of Cabrera, where hundreds of them died of starvation or disease. Shorn of his chief military support, Joseph and his remaining soldiers withdrew from Madrid to a line of defense along the Ebro, 170 miles northeast of the capital.

In the meantime the English government, confident that Junot's diminishing forces in Lisbon could no longer be reinforced from Spain, sent Sir Arthur Wellesley (the future Duke of Wellington) with a fleet and an army to Portugal. He landed his men at the mouth of the Mondego River on July 1, 1808, and was soon joined by bands of Portuguese infantry. Junot, who had allowed himself a life of pleasure and ease instead of keeping his forces in condition, led his 13,000 conscripts out from Lisbon to meet Wellesley's 19,000 soldiers at Vimeiro (August 21, 1808), and suffered a disabling defeat. Portugal returned to alliance with England, and the French invasion of the Peninsula appeared to be a complete disaster.

When Napoleon reached Paris on August 14, 1808, after his triumphal tour of his western provinces, he found his traditional enemies rejoicing over French setbacks, and already preparing another coalition against the now vincible consumer of nations. Metternich, Austrian ambassador to France, talked peace to Napoleon and planned war. Freiherr vom und zum Stein, brilliant chief minister in a Prussia eager for liberation, wrote to a friend in this August: "Here war between France and Austria is regarded as inevitable; it will decide the fate of Europe."[21] Napoleon, whose agents intercepted that letter, agreed. War, he wrote to brother Louis, "is postponed until spring."[22]

Napoleon pondered his choice. Should he lead his never defeated Grande Armée to Spain, suppress the revolt, chase Wellesley back to his ships, close the Portuguese gap in the blockade, and run the risk that Austria and Prussia would strike while his best troops were a thousand miles away? Alexander, at Tilsit, had promised to prevent such an attack upon him while Spain held him; but would the Czar keep his word under stress? Perhaps he should be additionally bribed. Napoleon invited him to a conference at Erfurt, where he would overwhelm him with a galaxy of political stars, and pin him to his pledge.

III. CONSTELLATION AT ERFURT: SEPTEMBER 27 – OCTOBER 14, 1808

He prepared for that conference with as much care as for a war. He invited all his vassal kings and dukes to attend in regal style and with their retinues. So many of them came that Talleyrand's printed memoirs took three pages to list them.[23] Napoleon took with him not only his family but most of his generals, and he asked Talleyrand to come out of his retirement and help Champagny to formalize the negotiations and results. He instructed the Comte de Rémusat to transport to Erfurt the best actors of the Comédie-Française—including Talma—with all the apparatus needed to produce the classic tragedies of the French drama. "I wish the Emperor of Russia," he said, "to be dazzled by the sight of my power. For there is no negotiation which it could fail to render easier."[24]

He reached Erfurt on September 27, and on the 28th he rode out five miles to greet Alexander and his Russian entourage. Every arrangement was made to please the Czar, except that Napoleon left no doubt that he was host, and in a German city that had become part of the French Empire. Alexander was not deceived by the gifts and flatteries that came to him, and he too put on all the signs and forms of friendship. His resistance to Napoleon's charms was furthered by Talleyrand, who secretly advised him to support Austria rather than France, arguing that Austria, not France, was the pivot of that European civilization which (in Talleyrand's view) Napoleon was destroying. "France," he said, "is civilized, but her sovereign is not."[25] Moreover, how could it be to Russia's advantage to strengthen France? When Napoleon sought to reinforce the alliance by marrying Alexander's sister the Grand Duchess Anna, Talleyrand counseled the Czar against agreement, and the wily Russian delayed replying to the proposal on the ground that the Czarina had charge of such affairs.[26] He rewarded Talleyrand by arranging the marriage of the diplomat's nephew to the Duchess of Dino, heiress to the duchy of Courland. Talleyrand later defended his treachery on the ground that Napoleon's appetite for nations was bound not only to exhaust Europe with war, but to lead to the collapse and dismemberment of France; his treachery to Napoleon, he claimed, was fidelity to France.[27] But henceforth his good manners left a bad odor everywhere.

During the conference the Duke of Saxe-Weimar invited his most famous subject to come to Erfurt. On September 29 Napoleon, seeing Goethe's name on a list of new arrivals, asked the Duke to arrange a meeting with the poet-philosopher. Goethe gladly came (October 2), for he judged Napoleon as "the greatest mind the world has ever seen,"[28] and he quite approved of uniting Europe under such a head. He found the Emperor at breakfast with Talleyrand, Berthier, Savary, and General Daru. Talleyrand included in his *Memoirs* what he claimed to be a careful recollection of this famous colloquy. (Felix Müller, a Weimar magistrate who accompanied Goethe, gave a report only slightly different.)

> "Monsieur Goethe," said Napoleon, "I am delighted to see you. . . . I know that you are Germany's leading dramatic poet."
>
> "Sire, you wrong our country. . . . Schiller, Lessing, and Wieland are surely known to Your Majesty."
>
> "I confess I hardly know them. However, I have read Schiller's *Thirty Years' War*. . . . You generally live in Weimar; it is the place where the most celebrated men of German literature meet!"
>
> "Sire, they enjoy greater protection there; but for the present there is only one man in Weimar who is known throughout Europe; it is Wieland."
>
> "I should be delighted to see Monsieur Wieland."
>
> "If Your Majesty will allow me to ask him, I feel certain that he will come immediately." . . .
>
> "Are you an admirer of Tacitus?"
>
> "Yes, Sire, I admire him much."
>
> "Well, I don't; but we shall talk of that another time. Write to tell Monsieur Wieland to come here. I shall return his visit at Weimar, where the Duke has invited me."[29]

As Goethe left the room (we are told) Napoleon remarked to Berthier and Daru, *"Voilà un homme!"*[30]

A few days later Napoleon, amid a host of notables, entertained Goethe and Wieland. Perhaps he had refreshed his recollections, for he spoke like a literary critic confident of his knowledge:

> "Monsieur Wieland, we like your works very much in France. It is you who are the author of *Agathon* and *Oberon*. We call you the Voltaire of Germany."
>
> "Sire, the comparison would be a flattering one if it were justified. . . ."
>
> "Tell me, Monsieur Wieland, why your *Diogenes*, your *Agathon*, and your *Peregrinus* are written in the equivocal style which mixes romance with history, and history with romance. A superior man like yourself ought to keep each style distinctly separate. . . . But I am afraid to say too much on this subject, because I am dealing with someone much more conversant with the matter than I am." [31]

On October 5, Napoleon rode out some fifteen miles to Weimar. After a hunt at Jena, and a performance of *La Mort de César* in the Weimar theater, the hosts and guests attended a ball where the splendor of the surroundings and the glamour of the women made them soon forget the verses of Voltaire. Napoleon, however, withdrew to a corner, and asked for Goethe and Wieland. They brought other literati with them. Napoleon spoke, especially to Wieland, on two of his favorite subjects—history and Tacitus:

> "A good tragic drama should be looked upon as the most worthy school for superior men. From a certain point of view it is above history. In the best history very little effect is produced. Man when alone is but little affected; men assembled receive the stronger and more lasting impressions.
>
> "I assure you that the historian Tacitus, whom you are always quoting, never taught me anything. Could you find a greater, and at times more unjust, detractor of the human race? In the most simple actions he finds criminal motives; he makes emperors out as the most profound villains. . . . His *Annals* are not a history of the Empire but an abstract of the prison records of Rome. They are always dealing with accusations, convicts, and people who open their veins in their baths. . . . What an involved style! How obscure! . . . Am I not right, Monsieur Wieland? But . . . we are not here to speak of Tacitus. Look how well Czar Alexander dances."[32]

Wieland was not overwhelmed; he defended Tacitus with both courage and courtesy. He pointed out, "Suetonius and Dio Cassius relate a much greater number of crimes than Tacitus, in a style void of energy, while nothing is more terrible than Tacitus' pen." And, with a bold hint to Napoleon: "By the stamp of his genius one would believe he could love only the Republic. . . . But when he speaks of the emperors who so happily reconciled . . . the Empire and liberty, one feels that the art of governing appears to him the most beautiful discovery on earth. . . . Sire, if it be true to say of Tacitus that tyrants are punished when he paints them, it is still more true to say that good princes are rewarded when he traces their images and presents them to future glory."

The assembled listeners were delighted by this vigorous riposte, and Napoleon was a bit confused. "I have too strong a party to contend with, Monsieur Wieland, and you neglect none of your advantages. . . . I do not like to say that I am beaten; . . . to that I would consent with difficulty. Tomorrow I return to Erfurt, and we shall continue our discussions."[33] We have no report of that further encounter.

By October 7 most of the visitors were back in Erfurt. Napoleon urged Goethe to come and live in Paris; "there you will find a larger circle for your spirit of observation, . . . immense material for your poetic creations."[34] On October 14 the Emperor conferred upon Goethe and Wieland the Cross of the Legion of Honor.

Meanwhile the foreign ministers of the two Powers had drawn up an agreement renewing their alliances, and pledging mutual aid in case either of them should be attacked. Alexander was to be left free to take Wallachia and Moldavia, but not Turkey; Napoleon could proceed to Spain with the Czar's blessing. On October 12 the document was signed. Two days later the Emperors left Erfurt; for a while they rode side by side; before they parted they embraced, and promised to meet again. (They did not.) Napoleon returned to Paris less sanguine than when he had come, but resolved to take his Grande Armée to Spain and reseat brother Joseph on his unwelcome throne.

IV. THE PENINSULAR WAR: II (OCTOBER 29, 1808 – JANUARY 16, 1809)

It was a typical Napoleonic campaign: swift, victorious, and futile. The Emperor sensed the rising opposition of the French people to the endless concatenation of his wars. They had agreed with him that his wars on the eastern front had been caused by governments conspiring to annul the Revolution; but they felt that their blood was being drained, and they resented especially its expenditure in Portugal and Spain. He understood that feeling, and feared that he was losing his hold on the nation, but (as he argued in retrospect) "it was impossible to leave the Peninsula a prey to the machinations of the English, the intrigues, hopes, and pretensions of the Bourbons."[35] Unless Spain should be securely tied to France it would be at the mercy of British armies coming through Portugal or Cádiz; soon England would gather the gold and silver of Portuguese or Spanish America, and pour it out in subsidies to finance a new coalition against France; there would have to be more Marengos, Austerlitzes, Jenas . . . Only a border-tight blockade of British goods could bring those London merchants to talk peace.

Leaving some fortresses garrisoned against Austrian or Prussian surprises, Napoleon ordered 150,000 men of the Grand Army to march over the Pyrenees and join the 65,000 men that Joseph had meanwhile assembled at Vitoria. He himself left Paris on October 29 with his plan of campaign already formed. The Spanish army was attempting to surround Joseph's troops; Napoleon sent instructions to his brother to avoid battle, and let the enemy advance in a spreading and thinning semicircle. When he neared

Vitoria, the Emperor deployed part of his forces to attack the Spanish center; it broke and fled. Another French division captured Burgos (November 10); others, under Ney and Lannes, at Tudela, overwhelmed a Spanish army under José de Palafox y Melzi. Perceiving that their soldiers and generals could not cope with the Grand Army and Napoleon, the Spaniards scattered again into the provinces, and on December 4 the Emperor entered Madrid. When some of his troops began to pillage, he had two of them publicly executed; the pillaging stopped.[36]

Leaving the city under a strong garrison and martial law, Napoleon took up his quarters three miles away at Chamartín. Thence, like some god creating a world, he issued (December 4) a series of decrees, including a new constitution for Spain. Some of its clauses show him still a "Son of the Revolution":

> To date from the publication of this decree, feudal rights are abolished in Spain. All personal obligations, all exclusive rights, . . . all feudal monopolies . . . are suppressed. Everyone who shall conform to the laws shall be free to develop his industry without restraint.
> The tribunal of the Inquisition is abolished, as inconsistent with the civil sovereignty and authority. Its property shall be sequestered and fall to the Spanish state, to serve as security for the bonded debt. . . .
> Considering that the members of various monastic orders have increased to an undue degree, . . . religious houses in Spain . . . shall be reduced to a third of their present number . . . by uniting the members of several houses of the same order into one. . . .
> In view of the fact that the institution which stands most in the way of the internal prosperity of Spain is that of the customs lines separating the provinces, . . . the barrier existing between the provinces shall be suppressed.[37]

Only martial mastery could enforce such a constitution over the active opposition of the entrenched nobility, the monastic clergy, and a population inured by time to feudal leadership and a consolatory creed. And that mastery was precarious. Wellesley was still triumphant in Portugal, and might invade Spain as soon as the Grand Army should be called back to face a challenging Austria. Moreover, a British army of twenty thousand men under Sir John Moore left Salamanca on December 13 and began a march northeastward, aiming to overwhelm Soult's division near Burgos. Responding quickly to this challenge, Napoleon led a substantial French force north over the Sierra de Guadarrama in the hope of attacking the rear of Moore's columns; now at last he would match his wits and soldiers against those hitherto sea-protected Englishmen. The passage through the Guadarrama Pass in midwinter was a much severer ordeal for his men than the crossing of the Alps in 1800; they suffered and grumbled, almost to mutiny, but Napoleon would not abandon the chase. Moore learned of his coming, and—fearing to be caught between two French armies—turned his troops westward on a hurried march over 250 miles of rugged snow-covered terrain toward Corunna, where they could find refuge in a British fleet.

At Astorga, January 2, 1809, Napoleon was close on their heels. But here he was stopped by disturbing news from two sources: in Austria the Arch-

duke Karl Ludwig was making active preparations for war; in Paris Talleyrand and Fouché were aiding a plan to replace Napoleon with Murat. The
Emperor left the pursuit of Moore to Soult, and hurried back to France.
Soult, the master gone, eased his pace, and did not reach Corunna until
most of the British had gained their ships. Moore led an heroic rearguard
action to protect the last stages of the embarkation; he was mortally
wounded, but did not die until the embarkation was complete. "If only I
had had time to follow the English," Napoleon mourned, "not a single man
jack of them would have escaped."[38] They not only escaped; they came
back.

V. FOUCHÉ, TALLEYRAND, AND AUSTRIA: 1809

When he reached Paris (January 23) Napoleon found conspiracies brewing amid public discontent. Letters from soldiers at the front revealed to hundreds of French families that Spanish resistance was re-forming and resolute,
and that Wellesley, his forces augmented, would soon move to oust Joseph
again from Madrid. Evidently war would go on, and French boys would be
conscripted year after year to force upon the Spaniards a government hostile
to their powerful Church and alien to their pride and blood. The royalists
of France, despite Napoleon's moves to appease them, had resumed their
plots to depose him; six such conspirators had been caught and shot in 1808;
another, Armand de Chateaubriand, was executed in February, 1809, despite
the appeals of his brother René, then the most acclaimed author in France.
Several Jacobins schemed for opposite reasons for the same end. Even in the
imperial government dissatisfaction with Napoleon was mounting: Fontanes
voiced it discreetly, Decrès openly: "The Emperor is mad, completely mad;
he will bring ruin upon himself and upon us all."[39]

Fouché, minister of police, had won compliments from Napoleon for exposing assassination plots, but he was increasingly doubtful of his master's
policies, and of his own future in the inevitable collapse. Sooner or later, he
felt, the beaten but proud governments of Austria and Prussia, and the superficially pro-French government of Russia, would unite again, fused with
British gold, to man another push against an uncomfortably dominant
France. Moreover, Napoleon in some coming battle might lose his life; why
should not some shot find and end him, as a shot, not long ago, had ended a
general standing at his side? Would not his sudden death, heirless, throw
France into a chaos that would leave it defenseless against its foes? Perhaps
Talleyrand could be persuaded to join in grooming Murat for a throne left
vacant by Napoleon's capture or death. On December 20, 1808, Fouché and
Talleyrand agreed that Murat was their man; and Murat concurred. Eugène
de Beauharnais got wind of the plan and told it to Madame Mère, who relayed it to her son in Spain.[40]

Napoleon would forgive Fouché more readily than he would Talleyrand;
Fouché's advice had often been on the saving side, but Talleyrand had rec-

ommended the execution of the Duc d'Enghien and the appropriation of Spain, and probably shared responsibility for the increasing coolness of Alexander. On January 24, 1809, seeing Talleyrand in the Council of State, Napoleon released his long-concealed resentment in a violent public reproof: "You have dared to maintain, sir, that you knew nothing about Enghien's death; you have dared to maintain that you knew nothing whatever about the Spanish war! . . . Have you forgotten that you advised me in writing to have Enghien executed? Have you forgotten that in your letters you advised me to revive the policy of Louis XIV [i.e., to establish his own family on the throne of Spain]?" Then, shaking his fist in Talleyrand's face, Napoleon cried, "Understand this: if a revolution should break out, no matter what part you had played in it, you would be the first to be crushed! . . . You are ordure in a silk stocking." That said, the Emperor hurriedly left the room. Talleyrand, limping after him, remarked to the councilors, "What a pity that so great a man should have such bad manners!"[41] On the morrow Napoleon ended Talleyrand's functions and salary as grand chamberlain. Soon, as was his wont, he regretted his outburst, and made no objection to Talleyrand's continued presence at court. In 1812 he could still say, "He is the most capable minister I ever had."[42] Talleyrand lost no chance to hasten Napoleon's fall.

Austria was doing her share. The whole country, from rich to poor, seemed eager for an attempt to free itself from the hard peace that Napoleon had laid upon it. Only Emperor Francis I hesitated, protesting that the appropriations for the army were bankrupting the state. Talleyrand sent encouraging words: the Grand Army was mired in Spain, French public opinion was strongly opposed to war, Napoleon's position was precarious.[43] Metternich, hitherto hesitant, argued that the time had come for Austria to strike. Napoleon warned the Austrian government that if it continued to arm he would have no choice but to raise another army at whatever cost. The Austrians continued to arm. Napoleon called upon Alexander to warn them; the Czar sent them a word of caution, which could be interpreted as counseling delay. Napoleon summoned two divisions from Spain, called up 100,000 conscripts, and ordered and received 100,000 troops from the Rhine Confederation, which feared for its life if Austria should overcome France; by April, 1809, Napoleon had 310,000 men under his command. A separate force of 72,000 French and 20,000 Italians was organized to protect Viceroy Eugène from an Austrian army sent to Italy under the Archduke Johann. On April 9 the Archduke Karl Ludwig invaded Bavaria with 200,000 men. On April 12 England signed a new alliance with Austria, pledging fresh subsidies. On April 13 Napoleon left Paris for Strasbourg, after announcing to his worried palace staff, "In two months I shall compel Austria to disarm." On April 17 he reached his main army at Donauwörth on the Danube, and gave final orders for the deployment of his forces.

The French won some minor engagements at Abensberg and Landshut (April 19 and 20). At Eckmühl (April 22) Marshal Davout led an irresistible attack upon Archduke Karl Ludwig's left wing while Napoleon's own divisions assaulted the center; after losing 30,000 men Karl retreated into Bohemia. Napoleon marched on to Vienna, which he entered on May 12 after a difficult and bravely contested crossing to the right bank of the Danube, there three thousand feet wide. In the meantime Karl reorganized his forces and brought them back to the left bank of the river at Essling. Napoleon tried to recross it, hoping to defeat the Archduke in a decisive engagement. But the Danube was in a rising flood, which swept away the principal bridges; part of the French army and much of the ammunition had to be left behind; and on May 22 Napoleon's 60,000 men found themselves embattled with 115,000 Austrian troops. After losing 20,000 men—the beloved Lannes among them—the Emperor ordered the remaining 40,000 to recross the Danube by whatever means they could find. The Austrians had lost 23,000, but the encounter was accepted throughout Europe as a disastrous defeat for Napoleon. Prussia and Russia watched the sequel eagerly, ready, at any further encouragement, to pounce upon the troublesome upstart who had so long eluded the lords of feudalism.

In Italy the fate of Viceroy Eugène had wavered in the balance of events. His Milan base, despite his genial rule, had been made insecure by the rising discontent of the people with Napoleon's treatment of the Pope. It was with considerable trepidation that Eugène led his army eastward to meet the Archduke Johann. He was defeated at the Tagliamento on April 16, and matters might have gone still worse for him had not Johann, on hearing of Napoleon's victory at Eckmühl, turned back in the vain hope of saving Vienna. Eugène, risking the loss of Italy to reinforce his adoptive father, also moved north, and reached him in time to be with him at Wagram.

After the repulse at Essling, Napoleon, reinforced in troops and artillery, had new bridges built across the Danube, and strongly fortified, as camp and arsenal, the island of Lobay, situated in the river only 360 feet from the left bank. On July 4 he bade his army cross again. Seeing himself outnumbered, Karl Ludwig retreated north; Napoleon pursued him, and at Wagram 187,000 Frenchmen and allies met 136,000 Austrians and allies in one of the bloodiest battles in history. The Austrians fought well, and were at times near victory; but Napoleon's superiority in manpower and tactics turned the tide, and after two days (July 5–6, 1809) of competitive homicide Karl, having lost 50,000 men, ordered a retreat. Napoleon had lost 34,000, but he had 153,000 left, while Karl had only 86,000; the odds were now two to one. The despondent Archduke asked for a truce, which Napoleon was glad to give.

He settled down in Schönbrunn with Mme. Walewska, and rejoiced to learn that she was pregnant; who now could say that it was his fault that Josephine had not borne him a child? Marie's aged husband was gallant enough to forgive her distinguished infidelity; he invited her back to his estate in Poland, and prepared to acknowledge the child as his own.[44]

Peace negotiations dallied for three months, partly because Karl Ludwig could not persuade his brother Francis I that further resistance could not be organized, and partly because Emperor Francis hoped that Prussia and Russia would come to his aid. Napoleon helped Alexander to resist the appeal by offering him part of Galicia, and promising not to restore the kingdom of Poland; on September 1 the Czar informed Austria that he was not prepared to break with France. The Austrian negotiators still held out, until Napoleon laid down an ultimatum. On October 14 they signed the Treaty of Schönbrunn, dictated by France in the royal palace of her ancient Hapsburg foes. Austria ceded the Innviertel and Salzburg to the Bavaria that she had so often invaded. Part of Galicia went to Russia, part of it to the grand duchy of Warsaw in partial return of territory taken by Austria in the partitions of Poland. Fiume, Istria, Trieste, Venezia, part of Croatia, most of Carinthia and Carniola were taken by France. Altogether Austria lost 3,500,000 taxable souls, and had to pay an indemnity of 85 million francs. Napoleon took all this as his due, and six months later he capped his spoils by getting an Austrian archduchess as his bride.

VI. MARRIAGE AND POLITICS: 1809–11

He left Vienna on October 15, 1809, and reached Fontainebleau on the 26th. He explained to intimate relatives and councilors his decision to seek a divorce. They were almost unanimous in approving, but not till November 30 did he summon up the courage to reveal his intention to Josephine. Despite his extramarital diversions, which seemed to him the legitimate privilege of a traveling warrior, he still loved her, and the break was to cause him months of emotional misery.

He knew her faults—her lazy, languid ways, her leisurely toilette, her extravagance in dress and jewelry, her inability to say no to milliners coming to display their wares. "She purchased all that was brought to her, at no matter what price."[45] Her debts repeatedly reached levels that brought storms from her husband; he drove the saleswomen from her rooms, scolded her, and paid the debts. He allowed her 600,000 francs per year for her personal expenses, and 120,000 more for her charities, for he knew that she was a compulsive giver.[46] He indulged her love for diamonds, perhaps because they made her fascinating despite her forty-two years. She was all feeling and no intellect, except the wisdom that nature gives to women for handling men. "Josephine," he told her, "you have an excellent heart and a weak head."[47] He seldom let her talk politics, and when she persisted he soon forgot her views. But he was grateful for the sensuous warmth of her embraces, for the "unfailing sweetness of her disposition,"[48] and for the modesty and grace with which she fulfilled her many functions as an empress. She loved him beyond idolatry, and he loved her this side of power. When Mme. de Staël accused him of not liking women, he replied, simply, "I like my wife."[49] Antoine Arnault marveled at "the empire exercised by the gentlest and most indolent of Creoles over the most willful and despotic of men. His determination, before which all men quailed, could not resist the tears of a woman."[50] As Napoleon put it at St. Helena, "I generally had to give in."[51]

She had long known his yearning for an heir of his blood as the legitimate and accepted inheritor of his rule; she knew his fear that without such a traditional transmission of power his capture, death, or serious illness would lead to a mad scramble of factions and generals for supremacy, and that in the resultant chaos the orderly, prosperous, and powerful France which he was building could disintegrate into another such terror—red or white—as that from which he had rescued it in 1799.

When, finally, he told her that they must part, she fainted, sincerely enough to be unconscious for many minutes. Napoleon carried her to her rooms, summoned his doctor, Jean-Nicolas Corvisart des Marets, and asked for Hortense's help in appeasing her mother. For a week Josephine refused consent; then, on December 7, Eugène arrived from Italy, and persuaded her. Napoleon comforted her with every tenderness. "I shall always love you," he told her, "but politics has no heart; it has only a head."[52] She was to have full title to the château and grounds of Malmaison, the title of empress, and a substantial annuity. He assured her children that he would be, to the end, their loving father.

On December 16 the Senate, after hearing the requests of both the Emperor and the Empress for the dissolution of their marriage, issued a decree of divorce, and on January 12 the Metropolitan Archbishop of Paris pronounced their marriage annulled. Many Catholics questioned the canonical validity of the annulment; in most of France the population disapproved of the separation; and many prophesied that from this time the good fortune that had so regularly followed Napoleon would seek other favorites.[53]

Politics having prevailed over love, Napoleon proceeded to seek a mate who not only would give promise of motherhood, but would bring with her some imperial connections helpful to the security of France and his rule. On November 22 (eight days before asking Josephine for a divorce) Napoleon instructed Caulaincourt, his ambassador in St. Petersburg, to present an official request to Alexander for the hand of his sixteen-year-old sister, Anna Pavlova. The Czar knew that his mother, who called Napoleon "that atheist," would never approve such a union, but he delayed replying, hoping to secure from Napoleon, as a *quid pro quo*, some territorial concessions in Poland. Impatient with the negotiations, and fearing a refusal, Napoleon acted on Metternich's hint that Austria would receive favorably a proposal for the Archduchess Marie Louise. Cambacérès opposed the plan, predicting that it would end the Russian alliance and lead to war.[54]

Marie Louise, then eighteen years old, was not beautiful, but her blue eyes, pink cheeks, and chestnut hair, her mild temper and simple tastes, were well adjusted to Napoleon's needs; all the evidence vouched for her present virginity and future fertility. She had considerable education, knew several languages, was skilled in music, drawing, and painting. From her childhood she had been taught to hate her suitor as the most wicked man in

Europe, but also she had learned that a princess was a political commodity, whose tastes in men must be subordinated to the good of the state. After all, this famous infamous monster must be an exciting change from the dull routine of a guarded girl longing for a wider world.

So, on March 11, 1810, at Vienna, she was formally married to the absent Napoleon, who was represented by Marshal Berthier. Repeating Marie Antoinette's bridal procession of 1770, she moved with eighty-three coaches and carriages through fifteen days and ceremonial nights to reach Compiègne on March 27. Napoleon had arranged to meet her there, but—curious or courteous—he drove out to welcome her at nearby Courcelles. On seeing her—but let him tell the story:

> I got out of the carriage quickly and kissed Marie Louise. The poor child had learned by heart a long speech, which she was to repeat to me kneeling. . . . I had asked Metternich and the Bishop of Nantes whether I could spend the night under the same roof with Marie Louise. They removed all my doubts, and assured me that she was now Empress and not Archduchess. . . . I was only separated from her bedroom by the library. I asked her what they had told her when she left Vienna. She answered me very naïvely that her father and Frau Lazansky had directed her as follows: "As soon as you are alone with the Emperor you must do absolutely everything that he tells you. You must agree to everything that he asks of you." She was a delightful child.
>   Monsieur Ségur wanted me to keep away from her for form's sake, but as I was already surely married, everything was all right, and I told him to go to the devil.[55]

The pair were united by a civil marriage at St.-Cloud on April 1, and, on the next day, by a religious marriage in the great hall of the Louvre. Nearly all the cardinals refused to attend this service, on the ground that the Pope had not annulled the marriage to Josephine; Napoleon exiled them to the provinces. Otherwise he was exuberantly happy. He found his bride sensually and socially pleasing—modest, obedient, generous and kind; she never learned to love him, but she was a cheerful companion. As empress she never achieved the popularity of Josephine, but she was accepted as symbolizing the triumph of France over the hostile royalties of Europe.

Napoleon did not forget Josephine. He visited her so often at Malmaison that Marie began to pout, whereupon he desisted; but then he sent Josephine comforting letters, nearly all addressed to "My love."[56] To one of these she replied from Navarre in Normandy on April 21, 1810:

> A thousand, thousand thanks for not having forgotten me. My son has just brought me your letter. With what ardor have I read it! . . . There is not a word in it which has not made me weep; but those tears were very sweet. . . .
>   I wrote to you on leaving Malmaison, and how many times thereafter did I wish to write! But I felt the reasons for your silence, and I feared to be importunate. . . .
>   Be happy, be happy as you deserve; it is my whole heart that speaks. You have given me too my share of happiness, and a share very keenly felt. . . . Adieu, my friend. I thank you as tenderly as I shall love you always.[57]

She consoled herself with finery and hospitality. He allowed her three million francs a year; she spent four million; after her death in 1814 some bills for her unpaid purchases pursued him to Elba.[58] At Malmaison she collected a gallery of art, and entertained without counting costs. Invitations to her receptions were valued next to Napoleon's. Mme. Tallien—now the fat and forty Princesse de Chimay—came, and together they recalled the days when they were queens of the Directory. Countess Walewska came; she was well received, and joined with Josephine in mourning their lost lover.

He was granted two years of happiness and relative peace. The Treaty of Schönbrunn had enlarged his realm, enriched his Treasury, and stimulated his appetite. He had annexed the Papal States (May 17, 1809), and had restored Joseph to his royal seat in Madrid. In January, 1810, Sweden, long an enemy, signed peace with France, and joined the Continental Blockade; in June, with Napoleon's solicited consent, she accepted Bernadotte as heir apparent to the Swedish throne. In December Napoleon absorbed Hamburg, Bremen, Lübeck, Berg, and Oldenburg into the French Empire. His anxiety to close all Continental ports to British trade made him, in the eyes of his foes, an insatiable conqueror accumulating debts to the jealous gods.

Domestically, matters were quiet and comforting; France was prosperous and proud; the only ripple on the stream was the final dismissal of Fouché for exceeding his powers. Savary succeeded him as minister of police, while Fouché retired to Aix-en-Provence to plan revenge. External affairs were not so smooth. Holland was cursing the embargo on British goods; Italy, proud of the Papacy, was losing patience with Napoleon; Wellington was building an army in Portugal for an invasion of Spain; and beyond the Rhine the German states under Bonapartist rule were complaining of impositions, and were only waiting for some imperial blunder to let them return to more congenial masters.

Nevertheless Marie Louise was with child, and the happy Emperor counted the days to her fulfillment. When the great event approached, he surrounded it with all the ceremony and solemnity that had traditionally greeted a Bourbon birth. Announcement was made that if the child was a daughter Paris would hear a salvo of twenty-one guns; if it was a son the salvos would continue to 101. The delivery was extremely painful; the fetus proposed to come into the world feet first. Dr. Corvisart told Napoleon that either the mother or the child might have to be sacrificed; he was told to save the mother at any cost.[59] Another physician used instruments to invert the fetus; Marie for some minutes was near death. Finally the child agreed to emerge head first; both mother and child survived (March 20, 1811). The 101 cannon shots sent their message over Paris, echoing through France; and there were not many persons in Europe who could begrudge the Emperor his happiness. All the rulers of Continental Europe sent their congratulations to the fond father and to the already proclaimed "King of Rome."[60] Now, for the first time in his career, Napoleon could feel tolerably secure; he had founded a dynasty that, in his hopes, would be as splendid and beneficent as any in history, and might even make Europe one.

CHAPTER X

Napoleon Himself

I. BODY

WE must not picture him as Gros painted him in 1796—standard in one hand, drawn sword in the other, costume ornate with colored sash and official insignia, long chestnut hair wild in the wind, eyes, brow, and lips fixed in determination; this seems too ideal to be true. Two years younger than his twenty-seven-year-old hero, Gros is said to have seen him planting that standard on the bridge at Arcole,[1] but the painting is probably the product of ardent idolatry—the man of art worshiping the men of deeds. And yet, two years later, Guérin portrayed Napoleon with essentially the same features: hair falling over forehead and shoulders, brows arched over eyes somber and resolute, nose going straight to the point like his will, lips closed tight as of a mind made up. This too is but one aspect of the man—the martial; there were many other moods that could relax those lineaments, as in his playful pulling of his secretary's ears, or in his paternal ecstasy over the infant "King of Rome." By 1802 he had discarded those long locks[2]—all but one which dangled over a receding forehead. He put on weight after forty years, and sometimes used his paunch to support his hand. Frequently, especially when walking, he clasped his hands behind his back; this became so habitual that it almost always betrayed him at a masquerade. Throughout his life his hands attracted attention by the perfection of their skin and the tapering fingers; indeed, he was quite proud of all four of his extremities. However, Las Cases, who thought him a god, could not help smiling at those "ridiculously handsome hands."[3]

He was absurdly short for a general, being only five feet and six inches in height;[4] the command had to be in the eyes. Cardinal Caprara, coming to negotiate the Concordat, wore "an immense pair of green spectacles" to soften the glare of Napoleon's eyes. General Vandamme, fearing their hypnosis, confessed, "That devil of a man exercises upon me a fascination that I cannot explain to myself; and in such degree that though I fear neither God nor devil, I am ready to tremble like a child when I am in his presence, and he could make me go through the eye of a needle to throw myself into the fire."[5] The Emperor's complexion was sallow, brightened, however, by facial muscles quickly reflecting—if he wished—each turn of feeling or idea. Napoleon's head was large for his stature, but was well shaped; his shoulders were broad, his chest well developed, suggesting a strong constitution. He dressed simply, leaving finery to his marshals; his complex hat, spreading like a folded waffle, had no adornment but a tricolor cockade.* Usually he wore

---

* One of Napoleon's hats, at a Paris auction on April 23, 1969, brought $30,840.[6]

a gray coat over the uniform of a colonel of his guard. He carried a snuffbox on his waistband, and resorted to it occasionally. He preferred knee breeches and silk stockings to pantaloons. He never wore jewelry, but his shoes were lined with silk and bound with buckles of gold. In dress, as in his final political philosophy, he belonged to the Ancien Régime.

He was "scrupulously neat in his person."[7] He had a passion for warm baths, sometimes lingering in them for two hours; probably he found in them some relief from nervous tensions, muscular pains, and an itching skin disease that he had contracted at Toulon.[8] He used eau-de-cologne on his neck and torso as well as on his face.[9] He was "exceedingly temperate" in food and drink; diluted his wine with water,[10] like the ancient Greeks; and usually gave only ten or fifteen minutes to his lunch. On campaigns he ate as chance allowed, and often hurriedly; sometimes this led to indigestion, and at the most critical moments, as at the battles of Borodino and Leipzig.[11] He suffered from constipation; in 1797 he added hemorrhoids, which he claimed to have cured with leeches.[12] "I never saw him ill," said Méneval, but he added: "He was only occasionally subject to vomiting bile, which never left any aftereffects. . . . He had feared, for some time, that he was affected with a disease of the bladder, because the keen air of the mountains caused him a kind of dysuria; but this fear was found to be without foundation."[13] However, there is considerable evidence that in his later life Napoleon was afflicted with inflammation of the urinary tract, sometimes leading to painful and inconveniently frequent urination.[14] His overstrung nerves sometimes (as at Mainz in 1806) collapsed into convulsions partly resembling epileptic seizures; but it is now generally agreed that he was not subject to epilepsy.[15]

There is no such agreement about the imperial stomach. "In all my life," he told Las Cases on September 16, 1816, "I never had either a headache or a pain in my stomach." Méneval corroborated him: "I have never heard him complain of pain in the stomach."[16] However, Bourrienne reported having more than once seen Napoleon suffering such stomach pains that "I would then accompany him to his bedchamber, and have often been obliged to support him." In Warsaw, in 1806, after violent stomach pains, he predicted that he would die of the same disease as his father—i.e., cancer of the stomach.[17] The doctors who performed an autopsy on him in 1821 agreed that he had a diseased—apparently a cancerous—stomach. Some students would add gonorrhea and syphilis to his woes, and suggest that some by-products remained with him to the end.[18]

He refused to treat his ailments with medicine. As a general accustomed to wounded soldiers, he admitted the need of surgery; but as for drugs, he distrusted their side effects, and preferred, when ill, to fast, drink barley water, lemonade, or water containing orange leaves, to take vigorous exercise to promote perspiration, and let the body heal itself. "Up to 1816," Las Cases reported, "the Emperor did not recollect having ever taken medicine";[19] but the imperial memory was then susceptible to wishful forgetting. "Doctor," he explained to the physician of the S.S. *Northumberland* on the way to

St. Helena, "our body is a machine for the purpose of life; it is organized to that end—that is its nature. Leave the life there at its ease; let it take care of itself; it will do better than if you paralyze it by loading it with medicines."[20] He never tired of teasing his favorite physician, Corvisart, about the uselessness of medicine; finally he led him to agree that, all in all, drugs had done more harm than good.[21] He amused his final physician, Francesco Antommarchi, by asking him which of the two groups, the generals or the doctors, would, at the Last Judgment, be found responsible for the greater number of deaths.

Despite his ailments, he had in him a fund of energy that never failed till Moscow burned. An appointment to service under him was no bureaucratic sinecure, but almost a sentence to slow death; many a proud official crept away exhausted after five or six years of keeping the Emperor's pace. One of his appointees complimented himself on not being stationed in Paris: there "I should die of application before the end of the month. He has already killed Portalis, Crétet, and almost Treilhard, who was tough; he could no longer urinate, nor the others either."[22] Napoleon admitted the high mortality among his aides. "The lucky man," he said, "is he who hides away from me in the depths of some province."[23] When he asked Louis-Philippe de Ségur what people would say of him after his death, and Ségur replied that they would express universal regret, Napoleon corrected him: "Not at all; they will say 'Ouf!' " in profound and universal relief.[24]

He wore himself out as he did others; the engine was too strong for the body. He crowded a century of events into twenty years because he compressed a week into a day. He came to his desk about 7 A.M., and expected his secretary to be available at any hour; "Come," he called to Bourrienne, "let us go to work."[25] "Be here tonight at one o'clock, or four, in the morning," he said to Méneval, "and we will work together."[26] Three or four days a week he attended the meetings of the Council of State. "I am always working," he told Councilor Roederer; "I work when I am dining, I work at the theater; in the middle of the night I wake up and work."

We might have supposed that these full and exciting days would be paid for by sleepless nights, but Bourrienne assures us that the Emperor slept well enough—seven hours at night, and "a short nap in the afternoon."[27] He boasted to Las Cases that he could go to sleep at will, "at any hour, and in any place," whenever he needed repose. He explained that he kept his many different affairs arranged in his head or memory as in a closet with several drawers; "When I wish to turn from a business, I close the drawer that contains it, and I open that which contains another. . . . If I wish to sleep I shut up all the drawers, and I am soon asleep."[28]

II. MIND

Goethe thought that Napoleon's mind was the greatest that the world had ever produced.[29] Lord Acton concurred. Méneval, awed by the nearness of power and fame, ascribed to his master "the highest intellect which has ever been granted to a human being."[30] Taine, the most brilliant and indefatigable opponent of Napoleolatry, marveled at the Emperor's capacity for long and intense mental labor; "never has a brain so disciplined and under such control been seen."[31] Let us agree that Napoleon's was among the most perceptive, penetrating, retentive, and logical minds ever seen in one who was predominantly a man of action. He liked to sign himself as a "member of the Institute," and he once expressed to Laplace his regret that "force of circumstances had led him so far from the career of a scientist";[32] at that moment he might have ranked the man who adds to human understanding above the man who adds to man's power.* However, he could be forgiven for scorning the "ideologues" of the Institute, who mistook ideas for realities, explained the universe, and proposed to tell him how to govern France. His mind had the defects of a romantic imagination, but it had the realistic stimulus of daily contact with the flesh and blood of life. His persistent mental activity was part and servant of persistent action at the highest level of statesmanship.

First of all, he was sensitive. He suffered from the keenness of his senses: his ears multiplied sounds, his nose multiplied odors, his eyes penetrated surfaces and appearances, and discarded the incidental to clarify the significant. He was curious and asked thousands of questions, read hundreds of books, studied maps and histories, visited factories and farms; Las Cases was amazed at the range of his interest, the scope of his knowledge about countries and centuries. He had a memory made tenacious and selective by the intensity and character of his aims; he knew what to forget and what to retain. He was orderly: the unity and hierarchy of his desires imposed a clarifying and directive order upon his ideas, actions, policies, and government. He required from his aides reports and recommendations composed not of eloquent abstractions and admirable ideals but of definite objectives, factual information, practical measures, and calculable results; he studied, checked, and classified this material in the light of his experience and purposes, and issued instructions decisive and precise. We know of no other government in history that worked with such orderly preparation to such orderly administration. With Napoleon the ecstasy of liberty yielded to the dictatorship of order.

By projecting his memories into anticipations, he became skilled in calculating the results of possible responses, and in predicting the plans and moves of his foes. "I meditate a great deal," he said. "If I seem equal to the occasion, and ready to face it when it comes, it is because I have thought the matter over a long time before undertaking it. . . . I have anticipated whatever might happen. It is no genie [*djinn*] which suddenly reveals to me what I ought to do or say, . . . but my own reflection."[34] So he prepared in detail the campaigns of Marengo and Austerlitz, and predicted not only the results

---

* If Napoleon had been wise, said Anatole France, "he would have lived in an attic and written four books"; i.e., he would have been another Spinoza.[33]

but the time they would require. At the summit of his development (1807) he was able to keep his wishes from obscuring his vision; he tried to antici- pate difficulties, hazards, surprises, and planned to meet them. "When I plan a battle no man is more pusillanimous than I am. I magnify to myself all the evils possible under the circumstances."[35] His first rule in case of unforeseen emergencies was to attend to them immediately, at whatever time of the day or night. He left permanent instructions with Bourrienne: "Do not wake me when you have good news to communicate; with such there is no hurry. But when you bring bad news rouse me instantly, for then there is not a moment to lose!"[36] He recognized that despite all foresight he might be surprised by some unexpected event, but he prided himself on having "the two-o'clock-in-the-morning courage"—the ability to think clearly and act promptly and effectively, after a sudden awakening.[37] He tried to be on his guard against chance, and repeatedly told himself that "it is only a step from victory to disaster."[38]

His judgment of men was usually as penetrating as his calculation of events. He did not trust appearances or protestations; a person's character, he thought, does not appear on his face until he is old, and speech conceals as often as it reveals. He studied himself ceaselessly, and on that basis he pre- sumed that all men and women were led in their conscious actions and thought by self-interest. He who was the object of so much devotion (from Desaix, Lannes, Méneval, Las Cases . . . and those soldiers who, dying, cried "*Vive l'Empereur!*") could not conceive of a selfless devotion. Behind every word and deliberate deed he saw the tireless grasp of the ego—the strong man's ambition, the weak man's fear, the woman's vanity or stratagem. He sought out each person's ruling passion or vulnerable frailty, and played upon it to mold him to imperial aims.

Despite all forethought and foresight he made (to our hindsight) an am- ple variety of mistakes, both in judging men and in calculating results. He might have known that Josephine could not bear a month of chastity, and that Marie Louise could not tie Austria to peace. He thought he had charmed Alexander at Tilsit and Erfurt, while the Czar, with Talleyrand's coaching, was deceiving him elegantly. It was a mistake to intensify British hostility in 1802 by so boldly extending his power over Piedmont, Lom- bardy, and Switzerland; a mistake to put his brothers on thrones too big for their brains; a mistake to suppose that the German states in the Confeder- ation of the Rhine would submit to French sovereignty when a chance came to break away; a mistake to publish a document that showed him thinking of conquering Turkey; a mistake (as he later confessed) to waste the Grand Army in Spain; a mistake to invade endless Russia, or remain there as winter neared. Supreme over so many men, he was subject, as he said, to the "nature of things," to the surprises of events, the frailties of disease, the inadequacies of his power. "I have conceived many plans," he said, "but I was never free to execute one of them. For all that I held the rudder, and with a strong hand, the waves were a good deal stronger. I was never in truth my own master; I was always governed by circumstance."[39]

And by imagination. His soul was a battleground between keen observation enlightening reason and vivid imaginings clouding it with romance, even with superstition; now and then he dallied with omens and horoscopes.[40] When he went to Egypt he took with him many books of science and many of sentiment or fancy—Rousseau's *La Nouvelle Héloïse*, Goethe's *Werther*, Macpherson's "Ossian";[41] he confessed later that he had read *Werther* seven times;[42] and in the end he concluded that "imagination rules the world."[43] Stranded in Egypt, he fed on dreams of winning India; struggling through Syria, he pictured himself conquering Constantinople with his handful of men, and then marching upon Vienna like a more invincible Suleiman. As power drove caution out of his blood he ignored Goethe's warning of *Entsagen*—the acknowledgment of bounds; his proliferating successes challenged the gods—violated the calculus of limitations; and in the end he found himself petulant and helpless, chained to a rock in the sea.

III. CHARACTER

His pride had begun with the self-centeredness natural to all organisms. In his youth it swelled defensively in the clash of individuals and families in Corsica, and then against the class and racial arrogance of students at Brienne. It was not by any means pure selfishness; it allowed devotion and generosity to his mother, to Josephine and her children; love for the "King of Rome"; and an impatient affection for his brothers and sisters, who also had selves to pamper and preserve. But as his successes widened, his power and responsibilities, his pride and self-absorption, grew. He tended to take nearly all the credit for his armies' victories, but he praised, loved, and mourned Desaix and Lannes. Finally he identified his country with himself, and his ego swelled with her frontiers.

His pride, or the consciousness of ability, sometimes descended to vanity, or the display of accomplishments. "Well, Bourrienne, you too will be immortal." "Why, General?" "Are you not my secretary?" "Tell me the name of Alexander's." "Hm, that is not bad, Bourrienne."[44] He wrote to Viceroy Eugène (April 14, 1806): "My Italian people must know me well enough not to forget that there is more in my little finger than in all their brains put together."[45] The letter *N*, blazoned in a thousand places, was occasionally graced with a *J* for Josephine. The Emperor felt that showmanship was a necessary prop of rule.

"Power is my mistress," he declared to Roederer in 1804, when Joseph was angling to be declared heir; "I have worked too hard at her conquest to allow anyone to take her away from me, or even to covet her. . . . Two weeks ago I would not have dreamed of treating him unjustly. Now I am unforgiving. I shall smile at him with my lips—but he has slept with my mistress."[46] (Here he did himself injustice; he was a jealous lover, but he was a forgiving man.) "I love power as a musician loves his violin."[47] So his ambition leaped from bound to bound: he dreamt of rivaling Charlemagne and uniting Western Europe, forcibly including the Papal States; then of follow-ing Constantine from France through Milan to the capture of Constanti-nople, building classic arches to commemorate his victories; then he found Europe too little, a mere "molehill,"[48] and proposed to rival Alexander by conquering India. It would be hard work, for himself and a million troops, but it would be repaid in glory, for him and them; and if death overtook them on the way it would not be too great a price to pay. "Death is nothing; but to live defeated and inglorious is to die daily."[49] "I live only for pos-terity."[50] *La gloire* became his ruling passion, so hypnotic that for a decade nearly all France accepted it as its guiding star.

He pursued his aims with a will that never bent except to leap—until he had exhausted the sublime and became pitiful. His unresting ambition gave unity to his will, direction and substance to every day. At Brienne, "even when I had nothing [assigned?] to do, I always felt that I had no time to lose."[51] And to Jérôme in 1805: "What I am I owe to strength of will, to character, application, and audacity."[52] Daring was part of his strategy; time and again he surprised his enemies by quick and decisive action at un-expected places and times. "My aim is to go straight toward my objective, without being stopped by any consideration";[53] it took him a decade to learn the old adage that in politics a straight line is the longest distance between two points.

Sometimes his judgment and conduct were clouded and perverted with passion. His temper was as short as his stature, and it shortened as his power spread. He had the heat and wilds of Corsica in his blood; and though he usually managed to check his wrath, those around him, from Josephine to his powerful bodyguard Roustam, watched their every word and move lest they incur his wrath. He became impatient with contradiction, tardiness, incompetence, or stupidity. When he lost his temper he would publicly berate an ambassador, swear at a bishop, kick philosopher Volney in the stomach, or, *faute de mieux*, boot a log on the hearth.[54] And yet his anger cooled almost as soon as it flared; often it was put on, as a move in the chess of politics; in most cases he made amends a day or a minute afterward.[55] He was seldom brutal, often kind, playful, good-humored,[56] but his sense of humor had been weakened by hardship and battle; he had little time for the pleasantries of leisure, the gossip of the court, or the wit of the salons. He was a man in a hurry, with a pack of enemies around him, and an em-pire on his hands; and it is difficult for a man in a hurry to be civilized.

He spent too much of his energy conquering half of Europe to have much left for the absurdities of coitus. He suspected that many forms of sexual desire were environmentally learned rather than hereditary: "Everything is conventional among men, even to those feelings which, one would sup-pose, ought to be dictated by Nature alone."[57] He could have had a covey of concubines in the full Bourbon tradition, but he made do with half a dozen mistresses spaced between campaigns. Women thought themselves immortal if they amused him for a night; usually he dispatched the matter with brutal brevity, and talked about his late partners with more coarseness than gratitude.[58] His infidelities caused Josephine many hours of worry and grief; he explained to her (if we may believe Mme. de Rémusat) that these *divertimenti* were natural, necessary, and customary, and should be over-looked by an understanding wife; she wept, he comforted her, she forgave him.[59] Otherwise he was as good a husband as his cares and wanderings would allow.

When Marie Louise came to him he accepted monogamy (so far as we know) with new grace, if only because adultery might lose him Austria. His devotion to her was doubled when he beheld her agony in giving him a son. He had always shown a fondness for children; his law code gave them especial protection;[60] now the infant King of Rome became the idol and bearer of his hopes, carefully trained to inherit and wisely rule a France giv-ing laws to a united Europe. So the great ego enlarged itself with marital and parental love.

He was too immersed in politics to have time for friends; besides, friend-ship implies a near-equality of give and take, and Napoleon found it hard to concede equality in any form. He had faithful servitors and devotees, some of whom gave their lives for his glory and their own; yet none would have thought of calling him a friend. Eugène loved him, but as a son rather than a friend. Bourrienne (never quite trustworthy) relates that in 1800 he often heard Napoleon say:

> "Friendship is but a name. I love nobody. I do not even love my brothers. Perhaps Joseph a little, from habit and because he is my elder; and Duroc,* I love him too. . . . I know very well that I have no true friends. As long as I continue what I am, I may have as many pretended friends as I please. Leave sensibility to women; it is their business. But men should be firm at heart and in purpose, or they should have nothing to do with war or government."[61]

This has the stoic Napoleonic ring, but is not easily reconciled with the lifelong devotion of men like Desaix, Duroc, Lannes, Las Cases, and a host of others. The same Bourrienne attests that "out of the field of battle Bona-parte had a kind and feeling heart."[62] And Méneval, close to Napoleon for thirteen years, agrees:

> I had expected to find him brusque and of uncertain temper, instead of which I found him patient, indulgent, easy to please, by no means exacting, merry with a merriness which was often noisy and mocking, and sometimes of a charming bonhomie. . . . I was no longer afraid of him. I was maintained in this state of mind by all that I saw of his pleasant and affectionate ways with Josephine, the assiduous devotion of his officers, the kindliness of his relations with the consuls and the ministers, and his familiarity with the soldiers.[63]

Apparently he could be hard when he thought that policy demanded it, and lenient when policy allowed; policy had to come first. He sent many men to jail, and yet a hundred instances of his kindness are recorded, as in the volumes of Frédéric Masson. He took action to improve conditions in the jails of Brussels, but conditions in French prisons in 1814 were unworthy

---

* Grand marshal of the palace; killed at Bautzen in 1813.

of the general efficiency of his rule. He saw thousands of men dead on the field of battle, and went on to other battles; yet we hear of his often stopping to comfort or relieve a wounded soldier. Véry Constant "saw him weep while eating his breakfast after coming from the bedside of Marshal Lannes,"[64] mortally wounded at Essling in 1809.

There is no question about his generosity, nor about his readiness to forgive. He repeatedly—and once too often—forgave Bernadotte and Bourrienne. When Carnot and Chénier, after years of opposition to Napoleon, appealed to him to relieve their poverty, he sent help immediately. At St. Helena he contrived excuses for those who had deserted him in 1813 or 1815. Only the British won his lasting resentment of their lasting enmity; he saw nothing but mercenary hardness in Pitt, was rather unfair to Sir Hudson Lowe, and found it impossible to appreciate Wellington.[65] There was a considerable justice in his self-estimate: "I consider myself a good man at heart."[66] No man, we are told, is a hero to his valet; but Véry Constant, Napoleon's valet through fourteen years, recorded his memories in numerous volumes "breathless with adoration."[67]

Persons brought up to the elegant manners of the Old Regime could not bear the blunt directness of Napoleon's style of movement and address. He amused such people by the awkward consciousness of his carriage and the occasional coarseness of his speech. He did not know how to put others at their ease, and did not seem to care; he was too eager for the substance to fret about the form. "I do not like that vague and leveling phrase *les convenances* [the proprieties]. . . . It is a device of fools to raise themselves to the level of people of intellect. . . . 'Good taste' is another of those classical expressions which mean nothing to me. . . . What is called 'style,' good or bad, does not affect me. I care only for the force of the thought."[68] Secretly, however, he admired the easy grace and quiet considerateness of the gentleman; he longed to win approval from the aristocrats who made fun of him in the salons of Faubourg St.-Germain. In his own way he could be "fascinating when he chose to be."[69]

His low opinion of women may have been due to his hurried carelessness of their sensitivity. So he remarked to Mme. Charpentier, "How ill you look in that red dress!"[70]—and he turned Mme. de Staël to enmity by ranking women according to their fertility. Some women rebuked his rudeness with feminine subtlety. When he exclaimed to Mme. de Chevreuse, "Dear me, how red your hair is!" she answered, "Perhaps it is, Sire, but this is the first time a man has ever told me so."[71] When he told a famous beauty, "Madame, I do not like it when women mix in politics," she retorted, "You are right, General; but in a country where they have their heads cut off, it is natural that they should want to know why."[72] Nevertheless Méneval, who saw him almost daily, noted "that winning charm which was so irresistible in Napoleon."[73]

He liked to talk—sometimes garrulously, almost always usefully and to the point. He invited scientists, artists, actors, writers, to his table, and surprised them by his affability, his knowledge of their field, and the aptness of his remarks. Isabey the miniaturist, Monge the mathematician, Fontaine the architect, and Talma the actor left reminiscences of these meetings, all testifying to the "grace, amiability, and gaiety" of Napoleon's conversation.[74] He much preferred talking to writing. His ideas advanced faster than his speeches; when he tried to write them down he wrote so rapidly that no one—not he himself—could then decipher his scrawl.[75] So he dictated, and as 41,000 of his letters have been published, and doubtless other thousands were written, we can begin to understand how the honor of being his secretary was a sentence to hard labor. Bourrienne, who took the post in 1797, had the good fortune to be dismissed in 1802, and so survived till 1834. He was expected to join Napoleon at 7 A.M., work all day, and be on call at night. He could speak and write several languages, knew international law, and, with his own method of shorthand, could usually write as fast as Napoleon dictated.

Méneval, who succeeded Bourrienne in 1802, labored still harder, for "I did not know any kind of shorthand." Napoleon was fond of him, often jested with him, but wore him out almost daily, after which he would tell him to go and take a bath.[76] At St. Helena the Emperor recalled: "I nearly killed poor Méneval; I was obliged to relieve him for a while from the duties of his situation, and place him, for the recovery of his health, near the person of Marie Louise, where his post was a mere sinecure."[77] In 1806 Napoleon authorized him to engage an assistant, François Fain, who served to the end, and on all campaigns. Even so Méneval was quite worn out when he escaped from his fond despot in 1813. It was one of those love affairs that thrive on inequality recognized and not abused.

IV. THE GENERAL

His body and mind, character, and career were in part molded by his military education at Brienne. There he learned to keep himself fit in any weather or place; to think clearly at any hour of day or night; to distinguish fact from desire; to obey without question as training for commanding without hesitation; to see terrains as possibilities for the open or hidden movement of masses of men; to anticipate enemy maneuvers and prepare to counter them; to expect the unexpected and meet it unsurprised; to inspire individual souls by addressing them en masse; to anesthetize pain with glory, and make it sweet and noble to die for one's country: all this appeared to Napoleon as the science of sciences, since a nation's life depends—other means having failed—upon its willingness and ability to defend itself in the final arbitrament of war. "The art of war," he declared, "is an immense study, which comprises all others."[78]

So he cultivated most those sciences that would contribute most to the science of national defense. He read history to learn the nature of man and the behavior of states; he surprised the savants, later, by his knowledge of ancient Greece and Rome, of medieval and modern Europe. He "studied and restudied" the campaigns of Alexander, Hannibal, Caesar, Gustavus Adolphus, Turenne, Eugene of Savoy, and Frederick the Great; "model yourself on them," he told his officers, "reject every maxim contrary to those of these great men."[79]

From the military academy he passed to the camp, and from the camp to control of a regiment. Perhaps from his stoic mother he had the gift of command, and knew its secret: that most persons would rather follow a lead than give it—if the leader leads. He had the courage to take responsibility, to stake his career again and again upon his judgment; and, with a daring that too often laughed at caution, he passed from one gamble to another—ever playing with more human pawns for higher stakes. He lost the last wager, but only after proving himself the ablest general in history.

His military strategy began with measures for winning the minds and hearts of his men. He interested himself in the background, character, and hopes of each officer directly under his command. He mingled now and then with the common soldiers, recalling their victories, inquiring about their families, and listening to their complaints. He good-humoredly rallied his Imperial Guard, and called them "*les grogneurs*" because they grumbled so much; but they fought for him to the last death. Sometimes he spoke cynically of the simple infantryman, as when, at St. Helena, he remarked that "troops are made to let themselves be killed";[80] but he adopted, and provided for, all the children of the French warriors who died at Austerlitz.[81] More than any other section of the French nation his soldiers loved him—so much so that, in Wellington's judgment, his presence on the battlefield was worth forty thousand men.[82]

His addresses to his army were an important part of his strategy. "In war," he said, "morale and opinion are more than half the battle."[83] No other general since Caesar at the Rubicon had ever exercised such fascination over his men. Bourrienne, who wrote some of those famous proclamations at Napoleon's dictation, tells us that the troops in many cases "could not understand what Napoleon said, but no matter, they would have followed him cheerfully barefoot and without provisions."[84] In several of his addresses he explained to them his plan of operations; usually they understood, and bore more patiently the long marches that enabled them to surprise or outnumber the foe. "The best soldier," he said, "is not so much the one who fights as the one who marches."[85] In a proclamation of 1799 he told his auditors: "The chief virtues of a soldier are constancy and discipline. Valor comes only in the second place."[86] He often showed mercy, but he did not hesitate to be severe when discipline was endangered. After his first victories in Italy, when he deliberately allowed his troops some pillage to make up for the Directory's skimping on their food, clothing, and pay, he forbade such conduct, and enforced the order so rigorously that it was soon obeyed. "Vienna, Berlin, Madrid, and other cities," says Méneval, "witnessed the condemnation and execution of soldiers belonging as well to the Imperial Guard as to other army corps, when these soldiers had been found guilty of pillage."[87]

Napoleon expressed part of his strategy in a mathematical formula: "The strength of an army, like the amount of momentum in mechanics, is estimated by the mass times the velocity. A swift march enhances the morale of an army, and increases its power for victory."[88] There is no authority for ascribing to him the aphorism that "an army travels on its stomach"—that is, on its food supply;[89] his view was rather that it wins with its feet. His motto was "*Activité, activité, vitesse*"[90]—action and speed. Consequently he placed no reliance on fortresses as defenses; he would have laughed at the Maginot Line of 1939. "It is axiomatic," he had said, far back in 1793, "that the side which remains behind its fortified line is always defeated"; and he repeated this in 1816.[91] To watch for the time when the enemy divides or elongates his army; to use mountains and rivers to screen and protect the movement of his troops; to seize strategical elevations from which artillery could rake the field; to choose a battleground that would allow the maneuvers of infantry, artillery, and cavalry; to concentrate one's forces—usually by swift marches —so as to confront with superior numbers a segment of the enemy too far from the center to be reinforced in time: these were the elements of Napoleonic strategy.

The final test of the general is in tactics—the disposition and maneuvering of his forces for and during battle. Napoleon took his stand where he could survey as much of the action as his safety would allow; and since the plan of operations, and its quick adjustment to the turn of events, depended upon his continued and concentrated attention, his safety was a prime consideration, even more in the judgment of his troops than in his actual practice; if he thought it necessary, as at Arcole, he did not hesitate to expose himself; and more than once we read of men being killed at his side in his place of observation. From such a point, through a staff of mounted orderlies, he dispatched instructions to the commanding officers in the infantry, the artillery, and the cavalry; and those messengers hurried back to keep him informed of the turn of events in every segment of the action. In battle, he believed, soldiers acquired their value chiefly through their position and maneuverability. Here too the aim was concentration—of massed men and heavy fire upon a particular point, preferably a flank, of the enemy, in the hope of throwing that part into a disorder that would spread. "In all battles a moment comes when the bravest troops, after having made the greatest efforts, feel inclined to run. . . . Two armies are two bodies that meet and endeavor to frighten each other; a moment of panic occurs, and that moment must be turned to advantage. When a man has been present in many actions, he distinguishes that moment without difficulty."[92] Napoleon was especially quick to take advantage of such a development, or, if his own men wavered, to send reinforcements, or change his line of operation in the course of a battle; this saved the day for him at Marengo. Retreat was not in his vocabulary before 1812.

It was natural that one who had developed such skill in generalship should come to find a macabre thrill in war. We have heard him lauding civilians as above soldiers; he gave precedence, at his court, to the statesmen over the marshals; and when conflicts arose between the civilian populations and the military he regularly took the civilian side.[93] But he could not conceal from himself or others that he experienced on the battlefield a pleasure keener than any that came from administration. "There is a joy in danger," he said, and he confessed to Jomini that he "loved the excitement of battle";[94] he was happiest when he saw masses of men moving at his will into actions that changed the map and decided history. He viewed his campaigns as responses to attacks, but he admitted, according to Bourrienne, "My power depends upon my glory, and my glory on my victories. My power would fall were I not to support it by new glory and new victories. Conquest has made me what I am, and conquest alone can maintain me."[95] We cannot quite trust the hostile Bourrienne for this pivotal confession; but Las Cases, to whom Napoleon was next to God, quoted him as saying (March 12, 1816), "I wished for the empire of the world, and, to ensure it, unlimited power was necessary to me."[96]

Was he, as his enemies put it, "a butcher"? We are told that he recruited a total of 2,613,000 Frenchmen for his armies;[97] of these about one million died in his service.[98] Was he disturbed by the slaughter? He mentioned it in his appeals to the Powers for peace; and we are told that the sight of the corpses at Eylau moved him to tears.[99] Yet, when it was all over, and he looked at the matter in retrospect, he told Las Cases: "I had commanded in battles that were to decide the fate of a whole army, and I had felt no emotion. I had watched the execution of maneuvers that were bound to cost the lives of many among us, and my eyes had remained dry."[100] Presumably a general must comfort himself with the thought that the premature deaths of those uprooted youths were insignificant displacements in space and time; would they not have come to an end anyway, obscurely, less gloriously, without the anesthesia of battle and the amends of fame?

Even so, he felt, as many scholars (Ranke, Sorel, Vandal . . .) felt, that he had been more sinned against than sinning; that he had fought and killed in self-defense; that the Allies had vowed to depose him as the "Son of the Revolution" and the usurper of a Bourbon throne. Had he not repeatedly proposed peace and been repulsed? "I only conquered in my own defense. Europe never ceased to war against France, against her principles, and against myself. The Coalition never ceased to exist, either secretly or openly."[101] He had taken, at his coronation, an oath to preserve the "natural boundaries" of France; what would France have said if he had surrendered them? "The vulgar have never ceased blaming all my wars on my ambition. But were they of my choosing? Were they not always determined by the ineluctable nature of things?—by the struggle between the past and the future?"[102] He was always weighed down, after the exuberant first years, by the feeling that no matter how many victories he might win, one decisive defeat would wipe them out and leave him at the mercy of his foes. He would have given half the world for peace, but on his own terms.

We may conclude that until Tilsit (1807) and the invasion of Spain (1808), Napoleon was on the defensive, and that thereafter, in the attempt to subjugate Austria, then Prussia, then Spain, then Russia, and to enforce his Continental Blockade, he brought additional wars upon an exhausted France and a resentful Europe. Though he had proved himself a superlative administrator, he abandoned the cares of state for the glory and ecstasy of war. He had won France as a general, and as a general he lost it. His forte became his fate.

V. THE RULER

As a civilian ruler he never quite forgot that he had been trained as a general. The habits of leadership remained, discouraging, except in the Council of State, objection or debate. "From my first entrance into [public] life I was accustomed to exercise command; circumstances and the force of my character were such that as soon as I possessed power I acknowledged no master and obeyed no laws except those of my own creating."[103] We have seen him, in 1800, emphasizing the civilian form of his rule—when the generals were plotting to depose him; but in 1816 he argued that "in the last analysis, in order to govern, it is necessary to be a military man; one can rule only in boots and spurs."[104] So, with a sharp eye to the secret and contradictory ideals of the French people, he declared himself a man of peace and a genius of war. Hence the relative democracy of the Consulate melted into the monarchy of the Empire, and finally into absolute power. The last of the Napoleonic codes—the penal (1810)—is a reversion to the barbaric severity of medieval penalties. Nevertheless he became almost as brilliant in government as in battle. He predicted that his achievements in administration would outshine his martial victories in human memory, and that his codes were a monument more lasting than his strategy and tactics (which are irrelevant to current war). He longed to be the Justinian as well as the Caesar Augustus of his age.

In the 3,680 days of his imperial rule (1804–14) he was in Paris for only 955,[105] but in these he remade France. When at home, and before 1808, he presided regularly, twice a week, over the Council of State; and then, said Las Cases (himself a member), "none of us would have been absent for the whole world."[106] He worked hard; in his eagerness to get things done he sometimes rose at 3 A.M. to begin his working day. He expected almost as much from his administrative aides. They were always to be ready to give him precise up-to-the-hour information on any matter falling within their jurisdiction; and he judged them by the accuracy, order, readiness, and adequacy of their reports. He did not consider his day finished until he had read the memoranda and documents that almost daily came to him from the various departments of his government. He was probably the best-informed ruler in history.

For major ministries he chose men of first-rate ability, like Talleyrand, Gaudin, and Fouché, despite their troublesome pride; for the rest, and generally for administrative posts, he preferred men of the second rank, who would not ask questions or propose measures of their own; he had no time or patience for such discussions; he would take a chance on his own judgment, assuming the responsibility and risk. He required of his appointees an oath of fidelity, not only to France but to himself; in most cases they readily agreed, feeling the mesmerism of his personality and the grandeur of his designs. "I aroused emulation, rewarded every merit, and pushed back the limits of glory."[107] He paid for his method of selecting aides by gradually surrounding himself with servitors who rarely dared to question his views, so that in the end there was no check upon his haste or pride except the power of his foreign foes. Caulaincourt in 1812 was an exception.

He was severe on his subordinates: stern to reprove and slow to praise, but ready to reward exceptional service. He did not believe in putting them confidently at their ease; some uncertainty of tenure would encourage diligence. He did not necessarily object to their liaisons, nor even to some shady elements in their past, for these gave him a hold on their good behavior.[108] He used his assistants to the limit, then let them retire with a generous pension, and perhaps some sudden title of nobility. Some of them did not survive to that denouement; Villeneuve, defeated at Trafalgar, killed himself rather than face reproof. Napoleon was not long moved by protests against his severity. "A statesman's heart must be in his head";[109] he must not let sentiment interfere with policy; in the operation of an empire the individual counts for little—unless he is a Napoleon. Perhaps he exaggerated his insensitivity to personal charms when he said, "I like only those people who are useful to me, and only so long as they are useful";[110] he continued to love Josephine long after she had become a hindrance to his plans. Of course he lied at need, like most of us; and, like most governments, he doctored his war bulletins to keep up public spirit. He had studied Machiavelli with pencil in hand; an annotated copy of *The Prince* was found in his carriage at Waterloo. He considered good anything that furthered his aims. He did not wait for Nietzsche to lead him "beyond good and evil" in "the will to power"; hence Nietzsche called him "that *Ens realissimum*," and the only good product of the Revolution. "The strong are good, the weak are wicked,"[111] said the Emperor. "Joseph," he mourned, "is too good to be a great man"; but he loved him.

Akin to these views—learned in Corsica and war—was his oft-repeated opinion that men are moved, and can be ruled, only by interest or fear.[112] So, year by year, these feelings became the levers of his government. In 1800, sending General Hédouville to suppress a rising in the Vendée, he advised him, "as a salutary example, to burn down two or three large communes [towns], chosen among those whose conduct is worst. Experience has taught him [the First Consul] that a spectacularly severe act is, in the conditions you are facing, the most humane method. Only weakness is inhuman."[113] He instructed his judicial appointees to pass severe sentences. "The art of the police," he told Fouché, "consists in punishing rarely and severely."[114] He not only employed a large force of police and detectives under Fouché or Régnier, but organized an additional secret police agency whose duty it was to help—and spy on—Fouché and Régnier, and to report to the Emperor any anti-Napoleonic sentiments expressed in the newspapers, the theater, the salons, or in books. "A prince," he said, "should suspect everything."[115] By 1804 France was a police state. By 1810 it had a new supply of minor Bastilles—state prisons in which political offenders could be "detained" by imperial order, without a regular procedure in the courts.[116] We should note, however, that the Emperor had moments of mercy. He issued many pardons, even to those who had plotted to kill him,[117] and sometimes he reduced the severity of a court penalty.[118] To Caulaincourt, in December, 1812, he mused:

> "They think I am stern, even hardhearted. So much the better—this makes it unnecessary for me to justify my reputation. My firmness is taken for callousness. I shall not complain, since this notion is responsible for the good order that is prevailing. . . . Look here, Caulaincourt, I am human. No matter what some people say, I too have entrails ['bowels of mercy'], a heart—but the heart of a sovereign. I am not moved by the tears of a duchess, but the sufferings of the people touch me."[119]

Unquestionably he was a despot, often enlightened, often hastily absolute. He confessed to Las Cases, "The state was myself."[120] Something of his tyranny might be excused as the usual control, by the government, of a nation's economy, theaters, and publications in time of war. Napoleon explained his omnipotence as necessary in the difficult transition from the licentious liberty of the Revolution after 1791 to the reconstructive order of the Consulate and the Empire. He recalled that Robespierre, as well as Marat, had recommended a dictatorship as needed to restore order and stability to a France verging on the dissolution of both the family and the state. He felt that he had not destroyed democracy; what he had replaced in 1799 was an oligarchy of corrupt, merciless, and unscrupulous men. He had destroyed the liberty of the masses, but that liberty was destroying France with mob violence and moral license, and only the restoration and concentration of authority could restore the strength of France as a civilized and independent state.

Until 1810 Napoleon could forgivably feel that he had been true to the Revolution's second goal—equality. He had upheld and spread the equality of all before the law. He had established not an impossible equality of abilities and merits, but an equality of opportunity for all talents, wherever born, to develop themselves in a society offering education, economic opportunity, and political eligibility to all; perhaps this *carrière ouverte aux talents* was his most lasting gift to France. He almost ended corruption in public life;[121] this alone should immortalize him. He gave to all the example of a man using himself up in administration when not called to the battlefield. He remade France.

Why did he fail? Because his grasp exceeded his reach, his imagination dominated his ambition, and his ambition domineered over his body, mind, and character. He should have known that the Powers would never be content to have France rule half of Europe. He succeeded measurably in leading

Rhineland Germany out of feudalism into the nineteenth century, but it was beyond him, or any man at that time, to bring into a lasting federation an area long since partitioned into states each with its jealous traditions, dialect, manners, creed, and government. Just to name those diverse realms, from the Rhine to the Vistula, from Brussels to Naples, is to feel the problem: kingdoms or principalities like Holland, Hanover, Westphalia, the Hanseatic cities, Baden, Bavaria, Württemberg, Illyria, Venice, Lombardy, the Papal States, the Two Sicilies—where could he find men strong enough to rule these areas, to tax them, finally to take their sons to war against nations more akin to them than the French? How could he forge a unity between those forty-four additional departments and the eighty-six of France, or between those proud and sturdy 16 million added people and these proud and volatile 26 million Frenchmen? *Perhaps* it was magnificent to try, but it was certain to fail. In the end imagination toppled reason; the polyglot colossus, standing on one unsteady head, tumbled back into difference, and the rooted force of national character defeated the great dictator's will to power.

VI. THE PHILOSOPHER

And yet, when imagination folded its wings, he could reason with the ablest of the savants in the French and Egyptian Institutes. Though he contrived no formal system of thought in which to imprison a universe that seemed to escape every formula, his realistic mind made short work of "ideologues" who mistook ideas for facts and built airy castles without foundations in biology and history. After trying Laplace and other scientists in administrative posts he concluded, "You can't do anything with a philosopher."[122] However, he encouraged the sciences, and recommended history. "My son should study much history, and meditate upon it," he said at St. Helena, "for it is the only true philosophy."[123]

Religion was one of the fields in which the ideologues had floated on a film of notions instead of grounding themselves in history. Only a logician, Napoleon felt, would bother long with the question, Does God exist? The real philosopher, schooled in history, would ask, why has religion, so often refuted and ridiculed, always survived, and played so notable a role in every civilization? Why did the skeptic Voltaire say that if God did not exist it would be necessary to invent him?

Napoleon himself lost his religious faith at the early age of thirteen. Sometimes he wished he had kept it; "I imagine it must give great and true happiness."[124] Everyone knows the story how, on the trip to Egypt, hearing some scientists discourse irreverently, he challenged them, pointing to the stars, "You may talk as long as you please, gentlemen, but who made all that?"[125] It is possible to quote him pro and con on this and many other subjects, for he changed his views and moods with time, and we tend to ignore their dates; yet what thoughtful person has not at fifty discarded the dogmas he swore by in his youth, and will not at eighty smile at the "mature" views

of his middle age? Generally Napoleon retained belief in an intelligence behind or in the physical world,[126] but he disclaimed any knowledge of its
character or purpose. "Everything proclaims the existence of a God," he
concluded at St. Helena,[127] but "to say whence I came, what I am, or where
I am going is above my comprehension."[128] At times he spoke like a materialistic evolutionist: "Everything is matter;[129] . . . man is only a more perfect
and better reasoning animal."[130] "The soul is not immortal; if it were it
would have existed before our birth."[131] "If I had to have a religion, I should
adore the sun, for it is the sun that fertilizes everything; it is the true god of
the earth."[132] "I should believe in religion if it had existed since the beginning
of the world. But when I read Socrates, Plato, Moses, or Mohammed, I have
no more belief. It has all been invented by men."[133]

But why did they invent it? To comfort the poor, Napoleon answered,
and to keep them from killing the rich. For all men are born unequal, and
become more unequal with every advancement in technology and specializa-
tion; a civilization must elicit, develop, use, and reward superior abilities, and
it must persuade the less fortunate to accept peaceably this inequality of rewards and possessions as natural and necessary. How can this be done? By
teaching men that it is the will of God. "I do not see in religion the mystery
of the Incarnation but the mystery of the social order. Society cannot exist
without inequality of [rewards and therefore] property, an inequality which
cannot be maintained without religion. . . . It must be possible to tell the
poor: 'It is God's will. There must be rich and poor in this world, but here-
after, and for eternity, there will be a different distribution.' "[134] "Religion
introduces into the thought of heaven an idea of equalization which saves
the rich from being massacred by the poor."[135]

If all this be true, it was a mistake of the Enlightenment to attack Christianity, and of the Revolution to make Catholic preaching difficult. "The
intellectual [moral?] anarchy which we are undergoing is the result of the
moral [intellectual?] anarchy—the extinction of faith, the negation of principles [beliefs] which have preceded."[136] Perhaps for this reason, and for
political use, Napoleon restored the Catholic Church as the "sacred gendarmerie [police] of the French nation."* He did not interpret the new
alliance as binding him to the Ten Commandments; he wandered from them
now and then, but he paid the priests to preach them to a generation weary
of chaos and ready for a return to order and discipline. Most parents and
teachers were glad to have the help of religious faith in rearing or training
children—to counter the natural anarchism of youth with a moral code based
upon religious and filial piety, and presented as coming from an omnipotent
God watchful of every act, threatening eternal punishments, and offering
eternal rewards. Most of the governing class were grateful for an educational process that would produce a public taught to accept, as natural and
inevitable, the inequality of abilities and possessions. The old aristocracy was
excused as cleansing its wealth with manners and grace; a new aristocracy

---

* So the Concordat was explained by Louis Bignon, who was designated by Napoleon's
will to write the history of Napoleon's diplomacy.[137]

was established; and revolution, for a generation, muted its voice and hid its guns.

In this regenerated society marriage and motherhood had to be resanctified, and property, not romantic love, had to be restored as their base and goal. Love generated by the physical attraction of boy and girl is an accident of hormones and propinquity; to found a lasting marriage upon such a haphazard and transitory condition is ridiculous; it is *une sottise faite à deux* —"a folly committed in pair."[138] Much of it is artificially induced by romantic literature; it would probably disappear if men were illiterate. "I firmly believe that [romantic] love does more harm than good, and that it would be a blessing . . . if it were banished" as a reason for uniting a man and a woman in the lifelong enterprise of rearing children and acquiring and transmitting property. "Marriage should be forbidden to individuals who have known each other less than six months."[139]

Napoleon had a Mohammedan view of marriage: its function is to produce abundant offspring under conditions of freedom for the man and protection for the faithful and obedient wife. The marriage ceremony, though it may be civil, should be ceremonious and solemn, as emphasizing the obligation undertaken.[140] The married couple should sleep together; this "exerts a singular influence upon married life, guarantees the position of the wife and the dependence of the husband, and preserves intimacy and morality";[141] Napoleon followed this old custom until he set his mind upon divorce.

However, even a faithful wife is not enough for a man. "I find it ridiculous that a man should not be able to have more than one legitimate wife. When she is pregnant it is as if the man had no wife at all."[142] Polygyny is better than divorce or adultery. There should be no divorce after ten years of marriage. A woman should be permitted only one divorce, and should not be allowed to remarry for five years afterward.[143] Adultery on the husband's part should not be sufficient ground for a divorce, unless there is the additional circumstance of the husband's keeping his concubine under the same roof with his wife.[144] "When a husband commits an act of unfaithfulness to his wife, he should confess it to her and regret his action; then every trace of guilt is wiped away. The wife is angry, forgives, and is reconciled to him; often she even gains through it. But that is not the case with the unfaithfulness of the wife. It is all very well for her to confess and regret, but who knows whether something else remains" in her mind or womb? "Therefore she must not, and cannot ever come to an understanding with him."[145] (But he had twice forgiven Josephine.)

He guarded himself against feminine charms by adhering to the Mohammedan view of women. "We treat women too well, and in this way have spoiled everything. We have done every wrong in raising them to our level. Truly the Oriental nations have more mind and sense than we in declaring the wife to be the actual property of the husband. In fact nature has made woman our slave. . . . Woman is given to man that she may bear him children; . . . consequently she is his property, just as the fruit tree is the property of the gardener."[146]

All this is so primitive (and so contrary to biology, where the female usually is the predominant sex, and the male is a tributary food-provider, sometimes himself eaten) that we should be glad to accept Las Cases' assurance that much of it was playful bravado, or the military man's dream of endless conscripts pouring from fertile wombs; but it was quite in harmony with the views of any Corsican *condottiere*. The Code Napoléon insisted on the absolute power of the husband over his wife, and over her property, as a necessity of social order. "I have always thought," Napoleon wrote to Josephine in 1807, "that woman was made for man, and man for country, family, glory, and honor."[147] On the day after the mutual massacre known as the battle of Friedland (June 14, 1807) Napoleon drew up a program for a school to be built at Écouen "for girls who have lost their mothers, and whose people are too poor to bring them up properly."

> What are the girls at Écouen to be taught? You must begin with religion in all its strictness. . . . What we ask of education is not that girls should think, but that they should believe. The weakness of women's brains, the instability of their ideas, . . . their need for perpetual resignation . . . all this can be met only by religion . . . I want the place to produce not women of charm but women of virtue; they must be attractive because they have high principles and warm hearts, not because they are witty or amusing. . . . In addition the girls must be taught writing, arithmetic, and elementary French; . . . a little history and geography; . . . not Latin . . . They must learn to do all kinds of women's work. . . . With the single exception of the headmaster, all men must be excluded from the school . . . Even the gardening must be done by women.[148]

Napoleon's political philosophy was equally uncompromising. Since all men are born unequal, it is inevitable that the majority of brains will be in a minority of men, who will rule the majority with guns or words. Hence utopias of equality are the consolatory myths of the weak; anarchist cries for freedom from laws and government are the delusions of immature and autocratic minds; and democracy is a game used by the strong to conceal their oligarchic rule.[149] Actually France had had to choose between an hereditary nobility and rule by the business class. So, "among nations and in revolutions, aristocracy always exists. If you attempt to get rid of it by destroying the nobility, it immediately reestablishes itself among the rich and powerful families of the Third Estate. Destroy it there, and it survives and takes refuge among the leaders of workmen and of the people."[150] "Democracy, if reasonable, would limit itself to giving everyone an equal opportunity to compete and obtain."[151] Napoleon claimed to have done this by making *la carrière ouverte aux talents* in all fields; but he allowed many deviations from this rule.

He was a bit equivocal about revolutions. They release the violent passions of the mob, since "collective crimes incriminate no one,"[152] and there is "never a revolution without a terror."[153] "Revolutions are the true cause of regeneration in public customs,"[154] but in general (he concluded in 1816) "a revolution is one of the greatest evils by which mankind can be visited. It is the scourge of the generation by which it is brought about; and all the advantages which it procures cannot make amends for the misery with which it embitters the lives of those who take part in it."[155]

He preferred monarchy to all other forms of government, even to defending hereditary kingship (i.e., his own) against doubts expressed by Czar Alexander. [156] "There are more chances of securing a good sovereign by heredity than by election."[157] People are happier under such a stable government than under a free-for-all, devil-take-the-hindmost democracy. "In regular and tranquil times every individual has his share of felicity: the cobbler in his stall is as content as the king on his throne; the soldier is no less happy than the general."[158]

His political ideal was a federation of European, or Continental, states, governed in their external relations from Paris as the "capital of the world." In that "Association Européenne" all the component states would have the same money, weights, measures, and basic laws, with no political barriers to travel, transport, and trade.[159] When Napoleon reached Moscow in 1812 he thought that only a just peace with Alexander remained in the way of realizing his dream. He had underestimated the centrifugal power of national differences; but he may have been right in believing that if Europe achieved unity it would be not through appeals to reason but through the imposition of a superior force continuing through a generation. War would then continue, but at least it would be civil.

As he approached his end he wondered whether he had been a free and creative agent or the helpless instrument of some cosmic force. He was not a fatalist, if this means one who believes that his success or failure, his health or illness, the character of his life and the moment of his death, have been determined by some hidden power, regardless of what he chooses to do;[160] nor was he clearly a determinist in the sense of one who believes that every occurrence, including his every choice, idea, or act, is determined by the composition of all the forces and history of the past. But he repeatedly talked of a "destiny"—a central stream of events, partly malleable by the human will, but basically irresistible as flowing from the inherent nature of things. At times he spoke of his will as strong enough to stem or bend the current—"I have always been able to impose my will upon destiny."[161] Too uncertain to be consistent, he also said: "I depend upon events. I have no will; I await all things from their issue"[162]—as they issue from their source. "The greater one is"—i.e., the higher he is in authority—"the less free will one can have"—the more and stronger will be the forces impinging upon him. "One depends upon circumstances and events. I am the greatest slave among men; my master is the nature of things."[163] He combined his fluctuating moods in the proud conception of himself as an instrument of destiny—i.e., the nature of things as determining the course and terminus of events. "Destiny urges me to a goal of which I am ignorant. Until that goal is reached I am invulnerable, unassailable"—as borne with the stream. "When destiny has accomplished its purpose in me, a fly may suffice to destroy me."[164] He felt himself bound to a destiny magnificent but perilous; pride and circumstance drove him on; "destiny must be fulfilled."[165]

Like all of us he frequently thought of death, and had moods defending or contemplating suicide. In youth he felt that suicide was the final right of every soul; at fifty-one he added: "if his death harms no one."[166] He had no faith in immortality. "There is no immortality but the memory that is left in the minds of men. . . . To have lived without glory, without leaving a trace of one's existence, is not to have lived at all."[167]

VII. WHAT WAS HE?

Was he a Frenchman? Only by the accident of time; otherwise he was French neither in body nor in mind nor in character. He was short, and later stout; his features were stern Roman rather than brightly Gallic; he lacked the gaiety and grace, the humor and wit, the refinement and manners of a cultured Frenchman; he was bent on dominating the world rather than enjoying it. He had some difficulty in speaking French; he retained a foreign accent till 1807;[168] he spoke Italian readily, and seemed more at home in Milan than in Paris. On several occasions he expressed dislike of the French character. "The Emperor," reported Las Cases, "dilated upon our volatile, fickle, and changeable disposition. 'All the French,' he said, 'are turbulent, and inclined to rail. . . . France loves change too much for any government to endure there.' "[169]

He spoke often—with the emphasis of one not sure—of his love for France. He resented being called "the Corsican"; "I wanted to be absolutely French";[170] "the noblest title in the world is that of having been born a Frenchman."[171] But in 1809 he revealed to Roederer what he meant by his love of France: "I have but one passion, one mistress, and that is France. I sleep with her. She has never been false to me. She lavishes her blood and treasure on me. If I need 500,000 men she gives them to me."[172] He loved her as a violinist can love his violin, as an instrument of immediate response to his stroke and will. He drew the strings of this instrument taut until they snapped, nearly all of them at once.

Was he the "Son of the Revolution"? So the Allies sometimes called him; but by this they meant that he had inherited the guilt of the Revolution's crimes, and had continued its repudiation of the Bourbons. He himself repeatedly said that he had brought the Revolution to an end—not only its chaos and violence but its pretenses to democracy. He was the Son of the Revolution insofar as he retained peasant emancipation, free enterprise, equality before the law, career open to talent, and the will to defend the natural frontiers. But when he made himself consul for life, then emperor, when he ended freedom of speech and the press, made the Catholic Church a partner in the government, used new Bastilles, and favored aristocracy old and new—then, surely, he ceased to be the Son of the Revolution. In many ways he remained so in the conquered lands; there he ended feudalism, the

Inquisition, and priestly control of life; there he brought in his Code and some rays of the Enlightenment. But, having so dowered these states, he gave them kings.

Was he rightly, despite his will, called "the Corsican"? Only in his family loyalty, his flair for combat, his passionate defense of France against its foes; but he lacked the Corsican spirit of feud, and his reading of the *philosophes* far removed him from the medieval Catholicism of his native isle. He was Corsican in blood, French in education, and Italian in almost everything else.

Yes, after all attempts to answer them, we must go back to Stendhal and Taine, and say that Napoleon was a *condottiere* of the Italian Renaissance, preserved in mold and type by the isolation, feuds, and wars of Corsica. He was Cesare Borgia with twice the brains, and Machiavelli with half the caution and a hundred times the will. He was an Italian made skeptical by Voltaire, subtle by the ruses of survival in the Revolution, sharp by the daily duel of French intellects. All the qualities of Renaissance Italy appeared in him: artist and warrior, philosopher and despot; unified in instincts and purposes, quick and penetrating in thought, direct and overwhelming in action, but unable to stop. Barring that vital fault, he was the finest master of controlled complexity and coordinated energy in history. Tocqueville put it well: he was as great as a man can be without virtue, and he was as wise as a man can be without modesty. Nevertheless he remained within the bounds of probability when he predicted that the world would not see the likes of him for many centuries.

CHAPTER XI

Napoleonic France

1800–1815

I. THE ECONOMY

THOUGH raised to be a soldier, Napoleon had a sound sense of economic realities as the fate of families, the subsoil of culture, and the strength and weakness of a state. Generally, despite an itch to regulate, he ranged himself on the side of free enterprise, open competition, and private property. He paid little attention to the socialistic plans of Charles Fourier and others for the communal production of goods and the equitable distribution of the product. He felt sure that in any society the abler minority will soon govern the majority, and absorb the greater part of the wealth; moreover, the inspiration of a communist ideal cannot long take the place of differential rewards in reconciling men to toil; in frank analysis, "it is hunger that makes the world move."[1] Moreover, communal ownership is a perpetual temptation to carelessness. "Whilst an individual owner, with a personal interest in his property, is always wide awake, and brings his plans to fruition, communal interest is inherently sleepy and unproductive, because individual enterprise is a matter of instinct, and communal enterprise is a matter of public spirit, which is rare."[2] So he opened all doors, all careers, to all men, of whatever fortune or pedigree; and until the later years of his rule France enjoyed a prosperity that brought peace to all classes; there was no unemployment,[3] no political revolt. "Nobody is interested in overthrowing a government in which all the deserving are employed."[4]

It was a prime principle with Napoleon that state "finances founded upon a good system of agriculture never fail."[5] Overseeing everything, overlooking nothing, he saw to it that protective tariffs, reliable financing, and well-maintained transport by roads and canals should encourage the peasants to labor steadily, to buy land, to bring more and more of it under cultivation, and to provide sturdy youngsters for his armies. Too many French farmers were sharecroppers or hired farm laborers, but half a million of them, by 1814, owned the acres that they sowed. An English lady traveling in France in that year described the peasants as enjoying a degree of prosperity unknown to their class anywhere else in Europe.[6] These tillers of the soil looked to Napoleon as a living guarantee of their title deeds, and remained loyal to him until their lands languished in the absence of their conscripted sons.

Industry too was a prime interest with Napoleon. He made it a point to visit factories, to show interest in processes and products, in the artisans and the managers. He aspired to bring science to the service of industry. He set up industrial exhibitions—in 1801 in the Louvre, and in 1806 under immense tents in the Place des Invalides. He organized the École des Arts et Métiers, and rewarded inventors and scientists. Experiments with steam propulsion were made in 1802 with a clumsy engine on a barge in a canal near Paris; their success was not convincing, but they spurred further efforts. In 1803 Robert Fulton offered a plan for applying steam power to navigation; Napoleon turned it over to the Institut National, where, after two months of experiment, it was rejected as impracticable. French industry developed more slowly than the British, having fewer markets, less capital, and less machinery. However, in 1801, Joseph-Marie Jacquard exhibited his new apparatus for weaving; in 1806 the French government bought the invention and distributed it; French textile industry became competitive with the British. The silk industry in Lyons, which in 1800 had 3,500 looms, used 10,720 in 1808;[7] and in 1810 one textile entrepreneur employed eleven thousand workers in his mills.[8] Meanwhile French chemists continued to meet the British exclusion of sugar, cotton, and indigo by making sugar from beetroot, dyes from woad, and linens superior to cotton;[9] also they turned potatoes into brandy.

Napoleon helped French industries with protective tariffs and the Continental Blockade, tided them over financial difficulties with loans on easy terms, opened up new markets for French products in his expanding empire, and took up any slack of employment by extensive public works. Some of these were monuments to the glory of Napoleon and his armies, like the Vendôme Column, the Madeleine, and the triumphal Arcs du Carrousel and de l'Étoile; some were military fortifications or facilities, like the fortress, dike, and port of Cherbourg; some were utilitarian structures artistically designed, like the Bourse, the Bank of France, the General Post Office, the Théâtre de l'Odéon, even the Halles des Blés or des Vins—the stately emporiums of corn or wines (1811). Some were aids to agriculture, like the draining of marshes; some to transport and trade. Here belong the opening of new streets in Paris, like the Rues de Rivoli, de Castiglione, de la Paix, and two miles of *quais*, like the Quai d'Orsay, along the Seine; more important, 33,500 miles of new roads in France, and countless bridges, including the Ponts d'Austerlitz and d'Iéna in Paris; add the deepening of river beds and the extension of France's magnificent system of canals. Major canals were dug connecting Paris with Lyons, and connecting Lyons with Strasbourg and Bordeaux. Napoleon fell before two other systems could be completed: canals binding the Rhine with the Danube and the Rhone, and binding Venice with Genoa.[10]

The workers who dug the canals, raised the triumphal arches, and manned the factories were not allowed to go on strike, or to form unions to bargain for better working conditions or higher pay. However, Napoleon's government saw to it that wages should keep abreast of prices, that bakers and butchers and manufacturers were under state regulation, and that—especially in Paris—the necessaries of life should be plentifully supplied. Until the last years of Napoleon's rule, wages rose faster than prices, and the proletariat, sharing modestly in the general prosperity and proud of Napoleon's victories, became more patriotic than the bourgeoisie. It gave scant hearing to bourgeois liberals, like Mme. de Staël or Benjamin Constant, preaching liberty.

Nevertheless there were sources and voices of discontent. As free enterprise progressively enriched the clever, some men perceived that equality withers under liberty, and that a *laissez-faire* government allows the concentration of wealth to exclude half of the population from the fruits of invention and the graces of civilization. In 1808 François-Marie Fourier issued his *Théorie des quatre mouvements et des destinées générales*—the first classic of utopian socialism. He proposed that those dissatisfied with the existing organization of industry should unite in cooperative communities (*phalanges*), each of some four hundred families, living together in a phalanstery, or common building; that all members should spend part of the working day in agriculture (collectively organized), part in domestic or group industry, part in leisure or cultural pursuits; that each individual should perform a variety of tasks, and should change his occupation occasionally; that each individual should share equally in the products or profits of the phalanx; and that each phalanx should have a community center, a school, a library, a hotel, and a bank. This plan inspired idealists in both hemispheres, and Brook Farm, near Boston, was only one of several utopian communities that were soon cut down by the natural individualism of men.

Napoleon himself was not very fond of capitalism. He called the Americans "mere merchants," who "put all their glory into making money."[11] He encouraged French commerce by the multiplication and maintenance of all avenues of transport and trade, and by the supply and steadiness of money; but he discouraged it by the thousand and one regulations of the Continental Blockade. Finally yielding to complaints, he issued (1810–11) licenses for the export of certain goods to Britain, and for the import of sugar, coffee, and other foreign products. He charged for these licenses, and a good deal of favoritism and corruption entered into their issuance.[12] Petty tradesmen fared better in France than wholesale merchants as industry grew; stores were stocked beyond French precedent as agriculture, industry, and transport expanded; and frequented streets blossomed with colorful boutiques; but the great port cities—Marseilles, Bordeaux, Nantes, Le Havre, Antwerp, and Amsterdam—were in decay, and the merchants were turning against Napoleon and his blockade.

His greatest success as an administrator was in finance. Strange to say, his wars, till 1812, usually brought in more than they cost; he put upon his enemies the onus of beginning the action; and when he defeated them he charged high fees—and Old Masters—for the lesson. Part of these gleanings he kept under his personal control as a *domaine extraordinaire*. He boasted in 1811 that he had 300,000,000 gold francs in the *caves des Tuileries*.[13] He used this fund to ease stringencies in the Treasury, to correct dangerous turns in the stock market, to finance public works or municipal improvements, to reward signal services, to distinguish artists and writers, to rescue embarrassed industries, to bribe a friend or an enemy, and to pay for his secret police. Enough remained to prepare for the next war, and to keep taxes far below their level under Louis XVI or the Revolution.[14]

"Before 1789," says Taine, "the peasant proprietor paid, on 100 francs' net income, 14 to the seignior, 14 to the clergy, 53 to the state, and kept only 18 or 19 for himself; after 1800 he pays nothing of his 100 francs of income to the seignior or the clergy; he pays little to the state, only 25 francs to the commune and *département*, and keeps 70 for his pocket."[16] Before 1789 the manual worker had labored from twenty to thirty-nine of his working days per year to pay his taxes; after 1800, from six to nineteen days. "Through the almost complete exemption [from taxes] of those who have no property, the burden of direct taxation falls almost entirely on those who own property."[16] However, there were many "extremely moderate" indirect or sales taxes, which fell upon all persons equally, and were therefore harder on the poor than on the rich. Toward the end of the imperial regime the costs of war far exceeded its returns; taxes and prices rose, and public discontent spread.

A crisis in finances in 1805 led Napoleon to reorganize the Bank of France, which had been established in 1800 under private management. While he was fighting for his political life at Marengo a group of speculators led by Gabriel-Julien Ouvrard secured control of army supplies. Running into difficulties, they appealed to the bank for a considerable loan; to raise this money the bank, with the permission of the Treasury, issued its own notes as legal currency; these failed to win acceptance in financial transactions, and fell to ninety percent of their face value; the company and the bank faced bankruptcy. On his return to Paris Napoleon rescued the bank with part of the indemnities received from Austria, but he insisted that henceforth it be "under control of the state, but not too much so." On April 22, 1806, he placed it under a governor and two vice-governors appointed by the government, and fifteen regents chosen by the shareholders. This new Banque de France opened branches at Lyons, Rouen, and Lille, and began a long career of service to the French economy and the state. The government still owns only a minority of the bank's shares.

Napoleon had small respect for the men who sold supplies to his army and ministries. He took it for granted that every contractor padded his bills, and that some of them offered shoddy materials at first-rate prices. He instructed his appointees to strictly check all bills presented to them, and sometimes he did this himself. "All the contractors," he told Bourrienne, "all the provision agents, are rogues. . . . They possess millions, roll in insolent luxury, while my soldiers have neither bread nor shoes. I will have no more of that!"[17] At Vienna in 1809 he received complaints of defective clothing and equipment sold to his army; he ordered an inquiry, which showed that the contractors had made large undue profits in these sales; he ordered a court-martial; this condemned the embezzlers to death. Every influence was made to save them, but Napoleon refused pardon, and the sentence was carried out.[18]

By and large, as hostile critics agree,[19] the first thirteen years of Napoleon's rule gave France the greatest prosperity she had ever known. When Las Cases, a titled and forgiven *émigré*, returned in 1805 from a tour of sixty *départements*, he reported that "France had at no period of her history been more powerful, more flourishing, better governed, and happier."[20] In 1813 the Comte de Montalivet, minister of the interior, claimed that this continuing prosperity was due to "the suppression of feudalism, titles, mortmain, and monastic orders; . . . to the more equal distribution of wealth, to the clearness and simplification of the laws."[21] In 1800 the population of France was approximately 28 million; in 1813 it was 30 million. It does not seem to be a startling gain, but if the same rate of growth (even uncompounded) had continued till 1870 Napoleon's nephew would have had 50 million men to meet the challenge of Bismarck's Germany.

II. THE TEACHERS

We have observed Napoleon, during his Consulate, trying to give a new order and stability to postrevolutionary France by a Code of Civil Law, and a Concordat of peace and cooperation between his government and the traditional religion of the people. To these formative forces he proposed to add a third by reorganizing the educational system of France. "Of all social engines, the school is probably the most efficacious, for it exercises three kinds of influence on the young lives it enfolds and directs: one through the master, another through con-discipleship, and the last through rules and regulations."[22] He was convinced that one reason for the breakdown of law and order during the Revolution was its inability to establish, amid the life-and-death conflicts of the time, a system of education adequately replacing that which the Church had previously maintained. Splendid plans had been formulated, but neither money nor time could be spared to realize them; primary education had been left to priests and nuns, or to lay schoolmasters maintained just above starvation by parents or communes; secondary education had barely survived in lycées dispensing courses in science and history, with scant attention to the formation of character. Napoleon thought of public education in political terms: its function was to produce intelligent but obedient citizens. "In establishing a corps of teachers," he said, with a candor unusual in governments, "my principal aim is to secure the means for directing political and moral opinions. . . . So long as one grows up without knowing whether to be republican or monarchist, Catholic or irreligious, the state will never form a nation; it will rest on vague and uncertain foundations; it will be constantly exposed to disorder and change."[23]

Having restored the Church to association with the government, he allowed semimonastic organizations, like the Frères des Écoles Chrétiennes, to attend to primary instruction, and nuns to teach well-to-do girls; but he refused to let the Jesuits reenter France. Nevertheless, he admired them for their strict organization as a dedicated guild of teachers. "The essential thing," he wrote (February 16, 1805), "is a teaching body like that of the Jesuits of old."[24] "While I was with him," Bourrienne recalled, "he often told me that it was necessary that all schools, colleges, and other establishments for public instruction be subject to military discipline."[25] In a note of 1805 Napoleon proposed that "a teaching order could be formed if all the managers, directors, and professors in the Empire were under one or more chiefs, like the generals, provincials, etc., of the Jesuits," and if it were the rule that no one could fill a higher position in the organization unless he had passed through various lower stages. It would be desirable, too, that the teacher not marry, or that he defer marriage "till he has secured an adequate position and income . . . to support a family."[26]

A year later (May 10, 1806) Antoine-François de Fourcroy, director general of public instruction, secured from the Corps Législatif a provisional decree that "there shall be established, under the name of the Imperial University, a body exclusively charged with the work of teaching throughout the Empire." (The University of Paris, founded c.1150, had been suppressed by the Revolution in 1790.) This new university was to be not merely a union of various faculties—theology, law, medicine, science, and literature; it was to be the sole producer of teachers for the secondary schools of France, and was to include all its living and teaching graduates. These "lycées" were to be established in one or more cities of each *département*, with a curriculum combining the classic languages and literatures with the sciences; they were to be financed by the municipality, but all their teachers were to be graduates of the university; and no one was to be promoted to a higher post unless he had previously held those below it,[27] and had obeyed his superiors like a soldier obeying an officer. To persuade French youths to enter this treadmill, Napoleon provided 6,400 scholarships, whose recipients pledged themselves to the teaching profession and promised to defer marriage at least to the age of twenty-five. As their final reward they were to "have clearly before them the prospect of rising to the highest offices of the state."[28] "All this," Napoleon told Fourcroy, "is only a commencement; by and by we shall do more, and better."[29]

He did better, from his point of view, by restoring (1810), as a branch of the university, the École Normale, where select students, living in common under military discipline, were given special training by a prestigious faculty including such masters as Laplace, Lagrange, Berthollet, and Monge. By 1813 all college teachers were expected to be graduates of the École Normale; science began to prevail over the classics in the college curriculum, and set the intellectual tone of educated France. The École Polytechnique, established during the Revolution, was changed into a military academy, where the physical sciences became the servants of war. Several provincial universities survived the Emperor's martial sweep, and private colleges were allowed to operate under license and periodical examination by the university. As the authoritarian mood relaxed, individual lecturers were permitted to use university halls to give special courses, and students were allowed to take these as they chose.

At the top of the intellectual pyramid was the Institut National de France. The French Academy, suppressed in 1793, had been restored in 1795 as Class II of the new Institute. Napoleon was proud of his membership in the Institute, but when its moral and political section, in 1801, presumed to discourse on how a government should be run, he ordered Comte Louis-Philippe de Ségur to "tell the Second Class of the Institute that I will have no political subjects treated at its meetings."[30] The Institute then contained many old rebels faithful to the Enlightenment and the Revolution, who privately laughed or wept at the official restoration of the Catholic Church. Cabanis and Destutt de Tracy had used the word *ideology* as the study of the formation of ideas; Napoleon called these psychologists and philosophers "ideologues" as men too immersed in ideas, and reveling in reason, to perceive and understand the realities of life and history. These intellectuals, spreading their notions through countless publications, were, in his judgment, obstacles to good government. "The men who write well and are eloquent," he said, "have no solidity of judgment."[31] He cautioned his brother Joseph, then (July 18, 1807) ruling Naples: "You live too much with literary people." As for the intellectuals who were buzzing in the salons, "I regard scholars and wits the same as coquettish women; one should frequent them and talk with them, but never choose one's wife from among such women, or one's ministers from among such men."[32]

On January 23, 1803, he reorganized the Institute into four classes, omitting the moral and political category. Class I, which he valued most, was to study the sciences. Among its sixty members were Adrien Legendre, Monge, Biot, Berthollet, Gay-Lussac, Laplace, Lamarck, Geoffroy Saint-Hilaire, and Cuvier. Class II had forty members, devoted to the language and literature of France; it replaced the old French Academy, and resumed work on the *Dictionnaire;* it included the old poet Delille, the famous dramatist Marie-Joseph de Chénier, the young historian Guizot, the Romantic stylist Chateaubriand, the philosophers Volney, Destutt de Tracy, and Maine de Biran. Class III, with forty members, dealt with ancient and Oriental history, literature, and art; here Louis Langlès pursued those studies of Persia and India that had already led to the École des Langues Orientales (1795); and Jean-Baptiste d'Ansse de Villoison discovered the Alexandrian commentators on Homer, so paving the way for F. A. Wolf's revealing theorem that "Homer" was many men. Class IV—the Académie des Beaux-Arts—included ten painters, six sculptors, six architects, three engravers, and three composers; here shone David, Ingres, and Houdon.

Aside from his distaste for ideologues, Napoleon supported the Institute heartily, eager to make it an embellishment of his reign. Every member of the Institute received from the government an annual salary of fifteen hundred francs; each permanent secretary of a class received six thousand. In February and March each class presented to the Emperor a report of the work done in its department. Napoleon was pleased with the total picture, for (Méneval claimed) "this general review of literature, science, and art . . . showed that human intelligence, far from going back, did not halt in its constant march toward progress."[33] We may question the "constant," but there is no doubt that the reorganization of science and scholarship under Napoleon placed their practitioners at the head of the European intellect for half a century.

III. THE WARRIORS

After education, conscription. War had been made more frequent, more homicidal, and more costly by the Revolution: the levy en masse in 1793 established the rule that war should be no longer the sport of princes using mercenaries, but a struggle of nations involving every class—though it was some time before the other governments followed the French in allowing commoners to become officers, even marshals. Rousseau had already laid down the principle that universal service was a logical corollary of universal suffrage: he who would vote should serve. Facing the European monarchies in a struggle to preserve its republic, France, which, before Louis XIV, had been a medley of proud regions with no national spirit binding the whole, was united in 1793 by a common fear. Its response was national and decisive. A large army, calling all men, became necessary; conscription began; and when masses of Frenchmen, inspired as armies had rarely been before, began to defeat the professional soldiers of the feudal monarchies, these countries too enforced conscription, and war became a conflict of masses competing in massacre. The glory of nationalism replaced the pride of dynasties as the tonic of war.

In 1803, faced with the rupture of the Peace of Amiens, and anticipating war with another coalition, Napoleon issued a new law of conscription: all males between twenty and twenty-five years of age were made subject to the draft. Many were exempted: young married men, seminarians, widowers or divorcés with children, anyone who had a brother already taken, and the eldest of three orphans. Moreover, a draftee could pay a substitute to take his place. At first this seemed to Napoleon to be unjust; then he allowed it, chiefly on the ground that advanced students should be left to continue their studies to fit themselves for administrative posts.[34]

This annual insistence that it is *dulce et decorum pro patria mori* was borne patiently by the French people in the ecstasy of Napoleon's victories; but when defeats began (1808), and left thousands of families grieving, resistance grew, evaders and deserters multiplied. By 1814 Napoleon had recruited 2,613,000 Frenchmen for his armies;[35] approximately a million of these died of wounds or disease;[36] add half a million enlisted or conscripted from foreign countries allied or subject to France. In 1809 Napoleon asked Czar Alexander to mediate between France and England, saying that a general peace would allow an end to conscription; that hope passed. As defeated enemies seemed to rise from their graves for new coalitions and campaigns, Napoleon kept many conscripts beyond their statutory five-year terms, and called up annual classes before their time, until in 1813 he summoned the class of 1815.[37] At last the patience of French parents gave way, and the cry of "Down with conscription!" rose everywhere in France.

By such methods grew the Grande Armée, which was Napoleon's love and pride. He fostered its spirit by giving each regiment its own colorful standard, which some brave youth would carry into the battle to lead and inspire its men; if he fell, another youth would rush up, pick up the flag, and carry it on. Usually this banner became the visible soul of the regiment; almost always it survived to display its remnants in victory parades, and at last to hang as a tattered but sacred trophy in the church of the Invalides. Nearly every regiment had its distinctive uniform and name, once famous from Brest to Nice, from Antwerp to Bordeaux: Grenadiers, Hussars, Chasseurs, Lancers, Dragoons . . . Above all there were the 92,000 men who formed the Imperial Guard, kept in protective reserve around the Emperor until some crisis called for their lives. Any conscript could rise to membership in the Guard, and even to wield a baton as one of the eighteen marshals of Napoleonic France.

The results of the wars were endless—biological, economic, political, and moral. The old figure of 1,700,000 Frenchmen dead in those campaigns[38] has been reduced by later calculations to a million men;[39] even so these presumably premature deaths may have weakened France for a generation, until her wombs made up the loss. Economically the wars, and the stimulus of blockaded ports and military needs, accelerated the growth of industry. Politically they strengthened the unification of regional governments and loyalties under a central rule. Morally the constant conflicts habituated Europe to the enlargement of wars, and to a code of slaughter unknown since the barbarian invasions. At the fronts, and then in the capitals, the rulers laid aside the Ten Commandments. "War justifies everything," Napoleon wrote to General Berthier in 1809;[40] "nothing has ever been established except by the sword";[41] and "in the last analysis there must be a military quality in government";[42] without an army there is no state.

To accustom the French people to this martial ethic Napoleon appealed to their love of glory. *La gloire* became a national fever generating enthusiastic concord and obedience; so Napoleon could say that "the wars of the Revolution have ennobled the entire French nation."[43] For ten years, with the help of the Allies, he kept his people in this hypnotic trance. Let Alfred de Musset, who was there, describe the mood of France in 1810:

> It was in this air of the spotless sky, where shone so much glory, where glistened so many swords, that the youth of the time breathed. They well knew that they were destined to the hecatomb, but they regarded Murat as invincible, and the Emperor had been seen to cross a bridge where so many bullets whistled that they wondered was he immune to death. And even if one must die, what did it matter? Death itself was so beautiful, so noble, so illustrious, in his battle-scarred purple! It borrowed the color of hope; it reaped

so many ripening harvests, that it became young, and there was no more old age. All the cradles of France, as well as its tombs, were armed with shield and buckler; there were no more old men; there were corpses or demi-gods.[44]

Meanwhile, at the front, Napoleon's soldiers stole and gambled, and drank their fears to sleep; his generals stole according to their station; Masséna amassed millions, and Soult was not far behind. Amiable Josephine, kindly Joseph, brave Lucien, and uncle Cardinal Fesch profited by investing in firms that were selling shoddy goods to French troops. Napoleon colored his war bulletins with exaggeration and concealment, bled the treasuries of defeated nations, appropriated their art, and pondered ways to effect the moral regeneration of France.

IV. MORALS AND MANNERS

The Revolution, by breaking down political and parental authority, and dismissing religious belief, had let loose the individualistic instincts of the French people—moderately in the provinces, catastrophically in the capital; the center of law found itself struggling within the center of chaos and crime. Napoleon, himself lawless, determined to restore stability to morals and manners as vital to the regeneration of France, the sanity and contentment of its people, and the success of his rule. He made it clear that he would keep a stern eye on all business relations in or with the government, and would punish severely all detected dishonesty. He set his face against immodest dress in society or on the stage; he reprimanded his brother Lucien and his sister Elisa for displaying too much of their flesh in private theatricals; and when, at a soiree, he found himself confronted by Mme. de Staël in low and ample décolleté, he remarked pointedly, "I presume that you nurse your children yourself?"[45] He insisted that Talleyrand marry his mistress. Mme. Tallien, who had directed Directory morals by the curve of her hips, disappeared into the provinces; Josephine said goodbye to adultery, and her frightened milliners cut their bills in half. The new Code gave the husband almost Roman powers over his wife and children; the family resumed its function of turning animals into citizens, at whatever cost to personal freedom.

The mood of the age suffered some darkening as part price of the new discipline. The reckless gaiety of the sexes and the classes under the Revolution yielded to bourgeois propriety and proletarian fatigue. The class barriers that had graded and steadied the population in Bourbon days gave way to a restless fever of competition as "career open to talents" built stairs between all tiers,[46] and set rootless youths climbing the slippery pyramids to power. Such deductions made, Napoleon was justified in feeling that under his rule morality returned to France, and manners regained some of the courtesy that had eased and graced prerevolutionary life in literate France.

He felt that despite all efforts to equalize opportunity some form of class distinction would inevitably develop from the natural diversity of abilities and environments. To keep this result from being merely an aristocracy of wealth, he established in 1802 the Legion of Honor, to be composed of men, chosen by the government, who had distinguished themselves by special excellence in their fields—war, law, religion, science, scholarship, art . . . It was to be half as democratic as life: all men were eligible, but no women. The members swore, on admission, to support the principles of liberty and equality; but they were soon graded into classes according to their merit or influence or tenure. Each received from the French government an annual stipend: 5,000 francs for a "grand officer," 2,000 to a "commander," 1,000 to an "officer," 250 to a "chevalier."[47] To distinguish them, the members were to wear a ribbon or a cross. When some councilors smiled at such "baubles," Napoleon replied that men are more easily led by decorations than by authority or force; "one obtains everything from men by appealing to their sense of honor."[48]

The Emperor took another step toward a new aristocracy by creating (1807) the "Imperial Nobility," conferring titles upon his relatives, his marshals, certain administrative officers, and outstanding savants; so, in the next seven years, he made 31 dukes, 452 counts, 1,500 barons, 1,474 chevaliers. Talleyrand became prince of Benevento, Fouché became Duc d'Otrante (Otranto); Joseph Bonaparte was suddenly grand elector, Louis Bonaparte was grand constable; Murat, cavalry leader, was surprised to find himself grand admiral; Marshal Davout was christened Duc d'Auerstedt; Lannes, Duc de Montebello; Savary, Duc de Rovigo; Lefebvre, Duc de Dantzig. Laplace and Volney became counts, and Napoleon's sisters blossomed into princesses. With each title went a colorful and distinctive uniform, an annual revenue, sometimes a substantial estate. Moreover—and here Napoleon frankly turned his back upon the republic—most of these titles were made hereditary. Only with transmissible property, in Napoleon's view, could his new aristocrats maintain their position and authority, and thereby serve as a support to the ruler. The Emperor himself, to keep a step or two ahead of the new aristocracy—which soon flaunted its titles, uniforms, and powers— guarded himself with chamberlains, equerries, prefects of the palace, and a hundred other servitors; and Josephine was equipped with ladies-in-waiting whose titles came from the Bourbons or beyond.

Still unsated, he turned to the survivors of the old nobility, and used every lure to draw them to his court. He had called many of them back to France as a foil to the still revolutionary Jacobins, and in the hope of establishing continuity between the old France and the new. This seemed impossible, for the returning émigrés scorned Napoleon as a parvenu usurper, denounced his policies, satirized his manners, looks, and speech, and made fun of his new aristocracy. Gradually, however, as his prestige mounted with his victories, and as France rose to such power and wealth as not even Louis XIV had won for her, this lofty attitude bent: the younger sons of the émigrés gladly accepted appointments in the Upstart's service;[49] grandes dames came to attend Josephine; and at last some nobles of ancient vintage—Montmorencys, Montesquious, Ségurs, Gramonts, Noailles, Turennes—added their aura to the imperial court, and were rewarded with partial restoration of their confiscated estates. After the marriage with Marie Louise the reconciliation seemed complete. But much of it was superficial; the newer sons and daughters of the Revolution did not relish the superior manners and prestige of the pedigreed; the Army, still fond of its revolutionary ideals, grumbled to see its idol exchanging bows with ancient foes; these looked down upon the tall generals, the nervous savants, and the ambitious Bonapartes, who had presumed to replace them.

To keep this den of lions from open war with words or swords, Napoleon insisted upon a code of etiquette. He commissioned some specialists to draw up, from the best Bourbon models, a manual of manners designed to meet every situation courteously; they did, to a bulk of eight hundred pages;[50] philosophers and grenadiers studied it; and the imperial court became a model of brilliant dress and empty speech. The courtiers played cards, but, as Napoleon forbade playing for money, the cards lost their value. Plays were performed, concerts were given, there were stately ceremonies and massive balls. When the excitement of comparing costumes and matching wit declined, the more intimate members of the court moved with Emperor and Empress to St.-Cloud, or Rambouillet, or Trianon, or, most happily, to Fontainebleau, where formality loosened its stays, and hunting warmed the blood.

No one was so irked by this regal ritual as Napoleon, and he avoided it as much as he could. "Etiquette," he said, "is the prison of kings."[51] And to Las Cases: "Necessity compelled me to observe a degree of state, to adopt a certain system of solemnity—in a word, to establish etiquette. Otherwise I should have been every day liable to be slapped on the shoulder."[52] As for ceremonies, they too had their rationale. "A newly established government must dazzle and astonish. The moment it ceases to glitter it falls."[53] "Display is to power what ceremony is to religion."[54] "Is it not a fact that the Catholic religion appeals more strongly to the imagination by the pomp of its ceremonies than by the sublimity of its doctrines? When you want to arouse enthusiasm in the masses you must appeal to their eyes."[55]

As usual in history, the manners of the court passed down, tapering, to the literate population. "It took only ten or twelve years," said the learned "Bibliophile Jacob" (Paul Lacroix) "to make of the grand monde of the Directory a decent, polished, and well-brought-up society."[56] This was especially true of Lyons and Bordeaux, not to speak of Paris where, said Mme. de Staël, "so many persons of intellect came together, . . . and so many were accustomed to employ that intellect in adding to the pleasures of conversation."[57] Napoleon, reported Las Cases, "rendered justice to the delicate tact which distinguished the inhabitants of the French capital; nowhere, he said, could be found so much wit, or more taste."[58] A hundred cafés gathered a gregarious people to sit and sip, to exchange news and repartees, while before them the mobile world passed in unwilling parade, each animalcule centering the world around itself. Fine restaurants had disappeared during the Terror, had reopened under the Directory, and began now their reign over the tastes and purses of the French people. It was during the Consulate and the Empire that Anthelme Brillat-Savarin accumulated the facts and legends that swelled his classic of gastronomy, *La Physiologie du goût*, which reached print only a year (1826) before his death.

Styles of speech and dress were changing. *Citoyen* and *Citoyenne* were being replaced by the prerevolutionary *Monsieur* and *Madame*. Men of fashion reverted to knee breeches and silk stockings, but pantaloons regained supremacy as the Empire waned. The ladies, abandoning the *style grecque* of the Directory, returned to skirts and bodices. Décolleté remained generous, with bare shoulders and arms; Napoleon opposed the fashion, Josephine approved of it; her pretty arms and shoulders and buttressed bosom won.[59]

The Emperor gave his approval to masked balls, for he was glad to see social life revive. He did not care for the salons that were flourishing in Paris. They were becoming a refuge of politicians, authors, and "ideologues" critical of his increasingly dictatorial regime. His brothers Joseph and Lucien organized frequent receptions where the talk was necessarily favorable to the Emperor and generally hostile to Josephine; Fouché and Talleyrand held their own courts, where criticism was polite; the returned *émigrés* excoriated all the Bonapartes in somber soirees in the Faubourg St.-Germain; and Mme. de Staël maintained her famous salon as part of her fifteen years' war against Napoleon. Mme. de Genlis, returning to France after seven years as an *émigrée*, devoted her salon and her writings to defending the Emperor against Bourbons, Jacobins, Mme. de Staël, and Mme. Récamier.

V. MME. RÉCAMIER

La Récamier's salon owed its success to her enticing beauty and her husband's complaisant wealth. Born in Lyons in 1777, named Jeanne-Françoise-Julie-Adélaïde Bernard, and known to her friends as Julie or Juliette, she was endowed with a loveliness of face and figure that survived even when she had become seventy and blind. She developed almost every charm of the feminine character—kindness, sympathy, tenderness, taste, grace, tact . . . She added to this a sensuous pliancy that stirred a hundred males without any known harm to her virginity. In 1793, aged sixteen, she married Jacques-Rose Récamier, who was forty-two but a banker. He was so pleased to contemplate her beauty, to hear her singing, to watch her delicate hands drawing sentiment from her piano or her harp, that he cushioned her in every comfort, financed her career as a *salonnière*, bore with paternal indulgence the conquests that she made, herself unconquered, and apparently did not insist on his marital rights.[60]

In 1798 he bought the Parisian home of Jacques Necker, on the Rue du Mont-Blanc. During that transaction Juliette, twenty-one, met Mme. de Staël, thirty-two; it was only a casual encounter, but it began a lifelong friendship that even rivalry in love could not end. Inspired by the success with which the older woman had brought to her salon the most prominent statesmen and authors of the time, Juliette in 1799 opened her new home to periodical gatherings of men and women prominent in the political, cultural, or social life of Paris. Lucien Bonaparte, the minister of the interior, lost little time in declaring to her his imperishable love. She showed his flaming letters to her husband, who advised her to treat Lucien with patience lest the Récamier bank incur the hostility of the rising dynasty. Napoleon extinguished Lucien's fire by sending him as ambassador to Spain. Perhaps he himself had cast an eye upon Juliette as a "morsel for a king."[61] She had quite other inclinations. Despite her husband's cautions, and her father's precarious position as postmaster general in the consular government, she welcomed to her salon royalists like Mathieu de Montmorency, anti-Napoleon generals like Bernadotte and Moreau, and others who resented the First Consul's increasingly imperial ways.

She was now in the prime of her beauty, and the leading painters were glad to have her sit for them. David portrayed her in the favorite pose of current goddesses—reclining on a couch, and loosely dressed in a Grecian gown that left bare her arms and feet. M. Récamier felt that David had not caught the demure loveliness of his wife; he challenged François Gérard, David's pupil, to rival his master; Gérard succeeded so well that David never forgave him.[62]

In 1802 Juliette and her mother visited England, where dignitaries like the Prince of Wales and belles like the Duchess of Devonshire received her with all the honors due to her beauty and her anti-Bonapartist sentiments. Soon after her return to France her father was arrested for having connived at secret negotiations between Parisian royalists and the rebel Chouans of the Vendée; he was arrested, and was in danger of being sentenced to death, when his distracted daughter persuaded Bernadotte to go to Napoleon and intercede for M. Bernard's release. Napoleon consented, but dismissed him from his post. "The government," Juliette admitted, "had a perfect right to remove him."[63]

In 1806 her husband appealed to the Bank of France to save him from bankruptcy by lending him a million francs. The directors referred the request to Napoleon, who, returning from Marengo, found the bank itself involved in difficulties; he forbade the loan. Récamier sold the house on the Rue du Mont-Blanc; Juliette sold her silver and jewelry, and, without complaint, accepted a simpler life. But she came close to a breakdown when, on January 20, 1807, her mother died. Hearing of this, Mme. de Staël invited her to come for a stay in the Necker château at Coppet in Switzerland. M. Récamier, absorbed in a struggle to regain solvency, gave her his permission to go. On July 10 she reached Coppet, and began the most amorous period of her career.

A succession of suitors attended upon her there, including Mme. de Staël's lover Benjamin Constant. She enjoyed and encouraged their attentions, all the while (we are told) guarding her citadel. Some critics have accused her of dealing recklessly with men's hearts, and Constant wrote bitterly: "She has played with my happiness, my life; may she be cursed!"[64] But Constant too played with hearts and lives, and the Duchesse d'Abrantès remembered Juliette as quite unblemished:

> One cannot expect to find, in future times, a woman like her—a woman whose friendship has been courted by the most remarkable persons of the age; a woman whose beauty has thrown at her feet all the men who have once set eyes upon her; whose love has been the object of universal desire, yet whose virtue has remained pure. . . . In her days of gaiety and splendor she had the merit of being always ready to sacrifice her own enjoyments to afford consolation . . . to any friend in affliction. To the world Mme. Récamier is a celebrated woman; to those who had the happiness to know and appreciate her she was a peculiar and gifted being, formed by Nature as a perfect model in one of her most beneficent moods.[65]

In October, 1807, Juliette came so close to commitment with Prince August of Prussia, nephew of Frederick the Great, that she wrote to her husband asking for release from their marriage. Récamier reminded her that he had through fourteen years shared his wealth with her, and had indulged her every wish; did it not seem wrong of her to desert him in his efforts for financial recovery? She returned to Paris and her husband, and the Prince had to comfort himself with her letters.

As Récamier grew rich again, and Juliette inherited a fortune from her mother, she resumed her salon, and her opposition to Napoleon. In 1811, when Mme. de Staël was in hot disfavor with the Emperor, and Mathieu de Montmorency had just been exiled for visiting her, Juliette dared fortune, and, over the warnings of Germaine, insisted on spending at least a day with her at Coppet. Napoleon, upset by bad news from Spain and Russia, forbade her to come within 120 miles of Paris. After his first abdication (April 11, 1814) she returned, reopened her salon, and entertained Wellington and other leaders of the victorious Allies. When Napoleon returned from Elba and recaptured France without a blow, she prepared to leave the capital, but Hortense promised to protect her, and she remained, temporarily subdued. After the second abdication (June 22, 1815) she resumed her hospitality. Chateaubriand, whom she had met in 1801, now reentered her life, and gave her a second youth in a strange and historic romance.

VI. THE JEWS IN FRANCE

The emancipation of the European Jews came first in France because France led in the emancipation of the mind, and because the Enlightenment had accustomed a rising proportion of adults to interpret history in secular terms. Biblical research had revealed Jesus as a lovable preacher critical of Pharisees but loyal to Judaism; and the Gospels themselves had shown him as gladly heard by thousands of Jews, and welcomed by thousands as he entered Jerusalem. How, then, could an entire people, through thousands of years, be punished for the crime of a high priest, and a handful of incidental rabble, demanding his death? Economic hostilities remained, and fed the

natural unease in the presence of strange speech and garb; but even that animosity was declining, and Louis XVI had encountered no popular resistance
to his removal of taxes that had specifically burdened the Jews. Mirabeau, in
an essay that barbed logic with wit, had pleaded for the complete emancipation of the Jews (1787), and the Abbé Grégoire had won a prize from the
Royal Society of Science and Arts in Metz, in 1789, for his treatise *The
Physical, Moral, and Political Regeneration of the Jews.* It seemed only a
logical consequence of the Declaration of Human Rights when the Constituent Assembly, on September 27, 1791, extended full civil rights to all the
Jews of France. The armies of the Revolution carried political freedom to
the Jews of Holland in 1796, of Venice in 1797, of Mainz in 1798; and soon
the Code Napoléon established it automatically wherever Bonaparte's conquests reached.

Napoleon himself came to the problem with the soldier's customary scorn
of tradesmen. Stopping at Strasbourg in January, 1806, on his return from
the Austerlitz campaign, he received appeals to help the peasants of Alsace
from their financial misery. Suddenly released from feudal servitude, they
had found themselves without employment or land to give them a living.
They had asked local bankers—mostly German Jews—to lend them the substantial sums they needed to buy acres, tools, and seed to set themselves up as
peasant proprietors. The bankers provided the funds, but at rates reaching
sixteen percent interest, which, to the lenders, seemed justified by the risks
involved. (Borrowers in America today pay similar rates.) Now some of the
farmers could not meet their payments of interest and amortization. Napoleon was informed that unless he interfered many peasants would face the
loss of their lands; he was warned that all Christian Alsace was up in arms
over the situation, and that an attack upon the Jews was imminent.

Arrived in Paris, he took up the matter with his Council. Some members
advised harsh measures; others pointed out that the Jews of Marseilles, Bordeaux, Milan, and Amsterdam were living in peace and respect in their communities, and should not be penalized by any general revocation of the rights
held by Jews in regions controlled by France. Napoleon compromised: he
ruled that the claims of Jewish creditors in certain provinces should not be
collected until a year had passed.[66] But at the same time (May 30, 1806) he
invited Jewish notables from throughout France to meet in Paris to consider
the problems affecting the relations of Christians and Jews, and to suggest
means of spreading the Jews more widely throughout France, and into a
greater variety of occupations. The prefects of the departments were to
choose the notables, but "on the whole their selection was fortunate."[67]

The rabbis and laymen most respected by their congregations gathered in
Paris in July, 1806, in number 111, and were given a hall in the Hôtel de
Ville for their deliberations. Napoleon, or his councilors, submitted to the
meeting some questions on which the Emperor solicited information: Are
Jews polygamous? Do they allow the marriage of Jews with Christians? Do
the rabbis claim the right to grant divorces independently of the civil authorities? Do the Jews consider usury lawful? The notables formulated an-

swers calculated to please Napoleon: polygamy was forbidden in the Jewish communities, and divorce was allowed only when confirmed by the civil courts; intermarriage with Christians was permitted; usury was contrary to Mosaic law.[68] Napoleon sent Count Louis Molé to express his satisfaction; and the Count, formerly critical, addressed the notables with spontaneous eloquence: "Who would not be astonished at the sight of this assembly of enlightened men, selected from among the descendants of the most ancient of nations? If an individual of past centuries could come to life, and if this scene met his gaze, would he not think himself transplanted within the walls of the Holy City?"[69] However, he added, the Emperor desired a religious sanction and surety to be given for the principles affirmed by this predominantly lay assembly, and proposed that the notables should call to Paris, for this and other purposes, the "Great Sanhedrin"—Israel's supreme rabbinical court—which, because of the dispersion of the Jews after the destruction of the Jerusalem Temple, had not met since A.D. 66. The notables were happy to cooperate. On October 6 they sent to all the leading synagogues of Europe the Emperor's invitation to elect delegates to the great "sitting together" (*Sanhedrin* was from the Greek *synedrion*) to consider means of mitigating the difficulties between Christians and Jews, and to facilitate the entry of French Jews into all the rights and advantages of French civilization. The notables accompanied their invitation with a proud and happy proclamation:

> A great event is about to take place, one which, through a long series of centuries our fathers, and even we in our own times, did not expect to see. The 20th of October has been fixed as the date for the opening of a Great Sanhedrin in the capital of one of the most powerful Christian nations, and under the protection of the immortal prince who rules over it. Paris will show the world a remarkable scene, and this ever memorable event will open to the dispersed remnants of the descendants of Abraham a period of deliverance and prosperity.[70]

The Great Sanhedrin could not live up to these enthusiastic expectations. Eight days after the invitations went out Napoleon and his troops fought the Prussians at Jena. All through that fall he remained in Germany or Poland, dismembering Prussia, creating the grand duchy of Warsaw, playing politics or war; all through the winter he remained in Poland, reorganizing his army, fighting the Russians to a draw at Eylau, overwhelming them at Friedland, and making peace with Czar Alexander at Tilsit (1807). He had little time left for the Great Sanhedrin.

It met on February 9, 1807. Forty-five rabbis and twenty-six laymen conferred, listened to speeches, and ratified the replies given to Napoleon by the notables. They proceeded later to issue recommendations to the Jews: to end any animosity to Christians, to love their country as now their own, to accept military service in its defense, to avoid usury, and to enter more and more into agriculture, handicrafts, and the arts. In March the Sanhedrin sent its report to the distant Napoleon, and adjourned.

Almost a year later, on March 18, 1808, Napoleon issued his final decisions. They ratified the religious freedom of the Jews, and their full political rights in all of France except Alsace and Lorraine; there, for the next ten years, certain restrictions were imposed upon bankers to lessen bankruptcies and racial animosities; the debts of women, minors, and soldiers were canceled; the courts were authorized to cancel or reduce arrears in payment of interest, and to grant a moratorium for payment; no Jew was to engage in trade without a license from the prefect; and further immigration of Jews into Alsace was forbidden.[71] In 1810 the Emperor added another request: that every Jew should take a family name—which he hoped would facilitate ethnic assimilation.

It was an imperfect settlement, but perhaps some allowance must be made for a ruler who insisted on ruling everything, and therefore found himself repeatedly inundated with problems and details. The Jews of Alsace felt unjustly injured by the Emperor's regulations; but most Jewish communities in France and elsewhere accepted them as a reasonable attempt to ease an explosive situation.[72] Meanwhile, in the constitution that he drew up for Westphalia, Napoleon declared that all the Jews of that new kingdom were to enjoy all the rights of citizenship on a complete level with other citizens.[73] In France the crisis passed, and the Jews entered fruitfully and creatively into French literature, science, philosophy, music, and art.

CHAPTER XII

Napoleon and the Arts

I. MUSIC

HAVING a continent to manage, Napoleon could not spare much time for music. It is hard to picture him sitting still and mute through one of the concerts at the Théâtre-Feydeau; nevertheless we hear of concerts given in the Tuileries, and we are assured that he took some pleasure in the intimate recitals arranged by Josephine in her apartments.[1] In any case Sébastien Érard and Ignaz Pleyel were making fine pianos, and every home in *le beau monde* had one. Many a hostess arranged a private musicale, at which, said the Goncourts, her guests listened heroically,[2] preferring spirited conversation. The Germans feasted on music without words; the French lived on words without music.

Napoleon liked opera better than concerts; he had little ear or voice for song, but it was part of the royal décor that the ruler should attend the opera occasionally, to meditate and be seen. He regretted that "Paris lacked . . . an opera house worthy of its high claims" as the capital of civilization;[3] it had to wait for his nephew and Charles Garnier to raise (1861–75) the sparkling gem that crowns the Avenue de l'Opéra. Even so, hundreds of operas were composed and produced during his rule. *La Dame blanche* of François-Adrien Boieldieu, master of comic opera, received a thousand performances in forty years.[4] Napoleon's Italian nature favored Italian operas, with their melodious arias and dramatic plots. Enthusiastic over Giovanni Paisiello's compositions, he invited him to come and direct the Paris Opéra and the Conservatory of Music. Paisiello came (1802), aged sixty-five; but the only opera he composed in Paris, *Proserpina* (1803), suffered a lukewarm reception; he withdrew into Masses and motets, and in 1804 he returned to Italy, where he served a more congenial audience in the Naples of Joseph Bonaparte and Joachim Murat.

Napoleon was more fortunate with Gasparo Spontini, who came in 1803, and earned the Emperor's support by treating historical subjects in such wise as to shed glory on the new Empire. His most famous opera, *La Vestale*, had difficulty in finding a company to stage it; Josephine interceded; it was produced; its "bizarre" and "noisy" theatrical emphasis combined with its love story to make it one of the most enduring successes in operatic record. When Napoleon was overthrown, Spontini composed music to celebrate the Bourbon Restoration.

Cherubini, who had dominated Parisian opera during the Revolution, continued to dominate it under Napoleon; however, the Emperor preferred lighthearted ariatic music to Cherubini's more stately presentations, and left him noticeably unrewarded. The composer accepted an invitation to Vienna (July, 1805), but Napoleon captured that city in November. Cherubini was not quite pleased when he was called upon to conduct music for the soirees given by Napoleon in the Palace of Schönbrunn. He returned to France, and found hospitality in the château of the Prince de Chimay, who had made Mme. Tallien respectable with marriage. On returning from Elba, Napoleon, amid all his distractions, took time to make Cherubini a chevalier of the Legion of Honor; but it was only under Louis XVIII that the somber Italian received due recognition and a comfortable income. From 1821 to 1841, as director of the Paris Conservatory of Music, he influenced an entire generation of French composers. He died in 1842, aged eighty-two, almost forgotten in the careless kaleidoscope of time.

II. VARIA

Napoleon closely rivaled Louis XIV in patronage of art, for, like him, he wished to proclaim the glory and grandeur of France, and he hoped that the artists would keep him fresh in human memory. His own taste was not of the best, as became one bred and bound to soldiering, but he did what he could to provide the artists of France with historic originals and personal stimulus. He pilfered masterpieces not only as negotiable wealth (as they are bought today), and as trophies and testimonials of victories, but as models for students in the museums of France; so the *Venus de' Medici* came from the Vatican, Correggio's lissome saints from Parma, Vermeer's *Marriage of Cana* from Venice, Rubens' *Descent from the Cross* from Antwerp, Murillo's *Assumption of the Virgin* from Madrid . . . ; even the bronze horses of St. Mark's made their perilous way to Paris. Altogether, between 1796 and 1814, Napoleon sent 506 works of art from Italy to France; of these, 249 were returned after his fall, 248 remained, 9 were lost.[5] Through such pillage Paris replaced Rome as the art capital of the Western world. As conquests multiplied, the spoils overflowed into the provinces; and to receive them Napoleon created museums in Nancy, Lille, Toulouse, Nantes, Rouen, Lyons, Strasbourg, Bordeaux, Marseilles, Geneva, Brussels, Montpellier, Grenoble, Amiens . . . Over all these collections, and particularly over the Louvre, Napoleon appointed Dominique Denon, who had served him in many lands, and who never forgot that the Emperor himself had gone to drag him to safety from a plateau swept by enemy fire during the battle of Eylau.

Napoleon established competitions and substantial prizes in several fields of art. He renewed the Prix de Rome, and restored the French Academy at Rome. He invited artists to his table, and played art critic, even during campaigns. He valued most those painters who could most effectively commemorate his deeds, and those architects who could help him make Paris the most beautiful of cities, and his reign the apex of its history. He commissioned sculptors to adorn fifteen new fountains for its squares.

Just as his taste in painting ran to the classical, so in architecture he admired the monumental style of ancient Rome, and aimed at strength and sublimity rather than at grace of relief or charm of detail. So he commissioned Barthélemy Vignon to design a Temple of Glory in honor of the Grande Armée; he bade its builders use nothing but marble, iron, and gold in its construction. The task proved so costly and difficult that, begun in 1809, it remained unfinished when Napoleon fell. His successors completed it (1842) as a church dedicated to Saint Mary Magdalen—La Madeleine. France has never taken to it; neither the piety nor the gaiety of Paris accords with that forbidding façade, whose columns might better express an advancing army than a tender sinner so penitent of her favors and so lavish in her love. — Monumental too is the Palais de la Bourse, or Stock Exchange, which Alexandre-Théodore Brongniart began in 1808, and which Étienne de La Barre continued in 1813; never elsewhere has Mammon been so majestically housed.

The preferred architects of the reign were Charles Percier and his usual associate, Pierre-François-Léonard Fontaine. Together they labored to unite the Louvre with the Tuileries, despite the unevenness in their structural lines; so they built the north wing (Cour Carrée) of the Louvre (1806). They repaired and renovated the exterior, and connected the floors with massive stairways. They designed the Arc de Triomphe du Carrousel (1806–08) in the style and proportions of the Arch of Septimius Severus in Rome. The more stately Arc de Triomphe de l'Étoile, at the farther end of the Champs-Élysées, was begun (1806) by Jean-François Chalgrin, but had merely emerged from its foundations when Napoleon fell; it was not completed till 1837, three years before his ashes passed under it in their triumphant procession to his tomb in the Hôtel des Invalides. Frankly imitating the Arch of Constantine in Rome, it surpassed it—and any Roman arch—in beauty, partly because of its marble bas-reliefs. At the left Jean-Pierre Cortot carved *The Crowning of Napoleon;* at the right François Rudé, in *The Marseillais* (1833–36), caught the martial ecstasy of the Revolution. This is one of the high moments of nineteenth-century sculpture.

That difficult art, under Napoleon, rested on the laurels it had earned before his rise. Houdon survived till 1828, and made a bust of him (now in the Museum of Dijon) which earned the artist a place in the Legion of Honor. Still remembering Roman emperors—this time the sculptured record of Trajan's victories—Napoleon commissioned Jean-Baptiste Le Père and Jacques Gondouin to tell the story of the Austerlitz campaign in bronze reliefs to be attached, plaque by plaque, in an ascending spiral on a column that would dominate the Place Vendôme. It was so done (1806–10), and in 1808 Antoine Chaudet crowned the shaft with a statue of Napoleon made from cannon captured from the enemy. Seldom had victorious pride mounted so high.

The minor arts—cabinetry, interior decoration, tapestry, needlepoint, pottery, porcelain, glass, jewelry, engraving, figurines—had almost died during the Revolution; they had begun recovery under the Directory; they flourished under Napoleon; Sèvres again produced fine porcelain. Furniture took on the solid, sturdy "Empire style." The miniatures in which Isabey portrayed, with microscopic brilliance, the leading characters of the age are among the finest of their kind in history. Joseph Chinard made delectable terra-cotta busts of Josephine and Mme. Récamier; the latter is especially fine, with one breast bared as a sample and as befitted a woman who was resolved to remain half a virgin to the end.

III. THE PAINTERS

Painting prospered now, for the country was prospering, and patrons could pay. Napoleon paid well, for he was playing to a gallery of centuries, and hoped to prolong their attention by the blandishments of literature and art. His admiration of Augustus' Rome and Louis XIV's Paris inclined him to favor classic norms of art—line, order, logic, proportion, design, reason, restraint; but the keenness of his senses, the range of his imagination, and the force of his passions gave him some understanding of the Romantic movement that was rising to liberate individualism, feeling, originality, imagination, mystery, and color from the bondage of tradition, conformity, and rule. So he made classic David his court painter, but he kept a corner of his favor for the sentiment of Gérard, the idyls of Prud'hon, and the explosive colors of Gros.

Jacques-Louis David took naturally to a patron who called himself a consul, who for a time tolerated a tribunate of popular orators, and who disguised his decrees as *senatus consulta*. He visited the triumphant Corsican soon after the 18th Brumaire. Napoleon won him at once by greeting him as the French Apelles, but gently reproved him for spending so much talent on ancient history; were there not memorable events in modern—even in contemporary—history? "However," he added, "do what you please; your pencil will confer celebrity upon any subject you may select. For every historical picture you may choose to paint you shall receive 100,000 francs."[6] This was convincing. David sealed the pact with *Bonaparte Crossing the Alps* (1801), which showed a handsome warrior with a charming leg, on a magnificent horse that appears to be galloping up a rocky mountainside—one of the most brilliant pictures of the age.

David had voted for the execution of Louis XVI; he must have winced when Napoleon made himself emperor and restored all the pomp and power of monarchy. But he went to see his new master crowned; the fascination of that scene overcame his politics; and after three years of intermittent devotion, he commemorated the event in the pictorial masterpiece of the period. Almost a hundred characters were portrayed in *The Coronation of Napoleon* (1807), even Madame Mère Letizia, who was not there; most of them faithfully, except for Cardinal Caprara, who complained that David had revealed him bald, without his usual wig. Everyone else was pleased. Napoleon, after examining the picture for half an hour, raised his hat to the artist, saying, "*C'est bien, très bien. David, je vous salue.*"[7]

David was not merely the official court painter; he was the unchallenged leader of French art in his time. Everyone of account came to him to sit for a portrait—Napoleon, Pius VII, Murat, even Cardinal Caprara, bewigged.[8] His pupils—especially Gérard, Gros, Isabey, Ingres—spread his influence even while deviating from his style. As late as 1814 English visitors to the Louvre were surprised to find young artists copying not the Renaissance masters, but the pictures of David.[9] A year later he was banished by the restored Bourbons. He went to Brussels, where he prospered with portraits. He died in 1825, having lived fully in all his seventy-seven years.

Of his pupils we leave Ingres (1770–1867) to later years; we bow in passing to Gérard and Guérin for their illuminating portraits; we stay longer with Antoine-Jean Gros because of his interesting passage through the styles. We have watched him at Milan, painting, or imagining, *Napoleon on the Bridge at Arcole;* here, so soon, classic David's heir is flirting with romance. Napoleon rewarded Gros's idolatry with a military commission that enabled the young artist to see war at close view. Like Goya a few years later, he saw not so much the fighting as the suffering. In *The Plague at Jaffa* (1804) he showed Napoleon touching the sores of a victim, but also he showed the terror and hopelessness of men, women, and children stricken by an obscene and undiscriminating fate. In *The Battle of Eylau* (1808) he pictured not the battle but the field stricken with the dying and the dead. He felt the living warmth of Rubens' colors, and poured into his paintings a flesh-and-blood vitality that raised the Romantic spirit of post-Napoleonic France. Then, feeling that he had betrayed his banished master, he tried to recapture in his work the calm of the classic style. He failed, and—lost and forgotten in an age wild with Hugo, Berlioz, Géricault and Delacroix—he succumbed to a melancholy that dried up in him the sap and love of life. On June 25, 1835, aged sixty-four, he left his home, walked out toward Meudon, and drowned himself in a tributary of the Seine.

Pierre-Paul Prud'hon (1758–1823) advanced the Romantic surge by preferring ideal beauty to reality, goddesses to gods, and Correggio to Raphael. He recognized with David the primacy of line, but felt that without color line was dead. He was feminine except in his love of women; his meditative tenderness and amorous sensitivity could forgive all faults that came in a gracious form. As youngest of thirteen children he was harassed with poverty in Cluny, and developed hesitantly; however, the local monks saw him drawing and painting, and persuaded a bishop to finance Pierre's art study in Dijon. He did well there, but, aged twenty, he married a goddess who was soon transformed into a rasping shrew. He won a scholarship, went to Rome without his wife, courted Raphael, then Leonardo, and finally surrendered to Correggio.

In 1789 he rejoined his wife, moved to Paris, and soon found himself stranded in a revolutionary chaos that had no time or taste for his Cupids and Psyches; obstinately he continued to paint them—with a loving delicacy that seemed to caress the flesh with the brush. He ate by producing bill heads, miniatures, and commercial illustrations. After ten years of such servitude he won from the Directory a commission to paint a picture—*Wisdom Descending to Earth*—which caught the attention of General Bonaparte. Later the First Consul centered on David, and could spare only transient favors to Prud'hon; Josephine, however, sat to him for the portrait that hangs in the Louvre. Meanwhile, tortured with monogamy, he and his wife agreed to part.

Not till 1808, when he was fifty, did he win acclaim. In that year he embodied his voluptuous dreams in *The Rape of Psyche*, and then balanced it with *Justice and Vengeance Pursuing Crime*. Impressed, Napoleon nominated him to the Legion of Honor, and gave him an apartment in the Sorbonne. In the next apartment the love-hungry painter found another artist, Constance Mayer, who became his mistress, housekeeper, and the solace of his old age. In 1821 Constance, apparently distracted with religious qualms, killed herself. The shock overwhelmed Prud'hon. In 1823 he died, almost unnoticed in the excitement of that Romantic movement which he had forwarded by going back from David to Watteau, and renewing the French worship of beauty and grace.

IV. THE THEATER

Napoleon was well acquainted with the classic drama of France, and only less so with the dramatic literature of ancient Greece. Corneille was his favorite because in him, far more than in Racine, he found what he felt was a just understanding of heroism and nobility. "A good tragedy," he said, at St. Helena, "gains upon us every day. The higher kind of tragedy is the school of great men: it is the duty of sovereigns to encourage and disseminate a taste for it. . . . Had Corneille lived in my time I would have made him a prince."[10] The Emperor did not care for comedy; he had no need to be amused; Talleyrand pitied M. de Rémusat because, as director of entertainments at the imperial court, he was expected to arrange some amusements for "*cet homme inamusable*."[11] But this unamusable man lavished funds upon the Comédie-Française and its "stars"; he welcomed Talma to his table, and Mlle. George to his bed.

In 1807 Napoleon restricted the number of Paris theaters to nine, and reinstituted the Théâtre-Français—the then and present home of the Comédie-Française—in almost exclusive right to perform the classic drama. On October 15, 1812, amid the ruins of burned Moscow, he found time to draw up for the Théâtre-Français an elaborate code of regulations which still govern it today.[12] So encouraged, the Comédie-Française staged, during the Empire, the finest productions of classic drama in French history. To supplement these activities the Théâtre de l'Odéon, built in 1779 and destroyed by fire in 1799, was rebuilt in 1808 on classic lines by Chalgrin. A court theater was set up in the Tuileries, and private theatricals of considerable excellence were staged in many rich homes.

Talma, after playing his parts in the Revolution, reached his zenith under Napoleon. His own character was so proud, distinctive, and intense that he must have found difficulty in shedding it for any assumed role. He mastered the subtle art by learning to control and coordinate all the movements of his limbs, all the muscles and features of his face, every inflection of his voice, to fit and convey any sensation, feeling, or idea, any wonder, doubt, or intention, in the personality he portrayed. Some playgoers went repeatedly to see him in the same role to relish and study the finesse of his art. He had discarded the oratorical style of the theater in the Old Regime; he spoke the alexandrine verses as if they were unmetered prose; he rejected any unnatural expression or sentiment; yet he could be as tender as any lover, as passionate as any criminal. Mme. de Staël, moved almost to terror by Talma's portrayal of Othello,[13] wrote to him, in 1807: "You are, in your career, unique in all the world, and no one, before you, has reached that degree of perfection where art unites with inspiration, reflection with spontaneity, and reason with genius."[14]

Napoleon too was enamored of the tragedian. He gave him substantial sums, paid his debts, and frequently invited him to breakfast; then the Emperor could so lose himself in discourse on the drama that he kept diplomats and generals waiting while he explained historical details that should determine the presentation of a character. On the morning after seeing *La Mort de Pompée* he told Talma, "I am not entirely satisfied. You use your arms too much. Monarchs are less prodigal of gestures; they know that a motion is an order, and that a look is death; so they are sparing of motions and looks." Talma, we are assured, profited from this counsel.[15] In any case he remained to the end of his life the ruler of the French stage.

It had its queens too, as Napoleon observed. Mlle. Duchesnois was plain of face but perfect in form. Accordingly, as Dumas *père* reported, "she was particularly fond of the part of Alzire, in which she could display her form almost naked." But also "she had a voice containing notes of such profound tenderness, such melodious sorrow, that to this day most people who have seen her in *Maria Stuart* prefer her to Mlle. Rachel."[16] Her forte was tragedy, in which she almost rivaled Talma; it was usually she who was chosen to play opposite to him. Mlle. George was a frailer beauty, whom the Comédie must have hesitated to cast in such demanding roles as Clytemnestra in Racine's *Iphigénie*. Her voice and figure charmed the First Consul; and like a feudal lord with the *droit de seigneur*, he called upon her for a command performance now and then.[17] Though this liaison ended after a year, she, like Talma, remained devoted to Napoleon through all his glory and defeats; consequently she lost her place at the Théâtre-Français when Napoleon fell; but she returned later to share in the excitement of the Romantic stage.

Napoleon believed, with some reason, that the Comédie-Française had in his reign raised the French stage to a higher excellence than ever before. Several times, to display its quality and his splendor, he bade the company, at the state's expense, come to Mainz, Compiègne, or Fontainebleau, and perform for the court, or, as at Erfurt and Dresden, to play *devant un parterre de rois*—"before an audience of kings."[18] Not even the Grand Monarque had shone in such theatrical glory.

CHAPTER XIII

Literature versus Napoleon

I. THE CENSOR

NAPOLEON was more interested in the stage than in literature. He noted carefully the programs of the Théâtre-Français, expressed his judgment on them, and was largely responsible for their discarding Voltaire and reviving Corneille and Racine. His taste in literature was not so respectable. He read fiction eagerly, and took many novels—mostly romantic—with him on his campaigns. His table talk at St. Helena contained some good literary criticism, showing knowledge of Homer, Virgil, Corneille, Racine, La Fontaine, Mme. de Sévigné, Voltaire, Richardson, and Rousseau; but he was quite dead to Shakespeare. "It is impossible to finish any of his plays; they are pitiful. There is nothing in them that comes anywhere near Corneille or Racine."[1] (French translations of Shakespeare were pitifully inadequate.)

Like most men of affairs he had no respect for writers on economics or government; he considered them phrasemongers with little corrective sense of reality, or of the nature and limits of man. He was sure that he knew better than they what the French people wanted and should have: efficiency and integrity in government, moderation in taxes, freedom of enterprise in business, regularity of provisions, security of remunerative employment in industry, peasant ownership, and a proud place for France in the parade of states; if this were given them the people would not insist on determining measures, or filling offices, by a count of noses after a contest of words. In his laborious pursuit of those ends—and of his own power or glory—he would not long tolerate interference by lords of the rostrum or the pen. If these gentry could be quieted by prizes, pensions, or political plums, such sedatives would be provided; otherwise disturbers of the consular or imperial peace should be barred from publication, or from Paris or France. "Unlimited freedom of the press," Napoleon wrote in 1802, "would very soon reestablish anarchy in a country where all the elements for such a condition are already present."[2]

To watch public opinion, Napoleon—following Directory precedents—ordered postmasters to open private mail, make note of hostile passages, reseal the envelopes, and send copies of the excerpts to himself or to the "Black Cabinet" in the General Post Office at Paris.[3] He instructed his personal librarian to make and bring to him, "daily between five and six o'clock," summaries of political material in current periodicals; "to submit to me, every ten days, an analysis of the brochures or books published within the previous ten days"; to report on the content and political tendencies of each play performed, within forty-eight hours after its premiere; and "every first and sixth day [of the ten-day week] between five and six o'clock, he will submit to me a bulletin on the posters, placards, or advertisements that may be worthy of attention; he will also report on whatever has come to his knowledge, and has been done or said, in the various lycées, literary assemblies, sermons, . . . that might be of interest from the point of view of politics and morals."[4]

On January 17, 1800—again continuing Directory custom—Napoleon ordered the suppression of sixty of the seventy-three newspapers then published in France. By the end of the year only nine survived, none of them radically critical. "Three hostile newspapers," he said, "are more to be feared than a thousand bayonets."[5] *Le Moniteur universel* regularly defended Napoleon's policies; sometimes he composed articles—even book reviews—for it, unsigned, but betraying their origin by their authoritative style. A wit renamed this government organ *Le Menteur* [liar] *Universel*.[6]

> I want you to write to the editor of *Le Journal des débats, Le Publiciste,* and *La Gazette de France*—these, I think, are the newspapers most widely read—in order to declare to them that . . . the Revolutionary times are over, and that there is but one single party in France; that I shall never tolerate newspapers that say or do anything against my interests; that they may publish a few little articles with just a little poison in them, but that one fine morning somebody will shut their mouths.[7]

On April 5, 1800, censorship was extended to the drama. The government argued that opinions individually and privately expressed might do little harm, but that the same opinions when put into the mouth of a famous historical character, and proclaimed from the stage with the force and eloquence of a popular actor, would have an influence explosively multiplied by the mutual reverberation of feelings—and by the irresponsibility of individuals—in a theatrical audience.[8] The censorship excluded from public performances any criticism of monarchy, and any praise of democracy. *La Mort de César* was banished from the boards because the audience applauded the speeches of Brutus against dictatorship.[9]

Finally the state took control of all printing. "It is very important that only those be allowed to print who have the confidence of the government. A man who addresses the public in print is like the man who speaks in public in an assembly";[10] he can scatter inflammatory material, and should be watched as a potential arsonist. Hence every printer must submit to a censor every accepted manuscript, either before or while he prints it, and, to secure the state's imprimatur, he must agree to delete objectionable matter, or accept substitutions proposed by the government. Even after the censor has given his consent, and the work has been printed, the minister of police is authorized to confiscate, and even to completely destroy, the published edition, no matter at what loss to the author or the publisher.[11]

It was in this prison of the mind that literature struggled to survive under Napoleon. The most heroic effort was made by a woman.

II. MME. DE STAËL: 1799–1817

1. Napoleon's Nemesis

The Committee of Public Safety had banished her from France; the Directory had reduced this to exclusion from Paris; the day after its fall she hurried back to the capital (November 12, 1799), and took an apartment in the Rue de Grenelle in the fashionable Faubourg St.-Germain. The new consular government—i.e., Napoleon—made no protest against her return.

Soon she had opened a new salon, partly because "conversing in Paris . . . has always been to me the most fascinating of all pleasures,"[12] partly because she was determined to play a part in the direction of events. She did not admit that such a role was unbecoming a woman; it seemed to her quite becoming if the woman (like her) had both money and brains; and particularly becoming to the heiress of Jacques Necker, whom she considered the unappreciated hero of the Revolution. Incidentally the government still owed him the twenty million francs he had loaned it in 1789; part of her resolve was to regain that sum for her father and her patrimony. Her ideal (like his) was a constitutional monarchy allowing freedom of press, worship, and speech, and protecting the property of the rich against the envy of the poor. In this sense she felt that she was faithful to the Revolution as defined by the National Assembly of 1789–91. She scorned the regicides, and welcomed to her salon her titled neighbors of the Faubourg, who daily prayed for a Bourbon restoration. Nevertheless she centered her gatherings around Benjamin Constant, who was all for a republic, and who, as a member of the Tribunate, opposed every move of Napoleon from consular to imperial power. She welcomed also the brothers of the First Consul, for they too were uncomfortable under his growing authority.

Indeed, most of the men of standing in the political and intellectual world of Paris in 1800 found their way to her soirees, eager to learn the latest political gossip, or to hear Madame sail off in such conversation as Paris had not heard from a woman since Mme. du Deffand. Mme. de Tessé declared: "If I were queen, I would order Mme. de Staël to talk to me all the time."[13] Germaine herself wrote that "the necessity of conversation is felt by all classes in France; speech is not there, as elsewhere, merely a means of communication; . . . it is an instrument on which they are fond of playing."[14]

She did not at once oppose Napoleon; indeed, if we may believe Bourrienne, she wrote him some flattering letters in the early Consulate, even to offering herself to his service.[15] But his resolute ignoring of her advances, his expanding censorship, his scorn of intellectuals in politics, his conception of women as breeders and charming toys not to be trusted with a thought, stung her to reply in kind. When he called her guests ideologues she called him an ideophobe; and as her ire warmed she described him as "Robespierre on horseback,"[16] or as the *bourgeois gentilhomme* on the throne.[17]

On May 7, 1800, she moved her household, and a small retinue of devotees, to Coppet for the summer. Napoleon had left Paris the day before to cross the Alps and meet the Austrians at Marengo. Germaine later confessed: "I could not help wishing that Bonaparte might be defeated, as that seemed the only means of stopping the progress of his tyranny."[18] In the fall of the year, bored with Coppet and Mont Blanc, she returned to the capital, for she lived on conversation, and "French conversation exists nowhere but in Paris."[19] Soon she gathered a bevy of geniuses in her salon, and their predominating topic was Napoleon's dictatorship. "She carries a quiver full of arrows," he complained. "They pretend that she speaks neither of politics nor of me; but how, then, does it come to pass that all who see her like me less?"[20] "Her home," he said at St. Helena, "became quite an arsenal against me. People went there to be dubbed knights in her crusade."[21] Yet he admitted: "That woman teaches people to think who never took to it before, or have forgotten how."[22]

He felt that as a man seeking to pull France out of chaos by giving her an efficient administration, and meanwhile leading her armies to victory against hostile coalitions, he had the right to expect, and, if necessary, enforce, some unity of morale in the public, some coordination of the national spirit with the national will to defend France's new republic and its "natural" frontiers; but this woman gathered and united against him both the royalists and the Jacobins, and comforted his enemies. Germaine's father here agreed with Napoleon; he reprimanded her for her persistent attacks upon the young dictator; some dictatorship, he told her, was necessary in time of crisis or war.[23] She replied that freedom was more important than victory. She encouraged Bernadotte in his opposition to Napoleon; she wrote some of the speeches that Constant made in the Tribunate against Napoleon's encroachment upon the powers of the legislature. She and Bonaparte were expanding and inflammable egoists, and France was not large enough to house them both and keep them free.

In the spring of 1801 Napoleon wrote to his brother Joseph: "Monsieur de Staël is in the most abject misery, and his wife gives dinners and balls."[24] Joseph relayed the rebuke, Germaine went to Monsieur's room in the Place de la Concorde, and found him in the last stages of paralysis. She attended to his care, and in May, 1802, she took him with her when she left Paris for Switzerland. He died on the way, and was buried in the cemetery of Coppet. In that year, increasingly excitable, Mme. de Staël began to take opium.

2. The Author

She was the greatest European authoress of her time, and the greatest French author, barring Chateaubriand. She had written fifteen books, now forgotten, before 1800; in that year she offered a major work, *De la Littérature;* thereafter she produced two novels—*Delphine* (1803) and *Corinne* (1807)—that made her famous throughout Europe; in 1810–13 she fought the battle of her life to publish her masterpiece, *De l'Allemagne;* at her death she left another major work, *Considérations sur ... la Révolution française,* and *Les Dix Années d'exil.* All of those here named were substantial and conscientious productions, some running to eight hundred pages. Mme. de Staël worked hard, loved assiduously, and wrote passionately; she fought to the end the strongest man of her time, and sadly triumphed in his fall.

De la Littérature considérée dans ses rapports avec les institutions sociales undertook a large and heroic theme: "I propose to examine the influence of religion, morals, and laws upon literature, and the influence of literature upon religion, morals, and laws."* It still breathes the spirit of the eighteenth century—freedom of thought, the individual versus the state, the progress of knowledge and morals; here is no supernatural myth, but faith in the spread of education, science, and intelligence. The first prerequisite of progress is the liberation of the mind from political control. With minds so freed, literature will embody, spread, and transmit the mounting heritage of the race. We must not expect art and poetry to progress like science and philosophy, for they depend chiefly on imagination, which is as keen and fertile in early as in later times. In the development of a civilization, art and poetry precede science and philosophy; so the age of Pericles preceded that of Aristotle, the Middle Ages preceded Galileo, the art of Louis XIV preceded the intellectual Enlightenment. The progress of the mind is not continuous; there are retrogressions, due to disturbances in nature or to the vicissitudes of politics; but even in the Middle Ages science and scientific method advanced, and made possible the appearance of Copernicus, Galileo, Bacon, and Descartes. In every age philosophy represents the accumulation and substance of the intellectual heritage. Perhaps (she mused) philosophy will in some future era be sufficiently comprehensive and mature to "be to us what the Christian religion has been in the past."[25] She defined *les lumières philosophiques* (philosophical enlightenment) as "the appreciation of things according to reason,"[26] and only in the face of death did she waver from her faith in the life of reason. "The triumph of the light [*les lumières*] has always been favorable to the greatness and betterment of mankind."[27]

But, she continues (having read Rousseau as well as Voltaire), the growth of the intellect is not enough; knowledge is only one element in understanding. The other is feeling. There must be a sensitivity of the soul as well as of the senses. Without it the soul would be a *tabula mortua,* a dead receiver of physical sensations; with it the soul enters into the life of other living beings, shares their wondering and suffering, feels the soul within the flesh, the God behind the material world. From this viewpoint the Romantic literature of the misty north—Germany, Scandinavia, Great Britain—is as important as the classic literature of the sunny south—Greece and Italy; the poems of "Ossian" are as important as Homer's epics, and *Werther* was the greatest book of its time.

Napoleon (in his youth) would have agreed with these evaluations, but

---

* We have not read this book since 1925. Most of the following analysis borrows from Herold's brilliant biography *Mistress to an Age,* pp. 205-13.

he must have been disturbed by the author's view of the relations between literature and government. Democracies (she held) tend to subject writers and artists to popular tastes; aristocracies lead them to write for an elite, encouraging deliberate thought and sobriety of form;[28] absolutism promotes art and science, thereby imposing itself through splendor and power, but it discountenances philosophy and historiography, for these make for a breadth and depth of view dangerous to dictatorship. Democracy stimulates literature and retards art; aristocracies impose taste but frown upon enthusiasm and originality; absolute government stifles freedom, innovation, and thought. If France could have a constitutional government—reconciling order and liberty—she might combine the stimulations of democracy with the judicious restraints of lawful rule.

All in all, this was a remarkable book for a woman of thirty-four years and several million francs. There are errors, of course, in these six hundred pages, for when the mind outgrasps its reach it is bound to risk a fall—though it may shake to the ground some elusive fruit. Madame was a bit vague in history and literature; she thought the Irish were Germans, and that Dante was a minor poet; but she argued bravely for a liberal government and a reasonable Christianity, and she spilled a hundred *aperçus* on her way. She foresaw that the development of statistics might make government more intelligent, and that political education might help prepare candidates for public office. She remarked prophetically that "scientific progress makes moral progress a necessity; for if man's power is increased, the checks that restrain him from abusing it must be strengthened."[29] "There is scarcely an idea of the eighteenth century which [the book] does not transmit, scarcely an idea of the twentieth century which it does not contain in germ."[30]

She had written, in this volume, her lifelong plaint—that "the entire social order . . . is arrayed against a woman who wants to rise to a man's reputation" in the realms of art and thought.[31] Now she had to make an exception; for, as she wrote twenty-one years later, "in the spring of 1800 I published my work on literature, and the success it met with restored me completely to favor with society; my drawing room became again filled."[32] The faint of heart who had shied away from her salon after Constant's blast against dictatorship returned penitent and adulant; and the Little Corporal in the Tuileries had to admit that he had found a foe to match his mettle.

In August, 1802, Jacques Necker sent to Consul Lebrun *Les Dernières Vues de politique et de finance*—his last views on politics and money. It excused the dictatorship of Napoleon, but as a necessary evil, presumably temporary; it warned against the continued concentration of power in the hands of the military; it expressed regret that the finances of the new government depended so heavily upon war indemnities; and it proposed a more liberal constitution of which Napoleon would be the "guardian." Lebrun showed the book to Napoleon, who, already half imperial, resented the notion that he should reduce his power. Convinced that Mme. de Staël had guided the pen of her father, he issued an order excluding her from Paris—i.e., in effect, closing her mischief-making salon. He forgot that she could write as well as speak. She spent the winter of 1802–03 in Geneva, but in December she again became the talk of Paris by publishing a novel, *Delphine*. No one reads it now; everyone of literary or political consciousness read it then, for it was part of a virile struggle between a woman and her time.

Delphine is a virtuous girl who longs and fears to yield; otherwise she is Mme. de Staël. Léonce (= Narbonne) is a handsome aristocrat who loves Delphine but abstains from her because a rumor accuses her of "affairs"; he cannot risk his social standing by making her his wife. He marries Matilde de Vernon, whose mother is a scheming witch who covers her lies with wit; Paris saw this lady as Talleyrand despite her skirts, and Talleyrand revenged himself by remarking of the masculine authoress that she had disguised both him and herself as women. Delphine, rejected, retires to a convent, where the abbess hurries her into a vow of lifelong chastity. When Léonce discovers her innocence he thinks of divorcing his unresponsive wife and courting Delphine, but he hesitates to ruin his career by violating the Catholic code of irrefragable monogamy. Matilde dies, a victim of dramatic convenience; Léonce persuades Delphine to elope with him and surrender to his passion; he deserts her, goes off to join the *émigrés*, is caught and condemned to death. Delphine, in love with his cruelty, rushes to save him, but arrives only in time to see him shot; whereupon she too falls dead.

This absurd and typically romantic plot served the authoress as a podium from which to discuss the legitimacy of divorce, the bigotry of Catholicism (she had inherited Protestantism), the moral rights of women as against the double standard, and the validity of the individual conscience as against the honor code of a class. Her arguments were well received by the intelligentsia of Paris, but they did not please Napoleon, who was turning to Catholicism as a cure for the mental and moral turmoil of France. On October 13, 1803, he issued an order forbidding Mme. de Staël to approach within forty leagues of Paris.

She thought it was just the right time to visit Germany. She had learned enough German to read it, though not to speak it; why not now sample the music of Vienna, the wit of Weimar, and the royal society of Berlin? On November 8, with son Auguste, daughter Albertine, two servants, and her now platonic *cavaliere servente* Constant, she crossed the Rhine at Metz into Germany.

3. The Tourist

Her first impression, at Frankfurt, was hostile; all the men seemed fat, lived to eat, and ate to smoke; she found it difficult to breathe when they were near. They wondered at this proud woman who could not appreciate the *Gemütlichkeit* of their pipes. Goethe's mother wrote to him: "She oppressed me like a millstone. I avoided her wherever I could, refused all invitations to go to things she was to attend, and breathed more freely when she left."[33]

Germaine, with her retinue, hurried on to Weimar, where she found the atmosphere purified by poetry. The town was dominated by writers, artists, musicians, and philosophers; the court was judiciously and tolerantly led by Duke Charles Augustus, his wife the Duchess Luise, and his mother the Duchess Dowager Anna Amalie. These people were well educated; they smoked with discrimination, and nearly all of them spoke French. Moreover, many of them had read *Delphine*, many more had heard of her war against Napoleon; and all noted that she had money and spent it. They feted her with dinners, theater parties, dances, and balls; they summoned Schiller to read scenes from *Wilhelm Tell*; they listened to her reciting long passages from Racine. Goethe, then at Jena, tried to play truant by pleading a cold; the Duke urged him to come to Weimar nevertheless; he came, and conversed with Madame uncomfortably. He was alarmed by her frank warning that she intended to print her report of his remarks.[34] She was disappointed to find that he was no longer Werther, having changed from a lover to a pontiff. He tried to confuse her with contradictions; "my obstinate contrariness often drove her to despair, but it was then that she was most amiable, and that she displayed her mental and verbal agility most brilliantly."[35] "Fortunately for me," she recalled, "Goethe and Wieland spoke French extremely well; Schiller struggled."[36] She wrote of Schiller with affection, of Goethe with respect; he and Napoleon were the only men she had met who made her realize her limitations. Schiller was fatigued by the rapidity of her thought and speech, but he ended by being impressed. "Satan," he wrote to a friend, "has led me to the female French philosopher who, of all creatures living, is the most animated, the most ready for contest, the most fertile in words. But she is also the most cultivated, the most *spirituelle* [intellectually alert] of women; and if she were not really interesting I would not be disturbed by her."[37] Weimar breathed a sigh of relief when, after a three months' stay, she left for Berlin.

She found the mists of Berlin depressing after the brilliance of Weimar. The leaders of the Romantic movement in Germany were absent or dead; the philosophers were immured in distant universities—Hegel at Jena, Schelling at Würzburg; Germaine had to content herself with the King, the Queen, and August Wilhelm von Schlegel, whose wide knowledge of languages and cultures delighted her. She engaged him to come with her to Coppet as tutor to her son Auguste; he agreed, and fell in love with her at the worst possible time.

At Berlin she received word that her father was dangerously ill. She hurried back to Coppet, but before reaching it she learned that he had died (April 9, 1804). It was a blow more desolating than any in her duel with Napoleon. Her father had been her moral as well as her financial mainstay; in her view he had always been right, and ever good; and not all her lovers could take his place. She found comfort in writing an idyl of adoration—*Monsieur Necker's Character and Private Life*—and in beginning work on her masterpiece, *De l'Allemagne*. She inherited most of her father's fortune, and now had an income of 120,000 francs per year.

In December she went to seek the sun in Italy. She took along her three children—Auguste, Albertine, and Albert—and Schlegel, who now tutored her also, for he found her poorly informed about Italian art. At Milan they were joined by a still better Baedeker—Jean-Charles-Léonard de Sismondi, who was beginning to write his learned *History of the Italian Republics*. He too fell in love with Germaine—or with her mind or her income—until, like Schlegel, he discovered that she never took a commoner seriously. Together they moved through Parma, Modena, Bologna, and Ancona to Rome. Joseph Bonaparte, always fond of her, had given her letters of introduction to the best society there. She was lionized by the aristocracy, but found the princes and princesses less interesting than the courtly cardinals, who, as men of the world, knew her books, her wealth, and her feud with Napoleon, and were not disturbed by her Protestant faith. She was received with an ovation, and with improvised poetry and music, into the Accademia dell' Arcadia; she used that experience in introducing *Corinne*.

In June, 1805, she was back in Coppet, soon again surrounded by lovers, friends, scholars, diplomats (Prince Esterházy of Vienna, Claude Hochet of Napoleon's Council of State), even a ruler—the Elector of Bavaria. Coppet's was now a more famous salon than any in Paris. "I just returned from Coppet," wrote Charles-Victor de Bonstetten, "and I feel completely stupefied . . . and exhausted by the intellectual debauches. More wit is expended at Coppet in a single day than in many a country during a whole year."[38] The assemblage was sufficiently numerous and talented to stage complete dramas; Germaine herself played the lead in *Andromaque* and *Phèdre*, and some guests thought her performances were surpassed only by the queens of the Paris stage. On other occasions there were recitals of music or poetry. Three times a day the table was set, sometimes for thirty guests; fifteen servants were kept busy; and in the gardens lovers might wander, and new friendships might be made.

Germaine's time-beaten lovers—Montmorency, Constant, Schlegel, Sismondi—had cooled considerably, exhausted by her demand for obedient devotion, and she was warming herself with passion for Prosper de Barante. He was twenty-three, she was thirty-nine, but her pace soon tired him, and he sought refuge in distance and the indecisiveness which she was satirizing in the Oswald of *Corinne*. That once famous novel was nearing completion, and called for a French printer, who would need the imprimatur of Napoleon's police. Prosper's father, prefect of the department of Leman, assured Fouché that Madame had been "reserved and circumspect" for the past year. She received permission to spend the summer of 1806 at Auxerre, 120 miles from Paris; she took a villa there; and in the fall she was allowed to move to Rouen for the winter. Several of her friends visited her in these cities, and some of them expressed hope that Napoleon would at last meet defeat in the arduous campaign that made him and his army spend the winter in the freezing north.[39] Napoleon's secret police opened Germaine's correspondence, and informed him of these sentiments. On December 31 he wrote angrily to Fouché: "Do not let that bitch of a Madame de Staël approach Paris. I know she is not far from it."[40] (Secretly and briefly she stole into Paris sometime in the spring of 1807.) Amid preparations for the battle of Friedland, Napoleon wrote to Fouché, April 19:

> Among the thousand and one things concerning Madame de Staël that come into my hands, here is a letter from which you can see what a fine Frenchwoman we have there. . . . It truly is difficult to restrain one's indignation at the spectacle of all the metamorphoses this whore, and an ugly one at that, is undergoing. I shall not tell you what projects this ridiculous coterie has already formed in case by a happy accident I should be killed, since a police minister may be assumed to be informed of this.

And on May 11, again to Fouché:

> This madwoman of a Madame de Staël writes me a six-page letter, in double Dutch. . . . She tells me she has bought an estate in the valley of Montmorency and draws the conclusion that this will entitle her to reside in Paris. I repeat to you that to leave such a hope to that woman is to torture her gratuitously. If I showed you the detailed evidence of everything she has done at her country place during the two months she resided there, you would be astonished. Indeed, although at five hundred leagues from France, I know better what happens there than does my Minister of Police.[41]

So, on April 25, 1807, Germaine unwillingly returned to Coppet. Constant, constant despite inconstancies, accompanied her partway, but diverged at Dôle to stay with his ailing father. Arrived at Coppet, she sent Schlegel to tell Constant that unless he rejoined her soon she would kill herself. Benjamin knew that this classic threat was a siren, not a swan, song, but he came, and silently bore her reproaches. He had long since ceased to love her, but "how can one tell the truth to one whose only answer consists in swallowing opium?" On July 10 Juliette Récamier came for a long visit; Germaine fell in love with her, and decided to live.

The police allowed *Corinne* to be printed, and its publication in the spring of 1807 gave its author a triumph that consoled her for Napoleon's victory at Friedland on June 14. The government-sponsored reviews were hostile, but thousands of readers were charmed, and said so. Today we are not enchanted by its form—an ecstatic romance interspersed with dull and dated essays on Italian scenery, character, religion, manners, literature, and art; and no one is thrilled by the hero's "manly face" (he turns out to be spineless), or "the divine inspiration enthroned in" the heroine's eyes.[42] But in 1807 Italy was not yet an overwritten land, more familiar to us, in history and art, than our own; romance was spreading its wings; romantic love was struggling to be freed from parental power, economic bonds, and moral taboos; the rights of women were beginning to find voice. *Corinne* had all these fascinations, embodied in a fair *improvatrice* who sings spontaneous poetry and strums a bewitching lyre. Corinne, in her prime, is visibly Germaine, with "an Indian shawl twined about her lustrous black curls; . . . her arms transcendently beautiful, . . . her figure rather robust"; moreover, her conversation "united all that is natural, fanciful, just, sublime, powerful, and sweet."[43] Strange to say, the unsentimental Emperor, stranded on St. Helena, took up the book and could not lay it down until he had read it to its end.[44]

4. Understanding Germany

To the task of overthrowing Napoleon and managing a menagerie of geniuses and epicures, Madame now added the delicate enterprise of explaining Germany to France. Even while her newborn *Corinne* was battling for life against a subjugated press, she was hiding in her secret self a bold and massive opus on the land beyond the Rhine. To prepare herself conscientiously she set out on another tour of Central Europe.

On November 30, 1807, she left Coppet with Albert, Albertine, Schlegel, and her valet Eugène (Joseph Uginet). At Vienna she heard music by Haydn, Gluck, and Mozart, but left no mention of Beethoven. During three of five weeks in Austria she carried on an amorous correspondence with an Austrian officer, Moritz O'Donnell; offered him money and marriage, lost him, and wrote to Constant letters of limitless devotion—"My heart, my life, everything I have is yours if you wish and as you wish";[45] he contented himself by borrowing some of her money. At Teplitz and Pirna she conferred with Friedrich von Gentz, an ardent anti-Bonaparte publicist; learning of these meetings, Napoleon concluded that she was aiming to disrupt the peace that he had recently signed at Tilsit in July. At Weimar she found neither Schiller (who had died in 1805) nor Goethe. She passed on to Gotha and Frankfurt; then, suddenly ill and depressed, she hurried back to Coppet.

Perhaps this intimation of mortality shared in her turn toward mysticism; Schlegel contributed to it; but a much stronger influence came from the ascetic Julie von Krüdener and the lecherous dramatist Zacharias Werner, both of whom sojourned at Coppet in 1808. By October of that year the guests and the language were predominantly German, and the *lumières* of the Enlightenment had yielded to a mystic religion. "There is no reality on this earth," Germaine wrote to O'Donnell, "except religion and the power of love; all the rest is even more fugitive than life itself."[46]

It was in this mood that she wrote *De l'Allemagne*. By 1810 it was nearing completion, and she longed to be in Paris for its printing. She wrote humbly to Napoleon, telling him that "eight years' [exile and] misery modify all characters, and destiny teaches resignation." She proposed to go to the United States; she asked for a passport, and permission for an interim stay in Paris. The passport was granted; the permission was not.[47] Nevertheless, in April, 1810, she moved with her family and Schlegel to Chaumont (near Blois), from which she superintended the printing of her three-volume manuscript in Tours. In August she moved to neighboring Fossé.

The proofs of the first two volumes were submitted by Nicolle, the printer, to the censors in Paris. They agreed to the publication after the deletion of a few unimportant sentences. Nicolle printed five thousand copies, and sent advance copies to influential persons. On June 3 the sympathetic Fouché was dismissed as minister of police, and was succeeded by the rigorous René Savary, Duc de Rovigo. On September 25 Juliette Récamier brought to the censor the proofs of Volume III, and to Queen Hortense a full set of proofs for transmission—with a letter from the authoress—to the Emperor. Savary, apparently with Napoleon's approval, decided that the book was so unfavorable to France and its ruler that its distribution could not be allowed. He ordered the printer to suspend the publication, and, on October 3, sent a stern notice to Mme. de Staël that she was to carry out at once her declared intention to go to America. On October 11 a detachment of gendarmes entered the printer's plant, smashed the type plates, and carried away all obtainable copies of the volumes; these were later crushed into pulp. Other officers demanded the manuscript; Germaine gave them the original, but her son Auguste secreted and preserved a copy. The authoress reimbursed the printer for his losses, and fled back to Coppet.

On Germany, as published in 1813, is an earnest attempt to survey, with brevity and sympathy, every aspect of German civilization in the age of Napoleon. That a woman with so many cares and lovers should have found the leisure, the energy, and the competence for such an enterprise is one of the marvels of that exciting time. Through the Swiss internationalism in her background, through her marriage with a Holstein baron, through her Protestant heritage and her hatred of Napoleon, she was prepared to give Germany the benefit of nearly every doubt, to use its virtues as an indirect criticism of Napoleon and tyranny, and to present it to France as a culture rich in sentiment, tenderness, and religion, and therefore well suited to correct the intellectualism, cynicism, and skepticism then current in literate France.

Strange to say, she did not care for Vienna, though, like her, it was both gay and sad—gay with wine and talk, sad with the mortality of love and the proliferation of Napoleon's victories. It was Catholic and southern with music, art, and almost childlike faith; she was Protestant and northern, heavy with food and sentiment, and floundering in philosophy. There was no Kant here, but there was Mozart; no ardor of controversy, no fireworks of wit, but there was the simple pleasure of friends and lovers, parents and children, promenading in the Prater and watching the Danube pass idly by.

Even the Germans disconcerted her; "stoves, beer, and the smoke of tobacco surround all the common folk with a thick and hot atmosphere from which they are never inclined to escape."[48] She deplored the monotonous simplicity of German dress, the complete domestication of the men, the readiness to submit to authority. "The separation into classes . . . is more distinct in Germany than anywhere else; . . . everybody keeps his rank, his place, . . . as if it were his established post."[49] She missed, in Germany, that cross-fertilization of aristocrats, authors, artists, generals, politicians, which she had found in French society; hence "the nobles have few ideas, the men of letters have too little practice in affairs";[50] the ruling class remains feudal, the intellectual class loses itself in airy dreams. Here Madame quoted Jean Paul Richter's famous epigram: "The empire of the seas belongs to the English, that of the land to the French, and that of the air to the Germans."[51]

She added, pertinently: "The extension of knowledge in modern times serves to weaken the character when it is not strengthened by the habit of business and the exercise of the will."[52]

She admired the German universities as then the best in the world. But she deplored the German language, with its massing of consonants, and she resented the length and structure of the German sentence, which kept the decisive verb to the end, and so made interruption difficult;[53] interruptions, she felt, were the life of conversation. She found too little in Germany of the lively but polite debate characteristic of Parisian salons; this, she thought, was due to lack of a national capital which could bring the country's wits together,[54] and partly to the German habit of sending the women away from the dinner table when the men proposed to smoke and talk. "At Berlin the men rarely converse except with each other; the military condition gives them a sort of rudeness, which prevents them from taking any trouble about the society of women."[55] In Weimar, however, the ladies were cultured and amorous, the soldiers minded their manners, and the Duke realized that his poets were giving him a niche in history. "The literary men of Germany . . . form in many respects the most distinguished assemblage which the enlightened world can present to us."[56]

Our guide had some trouble appreciating the nuances of German poetry, and even of German prose; she was accustomed to French clarity and found Teutonic depth a learned obscurity. But she took the side of the Germans in the Romantic revolt against classical models and restraints. She defined the classical style as one based upon the classics of ancient Greece and Rome; Romantic literature, by contrast, rose out of Christian theology and sentiment, spread its roots in the poetry of the troubadours, the legends of chivalry, the myths and ballads of the early medieval north. Basically, perhaps, the division lay in the classic subordination of the self to reality, and the Romantic subordination of reality to the self.

For this reason Mme. de Staël welcomed German philosophy despite its difficulty, for, like herself, it put the emphasis on the self; it saw in consciousness a miracle greater than all the revolutions of science. She rejected the psychology of Locke and Condillac, which reduced all knowledge to sensations, and so made all ideas the effects of external objects; this, she felt, led inevitably to materialism and atheism. In one of the longest chapters in her book she attempted, with modest disclaimers, to state the essence of Kant's *Critiques:* they restored the mind as an active participant in the conception of reality; free will as an active element in the determination of actions; and moral conscience as a basic ingredient in morality. By these theorems, she felt, "Kant had with a firm hand separated the different empires of the soul and the senses,"[57] and so had established the philosophical basis of Christianity as an effective moral code.

Though she had made a shambles of the Sixth Commandment, Madame was convinced that no civilization could survive without morality, and no moral code could dispense with religious belief. Reasoning about religion, she argued, is a treacherous procedure; "reason does not give happiness in place of that which it takes away."[58] Religion is "the solace of misery, the wealth of the poor, the future of the dying";[59] here the Emperor and the Baroness agreed. So she preferred the active Protestantism of Germany to the pretended Catholicism of upper-class France; she thrilled to the mighty hymns that resounded from German throats in choirs, homes, and streets, and she frowned upon the French way of watching the stock exchange and leaving the poor to attend to God.[60] She had a good word to say for the Moravian Brethren. Her final chapter was a plea for a mystic "enthusiasm" —an inner sense of an omnipresent God.

All in all, allowing for limitations imposed by temperament and time, *On Germany* was one of the outstanding books of the age, a heady leap from *Corinne* to Kant; and Napoleon would have been wise to disarm it with faint praise—as being excellent for a woman with no sympathy for the problems of government. She had strongly censured censorship, but to deny the book to France was to illustrate and strengthen her case. She had on many pages praised Germany at the expense of France, but she had often praised France at the expense of Germany, and a hundred passages revealed her love for her native and forbidden land. She had dealt lightly with abstruse subjects, but she had aimed to interest a wide audience in France, and thereby promote international understanding. She asked for a cross-fertilization of cultures, which would have helped Napoleon's union of the Rhenish Confederation with France. She wrote intelligently, sometimes wittily,[61] adorning her pages with illuminating perceptions and ideas. Ultimately she revealed Germany to France, as Coleridge and Carlyle were soon to reveal it to England. "This book," said Goethe, "ought to be considered as a powerful engine which made a wide breach in that Chinese wall of antiquated prejudice which divided the two countries; so that, beyond the Rhine, and afterward beyond the Channel, we [Germans] became better known—a fact that could not fail to procure for us a great influence over all Western Europe."[62] She was "a good European."

5. Imperfect Victory

Only another author can understand what it meant to Germaine de Staël that the culminating production of her life and thought had to remain hidden in the recesses of Coppet, apparently as dead as a child stifled at birth. She discovered that her home was surrounded by agents of the Emperor, that some of her servants had been bribed to report on her, and that any friend who dared to visit her would be marked for imperial revenge. Notables whose lives and fortunes had been saved by her during the Revolution took care not to come near her now.[63]

She had two consolations. In 1811 she met Albert-Jean Rocca, then close to twenty-three years old, a second lieutenant wounded in battle, permanently lamed, and suffering from tuberculosis. He fell in love with the heroic Germaine, who was then forty-five, physically unprepossessing, morally imperfect, intellectually brilliant, and not without financial charm.

"John" besieged her, and gave her a child. Germaine welcomed the new love as defying and delaying old age. — The other solace was her hope that if she could get to Sweden or England she might find a publisher for her hidden masterpiece. But she could not get to Sweden through any country under Napoleon's power. She resolved to take her manuscript secretly through Austria, then up through Russia to St. Petersburg, and thence to Stockholm, where Prince Bernadotte would help her. It was no easy matter for her to abandon the home that she had made famous, and the grave of her mother, whom she could now forgive, and of the father who still seemed to her to have been a political sage and a financial saint. — On April 7, 1812, she gave birth to Rocca's boy, who was sent to a nurse for safekeeping. On May 23, 1812, eluding all spies, and accompanied or followed by her daughter Albertine, her two sons, her old lover Schlegel and her new lover Rocca, she left for Vienna, hoping to secure there a passport to Russia, and then to find her way to St. Petersburg and a handsome, chivalrous, and liberal Czar. On June 22 Napoleon, with 500,000 men, crossed the Niemen into Russia, hoping to find there a beaten and penitent Czar.

Germaine told the story of this trip in her *Ten Years of Exile*. Contemplating now that strange conjunction of wills and events, one wonders at the courage that took this harassed woman through a thousand obstacles and a supposedly barbarous people, to reach Zhitomir, in Polish Russia, only eight days ahead of Napoleon's troops.[64] She hurried on to Kiev and thence to Moscow, where, challenging fate, she lingered to visit the Kremlin, to hear the church music, to visit the local leaders in science and literature. Then, a month before Napoleon's arrival, she left Moscow via Novgorod for St. Petersburg. Everywhere, in the cities on her route, she was received as a distinguished ally in the war against the invader. She flattered the Czar as the hope of European liberalism. Together they planned to make Bernadotte king of France.

In September she reached Stockholm, where she helped to bring Bernadotte into the coalition against Napoleon.[65] After a stay of eight months in Sweden, she crossed the sea to England. London acclaimed her as the first woman of Europe; Byron and other notables came to pay their respects, and she had no difficulty in arranging with Byron's publisher, John Murray, to issue her long-delayed volumes to the world (October, 1813). She remained in England while the Allies broke Napoleon at Leipzig, marched into Paris, and put Louis XVIII on the throne. Then (May 12, 1814) she hurried across the Channel, restored her salon in Paris after ten years of exile, and played host to dignitaries from a dozen lands—Alexander, Wellington, Bernadotte, Canning, Talleyrand, Lafayette. Constant rejoined her, and Mme. Récamier shone again. Germaine urged Alexander to remember his liberal pronouncements; Alexander and Talleyrand persuaded Louis XVIII to "grant" to his recaptured subjects a bicameral constitution based on the British model; at last Montesquieu had his way. But Madame did not like the word "grant"; she wanted the King to recognize the sovereignty of the people. In July, 1814, she went back to Coppet, triumphant and proud, but feeling the nearness of death.

Her adventures, her battles, even her victories, had brought her amazing vitality close to exhaustion. Nevertheless she devotedly tended the dying Rocca, arranged for the marriage of her daughter to the Duc de Broglie, and began to write her brilliant swan song, the 600-page *Considérations sur les principaux événements de la Révolution française*. The first part was a defense of Necker in all his policies; the second excoriated the despotism of Napoleon. After his seizure of the government his every move seemed to her an advance toward tyranny; and his wars were props and excuses for absolutism. Before Stendhal, long before Taine, she likened Napoleon "to the Italian despots of the fourteenth and fifteenth centuries."[66] He had read and accepted Machiavelli's principles of government, without feeling a comparable love for his country. France was not really his fatherland; it was his steppingstone. Religion was to him not the humble acceptance of a supreme being but an instrument for the conquest of power. Men and women were not souls but tools.[67] He was not sanguinary, but he was ever indifferent to the carnage of victory. He had the brutality of a *condottiere*, never the manners of a gentleman. And this crowned vulgarian made himself the judge and censor of all speech and thought, of the press that was the last refuge of liberty, and of the salons that were citadels of the free mind of France. He was not the son of the Revolution; but if he was, he was also its parricide.[68]

When she learned that a plan was forming to kill the dethroned Emperor, she hurried to notify his brother Joseph, and offered to go to Elba and protect her fallen foe; Napoleon sent her a word of appreciation. When he returned from Elba, and regained France without a blow, she could not help admire his courage: "I will not abandon myself to declamations against Napoleon. He did what was natural for the restoration of his throne, and his march from Cannes to Paris was one of the greatest conceptions of audacity that can be cited from history."[69]

After Waterloo she withdrew at last from the political arena. She did not relish the occupation of France by foreign troops, nor the rush of the old nobility to regain land, wealth, and power. However, she was glad to receive from Louis XVIII the twenty million francs owed to Necker or his heirs for his loan to the French Treasury. On October 10, 1816, she was privately married to Rocca. On October 16, though both were ailing, they went to Paris, and Germaine reopened her salon. It was her final triumph. The most famous names in Paris came: Wellington from England, Blücher and Wilhelm von Humboldt from Prussia, Canova from Italy; there Chateaubriand began his idyl with Mme. Récamier. But Germaine's health was fast failing, and her disillusionment with the Restoration grew as the royalists undertook to eliminate from the political life of France every vestige of the Revolution. This was not the dream that she had dreamed. Her *Considérations* defined despotism as the union of both the executive and the legislative powers in one person; and it insisted on a national assembly fully elected by a sovereign people.

She did not live to see that book published. Her body, weakened with passions, poisoned with drugs, winning sleep only through increasing doses of opium, broke down in its attempt to support her mind. On February 21, 1817, as she was mounting the stairs at a reception given by one of Louis XVIII's ministers, she swayed and fell, paralyzed by a cerebral stroke. For three months she lay on her back, unable to move but able to talk, and sensitive to a host of pains. At her urging her daughter took over the role of hostess in the salon. "I have always been the same, intense and sorrowful," she told Chateaubriand. "I have loved God, my father, and liberty."[70] She died on July 14, 1817, the anniversary of the Bastille. She was not yet fifty-one. Four years later her great enemy died, not yet fifty-two.

We can agree with Macaulay that she was "the greatest woman of her time,"[71] and the greatest name in French literature between Rousseau and Chateaubriand. Her work ranked higher in aim and range than in literary art, and her thought was more pervasive than profound. She shared many qualities with her chosen foe: forceful personality, courage against odds, domineering spirit, pride of power, and intolerance of dissent; but she lacked his realistic mind, and her imagination, as seen in her novels, was romantically childish compared with the reach of his political dreams. Let him sum her up from the perspective of his island isolation: "The home of Madame de Staël became a veritable arsenal against me. To her came many to be armed as her knights in her war. . . . And yet, after all, it is only true to say that she was a woman of very great talent, of high distinction, and of great strength of character. She will endure."[72]

III. BENJAMIN CONSTANT: 1767–1816

There were two Constants in Napoleon's stormy life: Véry Constant, his valet, who wrote about the great dictator's private life, voluminous memoirs disproving an old adage; and Benjamin Constant de Rebecque, who, born in Switzerland, educated in a dozen cities, and finally embattled in France, so littered his life with unpaid debts, discarded mistresses, and political somersaults that it would hardly be profitable to dally with him here had he not come close to history in many frays, been loved to distraction by notable women, and been able to describe his faults with such eloquence, subtlety, and impartiality as might help us to understand our own.

He chronicled his first twenty years of life in a *Cahier rouge* or *Red Notebook;* the next twenty in a short novel, *Adolphe;* and the years 1804–16 in a *Journal intime* that ranges from Paris to Coppet to Weimar to London with arresting snatches of history, literature, psychology, and philosophy. Only *Adolphe* was published in his lifetime (London, 1816); the *Journal* remained in manuscript till 1887, the *Cahier* till 1907; these scattered members, with a thousand contemporary references, constitute Constant today.

He came of a titled Swiss-German family that traced its pedigree through 800 years. We need go back no further than his father, who was so occupied with his own sins that he had little time left to supervise his son's. Baron Arnold-Juste Constant de Rebecque was an officer in a Swiss regiment serving the States-General of the Netherlands. He was handsome, well read, a friend of Voltaire. Early in 1767 he married Henriette de Chandieu, of French-Huguenot extraction. She was then twenty-five, he was forty. On October 25, at Lausanne, she gave birth to Benjamin; a week later she died, the first of many women who suffered from his irregularities. The father entrusted the boy to various tutors, carelessly chosen. One tried by beatings and fondlings to make the boy an infant prodigy in Greek. When the beatings endangered Benjamin's health he was transferred to a second tutor, who took him to a brothel in Brussels. His third tutor gave him a good knowledge of music, and, for the rest, relied on him to educate himself through reading. Benjamin read eight or ten hours a day, permanently injuring his eyes and his faith.[73] He spent a year at the University of Erlangen; then he was transferred to Edinburgh, where he felt the final flurry of the Scottish Enlightenment; but there too he took to gambling, which became second only to sex in disordering his life. After adventures in Paris and Brussels he settled in Switzerland, and began to write a history of religion, with a view to demonstrating the superiority of paganism to Christianity.

He passed from woman to woman, from casino to casino, until at last his father arranged (1785) to have him live in Paris with the family of Jean-Baptiste Suard, a literary critic of learning and goodwill.

> I was received with full acceptance by his set. My wit, which at that time entirely lacked solidity and accuracy, had an amusingly epigrammatic turn; my learning—which was very desultory but superior to that of most of the men of letters of the rising generation—and the originality of my character, all seemed novel and interesting. . . . When I remember the kind of things I used to say at that time, and the convinced disdain that I showed toward everyone, I am at a loss to know how I could have been tolerated.[74]

In 1787 he met "the first woman of superior intelligence whom I had hitherto known." "Zélide"—i.e., Isabella van Tuyll—had been the difficult *pièce de résistance* in Boswell's Holland days. She had rejected him and others to marry her brother's tutor, and was now living with him, in resigned discontent, in the town of Colombier near the Lake of Neuchâtel. When Constant came upon her she was in Paris seeing her novel *Caliste* through the press. She was forty-seven, but she had for the nineteen-year-old philanderer the charm of a woman still physically stimulating and intellectually brilliant and blasé to a degree that made his own proud sophistication seem sophomorically juvenile. "I still remember with emotion the days and nights we spent together, drinking tea, and talking with inexhaustible ardor on every possible subject." When she returned to Colombier he took up his own dwelling in nearby Lausanne. Her husband mistakenly believed that the disparity of their ages would limit Zélide and Constant to friendship. She set herself zealously to educating Benjamin in the wiles of women and the lies of men. "We intoxicated one another with our jests and our scorn of the human race."[75]

His father interrupted this semi-intellectual diversion by sending him to Brunswick to serve as a court functionary to the Duke who was soon to lead an army against the French Revolution. Between ceremonies he fell into the tender trap of the Baroness Wilhelmina von Cramm, married her (May 8, 1789), found husband-ry duller than philandering, concluded that Minna loved "cats, dogs, birds, friends, and a lover" more than her lawful mate, and sued for divorce. Feeling heart-free, he developed a passion for Charlotte von Hardenberg, wife of Baron von Marenholz. She refused Benjamin the consolation of adultery, but offered to marry him as soon as she could divorce the Baron. Frightened by the thought of another marriage, Constant fled to Lausanne (1793) and Colombier, where Zélide resumed his education. He was now twenty-six years old, and she felt that he should sacrifice the zest of variety for rest in unity. She told him, "If I knew a young and robust person who would love you as much as I do, and who is no more stupid than I am, I would have the generosity to say, 'Go to her!' "[76] To her surprise and indignation, he soon found a young and robust person.

On September 28, 1794, on the road between Nyon and Coppet, Benjamin met Germaine de Staël, aged twenty-eight, jumped into her carriage, and began a fifteen-year comedy of vows, tears, and words. He had never known a woman with an intellect so enriched, a will so strong, passions and senti-ments stronger still. Against these powers he was all weakness, for he had lost character through a permissive and fragmented youth, and had reduced his natural vitality through physiological campaigns without dignity or growth. Here too his ready triumph was a defeat, for though she accepted him as a lover, and allowed him to believe that he had fathered Albertine, she persuaded him to sign with her, at an unknown date, an oath of al-legiance which, aided by his debts to her, kept him in psychological bondage even after both had taken other mates to their beds.

> We promise to consecrate our lives to each other; we declare that we regard ourselves as indissolubly bound to each other; that we will share forever, and in every respect, a common destiny; that we will never enter into any other bond; and that we shall strengthen the bonds now uniting us as soon as lies within our powers.
> I declare that I am entering into this engagement with a sincere heart, that I know nothing on earth as worthy of love as Madame de Staël, that I have been the happiest of men during the four months I have spent with her, and that I regard it as the greatest happiness in my life to be able to make her happy in her youth, to grow old peaceably by her side, and to reach my term together with the soul that understands me, and without whose presence life on this earth would hold no more interest for me.
> BENJAMIN CONSTANT[77]

He followed her to Paris in 1795, merged his politics with hers, supported the Directory, accepted Napoleon's *coup d'état* as necessitated by the condi-tion of France, and served as spokesman for her as well as himself when, nominated by Napoleon, he became a member of the Tribunate. But as soon as the First Consul gave signs of desiring absolute power, the lovers jointly opposed him; she in her salon, he in his maiden speech (January 5, 1800), which demanded the right of the Tribunate to unshackled discussion. He won reputation as a forceful orator, but was marked for replacement as soon as the time should come (in 1802) for the Tribunate's periodic cleansing. When the lovers nevertheless carried on their war Napoleon banished them from Paris.

Constant went with her to Coppet, though their relations had apparently cooled to a platonic calm. "I need women," he told himself, "and Germaine is not sensual."[78] He offered to marry her; she refused, saying that this would sacrifice her rank and her daughter's marital prospects. In September, 1802, she fell in love with Camille Jordan, and invited him to accompany her to Italy, all expenses paid, vowing to "forget everything with you, whom I love profoundly."[79] Jordan refused. In April, 1803, Constant left Coppet for an estate he had bought near Mafliers, some thirty miles from Paris. In the fall, Germaine, risking Napoleon's ire, moved with her family to a country house in Mafliers. When Napoleon heard of this he bade her obey his order of banishment to 120 miles from Paris. She preferred to visit Germany. Constant, resenting the Consul's severity and touched by Germaine's grief, decided to accompany her.

He helped her and her children through the hardships of travel, rejoiced when he reached Weimar, and settled down there to work on his history of religion. On January 22, 1804, he began to keep a *Journal intime* with a buoyant entry: "I have just arrived in Weimar, I count on remaining some time, for there I shall find libraries, serious conversation after my taste, and, above all, peace for my work."[80] Some further entries reveal his mental growth:

January 23: I am working little and badly, but in revenge I have seen Goethe! Finesse, pride, physical sensitivity to the point of suffering; a remarkable spirit, a fine countenance, a figure slightly deteriorated. . . . After dinner I chat with Wieland—a French soul, cold like a philosopher, light like a poet. . . . Herder is like a warm, soft bed, where one has agreeable dreams. . . .

January 27: Johannes von Müller [the Swiss historian] has explained to me his plan for a universal history. . . . [With him] an interesting question arose: the creation or noncreation of the world. According to how we decide this question the course of the human race will appear diametrically opposite: if creation, deterioration; if no creation, amelioration. . . .

February 12: Have reread Goethe's *Faust* [Part I]. It is in derision of mankind and all scientists. The Germans find in it an unprecedented profundity, but as for me, I prefer *Candide.* . . .

February 26: A visit to Goethe. . . .

February 27: An evening with Schiller. . . .

February 28: Supper with Schiller and Goethe. I know no one in the world who has so much humor [*gaieté*], refinement, force, and range of spirit as Goethe.

February 29: . . . I depart tomorrow for Leipzig, and I do not leave Weimar without sadness. I have passed here three months very pleasantly: I have studied, lived secure, suffered little; I do not ask for more. . . .

> March 3: I visit the Museum at Leipzig. . . . The library has 80,000 volumes. . . . Why should I not remain here and work? . . .
> March 10: I have bought six louis [approximately $150.00] of German books.[81]

He left Mme. de Staël at Leipzig and made his way down to Lausanne to visit with his relatives. He arrived just in time to learn that Germaine's father had died—"this good Monsieur Necker, so noble, so affectionate, so pure. He loved me. Who now will guide his daughter?"[82] He rushed back to Germany, hoping to break the news to her gently; he knew that this loss would overwhelm her. He came back with her to Coppet, and stayed with her till she had raised her head again.

She needed him most in those days when he was longing to part from her, to be free to pursue his own political and personal career without tying it to her interest. He felt that he had ruined his political prospects by becoming a lieutenant in her war against Napoleon. In April, 1806, his diary analyzed his malady of will: "I always incline to break with Madame de Staël, but every time I feel this way, the next morning finds me in a contrary mood. Meanwhile her impetuosities and imprudences keep me in torment and perpetual danger. We must part . . . ; it is my sole chance for a peaceful life."[83] A month later his journal records: "In the evening a terrible scene—horrible, senseless, atrocious words. She is mad or I am crazy. How will it end?"[84]

Like so many authors unable to handle life, he took refuge in telling his side of the story in a fiction carefully disguised but transparently confessional. Hot with resentment of Germaine's domination and reproaches, angry at his own weak-willed hesitations, he wrote in fifteen days (January, 1807) and one hundred pages the first psychological novel of the nineteenth century, more probing and subtle than most, and merciless to both woman and man.

Adolphe traced the fictional author's aimless youth, his fragmentary education, his hasty and superficial amours, his eager reading—which replaced his faith with a cynicism that gnawed at the meaninglessness of his life. He brought his odyssey of irresponsible loves to a climactic catastrophe in the story of Ellénore, a noblewoman who had sacrificed home, honor, and future to be the mistress of Count P——. Adolphe notes the way in which society—founding its order and stability on laws and customs checking unsocial desires—punishes with gossip and contumely the woman (much less the man) who violates those protective norms. His pity for the ostracized Ellénore, his admiration for her courage, turn easily into love, or perhaps to the secret desire for one more conquest to sustain his pride. Just when his ardor is cooling to controllability she yields to him, leaves the Count and his money, takes a modest apartment, and tries to live on Adolphe's visits and funds. His interest in the surrendered citadel declines as her devotion mounts. He tries to break away from her; she reproaches him; finally they quarrel and part. She leaves him, and wastes away in poverty and lack of will to live. He rejoins her only to have her die in his arms.

Constant had sought to conceal any key that would unveil his fictional characters as denizens of Coppet; he had made his heroine Polish and sub-missive, and had made her die in despair. Nevertheless all who became acquainted with the book and its author identified him with Adolphe, and Mme. de Staël with Ellénore. Constant refrained for nine years from pub-lishing his book, but (vanity dulling caution) he read portions—sometimes all—of the manuscript to friends, and at last to Germaine herself, who fainted at its end.

Constant had received some passing strength by the return, into his life, of Charlotte von Hardenberg. She had divorced her first husband, and was tiring of the second, the Vicomte du Tertre; now she resumed her inter-rupted liaison with Constant. They were married on June 5, 1808, but when Benjamin, to quiet Mme. de Staël, returned to servitude at Coppet, Charlotte went back to Germany. Not till Madame discovered a new lover in John Rocca (1811) did Constant feel free. He went with Charlotte to live near Göttingen, and, helped by the university library, renewed his labor on his history of religion. The next two years were probably the happiest in his life.

But happiness was uncongenial to him. When (January, 1813) he heard from the Comte de Narbonne a firsthand story of Napoleon's disaster in Russia, and sensed the nearness of Napoleon's fall, his old restlessness re-turned. "Must I always be a spectator?" he asked himself in his journal. As the victorious Allies drove Napoleon back to the Rhine, Constant went to Hanover, met Bernadotte there, and was persuaded by him to write a pamphlet, *Esprit de conquête,* ascribing the collapse of France to Napoleon's despotism. Published in Hanover in January, 1814, at the height of the Allied push into France, it made him *persona grata* with the Allied leaders, and he followed their armies into Paris (April, 1814) in hopes of a personal restora-tion.

He visited Mme. de Staël's revived salon, and found that she had lost all interest in him. Since Charlotte was still in Germany, he announced in his journal (August 31, 1814) that he had fallen in love with Mme. Récamier, whose strategy of trembling but impregnable virginity he had long ridi-culed. He confided to the Duc de Broglie that he had tried to sell his soul to the Devil in exchange for the body of Juliette Récamier.[85] As she had been an ardent supporter of the Bourbons, she feared for her safety when she learned that Napoleon had escaped from Elba and had landed at Cannes. She inspired Constant to publish in the *Journal de Paris* (March 6, 1815) a call to the people of France to rise against the "Usurper." "Napoleon promises peace, but his very name is a signal for war. He promises victory; yet three times—in Egypt, Spain, and Russia—he deserted his armies like a coward."[86] La Récamier had lit in the inflammable Constant a fire that seemed to be burning all bridges behind him. On March 19 he proclaimed in the *Journal des débats* that he was ready to die for the restored King. That night Louis XVIII fled to Ghent; the next day Napoleon entered Paris; Constant hid in the United States Embassy. Napoleon issued a general amnesty; Constant emerged from hiding; on March 30 Joseph Bonaparte assured him that the Emperor was in a forgiving mood. On April 14 Napoleon received him and asked him to draft a liberal constitution. Napoleon revised the draft considerably, and then proclaimed it as the new charter of the French government. Constant was dizzy with glory.

On June 20, while he was reading *Adolphe* to Queen Hortense, the Duc de Rovigo entered to tell her that Napoleon had been defeated at Waterloo two days before. On July 8 Louis returned to the Tuileries; Constant sent him a humble apology; the King, judging him to be a wayward irresponsible adolescent who wrote excellent French, issued a pardon that surprised everyone. All Paris shunned Constant, and spun puns around his name. He wrote to Mme. Récamier forgiving her for having ruined "my career, my future, my reputation, and my happiness."[87] In October he left for Brussels, where he rejoined the patient Charlotte. Early in 1816 they crossed to England, where he had *Adolphe* published. In September he returned with his wife to Paris, plunged into politics, and began a new career.

IV. CHATEAUBRIAND: 1768–1815

1. Youth

For his French contemporaries François-René de Chateaubriand was the greatest writer of the time—"*le plus illustre* [said Sainte-Beuve in 1849] *de nos écrivains modernes*";[88] and another paragon of literary learning, Émile Faguet, wrote, about 1887 (forgetting Voltaire): "Chateaubriand is the greatest date in the history of French literature since the Pléiade" (*c.* 1550);[89] nearness lends enchantment to the view. Certainly his reign over French letters had been equaled only by Voltaire's. His ascendancy marked the triumph of religion over philosophy, just as Voltaire's had meant the triumph of philosophy over religion; and he lived long enough to see unfaith reborn. So one mood, passionately sustained, wears out its welcome, begets its opposite, and is revived, across the generations, through the embattled immoderation of mankind.

"My life and drama," he wrote, "is divided into three acts. From my early youth until 1800 I was a soldier and traveler; from 1800 till 1814, under the Consulate and the Empire, my life was devoted to literature; from the Restoration to the present day [1833] my life has been political."[90] There would be a fourth and subsiding act (1834–48), in which the triple hero was to be a living but fragile memory, sustained by kindly women, but fading in the mist of time.

"My name was first written Brien, . . . then Briand . . . About the beginning of the eleventh century the Briens gave their name to an important château in Brittany, and this château became the seat of the barony of Châteaubriand."[91] When the proud family lost almost everything but its château and its pride, the father went to America, and made a modest fortune. Returning, he married Apolline de Bedée, who gave him so many children that he withdrew into a somber introversion which passed down to his last and only remembered son. The mother soothed her labors and illnesses with an intense piety. Four of her children died before René was born, September 4, 1768, at St.-Malo, on the Channel coast. He later remarked that "after being born oneself, I know no greater misfortune than that of giving birth to a human being."[92] His sister Lucile, ever ailing, mingled her *mal-de-vie* with his in an intimacy so intense that it left them cold to marriage. The fog coming from the Channel, and the waves that beat upon their island and home added to their somber spirit, but became dear in memory.

When he was nine the family moved to an estate in Combourg, which brought with it the title of *comte*, and made René a *vicomte*. Now he was sent to a school at nearby Dol, taught by priests who, at his mother's urging, sought to inspire in him a vocation to the priesthood. They gave him a good grounding in the classics; soon he was making his own translations from Homer and Xenophon. "In my third year at Dol . . . chance put into my hands . . . an unexpurgated Horace. I obtained insight into . . . charms of an unknown nature in a sex in which I had seen only a mother and sisters. . . . My terror of the infernal shades . . . affected me both morally and physically. I continued, in my innocence, to fight against the storms of a premature passion and the terrors of superstition."[93] His sexual energy, without any known contact with the other sex, developed in him an image of an idealized woman, to whom he became mystically devoted with an intensity that may have diverted him from a normal development.

As the time for his First Communion neared, he feared to admit his secret agitations to his confessor. When he found courage to do so, and the kindly priest gave him comfort and absolution, he felt "the joy of the angels." "The next day . . . I was admitted to the sublime and moving ceremony which I vainly endeavored to describe in *Le Génie du christianisme*. . . . The Real Presence of the Victim in the Blessed Sacrament on the altar was as manifest to me as my mother's presence by my side. . . . I felt as though a light had been kindled within me. I trembled with veneration."[94] Three months later he left the Collège de Dol. "The memory of these obscure teachers will always be dear to me."[95]

That exaltation subsided as his reading raised questions to his faith. He confessed to his parents that he felt no vocation to the priesthood. At seventeen he was sent for two years to the Collège de Rennes to fit him for appointment to the Naval Guard at Brest. In 1788, aged twenty, he reported there for tests, but the prospects of life and discipline in the French Navy so frightened him that he returned to his parents at Combourg, and, perhaps to quiet their reproaches, agreed to enter the Collège de Dinan and prepare for the priesthood; "the truth is that I was only trying to gain time, for I

did not know what I wanted."[96] Finally he joined the Army as a commissioned officer. He was presented to Louis XVI, hunted with him, and saw
the taking of the Bastille; he sympathized with the Revolution until, in
1790, it abolished all ranks, titles, and feudal rights. When his regiment
voted to join the Revolutionary Army he resigned his commission, and—
fortified by a modest income left him at his father's death—he left on April 4,
1791, for the United States. He announced that he would try to find a
northwest passage through Arctic America. "I was an ardent freethinker at
the time."[97]

He reached Baltimore July 11, 1791, drove to Philadelphia, dined with
President Washington, amused him with his grandiose plans, made his way
to Albany, hired a guide, bought two horses, and rode proudly westward.
He marveled at the grandeur of the scenery, which mingled mountains,
lakes, and streams under a summer sun. He reveled in these open spaces and
their natural art, as a refuge from civilization and its cares. He recorded his
experiences in a journal which he later polished and published as *Voyage en
Amérique*, and which already displayed the scented beauty of his style:

> *Liberté primitive, je te retrouve enfin! Je passe comme cet oiseau qui vol
> devant moi, qui se dirige au hazard, et n'est embarrassé qu'au choix des
> ombrages. Me voilà tel que le Tout-Puissant m'a créé, souverain de la nature,
> porté triomphant sur les eaux, tandu que les habitants des fleuves accompagnent
> ma course, que les peuples de l'air me chantent leurs hymnes, que les bêtes de
> la terre me saluent, que les forêts courbent leurs cimes sur mon passage. Est-ce
> sur le front de l'homme de la société ou sur le mien qu'est gravé le sceau
> immortel de notre origine? Courez vous enfermer dans vos cités, allez vous
> soumettre à vos petites lois, gagnez votre pain à la sueur de votre front, ou
> dévorez le pain du pauvre; égorgez-vous pour un mot, pour un maître; doutez
> de l'existence de Dieu, ou adorez-le sous des formes superstitieuses; moi j'irai
> errant dans mes solitudes; pas un seul battement de mon coeur ne sera com-
> primé; pas un seul de mes pensées ne sera enchaînée; je serai libre comme la
> nature; je ne reconnaîtrai de souverain que celui qui alluma la flamme des
> soleils, et qui, d'un seul coup de sa main, fît rouler tous les mondes.**[98]

Here are all the paraphernalia of the Romantic movement: freedom,
nature, friendship for all living things; scorn of cities and the struggle of man
against man for bread or power; rejection of atheism and superstition; wor-

---

* "Primitive liberty, I recover you at last! I pass like this bird that flies before me, which
guides itself by free chance, and knows no embarrassment except in the choice of shade. Here
I am as the Almighty made me, sovereign of nature, carried triumphantly over the water,
while the denizens of the streams accompany me in my course, and the inhabitants of the
air sing their hymns to me, the beasts of the earth salute me, the forests bend their tree-tops
as I pass. Is it on the forehead of the man of society, or on mine, that the immortal seal of
our origin is engraved? Run, then, to shut yourself up in your cities; go subject yourself to
your petty laws; gain your bread by the sweat of your brow, or devour the bread of the
poor; kill one another for a word, for a master; doubt the existence of God, or worship him
under superstitious forms; as for me, I shall go wandering in my solitudes; not one beat of
my heart will be checked, not one of my thoughts shall be suppressed; I shall be as free as
nature; I shall recognize no sovereign except him who lit the flame of the suns, and who,
with one stroke of his hand, set in revolution all the worlds."

ship of God in nature; the escape from every law except that of God . . . It did not matter, for literature, that Chateaubriand had lost his religious faith, or that many of his descriptions were imaginary rather than factual, or that a hundred inaccuracies, exaggerations, or impossibilities were soon discovered in his *Voyage* by French or American critics;[99] here was a prose that set aflutter all female—many male—breasts; not since Rousseau or Bernardin de Saint-Pierre had French prose been so colorful, or nature so splendid, or civilization so absurd. All that the Romantic movement now awaited was a persuasive presentation of the American Indian as the lord of Eden and wisdom, and a panorama of religion as the mother of morals, art, and salvation. Chateaubriand would soon provide the one in *Atala* and *René*, the other in *The Genius of Christianity*.

The poet-explorer rode on through New York State, received hospitality from some Onondaga Indians, slept primitively on Mother Earth near Niagara, and heard the muffled roar of the falls. The next day, standing hypnotized by the river that hurried to its end, "I had an involuntary longing to throw myself in."[100] Eager to see the falls from below, he clambered down a rocky slope, lost his footing, broke an arm, and was hoisted to safety by Indians. Sobered, he surrendered his dream of a northwest passage, turned south, and reached the Ohio. At this point his narrative becomes dubious. He tells us that he followed the Ohio to the Mississippi, this to the Gulf of Mexico, then, over a thousand miles and a hundred mountains, to Florida. Critics, comparing distances, conveyances, and time, have judged his story incredible, and have branded his description of fauna and flora as quite unlike the landscapes and vegetation of those regions a hundred years later;[101] however, a century could have drastically changed the wildlife, and even, through cultivation and mining, the contour of the earth.

After a stay with the Seminole Indians, Chateaubriand made his way northwest to Chillicothe, in what is now Illinois. There he saw in an English journal news of Louis XVI's flight to Varennes (June 22, 1791). He worried that the captured King would now be daily in danger of his life. "I said to myself, 'Go back to France,' and abruptly brought my travels to a close."[102] On January 2, 1792, he reached France after an absence of nine months. He was still but twenty-three.

2. Development

He had exhausted nearly all his funds, and remained uncertain and insecure in a country hostile to viscounts and moving toward war and September Massacres. His sisters advised him to marry money, and found for him a moderately dowered bride, Céleste Buisson de La Vigne, aged seventeen. They married (February 21, 1792). The modest Céleste remained loyal to him through all his vicissitudes and mistresses, and through his decade of conflict with Napoleon, whom she admired; and after many years he learned to love her. They went to live in Paris, near his sisters Lucile and Julie. Part of his wife's fortune, invested in church securities, was lost in the confiscation of ecclesiastical property by the revolutionary government; part of it René gambled away in the casinos.

On April 20 the Legislative Assembly declared war upon Austria. French *émigrés* formed a regiment to join Austria in overthrowing the Revolution. Chateaubriand, though not quite certain that he desired this, felt bound to join his fellow nobles. Leaving wife and sisters in a Paris that would soon imprison and then massacre hundreds of the aristocracy, he rushed to Coblenz, enrolled in the *émigré* army, and shared in the abortive siege of Thionville (September 1, 1792); he was wounded in the thigh, and was honorably discharged. Unable to get back through mobilized France to his wife, he made his way, mostly on foot, to Ostend, found passage to the island of Jersey, was nursed back to health by an uncle, and, in May, 1793, crossed to England.

There he learned the ways of poverty, and bore them well despite "the sickly temperament to which I was subject, and the romantic notions of freedom which I cherished."[103] He refused the allowance offered to *émigré* nobles by the British government; he survived by teaching French privately and in a boarding school. He fell in love with a pupil, Charlotte Ives; she returned his affection; her parents proposed that he marry Charlotte; he had to confess that he already had a wife. Meanwhile his wife, his mother, and his sisters had been imprisoned in France; his elder brother, with his wife and her heroic grandfather Malesherbes, were guillotined (April 22, 1794); his own wife and his sisters were not released till the end of the Terror with the fall of Robespierre.

Lucile had often noted his facility with words, and had urged him to be a writer. During these years in England he began a vast prose epic, *Les Natchez*, into whose 2,383 pages he poured his romantic dreams and his idealization of the American Indian. Anxious to win fame as a philosopher, he published in London (1797) an *Essai historique, politique, et moral sur les révolutions anciennes et modernes*. This was a remarkable performance for a youth of twenty-nine; poor in organization, rich in garnered ideas. Revolutions, Chateaubriand argued, are periodic outbursts following always the same curve from rebellion through chaos to dictatorship. So the Greeks deposed their kings, established republics, and then submitted to Alexander; the Romans deposed their king, established a republic, and then submitted to the Caesars;[104] here, two years before the 18th Brumaire, was Chateaubriand's forecast of Napoleon. History is a circle, or an enlarged repetition of the same circle, with frills that make the old seem new; the same good and the same evil survive in men despite such mighty overturns. There is no real progress; knowledge grows, but merely to serve instincts that do not change. The faith of the Enlightenment in the "indefinite perfectibility of mankind" is a childish delusion. Nevertheless (a conclusion that startled most readers) the Enlightenment had succeeded in undermining Christianity; there is no likelihood that the religion of our youth can ever recover from that century of political peace and intellectual war. What religion, then, will replace the Christian? Probably none (the young skeptic concludes). Intellectual and political turmoil will undermine European civilization, and return it to the barbarism from which it emerged; peoples now savage will rise to civilization, go through successive grandeurs and revolutions, and sink into barbarism in their turn.[105]

The book made Chateaubriand famous in *émigré* circles, but shocked those who felt that aristocracy and religion must stand together or die divided. These criticisms left their mark on Chateaubriand, whose later works were largely an apology for this one; but he was now deeply moved by a letter sent him from France July 1, 1798, by his sister Julie:

> My friend, we have just lost the best of mothers. . . . If you knew how many tears your errors have drawn from our honorable mother, and how deplorable these errors seem to all who make profession not merely of piety but of reason—if you knew this pledge it would help to open your eyes, to make you give up writing; and if a Heaven touched by our prayers should permit our reunion, you would find, among us, all the happiness that we can taste on earth.[106]

When Chateaubriand received this letter it was accompanied by another to the effect that this sister Julie too had died. In the preface to *Le Génie du christianisme* he ascribed to these messages the complete change displayed by the later book: "These two voices from the tomb, this death serving to interpret death, were a blow to me; I became a Christian. . . . I wept, and I believed."

So sudden and dramatic a change invited skepticism, but in a less than literal sense it could be sincere. Probably Chateaubriand, in whom the philosopher was never distinct from the poet, ascribed to a moment, as by a figure of speech, the process by which he passed from unbelief to a view of Christianity as, first, beautiful, then morally beneficent, finally deserving, despite its faults, of private sympathy and public support. He was moved, in the last years of the dying century, by letters from his friend Louis de Fontanes, describing the moral disintegration then corroding France, and the rising desire of the people to return to their churches and their priests. Soon, in Fontanes' judgment, this hunger would compel a restoration of Catholic worship.

Chateaubriand resolved to be the voice of that movement. He would write a defense of Christianity in terms not of science and philosophy but of morals and art. No matter if those fascinating stories that were told us in our youth were legends rather than history; they entranced and inspired us, and in some measure reconciled us to those Hebraic Commandments upon which our social order, and therefore Christian civilization, had been built. Would it not be the greatest of crimes to take from the people the beliefs that had helped them to control their unsocial impulses and to bear injustice, evil, suffering, and the fatality of death? So Chateaubriand, in his final *Mémoires*, expressed both his doubts and his faith: "My spirit is inclined to believe in nothing, not even in myself, to disdain everything—grandeur, miseries, peoples, and kings; nevertheless it is dominated by an instinct of

reason that commands it to submit to everything evidently beautiful: religion, justice, humanity, equality, liberty, glory."[107]

Early in 1800 Fontanes invited Chateaubriand to return to France.
Fontanes was *persona grata* with the First Consul, and would see to it that
the young *émigré* should not be harmed. Napoleon was already thinking of
restoring Catholicism; a good book on the virtues of Christianity might
help him meet the inevitable gibes of the Jacobins.

On May 16, 1800, Chateaubriand rejoined his wife and Lucile in Paris.
Fontanes introduced him to a literary circle that gathered in the home of
the frail but beautiful Comtesse Pauline de Beaumont, daughter of Comte
Armand-Marc de Montmorin, once minister of foreign affairs under Louis
XVI, and then guillotined. Soon she became Chateaubriand's mistress. It
was in her country house, and under her prodding, that he finished *Le
Génie*. He did not think the time ripe for the complete publication of a book
so contrary to the skepticism prevailing in intellectual circles; but in 1801
he offered Paris a 100-page extract from it as an unpretentious idyl of
Christian virtue and romantic love. It made him at once the talk of literate
France, the idol of the women, and the favorite son of the reviving Church.

He called it *Atala, or The Loves of Two Savages in the Desert*. The
initial scene is in Louisiana as peopled by the Natchez Indians; the narrator
is the blind old chieftain Chactas. He tells how, in his youth, he was captured
by a hostile tribe, and was sentenced to be burned to death, but was saved
by the Indian maid Atala. They flee together through marshes and forests,
over mountains and streams; they fall in love by force of propinquity and
through dangers shared; he seeks—she refuses—consummation, having
pledged lifelong virginity to her dying mother. They meet an old missionary, who supports her piety by satirizing love as a form of inebriation,
and marriage as a fate worse than death.[108] Torn (like history) between
religion and sex, Atala solves her dilemma by taking poison. Chactas is
desolate, but the missionary explains that death is a blessed release from life:

> "Despite so many days gathered on my head, . . . I have never met a man
> who had not been deceived by dreams of happiness, no heart that did not hold
> a hidden wound. The spirit apparently most serene resembles the natural wells
> of Florida's savannas: their surface seems calm and pure, but when you see
> to the bottom . . . you perceive a large crocodile, which the well nourishes
> with its waters."[109]

Chateaubriand's description of Atala's funeral—priest and pagan mingling
their hands to cover her corpse with the soil—became a famous passage in
the literature of romance; it inspired also one of the great paintings of the
Napoleonic period—*The Burial of Atala*, with which Girodet-Trioson
brought half of Paris to tears in 1808. But the classical tradition was too
strong in the France of 1801 to win for the tale the full acclaim of critics.
Many of them smiled at the purple passages, and the ancient use of love,
religion, and death to stir hearts broken or young, and the conscription of
nature to serve, with her various moods, as an obbligato to human joys and

woes. But others praised—and a multitude of readers enjoyed—the simple words and quiet music of the style; the sounds, forms, and colors of the fauna and flora; the mountains, forests, and streams that supplied a living background to the tale. The mood of France was ready to hear a good word for religion and chastity. Napoleon was planning a reconciliation with the Church. It seemed a good time to publish *Le Génie du christianisme*.

3. The Genius of Christianity

The book appeared in five volumes on April 14, 1802, in the same week that saw the promulgation of the Concordat. "As far as I can judge," wrote Jules Lemaître in 1865, "the *Génie du christianisme* was the greatest success in the history of French literature."[110] Fontanes greeted it with a *Moniteur* article praising it with friendly superlatives. A second edition appeared in 1803, dedicated to Napoleon. From that moment the author felt that Bonaparte was the only man of the age whom he had to surpass.

The *génie* of the title did not quite mean genius, though it meant that too. It meant the distinctive character, the inherent creative spirit, of the religion that had begotten and nurtured the civilization of postclassical Europe. Chateaubriand proposed to annul the eighteenth-century Enlightenment by showing, in Christianity, such understanding tenderness toward human needs and griefs, such multifarious inspiration to art, and such powerful supports to moral character and social order, that all questions as to the credibility of the Church's dogmas and traditions became of minor importance. The real question should be: Is Christianity an immeasurable, inseparable, and indispensable support to Western civilization?

A more logical mind than Chateaubriand's might have begun with a picture of the moral, social, and political deterioration of that Revolutionary France which had divorced itself from Catholic Christianity. But Chateaubriand was a man of feeling and sentiment, and probably he was right in assuming that most of the French, of either sex, were more like him than like Voltaire and the other *philosophes* who had labored so ardently to "crush the infamy" of an authoritarian religion. He called himself an *anti-philosophe*; he carried far beyond Rousseau the reaction against rationalism, and he reproved Mme. de Staël for defending the Enlightenment. So he began with an appeal to feeling, and left reason to fall in line after feeling had led the way.

He proclaimed at the outset his belief in the fundamental mystery of Catholic doctrine, the Trinity: God as the Father creating, God as the Son redeeming, God as the Holy Spirit enlightening and sanctifying. One must not worry here about credibility; the important thing is that without a belief in an intelligent God, life becomes a merciless struggle, sin and failure become unforgivable, marriage becomes a fragile and precarious association, old age a somber disintegration, death an obscene but inescapable agony. The sacraments of the Church—baptism, confession, Communion, confirmation, matrimony, extreme unction (deathbed anointment), and sacerdotal ordination—transformed the chapters in our painful growth and ignominious decay into advancing stages of spiritual development, each deepened with priestly guidance and solemn ceremony, and strengthening the infinitesimal individual with membership in a powerful and confident community of believers in a redeeming and lovable Christ, a sinless and interceding Mother, a wise, omnipotent, watchful, punishing, forgiving, and rewarding God. With that faith man is redeemed from the greatest curse of all—to be meaningless in a meaningless world.

Chateaubriand proceeded to contrast the virtues recommended by the pagan philosophers with those taught by Christianity: on the one hand fortitude, temperance, and prudence—all directed toward individual advancement; on the other, faith, hope, and charity—a creed that ennobled life, strengthened the social bond, and made death a resurrection. He compared the philosopher's view of history as the struggle and defeat of individuals and groups with the Christian view of history as the effort of man to overcome the sinfulness original to his nature and to achieve a widening *caritas*. Better to believe that the heavens declare the glory of God than that they are accidental accumulations of rock and dust, persistent but senseless, beautiful but dumb. And how can we contemplate the loveliness of most birds and many quadrupeds without feeling that some divinity lurks in their resilient growth and their enchanting forms?

As for morality, the matter seemed to Chateaubriand painfully clear: our moral code must be sanctioned by God, or it will collapse against the nature of man. No code of confessedly human origin will carry sufficient authority to control the unsocial instincts of men; the fear of God is the beginning of civilization, and the love of God is the goal of morality. Moreover, that fear and love must be handed down, generation after generation, by parents, educators, and priests. Parents with no God to transmit, teachers with no support in religious creed and garb, will find the infinite inventiveness of selfishness, passion, and greed stronger than their uninspired words. Finally, "there can be no morality if there is no future state";[111] there must be another life to atone for the tribulations of virtue on the earth.

European civilization (Chateaubriand argued) is almost entirely due to the Catholic Church—to her support of the family and the school, to her preaching of the Christian virtues, to her checking and cleansing of popular superstitions and practices, to the healing processes of the confessional, to her inspiration and encouragement of literature and art. The Middle Ages wisely abandoned the unguided pursuit of truth for the creation of beauty, and they produced in the Gothic cathedrals an architecture superior to that of the Parthenon. Pagan literature has many excellences for the mind, many pitfalls for morality. The Bible is greater than Homer, the Prophets are more inspiring than the philosophers; and what fiction can compare, in tenderness and influence, with the life and teaching of Christ?

Obviously a book like the *Génie* could appeal only to those who, through the excesses of the Revolution or the trials of life, were emotionally ready to believe. So the philosopher Joubert, Chateaubriand's friend, said that he sought in Catholicism a refuge from a revolutionary world too horrible to bear.[112] Such readers may have smiled at the childish teleology which taught that "the song of birds is ordained expressly for our ears. . . . In spite of our cruelty [to them] they cannot forbear to charm us, as they are obliged to fulfill the decrees of Providence."[113] But those readers were so carried along by the elegance and music of the style that they passed over the use of the Three Graces to explain the Trinity, or of the Malthusian fear of overpopulation to defend ecclesiastical celibacy. If the arguments were sometimes weak, the charm was strong; even Nature would have been pleased if, after some earthquake, flood, or hurricane, she had heard Chateaubriand's litany of her loveliness.

Did he really believe? From 1801 to late in life, we are told,[114] he omitted his "Easter duty" of confession and Communion—the Church's minimal demand upon her children. Sismondi reported a conversation with him in 1813:

> Chateaubriand observed the universal decadence of religions both in Europe and in Asia, and compared these symptoms of dissolution with those of polytheism in the time of Julian. . . . He concluded from this that the nations of Europe would disappear along with their religions. I was astounded to find him so free a spirit. . . . Chateaubriand talked of religion; . . . he believes it [religion] necessary to sustain the state; he thinks that he and others are bound to believe.[115]

No wonder that, carrying with him through sixty years such a burden of secret doubt, he never recovered from the youthful pessimism that he described in *René*. In old age he said, "I ought not to have been born."[116]

4. René

The Genius of Christianity was a major expression of the Romantic movement in the religious field: it formulated the return of faith and hope, if not of charity; it exalted medieval poetry and art, and stimulated the revival of Gothic architecture in France. Within its five volumes it originally included not only *Atala* but, till 1805, *René*. This forty-page paean to pessimism reflected the despondency of *émigrés*, and Chateaubriand's youthful infatuation with his sisters. It became the fount and standard of a thousand moans of melodious despair.

René is a young French aristocrat who has fled from France and has joined the Natchez Indian tribe in the hope of forgetting an incestuous love. His adoptive father, Chactas, having told him the tale of Atala, persuades him to tell his own story. "Timid and constrained before my father, I found ease and contentment only with my sister Amélie." When he realized that his love for her was nearing incest, he sought release by losing himself in the Paris crowd—"vast wilderness of men"; or he sat for hours in an unfrequented church, begging God to free him from the crime of his love or from the incubus of life. He looked for solitude amid mountains and fields, but nowhere could he drive from his thoughts the tenderness and loveliness of Amélie. Tormented with desire to go to her and declare his love, he decided, in shame, to kill himself. Amélie divined this decision when she learned that he was making his will. She hurried to Paris, found him, embraced him wildly, and "covered my forehead with kisses." Three months of comradeship and restrained happiness followed. Then, overcome with remorse, she fled to a convent, leaving him a word of comfort and all her fortune. He sought her and begged permission to talk with her; she would not see him. When she was about to take the vows he made his way into the chapel, knelt near her, heard her, prostrate before the altar, begging, "God of mercy, let me never rise from this somber bed, and cover with your favors the brother who never partook of my criminal passion." They never saw each other again. He resumed his thoughts of suicide, but decided to bear the greater pain of life. "I found" (and this passage became a *locus classicus* of romantic grief) "a kind of satisfaction in my suffering. I discovered, with a secret movement of joy, that sorrow is not, like pleasure, a feeling that wears itself out. . . . My melancholy became an occupation which filled all my moments; my heart was entirely and naturally steeped in ennui and misery."[117] Sick of civilization, he decided to lose himself in America and live the simple life of an Indian tribe. A missionary reproved him for his self-centered mood, and bade him return to France and cleanse himself by services to mankind. However, "René perished afterward, with Chactas, . . . in the massacre of the French and the Natchez Indians in Louisiana."

It is a story well told, except that the events are improbable and the sentiment is overdone. But sentiment had been starved for a decade; grief had been dangerous and too deep for tears; now, the Revolution ended and security restored, sentiment was free, and tears might flow. The melancholy of René, echoing Werther's across a generation, became a pose for René de Chateaubriand, was echoed in Sénancour's *Obermann* in 1804, and was carried on in *Childe Harold's Pilgrimage* (1813); Chateaubriand reproached Byron for not acknowledging his debt.[118] The little book infected a generation with *mal de siècle*—the characteristic "illness of the time"; it became the model of a thousand, perhaps a hundred thousand, melancholy tales (*romans*); its hero was called a "storyteller," *un romancier*; so, perhaps, the Romantic movement derived its name. For half a century now it would dominate the literature and art of France.

5. Chateaubriand and Napoleon

The Genius of Christianity, said Napoleon, "is a work of lead and gold, but the gold predominates. . . . Everything great and national in character ought to acknowledge the genius of Chateaubriand."[119] For his part he welcomed the book as admirably concordant with the Concordat. He arranged a meeting with the author, recognized him as a valuable property, and appointed him (1803) first secretary to the French Embassy in Rome. The author recorded the meeting with modesty and pride: "It mattered little to him that I had no experience of public affairs, that I was entirely unfamiliar with practical diplomacy; he believed that some minds are capable of understanding, and have no need of apprenticeship." [120] He was soon followed to Rome by his mistress; however, she died in Rome (November 5), with Chateaubriand at her side, and after bidding him return to his wife.

He was soon *persona grata* to the Pope, and *ingrata* to the ambassador, Napoleon's uncle, Cardinal Fesch, who complained that the brilliant author was assuming ambassadorial authority. The Cardinal was not the man to allow this; he asked to be relieved of his aide; Napoleon recalled the Viscount by appointing him chargé-d'affaires in the little Swiss republic of Valais. Chateaubriand went to Paris to consider; but on hearing of the Duc d'Enghien's execution he sent to Napoleon his resignation from the diplomatic service.

> By daring to leave Bonaparte I had placed myself on his level, and he was turned against me by all the force of his perfidy, as I was turned against him by all the force of my loyalty. ... Sometimes I was drawn to him by the admiration with which he inspired me, and by the idea that I was witnessing a transformation of society and not a mere change of dynasty; but our respective natures, antipathetic in so many respects, always gained the upper hand; and if he would gladly have had me shot, I should have felt no great compunction about killing him.[121]

No immediate harm came to him. He was distracted from politics by the illness of his wife (whom he loved between liaisons) and the death of his sister Lucile (1804). Meanwhile he had taken as mistress Delphine de Custine. In 1806 he sought to replace her with Natalie de Noailles, but Natalie made her favors conditional on his undertaking a journey to the holy places in Palestine.[122] Leaving his wife in Venice, he went on to Corfu, Athens, Smyrna, Constantinople, and Jerusalem; he returned via Alexandria, Carthage, and Spain, and reached Paris in June, 1807. He had shown courage and stamina on this arduous tour, and on the way he had sedulously gathered material and background for two books that reinforced his literary fame: *Les Marytrs de Dioclétien* (1809), and *Itinéraire de Paris à Jérusalem* (1811).

While preparing these volumes he carried on his feud with Napoleon (then negotiating peace at Tilsit) by an article in the *Mercure de France* for July 4, 1807. It was ostensibly about Nero and Tacitus, but it could readily be applied to Napoleon and Chateaubriand.

> When, in the silence of abjection, no sign can be heard save that of the chains of the slave and the voice of the informer; when all tremble before the tyrant, and it is as dangerous to incur his favor as to merit his displeasure, the historian appears, entrusted with the vengeance of the nation. Nero prospers in vain, for Tacitus has already been formed within the Empire; he grows up unknown beside the ashes of Germanicus, and already a just Providence has delivered into the hands of an obscure child the glory of the master of the world. If the historian's role is a fine one it often has its dangers; but there are altars such as that of honor, which, though deserted, demand further sacrifices.

. . . Wherever there is a chance for fortune there is no heroism in trying it; magnanimous actions are those whose foreseeable result is adversity and death. After all, what do reverses matter if our name, pronounced by posterity, makes a single generous heart beat two thousand years after we have lived?[123]

On his return from Tilsit Napoleon ordered the new Tacitus to leave Paris. The *Mercure* was warned to take no further articles from his pen; Chateaubriand became a passionate defender of a free press. He retired to a property that he had bought in the Vallée-aux-Loups at Châtenay, and devoted himself to preparing *Les Martyrs* for publication. He deleted from the manuscript such passages as might be interpreted as derogatory of Napoleon. In that year (1809) his brother Armand was arrested for having transmitted dispatches from the *émigré* Bourbon princes to their agents in France. René wrote to Napoleon asking mercy for Armand; Napoleon found the letter too proud, and threw it into the fire; Armand was tried and found guilty, and was shot on March 31. René arrived a few moments after the execution. He never forgot the scene: Armand lying dead, his face and skull shattered by bullets, "a butcher's dog licking up his blood and his brains."[124] It was Good Friday, 1809.

Chateaubriand buried his grief in his valley solitude and in preparing his *Mémoires d'outre-tombe.* He began these reminiscences in 1811; he worked on them intermittently as a sedative from travel, liaisons, and politics; he wrote their last page in 1841, and forbade their publication till after his death; hence he called them *Memoirs from the Tomb.* They are bold in thought, childish in sentiment, brilliant in style. Here, for example, the parade of Napoleon's appointees hurrying to swear their eternal loyalty to Louis XVIII after Napoleon's collapse: "Vice entered leaning on the arm of crime [*le vice appuyé sur le bras du crime*]—Monsieur de Talleyrand walked in, supported by Monsieur Fouché."[125] In those leisurely pages are descriptions of nature rivaling those in *Atala* and *René;* and colorful episodes like the burning of Moscow.[126] Pages of sentiment abound:

The earth is a charming mother; we come forth from her womb; in childhood she holds us to her breasts, which are swollen with milk and honey; in youth and manhood she lavishes upon us cool waters, her harvests and her fruits; . . . when we die she opens her bosom to us again, and throws a coverlet of grass and flowers over our remains while she secretly transforms us into her own substance, to be reproduced in some new and graceful shape.[127]

And now and then a flash of philosophy, usually somber: "History is only a repetition of the same facts applied to diverse men and times."[128] These *Mémoires d'outre-tombe* are Chateaubriand's most enduring book.

He remained rurally quiet until 1814, when the successes of the Allied armies brought them to the frontiers of France. Would their advance, as in 1792, arouse the French people to heroic resistance? On the fifth anniversary of Armand's execution Chateaubriand issued a powerful pamphlet, *De Buonaparte et des Bourbons,* which was scattered through France as Napoleon retreated, fighting for life. The author assured the nation that "God himself marches openly at the head of the [Allied] armies, and sits in the Council of the Kings."[129] He reviewed the offenses of Napoleon—the execution of Enghien and Cadoudal, the "torture and assassination of Pichegru," the imprisonment of the Pope . . . ; these "reveal in Buonaparte" (spelled in the Italian way) "a nature foreign to France";[130] his crimes must not be charged to the French people. Many rulers had suppressed freedom of print and speech, but Napoleon had gone further, and had commanded the press to praise him at whatever cost to truth. The tributes to him as an administrator are undeserved; he merely reduced despotism to a science, turned taxation into confiscation, and conscription into massacre. In the Russian campaign alone 243,610 men died after experiencing every manner of suffering, while their leader, well sheltered and well fed, deserted his army to flee to Paris.[131] How noble and humane, by comparison, had Louis XVI been! As Napoleon had asked of the Directory in 1799, "What have you done with the France that was so brilliant when I left you?," so now the whole human race

> accuses you, calls for vengeance in the name of religion, morality, freedom. Where have you not spread desolation? In what corner of the world is there a family so obscure as to have escaped your ravages? Spain, Italy, Austria, Germany, Russia demand of you the sons that you have slaughtered, the tents, cabins, châteaux, temples that you have put to flame . . . The voice of the world declares you the greatest criminal that has ever appeared on the earth, . . . you who in the heart of civilization, in an age of enlightenment, wished to rule by the sword of Attila and the maxims of Nero. Surrender now your scepter of iron, descend from that mound of ruins of which you have made a throne! We cast you out as you cast out the Directory. Go, if you can, as your only punishment, to be witness of the joy that your fall brings to France, and contemplate, as you shed tears of rage, the spectacle of the people's happiness.

How now replace him? With the King who comes sanctified by his birth, a noble by his character—Louis XVIII, "a prince known for his enlightenment, his freedom from prejudice, his repudiation of revenge." He comes bearing in his hand a pledge of pardon to all his enemies. "How sweet it will be, after so many agitations and misfortunes, to rest under the paternal authority of our legitimate sovereign! . . . Frenchmen, friends, companions in misfortune, let us forget our quarrels, our hates, our errors, to save the fatherland; let us embrace over the ruins of our dear country, and call to our help the heir of Henry IV and Louis XIV . . . *Vive le roi!*"[132] Is it any wonder that Louis XVIII later said that those fifty pages had been worth to him 100,000 troops?[133]

Let us leave Chateaubriand here for a while. He was by no means finished; he still had thirty-four years of life in him. He was to play an active role in Restoration politics, was still to gather mistresses, ending at last in the arms of a Récamier who was graduating from beauty to benevolence. He spent more and more of his time on his *Mémoires;* and now that his enemy was immured in a distant island, itself imprisoned by the sea, he could write of him—as he did for 456 pages—in a mood made milder by time and victory. He lived till 1848, having seen three French Revolutions.

CHAPTER XIV

Science and Philosophy under Napoleon

I. MATHEMATICS AND PHYSICS

IN science the age of Napoleon was one of the most fruitful in history. He himself was the first modern ruler with a scientific education; and probably Aristotle's Alexander had not received so thorough a grounding. The Franciscan friars who taught him in the military school at Brienne knew that science is more helpful than theology in winning wars; they gave the young Corsican all the mathematics, physics, chemistry, geology, and geography that they knew. Arrived at power, he restored Louis XIV's practice of awarding substantial prizes for cultural achievements, and he revealed his background by giving most awards to scientists. Again following precedent, he extended his gifts to foreigners; so, in 1801, he and the Institute invited Alessandro Volta to come to Paris and demonstrate his theories of the electric current; Volta came; Napoleon attended three of his lectures, and moved the award of a gold medal to the Italian physicist.[1] In 1808 the prize for electrochemical discoveries was given to Humphry Davy, who came to Paris to receive it, though France and England were at war.[2] Periodically Napoleon invited the scientists of the Institute to meet with him and report on work done or in progress in their respective fields. At such a conference, on February 26, 1808, Cuvier spoke as the Institute's secretary, with almost the classic eloquence of a Buffon, and Napoleon could feel that the Golden Age of French prose had been restored.

The French excelled in pure science, and made France the most intellectual and skeptical of nations; the English encouraged applied science, and developed the industry, commerce, and wealth that made them the protagonists of world history during the nineteenth century. In the first decade of that century Lagrange, Legendre, Laplace, and Monge set the pace in mathematics. Monge developed with Napoleon a warm friendship that lasted till death. He regretted the deterioration of the consul into an emperor, but bore it with indulgence, and even consented to be made Comte de Péluse; perhaps it was a secret between them that Pelusium was an ancient ruin in Egypt. He mourned when Napoleon was banished to Elba, and openly rejoiced over the exile's dramatic return. The restored Bourbon ordered the Institute to expel Monge; it obeyed. When Monge died (1818) his students at the École Polytechnique (which he had helped to establish) wished to attend his funeral, but were forbidden; the day after his funeral they marched in a body to the cemetery, and laid a wreath upon his grave.

Lazare Carnot came under the influence of Monge when studying in the military academy at Mézières. After serving as "organizer of victory" on the Committee of Public Safety, and escaping with his life from the radical *coup d'état* of September 4, 1797, he found safety and sanity in mathematics. In 1803 he published *Réflexions sur la métaphysique du calcul infinitésimal;* and two later essays founded synthetic geometry. — In 1806 François Mollien made a revolution of his own by introducing double-entry bookkeeping in the Bank of France. — In 1812 Jean-Victor Poncelet, a pupil of Monge, joined the Grand Army in the invading of Russia, was captured, and adorned his imprisonment by formulating, at the age of twenty-four, the basic theorems of projective geometry.

Mathematics is both the mother and the model of the sciences: they begin with counting, and aspire to equations. Through such quantitative statements physics and chemistry guide the engineer in remaking the world; and sometimes, as in a temple or a bridge, they may flower into art. Joseph Fourier was not content with administering the *département* of Isère (1801); he wished also to reduce the conduction of heat to precise mathematical formulations. In epochal experiments at Grenoble he developed and used what are now the "Fourier Series" of differential equations—still vital to mathematics and a mystery to historians. He announced his discoveries in 1807, but gave a formal exposition of his methods and results in *Théorie analytique de la chaleur* (1822), which has been called "one of the most important books published in the nineteenth century."[3] Wrote Fourier:

> The effects of heat are subject to constant laws which cannot be discovered without the aid of mathematical analysis. The object of the theory which we are to explain is to demonstrate these laws; it reduces all physical researches on the propagation of heat to problems of the integral calculus whose elements are given by experiment. . . . These considerations present a singular example of the relations which exist between the abstract science of numbers and natural causes.[4]

More spectacular were the experiments that Joseph-Louis Gay-Lussac made to measure the effects of altitude on terrestrial magnetism and the expansion of gases. On September 16, 1804, he rose in a balloon to a height of 23,012 feet. His findings, reported to the Institute in 1805–09, placed him among the founders of meteorology; and his later studies of potassium, chlorine, and cyanogen continued the work of Lavoisier and Berthollet in bringing theoretical chemistry to the service of industry and daily life.

The most impressive figure in the physical sciences of Napoleon's reign was Pierre-Simon Laplace. It was not unknown to him that he was the handsomest man in the Senate, to which he had been appointed after his failure as minister of the interior. In 1796 he had presented in popular form but brilliant style (*Exposition du système du monde*) his mechanical theory of the universe, and, in a casual note, his nebular hypothesis of cosmic origins. More leisurely, in the five volumes of his *Traité de mécanique céleste* (1799–1825), he summoned the developments of mathematics and physics to the task of subjecting the solar system—and, by implication, all other heavenly bodies—to the laws of motion and the principle of gravitation.

Newton had admitted that some seeming irregularities in the movements of the planets had defied all his attempts to explain them. For example, the orbit of Saturn was continually, however leisurely, expanding, so that, if unchecked, it must, in the course of a few billion years, be lost in the infinity of space; and the orbits of Jupiter and the moon were slowly shrinking, so that, in the amplitude of time, the great planet must be absorbed into the sun, and the modest moon must be catastrophically received into the earth. Newton had concluded that God himself must intervene, now and then, to correct such absurdities; but many astronomers had rejected this desperate hypothesis as outlawed by the nature and principles of science. Laplace proposed to show that these irregularities were due to influences that corrected themselves periodically, and that a little patience—in Jupiter's case, 929 years —would see everything automatically returning to order. He concluded that there was no reason why the solar and stellar systems should not continue to operate on the laws of Newton and Laplace to the end of time.

It was a majestic and dismal conception—that the world is a machine, doomed to go on tracing the same diagrams in the sky forever. It had immense influence in promoting a mechanistic view of mind as well as matter, and shared with the kindly Darwin in undermining Christian theology; God, as Laplace told Napoleon, wasn't necessary after all. Napoleon thought the hypothesis somewhat nebulous, and Laplace himself came at times to doubt Laplace. Midway in his stellar enterprise he stopped to write a *Théorie analytique des probabilités* (1812–20) and an *Essai philosophique sur les probabilités* (1814). Nearing his term, he reminded his fellow scientists: "That which we know is a little thing; that which we do not know is immense."[5]

II. MEDICINE

The doctors might have said the same, with Napoleon's hearty consent. He never gave up hope of convincing his physicians that their drugs had done more harm than good, and that they would have more deaths to answer for, at the Last Judgment, than the generals. Dr. Corvisart, who loved him, heard his banter patiently; Dr. Antommarchi avenged and deserved Napoleon's taunts by giving him—then approaching death—one enema after another. That Napoleon appreciated the work of devoted and competent physicians is evident from his bequest of 100,000 francs to Dominique Larrey (1766–1842), the "virtuous" surgeon who accompanied the French army in Egypt, Russia, and at Waterloo, introduced the "flying ambulance" to give quick aid to the wounded, performed two hundred amputations in one day at Borodino, and left four volumes of *Mémoires de chirurgie militaire et campagnes* (1812–17).[5a]

The Emperor was not mistaken when he chose Jean-Nicolas Corvisart as his personal physician. The professor of practical medicine at the Collège de France was as careful in his diagnoses as he was skeptical of his treatments. He was the first French doctor to adopt percussion—chest tapping—as a diagnostic aid in ailments of the heart or lungs. He had found this method proposed in *Inventum novum ex Percussione* (1760) of Leopold Auenbrugger of Vienna; he translated the 95-page monograph, added to it from his own experience, and expanded it into a textbook of 440 pages.[6] His *Essai sur les maladies et les lésions organiques du coeur et des gros vaisseaux* (1806) established him as one of the founders of pathological anatomy. A year later he joined the imperial household as its resident physician. His difficult employer used to say that he had no faith in medicine, but full faith in Corvisart.[7] When Napoleon went to St. Helena Corvisart withdrew into rural obscurity, and he died faithfully in the year of his master's death (1821).

His pupil René-Théophile Laënnec carried further the experiments in auscultation (literally, listening), which, in his first attempt, consisted of two cylinders, each placed one end on the patient's body, the other end at the ear of the doctor, who was thereby "seeing the chest" (*stethos*) with his ears; so the sounds made by the internal organs—as in breathing, coughing, and digestion—could be heard unconfused by irrelevant noise. Helped by this instrument, Laënnec proceeded with investigations whose results he summarized in a *Traité de l'auscultation médiate* (1819); its second edition (1826) has been described as "the most important treatise on the thoracic organs ever written."[8] Its description of pneumonia remained an authoritative classic till the twentieth century.[9]

The outstanding achievement of French medicine in this period was in humanizing the treatment of the insane. When, in 1792, Philippe Pinel was appointed medical director of the famous asylum that Richelieu had founded at suburban Bicêtre, he was shocked to find that the rights of man so confidently declared by the Revolution had not been extended to the mentally deranged who were confined there or at a similar institution, the Salpêtrière. Many of the inmates were kept in chains lest they injure others or themselves; many more were quieted by frequent bloodletting or by stupefying drugs; any new arrival—not necessarily demented, but perhaps a nuisance to relatives or the government—was flung into the bedlam and left to deteriorate, by contagion, in body and mind. The result was a mess of maniacs whose antics, dull stares, or desperate appeals were occasionally exhibited to the public for a modest admission fee. Pinel went in person to the Convention to ask authority for trying a gentler regimen. He removed the chains, reduced to a minimum the bloodletting and the drugs, released the patients into the invigorating air, and ordered the guards to treat the insane not as secret criminals cursed by God but as invalids often amenable to improvement by patient care. He formulated his views and regimen in an enduring *Traité médico-philosophique sur l'aliénation mentale* (1801). The title was one more sign that Pinel had achieved, or aimed for, the Hippocratic ideal of the physician as combining the learning of the scientist with the sympathetic understanding of the philosopher. "A physician who is a lover of wisdom," Hippocrates had said, "is the equal of God."[10]

III. BIOLOGY

1. Cuvier (1769–1832)

The great Cuvier reached the top of his kind despite being a Protestant in a Catholic land. Like so many other scientists in Napoleon's France, he was raised to high political office, even to membership in the Council of State (1814); he kept that place under the restored Bourbons, and was made president of the Council, and a peer of France, in 1830. When he died

(1832) he was honored throughout Europe as the man who had founded paleontology and comparative anatomy, and had prepared biology to transform the mind of Europe.

His father was an officer in a Swiss regiment, who earned an Order of Merit and at fifty married a young wife. She watched with loving discipline over the physical and mental development of her son Georges-Léopold-Chrétien; she checked his work as a student, and had him read to her the classics of literature and history; Cuvier learned to be eloquent about molluscs and worms. He had the good fortune to be admitted to the Academy that Charles Eugene, duke of Württemberg, had founded at Stuttgart, where eighty masters taught four hundred select students. There he was enamored for a time by the works of Linnaeus, but permanently by the *Histoire naturelle* of Buffon.

Having graduated with an armful of prizes, but lacking any patrimony to finance further schooling, he took a post as tutor in a family living near Fécamp on the English Channel. Some fossils locally exhumed stirred his interest in geological strata as literal lithographs of prehistoric plant and animal life; and some shellfish gathered from the sea so fascinated him with their diversity of internal organs and external forms that he proposed a new classification of organisms according to their structural character and variations. From these beginnings he developed, by a curiosity and industry that never tired, a knowledge of fossil and living forms never equaled before him, and perhaps never since.

News of his learning and application reached Paris, won useful commendations from his future rivals Geoffroy Saint-Hilaire and Lamarck, and brought him, aged twenty-seven (1796), the professorship of comparative anatomy at the Muséum National d'Histoire Naturelle. At thirty-one he published one of the classics of French science, *Leçons d'anatomie comparée;* at thirty-three he was head professor at the Jardin des Plantes; at thirty-four he was made "perpetual secretary" (executive director) of the department of physical and natural sciences in the Institut National. Meanwhile (1802) he had traveled widely as a commissioner of the Institute in the reorganization of secondary education.

Despite his duties as teacher and administrator, he pursued his researches as if resolved, with some collaborators, to study and classify every species of plant or animal preserved in the strata or living on the earth or in the sea. His *Histoire naturelle des poissons* (1828–31) described five thousand species of fish. His *Recherches sur les ossements fossiles des quadrupèdes* (1812–25) almost created mammalian paleontology. It contained Cuvier's description of the woolly elephant—named by him the mammoth—whose remains had been found (1802) buried in a mass of permanently frozen earth in Siberia, and so well preserved that dogs ate its thawing flesh.[11] In one of these volumes Cuvier explained his principle of the "correlation of parts," by which he thought to reconstruct an extinct species from the study of a single surviving bone:

Every organized individual forms an entire system of its own, all the parts of which naturally correspond, and concur to produce a certain definite purpose, by reciprocal reaction or by combining toward the same end. Hence none of these separate parts can change their forms without a corresponding change in the other parts of the same animal; and consequently each of these parts, taken separately, indicates all the other parts to which it has belonged. Thus . . . if the viscera of an animal are so organized as to be fitted only to digest fresh flesh, it is requisite that the jaws should be so constructed as to fit them for devouring prey; the teeth, for cutting and devouring its flesh; the entire system of the limbs, or organs of motion, for pursuing and overtaking it; and the organs of sense, for discovering it at a distance. . . . In the same manner a claw, a shoulder blade, a condyle, a leg or arm bone, or any other bone separately considered, enables us to discover the description of teeth to which they have belonged; and so also reciprocally we may determine the forms of the other bones from the teeth. Thus, commencing our investigations by a careful survey of any one bone by itself, a person who is sufficiently master of the laws of organic structure may, as it were, reconstruct the whole animal to which that bone belonged.[12]

In 1817, in another mammoth work, *Le Règne animal distribué d'après son organisation,* Cuvier summed up his classification of animals into vertebrates, molluscs, articulates, and radiates, and proposed to explain the successive strata of fossils as due to the sudden extinction of hundreds of species by catastrophic convulsions of the earth. As to the origin of species, he accepted the then orthodox view that each species had been specifically created by God; that its variations had been produced by the divine guidance of each organism in its adaptation to its environment; and that these variations never produced a new species. On these and other points Cuvier engaged, two years before his death, in a famous debate which seemed to Goethe the most important event in the history of Europe in 1830. His living opponent in that contest was Etienne Geoffroy Saint-Hilaire, who built his case for the mutability and natural origin and evolution of species around the work of a still greater biologist, who had died a year before.

2. Lamarck (1744–1829)

It is easy to like Lamarck, for he struggled against poverty in youth, against the universally acclaimed Cuvier in maturity, and against blindness and poverty in old age; moreover, he left behind him a theory of the causes and methods of evolution much more agreeable to an amiable disposition than the merciless natural selection offered by the kindly Darwin.

Like most Frenchmen, he carried a heavy armament of names: Jean-Baptiste-Pierre-Antoine de Monet, Chevalier de Lamarck. He was the eleventh child of a martial father, who found military posts for all his sons except the last; him he sent to a Jesuit college at Amiens, with instructions to prepare himself for the priesthood. But Jean-Baptiste . . . envied his brothers their weapons and steeds; he left college, spent his allowance on an old horse, and rode off to war in Germany. He fought valiantly, but his heroic career was ended by a neck injury ignominiously received in barrack games. He went to work as a bank clerk, studied medicine, met Rousseau, was deflected into botany, pursued plants for nine years, and published in 1778 *Flore française*. Then, nearing the end of his economic resources, he accepted employment as tutor to the sons of Buffon, if only for the opportunity to meet that aging sage. When Buffon died (1788) Lamarck took the humble post of keeper of the herbarium in the Jardin du Roi—the royal botanical gardens in Paris. Soon the designation "of the King" fell from fashion, and at Lamarck's suggestion the garden was renamed Jardin des Plantes. Since it contained also a zoological collection, Lamarck gave to the study of all living forms the name *biologie*.

As his interest overflowed from plants to animals, Lamarck, leaving the vertebrates to Cuvier, took as his province the lowly backboneless animals, for which he coined the word *invertébrés* (invertebrates). By 1809 he had reached some original views, which he then expounded in *Système des animaux sans vertèbres* and in *Philosophie zoologique*. Despite failing eyesight, he continued his studies and his writing, helped by his eldest daughter and by Pierre-André Latreille. In 1815–22 he issued his final classifications and conclusions in a voluminous *Histoire naturelle des animaux sans vertèbres*. Thereafter he became totally blind, and almost destitute. His life was a tribute to his courage, and his old age was a disgrace to his government.

His "philosophy," or reasoned summary, of zoology began with contemplation of the endless and mysteriously originating variety in the forms of life. Every individual differs from all others, and within any species we can find so minute a gradation of differences as makes it difficult, perhaps unjust, to divide a species from its most similar and kindred neighbors in form and operation. Species, Lamarck concluded (unwittingly resuming the "conceptualism" of Abélard), is a concept, an abstract idea; in reality there are only individual beings or things; and the classes, kinds, or species into which we group them are merely (though invaluably) intellectual tools for thinking of similar objects which are, however, incorrigibly unique.

How did these different groups or species of plant or animal life arise? Lamarck replied with two "laws":

> *First Law:* In every animal which has not exceeded the term of its development, the more frequent and sustained use of any organ gradually strengthens that organ, develops and enlarges it, and gives it a strength proportioned to the length of time of such use; while the constant lack of use of such an organ perceptibly weakens it, causing it to become reduced, progressively diminishes its faculties, and ends in its disappearance.
>
> *Second Law:* Everything which nature has caused individuals to acquire or lose by the influence of the circumstances to which their race may be for a long time exposed, and consequently by the influence of the predominant use of such an organ, or by that of the constant lack of use of such part, it preserves by heredity and passes on to the new individuals which descend from it, provided that the changes thus acquired are common to both sexes, or to those which have given origin to these new individuals.[13]

The first law was obvious: the blacksmith's arm grows larger and stronger by use; the neck of the giraffe is elongated by efforts to reach higher levels of nutritive leaves; the mole is blind because its underground life makes eyes useless. In later works Lamarck divides his first law into two complementary elements: the environmental condition or challenge, and the organism's need and desire stimulating effort toward an adaptive response, as by the flow of blood or sap to the organ used. Here Lamarck tried to meet the difficult question, How do variations arise? Cuvier replied, Through the direct action of God. Darwin was to reply, Through "fortuitous variations" whose cause is unknown. Lamarck replied, Variations arise through the organism's need, desire, and persistent effort to meet an environmental condition. This explanation fell in well with the insistence of contemporary psychologists who stressed the originative action of the will.

But Lamarck's second law met with a thousand demurrers. Some thought to refute it by pointing out the lack of hereditary effect in the circumcision of Semitic foreskins and the compression of Chinese feet; such cavils, of course, failed to consider that these operations were external mutilations, not at all involving internal need and effort. Some other objections failed to allow for the "long time" admittedly required for an environmental condition to produce a change in the "race." With these provisos Charles Darwin and Herbert Spencer accepted, as a factor in evolution, the possible inheritance of "acquired characters"—i.e., of habits or organic changes developed after birth. Marx and Engels assumed such heritability, and relied upon a better environment to produce a natively better man; and the Soviet Union for a long time made the Lamarckian system a part of its defined creed. About 1885 August Weismann struck a blow at the theory by claiming that the "germ plasm" (cells carrying the hereditary characters) is immune to changes in the enveloping body, or somaplasm, and therefore cannot be affected by postnatal experiences; but this claim was invalidated when chromosomes (carriers of heredity) were found in the somatic as well as the germ cells. Experiments have returned a generally unfavorable report on the Lamarckian view,[14] but latterly some evidence has been produced of Lamarckian transmission in *Paramecium* and other protozoa.[15] Perhaps other positive instances would be found if experiments could be continued upon a longer succession of generations. Our laboratories suffer from an insufficiency of time; nature does not.

IV. WHAT IS MIND?

Lamarck's emphasis on felt need and consequent effort as factors in organic response harmonized with the retreat of the Institute's psychologists from the view of mind as a completely uninitiative mechanism of response to external and internal sensations. These internal explorers used the word "philosophy" as a summary of their findings; philosophy was not yet quite distinct from science; and, indeed, philosophy might be justly termed a summing up of science if science could successfully apply to mind and consciousness its methods of specific hypothesis, careful observation, controlled experiment, and mathematical formulation of verifiable results. That time had not yet come, and the psychologists of the early nineteenth century considered themselves philosophers as men reasoning tentatively about matters still beyond the reach and tools of science.

Despite Napoleon's opposition, the "ideologues" continued for a decade to dominate psychology and philosophy as taught in the Institute. His *bête noire* there was Antoine Destutt de Tracy, the firebrand who carried the torch of Condillac's sensationism through the years of the Empire. Sent as a deputy to the States-General of 1789, he worked for the liberal Constitution of 1791, but in 1793, revolted by the brutality of the mob and the terrorism of the "Great Committee," he subsided from politics into philosophy. In suburban Auteuil he joined the charmed circle that fluttered about the ever beautiful Mme. Helvétius, and there he came under the radical influence of Condorcet and Cabanis. He became a member of the Institute, where he rose to prominence in its Second Class, which specialized in philosophy and psychology.

In 1801 he began, and in 1815 completed, publication of his *Éléments d'idéologie*. He defined this as the study of ideas on the basis of Condillac's sensationism—the doctrine that all ideas are derived from sensations. This, he held, may seem untrue about general or abstract ideas like virtue, religion, beauty, or man; but in treating such ideas we should "examine the elementary ideas from which they are abstracted, and go back to the simple perceptions, to the sensations, from which they emanate."[16] Such an objective study, Destutt thought, could displace metaphysics, and end the reign of Kant. If we cannot reach a definite conclusion by this method "we must wait, suspend judgment, and renounce the attempt to explain what we do not really know."[17] This tough agnosticism displeased the agnostic Napoleon, who was at that time arranging a Concordat with the Church. Undeterred, Destutt classified ideology (psychology) as part of zoology. He defined consciousness as the perception of sensations; judgment as a sensation of relations; will as a sensation of desire. As for the idealists who argued that sensations do not indubitably prove the existence of an external world, Destutt admitted this concerning sights, sounds, odors, and tastes; but he insisted that we may certainly conclude to an external world from our sensations of touch, resistance, and movement. As Dr. Johnson had said, we can settle the question by kicking a stone.

In 1803 Napoleon suppressed the Second Class of the Institute, and Destutt de Tracy found himself without a podium or a printer. Unable to get permission to publish his *Commentaire sur L'Esprit des Lois de Montesquieu*, he sent the manuscript to Thomas Jefferson, President of the United States; Jefferson had it translated and printed (1811), without revealing the author's name.[18] Destutt lived to be eighty-two, and celebrated his old age by issuing a treatise *De l'Amour* (1826).

Maine de Biran (Marie-François-Pierre Gonthier de Biran), began his philosophical career by expounding sensationism with an obscurity that guaranteed his fame.* He began as a soldier and ended as a mystic. In 1784 he joined the royal Garde du Corps of Louis XVI, and helped to defend him from the "monstrous regiment of women"[20] besieging King and Queen at Versailles on October 5-6, 1789. Horrified by the Revolution, he returned to his estate near Bergerac. He was elected to the Corps Législatif in 1809, opposed Napoleon in 1813, and became treasurer of the Chamber of Deputies under Louis XVIII. His writings were asides from his political career, but they raised him to acknowledged leadership among the French philosophers of his time.

He stumbled into fame in 1802 by winning first prize in a competition sponsored by the Institute. His essay *L'Influence de l'habitude sur les facultés de penser* seemed to follow the sensationist views of Condillac, and even the physiological psychology of Destutt de Tracy. "The nature of the understanding," he wrote, "is nothing other than the sum of the principal habits of the central organ, which must be considered as the universal sense of perception";[21] and he thought that one might "suppose in reality each impression represented by the corresponding movement of a fiber in the brain."[22] But as he proceeded he moved away from the notion that the mind is merely the total of the body's sensations; it seemed to him that in efforts of attention or will the mind was an active and originative factor, not reducible to any combination of sensations.

This divergence from the ideologues was widened in 1805 with *Mémoire sur la décomposition de la pensée,* which chimed in with Napoleon's restoration of religion. The effort of will, Maine de Biran argued, shows that the soul of man is no passive recycling of sensations; it is a positive and will-full force which is the very essence of the self; the will and the ego are one. (Schopenhauer would stress this voluntarism in 1819, and it would continue in French philosophy and take brilliant form in Bergson.) This effortful will is added to the other factors that determine action, and gives them that "free will" without which man would be a ridiculous automaton. That internal force is a spiritual reality, not a conglomerate of sensations and memories. There is nothing material or spatial about it. Indeed (Maine de Biran proceeds), probably all force is likewise immaterial, and can be understood only by analogy with the willful self. From this point of view Leibniz was right in describing the world as a compound and battleground of monads each of which is a center of force, will, and individuality.

Perhaps Maine de Biran's double life of politics and philosophy, added to lively participation in weekly meetings at the Institute with Cuvier, Royer-Collard, Ampère, Guizot, and Victor Cousin, proved too arduous; his health broke down; his short life of fifty-eight years was nearing its close; he turned from mind-stretching speculation to a tranquilizing religious faith, and at last to a mysticism that raised him out of this painful world. Man, he said, should progress from the animal stage of sensation through the human stage of free and conscious will, to an absorption in the consciousness and love of God.

V. THE CASE FOR CONSERVATISM

The *philosophes* of the eighteenth century had weakened the French government by impairing the credibility and moral standing of the Church, and by calling for an "enlightened despotism" to mitigate the evils of ignorance, incompetence, corruption, oppression, poverty, and war. The French phi-

---

* "His bad style," said Taine, "has made him a great man; . . . if he had not been obscure we should not have believed him profound."[19]

losophers of the early nineteenth century replied to these "dreamers" by defending the necessity of religion, the wisdom of tradition, the authority of the family, the advantages of legitimate monarchy, and the constant need of maintaining political, moral, and economic dikes against the ever-swelling sea of popular ignorance, cupidity, violence, barbarism, and fertility.

Two men, in this period, drew up in angry detail an indictment of the eighteenth-century appeal from faith to reason, and from tradition to enlightenment. Vicomte Louis-Gabriel-Ambroise de Bonald was born (1754) to class comfort, and was schooled in a secure and obedient piety. Astonished and threatened by the Revolution, he emigrated to Germany, joined for a time the antirevolutionary army of the Prince de Condé, resented its suicidal disorder, and retired to Heidelberg to carry on the war with his disciplined pen. In his *Théorie du pouvoir politique et religieux* (1796) he defended absolute monarchy, hereditary aristocracy, patriarchal authority in the family, and the moral and religious sovereignty of the popes over all the kings of Christendom. The Directory condemned the book, but allowed him to return to France (1797). After a cautious pause he resumed his philosophic offensive with an *Essai analytique sur les lois naturelles de l'ordre social* (1800). Napoleon welcomed its defense of religion as indispensable to government. He offered Bonald a place in the Council of State; Bonald refused, then accepted (1806), saying that Napoleon had been appointed by God to restore the true faith.[23]

After the Restoration he occupied a succession of public offices, and issued a succession of conservative pronouncements, fervent but dull. He opposed divorce and the "rights of women" as disruptive of the family and social order, condemned freedom of the press as a threat to stable government, defended censorship and capital punishment, and proposed to punish with death the profanation of the sacred vessels used in Catholic services.[24] Some conservatives smiled at the enthusiasm of his orthodoxy; but he was consoled by his correspondence with Joseph de Maistre, who, from St. Petersburg, sent him assurances of complete support, and later published volumes that must have gladdened and maddened Bonald by the completeness of their conservatism and the brilliance of their style.

Maistre was born (1753) in Chambéry, where, twenty years earlier, Mme. de Warens had taught Rousseau the art of love. As capital of the duchy of Savoy, the city was subject to the kings of Sardinia; however, the Savoyards used French as their native language, and Joseph learned to write it with almost the verve and force of Voltaire. His father was president of the Savoy Senate, and he himself became a member in 1787; they had more than philosophical reasons for defending the status quo. Politically the son of his father, Joseph was emotionally akin to his mother, who transmitted to him a passionate loyalty to the Catholic Church. "Nothing," he later wrote, "can replace the education given by a mother."[25] He was schooled by nuns and priests and then in a Jesuit college at Turin; for them too his affection never waned; and after a brief flirtation with Freemasonry he accepted completely the Jesuit view that the state should be subordinate to the Church, and the Church to the pope.

In September, 1792, a French revolutionary army entered Savoy, and in November the duchy was annexed to France. The shock of this sudden transvaluation of all values, classes, powers, and creeds left Maistre with a hatred that darkened his mood, wrote his books, and heated his style. He fled with his wife to Lausanne, where he survived as official correspondent for Charles Emmanuel IV, king of Sardinia. He took some comfort in frequenting the salon of Mme. de Staël at nearby Coppet; but the intellectuals whom he met there, like Benjamin Constant, seemed to him infected with the scandalous skepticism of eighteenth-century France. Even the *émigrés* who were huddling in Lausanne were addicts of Voltaire; Maistre marveled at their unawareness that the anti-Catholicism of the *philosophes* had undermined the whole structure of French life by weakening the religious supports of the moral code, the family, and the state. Too old to shoulder arms against the Revolution, he resolved to fight the unbelievers and the revolutionists with his pen. He mingled vitriol with his ink, and left his mark upon the century. Only Edmund Burke, in that age, surpassed him in expounding the conservative view of life.

So in 1796, through a Neuchâtel press, he issued *Considérations sur la France*. He admitted that the government of Louis XVI had been vacillating and incompetent, and that the French Church needed moral renovation;[26] but to change the form, policies, and methods of the state so rapidly and drastically was to betray an adolescent's ignorance of the recondite foundations of government. No polity, he believed, could long survive which lacked roots in tradition and time, or supports in religion and morality. The French Revolution had shattered those supports by beheading the King and dispossessing the Church. "Never has such a great crime had so many accomplices. . . . Each drop of Louis XVI's blood will cost France torrents; perhaps four million Frenchmen will pay with their lives for the great national crime of an antireligious and antisocial insurrection crowned by regicide."[27] Soon, he predicted (in 1796), "four or five people will give France a king."[28]

In 1797 King Charles Emmanuel summoned Maistre to serve him in Turin; but shortly thereafter Napoleon took Turin, and the philosopher fled to Venice. In 1802 he was appointed Sardinian plenipotentiary at the court of Czar Alexander I. Expecting his mission to be brief, he left his family behind, but the service of his King kept him in St. Petersburg till 1817. He bore banishment impatiently, and drowned his cares in manuscript.

His basic production, *Essai sur le principe générateur des constitutions politiques* (1810), derived such constitutions from the conflict, in man, between good and evil (social and unsocial) impulses, and the need for an organized and lasting authority to maintain public order and group survival by supporting cooperative, as against individualistic, tendencies. Every man naturally longs for power and possession, and, until tamed, is a potential despot, criminal, or rapist. Some saints control earthly appetites, and a few philosophers may have accomplished this through reason; but in most of us virtue cannot of itself master our basic instincts; and to let every supposed adult judge all matters by his own reason (weak through inexperience, and slave to desire) is to sacrifice order to liberty. Such undisciplined liberty becomes license, and social disorder threatens the power of the group to unite against attack from without or disintegration from within.

Consequently, in Maistre's view, the ebullient Enlightenment was a colossal mistake. He compared it to the youth who, by his eighteenth year, has concocted or adopted schemes for the radical reconstruction of education, the family, religion, society, and government. Voltaire was a choice example of such jejune omniscience; he "talked of everything for a whole age without once piercing below the surface"; he was "so continually occupied with instructing the world" that he "had only very rarely time to think."[29] If he had studied history humbly as a transitory individual seeking instruction from the experience of the race, he might have learned that impersonal time is a better teacher than personal thought; that the soundest test of an idea is its pragmatic effects in the life and history of mankind; that institutions rooted in centuries of tradition must not be rejected without careful weighing of losses against gains; and that the campaign to écraser l'infâme—to destroy the moral authority of the Church which had disciplined adolescence and formed social order in Western Europe—would bring the collapse of morality, the family, society, and the state. The murderous Revolution was the logical outcome of the blind "Enlightenment." "Philosophy is an essentially destructive force"; it puts all its trust in reason, which is individual, in intellect, which is individualistic; and the liberation of the individual from political and religious tradition and authority endangers the state, and civilization itself. "Hence the present generation is witnessing one of the most dramatic conflicts humanity has ever seen: the war to the death between Christianity and the cult of philosophy."[30]

Since the individual lives too briefly to be fit to test the wisdom of tradition, he should be taught to accept it as his guide until he is old enough to begin to understand it; he will, of course, never be able to understand it fully. He should be suspicious of any proposed change in the constitution or the moral code. He should honor established authority as the verdict of tradition and racial experience, and therefore the voice of God.[31]

Monarchy—heredity and absolute—is the best form of government, for it embodies the longest and widest tradition, and makes for order, continuity, stability, and strength; while democracy, with its frequent changes in leaders and ideas, its periodical exposure to the whims and ignorance of the commonalty, makes for discontent, disorder, reckless experimentation, and an early end. The art of government includes mollifying the masses; the suicide of government lies in obeying them.

Leisurely (1802–16), in his most famous production, Les Soirées de Saint-Pétersbourg (1821), Maistre expounded some incidental aspects of his philosophy. He thought that science proved God, for it revealed in nature a majestic order that implied a cosmic intelligence.[32] We must not be disturbed in our faith by the occasional successes of the wicked or the misfortunes of the good. God allows good and evil to fall indifferently, like sun and rain, upon the criminal and the saint, for he is reluctant to suspend the laws of nature;[33] in some cases, however, he may be moved by prayer to change the incidence of a law.[34] Besides, most evils are penalties for faults or sins; probably every malady, every pain, is a punishment for some taint in ourselves, or our ancestry, or our living group.

If this is so, we should defend corporal punishment, execution for certain crimes, and even the tortures of the Inquisition. We should honor the public executioner instead of making him an outcast; his work, too, is the work of God, and is vital to social order.[35] The persistence of evil requires the persistence of punishment; relax this, and crime will grow. Moreover, "there is no punishment that does not purify, no disorder which Eternal Love does not turn against the principle of evil."[36]

"War is divine, since it is a law of the world"—permitted by God through all history.[37] Wild animals obey this rule. "Periodically an exterminating angel comes and clears away thousands of them."[38] "Humanity can be considered as a tree that an invisible hand is continually pruning, often to its benefit . . . A great deal of bloodshed is often connected with a high population."[39] "From the worm even to man there is accomplished the great law of the violent destruction of living beings. The whole earth, drinking blood, is merely an immense altar, where every living being must be immolated, time without end, without limit, without rest, even unto the destruction of all things, even to the death of death."[40]

If we object that such a world hardly moves us to worship its creator, Maistre answers that we must worship nonetheless, because all nations and generations have worshiped him, and so lasting and universal a tradition must contain a truth beyond the capacity of human reason to understand or refute. In the end, philosophy, if it loves wisdom, will yield to religion, and reason to faith.

In 1817 the King of Sardinia, restored to his Turin throne, recalled Maistre from Russia; and in 1818 he made him a chief magistrate and a councilor of state. In those two years the grim philosopher produced his last work, *Du Pape*, which was published soon after his death (1821). The book was his uncompromising answer to the question that had been raised by his exaltation of the monarch as society's protection against the individualism of the citizen: What if the monarch too, like Caesar or Napoleon, is as individualistic and self-centered as any citizen, and much more in love with power?

Maistre unhesitatingly replied that all rulers must accept subordination to an authority older, greater, and wiser than their own: they must submit, in all matters of religion or morality, to the verdict of a pontiff who inherits the power conferred upon the Apostle Peter by the Son of God. At that time (1821), when the states of Europe were struggling to recover from the brutality of the Revolution and the despotism of Napoleon, their leaders should recall how the Catholic Church had saved the remnants of Roman civilization by checking and taming the multiplying barbarians; how she had established, through her bishops, a system of social order and disciplined education which slowly, through the Dark and Middle Ages, begot a civilization based upon the agreement of kings to recognize the moral sovereignty of the pope. "Nations have never been civilized except by religion," for only the fear of an all-seeing and all-powerful God can control the individualism of human desire. Religion accompanied the birth of all civilizations, and the absence of religion heralds their death.[41] Therefore the kings of Europe must again accept the pope as their overlord in all moral or spiritual concerns. They should take education out of the hands of scientists and return it to the priests, for the ascendancy of science will coarsen and brutalize the people,[42] while the restoration of religion will give peace to the nation and the soul.

But what if the pope too should be selfish, and seek to turn every issue to the temporal advantage of the Papacy? Maistre had a ready answer: since the pope is guided by God, he is infallible when, on matters of faith or morals, he speaks as official head of the Church founded by Christ. So, half a century before the Church herself proclaimed it as an inseparable part of the Catholic faith, Maistre announced the infallibility of the pope. The Pope himself was a bit surprised, and the Vatican found it advisable to check the "ultramontanists" who were making embarrassing claims for the political authority of the Papacy.

Barring this final point, and some other exaggerations that could be passed with a smile, the conservatives of Europe welcomed Maistre's uncompromising defense of their views, and compliments came to him from Chateaubriand, Bonald, Lamennais, and Lamartine. Even Napoleon agreed with him on a number of items—the benevolence of Louis XVI, the vileness of the regicides, the excesses of the Revolution, the frailty of reason, the presumptuousness of the philosophers, the necessity of religion, the value of tradition and authority, the weaknesses of democracy, the desirability of hereditary and absolute monarchy, the biological services of war . . .

As for Napoleon's reigning enemies, they could feel that in Maistre's straightforward philosophy were some of the reasons why they had to overthrow this Corsican parvenu, this heir of a revolution that threatened every monarchy in the world. Here was the secret doctrine that they had never been able—never would be able—to explain to their subjects: the reasons why they, the hereditary kings, emperors, and aristocracies of Europe, had accepted the burdens, dangers, and ritual of rule, while the Marats, Robespierres, and Babeufs had accused them of mercilessly exploiting an innocent commonalty which claimed by divine right—really by assassination and massacre—all the benefits of social organization, and all the goods of the earth. Here was a doctrine on which the legitimate sovereigns of Europe could unite to restore an ancient order to their own lands and peoples, and even to barbarous, unforgivable, regicidal, God-betraying, Godforsaken France.

BOOK III

BRITAIN

1789–1812

CHAPTER XV

England at Work

A T the head of the opposition to the Revolution after 1792—at the head of the resistance to Napoleon when his other enemies were collapsing in unwilling alliance or ruinous defeat—stood the government and the people, the expanding industries and commerce, the Navy and its Nelson, the mind and will, of England. Not at once, nor all together; at the outset of the conflagration the leaders and formative voices were uncertain and divided, frightened or inspired; the poets and philosophers responded with enthusiasm to the early idealism of the Revolution, the ardor and courage of its armies; but soon they were chastened by the angry eloquence of Burke and the news of massacre and terror in utopia; and as the liberators became conquerors, subjecting half of Europe to the ambitions of France, England saw, as hinging on the result of the conflict, that balance of Continental Powers upon which the little island had for centuries depended for its security and freedom.

Slowly the nation came together. Despite the surrender of its allies, the obstruction of its trade, the bankruptcy of firms and financiers, the exhaustion of its toilers, the daily temptation to accept the terms of that brilliant and terrible Corsican bestriding the Continent and threatening to cross the Channel with half a million undefeated warriors—despite this greatest challenge to England since 1066, the King and Parliament stood firm, the nobles and merchants paid heavy taxes, the man with only a body to give suffered impressment into the Army or Navy, the incomparable seamen of England passed from mutinies to victories; and the beloved "spot of earth" emerged from the destitution and near-starvation of 1810–11 to build, within half a century, the most powerful and civilizing empire since the fall of Rome.

We must stand aside for a while from the drama and conflict to consider the resources of soil and labor, science and letters and art, mind and creed and character that made possible this victory, this transformation.

I. A DIFFERENT REVOLUTION

Geography had something to do with it. The climate was not ideal: the warm air brought by the Gulf Stream's North Atlantic current fought an unremitting war with Arctic winds, and the conflict deposited frequent mists and rains upon Ireland, Scotland, and England, making the soil fertile, the parks green, the trees majestic, the streets wet; so that a nasty wit mourned that though the sun never sets upon the British Commonwealth it never rises on England. Napoleon too succumbed to that hyperbole; "You have no sun in England," he told his British physician Dr. Arnott, who corrected him,

"Oh yes we do; . . . in July and August the sun shines warmly in England."[1] The mists of their habitat may have clouded the poetry of Blake and enveloped Turner, and may have shared in fortifying the character and institutions of the English people. Their island made them insular, but it protected them against the shifting winds of doctrine, the fads of art, the manias of revolution, and the massacres of war that so often raged across the Continent. They stood steady on their foot of earth.

If their island was small, the seas that stormed or caressed its shores called them to far-reaching adventures; a thousand liquid roads invited men who could pitch and roll and always stand erect. A hundred distant lands were waiting, with products and markets, to help transform England from agriculture to industry, commerce, and worldwide finance. Innumerable quirks of shoreline offered inlets to oceans seeking peace, and safe harbors to vessels from all the world. In the island itself there were a dozen navigable rivers, and a hundred canals leading to one or another of those streams. No Englishman was more than seventy-five miles from waters that would take him to the sea.

Britain rose to the geographic challenge by making and bearing the Industrial Revolution.* She built merchant ships of a size never before known, some of them huge "East-Indiamen" for half-a-year voyages to India and China. She loved the sea possessively as an extension of England, and fought to the verge of exhaustion for control of that *altera patria* against the Spanish, then the Dutch, now the French. She cut new paths through the water to and around continents, to the resources and markets of Africa, India, the Far East, Australia, the South Pacific, and the two Americas, alien or revolted, but eager for trade. Only the Northwest Passage defied these insatiably seeking Britons, and sent them home shivering but unbowed.

Those merchant fleets, however, and the roving Navy that protected them, had to be built with mostly imported lumber; those colonies and customers had to be requited for their raw materials, their silver and gold, their spices, victuals, and exotic fruits, with the products of British industry; that flourishing commerce had to be cargoed and financed by the Industrial Revolution. Gradually England, especially middle and northern, and Scotland, especially southern, reorganized their economic life by drawing more and more of their population from the fields and villages into towns and factories, and from the slow crafts of home or guild into confined collections of disciplined men, women, and children, tending and paced by machinery, and producing manufactured goods for the world.

Enclosures helped the transition. As far back as the twelfth century, clever Englishmen had reckoned that they could use land more profitably in large tracts than in small. They bought up individual farms and the "commons"— those common fields and woods where peasants had traditionally grazed their cattle and cut their fuel; they worked their extended properties with hired "hands" under an overseer. In the fifteenth century they decided that

---

* This has been briefly described in *Rousseau and Revolution*, 669–82.

they could glean more profit by raising livestock, or, still better, pasturing sheep, than by plowing the earth; for now they needed fewer human beings, and found ready markets for carcasses and wool in chilly, meat-loving Britain, and abroad. More and more peasant proprietors sold or lost their farms and drifted to the towns; the sturdy yeomanry slowly disappeared, taking with it some strength and pride from the English character. By 1800 there were 15 million souls in Britain, and 19 million sheep; the sheep, said a wit, are devouring the men. To this day, traveling in the middle and northern counties of England, one is struck by the scarcity of farms and tillage, and the number of green and fenced enclosures where the only visible inhabitants are sheep idly transforming grass into wool, and rewarding with their end products a grateful soil.

We must not exaggerate; throughout this period (except for the near-starvation crisis brought on in 1811 by Napoleon's Continental Blockade) English agriculture, increasingly capitalistic and mechanized, succeeded in feeding England without foreign aid.[2] So confident were the growers that they persuaded Parliament to pass "Corn Laws" checking, by severe tariff duties, the import of competing grain. ("Corn" then meant any grain; in England it usually denoted wheat; in Scotland, oats.) Even so, by 1790, the townward migration of displaced peasants, aided by impoverished immigrants from Scotland and Ireland, provided the labor force that made industrialization possible.

Industry was still mostly in homes and craft shops, but most of it was locally determined and consumed; it was not organized for wholesale production that could supply diverse markets spreading across frontiers. The home or shop worker was at the mercy of the middlemen who sold him material and bought his product; his payment was determined by supply and demand and the hungriest of his competitors; usually his wife and children had to work with him, from dawn to dark,[3] to keep the wolf from the door. Some more efficient way had to be found to finance and organize industry if it was to meet the needs of multiplying townsfolk, or fill the holds of merchantmen seeking foreign goods or gold.

Inspired by Adam Smith but forgetful of his cautions, English industry was geared to private enterprise, spurred by the profit motive, and largely free from governmental regulation. It obtained capital from its own unspent earnings, from prosperous merchants, from landlords gathering agricultural revenues and urban rents, and from bankers who knew how to make money breed by hugging it, and who lent money at lower rates of interest than their French compeers. So individuals and associations provided funds for entrepreneurs who proposed to unite the products of farm and field with the service of machines and the labor and skills of men, women, and children on a larger scale and to greater gains than England had ever known. The providers of capital kept watch on its use, and gave its name to the economic system that was about to transform the Western world.

It was a risky game. An investment might be ruined by bad management, price or market fluctuations, style changes, overproduction for underpaid consumers, or some new invention cornered by a competitor. The fear of loss sharpened the greed of gain. The cost of labor had to be kept minimal; rewards must be offered for inventions; machines must as far as possible replace men. Iron must be mined or imported to make machines, ironclads, bridges, guns. Coal (luckily abundant in England) must be mined to fuel smelters, purify ores, and toughen iron into steel. As many machines as possible must be tied to one strong source of power; that source might be wind, or water, or animals walking a treadmill or turning a screw; but the best power plant would be a steam engine like those that James Watt had set up in Matthew Boulton's plant near Birmingham (1774). Given enough capital and careful organization, any number of machines could be operated by one or a few engines; and to each machine could be attached a man, or a woman, or a child, who would tend it from twelve to fourteen hours a day for a subsistence wage. The factory system took form.

Soon a thousand smokestacks belched their fumes over rising industrial centers—Manchester, Birmingham, Sheffield, Leeds, Glasgow, Edinburgh. In the Britain of 1750 there had been two cities with fifty thousand inhabitants; in 1801 there were eight; in 1851 there would be twenty-nine. Roads were paved to ease the transit of materials, fuels, and products to factories, markets, and ports. Stagecoaches were built to withstand eight passengers and ten miles an hour.[4] About 1808 Thomas Telford, about 1811 John McAdam (both Scottish engineers) devised new road surfaces essentially like the macadamized highways of today. In 1801 George Trevithick built the first steam locomotive to draw a passenger car on rails. In 1813 George Stephenson built a better one; in 1825 he opened the first regular steam railway service—between Stockton and Darlington. In 1801 a small steamboat began to operate on a Scottish canal; in 1807 the Boulton and Watt factory constructed a passenger steamboat on a model offered by Robert Fulton, who ran his *Clermont* from New York to Albany in August of that year. Meanwhile London, Harwich, Newcastle, Bristol, Liverpool, Glasgow were developing ports and facilities for ocean commerce; and Nelson, at Abukir and Trafalgar, was winning for England the command of the sea.

In 1801 the government took the first scientific census of Great Britain (England, Wales, and Scotland), to the dismay of citizens who resented the invasion of privacy as a prelude to regimentation.[5] The recorded total showed 10,942,646 souls (the United States then had some 6,000,000). By 1811 this had grown to 12,552,144.[6] Probably the rise reflected an increase in the food supply, an improvement in medical service, and a consequent decline in infantile and senile mortality. London had grown to 1,009,546 inhabitants in 1811, but the largest and most significant expansion had been in the industrial north and west. In 1811 the number of British families engaged in farming or herding was recorded as 895,998; in trade or manufactures, 1,128,049; 519,168 in other occupations.[7] The government had depressed agriculture by sanctioning enclosures; it had encouraged industry by favoring free enterprise and a protective tariff, and by forbidding labor unions to agitate for better wages (1800). It had favored commerce by improving roads and canals, and by building an invincible British Navy. Merchants, manufacturers, and financiers had acquired great wealth, and some had earned or bought seats in Parliament.

The economic picture of Britain in 1800 showed, at the top, an aristocracy still, but decreasingly, masters of the economy through ownership of the land; cooperating with them was a Parliament overwhelmingly noble or genteel; swelling below and around them was a ruthless and enterprising bourgeoisie of merchants and manufacturers displaying their new riches and bad manners, and clamoring for more political power; below these the professions, from the most learned physician to the most courageous or virulent journalist; below them all a peasantry progressively dispossessed and dependent upon relief, and sunless miners stripping or gutting the earth, and "navvies" engaged in movable gangs to level roads and dig canals, and a labor pool of hungry, disorganized, demoralized factory workers writing their tragedy in polluted skies.

II. AT THE BOTTOM

If now we review again the condition of the factory workers in the Britain of 1800, we must not exaggerate their prominence in the total picture of the time. Presumably there were many more pleasant scenes in "Merrie England." Factory labor itself was not then the main feature of British industry; most industrial production was still carried on in rural or urban homes at individual looms or lathes, or by craftsmen in their independent shops. The factory system was for the most part confined to the processing of cotton, linen, or wool. Even as so limited, its role in the panorama of the age is one of the saddest episodes in English history.

The factories themselves were rooted in slums and shrouded in their own effluvia of bilge and fumes. Their interiors were generally dusty and dirty, ill-ventilated, and ill-lit—till 1805, when, here and there, gaslighting was installed. The machines were geared to a speed that required their human attendants to keep eyes alert and hands busy through the twelve or fourteen hours of the working day; like some latter-day inventions the machine saved labor and spent men. An hour was allowed for luncheon; thereafter the toil continued, in most cases till eight o'clock.[8] The labor force was replenished at need from a human reservoir continually replenished by displaced peasants or careless wombs.

Between deliveries women were preferred to men as factory workers, and children were preferred to women, as requiring less pay. In 1816, of 10,000 employees in forty-one Scottish mills, 3,146 were men, 6,854 were women, 4,581 were under eighteen.[9] Still cheaper, and widely favored, was the labor of orphaned or destitute children sent to the factories by the Poor Relief administrators. The Factory Act of 1802 tried to establish some minimal standard for the use of such "apprentices," forbidding their employment for more than twelve hours a day; but Parliament refused to pay the commissioners appointed to enforce the act.[10] Generally, child labor continued in British mills till 1842.[11]

In 1800 the average wage of a London adult male worker was eighteen shillings per week (about $23.00 in the United States in 1960); in the country it was about one-third less.[12] By and large, the wages of a family were determined by the amount needed to maintain the strength needed for work; but this was predicated on the wife and child joining the factory force.[13] Employers argued that wages had to be kept low to get the workers to come to work; some laborers took weekends of two or three days, and when they returned they might be still drowsy with alcohol in their blood.[14] Only hunger would bring them back to the machines.

There were certain mitigations. Some employers paid the rent and fuel expenses of their employees. Commodity prices were low—approximately a third of their average in the Great Britain of 1960.[15] Wages generally rose and fell with prices, until 1793, when war began with France; then all classes suffered in their incomes, but as the workers had been kept down to a subsistence wage they suffered most.

They lived in towns where air was poisonous, in ghettos that nurtured disease, in crowded homes—sometimes damp cellars—where sunlight was a rare intruder, lighting was dim, cleanliness was a mirage, domestic strife rasped tired nerves, privacy was impossible, and the only refuge for the woman was piety, and, for the man, the pub. Drunkenness was hebdomadal. Houses took water from wells and public pumps; when these ran short the women carried water from the nearest river or canal, which, as like as not, was polluted by industrial, domestic, or human waste.[16] Sanitation was primitive, sewers were rare: "I am convinced," wrote Thorold Rogers in 1890 (when he was professor of political economy in Oxford), "that at no period of English history for which authentic records exist, was the condition of manual labor worse than in the forty years from 1782 to 1821, the period in which manufacturers accumulated fortunes rapidly, and in which the rent [receipts] of agricultural land was doubled."[17] This condition lasted till the 1840s. Carlyle, who grew up in Scotland and England between 1795 and 1840, summed up the condition of the British factory worker in that period by concluding that Britons had been better off when they were medieval serfs. Industrial progress had left the proletaire so slight a share in the growing wealth that he was reverting to barbarism in manners, dress, amusements, and speech. "Civilization works its miracles," wrote Alexis de Tocqueville on visiting Manchester; "civilized man is turned back almost into a savage."[18] Honor to Manchester and her fellow cities for the immense advances they have made since those bitter days.

The Poor Law, first enacted in 1601, often thereafter reformed, offered some help for the destitute. It was administered by parish officials who usually gathered the recipients into workhouses. It was financed by a specific tax on householders, who complained that their payments were wasted on ne'er-do-wells, encouraging reckless fertility; they submitted to the impost as insurance against social disorder. In many districts, after 1795, the rate of relief was adjusted to supplement wages deemed inadequate to subsistence; some employers took advantage of this to keep wages low.

Despite such middling mercies the discontent of the workers reached a danger point as the nineteenth century began. Forbidden, till 1824, to organize for better pay, they secretly organized; forbidden to strike, they struck; defeated, they struck again.[19] Reformers like Robert Owen warned Parliament that unless factory conditions improved, costly violence would increase. Discontent was checked by the renewal of hostilities with France (1803); it increased as the war dragged on, and came to open revolt in 1811. It was led not by factory employees but by lace and stocking weavers operating "frames" in homes and small shops in or near Nottingham. These men and women could still recall the open-air life on the farms, and perhaps they idealized it in contrast with confined work at their looms. They resented their subjection to the "hosier" who leased them the frames, sold them raw material, and bought their product at rates determined by him and the suppliers of his stock or capital. Moreover, they feared that even their present jobs would soon be lost to the spreading factories and their multiple, power-driven looms. In their mounting fury they resolved to smash, wherever they could, the machines that symbolized their serfdom.

An obscure and perhaps mythical individual named Ned or King Ludd organized the angry weavers, and drew up plans for their raids. In the fall of 1811 separate bands of "Luddites" invaded one district after another and destroyed all the textile frames they found. The movement spread from Nottinghamshire to Lancashire, Derbyshire, and Leicestershire, and continued through 1812. The machine-wreckers abstained from injuring persons except in the case of an employer who ordered his men to fire upon them; the strikers sought him out and killed him. Half of England shivered with fright, remembering the French Revolution. "At this moment," wrote Robert Southey, "nothing but the Army preserves us from that most dreadful of all calamities, an insurrection of the poor against the rich; and how long the Army can be depended upon is a question which I scarcely dare to ask myself. . . . The country is mined beneath our feet."[20] William Cobbett, a lusty liberal journalist, defended the raiders in the House of Commons; the poet Byron delivered a fervent address in their favor in the House of Lords. The Prime Minister, Lord Liverpool, put through Parliament some severe legislation, and sent a regiment to suppress the revolt. The leaders were rounded up, and were summarily condemned in a mass trial at York (1813); some were deported, some were hanged. The machines multiplied. No legislative relief came to adult British labor till 1824.

III. THE DISMAL SCIENCE

The economists gave little comfort to the workers. Thomas Malthus, in *An Essay on the Principle of Population* (1798), explained that it is useless to raise wages, for this would lead to larger families, increasing the pressure of population upon the food supply, and would soon restore the poverty that must forever result from the natural inequality of men.[21] In a revised but impenitent form (1803) of his famous essay Malthus laid down his own "iron law of wages": "The wages of labour will always be regulated by the proportion of the [labor] supply to the demand."[22] In *Principles of Political Economy* (1820) he warned that thrift might be carried to excess, since it would reduce investment and production; he defended "rents" (the returns from property investments) as "the reward of present valour and wisdom, as well as of past strength or cunning;"[23] and he agreed with Voltaire that the luxuries of the rich have the good effect of providing employment for skilled artisans. In a liberal moment he recommended public works as a mitigation of unemployment in periods of reduced production.

David Ricardo accepted the theorems of his friend Malthus, and built upon them his own *Principles of Political Economy and Taxation* (1817), which remained for half a century the classical text of what Carlyle was to call "the dismal science."[24] Son of a Dutch Jew who had prospered on the London Stock Exchange, he was converted to Unitarian Christianity, married a Quaker girl, established his own brokerage firm, made a fortune, retired from business (1815), and wrote several recondite treatises, especially on finance. In 1819 he was elected to the House of Commons, where he denounced Parliamentary corruption, defended free assembly, free speech, free trade, trade unions, and warned the capitalists to watch out lest the landlords of Britain, by their power to raise rentals, should sooner or later absorb the gains of industry. In his epochal treatise he argued that a rise in wages is never real, since it will soon be canceled by a rise in prices due to the increased cost of production; that the proper wage of the laborer is the amount he needs to subsist and perpetuate (without increasing) his species. Ricardo left a mite for Marx by defining the value (not the price) of a commodity by the amount of labor required for its production.

He was not as dismal as his science. He and Malthus remained fast friends to the end, though often disagreeing in private and in print. When both of them had died (Ricardo in 1823, Malthus in 1834), Sir James Mackintosh (a surviving gleam of the Scottish Enlightenment) said of them, and of their common source: "I have known Adam Smith slightly, Ricardo well, and Malthus intimately. Is it not something to say for a science that its three greatest masters were about the three best men I ever knew?"[25]

IV. ROBERT OWEN: 1771–1858

We turn with pleasure to Robert Owen, the successful manufacturer who tried to make the British economy a love affair between capitalism and socialism.

He was born in Newtown, Wales, where his father was successively saddler, ironmaster, and postmaster. Robert in boyhood was a physical weakling, but he learned to care for his health, and lived to be eighty-seven. He was put to work at the age of nine; at ten he was apprenticed to a draper in Stamford; at fourteen he became assistant to a draper in Manchester; at nineteen he was made manager of one of the largest mills in Lancashire, at an annual salary of three hundred pounds ($7,500?). There he remained for eight years, earning a reputation for ability and integrity. He saved, studied, read with discriminating eagerness, and made stimulating friendships: with John Dalton and his atomic chemistry, Robert Fulton with his steamboats, Samuel Coleridge with his radical ideas and haunting verse. In 1799, aged twenty-eight, he bought from David Dale, for himself and two partners, a group of textile mills at New Lanark, near Glasgow, and received as a bonus Dale's daughter, who became his loving wife. She gave him seven children.

New Lanark was a town of about two thousand souls, including some five hundred children sent there from the poorhouses of Glasgow and Edinburgh. As Owen later recalled, "the population lived in idleness, poverty, and almost every kind of crime; consequently in debt, out of health, and in misery. . . . The ignorance and ill-training of these people had given them habits of drunkenness, theft, falsehood, and uncleanliness, . . . with strong national prejudices, both political and religious, against all attempts on the part of a stranger to improve their condition."[26] The little mill town had almost no public sanitation; the houses were dark and dirty; crime seemed an exciting relief from dulling labor, and the "pub" was a warm and jolly refuge from the quarrelsome home. Owen had lost all supernatural belief, but had clung all the more devotedly to the ethical idealism of Christ; and he was repelled by the combination of the new industrial serfdom with the old Christian theology. He resolved to seek some reconciliation between successful capitalism and Christian morality.

He contented himself—alarmed his partners—with a five percent return on their invested funds. He raised wages, and forbade the employment of children under ten years of age. He rejected the argument of Malthus that a rise in wages would increase the pressure of population upon the food supply, would raise prices, and leave real wages unchanged; he argued that limitless edibles from the sea, the spread of cultivation by increased population, and the multiplication of inventions and labor productivity would enable the population to eat and grow and prosper—if the government would adopt the reforms that he would propose.[27] He opened at New Lanark a company store, which sold the staples of life practically at cost. He patiently instructed his employees not only in the techniques of production but in the art of life; he assured them that if they would practice mutual consideration and aid they would enjoy a peace and content such as they had never experienced before. He seems to have won many of his workers to habits of order, cleanliness, and sobriety. When his partners complained that he was spending on charity and education money that might have made higher profits, he dissolved the partnership and formed a new firm (1813), whose members (one of them Jeremy Bentham) applauded his experiment and were content with a five percent return on their investment.

The mills at New Lanark acquired a national—even an international—reputation. The town was far off the main roads—a full day's ride by post from Glasgow through mountains and mists; nevertheless thousands of visitors came to examine the incredible phenomenon of a factory operated on Christian principles; twenty thousand signed the guest book between 1815 and 1825. They included writers, reformers, realistic businessmen, princes like Archdukes Johann and Maximilian of Austria, and, in 1815, Grand Duke Nicholas (soon to be czar), who approved the operations and the results, and invited Owen to establish similar factories in Russia.[28]

After fourteen years of his experiment Owen felt warranted in proclaiming it to the world, for he was confident that its universal adoption would "give happiness to every human being through all succeeding generations."[29] So in 1813 he issued the first of four essays which, under the general title *A New View of Society*, became a major classic in the literature of reform. He offered his proposals in no combative spirit; he assured the rulers and manufacturers of Britain that he had no desire for—and no faith in—any violent change; that his plan threatened no loss to anyone; that, in fact, it would swell the employer's returns; and that it might save England from revolution.

He began with a proposition almost fundamental to any basic reform— that the character of man, supposedly fixed by an ancient and immutable heredity of competition and conflict, is substantially molded through childhood experiences and beliefs. "The greatest of all errors [is] the notion that individuals form their own characters."[30] On the contrary, an individual's character is formed for him by the thousand influences impinging upon him [before his birth and] from his birth to his death. Owen concluded, with an enthusiasm that rejected modifiers: "Any character, from the best to the worst, from the most ignorant to the most enlightened, may be given to any community, even to the world at large, by applying certain means; which are to a great extent at the command, under the control, of those who possess the government of nations."[31] From this principle Owen drew two propositions: one, that the present possessing classes were not to blame for their practices and beliefs, since they too were the product of their past and present environments; the other, that reform must begin with the children, and with the improvement and multiplication of schools. Every effort must be made to bring up children to understand that since no one individual is to blame for his character or for the condition of society and industry, each must be considerate of all others: must cooperate willingly, and must be undiscourageably kind. So, at a time when there were very few schools in England for the children of commoners, Owen proposed that "the governing power of all countries should establish national plans for the education, and general formation of the character, of their subjects; . . . and that without . . . exception for sect or party or country."[32]

David Dale had already done much for the education of children in New Lanark. Owen carried this further by establishing, in one of his buildings, his "New Institution" (1816) for the transformation of angels and barbarians into Christians without theology. He asked for them "as soon, almost, as they could walk";[33] like Plato he feared that the parents, already formed or deformed, would transmit to their children the aggressive and competitive spirit of the existing regime. He yielded to mothers who insisted that children, in their early years, needed maternal affection and care. Usually he took them at the age of three, and let them, weather permitting, play and learn in the open air. The girls, as well as the boys, were to get the three R's, but also they would be instructed in the household arts. The boys would be trained in military exercises, but, like the girls, they would be taught to sing, dance, and play some instrument. All this would be subordinated to the formation of moral character, with emphasis on courtesy, kindness, and cooperation. There would be no punishments.[34] At the close of each schoolday the children would be returned to their parents. They would not be allowed to work in the factory before they were ten years old.

Apparently there was no religious instruction in Owen's school, nor in the evening lectures offered to adults. As a child of the Enlightenment he was convinced that religion dulled the mind of the child with superstitions; that intelligence is the supreme virtue; that widespread education is the only solution to social problems; and that progress, given this aid, is inevitable and limitless.[35] In his mills and his school no distinction of race or creed was made; "charity and kindness admit of no exception."[36] He believed that the methods he advocated were an attempt to move in the direction of the ethics of Christ, and he looked forward fervently to the moral utopia that he expected his principles to bring.

In his fourth essay (1816), dedicated to the Prince Regent, he offered some proposals for legislation. He asked Parliament to progressively reduce the importation of "spirits" (liquor), to raise taxes on their consumption, and finally to end the licensing of "gin-shops" and alehouses, so that drunkenness would become the luxury of moneyed fools. He recommended the spread and financing of elementary schools for the moral betterment of the coming generations. He pleaded for a "factory act" that would forbid the employment of children under ten years of age, and the night labor of persons under eighteen; that would regulate the hours and conditions of labor, and would maintain a system of regular inspection of factories. A governmental Department of Labor should periodically collect statistics of local variations in the supply and need of labor, and should use this information to alleviate unemployment.[37] He called for the abolition of the state lottery as a disgraceful scheme to "entrap the unwary and rob the ignorant."[38]

He agreed with Malthus that the Poor Laws—which kept the unemployed and impoverished at a level of subsistence just a step from starvation—degraded the recipients of relief, and left them fit for only fertility and crime. Instead of the workhouses maintained by this system, Owen proposed (1817) that the state should set up communities, each of which, with five hundred to fifteen hundred souls, would be organized by a self-sustaining division of labor to produce its own food and clothing, and maintain its own school.[39]

Having appealed to Parliament with scant result, Owen issued (1818) an address "To the British Manufacturers,"[40] describing the success of his system at New Lanark, and urging them to dispense with the employment of children under twelve years of age. They could not see their way to doing this; and they resented Owen's analysis of economic depression as due to inventive productivity outrunning the purchasing power of the people. They dismissed him as an atheistic visionary who had no real understanding of the problems that employers had to meet, or of the human needs that only religion could satisfy.

Finally Owen turned to the laborers themselves, and sought their support in an "Address to the Working Classes" (1819). He pleased them by acclaiming "manual labor, properly directed," as "the source of all wealth, and of national prosperity."[41] But he cautioned them that England, and its working classes, were not ready for socialism; he disclaimed any intent to propose that the British government should now give direct employment to all its working population.[42] He discountenanced any precipitate measures, and he rejected revolution as "calculated to generate and call forth all the evil passions of hatred and revenge."[43] However, in his 1820 *Report to the County of Lanark* (a body of landowners), he declared that what England now needed was not piecemeal reforms but a basic transformation of the social order.[44]

Frustrated in England, he turned hopefully to the United States, where several religious sects had made some communistic experiments. In 1814 a group of German-American Pietists bought thirty thousand acres along the Wabash River in the southwestern part of the Indiana Territory, and developed there a town called Harmonie. By 1825 they faced bankruptcy. Owen rescued them, and ruined himself, by giving them forty thousand pounds for the acres and the town, which he renamed New Harmony. He invited men and women of goodwill to join him there in establishing a cooperative community. He paid all expenses except for the school, which was financed by William Maclure. A thousand enthusiasts came, ate for a year at Owen's expense, slowly reconciled themselves to disciplined work, and fell to quarreling about religion and politics. In 1827, having lost most of his forty thousand pounds,[45] Owen turned over the colony to Maclure, and returned to Britain.

He was not quite finished. He led a movement for the development of trade unions into guilds that would compete with private enterprise in productive industry. The National Operative Builders Union accepted contracts for construction. Other unions followed suit, and in 1833 Owen organized them into a Grand National Consolidated Trades-Union, which he hoped would gradually supplant British capitalism, and finally replace the state. Parliament intervened with repressive laws, which were rigorously enforced; the banks refused loans; and in 1834 Owen acknowledged defeat.

His life, which had been so successful in industry, seemed now to have reached an almost total failure. Religious differences had darkened his marriage; his wife was a fervent Calvinist; when she discovered that he was an agnostic she worried daily about his inevitable damnation. Later she urged their son Robert to undertake his father's conversion to Calvinism; the re-

sult was that the son's religious faith suffered considerable dilution.[46] After
returning from America, Owen lived apart from his wife, though remaining
on friendly terms with her. He believed in divorce, but did not seek one;
his devotion was absorbed in his mission.

He gave his active encouragement to several communities that tried to
practice his principles: at Orbiston in Scotland, at Ralahine in Ireland, at
Queenwood in England. The first disbanded in two years, the second in
three, the third in six. He continued to spread his ideas through addresses
and writings, and lived to see the development of many consumers' cooper-
atives in the British Isles. He kept busy writing recommendations for reform
to learned bodies, to governmental personnel, to Queen Victoria. Finally, in
1853, he turned to spiritualism, became the dupe of various mediums, and
held intimate conversations with Franklin, Jefferson, Shakespeare, Shelley,
Napoleon, and the Prophet Daniel.[47] In 1858, having long outlived his era
and himself, he returned to his native Newtown, and died there in his eighty-
eighth year.

He was a good man, as near to selflessness as any self can be who is completely certain. He could not quite transcend his ego; he had his secret pride
in power, success, and intellect; his enterprises were predicated on his personal rule; but he was right in assuming that competent cooperation requires
discipline and authority. The best a man can do is enlarge his ego to include
his kin, his country, his kind, and so find satisfaction in a widening beneficence. This, after all, is what Robert Owen did, on a bravely broadening
scale; and that is enough to range him among the inspiring prophets of a
better life.

CHAPTER XVI

English Life

I. CLASSES

A CIVILIZATION is a people given social order by government, law, religion, morals, customs, and education, and left sufficiently free to invent and experiment, to develop friendship, charity, and love, and to beget art, literature, science, and philosophy. How did these forms of order and liberty operate in the England of 1789 to 1815, and what did they produce?

First, the natural diversity of men—in heritage, opportunity, and skills—arranged them into classes each of which contributed a supporting share to the corporate life. There were no castes in England, for an individual of outstanding wealth or excellence might rise from one class to another, even to the peerage; and the relationship of peer to peasant was often one of friendly intercourse, rarely that of Brahmin to Untouchable. Serfdom had disappeared, though only a small minority of peasants owned the land they tilled. The noble paid taxes like the rest, and sometimes (unlike their French compeers) engaged in commerce or industry. Only the eldest living son of a nobleman shared in his nobility; the other children were legally (not socially) commoners.

Many unnatural inequalities remained. The concentration of wealth was unusually high. Equality before the law was nullified by the cost of litigation. Accused lords could be tried only by the House of Lords (a jury of their peers); this "privilege of peerage" survived till 1841. Careless men of no pedigree might be forcibly impressed into the Navy. Commoners rarely reached high office in the Navy or the Army, in the civil service, the universities, or the law. A ruling class of nobles and gentry seldom allowed to the undistinguished mass any share in determining the personnel or policies of the government.

Perhaps class consciousness was keenest in the bourgeoisie, which remained proudly aloof from the peasantry and the proletariat, and dreamed of peerages. Within itself there were jealous strata: the industrial capitalist looked down upon the neighborhood shopkeeper;* the great merchant who had graced money with adventure stood aloof from the industrialist; and the swelling nabobs, who had gilded their colonial gleanings with patriotism and religion, were forming a class of their own. As in France, so in England, no one seemed content anymore with the place to which Providence, capacity, or chance had assigned him; everyone was busy climbing or falling; the restlessness of modernity began. The basic struggle was of the capitalist

---

* Samuel Adams in 1748 had called England "a creation of shopkeepers";[1] Napoleon repeated it; it was hardly true.

to replace the aristocrat at the helm of state; in France it took a generation; in England it took centuries.

So, till 1832, the nobility was supreme, and smiled at its challengers. In its strictest sense it consisted, in 1801, of 287 "temporal" peers or peeresses, and twenty-six Anglican bishops, who, as "spiritual lords," were entitled to sit in the House of Lords. The temporal peers were ranked, in descending order, as princes of the (royal) blood, dukes, marquesses, earls, viscounts, and barons. To all of these except princes and dukes the appellation "lord" could be properly applied; and their titles carried down, generation after generation, to the eldest son. Their wealth was based upon the ownership of vast areas, tilled by tenant farmers and hired laborers, and bringing such rents as the Duke of Newcastle's £120,000, or Viscount Palmerston's more usual £12,000, a year.[2] The combined estates of the Dukes of Bedford, Norfolk, and Devonshire could have covered an average county.[3] Below these lords temporal and spiritual England ranked 540 baronets and their wives, entitled to prefix "Sir" or "Lady" to their Christian names, and to transmit these titles in their families. Next were 350 knights and their wives, entitled to the same prefixes, but not to transmit them. Below these came some six thousand squires or "gentry"—landowners born in old and accepted families, and authorized to bear a coat of arms. All these groups below the "lords" constituted the lesser nobility, but they were generally included in the "aristocracy" that ruled England.

It does not seem to have felt that there was anything wrong in minority rule. Its members bore with stoic equanimity the poverty of the peasants, the degradation of the factory workers, and the spoliation of Ireland. Poverty, they believed, was the natural and necessary penalty of incompetence or sloth, and weak-kneed theorists must not be allowed to transform Britain into a democracy resting on a degenerative dole. Despite anarchist dreamers like William Godwin or Percy Shelley, some government is necessary; without it the people become a mob, dangerous to every individual and every liberty. Napoleon was not prejudiced in favor of England, yet he said at St. Helena, "It would be a European disaster if the English aristocracy were to disappear, if it were handed over to a London mob."[4] All government is by a minority or by a despot, and the ruling minority is either an aristocracy of birth or a plutocracy of wealth. Democracy, of course, is the latter, for only wealth can finance campaigns, or pay the cost of persuading the people to vote for the moneyed minority's candidate. Men democratically chosen are rarely equipped, by birth and training, to deal successfully with the problems of government, much less with international relations. An aristocracy of birth is a school of statesmanship. Some of its graduates may become worthless wastrels, but a saving few acquire, by long association with the problems and personnel of rule, the ability to deal with critical affairs without endangering the nation by their bungling. Moreover, a properly functioning aristocracy wins from the people a habit of obedience, and a respect for authority, which are boons to public order and security.

Such arguments, subtly phrased and obscurely felt, seem to have persuaded the majority of the English nation. But they did not convince the rising bourgeoisie, which resented the power of landed wealth to control ministries and Parliament; they were angrily repudiated by rebellious labor; and they were sharply questioned by an intelligentsia shocked to observe, and resolved to reveal, the means by which a self-serving aristocracy was governing England.

II. THE GOVERNMENT

1. The Legislature

The Constitution of England is the whole body of unrepealed enactments of Parliament and unrevoked decisions of the courts. By such precedents the full authority of the government resided in the Crown (king or queen) and the Parliament acting in concert; usually, since 1688, the monarch accepted what Parliament legislated. No written document limited the power of Parliament to pass any law that pleased both its chambers. The upper chamber, the House of Lords, consisted of the temporal and spiritual lords, sitting by right of birth and tradition, requiring no election, empowered to reject any measure voted by the House of Commons, and serving as a supreme court in appeals from judicial decisions, in impeachments of governmental personnel, and in all actions brought against its secular members on charge of a major crime. It was a bastion of the aristocracy fighting rearguard actions against the advancing bourgeoisie.

The House of Commons numbered 558 members: two each from the Universities of Oxford and Cambridge, one from Trinity College, Dublin, forty-five from Scotland; the rest chosen by forty counties ("shires") and twenty boroughs (townships) by electors holding limited franchises too varied to be specified here.[5] Excluded from the electorate were women, paupers, Roman Catholics, Quakers, Jews, agnostics, and, in general, anyone who could not swear allegiance to the authority and doctrines of the Church of England. All in all, there were 245,000 eligible voters in England's nine million souls. Since voting was public, few voters dared support any candidate but the principal landowner's nominee; many eligible citizens did not bother to vote; and some elections were decided by arrangement among the leaders, without any voting at all. The number of Parliamentary representatives allowed to each borough had been fixed by tradition, and took little account of growth or decline in the borough's population; some boroughs with a mere handful of voters returned one or more members, while London, with six thousand voters, was allowed only four. The new industrial centers were poorly represented in Parliament, if at all; Manchester, Birmingham, and Sheffield had no member there, while the old county of Cornwall had forty-two. We should add, however, that in local affairs many towns and villages retained considerable self-rule; so the city of London, through a property-limited suffrage, chose its own government, and maintained a proud independence of Parliament.

About half the seats in the Commons were filled by these semipopular elections; the other half were filled through uncontested nomination by local or distant proprietors; and these nominations were in many cases offered by the boroughs to the highest bidder. "Boroughs, in other words seats in the House of Commons, were bought and sold as openly as any article of commerce; and the King himself was at times the great purchaser of boroughs."[6]

The chosen members were loosely divided between two parties—Tories and Whigs. These had largely forgotten the issues that had once divided them; their leaders were in both cases members of old aristocratic families; but the Whigs were more inclined than the Tories to listen to the upcoming and affluent lords of commerce and industry, while the Tories defended— the Whigs challenged—the traditional "prerogative" of royal power. The bone of contention was not principle but power: which party was to form the ruling ministry, divide the lucrative offices, and oversee the developing, fee-splitting bureaucracy.

Despite its aristocratic base, the British government was considerably more democratic in its lawmaking than most Continental states; whereas in these (including France after 1804) the supreme power was wielded by an emperor or a king, in Britain the actual ruler, since 1688, was not the king but the Parliament; and in the bicameral Parliament the authority lay chiefly with the Commons through its "power of the purse": no disbursement of public funds could be made without its consent. Theoretically the king could veto any measure passed by Parliament; actually George III never stretched his prerogative to this testing point. The king, however, could dissolve the Parliament and "go to the country" for a new election; in that case the candidates he favored and financed had a good chance of winning seats, for the indigenous King (after two alien Georges) had become again the nation embodied, the central object of patriotic loyalty and pride.

2. The Judiciary

The English judiciary was as haphazard, chaotic, and competent as the legislature. First of all, it had to administer a body of laws that had grown almost daily through hundreds of years, that had long remained unsystematized, and that was so brutal in its traditional penology that judges had often to amend it or ignore it. The law was heavy with relics of its feudal origins and its Christian emendations: accused lords still demanded to be tried by lords, and "benefit of clergy" still (till 1827) exempted Anglican ministers from secular courts. Hundreds of laws (against public gambling, nocturnal amusements, unlicensed assemblies . . .) remained in the statutes, though rarely enforced. Some improvements were made in this period: the number of crimes (some two hundred) for which, in 1800, death was prescribed was repeatedly reduced; and a true account of assets and liabilities could avert imprisonment for debt. But the law of bankruptcy remained so cumbersome that businessmen avoided it as the road to double bankruptcy. The Habeas Corpus Act of 1679, which aimed to end undue imprisonment before trial, had been so often suspended that it lost its force in crises like the French Revolutionary Wars. The confusion, contradictions, and barbarities of British law continued until Bentham slashed at them with his persistent and detailed demands for reform.

The capture of criminals was made additionally difficult by the scarcity of police in the towns, and their almost total absence in the countryside; citizens were driven to form voluntary associations to protect their lives and property. Even if arrested, the criminal might delay or escape imprisonment by hiring lawyers to find or forge reasons for appeal, or loopholes in the law; "it was the boast of the lawyers that there was not a single statute through which they could not drive a coach and six."[7]

At the lowest rung of the legal profession were the attorneys or solicitors, who acted as legal agents for a client, or researched and prepared briefs for the barristers, who were the only lawyers admitted to the bar. From them the king, usually on recommendations by the lord chancellor, chose the judges.

Once or twice a year the judges of the Common Law Courts toured the counties to try, locally, civil and criminal cases. As their stay in any one place was brief, the administration—in some measure the creation—of the law in each county or borough was left to local "justices of the peace." These were chosen by the central government from among the richer landowners of the district; they were unpaid, but their wealth was expected to keep them from corruption. They were not above class prejudice, and some became famous for severe sentences against radicals; but, all in all, they provided fair and competent local administration, almost equal to that of the prefects in Napoleonic France.

The best feature of English law was the right of the accused to trial by jury. Apparently this institution of the Carolingian Franks had come to England in primitive form with the Norman Conquest. The size of the jury was not fixed at twelve members until 1367; and only about that time was a unanimous verdict required. The jurors were chosen—usually from the middle class—from a panel of forty-eight to seventy-two men, after extensive rights of challenge by the contending parties. Periodically the justices of the peace were assisted in each county by a grand jury, upon whose recommendations the court was expected to act. In trials the jurors heard the evidence, the speeches of contending counsel, and the judge's summing up; after this they retired to an adjoining room, where, "in order to avoid intemperance and causeless delay," they were kept without meat, drink, fire, or candle (unless by permission of the judge) "till they were unanimously agreed."[8]

3. The Executive

Theoretically the executive power was vested in the monarch; actually it lay in his cabinet of ministers; and these had to be members of Parliament, responsible to it for their actions, and dependent upon it for their funds.

Theoretically the king appointed these ministers; in practice he was expected to choose as their head the leader of the party victorious in the latest election; and this prime minister, with others prominent in his party, nominated, for the ruler's formal appointment, the secretaries of the various ministries. In his first administration (1783–1801) William Pitt took a double role as chancellor of the exchequer and first lord of the treasury; that is, he controlled, subject to Parliamentary approval, both the collection and the disbursement of the national revenue. In the Cabinet, as well as in the government as a whole, the power of the purse was the chief instrument of discipline and rule.

George III did not admit his subordination to Parliament. From his accession in 1760, at the age of twenty-two, he had sought to enforce the royal prerogatives. But the costly collapse of his leadership in the War of American Independence, and his repeated intervals of insanity (1765, 1788, 1804, 1810–20), weakened his body, mind, and will, and after 1788 he allowed William Pitt to govern except for three provisos: slavery must not be finally condemned, the British Catholics must not be allowed to vote, and there should be no peace with France until Louis XVIII was securely placed on his rightful throne.

George III was a good man within the limits of his vision and his creed. Napoleon, in captive retrospect, described him as "the honestest man in his dominions."[9] He distinguished himself from his Hanoverian predecessors by obeying all the Commandments except the fifth, and by falling far short of the Leviticean injunction to "love thy neighbor as thyself"; but he loved the English people. Despite his faults, and because of his misfortunes, they loved him in return—for loving his inherited religion, for loving his wife and daughters, and for giving the nation an inspiring picture of a simple and devoted life. Their hearts went out to him when, despite his example, most of his sons tarnished their princely titles with marital chaos, conscienceless gambling, reckless extravagance, and visible deterioration of body and character. Wellington was to describe them as "the damnedest millstones, about the neck of any government, that can be imagined."[10]

The oldest of them—George, Prince of Wales—was the most impossible, troublesome, and charming. He was handsome and knew it. He had received a good education, could speak French, German, and Italian fluently, sang well, played the violoncello, wrote poetry, kept in touch with contemporary English literature, numbered Richard Sheridan and Thomas Moore among his intimate friends, and was an intelligent patron of art. He set up at Carlton House a princely establishment, furnished it elegantly at the nation's cost, favored the politics and rivaled the thirst of Charles James Fox, and, to the horror of his father, became the idol of the Whigs. He liked, too, the young dandies who spent their wealth on fancy clothing, women, horses, and dogs;[11] he accompanied such Britons to prizefights, and outpaced everyone in expenditure and debts. Parliament repeatedly voted a hundred thousand pounds to restore his solvency,[12] for none could tell when this good-natured wastrel would, as king, be the generous donor of lucrative sinecures.

At seventeen he had confessed to being "rather too fond of women and wine." Among his early mistresses was Mary Robinson, who fascinated him by her playing of Perdita in *A Winter's Tale;* for three years he maintained her in precarious luxury. Then he entered upon a more serious affair with Maria Anne Fitzherbert, twice widowed, Roman Catholic, six years his senior, and unmanageably decent; she refused to become his mistress, but consented to marry him. The Act of Settlement that had given the throne of England to the house of Hanover had excluded from the succession any husband or wife of a Roman Catholic; and a law of 1772 prohibited any member of the royal family under twenty-five years of age from marrying without the ruler's consent. Nevertheless, the Prince married Mrs. Fitzherbert (1785), paying a young Anglican curate five hundred pounds to perform the illegal ceremony; the illegality preserved the Prince's right of succession. He assumed this right in 1788, when his father lapsed into insanity; he waited impatiently for him to die; but father and son could seldom agree.

They agreed, however, that if the King (actually Parliament) would pay the Prince's new debts (£110,000), the heir apparent would leave his morganatic wife and marry his father's niece, Princess Caroline of Brunswick. He found her discouragingly ugly, she found him disgustingly fat; but they married, April 8, 1795. Caroline later averred that he had spent the wedding night in a drunken torpor;[13] however, she gave him a daughter, Princess Charlotte, January 7, 1796. Soon thereafter he left her, and returned, for a time, to Mrs. Fitzherbert, who was apparently the only woman whom he ever deeply loved. (When he died, a miniature with a portrait of her was found pendant from his neck.[14])

In November, 1810, George III—breaking under Parliamentary opposition, shame for his son, and grief for his dead daughter Amelia—went finally insane. For nine years thereafter the King of England was a raving, straitjacketed lunatic, pitied and beloved by his people; and the Regent, assuming all royal pomp and power, was a degenerate ruin, fat, fifty, kindly, cuckolded, and despised.

III. RELIGION

The government and the intelligentsia of England had by this time reached a gentlemen's agreement about religion. The deistic attack upon the orthodox creed had subsided as the skeptics came to realize that they had nothing to put in its place as an aid to individual morality and public peace. William Godwin, Robert Owen, Jeremy Bentham, and James Mill were surviving examples of unbelief, but they made no propaganda thereof; Tom Paine was an exception. The English aristocracy, which had found some charm in the young Voltaire, was now carefully conspicuous in Sabbath observance. "It was a wonder to the lower orders throughout all parts of England," noted the *Annual Register* in 1798, "to see the avenues to the churches filled with carriages" on Sundays.[15] John Stuart Mill remarked in 1838:

> There is, in the English mind, both in speculation and in practice, a highly salutary shrinking from all extremes. . . . *Quieta non movere* [not to disturb the quiet] was the favourite doctrine of those times; . . . therefore, on condition of not making too much noise about religion, or taking it too much in earnest, the Church was supported even by philosophers as a bulwark against fanaticism, a sedative to the religious spirit, to prevent this from disturbing the harmony of society or the tranquillity of the state. The clergy of the Establishment thought they had a good bargain on these terms, and kept its conditions very faithfully.[16]

The Established Church was officially the "United Church of England and Ireland." Though it accepted the Thirty-nine Articles of the Calvinist creed, it kept many features of the Catholic ritual. It had archbishops and bishops, but these usually married, and they were appointed by the Crown. Local parsons were generally chosen by the local squires, and helped them in maintaining social order. The Anglican clergy acknowledged the king as their head and ruler, and depended upon the state to collect from all families in England the tithe that supported the Church. Burke described Britain as a Christian Commonwealth in which Church and state were "one and the same thing, being different integral parts of the same whole"; and John Wilson Croker called Westminster Abbey "a part of the British Constitution."[17] The relationship resembled that between the Catholic Church and the government of France under Louis XIV, except that there was almost no persecution for heresy.*

The dissenting sects—Methodists, Presbyterians, Baptists, Independents, Congregationalists, Quakers, and Unitarians—were allowed to preach their doctrines on one condition: that they declare themselves Christians.[19] Some Dissenters sat in the House of Lords. Methodist preachers gathered great audiences by their frightening eloquence. The oppressed workers of the towns, losing earthly hopes, returned to their childhood faith, and with such ardor that when revolutionary ideas swept over the Channel from France, they resisted all efforts to make them revolt. In 1792 the leaders of Wesleyan Methodism required of each adherent an oath of loyalty and obedience to the king.[20]

Within the Established Church itself the influence of Methodism inspired an "Evangelical Movement": many of the younger clergy and laity resolved to revitalize the Anglican creed by taking the Gospel to heart, and devoting themselves to simple living, piety, charity, and church reform. One of them, William Wilberforce, led the English campaign against slavery; another, Hannah More, spread a fresh Christian fervor by her lectures, books, and Sunday schools.

---

* In the letter of the law an atheist was an outlaw, and might be hunted down like a criminal. Blasphemy—any indignity offered to God by word, writing, or sign—could be punished by eighteen two-hour periods of standing in the pillory.[18] These laws were rarely enforced.

Two religious groups remained outside the circle of full toleration: Catholics and Jews. English Protestants had not forgotten Guy Fawkes and his attempt to blow up the Parliament (1605), nor the flirtations of Stuart kings —Charleses I and II, James II—with Catholic powers, mistresses, and ideas; they tended to look upon a Catholic as one who had given his allegiance to a foreign potentate (the popes were temporal sovereigns as rulers of the Papal States), and they wondered how a Catholic would behave in a conflict between a Roman pontiff and a British king.

There were some sixty thousand Catholics in the England of 1800. Most of them were of Irish origin, but some were indigenous descendants of pre-Reformation British Catholics. The laws against them had by this time been much relaxed. Various enactments between 1774 and 1793 had restored to them the right to own land, to hold their own services, and to transmit their faith through their own schools; and a specially worded oath enabled them to swear allegiance to the king and the government without repudiating the pope. However, they could not vote, and could not be elected to Parliament.

Toward the end of the eighteenth century the movement for the full emancipation of English Catholics seemed on the verge of success. Prominent Protestants—Wesley, Canning, Wilberforce, Lord Grey—supported it. The French Revolution aroused in England a reaction against Voltaire and the Enlightenment, and some sympathy for a religion so opposed by the revolutionary government. After 1792 the French *émigrés*, including Catholic priests and monks, received a warm welcome, and financial aid, from the British state; the exiles were allowed to establish monasteries and seminaries. The notion that a Church so weakened and despoiled could be a danger to England now seemed absurd, and in a war against France that Church could be a valuable ally. In 1800 Pitt introduced a bill for the emancipation of Catholics in England. The Tories and the High Church Anglicans opposed it, and George III stood resolutely with them. Pitt withdrew his motion, and resigned. Catholic emancipation in England had to wait till 1829.

Still tardier (1858) was the removal of civil disabilities from the Jews in England. They numbered some 26,000 in 1800: most of them in London, some in the provincial cities, almost none in the countryside. The long war interrupted further immigration, and allowed the English Jews to adjust themselves to British ways, and to break down some racial barriers. The law still barred them from the franchise, and from major offices, by requiring an oath "on the faith of a Christian," and taking of the sacrament according to the rites of the Established Church. Otherwise they were free, and might worship unhindered in their homes and synagogues. Several prominent Jews accepted conversion to Christianity—Sampson Gideon the banker, David Ricardo the economist, Isaac Disraeli the author. The last, besides fathering the incomparable Benjamin, published anonymously and casually, between 1791 and 1834, *Curiosities of Literature*, which can still please an educated and leisured mind.

The long experience of the Jews in banking, and their family connections across frontiers, enabled them to come to the aid of the British government in the Seven Years' War and the long duel with France. The brothers Benjamin and Abraham Goldsmid helped Pitt to break the ring of extortionate brokers who had monopolized the transactions in Treasury issues. In 1810 Nathan Rothschild (1777–1836) established in London a branch of the firm that his father, Meyer Amschel Rothschild, had founded in Frankfurt-am-Main. Nathan seems to have been the ablest of the financial geniuses who distinguished the family through several centuries and in many states. He became the favorite intermediary of the British government in its financial relations with foreign powers; it was he or his agents who transmitted from England to Austria and Prussia the subsidies that enabled them to fight Napoleon; and he played a leading role in the industrial and commercial expansion of England after 1815.[21]

IV. EDUCATION

England seemed resolved to show how a government could get along without sending its children to school. The aristocracy was not interested in education except for its own sons. It seemed better for the status quo that the peasant and the proletaire, and probably the bourgeois too, should be unable to read, especially now that Godwin, Owen, Cobbett, Paine, Coleridge, and Shelley were printing such nonsense about exploitive aristocracies, agricultural communes, factory slaves, and the necessity of atheism. "The resolute advocates of the old system," wrote Godwin about 1793, "have, with no contemptible foresight, opposed the communication of knowledge as a most alarming innovation. In their well-known observation—that 'a servant who has been taught to write and read ceases to be any longer the passive machine they require'— is contained the embryo from which it would be easy to explain the whole philosophy of European society."[22] Besides (argued the upper echelon), the lower classes would be unable to judge with wisdom and caution the notions presented to them in lectures, journals, or books; ideas would be explosives; given nationwide schooling, the "monstrous regiment" of dreamy simpletons would try to tear down the necessary privileges and powers of the only classes that can preserve social order and civilization. And manufacturers, worried by competitors, pressed by investors, and looking for cheap labor, saw no sense in teaching child laborers the Rights of Man and the splendors of utopia. "These principles," said an anonymous conservative quoted by Godwin, "will inevitably ferment in the minds of the vulgar, . . . or the attempt to carry them into execution will be attended with every species of calamity. . . . Knowledge and taste, the improvements of the intellect, the discoveries of the sages, the beauties of poetry and art, are trampled under foot and extinguished by barbarians."[23]

In 1806 Patrick Colquhoun, former police magistrate in London, estimated that two million children in England and Wales received no education; in 1810 Alexander Murray, philologist, calculated that three fourths of the agricultural laborers were illiterate; in 1819 official statistics reported 674,883 children attending schools in England and Wales—a fifteenth of the population.[24] When, in 1796, Pitt proposed that the government set up schools for industrial education, his measure did not come to a vote; when, in 1806, Samuel Whitbread offered a bill for the governmental establishment of an elementary school in every parish (such as already existed in Scotland), it was passed by the Commons, but was rejected by the Lords on the ground that it did not place education on a religious basis.

Religious groups taxed themselves to provide some education for some of their children. The Society for Promoting Christian Knowledge maintained "charity schools," but their total enrollment of children did not exceed 150,000.[25] Hannah More's schools were almost confined to religious instruction. The Poor Law administration opened "Industry Schools" to 21,600 of its 194,914 children to fit them for employment. One thing the children in the religious schools learned well—the Bible; it became their faith, their literature, and their government, a precious possession amid the misfortunes, injustices, and bewilderment of life.

In 1797 Dr. Andrew Bell, to meet a shortage of teachers, established a "monitorial system" of using older students as assistant instructors in elementary schools connected with the Anglican worship. A year later Joseph Lancaster introduced a similar system on principles accepted by all Christians. The churchmen refused to operate with this undenominational plan; Lancaster was denounced as a deist, an apostate, a tool of Satan, and Coleridge joined in the condemnation.[26] In 1810 James Mill, Lord Brougham, Francis Place, and Samuel Rogers founded the Royal Lancastrian Association to spread unsectarian schools. Alarmed by the progress of the plan, the Anglican bishops organized a rival "Society for the Education of the Poor in Accordance with the Principles of the Established Church." Not till 1870 was a national system of undenominational elementary schools established in England.

Higher education was provided, for those who could afford it, by domestic tutors, "public" schools, lecturers, and two universities. The public schools—Eton, Harrow, Rugby, Winchester, Westminster, and Charterhouse—were open, for a fee, to the sons of the nobility and the gentry, with occasional additions from affluent bourgeois. The course of studies was primarily classical—the languages and literatures of ancient Greece and Rome. Some sciences were added on the side, but the parents wanted their sons trained for government and polite company, and they were convinced that a youth could better prepare for these by Greek and Roman history, literature, and oratory than by physics, chemistry, and English poetry; Milton, however, was admitted as a displaced Roman who wrote Latin almost as readily as English.

Discipline in the public schools was a mixture of flogging and fagging. Major offenders were flogged by the masters; fagging was the provision of menial services by boys of the lower "forms" or classes for those of the upper forms: to run errands for them, shine their shoes, prepare their tea, carry their cricket bats and balls, and bear their bullying silently; the theory was that one must learn to obey before he is fit to command. (A like theory prevailed in the Army and the Navy, which were also organized on flogging and fagging and silent obedience; in this sense the victories of Trafalgar and Waterloo were won not only on "the playing fields of Eton and Harrow" but as well in the halls and rooms of the public schools.) Once a fag reached the upper forms, he was ready to defend the system. There was some democracy in these nurseries of aristocracy: all fags were equal, regardless of wealth or pedigree, and all graduates (if they avoided commerce) looked upon one another as equals—and upon all others as inferiors, however talented.

From such schools the graduate—usually at the age of eighteen—went on to become an "undergraduate" at Oxford or Cambridge. These universities had declined from their late-medieval and Renaissance excellence; Gibbon was not alone in regretting his Oxford days as mostly wasted in irrelevant studies (though he profited hugely from the Latin and Greek), and student competition in gambling, drinking, wenching, and warfare with the town. Admission required acceptance of the Established Church. Instruction was by dons, each of whom took charge of one or more pupils, and transmitted his lore to them by lectures or tutoring. There too the classics dominated the curriculum, but mathematics, law, philosophy, and modern history had won a place, and lectures were available—though sparsely attended—in astronomy, botany, physics, and chemistry.

Oxford was Tory, Cambridge was Whig. In the latter, subscription to the Thirty-nine Articles had been removed as a condition for entrance, but only members of the Church of England could take a degree. The campaign against slavery had been waged there since 1785. Science found at Cambridge better teachers and more students than at Oxford, but both universities lagged behind the German and the French. Oxford taught philosophy from the works of Aristotle; Cambridge added Locke, Hartley, and Hume. Cambridge was producing scholars of international renown; Oxford aimed rather to fit men for eloquence and strategy in Parliament, and then, after trials and experience, and with proper connections, for a role in the government of Britain.

V. MORALITY

1. Man and Woman

What kind of moral life evolved from this class government, this changing economy, this union of state and Church, this education so limited in content and spread, this national heritage once strengthened by isolation, now challenged by communication, revolution, and war?

Men and women are not naturally moral, for their social instincts, which favor cooperation, are not as strong as their individualistic impulses, which serve the self; so these must be weakened, and those strengthened, by law expressing the will and power of the group, and by a moral code transmitted through the family, the church, the school, public opinion, custom, and taboos. Inevitably, then, there was considerable crime in the England of 1789–1815, a deal of dishonesty, and a flow of premarital sex. If we may believe Hogarth and Boswell, brothels and streetwalkers abounded in London and the factory towns. The aristocracy had found prostitutes less expensive than mistresses. Lord Egremont, open-handed host to Turner and other artists, "was said to have had a series of mistresses, by whom he sired many children. . . . The gossip, however, only added to the warmth his friends felt for him."[27] We may judge the morals of the upper classes by the amiability with which they adjusted themselves to those of the Prince of Wales. "The Prince grew up amidst the most licentious aristocracy that England had known since the Middle Ages."[28] The peasantry may be presumed to have respected the old moral code, for the family organization of agriculture required a strong parental authority, and allowed almost inescapable surveillance of the young by the old. The growing proletariat, however, released from such controls, imitated its exploiters as well as its income would allow. "Low wages in unregulated sweatshop industries made temptation strong"[29] for women factory workers to sell themselves for an added pittance to their minimal wage.

Until 1929 the legal age of marriage was fourteen for the male, twelve for the female. Normally marriage was mercenary. A man or a woman was maritably desirable according to his or her actual or prospective income; mothers schemed night and day (as in Jane Austen's novels) to marry their daughters to money. Love marriages were still exceptional, though literature was exalting them. Common-law marriage was legally recognized; formal marriage required a clergyman. Families were large, for children were economic assets, only a little less so in factories than on farms. Contraception was primitive. The rate of population growth was rising, but was slowed by infantile and senile mortality, and the inadequacy of nourishment, medical care, and public sanitation. Adultery was widespread. Divorce could be obtained by the husband or (after 1801) by the wife, but only by an act of Parliament, which cost so much that only 317 divorces were granted before the law was liberalized in 1859. Until 1859 a woman's movable property became her husband's at marriage, and he automatically acquired whatever such property came to her after marriage. She retained her property in land, but the income therefrom belonged to her husband. If she predeceased him all her property passed to him.[30]

We hear of wealthy women, but they were few. By the custom of entail a father who had no living son could—and in many cases did—bequeath his estate to a male relative, leaving his daughters dependent on friendship or courtesy. It was a man's world.

2. Mary Wollstonecraft

Custom had inured most British women to these inequities, but the winds now blowing from Revolutionary France aroused some sufferers to protest. Mary Wollstonecraft felt them, and raised her voice in one of the ablest appeals ever made for women's liberation.

Her father was a Londoner who decided to try farming; he failed, lost his fortune and his wife, took to drink, and left his three daughters to earn their own living. They opened a school, won praise from Samuel Johnson, and went bankrupt. Mary became a governess, but was dismissed after a year because "the children loved their governess better than their mother."[31] Meanwhile she wrote several books, including, in 1792, at the age of thirty-three, *A Vindication of the Rights of Woman*.

She dedicated it to "M. Talleyrand-Perigord, Late Bishop of Autun," with a hint that since the Constituent Assembly had proclaimed the Rights of Man, it was morally obligated to issue a Declaration of the Rights of Woman. Perhaps to ease her way she took a high moral tone, professing loyalty to country, virtue, and God. She said little of woman suffrage, for "as the whole system of representation is now in this country only a convenient handle for despotism, they [women] need not complain; for they are as well represented as a numerous class of hardworking mechanics, who pay for the support of royalty when they can scarcely stop their children's mouths with bread." Nevertheless, "I really think that women ought to have representatives [in Parliament], instead of being governed without having any direct share allowed them in the deliberations of government."[32] As an example of sexually based legislation she pointed to the laws of primogeniture and entail. And custom was even crueler than law, for it branded and punished a woman through life for one moment's departure from chastity, "though men preserve their respectability during the indulgence of vice."[33]

Probably some readers were shocked by Mary's declaration of a woman's right to feel, or to confess, physical satisfaction in coitus.[34] But she warned both sexes that "love considered as an animal appetite cannot long feed itself without expiring";[35] indeed, in that sense "it is the most evanescent of all passions."[36] Love as a physical relationship should be gradually replaced by friendship. This requires mutual respect, and respect requires that each mate should find in the other an individual and developing character.[37] Hence the best beginning of woman's liberation lies in recognizing her faults, and realizing that her freedom will depend upon her education in mind and conduct.

The *Vindication* proceeded to list some feminine faults of that time: the affectation of weakness and timidity, which feeds and pleases the male's assumption of superiority; the addiction to cards, gossip, astrology, sentimentality, and literary trash; the absorption in dress and self-admiration.

> Nature, music, poetry, and gallantry all tend to make women the creatures of sensation, . . . and this overstretched sensibility naturally relaxes the other powers of the mind, and prevents intellect from attaining that sovereignty which it ought to attain; . . . for the exercise of the understanding, as life advances, is the only method pointed out by Nature to calm the passions.[38]

Nearly all these faults, Mary felt, were due to inequalities of education, and to man's success in making women think that (as a lady authoress had told them), "Your best, your sweetest empire is to please."[39]

Mary resented these fripperies and artifices, and looked with envy upon those Frenchwomen who insisted on getting an education, and who learned to write letters that are among the fairest products of the French mind. "In France there is understandably a more general diffusion of knowledge than in any other part of the European world, and I attribute it, in part measure, to the social intercourse that has long subsisted between the sexes."[40] A generation before Balzac, Mary Wollstonecraft noted that

> the French, who admit more of mind into their notions of beauty, give the preference to women of thirty. . . . They allow women to be in their most perfect state when vivacity gives place to reason, and to that majestic seriousness of character which marks maturity. . . . In youth, till twenty, the body shoots out; till thirty the solids are attaining a degree of density, and the

flexible muscles [of the face], growing daily more rigid, give character to the countenance—that is, they trace the operation of the mind with the iron pen of fate, and tell us not only what powers are within, but how they have been employed.[41]

The faults of women, Mary believed, were nearly all due to the denial of educational opportunities, and to the male's success in getting women to think of themselves as sex toys before marriage, and as decorative ornaments, obedient servants, and maternity machines afterward. To give both sexes an equal chance to develop mind and body, boys and girls—up to the time of technical vocation—should be educated together, with the same curriculum and, when possible, the same or equivalent sports. Every woman should be made sufficiently strong in body and competent in mind to earn her own living if necessary,[42] but "whatever tends to incapacitate the maternal character takes woman out of her sphere";[43] sooner or later the biological functions and physiological differences will have their say. Maternal nursing is good for maternal health, and might make families smaller and stronger.[44] The ideal of woman's emancipation should be the educated mother in equal union with an educated male.[45]

Having seen her book through the press, the brilliant young author crossed the Channel to France, fascinated by the creative years of the Revolution, but just in time for the Massacres and the Terror. She fell in love with an American in Paris, Captain Gilbert Imlay, and agreed to live with him in unsanctioned union. After making her pregnant, Imlay took to absenting himself for months at a time, on business or otherwise. Her letters begging him to come back[46] are almost as eloquent, and were as futile, as those of Julie de Lespinasse a generation before. In 1794 she bore her child, but this did not hold the father. He offered to send her a yearly fund for her support; she refused it, and returned to England (1795). She tried to drown herself in the Thames, but was dragged back to life by solicitous watermen.

A year later she met William Godwin and became his common-law wife; neither of them believed in the right of the state to regulate marriage. However, for the sake of their expected child, they decided to submit to a religious ceremony (March 29, 1797). Ashamed of their legality, they concealed from their radical friends the fact that they were no longer living in sin. For a while she shone in the rebel circle that gathered around the publisher Joseph Johnson: Godwin, Thomas Holcroft, Tom Paine, William Wordsworth, and William Blake (who illustrated some of her writings). On August 30, 1797, amid intense suffering, she gave birth to Shelley's future wife. Ten days later she died.

3. Social Morality

By and large, despite those steady and decent lives that history fails to record, each class of the English population in this period shared in a general moral deterioration. Gambling was universal; the government itself (till

1826) took a hand in it with a national lottery. Drunkenness was endemic, as an escape from cold mists and rains, brutalizing poverty, family warfare, political strains, philosophical despair; Pitt and Fox, otherwise so different, agreed in favoring this anesthesia. Taverns were allowed to remain open through Saturday night till 11 A.M. Sunday,[47] for Saturday was pay day, and time had to be allowed the "pub" to get its prime cut of the weekly wage. The middle classes drank more moderately; the upper classes drank heavily, but had learned to carry their liquor steadily, like a leaking tub.

A special indulgence allowed political corruption at every stage of government. In many cases, as already noted, votes, boroughs, nominations, offices—in some cases peerages—were bought and sold as openly as shares on the stock exchange. George III, whose virtues were domestic, saw no wrong in laying out money for the procurement of votes for or in Parliament, or distributing offices for political support. In 1809 seventy-six M.P.s held such sinecures. "A favored few connected by relationship or interest with the rich and the powerful received huge salaries for doing nothing, whilst the men who actually did the work were in many cases grossly underpaid."[48] Judges sold the subordinate posts in their jurisdiction, and exacted from their holders a share of the fees which the public paid for official services.

The government could be cruel as well as venal. We have mentioned the severity of its penal code. The forcible impressment of wayfarers into the Navy was a prelude to low pay, bad food, and merciless discipline.[49] On several occasions the crews mutinied; one such strike blockaded the port of London for a month. Nevertheless, the English sailors were the best seamen and naval warriors in history.

Many efforts were made for moral reform. In 1787 George III issued a condemnation of Sabbath-breaking, blasphemy (cursing), drunkenness, obscene literature, and immoral amusements; the effect is not recorded. Jeremy Bentham, with his *Parliamentary Reform Catechism* (1809), led a dozen able disciples in exposing political venality and incompetence. Methodist and Evangelical preaching had some effect, which was doubled when the Revolution raised fears that a nation so morally unhinged could successfully combat French invasion or internal revolt. A Society for the Suppression of Vice campaigned against dueling, brothels, and pornography. Other reformers attacked child labor, the use of children as chimneysweeps, the horrors of the prisons, the ferocity of the penal code. A wave of humanitarianism, stemming partly from religion, partly from the Enlightenment, spread works of philanthropy and charity.

William Wilberforce was the most tireless of the English reformers. Born in Hull (1759) of a family rich in both land and commerce, and going through Cambridge as a comrade of William Pitt, he had little trouble in getting elected to Parliament (1774) a year after Pitt became prime minister. Feeling the influence of the Evangelical Movement, he helped to establish the Society for the Reformation of Manners (1787). Above all he protested that a nation officially Christian still tolerated the trade in African slaves.

England was now leading in this traffic. In 1790 British vessels transported

38,000 slaves to America, French ships 20,000, Portuguese 10,000, Dutch 4,000, Danish 2,000; each nation contributed according to its ability in what was probably the most criminal action in history. From Liverpool and Bristol the ships carried liquor, firearms, cotton goods, and diverse trinkets to the "Slave Coast" of Africa. There, often with the purchased help of native chieftains, the Christian chieftains exchanged their cargo for Negroes, who were then taken to the West Indies and the Southern colonies in North America. The captives were closely packed in the hulls of the vessels, and in many cases were chained to prevent rebellion or suicide. Food and water were just enough to keep them alive, ventilation was poor, sanitation minimal. To reduce the load in a severe storm, sick slaves might be thrown overboard; sometimes the not sick too, for every slave was insured, and might be worth more dead than alive. It has been calculated that of the approximately twenty million Negroes transported to the British West Indies only twenty percent survived the voyage.[50] On the return trip the ships carried molasses; in Britain this was distilled into rum, which was used to purchase slaves for the next run.

The Quakers, on both continents, took the lead in attacking the trade as the first step in the abolition of slavery. A score of writers joined in the English campaign: John Locke, Alexander Pope, James Thomson, Richard Savage, William Cowper, and, not least, Mrs. Aphra Behn, whose novel *Oroonoko* (1678) had given a revolting description of the West Indian economy. In 1772 the Quaker Granville Sharp secured from the Earl of Mansfield, lord chief justice, a decree forbidding the importation of slaves into Britain; any slave was to become automatically free the moment he set foot on British soil. In 1786 another Quaker, Thomas Clarkson, published an *Essay on the Slavery and Commerce of the Human Species*, presenting in impressive total the results of almost a lifetime of research. In 1787 Clarkson, Sharp, Wilberforce, Josiah Wedgwood, and Zachary Macaulay (father of the historian) formed the Society for the Abolition of the Slave Trade. In 1789 Wilberforce offered the Commons a bill to end the evil; it was outvoted by mercantile funds. In 1792 Pitt made one of his greatest speeches to defend a similar measure; this too failed. Wilberforce tried again in 1798, 1802, 1804, 1805, and was repeatedly repulsed. It remained for Charles James Fox, in his brief ministry (1806–07), to press the matter to victory; Parliament yielded, and forbade any participation, by British merchants, in the slave trade. Wilberforce and "the Saints" who supported him knew that this victory was but a beginning; they pressed on with a campaign for the emancipation of all the slaves still on British soil. Wilberforce died in 1833; a month later, August 28, slavery was abolished in all territories under British rule.

VI. MANNERS

One of the most startling events of 1797 was the first appearance of the silk top hat; apparently it was worn by a London haberdasher who claimed the Englishman's inborn right to be unique. Crowds gathered about him; some women, we are told, fainted at the alarming sight. But there is nothing so absurd that couturiers and haberdashers cannot make it an imperative fashion; soon all upper-class London males were carrying stovepipes on their heads.

Swords on the hip and wigs on the head were disappearing. Beards were shaved. Most males let their hair grow to their shoulders, but some youngsters expressed their defiant individuality by having their hair clipped short.[51] Pantaloons were winning the battle for men's legs; by 1785 trousers reached to midcalf; by 1793 they fell to the ankles. Shoestrings were displacing buckles and beginning their irksome reign. Coats were long, and now dispensed with embroidery, but art and income were lavished on waistcoats.

As in contemporary France under the Directory, the crossing of noble and commoner produced the dandy—the "buck" or "beau." George Bryan "Beau" Brummel (1778–1840) specialized in adorning himself, and spent half the day in dressing and undressing. At Eton, where the students called him "Buck," he became the intimate friend of the Prince of Wales, who felt that clothing is half the art of rule. Having inherited thirty thousand pounds, Brummel hired separate tailors for each part of his body, and made himself *arbiter elegantiarum* for London's males. He was good-humored and kindly, and made cleanliness next to cravats; but he loved gambling even more than finery, ran up debts, fled across the Channel to escape his creditors, lived for twenty years in dingy poverty and slovenly dress, and died, aged sixty-two, in a French asylum for the insane.

Women were abandoning hoops, but they still corseted themselves to keep their breasts poised and full. The waistline was raised, and a generous décolleté attended to the rest. During the Regency (1811–20), fashions drastically changed: corsets were discarded, petticoats were left unused, and gowns were transparent enough to reveal the lines of thighs and legs. Byron thought these revelations were dulling the fascination of pursuit, and, in a rare excursion into morality, complained: "Like Mother Eve our maids may stray unblamed, / For they are naked, and are not ashamed."[52]

Nevertheless, there was more modesty in dress than in eating. Meals were immense, not so much through gluttony as because the climate encouraged adipose tissue as a help to body heat. The poor relied basically on bread and cheese, ale or tea, but in the money classes the main meal—sometimes lasting from nine to midnight—could run to several courses: soup, fish, poultry, meat, venison, dessert, plus properly adjusted wines. After dessert the ladies disappeared, so that the men might freely discourse on politics, horses, and women. Mme. de Staël protested that this sexual dichotomy removed a main stimulant to the refinement of manners and the enjoyment of society. Table manners were not as elegant as in France.

Manners in general were hearty and rough. Speech was peppered with profanity; the Archbishop of Canterbury complained, "The torrent of profanity every day makes more rapid advances."[53] Fisticuffs were frequent in the lower classes. Boxing was a favorite sport, and prizefighting drew avid patrons from all ranks. A doubly contemporary description has come down to us from Robert Southey (1807):

> When a match is made between two prize-fighters, the tidings are immediately communicated to the public in the newspapers; a paragraph occasionally appears saying the rivals are in training, what exercise they take, what diet—for some of them feed upon raw beef as a preparative. Meantime the amateurs and the gamblers choose their party, and the state of the bets appears also in the newspapers; not infrequently the whole is a concerted scheme, that a few rogues may cheat a great many fools.[54]

Large crowds—sometimes twenty thousand—gathered for such vicarious violence. Lord Althorp recommended the sport as a purification of the aggressive instincts among the people, but the managers saw it as a purgation of pocketbooks.

Poorer people sought catharsis by tying a bull or a bear to a post, and baiting it with sticks and dogs—in some cases for two or three days—till, in a moment of mercy, they put the victim to death or sent it to the slaughterhouse.[55] Cockfighting continued as a diversion until forbidden in 1822. Cricket, which had been played in England as far back as 1550, submitted to formal rules in the eighteenth century, and offered the most stirring matches in the sporting year, with heavy betting and wild partisanship in the immense crowds. Horse racing provided another purge for gamblers, but there was in it, too, an ancient affection for horses, and a loving care in breeding and training them. The hunt was the summit of fashion in sports: the hunters riding to the grounds in handsome coaches, the swift flight over fields and crops, hedges, fences, and streams, on horses and after dogs breathing pleasure in the game.

Every class had its social gatherings, from the coffeehouses—where simple men drank beer, smoked pipes, read newspapers, and talked politics and philosophy—to the sumptuous Royal Pavilion at Brighton, where lucred folk engaged in festivities "almost as gay in winter as in summer."[56] At home gatherings people played cards or other games, heard music, or danced. The waltz had come in from Germany, and had been named from *walzen*, to revolve. Moralists helped to make it popular by branding it as sinful intimacy. Coleridge, about 1798, complained convincingly: "I am pestered every ball night to dance, which very *modestly* I refuse. They dance a most infamous dance called the Waltzen. There are perhaps twenty couples—the Man and his Partner embrace each other, arms and waists, and knees almost touching, and then whirl round and round . . . to lascivious music."[57]

The upper classes could arrange dances or other parties at one of the fashionable clubs—Almack's, White's, Brook's; there too they could gamble for high stakes, and discuss the latest performance of Mrs. Siddons, the frolics of the Prince, the novels of Jane Austen, the engravings of Blake, the storms of Turner, the landscapes of Constable. Among the Whigs the social pinnacle was Holland House, where Lady Holland held soirees at which one could meet such dignitaries as Lord Brougham, Philippe Duc d'Orléans, Talleyrand, Metternich, Grattan, Mme. de Staël, Byron, Thomas Moore, or the noblest Whig of them all, Charles James Fox.[58] No salon in France could rival Holland House at the end of the eighteenth century.

VII. THE ENGLISH THEATER

Add to all this varied life the English passion for the theater, which rages to this day. And even as now the dramatists were of but minor worth, and the actors were the play. The inescapable competition of Shakespeare seemed to discourage the writing of tragedies; after the heyday of Sheridan and Goldsmith the best new comedies were mortal efforts like Thomas Holcroft's *The Road to Ruin* (1792) and Elizabeth Inchbald's *Lovers' Vows* (1798), which clung to the frail line of middle class sentiment rather than the virile strain of Jonson's lethal laughter or Shakespeare's philosophic fun. Only the actors were still at the top of their form.

They seemed at first glance to be all of a family, which walked the boards from Roger Kemble, who died in 1802, to Henry Kemble, who died in 1907. Roger sired Sarah Kemble, who became Mrs. Siddons; John Philip Kemble, who joined the Drury Lane company in 1783 and became its manager in 1788; and Stephen Kemble, who managed the Edinburgh Theatre from 1792 to 1800.

Sarah was born in 1755, in the Shoulder-of-Mutton Inn at Brecon, Wales, as an incident in the tour of her father's troupe. As soon as she could act she was given a role; she became a seasoned actress by the age of ten. Amid her hectic life she managed to get considerable education; she became a woman of mature and cultivated mind as well as professional excellence and ageless charm. At eighteen she married William Siddons, a minor member of her company. Two years later Garrick, having heard of her success in the provinces, sent an agent to watch her perform. The report being favorable, Garrick offered her an engagement at Drury Lane, and she appeared there as Portia on December 29, 1775. She did not do well, partly through nervousness, partly, perhaps, because she had recently given birth. She was thin, tall, and grave; classic in features and restraint; and her voice, accustomed to smaller theaters, failed to fill the immense theater. After a disappointing season she returned to the provincial circuit, and for seven years she labored patiently to improve her art. In 1782 Sheridan, who had succeeded Garrick as manager, persuaded her to return to London. On October 10, 1782, she took the lead in Thomas Southerne's century-old *The Fatal Marriage;* and her success was so complete that from that evening she moved on to become the finest tragedienne in British history. For twenty-one years she ruled at Drury Lane, and for ten more she was the undisputed queen at Covent Garden. To see her there as Lady Macbeth was the culminating experience of a theatergoer's life. When she retired from the stage, on June 29, 1812, at the age of fifty-seven, she played that role, and the audience was so moved by her performance of the sleepwalking scene that it preferred to applaud her through the rest of the evening rather than let the play go on.[59] For nineteen years thereafter she lived in quiet retirement, cheating town gossipers by her marital fidelity. Gainsborough triumphed with his painting of her, and she reigns to this day in the National Portrait Gallery.

Her brother John Philip Kemble, born like her in a provincial inn, was destined by his parents for the Catholic priesthood, perhaps in the popular theory that a member in holy orders would gain heaven for all the family. He was sent to Douai to study in its Catholic college and seminary; there he received a good classical education, and there he acquired a clerical solemnity that later clung to nearly all his roles. But in that quiet environment the exciting career of his father kept a secret fascination for him. At eighteen (1775) he left Douai and returned to England; a year later he joined a theatrical troupe; by 1781 he was playing Hamlet in Dublin. There for a time his sister Sarah joined him, and thence she brought him with her to Drury Lane.[60] His debut there as Hamlet (1783) was only a moderate success; the London public found him too sedate for its taste, and the critics condemned him for not only abbreviating but emendating Shakespeare's text. However, when he joined Mrs. Siddons in *Macbeth* (1785) their performance was hailed as an event in the history of the English theater.

In 1788 Sheridan, then chief owner of the Drury Lane, appointed Kemble manager of the company. He continued to fill the leading roles, but Sheridan's gay despotism and financial unreliability made the sensitive actor uncomfortable. In 1803 he accepted the management of the Covent Garden Theatre, and bought a sixth share of the enterprise for £23,000. In 1808 the edifice burned down. After a costly idleness Kemble assumed management of the rebuilt theater; but when he tried to offset the unexpectedly high cost of the new structure by raising the price of admission, the audience stopped his next performance by persistent cries of "Old prices!"; he was not allowed to continue until he promised to restore them.[61] The Duke of Northumberland saved the company with a gift of £10,000. Kemble struggled on, increasingly challenged by younger actors. With a final triumph in *Coriolanus*, when the same public that had hooted him in 1809 shook the theater with acclaim, he left the British stage, and surrendered his crown to Edmund Kean. The classic style of acting disappeared from England with him, as it was disappearing from France with his friend Talma; and the Romantic movement triumphed in the theater as it was doing in painting, music, poetry, and prose.

Kean's life included all the vicissitudes of his high-strung profession, all its humors and tragedies. He was born in a London slum in 1787, as one result of a night's outing between Aaron (or Edmund) Kean, a stagehand, and Ann Carey, who earned a minimal living on the stage and the street. Deserted in early childhood by his parents, he was brought up by his father's brother, Moses Kean, a popular entertainer, and more formally by Moses' mistress, Charlotte Tidswell, a minor actress at Drury Lane. She trained him in histrionic art and tricks, while Moses made him study Shakespearean roles; the boy learned everything that could hold a provincial audience, from acrobatics, ventriloquism, and boxing to Hamlet and Macbeth. But he had waywardness in his blood, and ran away repeatedly; at last Charlotte bound a dog collar around his neck, inscribed "Drury Lane Theatre." By the age of fifteen he had shed the collar, and strayed off to an independent career as an actor of any part, for fifteen shillings a week.

For ten years he lived the hectic, exhausting life of a strolling player, nearly always poor and humiliated, but burning with confidence that he could outperform any man on the English stage. Soon, to forget his toil and torments, he took to alcohol as favoring his dreams of his supposedly noble birth and his forthcoming victories. In 1808 he married Mary Chambers, a fellow trouper; she gave him two sons, and clove to him through all his bouts with whiskey and women. Finally, after many years of degrading alternations between Shakespearean parts and impersonating an agile chimpanzee, he received an invitation to a trial appearance at Drury Lane.

For his debut there (January 26, 1814) he chose the difficult role of Shylock. He poured into the role some of the resentments that life's indignities had stored up in him. When Shylock said, in scorn and sarcasm, to the Christian Venetian merchant asking for a loan,

> Hath a dog money? Is it possible
> A cur can lend three thousand ducats?,

Kean seemed to have forgotten that he was anyone other than Shylock; and the passion, the violence, that he poured into the part put an end, almost in two lines, to the classic era in English acting, and opened on the London boards the era of feeling, imagination, and romance. Gradually the audience, sparse and skeptical, was carried away by this unknown actor, himself carried away by immersion in his part. Scene by scene the response and applause grew, until, at the close, that half-audience surrendered to him ecstatically. William Hazlitt, ablest critic of the age, hurried off to write an enthusiastic review. Kean, rushing home to his family, embraced his wife and child, saying to the one, "Now, Mary, you shall ride in your carriage," and to the boy, "My son, you shall go to Eton!"[62]

At Kean's second performance in *The Merchant of Venice*, the house was full. After the third the reigning manager, Samuel Whitbread, gave Kean the contract they had agreed upon for a three years' engagement at eight pounds a week; Kean signed; Whitbread took it and changed the eight pounds to twenty. The time would come when Kean's contract would call for fifty pounds per night. He played almost all the famous Shakespearean roles—Hamlet, Richard III, Richard II, Henry V, Macbeth, Othello, Iago, Romeo. He succeeded in all but the last; the delicate shades of Romeo's aristocratic character eluded an actor too hardened and embittered by the ruthless inequalities of life.

When it came his turn to see young actors waiting eagerly to take his place, he squandered his earnings in drink, fed on the idolatry of tavern habitués,[63] joined a secret movement for "the damnation of all lords and gentlemen," and was successfully sued for adultery with the wife of a city alderman (1825).[64] He paid the charges, and labored to win back his place in the theater; but his mind lost hold of the parts he played, and more than once he forgot his lines. The audience was as merciless as it had been idolatrous; it shouted insults at him, asked him why he drank so heedlessly. He left England, toured America triumphantly, made another fortune, squandered it. He returned to London, and agreed to play Othello to his son's Iago at Covent Garden (1833). The audience acclaimed Iago, received Othello silently. The effort, unsupported by applause, was too much for Kean; his strength ran out, and he neared collapse. After speaking the line "Farewell! Othello's occupation's gone" he fell into the arms of his son, and whispered to him, "Charles, I am dying; speak to them for me."[65] He was taken home; the wife whom he had once abandoned took loving care of him. Two months later he died, May 15, 1833, only forty-six years old. Life had broken in midlife the greatest actor—barring Garrick—in English history.

VIII. IN SUM

All in all, it was a virile and fruitful England. There were many weak spots in the picture, as in every picture true to life: the yeomanry disappearing, the proletariat enslaved, drink and gambling ruining fortunes and breaking up homes; government frankly a class privilege, and law made by a few men for other men and all women. And yet amid these faults and crimes science was developing, philosophy was ruminating, Constable was revealing English landscapes, Turner was chaining the sun and stilling the storm, and Wordsworth, Coleridge, Byron and Shelley were giving England a feast of poetry unequaled anywhere since the first Elizabeth. Under all the turbulence there lay a saving order and stability that allowed many freedoms —more than in any other European state except in France, where excessive freedom had committed suicide. There was freedom of movement and travel except in war, freedom of worship this side of blasphemy, freedom of the press this side of treason, freedom of opinion this side of advocating a violent revolution which would, by all precedents, involve a decade or more of bewildering lawlessness and insecurity.

It was not a highly educated public opinion; it often expressed Mrs. Gump, and upheld outworn taboos; but it had the courage to boo a degenerate prince and applaud his cruelly discarded wife.[66] It expressed itself also in a hundred associations and societies dedicated to education, science, philosophy, and reform. On critical issues it expressed itself in public assemblies and exercised the right of petition guaranteed by English law; and when it felt too heavily the hand of an oligarchic state it took to resistance as the final stand of patient Englishmen; more than once a healthy riot ran through the countryside and city streets.

The government was an aristocracy, but it was at least polite; it transmitted manners, checked fads, and maintained standards of taste against barbarism in art and superstition in belief; it supported several good causes, and kept its great poets from starvation. There was an occasionally insane King,

but his claws had been cut, he had become helplessly lovable, and he served
as a symbol of national unity, a focus of national fervor and pride; there
seemed no sense in killing a million people to depose so useful a master of
ceremonies. After a bow or two an Englishman might follow his own mood,
go his own way, provided he did not insist upon the equal rights of boot-
blacks and baronets to make the laws of the land. "In England," Mme.
de Staël noted, "originality is allowed to individuals, so well regulated is the
mass";[67] it was the superimposed order that allowed the burgeoning of freedom.

   Let us see this combination at work in art, science, philosophy, literature,
and statesmanship. Only then will the picture of English life, A.D. 1800, be,
within our limits, just and complete.

CHAPTER XVII

The Arts in England

I. THE ARTISTS

THE words *art* and *artist*, which in guild days had been applied to any craft or craftsman, changed their meaning in the eighteenth century as crafts and guilds were replaced by industries and workingmen; now they were applied to the practice and practitioners of music, decoration, ceramics, drawing, engraving, painting, sculpture, and architecture. Likewise the word *genius*, which had signified some innate and characteristic quality, or some supernatural spirit, now increasingly denoted a transcendent native ability, or its possessors; like *miracle* and *act of God*, it became a convenient substitute for a natural and specific explanation of an unusual person or event.

The transition to industry, commerce, and city life brought a further decline in aristocratic patronage of art; however, we must note that moneyed men supported Wordsworth and Coleridge, and Lord Egremont opened his manor house at Petworth to Turner as a refuge from London. George III had helped to establish (1768) the Royal Academy of Art with a gift of five thousand pounds and handsome quarters in Somerset House. Its forty members were not made automatically immortals like their French models, but they were raised to the gentry with the title of (e)squire, and though their new dignity could not be passed on to their offspring, it helped to improve the social standing of major artists in Britain. The Academy organized classes in anatomy, drawing, painting, sculpture, and architecture. Inevitably an institution supported by a conservative monarch became a citadel of tradition and respectability. Innovative artists denounced it, and became so numerous, and won such acclaim, that in 1805 some nobles and bankers financed the organization of the British Institution for the Development of the Fine Arts, which held periodic exhibitions, awarded prizes, and provided a lively competition for the Royal Academy. Guided, angered, and nourished by these rival forces, British art produced excellent works in every field.

No; music was an exception; it was barren of memorable compositions in this period. England was keenly conscious of this dearth, and made up for it in some measure by generous appreciation of composers coming to her from the Continent; so she gave Haydn a warm welcome in 1790 and again in 1794. The Royal Philharmonic Society was founded in 1813, survived the Industrial Revolution, the French Revolution, two Napoleons, and two World Wars, and still exists as one element of permanence in an incalculable flux.

The minor arts flourished without flair. They continued to produce elegant but sturdy furniture, powerful or fanciful metalware, quietly beautiful ceramics. Benjamin Smith molded iron into an ornate candelabrum for presentation by the city of London to the Duke of Wellington.[1] John Flaxman, besides making classical designs for Wedgwood pottery, fashioned the famous Trafalgar Cup to commemorate Nelson's victory,[2] and he was both sculptor and architect of the massive monument to Nelson in St. Paul's.

Sculpture, however, was almost a minor art in England, perhaps because it favored a nudity uncongenial to the national climate and morality. In 1801 Thomas Bruce, seventh Earl of Elgin, while serving as British envoy to the Porte, persuaded the Turkish authorities in Athens to let him remove from the Acropolis "any pieces of stone with old inscriptions or figures thereon." Interpreting this like a lord, Lord Elgin removed the great frieze of the Parthenon, and many marble busts, and transported them, in ship after ship, 1803–12, to England. He was denounced by Byron and others as a rapacious vandal, but he was vindicated by a committee of Parliament, and the "Elgin marbles" were bought by the nation for £35,000 (much less than Elgin paid for them), and were deposited in the British Museum.[3]

II. ARCHITECTURE

The marbles shared in supporting the classic wave against the Gothic ripples in the war of architectural styles; a thousand columns—Doric, Ionic, or Corinthian—advanced to oppose the amateur efforts of Walpole and Beckford to restore the pointed arches and towered battlements so dear to medieval knights and saints. Even in secular structures the columns won; Sir William Chambers' Somerset House (1775 ff.) is a spreading Parthenon, and many a country house looks like a Greek peristyle guarding a Roman palace; let James Wyatt's Ashridge Park mansion (1806–13) serve as a stately instance of the kind. In 1792 the future Sir John Soane, son of a bricklayer, began to rebuild the Bank of England behind a Corinthian portico, combining the Arch of Constantine with the Temple of the Sun or Moon.

The Gothic revival inaugurated by Horace Walpole's Strawberry Hill (1748–73) could not maintain itself against the avalanche of pillars, domes, and pediments. William Beckford was the romantic hero of this medieval trance. Born rich of a father who twice became mayor of London, he was given more education than he could stand: he received piano lessons from the young Mozart, architectural training from Sir William Chambers, and history via the Grand Tour. At Lausanne he bought the library of Edward Gibbon. After some ambisexual scandals he married Lady Margaret Gordon, who died in childbirth. Meanwhile he had written *Vathek*, the most powerful of the Oriental mystery novels that were swelling the Romantic wave; it was published in English and French (1786–87), and won high praise from Byron. Helped by Wyatt, Beckford began in 1796 to build a Gothic abbey at his Fonthill estate in Wiltshire, filled it with art and books, and lived there, hermitically sealed, from 1807 to 1822. Then he sold it, and shortly afterward its collapse revealed basic faults in its structure and design. He died at Bath in 1844, aged eighty-five. John Hoppner's sympathetic portrait (*c.* 1800) preserves a spirit poetic, mystic, and humane.

John Nash lightened the heaviness of British architecture by adding a bit of rococo gaiety. Well seconded by Humphry Repton as landscape gardener, he designed country estates with a distribution of cottages, bowers, dairies, in French, Indian, Chinese styles. They pleased the bored nobles and gentry; Nash became rich, and won the patronage of the lavish Prince. In 1811 he was commissioned to rebuild a mile of Regent Street to run from the Regent's Carlton House in a sweeping curve out to the countryside. Nash varied the lines with crescents and terraces, interspersed open spaces of grass and trees between the building groups, and used Ionic columns to grace the curve of the avenue. (Most of the work has been demolished to allow more buildings and less grass.) It was a brilliant essay in town planning, but its cost shocked a nation that was half starving itself to defeat Napoleon.

Nevertheless the delighted Regent engaged Nash to restore the Royal Pavilion at Brighton, which had been a favorite resort of the Prince and his friends. Nash accomplished the task between 1815 and 1823, at a cost of £160,000. He rebuilt the pavilion in Hindu-Moorish style, with tentlike domes and flanking minarets. Its banquet hall was remodeled with a convex ceiling and Chinese decoration, including lotus-and-dragon chandeliers costing £4,290.[4] The first impression was one of bizarre splendor; the final judgment condemned the excess in ornament and cost.

In 1820 the Regent became George IV. Soon he commissioned Nash to rebuild Buckingham House as a royal palace. Amid the destitution and near-bankruptcy that had followed the victory over Napoleon, Nash labored and spent until the royal wastrel died (1830). Then the exuberant architect was summoned by the new government to explain his expenditures and some alleged defects in the construction. Seldom had England been so splendid, or so poor.

III. FROM CARTOONS TO CONSTABLE

During twenty years of war a thousand British artists had struggled to feed their families and their dreams. Not the humblest of them in reward and fame were the caricaturists who filled the press with cartoons of the passing scene. Napoleon was a blessing to these impish geniuses, for their daily satires of "Little Boney"—or the "Mediterranean mulatto," as the *Morning Post* called him[5]—were shots in the arm to a weary "war effort," and pricks in the pride of the fuming Emperor.

Greatest of these acupunctors was Thomas Rowlandson (1756–1827). Born to a rich but speculative trader, he was amply encouraged in his talent for drawing. After studying at the Royal Academy, he enrolled in the École de l'Académie Royale in Paris, returned to England, and soon won acclaim by his drawings. Suddenly impoverished by the ruin of his father in gambling, he was reanimated by a French aunt who sent him £35,000. Free to satirize the absurdities and hypocrisies of his time, he drew caricatures of a duchess kissing a butcher for his vote, a fat parson receiving a pig as tithe from a half-starved peasant, a group of naval officers hunting whores ashore. He went on to draw extensive and complex pictures—*Vauxhall Gardens*, *Comforts of Bath*, and a hilarious series, nationally famous, *The Tours of Dr. Syntax*. His anger at politicians, roisterers, and dolts led him to exaggerate the forgivable exaggerations of caricature. Many of his drawings had to be cleansed of their obscenity; his satire lost all healing pity; his later work breathed scorn of the human race, as if there had never been a loving mother or a generous man.

Even more popular were the caricatures of James Gillray (1757–1815); people fought at the bookstores to get the first copies of his cartoons.[6] Like Rowlandson he studied at the Royal Academy, and became a finished artist, vivid in imagination but firm in line. He put nearly all his art at the service of the war: he pictured Napoleon as a pygmy, and Josephine as a fishwife; he represented Fox, Sheridan, and Horne Tooke (supporters of the French Revolution) as waiting, in a London club, upon a victorious Revolutionary general. Reprints of his satires—crude in concept, finished in form—circulated throughout Europe, and shared in dethroning Napoleon.[7] He died seventeen days before Waterloo.

There were many good engravers in that generation, but William Blake cut deeply enough to survive time's obliterations. He developed his own methods, and even tried to replace print by etching text and illustration together into copper plates. But his pen outran his graver, and in the end he spoke through poetry.

He was a rebel because he resented his poverty; because the Academy refused to recognize engravers as artists as well as artisans, or to admit their works to its exhibitions; and because he heartily rejected its injunctions to cleave to the rules, traditions, and proprieties of art. "The Enquiry in England," he declared (*c.* 1808), "is not whether a Man has talents and genius, but whether he is Passive and Politic and a Virtuous Ass and obedient to Noblemen's Opinions in Art. If he is, he is a God Man. If not, he must be starved."[8] He neared this at times, since he received only pittances for drawings and engravings that in the London of 1918 fetched $110,000.[9] His twenty-two plates illustrating the Book of Job kept him alive at two pounds per week from 1823 to 1825; they were sold to J. Pierpont Morgan (1907) for £5,600; they are among the finest engravings in history.

Blake was a complex cross between pagan and puritan, classic and romantic. He was enthralled by Michelangelo's statuary and Sistine Chapel ceiling. He too felt the splendor of the healthy human body; he symbolized it in the print (1780) entitled "Glad Day"—a youth diaphanously clothed, knowing the joy of bounding vitality. Sex plays only a modest part in his art; it entered assertively in his poems, but moderately in his life; he had a helpful and loving wife, who made fidelity bearable. His drawings were at first strictly classical, rating line above color, and form over fancy; but as he advanced in years, and in love with the Old Testament, he let his pencil roam into imaginary figures overwhelmingly robed, and faces worn by the riddles of life.[10]

In his last years he engraved seven plates for an edition of Dante; on his deathbed (1827) he made one more print of God as "The Ancient of Days" creating the world. It was through his almost supernatural imagination, as well as through the finesse of his line, that he became, a generation after his death, the proclaimed progenitor of the Pre-Raphaelite School. We shall meet him again.

Among the painters the vital question, sometimes involving bread and butter, was: How far should they conform to the advice and tastes of the Academy? Some of its professors gave their highest approval to historical subjects, as revealing famous characters in memorable events. Others praised portraiture as probing and revealing character—and as pleasing contributory notables who wished to be preserved in oil. Very few of the Academic fraternity cared for genre pictures, for these smelled of the commonalty. Least approval of all was accorded to landscape paintings; a Constable, who had lost his heart to them, had to labor in obscurity till he was fifty-three before the Academy allowed him full membership.

In 1792 Sir Joshua Reynolds died, and the Academy chose as its president an American domiciled in England. Benjamin West had been born in Springfield, Pennsylvania, in 1738. He showed such artistic talent in youth that generous neighbors sent him to study in Philadelphia, then to Italy. After imbibing the classical tradition there in galleries and ruins, he moved to London (1763), painted some lucrative portraits, pleased George III, and advanced to historical themes. His *Death of Wolfe* (1771), who had snatched Canada from Montcalm and France, shocked the Academy by picturing modern figures in modern dress; but the elders admitted that half a continent was worth an obeisance to pantaloons.

Another American, John Singleton Copley, born near Boston in 1738, won fame with his portraits of John Hancock, Samuel Adams, and the Copley family. In 1775 he moved to London, and soon reached his peak with *The Death of Chatham* (1779). To escape from the neoclassical idealization of historical figures, he painted the scene with a courageous realism which —though it troubled the Academy—effected a revolution in English painting.

The education of the Academy was continued by Johann Heinrich Füssli of Zurich, who in 1764, aged twenty-three, became Henry Fuseli of London. Encouraged by Reynolds, he left England in 1770 for eight years of study in Italy. His flair for heterodox flights of the imagination was not quite cured by classic models and norms. When he returned to London he disturbed some sleeping beauties with *The Nightmare* (1781), in which a lovely woman dreams that she is approached by a terrifying fiend. (A copy of this hung in Sigmund Freud's study.) Despite himself and his sarcastic wit, Fuseli became a professor in the Academy, where his lectures eased the transition to Romance and the Pre-Raphaelites.

The difficulty of making a living by painting nature was illustrated by the careers of John Hoppner (1758–1810) and John Crome (1768–1821). Hoppner starved as a lover of landscapes, and then flourished as a painter of portraits, almost rivaling Lawrence in sitters and fees. Nelson sat for him; so did Wellington, Walter Scott, and sundry lords; St. James's Palace is rich with Hoppner's legacy. — Crome remained in his native Norwich nearly all his fifty-three years. He worked for a time as a sign painter; studied the pictures of Hobbema and other Dutch masters; and learned from them to relish the simple scenes of common life. Too poor to travel, he sought his subjects in the rural hinterland of Norwich. There he found the perspective which he painted in his finest landscape, *Mousehold Heath*. Art and philosophy needed no more.

Sir Thomas Lawrence (1769–1830) followed the primrose path of portraiture. The son of an innkeeper, he received little schooling, little artistic training; it must have disconcerted the Academy to observe how well he succeeded without them. He had an almost natural flair for quickly catching a likeness and putting it down—in boyhood at Bristol with his pencil, in youth at Bath with pastel; only when he moved to London (1786) did he work with oils. Perhaps his physical charm and happy spirits opened hearts and doors to him. While still but twenty he was commissioned to go to Windsor and portray Queen Charlotte Sophia. He succeeded so diplomatically (for she was no beauty) that he was elected to associate membership in the Academy at twenty-two, and to full membership at twenty-five. A hundred notables competed to sit for him. He rejected Cromwell's advice to paint the warts as well as the dimples; there was no gold in warts. He improved the features of his sitters, who protested not; and what his ladies lacked in beauty he made up by clothing them in gossamer finery, endowing them with lovely hands and fascinating eyes, and casting them in some dramatic pose. Typical of his work is the handsome and striking figure he made of the Prince Regent in 1815. Sometimes, as in the *Pinkie* of the Huntington Gallery, he achieved a pleasant whimsy, but we miss in his male portraits the strong character that Reynolds had found or fashioned in his sitters. Lawrence earned much, gave generously, and became the idol of his age. When he died a distinguished cortege escorted him to St. Paul's.

John Constable (1776–1837) insisted on painting landscapes, and earned no bride till forty. His father was a Sussex miller who indulged his son's talent for drawing and painting, and financed two years of study for him in London. But John's development was slow; by 1797 he felt that he deserved no further keep; he returned to Sussex to work in his father's mill. In his spare time he continued to paint. He sent some of his work to the Academy, which offered him admission to its school. So in 1799 he was back in London, supported by a paternal allowance, and encouraged by Benjamin West. A fellow artist, Richard Reinagle, painted an engaging portrait of him in that year.

Perhaps he read Wordsworth's poems about the scenery around Lake Windermere, for he too saw God in every leaf. In 1806 he toured the Lake District, which let him study mountains embraced by mists, and fields happy under tranquil rains. He returned to London strengthened in his resolve to devote his art to nature. He said of his landscapes that he hoped "to give to one brief moment, caught from fleeting time, a lasting and sober existence."[11] Meanwhile he received incidental commissions that kept him in food and lodging. In 1811, at last, he produced his first acclaimed masterpiece—*Dedham Vale*, an Essex panorama under a midday sun.

In that year, it seems, he fell in love with Maria Bickell, who welcomed his attentions; but her father forbade her to stoop to so low an income as Constable then earned. Not till five years later, when his father's death left him an assuring income, did he venture to press his suit. Her father relented, Constable carried off his bartered bride, and flattered her with a portrait that now brightens a Tate Gallery wall. Thereafter he painted the finest landscapes that English art had yet produced—not as exciting as Turner's, but conveying, with a loving detail that honored every leaf, the peace and green wealth of the English countryside. In that happy period he submitted to the Academy *Flatford Mill* (1817), *The White Horse* (1819), *The Hay Wain* (wagon) (1821), *Salisbury Cathedral* (1823), and *The Cornfield* (1826). Each was a masterpiece, and won faint praise.

In 1824 he submitted *The Hay Wain* for exhibition in the Paris Salon, and in 1825 *The White Horse* was shown at Lille. Each won a gold medal, and French critics hailed Constable as a master. The London Royal Academy, caught short, at last gave him full membership (1829).

The honor came too late to mean much to him, for in that year his wife died, of tuberculosis probably aggravated by London's soot. Constable continued to produce such arresting landscapes as *Valley Farm* and *Waterloo Bridge*, but nearly all his later work reflected an enduring grief. He wore mourning until his sudden death.

IV. TURNER: 1775–1851

Joseph Mallord William Turner was as proud as his name, and never allowed a hostile critic or a shattered love to disturb his march to unquestioned mastery.

He was born on April 23, 1775, perhaps sharing the day and the month with Shakespeare. His father was a barber whose shop in Maiden Lane, behind Covent Garden, was hardly a fit spot for a landscape artist's growth. According to an early biographer,[12] Maiden Lane was a "dim defile," paved with mud, crowded with noisy traffic, and torn with vendors' cries. Across from the barbershop was an inn, the Cider Cellar, whose habitués sang in prophetic atonality. Add that William's sister was soon to die, and his mother was going mad. Nature and circumstances made some amends by giving the boy a tough frame and will, a realistic mind, and an unshakable self-confidence, which, conjoined, withstood, for seventy-six years, crises, critics, and germs.

His father saw in him signs of a talent ill-adjusted to Maiden Lane. He

sent William, aged ten, to live with an uncle—and attend school—in Brent-
wood, Middlesex. Within two years the boy had produced drawings that his
proud father hung in and around the barbershop, and offered for sale. A
clergyman customer recommended some of them to an Academic friend.
Soon William was given a trial at the Academy; he did well; he was accepted as a student at the age of fourteen, and, a year later, was allowed to
display a watercolor at the exhibition.

In vacation time, during the years 1789–92, he toured the countryside
with his sketchbook, going as far afield as Oxford, Bristol, Wales; those
eager sketches of land, sun, and sea are still visible in the British Museum.
At nineteen he was selling his drawings to magazines; at twenty-one he began to exhibit his oil paintings at the Academy; at twenty-four he was
elected an associate, at twenty-seven a full, member. Made economically independent by his sales, he opened (1800) a spacious studio at 64 Hurly
Street; and there his father came to live with him as his attendant and business agent. This love affair harmonized well with the artist's disinclination
for marriage. He was not physically or facially attractive, and had little
charm of manner. He was a man absorbed. For almost half a century he
dominated English art, overwhelming competition with the abundance and
brilliance of his work.

Biographers ease their task of understanding him by dividing him into
three periods. In the first (1787–1820) he inclined to historical subjects, but
transformed them into studies of sun and sea. In 1799 he was among the four
painters who, in the Academy exhibition, celebrated Nelson's demolition of
Napoleon's fleet at Abukir. In 1802 he made his first trip abroad. As the
packet neared Calais it found the waves too high and violent to allow dock-
ing. Turner and some other passengers managed to reach shore in a rowboat.
There he took out his sketchbook and outlined the complex scene of the
vessel struggling against the storm; a year later he exhibited in London his
massive canvas, *Calais Pier*, in which he gave full play to his fondness for
dark clouds, angry seas, and brave men. From France he hurried on to
Switzerland to make four hundred drawings of mountains challenging the
sky. His sketchbooks became his second memory.

When he returned to London he found the Academic critics complaining
that he laid colors down too thickly, recklessly, confusedly, and in combinations violating all sane precedent; that his methods ignored the norms
taught by the late Sir Joshua Reynolds for following Old Masters and ob-
serving traditional rules. Turner honored the memory of the kindly dictator,
but he obeyed the dictates of his own character. Henceforth he was in art
the clearest voice of the Romantic revolt against age-old subjects, obsolete
rules, and the stifling of experiment and imagination by custom and reality.
He replied to his critics by exhibiting in his studio *The Shipwreck* (1804)—
a merciless visualization of nature's mastery over man. It was acclaimed. A
year later he won British hearts by celebrating Nelson's victory at Trafalgar.
The picture was a confusion of ships, the elements, and men; but so had the
battle been. Nevertheless, the critics voiced a widely felt bewilderment:

Turner was all color, no line; even the color seemed to have been splashed about formlessly, and yet made a subject in itself; the edifices and the human beings on his canvases were blotches of obscurity, dots denoting insignificance, as if the artist had been obsessed by the helplessness of man against a nature enraged. There were pleasant exceptions, as in *The Sun Rising through Mist* (1807); but in *Hannibal Crossing the Alps* (1812) all sense of man's heroism seemed lost in the black and yellow clouds swirling above soldiers cringing in fear. Was this wild artist an enemy of the human race?

Turner went on his way wielding his brush with force and verve, apparently resolved to sweep man and life from the earth, leaving nothing but sun, clouds, mountains, and raging seas. He was not entirely a misanthrope; he was capable of warm affection, and developed a quiet friendship with Sir Thomas Lawrence, his opposite in practice and theory. But he recognized no nobility except genius, and had few delusions about the common man. He liked his work and his privacy, feeling, like Leonardo, that "if you are all alone you will be all yourself." He had no ascertainable faith in any supernatural world. His god was nature, and he gave it his kind of adoration—not of its wisdom and beauty, as in Wordsworth, but of its pertinacity and power; and he knew that it would engulf him too, and man, in its own grim time. He did not bother much about morality. He had a mistress or two, but kept them decently private. He made some nude drawings of an erotic character; these, falling into Ruskin's hand, were at once destroyed. He loved money, commanded high fees, and left a fortune. He was a rough diamond, solitaire.

His middle period (1820–33) began with a sun-pursuing trip to Italy. During those six months he made fifteen hundred drawings; after his return to England he turned some of them into new essays in color, light, and shade, like *The Bay of Baiae* (1823), where even the shadows speak. Again in France (1821), he made illuminating watercolors of the Seine. In 1825–26 he wandered through Belgium and Holland and brought home sketches, some of which became the paintings *Cologne* and *Dieppe*, now in the Frick Collection in New York. Occasionally, in the 1830s, he enjoyed the hospitality of Lord Egremont at Petworth; as usual he hid himself with his work, but he gave his host a moment's immortality with *The Lake at Sunset*.

In the final period (1834–45) of his fertility he surrendered more and more to the lure of light; recognizable objects almost disappeared; what remained was a fascinated study of color, radiance, and shade. Occasionally he let objects play a leading role, as in *The Fighting Téméraire Towed to Her Last Berth* (1839) after many a blast for Britain; or the proud locomotive announcing a century of iron horses in *Rain, Steam, and Speed* (1844). When the Houses of Parliament burned down in 1834 Turner sat nearby, making sketches for his later painting of the spectacle. Crossing from Harwich his ship ran into a madness of wind and snow; the aging artist had himself lashed to the mast for four hours that he might burn into his memory the details and terror of the scene;[13] later he fused the confusion into a fury of white paint called *The Snowstorm* (1842). Then (1843), as a final triumph, he pictured *The Sun of Venice Going Out to Sea.*

His last years were darkened by a mounting consensus of condemnation, mitigated by a paean of praise from a master of English prose. One critic dismissed *The Snowstorm* as "soapsuds and whitewash";[14] another summed up the artist's final period as the work of "a diseased eye and reckless hand"; and *Punch* proposed a general title for any picture by Turner: "A Typhoon Bursting in a Simoon over the Whirlpool of Maelstrom, Norway, with a Ship on Fire, an Eclipse, and the Effect of a Lunar Rainbow."[15] After half a century of labor, the grand and brilliant oeuvre seemed to be despised and rejected by the merciless judgment of conservative taste.

Then, in May, 1843, John Ruskin, aged twenty-four, issued the first volume of *Modern Painters*, whose persistent and enthusiastic themes were the superiority of William Turner over all other modern landscape painters, and the complete veracity of Turner's pictures as a report on the external world. Turner was not offended to find himself exalted above Claude Lorrain, who had been the inspiration of his youth; but as he read on he began to wonder would not this eulogy harm him by its elongation and excess. For a time it did; critics lauded Ruskin's prose but questioned his judgment and counseled a more balanced view. Ruskin was not to be restrained; he returned again and again, in volume after volume, to the enterprise of defending and expounding Turner, until he had given the artist almost a third of the book's two thousand pages. In the end he won his battle, and lived to see his idol acclaimed as one of the creative enlargers of modern art.

Meanwhile Turner died, December 19, 1851, and was buried in St. Paul's. His will left his artistic remains to the nation—three hundred paintings, three hundred watercolors, nineteen thousand drawings—and left his unspent earnings, £140,000, to a fund for needy artists. (His surviving relatives obtained annulment of the will, and divided the money among themselves and their lawyers.)

Perhaps his greatest legacy was his pictorial discovery of light. In that same generation that heard Thomas Young formulate his wave theory of light, Turner spread over Europe luminescent paintings and watercolors proclaiming that light is an object as well as a medium, and that it deserves representation in its diverse forms, colors, components, and effects. This was impressionism before the Impressionists; and perhaps Manet and Pissarro, when they visited London in 1870, saw some of Turner's spectacular illuminations.[16] Seven years later Degas, Monet, Pissarro, and Renoir sent to a London art dealer a letter saying that in their studies of "the fugitive phenomena of light" they did not forget that they had been "preceded in this path by a great master of the English School, the illustrious Turner."[17]

CHAPTER XVIII

Science in England

I. AVENUES OF PROGRESS

IT was natural that England, having led the way from agriculture to industry, should favor those sciences that offered practical possibilities, leaving theoretical studies to the French; and it was to be expected that her philosophers in this period—Burke, Malthus, Godwin, Bentham, Paine— should be men of the world, facing the living problems of morality, religion, population, revolution, and government, and abandoning to German professors the airy flights into logic, metaphysics, and the "phenomenology of mind."

"The Royal Society of London for Improving Natural Knowledge," as organized in 1660, had announced its "designs of founding a Colledge for the promotion of Physico-Mathematical Experimentall Learning." But it had not become a college in the sense of an organization of teachers for the secondary education of youth; it had developed into a restricted club of fifty-five gentlemen scientists, periodically meeting for consultation, gathering a library of science and philosophy, providing a special audience for addresses and experiments, awarding medals for contributions to science, and occasionally publishing its *Philosophical Transactions*. "Philosophy" still included the sciences, which were budding from it one by one as they replaced logic and theory with quantitative formulations and verifiable experiments. The Royal Society arranged, usually with governmental subsidies, various scientific undertakings or expeditions. In 1780 the government assigned to it elegant quarters in Somerset House, where it remained till 1857, when it moved to its present home in Burlington House, on Piccadilly. Its president from 1778 to 1820, Sir Joseph Banks, spent much of his fortune in the promotion of science and the patronage of scientists.

Only less famous than the Royal Society, and more designed for education, was the Royal Institution of London, established in 1800 by Count Rumford, "for directing, by regular courses of philosophical lectures and experiments, the application of the new discoveries in science to the improvements of arts and manufactures." It provided, in Albemarle Street, a spacious auditorium where John Dalton and Sir Humphry Davy gave lectures in chemistry, Thomas Young on the nature and propagation of light, Coleridge on literature, Sir Edwin Landseer on art . . . More specific were the Linnaean Society, incorporated in 1802 for botany, the Geographical Society (1807), and soon thereafter societies for zoology, horticulture, animal chemistry, and astronomy. Manchester and Birmingham, happy to apply science to their industries, established their own "philosophical" societies, and Bristol set up a "Pneumatic Institute" for the study of gases. Academies were formed to expound science to general audiences; to one of these Michael Faraday, aged twenty-five (1816), gave a course of lectures that shared for half a century in stimulating electrical research. Generally, in scientific education, the business community was ahead of the universities, and many epochal advances in science were made by independent individuals self-supported or financed by friends.

Surrendering mathematics to the French, British science concentrated on astronomy, geology, geography, physics, and chemistry. Astronomy was placed under royal protection and subsidies, as vital to navigation and control of the seas. Greenwich Observatory, with the finest equipment that the money of Parliament could buy, was generally recognized as at the top of its class. James Hutton, two years before his death, published in 1795 *Theory of the Earth*, a classic in geology: it summarized our planet's public life as a uniform cyclical process by which rains erode the surface of the land, rivers rise with erosions or bear them to the sea, the waters and moisture of the earth evaporate into clouds, these condense into rain ... At the other end of this age (1815) William Smith—nicknamed "Strata Smith"—won fame with the fifteen immense sheets of his *Geological Map of England and Wales*. They showed that strata regularly slant eastward in a slight ascending grade until they end at the earth's surface; and they advanced paleontology by identifying strata according to their organic deposits. For revealing such subterranean secrets the British government, in 1831, awarded him a life annuity of £100. He died in 1839.

British navigators continued to explain the nooks and crannies of lands and seas. In the years 1791–94 George Vancouver charted the coasts of Australia, New Zealand, Hawaii, and the Pacific Northwest of America; there he circumnavigated the enchanting island that bears his name.

II. PHYSICS: RUMFORD AND YOUNG

It is difficult to place nationally the Benjamin Thompson who was born (1753) and reared in America, knighted in England, and made Count Rumford in Bavaria, and who died in France (1814). In the War of American Independence he sided with Britain, and moved to London (1776). Sent back to serve as British secretary in the colony of Georgia, his interest overflowed from politics to science, and he made researches which won him a fellowship in the Royal Society. In 1784, with the permission of the British government, he entered the service of Bavaria under Prince Maximilian Joseph. In the next eleven years, as Bavarian minister of war and police, he reorganized the Army, improved the condition of the working class, ended mendicancy, and found time to contribute papers for the *Philosophical Transactions* of the Royal Society. The grateful Maximilian made him (1791) a count of the Holy Roman Empire; he took for his title the name of his wife's birthplace (now Concord) in Massachusetts. During a year in Britain (1795) he labored to better the heating and cooking arrangements of the people, with a view to reducing domestic pollution of the air. After another year of service in Bavaria, he returned to England, and, with Sir Joseph Banks, established the Royal Institution. He founded—and was the first to receive—the Rumford Medal of the Royal Society. He provided funds for the award of a similar medal by academies of arts and sciences in Bavaria and America, and for the Rumford professorship in Harvard University. After the death of his wife he moved to Paris (1802), took a house in Auteuil, married the widow of Lavoisier, and remained in France despite the renewal of war with England. Active to the end, he labored, in his final year, to feed with "Rumford soup" the French populace nearing destitution as Napoleon, taking all available sons, marched to his doom.

Rumford's contributions to science were too varied and incidental to be spectacular, but, taken altogether, they formed a remarkable counterpoint to a busy administrative life. While watching the boring of cannon in Munich he was struck by the heat which the operation produced. To measure this he arranged to have a solid metal cylinder rotate with its head against a steel borer, all in a watertight box containing eighteen and three-quarter pounds of water. In two and three-quarter hours the temperature of the water rose from 60 degrees Fahrenheit to 212 degrees—the boiling point. "It would be difficult," Rumford later recalled, "to describe the astonishment expressed in the countenances of the bystanders on seeing so large a quantity of water heated, and actually made to boil, without any fire."[1] This experiment proved that heat was not a substance but a mode of molecular motion roughly proportioned in degree to the amount of work done to produce it. This belief had been held long before, but Rumford's device provided its first experimental proof, and a method of measuring the mechanical equivalent of heat—i.e., the amount of work required to heat one pound of water one degree.

Thomas Young was almost as "undulant and diverse" as Rumford and Montaigne. Born (1773) of Quaker parentage in Somerset, he began with religion, and then passed, with undiminished devotion, to science. At the age of four, we are assured, he had read the Bible through twice, and at fourteen he could write in fourteen languages.[2] At twenty-one he was elected a fellow of the Royal Society; at twenty-six he was an established physician in London; at twenty-eight he was teaching physics in the Royal Institution; and in 1801 he began there the experiments that confirmed and developed Huyghens' conception of light as undulations of a hypothetical ether. After much debate this view generally—not universally—displaced Newton's theory of light as the emanation of material corpuscles. Young also offered the hypothesis, later developed by Helmholtz, that the perception of color depends upon the presence in the retina of three kinds of nerve fibers, respectively responsive to red, violet, and green. For good measure he gave the first descriptions of astigmatism, blood pressure, capillary attraction, and tides, and shared actively (1814) in the decipherment of the Rosetta Stone. He was, said a learned historian of medicine, "the most highly educated physician of his time," and, added Helmholtz, "one of the most clear-sighted men who ever lived."[3]

III. CHEMISTRY: DALTON AND DAVY

In that same decade, and also at the Royal Institution, John Dalton revolutionized chemistry with his atomic theory (1804). Son of a Quaker weaver, he was born (1766) at Eaglesfield, near Cockermouth, at the northern end of that misty magnificent Lake District which was soon to harbor Wordsworth, Coleridge, and Southey. Later, writing in the third person, he summarized his early career in a bald chronology that does not quite hide the hot ambition that burns a path to accomplishment:

> The writer of this . . . attended the village school . . . till 11 years of age, at which period he had gone through a course of Mensuration, Surveying, Navigation, etc.; began about 12 to teach the village school; . . . was occasionally employed in husbandry for a year or more; removed to Kendal at 15 years of age as assistant in a boarding school, remained in that capacity for 3 or 4 years, then undertook the same school as a principal, and continued for 8 years, and while at Kendal employed his leisure in studying Latin, Greek, French, and the Mathematics with Natural Philosophy, removed thence to Manchester in 1793 as Tutor in Mathematics and Natural Philosophy in the New College.[4]

Whenever time and funds permitted he carried on observations and experiments, despite color blindness and crude instruments, many of them made by himself. Amid his many interests he found time to keep a meteorological record from his twenty-first year to a day before his death.[5] His vacations were usually spent foraging for facts in those same mountains where Wordsworth would roam a few years later; however, while Wordsworth was looking and listening for God, Dalton was, for example, measuring atmospheric conditions at different altitudes—much as Pascal had done a century and a half before.

In his experiments he accepted the theory of Leucippus (c. 450 B.C.) and Democritus (c. 400 B.C.) that all matter consists of indivisible atoms; and he proceeded on the assumption of Robert Boyle (1627–91) that all atoms belong to one or another of certain ultimate indecomposable elements—hydrogen, oxygen, calcium . . . In A New System of Chemical Philosophy (1808) Dalton argued that the weight of any atom of an element, as compared with any atom of another element, must be the same as the weight of a mass of the first element as compared with an equal mass of the other. Taking the weight of a hydrogen atom as one, Dalton, after many experiments and calculations, ranged each of the other elements by the relative weight of any one of its atoms with an atom of hydrogen; and so he drew up, for the thirty elements known to him, a table of their atomic weights. In 1967 chemists recognized ninety-six elements. Dalton's conclusions had to be corrected by later research, but they—and his complex "law of multiple proportions" in all combinations of elements—proved of immense help in the progress of the science in the nineteenth century.

More varied and exciting were the life, education, and discoveries of Sir Humphry Davy. Born in Penzance (1778) of a well-to-do middle-class family, he received a good education, and supplemented it with expeditions that combined geology, fishing, sketching, and poetry. His happy nature won him a miscellany of friends, from Coleridge, Southey, and Dr. Peter Roget—the ingenious and indefatigable compiler of the *Thesaurus of English Words and Phrases* (1852)—to Napoleon. Another friend allowed him free use of a chemical laboratory, whose bubbling retorts charmed Davy into dedication. He organized his own laboratory, sampled diverse gases by inhaling them, persuaded Coleridge and Southey to join his inhaling squad, and almost killed himself by breathing water gas, a powerful poison.

At the age of twenty-two he published an account of his experiments as *Researches Chemical and Philosophical* (1800). Invited to London by Count Rumford and Joseph Banks, he gave lectures and demonstrations on the wonders of the storage battery (Volta's "pile"), bringing new fame to the Royal Institution. Using a battery of 250 pairs of metal plates as an agent of electrolysis, he decomposed various substances into their elements; so he discovered and isolated sodium and potassium; soon he went on to isolate barium, boron, strontium, calcium, and magnesium, and add them to the list of elements. His achievements established electrochemistry as a science endless in its theoretical and practical possibilities. The news of his work reached Napoleon, who sent him in 1806, across the frontiers of war, a prize awarded by the Institut National. Berthollet in 1786 had explained to James Watt the bleaching power of chlorine; England had been slow to use the suggestion; Davy renewed it effectively. In him science and industry developed that mutual stimulation which was to play a leading role in the economic transformation of Great Britain.

In 1810, before an audience at the Royal Institution, Davy performed experiments demonstrating the power of an electric current, in passing from one carbon filament to another, to produce both light and heat. He described the operation:

> When pieces of charcoal about an inch long and one-sixth of an inch in diameter were brought near each other (within the thirtieth or fortieth of an inch), a bright spark was produced, and more than half the volume of the charcoal became ignited to whiteness; and, by withdrawing the points from each other, a constant discharge took place through the heated air, in a space equal to at least four inches, producing a most brilliant ascending arch of light. . . . When any substance was introduced into this arch, it instantly became ignited; platina melted as readily in it as wax in a common candle; quartz, the sapphire, magnesia, lime, all entered into fusion.[6]

The potentialities of this process of generating light and heat were not developed until cheaper ways of producing electric current were invented; but in that brilliant experiment lay the electric blast furnace, and the transformation of night into day for half the population of the earth.

In 1813, accompanied by his young assistant Michael Faraday, and armed with a safe-conduct issued by Napoleon while nearly all Europe was at war, Davy traveled through France and Italy, visiting laboratories, making experiments, exploring the properties of iodine, and proving that the diamond is a form of carbon. Returning to England, he studied the causes of mine explosions, and invented a safety lamp for miners. In 1818 the Prince Regent made him a baronet. In 1820 he succeeded Banks as president of the Royal Society. In 1827, his health having begun to fail, he gave up science for fishing, and wrote a book thereon, illuminated by his own drawings. In 1829, partly paralyzed, he went to Rome to be "a ruin amongst ruins,"[7] but he died before the year was out. He had been allowed only fifty-one years, but he had crowded many lives into that half century. He was a good great man and one of those redeeming men and women who must be weighed in the balance against our ignorance and sins.

IV. BIOLOGY: ERASMUS DARWIN

Biology did not, as yet, do as well in England as physics, chemistry, and geography; these were akin and helpful to industry and commerce; but biology revealed the tragedy as well as the splendor of life, and troubled religious belief.

Erasmus Darwin, grandfather of Charles, has already received our homage,* but he was a spark in the brilliance of this age, since it saw the publication of his *Botanic Garden* (1792), *Zoonomia* (1794–96), and *The Temple of Nature* (1803). These books were all written from an evolutionary point of view. They agreed with Lamarck in basing the theory upon the hope that adaptive habits and organs, developed by desire and effort, might, if strengthened through many generations, be written transmissibly upon nerves and flesh. The genial doctor, who bore a great name fore and aft, sought to reconcile evolution with religion by suggesting that all animal life had begun with "one living filament which the first great Cause imbued with animality," leaving it to "improve by its own inherent activity, and to deliver down these improvements by generation to posterity, world without end."[8]

The perennial debate between religion and science, though muted in this age, entered into the once guarded realm of psychology as Hartley and Priestley prepared a physiological interpretation of the association of ideas, and as anatomists progressively revealed the correlation between body and mind. In 1811 Charles Bell published *A New Idea of the Anatomy of the Brain*, in which he seemed to prove that specific parts of the nervous system convey sense impressions to specific parts of the brain, and specific nerves carry motor impulses to specific organs of response. The phenomena of hypnotism, increasingly abundant, seemed to indicate a physiological trans-

* *The Age of Voltaire*, 579–81.

formation of sensation into idea into action. The effects of opium and other drugs in inducing sleep, affecting dreams, stimulating the imagination and weakening the will (as in Coleridge and De Quincey) further called in question the freedom of the will, reducing it to the algebraic sum of competing images or impulses. And the rising status, scientific dispute, and social standing of the medical profession, compared with the lowered status and reduced vitality of the Anglican clergy, seemed to reflect the secret spread of religious indifference, or doubt, or unbelief.

V. MEDICINE: JENNER

The medical fraternity hardly deserved that name, for it fully reflected the British penchant for class or grade distinctions. The Royal College of Physicians, proud of its establishment by Henry VIII in 1518, limited its "associate" memberships to some fifty men who had taken a degree at Oxford or Cambridge, and its "licentiate" memberships to about fifty other distinguished practitioners. These hundred men served as a kind of House of Lords to the medicos of England. They earned substantial incomes, sometimes as high as twenty thousand pounds a year. They could not become peers, but they could be knighted, and might aspire to a baronetcy. Of markedly lower status was the Royal College of Surgeons, established in 1800. Below these were the *accoucheurs*, male midwives, who specialized in drawing embryos out of their warm security into the competitive world. At the bottom of the healers were the apothecaries, who provided nearly all the medical care available in rural areas.

Neither of these "colleges" offered medical education except for occasional lectures by famous physicians. Neither Oxford nor Cambridge had a school of medicine; students who desired university training in medicine had to seek it in Scotland. Otherwise the training of English doctors was left to the private schools that grew in the neighborhood of the great hospitals raised by private philanthropy. Sir Thomas Bernard spent much of his wealth in reforming the famous "Foundlings' Hospital" in the north of London, and shared with other wealthy men in financing, in London and elsewhere, free clinics for the treatment of cancer, ophthalmia, and hernia. But the poor sanitation of the cities spread diseases, or generated new ones, as fast as medicine could cure them.

In 1806 London recorded a singular event: it had gone a full week without a death from smallpox—that pustulous, feverish, face-marring, and infectious disease which had once been epidemic in England, and might at any time swell again into a deadly plague.

A modest English physician, Edward Jenner—addicted to hunting, botany, composing poetry, and playing the flute or the violin—made the miracle week possible by a decade of inoculations that finally overcame the conservatism of British society. The prevention of smallpox by inoculation with weakened virus from a smallpox-infected human being had been practiced by the ancient Chinese; Lady Mary Wortley Montagu had found it customary in the Constantinople of 1717; on her return to England she recommended the procedure there. It was tried upon criminals, then upon orphans, with considerable success. In 1760 Drs. Robert and Daniel Sutton reported that in thirty thousand cases of smallpox inoculation they had had twelve hundred fatalities. Could a surer method of preventing smallpox be found?

Jenner was led to a better way by noting that many milkmaids in his native Gloucestershire contracted cowpox from infected nipples of cows, and that these women were thereafter immune to smallpox. It occurred to him that a like immunity might be established by inoculating with a vaccine (*vacca* is Latin for *cow*) made from virus of a pox-infected cow. In a paper published in 1798 Jenner recounted a venturesome procedure which laid the foundations of experimental medicine and immunology.

> . . . I selected a healthy boy, about eight years old, for the purpose of inoculation for [with] the Cow Pox. The matter was taken from a sore on the hand of a dairymaid who was infected by her master's cows, and it was inserted, on the 14th of May, 1796, in the arm of the boy. . . . On the seventh day he complained of uneasiness, . . . and on the ninth he became a little chilly, lost his appetite, and had a slight headache. . . . On the following day he was perfectly well. . . .
>
> In order to acertain whether the boy, after feeling so slight an affection of the system from the Cow Pox virus, was secure for the contagion of the Small Pox, he was inoculated, the 1st of July following, with variolous matter [*variola* is Latin for smallpox] immediately taken from a pustule. . . . No disease followed. . . . Several months afterwards he was again inoculated with variolous matter, but no sensible effect was produced in the constitution.[9]

Jenner went on to describe twenty-two other cases of similar procedure with completely satisfactory results. He met with condemnation for what seemed to be human vivisection, and he tried to atone for using a consenting minor by building a cottage for him and planting a rose garden for him with his own hands.[10] In 1802 and 1807 Parliament voted Jenner £30,000 to improve and spread his methods. In the course of the nineteenth century smallpox almost disappeared from Europe and America, and when it occurred it was in unvaccinated individuals. Vaccination was applied to other ailments, and the new science of immunology shared with other medical advances, and with public sanitation, in giving modern communities as much health as is allowed by the harassments of poverty, the fertility of ignorance, the recklessness of appetite, and the patient inventiveness of disease.

CHAPTER XIX

English Philosophy

SCIENCE in the Britain of 1789–1815 had little influence on philosophy. "Natural philosophy"—i.e., the physical sciences—could be reconciled with a liberal theology, and even the idea of evolution could be domesticated by interpreting the six "days" of Creation as elastic aeons of development. The upper classes, now that their flirtation with Voltaire and the Encyclopedists had been ended by the Revolution, had come to distrust ideas as an infectious disease of youth; they considered weekly worship a wise investment in social order and political stability, and they complained that Prime Minister Pitt found no time to go to church. There were some privately skeptical bishops, but they were known for their public piety. Nevertheless, the old conflict continued. In the same year 1794 two opposite voices proclaimed it: Thomas Paine in *The Age of Reason*, and William Paley in *A View of the Evidences of Christianity*. A glance at both of them will suggest the temper of the time.

I. TOM PAINE ON CHRISTIANITY

"Tom" Paine, as two continents came to call him, was an Englishman, born to a Quaker family at Thetford, Norfolk, in 1737; but, on the advice of Benjamin Franklin, he emigrated to America in 1774, and took an active part in the American Revolution. General Washington credited Paine's booklet *Common Sense* (January, 1776), with having "worked a powerful change in the minds of many men."[1] During the Revolutionary War, as an aide-de-camp to General Nathanael Greene, he issued a series of tracts—*The Crisis*—to keep up the spirit of the rebel army and citizenry; one of these began with a famous line—"These are the times that try men's souls." From 1787 to 1802 he lived chiefly in Europe, working for the French Revolution both in France and in England. We have seen him risking his head by voting for commuting the sentence of Louis XVI from death to exile. In December of that year 1793, apparently at the instigation of Robespierre,[2] the Convention decreed the expulsion of all foreigners from its membership. There were only two: Anacharsis Cloots and Thomas Paine. Expecting arrest, Paine wrote hurriedly what is now Part I of *The Age of Reason*. He sent the manuscript to America with the following dedication.

> To my Fellow-Citizens of the United States of America: I put the following work under your protection. It contains my opinions on religion. You will do me the justice to remember that I have always strenuously supported the Right

of every Man to his own opinion, however different that may be to mine. He who denies to another his right, makes a slave of himself to his present opinion, because he precludes himself the right of changing it.

The most formidable weapon against error of every kind is Reason, and I have never used any other, and I trust I never shall.

Your affectionate friend and fellow-citizen.

THOS. PAINE
Paris, Jan. 27, 1794

At the outset Paine gave an unexpected reason why he had written the book: not to destroy religion, but to prevent the decay of its irrational forms from undermining social order, "lest in the general wreck of superstition, of false systems of government, and false theology, we lose sight of morality, of humanity, and of the theology that is true." And he added, reassuringly: "I believe in one God, and no more; and I hope for happiness beyond this life."[3]

Then he drew his Occam's razor:

> I do not believe in the creed professed by the Jewish church, by the Roman church, by the Greek church, by the Turkish church, by the Protestant church, nor by any church that I know of. My own mind is my own church. All national institutions of churches . . . appear to me no other than human inventions, set up to terrify and enslave mankind, and monopolize power and profit.[4]

He admired Christ as "a virtuous and an amiable man," and "the morality that he preached and practiced was of the most benevolent kind"; but the story of his being fathered by a god was just a variation of a myth common among the pagans.

> Almost all the extraordinary men that lived under the heathen mythology were reputed to be the sons of . . . gods . . . The intercourse of gods with women was then a matter of familiar opinion. Their Jupiter, according to their accounts, had cohabited with hundreds. The story, therefore, had nothing in it either new, wonderful, or obscene; it was conformable to the opinions that then prevailed among the people called Gentiles, . . . and it was those people only that believed it. The Jews, who had kept strictly to the belief of one God and no more, and had always rejected the heathen mythology, never credited the story.[5]

So the Christian mythology was merely the pagan mythology in a new form.

> The trinity of the gods that then followed was no other than a reduction of the former plurality, which was about twenty or thirty thousand; the statue of Mary succeeded that of Diane of Ephesus; the deification of heroes changed into the canonization of saints. The mythologists had gods for everything; the Christian mythologists had saints for everything; the Church had become as crowded with one as the pantheon had been with the other . . . The Christian theory is little else than the idolatry of the ancient Mythologists, accommodated to the purposes of power and revenue; and it yet remains to reason and philosophy to abolish the amphibious fraud.[6]

Paine then played his searchlight of reason upon the Book of Genesis, and, having no patience with parables, fell heavily upon Eve and the apple. Like Milton, he was fascinated by Satan, the first of all rebels. Here was an angel who, for trying to depose a monarch, had been plunged into hell, there to suffer time without end. Nevertheless he must have escaped those inextinguishable fires now and then, for he had found his way into the Garden of Eden, and could tempt most sinuously; he could promise knowledge to Eve and half the world to Christ. The Christian mythology, Paine marveled, did Satan wondrous honor; it assumed that he could compel the Almighty to send his son down to Judea and be crucified to recover for him at least a part of a planet obviously in love with Satan; and despite that crucifixion, the Devil still retained all non-Christian realms, and had millions of servitors in Christendom itself.

All this, said our doubting Thomas, was offered us most solemnly, on the word of the Almighty himself, through a series of amanuenses from Moses to Saint Paul. Paine rejected it as a tale fit for nurseries, and for adults too busy with bread and butter, sickness and mortality, to question the promissory notes sold to them by the theologians. To stronger souls he offered a God not fashioned like man, but conceived as the life of the universe.

> It is only in the Creation that all of our ideas . . . of God can unite. The Creation speaketh an universal language; . . . and this *word of God* reveals to man all that is necessary for man to know of God.
> Do we want to contemplate his power? We see it in the immensity of the Creation. Do we want to contemplate his wisdom? We see it in the unchangeable order by which the incomprehensible whole is governed. Do we want to contemplate his munificence? We see it in the abandon with which he fills the earth. Do we want to contemplate his mercy? We see it in his not withholding that abundance even from the unthankful. In fine, do we want to know what God is? Search not the book called the Scripture, . . . but the Scripture called the Creation.[7]

He was imprisoned from December 28, 1793, till the fall of Robespierre, July 27, 1794. On November 4 "the Convention, to repair as much as lay in their power the injustice I had sustained, invited me, publicly and unanimously, to return to the Convention, . . . and I accepted."[8] Amid the turmoil of the Thermidorean reaction he composed Part II of *The Age of Reason;* it was devoted to a laborious critique of the Bible, and added little to what more scholarly studies—many of them by clergymen—had already provided. Both in England and in America his protestations of belief in God were lost in his impassioned rejection of a Bible dear to the people and precious to the government, and he found himself without honor in both his native and his adoptive land. When, in 1802, he returned to New York (which had formerly rewarded his services to the American public by giving him a 300-acre estate at New Rochelle), he received a cool reception, only partly countered by Jefferson's faithful friendship. His last seven years were darkened by addiction to drink. He died in New York in 1809. Ten years later William Cobbett had Paine's bones removed to England. There his undiscourageable spirit, through his books, played a part in the long campaigns that produced the Reform Act of 1832.

Though Paine was a deist rather than an atheist, many believers in Christianity felt that his deism was only a polite cover for disbelief in a personal God. William Paley, rector of Bishop-Wearmouth, gave so able a defense of his faith in *A View of the Evidences of Christianity* (1794) that a reading of this book remained till 1900 a prerequisite for admission to Cambridge University. Still more famous was his *Natural Theology* (1802), which sought to prove the existence of a Supreme Intelligence by accumulating, from the sciences themselves, evidences of design in nature. If, he argued, a man who had never seen a watch came upon one and examined its mechanism, would he not take for granted that some intelligent being had designed it? But are there not in nature hundreds of operations indicating the arrangement of means to a desired effect?

> At one end we see intelligent Power arranging planetary systems; . . . at the other, . . . providing an appropriate mechanism for the clasping and unclasping of the filaments of the feather of a humming bird. . . . Every organized natural body, in the provisions which it contains for its sustentation and propagation, testifies a care, on the part of the Creator, expressly directed to these purposes.[9]

Half of literate England began to discuss Paley's books and watch; Coleridge, Wordsworth, and Hazlitt talked about them in a lively debate at Keswick. The *Natural Theology* had a long life; the great Darwin himself studied it carefully[10] before formulating his rival theory that the adjustment of organs to desirable ends had come about through natural selection. A century after Paley, Henri Bergson eloquently rephrased the "argument from design" in *L'Évolution créatrice* (1906). The debate goes on.

II. GODWIN ON JUSTICE

Quite forgotten today, William Godwin (1756–1836) was the most influential English philosopher of his generation. "No work in our time," wrote Hazlitt toward 1823, "gave such a blow to the philosophical mind of this country as the celebrated *Enquiry Concerning Political Justice*."[11] "Throw away your books of chemistry," Wordsworth told a young student, "and read Godwin on Necessity";[12] and in Godwin's old age, when he had come to doubt himself, he saw his ideas broadcast on the wings of song by his son-in-law Shelley. He would probably have been put in jail except for the high price he charged for his book.

His parents were devout Calvinists, dedicated to the predestinarianism that in Godwin became determinism. His father was a Nonconformist minister; he himself was educated for the pulpit, and served as clergyman in divers towns. While so functioning at Stowmarket he was introduced by a young republican to the French philosophers, who soon upset his faith. He took atheism from d'Holbach, though in later years he graciously made a place

for God in his congested volume. He took from Helvétius the belief in education and reason as the progenitors of utopia. He followed Rousseau in accepting the native goodness of men, but he preferred philosophical anarchism
to Rousseau's omnipotent state. He abandoned the Christian ministry, and
set out to butter his bread with pen and ink. He joined Lord Stanhope and
Thomas Holcroft in a club of "revolutionists," but for the most part he gave
himself to arduous study and difficult writing; and in 1793, aged thirty-
seven, he issued the most radical major work of his time.

He called it *Enquiry Concerning Political Justice and Its Influence on
General Virtue and Happiness.* Apparently a book on government, it covered nearly all the problems of philosophy, from perception to statesmanship, stopping just short of God. He scorned the fables of heaven and hell as
transparent devices to promote obedience and facilitate government.[13] He
condemned clergymen who swore acceptance of the Thirty-nine Articles of
the official faith while privately discarding them.[14] He rejected free will,
and the will itself if understood as a distinct faculty; it was for him merely
an abstract term for conscious responses to stimuli, situations, or desires.[15]
Since actions are determined by heredity, individual experience, and present
circumstances, we should meet the wrongdoings of others without anger or
recrimination, and we should reform our penal system to rehabilitate rather
than punish; however, it may be necessary to use praise, blame, and punishment as providing corrective memories in future temptations.[16]

What should we praise, and what condemn? The morally good, and
morally bad? And what is good? Following Helvétius (1758) and Bentham
(1789), Godwin defined the good as that which promotes individual or
group happiness, and he defined happiness as consistent pleasure of body,
mind, or feeling. This ethical philosophy is not hedonistic or sensual, for it
ranks intellectual pleasures above those of the senses. It is not egoistic or
selfish, for it recognizes that the individual is part of a group; that the good
of the group is prerequisite to the security of its constituent individuals; and
that among the highest of all pleasures are those that an individual may derive
from contributing to the happiness of his fellow men. Our social instincts
generate altruistic actions, and these actions can give us a pleasure keener
and more lasting than any delight of sense or intellect.[17] To be kind is to be
happy; to be unkind is to be miserable. "Morality, the science of human
happiness," is "the principle which binds the individual to the species, and
the inducements which are calculated to persuade us to model our conduct
on the way most conducive to the advantage of all."[18]

Justice, then, is the regulation of conduct, in the individual and the group,
for the greatest happiness of the greatest number. "The immediate object of
government is security for the group or the individual." Since the individual
desires as much freedom as comports with his security, "the most desirable
state of mankind is that which maintains general security with the smallest
encroachment upon individual independence."[19] Hence there is no need for
governmental or religious sanctions for marriage; the mutual agreement of

two adults to live together should suffice; and the union should be dissoluble at the desire of either party.[20] (This line especially pleased Shelley.)

Godwin did not like governments. Whatever their form or theory, they were, in practice, the domination of a majority by a minority. He repudiated the conservative contention that the masses were congenitally inferior and always potentially murderous, and therefore had to be ruled by fable, terror, or force. Like Owen, he thought that most inferiorities were due to inadequate education, narrow opportunities, or environmental blight.[21] He laughed at equality before the law, when every day saw a moneyed wrong-doer freed, by legal trickery or judicial favor, from the penalty of his crime.[22] He was not a socialist; he accepted the institution—and the inheritance—of property,[23] and opposed governmental control of production or distribution;[24] but he insisted that private property should be considered a public trust,[25] and warned that the concentration of wealth was inviting revolution.[26]

However, he had no taste for revolution. "Till the character of the human species is essentially altered," any forcible overthrow of the existing system, any violent attempt to redistribute wealth, would cause a social disruption "more injurious to the common welfare than the inequality it attempted to remove."[27] "A revolution of opinion is the only means of attaining a better distribution of wealth,"[28] and this will require a long and patient process of education through schools and literature.

Nevertheless, to require a general education through a national system of schools would be a mistake, for these would be tools of national chauvinism leading to war, and of governmental propaganda aimed to instill a blind obedience.[29] Education should be left to private enterprise, should always tell the truth, and should habituate the student to reason. "Reason is not an independent principle" or faculty, "and has no tendency to incite us to action; in a practical view it is merely a comparison and balancing of different feelings. Reason . . . is calculated to regulate our conduct according to the comparative worth it ascribes to different excitements" or impulses. "Morality is nothing but a calculation of consequences,"[30] including the consequences to the group. "It is therefore to the improvement of reason that we are to look for the improvement of our social condition."[31]

The road to utopia through education is long and arduous, but man has made some progress on that road, and there is no visible limit to his further advance. The goal is a humanity sufficiently instructed and foresightful to act reasonably and freely. Anarchism is the distant ideal, but for many generations to come it will remain an ideal, and the nature of man will necessitate some form of government. We must continue to hope that, in our distant and cleansed descendants, intelligence will graduate into orderly freedom.

There must have been a rich fount of intellectual energy in Godwin, for in 1794, only a year after publishing his ponderous *Enquiry*, he issued what many judged to be the outstanding novel of the time, *Caleb Williams*, which showed "the spirit and character of the government intruding itself in every rank of society." To this story the author added his own living romance: he married Mary Wollstonecraft (1797), adopted her free-love daughter Fanny Imlay, and lived with Mary for a year in stimulating companionship. "I honored her intellectual powers," he said, "and the noble generosity of her propensities; mere tenderness would not have been adequate to produce the happiness which we experienced."[32] She died, as we have seen, shortly after giving birth to Mary Godwin Shelley.

In 1801 he married Mrs. Mary Jane Clairmont, whose daughter (by her first husband) was to be one of Byron's mistresses. Godwin and his wife supported their complex brood by publishing books, among them the *Tales from Shakespeare* (1807) of Charles and Mary Lamb. In the reaction which drew Wordsworth and Coleridge from his friendship Godwin fell upon hard times, and he too shared in the natural conservatism of old age. Shelley, himself in straits, helped him; and in 1833, by the irony of history, the government, which he had tolerated as a necessary evil, made him a "yeoman usher of the Exchequer," with a modest pension that fed him till he died (1836).

III. MALTHUS ON POPULATION

Godwin's *Enquiry* provoked into print a book far more famous than his own. The process was aided by the unusual reaction of a son against his father's liberal philosophy.

Daniel Malthus (died 1800) was an amiable eccentric, a personal friend of David Hume and Jean-Jacques Rousseau. He shared the skepticism of the Scot and the pessimism of the Swiss about civilization. He attended personally to his son's pre-college education, and trusted that Thomas Malthus (1766–1834) would be a law-abiding radical like himself and Godwin. Thomas went through Cambridge, and entered the Anglican ministry in 1797. When Godwin's book appeared (1793), father and son had many fond debates over its contents. Thomas did not share his father's enthusiasm about it. This utopian fancy of triumphant reason, he felt, would be repeatedly stultified by the simple fact, so pithily declared in the Book of Ecclesiastes, that when the supply of food rises its beneficence is soon annulled by an increase in population. As the fertility of the earth is limited, and there is no bound to the sexual mania of men, the multiplication of mouths—through earlier marriage, reckless reproduction, lowered infantile and senile mortality—must soon consume the augmented food. The father did not accept this conclusion, but he admired the force with which it had been argued, and he asked his son to write out his views. Thomas did, and the result was published in 1798 as *An Essay on the Principle of Population as It Affects the Future Improvement of Society*.

It began with a disarming apology to the two writers whose optimism it challenged:

> I cannot doubt the talents of such men as Godwin and Condorcet. . . . I have read some of their speculations, on the perfectibility of men and society, with great pleasure. I have been warmed and delighted with the enchanting picture which they hold forth. I ardently wish for such happy improvements. But I see great and, to my understanding, unconquerable difficulties in the way to them. These difficulties it is my present purpose to state; declaring, at the same time that so far from exulting in them as a cause of triumph over the friends of innovation, nothing would give me greater pleasure than to see them completely removed.[33]

Malthus tried to put his argument in mathematical form. Allowing that the food supply may increase arithmetically every twenty-five years (from 1 to 2 to 3 to 4 to 5 to 6, etc.), the population, if unchecked—and allowing four surviving children to every couple—would increase geometrically every twenty-five years (from 1 to 2 to 4 to 8 to 16 to 32 . . .). At this rate "in two centuries the population would be to the means of subsistence as 25 to 9; in three centuries it would be 4,096 to 13; and in 2,000 years the difference would be incalculable."[34] The reason why population has not risen so rapidly is that it was limited both by negative and by positive checks on reproduction. The negative checks were preventive: the deferment of marriage by poverty or other causes; "vice" (by which Malthus meant extramarital sex), "unnatural passions" (homosexuality, sodomy, etc.), and the various means of contraception in or outside of marriage. When these negative factors failed to keep population in balance with the food supply, nature and history provided positive checks operating upon individuals already existing: infanticide, disease, famine, and war, painfully balancing births with deaths.

From this somber analysis Malthus drew surprising conclusions. First, there is no use raising the wages of workingmen, for if wages are increased the workers will marry earlier and will have more children; the population will grow; the mouths will increase faster than the food, and poverty will be restored. Likewise it is useless to raise the "poor rates" (taxes for the care of the unemployed); this will be an incentive to idleness and larger families; mouths will again multiply faster than goods; the competition among buyers will allow sellers to raise the prices of their diminishing stocks; and soon the poor will be as poor as before.[35]

To complete his demolition of Godwin, Malthus went on to consider the "dream" of philosophical anarchism. If government were to disappear, "every man would be obliged to guard with force his little store," as we bar our doors and windows when law and order fail. "Selfishness would be triumphant . . . , contention perpetual."[36] With all restraints removed from mating and coitus, reproduction would advance faster than production, overpopulation would reduce each individual's allotment of goods, and utopia would collapse in desperate competition, price and wage spirals, inevitable chaos, spreading misery.[37] Government would have to be restored; private property would have to be protected to encourage production and investment; private violence would have to be suppressed by public force. History would return to its traditional formula: the products of nature divided by the nature of man.

In a revised and much extended form of the *Essay*, Malthus laid down, more clearly and harshly than before, the preventive remedies that might render unnecessary the catastrophic cures used by nature and history. He proposed a halt to poor relief, and a check on interference with free enterprise; the law of supply and demand should be left to operate in the relations of producers and consumers, employers and employees. Early marriage must be discouraged to keep the birth rate down. "Our obligation" is "not to marry till we have a fair prospect of being able to support our children."[38] Above all, men must learn moral restraint before and after marriage. "The interval between the age of puberty and . . . marriage must . . . be passed in strict chastity."[39] Within marriage there must be no contraception in any way or form. If these or equivalent regulations are not observed we must resign ourselves to periodical reductions of overpopulation by famine, pestilence, or war.

The *Essay on Population* was received as a divine revelation by the conservative elements of the British people. Parliament and the employers felt warranted in resistance to the demands of liberals like Robert Owen for legal mitigations of the "laws" of supply and demand. William Pitt withdrew the bill he had introduced for extending poor relief.[40] The measures already taken by the government against British radicals seemed justified by Malthus' contention that these peddlers of utopia were seducing simple souls to tragic delusions. British manufacturers were strengthened in their belief that low wages made for disciplined labor and obedience. Ricardo made the Malthusian theory the foundation of his "dismal science." (It was after reading Malthus that Carlyle gave that name to economics.) Now nearly all the evil incident to the Industrial Revolution could be ascribed to the reckless fertility of the poor.

The liberals were at first thrown into dismay and disarray by Malthus' *Essay*. Godwin took twenty years to draw up his answer, and then his book *Of Population, an Answer to Malthus* (1820) was mostly a reiteration of his hopes, and a complaint that Malthus had converted the friends of progress into reactionaries by the hundred.[41] William Hazlitt was an exception: in an essay on Malthus in *The Spirit of the Age* (1824), he attacked the merciless divine with all the sharp edge of his intellect. The fertility of plants, he thought, could be relied upon to outrun the fertility of women. "A grain of corn will multiply and propagate itself much faster even than the human species. A bushel of wheat will sow a field; that field will furnish seed for 20 others."[42] There will be "green revolutions."

Later writers brought up an array of facts to calm Malthusian fears. In Europe, in China, in India, population has more than doubled after Malthus; yet their people are better fed than before. In the United States the population has doubled several times since 1800; nevertheless, despite an ever lower percentage of the people required for it, agriculture produces more adequately than ever before, and has an immense surplus for export. Contrary to Malthus, the rise in wages has brought not an increase but a lowering of the birth rate. The problem is no longer a deficiency of seeds or fields but a shortage in the supply of nonhuman energy to operate the mechanisms of agriculture and industry, of villages and towns.

Of course the real answer to Malthus has been contraception—its moral acceptance, its wider dissemination, its greater efficacy, its lower cost. The general secularization of thought broke down the theological barriers to birth control. The Industrial Revolution transformed children from the economic assets they had been on the farm to the economic handicaps they became in cities as child labor slowly diminished, as education became expensive, as urban crowding rose. Intelligence spread: men and women realized that changed conditions no longer required large families. Even war now demanded technical inventiveness for competition in material destruction rather than masses of young men deployed in competitive homicide.

So the answer to Malthus came not from Godwin's theories but from the "Neo-Malthusians" and their propaganda for birth control. In 1822 Francis Place published *Illustrations and Proofs of the Principle of Population*. He accepted Malthus' principle that population tends to increase faster than the food supply. Restraint, he agreed, is necessary, but not by postponing marriage; better would be the acceptance of contraception as a legitimate and relatively moral substitute for nature's blind fertility and war's wholesale destruction. (He himself had fifteen children, of whom five died in childhood.) He scattered through London handbills printed at his own expense, advocating birth control; and he continued his campaign till his death at the age of eighty-three (1854).

Malthus lived long enough to feel the force of Place's arguments. In 1824 he contributed to the *Encyclopaedia Britannica* an article revising his theory, withdrawing his frightening mathematical ratios, and laying new stress upon overpopulation as a factor in the struggle for existence. Many years later Charles Darwin wrote in his *Autobiography*:

> In October, 1838, fifteen months after I had begun my systematic enquiry, I happened to read for amusement *Malthus on Population*; and being well prepared to appreciate the struggle for existence . . . from long-continued observation of the habits of animals and plants, it at once struck me that under these circumstances favorable variations would tend to be preserved, and unfavorable ones to be destroyed. The result of this would be the formation of a new species. Here then I had at last got hold of a theory by which to work.

So, after almost a generation of further research and thought, Darwin published (1859) *The Origin of Species*, the most influential book of the nineteenth century. The Chain of Ideas adorns the "Great Chain of Being," and underlies the history of civilization.

IV. BENTHAM ON LAW

Bentham is a harder nut to milk than Godwin or Malthus, for Godwin offered tempting ideals and Malthus some fascinating terrors, while Jeremy Bentham (1748–1832) wrote on economics, usury, utility, law, justice, and prisons—none of which is very charming; besides, he himself was a seclusive giant, endlessly learned, pondering imponderables, publishing little, reforming everything, and crying out for the marriage of two ogres—logic and law. Yet his influence, rising through his eighty-four years, surmounted his time and pervaded a century.

He was the son of a wealthy attorney, who almost crushed him with education. We are told that by the age of three he had read Paul de Rapin's eight-volume *History of England*, and had begun the study of Latin. (This suffocating pedagogy was passed on to Bentham's disciple James Mill, who used it on his son John.) At Westminster School Jeremy excelled in writing Greek and Latin poetry. At Oxford he specialized in logic, and took his degree at fifteen. He went on to study law at Lincoln's Inn, but the chaos of the lawbooks aroused his ire, and he resolved, at whatever cost, to bring reason and order into British jurisprudence and legislation. In December, 1763, aged fifteen, he heard Sir William Blackstone's eulogy of English law; he was astonished and repelled by this unquestioning adulation, which could only delay legal reform. From that time almost to his death he thought of bringing rationality, consistency, and humanity into English law. "Have I," he asked himself, "a genius for anything? What can I produce? . . . What, of all earthly pursuits, is the most important? Legislation. Have I a genius for legislation? I gave myself the answer, fearfully and tremblingly: 'Yes' "[43] This *timid* pride can be the fount of achievement.

He brought to his task a mind realistic, sworn to order and reason. He resented such oppressive abstractions as duty, honor, power, and right; he liked to break them down into specific realities, and to examine each part with a persistent view to fact. What, for instance, is a right? Is it "natural"—something due us from birth, as the French Revolution's Declaration of the Rights of Man supposed?—or is it merely an individual liberty subordinate to public good? What is equality? Is there any such thing outside of a mathematical abstraction? Is inequality of ability, possessions, and power the inevitable fate of every living thing? What is "common sense" or "natural law"? All these abstractions, in Bentham's opinion, were "nonsense on stilts,"[44] strutting obstructively in universities, Parliaments, and courts.

We may imagine what such an impatient realist did to the theology current in his time and place. He found no use for the traditional deity in his attempt to see with impartial eye the world of science, history, economics, law, or government.[45] He tried to hold his sharp tongue about these matters, for he felt that the Anglican Church was comparatively rational, and might be made beneficent; but the clergy felt his silent hostility, and denounced his utilitarianism, quite justly, as a "godless philosophy."[46]

He began by trying to depose Blackstone as the web-weaving encomiast of the British Constitution. That mystical entity appeared to him as a patchwork and antiquated product of casual contingencies, contradictory compromises, hasty amendments, and passing inspirations, bound with no logic and rooted in no principle. So (while the American colonies were ignoring that landed gentlemen's agreement) Bentham issued, as one spark from his anvil, *A Fragment on Government* (1776)—the first blow of that "philo-sophical radicalism" which was to struggle for half a century before win-ning half a victory in 1832.

The twenty-eight-year-old challenger, while praising Blackstone for hav-ing "taught jurisprudence to speak the language of scholars and gentlemen," reproved him for reducing the constitution to the sovereignty of the king. *É contra*, a sane constitution will distribute the powers of government among the different parts thereof, and will facilitate their cooperation and mutual restraint. The guiding principle of legislators must be not the will of a superior but "the greatest happiness of the greatest number" of those for whom they legislate; and the proper test of a proposed law is its utility to that end.[47] Here, in the famous "principle of utility," was the essence of Bentham's legal and ethical teaching. It was a remarkable correlate of the Declaration of Independence that Thomas Jefferson had issued in that same year; philosophy and history briefly embraced; and the Christian tradition—Bentham unwitting—warmed and blessed the union.

The little book had been written in a style more intelligible, and in a spirit more attractive, than those of Bentham's later treatises. He spent some time now in travel. From Russia, in 1787, he sent to England a *Defence of Usury*—i.e., interest. He opposed the theological condemnation of interest; in economics, as in politics, the individual should be left as free to use his own judgment as the good of the community would allow. Bentham was a liberal, but in the eighteenth-century understanding of that word as mean-ing a defender of liberty; he agreed with the Physiocrats and Jefferson that the state should keep to a minimum its interference with individual freedom. He was a radical—a get-to-the-root man; but he was not in favor of national-izing industry. In 1787 there was not much industry to nationalize.

On his return from Russia, Bentham prepared for publication his major work: *The Principles of Morals and Legislation* (1789; his press inclined to revolutionary dates). It is a difficult book, sternly propped with a hundred definitions, yet leaving the unprofessional reader considerably confused at the close. But Bentham was undertaking a mind-breaking task: to replace a theological with a natural ethic; to base conduct and law upon group or national need rather than upon the will of an executive or a class; and to lib-erate law and conduct from religious decrees at one end and revolutionary dreams at the other. A man undertaking such tasks might be allowed an oc-casional sin against a writer's moral obligation to be clear.

The new basis, of both morality and law, was to be the principle of utility —the usefulness of an act to the individual, of a custom to the group, of a law to the people, of an international agreement to mankind. Bentham took it for granted that all organisms seek pleasure and shun pain. Pleasure he de-fined as any satisfaction, pain as any dissatisfaction, of body or mind. Utility is the quality of producing pleasure or avoiding pain; happiness is the conti-nuity and consistency of pleasures. The utility need not be entirely to the individual agent; it may be, partly or primarily, to the family, the commu-nity, the state, or mankind. The individual may (through his social instincts) find pleasure—or avoid pain—in subordinating his satisfaction to that of the group to which he belongs.[48] Consequently, aside from its immediate purpose, the final object and moral test of all actions and laws is the degree in which it contributes to the greatest happiness of the greatest number. "I would have the dearest friend I have to know that his interests, if they come in competition with those of the public, are as nothing to me. Thus I would serve my friends—thus would I be served by them."[49]

Bentham did not pretend to have originated his utilitarian formula. He declared, with his usual candor, that he had found it in Joseph Priestley's *Essay on the First Principles of Government* (1768). He could have found it in Francis Hutcheson's *Enquiry Concerning Moral Good and Evil* (1725), which defined the good citizen as one who has promoted "the greatest happiness of the greatest number";[50] or in Beccaria's *Trattato dei delitti e delle pene* (1764), which described the moral test and goal as "*la massima felicità divisa nel maggior numero*"; or, most clearly, in Helvétius' *De l'Esprit* (1758): "Utility is the principle of all human virtues, and the foundation of all legislation. . . . All laws should follow a single principle, the utility of the public—i.e., of the greatest number of the persons under the same government."[51] Bentham was merely giving a quantitative form to the Biblical injunction "Thou shalt love thy neighbor as thyself."[52]

His achievement was to apply "the principle of the greatest happiness" (his final formula) to the laws of England. He now had a moral imperative of clear import, and a test by which to judge the injunctions of preachers, the exhortations of teachers, the principles of parties, the laws of legislators, the edicts of kings. The law must admit no mystical entities like "rights," natural, popular, or divine; no revelations from God to Moses or Mohammed or Christ; no punishments for vengeance' sake. Every proposal must answer the question *Cui bono?*, For whose good will it be?— for one, or a few, or many, or all? Law must adjust itself to the ineradicable nature and limited capacities of men, and to the practical needs of society; it must be clear, and permit of practical enforcement, expeditious trial, prompt judicial judgment, and penalties corrective and humane. To these ends Bentham devoted the last ten chapters of his book, and the final years of his life.

Meanwhile he applied his testing rod to the issues of the day. He upheld the Physiocratic doctrine of *laissez-faire* in industry and politics. Generally the individual is the best judge of his own happiness, and should be left as free as socially practicable to seek it in his own way; however, society should encourage voluntary associations, whose members would surrender part of their liberties to united effort for a common cause. From the same principles Bentham argued that representative government, with all its faults and multiple corruption, is best.

The Principles of Morals and Legislation received a wider acclaim than might have been expected from the difficulties of its form and style, its critical spirit, and its strongly secular bent. Its welcome abroad was warmer than at home. France translated him, and made him a French citizen in 1792. Political leaders and thinkers corresponded with him from various capitals and universities on the Continent. In England the Tories condemned utilitarianism as unpatriotic, un-Christian, and materialistic. Some writers urged that many actions—romantic or parental love, self-sacrifice, mutual aid—involve no conscious calculation of egoistic satisfactions. Artists balked at judging works of art according to their usefulness. But all except officeholders agreed that self-interest is the ethic and policy of all governments, when disguise and pretense have been removed.

Bentham lived up to his philosophy, and made his years unremittingly useful. In *Rationale of Judicial Evidence* (1825), and elsewhere, he strove to clarify old laws and present cases, and succeeded in moderating the barbarous excesses of traditional penology. He began in 1827, aged seventy-nine, to codify English law, but death caught him between Volumes I and II. He took part in establishing *The Westminster Review* (1823) as an organ of liberal ideas. He gathered about him a band of disciples who recognized the warm heart behind the crusty exterior. Pierre-Étienne Dumont was his apostle in France; James Mill, himself an outstanding thinker, edited the master's manuscript into readability; John Stuart Mill raised the cause from calculus to humanity.

Led by Bentham, these "philosophical radicals" worked for adult male suffrage, secret ballot, free trade, public sanitation, the improvement of prisons, the cleansing of the judiciary, the chastening of the House of Lords, and the development of international law. Till the 1860s the individualistic and freedom-oriented elements in Bentham's philosophy were stressed by his followers; thereafter the socialism lurking in "the greatest happiness of the greatest number" turned the current of reform toward the use of government as an agent of the public will in attacking public ills.

Dying, Bentham puzzled over the problem of making his corpse fully useful to the greatest number. He directed that it should be dissected in the presence of his friends. It was. Then the cranium was filled and faced with wax, the skeleton was dressed in Bentham's somber and habitual garb, and was set upright in a glass case in University College, Cambridge, where it remains to this day.

CHAPTER XX

Literature in Transition

I. THE PRESS

I F France held the political stage in this era, England led in literature. What, except for Chateaubriand's prose, has France to compare with Wordsworth, Coleridge, Byron, and Shelley?—not to include Keats (1795–1821), whose masterpieces slip out of our present range. Next to the age of Elizabeth I, this was the brightest flowering in the four centuries of English poetry.

Even correspondence could then be literature, for the letters of Byron and Coleridge seem more contemporary with us than their verse. In those days, when, usually, the recipient paid the postage, he demanded substance or style for his stamp; but to receive a letter from such ebullient spirits could be a passport to life after death.

The newspapers, however, were not literature. Normally each was a sheet folded into four pages; the first and fourth of these were taken up by advertisements, the second went to politics, including a summary of yesterday's Parliamentary doings. London had several dailies: chiefly the *Times*, founded in 1788, and having some five thousand purchasers; the *Courier*, with ten thousand; the *Morning Post*, organ of the Whigs, and featuring "leaders" by Coleridge; and the *Examiner*, voice of liberals like Leigh Hunt. County or borough centers had each its own paper, sometimes two, one for the Ins and one for the Outs. There were several weeklies, of which the most popular was William Cobbett's *Political Register*. And there were several periodicals of political, social, and literary comment. The most powerful of these were the quarterly *Edinburgh Review*, founded in 1802 by Francis Jeffrey, Henry Brougham, and Sydney Smith* to defend progressive ideas; and the *Quarterly Review*, established in 1807 by John Murray, Robert Southey, and Walter Scott to plead the Tory cause.

The power of the press was a prominent element in the British scene. It was no longer a vehicle of literature as in the leisurely days of Addison and Steele; it had become an outlet for advertisers and an organ of political groups. Since the advertisers paid according to circulation, the editor and the publishers had to consider public opinion, often at the expense of the party in power; so the press lampooned the wastrel sons of the King despite all efforts of the government to shield them. Gradually, as the nineteenth century advanced, the press became an instrument, finally an indispensable constituent, of the rising democracy.

---

* To be distinguished from Sir William Sidney Smith, who foiled Napoleon at Acre.

II. BOOKS

Books multiplied as the middle class and the reading public grew. Publishing became sufficiently profitable to be an independent business, separate from bookselling. Publishers competed for authors, paid them better, feted them at literary salons. So Joseph Johnson wined and published Godwin, Paine, and Blake; Archibald Constable shared his debts with Walter Scott; Thomas Norton Longman took Wordsworth; Joseph Cottle, at Bristol, kept Coleridge and Southey; and John Murray, from London, held wandering Byron in leash. Meanwhile the old firm of Longmans spent three hundred thousand pounds publishing a new edition (1819) of Chambers' *Cyclopoedia*, in thirty-nine volumes; and the *Encyclopaedia Britannica* issued three new editions in this brief period—the third, in eighteen volumes, in 1788–97, the fourth in twenty volumes in 1810, the fifth in twenty-five volumes in 1815.

Instead of royalties, publishers paid lump sums for manuscripts, and added something if further editions were printed and sold; nevertheless very few authors lived by their pens—Thomas Moore comfortably, Southey and Hazlitt precariously, Scott through riches and ruin. Publishers succeeded patricians as patrons of literature, but some moneyed men still held out a hand; so the Wedgwoods subsidized Coleridge, and Raisley Calvert bequeathed nine hundred pounds to Wordsworth. The government sent occasional honorariums to well-behaved authors, and maintained a poet laureate at a hundred pounds; for this he was expected to compose on the instant a poem celebrating a victory of the armed forces, or a royal birth, marriage, or death.

The growth of the reading public was checked by the high price of books, but was promoted by book clubs and lending libraries. Best of the latter were the Athenaeum and the Lyceum, both at Liverpool, the one with eight thousand volumes, the other with eleven thousand. Subscribers paid an annual fee, from one to two and a half guineas, for the right to borrow any book on the shelves. Every town had its lending library. Something was lost in taste and standards as reading spread from the aristocracy through the commonalty. The transition from classic tradition to Romantic sentiment was fed by this spreading audience, and by the growing emancipation of youthful love from parental control and property bonds; and one love affair could do for a hundred plots. Richardson's tearful themes were gaining ground from Fielding's lusty lovers and Smollett's virile adventurers.

Women predominated among the novelists, except for Matthew "Monk" Lewis and his chamber of horrors, *Ambrosio, or The Monk* (1795). Next only to him in the terror and mystery school was Mrs. Ann Radcliffe, with her succession of successes: *A Sicilian Romance* (1790), *The Romance of the Forest* (1791), and *The Mysteries of Udolpho* (1794). Usually the English public called such books romances (from the French word *roman*, meaning a story), and kept the term *novel* for extended narratives of natural happenings in ordinary life, as in Fielding and Jane Austen; Scott's Waverley Novels bridge the definitions. In Romantic fiction the women authors naturally excelled. Frances (Fanny) Burney, who, at twenty-six, had made a stir with *Evelina* (1778), went on to sparkle with *Cecilia* (1782), *Camilla* (1796), and *The Wanderer* (1814); and after her death (1840) her *Diary* (1842) charmed another generation.

Even more famous was Maria Edgeworth, whose *Castle Rackrent* (1800) and *The Absentee* (1812?) gave in fictional but realistic form such powerful descriptions of Irish exploitation by English landlords that England itself was stirred to mitigate these evils. Only one woman writer of her generation surpassed her, and that woman surpassed the men as well.

III. JANE AUSTEN: 1775–1817

All her adventures were by proxy, through her pen; and even there she needed few, since she found sufficient fascination in the ordinary life of genteel, but educated and sensitive, women like herself. Her father was rector of Steventon parish in Hampshire. She was born in the parsonage, and lived there till she was twenty-six. In 1809 her brother Edward provided his mother and sisters with a home in Chawton. There she lived till her final year, varying her simple routine with visits to her brothers and a stay in London. In May, 1817, she went to Winchester for medical treatment, and there, on July 18, she died, unmarried, aged forty-one.

She gave suspense and meaning to her life by the sisterly love that warms her letters; by her subtle and slightly sardonic humor, which caught the absurdities and hidden anxieties of life, and portrayed them without bitterness; and by her enjoyment of the rural scenery and easy tempo of provincial days. She had enough of London to dislike it; she gave no fond picture of it, as a cross between dingy poverty and well-bred decay; it was a place where bored country girls came to be seduced. The finer sort of English living, she felt, was in the lower aristocracy of the countryside; in their homes family discipline and a treasured tradition generated stability and a quiet content. In those pockets of peace one seldom heard of the French Revolution, and Napoleon was too distant a bogey to take one's mind off the more urgent business of getting a fit partner for the dance or for life. Religion had its place in those homes, but kept it, and had been pared of its terrors by a secret sophistication, such as might well flourish in a parsonage. The Industrial Revolution had not yet reached into the countryside to embitter the classes and sully scene and air. We hear Jane Austen's authentic voice in her commiseration with Fanny Price, who had to spend some unwilling months in London:

> It was sad to Fanny to lose all the pleasures of spring. . . . She had not known before how much the beginnings and progress of vegetation had delighted her. What animation, both of body and mind, she had derived from

watching the advance of that season which cannot, in spite of its capricious-
ness, be unlovely, seeing its increasing beauties from the earliest flowers in the
warmest divisions of her aunt's garden, to the opening leaves of her uncle's
plantations and the glory of his woods.[1]

It was such an environment—a comfortable home, a fragrant garden, an
evening walk with gay sisters, an encouraging word from a father who
praised and peddled her manuscripts—that put into Jane Austen's novels a
fresh air of peace, health, and goodwill, and that gives to her unhurried
readers a quiet satisfaction hardly to be found in any other novels. She had
learned that the day itself is blessing enough.

So she wrote her six novels, and waited patiently for that unhurried public. In 1795, aged twenty, she composed the first form of *Sense and Sensibility*, but it did not satisfy her, and she laid it aside. In the next two years
she labored over *Pride and Prejudice*, revised it and revised it, and sent it to
a publisher, who returned it as promising no profit. In 1798–99 she put into
shape *Northanger Abbey;* Richard Crosby bought it, but let it lie unpublished. Then came a barren interlude, disturbed by change of residence, and
perhaps by discouragement. In February, 1811, she began *Mansfield Park;*
and in November *Sense and Sensibility*, rewritten, reached print. Then, in
her last five years, came a rich harvest: *Pride and Prejudice* found a publisher in 1813, *Mansfield Park* in 1814, *Emma* in 1816; and in 1817, after her
death, *Northanger Abbey* surfaced, and soon *Persuasion* appeared.

Pride and Prejudice offers at the outset a bevy of five sisters, all ready and
eager for marriage. Mrs. Bennet is a flighty, exclamatory soul, whose morning prayer and hourly thought are to find husbands for her brood. Mr. Bennet has learned to retire from his wordy wife to his library, where the
words make no noise, and he has quite given up the problem of providing
five dowries of land or pounds. He holds his home only till his death; thereafter it goes by entail to the Reverend Mr. Collins, the still unmarried parson of a nearby town. If one of those five sisters could snare that dominie!

The oldest and loveliest, Jane, has set her aim on the rich and handsome
Mr. Bingley, but he seems to prefer another candidate, and Jane hardly
hides her grief. Elizabeth, next in age, is proud not of her face or form but
of her independent, self-reliant character; she thinks for herself, and is not
to be auctioned off; she has read widely, and can handle any man in a duel
of mind or wit, without being aggressively intellectual; her author frankly
admires her. The third sister, Mary, is eagerly nubile, and frets over the long
time her predecessors are taking in clearing her way. Lydia, the youngest,
wonders why a girl has to wait for the magic formula of marriage before
being allowed to explore the mysteries of sex.

The household is brightened by the news that Mr. Collins is planning to
pay it a visit. He is a man proudly conscious of his sanctity, but carefully
cognizant of class distinctions and material interests; in him the author presents a merciless picture of the caste subservience into which the lower
Anglican ministry had fallen; the satire seems extreme, but it is as clean and
thorough as a guillotine.

The young reverend comes, sees that lovely Jane is immune, and offers his hand to Elizabeth, who demoralizes the family by refusing him, loath to be imprisoned in his perfections. Mary, feeling that for the third of five sisters to be first to get a husband would be quite a trick, sets her eyes and smiles and delicate attentions upon the fated heir to the property, and charms him into asking Mr. and Mrs. Bennet for her hand.

All seems well, but Lydia, fearing senile virginity, runs off, unwed, with the dashing Mr. Wickham. The entire family is tarnished with her sin, and is shunned by nearly all the neighbors. The Reverend Mr. Collins sends a reproving word to Mr. Bennet: "The death of your daughter would have been a blessing compared with this. . . . Who will connect themselves with such a family?"[2] Elizabeth saves all by alluring the class-prejudiced Mr. Darcy with her proud inaccessibility; he lays his millions at her feet, compels Wickham to cleanse Lydia with marriage, and, by the magic hand of the authoress as a *dea ex machina*, all problems are solved; even Mr. Bingley discovers that he has always loved Jane.

Mansfield Park is better built: the final solution is forecast near the outset, and is step by step prepared by almost every incident. The characters are not puppets in a plot but souls wondering their way through life, and properly illustrating the remark of Heracleitus (which should be the guide of all fiction), that "a man's character is his fate." The Park is the handsome domain of Sir Thomas Bertram, who is a much more solicitous father than Mr. Bennet. He too, however, makes surprising mistakes: absorbed in pursuit of wealth and honor, he lets his eldest son disintegrate morally and physically, and allows his daughter to prolong their vacation in a London society where all the morals of the countryside are the butt of humor instead of the staff of life. It is to his credit that he adopts into his family the modest and sensitive Fanny Price, the impoverished niece of his wife. His consoling pride is his younger son Edmund, who is dedicated to the Church, and is described as all that a future clergyman should be; he is an apology for Mr. Collins. It takes Edmund several hundred pages to realize that his affection for Fanny is more than brotherly love; but in its leisurely course their rising attachment is a pleasant romance in a classic tale.

For even in her studies of love Jane Austen is and was a classic—a lasting excellence and a sober mind. In an age of Udolphian mysteries and Walpolian castles she remained a realistic and rational observer of her time. Her style is as chaste as Dryden's; her piety is as unemotional as Pope's. Her scope is narrow, but her probe is deep. She perceives that the basic aspect of life is the conscription of the individual into the service of the race; that the crises of government, the conflicts of power, even the cries for social justice are not as fundamental as the repeated, unconscious effort of youth to mature and be used and consumed. She takes both aspects—female and male —of the human mystery quietly; its ills beyond her curing, its goal beyond her ken. She never raises her voice, but we follow it willingly, so far as the rapids of life will allow; and we can be captured by her calm. Today there is hardly a village in England but has her worshipers.

IV. WILLIAM BLAKE: 1757–1827

Born eighteen years before her, enduring ten years after her, William Blake spanned the transition to Romanticism; he lived on mystery, rejected science, doubted God, worshiped Christ, transformed the Bible, emulated the Prophets, and called for a utopia of earthbound saints.

He was the son of a London hosier. At the age of four he was frightened by seeing God looking at him through a window. A little later he saw angels fluttering in a tree, and the Prophet Ezekiel wandering in a field.[3] Perhaps because his imagination mingled lawlessly with his sensations, he was sent to no school till the age of ten; and then it was to a drawing school in the Strand. At fifteen he began a seven-year apprenticeship to the engraver James Basire. He read much, including such romantic lore as Percy's *Reliques of Ancient English Poetry* and Macpherson's "Ossian." He himself wrote verses, and illustrated them. At twenty-two he was accepted as a student of engraving at the Royal Academy, but he rebeled against Reynolds' classical injunctions; later he lamented that he had "spent the vigor" of his "Youth and Genius under the incubus of Sir Joshua and his Gang of cunning Hired Knaves."[4] Despite them he developed his own imaginative style of drawing, and was able to support himself with his watercolors and engravings.

He was not strongly sexual; he once expressed the hope that "sex would vanish and cease to be."[5] Nevertheless, aged twenty-five, he married Catherine Boucher. He often tried her with his tantrums and wearied her with his visions; but she recognized his genius, and cared for him faithfully to his end. He had no known children, but loved to play with those of his friends. In 1783 John Flaxman and the Reverend A. S. Mathews paid for the private printing of Blake's early verses; these *Poetical Sketches,* when reprinted in 1868, shared in the belated expansion of his fame. Some of them, like the rhymeless rhapsody "To the Evening Star," raised an original note in English poetry.[6]

Like any feeling soul, he resented England's concentrated wealth and festering poverty. He joined Tom Paine, Godwin, Mary Wollstonecraft, and other radicals grouped around the publisher Joseph Johnson; together they drank the strong wine of the French Enlightenment, and sang of justice and equality. His appearance befitted a spirit allergic to any imposed order. He was short and broad, with a "noble countenance full of expression and animation. His hair was of a yellow brown, and curled with the utmost crispness and luxuriance; his locks, instead of falling down, stood up like a curling flame, and looked at a distance like radiations, which, with his fiery eye and expansive forehead, his dignified and cheerful physiognomy, must have made his appearance truly prepossessing."[7]

In 1784 he opened up a print shop on Broad Street. He took in, as assistant, his young brother Robert. It was a happy relationship, for each was devoted to the other; but Robert was consumptive, and his death in 1787 deepened a somber strain in William's mood, and the mystic element in his thought. He was convinced that he had seen Robert's soul, at the moment of death, rise through the ceiling, "clapping its hands for joy."[8] To Robert's ghost he attributed a method of engraving both text and illustration upon one plate. Nearly all of Blake's books were so engraved, and were sold for prices ranging from a few shillings to ten guineas. Hence his audience was narrowly limited during his life.

In 1789 he issued his first masterpiece, nineteen little *Songs of Innocence.* Apparently he meant, by "innocence," the pre-pubetic period in which the pleasantest legends that had gathered about Christ were happily believed, brightening and guiding growth; however, Blake was thirty-two when the poems appeared, and we sense in them that experience is already mourning the death of innocence. We must recall his famous lines, that we may contrast them with lines addressed to a tiger five years later.

> Little Lamb, who made thee?
> Dost thou know who made thee?
> Gave thee life and bid thee feed
> By the stream and o'er the mead;
> Gave thee clothing of delight,
> Softest clothing, woolly, bright;
>   Little Lamb, who made thee?
>   Dost thou know who made thee?
>
> Little Lamb, I'll tell thee,
> Little Lamb, I'll tell thee;
> He is calléd by thy name
> For he calls himself a Lamb;
> He is meek and he is mild;
> He became a little child;
> I a child and thou a lamb,
> We are calléd by his name.
>   Little Lamb, God bless thee.
>   Little Lamb, God bless thee.

Perhaps still finer is the next poem, "The Little Black Boy," in which a Negro child wonders why God has darkened his skin, and dreams of the time when black child and white child will play together without the shadow of color crossing their games. And, two poems later, "The Chimney Sweeper" imagines an angel coming down to free all chimneysweeps from the coat of soot in which they work and sleep. "Holy Thursday" ends with a warning: "Then cherish pity, lest you drive an angel from your door."

Five years passed: the years in which the French Revolution exploded, burned brightly with idealism (1791), and then turned into massacre and terror (1792–94). In 1789, according to one report, Blake publicly wore the red cap of revolution, and joined Paine in attacking the Established Church. Excited to confusion, he broke out of the ballad form into "prophecies" echoing Jeremiah and Hosea, ominous proclamations to a sinful world.

These are not recommended reading to those who resent manufactured obscurity, but we note in passing that in *The Marriage of Heaven and Hell* (a satire of Swedenborg) Blake equates these realms with innocence and experience. Some of the "Proverbs from Hell" suggest a temporarily vegetarian-Whitmanic-Freudian-Nietzschean radicalism:

All wholesome food is caught without a net or a trap. . . .
The most sublime act is to set another before you. . . .
The pride of the peacock is the glory of God. . . . The nakedness of women is the work of God. . . .
Sooner murder an infant in its cradle than nurse unacted desires. . . .
God only Acts and Is, in existing beings or Men. . . .
All deities reside in the human breast. . . .
The worship of God is, Honoring his gifts in other men, . . . and loving the greatest man best. Those who envy or calumniate great men hate God, for there is no other God.

In *Songs of Experience* (1794) the poet countered his *Songs of Innocence* with odes of doubts and condemnation.

Tyger, Tyger, burning bright
In the forests of the night,
What immortal hand or eye
Could frame thy fearful symmetry? . . .

And what shoulder, and what art,
Could twist the sinews of thy heart?
And when thy heart began to beat,
What dread hands and what dread feet? . . .

When the stars threw down their spears
And watered heaven with their tears,
Did he smile his work to see?
Did he who made the Lamb make thee?

Whereas in *Songs of Innocence* "A Little Boy Lost" is rescued by God and brought back rejoicing to his home, a corresponding "song of experience" tells of a boy burned by the priests for acknowledging that he has no religious faith. In *Innocence* "Holy Thursday" described St. Paul's Cathedral as crowded with happy children singing hymns; "Holy Thursday," in *Experience*, asks:

Is this a holy thing to see
In a rich and fruitful land,
Babes reduced to misery,
Fed with cold and usurous hand?
Is that trembling cry a song?
Can it be a song of joy?
And so many children poor?
It is a land of poverty.

Against such evils revolution no longer seemed a valid cure; for "The iron hand crushed the Tyrant's head, And became a Tyrant in his stead."[9] Disappointed with violent revolt, Blake sought solace in his residual religious belief. He now distrusted science as the handmaid of materialism, the tool of the clever against the innocent, of power against simplicity. "Art is the Tree of Life, Science the Tree of Death; God is Jesus."[10]

After 1818 Blake wrote little poetry, found few readers, and supported himself by his art. At times, in his sixties, he was so poor that he had to engrave advertisements for Wedgwood pottery. In 1819 he found a saving patron in John Linnell, who commissioned him to illustrate the Book of Job and Dante's *Divine Comedy*. He was working on this final task when death came to him (1827). No stone marked his grave, but, a full century later, a tablet was erected on the spot; and in 1957 a bronze bust by Sir Jacob Epstein was placed in Westminster Abbey.

At his death the transition to Romanticism was complete. It had begun timidly, in the very heyday of classicism, with Thomson's *Seasons* (1730), Collins' *Odes* (1747), Richardson's *Clarissa Harlowe*(1747), Gray's *Elegy* (1751), Rousseau's *Julie, ou La Nouvelle Héloïse* (1761), Macpherson's *Fingal* (1762), Walpole's *Castle of Otranto* (1764), Percy's *Reliques of Ancient English Poetry* (1768), Scottish and German ballads, Chatterton's remarkable forgeries (1769), Goethe's *Werther* (1774). In truth there had been romantics in every age, in every home, in every lass and youth; classicism was a precarious structure of rule and restraint overlaid upon impulses and passions running like liquid fire in the blood.

Then the French Revolution came, and even its collapse brought liberation. Old forms of law and order lost prestige and force; feeling, imagination, aspiration, old impulses of violence in word and deed were set free; youth started fires of poetry and art under every literary rule, every moral prohibition, every constricting creed, every law-encrusted state. In 1798 Wordsworth and Coleridge came together in writing the poems and prefaces of *Lyrical Ballads;* Burns and Scott were singing of love, revolt, and war in Scotland; Napoleon's armies were shattering shibboleths faster than revolution could spread its dream. Everywhere literature had become the voice of freedom in revolt. Seldom had the future seemed so open, hope so limitless, or the world so young.

CHAPTER XXI

The Lake Poets

1770–1850

I. AMBIENCE

WE here gather Wordsworth, Coleridge, and Southey into one awkward and concurrent chapter, not because they established a school —they did not; nor because they displayed any shared spirit in their characters or works. Coleridge's magic verse was wrapt in mystery, strange souls and secrets, while Wordsworth's proseful poetry rambled contentedly with common men, women, children, and things. Coleridge lived and died a romantic—a creature of feeling, fancies, hopes and fears; Wordsworth, except for a romantic interlude in France, and a rebellious pronouncement in 1798, was as classic as Crabbe, and conservatively calm. As for Southey, his poetry was Romantic while it paid; his prose was restrained and worthy of Dryden; his mature politics hugged the status quo; and his life of marital stability and generous friendship safely balanced the emotional, philosophical, financial, and geographical wanderings of the fellow poet with whom he had once dreamed of a communal utopia on Susquehanna's shores.

These men constituted a school only in the sense that they dwelt through many years in the Lake District of northwest England—the misty, rainy, mystic assemblage of cloud-capped mountains and silver "meres" that makes the area from Kendal through Windermere, Ambleside, Rydal Water, Grasmere, Derwentwater, and Keswick to Cockermouth one of the fairest regions of our planet. Not toweringly majestic—the tallest mountain reaches only to three thousand feet; not congenial to consumptives—the rain falls there almost daily; but the mists embrace the mountains amicably, the sun breaks out nearly every day, and accustomed denizens bear the wanderings of the weather because of the peace of the villages, the evergreen foliage, the abounding flowers happy in the dew, and the spirits of mad Coleridge and steady Wordsworth echoing through the hills. There at Cockermouth Wordsworth was born, and at Grasmere died; there at Keswick Coleridge lived intermittently, and Southey forty years; there, for diverse periods, stayed De Quincey, Arnold of Rugby, Ruskin; there, briefly, Scott and Shelley, Carlyle and Keats came to sample Eden, and recall its laureates.

417

II. WORDSWORTH: 1770–97

His mother, nee Ann Cookson, was the daughter of a linen draper in Penrith. His father, John Wordsworth, was a lawyer, prospering as business agent of Sir James Lowther. In their comfortable home at Cockermouth John and Ann brought up five children: Richard, who became an attorney and managed the poet's finances; William and Dorothy, who are our chief present concern; John, who went to sea and died in a shipwreck; and Christopher, who became a scholar and rose to be master of Trinity College, Cambridge. For reasons now forgotten William was not baptized till after the birth of Dorothy a year after him, in 1771; brother and sister were christened on the same day, as if to sanction and bless their lifelong love.

Dorothy, more than any of his brothers, became William's childhood friend. She shared his fascination with the varied nature that surrounded them. He was keen and sensitive, she was more so, quicker to catch the forms and colors of the vegetation, the moods and exhalations of the trees, the lazy wanderings of the clouds, the moon benignly shedding silver on the lakes. "She gave me eyes, she gave me ears," the poet was to say of his sister. She tamed his hunting impulses to chase and kill; she insisted that he should never hurt any living thing.[1]

When she was seven they bore the bereavement of their mother's death. Their father, stunned, refused to take another wife; he buried himself in his work, and sent his children to live with relatives. Dorothy went off to an aunt in Halifax in Yorkshire, and could now see William only on his vacations. He was sent in 1779 to a good school at Hawkshead, near Lake Windermere; there he studied the Greek and Latin classics, and began, as he said, to "spin verses."

But the woods and waters of the vicinity seemed to have played a greater role than his books in the formation of his style and character. He was not unsocial; he took part with the other boys in the games of youth, and sometimes joined in a boisterous evening at the local inn; but many times he walked off alone into the hills, or along the shores of Esthwaite Water or Lake Windermere. Now and then, careless of weather and friendly to its forms, he wandered too far for security, and knew the fears that can come to youths invading the appropriated haunts of "lower" life; but gradually he came to feel a hidden spirit in the growth of plants, the play and struggle of animals, the pride of the mountains, the smiles and frowns of the kaleidoscopic sky. All these voices from field, forest, peak, and cloud seemed to speak to him in their own language, too secret and subtle for words, but felt by him as assurance that the incredible multiform multitude of things about him was no helpless mechanism of matter, but the frame of a God greater and nearer than the distant, silent, formless deity of his prayers. He developed a mood of somber inwardness as well as outgoing adoration.

In 1783 the father suddenly died. His disordered assets passed into such prolonged and expensive litigation, and the £4,700 owed him by Sir James Lowther were so long held back, that the available bequest, amounting to six hundred to each of the children, fell far short of providing for their continued education.[2] Brother Richard nevertheless found means to see William through Hawkshead.

In October, 1787, Wordsworth "went up" to Cambridge and entered St. John's College. One of his uncles had persuaded the headmaster to give the youth a scholarship, in the hope that he would prepare himself to receive holy orders in the Anglican Church—and so cease to be a financial burden on his relatives. Instead of taking courses leading to the ministry, he read for his own pleasure—specializing in Chaucer, Spenser, Shakespeare, and Milton —and protested against compulsory chapel attendance twice a day; apparently his reading had rubbed off some of his inherited faith. Much of it must have remained, for he found Voltaire dull.

In July, 1790, he persuaded a Welsh classmate, Robert Jones, to pool savings with him to a total of twenty pounds and join him in a walking tour on the Continent. They made their way to Lake Como, turned east into Switzerland, ran short of funds, and hurried back to England and Cambridge in time to appease the wrath of their financiers. Wordsworth made up for a year's neglect of Dorothy by spending the Christmas holidays with her at Fornsett Rectory near Norwich. "We used to walk every morning about two hours," she wrote to Jane Pollard, "and every evening we went into the garden at four . . . to pace backwards and forwards till six. . . . Ah, Jane! I never thought of the cold when he was with me."[3] She hoped that he would become a clergyman, and that she would be allowed to keep house for him.

When he graduated from Cambridge (January, 1791) he disappointed many hopes by going to London, "where for four months he lived in an obscurity which remains almost complete."[4] In May he took off with Jones on a walking tour through Wales; they climbed Mount Snowdon (1,350 feet) to see the sunrise. On November 27, alone, he crossed again to France.

The Revolution was then in its finest phase: a liberal constitution had been formulated, a Declaration of the Rights of Man had been proclaimed to the world; how could any sensitive youth, still a fledgling in philosophy, resist that call to universal justice and brotherhood? It was too hard for a poor scholar who had known some hurt from titled overlords (Sir James Lowther) to condemn those Frenchmen who, as he would put it in his autobiographical *Prelude,*

> held something up to view
> Of a Republic where all stood thus far
> Upon equal ground; that we were brothers all
> In honor, as in one community,
> Scholars and gentlemen; where, furthermore,
> Distinction open lay to all that came,
> And wealth and titles were in less esteem
> Than talents, worth, and prosperous industry.[5]

Arrived in France, he was stirred by the ardor of the nation rising spontaneously to arms to meet the threat of the Duke of Brunswick to suppress
the Revolution, and, if Paris resisted him, to burn it to the ground. He became friends with an officer in the Revolutionary Army, Michel de Beau-
puis, who "by birth ranked with the most noble," but now felt obliged to
defend France against invaders. This classless dedication moved Wordsworth to consider how he himself could be useful in the cause. But he felt
too frail to bear arms, and knew too little French to serve in a civilian or
political post. He settled down at Orléans to study the language, so bewitching on a woman's lips, so bewilderingly deceptive in orthography.

He found it most charming, but largely superfluous, in Annette Vallon, a
warmhearted, warm-blooded young woman who gave him not only instruction but herself. In return he could give her nothing but his youthful seed.
He was twenty-one, she was twenty-five. When the result announced itself, Annette thought she deserved a wedding ring, but William wondered:
could he, who knew more Latin than French, survive as a husband in France;
or could she, as a pagan Catholic, survive in Puritan England?

On October 29, 1792, he left her in Orléans and moved to Paris. Before
parting he signed a paper authorizing a M. Dufour to represent him as the
absent father at the christening of Annette's expected child.[6] It was born on
December 15, and was named Caroline.

By that time Wordsworth, in Paris, was immersed in the Revolution. He
attended meetings of the Jacobin Club, visited the Legislative Assembly,
made friends of Girondins. The fever of the day came upon him; he felt
himself at the center of world-shaking, history-making events:

> Bliss was it in that dawn to be alive;
> But to be young was very Heaven![7]

Then a letter reached him from brother Richard refusing further funds, and
insisting upon his immediate return. As the Revolution did not offer to support him, he crossed to London, and tried to thaw the frozen arteries of
familial finance. Brother Richard remained lovingly stern. Uncle William
Cookson, rector of Fornsett and host of Dorothy, closed his purse and doors
to the youngster whose education had been paid for as a prelude to sacerdotal services, but who now seemed to have turned into a shiftless Jacobin.

William was sorely hurt; he had adopted poetry as a profession, and felt
entitled, as a consecrated devotee of a Muse, to fraternal and avuncular support. Defiantly, he associated with the radicals who frequented Johnson's
bookshop, and he continued his public support of the Revolution. In the
last fifty lines of *Descriptive Sketches*, which he wrote and published in
1793, he praised the Revolution as the liberation not of one nation only, but
potentially of all mankind; and privately, as he posthumously confessed, he
rejoiced in French victories even "when Englishmen by thousands were
o'erthrown, left without glory on the field."[8] On February 1, 1793, France
declared war on England; in March a letter reached Wordsworth from Annette begging him to come back to her, but the Channel was closed to civil-

ian travel. He did not forget her, the thought of her burned his conscience; we shall see him, nine years later, trying to make some amends. During those years Annette became an ardent royalist, and William slowly discovered the virtues of the British Constitution.

His faith in the Revolution waned when the Terror guillotined the Girondins whom he had admired (1794). About this time he was much impressed by Godwin's *Enquiry Concerning Political Justice;* it encouraged his radicalism, but it warned against revolutions as feeding on revolutionists. In 1795 he met Godwin himself, and was charmed; seven times in that year he called upon the famous philosopher in his home. Even when he himself had become an ardent conservative he remained Godwin's friend till death intervened (1836).

An added inducement to sobriety came when, in 1795, Raisley Calvert bequeathed Wordsworth nine hundred pounds. Recklessly the poet lent three hundred of this legacy to his notoriously improvident friend Basil Montagu, and two hundred to Montagu's intimate, Charles Douglas—in both cases on mortgages hopefully paying ten percent. Wordsworth reckoned that the fifty-pounds-a-year interest (it was very irregularly paid), plus the remaining four hundred, would not suffice, even with Dorothy's annuity of twenty pounds, to finance his sister's dream of a cottage where they might live in a modest condominium of poetry and love. But just then another friend, John Pinney of Bristol, offered them, furnished and free, his Racedown Lodge in Dorset. So, on September 26, 1795, Wordsworth and Dorothy set up housekeeping there, and there they remained till June, 1797, in unexpected comfort and bliss.

We picture him, now twenty-five, as of middle height, gaunt and slightly stooped; his thin careless hair falling around his collar and his ears; his dark and somber eyes looking down along an inquiring and slightly aggressive nose; his trousers of pastoral plaid, his coat a loose brown frock, a black handkerchief serving as a tie. He was frail in body, strong in energy, spirit, and will; he could outwalk the sturdiest of his guests, and could with his own arms and axe keep his fires burning with cut or gathered wood. He was as sensitive as a poet, as nervous as a woman; he suffered from headaches, especially when he composed. He was often moody, inclined to hypochondria, easily moved to tears; once he thought of killing himself[9]—but that is a universal bravado. He was acquisitive, proud, self-centered, sure of his superior sensitivity, understanding, and (forgiving that carelessly fallen seed) moral excellence. But he was modest before Nature, holding himself her servant and her voice for the instruction of mankind.

Dorothy was his opposite: small and frail; earning her face of tan with many walks under the sun; selflessly absorbed—or selfishly delighted—in serving her brother, never doubting his genius, keeping their shelter clean and warm for him, tending him in his illnesses, searching out the subtlest beauties and wonders in nature with what he called "the shooting lights of thy wild eyes,"[10] and jotting down those percepts in her journals for her remembrance and his use. She gave ears and hands as well as eyes; she never (visibly) tired of hearing him recite his verses, or of copying them readably. He loved her in return, deeply but without forbidden passion, as the dearest and least demanding of his acolytes, as a precious delicate lateral tendril of himself.

To turn their home into a family, and add £50 to their annual revenue, they took under their care the three-year-old Basil, son of Basil Montagu; and they rejoiced to see their young ward "metamorphosed from a shivering, half-starved plant into a lusty, blooming, fearless boy."[11] In the spring of 1797 Dorothy's friend Mary Hutchinson came down from Penrith to stay with them till June 5. And on June 6, answering in his own exuberant way an invitation sent him by Wordsworth, a youth of twenty-five, pregnant with poetry, leaped over a gate, bounded over a field, and entered powerfully into the lives of William and Dorothy Wordsworth. It was Coleridge.

III. COLERIDGE: 1772–94

He is the most interesting of our conglomerate, the most varied in his talents, charms, ailments, ideas, and faults. He ran the gamut from idealism to disaster in love and morals, in literature and philosophy. He plagiarized from as many authors as he inspired. No aliquot portion of a chapter can do him justice.

Samuel Taylor Coleridge was born October 21, 1772, the tenth and final child of John Coleridge, schoolmaster and then vicar at Ottery St. Mary in Devonshire, an advanced mathematician, a scholar in classical and Oriental languages, the author of *A Critical Latin Grammar*. "S. T. C.," as the son would later sign himself, stumbled under this learned heritage, and lightened it by shedding Greek or Latin tags in almost every paragraph.

From his third to his seventh year, he later recalled,

> I became fretful and timorous, and a tell-tale; the schoolboys drove me from play, and were always tormenting me, and hence I took no pleasure in boyish sports, but read incessantly. . . . At six years old I had read Belisarius, Robinson Crusoe, . . . and the Arabian Nights Entertainments. . . . I was haunted by specters; . . . I became a dreamer, and acquired an indisposition to all bodily activity; and I was fretful, and inordinately passionate, . . . slothful . . . , hated by the boys;—because I could read and spell, and had . . . a memory and understanding forced into almost an unnatural ripeness, I was flattered and wondered at by all the old women. And so I became very vain, . . . and before I was eight years old I was a *character*. Sensibility, imagination, vanity, sloth, and feelings of deep and bitter contempt for all who traversed the orbit of my understanding, were even then prominent.[12]

The death of his father (1779), whom he had loved passionately, was an unsettling blow to Samuel. Two years later he was sent for further education to Christ's Hospital, which kept a charity school in London. The food was poor, the discipline was severe; he spoke in later life of the ignominious punishments that fell doubly hard upon a lad who felt that he had been forgotten by his family. They wanted him to be a clergyman; he longed to be a shoemaker. In 1830 (by which time his memory had become especially unreliable) he told of his one "just" flogging:

> When I was about thirteen, I went to a shoemaker, and begged him to take me as his apprentice. He, being an honest man, immediately brought me to Bowyer [headmaster], who got into a great rage, knocked me down, and . . . asked me why I had made myself such a fool? to which I answered that I had a great desire to be a shoemaker, and that I hated the thought of being a clergyman. "Why so?" said he.—"Because, to tell you the truth, sir," said I, "I am an infidel." For that, without more ado, Bowyer flogged me.[13]

Obviously he had plucked some forbidden fruit, perhaps from the circulating library in King Street. There, he later claimed in his monumental way,

> I read through [all the books in] the catalogue, folios and all, whether I understood them or not, . . . running all risks in skulking out to get the two volumes which I was entitled to have daily. Conceive what I must have been at fourteen; I was in a continual fever. My whole being was, with eyes closed to every object of present sense, to crumple myself up in a sunny corner, and read, read, read.[14]

There is, of course, some vain enlargement here. In any case he did so well at Christ's Hospital School that his family arranged to have him accepted as a "sizar" (on a work-and-study scholarship) at Jesus College, Cambridge (1791). There he attempted higher mathematics, and the most difficult Greek. "I am reading Pindar, and composing Greek verses like a mad dog. . . . At my leisure hours I translate Anacreon. . . . I am learning to play the violin."[15]

As always in Coleridge, we must allow for hyperbole. In any case he neglected his health, and came down (1793) with rheumatic fever. He found relief from the pain by taking opium. It was at that time a common anodyne, but Coleridge fell into its habitual use. His scholastic pace slowed, and he allowed himself more interest in current affairs. However, he outran the allowance sent him by his family, fell into debt, was harried by his creditors, and, in a desperate effort to escape them, suddenly left Cambridge, and (December, 1793) enlisted in the army that was being formed to fight France. His brother George bought Samuel's release for forty guineas, and persuaded him to return to Cambridge. He managed to graduate in 1794, but without a degree. This hardly disturbed him, for meanwhile he had discovered utopia.

He had been prepared for this by losing his religious faith; heaven and utopia are compensatory buckets in the well of hope. The French Revolution had stirred him as it stirred almost every literate and unmoneyed youth in England. Now, in the spring of 1794, word came from his friend Robert Allen at Oxford that several of the students there were eager to reform British institutions and ways. One student, reported Allen, was especially brilliant and had written verses celebrating social revolt. Could Coleridge come down to Oxford and meet these youths? In June, 1794, Coleridge came.

IV. SOUTHEY: 1774-1803

Of the Lake triad Robert Southey was the worst poet and the best man. He was born at Bristol, son of a clothier; but from that mercantile environment his wealthy aunt, Elizabeth Tyler, often borrowed him to be polished in the genteel society of Bath. At fourteen he was sent to the prestigious Westminster School in London, where, doubtless surreptitiously, he read Voltaire, Rousseau, Gibbon, and Goethe's *Werther*, and wrote some epic poetry and rebellious prose. His attack upon corporal punishment, in the school magazine called *The Flagellant*, infuriated the headmaster, who felt that he had been disarmed. Robert was expelled just as graduation neared, but somehow he was admitted into Balliol College, Oxford, in December, 1792. There he continued his secret operations—writing an epic, *Joan of Arc*, in which he praised the French Revolution. He was engaged upon a verse drama about Wat Tyler, the English revolutionist of 1381, when Coleridge arrived.

The older found the younger man in a brown study, for Robespierre had sent the lustiest leaders of the Revolution—Danton and Desmoulins—to the guillotine; were the Rights of Man ending in competitive homicide? Coleridge comforted him: Europe, he explained, was decadent, worn out with history; but every week or so, from Southey's native Bristol, a ship sailed to an America spacious, fertile, and republican. Why should not Coleridge and Southey organize a group of stout English lads and lasses, get them soundly married, migrate with them to Pennsylvania, and set up a communal colony on the lovely shores of the Susquehanna's unpolluted stream? All that was necessary was that each male should contribute £125 to the common fund. Each couple should have an equal voice in ruling the colony, and so Coleridge named it a "pantisocracy."

To raise their own shares of the cost the two founding fathers joined in writing a verse drama, *The Fall of Robespierre*; it was published, but had no sale. Southey sold *Joan of Arc* to Cottle of Bristol for fifty guineas. The degreeless graduates lectured in Bristol, and earned enough to raise Southey to proposal point; Edith Fricker accepted him, and they were married (November 14, 1795). Edith's sister Mary had already accepted Robert Lovell and pantisocracy. Now, said Southey, it was extremely desirable that Coleridge should love and marry the third sister, Sara.

When Elizabeth Tyler disowned him as lost to gentility by his lowly marriage and subversive ideas, Southey accepted an invitation to visit Lisbon as companion to an uncle who was chaplain to the British Embassy there. The trip broadened the young pundit's borders; he traveled in Spain as well as Portugal; when he returned to England (May, 1796) he discovered that he loved it, and pantisocracy faded with his youth. He studied law, found work as a journalist, and time to write more unmemorable epics, and some famous ballads, like "The Battle of Blenheim." In 1803, armed with a friendly annuity of £160, he settled down in Greta Hall, Keswick, hardly suspecting that he would stay there to the end of his life.

V. COLERIDGE: 1794-97

He was a cross between lively nerves and hesitant will. He loved Mary Evans of London, but shrank from the task of maintaining her in her wonted style; she liked his rich and ebullient spirit, but had no faith in its earning power. She turned away, and he resigned himself to Sara Fricker, who, plain and penniless, could keep house and bear children, but could not inspire odes.

To finance his prospective marriage and his lingering dream, he delivered more lectures in Bristol, charging a shilling for each admission (January to June, 1795). These *Conciones ad Populum* were recklessly radical: they denounced the Established Church as the servant of the rich and knowing no Lord but the lord of the manor. They condemned the war with France as an attempt to suppress the Revolution and turn back the march of history. They excused the Terror as a response to "Pitt's War," and they denounced the "Gag Bills" as governmental efforts to silence the public will. They drew small though enthusiastic audiences, but on the proceeds Coleridge took Sara Fricker to the altar (October 4, 1795).

In that same autumn he first met Wordsworth. William was only two years older than Samuel, but he had experienced the Revolution, had seen utopia in the flesh. He shared the younger man's dread of a Bourbon restoration, but he could not interest himself in Pennsylvania; the battlefield of ideas was in Europe; and as to the splendor of the Susquehanna, why not be satisfied with the glory of the English Lakes? Coleridge was only half convinced, but he put it in his tablets to watch this William grow, and perhaps learn from him how to ride the rapids of life.

He filled many tablets with gleanings from the books and souls he met. He read widely, eagerly, and in a dozen fields, about men, animals, plants, sciences, religions, philosophies, nations, literatures, arts. His was one of the hungriest, most absorbent, and most retentive minds of which we have any record. His memory became a storehouse from which he drew, to the end of his life, for images, ideas, phrases, arguments, even paragraphs. Too often he neglected to mention, or pleasantly forgot, the source of his catch, and carelessly mingled his own notions with borrowed goods. In the end the weight of his stores, and their unmanageable variety, were too great for a mind wedded to freedom and divorced from order. The storeroom nearly collapsed under its stores.

Perhaps to relieve his memory, or to feed his wife, he hit upon the idea of printing and selling a magazine almost entirely written by himself. He buttonholed his acquaintances, and conscripted his lecture auditors, as potential subscribers, and scattered a "Prospectus: That all may know the TRUTH, and that the TRUTH may make us FREE. On Friday the 5th day of

February 1796 will be published No. 1 (price four pence) of a miscellany to be published every eighth day, under the name of *The Watchman*, by S. T. Coleridge, author of Addresses to the People."[16] Here in print, as in his lectures, he spoke as a bridge-burning radical against the war, slavery, shackling of the press, and especially against sales taxes as falling cruelly upon the common man.[17] But he did not recommend universal adult suffrage, male or female. "We should be bold in the avowal of political truth among those only whose minds are susceptible of reasoning; and never to the multitude, who, ignorant and needy, must necessarily act from the impulse of inflamed passions."[18] — Coleridge found it unbearable to fill thirty-two pages every eight days with his own pen; increasingly they depended upon alien gleanings not always acknowledged. Some watchful readers protested. Circulation fell, debts rose. After ten numbers *The Watchman* died.

On September 1, 1796, Coleridge's first child was born. He named him David Hartley, from the English protagonist of the associationist psychology. Here was a delectable face, but another mouth to feed. Meanwhile he himself was feeling ailments of heart and lungs, and was relying more and more upon opium to ease the pain. He was near the end of his resources when a friendly liberal, Thomas Poole, offered him, at the nominal rent of seven pounds a year, a small house near his own at Nether Stowey, near Bridgewater. On December 31, 1796, Coleridge, Sara, and David moved in. Sara made the place comfortable and clean. "S. T. C." worked in an adjoining garden, helped to care for Poole's poultry and pigs, and wrote memorable, nonnegotiable poetry.

About this time, according to a memory always rich and adorned, "Kubla Khan" was conceived, and for the most part written, in a miraculous dream:

> In the summer of 1797 the Author, then in ill-health, had retired to a lonely farm-house between Porlock and Linton. . . . In consequence of a slight indisposition, an anodyne had been prescribed, from the effects of which he fell asleep in his chair at the moment that he was reading . . . in *Purchas's Pilgrimage:* "Here the Khan Kubla commanded a palace to be built, and a stately garden thereunto. And thus ten miles of fertile ground were enclosed with a wall." The Author continued for about three hours in a profound sleep, at least of the external senses, during which time he has the most vivid confidence, that he could not have composed less than from two to three hundred lines, . . . without any sensation or consciousness of effort. On awakening he appeared to himself to have a distinct recollection of the whole, and taking his pen, ink, and paper, instantly and eagerly wrote down the lines that are here preserved.

This famous preface has been interpreted as a fable with which Coleridge deceived himself or others into accepting the immaculate conception and brief continuance of "Kubla Khan." However, it is not unknown that an author, after manufacturing phrases during the day, should continue to do so in a dream; but almost always these jewels sink into unconsciousness as the sleeper wakes. Perhaps in this case the opium induced not only the dream but the delusion that the composition was part of the dream. In any case Coleridge, with his characteristic skill of rhyme and alliteration, transformed Purchas' prose into one of the most tempting torsos in the English language.

Perhaps a more important event than "Kubla," in Coleridge's year 1797, was an invitation to visit the Wordsworths at Racedown. He excused himself to Sara and David, and started off to walk nearly all the intervening miles. He sighted his goal on June 6, and ran excitedly across a field to his brother poet's door. When William and Dorothy opened it, and their hearts, to him, a new epoch began in these three lives, and one of the most fruitful collaborations in literary history.

VI. A THREESOME: 1797–98

Coleridge was then at the height of his charm. His whole body, despite its secret pains and poisons, was responsive to the lively interests of his mind. His handsome face—sensual mouth, finely formed nose, gray eyes sparkling with eagerness and curiosity, his careless black hair curling about his neck and ears—made him immediately attractive, especially to Dorothy. It did not take her long to fall in love with him in her shy way, always keeping William unchallengeable on his pedestal. Coleridge was taken aback by her tininess, yet was drawn to her by her quiet sympathy; this was a friend who would take him with all his faults, and would overlook his shiftlessness to see his warm feeling, his strangely recondite fancies, his shaken and bewildered faith, the frightened malaise of a poet lost amid factories and wars. For the present, however, he hardly saw this timid sprite of a girl, being overwhelmed by her brother.

Here, he realized, in this man with calm, grave face, high forehead, meditative eyes, was a real and living poet, sensitive to every vibration of things and souls, shunning the economic maelstrom, quietly making it his life task to find fit evocative words for his insights and dreams. Coleridge, who *at that time*—with *The Ancient Mariner* already growing in him—was the greater poet of the two, felt the dedication in this man, envied him his freedom to give himself totally to poetry, and may have wondered whether a sister is not better than a wife. "I feel myself *a little man by his side*," he wrote, soon after his coming; "and yet I do not think myself the less man than I formerly thought myself. William is a very great man, the only man to whom at all times and in all modes of excellence I feel myself inferior."[19]

So began three weeks of mutual stimulation. Each read his poems to the other. Wordsworth read more, Coleridge talked more. "His conversation," Dorothy wrote, "teemed with soul, mind, and spirit. Then he is so benevolent, so good-tempered and cheerful. His eye . . . speaks every emotion of his animated mind."[20]

Usually such a triune love affair cools after three weeks, but then Coleridge, loath to let it end, begged William and Dorothy to accompany him to Nether Stowey for some return of their hospitality. They went with him, expecting to come back to Racedown soon; but friend Poole, learning that their lease would soon expire and could not be renewed, found for them a handsome cottage, furnished, for £23 a year, in Alfoxden, four miles from

Coleridge; and there William and Dorothy took comfort and inspiration for the next fifteen months.

In that happy period there was much walking between one nucleus and the other of the poetic ellipse: sometimes the two men, sometimes Coleridge and Dorothy, sometimes the three. There was a triple exchange of feelings, observations, and ideas: Wordsworth encouraged Coleridge to let imagination be his guide; Coleridge enlarged Wordsworth's acquaintance with the philosophers, and challenged him to undertake an epic. Years later, in *The Prelude*, Wordsworth reminded his wandering friend of "the buoyant spirits / That were our daily portion when we first / Together wantoned in wild Poesy."[21] Dorothy was their bond and catalyst; she warmed them with her praise and eager listening, challenged them with the keenness and depth of her perceptions, and united them as their spiritual bride. They were, said Coleridge, three persons in one soul.[22]

Both Wordsworth and Coleridge must have looked into the journal that Dorothy began at Alfoxden on January 20, 1798. They must have been struck by a line on its second page: "The hum of insects, that noiseless noise which lives in the summer air." But Sara Coleridge would have been struck rather with entries for February 3 to 12:

> Feb. 3rd: Walked with Coleridge over the hills. . . .
> Feb. 4th: Walked a great part of the way to Stowey with Coleridge. . . .
> Feb. 5th: Walked to Stowey with Coleridge. . . .
> Feb. 11th: Walked with Coleridge near to Stowey.
> Feb. 12th: Walked alone to Stowey. Returned in the evening with Coleridge.[23]

Sara was not happy over this ambulatory romance; it seemed sexually innocent, but where would it end?

VII. *LYRICAL BALLADS:* 1798

Another stimulant came to Coleridge in January, 1798: Josiah and Thomas Wedgwood—sons and heirs of the Josiah Wedgwood (1730–95) who had made his pottery famous throughout Europe—offered the almost penniless poet an annuity of one hundred fifty pounds ($3,750) on condition that he devote himself wholly to poetry and philosophy. Coleridge welcomed the gift in a letter of January 17, and proceeded, in an ecstasy of creation, to complete *The Rime of the Ancient Mariner*.

Armed with this proof of potency, he proposed to Wordsworth that they should pool their new poems in collaborative volumes that would earn them enough money to finance a trip to Germany. He hoped that a year in Germany would teach him enough of the language and the culture to let him read in the original, and with understanding, those masterpieces which, from Kant to Goethe, had given Germany the unquestioned lead in European philosophy, and had brought it at least to rivalry with England and France in literature. Wordsworth was not enthusiastic about Germany, but France and north Italy were controlled by the Revolution; he fell in with Coleridge's plan.

In April, 1798, they invited publisher Cottle to come over from Bristol to hear their latest verses. He came, listened, and advanced thirty pounds for the copyright. He wished to publish also the names of the authors, but Coleridge refused. "Wordsworth's name," he said to Cottle, "is nothing, and mine stinks."[24]

Eighteen years later Coleridge explained the theory behind the collaboration:

> It was agreed that my endeavours should be directed to persons and characters supernatural, or at least romantic; . . . Mr. Wordsworth, on the other hand, was to propose to himself, as his object, to give the charm of novelty to things of every day, and to excite a feeling analogous to the supernatural, by awakening the mind's attention to the lethargy of custom, and directing it to the loveliness and the wonders of the world before us. . . . With this view I wrote "The Ancient Mariner," and was preparing, among other pieces, "The Dark Ladie" and the "Christabel," in which I should have more nearly realised my ideal.[25]

Probably the theory took form after the poems had been written. So with Wordsworth's explanation, prefixed to the first edition:

> The majority of the following poems are to be considered as experiments. They were written chiefly with a view to ascertain how far the language of conversation in the middle and lower classes of society is adapted to the purposes of poetic pleasure. Readers accustomed to the gaudiness and inane phraseology of many modern writers, if they persist in reading this book to its conclusion, will perhaps frequently have to struggle with feelings of strangeness and awkwardness; they will look round for poetry, and will be induced to inquire by what species of courtesy these attempts can be permitted to assume that title. It is desirable that such readers . . . should not suffer the solitary word *Poetry*, a word of very disputed meaning, to stand in the way of their gratification. . . .
> Readers of superior judgement may disapprove of the style in which many of these pieces are executed. . . . It will appear to them that, wishing to avoid the prevalent faults of the day, the author has sometimes descended too low, and that many of the expressions are too familiar and not of sufficient dignity. It is apprehended that the more conversant the reader is with our elder writers, . . . the fewer complaints of this kind will he have to make.[26]

Prose interfered with their poetry: the owner of the Alfoxden house notified the Wordsworths that their lease could not be renewed beyond June 30, 1798. On June 25 William and Dorothy left for Bristol to negotiate with Cottle. On July 10 they took a ferry across the River Severn, and walked ten miles in Wales to Tintern Abbey. Near this "very beautiful ruin," and on the way back to Bristol, Wordsworth composed the first draft of the poem that was added as the concluding piece of the *Lyrical Ballads*.

The little book was published on October 4, 1798, nineteen days after the unavowed authors had left for Germany. The title was fitting: Coleridge's main contributions were lineal descendants of old English ballads—tales in songlike verse; and most of Wordsworth's contributions were simple lyrics of simple life, in the almost monosyllabic language of the English peasantry.

The book opened with *The Rime of the Ancient Mariner;* this occupied fifteen of the 117 pages; it was the longest entry, and perhaps the best, though England came only slowly to realize this, and Wordsworth never.

The *Rime* has indeed many faults, but we must not stress, among these, the absurdity of the tale; Coleridge had entered a realm of mystery and imagination in which anything could happen, and mighty events might flow from trifling incidents. He had to depend upon imagination, for he had never been to sea,[27] and he had to borrow from travel books for maritime terms and moods. Nevertheless he caught the mystic aura of old legends, the marching rhythm of old ballads; and the old mariner carries us with him almost to the end. It is, of course, one of the greatest lyrics in the English language.

Wordsworth's contributions were mostly examples of his finding wisdom in simple souls. Some of these poems, like "The Idiot Boy" and "Simon Lee," were hilariously satirized by reviewers; but which of us has not sympathized with a mother's patient love for her harmlessly feeble-minded child? (One line of that understanding poem tells of "the green grass—you almost hear it growing";[28] was this snatched from Dorothy?) Then, after lingering with his rural types, Wordsworth concluded the book with the meditative "Lines Composed a Few Miles above Tintern Abbey." Here he gave supreme expression to his feeling that nature and God (Spinoza's *Deus sive Natura*) are one, speaking not only through the miracles of growth but also through those awesome and (to human short sight) seemingly destructive forces that Turner was then worshiping in paint. To his wanderings in woods and fields, his rowing on placid lakes and scrambling over massive rocks, to a thousand cries or whispers from a thousand forms of life, even from the supposedly inanimate world—

> To them I may have owed . . . that blessed mood,
> In which the burthen of the mystery,
> In which the heavy and the weary weight
> Of all this unintelligible world,
> Is lightened . . .
> While with an eye made quiet by the power
> Of harmony, and the deep power of joy,
> We see into the life of things.[29]

And then he rose to his finest profession of faith:

> I have learned
> To look on Nature, not as in the hour
> Of thoughtless youth, but hearing oftentimes
> The still, sad music of humanity,
> Not harsh nor grating, though of ample power
> To chasten and subdue. And I have felt
> A presence that disturbs me with the joy
> Of elevated thoughts: a sense sublime
> Of something far more deeply interfused,
> Whose dwelling is the light of setting suns,
> And the round ocean, and the living air,

> And the blue sky, and in the mind of man;
> A motion and a spirit, that impels
> All thinking things, all objects of all thought,
> And rolls through all things. Therefore am I still
> A lover of the meadows and the woods,
> And mountains; and . . . recognize,
> In nature and the language of the sense,
> The guide, the guardian of my heart, and soul
> Of all my moral being.[30]

Dorothy too had reached this healing, unifying creed, and found it not inconsistent with her Christian faith. At the close of his hymn Wordsworth added a paean to her as his sister soul, and bade her keep to the end

> Our cheerful faith, that all which we behold
> Is full of blessings. Therefore let the moon
> Shine on thee in thy solitary walk;
> And let the misty mountain winds be free
> To blow against thee; . . . and, in after years,
> When these wild ecstasies shall be matured
> Into a sober pleasure, when thy mind
> Shall be a mansion for all lovely forms,
> Thy memory be as a dwelling place
> For all sweet sounds and harmonies . . .[31]

Lyrical Ballads was not favorably received. "They are not liked by any," reported Mrs. Coleridge—a wife forgivably envious of her husband's Muse. The reviewers were so busy exposing loose joints in *The Mariner*, and loose sentiment in Wordsworth's ditties, that none of them seems to have recognized *The Mariner* as a future fixture in all anthologies, though some noticed the devout pantheism of "Tintern Abbey." The little book sold five hundred copies in two years, and Coleridge ascribed some of these sales to a sailor who thought, from the *Rime*, that the volume was a naval songbook. Wordsworth ascribed the tardiness of the sale to the inclusion of *The Ancient Mariner*.

In 1799, while Coleridge was in Germany, Wordsworth prepared a second edition of the *Ballads*. On June 24 he wrote to Cottle: "From what I gather it seems that *The Ancyent Marinere* has upon the whole been an injury to the volume. [This may have been true.] . . . If the volume should come to a second edition I would put in its place some little things which would be more likely to suit the common taste."[32] *The Mariner* was admitted to the second edition, with a (disarming?) note from Wordsworth admitting its faults but pointing out its excellences.

This edition (January, 1801) contained a new poem by Wordsworth, "Michael"—a tale leisurely told, in blank verse, of an eighty-four-year-old shepherd, loyal in labor, firm in morals, loved in his village, and of his son, who moved to the city and became a dissolute degenerate. A new preface by Wordsworth announced in detail, and in sentences now famous, his theory of poetry: Any object or idea may generate poetry if it is borne on feeling and carries significance; and any style or language can be poetic if it transmits such feeling and significance. "Poetry is the spontaneous overflow of powerful feelings; it takes its origin from emotion recollected in tranquillity";[33] the artist himself must have controlled his emotion before he can give it form. But such emotions are not confined to the literate or the elite; they can appear in the unlettered peasant as well as in the scholar or the lord; and perhaps in greater purity and clarity in the simpler soul. Nor does the expression need a special poetic vocabulary or style; the best style is the simplest, the best words are the least discolored with pretense or pomp. Ideally the poet should speak in the language of the common man; but even learned words may be poetic if they convey the feeling and the moral force.

For in the end it is the moral import that counts in every art. Of what use is our own skill with sound or form if it be not to seek readier acceptance of a clarifying, healing, or ennobling thought? "A great poet ought, to a certain degree, to rectify men's feelings, . . . to render them more sane, pure, and permanent, in short, more consonant to nature—that is, to eternal nature and the great spirit of things. He ought to travel *before* men occasionally, as well as at their sides."[34] The ideal poet, or painter, or sculptor is a philosopher clothing wisdom in art, revealing significance through form.

That preface played a part in history, for it helped to put an end to the fancy language, the class prejudices, the classical references, the mythological frills that had often littered the poetry and oratory of the English Augustan Age. It declared the rights of feeling, and—in the most unromantic style—gave another welcome to romance. Wordsworth himself was of classic mold and mood, given to thought and rule; he provided the tranquillity of recollection, while Coleridge brought emotion and imagination. It was an excellent collaboration.

VIII. THE WANDERING SCHOLARS: 1798–99

Not waiting to see their book published, and helped by an additional gift to Coleridge by Josiah Wedgwood, and an advance to Wordsworth by his brother Richard, the two poets and Dorothy sailed on September 15, 1798, from Yarmouth to Hamburg. There, after an uninspiring visit to the aging poet Klopstock, they separated: Coleridge went to study in the University of Göttingen, and Wordsworth and Dorothy took a diligence to the "free Imperial city" of Goslar, at the northern foot of the Harz Mountains. There, contrary to plan but immobilized by the cold, the Wordsworths remained for four months. They tramped the streets, fed the stove, wrote or copied poetry. Warming himself with memories, Wordsworth composed Book 1 of *The Prelude*, his autobiographical epic. Then, suddenly realizing how much they loved England, they set out on foot, on a cold February 23, 1799, to bid Coleridge goodbye at Göttingen, and then hurry back through the rough North Sea to Yarmouth and on to Sockburn on the Tees, where Mary Hutchinson waited quietly for William to marry her.

Meanwhile Coleridge did his best, at Göttingen, to become a German. He learned the language, and became entangled in German philosophy. Finding no explanation of mind in the psychology of materialism, he abandoned the mechanistic associationism of Hartley, and adopted the idealism of Kant and the theology of Schelling, who presented Nature and Mind as two aspects of God. He heard or read the lectures of August Wilhelm von Schlegel on Shakespeare, and took from them many a notion for his own later lectures on the Elizabethan drama. Drunk with ideas and abstractions, he lost his old flair for feeling and imagery, and abandoned poetry for philosophy. "The poet in me is dead," he wrote, "I have forgotton how to make a rhyme."[35] He became the bearer of German philosophy to England.

In July, 1799, he left Germany and returned to Nether Stowey. But a year's absence from his wife had dulled the edge of husbandry; Sara Coleridge was no longer a romance, and both husband and wife were darkened by the recent death of their second child, Berkeley. In October, restless, he went north to see Wordsworth at Sockburn. On that visit he held too long the hand of Sara Hutchinson, Mary's sister; some mystic current passed from the woman to the man, and Coleridge plunged into his third unhappy love affair. This Sara, mindful of his obligations to the other, gave him affection, but no more. After two years of vain wooing he resigned himself to defeat, and wrote a touching ode, "Dejection," as almost the last flash of his poetry.

He accompanied Wordsworth on a walking tour of the Lake District, each looking for a home. At Keswick he thought he had found one, but an offer of employment on the *Morning Post* deflected him to London. Meanwhile Wordsworth had leased a cottage thirteen miles farther south at Grasmere. He returned to Sockburn and won Dorothy's consent to the move; and on December 17, 1799, brother and sister began their long passage, mostly on foot, from Sockburn to Grasmere, over many miles of winter-hardened and rutted roads. On December 21 they made their hearth in what Wordsworth called "Town's End," and what came later to be called Dove Cottage. There they lived the hardest and happiest years of their lives.

IX. IDYL IN GRASMERE: 1800–03

From May 14, 1800, to January 16, 1803, Dorothy kept her "Grasmere Journal." Through those 150 pages we are enabled to see and feel the daily life of brother and sister, and later, briefly, of brother, sister, and wife. The climate of Grasmere was not made for health: rain or snow fell almost every day, and the winter's cold—even with snow—might reappear in June or July.[36] Sunny days were ecstasies, and the occasional emergence of the moon was a transfiguring revelation. The cottage was heated with coal in fireplace and stove, but sometimes, Dorothy noted, "I could not sleep for sheer cold." They took the weather stoically, grateful for spring and the usual gentleness of the rain; "it rained very mildly and sweetly" occurs repeatedly in the journal. "Sometimes Grasmere looked so beautiful that my heart almost melted away."[37]

Many a walk they took, together or apart, sometimes a mile to Ambleside for mail, sometimes half a day's journey to Keswick after Coleridge had settled there. Wordsworth seemed content with his sister-bride, calling her

> The dear companion of my lonely walk,
> My hope, my joy, my sister, my friend,
> Or something dearer still, if reason knows
> A dearer thought, or, in the heart of love,
> There is a dearer name.

And as late as 1802 (the year of his marriage) he referred to her as "my love."[38] She was content to call him "Sweet brother." [39]

She now had an income of forty pounds, he seventy; this (added to some dribblings from his publications), amounting to some one hundred forty pounds ($3,500?), was their yearly income. They had one or two servants, for poverty was so general that many a woman, spouseless, was willing to work for bed and board. Poet and sister dressed simply: Dorothy in garments usually made by herself, even to shoes;[40] William in peasant garb, or in cast-off clothing sent him by friends.[41] But they kept a vegetable garden, and sometimes caught fish in the lake. Moreover, the journal records, "I made tarts and pies,"[42] "bread and pies,"[43] "pies and cakes."[44] William was pampered.

But he worked too. Part of each normal day he composed, usually on his solitary walks, from which he returned to dictate lines to Dorothy. Also he chopped wood; dug and planted in the garden; and "William cleared a path to the necessary,"[45]—i.e., through the snow to the outdoor privy. Add that Dorothy brewed ale,[46] and "we borrowed some bottles for bottling rum."[47] Despite the vegetables, William suffered from hemorrhoids,[48] and (after 1805) from weakened sight, and insomnia; many an evening Dorothy had to read him to sleep.[49]

Those Theocritean days were suddenly confused by money and marriage. On May 24, 1802, Sir James Lowther, Earl of Lonsdale, died, leaving his property and title to his nephew, Sir William Lowther, who arranged to pay the money owed by Sir James to the heirs of John Wordsworth, Sr. Apparently four thousand pounds was divided among the children. Though the shares of William and Dorothy were not paid till 1803, William felt that his reasonable expectations warranted him in at last offering his hand to Mary Hutchinson.

But the memory of Annette Vallon rankled in his conscience. Should he not clear up his relation with her before asking Mary to take him? On July 9, 1802, he and Dorothy left Grasmere by coach and foot for Mary's present home at Gallow Hill. On July 26 they left Gallow Hill by coach for London. There, awed by the majesty of the city as seen in the early morning from Westminster Bridge, Wordsworth composed one of his many memorable sonnets—"Earth has not anything to show more fair."[50] They went on to Dover, took the packet across the Channel, and on July 31 found Annette and her nine-year-old daughter, Caroline, in waiting for them in Calais.

We do not know what agreement they came to; we know only that fourteen years later, when Caroline married, Wordsworth, then prospering, settled upon her an annuity of thirty pounds ($750?). The four remained at Calais for four weeks, walking the seashore in apparent accord. Wordsworth spun off another excellent sonnet—"It is a beauteous evening, calm and free, / The holy time is quiet as a Nun / Breathless with adoration,"— ending with a benediction for Caroline. On August 29 Wordsworth and Dorothy left for Dover and London. Apparently he was in no hurry, for not until September 24 did brother and sister get back to Gallow Hill.

On October 4, 1802, William and Mary were married. No presents came to the bride, for her relatives disapproved of Mary's marrying "a vagabond."[51] Dorothy, who only recently had written of William in her journal as "my Beloved," could not trust herself to attend the ceremony. "Her feelings were wrought to an almost uncontrollable pitch."[52] She went upstairs and lay "almost insensible" until Sara Hutchinson called to her that "they are coming" back from the church. "This," she wrote in her journal that afternoon, "forced me from my bed where I lay, and I moved, I knew not how, . . . faster than my strength could carry me, till I met my beloved William and fell upon his bosom. He and John Hutchinson led me to the house, and there I stayed to welcome my dear Mary."

That same day, in a chaise, the poet, his wife, and his sister began the long ride to Grasmere. Dorothy gradually adapted herself to the *ménage à trois*, and soon learned to love Mary as a sister and confidante. Besides, Mary brought to the household her own income of twenty pounds a year. When the Lowther payment finally arrived, it lifted the family to bourgeois comfort. William became an ardent patriot, and enlisted in the Grasmere Volunteers for the domestic defense of England against Napoleon.

To the Grasmere idyl belong some of Wordsworth's finest lyrics ("To a Butterfly"); the powerful sonnet to Milton; the ode "Resolution and Independence," chiding his own melancholy; and (between 1803 and 1806) the most famous of all his compositions—"Intimations of Immortality from Recollections of Early Childhood." Seldom has a philosophic fantasy been so beautifully expressed.

It begins on a somber note about his dimming eyesight: "Turn wheresoe'er I may, / By night or day, / The things which I have seen I now can see no more." He makes this a symbol of our idealistic visions vanishing with our youth—"Where is it now, the glory and the dream?"—and he wonders may not the helpless miracles that we are at birth have come from a heavenly home whose memory brightens our childhood and fades as we grow:

> Our birth is but a sleep and a forgetting;
> The soul that rises with us, our life's star,
>   Hath had elsewhere its setting,
>   And cometh from afar;
>   Not in entire forgetfulness,
>   And not in utter nakedness,
> But trailing clouds of glory do we come
>   From God, who is our home;

> Heaven lies about us in our infancy!
> Shades of the prison-house begin to close
>   Upon the growing Boy,
> But he beholds the light, and whence it flows,
>   He sees it in his joy; . . .
> At length the Man perceives it die away,
> And fade into the light of common day.

Therefore the poet hails the child as

> Thou best Philosopher, who yet dost keep
> Thy heritage, . . .
> Thou, over whom thy Immortality
> Broods like the Day . . .

But even we adults have some dim consciousness of that lost horizon—

> Blank misgivings of a Creature
> Moving about in worlds not realized . . .
> Our souls have sight of that immortal sea
>   Which brought us hither,
>   Can in a moment travel thither,
> And see the children sport upon the shore,
> And hear the mighty waters rolling ever more.

This is anthropology theologized: the child, still an animal, rejoicing in its animal motions, limbs, and freedom; resenting every garment, prohibition, and restraint; inwardly longing for the freedom of animal life and movement in fields or woods, in seas or the air, and slowly, resentfully losing those liberties as the child becomes adult and the youth submits to civilization. But Wordsworth would have none of this; he was recalling Pythagoras, and hoping to find in him some bridge back to his childhood creed. The aging man seeks the womb of his feelings as of his life.

X. LOVE, LABOR, AND OPIUM: 1800–10

In April, 1800, having completed his assignment with the *Morning Post*, Coleridge came to Grasmere for a three-week stay with the Wordsworths. Dorothy told him that she had found a pleasant haven for him and his family in a large house called Greta Hall, some three miles out of Keswick. Coleridge went, saw the place in the glory of summer, found in one room a library of five hundred volumes, many of them grist to his mill, and enthusiastically signed the lease. In August, 1800, he took his wife Sara and son Hartley from Nether Stowey to their new home. There, on September 14, Sara gave birth to another boy, whom they named Derwent from a nearby lake and stream. Soon the winter revealed to them their mistake: the cold and rain aggravated Coleridge's tendencies to asthma and rheumatic fever, and the geographical separation from her relatives deepened the melancholy of his wife, so often left alone by her husband's wanderings of body and mind.

Frequently he left her to walk the three plus thirteen miles to Keswick and Grasmere to enjoy the stimulus of Wordsworth's conversation and Dorothy's affectionate attentions; and only less frequently Wordsworth and Dorothy walked north to brighten Coleridge's day. In November, 1800, Sara Hutchinson came down from Gallow Hill for a stay of several months with Mary, William, and Dorothy at Dove Cottage; and there Coleridge resumed his pursuit of her. With unintentionally cruel simplicity, he confessed to his wife his love for the second Sara, and asked for permission to love them both. Day by day she retreated from him into motherly cares, and he into his brooding and his books.

He tried to complete the ballad-story "Christabel," which he had begun in 1797; but he found no "fine frenzy" in him, and left the tale unfinished. Scott and Byron praised it in its manuscript form, and may have taken some hints from it in theme, meter, and mood; finally (1816), at Byron's urging, Murray printed it. It is a haunting relic of a vanished charm.

After a year at Greta Hall, Coleridge, his health and funds exhausted, felt that he could not survive another winter at the Lakes. He was glad to receive an invitation to join the staff of the *Morning Post* as an editorial writer. On October 6, 1801, he went to Grasmere to say goodbye; on the 9th Dorothy and Mary walked with him to Greta Hall; on the 10th he left for London, and Mary and Dorothy walked back to Grasmere. Dorothy wrote in her journal: "C. had a sweet day for his ride. Every sight and every sound reminded me of him, dear dear fellow . . . I was melancholy and could not talk, but at last I eased my heart by weeping—nervous blubbering, says William. It is not so. O how many, many reasons I have to be anxious for him."[53]

Arrived in London, Coleridge worked hard writing "leaders," in which his growing conservatism went well with the policy of the *Post*, the chief organ of the semiliberal Whigs—anti-ministry but pro-property. He condemned slavery and the "rotten boroughs" (which regularly sent Tories to Parliament), denounced the government for rejecting Napoleon's offer of peace (1800), and almost ruined Pitt with a merciless analysis of the Prime Minister as a statesman and as a man. However, he defended private property as the necessary base of a progressive but orderly society, and argued that that government is best which makes "each man's power proportionate to his property."[54] He wrote vigorously and effectively; the circulation of the *Post* rose substantially during his stay.[55] But that year of hectic work contributed to the breakdown of his health. When he returned to Greta Hall (1802) he was physically and morally exhausted—the body ailing, the husband alienated, the lover rejected, the will a slave to opium.

He had begun to take the drug as early as 1791, aged nineteen.[56] He used it to quiet his nerves, to reduce pain, to induce sleep, to retard—or conceal from himself—the deterioration of his heart and lungs, perhaps to resign himself to defeat. And when elusive sleep came at last, it became a host to frightening dreams, which he hinted at in "The Pains of Sleep" (1803):

> the fiendish crowd
> Of shapes and thoughts that tortured me; . . .
> Desire with loathing strangely mixed,
> On wild or hateful objects fixed;
> Fantastic passions, maddening brawl!
> And shame and terror over all.[57]

His notebooks tell of an imaginary people on the moon "exactly like the people of this world in everything except indeed that they eat with their Backsides, and stool in their mouths; . . . they do not kiss much."[58] Like most of us he had dreams of fear, but in his case so vivid that sometimes he wakened the household with his screams.[59]

Perhaps his ailments and drugs, though sometimes confusing his thought and weakening his will, opened to him areas and vistas of perception and imagination closed to normal minds. In any case his range of knowledge was unsurpassed in his generation, leaving Wordsworth, in this respect, far behind. He humbled himself before Wordsworth, but Wordsworth could seldom talk about anything but his poems, while Coleridge's conversation, even in his decay, had a range, vivacity, and interest that impressed Carlyle, and might even have silenced Mme. de Staël. What awed him in Wordsworth was the older man's concentration of purpose and steadiness of will; Coleridge was more and more substituting the wish for the will and imagination for reality.

He marveled at his modesty, but he was intensely self-conscious, found himself (but in this like Wordsworth and ourselves) the most interesting of all subjects, and was secretly and aggressively proud. He called attention to his honesty, his austere moral code, his indifference to money or fame; but he longed for honors, plagiarized happily,[60] borrowed money forgetfully, left his wife and children, and allowed his friends to support them. Perhaps opium weakened his sexual capacity, and allowed him to mistake fancy for performance.

In April, 1804, seeking to reduce his asthma and rheumatic fever with the Mediterranean air and sun, he accepted a loan of a hundred pounds from Wordsworth,[61] and sailed to Malta, then a crucial but disputed bastion of British power. He took with him an ounce of crude opium and nine ounces of laudanum. On the voyage, May 13, he wrote in his notebook a desperate prayer:

> O dear God! give me strength of soul to make one thorough Trial—if I land at Malta / spite of all horrors to go through one month of unstimulated Nature. . . . I am loving and kind-hearted and cannot do wrong with impunity, but O! I am very, very weak—from my infancy have been so—and I exist for the moment!—Have mercy on me, have mercy on me, Father and God![62]

For almost a year he seemed to recover his self-control. In July he was appointed private secretary to Sir Alexander Ball, governor of Malta, and in January, 1805, he was advanced to the more responsible post of public secretary. He worked hard, and revealed surprising powers of judgment and application. Then, after a year of service, he was so exhausted that he relapsed into drug addiction. He left Malta, traveled in Sicily and Italy, and returned to England (1806). By that time he was more than ever dependent upon opium, checking its soporific action with brandy.

On October 26, 1806, he met the Wordsworths at an inn in Kendal. "Never," wrote Dorothy under that date, "did I feel such a shock as at first sight of him"; so fat that "his eyes are lost" in his swollen face, and only a momentary gleam appeared of the former "divine expression of his countenance."[63] He went on to Keswick, and asked his wife for a separation. She refused. He left her, taking with him son Derwent, six years old. He transferred to his wife his Wedgwood annuity,[64] but Josiah Wedgwood withdrew his share of this in 1813. Southey, established in Greta Hall since 1803, took over the care of his sister-in-law. Coleridge was tided over the crisis by a gift of a hundred pounds sent anonymously by his fellow addict De Quincey, and by the lectures that he gave at the Royal Institution in 1808, 1809, and 1810.

In that year the great friendship ended. Its basis had been mutual inspiration to poetry; that ceased when the font of poesy dried up in Coleridge after 1800 through physical weakening, soporific opiates, marital alienation, and enthrallment by philosophy. Wordsworth had encouraged the exchange of Muses by suggesting to Coleridge that his genius favored prose. Coleridge had been offended by learning that all three Wordsworths had cautioned Sara Hutchinson against encouraging his advances. The divergence became a chasm when, in a letter of May 31, 1809, Wordsworth warned Poole not to involve himself too heavily in Coleridge's new magazine (1809–10), *The Friend*. "As one of Coleridge's nearest and dearest friends," Wordsworth wrote:

> I give it to you as my deliberate opinion, formed upon proofs that had been strengthening for years, that Coleridge neither will nor can execute anything of important benefit either to himself, his family, or mankind. Neither his talents nor his genius, mighty as they are, nor his vast information, will avail him anything; they are all frustrated by a derangement of his intellectual and moral constitution. In fact he has no voluntary power of mind whatsoever, nor is he capable of acting under any *constraint* of duty or moral obligation.[65]

This is merciless and extreme, but Wordsworth had told Coleridge as much in a letter a few weeks before.[66] The matter was made worse when, according to Coleridge, Basil Montagu told him that Wordsworth had advised him not to let Coleridge lodge with him, since Coleridge, by heavy drinking and otherwise, had made himself "a nuisance" at Grasmere.[67] Wordsworth later (1812) assured Coleridge that Montagu had misquoted him. Coleridge pretended to accept the explanation, but the broken strings could not be repaired, and the historic friendship died.

XI. COLERIDGE PHILOSOPHER: 1808–17

Perhaps we have exaggerated Coleridge's collapse; we must note that between 1808 and 1815 he delivered lectures—at Bristol and at the Royal

Institution in London—which suffered somewhat from confusion of thought
and expression, but impressed such auditors as Charles Lamb, Lord Byron,
Samuel Rogers, Thomas Moore, and Leigh Hunt; as if by some spontaneous
esprit de corps, these and other scribes came to the support of their maimed
compeer. Henry Crabb Robinson, who numbered a dozen English or German notables among his friends, described the third of the London lectures
as "excellent and very German." "In the fourth," he reported, "the mode of
treating the subject was very German, and much too abstract for his audience, which was thin."[68] Coleridge's accumulation of facts, ideas, and
prejudices was too abundant to let him cleave to his announced subject;
he wandered wildly but inspired. Charles Lamb, who summarized him in a
famous phrase as an "archangel, a little damaged,"[69] concluded that it was
"enough to be within the whiff and wind of his genius for us not to possess
our souls in quiet."[70]

During the years 1815–17, when Coleridge was again nearing a breakdown, he poured his aging conclusions into print. In *Theory of Life* (1815)
he showed a surprising knowledge of science, especially of chemistry, which
he knew through friendship with Humphry Davy; but he rejected all attempts to explain mind in physicochemical terms. He called "absurd the
notion of [Erasmus] Darwin, . . . of man's having progressed from an
orang-outang state."[71]

In *The Statesman's Manual* (1816) he offered the Bible as "the best guide
to political thought and foresight."

> The historian finds that great events, even the most important changes in the
> commercial relations of the world, . . . had their origin not in the combinations
> of statesmen, or in the practical insights of men of business, but in the closets of
> uninterested theorists, in the visions of recluse geniuses. . . . All the epoch-
> forming revolutions of the Christian world, the revolutions of religion, and
> with them the civil, social, and domestic habits of the nations concerned, have
> coincided with the rise and fall of metaphysical systems.[72]

(He may have been thinking of the results of the thoughts of Christ, Copernicus, Gutenberg, Newton, Voltaire, Rousseau.) After a fair summary
of the factors that led to the French Revolution, Coleridge concluded that
the voice of the people is not the voice of God; that the people think in
passionate absolutes, and cannot be trusted with power;[73] and that the best
road to reform is through the conscience and action of an educated and
propertied minority.[74] Generally the best guide to right action, in politics
as elsewhere, is the Bible, for this contains all the important truths of history
and philosophy. "Of the laboring classes more than this is not demanded,"
and "not perhaps generally desirable. . . . But you, . . . as men moving
in the higher classes of society," should also know history, philosophy, and
theology. The antidote to false statesmanship is history, as "the collation of
the present with the past, and the habit of thoughtfully assimilating the
events of our own age to those of the time before."[75]

A Lay Sermon (1817) continued this appeal to the "higher and middle
classes" as the best vehicles of sane reform, and as guards against the "soph-

ists and incendiaries of the revolutionary school."[76] But the book recognized some current evils: the reckless swelling of the national debt, a peasantry sinking into pauperism, the labor of children in the factories. Coleridge noted "the folly, presumption, and extravagance that followed our late unprecedented prosperity; the blind practices and blinding passions of speculation in the commercial world, with the shoal of ostentatious fooleries and sensual vices." He mourned the liability of the new business economy to periodical exaltations and depressions, leading to breakdowns and general suffering.[77]

He recommended some basic reforms. "Our manufacturers must consent to regulation,"[78] especially of child labor. The state should recognize as its "positive ends: 1. To make the means of subsistence more easy to each individual. 2. To secure to each of its members the hope of bettering his own condition and that of his children. 3. The development of those faculties which are essential to his humanity; i.e., to his rational and moral being."[79] He called for an organization of the leaders in every profession to study the social problem in the perspective of philosophy, and to offer recommendations to the community; and this "national church should be financed by the state."[80]

Coleridge ended his *Lay Sermon* by conceding to the theologians that no purely lay or secular wisdom can solve the problems of mankind; only a supernatural religion and a God-given moral code can check the inherent cupidity of men.[81] Evil is so inborn in us that "human intelligence . . . alone" is "inadequate to the office of restoring health to the will."[82] He called for a humble return to religion, and to full faith in Christ as God dying to redeem mankind.[83]

In 1815–16 Coleridge composed or dictated certain "Sketches of my Literary Life and Opinions" for use in a projected autobiography. That volume was never completed, and Coleridge published the sketches in 1817 as *Biographia Literaria*, which is now our most manageable source for Coleridge's thought in philosophy and literature. It is remarkably coherent and clear, considering that most of it was produced during despondency about his addiction to opium, his accumulating debts, and his inability to provide for the education of his sons.

He began by repudiating the associationist psychology that had once fascinated him; he rejected the notion that all thought is the mechanical product of sensations; these, he now held, give us merely the raw materials which the self—the remembering, comparing, continuing personality—remolds into creative imagination, purposive thought, and conscious action. All our experience, conscious or not, is recorded in the memory, which becomes the storehouse from which the mind—consciously or not—draws up material for the interpretation of present experience and for the illumination of present choices. Here, of course, Coleridge was following Kant. His ten months in Germany had transformed him not only from a poet into a philosopher but from a determinist Spinozist into a free-will Kantian. Here he fully acknowledged his debt. "The writings of the illustrious sage of

Königsberg, . . . more than any other work, at once invigorated and disciplined my understanding."[84]

From Kant Coleridge proceeded to Fichte's exaltation of the self as the only reality directly known, through Hegel's contrast and union of nature and the self, to Schelling's subordination of nature to mind as two sides of one reality, in which, however, nature acts unconsciously, while mind may act consciously and reaches its highest expression in the conscious creations of the genius. Coleridge borrowed freely from Schelling, and often neglected to mention his sources;[85] but he confessed his general debts, and added: "To me it will be happiness and honor enough, should I succeed in rendering the system itself [of Schelling] intelligible to my countrymen."[86]

The last eleven chapters of the *Biographia* offered a philosophical discussion of literature as a product of imagination. He distinguished between fancy and imagination: fancy is fantasy, as in imagining a mermaid; Imagination (capitalized by Coleridge) is the conscious unification of parts in a new whole, as in the plot of a novel, the organization of a book, the production of a work of art, or the molding of the sciences into a system of philosophy. This conception became a tool for the understanding and criticism of any poem, book, painting, symphony, statue, building: how far does the product have, or lack, structure—the weaving of relevant parts into a consistent and significant whole? In those pages Coleridge offered a philosophical basis for the Romantic movement in literature and art.

He completed his complex *Biographia* with an acute criticism of Wordsworth's philosophy and practice of poetry. Is it true that the highest philosophy of life can be found in the ways and thoughts of the simplest men? Is the language of such men the best medium of poetry? Is there no basic difference between poetry and prose? On all these points the poet become critic differed courteously but pointedly and effectively. Then he concluded with a healing homage to the Grasmere sage as the greatest poet since Milton.[87]

XII. WORDSWORTH: CLIMAX, 1804–14

After some minor wanderings, the Wordsworth ménage moved (1808) from Dove Cottage to a larger house at nearby Allan Bank. There the poet blossomed out as a landscape gardener, surrounding the house with plants and flowers that frolicked in the Grasmere rains. In 1813 the family moved finally to a modest estate at Rydal Mount in Ambleside, a mile south of Grasmere. They were now prosperous, with several servants and some titled friends. In this year Lord Lonsdale arranged Wordsworth's appointment as distributor of stamps for Westmorland County; this post, retained till 1842, brought the poet an additional two hundred pounds per year. Freed from economic worry, he spent more time in his garden, making it the paradise of rhododendra and other flowering plants which it still is.

From his window on the second floor he had an inspiring view of Rydal Water (i.e., Lake) two miles away.

Meanwhile (1805) he completed *The Prelude*, begun in 1798; "every day," Dorothy noted, he "brings us in a large treat" of it from his morning walk.[88] She and Sara Hutchinson were kept busy taking dictation; Wordsworth had learned to think in blank verse. He subtitled the leisurely epic "The Growth of a Poet's Mind"; it was intended as a mental autobiography, and as a prelude to *The Excursion*, which would expound in detail the philosophy reached in that growth. He gave the record an added intimacy by repeatedly addressing his memories to Coleridge. He apologized for the surface egotism of the poem; it was, he confessed, "a thing unprecedented that a man should talk so much about himself."[89] Perhaps for that reason he kept it unpublished during his life.

It is quite tolerable if taken in small doses. Most pleasant are the scenes of his childhood (Books I and II), his solitary woodland rambles, when it seemed to him that in the chatter of the animals, the rustling of the trees, even in the resonance of rocks and hills, he heard the voice of a hidden and multiform god. So, as he sat

> Alone upon some jutting eminence,
> At the first gleam of dawnlight . . .
> Oft in these moments such a holy calm
> Would overspread my soul, that bodily eyes
> Were utterly forgotten; and what I saw
> Appeared like something in myself, a dream,
> A prospect in the mind. . . .
>   I, at this time,
> Saw blessings spread around me like a sea . . .
>   with bliss ineffable
> I felt the sentiment of Being spread
> O'er all that moves and all that seemeth still,
> O'er all that, lost beyond the reach of thought
> And human knowledge, to the human eye
> Invisible, yet liveth to the heart;
> O'er all that leaps and runs, and shouts and sings,
> Or beats the gladsome air; o'er all that glides
> Beneath the wave, yea, in the wave itself,
> And mighty depth of waters. Wonder not
> If high the transport, great the joy I felt,
> Communing in this sort through earth and Heaven
> With every form of creation, as it looked
> Towards the Uncreated . . .

(There may be a flaw or retrogression here; the last line suggests a division of reality between creation and its creator; we had supposed that in Wordsworth's pantheistic vision God and nature, as in Spinoza, were one.)

At Cambridge (III) he sometimes joined in student frolics or forays, but he was disturbed by the reckless and undisciplined superficiality of undergraduate life; he took more pleasure in the English classics, or in boating on the Cam. In vacation time (IV) he returned to his early haunts, ate at the family table, nestled in his accustomed bed—

> That lowly bed whence I had heard the wind
> Roar, and the rain beat hard; where I so oft
> Had lain awake on summer nights to watch
> The moon in splendor couched among the leaves
> Of a tall ash that near our cottage stood;
> Had watched her with fixed eyes, while to and fro
> In the dark summit of the waving tree
> She rocked with every impulse of the breeze.

At Cockermouth he could walk with his old dog, who let him compose verses aloud and did not therefore think him "crazed in brain."

> Ah! need I say, dear Friend, that to the brim
> My heart was full; I made no vows, but vows
> Were then made for me, . . . that I should be . . .
> A dedicated spirit,

living for poetry.

Pleasant, too, was that stolen jaunt across the Channel (VI), to feel the happy madness of France in revolution, the exaltation of the Alps, and then, returning, to see the "monstrous ant-hill" called London, with old Burke intoning in Parliament the virtues of tradition, and "with high disdain Exploding upstart Theory"; to watch the crowds frolicking at Vauxhall or worshiping at St. Paul's; to see or hear the moving multitudes, the varied races, faces, garbs, and speech, the clatter of traffic, the smiles of prostitutes, the vendors' cries, the flower women's appeals, the street singer's hopeful serenade, the artist chalking pictures on the flagstones, "the antic pair of monkeys on a camel's back"—all this the poet felt as keenly as the woods, but he liked them not, and fled (VIII) to calmer scenes where love of all-embracing nature could teach him to understand and forgive.

Then again to France (IX), where old despotism and ancient misery seemed to have justified and ennobled revolt, and even a Briton could join in its wild ecstasy (XI).

> Not favoured spots alone, but the whole earth
> The beauty wore of promise . . .
> What temper at the prospect did not wake
> To happiness unthought of?

From that high rapture France descended to crime, and Wordsworth to prose:

> But now, become oppressors in their turn,
> Frenchmen had changed a war of self-defence
> For one of conquest, losing sight of all
> Which they had struggled for . . .

Slowly, hesitantly, the poet drew his *Prelude* to a close (XIV), calling upon his friend to return (from Malta) and join in the effort to win mankind back from war and revolution to love of nature and mankind. He was discontent with his poem,[90] knowing that there were spacious deserts around the oases. He had confessedly seen little difference between prose and poetry, and he too often mingled them in the steady, dulling march of his blank verse. He had made "emotion remembered in tranquillity" the essence of poetry, but an emotion tranquilized through fourteen cantos becomes an irresistible lullaby. Generally, the character of an epic is a great or noble action told; and thought is too private to be epical. Even so, *The Prelude* leaves the resolute reader with a sense of healthy acceptance surviving reality. Wordsworth, sometimes as childish as a nursery rhyme, cleanses us with the freshness of woods and fields, and bids us, like the imperturbable hills, bear the storm silently, and endure.

Before leaving for Germany in 1798 Wordsworth had begun *The Recluse*, on the theory that only a man who had known life and had then withdrawn from it could judge it fairly. Coleridge urged him to develop this into a full and final statement of his philosophy. More specifically Coleridge suggested: "I wish you would write a poem in blank verse, addressed to those who, in consequence of the complete failure of the French Revolution, have thrown up all hopes for the amelioration of mankind, and are sinking into an almost epicurean selfishness."[91] They agreed that the summit of literature would be a happy marriage of philosophy and poetry.

On second thought Wordsworth felt that he was not ready to meet this challenge. He had made considerable progress with *The Prelude*, which proposed to be a history of his mental development; how could he, before completing this, write an exposition of his views? He put *The Recluse* aside, and pursued *The Prelude* to its apparent end. Then he found his energy and confidence waning, and the passage of the once exuberant Coleridge out of his life had removed the living inspiration that once had spurred him on. In this condition of depleted vigor and prosperous ease he wrote *The Excursion*.

It begins well, with a description—apparently taken from the abandoned *Recluse*—of the ruined cottage where lives the "Wanderer." This replica of Wordsworth leads the excursionist to the Solitary, who tells how he lost his religious faith, became sated with civilization, and retired to the peace of the mountains. The Wanderer offers religion as the only cure for despair; knowledge is good, but it increases our power rather than our happiness. Then he leads on to the Pastor, who submits that the simple faith and family unity of his peasant flock are wiser than the attempt of the philosopher to replace the wisdom of the ages with the webs of intellectual argument. The Wanderer deplores the artificial life of the city, and the evils of the Industrial Revolution; he advocates universal education, and prophesies its "glorious effects." The Pastor, however, having the last word, entones a paean to a personal God.

The Excursion, being a Portion of the Recluse, a Poem, was published in

1814 at two guineas a copy. (Its supposed preface, *The Prelude*, was not printed till 1850.) Wordsworth asked his neighbors, the Clarksons, to help its sale among their Quaker friends, "who are wealthy and fond of instructive books"; he gave a copy to the novelist Charles Lloyd on the understanding that it should not be lent to anyone who could afford to buy it; and he refused to lend it to a rich widow, who considered two guineas as rather high a price for "part of a work."[92] Eight months after publication only three hundred copies had been sold.

The reviews were mixed. Lord Jeffrey, in the November, 1814, issue of the *Edinburgh Review*, condemned the poem with an ominous beginning: "This will never do." Hazlitt, after praising "delightful passages, both of natural description and of inspired reflection," found the poem as a whole "long and labored," repeating "the same conclusions till they become flat and insipid."[93] And Coleridge, who had called for a masterpiece, saw in *The Excursion* "prolixity, repetition, and an eddying, instead of progression, of thought."[94] But in his later *Table Talk* Coleridge praised Books I and II ("The Deserted Cottage") as "one of the most beautiful poems in the language."[95] Shelley disliked *The Excursion* as marking Wordsworth's surrender of a naturalistic pantheism to a more orthodox conception of God; but Keats found many inspirations in the poem, and ranked Wordsworth, all in all, above Byron.[96] Time has agreed with Keats.

XIII. THE SAGE OF HIGHGATE: 1816–34

In April, 1816, Coleridge, nearing physical and mental collapse at the age of forty-three, was received as a patient by Dr. James Gillman, of Highgate, London. Coleridge was then consuming a pint of laudanum per day. Southey, about this time, described him as "half as big as the house"; his frame loose and bent; his face pale, round, and flabby; his breath short; his hands so shaky that he could hardly bring a glass to his lips.[97] He had some loyal friends, like Lamb, De Quincey, and Crabb Robinson, but he rarely saw his wife or children, lived mostly on pensions or gifts, and was losing his last hold on life. Perhaps the young physician had heard that Byron and Walter Scott had ranked this broken man as England's greatest man of letters;[98] in any case he saw that Coleridge could be saved only by constant and professional surveillance and care. With the consent of his wife, Dr. Gillman took Coleridge into his home, fed him, treated him, comforted and cured him, and kept him till death.

The recovery of Coleridge's mind was astonishing. The doctor so marveled at the extent of his patient's knowledge, the wealth of his ideas, and the brilliance of his conversation that he opened his doors to a growing circle of old and young men to whom the "damaged archangel" talked at random, seldom with full clarity or logical order, but with unfailing wit, zest, and effect. Fragments of these conversations, preserved as *Table Talk*, still strike a spark: "Every man is born an Aristotelian or a Platonist."

"Either we have an immortal soul, or we have not. If we have not we are beasts; the first and wisest of beasts, it may be, but still true beasts."[99]

He was not content to be among the first and wisest of beasts. As he neared death he sought comfort in religion, and, as if to make sure of his bargain, embraced it in its most orthodox available form, the Church of England, as the pillar of English stability and morality; and hopefully he wished it everlasting life: *Esto perpetua!* His essay *On the Constitution of the Church and the State* (1830) presented them as two mutually necessary forms of national unity, each protecting and helping the other.[100] He (and Wordsworth) opposed the political emancipation of British Catholics, on the ground that the growth of "popery" would endanger the state by developing a conflict of loyalties between patriotism and religion.

He took full advantage of the conservatism natural to old age. In 1818 he had supported Robert Owen and Sir Robert Peel in their campaigns for restrictions on child labor, but in 1831 he opposed the Reform Bill that was to break the hold of the Tories upon Parliament. He advised against the abolition of West Indian slavery.[101] He who, more than most philosophers, had studied and supported science, rejected the idea of evolution, preferring "the history I find in my Bible."[102] In the end his capacious and far-reaching intellect yielded to ailments of body and will, and he fell into a timid fear of every innovation in politics or belief.

He lacked the steady patience to achieve constructive unity in his work. In the *Biographia Literaria* (1817), he had announced his intention to write an *opus magnum*—the *Logosophia*—that would be the sum, summit, and reconciliation of science, philosophy, and religion; but all that flesh and soul would let him contribute to that enterprise was a medley of fragments labored, chaotic, and obscure. To such a pass had come the mind that De Quincey had described as "the most capacious, . . . subtlest, and most comprehensive . . . that has yet existed among men."[103]

In July, 1834, Coleridge began his adieus to life. "I am dying, but without expectation of a speedy release. . . . Hooker wished to live to finish his Ecclesiastical Polity,—so I own I wish life and strength had been spared me to complete my Philosophy. For, as God hears me, the originating, continuing, and sustaining wish and design in my heart were to exalt the glory of his name; and, which is the same thing in other words, to promote the improvement of mankind. But *visum aliter Deo* [God saw otherwise], and his will be done."[104] Coleridge died on July 25, 1834, aged sixty-two. Wordsworth was shaken by the passing of "the most wonderful man he had ever known"; and Lamb, best friend of all, said, "His great and dear spirit haunts me."[105]

XIV. ON THE FRINGE

Charles Lamb (1775–1834) was one of several keen spirits whose principal publications place them after 1815, but who in our period entered intimately into the lives of the Lake Poets. Lamb was the closest of Coleridge's London friends. They had known each other as schoolboys at Christ's Hospital. There Lamb's incurable stammering kept him from scholastic honors. He left school at fourteen to support himself; at seventeen he became an accountant in the East India House; and he remained there until he was retired on a pension at the age of fifty.

There was a strain of insanity in his heritage; he himself spent six weeks in an asylum (1795–96); and in 1796 his sister Mary Ann (1764–1847), in an insane mania, killed their mother. For several periods Mary had been confined, but for the most part Lamb, renouncing marriage, had her live with him till his death. She recovered sufficiently to collaborate with him in writing *Tales from Shakespeare* (1807). His own unique product was the *Essays of Elia* (1820–25), whose genial style, modesty, and art revealed one of the most lovable characters in that not too gracious age.

In June, 1797, still shaken by the tragedy of the previous year, he accepted an invitation from Coleridge to visit him at Nether Stowey. As a stammerer he hardly dared talk when he found himself before two poets—Wordsworth and Coleridge—in rival volubility. Five years later he and his sister visited the Coleridge family in Greta Hall. "He received us with all the hospitality in the world."[106] Though he himself remained a skeptic to the end, Lamb never allowed Coleridge's theological diversions to interfere with an affection and an admiration that withstood every discouragement.

The National Portrait Gallery contains a tender portrait of Lamb by his friend William Hazlitt (1778–1830), the liveliest and sharpest literary critic of the time. Hazlitt visited Coleridge in 1798, and again, at Greta Hall, in 1803. On the second occasion Wordsworth joined them, and the three set about determining whether God existed. William Paley, as we have seen, had recently defended the affirmative with the argument from design; Hazlitt countered it; Wordsworth took a middle ground, affirming God not as external to the universe and guiding it from without, but as inherent in it as its life and mind. On that visit Hazlitt incurred the wrath of the neighbors by seducing a schoolgirl. Fearing arrest or worse, he fled to Grasmere, where Wordsworth gave him a night's lodging and, the next morning, advanced him funds to pay coach fare to London.

When Coleridge and Wordsworth turned against the Revolution, and denounced Napoleon in fervent verse, Hazlitt set them down as turncoats, and wrote a four-volume *Life of Napoleon Buonaparte* (1828–30) from Napoleon's point of view. Meanwhile he had made his mark as a critic with his lectures (1820) on the Elizabethan drama, and his contemporary portraits in *The Spirit of the Age* (1825); Wordsworth did not enjoy its satirical attack on the "peasant school" in literature.[107]

The aging poet liked better Thomas De Quincey (1785–1859), who offered him a continuo of admiration. Thomas was a genius in his own right, who was to alarm Britain in 1821 with *Confessions of an English*

Opium Eater. Beginning as a prodigy, speaking classic Greek readily at fifteen, running away from school and Oxford as too slow for his pace, he must have surprised himself by his delight with the unpretentious simplicity of the *Lyrical Ballads*. In May, 1803, he wrote to Wordsworth such a letter as might have turned the solitary poet's head:

> I have no other motive in soliciting your friendship than what (I should think) every man who has read and felt the "Lyrical Ballads" must have in common with me. The whole aggregate of pleasure I have received from eight or nine other poets that I have been able to find since the world began falls infinitely short of what these two enchanting volumes have singly afforded me;—that your name is with me forever linked to the lovely scenes of nature. . . . What claim can I urge to a fellowship with such a society as yours, beaming (as it does) with genius so wild and so magnificent?

He added that Wordsworth would never find anyone "more ready . . . to sacrifice even his life whenever it would have a chance of promoting your interest and happiness."

Wordsworth's reply was a model of kindly instruction. "My friendship," he wrote, "is not in my power to give; this is a gift which no man can make. . . . A sound and healthy friendship is the growth of time and circumstance; it will spring up like a wildflower when these favour, and when they do not it is in vain to look for it." He tried to deter the youth from seeking a regular correspondence: "I am the most lazy and impotent letter writer in the world." But he added: "I shall indeed be very happy to see you at Grasmere."[108]

Despite his ardor, De Quincey let three years pass before accepting the invitation. Then, reaching sight of Wordsworth's cottage, he lost courage, and, like the fabled pilgrim nearing Rome, turned back as unworthy. But late in 1807, at Bristol, Coleridge accepted his offer to escort Mrs. Coleridge and her children to Keswick. On the way she stopped with him at Dove Cottage, and now, at last, De Quincey saw Wordsworth "plain," as Browning was soon to see Shelley. "Like a flash of lightning I saw the figure emerge of a tallish man, who held out his hand and saluted me with most cordial expressions of welcome."[109]

XV. SOUTHEY: 1803–43

Meanwhile, at Greta Hall and London, Southey, with his industrious but uninspired pen, supported his wife Edith, his five daughters (born between 1804 and 1812), and a fondly idolized son who died in 1816 at the age of ten. After Coleridge's passage to Malta Southey took over responsibility for Mrs. Coleridge and her children. Even Wordsworth sometimes leaned on him: when William's brother John was lost at sea (1805) the news threw the Grasmere household into such grief that Wordsworth sent a message to Southey begging him to come down and help him comfort Dorothy and Mary. He came, and "he was so tender and kind," Dorothy wrote, "that I loved him at once; he wept with us in our sorrow, and for that cause I think I must always love him."[110]

Vanity misled him for a while; he composed epic after epic, each a failure; the times were their own epic. He resigned himself to prose, and fared better. In 1807 he published *Letters from England: By Don Manuel Alvarez Espriella*, and put into the mouth of this imaginary Spaniard a strong denunciation of child labor and other conditions in British factories. E.g.,

> I ventured to inquire concerning the morals of the people who were trained up in this monstrous manner, and found . . . that in consequence of herding together such numbers of both sexes, utterly uninstructed in the commonest principles of religion and morality, they were as debauched and profligate as human beings under the influence of such circumstances must inevitably be; the men drunken, the women dissolute; that however high the wages they earned, they were too improvident ever to lay by for a time of need; and that, though the parish was not at the expense of maintaining them as children, it had to provide for them in diseases induced by their mode of life, or in premature disability or old age.[111]

The aristocrat's conclusion on the English economy: "In commerce, even more than in war, both men and beasts are considered mainly as machines, and sacrificed with even less compunction."[112]

Southey soon found that he could not live by his pen, much less support his dependents, especially in time of war, unless he adopted a more conservative line. The change was smoothed by a governmental pension of one hundred sixty pounds a year (1807), and an invitation to contribute articles regularly to the Tory *Quarterly Review*. In 1813 he raised his status both as an author and as a patriot by issuing his *Life of Nelson*—a clear and vivid narrative based on laborious research, and written in an eighteenth-century style so simple, clear, and smooth that it carries the reader along despite obtrusions of the writer's natural bias in favor of his hero and his country. Nelson's infatuation with Emma Hamilton is reduced from a decade to a paragraph.

Byron, Shelley, and Hazlitt mourned when Southey seemed to lower the prestige of poetry by accepting the laureateship of England. This distinction had fallen in prestige when Pitt (1790) gave it to Henry Pye, an obscure justice of the peace. At Pye's death (1813) the government offered the post to Walter Scott, who refused it and recommended Southey as a deserving laborer. Southey accepted it, and was rewarded by an increase of his pension to three hundred pounds a year. Wordsworth, who should have had the appointment, remarked handsomely: "Southey has a little world dependent on his industry."[113]

Byron, who was later to condemn Southey to obloquy and oblivion, spoke well of him after a meeting with him at Holland House in September, 1813: "The best-looking bard I have seen in some time."[114] And to Thomas Moore: "To have that poet's head and shoulders I would almost have written his sapphics. He is certainly a prepossessing person to look at, a man of talent. . . . His manners are mild. . . . His prose is perfect."[115] But Southey's evident anxiety to please the holders of wealth or power brought Byron into open war against him in 1818. The unkindest cut of all came when a group of rebels secured the manuscript of Southey's radical drama *Wat Tyler* (which he had written in 1794 and left unprinted), and published it with joy in 1817.

Southey retired to Greta Hall, his library, and his wife. She had more than once neared insanity; in 1834 her mind gave way, and in 1837 she died. Southey himself gave up the battle in 1843; and then, by almost universal consent, and over his own protests, Wordsworth was made poet laureate.

XVI. WORDSWORTH EPILOGUE: 1815–50

Poetry belongs to youth, and Wordsworth, living eighty years, died as a poet about 1807, when, aged thirty-seven, he composed *The White Doe of Rylstone*. By that time Walter Scott had published *The Lay of the Last Minstrel* (1805); Wordsworth envied its flowing style, and used the meter for his own "lay"—a narrative ballad about the religious wars of north England in the twelfth year of Elizabeth I. Almost an entire family—father and eight sons—was wiped out in one campaign. Emily, the surviving sister, spends the rest of her life in mourning; a white doe comes daily to comfort her, and it accompanies her in her Sabbath visits to the tomb of the youngest brother in Bolton churchyard. When Emily dies the doe continues, alone, those weekly trips from Rylstone to Bolton, and lies quietly beside the grave till the Sabbath service in the church is over, then quietly returns, through woods and streams, to its Rylstone haunts. It is a pretty legend, gracefully and melodiously told.

This was the last triumph of Wordsworth's art. Aside from some sonnets, which he emitted at the slightest provocation, he did no more for poetry. Physically fifty, he looked every inch a sage, tall and stately, wrapped in warm garments against the incalculable cold, hair receding and carelessly tangled, head bent, eyes grave in contemplation, as of one who, having seen Shelley and Byron pass from infancy through ecstasy to death, now calmly awaited his turn, confident that he would leave a monument more lasting than passionate utopias or sardonic rhymes.

He had the defects of his virtues, for it takes much egotism to preach to mankind. "Milton is his greatest idol," wrote Hazlitt, "and he sometimes dared to compare himself with him."[116] He accepted praise as unavoidable, and resented criticism as ingratitude. He loved to recite his own poetry, as was slyly noted by Emerson, who visited him in 1833; but he had said, in a preface of 1815, that his poems were meant to be read aloud; and in fact they were music as well as meaning, and a lyric deserves a lyre.

Of course he became conservative as he aged; it was a privilege—perhaps a duty—of years; and if Byron and Shelley did not recognize this it may have been because they died in the dementia praecox of youth. The deterioration of the French Revolution from constitution to dissolution gave Wordsworth some excuse for caution; and the brutality of the Industrial Revolution seemed to justify his feeling that something wholesome and beautiful had passed from England with the replacement of the sturdy yeomanry by the factory "hand." In 1805 and later, by gift or purchase, he had become the owner of several modest properties; and as a landholder he readily sympathized with the "landed interest" as the cement of economic order and social stability. Hence he opposed the reform movement as a plan of the manufacturers to reduce the cost of corn, and therefore of labor, by repealing those "Corn Laws" that impeded, with high tariff dues, the import of foreign grain.

He, who had been through many years an admirer of Godwin, now rejected Godwin's free individualism on the ground that individuals can survive only through a communal unity maintained by general respect for tradition, property, and law. After 1815 he supported the government in all its repressive measures, and was branded as an apostate from the cause of liberty. He held his ground, and countered with his final diagnosis of the age: "The world is running mad with its notion that its evils are to be relieved by political changes, political remedies, political nostrums, whereas the great evils—civilization, bondage, misery—lie deep in the heart, and nothing but virtue and religion can remove them."[117]

So he appealed to the English people to support the Church of England. He versified some English history in forty-seven "Ecclesiastical Sonnets" (1821), which bore us with their forgotten heroes and sometimes surprise us by their excellence. According to Henry Crabb Robinson, "Wordsworth said he would shed his blood, if necessary, to defend the Established Church. Nor was he disconcerted by a laugh raised against him on account of his having before confessed that he knew not when he had been in a church in his own country."[118]

We do not find that he sought comfort in religion when the world of love around him began to crumble. In 1829 Dorothy suffered a severe attack of stone, which permanently weakened her health and spirit. Further attacks damaged her nervous system; after 1835 she lost the use of her legs, and her memory failed except for events in the distant past, and for her brother's poems, which she could still recite. For the next twenty years she remained in the household as helpless and quietly insane, sitting silent in her chair near the fire, and waiting patiently for death. In 1835 Sara Hutchinson died, and Wordsworth was left with his wife Mary to care for his sister and his children. In 1837 he had still sufficient fortitude to undertake, with the omnipresent Robinson, a six months' tour of France and Italy. In Paris he met again Annette Vallon and his daughter Caroline, now securely wed.

He died on April 23, 1850, and was buried among his neighbors in Grasmere churchyard. Dorothy lingered five years more, patiently tended by

Mary, who was now nearly blind. Mary herself died in 1859, aged eighty-nine, after a long life of duties faithfully performed. There must have been something in Wordsworth greater than his poetry to have won the lasting love of such women. They too, and their like in a million homes, should be remembered as part of the picture of England.

CHAPTER XXII

The Rebel Poets

1788–1824[*]

I. THE TARNISHED STRAIN: 1066–1809

TO understand Byron we should have to know with some fullness the history and character of the ancestors whose blood ran like an intermittent fever in his veins. Some of that blood, like his name, may have come from France, where several Birons were remembered by history; Byron himself proudly mentioned, in *Don Juan* (Canto x, line 36), a supposed progenitor, Radulfus de Burun, as having come over to England with William the Conqueror. In the twelfth century the Buruns became Byrons. A Sir John Byron served Henry VIII so well that, on the dissolution of the monasteries, the King transferred to him, for a nominal sum, the abbey (founded about 1170) and lands of "the late Monastery and Priory of Newstede . . . within our County of Nottingham."[1] A succession of baronial Byrons thereafter played minor parts in English history, supporting the Stuart kings, following Charles II into exile, forfeiting Newstead Abbey, regaining it at the Restoration.

The poet's great-uncle William, the fifth Lord Byron (1722–98), handsome and reckless, served in the Navy; earned the name "Wicked Lord" by living as a rake in the Abbey; squandered much of his wealth; killed his relative William Chaworth in an impromptu duel in a darkened room of a tavern; was sent to the Tower on a charge of murder; was tried by the House of Lords (1765), was declared "not guilty of murder, but guilty of manslaughter"; retired to the Abbey, and lived there in somber isolation till his death.

His brother John Byron (1723–86) became a midshipman, suffered shipwreck, and published a *Narrative* from which his grandson took the vivid shipwreck scene in *Don Juan*. As commander of the *Dolphin* John circumnavigated the globe. Finally he retired to a home in west England, where he was known as "the Nautical Lover" because he had a wife or a mistress in every port.

His eldest son, Captain John Byron (1756–91), father of the poet, crowded so many deviltries into his thirty-five years that he was called "Mad Jack." After service in the American colonies he spent some time in

---

[*] This chapter is, throughout, indebted to Leslie Marchand's *Byron* (3v., New York: Knopf, 1957), a masterpiece of impartial scholarship.

London, making his mistresses pay his debts. In 1778 he eloped with the Marchioness of Carmarthen; her husband the Marquess divorced her, Captain Byron married her and enjoyed her income. She bore him three children, of whom one, Augusta Leigh, became the poet's half sister and sometimes mistress.

In 1784 the former Lady Carmarthen died. A year later the dashing widower married a Scotch girl of twenty years and £23,000—Catherine Gordon of Gight, plain but fiercely proud, with a pedigree going back to James I of Scotland. When she bore the poet she gave him another line of distinguished and hectic heredity: French in origin, stormy in character, with a turn for robbery, murder, and feud. The mother herself was a medley of wild love and hate. These she spent upon her husband, who squandered her fortune and then deserted her; and then upon her only son, whom she pampered with affection, bruised with discipline, and alienated with such epithets as "lame brat." Said Childe Harold (i.e., Byron), "I should have known what fruit would spring from such a seed."[2]

George Gordon Byron was born in London January 22, 1788. His right foot, at birth, was deformed by an inward turn of the sole and an upward tension of the heel. The deformity might have been cured by daily manipulation of the foot; but the mother had neither the patience nor the hardihood for a procedure that would have seemed to the child intentionally cruel; nor were the physicians inclined to recommend it. By the age of eight the misshapen foot had so far improved that the boy could wear a common shoe over an inner shoe designed to balance and diminish the distortion. In daily life and in sports he became agile on his feet, but he could not cross a drawing room without painful consciousness of his limp. In youth he flared up at any mention of his handicap. It shared in sharpening his sensitivity and temper; but it probably spurred him on to victories—in swimming, courtship, and poetry—that might divert attention from his deformity.

In 1789 the mother moved with her child to Aberdeen. A year later her husband fled to France, where he died in 1791, dissolute and destitute. Left with only a fragment of her fortune, Mrs. Byron did her best to give her son an education fit for a lord. She described him fondly, when he was six, "as a fine boy, and walks and runs as well as any other child."[3] At seven he entered Aberdeen Grammar School, where he received a good grounding in Latin. Through further education and much travel in Greece, Asia Minor, and Italy, he became so familiar with Latin and Greek literature that only an accomplished scholar in classical antiquity can understand the quotations and historical allusions that emerge through the playfulness of *Don Juan*. Byron loved history—cleansed of nationalism and mythology—as the only truth about man; Shelley ignored it, being wedded to an ideal uncomfortable with history.

In 1798 Byron's great-uncle, "the Wicked Lord," died at Newstead, leaving the ten-year-old boy his baronial title, the Abbey, his 3,200 acres, and his debts. These were so profuse that only enough income remained to enable the widow to move from Aberdeen to the Abbey, and live there in middle-class comfort. She sent her boy to a school at Dulwich, and, in 1801, to the famous "public" school at Harrow, eleven miles from London. There he resisted the "fagging" services usually required of the younger by the older students; and when he himself, as an upper-class man, used a "fag," it was with a quite revolutionary courtesy. He was a troublesome pupil, disrupted discipline, committed pranks, and neglected the studies assigned; but he did much reading, often of good books, and rising to Bacon, Locke, Hume, and Berkeley. Apparently he lost his religious faith, for a fellow student called him a "damned atheist."[4]

At seventeen he entered Trinity College, Cambridge. There he took expensive quarters, with servants, a dog, and a bear as room-mates. He patronized the local prostitutes and physicians, and occasionally sought more distinguished service in London. On a vacation at Brighton (1808) he kept with him a girl disguised as a boy; but, with due impartiality, he developed at Cambridge what he described as "a violent, though *pure*, love and passion" for a handsome youth.[5] Also, by his exuberance, generosity, and charm, he made several lasting friendships; best of all with John Cam Hobhouse, who, almost two years his senior, contributed some momentary sense and caution to Byron's often lawless life. For the young poet seemed bent on ruining himself with a moral freedom that would not wait for intelligence to replace the prohibitions of a lost religious faith.

In June, 1807, aged nineteen, he published a volume of poems—*Hours of Idleness by George Gordon, Lord Byron, a Minor*. He went to London to arrange for favorable notices of the book. The *Edinburgh Review* for January, 1808, greeted it with sarcastic comments on the title as a pose, and on the signature as an excuse; why had not the adolescent peer waited a decent time for some measure of maturity?

He reached his majority on January 22, 1809. He paid off the more pressing of his debts, and incurred more by gambling. He took his seat in the House of Lords, and suffered under the silence recommended to novices; but three days later he blasted the critics of his book in *English Bards and Scotch Reviewers*, a clever and slashing satire imitating, and almost rivaling, Pope's *Dunciad*. He ridiculed the sentimental Romantic movement (of which he was soon to be a leader and a god), and called for a return to the masculine vigor and classic style of England's Augustan Age:

> Thou shalt believe in Milton, Dryden, Pope;
>   Thou shalt not set up Wordsworth, Coleridge, Southey. . . .
> We learn from Horace, "Homer sometimes sleeps";
>   We feel, without him, Wordsworth sometimes wakes.[6]

Then, after taking his M.A. degree at Cambridge, befriending pugilists, practicing fencing, and taking an additional course in London's night life, he sailed with Hobhouse, July 2, 1809, for Lisbon and points east.

II. THE GRAND TOUR: BYRON, 1809–11

It was not traditionally grand: England was at war, and Napoleon controlled France, Belgium, Holland, Germany, and Italy; so Byron spent most of his two-year trip in Albania, Greece, and Turkey, with considerable effect on his politics, his views of women and marriage, and his death. He left £13,000 of debts behind him, and took four servants with him. He found Lisbon impoverished even beyond wont by the Peninsular War; every native seemed hostile, and Byron carried two pistols wherever he went. His party moved on horseback to Seville and Cádiz, and thence by a British frigate to Gibraltar (where he released all of his servants except his accustomed valet, William Fletcher), and on to Malta. There (September 1–18, 1809) he fell in love with Mrs. Spencer Smith, and so conspicuously that a British captain commented on his precipitance. Byron sent him a challenge, with an added flourish: "As the vessel on which I am to embark must sail with the first change of wind, the sooner our business is arranged, the better. Tomorrow at six will be the best hour." The captain sent his regrets.

On September 19 Byron and Hobhouse left Malta on the brig *Spider*. A week's sail brought them to Patras. There they went on shore briefly, if only to set foot on Greek soil; but on the same evening they reboarded the *Spider* and continued past Missolonghi and Penelope's Ithaca, and debarked at Preveza, near the Actium so fatal to Anthony and Cleopatra. Thence they moved north on horseback through Epirus and into Albania, from whose capital the terrible Turk, Ali Pasha, ruled Albania and Epirus with sword and style. He accorded Byron all the honors judiciously due to a British lord; for (he told the poet) he knew him to be of aristocratic lineage by his small hands and ears.

On October 23 Byron and company turned back, and on the 27th they reached Janina, capital of Epirus. There he began to record his impressions of his tour in the autobiographical *Childe Harold's Pilgrimage*. On November 3 the party traveled south through the modern Aetolia, escorted (by order of the Pasha) by a band of Albanian mercenaries each noted for his skill in murder and robbery. They fell in love with their new master, partly because he seemed fearless of death. When Byron came down with a fever they threatened to kill the doctor if his patient died; the doctor ran away, and Byron recovered. On November 21 the party took ship from Missolonghi to Patras; thence, with a new guard, they proceeded on horseback through the Peloponnesus and Attica, saw Delphi and Thebes, and entered Athens on Christmas Day of 1809.

It must have been for the two pilgrims a day of mingled joy and gloom. The evidences of ancient grandeur and modern decay, and the apparently humble acceptance of Turkish rule by a once proud people now reduced from strength to subtlety, and content with the business and gossip of the day, amused Hobhouse but saddened Byron, who incarnated the spirit of independence and the pride of race. The poet made Childe Harold cry out for revolt, and thought of how he might help these heirs of greatness to be free.

In any case their women were beautiful, with their dark, inflammatory eyes and their yielding grace. Byron and Hobhouse were housed and served by the widow Macri, who had three daughters, all of them under fifteen. The young roué learned to feel for them an affection that rejoiced in their innocence. Apparently it was Theresa, aged twelve, who taught him the melodious greeting *Zoé mou sas agapo*—"Life of my life, I love you." Around that tender phrase he wrote his famous song: "Maid of Athens, ere we part, / Give, oh give me back my heart!"

On January 19, 1810, Byron and Hobhouse set out, with a servant and a guide, and two men to care for the horses, to visit one of the most inspiring sights in Greece. The ride took them four days, but the end justified the means: they came in sight of the surviving columns of a temple to Poseidon raised, in the heroic past, on Sunium Promontorium (Cape Colonna) to tell mariners that they had sighted Greece. It was in remembering that shattered perfection, and the seemingly smooth Aegean far below, that Byron composed "The Isle of Greece," later inserted into the third canto of *Don Juan*. From Sunium it was but a day's ride to Marathon, where the poet was moved with feelings that soon took form in famous lines:

> The mountains look on Marathon,
>   And Marathon looks on the sea;
> And musing there an hour alone,
>   I dreamed that Greece might still be free;
> For standing on the Persians' grave
>   I could not deem myself a slave.

On March 5 Byron and Hobhouse left Athens on an English vessel, the *Pylades*, for Smyrna. Forced to wait there for a month, the poet completed Canto II of *Childe Harold*. A side trip of three days to Ephesus revealed the ruins of a city that had lived through three zeniths—Greek, Christian, and Mohammedan. "The decay of three religions," Hobhouse remarked, "is there presented to one view."[7]

On April 11 they took passage on the frigate *Salsette* for Constantinople. Contrary winds and diplomatic obstructions kept the vessel anchored for a fortnight at the Asiatic side of the Dardanelles. Byron and Hobhouse trod the Troad plain, hoping that it covered Homer's Ilium, but Schliemann had not yet been born. On April 15 Byron and an English naval officer, Lieutenant William Ekenhead, had themselves conveyed across the Hellespont to the European side, and then tried to swim back; but the strength of the current and the coldness of the water were too much for them. On May 3 they tried again, crossing from Sestos in European Turkey to Abydos in Asia Minor; Ekenhead accomplished the feat in sixty-five minutes, Byron in seventy. At that point the channel is one mile wide, but the current forced the new Leanders to swim over four miles.[8]

The tourists reached Constantinople on May 12, admired the mosques, and left on July 14. On the 17th their vessel anchored in the harbor of Zea on the island of Keos, where they parted; Hobhouse continued to London, Byron and Fletcher changed to a boat bound for Patras. Again they crossed overland to Athens. There Byron resumed his long inquiry into feminine differences; he boasted of his conquests, contracted gonorrhea, and adopted melancholy as a career. On November 26 he wrote to Hobhouse: "I have now seen the world. . . . I have tested all sorts of pleasure; . . . I have nothing more to hope, and may begin to consider the most eligible way of walking out of it. . . . I wish I could find some of Socrates' Hemlock."[9] In January, 1811, he took rooms for himself and some servants in a Capuchin monastery at the foot of the Acropolis, and dreamt of monastic peace.

On April 22 he left Athens for the last time, stayed a month in Malta, and went on to England. He reached it on July 14, two years and twelve days after leaving it. While busy renewing contacts in London he received news that his mother had died, aged forty-six. He rushed up to Newstead Abbey, and spent a night sitting in the dark beside her corpse. When a maid begged him to retire to his room, he refused, saying, "I had but one friend in the world, and she is gone!" He had said the same thing in an epitaph for his Newfoundland dog Boatswain, who had died in November, 1808, and had been buried in the Abbey garden vault:

> To mark a friend's remains these stones arise;
> I never had but one,—and here he lies.

In August, 1811, Byron drew up a will entailing the Abbey to his cousin George Byron, specifying gifts for his servants, and leaving directions for his burial: "I desire that my body may be buried in the vault of the garden of Newstead, without any ceremony or burial service whatever, and that no inscription, save my name and age, be written on the tomb tablet; and it is my will that my faithful dog may not be removed from the said vault."[10] Having arranged his death, he proceeded to conquer London.

III. THE LION OF LONDON: BYRON, 1811–14

He made friends readily, for he was attractive in person and manners, fascinating in conversation, widely informed in literature and history, and more faithful to his friends than to his mistresses. He took rooms at 8 St. James's Street, where he welcomed Thomas Moore, Thomas Campbell, Samuel Rogers, Hobhouse . . . ; and they welcomed him in turn. Through Rogers and Moore he entered the famous circle at Holland House. There he met Richard Brinsley Sheridan, who was declining in political influence, but had not lost his conversational flair. "When he talked," Byron recalled, "we listened, without one yawn, from six till one in the morning. . . . Poor fellow! he got drunk very thoroughly and very soon. It occasionally fell to my lot to convey him home."[11]

Stimulated by these Whiggish wits, Byron took up the cause of the "Luddite" frame-breakers of Nottinghamshire, his own county. On February 20, 1812, the Commons passed a bill condemning any captured frame-breaker to death. The measure moved to the House of Lords, and on February 27 Byron rose to speak against it. He had written his address in advance, in excellent English, and he began in a tone of modesty expected of a maiden speech. He admitted that some workers had been guilty of violence involving considerable losses to property, and that the shattered machines might in the long run have been a boon to the national economy; but meanwhile they had thrown out of work hundreds of men who had through time and labor acquired a skill suddenly made useless to them in supporting their families; they were now reduced to poverty and charity, and their despair and bitterness could be gauged from their violence. As he proceeded the young orator lost caution and support by attacking the war as the source of unprecedented misery among English laborers. The Lords frowned, and passed the bill. On April 21 Byron made a second speech, denouncing British rule in Ireland, and called for the emancipation of Catholics throughout the British Empire; the Lords praised his eloquence, rejected his plea, and set him down as a political innocent useless to his party. He abandoned politics, and decided to plead his case through poetry.

Twelve days after his maiden speech the first two cantos of *Childe Harold's Pilgrimage* were offered to the public. Their almost unprecedented success— the first edition (five hundred copies) sold out in three days—encouraged the author to believe that he had found a medium more enduring than forensic speech. Now he made the exuberant remark "I awoke one morning and found myself famous."[12] Even his old enemies at the *Edinburgh Review* praised him, and, in gratitude, he sent an apology to Jeffrey for having bruised him in *English Bards and Scotch Reviewers*.

Almost every door was now opened to him; almost every prominent hostess invited him; a dozen women, warming to his handsome face, fluttered about him, hoping to snare the young lion in their varied charms. They were not repelled by his reputation for sexual voracity, and his lordly title made him seem a precious prize to those who did not know his debts. He enjoyed their attentions, being readily excited by their mysterious radiation. "There is," he said, 'something to me very softening in the presence of a woman—some strange influence, even if one is not in love with them—which I cannot account for, having no very high opinion of the sex."[13] Despite all his skeptical intelligence he succumbed again and again to the magnet that every healthy woman is to any healthy man.

One of his first conquerors was Lady Caroline Lamb (1785–1828). Daughter of the third Earl of Bessborough, she married, at twenty, William Lamb, second son of Lord and Lady Melbourne. After reading *Childe Harold's Pilgrimage* she resolved to meet the author; but on being presented to him she took fright and quickly turned away from him as "dangerous to know." The rejection stimulated him; when they met again "he begged permission to see me." He came. She was three years his senior and already a mother; but she made herself pleasant and fragrant, and she was heiress to a great fortune. He came again, almost every day. Her husband, busy with his own affairs, accepted him as the British equivalent of an Italian *cavaliere servente*. She grew more and more attracted to him; went to his rooms, openly or dressed as a page; she wrote him passionately amorous letters. For a time his temperature rose with hers, until he proposed to elope with her;[14] but when her mother and her husband took her off to Ireland (September, 1812), he readily resigned himself, and was soon entangled in a liaison with Lady Oxford.

Amid such exaltations Byron kept some stability by writing rapidly, in fluent verse, a series of Oriental tales of adventure, violence, and love. They made no pretense to greatness; they were romantic imaginations, echoing the poet's travels in Albania, Epirus, and Greece; they required little thought from the author, and none from the reader, and sold excitingly well. First came *The Giaour*, in March, 1813; soon, in December, *The Bride of Abydos*, of which six thousand copies were bought in a month; better still, *The Corsair* (January, 1814), which shattered all precedents by selling ten thousand copies on the day of its publication; then *Lara* (1815) and *The Siege of Corinth* (1816). The publisher gathered his guineas, and offered a share to Byron, who, proud as a lord, refused to take payment for his poems.

Even while composing these tales of dashing outlaws, the author was wearying of his lawless life. He could not go on philandering until he had worn out his health, his welcome, and his funds. He and Hobhouse had vowed to shun marriage as a prison of the spirit as well as the flesh; now he wondered whether marriage might not be a necessary mooring for desires which, let loose, could derange not only the individual but society itself. He felt that he might be persuaded to surrender his freedom for stability and calm, or for a surer income than his crumbling Abbey could provide.

Annabella Milbanke seemed to meet all his requirements. She had beauty and education, and was the only child of a substantial fortune. When he first met her, March 25, 1812, at the home of her aunt, Lady Melbourne, he was favorably impressed: "Her features were small and feminine, though not regular. She had the fairest skin imaginable. Her figure was perfect for her height, and there was a simplicity, a retired modesty about her, . . . that interested me exceedingly."[15] He did not speak to her, for each waited for the other to take the initiative. But she too was interested, for in her diary and letters she spent some time analyzing his character: "Acrimony of spirit, . . . dissimulant, the violence of its scorn. . . . Sincere and independent. . . . It is said that he is an infidel, and I think it probable from the general character of his mind. His poem [*Childe Harold*] sufficiently proves that he can feel nobly, but he has discouraged his own goodness."[16] This was a perceptive phrase; perhaps the thought came to her how interesting, though dangerous, it would be to try to save this sensitive man from his senses, to release his shy virtues, and, incidentally, to capture the young lion of London from all those women who were enthralled by his scandalous reputation.

Months passed, during which Lady Caroline Lamb held the stage. Then

that flame was cooled by the Irish Channel; and on September 13, 1812, Byron wrote to Lady Melbourne a strange letter that opened a fatal direction
in his life: "I was, am, and shall be, I fear, attached to . . . one to whom I
never said much, but have never lost sight of; . . . one whom I wished to
marry, had not this [Lamb] affair intervened. . . . The woman I mean is
Miss Milbanke. . . . I never saw a woman whom I esteemed so much."[17] Lady
Melbourne, well pleased, told her niece of Byron's confession, and asked
would she consider a proposal. On October 12 Miss Milbanke sent a reply
worthy of Talleyrand:

> Believing that he never will be the object of that strong affection which
> would make me happy in domestic life, I should wrong him by any measure
> that might, even indirectly, confirm his present impressions. From my limited
> observation of his conduct, I am predisposed to believe your strong testimony
> in his favour, and I willingly attribute it more to the defect of my own feelings
> than of his character, that I am not inclined to return his attachment. After
> this statement, which I make with real sorrow from the idea of its giving pain,
> I must leave our future intercourse to his judgement. I can have no reason for
> withdrawing from an acquaintance that does me honour and is capable of im-
> parting so much rational pleasure, except the fear of involuntarily deceiving
> him.[18]

Byron, who had not felt any basic urge toward this learned and conscientious lady, took the refusal amiably, and readily found comfort in the
arms of the Countess of Oxford, then of Lady Frances Webster, and, concurrently, of his half sister Augusta Leigh. Born in 1783, she was her half
brother's elder by five years. She had now (1813) been six years married to
her first cousin, Colonel George Leigh, and had three children. At this juncture she came to London from her home in Six Mile Bottom, Cambridgeshire,
to ask Byron's financial help in difficulties caused by her husband's losses, and
prolonged absences, at racetracks. Byron could not give her much, for his
income was precarious, but he entertained her with genial conversation, and
discovered that she was a woman.

She was thirty; not quite the *femme de trente ans* that Balzac praised, for
she lacked intellectual background and vivacity; but she was affectionate,
accommodating, perhaps a bit awed by her brother's fame, and inclined to
give him whatever she could command. Her long separation from him,
added to her husband's neglect, left her emotionally free. Byron, who had
rashly discarded any moral taboo that had not met the test of his young reason, wondered why he should not mate with his sister, as the Pharaohs had
done. Later developments indicate that he now, or soon, had sexual relations
with Augusta.[19] In August of this year 1813 he thought of taking her with
him on a Mediterranean voyage.[20] That plan fell through, but in January he
took her to Newstead Abbey. When, on April 15, 1814, Augusta gave birth
to a daughter, Byron wrote to Lady Melbourne that "if it is an ape, that
must be my fault"; the child herself, Medora Leigh, came to believe herself
his daughter.[21] In May he sent Augusta three thousand pounds to clear her
husband's debts. In July he was with her in Hastings. In August he took her
to his Abbey.

While he was becoming more and more deeply involved with his half sister, Miss Milbanke was sending him letters whose rising cordiality prompted him to write in his journal under December 1, 1813:

> Yesterday a very pretty letter from Annabella, which I answered. What an odd situation and friendship is ours!—without one spark of love on either side. . . . She is a very superior woman, and very little spoiled, which is strange in an heiress—a girl of twenty—a peeress that is to be, in her own right—an only child, and a *savante*, who has always had her own way. She is a poetess—a mathematician, a metaphysician, and yet, withal, very kind, generous, and gentle, with very little pretension. Any other head would be turned with her acquisitions, and a tenth of her advantages [22]

As if she had read this astonishing tribute, her letters in 1814 became increasingly tender, assuring him that she was heart-free, asking for his picture, and signing herself "Affectionately." Melting in her epistolary warmth, he wrote to her on August 10: "I did—do—always still love you." She answered that she was unfit for marriage, being absorbed in philosophy, poetry, and history.[23] Responding to this challenge, he sent her, on September 9, a second proposal, rather dispassionate, as in a game of chess. If she again refused he planned to leave with Hobhouse for Italy. She accepted.

He approached his fate in alternating order: fear that he was losing the liberty that he had become accustomed to in friendship, sex, and ideas; hope that marriage would rescue him from an entangling web of dangerous and degrading alliances. He explained to his friends: "I must, of course, reform, reform thoroughly. . . . She is so good a person." And to his fiancée: "I wish to be good. . . . I am whatever you please to make me."[24] She accepted her task piously. To Emily Milner she wrote, about October 4, 1814:

> It is not in the great world that Lord Byron's true character must be sought; but ask of those nearest to him—of the unhappy whom he has consoled, of the poor whom he has blessed, of the dependents to whom he has been the best of masters. For his despondency I fear I am too answerable for the last two years. I have a calm and deep security—a confidence in God and man.[25]

As the time came for Byron to go to Annabella's family at Seaham (near Durham) and claim her in marriage, his courage sank. He tarried on the way at Augusta's home, and there wrote a letter to his fiancée withdrawing from the engagement. Augusta persuaded him to destroy the letter,[26] and to accept marriage as a saving tie. On October 29 he continued to Seaham, with Hobhouse, who noted in his diary: "Never was lover less in haste." The bridegroom found the bride's family cordial, put on his best manners to please them, and, on January 2, 1815, led her to the altar.

IV. TRIAL BY MARRIAGE: BYRON, 1815–16

After the ceremony they rode on a gloomy winter day to a honeymoon at Halnaby Hall, in a suburb of Durham. He was now nearing twenty-seven, she was twenty-three. He had had eight or more years of irresponsible and

almost promiscuous sex, and had seldom associated coitus with love. According to Moore's report of a passage he had seen in Byron's memoirs (burned
in 1824), the husband did not wait for the night to shroud their consummation; he "*had* Lady Byron on the sofa before dinner on the day of their
marriage."[27] After dinner, if we may trust his recollection, he asked her
whether she intended to sleep in the same bed with him, and added, "I hate
sleeping with any woman, but you may if you choose."[28] He accommodated
her, but he later told Hobhouse that on that first night "he had been seized
with a sudden fit of melancholy, and had left his bed." The next day (the
wife claimed) "he met me repellently, and uttered words of blighting irony:
'It is too late now; it is done, and cannot be undone.' "[29] A letter was handed
to him from Augusta Leigh; he read to Annabella its superscription: "Dearest, first and best of human beings."[30] According to the wife's memory, he
complained "that if I had married him two years before, I should have spared
him that for which he could never forgive himself. He said he could tell me
but it was another person's secret. . . . I asked . . . if —— [Augusta] knew
it. He appeared terrified."[31] However, Annabella seems to have had no suspicion of Augusta at this time.

After three weeks at Halnaby Hall the newlyweds returned to Seaham for
a stay with the Milbanke family. Byron adjusted himself and became popular with everybody, including his wife. After six weeks of this he began to
long for the excitement of London and the voices of his friends. Annabella
agreed. In London they settled in luxurious rooms at 13 Piccadilly Terrace.
On the day after their arrival Hobhouse came and Byron recovered his good
humor. "For ten days," his wife related, "he was kinder than I had ever
seen him."[32] Perhaps in gratitude, or fearing loneliness, she invited Augusta
to spend some time with them. Augusta came in April, 1815, and stayed till
June. On June 20 George Ticknor, the American historian of Spanish literature, visited the new ménage, and gave a quite favorable report of Byron's
behavior. On that occasion an uncle of Annabella entered joyfully with the
news that Napoleon had just been defeated at Waterloo. "I'm damned sorry
for it," said Byron.

He resumed the writing of poetry. In April, 1815, he joined two Jewish
composers in issuing *Hebrew Melodies*, of which they had written the music and he the words. The collaboration, despite the guinea price, soon sold
ten thousand copies. Murray brought out an edition of the poems alone, and
this too found a wide sale. In October Byron finished *The Siege of Corinth;*
Lady Byron made the fair copy for the printer. "Annabella," Byron told
Lady Blessington, "had a degree of self-control that I never saw equaled.
. . . This produced an opposite effect on me."[33]

He had some excuse for irritability. Assuming that he had sold Newstead
Abbey, he had taken expensive lodgings for himself and his wife, and had
spent lavishly in furnishing them; but the sale fell through, and Byron found
himself literally besieged. In November, 1815, a bailiff entered the apartment, placed attachments on some furniture, and threatened to spend the
night there until Byron paid his bills. Annabella's rich parents, Byron felt,

should have contributed more generously to the expenses of the new ménage.

His worries tinged even his spells of tenderness with bitterness or gloom. "If any woman could have rendered marriage endurable to me," he told his wife, "you would." But then, "I believe you will go on loving me until I beat you." When she expressed the hope and faith that he would learn to love her, he repeated, "It is too late now. If you had taken me two years ago . . . But it is my destiny to ruin all I come near."[34] Having accepted a place on the governing board of the Drury Lane Theatre, he joined Sheridan and others in much drinking, and took one of the actresses to bed.[35] Annabella appealed to Augusta to come again and help her manage him; Augusta came (November 15, 1815), reproved her brother, and found herself joined with Annabella as victim of his rage. "Augusta was filled with pity for her sister-in-law."[36]

Through most of those difficult months Lady Byron had been carrying his child. On December 10, 1815, she gave birth to a daughter, who was named Augusta Ada—later just Ada. Byron rejoiced, and became fond of the infant, and, passingly, of the mother. "My wife," he told Hobhouse in that month, "is perfection itself—the best creature breathing. But mind what I say—don't marry."[37] Soon after Ada's birth his furies returned. In one tantrum he threw into the fireplace a precious watch which he had carried since boyhood, and then shattered it with a poker.[38] On January 3, 1816, according to Annabella's account to her father, Byron came to her room and talked with "considerable violence" of his affairs with women of the theater. On January 8 she consulted Dr. Matthew Baillie as to Byron's sanity; he came, watched the caged poet, but declined to give an opinion.

Apparently Byron consented that Annabella should go, with her child, for a stay with her mother, Lady Milbanke, nee Noel, at the Noel property in Kirkby, Leicestershire. Early on January 15 she left with Ada while Byron was still asleep. At Woburn she stopped to send him a strange hortatory but inviting note:

> DEAREST B: The child is quite well and the best of travellers. I hope you are *good*, and remember my prayers and injunctions. Don't give yourself up to the abominable trade of versifying—nor to brandy—nor to anything or anybody that is not *lawful* and *right*. Though *I* disobey in writing to you, let me hear of *your* obedience at Kirkby. Ada's love to you, and mine.
>
> PIP[39]

From Kirkby she wrote again, humorously and affectionately, telling him that her parents were looking forward to seeing him. On the same day she wrote to Augusta (who was still with Byron) with Lady Milbanke's recommendation that she should dilute Byron's laudanum (opium) with three-quarters water.

Gradually, then fully, Annabella told her parents how, in her view, Byron had treated her. Shocked, they insisted on her complete separation from her husband. Lady Milbanke rushed down to London to consult a medical examiner who had watched Byron's behavior; if she could establish Byron's

insanity the marriage might be annulled without Byron's consent. The examiner reported that he had seen no signs of insanity in the poet, but had
heard of some neurotic outbreaks, as when Byron was seized by a convulsive fit in his enthusiasm over the acting of Edmund Kean. Annabella
sent a caution to her mother not to involve Augusta Leigh in the matter, for
Augusta had been "the truest of friends to me. . . . I very much fear that she
may be supposed the cause of separation by many, and it would be a cruel
injustice."[40]

On February 2, 1816, Annabella's father, Sir Ralph Milbanke, dispatched
to Byron a proposal for peaceful separation. The poet replied courteously
that he saw no reason why the wife who had so recently sent him messages
of affection should have so completely changed her mind. He wrote to
Annabella, asking if she had freely agreed to her father's action. She was
moved to "distress and agony" by his letter, but her parents refused to let
her reply. Augusta added her own appeal for reconsideration; to which
Annabella replied: "I will only recall to Lord Byron's mind his avowed in-
surmountable aversion to the married life, and the desire and determination
he has expressed, ever since its commencement, to free himself from that
bondage, as finding it quite insupportable."[41]

On February 12 Hobhouse went to see Byron. On the way he heard some
of the gossip circulating in London's social and literary circles, and implying
that Byron had been brutal and unfaithful to his wife. Some items from
Hobhouse's diary for that day:

> Saw Mrs. L[eigh] and George B[yron, the poet's cousin], and from them
> learnt what I fear is the real truth that B has been guilty of very great tyranny
> —menaces—furies—neglects, and even real injuries such as telling his wife he was
> *living* with another woman— . . . locking doors—showing pistols . . . everything
> she [Lady Byron] seems to believe him to have been guilty—but they acquit
> him—how? by saying that he is mad. . . . Whilst I heard these things Mrs. L
> went out and brought word that her brother was crying bitterly in his bed-
> room—poor, poor fellow. . . .
> I now thought it my duty to tell Byron I had changed my opinion. . . . When
> I told him what I had heard in the streets that day he was astounded—he had
> heard he was to be accused of cruelty, drunkenness, and infidelity—I got him to
> own much of what I had been told in the morning—he was dreadfully agitated
> —said he was ruined and would blow out his brains. . . . Sometimes says, "and
> yet she loved me once," and at other times that he is glad to be rid of such a
> woman—he said if I would go abroad he would separate at once.[42]

About this time Byron received a bill for two thousand pounds for the
coach he had bought for himself and his wife. He could not meet the debt,
and had only one hundred fifty available; yet, with his characteristically
reckless generosity, about February 16, 1816, he sent a hundred pounds to
Coleridge.

On February 22 Annabella came to London and gave to Dr. Stephen
Lushington an account that in his judgment made separation necessary. In
that week public gossip mentioned Mrs. Leigh, and accused Byron of
sodomy. He perceived that any further refusal of a quiet separation would

bring a court action in which Augusta would be irrevocably ruined. On March 9 he gave his consent, and offered to resign all rights to his wife's fortune, which had been bringing the couple a thousand pounds a year; she agreed that half of this sum should be paid to him annually. She promised to publicly renew her friendship with Augusta, and she kept that promise. She did not seek a divorce.

Soon after the separation he composed a poem—"Fare thee well, and if for ever, / Still fare thee well"—and sent it to her. A group of his friends— Hobhouse, Scrope Davies, Leigh Hunt, Samuel Rogers, Lord Holland, Benjamin Constant—came to his rooms to make him forget the collapse of his marriage. Alone and uninvited, Godwin's stepdaughter "Claire" Clairmont brought him word of admiration from a rival poet, Percy Shelley, and offered her person as a balm for his wounds. He accepted her offer, opening a long concatenation of new griefs. On April 25, 1816, with three servants and a personal physician, he sailed for Ostend, never to see England again.

V. THE YOUTH OF SHELLEY: 1792–1811

Percy commended his grandfather, Sir Bysshe Shelley, for having "acted very well to three wives"; moreover, "he is a complete atheist, and he builds all his hopes on annihilation."[43] Sir Bysshe took his unusual "Christian" name from his grandmother's maiden name. He had a long pedigree, which (like Byron) he traced back to the Norman Conquest; in that distinguished line one Shelley had been hanged for supporting Richard II, another for plotting to kill Elizabeth I. Sir Bysshe eloped with his second wife, buried her, and eloped with a third, who was descended from Sir Philip Sidney. Her fortune swelled that of her husband, and helped him to a baronetcy in 1806. He lived to be eighty-three, much to the annoyance of his children. The eldest of these was Timothy Shelley, who passed through Oxford and into Parliament, where he voted the mildly liberal Whig line. In 1791 he married Elizabeth Pilfold, a woman of great beauty, considerable temper, and some agnosticism,[44] all of which reappeared in her eldest son.

Percy Bysshe Shelley was born on August 4, 1792, at the family property known as Field Place—a spacious home and estate near Horsham in Sussex. Four sisters were born later, and much later a brother. Percy was brought up in close companionship with his sisters; he may have taken from them some habits of tenderness, excitability, and imagination; and for the eldest of them he developed an intense affection.

At Eton he suffered agonies of injured pride from fagging. He shunned most sports except rowing; fatefully he never learned to swim. He was soon proficient in Latin, and changed bullies into friends by helping them with their lessons. His extracurricular reading included many tales of mystery and terror, but also he relished the materialism of Lucretius' *De rerum natura*, the science of Pliny's *Natural History*, the optimism of Condorcet's *Sketch of a Tableau of the Progress of the Human Mind*, and the philosophical anarchism of Godwin's *Enquiry Concerning Political Justice*. This book, he later wrote, "opened my mind to fresh and more extensive views; it materially influenced my character; I rose from its perusal a wiser and better man. . . . I beheld that I had duties to perform."[45]

During vacations he fell in love, aged sixteen, with a cousin, Harriet Grove, who often visited Field Place. They began a correspondence whose ardor raised them in 1809 to mutual pledges of eternal fidelity. But he confessed to her his doubts about God; she showed his agnostic letter to her father, who advised her to set Percy adrift. When, in January, 1811, Harriet transferred her troth to William Helyer, Shelley wrote to his friend Thomas Jefferson Hogg a letter worthy of Byron's wildest heroes: "She is no longer mine, she abhors me as a deist, as what she was before. Oh! Christianity, when I pardon this last, this severest of thy persecutions, may God (if there be a God) blast me! . . . Is suicide wrong? I slept with a loaded pistol and some poison last night, but did not die."[46]

Meanwhile (1810) he had passed from Eton to University College, Oxford. He avoided there, except for an exploratory night or two,[47] the sexual riot that seemed to most undergraduates a necessary course to manhood. He listened now and then to lectures by the dons, who kept only a step ahead of him in Latin and Greek; soon he was composing Latin poetry, and he never forgot Aeschylus. His quarters were disordered with scattered books and manuscripts, and the abracadabra of amateur science; in one experiment he nearly blew up his room. He trusted to science to remake the world and man. He did not care for history, having taken the word of Voltaire and Gibbon that it was mainly the record of the crimes and follies of mankind; nevertheless he read these two skeptics fondly. He thought that he had found an answer to the riddle of the universe in Lucretius and the *philosophes:* it was a choreography of atoms following necessary laws. Then he discovered Spinoza, and interpreted him as a monistic dualist who saw matter and mind as two aspects of one divine substance—a something like mind in all matter, and a something like matter clothing all mind.

He read passionately. His classmate Hogg described him as "having a book in hand at all hours; reading . . . at table, in bed, and especially during a walk . . . not only at Oxford . . . in High Street, but in the most crowded thoroughfares of London. . . . I never beheld eyes that devoured the pages more voraciously."[48] Eating seemed to him a waste of time, if unaccompanied by reading; and the simplest food was best, if only as least distracting from the digestion of ideas. He was not yet a vegetarian, but bread in one pocket and raisins in another seemed to him a well-balanced meal. However, he had a sweet tooth, savored honey on gingerbread, and liked to adorn his drinking water with wine.[49]

He is represented to us, in his Oxford days, as a tall, slender, stooping bundle of nerves, theories, and arguments; careless of his dress and hair; shirt collarless and open at the throat; face almost femininely fair; eyes brilliant but restless; manners awkward but courteous. He had a poet's organism, sensitive at every nerve end, warm with unchecked feelings, receptive to a chaos of ideas, but allergic to history. He had a poet's moral code, naturally stressing individual liberty and suspicious of social restraints. Wonderful, Hogg reported, were the nights in Shelley's room, when they read poetry and philosophy to each other, demolished laws and creeds, exchanged certainties till 2 A.M., and agreed on one point above all others—that there was no God.

On that subject the young rebels concocted a collaboration which they entitled *The Necessity of Atheism*. That term was then proscribed in polite society; gentlemen skeptics called themselves deists, and spoke respectfully of God as an unknowable spirit, inherent in nature as its life and mind. Shelley himself would later come to this view; but, in brave and uncalculating youth, the authors preferred to call themselves atheists as a challenge to a taboo and a call to attention. The argument of the essay was that neither our senses nor reason nor history reveal a God. The senses reveal only matter in motion according to law. Reason rejects the idea of a creator evoking the universe out of nothing. History offers no example of divine action, nor of a divine person appearing on the earth. The authors did not sign their names, but, on the title page, ascribed it to, "Through deficiency of proof, An Atheist."

The *Oxford University and City Herald* for February 9, 1811, contained an advertisement for the pamphlet. It appeared on February 13, and Shelley at once placed copies of it in the window or on the counter of an Oxford bookstore. The Reverend John Walker, fellow of New College, saw the display, and called upon the bookseller to destroy all copies of it in his possession; this was done. Meanwhile Shelley had sent copies to many bishops, and to several university dignitaries.[50] One of these brought the pamphlet to the master and fellows of University College. These summoned Shelley to appear before them on March 25. He came, was shown the pamphlet, and was asked was he the author. He refused to answer, and made an appeal for freedom of thought and the press. He was told to leave Oxford by the next morning. Hearing of this, Hogg confessed himself co-author, and asked for equal punishment; it was granted. That afternoon a college bulletin announced that Shelley and Hogg were being expelled "for contumacy in refusing to answer certain questions put to them." Privately the master sent word to Shelley that if it should prove difficult for him to leave at such short notice, a request for a few days' delay would be granted. The message was ignored. On March 26 Shelley and Hogg proudly left on the top of the coach for London.

VI. ELOPEMENT I: SHELLEY, 1811–12

They took rooms at 15 Poland Street. Shelley's father, in town for a session of Parliament, came to them there, and appealed to them to renounce their views. Finding Shelley unmoved, he bade him dismiss Hogg as an evil influence, return to the family home, and stay there "under such gentleman

as I shall appoint, and attend to his instructions and directions." Shelley refused. The father departed in anger and despair. He recognized Shelley's
abilities, and had looked forward to his taking an honorable place in Parliament. Hogg left for York to study law. Soon Shelley's funds ran out. His
sisters, then studying at Mrs. Fenning's School in the Clapham district of
London, sent him their pocket money. In May his father relented, and
agreed to allow him £200 a year.

Among his sisters' fellow students at Clapham was sixteen-year-old Harriet Westbrook, daughter of the prosperous owner of a tavern in Grosvenor
Square. When she met Percy she was awed by his pedigree, his fluency of
language, the range of his studies, the fascinating deviltry of his views. She
soon agreed that God was dead and that laws were unnecessary nuisances.
She read with fond tremors the rebel texts he lent her, and the translated
classics revealing a wonderful civilization that had never heard of Christ.
She invited him to her home. "I spend most of my time at Miss Westbrook's," Shelley wrote to Hogg in May, 1811. "She is reading Voltaire's
Dictionnaire philosophique."[51] When her schoolmates discovered that her
strange friend was an atheist they boycotted her as already smelling of hell.
When she was caught with a letter from him she was expelled.

Early in August Shelley reported to Hogg: "Her father has persecuted
her in a most horrible way, by endeavoring to compel her to go to school.
She asked my advice; resistance was the answer, at the same time that I es-
sayed to modify Mr. Westbrook in vain! And in consequence of my advice
she has thrown herself on my protection."[52] Later he recalled the result:
"She became evidently attached to me, and feared that I should not return
her attachment. . . . It was impossible to avoid being much affected; I promised to unite my fate with hers."[53] Apparently he proposed a free-love
union; she refused; he proposed marriage; she agreed. Her father refused
consent. On August 25 the couple eloped, took the coach to Edinburgh, and
there were married by the rites of the Scottish Church (August 28, 1811).
Her father yielded to the *fait accompli,* and settled upon her an annuity of
two hundred pounds. Her older sister Eliza came to live with her in York
and (Shelley confessing himself a poor hand at practical matters) took
charge of the new family's funds. "Eliza," he reported, "keeps our common
stock of money, for safety, in some hole or corner of her dress," and "gives
it out as we want it."[54] Shelley was not quite happy at Eliza's mastery, but
took comfort in Harriet's docility. "My wife," he later wrote to Godwin, "is
the partner of my thoughts and feelings."[55]

Harriet and Eliza, with Hogg nearby, stayed in York while Shelley went
to London to soften his father. Mr. Shelley had stopped his allowance on
hearing of the elopement; now he renewed it, but forbade his son ever to
enter the family home. Returning to York, Shelley found that his dear friend
Hogg had attempted to seduce Harriet. She said nothing of this to her husband, but Hogg confessed, was forgiven, and departed. In November the
trio left for Keswick, where Shelley became acquainted with Southey.

"Here," wrote Southey (January 4, 1812), "is a man who acts upon me as my own ghost would do. He is just what I was in 1794. . . . I told him that all the difference between us is that he is nineteen and I am thirty-seven."[56] Shelley found Southey amiable and generous, and read the older man's poetry with pleasure. A few days later he wrote: "I do not think as highly of Southey as I did. It is to be confessed that to see him in his family . . . he appears in a most amiable light. . . . How he is corrupted by the world, contaminated by custom; it rends my heart when I think what he might have been."[57]

He found some balm in reading Godwin's *Political Justice*. When he learned that this once famous philosopher was now living in poverty and obscurity, he wrote to him a letter of worship:

> I had enrolled your name in the list of the honorable dead. I had felt regret that the glory of your being had passed from this earth of ours. It is not so. You still live, and, I firmly believe, are planning the welfare of human kind. I have just but entered on the scene of human operations, yet my feelings and my reasonings correspond with what yours were. . . . I am young; I am ardent in the cause of philosophy and truth. . . . When I come to London I shall seek for you. I am convinced I could represent myself to you in such terms as not to be thought unworthy of your friendship. . . .
> Adieu. I shall earnestly await your answer.[58]

Godwin's reply is lost; but we may judge its tenor from his letter of March, 1812: "As far as I can yet penetrate into your character, I conceive it to exhibit an extraordinary assemblage of lovely qualities, not without considerable defects. The defects do and always have arisen chiefly from this source—that you are still very young, and that in certain essential respects you do not sufficiently perceive that you are so." He advised Shelley not to publish every ebullition, and, if he published anything, not to put his name to it. "The life of a man who does this [publishes and signs] will be a series of retractions."[59]

Shelley had already practiced restraint by keeping in manuscript, or in some privately printed copies, his first important composition—*Queen Mab*. "It was written by me at the age of eighteen—I dare say in a sufficiently intemperate spirit—but . . . was not intended for publication."[60] In 1810 he was still aflame with the French *philosophes;* he prefaced the poem with Voltaire's angry motto *Écrasez l'infâme!*, and he borrowed many ideas from Volney's *Les Ruines, ou Méditations sur les révolutions des empires* (1791).

As the poem begins, the maiden Ianthe is asleep. In a dream the Fairy Queen Mab comes down to her from the sky, takes her up to the stars, and asks her to contemplate, from that perspective, the past, present, and future of the earth. A succession of empires passes before her—Egypt, Palmyra, Judea, Greece, Rome . . . Leaping to the present, the Queen pictures a king (obviously the Prince Regent) who is "a slave even to the basest appetites";[61] she wonders that not one of the wretches who famish while he feasts "raises an arm to dash him from the throne"; and she adds a now famous verdict:

> The man
> Of virtuous soul commands not, nor obeys.
> Power, like a desolating pestilence,
> Pollutes whate'er it touches.[62]

The Queen also dislikes commerce and Adam Smith: "the harmony and happiness of man yields to the wealth of nations"; "all things are sold, even love."[63] She pictures the burning of an atheist; this frightens Ianthe; the Queen comforts her by assuring her, "There is no God."[64] Ahasuerus, the Wandering Jew, enters, and berates the God of Genesis for punishing billions of men, women, and children through thousands of years for one woman's unintelligible sin.[65] (Byron may have found suggestions here for his *Cain*; Shelley had sent him a privately printed copy.) Finally the Queen pictures a rosy future: love unbound by law, prisons empty and needless, prostitution gone, death without pain. Then she bids Ianthe return to the earth, preach the gospel of universal love, and have undiscourageable faith in its victory. Ianthe awakes. — It is a powerful poem, despite its juvenile thought and sometimes bombastic style; in any case a remarkable product for a lad of eighteen years. When, without the poet's consent, *Queen Mab* was published in 1821, the radicals of England welcomed it as their plaint and dream. Within twenty years fourteen editions were issued by piratical firms.[66]

After a stay (February–March, 1812) in Ireland, where, with heroic impartiality, he worked for both Catholic and proletarian causes, Shelley and Harriet passed into Wales. Oppressed by the poverty there, they went to London to raise funds for Welsh charities. He took this opportunity to pay his respects to Godwin, who was so pleased with him that the two families frequently played host to each other. After short return visits to Ireland and Wales, the younger couple settled in London. There, March 24, 1814, to insure the legitimacy of any son and heir they might have, Shelley and Harriet were remarried, now by a Church of England rite. Some time before, on her birthday, he had addressed to her a poetic renewal of his vows:

> Harriet! let death all mortal ties dissolve;
> But ours shall not be mortal! . . .
> Virtue and Love! unbending Fortitude,
> Freedom, Devotedness, and Purity!
> That life my spirit consecrates to you.[67]

VII. ELOPEMENT II: SHELLEY, 1812–16

Through all his wanderings Shelley seems never to have thought of earning his own living. Perhaps he shared Wordsworth's view that a dedicated poet should be excused from labors or concerns that might stifle the poetry in his blood. He saw no contradiction between his propaganda for equal rights under a republic and his efforts to get his share of the wealth that his grandfather bequeathed to his father. He added to the paternal annuity by selling "post-obits" to moneylenders; so, in 1813, he pledged two thousand pounds of his expected inheritance in exchange for six hundred in hand.

Perhaps the moneylenders were encouraged by his frail physique and recurrent illnesses. A constant pain in his left side (his second wife would report) "wound up his nerves to a pitch of sensibility that rendered his views of life different from those of a man in the enjoyment of healthy sensations. Perfectly gentle and forbearing in manner, he suffered a good deal of irritability, or rather excitement, and his fortitude to bear was almost always on a stretch."[68]

He thought he might ease his pains by a vegetarian diet. He was confirmed in this hope by experiments described in John Newton's *Return to Nature, or Defence of a Vegetable Regimen* (1811). By 1812 he and Harriet were confirmed vegetarians. By 1813 he was so enthusiastic about what she called "the Pythagorean system"[69] that he interpolated in his notes to *Queen Mab* an appeal to all and sundry:

> By all that is sacred in our hope for the human race, I conjure those who love happiness and truth to give a fair trial to the vegetable system! . . . There is no disease, bodily or mental, which adoption of a vegetable diet and pure water has not infallibly mitigated, wherever the experiment has been tried. Debility is gradually converted into strength, disease into healthfulness.[70]

In *Vindication of Natural Diet* (1813) he traced man's evil impulses, and most wars, to a meat diet, and pleaded for a return from commerce and industry to agriculture:

> On a natural system of diet we should require no spices from India, no wines from Portugal, Spain, France, or Madeira. . . . The spirit of the nation, that should take the lead in this great reform, would insensibly become agricultural; commerce, with all its vices, selfishness, and corruption, would gradually decline; more natural habits would produce gentler manners.[71]

A strange concatenation of circumstances led from his vegetarianism to the breakup of his first marriage. Through his admiration for John Newton he met Newton's sister-in-law, Mrs. John Boynton, a vegetarian, a republican, charming despite her white hair, and capable of educated conversation in two languages. In June, 1813, Harriet had given birth to a pretty daughter, whom Shelley named Ianthe; that summer he moved with them, and sister Eliza, to Bracknell, a pleasant place thirty miles from London. Shortly thereafter Mrs. Boynton took a house there, and gathered about her a circle of French *émigrés* and English radicals whose views on government and diet pleased Shelley. More and more frequently he left Harriet and Ianthe with Eliza, and went off to enjoy the company of Mrs. Boynton, her friends, and her married daughter.

Several shadows had fallen across his relations with his wife. He seems to have felt a certain retardation in her intellectual growth: she was increasingly absorbed in her child, and careless about politics, and yet she had developed a liking for gay comforts and fine clothes; partly for her sake he had bought an expensive carriage. At this critical juncture in his affairs (May 26, 1813) he received notice from his father that unless he retracted his atheism and apologized to the master of his college at Oxford, he would disinherit him and end all financial aid. In expectation of a substantial bequest on his coming of age (August 4, 1813), Shelley had contracted debts that mortgaged his future. Harriet and Eliza panicked, and obviously wondered whether Paris was not worth a Mass. Shelley refused to recant, and continued to frequent the soirees of Mrs. Boynton. Godwin sent word that he was facing arrest by his creditors, and implied that he would welcome aid. In June, 1814, Harriet moved with her child to Bath, apparently in the expectation that her husband would soon join her there. Shelley went to London, took a room in Fleet Street, tried to raise money for Godwin, and almost daily dined at the philosopher's home in Skinner Street. There he met Mary Godwin.

She was the child in whose birth, seventeen years back, the gifted but unfortunate vindicator of the rights of woman had lost her life. Mary's fresh youth, her alert mind, her pale and thoughtful face, her unconcealed admiration for Shelley, were too much for the poet, who was still a lad of twenty-one. Again pity mingled with desire. He had often heard of Mary Wollstonecraft and her remarkable book; here was her daughter who, unhappy under a stern stepmother, went often to sit alone beside her mother's grave. Here—Shelley felt—with her double heritage of sensitivity and intellect, was a finer mind and spirit than Harriet. Within a week he was in the throes of a passion such as he seems never to have experienced before. On July 6 he asked Godwin for the hand of his daughter. The astonished philosopher denounced his acolyte as "licentious," forbade him the house, and put Mary under the custody of her stepmother.[72]

Soon afterward Thomas Love Peacock found the poet almost delirious in his Fleet Street room. "Nothing that I have ever read, in tale or history, could present a more striking image of a sudden, violent, irresistible . . . passion, than that under which I found him labouring, when, at his request, I went up from the country to call on him. . . . His eyes were bloodshot, his hair and dress disordered. He caught up a bottle of laudanum, and said, 'I never part from this.' "[73]

Despite all obstacles, Shelley arranged to meet Mary at her mother's grave. He reduced her resistance by telling her that Harriet had been unfaithful to him with a Mr. Ryan.[74] He continued for some time to deny the legitimacy of the child that Harriet was now carrying (later he claimed it was his own). She denied his charge, and Shelley's friends Peacock, Hogg, Trelawny, and his publisher Hookham supported her; Godwin later rejected it.[75]

Shelley wrote to Harriet (still at Bath) and asked her to come to London. She came (July 14, 1814), and was received into her father's house. The poet visited her there, and found her alarmingly ill. He begged her to give him a separation; she refused. On returning to his room he wrote to her a hectic letter assuming some kind of agreement:

My Dearest Friend:

Exhausted as I am with our interview, and secure of seeing you tomorrow, at 12, I cannot refrain from writing to you.

I am made calm and happier by your assurances. . . .

For this, dearest Harriet, from my inmost soul I thank you. This is perhaps the greatest among the many blessings which I have received, and still am destined to receive, at your hands. I loathed the very light of day, and looked upon my own being with deep and unutterable abhorrence. I lived in the hope of consolation and happiness from you and have not been deceived.

I repeat (believe me for I am sincere) that my attachment to you is unimpaired: I conceive that it has acquired even a deeper and more lasting character, that it is now less exposed than ever to the fluctuations of phantasy or caprice. Our connection was not one of passion and impulse. Friendship was its basis, and on this basis it has been enlarged and strengthened. It is no reproach to me that you have never filled my heart with an all-sufficing passion. . . .

Shall I not be more than a friend? Oh, far more Brother, Father of your child, so dear as it is to us both. . . .

If you want to draw on the Bankers before I see you, Hookham will give you the cheques.

Adieu. Bring my sweet babe. I must ever love her for your sake.

Ever most affectionately yours,
P. B. Shelley.[76]

Harriet gave her own account in a letter of November 20, 1814, to Catherine Nugent:

. . . Mary was determined to seduce him. . . . She heated his imagination by talking of her mother, and going to her grave with him every day, till at last she told him she was dying in love for him. . . . Why [Mary asked] could we not all live together? I as his sister, she as his wife? He had the folly to believe this possible, and sent for me, then residing at Bath. You may suppose how I felt at the disclosure. I was laid up for a fortnight after. I could do nothing for myself. He begged me to live. . . . Here I am, my dear friend, waiting to bring another infant into this woeful world. Next month I shall be confined. He will not be near me.

H. Shelley.[77]

Godwin gave some details in a letter of August 27, 1814, to John Taylor:

I had the utmost confidence in him [Shelley]; I knew him susceptible of the noblest sentiments; he was a married man, who had lived happily with his wife for three years. . . . On Sunday, June 26th, he accompanied Mary, and her sister Jane Clairmont, to the tomb of Mary's mother. . . . There, it seems, the impious idea occurred to him of seducing her, playing the traitor to me, and deserting his wife. . . . On Wednesday, the 6th of July, . . . he had the madness to disclose his plans to me and to ask my consent. I expostulated with him, . . . and with so much effect that for the moment he promised to give up his licentious love. . . . They both deceived me. In the night of the 27th Mary and her sister Jane escaped from my home; and the next morning I found a letter informing me what they had done.[78]

Jane Clairmont was only stepsister to Mary, being the daughter of the second Mrs. Godwin by a former husband. Originally named Clara Mary Jane, she preferred to be called Clara, and became Clare or Claire. Born April 27, 1798, she was now sixteen years old, and was quite consciously nubile. Talented and generous, sensitive and proud, she fretted under the authority of a worried and irritable mother, and a stepfather too burdened and bankrupt to spare her any love. She appealed to Mary and Shelley to take her with them. They did, and on July 28, 1814, the three fled from London to Dover, and thence to France.

On August 20 the pilgrims reached Lucerne. There Shelley found no message for him, and no money from London. He had in his purse only twenty-eight pounds. Sadly he told his comrades that he must return to England and settle his finances. By boat and carriage they hurried north, and on September 13, 1814, they were again in London. He spent the next twenty months hiding from his creditors, and raising more loans to feed himself, Mary, Claire, and Godwin, who still refused to see him but welcomed cash remittances. Meanwhile Harriet gave birth to her second child, Charles; Mary gave birth to her first, William; and Claire leaped into Byron's bed. Finally the poet's grandfather died, leaving to Shelley's father, now Sir Timothy Shelley, property valued at eighty thousand pounds. Shelley was now heir apparent, but not so recognized by his father. He offered to resign his rights in exchange for a life annuity of a thousand pounds; it was agreed; and Shelley pledged two hundred a year to Harriet. On May 4, 1816, he, Mary, William, and Claire left again for Dover and France. Nine days before them Byron had "kicked the dust of England from his feet."

VIII. SWISS HOLIDAY: BYRON AND SHELLEY, 1816

Both poets, independently, had chosen Switzerland as their haven, and Geneva as their center of operations. Shelley's party arrived on May 15, and took lodgings in suburban Sécheron. Byron and his retinue boarded at Ostend a sumptuous coach which he had ordered built, at a cost of five hundred pounds, on the model of one used by Napoleon and captured at Genappe as part of the trophies of Waterloo; it had a bed, a library, and all facilities for dining. Byron made a special tour of the ground and the remains of the battle; and probably at Brussels that evening composed the stanzas 21 to 28 that were to be especially memorable in Canto III of *Childe Harold's Pilgrimage*.

Late on May 25 he checked in at the Hotel d'Angleterre, a mile north of Geneva center. The entry register required him to give his age; he wrote "100." Claire Clairmont, who had been eagerly checking arrivals, discovered this, and sent him a note commiserating on his age and suggesting a rendezvous. On May 27 he came across Shelley, Mary, and Claire at a boat landing; this was the first meeting of the poets. Byron had read *Queen Mab*, had praised its poetry, but had been politely silent about its politics; it was too much to expect a youth of twenty-four to understand the virtues of aristocracy—though they might have agreed on the convenience of inheritance. Shelley to the end considered Byron his superior in poetry.

On July 4 he leased a home at Montallègre, two miles from Geneva, on the southern shore of Lake Geneva. On July 7 Byron rented the Villa Diodati, ten minutes' walk from Shelley. They united in leasing a small sailboat, and the two families often joined in sailing on the lake, or in an evening of discussion at the Villa Diodati. There, on June 14, Byron suggested that each write a ghost story. They tried; all confessed failure except Mary, who, aged nineteen, produced one of the most famous novels of the nineteenth century—*Frankenstein, or The Modern Prometheus;* it was published in 1818, with a preface by Shelley. Among many other remarkable features it posed two problems still of basic interest: Can science create life? And can it keep its powers from producing evil as well as good?

Byron also suggested that he and Shelley undertake to circumnavigate the lake in their modest boat, stopping at historic spots, especially those made famous by Rousseau's *Julie, ou La Nouvelle Héloïse.* Shelley agreed, though he still had not learned to swim. They set out, with two boatmen, on June 22, and took two days to reach Meillerie (in Savoy). There they lingered on the spot where, in the novel, Saint-Preux, banished from Julie, had supposedly written her name upon the rocks. Resuming their voyage, the poets ran into a sudden storm; the waves repeatedly climbed over the prow into the boat, threatening to capsize it. Byron later recalled the scene: "I stripped off my coat, made him strip off his and take hold of an oar, telling him that I thought . . . I could save him if he would not struggle when I took hold of him. . . . He answered with the greatest coolness that he had no notion of being saved, that I would have enough to do to save myself, and begged not to trouble me."[79]

The storm subsided, the poets landed and rested, and on the next morning they visited Chillon and the castle where François de Bonnevard had been imprisoned (1530–36) by the Duke of Lausanne. At Clarens—Shelley holding Rousseau's novel in his hands as a guide—the poets walked over the ground made memorable as a sanctuary of French Romanticism. On June 27 they docked at Ouchy, port of Lausanne; that night Byron wrote *The Prisoner of Chillon* and sketched the stanzas on Rousseau in *Childe Harold.* On June 28 the poets visited the Lausanne home in which Gibbon had written *The Decline and Fall of the Roman Empire.* On July 1 the wanderers were back at Montallègre and Diodati. During the next two weeks Byron wrote the third canto of *Childe Harold's Pilgrimage,* and Claire Clairmont copied it for him, knowing now one of the few happy moments in her life.

It was her fate to bring misfortune with her. Her open devotion to Byron raised Swiss gossip to a point where it hurt: the two poets, it charged, were living in promiscuous relations with two sisters. Some imaginative souls called Byron and Shelley incarnate devils; and one English lady traveling in Switzerland fainted when Byron appeared at Mme. de Staël's Coppet salon.[80] Perhaps the gossip shared in Byron's determination to end his relations with Claire. He asked Shelley not to let her come to the Villa Diodati anymore. Claire, now three months pregnant with Byron's child, pleaded to be allowed one more visit, but was dissuaded.

On July 24 Shelley took Claire and Mary on a trip to Chamonix in Savoy.

They failed that day—succeeded on the next—in their attempt to reach the Mer-de-Glace. Returning to Switzerland, they stopped at a Chartreuse monastery in Montenvers. Under his signature in the guest book—irritated by the pious entries before his own—he wrote, in Greek: "*Eimi philanthropos demokratikos t'atheos te—*" (I am a lover of mankind, a democrat, and an atheist).[81] When Byron, shortly thereafter, stopped at the same place, he blotted out the "*atheos*," fearing that it would be used against Shelley in England. It was.[82]

On August 29 Shelley, Mary, and Claire left for England. Byron gave Shelley the manuscript of *The Prisoner of Chillon* and Cantos III and IV of *Childe Harold* for delivery to the publisher John Murray. Shelley himself, busy with Mary and Claire, brought only the "Hymn to Intellectual Beauty," and the ode "Mount Blanc: Lines Written in the Vale of Chamouni [Chamonix]." This ode is almost as confused as the rivulets of ice that curl down the mountain slopes to the Mer-de-Glace. Shelley found his impressions so many and so diverse that he was unable to give them any clear expression; and while for a time he thought of the towering mass as voicing Wordsworth's Nature God, he fell back upon the feeling of a cold immensity disdainfully silent before all human judgments.

The "Hymn to Intellectual Beauty" also shows some influence of Wordsworth, but Shelley's "intimations of immortality" soon fade. He wonders why there is darkness as well as light, evil as well as good. He dreams that man might yet be saved by a deepening and broadening of the aesthetic sense, and the pursuit of the beautiful in thought and deed as well as in flesh and form:

> I vowed that I would dedicate my powers
>   To thee and thine—have I not kept the vow? . . .
>   . . . never joy illumed my brow
>   Unlinked with hope that thou wouldst free
>   This world from its dark slavery,
>   That thou—O awful Loveliness,
> Wouldst give whate'er these words cannot express.[83]

In the end the attempts of Wordsworth, Byron, and Shelley to find a benevolent friend in nature failed before its calm neutrality. Wordsworth surrendered to the Church of England; Byron and Shelley surrendered to despair.

IX. DECAY IN VENICE: BYRON, 1816–18

In September, 1816, Hobhouse came down from England, and joined Byron in an extensive tour of the Swiss Alps. In October they crossed them into Italy. They were well received at Milan; the educated Italians honored Byron as England's greatest living poet, and appreciated his evident distaste for Austrian rule in Lombardy. He took a box at La Scala. Stendhal saw him there, and described him ecstatically: "I was struck by his eyes. . . . I have never in my life seen anything more beautiful or more expressive. Even today, if I come to think of the expression which a great painter should give to a genius, this sublime head at once appears before me. . . . I shall never forget the divine expression of his face; it was the serene air of power and genius."[84]

Poet and friend reached Venice on November 16, 1816. Hobhouse left him for hurried sightseeing, and soon went on to Rome; Byron took lodgings in a side street off the Piazza San Marco, and made a mistress of his landlord's wife, Marianna Segati. Even so he found time to complete *Manfred* and (September, 1818) to begin *Don Juan*, in which he passed from gloomy, romantic, self-indulgent brooding to rollicking, humorous, realistic satire.

Manfred, of course, is Byron again, now disguised as a melancholy misanthrope in a Gothic castle. Feeling "a strong curse upon my soul," and brooding over his sins, he summons the witches from their Alpine lairs, and asks from them one gift—forgetfulness. They answer that forgetfulness comes only with death. He climbs the Jungfrau, and sees in a lightning-blasted pine tree a symbol of himself—"a blighted trunk upon a cursèd rock, which but supplies a feeling to decay." He seeks death by trying to jump from a cliff; a hunter stops him, leads him to a mountain cottage, offers him a warming wine, and asks the reason for his despair. Manfred, taking the wine for blood, replies in words that might be taken as a confession of incest:

> I say 'tis blood! the pure warm stream
> Which ran in the veins of my fathers, and in ours
> When we were in our youth, and had our heart,
> And loved each other as we should not love;
> And that was shed; but still rises up,
> Coloring the clouds that shut me out from heaven.

He envies the hunter's free and healthy life

> By danger dignified, yet guiltless; hopes
> Of cheerful old age and a quiet grave,
> With cross and garland over its green turf,
> And thy grandchildren's love for epitaph;
> This do I see—and then I look within—
> It matters not—my soul was scorched already.

He gives the hunter gold, and departs. Using his unsanctioned science, he summons Astarte, in whom he sees the figure of his forbidden love. His appeal to her to forgive him—"Astarte, my beloved, speak to me!"—is one of the high flights of Byronic passion and sentiment. Like the major criminals in Gulliver's land of the Luggnaggians, he has been condemned to immortality, and thinks it the greatest possible penalty; he begs her, out of her mystic power, to grant him the gift of death. She accommodates him: "Manfred, tomorrow ends thy earthly life." An attendant witch applauds his courage: "He mastereth himself, and makes his torture tributary to his will. Had he been one of us he would have made an awful spirit." Milton's Satan may have left here one of many echoes in Byron's works. — To the abbot who, on the following evening, seeks to win him back to Christ, Manfred answers that it is too late, and adds:

> There is an order
> Of mortals on the earth, who do become
> Old in their youth, and die ere middle age,
> Without the violence of warlike death.

And when Manfred leaves for his last rendezvous, the abbot mourns:

> This should have been a noble creature; he
> Hath all the energy which would have made
> A goodly frame of glorious elements,
> Had they been wisely mingled.

As if challenging the world to think that its darkest suspicions of him were now confessed, Byron sent *Manfred* to England, and Murray published it on June 16, 1817. A week later a review in a London paper called for an end to all sympathy for Byron, who "has coloured Manfred into his own personal features. . . . Manfred has exiled himself from society, and what is to be the ground of our compassion for the exile? Simply the commission of one of the most revolting crimes. He has committed incest!"[85]

On April 17, 1817, Byron left Venice to spend a month with Hobhouse in Rome. His foot deterred him from touring the museums, but he saw the massive relics of classical Rome, and visited Pompeii; "I stand a ruin amidst ruins," said Childe Harold.[86] By May 28 he was back in Venice.

In December he succeeded, after many trials, in selling Newstead Abbey and its lands for £94,500; he instructed his London banker, Douglas Kinnaird, to pay all the poet's debts, and send him £3,300 annually from the earnings of the residue; in addition to this he now agreed to receive payment for his poems. Flush, he bought the sumptuous Palazzo Mocenigo on the Grand Canal. He peopled it with fourteen servants, two monkeys, two mastiffs, and a new mistress—Margarita Cogni, proud wife of a local banker. He was not monogynous; he boasted of having had two hundred women, seriatim, in Venice.[87] On January 20, 1817, he informed Kinnaird that "in the evenings I go out sometimes, and indulge in coition always"; and on May 9, 1818, he wrote to the banker, "I have a world of harlotry."[88] By midsummer he had fallen far from the divinity described by Stendhal two years before; he was fat, his hair was turning gray, and he looked older than his thirty years. Shelley was shocked to find him so when they met again.

X. SHELLEY *PATER FAMILIAS*: 1816–18

On September 8, 1816, Shelley, Mary, their child William, his Swiss nurse Elise Foggi, and Claire Clairmont reached England. All but Shelley went to Bath; he hurried to London, expecting to find there five hundred pounds from his father. None came, and he had to default on his promise to give three hundred pounds to his desperate father-in-love. Godwin fumed; Shelley fled to his lawless mate in Bath.

There, on September 26 and October 3, Mary received tender letters from her half sister Fanny Godwin. Born in France in 1794, Fanny was the "natural" daughter of Captain Imlay and Mary Wollstonecraft. She had been adopted by Godwin on his marriage to her mother. Despite his kindness she had been unhappy under the unwilling care of his second wife, Mrs. Clairmont. Her letters reveal a gentle soul, bearing misfortune bravely, blaming no one, and timidly eager to please. Mary had been sisterly to her, but after Mary and Claire went off with Shelley Fanny had no protection against her stepmother. When the elopers returned to England their precarious finances did not encourage them to add Fanny to their fold. On October 12 Shelley brought to Mary and Claire the news that Fanny had gone to Swansea, secluded herself in a hotel room, and killed herself with opium.

The Furies had little mercy on Shelley. On returning to England he had inquired about his wife, to whom he was still legally bound. He learned that she was living with her father, and was regularly receiving four hundred pounds a year. In November he sought to visit her, but was told that she had disappeared. On December 12, 1816, the *Times* reported that her body had been recovered, two days before, from the Serpentine Lake in Hyde Park.

Anxious to get custody of his offspring by Harriet—daughter Ianthe and son Charles—Shelley hurried to legalize with marriage his union with Mary (December 30, 1816). Through three months his claim for the children dragged on in the Court of Chancery. Mary assured him that she would be "very happy to receive those darling treasures"—the children of Harriet—under her care. But Harriet's father and sister contested Shelley's claim on the grounds that he was an avowed atheist and a disbeliever in legal marriage, who had deserted his wife and eloped with an unmarried woman; such a man, they argued, was not likely to bring up the children in a manner fit for life in England. The court disallowed the argument from theology, but recognized the others, and decided against Shelley (March, 1817). However, his choice of foster parents was sanctioned by the court, and he agreed to contribute one hundred twenty pounds a year for their maintenance.

While her husband was litigating in London, Mary watched over Claire Clairmont, who, still only nineteen, gave birth (January 12, 1817) to a daughter ultimately named Allegra. Claire's letters to Byron, since leaving Switzerland, had not been answered, though Shelley's were; and the thought that Byron would never acknowledge the child drove the mother to despair. Shelley appealed to Byron for instructions, taking care to stress Allegra's beauty. Byron agreed to take and care for the child if she were brought to him. Mary complicated matters (September, 1817) by giving birth to her second child, who was baptized Clara Everina. Mother and child ailed, and soon all the adults agreed that what the family needed was the warmth and sky and fruits of Italy. On March 11, 1818, they crossed to France, and began the long ride, by *mal-de-mer* coaches, to Milan.

Thence Shelley sent Byron an invitation to come and see Allegra. Fearing that this might lead to a renewed liaison with Claire, Byron refused; instead, he suggested, her nurse should take the child to Venice, and if the adoption plan proved satisfactory, the mother should be free to visit Allegra now and then. Claire reluctantly consented. Byron found the little girl so lovely and lovable that he took her into his palace; but Allegra was so frightened by his animals and concubines that Byron soon paid Richard Hoppner, British consul, and his wife, to take the child into their home.

Hearing of this, Shelley and Claire (leaving Mary and her children at Lucca) went to Venice, and found Allegra reasonably well treated. Byron received Shelley cordially, took him on a gondola ride to the Lido, and invited him and his family, with Claire and Allegra, to stay as long as they liked in Byron's villa, I Cappuccini, at Este. Mary came from Lucca with her children, but Clara Everina sickened on the way, and died in Venice (September 24, 1818). On October 29, after a month's stay in I Cappuccini, they bade goodbye to Allegra, and headed south for Rome.

XI. SHELLEY: ZENITH, 1819–21

Between his arrival in Rome (1819) and his reunion with Byron in Pisa (1821) the great events in Shelley's life were his poems. There had been flashes of high excellence before, as here and there in *Queen Mab*, and latterly as in "Ozymandias" (1817)—a sonnet of compact thought and startling force. The "Lines Written in the Euganean Hills" (1818) lack such concentration of thought and chiseled form; and the "Lines Written in Dejection near Naples" (1818) are too self-pitying to invite condolence; a man should not wear his grievances on his sleeve. But now, in three years, came *Prometheus Unbound*, "Ode to the West Wind," "To a Skylark," "The Cloud," *Epipsychidion*, and *Adonais*. We pass by *The Cenci* (1819), in which Shelley, with some success, tried to rival John Webster and other Elizabethan-Jacobean dramatists in a dark and bloody story of incest and murder.

Prometheus Unbound, according to the author's preface, was written atop the Baths of Caracalla in Rome in 1820. He had challenged the Elizabethans with *The Cenci;* now he risked the farthest grasp of his ambition by challenging the Greeks. In *Prometheus Bound* Aeschylus had shown the "Foreknower" as a rebellious Titan chained to a rock in the Caucasus for revealing to mankind too much of the tree of knowledge. In the lost remainder of the trilogy, according to tradition, Zeus had relented and had freed Prometheus from the rock, and from the eagle which, by divine command, had continually pecked at the hero's liver, like doubt at a rebel's certainties. Shelley's "lyrical drama" (as he called it) pictures Zeus as a crusty old Bourbon cruelly responsible for the misfortunes of mankind and the misbehavior of the earth; Prometheus blasts him with all the ardor of an Oxford undergraduate summoning bishops to the obsequies of God. Then the Titan regrets the intensity of his curse: "I wish no living thing to suffer pain."[89] He returns to his chosen task—to bring wisdom and love to all mankind. The Spirit of the Earth, rejoicing, hails him: "Thou art more than God, being wise and kind."[90]

Through Act I the speeches are bearable, and the lyrics of the attendant spirits rumble with elemental power, sparkle with ambrosial metaphors, and ride on melodious rhymes. But speeches, theological or atheological, are not the lightning of poetry; odes become odious and lyrics lose their lure when they fall upon the reader with confusing profusion; beauty unending becomes a bore. Too much of Shelley's poetry is emotion remembered *without* tranquillity. As we proceed we sense something of weakness in these verses, too many sentiments for too few deeds; too many moods and lines of hearts and flowers ("I am as a drop of dew that dies," says the Spirit of the Earth[91]). It is a style that can adorn a lyric but slows a drama—which, by its name, should move with action; a "lyrical drama" is a contradiction in terms.

By contrast the "Ode to the West Wind" (1819) stirs us throughout, for its powerful inspiration is compressed into seventy lines. Here Shelley's richness of rhymes has no time to cloy; the emotion is not spread thin, but is centered on one idea—that the winter of our discontent may hopefully be followed by some spring of growth. This time-honored metaphor repeatedly occurs in Shelley; it sustained him when his world of hopes and dreams seemed to fall in ruins before the onset of experience. He prayed that his ideas, like fallen leaves before the wind, might be preserved and spread through the "airy incantation of his verse." They were.

That ode, which touches the peaks of poetry, was "conceived and chiefly written" (Shelley tells us) "in a wood that skirts the Arno near Florence, and on a day when that tempestuous wind . . . was collecting the vapours which pour down the autumnal rains."[92] Why had he left Rome? Partly because he had either to seclude himself or to bear the nearness of British tourists who thought of him not as a great poet but as an adulterous atheist. More keenly he and Mary felt the death of their child William (June 7, 1819), after only four years of life. Neither parent ever fully recovered from the loss of both their children within nine months. Gray hairs appeared among Shelley's brown, though he was only twenty-seven.

After burying William in the English cemetery at Rome, the family moved north to Livorno, *Anglice* Leghorn. Wandering in a garden there, Shelley felt hurt, as any poet might, at the frightened flight of birds on his approach. One especially fascinated him by its singing as it soared. Going back to his room, he composed the first form of "To a Skylark," with its haunting, brooding hexameters. Those airy stanzas offend not with their rhymes, for every line is warm with feeling and solid with thought.

On October 2, 1819, the Shelleys moved to Florence, where Mary gave birth to her third child, soon named Percy. In Florence Claire Clairmont found employment as a governess, and at last freed Shelley from her care.

On October 29, 1820, he moved his family to the Hotel Tre Palazzi in Pisa, where he had perhaps the strangest adventure of all.

Despite his repeated illnesses he had not lost his sensitivity to sexual gravitation; and when he found a woman not only beautiful but unfortunate the double attraction overwhelmed him. Emilia Viviani was a girl of high family, who had been, against her will, placed in a convent near Pisa to safeguard her virginity till a financially proper husband could be found for her. Shelley, Mary, and sometimes Claire went to see her, and all were charmed by her classic features, her modest manners, and her confiding simplicity. The poet idealized her, made her the object of his waking dreams, and wrote some of them out in *Epipsychidion* ("To a soul unique"?), which was published under a pseudonym in 1821. Some surprising lines:

> I never thought before my death to see
> Youth's vision thus made perfect. Emily,
> I love thee; though the world by no thin name
> Will hide that love from its unvalued shame.
> Would we two had been twins of the same mother!
> Or, that the name my heart lent to another
> Could be a sister's bond for her and thee,
> Blending two beams of one eternity!
> Yet were one lawful and the other true,
> These names, though dear, could paint not, as is due,
> How beyond refuge I am thine. Ah me!
> I am not thine: I am a part of *thee*.

And so from ecstasy to ecstasy:

> Spouse, Sister! Angel! Pilot of the Fate
> Whose course has been so starless! O too late
> Belovèd! O too soon adored, by me!
> For in the fields of immortality
> My spirit should at first have worshipped thine,
> A divine presence in a place divine.

Clearly the youth of twenty-eight was in a condition favoring idealization; our laws and morals cannot quite regulate our glands; and if one is a genius or a poet, he must find outlet and relief in act or art. In this case the ailment was cured or redeemed by a poem that oscillates between absurdity and excellence:

> The day is come, and thou wilt fly with me. . . .
> A ship is floating in the harbour now,
> A wind is hovering o'er the mountain's brow

to take them to an island in the blue Aegean;

> It is an isle 'twixt Heaven, Air, Earth, and Sea,
> Cradled, and hung in clear tranquillity . . .
> This isle and house are mine, and I have vowed
> Thee to be lady of the solitude.

There she shall be his love, and he be hers:

> Our breath shall intermix, our bosoms bound,
> And our veins beat together; and our lips
> With other eloquence than words, eclipse
> The soul that burns between them, and the wells
> Which boil under our being's inmost cells,
> The fountains of our deepest life, shall be
> Confused in Passion's golden purity . . .
> I pant, I sink, I tremble, I expire![93]

Can this be "Shelley plain"? Poor Mary, left to her baby Percy and her own dreams, did not see these effusions for some time. Meanwhile the vision faded; Emilia married, and (according to Mary) led her husband "a devil of a life";[94] Shelley repented his melodious sin, and Mary nursed his desolation with motherly understanding.

He was roused to better poetry when he heard that Keats had died (February 23, 1821). He may not have cared much for *Endymion*, but the "savage criticism" with which the *Quarterly Review* had greeted Keats's major effort so angered him that he called upon their common Muse to inspire in him a fitting threnody. On June 11 he wrote to his London publisher: " 'Adonais' is finished, and you will soon receive it. It is little adapted for popularity, but is perhaps the least imperfect of my compositions."[95] He had chosen as its form the difficult Spenserian stanza so recently used with a better font of rhymes by Byron in *Childe Harold's Pilgrimage;* and he worked on the requiem with all the care of a sculptor carving a monument to a friend; but the demands of the rigid mold gave to some of the fifty-five stanzas an air of artificiality that a less hurried art might have concealed. The theme too hastily assumed that a review had killed Keats, and the mourner asked that "the curse of Cain light on his head who pierced thy innocent breast";[96] but the autopsy of Keats showed that he had died of acute tuberculosis.

In the final stanzas Shelley welcomed his own death as a blessed reunion with the undying dead:

> The One remains, the many change and pass;
> Heaven's light forever shines, Earth's shadows fly;
> Life, like a dome of many-coloured glass,
> Stains the white radiance of Eternity,
> Until Death tramples it to fragments.—Die,
> If thou wouldst be with that which thou dost seek! . . .
>
> Why linger, why turn back, why shrink, my Heart?
> Thy hopes are gone before; from all things here
> They have departed; thou shouldst now depart! . . .
> 'Tis Adonais calls! Oh! hasten thither,
> No more let Life divide what Death can join together. . . .
>
> I am borne darkly, fearfully, afar;
> Whilst, burning through the inmost veil of Heaven,
> The soul of Adonais, like a star,
> Beacons from the abode where the Eternal are.[97]

Keats might have answered with his unforgettable lines:

> Now more than ever seems it rich to die,
>   To cease upon the midnight with no pain,
>   Whilst thou art pouring forth thy soul abroad
>   In such an ecstasy![98]

XII. LOVE AND REVOLUTION: BYRON, 1818–21

Shelley retained varied memories of Byron in their last meeting—his fine manners, candid conversation, generous impulses—and his apparent content with a degrading promiscuity of companions and courtesans. "The Italian women with whom he associates are perhaps the most contemptible of all who exist under the moon. . . . Byron is familiar with the lowest sort of these women, the people his gondoliers pick up in the streets. He allows fathers and mothers to bargain with him for their daughters. . . . But that he is a great poet I think his address to the ocean proves."[99] Byron was well aware of his abandonment of English morals and tastes; the English code had outlawed him, and he would reject it in return. Yet he told a friend in 1819, "I was disgusted and tired with the life I led in Venice, and was glad to turn my back on it."[100] He succeeded, with the help, patience, and devotion of Teresa Guiccioli.

They first met on her visit from Ravenna to Venice in April, 1819. She was nineteen, petite, pretty, vain, convent-educated, warmhearted, passionate. Her husband, Count Alessandro Guiccioli, fifty-eight, had had two previous marriages, and was often immersed in business. It was for precisely such a situation that the current moral code of the upper-class Italians allowed a woman to have a *cavaliere servente*—a gentleman servitor who would be always within call to admire, amuse, or escort her, and be rewarded with a kiss of her hand—or something more if they were discreet and the husband was preoccupied or tired. There was moderate danger of a duel, but sometimes the husband would appreciate the aid, and would absent himself a while. So the Contessa felt free to be drawn to the Englishman's handsome face, intriguing conversation, and charming limp. Or in her later words:

> His noble and exquisitely beautiful countenance, the tone of his voice, his manners, the thousand enchantments that surrounded him, rendered him so different, and so superior a being to any whom I had hitherto seen, that it was impossible that he should not have left the most profound impression upon me. From that evening, during the whole of my subsequent stay in Venice, we met every day.[101]

Those days of reckless happiness ended when the Count took Teresa back to Ravenna. Byron sent her some promissory notes, as on April 22, 1819: "I assure you that you shall be my last passion. Before I knew you, I felt an interest in many women, but never in one only. Now I love *you*; there is no other woman in the world for me." So far as we know, he kept that pledge.

On June 1, in his "heavy Napoleonic carriage," he left Venice for Ravenna as a tourist seeking Dante's remains. Teresa welcomed him; the Count was complaisant; Byron wrote to a friend: "They make love a good deal here, and assassinate a little."[102] He was allowed to take Teresa to La Mira (seven miles south of Venice), where he had a villa; there the love affair advanced unhindered even by Teresa's hemorrhoids.[103] Allegra joined them there and made the party respectable. Tom Moore dropped in, and now received from Byron the manuscript of "My Life and Adventures," which was to cause so much commotion after the author's death.

From La Mira Byron took Teresa to Venice, where she lived with him in his Palazzo Mocenigo. There her father reclaimed her, and—forbidding Byron to follow—took her back to Ravenna. On arrival Teresa fell so convincingly ill that the Count hurriedly sent for her lover. Byron came (December 24, 1819), and, after some wandering, settled down as a paying tenant on the third floor of the Count's palace. He brought with him into his new quarters two cats, six dogs, a badger, a falcon, a tame crow, a monkey, and a fox. Amid this life of varied dedications he wrote more of *Don Juan*, some rhetorical and unstageable plays on Venetian doges, a more presentable drama about Sardanapalus, and, in July, 1821, *Cain: A Mystery*, which completed the abomination of his name in England.

The opening scene shows Adam and Eve, Cain and his sister-wife Adah, Abel and his sister-wife Zillah, preparing to offer sacrifices and prayers to Jehovah. Cain asks his parents some of the questions that had puzzled Byron in his schooldays: Why did God invent death? If Eve ate of the tree of knowledge, why had God planted that forbidden tree so prominently in the Garden of Eden; and why should the desire for knowledge be accounted a sin? Why, in punishment for Eve's modest collation, had the Omnipotent decreed labor as the lot and death as the fate of all living things? What is death? (No one had yet seen it.) Cain is left rebelliously brooding while the rest go to their tasks of the day. Lucifer (Lightbearer) appears, takes over the stage as in Milton, and calls himself proudly one of those

> Souls who dare look the Omnipotent tyrant in
> His everlasting face, and tell him that
> His evil is not good.

Adah returns and pleads with Cain to rejoin his relatives in the field; he has neglected his share of the day's work; she has done it for him, and now invites him to an hour of love and rest. Lucifer taunts her by describing love as a lure to reproduction, and predicts the centuries of toil, strife, suffering, and death awaiting the multitudes that will trace their existence to her womb. . . . Cain and Abel prepare their altars; Abel sacrifices the first of his flock; Cain offers fruit, but, instead of a prayer, asks again why the Omnipotent has permitted evil. Abel's sacrificial lamb is consumed in a bright flame that ascends to heaven; Cain's altar is overthrown by an angry wind that scatters his fruit in the dust. Furious, he tries to demolish Abel's altar. Abel resists; Cain strikes him; Abel dies. Adam reproaches Eve as the primal source of sin; Eve curses Cain; Adah pleads for him: "Curse him not, mother, for he is my brother / And my betrothed." Adam bids Cain leave them and never return; Adah accompanies Cain into banishment. Since Abel had died childless, all humanity (Byron concludes) was Cain's progeny, and bears his mark in secret instincts finding vent in violence, murder, and war.

Cain seems at times an essay in defiance by a schoolboy atheist who has not read Ecclesiastes; and yet at times the drama rises to an almost Miltonic power. Walter Scott, to whom the *Mystery* was dedicated, praised it; as Goethe, losing for a moment his Olympian perspective, said, "Its beauty is such as we shall not see a second time in the world."[104] In England its publication was met with a furor of criticism and horror: here, it seemed, was another Cain, but a worse murderer—killing the faith that had sustained a thousand generations. Murray warned Byron that he was rapidly losing readers for his works.

The portrait of Cain's faithful Adah gave another proof of tender elements in Byron's character; but his treatment of Allegra and her mother showed a tougher strain. The once happy child, now four years old, had been saddened by the distances that separated her from both her parents; and she felt that the Hoppners were wearying of her. Byron sent for her to come to Ravenna; and yet he could hardly ask her to live with him and his menagerie in the palace of the man who was becoming audibly uncomfortable with his horns. After much thought he put her into a convent at Bagnacavallo, twelve miles from Ravenna (March 1, 1821). There, he presumed, she would have companionship, be out of his way, and receive some education. That this would be Catholic did not disturb him; on the contrary he felt that it would be a tragedy for the girl to grow up without a religion in an Italy where every woman was a pious Catholic even in her amours. After all, if one must be a Christian, better go all the way, take the Apostles' Creed, the Mass, and the saints, and be a Catholic. "It is my wish," he wrote on April 3, 1821, "that Allegra should be a Roman Catholic, which I look upon as the best religion."[105] When Allegra was ready for marriage he would settle upon her a fortune of four thousand pounds, and she would have no difficulty in finding a husband.

This was convenient for Byron, but when the news of it reached Claire Clairmont she protested passionately, and begged that Shelley get the child restored to her. Shelley undertook to go to Ravenna and see how Allegra was faring. He arrived there on August 6, 1821, and was cordially received by Byron. He wrote back to his wife: "Lord Byron is very well, and was delighted to see me. He has . . . completely recovered his health, and lives a life totally the reverse of that which he led in Venice."[106] Byron told him that political conditions would soon compel him to move to Florence or Pisa; he would take Allegra with him, and she would be close to her mother. Shelley was content with this, and turned his attention to something more immediately affecting himself.

He was dismayed to learn that Allegra's nurse Elise (whom he had dismissed from his service in 1821) had told the Hoppners that he had had secret sexual relations with Allegra's mother; that Claire, in Florence, had borne his child, which he had at once placed in a foundling asylum; furthermore, that Shelley and Claire had treated Mary shamefully, even to his beating her. The astonished poet wrote at once to Mary (August 7), asking her to write to the Hoppners denouncing these tales; Mary did, but sent her letter to Shelley for his approval; he showed it to Byron, and apparently relied on him to give it to Hoppner. Shelley was disappointed to find that Byron had known of the rumors, and had apparently believed them. The famous friendship began to cool, and cooled further when Byron moved from Ravenna to Pisa, leaving Allegra in her convent.

That change was the result of mixing love and revolution. In July, 1820, Teresa's father, Count Ruggero Gamba, had secured from the Papal Curia a writ awarding her a separation from her husband, with regular payments of alimony from him, on condition that she live with her parents. She moved accordingly, and Byron, still living in the Guiccioli palace, became a frequent visitor to the Gamba household. He was delighted to find that Gamba and his son Pietro were leaders in the Carbonari, a secret organization plotting to overthrow Austrian rule in north Italy, papal rule in middle Italy, and Bourbon rule at Naples over the "Kingdom of the Two Sicilies"— i.e., south Italy and Sicily. Byron, in "The Prophecy of Dante" (1819), had already appealed to the Italian people to rise and free themselves from Hapsburg or Bourbon rule. By 1820 Austrian spies suspected him of paying for weapons to be delivered to the Carbonari; and a royalist poster set up in Ravenna called for his assassination.[107] On February 24, 1821, the Carbonari insurrection failed; its leaders fled from those parts of Italy under Austrian, papal, or Bourbon rule. Count Gamba and son went to Pisa; on Byron's advice Teresa soon followed them; and on November 1, 1821, Byron arrived there, and settled in the Casa Lanfranchi on the Arno, where Shelley had already rented rooms for him. Now would come the final test of their friendship.

XIII. CONTRASTS

The two poets had now reached the fullness of their development. The elder had still some cantos of *Don Juan* to compose; these are so bitter in their hostility to England that even a Gallic taste can find them immoderate. *The Vision of Judgment* (October, 1821) is also mercilessly satirical, but Southey's prior *A Vision of Judgment* (April, 1821) had provoked retaliation by calling Byron the leader of the "Satanic" school in English poetry; Byron cut him up with gusto and skill. In these final compositions he moved away from the romantic self-pitying melancholy of Childe Harold toward a more classic pose of reason and humor judging all—but moderation still escaped him. His letters—especially those to Murray—show a maturer mood, for there his caustic wit was tempered with critical self-scrutiny, as if he had discovered that modesty opens a door to wisdom.

He was modest about his poetry. "I by no means rank poetry or poets high in the scale of intellect. This may look like affectation, but it is my real opinion. . . . I prefer the talents of action—of war, or the senate, or even of science—to all the speculations of those mere dreamers."[108] He praised Shelley as a man, but thought much of his verse to be childish fantasy. He was anxious to be valued as a man rather than as a poet. He was painfully conscious of his appearance. He preferred riding to walking, for his right foot distracted attention from his handsome face. Dietetically his life was an alternation between eating to obesity and dieting to debility; so in 1806 his five feet eight and a half inches weighed 194 pounds; by 1812 he was down to 137; by 1818 he had swelled to 202. He was proud of his sexual achievements, and sent mathematical reports of them to his friends. He was a man of emotion; often lost his temper or self-control. His intellect was brilliant but unsteady; "the moment Byron reflects," said Goethe, "he is a child."[109]

In religion he began as a Calvinist; in *Childe Harold* he spoke of the Papacy with old-Protestant vigor as "the Babylonian whore."[110] In his twenties he read philosophy, liked Spinoza, preferred Hume, and declared, "I deny nothing, but doubt everything."[111] In 1811 he wrote to a proselytizing friend, "I will have nothing to do with your immortality"; ten years later he wrote, "Of the immortality of the soul it appears to me that there can be little doubt."[112] In Italy he fell in with the climate and the people, and began to think Catholically; when the Angelus rang he longed to share the peace that seemed for a moment to settle upon all native souls; "I have often wished that I had been born a Catholic."[113] Toward the end (1823) he talked, as in boyhood, of predestination and God.[114]

Having in adolescence lost his religious belief, and having found no moral mooring in literature or philosophy, he had no fulcrum from which to offer resistance to the sensations, emotions, or desires that agitated him. His free and agile intellect found persuasive reasons for yielding, or his temperament gave reason no time to display the wisdom of social restraints. Apparently he curbed his homosexual inclinations, and satisfied them with warm and faithful friendships; but he yielded to the charms of his sister; and in *Childe Harold* he boldly told of his love for

> one soft breast
> Which unto his was bound by stronger ties
> Than the Church links withal.[115]

Condemned by English society for exceeding its permitted indulgences, or failing to cover them gracefully, he declared war upon British "hypocrisy" and "cant." He satirized the upper classes as "formed of two mighty tribes, the Bores and Bored." He condemned the exploitation of labor by the factory owners, and sometimes he called for revolution:

> "God save the King!" and kings,
> For if he don't I doubt if *men* will longer.
> I think I hear a little bird, who sings,
> The people by and by will be the stronger, . . .
>   and the mob

> At last all sick of imitating Job. . . .
>   I would fain say, "Fie on't."
> If I had not perceived that revolution
> Alone can save the earth from hell's pollution.[116]

However, on second thought, he felt no attraction to democracy. He distrusted mobs, and feared that a revolution would bring a dictatorship worse than that of king or parliament. He saw some virtue in rule by an aristocracy of birth, and longed for an aristocracy purged, reasonable, trained, and competent. He himself never forgot that he was a lord; he soon checked any assumption of egalitarian familiarity; he knew that in social relations distance lends enchantment to the view.

His view of Napoleon changed with events. Till Bonaparte crowned himself emperor, and armed and surrounded himself with titles, Byron saw him as an excellent compromise between kings and mobs. Even with baubles, and those questionable invasions of Spain and Russia, Byron prayed for Napoleon to win against the Continental monarchies. He scolded the defeated Emperor for not killing himself instead of abdicating; but when Napoleon returned from Elba the poet again prayed for his victory against the Allies. Six years later, hearing of Napoleon's death, he mourned: "His overthrow was a blow on the head to me. Since that period we have been the slaves of fools."[117]

He was a baffling mixture of faults and virtues. He could in a rage be coarse and cruel; normally he was courteous, considerate, and generous. He gave recklessly to friends in need; to Robert Dallas he transferred copyrights worth a thousand pounds; another thousand enabled Francis Hodgson to avoid bankruptcy. Teresa Guiccioli, who saw him almost daily through four years, described him as a veritable angel through nine hundred pages.[118] He, far more than Coleridge, was a "damaged archangel," carrying in his flesh the flaws of his heritage, illustrating and redeeming them with an audacity of conduct, a profusion of verse, and a force of rebel thought that overwhelmed old Goethe into calling him "the greatest [literary] genius of our century."[119]

By comparison Shelley was the "ineffectual angel" of historic phrase. Not quite ineffectual; who shall say that the leaves scattered by the incantation of his verse did not deposit some of the seeds that grew into religious toleration, the liberation of woman, the victories of science in technology and philosophy, the extension of the franchise, and the reform of Parliament that made the nineteenth a "wonderful century"?

And he was a quite human angel. He had a body, and yielded to its demands at least for two elopements, not to speak of Emilia Viviani. He was thin, troubled with ailments, and with a persistent pain in the back. Of course he was exceptionally sensitive—even more than Byron—to external and internal stimuli. Recall his letter to Claire Clairmont (January 16, 1821): "You ask me where I find my pleasures. The wind, the light, the air, the smell of a flower, affect me with violent emotions."[120]

Like all of us, he was especially fond of himself. He confessed to Godwin (January 28, 1812): "My egotism seems inexhaustible."[121] In taking Mary Godwin, and asking his wife Harriet to subside into a sister, he pleased his desires like any other mortal, and revealed more of himself in explaining that Harriet accorded less than Mary with his philosophy and ideals. He was modest about his poetry, rating it below Byron's. In friendship he was faithful and considerate to the end. Byron, in reporting Shelley's death to Murray, wrote: "You were all brutally mistaken about Shelley, who was, without exception, the best and least selfish man I ever knew. I never knew one who was not a beast by comparison."[122] Hogg reported the poet as erratic, forgetting appointments and promises, and readily slipping into a meditation oblivious of time and place.[123] He was generally accounted impractical, but he was not easily cozened in money matters, and he did not surrender his hereditary rights without a long struggle.

He was too high-strung to be a quite rational thinker, and too lacking in a sense of humor to question his own ideas. His constant lure was imagination; reality seemed so drear and gross compared with conceivable improvements that he tended to take refuge from reality in the Elysian Fields of his waking dreams. He proposed to do away with kings, lawyers, and priests; to convert to vegetarianism a world still in the hunting stage, and to free the love of the sexes from all trammels of law. He saw no obstacles to all this in the nature of man or in man's biological past. "Shelley believed," said his loving widow, "that mankind has only to will that there should be no evil, and there would be none. . . . This opinion he entertained . . . with fervent enthusiasm."[124] He almost ignored history, except to idealize the Greeks, and there he ignored the slaves.

We tend to exaggerate Shelley's simplicity because we forget that death never allowed him to mature. Because of their premature end Byron and Shelley have come down to us as Romantic poets, as very gods of the Romantic movement in England; had they lived to be sixty they would probably have become conservative citizens, and might have come down to us with a humbler place in history than their early romantic deaths have earned for them.

Indeed, by the age of twenty-eight Shelley had already cooled to a respectable moderation. In 1820 he wrote a substantial essay called *A Philosophical View of Reform*, which was published a year later. "Poets and philosophers," he announced, "are the unacknowledged legislators of the world":[125] poets because they are the voices of imagination, which, amid many absurdities, conceive new ideas that in time stir men to experiment and advance; philosophers because they bring to social problems the habit of calm reason and the perspective of years. Like Byron and every humane spirit of the time, Shelley had been revolted by the condition of the factory workers in England, and by the cold recipes of Malthus for controlling the population but leaving wages to be dictated by the law of supply and demand—i.e., by the number of unemployed competing for available jobs.[126]

He denounced both Protestantism and Catholicism for having failed to apply the spirit of Christ to the relations between rich and poor.[127] He proposed to eliminate, by a levy on the rich, the national debt whose yearly interest charges required heavy taxes upon the general public.[128] He pointed out that the increase of population between 1689 and 1819 had changed the proportion of voters to nonvoters, leaving the election of Parliament to an even smaller minority, practically disenfranchising the people.[129] He forgave the landed aristocracy as rooted in law and time, and (perhaps with an eye to future Shelleys) he sanctioned a moderate transmission of wealth; but he scorned the rising plutocracy of manufacturers, merchants, and financiers.[130] He repudiated Machiavelli's exemption of governments from morality: "Politics are only sound when conducted on principles of morality. They are, in fact, the morality of nations."[131] He called for "a republic governed by one assembly," but, like his mentor Godwin, advised against violent revolution.[132] He defended the French Revolution, praised Napoleon Consul, repudiated Napoleon Emperor, deplored the French defeat at Waterloo.

Shelley's *Defence of Poetry*, written in 1821, did not find a publisher till 1840. Here the self-exiled poet, now omitting philosophers, exalted poets as the "supreme lawgivers of the world."[133] He had expressed this comforting opinion in his preface to *Prometheus Unbound:* "The great writers of our age are, we have reasons to suppose, the companions and forerunners of some unimagined change to our social condition or the opinions which cement it. The cloud of mind is discharging its collected lightning, and the equilibrium between institutions and opinions is now restoring, or is about to be restored."[134] Now he added: "Our own will be a memorable age in intellectual achievements, and we live among such philosophers [Kant, Fichte, Hegel, Schelling—and Godwin] and poets [Goethe, Schiller, Wordsworth, Coleridge, Byron, Shelley] as surpass beyond comparison any who have appeared since the last national struggle for civil and religious liberty" (1642).[135]

By contrast Shelley underestimated the role that science was beginning to take in remolding ideas and institutions. He warned against letting the progress of science, which merely improves our tools, outrun the development of literature and philosophy, which consider our purposes;[136] so the "unmitigated exercise of the calculating faculty" had further enriched the clever few, and had added to the concentration of wealth and power.[137]

Shelley's discontent with his second father-in-law's finances spread to Godwin's philosophy. Having rediscovered Plato (he had translated the *Symposium* and the *Ion*), he passed from a naturalistic to a spiritual interpretation of nature and life. He now doubted the omnicompetence of reason, and had lost his enthusiasm for atheism. As he neared thirty he ceased to attack supernatural religion; now he thought, very much like the young Wordsworth, that nature was the outer form of a pervading inner soul. There might even be a kind of immortality: the vital force in the individual passes, at his death, into another form, but never dies.[138]

XIV. PISAN CANTO: 1821–22

Byron, when he reached Pisa, had almost outlived his sexual history, except for an idealizing memory as in the Haidee episodes in *Don Juan*. At Pisa Teresa Guiccioli lived with Byron, but in diminishing intimacy; he spent most of his time with his friends and Shelley's. For them he arranged weekly dinners, where discussion ran freely. Shelley attended, stood his ground politely but firmly in argument, but slipped away before strong drinking began. Teresa tried to give substance to her quiet life by becoming friends with Mary Shelley and reading history to keep up with Mary's intellectual interests. Byron disapproved of Teresa's studies, preferring women whose intellect was modestly subordinated to their charms.

He had almost forgotten Allegra. Her mother pleaded with Mary Shelley to come to Florence to join her in a plan to go to Ravenna, abduct the girl, and bring her to a healthier climate and wider life. Shelley refused to allow this. Then came the news that on April 20, 1822, Allegra, five years old, had died of malaria in her convent. The event shared in the cooling of Shelley's friendship with Byron. Earlier in this spring he had written to Leigh Hunt: "Particular dispositions in Lord Byron's character render the close and exclusive intimacy with him, in which I find myself, . . . intolerable to me. Thus much, my best friend, I will confess and confide to you."[139]

He tried to conceal his discomfort, for he had persuaded Byron to invite Hunt to come to Pisa and edit a new magazine, *The Liberal*, which Byron and Shelley planned to launch as an offset to the conservative *Quarterly Review*. Byron sent the bankrupt Hunt two hundred fifty pounds; Hunt and family sailed from London, hoping to reach Leghorn on July 1, 1822. Shelley promised to meet him.

Externally the first six months of that fatal year were a pleasant time for the two poets. They went riding together almost daily, and matched their marksmanship in a pistol club; Shelley almost equaled Byron's accuracy of aim. "My health," he wrote to Peacock, "is better; my cares lighter; and tho' nothing will cure the consumption of my purse, yet it drags on a sort of life in death, very like its master, and seems, like Fortunatus' purse, always empty, yet never quite exhausted."[140] In January Byron's mother-in-law died, leaving him (despite the separation from his wife) properties that brought him an additional three thousand pounds per year. Flush, he ordered a commodious yacht to be built for himself at Leghorn, appointed John Trelawny its skipper, named it *Bolivar* in honor of the South American revolutionist, and invited Shelley and his new friends Edward Williams and Thomas Medwin to join him and the Gambas in a yachting trip in the coming summer. Shelley and Williams shared in having a smaller sailboat, eighty-four feet long, eight in the beam, to be built for them at a cost of eighty pounds. Trelawny named it *Don Juan*, Mary renamed it *Ariel*.[141]

Looking forward to a summer of boating, Byron engaged the Villa
Dupuy near Leghorn. Shelley and Williams rented for their families the
Casa Magni, near Lerici, on the shores of the Bay of Spezia, some forty
miles north of Leghorn. On April 26, 1822, the Shelleys and Williams transferred their ménages to the Casa Magni, and there awaited the delivery of
their boat.

XV. IMMOLATION: SHELLEY, 1822

Only some poetic trance could have chosen so lonely a place, or so wild
an environment, for a vacation. Casa Magni was large enough for two
families, but it was unfurnished, and was approaching disintegration. It was
surrounded on three sides by forest, and in front by the sea, whose waves
sometimes reached the door. "Gales and squalls hailed our first arrival,"
Mary Shelley later recalled, and "the natives were wilder than the place.
Had we been wrecked on an island of the South Seas we could scarcely
have felt ourselves farther from civilization and comfort."[142]

On May 12 the *Ariel* arrived from Genoa. Williams, who had been in
the Navy, and Shelley, still unable to swim, were delighted with the boat,
and spent many an afternoon or evening sailing along the coast. Seldom
had Shelley been so happy or so well. Sometimes the women joined them;
but Mary was pregnant again, frequently ill, and unhappy because her
husband would not let her see her father's plaintive letters.[143]

In the house or on the boat Shelley wrote his final poem, "The Triumph
of Life," which was cut short at line 544 by his final voyage. There is no
triumph in it, for it describes a procession of various human types, all failures and decayed, hurrying to death. At line 82 the shade of Rousseau rises
to explain the stupidity of civilization; he shows history's famous figures—
Plato, Caesar, Constantine, Voltaire, Napoleon—caught in the same mad
rush for wealth or power; and recommends, as the only escape, a return to
a simple and natural life.

Not yet thirty, Shelley, after thought of suicide on June 18, 1822, wrote
to Trelawny:

> Should you meet with any scientific persons capable of preparing the Prussic
> acid, or essential oil of bitter almonds, I should regard it as a great kindness if
> you would procure me a small quantity. . . . I would give any price for this
> medicine. . . . I need not tell you I have no intention of suicide at present, but
> I confess it would be a comfort to me to hold in my possession that golden key
> to the chamber of perpetual rest.[144]

Perhaps to help his sick wife, Shelley had invited Claire Clairmont to
come from Florence and spend the summer at Casa Magni. She came early
in June, in time to help Mary through an almost fatal miscarriage. On June
22 Shelley, nearing a nervous breakdown, suffered a nightmare so terrifying
that he ran from his room to Mary screaming.

On July 1 news reached them that Leigh Hunt and family had reached Genoa, and were preparing to leave it by a local transport vessel to join Byron at Leghorn. Shelley, anxious to welcome his faithful friend, to ease Byron's reception of him, and to strengthen his partner's fading interest in their new magazine, decided to sail at once in the *Ariel* with Williams for Leghorn. Mary had premonitions of disaster. "I called Shelley back two or three times. . . . I cried bitterly when he went away."[145]

The *Ariel* left Casa Magni at noon July 1, and reached Leghorn safely at nine that evening. Shelley greeted Hunt joyfully, but was depressed to learn that the Tuscan authorities had ordered the Gambas to leave their territory at once, and that Byron, resolved to follow Teresa, was planning to leave Leghorn soon to join her in Genoa. Nevertheless Byron agreed to honor his agreement with Hunt, and to have the Hunts occupy rooms in the Casa Lanfranchi at Pisa. Shelley accompanied them to Pisa, saw them settled, and drove back to Leghorn on July 7.

He spent the morning of Monday, July 8, shopping for the family at Casa Magni. Williams urged him to hurry, to catch the favorable wind then blowing toward Lerici. Captain Roberts of the *Bolivar* predicted a storm for that afternoon, and advised a day's delay; Williams urged immediate departure; Shelley agreed; and about half past one that afternoon the *Ariel* sailed from Leghorn with Shelley, Williams, and a young sailor, Charles Vivian.

About six-thirty that evening a heavy storm, with thunder, wind, and rain, fell upon the Bay of Spezia, and hundreds of vessels hurried into harbor. At Casa Magni the storm was so severe that the three women waiting anxiously there comforted themselves with the conclusion that the two husbands had waited out the storm at Leghorn. Then Tuesday, Wednesday, and Thursday passed. "The real anguish of these moments," Mary later wrote, "transcends all the fictions that the most glowing imagination ever portrayed. Our seclusion, the savage nature of the inhabitants of the neighboring village, and our immediate vicinity to the troubled sea, combined to imbue with strange horror our days of uncertainty."[146] On Friday a letter came from Hunt to Shelley, including lines that brought terror to the waiting women: "Pray tell us how you got home, for they say you had bad weather after you sailed on Monday, and we are anxious." Jane Williams and Mary rode all day to Pisa. By midnight they reached Casa Lanfranchi, found Byron and Hunt there, and were assured that Shelley and Williams had left Leghorn on Monday. They rode on through the night, and reached Leghorn at two o'clock on the morning of Saturday, July 13. There Trelawny and Roberts tried to calm them with the possibility that the *Ariel* had been blown to Corsica or Elba. Byron commissioned Roberts to use the *Bolivar* to search the sea and shore between Leghorn and Lerici. Trelawny accompanied Mary and Jane on a futile search along the coast for signs or news of the missing men. He stayed with the mourning women at Casa Magni till July 18, and then left to make further inquiries. On July

19 he returned to them, and revealed to them, as gently as he could, that the corpses of their husbands had been found washed upon the shore near Viareggio on July 17 or 18. (About July 30 the mutilated body of Charles Vivian was found four miles farther north, and was buried on the shore.) He took Mary and Jane to Pisa, where Byron offered them rooms in the Casa Lanfranchi, but they took quarters nearby. Mary wrote to a friend: "Lord Byron is very kind to me, and comes with the Guiccioli to see us often."[147]

The bodies had already been buried in the sands by natives. Tuscan law forbade such buried corpses to be exhumed or reburied; but Trelawny knew that Mrs. Shelley wished Shelley's remains to be interred near those of their son William in Rome. He persuaded the Tuscan authorities to allow exhumation, on condition that the remains be burned on the shore. The bodies had been mutilated or consumed almost beyond recognition; but in one jacket a volume of Sophocles was found in one pocket and a volume of Keats in the other.[148]

On August 15 Byron, Hunt, and Trelawny, with a quarantine official and an English officer, Captain Shenley, stood by as a squad of soldiers burned the remains of Williams. The next day, at a spot across from Elba, the remains of Shelley were exhumed and burned in the presence of Byron, Hunt, Trelawny, and some neighboring villagers. Into the flames Trelawny threw incense, wine, and oil, and pronounced incantations consigning the ashes to "the Nature which he worshipped."[149] Byron, unable to bear the spectacle to the end, swam off to the *Bolivar*. After three hours nearly all of the body had fallen away except the heart. Trelawny, at the cost of a burned hand, snatched the heart from the fire. A casket containing the ashes was taken to Rome, and was buried in a new cemetery close by the old Protestant cemetery that held the remains of child William. Shelley's heart was given by Trelawny to Hunt, and by him to Mary. At her death in 1851 the ashes of the heart were found in her copy of *Adonais*.

XVI. TRANSFIGURATION: BYRON, 1822–24

In September, 1822, Byron and the Gambas moved from Pisa to Albaro, a suburb of Genoa. The several moves of body, mind, and mood that he had made since leaving England had tired him, and he had begun to tire even of Teresa's untiring love. His sharp eyes and sardonic spirit had removed the veils of life, and apparently had left no reality that could stir him to idealism or devotion. He was the most famous living poet, but he was not proud of his poetry; the febrile plaints of *Childe Harold* seemed unmanly now, and the clever cynicism of *Don Juan* left author and reader naked in a disillusioned world. "A man," he now felt, "ought to do something more for mankind than write verses."[150] At Genoa he asked his physician to tell him "which is the best and quickest poison?"[151]

Greece offered him a redeeming death. It had fallen subject to the Turks in 1465, and had become somnolent under alien domination. Byron, in *Childe Harold* (Canto II, lines 73–84), had called upon it to revolt: "Heredi-tary bondsmen! Know ye not / Who would be free themselves must strike the blow?" Greece had revolted in 1821, but it was without arms, without money, without unity; it was crying out for help from the nations to which it had transmitted its rich inheritance. It had sent a committee to London to seek funds; the committee sent representatives to Genoa with a challenge to Byron to use some of his wealth in furthering the revolution he had sought to inspire. On April 7, 1823, he told the emissaries that he was at the service of the Greek Provisional Government.

He was transformed. He was now all action. Cynicism gave way to dedi-cation; poetry was laid aside; romance graduated from rhymes to resolution. After putting aside some funds for the Hunts and above all for Teresa, he devoted the remainder of his fortune to the Greek Revolution. He instructed his agents in London to sell everything of his in England that could bring money, and to send him the proceeds. He sold the *Bolivar* for half its cost, and engaged an English vessel, the *Hercules*, to take him, Pietro Gamba, and Trelawny to Greece with some cannon and ammunition, and with medical supplies for a thousand men for two years. Teresa Guiccioli strug-gled to keep him with her; he resisted her affectionately, and had the con-solation of knowing that she and her parents had received permission to return to their home in Ravenna. He told Lady Blessington: "I have a presentiment that I shall die in Greece. I hope it may be in action, for that would be a good finish to a very triste existence."[152]

On July 16, 1823, the *Hercules* left Genoa for Greece. After exasperating delays it anchored (August 3) at Argostólion, the port of Cephalonia, largest of the Ionian Islands. This was still fifty miles from Greece, but Byron was forced to fret away months there; he had hoped to join, at Missolonghi, the most inspiring of the Greek leaders; but Marco Bozzaris had been killed in action, Missolonghi was in Turkish hands, and Turkish warships controlled all western approaches to the Greek mainland. Early in December Prince Alexandros Mavrokordatos recaptured Missolonghi, and on the 29th Byron left Cephalonia. Colonel Leicester Stanhope, agent of the Greek committee that was raising funds in England to aid the revolu-tion, wrote from Missolonghi: "All are looking forward to Lord Byron's arrival as they would be to the coming of the Messiah."[153] After several adventures and delays the young savior reached Missolonghi, January 4, 1824, and received a joyous welcome from prince and people scenting gold.

Mavrokordatos commissioned him to pay, provision, and lead a squad of six hundred Suliotes—bellicose barbarians part Greek, part Albanian. He was not inspired by their appearance, and he knew that the Greek revolu-tionists were divided into rival factions under leaders more political than martial. Nevertheless he was happy to have been assigned an active role, and did not delay in dispensing aid; to Mavrokordatos alone he gave some two thousand pounds a week to keep the Missolonghians in food and spirit. Meanwhile he lived in a villa north of the town and near the shore, "on the verge," said Trelawny, "of the most dismal swamp I have ever seen." The Suliotes proved disorderly and rebellious, more anxious to get his money than his leadership; the young Lochinvar's hope for martial action had to wait till order and morale had been restored. Trelawny, never good at waiting, went off to seek adventure elsewhere. Only Pietro Gamba remained close to Byron, watching over him anxiously as he saw him failing under the heat, the worry, and the malarial air.

On February 15, visiting Colonel Stanhope, Byron suddenly grew pale and fell to the ground in convulsions, unconscious, and foaming at the mouth. He recovered consciousness, and was taken to his villa. Doctors gathered around him, and applied leeches to bleed him. When these were removed the bleeding could not be soon stopped, and Byron fainted from loss of blood. On February 18 his Suliotes rioted again, threatening to invade his villa and kill all available foreigners. He rose from his bed and calmed them, but his hope to lead them against the Turks at Lepanto faded, and with it his dream of a fruitful and heroic death. He was comforted by a letter from Augusta Leigh, enclosing a picture of his daughter Ada and Annabella's description of the child's habits and temperament. His eyes lighted with a moment's happiness. Everything normal had been denied him.

On April 9 he went out riding with Pietro. They were caught in a heavy rain on their way back, and Byron that evening suffered chills and fever. On the 11th his fever grew worse; he took to his bed, felt his strength ebbing, and recognized that he was dying. Sometimes, in those last ten days, he thought of religion, but "to say the truth," he remarked, "I find it equally difficult to know what to believe in this world and what not to believe. There are so many plausible reasons for inducing me to die a bigot, as there have been to make me hitherto live a freethinker."[154] Dr. Julius Millingen, his chief physician, recorded:

> It is with infinite regret that I must state that, although I seldom left Lord Byron's pillow during the latter part of his illness, I did not hear him make any, even the smallest, mention of religion. At one moment I heard him say, "Shall I sue for mercy?" After a long pause he added: "Come, come; no weakness! Let's be a man to the end."

The same doctor quotes him as saying, "Let not my body be sent to England. Here let my bones molder. Lay me in the first corner without pomp or nonsense."[155]

On April 15, after another convulsion, he allowed the doctors to bleed him again. They took two pounds of blood, and, two hours later, another. He died on April 19, 1824. The unusually incompetent autopsy showed uremia—the poisonous accumulation, in the blood, of elements that should have been eliminated in the urine. There was no sign of syphilis, but much evidence that repeated bleedings and strong cathartics had been the final causes of death. The brain was one of the largest ever recorded—710 grams above the top range for normal men.[156] Perhaps years of sexual excess, and alternate periods of heavy eating and reckless fasts, had weakened the body's resources against strain, anxiety, and miasmic air.

News of the death did not reach London till May 14. Hobhouse brought it to Augusta Leigh; the two broke down together. Hobhouse then turned to the problem of Byron's secret memoirs. Moore had sold these for two thousand guineas to Murray, who was tempted to send them to the press despite warning from his chief adviser, William Gifford, that (in Hobhouse's words) they were "fit only for the brothel, and would doom Lord Byron to everlasting infamy if published."[157] Murray and Hobhouse proposed to destroy the manuscript; Moore protested, but agreed to let Mrs. Leigh decide; she asked that it be burned; it was done. Moore returned two thousand guineas to Murray.

Byron's old servant, Fletcher, insisted that his master, shortly before death, had expressed a wish to be buried in England. The Greek authorities and populace protested, but they had to be content with parts of the viscera removed before embalming. The body, preserved in 180 gallons of spirits, reached London on June 29. A request was made to the authorities of Westminster Abbey to let the corpse be buried in the Poets' Corner there; permission was refused. On July 9–10 the public was allowed to view the coffined remains; many people came, very few of note; but some dignitaries allowed their empty carriages to take part in the procession that carried the corpse from London, July 12–15, to Nottingham. From a window Claire Clairmont and Mary Shelley saw the funeral move by. Farther along it passed an open carriage bearing Caroline Lamb; her husband, riding ahead, learned the name of the dead, but did not, till days later, reveal it to his wife. On July 16 the poet was buried in the vault of his ancestors, beside his mother, in the parish church of Hucknall Torkard, a village near Newstead Abbey.

XVII. SURVIVORS

Of those who had played a part in Byron's drama, most survived far into the next epoch of history. Soonest to pass was Pietro Gamba; after escorting his hero's body to London he returned to Greece, remained faithful to the revolution, and died there of fever in 1827. — Lady Caroline Lamb became "very ill" when her husband told her that Byron's corpse had passed her; she had satirized him in a novel, *Glenarvon* (1816), but now she said, "I am very sorry I ever said one unkind word against him."[158] She survived him by less than four years. — Augusta Leigh inherited, by Byron's will, nearly all (some one hundred thousand pounds) that remained of his fortune; spent most of it paying the gambling debts of her husband and her sons, and died in poverty in 1852.[159] — Lady Byron kept to the end some tenderness for the man whose inherited devils had cursed her marriage; "As long as I live," she wrote, "my chief difficulty will probably be not to remember him too kindly."[160] "Can I not be believed when, after all which I have disclosed, I say there was a higher better being in that breast throughout, . . . one which he was always defying, but never could destroy?"[161] Their daughter Ada, on whose development Byron had set such hopes, married the second Earl of Lovelace, lost a fortune gambling on horses, was saved from financial disaster by her mother, lost hope and health, and died, like her father, at the age of thirty-six (1852); Lady Byron, trying to fill her lonely life with social services, died in 1860.

John Cam Hobhouse entered Parliament as a radical, rose to be secretary at war (1832–33), became a baron, and died in 1869 at the age of eighty-three. Teresa Guiccioli, after Byron's death, returned to her husband, but soon applied for, and received, a second separation. She had brief affairs with Byron's lame friend Henry Fox, and with Byron's admirer the French poet Lamartine. Falling with light grace from suitor to suitor, she married, at forty-seven, the wealthy and amiable Marquis de Boissy, who (according to a slightly prejudiced English view) proudly introduced her as "my wife, the former mistress of Byron." When the Marquis died she took up spiritualism, talked with the spirits of Byron and her late husband, and reported that "they are together now, and are the best of friends."[162] She died in 1873, aged seventy-two, after writing several books portraying Byron as an almost flawless genius and gentleman. — Claire Clairmont died in 1879, aged eighty-one, carrying to the end a view of Byron as "the merest compound of vanity, folly, and every miserable weakness that ever met together in one human being."[163]

Mary Shelley, despite some hurts, kept a more favorable view of "Albé" (as his circle had nicknamed Byron); when she learned of his death she wrote: "Albé—the dear, capricious, fascinating Albé—has left this desert world! God grant that I may die young!"[164] She spent much of her remaining twenty-seven years editing her husband's works with love and care, and a quiet eloquence of her own.

Leigh Hunt, who had dared to praise Shelley's poetry when nearly all critics condemned it as the vagaries of an unfinished adolescence, remained faithful to his youthful radicalism, wrote hostile memories of Byron, and lasted till 1859. Thomas Jefferson Hogg, after outliving various infatuations, married Williams' widow Jane, and lived with her the last thirty-five years of his life. The most remarkable of these epigoni was Edward John Trelawny, who came into Shelley's life at Pisa, when both were entering their thirtieth year. Shelley was nearing his end, Trelawny had still fifty-nine years to live. But already this "knight-errant, . . . dark, handsome, and mustachioed" (as Hunt described him), had had so many adventures, in so many countries, that his reminiscences never bored his new friends. Though Byron made him master of the horse and of *Bolivar*, it was Shelley, this "mild-mannered, beardless boy," whom this man of action learned most to love. After seeing Byron safely arrived but immobilized at Missolonghi, he went off to seek his own fate, expecting to die in the cause of Greece. He saw Greece liberated, resumed his wandering, lived till 1881, and was buried in the grave that he had bought in 1822, next to Shelley's ashes in the English cemetery at Rome.

CHAPTER XXIII

England's Neighbors

1789–1815

I. THE SCOTS

THEY had been under British rule since the Union of 1707, enjoying freedom of movement and trade within the island, but never reconciled to government by a distant Parliament in whose House of Commons Scotland's 1,800,000 souls were represented by forty-five delegates against the 513 representing the 10,164,000 population of England and Wales. Of the Scottish members, fifteen were appointed by self-perpetuating and corrupt town councils whose members were chosen by a total of 1,220 electors in all the boroughs. The remaining thirty were elected by the rural counties on a franchise limited to influential landholders; so the county of Bute, with 14,000 inhabitants, had twenty-one voters, and all the counties together had 2,405.[1] Most of the successful candidates had been selected by the great nobles of the old and spacious estates. Feudalism had been abolished throughout Scotland in 1748, but poverty remained, since greed and inequality are in the structure of man. By and large, Scotland, like England, accepted this form of representative government as the best that could be established among a people fondly tied to tradition, and too harassed by daily needs to acquire the knowledge and experience needed for voting intelligently on national issues.

Religion was stronger than the state. The Sabbath was a day of somber worship and remembrance of sin; the clergy preached Adam's fall, a personal Devil, and a vengeful God; and the congregations were more hardened in doctrine and morals than their pastors. David Deans, in *The Heart of Midlothian*, is sure that a girl who goes to a dance will go to hell.[2]

Nevertheless Scotland was in many ways ahead of England. She had a national system of really public schools: every parish was required to maintain a school where boys and girls together were taught reading and arithmetic. For this instruction the parents paid two shillings per quarter-year per student; and for two shillings more the student would get a touch of Latin. The children of paupers were paid for by the parish, and when the parish was too widespread to gather its children together, an itinerant schoolmaster brought some schooling to each section in turn. The teachers were strictly subject to the parish clergy, and were expected to help in transmitting a terrifying theology; for the elders had found that Calvinism was an economical way of installing a sheriff in every soul. A goodly number of undaunted spirits survived to produce the Scottish Enlightenment in the generation before the French Revolution, and to continue it, somewhat subdued, in the age of Napoleon.

Scotland was proud of its universities, at St. Andrews (founded in 1410), Glasgow (1451), Aberdeen (1494), and Edinburgh (1583). These considered themselves superior in many respects to Oxford and Cambridge, and some modern scholars admit the claim;[3] in medical instruction the University of Edinburgh was the acknowledged leader.[4] The *Edinburgh Review*, founded in 1802, was by common consent the most brilliant periodical in Great Britain, and the brave liberal lawyer Thomas Erskine (1750–1823) outshone nearly all other advocates before the London bar. It must be acknowledged, however, that when it came to suppressing freedom of thought—especially when this favored revolutionary France—no English jurist could rival the Scotch. Otherwise the intellectual climate in Edinburgh and Glasgow continued to favor the freedom that had protected David Hume, William Robertson, James Boswell, Robert Burns, and Adam Smith. We are told that not only the students but the entire intelligentsia of Edinburgh were to be seen taking notes at Dugald Stewart's lectures on philosophy.

Stewart is almost forgotten today outside Scotland; but one of the stateliest monuments in Edinburgh is a small classic temple erected to his memory. He followed Thomas Reid in subjecting the skeptical conclusions of Hume and the mechanistic psychology of David Hartley to the scrutiny of "common sense."[5] He rejected metaphysics as a vain attempt of the mind to fathom the nature of the mind. (Only Baron Munchausen could pull himself up by his bootstraps.) In place of metaphysics Stewart proposed inductive psychology, which would practice patient and precise observation of mental processes without pretending to explain mind itself. Stewart was a man of wit and style, who gave acute accounts of wit, fancy dreams, and the poetic faculty. (His country was still a fount of loving songs, and some of the tenderest tunes that warmed our youth came from the banks and braes of Scotland.)

James Mill—though he surfeited his son with education—was a man of good will and spacious intellect. Son of a shoemaker, he won honors in Greek at the University of Edinburgh. Having graduated, he moved to London, lived dangerously by journalism, married, and begot a son whom he named after his M.P. friend John Stuart. Between 1806 and 1818 he wrote a *History of British India* which contained so convincingly documented a critique of misrule that it advanced major reforms in the government of India.

Meanwhile (1808) he met Jeremy Bentham, and enthusiastically accepted the utilitarian proposal that ethical and political customs and concepts should be judged according to their ability to advance the happiness of mankind. Overflowing with energy and ideas, Mill made himself the apostle of Bentham to Britain. For the fourth (1810), fifth (1815), and sixth (1820) editions of the *Encyclopaedia Britannica* (itself a Scottish enterprise) he wrote articles—on government, jurisprudence, prison reform, education, and freedom of the press—which, republished, won wide circulation and influence. These essays, and his contributions to the *Westminster Review*, became a force in the movement that led to the Reform Act of 1832. Under such leadership the British radicals turned from total revolution to progressive reform through a government based on a widening franchise and a utilitarian philosophy. In *Elements of Political Economy* (1821) Mill warned against letting population grow faster than capital, and proposed taxation of the "unearned increment"—the laborless rise in the value of land. In an *Analysis of the Phenomena of the Human Mind* (1829) he sought to explain all mental operations through the association of ideas. And in 1835, a year before his death, he published a *Fragment on Mackintosh*.

Sir James Mackintosh continued the Scottish education of England. After acquiring the tools of thought at the universities of Aberdeen and Edinburgh, he migrated to London (1788). Soon he thrilled to the news that a popular uprising had captured the Bastille; in 1790 he resented Edmund Burke's hostile *Reflections on the French Revolution*; and in 1791 he answered that historic diatribe with *Vindiciae Gallicae*, a vindication of Gallic democracy. The twenty-six-year-old philosopher saw, in the early stages of the cataclysm, the noble voice and fruit of a humanitarian philosophy; whereas the threatened monarchies were not, as Burke supposed, the tested wisdom of tradition and experience but the chaotic residue of haphazard institutions, unforeseen events, and patchwork repairs.

> All the governments that now exist in the world (except the United States of America) have been fortuitously formed. . . . It was certainly not to be presumed that these fortuitous governments should have surpassed the works of intellect. . . . It was time that men should learn to tolerate nothing ancient that reason does not respect, and to shrink from no novelty to which reason may conduct. It was time that the human powers . . . should mark the commencement of a new era in history by giving birth to the art of improving government, and increasing the civil happiness of man.[6]

As the Revolution declined from the ideals of philosophers to the chaotic tyranny of terrified men, Mackintosh revised his theorems, and adjusted himself to the social forces impinging upon him. His lectures on "The Laws of Nature and of Nations" (1799) discoursed, in a way that would have pleased Burke, on how social organization can generate—in the individual's development—habits of action and judgments of conscience which acquire all the appearance of being innate; so the adult, through civilization, is a product not of nature only but of nurture as well. — In his final years Mackintosh wrote, from original researches and documents, a *History of the Revolution in England* (1832).

We may judge from these instances that Scottish civilization was not resting on its past glories at the turn of the eighteenth into the nineteenth century. Agriculture was prospering, especially in the Lowlands. There, too, the textile mills were busy, and Robert Owen was opening up new visions of human cooperation. Glasgow was proud of its scientists, and Edinburgh was throbbing with lawyers, doctors, and clergymen in the van of their time. In art Sir Henry Raeburn was painting portraits that made him the Reynolds of Scotland. In literature Boswell was publishing (1791) that inexhaustible fountain of delight, *The Life of Samuel Johnson;* and at Abbotsford on the Tweed, mediating between ancient enemies, singing melodious lays, and writing world-famous novels to pay debts only partly his own, was the finest Scot and gentleman of them all.

Walter Scott was by temperament well suited to be a leader in the Romantic flowering of British literature, for he liked to think of himself as descended from the Scottish border chieftains whose feuds and wars had provided stirring matter for the ballads that were fed him in his childhood. His immediate ancestors, however, were an Edinburgh solicitor and the daughter of a professor of medicine in the University of Edinburgh. He was born there in 1771, one of twelve children, six of whom, after the custom of that time, died in infancy. In his eighteenth month he was stricken with poliomyelitis, which left him permanently lame in his right leg. Byron's kindred disability may have helped Scott to maintain an undiscourageable friendship with the younger poet through all divergences of morals and belief.

After attending Edinburgh's Old College, Scott began a five-year apprenticeship in law under his father, and in 1792 he was admitted as an advocate to the Scottish bar. His marriage with Charlotte Charpentier (1797) and a legacy from his father (1799) gave him a comfortable income. He was sociable and likable, and won many influential friends, through whom, in 1806, he was appointed clerk of session at Edinburgh. The emoluments of office, and some bequests from relatives, allowed him to neglect, and soon abandon, his law practice in order to indulge his taste for literature.

A chance meeting with Robert Burns, a fondness for Thomas Percy's *Reliques of Ancient English Poetry,* and an acquaintance with the lyrics— especially *Lenore*—of Gottfried Bürger, refreshed his adolescent interest in old British ballads. In 1802–03 he brought out, in three volumes, *The Minstrelsy of the Scottish Border.* Stimulated by these lively tales, he tried his own hand at the form, and in 1805 he issued *The Lay of the Last Minstrel.* Its sale was a landmark in the annals of British poetry. When he went to London in 1807 he found himself the lord of the salons. He decided to make literature his profession and almost his business, and began a perilous investment of his time and money in composing, printing, and publishing.

In the rhymed octosyllabic couplets of Coleridge's *Christabel* he found an easy medium for his swiftly moving, romantic narratives of love and war, of mystery and the supernatural, in Scottish legend and history. He exploited the new field with *Marmion* (1808), *The Lady of the Lake* (1810), *Rokeby* (1813), and *The Lord of the Isles* (1815). He did not claim to be a great poet; he wrote to entertain the public profitably, not to entertain the Muses, who, after all, were weary of epics and hexameters. His readers followed him breathlessly from knight to fair lady to heroic fray; and they sang with zest such interspersed songs as "O, young Lochinvar is come out of the west, / Through all the wide Border his steed was the best."[7] Then, in 1813, Byron issued *The Giaour* and *The Bride of Abydos*, and in 1814 *The Corsair* and *Lara*. Scott saw his audience leaving border for Oriental mysteries and desperate misanthropes; he recognized that the young lord of Newstead Abbey could outrhyme and outpace the laird of Abbotsford; and in 1814, with *Waverley*, he turned from poetry to prose, and struck new ore.

It was most opportune. In 1802 he had advanced money to James Ballantyne, a printer at Kelso, to move his press to Edinburgh; in 1805 he became privately a partner in James and John Ballantyne's printing and publishing firm; and henceforth he arranged that his compositions, by whomever published, should be printed at the Ballantyne press. With his earnings and profits Scott bought in 1811 the estate of Abbotsford (near Melrose), expanded its 110 acres to 1,200, and replaced the old farmhouse with a château expensively furnished and beautifully adorned; it is one of the showplaces of Scotland. But in 1813 the Ballantyne firm neared bankruptcy, partly due to publishing, at a loss, various projects edited by Scott. He set himself to restore the Ballantynes to solvency with loans from his rich friends and with the proceeds from his writings. By 1817 the firm was solvent, and Scott was immersed in one of the most famous series of novels in literary history.

Waverley was published anonymously in 1814, and earned some two thousand pounds—much of which was soon spent on Abbotsford. Scott concealed his authorship, feeling it a bit unseemly for a clerk of sessions to write fiction for sale. His pen moved almost as fast in prose as it had done in verse. In six weeks he wrote *Guy Mannering* (1815); in 1816 *The Antiquary*; in 1816–19 (under the general title of *Tales of My Landlord*) he presented an engaging panorama of Scottish scenes—*Old Mortality, The Heart of Midlothian, The Bride of Lammermoor*, and *The Legend of Montrose;* from one of these Donizetti made another fortune. Scott traveled extensively through Scotland and England and the neighboring islands; he called himself an antiquary rather than a novelist; and he was able to give his stories a local color and dialectic tang that delighted his Scottish following. *Ivanhoe, The Monastery*, and *The Abbot*—all in 1820—took medieval England as their scene, not quite so realistically as the Scottish tales had done. In 1825 Scott ventured into the medieval East, and in *The Talisman* he gave so flattering a picture of Saladin that pious Scots began to doubt the thoroughness of the author's orthodoxy. When George Eliot was asked what first had shaken her Christian faith, she answered, "Walter Scott."[8]

Those of us who relished the "Waverley Novels" in youth are now too fevered with our modern pace to enjoy them today; but even a hurried immersion in one of them—say *The Heart of Midlothian*—renews our sense that the man who could produce such a book every year for a decade must have been one of the wonders of his time. We see him playing the feudal baron at Abbotsford (he was knighted in 1820), yet meeting all men with kindness and simplicity; the most famous author of the age—known from Edinburgh to St. Petersburg (where Pushkin revered him), but laughing heartily on hearing himself compared to Shakespeare. His poems and novels were potent factors in the Romantic movement, though he harbored few romantic delusions. He shared in reviving interest in medieval ways; nevertheless he pleaded with the Scots to put aside their idealization of their violent feudal past, and to adjust themselves to that Union which was slowly merging two peoples into one. In his old age he warmed himself with a Tory patriotism that would admit no fault in the British Constitution.

Meanwhile his printers, the Ballantynes, and his publisher, Archibald Constable, were both approaching bankruptcy. In 1826 they surrendered their remaining assets to the court, and Sir Walter, as partner, became liable for the Ballantynes' debts. Now at last Europe learned that the author of the Waverley Novels was the lord of Abbotsford. The court allowed him to keep his home and some acres, and his official salary as clerk of session, but all his other assets were forfeited. He could still live comfortably, and he continued to pour forth novel after novel in the hope that his earnings could annul his debts. In 1827 he sent forth a laborious *Life of Napoleon*, which a wit called "a blasphemy in ten volumes." It denuded the Corsican of almost every virtue, but it pleased the British soul, and moderately reduced the author's debts.

The quality of his remaining product reflected his haste and unease. In 1830–31 he suffered several strokes. He recovered, and the government assigned a frigate to take him for a cruise under the Mediterranean sun; but new strokes disabled him, and he was hurried back so that he might die in his beloved Abbotsford (1832). Another publisher, Robert Cadell, took over his remaining debts (£7,000) and copyrights, and made a fortune out of the combination, for the novels of Walter Scott remained popular till the end of the century. Wordsworth thought him "the greatest spirit of his generation."[9]

II. THE IRISH

Ireland in 1800 had approximately 4,550,000 souls, of whom 3,150,000 were Roman Catholics, 500,000 were Episcopal Protestants, and 900,000 (chiefly in Ulster) belonged to Dissenting Protestant sects. Catholics were granted the vote in 1793, and then became eligible to most civil-service posts; but they were still debarred from the highest offices, from the judicial bench, and from the Irish Parliament; in effect Catholics were allowed to choose among Protestant candidates to rule Catholic Ireland. The king or his ministers appointed a Protestant lord lieutenant, or viceroy, as chief executive over Ireland, and allowed him to rule the bureaucracy—and in considerable measure the Irish Parliament—through bribery and the distribution or sale of patronage.[10]

Till 1793 all the soil of Ireland was owned by British or Irish Protestants. After 1793 a small number of Catholics were allowed to purchase land; the rest were tenant farmers tilling small tracts, or were laborers on farms or in factories. Rents and tithes were collected with stern regularity, with the result that most Irish farmers lived in hopeless poverty. They were too poor, and too shorn of incentive, to buy the new machinery that was multiplying rural products in Britain; Irish agriculture remained static. "The greatest landlords were absentees living in England, who drew what they could from Ireland without nursing its capacity."[11] In the factory districts of Dublin poverty was even worse than on the land. Irish industry was choked by high duties that prevented the import of raw cotton, and by commercial regulations that to a large extent prevented Irish products, except linen, from competing with British products within the Empire.[12] Shelley, seeing the condition of the Dublin factory workers in 1812, wrote: "I had no conception of the depths of human misery until now."[13]

The Irish Catholics, like all the population, paid tithes to support the Established Protestant Church in Ireland; but in addition they maintained, by voluntary contributions, their Catholic clergy, who had been stripped of their former wealth. The Roman Church naturally supported the movement for Irish independence, and consequently won the loving loyalty of the Catholic population. Here the social rebel was usually a religious conservative; and liberals like Thomas Moore, though they might be friends with skeptics like Byron, never openly wandered from Catholic orthodoxy.

It was a Protestant who, in the second half of the eighteenth century, led the revolt against the exploitation of Ireland. Henry Grattan (1746–1820) belonged to the school of two other Irishmen—Burke and Sheridan; he believed in the power of reason expressed with eloquence. With this weapon he achieved some limited but significant victories: repeal of the Test Act, which had required submission to the Church of England as a prerequisite to membership in Parliament; the removal of the more stifling restrictions on Irish trade; and the recognition that (as he delicately put it) only the king of England, with the consent of the Parliament of Ireland, could legislate for Ireland—i.e., the acts of the Irish Parliament need no longer secure the approval of the Parliament of Great Britain. However, when Grattan tried to win for Ireland's Catholics full eligibility to the Irish Parliament, he failed; Ireland remained a Catholic country ruled by a Protestant government.

Theobald Wolfe Tone (1763–98) took up the battle. A graduate, like Grattan, of Trinity College, Dublin, he went to London to study law. Returning, he helped to organize the Society of United Irishmen (1791), whose aim was the cooperation of Protestants and Catholics in pursuit of social and political reform. Pushing ahead with passion and energy, Tone arranged a Catholic convention, whose program of action frightened the Irish Parliament into passing the Relief Act of 1793, extending the franchise to Catholics.

Tone was not satisfied. In 1794 he entered into negotiations with William Jackson, who secretly represented the Committee of Public Safety, then ruling a France at war with Britain. Jackson was detected and arrested; Tone fled to the United States, and thence to France. There he persuaded

Lazare Carnot, of the Committee, to sanction a French invasion of Ireland. General Lazare Hoche received command, made Tone an adjutant general, and sailed for Ireland on December 15, 1796, with forty-six ships and fourteen thousand men. The expedition encountered a storm off the English coast, and was almost totally wrecked. Tone survived, and accompanied a smaller expeditionary force aimed to help Ireland. This was captured by the British. Tone was sentenced to be hanged, but escaped the noose by cutting his throat in jail (November, 1798).

Meanwhile Irish resentment of English rule had grown into widespread revolt. Pitt, Britain's prime minister, thought to quiet the movement by conciliation. He allowed the Duke of Portland, home secretary (including Irish affairs), to appoint as lord lieutenant William Wentworth, second Earl Fitzwilliam, who frankly confessed his sympathy with the Irish. After three months of service (January–March, 1795), in which he made more concessions to the Catholics than Pitt thought wise, he was recalled, and the Irish resistance became open war. For a time Irish Protestants joined Catholics in attacking foreign rule; but in Ulster, where Protestants were in the majority, they soon changed from cooperation to opposition, fearing that the success of the rebellion would bring Ulster under Catholic domination. In September, 1795, Ulster Protestants formed the Orange Society, and joined the "Peep-of-Day Boys" in burning or wrecking Catholic houses and chapels; hundreds of Catholics fled from Ulster, fearing massacre. More and more Protestants seceded from the United Irishmen. The Catholic remainder took to arms, captured control of several counties, and advanced upon government citadels in Dublin. Grattan, in the Irish Parliament, thought to bring peace by proposing the eligibility of Catholics to Parliament; this was overwhelmingly rejected as involving (the Catholics now having the vote) the early transformation of the Irish Parliament into a Catholic power. The British general asked for and received reinforcements, and declared martial law; for weeks the once gay capital became a hell of hatred and killing. The count of corpses gave victory to the government; by the fall of 1798 the rebellion had been suppressed.

Pitt knew that suppression was not solution, and that the smoldering discontent in Ireland had become a vital danger to Britain. By 1800 England had had seven years of war with France, during which she had profited from the chaos produced in France by the Revolution. Now, however, Napoleon was bringing order to France and power to her armies; he was building a fleet that would soon challenge British control of the seas. A disaffected Ireland always on the verge of revolt was a daily invitation to Napoleon to lead his troops across the Channel, and—Catholics with Catholics—organize most of Ireland into a hostile force on Britain's flank. Some way, Pitt felt, must be found to bring the Irish people into a safe union with Britain under one Parliament and king. If this could be done Pitt proposed to give the full franchise—the vote and eligibility to office—to all adult male Catholics not only in Ireland but throughout England, Scotland, and Wales; to admit Catholics to one united Parliament in London; and to provide governmental salaries to dissenting ministers and Catholic priests as well as to the clergy of the Established Church.[14] In such an arrangement religion could become not a revolutionary ferment but a force for national unity and public content.

This statesmanlike plan, preceding by a year Napoleon's Concordat with the Catholic Church, met with a varied opposition. Irish Catholics suspected it as a disguise for the continued domination of Ireland by England; Irish Protestants protested that it would subject them to rule—perhaps vengeance and expropriation—by victorious Irish Catholics; and the Irish Parliament was unwilling to die. Pitt hoped that in the long run union with England—involving free trade with all parts of the Empire—would ultimately benefit the Irish economy and reunite the Irish as the Scots were reconciled. The Catholic majority in Ireland might be tempered and controlled by the immense Protestant majority in Britain. By a lavish use of money, sinecures, and peerages,[15] and the support of Irish merchants, the Irish Parliament was persuaded to vote its own death (August 1, 1800). Henceforth, till 1921, Ireland was to be ruled by the British Parliament, in which it would be represented by four spiritual and twenty-eight temporal peers in the House of Lords, and one hundred members in the Commons.

Pitt's apparent success was darkened by his inability to win the King to his design. When he proposed to carry out his implied promise of complete political emancipation to Catholics in the new "United Kingdom of Great Britain and Ireland," George III refused consent, on the ground that his coronation oath bound him to protect the Established Church of England. When Pitt pressed him, the King gave signs of relapsing into insanity. Pitt yielded, and, feeling compromised, he resigned from the King's ministry (February 3, 1801). Catholic emancipation was shelved, and had to wait till 1829.

Most of the Irish leaders concluded that they had been deceived, and that Pitt had never intended to implement his promise. Resistance to the Union as actually annexation rose to violence. In 1803 Robert Emmet led a forlorn revolt that made him one of the best-loved figures in Irish history and song. He was born in Dublin (1778) as the youngest son of a physician to the Lord Lieutenant. As a student in Trinity College he was nearing graduation with honors when he removed his name from the roll of undergraduates in protest against official inquisition into their political views. He joined the United Irishmen, where his older brother Thomas was secretary of the supreme council. Thomas advised against revolutionary violence, but Robert went to France, found access to Napoleon, and pleaded for another French attempt in Ireland. Unable to persuade Napoleon, Emmet returned to Dublin, gathered weapons and allies, and planned an attack upon Dublin Castle. When he learned that the government had discovered his plot and had ordered his arrest, he formed an impromptu force of 160 men, and marched toward the castle. On their way they encountered Lord Kilwarden, chief justice of Ireland; the excited and unmanageable crowd killed him and his nephew on the spot. Realizing that his effort must now fail, Emmet fled, and hid for a while among the Wicklow Mountains. He risked discovery by moving nearer to the home of his fiancée, Sarah Curran, daughter of John Philpot Curran, Protestant defender of Catholic causes. Robert was discovered, captured, tried for treason, and sentenced to death. His speech to the jury is one of the classics of Irish eloquence:

> I have but one request to make at my departure from the world: it is the charity of its silence. Let no man write my epitaph; for as no man who knows my motives dares now vindicate them, let not prejudice or ignorance asperse them. Let them and me rest in obscurity and peace, and my tomb remain un-inscribed, and my memory in oblivion, until other times and other men can do justice to my character. When my country takes her place among the nations of the earth, then, and not till then, let my epitaph be written.[16]

CHAPTER XXIV

Pitt, Nelson, and Napoleon

1789–1812

I. PITT AND THE REVOLUTION

WILLIAM Pitt II had taken office in 1783 as chancellor of the exchequer and first lord of the treasury. He who gathered and dispensed the money of the realm was to be lord of the isles and the Maecenas of coalitions.

He had enjoyed almost every advantage available to a Briton. He came of a prominent family, and absorbed world politics, high finance, and good manners from the conversation and entourage of his brilliant father, the Earl of Chatham. He had the best private education, much of it directly from that father himself. He entered Parliament at twenty-one, and took charge of England at twenty-four. He overwhelmed opposition by his proud reserve, his intellectual equipment, the logic, rather than passion, of his oratory, the firmness and penetration of his eye, his knowledge and manipulation of public finance. He had read and admired Adam Smith's *Wealth of Nations;* he accepted Smith's philosophy of free enterprise and free trade. He, the aristocrat, supported the claim of the rising mercantile and industrial bourgeoisie to fuller representation in Parliament and policy; with their fluid wealth he fought Napoleon, while the aristocracy, with their wealth in immobile land, contributed counsel, diplomacy, and protocol. He established a sinking fund for paying the national debt, and succeeded in reducing that debt until war took every shilling that could be drawn from the nation. He tried manfully but in vain to eliminate "rotten boroughs," though he had used them in his rise. He supported a measure that transferred from the judge to the popular jury the decision in cases of alleged libel—i.e., he protected the press in its exposure of official misconduct. He supported Wilberforce in the long campaign against the trade in slaves. Napoleon defeated him and broke his spirit, but it was the Britain that he had reorganized, financed, and inspired that defeated Napoleon.

The British King was almost as much of a problem as the French Consul. George III followed Pitt's advice in almost everything but the emancipation of the Catholics; but the aging monarch was at any moment liable to relapse into insanity—as he did in 1788–89; and when such breakdowns came, the Prince of Wales always hovered near the throne—the Prince who was the idol of the Whigs and the friend of Charles James Fox, who agreed with Pitt only in loving wine this side of paralysis. For a while George III was

512

relied upon to die (1787); he recovered, but remained weak and hesitant; and generally thereafter submitted, wondering, to Pitt's rule.

When the young statesman took the reins England was just beginning to recover from the disastrous war with her American colonies. Britain seemed militarily ruined in face of a France bankrupt but victorious, a Spain prospering and enlightened under Charles III, and a Russia swelling its borders under Catherine II, organizing vast armies, swallowing half of Poland, and plotting to divide European Turkey between herself and Joseph II of Austria. Now the safety of England depended on two conditions: her control of the seas, and the balance of political power in Continental Europe. If either end of that balance became supreme, it could dictate to England, simply by closing Continental markets to British goods. The death of Joseph II (1790) eased the Eastern threat; Catherine hesitated; and Pitt was about to turn from foreign to domestic affairs when the French Revolution announced that it had come to give a constitution to monarchies, or destroy them. Day by day the astonishing news crossed the Channel: the Bastille had been stormed by a city mob; feudal rights had been surrendered; church property had been confiscated by an impious state; a horde of women had marched on Versailles, and had forced Louis XVI and Marie Antoinette to come and live in Paris under popular surveillance.

At first Pitt was not as disturbed as his upper-class friends. After all, England already had a constitution, which any number of famous Frenchmen had praised and envied. A little turmoil in France would be appreciated: England could then work in peace on her internal problems while France disordered and then reconstituted its political life.[1] While aristocrats trembled, British men of letters rejoiced—Godwin, Wordsworth, Coleridge, Southey, Cowper, Burns. On November 4, 1789, a "Society for Commemorating the Revolution" (of 1688), was so stirred by a Unitarian preacher, Richard Price, that it sent an address of congratulations to the National Assembly in Paris, expressing the hope that "the glorious example given in France" might encourage other nations to assert the "inalienable rights of mankind."[2] The message was signed for the Society by its president, the third Earl Stanhope, brother-in-law of William Pitt. Price's address, circulated as a pamphlet throughout England, almost called for revolution:

> Be encouraged, all ye friends to freedom, and writers in its defence! The times are auspicious. Your labours have not been in vain. Behold kingdoms, admonished by you, starting from sleep, breaking their fetters, and claiming justice from their oppressors! Behold the light you have struck out—after setting America free—reflected to France, and there kindled into a blaze that lays despotism in ashes, and warms and illuminates Europe!
>
> Tremble, all ye oppressors of the world! Take warning, all ye supporters of slavish governments and slavish hierarchies! . . . You can not now hold the world in darkness. . . . Restore to mankind their rights, and consent to the correction of abuses, before they and you are destroyed together.[3]

This was more than Edmund Burke could stomach. He was no longer the fiery orator who had pleaded the cause of the American colonies before Parliament; he was sixty now, he had mortgaged himself to a large estate, and had regained the religion of his youth. On February 9, 1790, in the House of Commons, he began a debate which ended his old friendship with Charles James Fox:

> Our present danger is . . . from anarchy: a danger of being led, through an admiration of successful fraud and violence, to an imitation of the excess of an irrational, unprincipled, proscribing, confiscatory, plundering, ferocious, bloody, and tyrannical democracy. On the side of religion the danger is no longer from intolerance but from atheism—a foul, unnatural vice, a foe to all the dignity and consolation of mankind—which seems in France, for a long time, to have been embodied into a faction, accredited, and almost avowed.[4]

In November, 1790, Burke issued his *Reflections on the French Revolution.* He gave them the form of a letter to "a gentleman in Paris"—a letter 365 pages long. He denounced Dr. Price and the Society for Commemorating the Revolution: clergymen, he felt, should mind their business, which is to preach Christian virtues, not political reforms; the virtues reach to the heart of the matter, which is the evil tendencies of human nature; the reforms change only the surface forms of evil, for they effect no change in the nature of man. Universal suffrage is a fraud using a delusion; a count of noses will not affect the distribution and decisions of power. Social order is indispensable to individual security, but it cannot survive if every individual is free to violate any law that he does not like. An aristocracy is desirable, for it allows a nation to be ruled by trained and selected minds. Monarchy is good because it gives a psychological unity and historical continuity helpful in the difficult reconciliation of order with liberty.

Two months after this historic blast Burke published a *Letter to a Member of the National Assembly* of France. In this—and more fully in a *Letter to a Noble Lord* (1796)—he offered a philosophical basis for conservatism. No individual, however brilliant and well informed, can in one lifetime acquire the knowledge and wisdom that would warrant him to sit in judgment upon those complex, subtle, and persisting traditions that embody the experience and judgment of the community, the nation, or the race after thousands of experiments in the great laboratory called history. Civilization would be impossible "if the practice of all moral duties, and the foundations of society, rested upon having their reasons made clear and demonstrative to every individual."[5] So religion can only with great difficulty be explained to the youth who has acquired a little knowledge, and is delighting in his liberated reason; not until he has much experience of human nature, and has seen the power of primitive instincts, will he appreciate the services of religion in helping society to control the innate individualism of men. "If we should uncover our nakedness [release our instincts] by throwing off the Christian religion, which has been . . . one great source of civilization amongst us, . . . we are apprehensive . . . that some uncouth, pernicious, and degrading superstition might take the place of it."[6] Likewise it is difficult to explain to the youngster newly enreasoned, and envious of his neighbor's goods, that a man of exceptional ability will not go through long and expensive training to acquire a socially useful skill, or bestir himself to practice it, unless he is allowed to keep a portion of his earnings as a gift to his chidren. Furthermore, human society is not merely an association of persons in space, it is also a succession of persons in time—of persons dead, living, or unborn, in a continuity of flesh and blood through generations. That continuity lies more deeply in us than our association on a given spot of earth; it can persist through migrations across frontiers. How can this be made clear to boys bursting with individual ambition and sophomoric pride, and recklessly ready to snap family ties or moral bonds?

Burke's dirge for a dying world was greeted with gratitude and delight by the conservative leaders of Britain; and men of seasoned judgment accepted the three publications as a distinguished contribution to social and political philosophy. Coleridge, in his later years, enthused over them as once he had rejoiced over the Revolution. "I cannot conceive," he wrote in 1820, "a time or a state of things in which the writings of Burke will not have the highest value. . . . There is not one word I would add or withdraw."[7]

Two Britons, among many, came to the defense of the Revolution: Sir James Mackintosh with *Vindiciae Gallicae*, and Thomas Paine with *The Rights of Man*—both in 1791. The Revolution was then only two years old, but it had already done its basic work—given France a liberal constitution, ended feudal privileges, established freedom of speech, press, and assemblage, and appropriated the wealth of the Church to rescue a bankrupt state; the destructive excesses of the Revolution had not yet come. Under the circumstances Mackintosh could reply to Burke that the Revolution was a legitimate protest against an unjust and incompetent government. Paine could argue that no tradition should be suffered to deny all efforts at reform, and that the rights proclaimed by the Revolution were the proper charter of a modern state.

But Paine went much further. He demanded the replacement of monarchy and aristocracy by a republic; a steeply graduated income tax that would redistribute concentrated wealth, and would use it to wipe out unemployment and poverty, and provide education for every child, and a pension for the old. And he restated the rights of man in terms of Rousseau:

> 1. Men are born, and always continue, free and equal in respect of their rights. Civil distinctions, therefore, can be founded only on public utility.
> 2. The end of all political associations is the preservation of the natural and imprescriptible rights of man; these rights are liberty, property, security, and resistance of oppression.
> 3. The Nation is essentially the source of all sovereignty; nor can *any individual*, or *any body of men*, be entitled to any authority which is not expressly derived from it.[8]

The Rights of Man sold fifty thousand copies in a few weeks; this may indicate the strength of the radical movement in England in 1791. Societies more or less radical flourished: the Society for Constitutional Information, the Corresponding Society of London, the Scottish Friends of the People, the Society for Commemorating the Revolution. Some of these sent compliments to the French Revolution; two of them helped to give Paine's book a wide distribution.

Pitt observed, and was disturbed. Privately he was impressed by Paine's book: "Paine is no fool," he said to his niece; "he is perhaps right; but if I did what he wants I should have thousands of bandits on my hands tomorrow, and London burned."[9] He issued an order for Paine's arrest; Paine fled to France; he was tried in absence, and was declared guilty of treason (December, 1792).

The English had many reasons for not following France into revolution. They had had their 1789 in 1642. They had had their intellectual revolt before the French: the deist erosion of orthodox belief had preceded the French Enlightenment, and had been absorbed into British equanimity by the time Voltaire reached England in 1726. The Methodist movement diverted some discontent into piety. The Anglican Church was comparatively liberal, and had not acquired enough wealth to arouse the envy and hostility of the laity. Feudalism had disappeared; there were no feudal dues; a large proportion of the peasantry owned the land that it tilled. The middle class had already entered Parliament, and found effective voice in national policy; the Prime Minister often supported its claims. The workers were badly treated by employers and legislators, and some rebelled violently, but the Army could be depended upon to suppress them, and the judiciary to hang their leaders. When England and France went to war, patriotism diverted class hatred into nationalist fervor. Revolution subsided into reform, and spread itself out through the nineteenth century.

Meanwhile the French Revolution had passed from legislation to the September Massacres; its army had defeated the Prussians and the Austrians at Valmy (September 20, 1792); and the revolutionary fever had spread into Rhineland Germany. The citizens of Mainz and Darmstadt, having thrown off feudal rule and set up a popular government, and fearing invasion and punishment by monarchical troops, had sent emissaries to France, asking protection. After some debate the French government issued (November 19, 1792) the most revolutionary of all its decrees:

> The National Convention declares, in the name of the French Nation, that it will accord fraternity and aid to all peoples who wish to recover their liberty, and charges the executive power to give the generals the orders necessary for bringing aid to these peoples, and to defend the citizens who shall have been, or may be, troubled for the cause of freedom.[10]

This recklessly generous announcement set every European monarchy on edge. The government of Great Britain was further alarmed by the advance of French troops into Belgium, and the demands of France upon Holland for the opening of the River Scheldt to all trade. This navigable river, 270 miles long, rises in eastern France, and wanders through Belgium (passing close to Antwerp) into Holland, where it divides into two estuaries and empties into the North Sea. Holland, by permission of the Peace of Westphalia (1648), had closed both estuaries to all trade except of its own choice, which favored Britain and excluded Belgium; so Antwerp declined and Amsterdam flourished. On November 27, 1792, the French government notified England of its resolve to force open the outlets of the Scheldt. Pitt replied that Britain was bound, by a treaty of 1788, to protect Holland from any foreign attack. Furthermore, since the Rhine also emptied into the North Sea through Dutch estuaries, the control of Holland by France would mean French control of the mouths of the Rhine, and therefore of British trade reaching central Germany by the Rhine. On December 31, 1792, the British government notified France that

> England will never consent that France should arrogate the power of annulling at her pleasure—and under the pretence of a pretended natural right of which she makes herself the only judge—the political system of Europe, established by solemn treaties and guaranteed by the consent of all the Powers. This government, adhering to the maxims which it has followed for more than a century, will also never see with indifference that France shall make itself, either directly or indirectly, the sovereign of the Low Countries, or general arbiter of the rights and liberties of Europe.[11]

January 21, 1793, the French government beheaded Louis XVI. News of this reached London on the 23rd, shocking George III, and, soon thereafter, most of the British people. On January 24 the British government ordered the French minister, Marquis François-Bernard de Chauvelin, to leave the kingdom. On February 1 France declared war on both England and Holland.

George III welcomed the war, believing that it would unify the nation. Pitt regretted it, but gave it all his energies. He opened negotiations that led to the First Coalition (1793): Britain, Portugal, Spain, Sardinia, Naples, Austria, Prussia, and Russia. He levied high taxes upon every class and group in the kingdom, and sent repeated subsidies to his allies. He tightened the laws against any propaganda defending France or the Revolution. He suspended the freedom of the press, and (1794) the Habeas Corpus Act, which had secured the right of every arrested person to early trial or speedy release; political suspects could now be held without trial. (France did the same.) After an antiwar demonstration in which a stone was thrown at the King, the Seditious Meetings Act (1796) forbade meetings of over fifty people except under governmental license and control. Critics of the British Constitution were liable to seven years' exile in Australia's Botany Bay. Prominent radicals—John Horne Tooke, philologist, John Thelwall, friend of the early Coleridge, and shoemaker Thomas Hardy, founder of the London Corresponding Society—were tried on charges of treason (May, 1794), were defended by Thomas Erskine, and were acquitted.

These trials revealed the panic that had struck the upper classes of Britain when they found themselves faced by another revolution so soon after the costly revolt of the American colonies. The thousand-year-old world of kings and aristocracies seemed to be collapsing, besieged by peasants burning feudal châteaux and title deeds, and by city mobs imprisoning the royal family and cutting off hundreds of noble heads. All this, many Britons felt, was the result of atheistic French "philosophers," and of their English imitations, Godwin and Paine. Any time now the godless French troops would take Holland and the Rhineland; in a year or two they might try to invade England. How could Britain, with only 15 million men and no standing army, defeat in war a France with 28 million men and an army already proud with victory?

Pitt knew all this, but he thought in terms of money rather than of men; men could be bought for money, if not in England, then in Austria, Prussia, Russia; and England had money, coming in every day from commerce, industry, land, colonies, loans, taxes on every article of consumption, on every form of income. These revenues could equip a small army for defense against an improbable invasion; they could keep Britain's factories humming, her press patriotic and her caricaturists at the top of their form; they could pay for new armies provided by allies short of money and long of men. Above all, they could build and man ships numerous enough, armed enough, to control the oceans, blockade every French port, capture any French vessel at sea, annex to the British Empire any French colony. Every month that Navy was growing in sturdy ships and disciplined, incomparable seamen. And it had one of the greatest admirals in history.

II. NELSON: 1758–1804

The Nelsons were originally Nielsens, of East Anglian Viking stock; perhaps Horatio had ships in his blood. He was born September 29, 1758, in Burnham Thorpe, Norfolk, which neighbors the sea. His father was rector of the parish. His mother was related to Robert Walpole, prime minister. Her brother, Captain Maurice Suckling, was assigned in 1770 to H.M.S. *Raisonnable* in expectation of war with Spain. Horatio, aged twelve, begged and received permission to serve under him; thereafter the boy's school was the sea.

He was not physically strong; he was often sick; but he was resolved to seize every opportunity for instruction, development, and honor. He served in various vessels on a variety of missions, repeatedly risking his life; was promoted step by step, and at twenty was made captain of the frigate *Hinchinbrook*. He was as vain as he was competent, and never doubted that he would someday reach the top in post and fame. He was as tardy in obeying his superiors as they were in rewarding his services; but he gave an arm, then an eye, then his life for Britain, and could be indulged in a pride as lofty as his monument.

Sensitive to every sight and touch, he readily surrendered to the beauty, grace, and tenderness of women. At Quebec in 1782, as captain of the *Albemarle*, he was on the verge of leaving his post at the cost of his career, to return to the city with an offer of marriage to a woman who had given him her warmth the night before; a resolute friend barred his way and called him back to his duty and destiny.[12] In 1787, as captain of the cruiser *Boreas*, he dallied at Antigua, in the West Indies, and married Mrs. Frances Nisbet, a pretty young widow with a rich uncle. He brought her to England, set her up on a small but comfortable estate, and spent a happy interbellum with her in the country. When war with France became likely he was made captain (1793) of the *Agamemnon*—one of the most highly rated ships in the Navy—with instructions to join Lord Hood's fleet in the Mediterranean, and incidentally take a note to Sir William Hamilton, British minister at the court of Naples. He delivered the message, and met Lady Hamilton.

Amy Lyon, born in 1761 to a Welsh blacksmith, had in youth earned her bread with her body, and had borne two illegitimate children by the time she was nineteen. In that year she settled down as the mistress of the Honorable Charles Greville, second son of the Earl of Warwick. He rechristened her Emma Hart, taught her the arts of ladyship—singing, dancing, harpsichord, entering a room gracefully, exchanging nougats of conversation, and pouring tea. When he had refashioned everything but her soul, he took her to George Romney, who painted thirty portraits of her. When Greville found a chance to marry an heiress, he had to find another berth for his fair lady, who had now learned to love him. Luckily his uncle Sir William Hamilton, a childless widower, was then in England. He was rich, a foster brother of George III, a fellow of the Royal Society, a distinguished collector of Herculanea and classic art. He found Emma to his liking, and agreed to take her off his nephew's hands. After returning to Naples, he sent Emma an invitation to come to Naples with her mother and there complete her education in music. She accepted, on the understanding that Charles Greville would soon follow her. He did not come.

Sir William gave her and her mother four rooms in the British Legation. He comforted her with luxuries and tactful admiration; he arranged for her instruction in music and Italian; he paid her milliners without complaint. She wrote fond letters to Greville, begging him to come; he bade her "oblige Sir William"; his letters became rarer, shorter, and ceased. She became Sir William's mistress, for she relished love only next to luxury. Otherwise she behaved modestly and discreetly, spread charity, became a favorite with the nuns, the King, and the Queen. She sat for her portrait to Raphael Mengs, Angelica Kauffmann, Mme. Vigée-Lebrun. Pleased with her, Sir William made her his wife (1791). When France declared war on England she became an active and passionate patriot, and labored to keep Naples in the coalition with England.

In the summer of 1794 Nelson was ordered to lay siege to Calvi, a seaport of Corsica, then held by the French. He captured the stronghold, but during the battle an enemy shot, striking near him, spattered sand into his right eye. The wound healed without disfigurement, but the eye was left permanently blind.

That victory meant little in the perspective of events, for their course in the next two years was strongly against England. Napoleon entered Italy, scattered the Sardinian and Austrian armies, and compelled the governments of Sardinia, Austria, and Naples to leave the First Coalition and accept terms of peace with France. In October, 1796, Spain, angered by British actions in the West Indies, declared war against England. With the Spanish fleet ready to join the French in the Mediterranean, that sea became unsafe for the British. On February 14, 1797, a British force of fifteen ships under Admiral Sir John Jervis, then commander of the Mediterranean fleet, came upon a Spanish armada of twenty-seven vessels some thirty miles out from Cape St. Vincent, the extreme southwest coast of Portugal. Nelson, commanding H.M.S. *Captain,* directed this and other vessels to attack the rear guard of the enemy flotilla, and himself led his men in boarding and capturing the *San Josef* and then the *San Nicolas.* The Spanish ships, poorly armed and poorly managed, with untrained men at the guns, surrendered, one after another, giving the English so complete a victory that Jervis was made Earl of St. Vincent, and Nelson was made a knight of the Bath. The British Navy was again master of the Mediterranean.

In July, 1797, Nelson—now a rear admiral—was sent to capture Santa Cruz, on one of the Canary Islands. The town had been strongly fortified by the Spanish as strategically vital for protection of their trade with the Americas. It offered an unexpectedly able resistance, helped by a rough surf that made the British landing boats almost unmanageable; some were smashed on rocks, some were disabled by Spanish guns; the attack failed. Nelson himself was shot in the right elbow; the arm was incompetently amputated, and Nelson was sent home to recuperate under the care of his wife.

He fretted at the thought that the Admiralty would list him—with only one arm and one eye—as permanently disabled. He begged for a new commission. In April, 1798, he was assigned as rear admiral to H.M.S. *Vanguard,* with orders to join Lord St. Vincent's fleet near Gibraltar. On May 2 he was given command of three ships of the line and five frigates, with instructions to watch outside Toulon, where Napoleon was preparing a mysterious expedition under the shelter of the harbor's forts. On May 20 Nelson's squadron was so badly damaged by a storm that it had to retire to Gibraltar for repairs. When the ships returned to their watch Nelson learned that the French flotilla, under cover of darkness, had left Toulon and sailed east, destination unknown. He set sail in pursuit, spent much time following false clues, ran out of supplies, and put in at Palermo to provision and recondition his fleet. This was allowed him through the intercession of Lady Hamilton with the Neapolitan government, which, being then at peace with France, had hesitated to allow this violation of its neutrality.

His ships again in good order, Nelson led them back to the search for Napoleon's fleet. He found it at last at Abukir, near Alexandria. Now again he risked everything. On the night of July 31, 1798, he bade his officers put all their ships in readiness for battle at dawn. "By this time tomorrow," he said, "I shall have gained a peerage or Westminster Abbey"—a hero's tomb.[13] In the battle he exposed himself as usual. A fragment of shot struck him in the forehead; he was taken below deck in expectation of death, but the wound proved superficial, and soon Nelson, head bandaged, was back on deck, and remained there till the British victory was complete.

With the dangerous "Little Corporal" apparently bottled up, Pitt was able to form a Second Coalition with Russia, Turkey, Austria, Portugal, and Naples. The Neapolitan Queen Maria Carolina, sister of the guillotined Marie Antoinette, happy to see her chaotic kingdom once more engaged on the side of the Hapsburg dynasty and the Catholic Church, joined with her lackadaisical King Ferdinand IV in preparing a royal welcome for Nelson's victorious but damaged fleet, which anchored in Naples' harbor on September 22, 1798. Lady Hamilton, seeing the wounded admiral, rushed forward to greet him, and fainted in his arms.[14] She and her husband took him into their legation, the Palazzo Sassa, and did everything for his comfort. Emma made no effort to conceal her infatuation, and the famished hero warmed to her under her smiles and care. He was forty, she was thirty-seven; she was no longer ravishing, but she was near and fed the Briton with the adulation which had become to him, next to battle, the wine of life. Sir William, now fifty-eight, running short of funds and absorbed in art and politics, accepted the situation philosophically, and may have felt relieved. By the spring of 1799 Nelson was paying a large part of Emma's expenses. The British Admiralty, after voting him the highest honors and substantial sums, and allowing him due rest, bade him go to the aid of other admirals; he excused himself on the ground that it was more important for him to stay and protect Naples from the spreading revolution.

Late in 1799 Hamilton was replaced by Arthur Paget as British minister at Naples. On April 24, 1800, Sir William and Emma left Naples for Leghorn, where they were joined by Nelson; thence they traveled overland to the Channel, and across the Channel to England. All London feted him, but public opinion condemned his continued attachment to another man's wife. Mrs. Nelson came to reclaim her husband, and demanded that he divest himself of Emma; when he refused, she left him. On January 30, 1801, Emma, at Sir William's estate, gave birth to a daughter, whom she named Horatia Nelson Thompson, presumably a product of "the Nelson touch." In that month Nelson, who had meanwhile become a vice-admiral, set out on his next assignment—to capture or destroy the Danish fleet; we shall see him there. On his return, and during the Peace of Amiens, he lived on his estate at Merton in Surrey, with the Hamiltons as his guests. On April 6, 1803, Sir William died, in his wife's arms and holding Nelson's hand. Thereafter, with an inheritance of eight hundred pounds a year, she lived with Nelson at Merton till he was called to his greatest victory and his death.

III. TRAFALGAR: 1805

When Pitt resigned his first ministry (February 3, 1801) he readily supported the appointment of his friend Henry Addington as his successor. Addington shared Pitt's dislike of the war. He noted its unpopularity with the country, especially with exporters; he saw how readily Austria had dissolved the Second Coalition after her defeat at Marengo; he saw no sense in wasting subsidies on such weak-kneed allies; he resolved to end the war as soon as face-saving would permit. On March 27, 1802, his agents signed with Napoleon the Peace of Amiens. For fourteen months the guns were silent; but Napoleon's expansion of his power in Italy and Switzerland, and England's refusal to leave Malta, ended this lucid interval, and hostilities were resumed on May 20, 1803. Addington commissioned Nelson to command and prepare a fleet whose mission was simple: to locate the main French armada and destroy it to its last ship. Meanwhile Napoleon was filling with men and matériel vast camps, harbors, and arsenals at Boulogne, Calais, Dunkirk, and Ostend, and was building hundreds of vessels designed to ferry his legions across the Channel for the conquest of England. Addington struggled to meet this challenge, but he vacillated rather than commanded, while the organization of home defense stumbled into chaos. When his party supporters fell from 270 to 107 he signified his willingness to resign; and on May 10, 1804, Pitt began his second ministry.

He set himself at once to form a Third Coalition (1805), with Russia, Austria, and Sweden, and gave them subsidies raised in part by an increase of twenty-five percent in taxes. Napoleon responded by ordering his Channel army to march across France and give Austria another lesson; and to his vice-admiral, Pierre de Villeneuve, he sent instructions to prepare the best ships of the French Navy to meet Nelson in a fight to end British control of the seas.

Nelson's flagship, the *Victory*, had 703 men, averaging twenty-two years old; some were twelve or thirteen, a few were ten. About half of them had been captured by press gangs; many were convicts condemned to naval service as a penalty for crime. Their pay was minimal, but they shared, according to their station and behavior, in the cash realized from captured vessels or stores. Shore leave was rare, through fear of desertions; to meet the needs of the men, cargoes of prostitutes were brought on board; at Brest, one morning 309 women were afloat, with 307 men.[15] The conscripts soon learned, through hard discipline, to adjust themselves to their condition, and usually to take pride in their work and their courage. Nelson, we are told, was popular with his men because he never punished except through obvious necessity and with visible regret; because he knew a seaman's business, and seldom erred in tactics or command; because he himself faced the guns of the enemy; and because he made his men believe that they would never fail him or England, and would never be defeated. This was the "Nelson touch" that made these condemned men love him.[16]

On July 8, 1803, he joined his eleven ships in the Mediterranean off Toulon, in whose spacious harbor Villeneuve and his fleet were finding protection by the guns of the forts. The French admiral had lately received new orders from Napoleon: to escape from Toulon, force a passage by Gibraltar, sail to the West Indies, join another French squadron there and attack British forces wherever encountered. While Nelson's ships were taking on water at a Sardinian port, Villeneuve escaped from Toulon (March 30, 1805), and made full sail for America. Nelson belatedly pursued him, and reached Barbados on June 4. Hearing of this, Villeneuve headed back across the Atlantic, and effected union, at Corunna, with a Spanish squadron of fourteen vessels under Admiral Federico de Gravina.

Revised orders from Napoleon bade him sail north, join another French force at Brest, and attempt to wrest control of the Channel before Nelson could come up from the West Indies. But Villeneuve's ships, after their Caribbean cruise, were in no condition to face battle. On August 13 he led his enlarged fleet in a dash south to the well-equipped and well-fortified harbor of Cádiz, and began there the reconditioning of his ships and men. Late in August a British squadron under Vice-Admiral Cuthbert Collingwood took up the task of keeping watch on Villeneuve. Nelson, after completing his comedy of crossings, thought that he too, and his men, needed repairs and rest, and he was allowed some weeks with his mistress at Merton. On September 28 he and his ships joined Collingwood off Cádiz, and waited impatiently for the French to come out and fight.

Napoleon again changed his instructions: Villeneuve was to leave Cádiz, try to elude the British fleet, and go to cooperate with Joseph Bonaparte in the French control of Naples. On October 19 and 20 the reluctant admiral led his thirty-three ships out of Cádiz and headed for Gibraltar. On the 20th Nelson sighted them, and at once ordered his twenty-seven vessels to clear their decks for battle. That night he began, and the next morning finished, a letter to Lady Hamilton:

> My Dearest beloved Emma, the dear friend of my bosom the signal has been made that the Enemy's combined fleet are coming out of port. We have very little wind so that I have no hopes of seeing them before tomorrow. May the God of Battles crown my endeavours with success at all events I will take care that my name shall ever be most dear to you and Horatia both of whom I love as much as my own life. . . . May God Almighty give us success over these fellows and enable us to get peace.[17]

And in his diary, on the day of battle, he wrote:

> . . . May the Great God . . . grant to my country, and for the benefit of Europe in general, a great and glorious Victory, and may no misconduct in any one tarnish it; and may humanity after victory be the predominant feature in the British fleet. For myself, . . . I commit my life to Him who made me; and may his blessing light upon my endeavours for serving my Country faithfully. To him I assign myself and the just cause which is entrusted to me to defend. Amen. Amen. Amen.[18]

The rival armadas met on October 21, 1805, off Cape Trafalgar, on the coast of Spain shortly south of Cádiz. Villeneuve, from his flagship *Bucentaure*, signaled to his ships to form in a single line from north to south, their port sides to the oncoming enemy; the vessels, imperfectly handled, had barely completed this maneuver when they found themselves the target of the British forces advancing northeastward in a double line. At 11:35 A.M. Nelson, from his flagship *Victory*, sent flashing throughout his fleet the famous signal "England expects that every man will do his duty." At 11:50 Admiral Collingwood, commanding fifteen ships, led the attack by ordering his flagship, the *Royal Sovereign*, to sail directly through the gap between the first and second of Admiral Gravina's men-of-war, the *Santa Ana* and the *Fougueux*. By this move his men were in a position to fire broadsides against both the Spanish vessels, which could not return the fire—battleships were then designed with few or no guns fore or aft. The British gunners had an additional advantage: they could ignite their cannon with flintlocks (pistol locks having a flint in the cock to strike a spark); this method was twice as quick as the French way of igniting cannon by slow-acting matches; and the firing could be better synchronized with the roll of the ship.[19] The remainder of Collingwood's squadron followed his example by piercing the enemy's line, then veering, and concentrating their attack upon Gravina's ships, where morale was low. At the northern end of the battle line the French met bravely the fury of Nelson's attack; some of them cried, *"Vive l'Empereur!"* as they died; nevertheless, as at Abukir, the superior training and skill of the British crews, in seamanship and gunnery, carried the day.

But the issue was decided when a sniper in the topmast of the *Redoutable* directed a fatal shot at Nelson. The admiral had not only exposed himself as usual; he had doubled his peril by refusing to remove from his chest the distinguishing badges of honor that England had conferred upon him. The ball went through his breast and shattered his spine. His devoted aide, Captain Thomas Masterman Hardy, carried him down into the hold, where Dr. Beatty confirmed Nelson's conviction that he had only a few hours of life left to him. He remained conscious another four hours, long enough to learn that his fleet had won a complete victory, that nineteen of the enemy's ships had surrendered, not one of the British. Almost his last words were, "Take care of my dear Lady Hamilton, Hardy; take care of poor Lady Hamilton." Then, "Kiss me, Hardy. Now I am satisfied. Thank God, I have done my duty."[20]

All of Nelson's ships, anchored by Nelson's deathbed command, survived the gale that he had foreseen, and reached England in time to let their crews share in the national celebration of their victory. The hero's corpse, immersed in brandy to delay decomposition, was carried upright in a cask to England, where it received the most splendid funeral in living memory. Captain Hardy delivered to Lady Hamilton her dead lover's farewell letter. She treasured it as her only consolation. At the end of it she wrote:

Oh miserable wretched Emma,
Oh glorious and happy Nelson.

His will left all his property and governmental rewards to his wife except for the house at Merton, which Emma Hamilton retained. Worried lest this —and her annuity from her husband—should not keep her in comfort, he wrote a codicil to his will on the day of battle: "I leave Emma Lady Hamilton as a legacy to my King and Country, that they will give her an ample provision to maintain her rank in life"; and in his dying hours, as reported by Dr. Scott, he asked that his country should take care also of "my daughter Horatia."[21] King and country ignored these requests. Emma was arrested for debt in 1813, and soon released, and fled to France to escape her creditors. She died in poverty at Calais, January 20, 1815.

Admiral Gravina, after an honorable resistance, escaped with his flagship to Spain, but so severely wounded that he died a few months later. Villeneuve had not led wisely but had fought bravely, exposing himself as recklessly as Nelson; he surrendered his ship only after nearly all his men were dead. He was taken to England, was released, and left for France. Unwilling to face Napoleon, he killed himself in a hotel at Rennes, April 22, 1806. His final letter apologized to his wife for deserting her, and thanked the fates that he was leaving no child "to be burdened with my name."[22]

Trafalgar was one of the "decisive battles" of history. It decided for a century Britain's mastery of the seas. It ended Napoleon's chance to free France from the cordon that the British fleet had drawn along her shores. It forced him to give up all thought of invading England. It meant that he must fight land battles ever more costly, and ever leading to more. He thought to cancel Trafalgar by his massive victory at Austerlitz (December 2, 1805); but this led to Jena, Eylau, Friedland, Wagram, Borodino, Leipzig, Waterloo. Sea power would win.

Even so, Pitt, who had lived through a hundred crises to rejoice over Trafalgar, agreed with Napoleon in thinking that Austerlitz had matched and canceled Nelson's victory. Worn out by a succession of crises in domestic as well as foreign affairs, he withdrew from London for a rest in Bath. There he received the news that Austria, the pivot of his coalitions, had again collapsed. The shock gave the finishing touch to physical ailments deadened and doubled by brandy. On January 9, 1806, he was taken to his home in Putney. In that house, on January 23, 1806, he died, aged forty-seven, after having been prime minister of Great Britain through nearly all his adult life. In those nineteen years he had helped to guide his country to industrial, commercial, and maritime supremacy, and had reformed its financial system masterfully; but he had failed either to chasten and confine the French Revolution or to check the dangerous expansion of Napoleon's authority in Europe. The Continental balance of power, so precious to England, was disappearing, and hard-won domestic liberties of speech, assemblage, and press had been lost for the duration of a war that had now gone on for twelve years, and gave no sign of an end.

IV. ENGLAND MARKS TIME: 1806–12

The scope of our canvas will not allow us to describe in detail the four ministries that succeeded Pitt's. Barring a year of Fox, their energies went to personal and party problems rather than to statesmanship and policy, and their sum total, internationally, was more of the same to the same result: the descent from prosperity to destitution, and from enterprise into procrastination.

The brief "Ministry of All the Talents" (1806–07) was brightened by the efforts of Charles James Fox, as secretary for foreign affairs, to arrange peace with France. His unsteady career had been marked by a patient liberalism and his capacity to accept the French Revolution, and even Napoleon, into the tolerable eccentricities of history. Unfortunately he came to power when his strength of body and mind had suffered from his reckless enjoyment of food and drink. He made a handsome approach to negotiations by sending word to Talleyrand (February 16, 1806) that a British patriot had come to the Foreign Office with a plan for assassinating Napoleon, and adding assurances that the zany was being carefully watched. The Emperor appreciated the gesture, but he was so elated with his triumph over Austria, and Britain was so exalted by Nelson's victory at Trafalgar, that neither would make the concessions required as preparatory to peace. Fox succeeded better with his proposal to Parliament for ending the traffic in slaves; after a generation of effort by Wilberforce and a hundred others, the measure became law (March, 1807). By that time Fox had died (September 13, 1806), aged fifty-seven, and British politics fell into a treadmill of hopeful inertia.

This, however, would hardly be the just word for the dominant figures in the ministry (1807–09) of William Cavendish Bentinck, Duke of Portland. George Canning, secretary for foreign affairs, sent a fleet to bombard Copenhagen (1807); and Robert Stewart, Viscount Castlereagh, secretary for war, sent a disastrous expedition to Walcheren in an attempt to capture Antwerp (1809). The two secretaries, matched in ability and passion, quarreled over each other's enterprises, and fought a duel, which scratched Canning. Doubly tarnished by internal comedy and external tragedy, the Portland ministry resigned.

Spencer Perceval, as minister (1809–12), had the double misfortune of seeing Britain reach its nineteenth-century nadir, and of being assassinated for his pains. By the fall of 1810 Napoleon's Continental Blockade had so injured British industry and commerce that thousands of Britons were unemployed, and millions were on the edge of destitution. Unrest had come to revolutionary violence; the Luddite weavers began to smash machines in 1811. In 1810 British exports to northern Europe had brought in £7,700,000; in 1811 they brought in £1,500,000.[23] In 1811 England was slipping into a second war with America; as part of the cost her exports to the United States fell from £11,300,000 in 1810 to £1,870,000 in 1811. Meanwhile taxes were rising for every Briton, until, by 1814, their burden threatened the collapse of Britain's financial system, and the credit of her currency abroad. Hungry Britons cried out for a lowering of import duties on foreign grain; agricultural Britons opposed such a move lest it reduce the price of their product; Napoleon eased the crisis for England (1810–11) by selling export licenses to French grain producers; he needed cash for his campaigns. When the Grand Army set out for Russia in 1812 England knew that victory for Napoleon would mean the more rigid closing of all Continental ports against British goods, and Napoleon's fuller control of Continental shipments to Britain. All England watched and worried.

Except George III. He was spared awareness of these events by his final lapse into deafness, blindness, and insanity. The death of his best beloved daughter Amelia (November 1810) was the last blow, snapping all connection between his mind and reality; now he was privileged to live in a world of his own, in which there were no rebel colonies, no ministerial Foxes, no unmannerly, murderous Napoleons. He must have found some satisfaction in this condition, for otherwise his health improved; he lived on for ten years more, talking cheerfully, without bond or burden of logic or grammar, amid every comfort and service, and through a postwar depression worse than that of 1810–12. His popularity grew with his disease. His starving people pitied him, and wondered, with old myths, had he not been touched and taken by God.

On May 11, 1812, in the lobby of the House of Commons, Prime Minister Perceval was shot dead by a bankrupt broker, John Bellingham, who felt that his commercial enterprises had been ruined by the policies of the government. In June, under the Earl of Liverpool, a new cabinet was formed, which, by miracles of tact and circumstance, endured till 1827. In that same June the United States declared war upon England, and Napoleon's 500,000 men crossed the Niemen into Russia.

Fig. 47—Sir Thomas Lawrence: *Arthur Wellesley, 1st Duke of Wellington*. Wellington Museum, Apsley House, London.   PAGE 535

FIG. 48—GEORGE ROMNEY: *William Pitt the Younger*. The Tate Gallery, London.

FIG. 49—SIR THOMAS LAWRENCE: *George IV as Prince Regent* (1814). The National Portrait Gallery, London. PAGE 357

Fig. 50—George Romney: *Lady Hamilton as Ariadne*. Reproduced by courtesy of the Trustees, the National Maritime Museum, London.

PAGE 519

Fig. 51—L. F. Abbott: *Nelson after Losing His Arm at Teneriffe*. Reproduced by courtesy of the Trustees, the National Maritime Museum, London.   PAGE 518

FIG. 52—HENRY SCHEFFER: *Prince Eugène de Beauharnais, Viceroy.* (The Bettmann Archive)

FIG. 53—*Portrait of Pauline Bonaparte*. (The Bettmann Archive)   PAGE 220

Fig. 54—Jacques-Louis David: *Pope Pius VII*. Louvre, Paris. (Cliché des Musées Nationaux)

PAGE 548

FIG. 55—ENGRAVING AFTER A PAINTING BY SIR THOMAS LAWRENCE: *Prince Klemens Wenzel von Metternich*. (The New York Society Library)

PAGE 560

FIG. 56—PAINTING AFTER A PORTRAIT BY DROUAIS: *Emperor Joseph II.* (The Bettmann Archive)   PAGE 558

FIG. 57—ENGRAVING: *Queen Louise of Prussia.*
(The Bettmann Archive)   PAGE 595

FIG. 58—*Karl Friedrich Gauss.* (The Bettmann Archive)   PAGE 607

FIG. 59—*Statue of Alessandro Volta*
at Como, Italy. (The Bettmann
Archive)   PAGE 551

FIG. 60—*The Brandenburg Gate*, DESIGNED BY KARL GOTTHARD LANGHANS, WITH THE *Quadriga* BY JOHANN GOTTFRIED SCHADOW. (The Bettmann Archive)   PAGES 610—11

FIG. 61—WOODCUT AFTER A DRAWING BY JOHANNES VEIT: *Friedrich von Schlegel.* (The Bettmann Archive)　　PAGE 632

FIG. 62—ENGRAVING BY F. HUMPHREY: *August Wilhelm von Schlegel.* (The Bettmann Archive)　　PAGE 632

FIG. 63—PORTRAIT AFTER AN 1808 PAINTING BY DAHLING: *Johanh Gottlieb Fichte*. (The Bettmann Archive)

FIG. 64—DRAWING: *Johann Christian Friedrich von Schiller.* (The Bettmann Archive)

PAGE 621

FIG. 65—CHARCOAL DRAWING BY GEBBERS: *Johann Wolfgang von Goethe, age 77.* (The Bettmann Archive)

PAGE 622

FIG. 66—WOODCUT: *Ludwig van Beethoven.* (The Bettmann Archive)

PAGE 567

FIG. 67—JOHN CAWSE: *Carl Maria von Weber* (1826). Reproduced by
permission of the Royal College of Music, London. PAGE 613

Fig. 68—Engraving by H. P. Hansen after a painting by Riepenhausen: *Adam Gottlob Oehlenschläger.* (The Bettmann Archive) PAGE 666

Fig. 69—Sketch: *Esaias Tegnér.* (The Bettmann Archive) PAGE 662

FIG: 70—ENGRAVING BY X. A. VON R. CREMER AFTER A PAINTING BY
GEBBERS: *Hegel in His Study*. (The Bettmann Archive) PAGE 645

FIG. 71—ENGRAVING: *The Winter Palace, St. Petersburg.* (The Bettmann Archive)

PAGE 681

FIG. 72—FRANÇOIS GÉRARD: *Czar Alexander I.* The Victoria and Albert Museum, Lond▪

PAGE ▪

Fig. 73—Engraving: *Marshal Michel Ney*. (The New York Society Library) PAGES 704, 708

FIG. 74—PAINTING AFTER AN EYEWITNESS SKETCH BY J. A. KLEIN: *The Retreat from Moscow*. (The Bettmann Archive)

PAGE 707

FIG. 75—DRAWING BY ALFRED CROQUIS: *Talleyrand, author of "Palmerston, une Comédie de Deux Ans."* (The Bettmann Archive)   PAGES 731, 753

FIG. 76—JEAN-BAPTISTE ISABEY: *Louis XVIII*, SEPIA DRAWING. Louvre, Paris. (Cliché des Musées Nationaux)

FIG. 77—GEORGE DAWE: *Field Marshal Gebhard Leberecht von Blücher*. The Victoria and Albert Museum, London.

PAGE 743

FIG. 78—J. JACKSON: *Arthur Wellesley, 1st Duke of Wellington* (c. 1827). The National Portrait Gallery, London. PAGE 744

FIG. 79—MARCHAND: *View of Longwood*, WATERCOLOR. Musée de Malmaison, Paris.
(Cliché des Musées Nationaux)   PAGE 758

FIG. 80—LITHOGRAPH BY JOSEF KRIEHUBER
AFTER A PAINTING BY MORITZ MICHAEL
DAFFINGER: *Napoleon II, the Duke of
Reichstadt*. Österreichische Nationalbiblio-
thek.   PAGE 772

FIG. 81—*Napoleon at St. Helena.* (The New York Society Library)   PAGE 758

FIG. 82—*Napoleon's Tomb in the Hôtel des Invalides, Paris.* (Photo Hachette)   PAGE 776

BOOK IV

THE CHALLENGED KINGS

1789–1812

CHAPTER XXV

Iberia[*]

I. PORTUGAL: 1789–1808

NEWS of the French Revolution came to a Portugal that was struggling to return to the quiet order of the Middle Ages after the violent and scandalous attempt of the Marquês de Pombal to bring it abreast, in culture and law, with the France of Louis XV and the Spain of Charles III. The Pyrenees obstructed the flow of ideas between France and the Peninsula; the movement of ideas from Spain was hindered by Spain's recurrent eagerness to swallow her sister state; and in both countries the agents of the Inquisition loomed like lions at a palace gate to repel any word or thought that might question the ancient creed.

At the bottom of the social scale stood other guardians of the past: the simple, mostly unlettered commoners—peasants, craftsmen, tradesmen, soldiers—who were fondly habituated to their transmitted faith, comforted by its legends, awed by its miracles, thrilled by its ritual. At the top were the feudal barons, models of manners and owners of the soil; a timid, feeble-minded Queen Maria Francisca, and her son John, regent (1799) and then (1816–26) king; all dependably protective of the Church as the indispensable support of private morals, social order, and absolute, divine-right monarchy.

Amid these diverse sentinels lurked a small minority—students, Freemasons, scientists, poets, businessmen, a few officials, even a noble or two—who were irked by the despotism of the past, furtively flirted with philosophy, and dreamed of representative government, free trade, free assembly, free press, free thought, and a stimulating participation in the international of the mind.

Upon that timid minority, those shocked commoners, those startled dignitaries and Inquisitors, the news of the French Revolution, however dulled by delay, came as an exhilarating or terrifying revelation. Some reckless spirits openly rejoiced; Masonic lodges in Portugal celebrated the event, the Portuguese ambassador in Paris, who may have read Rousseau or heard Mirabeau, applauded the French National Assembly; the Portuguese Minister for Foreign Affairs allowed the official gazette to salute the fall of the Bastille; copies of the Revolutionary Constitution of 1791 were sold by French booksellers in Portugal.[1]

But when Louis XVI was deposed by a Paris uprising (1792), Queen Maria felt her throne tremble, and surrendered the government to her son.

---

[*] This name was given by the ancient Greeks to the region along the River Iberus (now Ebro), and was subsequently extended to the whole Spanish-Portuguese Peninsula.

The future John VI turned with fury upon the liberals of Portugal, and encouraged his intendant of police to arrest, or expel, or keep under unremitting surveillance, every Freemason, every important alien, every writer who advocated political reform. Francisco da Silva, leader of the liberals, was imprisoned; liberal nobles were banished from the court; Manuel du Bocage (1765–1805), leading Portuguese poet of the age, who had written a powerful sonnet against despotism, was jailed in 1797, and supported himself in prison by translating Ovid and Virgil.[2] In 1793, infuriated by the execution of Louis XVI, the Portuguese government followed Spain in a holy war against France, and sent a squadron to join the British fleet in the Mediterranean. Soon Spain negotiated a separate peace (1795); Portugal asked for a like accommodation, but France refused, alleging that Portugal was in effect a colony and ally of England. The quarrel simmered till Napoleon, after conquering half of Europe, reached out for the little state that was refusing to join in his Continental Blockade of Britain.

Behind the military and political situation of Portugal lay the precarious structure of its economic life. As with Spain, the nation's wealth depended upon the importation of precious metals from its colonies; this gold and silver, rather than domestic products, went to pay for imported articles, to gild the throne, enrich the rich, and purchase luxuries and slaves. No middle class grew to develop natural resources with progressive agriculture and technological industry. When command of the seas passed to England, the supply of gold became subject to evading the British Navy or making terms with the British government. Spain chose to fight, and almost exhausted her resources to build a navy excellent in everything but seamanship and morale. When that navy, reluctantly merged with the French, was defeated at Trafalgar, Spain became dependent upon France; and Portugal, to avoid absorption by France and Spain, became dependent upon England. Enterprising Englishmen filled important posts in Portugal, opened or managed factories there. British goods dominated Portugal's import trade, and Britons agreed to drink port wine from Oporto ("the port") in Portugal.

The situation irritated and tempted Napoleon. It defied his plan to bring England to peace by excluding her products from Continental markets; it gave him an excuse for conquering Portugal; a conquered Portugal could share with France in imprisoning Spain within French policy; and a subject Spain might provide another throne for another Bonaparte. So, as we have seen, Napoleon persuaded the Spanish government to join with France in invading Portugal; the Portuguese royal family fled in an English vessel to Brazil; and on November 30, 1807, Junot led a French-Spanish army, almost unresisted, into Lisbon. Liberal leaders in Portugal flocked to the new government, hoping that Napoleon would annex their country and give it representative institutions.[3] Junot humored these men, secretly laughed at them, announced (February 1, 1808) "that the House of Braganza has ceased to reign," and more and more behaved like a king.

II. SPAIN: 1808

Spain was still in the Middle Ages, and preferred it so. It was a God-intoxicated country, crowding its somber cathedrals, making devout pilgrimages to sacred shrines, multiplying monks, comforted with indulgences and absolutions, fearing and revering the Inquisition, kneeling as the consecrated Host was borne in awesome processions through the streets, cherishing above all else the faith that brought God into every home, disciplined children, guarded virginity, and offered Paradise at the end of the burdensome testing called life. A generation later George Borrow found "the ignorance of the masses so great," at least in León, "that printed charms against Satan and his host, and against every kind of misfortune, are publicly sold in the shops, and are in great demand."[4] Napoleon, still a son of the Enlightenment while signing concordats with the Church, concluded that "the Spanish peasants have even less share in the civilization of Europe than the Russians."[5] But the Spanish peasant, as Byron testified, could be as "proud as the noblest duke."[6]

Education was almost confined to the bourgeoisie and the nobility; literacy was a distinction; even the hidalgos seldom read a book. The ruling class distrusted print;[7] and in any case widespread literacy was not needed in the existing economy of Spain. Some commercial cities, like Cádiz and Seville, were fairly prosperous, and Byron, in 1809, thought Cádiz "the prettiest city in Europe."[8] Some industrial centers prospered; Toledo was still famous for its swords.[9] But the country was so mountainous that only a third of the soil could be profitably cultivated; and the roads and canals were so few, so difficult and ill-kept, so obstructed with provincial or feudal tolls, that corn could be more cheaply imported than domestically produced.[10] Disheartened by a difficult soil, the peasants preferred the pride of conspicuous leisure to the precarious fruits of tillage; and the townsmen found more pleasure in smuggling than in ill-paid toil. Over all the economic scene lay the burden of taxes rising faster than income, and demanded by a widening officialdom, a pervasive police, and a degenerating government.

Despite these difficulties the high spirit of the nation survived, supported by traditions of Ferdinand and Isabella and Philip II, of Velásquez and Murillo, by the spread and potential wealth of Spain's empire in the Americas and the Far East. Spanish art enjoyed a repute rivaling the Italian and the Dutch. Now the nation gathered its treasures in painting and sculpture into the Museo del Prado, built at Madrid (1785–1819) by Juan de Villanueva and his successors and aides. There, among its greatest glories, are the frightening masterpieces of the supreme painter of that age, Francisco José de Goya y Lucientes (1746–1828).* Vicente López y Portaña handed

---

* See *Rousseau and Revolution*, 300–09. That volume, thinking itself the last of its series, accompanied Goya and Goethe to their end, whereas, of course, they belonged to, and enclosed, the age of Napoleon, whom they both admired through his rise and fall.

him down to us in an uncompromising portrait fully in accord with the powerful and somber spirit who showed war in all its gory savagery, and who loved his country and scorned its king.

Spanish literature—till civil and foreign war consumed the nation—flourished under the double impulse of Catholic scholarship and the French Enlightenment. A Jesuit priest, Juan Francisco de Masdeu, issued, in installments from 1783 to 1805, a learned *Historia crítica de España y de la cultura española*, which achieved integral history by weaving cultural history into the general record of a civilization.[11] Juan Antonio Llorente, who had been general secretary of the Spanish Inquisition from 1789 to 1801, received from Joseph Bonaparte (1809) a commission to write a history of that institution; he thought it safer to do this in Paris, and in French (1817–18). The flowering of prose and poetry that had adorned the age of Charles III had not quite faded at his death: Gaspar Melchor de Jovellanos (1744–1811) continued to be the voice of liberalism in education and government; Leandro Fernandez de Moratín (1760–1828) still dominated the stage with comedies that earned him the title of the Spanish Molière. During the War of Liberation (1808–14) Manuel José Quintana and the priest Juan Nicasio Gallego poured out passionate poetry to stimulate the revolt against the French.

Till that struggle tore them apart, most of the leading writers had been won to French ideas of intellectual and political liberty; they and the Freemasons were *afrancesados*—Frenchified; they deplored the monarchical emasculation of the provincial *cortes* that had once kept Spain alive in all its parts; they hailed the French Revolution, and welcomed Napoleon as challenging Spain to free itself from a feudal aristocracy, a medieval Church, and an incompetent government. Let a masterly Spanish historian sing a powerful dirge to a dying dynasty:

> In 1808, when the Bourbon monarchy was working toward its own destruction, the political and social situation of Spain might have been summed up as follows: An aristocracy, especially the courtiers, which had lost respect for the kings; rotten politics, ruled by personal animosities and reciprocal fears; absolute lack of patriotism among the upper classes, who subordinated everything else to passions and greed; the delirious hope of the masses, centered upon a Prince—Ferdinand—who had already shown himself to be both false and vengeful; and finally the profound influence, in intellectual circles, of the ideas of the Encyclopedists and the French Revolution.[12]

An earlier chapter has described, from Napoleon's corner, the collapse of the Spanish monarchy: Charles IV (r. 1788–1808) allowed his wife Maria Luisa and her paramour Godoy to take the government out of his hands; Prince Ferdinand, heir apparent, maneuvered his father into abdicating; Godoyistas fought Fernandistas; Madrid and its environs were in chaos. Napoleon saw in the confusion an opportunity to bring the entire Peninsula under French rule and security within the Continental Blockade. He sent Murat and a second French army into Spain, with instructions to maintain order. Murat entered Madrid (March 23, 1808), and suppressed a popular insurrection on the historic Dos de Mayo—the Second of May. Meanwhile Napoleon had invited both Charles IV and Ferdinand to meet him in Bayonne, in France near the Spanish border. He frightened the Prince into restoring the throne to his father, and then persuaded the father to abdicate in favor of Napoleon's appointee, provided Catholicism should be recognized and protected as the national religion. Napoleon bade his brother Joseph to come and be king of Spain. Joseph, unwilling, came, and received from Napoleon a new constitution for Spain, granting much of what the Spanish liberals had hoped for, but requiring them to make their peace with a chastened Church. Joseph went sadly to his new responsibilities, and Napoleon returned to Paris happy with his absorption of Spain.

He had reckoned without the Spanish masses and Wellington.

III. ARTHUR WELLESLEY: 1769–1807

He would not be Wellington till 1809; till 1798 he was Wesley, though far removed from Methodism. He was born in Dublin, May 1, 1769 (105 days before Napoleon), being the fifth son of Garret Wesley, first Earl of Mornington, the English proprietor of an estate north of the Irish capital. He was sent to Eton at the age of twelve, but was called home after "three inglorious years."[13] There is no indication that he did better in sports than in studies, and he later disclaimed authorship of the now anonymous remark that "the battle of Waterloo was won on the playing fields of Eton."[14] He did better with tutors, but still his mother mourned, "I vow to God I don't know what I shall do with my awkward son Arthur."[15] So he was surrendered to the Army, and was sent, aged seventeen, to the Académei Royale de l'Équitation at Angers, where noble sons learned mathematics, a touch of the humanities, and much of the horsemanship and swordsplay useful to officers.

When he had won his spurs he was appointed—through family influence or plain purchase—to be aide-de-camp to the Lord Lieutenant of Ireland, and to a seat in the Irish House of Commons as representative of the borough of Trim. In 1799 he was made lieutenant colonel and led three regiments in the Duke of York's invasion of Flanders. He came back from that aborted venture so disgusted with war, mud, and titled incompetence that he thought of abandoning the Army for civil life. He preferred the violin to the barracks, suffered a succession of ailments, and impressed his brother Mornington as so deficient in ability that not much could be expected of him.[16] A portrait of him, aged twenty-six, by John Hoppner made him look like a poet, as handsome as Byron. Like Byron, he proposed to a noble lady, was rejected and sampled surfaces incontinently. In 1796 he went to India as a colonel under his brother Richard, who, now Marquess Wellesley, became governor of Madras, then of Bengal, and added some Indian principalities to the British Empire. Arthur Wellesley (as the future Duke now spelled himself) won some profitable victories in these campaigns, and was knighted in 1804. Returning to England, he secured a seat in the British Parliament, proposed again to Cathey Pakenham, was accepted (1806), and lived unhappily with her until they learned to live mostly apart. She gave him two sons.

He continued to rise from post to post, now not so much by purchase as by earning a reputation for careful analysis and competent performance. William Pitt, near death, marked him out as a man who "states every difficulty before he undertakes any service, but none after he undertakes it."[17] In 1807 he became chief secretary for Ireland in the ministry of the Duke of Portland; in 1808 he was made lieutenant general; in July he was commissioned to lead 13,500 troops and expel Junot and the French from Portugal.

On August 1 he landed his men at Mondego Bay, a hundred miles north of Lisbon. There he received some 5,000 Portuguese allies, and a letter from the War Ministry promising him another 15,000 men at an early date, but adding that Sir Hew Dalrymple, aged fifty-eight, would accompany these reinforcements and assume supreme command of the entire expedition. Wellesley had already designed his campaign, and did not enjoy subordination. He decided not to wait for those 15,000 men, but to march north with his 18,500, and seek a battle that would decide Junot's fate and his own. Junot, who had allowed his army to deteriorate with all the pleasures of a capital, led his 13,000 men out to meet the challenge, and suffered a costly defeat at Vimeiro, near Lisbon (August 21, 1808). Dalrymple arrived after the battle, took command, stopped pursuit, and arranged with Junot the Convention of Cintra (September 3) by which Junot surrendered all the towns and fortresses that the French had occupied in Portugal, but obtained consent for the unhindered exit of his surviving forces; the British agreed to provide shipping for those who wished to return to France. Wellesley signed the document, feeling that the liberation of Portugal by one battle justified some British courtesies.

This was the convention that Wordsworth and Byron, agreeing now and rarely afterward, denounced as an incredible stupidity; those released Frenchmen, if able to walk, would soon be conscripted to fight Britain or her allies again. Wellesley was summoned to London to face a court of inquiry. He was not entirely sorry to go; he did not relish the prospect of serving under Dalrymple; and—incredible as it may seem—he hated war. "Take my word for it," he was to say after many victories, "if you had seen but one day of war you would pray to Almighty God that you might never again see an hour of it."[18] He seems to have convinced the court of inquiry that the Convention of Cintra, by dissuading further resistance, had saved thousands of British and Allied lives. Then he retired to Ireland, and waited for a better opportunity to serve his country and his good name.

IV. THE PENINSULAR WAR: III (1808–12)

Joseph Bonaparte, king of Spain, was in multiple trouble. He labored to win a wider acceptance than that given him by a sprinkling of liberals. These favored confiscatory measures against the wealthy Church, but Joseph, already hampered by his reputation as an agnostic, knew that every move against the clergy would further inflame resistance to his alien rule. The Spanish armies that Napoleon had defeated had re-formed in scattered divisions, undisciplined but enthusiastic; the guerrilla war of the peasantry against the usurpers went on between sowing and reaping annually; the French army in Spain had to divide itself into separate forces under jealous generals in a chaos of campaigns that defied the efforts of Napoleon to co-ordinate them from Paris. Napoleon learned, said Karl Marx, that "if the Spanish State was dead, Spanish society was full of life, and every part of it was overflowing with power of resistance. . . . The center of Spanish resistance was nowhere and everywhere."[19] After the collapse of a major French army at Bailén a major part of the Spanish aristocracy joined the revolution, diverting popular hostility from themselves to the invaders. The active support of the revolt by the clergy helped to turn the movement from liberal ideas; on the contrary, the success of the War of Liberation strengthened the Church and the Inquisition.[20] Some liberal elements survived in the provincial juntas; these were sending delegates to a national Cortes at Cádiz; and this was writing a new constitution. The Iberian Peninsula was alive with insurrection, hope, and piety, while Joseph longed for Naples, Napoleon fought Austria, and Wellesley-Wellington—a thoroughly modern man —was preparing to come down again from England and aid in restoring medieval Spain.

Sir John Moore, before his death at Corunna (January 16, 1809), had advised the British government to make no further attempt to control Portugal. The French, he thought, would sooner or later carry out Napoleon's order to make Portugal a vassal of France; and how was England to find transport, and provision enough soldiers to face the 100,000 seasoned French troops then in Spain? But Sir Arthur Wellesley, restless in Ireland, told the War Ministry that if it would give him undivided command of twenty to thirty thousand British troops, and native reinforcements, he would undertake to hold Portugal against any French army not exceeding 100,000 men.[21] His government took him at his word, and on April 22, 1809, he reached Lisbon with 25,000 Britishers, whom he was later to describe as "the scum of the earth, . . . a pack of rascals, . . . a crowd who only enlist for drink, and can only be managed with the whip";[22] but they could fight lustily when faced with a choice of killing or being killed.

Anticipating their arrival, Marshal Soult had marched 23,000 Frenchmen

—doubtless themselves poor devils more familiar with taverns than salons— down the coast to Oporto; while from the west another French army, under Marshal Claude Victor, was advancing along the Tagus. Wellesley, who had carefully studied Napoleon's campaigns, resolved to attack Soult before the two marshals could join their forces in an attack on British-held Lisbon. Having added to his 25,000 men some 15,000 Portuguese under William Carr Beresford (Viscount Beresford to be), he led them to a point on the River Douro opposite Oporto. On May 12, 1809, he crossed the stream, and attacked Soult's unsuspecting army in the rear in a battle that drove the French into a disorderly retreat, having lost 6,000 men and all their artillery. Wellesley did not pursue them, for he had to hurry south to halt Victor; but Victor, informed of Soult's disaster, turned back to Talavera, where he received from Joseph reinforcements that increased his army to 46,000 men. Against these Wellesley had 23,000 Britons and 36,000 Spaniards. The hostile masses met at Talavera on July 28, 1809; the Spanish troops soon had enough, and fled from the field; nevertheless Wellesley drove off repeated French attacks until Victor withdrew with a loss of 7,000 men and seventeen guns. The British had suffered 5,000 casualties, but held the field. The British government credited Wellesley with his courageous leadership, and made him Viscount Wellington.

Nevertheless his support in the War Ministry was weakening. The victory of Napoleon at Wagram (1809), and his marriage with the Austrian Emperor's daughter (March, 1810), had ended the Austrian fealty to England; Russia was still an ally of France; and an additional 138,000 French troops were now available for service in Spain. Marshal André Masséna, with 65,000 men, was planning to lead them out of Spain to the definite conquest of Portugal. The British government informed Wellington that if the French again invaded Spain he would be excused if he withdrew his army to England.[23]

This was a crucial moment in Wellington's career. Withdrawal, however permitted, would tarnish his record unless some major future victory, not to be reckoned upon, could lend glamour even to his defeats. He decided to risk his men, his career, and his life on one more throw of the dice. Meanwhile he had his men build, from the Tagus through Torres Vedras to the sea, a line of fortifications twenty-five miles north of his base at Lisbon.

Masséna began his campaign by capturing the Spanish stronghold of Ciudad Rodrigo, and then crossed into Portugal with 60,000 men. Wellington, commanding 52,000 Allies (i.e. British, Spanish, and Portuguese), met him at Bussaco (north of Coimbra) on September 27, 1810. In the battle he lost 1,250 in dead and wounded; Masséna lost 4,600. Nevertheless Wellington, feeling that he could not rely, like Masséna, on reinforcements, retired to the Torres Vedras fortifications, ordered a policy of "scorched earth" as his army retreated, and waited for Masséna's army to grow hungry and disappear. It did. On March 5, 1811, Masséna led his starving men back to Spain, and yielded his command to Auguste Marmont.

After a winter of resting and training his men, Wellington took the initiative, marched into Spain, and with 50,000 troops attacked Marmont's 48,000 near Salamanca on July 22, 1812. Here the wholesale execution cost the French 14,000 casualties, the Allies 4,700; Marmont gave way. On July 21 King Joseph, with 15,000 soldiers, had left Madrid to go to Marmont's aid; en route he learned of Marmont's defeat. Not daring to return to the capital, he led his army to Valencia, to join a larger French force there under Marshal Suchet. He was followed in chaotic haste by his court and officials and some 10,000 *afrancesados*. On August 12 Wellington entered Madrid, and was welcomed ecstatically by a populace that had remained immune to French charm and Napoleon's constitution. "I am among a people mad with joy," Wellington wrote to a friend. "God send my good fortune may continue, and that I may be the instrument of securing their independence."[24]

God hesitated. Marmont reorganized his army behind the fortifications of Burgos; Wellington besieged him there; Joseph marched from Valencia with 90,000 men to face the Allies, Wellington retreated (October 18, 1812) past Salamanca to Ciudad Rodrigo, losing 6,000 men on the way. Joseph re-entered Madrid, to the grim displeasure of the populace and the delight of the middle class. Meanwhile Napoleon was shivering in Moscow, and Spain, like the rest of Europe, awaited the result of his gamble for a continent.

V. RESULTS

Even at this resting point in the Peninsular War, some results had taken form. Geographically, the largest result was that the South American colonies of Spain and Portugal had freed themselves from their weakened motherland, and had begun their own lusty and unique career. All Spain south of the Tagus had been cleared of French troops. Militarily Wellington had proved that France could not take Portugal—and probably could not hold Spain—without risking the loss of all her conquests east of the Rhine. Socially, the popular resistance, however chaotic, had achieved a victory for the peasantry and the Church. Politically, the provincial juntas had won back some of their old power of local rule; each had built its own army, minted its own coinage, formed its own policy—even, in some cases, signing a separate peace with Britain. And most significantly of all, the juntas had sent delegates to a national Cortes, with instructions to formulate a new constitution for a new Spain.

This supreme Cortes, fleeing from French armies, had met first on the Isla de León in 1810; when the French withdrew, it moved to Cádiz; and there, on March 19, 1812, it promulgated a proudly liberal constitution. Since most of the delegates were good Catholics, Article XII declared that "the religion of the Spanish nation is and shall perpetually be Catholic, Apostolic, and Roman, the only true religion. The nation protects it by wise and just laws, and prohibits the exercise of any other [religion] whatever"; however, the constitution abolished the Tribunal of the Inquisition,

and restricted the number of religious communities. In nearly all other matters the Cortes accepted the leadership of the 184 delegates from the middle
class. Most of these called themselves "Liberals"—the first known use of the
term as a political designation. Under their lead the Constitution of 1812
rivaled the Constitution of 1791 in revolutionary France.

It accepted the Spanish monarchy, and acknowledged the absent Ferdinand VII as the rightful king; however, it placed the sovereignty not in the
king but in the nation acting through its elected delegates. The king was to
be a constitutional ruler, obeying the laws; and adding to them, and making
treaties, only in conjunction with the national Cortes, which was to be a
single chamber. A new Cortes was to be chosen every second year, by the
adult males of the nation, through three stages of election: parochial, district, and provincial. Laws were to be made uniform throughout Spain; all
citizens were to be equal before the law; and the judiciary was to be independent of both the Cortes and the king. The constitution called for the
abolition of torture, slavery, feudal courts, and seignorial rights. The press
was to be free, except in matters of religion. Uncultivated communal lands
were to be distributed to the poor.

Under the circumstances—which included the religious traditions of Spain
—it was a brave and progressive constitution. Now, it seemed, Spain would
enter the nineteenth century.

CHAPTER XXVI

Italy and Its Conquerors

1789–1813

I. THE MAP IN 1789

IN this period Italy was not a nation but a battleground. Split into jealously separate regions and dialects, the country was too fragmented to stand united against foreign attack, and (north of Naples) too blessed with sun and a fruitful, well-watered soil—beneficent streams curling down from Alps or Apennines—to shoulder arms repeatedly for the difference between native and foreign taxgatherers.

Most of Italy had fallen under the rule or influence of the Austrian Hapsburg dynasty by the Treaty of Utrecht (1713), which assigned Milan, Mantua, Naples, Sardinia, and their dependencies to the Emperor Charles VI. In the northwest corner of the peninsula Savoy and Piedmont were ruled by the kings of Sardinia. In 1734 the "Kingdom of the Two Sicilies," with its foci at Naples and Palermo, was transferred from the Hapsburgs to the Bourbons by the able warrior and ruler who became Charles III of Spain. Before passing to Spain he bequeathed the Neapolitan realm to his son Ferdinand IV, who married the Archduchess Maria Carolina; and her domination of her husband brought the entire kingdom of Naples under Austrian influence. When the Empress Maria Theresa died (1780) her sons governed Lombardy, Tuscany, and Modena; her daughters were married respectively to the rulers of Naples and Parma; and Savoy, Piedmont, and Sardinia had fallen under an Austrian protectorate. The only independent regions in Italy were then Venice, Lucca, San Marino, and Genoa. In this division of Italy between the Austrian Hapsburgs in the north and the Spanish Bourbons in the south the Papal States remained papal only because the rival dynasties that embraced them with possessive ardor were restrained by their mutual jealousy and that Catholic piety which alone made Italy one.

Austrian rule in northern Italy was excellent in terms of the time. In Lombardy the feudal and ecclesiastical proprietors were taxed, and their privileges had been considerably reduced; a hundred monasteries were closed, and their revenues were devoted to education or charity; under the scholarly prodding of Cesare Beccaria's *Dei delitti e delle pene* (1764) judicial procedure was reformed, torture was abolished, and the criminal law was made more humane. In Tuscany, between 1765 and 1790, Grand Duke Leopold gave the former territory of the Medici "perhaps the best government in Europe."[1] Florence, his capital, remained a citadel of civilization through all the fluctuations of power and ideas.

Venice, rich, corrupt, and beautiful, was now (1789) visibly nearing her end as a sovereign state. Her eastern empire had long since been lost to the Turks, but her rule was still acknowledged between the Alps and Padua, and between Trieste and Brescia. Formally a republic, actually a closed aristocracy, its government had become listless, oppressive and incompetent. It had the best spies in Christendom, but no army. It had become the playground of Europe, pledged to pleasure, and trusting to its courtesans to keep her enemies amiable. Caught between Austria on the north and Austrian Lombardy on the west, it was clearly fated to be absorbed by Austria whenever France ceased to protect her.

South of Tuscany and the Po the Papal States began their sinuous contour with the Romagna and its "Legations"—Ferrara, Bologna, and Ravenna, each administered by a papal legate; then southward with the "Marches," or borderlands near the Adriatic—Rimini, Ancona, and Urbino; then across the Apennines through Umbria's Perugia and Spoleto, and through Latium's Orvieto and Viterbo to Rome. All this historic region was under the popes, according to the "donations" made to the Church by Pepin, king of the Franks, in 754, and by Charlemagne in 774. After a decisive victory in the Council of Trent (1545–63), the popes had enlarged their authority over the bishops, as the contemporary kings were doing over the feudal lords; power is centripetal.

But soon thereafter the Papacy entered into a slow decay as the advances of science and the inroads of philosophy left the Church with a dangerously reduced support in the influential classes of Western Europe; and it was meeting open opposition not only from Protestant rulers but as well from Catholic sovereigns like Joseph II of Austria and Ferdinand IV of Naples. Even in the states of the Church a growing minority of secret skeptics weakened the hold of the clergy upon the people. The Curia or papal court (wrote Joseph II in 1768) "has become almost an object of scorn. Internally its people exist in the deepest misery, wholly depressed, while its internal finances are in complete disorder and discredit." Joseph, an unbeliever, may have been prejudiced, but the Venetian ambassador reported in 1783 that "the internal affairs of the pontifical state are in the greatest disarray; it is in a progressive decline, and the government daily loses force and authority."[2] Despite their poverty, and the malarial infection of the summer air, the people of Rome made life tolerable by taking full advantage of the churchly indulgence given to their perennial amours and Carnival games; and the clergy itself relaxed under the Italian sun.

Both of the popes in this critical period were pious and honorable men. Pius VI (r. 1775–99), despite his arduous trip to Vienna, failed to win Joseph II of Austria to obedience; and all his culture and gentleness did not save him from losing Avignon to France and dying a prisoner of the Directory. Pius VII (r. 1800–23) did his best to restore Catholicism in France, suffered a long imprisonment under Napoleon, and lived to triumph humbly over the fallen Emperor (1814).

South of the Papal States the Spanish Bourbons grew rich with the prosperity of Gaeta, Capua, Caserta, Naples, Capri, and Sorrento. But there Italian prosperity ceased. Cities like Pescara, Aquila, Foggia, Bari, Brindisi, Taranto, and Crotone remembered Milo, Caesar, Frederick II (Holy Roman emperor, "*stupor mundi*"), even Pythagoras; but they were burned by an immoderate sun, despoiled with taxes, and comforted only by their creed. Then the taxgatherer crossed from Reggio Calabria to Messina in Sicily ("from Scylla to Charybdis"); and there too the cities dignified their poverty under memories of Phoenicians, Greeks, Carthaginians, Romans, Vandals, Moslems, Normans, Spaniards, until the taxgatherers stopped at Palermo and attended to the needs and luxuries of kings and queens, merchant princes, brigands, and saints. Such was the colorful realm which the eight-year-old Ferdinand IV inherited in 1759. He grew into a handsome athlete who preferred pleasure and sports to the burdens of power, and mostly left the government to his wife Maria Carolina.

Under the guidance of her Prime Minister and paramour, Sir John Acton, Maria oriented Neapolitan policy from pro-Spain to pro-Austria, and, in 1791, to pro-England. Meanwhile feudal barons exacted every due from an exhausted peasantry; corruption reigned in the court, the bureaucracy, and the judiciary; taxes were high, and fell chiefly upon the lower classes; the city populace was barbarized by poverty, habituated to disorder and crime, and held in check by a numerous police and by an obscurantist clergy skilled in miracles. (In a chapel of the cathedral the relics of Saint Januarius bled annually.) As usual, the Church was lenient with sins of the flesh; after all, these were the only luxury allowed to the poor; and in Carnival days the Sixth Commandment was looked upon as an unwarranted imposition upon human nature.

Nevertheless the Queen was jealous of Catherine II of Russia, who had so many philosophers at her call or knee. So she patronized artists, scholars, and professors of wisdom; and though she probably did not know it, Naples had "more educated men and women of modern ideas than any other city in Italy."[3] Many of these men followed with silent hope the news that came from Paris that the people had stormed and taken the Bastille.

II. ITALY AND THE FRENCH REVOLUTION

An impressive scattering of liberals had prepared the educated classes of Italy for some basic transformation in France. Beccaria and Parini in Milan, Tanucci, Genovesi, and Filangieri in Naples, Caraccioli in Sicily, had already labored, in prose and poetry, in legislation and philosophy, for some of the measures that were now being passed by a French National Assembly apparently pledged to reason and moderation. In Tuscany the Grand Duke

Leopold himself hailed the Revolution as promising precious reforms in every country in Europe.[4]

When Napoleon, as son and general of the Revolution, rushed into Italy (1796), like some wild west wind, and drove the Sardinian and Austrian armies out of Piedmont and Lombardy, nearly all the population welcomed him as an Italian leading French troops to the liberation of Italy. For a while, despite local insurrections at Pavia, Genoa, and Verona, he was able to dispose of Italian states and principalities as if they had fallen into his hands as unconditional gifts. So in July and August, 1797, he bundled Milan, Modena, Reggio Emilia, Bologna, and a slice of Switzerland into a medley called the Cisalpine Republic, and gave it a constitution like that of Revolutionary France.

The liberalism of his early rule in north Italy quieted for a time the local dreams of liberty. The native leaders, softened with sinecures and dignities, recognized that on a continent divided among wolves, one or another of the wolves must be accepted as protector; and better one that spoke excellent Italian and eased taxation and art raids with enlightened laws. But the advancing legislation of the Revolution against the Catholic Church in France checked this Italian sympathy; their religion proved more precious to the Italian populace than a political liberty persecuting priests and smelling of September Massacres.

In Rome, January 13, 1792, a diplomatic agent of France was attacked by a mob, and so severely handled that he died the next day. This created a new crisis for Pope Pius VI, who had already suffered from the Edict of Toleration (1781) of Joseph II in Austria. Now he found himself faced by the Revolution's expropriation of French Church property, and the Civil Constitution of the Clergy (July 12, 1790). Brought up to complete orthodoxy and a trustful respect for tradition, Pius denounced the Revolution, and supported the challenged kings in their efforts to suppress it. At the Peace of Tolentino (February 19, 1797) he was compelled, by the victories and threats of Napoleon, to cede to France the papal enclaves of Avignon and Venaissin, and to the new Cisalpine Republic the city-states of Ferrara, Bologna, and Ravenna.

In December, 1797, a Roman mob killed the French General Léonard Duphot. General Louis Berthier, who had succeeded Napoleon (then in Egypt) in command of the Army of Italy, seized the opportunity to invade Rome and set up a Roman Republic under French rule. Pius VI protested, was arrested, resisted, and was transported from place to place until he died at Valence, as a prisoner of the Directory, on August 29, 1799. Observers innocent of history wondered whether the Papacy had come to an end.[5]

The situation offered Ferdinand IV of Naples a triple opportunity: to test the new army that had been organized for him by Sir John Acton, to prove himself a loyal son of the Church, and to take a slice of papal territory as an honorarium. Admiral Nelson, who was then tarrying in Naples in thrall to Emma Hamilton, agreed to help by landing a naval force at Leghorn. The King gave command of his army to the Austrian General Karl Mack, and rode with it to the easy conquest of Rome (November 29, 1798). The French regiments left there decided that they were no match for the whole Neapolitan Army, and readily evacuated the city.

While the scattered cardinals were choosing a new pope in Venice, Ferdinand's troops sampled the art and belles of Rome. Meanwhile a brilliant general, Jean-Étienne Championnet, came down from the north with a fresh French army, led it to a victory over Mack's disordered troops at Civita Castellana (December 15, 1798), pursued them all the way to Naples, took that city to the joy of its intelligentsia, and set up there the Parthenopean Republic (January 23, 1799). Ferdinand and his Queen, Sir William Hamilton and his Bovary, fled to Palermo on Nelson's flagship *Vanguard*.

The new republic lasted less than five months. Championnet and many of his men were summoned north to repel the Austrians; he died in that campaign (1800). Cardinal Fabrizzio Ruffo, aided by the English Captain Edward Foote, organized a new army for Ferdinand, and recaptured Naples with the help of the populace, which looked upon the French garrison as verily damned atheists. The French, with the assistance of a Neapolitan admiral, Francesco Caracciolo, took refuge in two of the harbor's forts. Cardinal Ruffo and Captain Foote offered them unhindered departure for France if they would surrender. They agreed, but before the pact could be carried out Nelson and his fleet, bearing the royal party, arrived from Palermo; Nelson took command, and, over the protests of the Cardinal, turned his guns upon the forts.[6] The French surrendered unconditionally. Caracciolo was caught while trying to sail away; he was hastily tried before a military court on Nelson's ship, and was hanged from the yardarm of his flagship, *La Minerva* (June 29, 1799). King and Queen, restored to power, imprisoned hundreds of liberals, and put their leaders to death.

III. ITALY UNDER NAPOLEON: 1800–12

For nine months after his return from Egypt Napoleon devoted himself to reconciling the French nation to his definition of political liberty as periodical plebiscites foreseeably approving enlightened despotism. France was tiring of democratic liberty just when Italian liberals, fretting under restored Austrian rule, were longing for it. When would that brilliant Italian-become-Frenchman come again to Italy, boot out those Austrians, and give Italy an Italian government?

The crafty Consul took his time, for careful preparation was the first principle of his strategy. When at last he came it was by a dash more brilliant even than the onrush of 1796: a climb up and slide down the Alps, dividing the Austrians in two, taking their main army in the rear, hemming it in, holding it and its old commander prisoners until the Austrian wolf surrendered to the Gallic fox all of its Italian possessions west of Venezia (1801). Napoleon juggled his winnings into something much like the configuration that he had made in 1797. The Cisalpine Republic, centering around Milan, and the Ligurian Republic at Genoa were given relative independence, with Italian governors under a French protectorate. The Papal States were as yet left undisturbed. Concordats were being prepared with the Church, and Napoleon had ceased to be a Mohammedan. By a treaty of March 18, 1801, Ferdinand IV of Naples agreed to close Neapolitan ports to British shipping; Nelson could not help, for he was busy attacking Copenhagen (April 2, 1801). Italians sensed a fine Italian hand behind the consummations, and rejoiced.

Then the hand closed in the grasp of power. In January, 1802, a delegation of 454 delegates from the Cisalpine Republic met in Lyons, adopted a new constitution drawn up by Napoleon, and accepted Talleyrand's inspired proposal to elect Napoleon president of the new Republica Italiana. After he made himself emperor of the French (1804), the title President of Italy seemed incongruously modest; so, on May 26, 1805, Napoleon received in Milan the old and revered Iron Crown of the Lombard kings, and became sovereign of (north) Italy. He introduced the Code Napoléon, equalized educational opportunity by milking the richer provinces to help the poorer, and promised to keep "my people of Italy . . . the least heavily taxed of all the nations of Europe." Departing, he left with them, as his viceroy and a pledge of solicitude, his beloved stepson Eugène de Beauharnais.

For the next eight years the new kingdom (mainly Lombardy) enjoyed a general prosperity, and a vigorous political life, which would long be blessed in Italian memory. The government made no pretense to democracy; Napoleon had no faith in the ability of the populace, there or elsewhere, to wisely choose its leaders and its policy. Instead he advised Eugène to gather about him the most experienced and competent administrators. They served him with enthusiasm and skill. They organized a competent bureaucracy; they set on foot extensive public works—roads, canals, parks, housing, schools; they reformed sanitation, prisons, and the penal code; they spread literacy and fostered music and art. Taxes rose from 82 million francs in 1805 to 144 million in 1812, but part of this reflected inflation of the currency to finance war, and part of it was a redistribution of concentrated wealth for the public good.

Meanwhile the Emperor continued to Napoleonize Italy. In September, 1802, he annexed Piedmont to France. In June, 1805, he charmed the government of Genoa into asking for the incorporation of its Ligurian Republic into the French Empire. In September, 1805, he absorbed the duchies of Parma, Piacenza, and Guastalla. In December, 1805, after almost annihilating the Austrian Army at Austerlitz, he persuaded the Emperor Francis II to surrender Venezia to Eugène's new kingdom. Venice was so grateful for this partial atonement of Napoleon's disgraceful bartering of her in 1797 that when he visited the city in 1807 it exhausted itself in festivities.[7] In May, 1808, he took over the grand duchy of Tuscany, where Austrian administration had been at its best. His sister Elisa had ruled Lucca so well that Napoleon transferred her to Tuscany, where, under her wise and conciliatory government, Florence became a haven of letters and arts reminiscent of its Medicean days.

On March 30, 1806, Napoleon proclaimed his brother Joseph king of Naples, and sent him, with French troops, to evict the unmanageable Ferdinand IV and his demanding Queen. The Emperor seems to have reserved the most difficult assignments for the genial Joseph, and to have judged his performance with small consideration of the difficulties involved. Joseph was a man of culture, who liked the company of educated men, and of women whose education had not ruined their charm.[8] With such a *modus vivendi*, Bonaparte felt, a man could never successfully govern a kingdom. Why appoint him, then? Because the conqueror had more kingdoms than brothers, and felt that he could trust no one but his close relatives.

Joseph was readily accepted as king of Naples by leaders of the middle class, restless under feudalism; but the populace rejected him as a usurper and an infidel, and Joseph had to steel himself to severe measures to subdue their resistance. The Queen had taken to Sicily all funds in the state bank; a British fleet blockaded the port and stifled maritime trade; and the French troops, victorious but ill-paid, were dangerously insubordinate. Joseph appealed to his brother for some negotiable currency; Napoleon bade him make Naples pay for its liberation. Joseph negotiated a loan from Dutch bankers, and laid a tax upon all incomes, noble or plebeian, clerical or lay. He brought in from Paris Comte Pierre-Louis Roederer, one of Napoleon's favorite economists, to take charge of the fisc; and soon the state's finances were in good order. Other experienced administrators established a free school in every commune of the kingdom, and a college in every province. Feudalism was abolished; the lands of the Church were nationalized and sold to the peasantry and to a growing middle class. Laws were harmonized under a variant of the Napoleonic Code. The judiciary was cleansed, procedure was expedited, prisons and penal code were reformed.[9]

Joseph was nearing success and public approval when he was suddenly summoned to a throne and task still more difficult and dangerous—to be king of Spain (June 10, 1808). In his place Napoleon, running out of brothers, set up, as king of Naples, Joachim Murat, who was his brother-in-law by marriage with Caroline Bonaparte.

Murat is remembered chiefly for his showy costumes and his fearless initiative in battle; let us honor him for his reconstruction of the Neapolitan government. He was a man with all the peasant virtues except patience, fitter for herculean tasks than for cunning diplomacy or farsighted statesmanship; a loving husband between squalls, and faithful to his imperious brother-in-law till he thought him mad. We can understand his complaint that the Continental Blockade demanded by Napoleon was ruining Naples' economic life. Nevertheless, perhaps because of his impatience, he and his aides accomplished much in his four-year reign. They completed the reform of taxation, established a national bank, paid off the national debt (mostly through the sale of ecclesiastical property), abolished internal traffic tolls, and financed substantial public works. Altogether, the administrations of Joseph and Murat, lasting less than eight years, transformed the political, economic, and social life of Naples so fundamentally that when Ferdinand IV was restored to his throne in 1815 he accepted nearly all the reforms that the French had made.

Dearer than these accomplishments to Joachim's heart was the army of sixty thousand men which he had organized and trained, and with which he hoped to unite Italy and be its first king. From that dream, and from the sun of Italy, he was peremptorily summoned, in 1812, to join his brother-in-law in the conquest of Russia.

IV. EMPEROR AND POPE

Napoleon felt that he had taken substantial steps in transforming Italy from a geographical expression into a nation by organizing the Cisalpine Republic in the north and the kingdom of Naples in the south. But the Austrians, during his absence in Egypt, had put an end to the Roman Republic established by the French only a year before; the Papacy had regained its historic capital, and most of its Papal States; and on March 13, 1800, a conclave of cardinals had elected a new pontiff, Pius VII, to whom nearly all Catholics looked for a firm defense of the "temporal power"—the territorial possessions—of the popes.

Napoleon found Pius reasonable enough in negotiating concordats in Paris and Rome, and in blessing his assumption of imperial powers. But those Papal States (though not, as once claimed, deeded to the Church by the supposed "Donation of Constantine"*) had been given to Pope Stephen II in 754 by Pepin the Short, king of the Franks. Charlemagne in 774 confirmed this "Donation of Pepin," but "interfered in the government of the Papal States," and "considered himself Christendom's head, to whom the Pope had to listen, even in matters theological."[10] Napoleon had developed similar ideas. He had set his heart on countering England's blockade of France with a Continental Blockade against the entry of British goods; but the Papal Curia, or administrative court of the popes, insisted on keeping the ports of the Papal States open to all trade. Moreover, these states stood as a divisive barrier between north and south Italy. Now the desire to unify Italy under his own hat had become a ruling passion in Napoleon; "this," he told Joseph, "is the chief and constant goal of my policy."[11] In accord with that policy French troops had occupied Ancona (1797), a strategic port on the Adriatic, commanding a main road between north and south Italy. Now, November 13, 1805, as Napoleon was preparing to face Austria and Russia in battle, Pius VII, stung to uncharacteristic audacity by his Curia, sent to Napoleon a startling challenge: "We owe it to ourselves to demand from

---

* See *Encyclopaedia Britannica*, VII, 580, or *The Renaissance*, 352.

Your Majesty the evacuation of Ancona; and if we are met with a refusal, we fail to see how we can reconcile it with the maintenance of friendly relations with Your Majesty's minister."[12] Hotly resenting the timing of this ultimatum, which he received at Vienna on the eve of Austerlitz, Napoleon answered the Pope with a counterchallenge: "Your Holiness is the sovereign of Rome, but I am its emperor."[13] Having spoken like Charlemagne, he advanced like Caesar, and overwhelmed the Austrians and the Russians at Austerlitz.

A year later (November 12, 1806), having destroyed the Prussian Army at Jena, Napoleon sent from Berlin to the Pope a demand that the English be expelled from Rome, and that the Papal States join the "Italian Confederation"; for, he said, he could not tolerate, "between his Kingdom of Italy and his Kingdom of Naples," the existence of "ports and fortresses which, in the event of war, might be occupied by the English, and compromise the safety of his states and his peoples."[14] Pius was given till February, 1807, to obey; he refused, and allowed the British minister to remain in Rome. On his triumphant return from Tilsit Napoleon again demanded the expulsion of the English agents from Rome; Pius again refused. On August 30 Napoleon threatened to seize the Papal Marches. Frightened, Pius agreed to close his ports to the British. Napoleon now demanded that the Pope make common cause with him against the enemies of France. Pius refused. On January 10, 1808, Napoleon ordered General Miollis (then heading a French division in Florence) to march upon Rome.

From that day events moved forward in one more historic conflict between Church and state. On February 2 Miollis and his troops took Civitavecchia; the next day they entered Rome, and surrounded the Quirinal—the hill that held the papal palace and the offices of the Curia. From that time till March, 1814, Pius VII was a prisoner of France. On April 2, 1808, Napoleon ordered the annexation of the Papal Marches to the kingdom of Italy. Now there was an open corridor between the kingdom of Naples and the kingdom of Italy—between Joseph and Eugène.

A year intervened, in which Napoleon was busy with Spain. On May 17, 1809, from Vienna again conquered, Napoleon proclaimed the absorption of the Papal States into the French Empire, and the end of the temporal power of the popes. On June 10 the Pope excommunicated Napoleon. On July 6 General Radet led some French troops into the Pope's audience chamber and gave him a choice of abdication or exile. Pius took only his breviary and a crucifix, and followed his captors to a waiting carriage, which bore him along the Italian coast past Genoa to Savona. There he was kept in polite imprisonment until Napoleon—after publishing an alleged plot to abduct the Pontiff to England—had him transferred to Fontainebleau (June, 1812). On February 13, 1813, Pius signed a new agreement with Napoleon; on March 24 he revoked his signature. In his palatial jail he lived simply, even to mending his own shirt.[15] He remained there through all the events of 1812 and 1813, until, on January 21, 1814, Napoleon, himself facing imprisonment, had him returned to Savona. In April, the Allies, having taken Paris and Napoleon, sent word to the Pope that he was free. On May 24 Pius VII, worn out with physical and mental suffering, re-entered Rome. Nearly all the population welcomed him with fervor and acclaim; young Romans competed for the privilege of replacing the horses and drawing his carriage to the Quirinal.[16]

In their brief control of the Papal States Napoleon's French administrators, helped by native liberals, transformed the economic and political scene with perhaps painful vigor and speed. Feudalism and the Inquisition were ended. Over five hundred religious houses were closed, giving an uncomfortable freedom to 5,852 monks and nuns. Corrupt officials were dismissed; public accountancy was introduced. Roads were repaired and policed; brigandage was almost stopped. Streets were cleaned and lighted; a quarter of the Pontine Marshes was drained and put under cultivation. Religious liberty was proclaimed; the Jews moved freely from their ghetto; Masonic lodges flourished. Hospitals multiplied; prisons were improved; schools were built and manned; a new university was opened in Perugia. The excavation of classic remains was continued, and Canova was put in charge of a museum that housed the findings. But taxes were collected with unheard-of insistence, and men were conscripted into the national Army. The merchants complained of the restrictions laid upon trade with England. The majority of the population frowned upon the sudden transformation of their traditional institutions, and the scandalous treatment of a Pope whom even the atheists had begun to love. "The populace looked back with regret to the soft and indolent rule of the Pope."[17]

All in all, Napoleon's imprisonment of Pius VII was an astonishing blunder for so astute a ruler. The concordats and the coronation had brought to the Consul and the Emperor a helpful reconciliation with Catholics throughout Europe, and even a formal acceptance of his rule by nearly all the kings of Europe; but his later treatment of the Pope alienated nearly all Catholics and many Protestants. The Papacy was strengthened by Napoleon's attempt to make it his political instrument; the French Catholic Church, which till his time had been "Gallican"—i.e., antipapal—now gave its reverence and loyalty to the Papacy. The Jesuits, who had been expelled by a politically intimidated Pope, were restored throughout Christendom by the gentle but resolute Pius VII in 1814. The temporal power of the Papacy was renewed in that year, and its spiritual power was increased by the quiet resistance of the imprisoned Pope. Napoleon himself, between abdications, admitted his misjudgment of Pius VII. "I always believed the Pope to be a man of very weak character. . . . I treated him harshly. I was wrong. I was blind."[18] Pius, on the other hand, had never underestimated Napoleon, had in many ways admired him, and showed a certain tenderness for him when his former jailer became a prisoner in turn. When Napoleon's mother complained to the Pope that the English were mistreating her son on St. Helena, Pius begged Cardinal Consalvi to intercede for his fallen foe.[19] The Pope outlived the Emperor by two years. He died in 1823, murmuring, in delirium, "Savona, Fontainebleau."[20]

V. BEHIND THE BATTLES

Battles are the technical fireworks of the historic drama; behind them are the loves and hates of men and women, the toil and gambles of economic life, the defeats and triumphs of science, literature, and art, the desperate longings of religious faith.

The Italian may have been a hurried lover, but he attended lustily to the continuance of the species, and so littered the golden peninsula with his like that one function of the battles was to reduce the pullulating crowd. The Church discouraged childlessness more than adultery, for so she could disarm dissent with multiplication. She smiled on Eros, and laid no puritan pall upon Carnival ecstasies. Girls were almost always virginal, for marriage came early, and premarital surveillance was severe; but after marriage—since this was usually a union of properties—a woman might take a *cavaliere servente*, or even a lover, and still be respectable; if she employed two or three lovers she was accounted "a little wild." This, however, is the testimony of Byron,[21] who liked to believe every woman accessible. Perhaps he meant to speak only of Venice, where Venus seemed especially at home, but Stendhal gave a similar picture of Milan in his *Chartreuse de Parme*.

Despite such easy morals, the life of the Milanese in 1805 seemed dull to Mme. de Rémusat, who mourned "the absolute nonexistence of family life—the husbands strangers to their wives, leaving them to the care of a *cavaliere servente*";[22] and Mme. de Staël, who shone in bisexual discourse, was displeased with what she considered the superficiality of conversation dominated by males; "the Italians," she thought, "shrink from the fatigue of thinking."[23] The Italians could have reminded her that the Church frowned upon audible thinking; and the great majority of them agreed with the Pope that a religion with a settled creed and transalpine revenues was a beneficent institution in Italy. Even so, there was much quiet free thought among the educated minority,[24] and considerable political heresy. Alfieri could rhapsodize over the French Revolution until it confiscated his property, and hundreds of Italians applauded the news of the fallen Bastille. Italy had bisexual societies of polite learning like the Accademia dell' Arcadia; and that once famous congregation of learned men and women, the Accademia della Crusca, was reconstituted in 1812. In 1800 a woman, Clotilda Tambroni, was teaching Greek in the University of Bologna.

There and in other Italian universities science and medicine were flourishing. In 1791, at the University of Bologna, Luigi Galvani (1737–98) showed that if the muscle of a frog's leg is connected with a piece of iron, and its nerve is connected with a piece of copper, an electric current will be generated and will cause the muscle to contract. In 1795, at the University of Pavia, Alessandro Volta (1745–1827) invented the "Voltaic pile," or storage battery, which so astonished Europe that he was called to Paris in 1801 to demonstrate it at the Institute; and on November 7, before an audience that included Napoleon, he read a paper "On the Identity of the Electric Fluid with the Galvanic Fluid." In 1807 Luigi Rolando published his epochal researches in the anatomy of the brain. "Thoughtless" Italy was teaching Europe a revolution greater than the French.

The Italian theater languished because Italians found it so natural to transform speech into song, and drama into opera. The populace flocked to simple plays in the style of the *commedia dell' arte;* the maturer spirits went to such dramas as those in which Vittorio Alfieri (1749–1803) had proclaimed his hatred of tyranny and his longing for the liberation of Italy from foreign rule. Nearly all his plays antedated the French Revolution;[25] but his passionate treatise *Della tirannide,* written in 1777, published in Baden in 1787, and at last in Italy in 1800, became one of the classics of Italian philosophy and prose. Finally, in *Misogallo* (1799), nearing the end of his troubled life, he appealed to the Italian people to rise and throw off all alien rule and become a united nation. Here the Risorgimento of Mazzini and Garibaldi found its first clear voice.

The extroverted ardor, the melodious language, and the musical bent of the Italians lent themselves to poetry. This brief age—even after surrendering Alfieri to the past and Leopardi to the future—had a hundred poets climbing Parnassus. Happiest of them was Vincenzo Monti (1754–1828), who had a good word to say for every promising subject. *La Bassevilliana* (1793) defended religion against the French Revolution, and won him acceptance at the papal court; in *Il bardo della Selva Nera* (1806) he gloried in Napoleon's liberation of Italy, and he was appointed by the conqueror to a professorship in the University of Pavia; after the fall of Napoleon he discovered and proclaimed the faults of the French and the virtues of the Austrians. Through all these leaps he continued to praise *La bellezza dell' universo.* He surpassed these flights in his translation of the *Iliad* (1810); he knew no Greek, but merely versified a prose version, so that Foscolo called him *gran traduttor dei traduttore d'Omero.*

Ugo Foscolo (1778–1827) was a greater poet and sadder man. Being a poet, he was sensuous passion rather than ordered thought; he indulged his desires, passed from one romance to another, from one country or gospel to another, and ended with a longing for old dreams. But through all his phases he was a patient craftsman, seeking perfect form for his verses, even when discarding, as specious ornaments, not only rhyme but rhythm, and seeking perfection in a language-music all his own.

He was born between two worlds—on the Ionian island of Zante between Greece and Italy, from an Italian seed in a Greek womb. After fifteen years in Zante he moved to Venice, sampled its frail beauties, fell in love with its decadent charm, and learned to hate the neighborly grasp of Austria. He rejoiced when Napoleon came like a torrent from Nice to Mantua; he hailed the hero of Arcole as *Buonaparte liberatore;* but when the unprincipled savior surrendered Venice to Austria he turned upon him in a romantic novel, *Le ultime lettere di Iacopo Ortis* (1798)—the last letters of a Venetian Werther who recounts, in letters to a friend, the double loss of his inamorata to a rival, and of his beloved Venice to a Teutonic ogre.

When the Austrians set out to reconquer north Italy, Foscolo joined the French Army, fought bravely at Bologna, Florence, Milan, and served as a captain in the forces that Napoleon prepared for the invasion of England. When that dream faded, Foscolo abandoned the bayonet for the pen, returned to Italy, and published there his finest work, *I sepolcri* (1807). In these classically polished, romantically emotional three hundred pages he defended tomb inscriptions as the inspiring remembrance of great men; he honored the Church of Santa Croce in Florence for carefully preserving the remains of Machiavelli, Michelangelo, and Galileo; he asked how a people that had through many centuries produced so many heroes of thought and action, so many masterpieces of philosophy, poetry, and art, could rest content with alien masters; and he exalted the legacy of great men as their real immortality, and as the soul and spiritual life of the nation and the race.

When, in 1814–15, the Austrians again became masters of northern Italy, Foscolo exiled himself to Switzerland, and thence to England. He supported himself by giving lessons and writing articles, and died in great poverty in 1827. In 1871 his remains were brought from England to Florence, and were buried in Santa Croce, in an Italy at last free.

"In Italy," said Byron (who loved it nonetheless), "a man must be a cicisbeo [a "serving cavalier"], or a singer in duets, or connoisseur of operas, or nothing."[26] Italian opera, generated especially in Venice and Naples, still dominated the sounding boards of Europe, after a brief challenge by Gluck and Mozart; soon (1815) Rossini's engaging melodies and tempestuous arias would steal the stage, even in Vienna. Piccini, after his bout with Gluck in Paris, returned to Naples, and was placed in house arrest for sympathizing with the French Revolution; after Napoleon's conquest of Italy he was again invited to France (1798), but died there two years later. Paisiello, as composer and conductor, triumphed in St. Petersburg, in Vienna, in Paris, and in Naples under Ferdinand IV, then under Joseph, then under Murat. Domenico Cimarosa succeeded Antonio Salieri as *Kapellmeister* in Vienna, and produced there the most famous of his operas, *Il matrimonio segreto* (1792). In 1793 he was called back to Naples as *maestro di capella* by Ferdinand; when the French took Naples he received them gladly; when Ferdinand was restored he sentenced the composer to death, but was induced to commute this to exile. Cimarosa set out for St. Petersburg, but died at Venice on the way (1801). Meanwhile Muzio Clementi was composing and performing piano music in various capitals, and was preparing the once famous *Gradus ad Parnassum* (1817) for the instruction of young pianists everywhere.

Niccolò Paganini (1782–1840) began at Geneva in 1797 his long career as a concert violinist. Loving his violin more passionately and faithfully than he loved any of the many women who throbbed to his music, he developed the possibilities of the instrument to unprecedented complexities of composition and performance. He composed twenty-four *capricci*, which astonished with the whimsicality of their developments. Elisa Bonaparte Bacciocchi appointed him music director at Piombino (1805), but that could not long keep him from the tours where his concerts were sure to bring him large audiences and pleasant wealth. In 1833 he settled in Paris. He gave twenty thousand francs to Berlioz, who was struggling with poverty, and encouraged him to compose *Harold in Italy*. Paganini's strenuous working and playing brought him to exhaustion. He decided to leave the excitement of a capital that was frantic with genius and bubbling with revolution. He died at Nice in 1840, leaving—besides his *capricci*—eight concertos and numerous sonatas to challenge the violin virtuosi of the advancing century. The art of the violin is only now recovering from his antic pranks.

VI. ANTONIO CANOVA: 1757–1822

Italy in the age of Napoleon was too absorbed in war and politics, too poor in public spirit or private philanthropy, to generate such art, and particularly such architecture, as had exalted Italy when all Europe was sending "Peter's pence" to the popes, and Florence, Venice, and Milan, as well as Rome and Naples, were rich and self-ruled. Some outstanding structures were raised: Luigi Cagnola's Arco della Pace in Milan (1806–33); Antonio Selva's Teatro la Fenice in Venice (1792); Cosimo Morelli's Palazzo Braschi at Rome (1795), with its stately staircase; and Antonio Niccolini's imposing façade (1810–12) of the Teatro San Carlo in Naples. There was no memorable painting, but Italy's sculptors were inspired by the excavations at Herculaneum to discard the eccentricities of baroque and the exuberance of rococo, and to seek the grace and calm and simple line of classic statuary. One of these sculptors left us work that still stops the eye, tempts the touch, and lives in the memory.

Antonio Canova was born in Possagno, at the foot of the Venetian Alps. Both his father and his grandfather were sculptors, specializing in altars and religious monuments. When the father died (1760) the grandfather took Antonio into his home, and later into his studio. The boy's willingness to work and eagerness to learn caught the attention of Giovanni Falier, a patrician of Arsolo. Falier provided funds for Antonio's study in Venice, and was rewarded with the youth's first notable production, *Orpheus and Eurydice*.[27] In 1779, with Falier's approval, he set out for Rome. From that center he studied the remains of ancient art. More and more he was won to Winckelmann's interpretation of Greek sculpture as aiming to represent ideal beauty through perfect form and line. He dedicated himself to the revival of the classic style.

His friends in Venice persuaded the government to send him an annuity of three hundred ducats for the next three years. This neither spoiled him

te the art of antiquity; soon the Romantic movement subordinated line
d form to color and feeling, and Canova's fame faded.

It should not be irrelevant to add that Canova was a good man, known for
odesty, piety, and charity, and capable of appreciating his competitors. He
orked hard, and suffered from the malarial air of Rome, and from carving
assive monuments. In the summer of 1821 he left Rome, and sought clearer
r and a quieter life in his native Possagno. There, on October 13, 1822, he
ied, aged sixty-four, mourned by all literate Italy.

VII. *VALE ITERUM ITALIA*

What was the algebraic total of the good and the evil done by France in
Italy in this age? To a nation drugged into lassitude by foreign rule it
brought the arousing cry and example of a nation rising in wrath and
achieving freedom by its own will and deed. It brought a new and challenging spirit into the relations of the citizens to the state. It brought a Code
Napoléon severe but constructive and defined, promoting order and unity,
and legal equality in a people long divided by class and allergic to law. Napoleon and his hard-working administrators improved and cleansed the processes of government, expediting performance, multiplying public works,
adorning the cities, opening boulevards and parks, clearing roads, marshes,
and canals, establishing schools, ending the Inquisition, encouraging agriculture and industry, science and literature and art. The religion of the people
was protected by the new regime, but lost the power to suppress noncon-
formity, and was made to contribute to the expenses of the state. Conversely
it was the skeptic Napoleon who allotted funds to complete the Cathedral
of Milan. The whole procedure of law was quickened and reformed; torture
was outlawed, Latin was no longer required in the courts. In this period
(1789–1813) Joseph and Murat in Naples, Eugène in Milan, were blessings
to their realms, and would have been loved if they had been Italians.

The other side of the picture was conscription, taxation, and expert pil-
fering. Napoleon put an end to brigandage, but he appropriated works of
art with such appreciation as perhaps they had ceased to receive in an Italy
saturated with masterpieces. In Napoleon's view conscription was the most
rational and equitable method of protecting the new nations from domestic
disorder and foreign rule. "The Italians," he said, "should remember that
arms are the principal support of a state. It is time that the youths who live
in idleness in the great towns should cease to fear the fatigues and dangers of
war." Probably conscription would have been accepted as a necessary evil
had not Italian conscripts found that they were expected to go anywhere to
protect the interests of Napoleon or France; so six thousand of them were
moved to the English Channel in 1803 to join in a problematical invasion of
England; eighty thousand of them [32] were pulled out of their native sunshine
to sample the plains and snows and Cossacks of Russia.

Nor did the Italians agree about the patriotism of taxation. Here too the

nor deterred him. He frankly imitated classic models, and s
to equal them; so his *Perseus* and *The Pugilist*, both done i
only modern works deemed worthy to stand in the Belveder
beside world-acclaimed productions of classical antiquity
Slaying the Centaur (1805)—a colossal marble group now in
rial Gardens of Vienna—could easily be mistaken for an anci
were it not for the exaggeration of muscles and fury. Canova
in softer moods congenial to his character, as in the *Hebe*
Gallery in Berlin; here the daughter of Zeus and Hera is
youth, caught in the mobile grace of dispensing wine to the go

In this fruitful year 1805 Canova began the most famous
the *Venus Victrix* of the Galleria Borghese in Rome. He per
Borghese, sister of Napoleon, to pose for this sensuous figure.
twenty-five, at the perfection of her form; but we are told[29]
used only her face as his model; for the drapery and the limbs
his imagination, his dreams, and his memories. He finished the
years, and then exposed it to the judgment of the public and hi
marveled at its proud beauty and loving finish; here was no mer
some ancient masterpiece, but a living woman of her time,
brother's judgment, the fairest. Canova made her a gift to the gen

In 1802 Napoleon asked Canova to come from Rome to
Pius VII, having just signed a concordat with the Consul, adv
to go, if only as one more Italian conqueror of France. Of the
trait busts that the sculptor made of Napoleon, the most pleasi
modest Musée Napoléon at Cap d'Antibes; there the young v
veritable Aristotle of meditation. Unreasonably more famous
length statue which Canova made in plaster and then carved in or
Carrara marble on his return to Rome. It was sent to Paris in 181
set up in the Louvre; but Napoleon objected to it, allegedly b
little Winged Victory placed in his right hand seemed to be fly
from him. The figure was packed away out of sight. In 1816 t
government bought it, and presented it to Wellington. It now stan
feet high, at the foot of the stairway in Wellington's London palac
House. Canova came to Paris again in 1810 to make a seated statue
Louise. The result was not prepossessing, but Napoleon gave the
artist funds to repair the Florence Cathedral, and for financing S
Academy (for artists) in Rome. After Napoleon's fall Canova w
head of the commission appointed by the Pope to restore to their
owners the art works that had been sent to Paris by French generals

He stood at the top of the Italian sculptors of his time, and was su
in Europe only by the now venerable Houdon (1741–1828). Byro
was more at home in Italy than in France, thought that "Europe—th
—has but one Canova,"[30] and "Such as the great of yore, Canova
day."[31] Part of his acclaim may have been due to the neoclassic wa
brought him, like David—both helped by Napoleon—to acknowledge
ership in his art. But Europe could not long be content to imitate or

labor of Italy went not only to protect, govern, and embellish Italy, but also to help Napoleon meet the expenses of his expanding and precarious empires. Eugène was expected to win the love of his subjects while he was picking their pockets; taxes in his little kingdom rose from 82 million francs in 1805 to 144 million in 1812. The Italians added that such levies might have been more easily borne if the Emperor's Continental Blockade had not deprived Italian industry of its English market, while export and import duties favoring France were hurting Italian commerce with France and Germany.

So, even before the Austrians came back, the Italians had tired of Napoleon's protectorate. They felt that they were not only losing great art, but were being drained of the wealth they were creating in order that France might invade England and conquer Russia. This was not the dream their poets had dreamed. They admitted that the Pope's functionaries had allowed a high degree of corruption to enter into the administration of the Papal States, but they did not like the rough handling of Pius VII by French officers, nor his long imprisonment by Napoleon's command. At last they lost love even for the lovable Eugène, for it was through his hands that many of Napoleon's most unwelcome edicts had been imposed; and when, after Leipzig, Napoleon was in danger of complete defeat (1813), they refused to support Eugène's efforts to send him aid. The effort to liberate Italy through alien arms and rule failed; liberation awaited the development of national unity through native literature, statesmanship, and arms.

Napoleon himself, amid his many miscalculations, had foreseen these difficulties. In 1805—the year of his coronation as king of Italy—he said to Bourrienne:

> The union of Italy with France can only be temporary, but it is necessary in order to accustom the nations [states] of Italy to live under common laws. The Genoese, the Piedmontese, the Venetians, the Milanese, the inhabitants of Tuscany, the Romans, the Neapolitans, hate one another. . . . Yet Rome is, from the recollections connected with it, the natural capital of Italy. To make it so, however, it is necessary that the power of the pope should be confined within limits purely spiritual. I cannot now think of this, but I will reflect upon it hereafter. . . . All these little states will insensibly become accustomed to the same laws; and when manners have been assimilated, and enmities extinguished, then there will be an Italy, and I will give her independence. But for that I must have twenty years, and who can count on the future?[33]

We cannot always trust Bourrienne, but Las Cases quotes Napoleon as having spoken to the same effect at St. Helena: "I have planted in the hearts of the Italians principles that can never be rooted out. Sooner or later this regeneration will be accomplished."[34] It was.

CHAPTER XXVII

Austria

1780–1812

I. ENLIGHTENED DESPOTS: 1780–92

IN 1789 Austria was one of the major states of Europe, proud of its history, its culture, and its power, with an empire far wider than its name. That name, from *Auster*, the south wind, justly conveyed the sense of a people Teutonically tough but good-natured and good-humored, sharing happily the *joie de vivre* and music madness of Italy. It had been a Celtic nation when, shortly before Christ, the Romans conquered it, and it seemed to have retained, across two millenniums, some Celtic vivacity and wit. At Vindobona (which became Vienna and then Wien) the Romans built an outpost of their civilization against intrusive barbarians; there Marcus Aurelius, between golden thoughts, held back the Marcomanni about A.D. 170; there Charlemagne placed the East Mark, or eastern boundary, of his realm; there in 955 Otto the Great set up his Österreich, or Eastern Kingdom, against the Magyars; and there in 1278 Rudolf of Hapsburg established the rule of a dynasty that continued till 1918. In 1618–48 the south wind blew strongly Catholic, leading the old faith against the new in thirty years of war; and that faith was fortified when, in 1683, Vienna for a second time served as a bulwark of Christendom, throwing back the Turks. Meanwhile the Hapsburg monarchy spread the rule of Austria over the adjacent duchies of Styria, Carinthia, Carniola, and the Tirol; over Bohemia (Czechoslovakia), Transylvania (Romania), Hungary, Polish Galicia, Lombardy, and the Spanish Netherlands (Belgium). Such was the scattered realm that Europe knew as the Austrian Empire when, in 1797, Napoleon first knocked at Vienna's gates.

The Hapsburg dynasty reached its final peak in the reign of Maria Theresa (r. 1740–80), that willful and wonderful matriarch who rivaled Catherine II and Frederick the Great among the monarchs of her time. She lost Silesia to Frederick's Machiavellian grasp, but thereafter, with her people and her allies, she fought him to a deadlock of exhaustion. Surviving that conflict, she lived to place five of her sixteen children upon thrones: Joseph in Vienna, Leopold in Tuscany, Maria Amalia in Parma, Maria Carolina in Naples, Marie Antoinette in France. She reluctantly transmitted her realm to her oldest son, for she distrusted his agnosticism and reforms, and foresaw that her people, immovably in love with her, would be unhappy under any disturbance of their traditional beliefs and ways.

Her judgment seems justified by the troubles that bewildered Joseph, who shared the throne with her from 1765 to 1780, and then held it for ten years more. He shocked the aristocracy by freeing the serfs, and shocked the strongly Catholic population by flirting with Voltaire, allowing Protestant worship, and harassing Pius VI. Unsupported by the bureaucracy that enveloped him, he had to confess, in his last days, that the peasants, suddenly separated from their feudal lords, had made a mess of their liberty; that he had disrupted the economy; that he had driven the upper classes in Hungary and the Austrian Netherlands to revolt, threatening the very existence of the Empire. His purposes were benevolent, but his methods were to rule by innumerable decrees which dictated the end without preparing the means. Frederick the Great said of him· "He invariably takes the second step before he takes the first."[1] He died (February 20, 1790) regretting his impetuous procedure, and mourning the popular conservatism that loved habit too much to bear reform.

His brother Leopold shared his aims but avoided his haste. Though he was only eighteen when made grand duke of Tuscany (1765), he tempered his power with caution, gathered about him mature Italians (e.g., Cesare Beccaria) familiar with the people, needs, and possibilities of the duchy, and, with their help, gave his historic realm a government that was the envy of Europe. When the death of his brother raised him to imperial leadership he had had twenty-five years of experience. He moderated some of Joseph's reforms, and canceled others, but fully acknowledged the obligation of an "enlightened despot" to raise the educational and economic opportunities of his people. He withdrew the Austrian Army from Joseph's ill-considered attack on Turkey, and, with some use of it, persuaded Belgium to return to the Austrian allegiance. He pacified the Hungarian nobles by recognizing the national authority of their Diet and constitution. He appeased the Bohemians by restoring to Prague the crown of Bohemia's ancient kings, and accepting coronation there in St. Vitus' Cathedral. He knew that in government the substance can be withdrawn if the form is retained.

Meanwhile he resisted the attempt of French *émigrés* and European kings to involve him in war with Revolutionary France. He felt for the plight of his younger sister, Marie Antoinette, but he feared that war with France would mean his loss of still unreconciled Belgium. Nevertheless, when the flight of Louis XVI and Marie Antoinette was stopped at Varennes, and they were led back to Paris to live in daily danger of their lives, Leopold proposed to his fellow monarchs that they take united action to control the Revolution. Frederick William II of Prussia met with Leopold at Pillnitz, and signed with him a declaration (August 27, 1791) threatening intervention in France. Louis XVI made this awkward by accepting the Revolutionary constitution (September 13). But disorder continued and rose, again endangering King and Queen; Leopold ordered the mobilization of the Austrian Army; the French Assembly demanded an explanation; Leopold died (March 1, 1792) before the message arrived. His son and successor, Em-

peror Francis II, aged twenty-four, rejected the ultimatum; and on April 20
France declared war.

II. FRANCIS II

That story has been told from the French corner; how did the Austrians
view it and feel it? They heard of their Archduchess—whose beauty had
sent Edmund Burke into a delirium of eloquence—being scorned by the
Parisians as "L'Autrichienne," being in effect imprisoned in the Tuileries by
the mob, and then deposed and imprisoned by the Assembly. They heard of
the September Massacres, and how the severed head of the Princesse de
Lamballe was paraded on a pike in view of the Queen who had loved her.
They heard of her, white-haired, riding captive in a tumbril through a
taunting crowd to her death under the guillotine. Nothing more was needed
to make the people of Austria rally to the young Emperor who was to lead
them in war against those French murderers. It did not matter that he was
a middling mind, a bungling though benevolent despot, choosing incompetent
generals, losing battle after battle, surrendering part after part of the body of
Austria, and leaving his capital to the mercy and use of the conqueror.
These defeats made the Austrians love Francis all the more; he seemed to
them their appointed ruler by divine right, by papal consecration, and by
the unchallenged legitimacy of royal descent; and he was defending them as
well as he could against murderous barbarians and then against a Corsican
devil. His repudiation of every liberal measure left by his uncle and his
father, his restoration of feudal dues and the *corvée*, his rejection of any
move away from autocracy to constitutional government—all this seemed forgotten when, after Austerlitz and Pressburg, he reentered his capital beaten
and despoiled. He was acclaimed with wild devotion by his people.[2] In all
the crowded events of the next eight years they saw only the triumph of the
wicked, and the scandalous humiliation of a God-given ruler, who, as surely
as God existed, would in due time be revenged upon Austria's enemies, and
be restored to his full birthright of possessions and power.

III. METTERNICH

The man who guided him to that fulfillment was born at Coblenz on the
Rhine May 15, 1773, and was christened Klemens Wenzel Lothar von Metternich. He was the eldest son of Prince Franz Georg Karl von Metternich,
Austria's representative at the courts of the Prince-Archbishop Electors of
Trier, Mainz, and Cologne. The boy received his first two names from the
first of these ecclesiastical rulers, and he never forgot his religious connections and loyalties through all his Voltairean youth and Machiavellian ministries. He was given also the name Lothar to remind Europe that an ancestor
so called had ruled Trier in the seventeenth century. Sometimes he added

"Winneburg Beilstein" to indicate the properties that had belonged to the family for eight centuries, and whose seventy-five square miles provided ground for the noble preposition *von*. Obviously he was not made to love or guide revolutions.

He received the education normal to his status from a tutor who initiated him into the French Enlightenment,[3] and then from the University of Strasbourg. When this institution felt some tremors from the fall of the Bastille, Klemens was transferred to the University of Mainz, where he studied law as the science of property and precedent. In 1794 the French seized Coblenz as a hive of buzzing *émigrés*, and nearly all the Metternich estates were "nationalized." The family found refuge and comfort in Vienna. Tall, athletic, elegant, Klemens wooed and won Eleonore von Kaunitz, rich granddaughter of the statesman who had married Hapsburg Austria to Bourbon France. Almost inheriting from his bride the diplomatic arts of noncommittal courtesy and of gracing appropriation with righteousness, he was soon fit for stratagems and spoils.

In 1801, aged twenty-eight, he was appointed minister to the court of Saxony. There he met Friedrich von Gentz, who became his mentor and mouthpiece for the next thirty years, arming him with the most telling arguments for the *status quo ante* revolution. Faithful to the mores of the Ancien Régime, he took a mistress, Katharina Bagration, the eighteen-year-old daughter of a Russian general whom we shall meet again. In 1802 she bore Klemens a daughter, who was acknowledged to be his by his wife.[4] Impressed by his progress, Vienna promoted him (1803) to the Austrian Embassy at Berlin. During his three years in Prussia he met Czar Alexander I, and formed with him a friendship that lasted till they had overthrown Napoleon. This, however, was not in Bonaparte's vision when, after Austerlitz, he asked the Austrian government to send him "a Kaunitz" as ambassador to France. Count Philipp von Stadion, then head of the Foreign Ministry, sent him Metternich. The thirty-three-years-young Kaunitz-in-law reached Paris on August 2, 1806.

Now began a nine-year battle of wits between diplomacy and war, in which the diplomat won by the cooperation of the general. For relaxation from encounters with Napoleon's penetrating eyes—and finding his illustrious wife intellectually unstimulating and physically *toujours la même*—Metternich amused himself with Mme. Laure Junot, wife of the then governor of Paris. But he did not forget that he was expected to probe Napoleon's mind, discover his aims, and explore all possibilities of guiding them to Austria's advantage. Each man admired the other. Napoleon, Metternich wrote to Gentz in 1806, "is the only man in Europe who wills and acts"[5]; and Napoleon found in Metternich an intellect as penetrating as his own.[6] Meanwhile the Austrian learned much by studying Talleyrand.

He spent some three years as ambassador in Paris. He saw with concealed satisfaction the ensnarement of the Grande Armée in Spain. He tried and failed to hide from Napoleon the rearming of Austria for another attempt to unseat him. He left Paris on May 25, 1809, joined Francis II at the front, and witnessed the Austrian defeat at Wagram. Stadion, his martial venture thwarted, resigned his leadership of policy. Francis offered the post to Metternich, and on October 8, 1809, Metternich, aged thirty-six, began his thirty-nine years' career as minister of the imperial household and of foreign affairs.

In January, 1810, General Junot found in his wife's desk some love letters from Metternich. He nearly strangled her, and vowed he would challenge the mettlesome Minister to meet him in a duel at Mainz. Napoleon ended the fracas by dispatching the general and his wife to Spain. The story apparently did no damage to Metternich's reputation, nor to his marriage, nor to his position in the Austrian government. He shared in arranging the marriage of Napoleon with the Austrian Archduchess Marie Louise. He was delighted to hear that this sudden *rapprochement* between France and Austria had angered Russia. He watched the tension grow between those opposed nuclei of European force. He hoped and planned that some weakening of both empires would let Austria regain the lands she had lost, and the high place she had held in the clashing concert of the Powers.

IV. VIENNA

Behind the walls of war lived the peaceable and amiable people of Vienna, a reasonably tolerant mixture of Germans, Hungarians, Czechs, Slovaks, Croats, Moravians, French, Italians, Poles, and Russians—190,000 souls. The great majority were Roman Catholic, and, when they could, worshiped the city's patron saint in St. Stephen's Church. The streets were mostly narrow, but there were some spacious and well-paved boulevards. A congeries of majestic buildings focused on the palatial Schönbrunn, which housed the Emperor, his family, and the main offices of the government. The "blue" Danube passed along the edge of the city, carrying commerce and pleasure in amiable confusion. Sloping toward the river, the park called the Prater (meadow) gave old and young a place for carriage drives or promenades. And just outside the city gates the Wienerwald, or Vienna Woods, invited those lucky walkers who loved trees and trysts, the smell of foliage, the song and chatter of winged residents.

All in all the Viennese were a docile and well-behaved people, quite unlike the Parisians, who, with or without revolution, lived on excitement, resented marriage, hated their nobles, suspected their King, and doubted God. There were nobles here too, but they danced and musicked in their palaces, respected pedestrians, indulged in no snobbery, and died gallantly, however ineffectually, before Napoleon's businesslike warriors. Class consciousness was keenest in the upper middle class, which was making fortunes by supplying the Army, or lending to aristocrats impoverished by a feudalism without stimulus, or to a state always fighting and losing wars.

A proletariat was beginning to form. By 1810 there were over a hundred factories in or near Vienna, employing in all some 27,000 men and women, nearly all at wages that sufficed to keep them alive and multiplying.[7] As early as 1811 there were complaints that oil refineries and chemical plants were polluting the air.[8] Commerce was developing, helped by access to the Adriatic at Trieste, and by the Danube that touched a hundred towns plus Budapest and reached the Black Sea. After 1806 Napoleon's attempt to exclude British goods from the Continent, and French control of Italy, hampered Austrian commerce and industry, and left hundreds of families to unemployment and penury.

Finance was mostly managed by Jews, who, excluded from agriculture and most industry, became experts in the handling of money. Some Jewish bankers in Austria rivaled the Esterházys in the splendor of their establishments; some became the cherished friends of emperors; some were honored as saviors of the state. Joseph II ennobled certain Jewish bankers in appreciation of their patriotism. The Emperor liked especially to visit the home of the financier Nathan von Arnstein, where he could discuss literature and music with the banker's pretty wife. This was the versatile and cultivated Fanny Itzig, who maintained one of the most favored salons in Vienna.[9]

The government was administered by the nobility with middling competence and inconsiderable honesty. Jeremy Bentham, in a letter of July 7, 1817, mourned this "utter moral rottenness of the Austrian state," and he despaired of finding "an honorable person." No commoner could rise to a commanding post in the armed services or the government; consequently there was little stimulus to soldiers or bureaucrats to take pains or risks for promotion's sake. The ranks of the Army were filled by shiftless volunteers, or by conscription through lottery, or by the impressment of beggars, radicals, or criminals;[10] no wonder these Austrian armies were periodically routed by French legions in which any private might rise to leadership, and even join Napoleon's covey of dukes.

Social order was maintained by the Army, the police, and religious belief. The Hapsburg rulers rejected the Reformation, remained loyal to the Catholic Church, and depended upon its well-trained clergy to man the schools, censor the press, and bring up every Christian child in a creed that sanctified hereditary monarchy as a divine right, and comforted poverty and grief with the consolations and promises of the faith. Great fanes like the Stefanskirche and the Karlskirche offered a ritual solemn with song and censer and collective prayer, and exalted by Masses that Protestants like Bach and skeptics like Beethoven were eager to provide. Religious processions periodically brought drama to the streets, renewing the public memory of martyrs and saints, and celebrating the merciful mediation of Vienna's queen, the Virgin Mother. Aside from the disciplinary fear of hell, and some unpleasant pictures of saintly tortures, it was as comforting a religion as has ever been offered to mankind.

Education, primary and secondary, was left to the Church. The Universities of Vienna, Ingolstadt, and Innsbruck were manned by learned Jesuits. The press was strictly controlled; all Voltaireana were stopped at the nation's borders or the city gates. Freethinkers were rarities. Some Freemason lodges had survived Maria Theresa's attempt to destroy them; but they confined themselves to a moderate anticlericalism which even a good Catholic might allow, and a program of social reform which an emperor could endorse. So Mozart, a firm Catholic, was a Freemason; and Joseph II joined the secret order, approved the principles of reform, and made some of them laws. A more radical secret society, the Illuminati—which Adam Weishaupt, an ex-Jesuit, had founded at Ingolstadt in 1776—survived, but in comparative decay. Leopold II renewed his mother's prohibition of all secret societies.

The Church accomplished well the task of training the people to patriotism, charity, social order, and sexual restraint. Mme. de Staël reported in 1804: "You never met a beggar. . . . The charitable establishments are regulated with great order and liberality. Everything bears the mark of a parental, wise, and religious government."[11] Sexual morals were fairly firm among the commonalty, much looser in the upper classes, where the men had mistresses and the wives had lovers. Beethoven, Thayer tells us, protested against "the practice, not uncommon in the Vienna of his time, of living with an unmarried woman as a wife."[12] But family unity was usual, and parental authority was maintained. Manners were genial, and gave little welcome to revolutionary sentiments. Beethoven wrote, on August 2, 1794: "It is my belief that as long as the Austrian has his dark beer and sausage he will not revolt."[13]

The typical Viennese preferred to be entertained rather than reformed. He readily surrendered his kreuzers or groschen (pennies) for simple amusements, such as watching Niklos Roger, "the incombustible Spaniard," who claimed to be immune to fire.[14] If he could spare a bit more he might play billiards or bowl. Vienna and its outskirts abounded in cafés—so called from the coffee that was now rivaling beer as the favorite drink. These were the clubs of the poor; Viennese of ascending status went to *Bierhallen*, which had gardens and fine rooms; the well-to-do could lose their money in gambling halls, or go to a masquerade ball—perhaps in the Redoutensaal, where hundreds of couples could dance at the same time. Even before the days of Johann Strauss (1804–49) the men and women of Vienna lived to dance. The restrained and stately minuet was yielding to the waltz; now the man might enjoy electric contact with his severed half, and lead her into the exciting whirl that had given the dance its name. The Church protested, and forgave.

V. THE ARTS

The theater flourished in Vienna, in all degrees from twopenny sketches on impromptu stages to classic dramas in sumptuous housing and décor. The oldest regular playhouse was the Kärntnerthor, which had been built by the municipality in 1708; here the actor-playwright Joseph Anton Stranitsky

(d. 1726), building on the Italian Arlecchino (Harlequin), created and developed the character of Hanswurst, or John Boloney, the hilarious buffoon in whom the Germans, north and south, satirized their own beloved absurdities. In 1776 Joseph II sponsored and financed the Burgtheater, whose classic façade promised the best ancient and modern plays. Most sumptuous of all was the Theater-an-der-Wien (on the River Wien), built in 1793 by Johann Emanuel Schikaneder, who wrote the libretto for—and acted Papageno in —Mozart's *Magic Flute* (1791). He equipped his theater with every mechanical device known to the scene shifters of his time; he astonished his audiences with dramatic spectacles outmatching reality; and he won for his playhouse the distinction of presenting the premiere of Beethoven's *Fidelio*.

Only one art now rivaled drama in Vienna. It was not architecture, for Austria had finished by 1789 its golden age of baroque. It was not literature, for the Church weighed too heavily on the wings of genius, and the age of Grillparzer (1791–1872) had yet to come. In Vienna, Mme. de Staël reported, "the people read little";[15] as in some cities today a daily newspaper supplied their literary needs; and both the *Wiener Zeitung* and the *Wiener Zeitschrift* were excellent.

Of course the supreme art of Vienna was music. In Austria and Germany —as befitted a people who cherished the home as the fount and citadel of civilization—music was more a domestic and amateur art than a public performance by professionals. Almost every educated family had musical instruments, and some could offer a quartet. Now and then a concert was organized for prepaying subscribers, but concerts open to the general public for an admission charge were rare. Even so, Vienna was crowded with musicians, who starved one another by their number.

How did they survive? Mostly by accepting invitations to perform in private homes, or by dedicating their compositions—with or without prearranged payment—to wealthy nobles, clerics, or businessmen. The love, practice, and patronage of music had been a tradition with Hapsburg rulers for two centuries; it was actively continued in this period by Joseph II, Leopold II, and Leopold's youngest son, the Archduke Rudolf (1788–1831), who was both a pupil and a patron of Beethoven. The Esterházy family provided a succession of generations supporting music; we have seen Prince Miklós József Esterházy (1714–90) keeping Haydn for thirty years as conductor of the orchestra maintained in the Schloss Esterházy, the "Versailles of Hungary." His grandson Prince Miklós Nicolaus Esterházy (1765–1833) engaged Beethoven to compose music for the family orchestra. Prince Karl Lichnowsky (1753–1814) became an intimate friend and patron of Beethoven, and for a time gave him lodging in his palace. Prince Jose Fran Lobkowitz, of an old Bohemian family, shared with Archduke Rudolf and Count Kinsky the honor of subsidizing Beethoven till his death. To these we should add Baron Gottfried van Swieten (1734–1803), who helped musicians not so much with money as with his energy and skill in getting engagements and patrons; he opened London to Haydn and received the dedication of Beethoven's First Symphony; and he founded in Vienna the Musikalische Gesellschaft—twenty-five nobles pledged to help bridge the gaps between composers, music publishers, and audiences. It was in part due to such men that the most disagreeable composer in history survived to make himself the unchallenged music master of the nineteenth century.

CHAPTER XXVIII

Beethoven

1770–1827

I. YOUTH IN BONN: 1770–92

HE was born on December 16, 1770. Bonn was the seat of the prince-archbishop elector of Cologne, one of those Rhineland principalities which, before Napoleon "secularized" them, were ruled by Catholic archbishops engagingly secular and inclined to support well-behaved artists. A considerable part of Bonn's 9,560 population was dependent upon the electoral establishment. Beethoven's grandfather was a bass singer in the Elector's choir; his father, Johann van Beethoven, was a tenor there. The family, of Dutch stock, had come from a village near Louvain. The Dutch *van* indicated place of origin, and did not, like the German *von* or the French *de*, indicate titled and propertied nobility. Grandfather and father were inclined to excessive drinking, and something of this passed down to the composer.

In the year 1767 Johann van Beethoven married the young widow Maria Magdalena Keverich Laym, daughter of a cook in Ehrensbreitstein. She developed into a mother much beloved by her famous son for her soft heart and easy ways. She gave her husband seven children, four of whom died in infancy. The survivors were the brothers Ludwig, Caspar Karl (1774–1815), and Nikolaus Johann (1776–1848).

The father's salary of three hundred florins as "Electoral Court tenorist" was apparently his sole income. The family lived in a poor quarter of Bonn, and the young Beethoven's surroundings and associations were not of a kind to make him a gentleman; he remained a roughhewn rebel to the end. Hoping to improve the family income by developing a son into a child prodigy, Beethoven's father induced or compelled the four-year-old boy to practice at the clavier or on the violin many hours in the day, occasionally at night. Apparently the boy had no spontaneous urge to music,[1] and (according to divers witnesses) he had to be urged on by a severe discipline that sometimes brought him to tears. The torture succeeded, and the boy came to love the art that had cost him so many painful hours. At the age of eight, with another pupil, he was displayed in a public concert, March 26, 1778, with financial results unrecorded. In any case the father was encouraged to engage teachers who could lead Ludwig into the higher subleties of music.

Aside from this he received little formal education. We hear of his attending a school where he learned enough Latin to salt some of his letters with

humorous Latin inventions. He picked up enough French (which was the
Esperanto of the time) to write it intelligibly. He never learned to spell
correctly in any language, and seldom bothered to punctuate. But he read
some good books, ranging from Scott's novels to Persian poetry, and copied
into his notebooks morsels of wisdom from his reading. His only sport was
in his fingers. He loved to improvise, and in that game only Abt Vogler
could match him.

In 1784 Maria Theresa's youngest son, Maximilian Francis, was appointed
elector of Cologne, and took up his residence in Bonn. He was a kindly
man, enthusiastic about food and music; he became "the fattest man in Europe,"[2] but also he brought together an orchestra of thirty-one pieces. Beethoven, aged fourteen, played the viola in that ensemble, and was also listed
as "deputy court organist," with a salary of 150 gulden ($750?) per year.[3]
A report to the Elector in 1785 described him as "of good capability, . . . of
good, quiet behavior, and poor."[4]

Despite some evidence of sexual ventures,* the good behavior and growing competence of the youth led to his receiving from the Elector (1787)
permission and funds for a trip to Vienna for instruction in musical composition. Soon after his arrival he was received by Mozart, who heard him play,
and praised him with disappointing moderation, apparently thinking that the
piece had been long rehearsed. Suspecting this suspicion, Beethoven asked
Mozart to give him, on the piano, a theme for variations. Mozart was astonished at the youth's fertility of invention and sureness of touch, and said
to his friends, "Keep your eyes on him; someday he will give the world
something to talk about";[6] but this story has too familiar an air. Mozart appears to have given the boy some lessons, but the death of Mozart's father,
Leopold (May 28, 1787), and news that Beethoven's mother was dying, cut
this relationship short. Ludwig hurried back to Bonn, and was at his mother's
bedside when she died (July 17).

The father, whose tenor voice had long since decayed, wrote to the
Elector, describing his extreme poverty, and appealing for help. No answer
is recorded, but another singer in the choir came to the rescue. In 1788
Ludwig himself added to the family income by giving piano lessons to
Eleonore von Breuning and her brother Lorenz. Their widowed, wealthy,
cultured mother received the young teacher into full equality with her children, and the friendships so formed helped in some measure to smooth the
sharp corners of Beethoven's character.

Helpful, too, was the kindness of Count Ferdinand von Waldstein (1762–
1823), himself a good musician, and a close friend of the Elector. Learning
of Beethoven's poverty, he sent him occasional gifts of money, pretending

---

* The post-mortem examination of Beethoven revealed various internal disorders which
Grove's Dictionary of Music and Musicians (3d ed., I, 271b) described as "most probably
the result of syphilitic affections at an early period of his life." Thayer, biographer par
excellence of Beethoven, put the matter politely: Beethoven "had not escaped the common
penalties of transgressing the laws of strict purity."[5] The matter is still debated.

that they were from the Elector. Beethoven later dedicated to him the piano sonata (Opus 53 in C Major) that bears his name.

Ludwig needed help more than ever now, for his despondent father had surrendered to alcohol, and had been with difficulty rescued from arrest as a public nuisance. In 1789 Beethoven, not yet nineteen, took upon himself the responsibility for his younger brothers, and became legal head of the family. A decree of the Elector (November 20) ordered that the services of Johann van Beethoven should be dispensed with, and that half of his annual salary of two hundred reichsthalers should be paid him, and the other half to his eldest son. Beethoven continued to earn a small sum as chief pianist and second organist in the Elector's orchestra.

In 1790, flush with a triumph in London, Franz Joseph Haydn stopped at Bonn on his way home to Vienna. Beethoven presented to him a cantata that he had recently composed; Haydn praised it. Probably some word of this reached the Elector's ear; he listened favorably to suggestions that he allow the youth to go to Vienna for study with Haydn, and to continue for some months to receive his salary as a musician on the Elector's staff. Probably Count von Waldstein had won this boon for his young friend. He wrote in Ludwig's album a farewell note: "Dear Beethoven, you are traveling to Vienna in fulfillment of your long-cherished wish. The genius of Mozart [who had died on December 5, 1791] is still weeping and bewailing the death of her favorite. . . . Labor assiduously and receive Mozart's spirit from the hands of Haydn. Your true friend Waldstein."

Beethoven left Bonn, father, family, and friends on or about November 1, 1792. Soon afterward French Revolutionary troops occupied Bonn, and the Elector fled to Mainz. Beethoven never saw Bonn again.

II. PROGRESS AND TRAGEDY: 1792–1802

Arrived in Vienna, he found the city alive with musicians competing for patrons, audiences, and publishers, looking askance at every newcomer, and finding no disarming beauty in the youth from Bonn. He was short, stocky, dark-complexioned (Anton Esterházy called him "the Moor"), pock-marked, front upper teeth overlapping the lower, nose broad and flat, eyes deepset and challenging, and head "like a bullet," wearing a wig and a *van*. He was not designed for popularity, with either the public or his competitors, but he was rarely without a rescuing friend.

Soon came news that his father had died (December 18, 1792). Some difficulty having developed about Beethoven's share in his father's small annuity, he petitioned the Elector for its continuance; the Elector responded by doubling it, and adding: "He is further to receive three measures of grain . . . for the education of his brothers" (Karl and Johann, who had moved to Vienna).[7] Beethoven, grateful, made some good resolutions. In a friend's album, May 22, 1793, he wrote, using the words of Schiller's *Don Carlos*: "I am not wicked—Hot blood is my fault—my crime is that I am young. . . .

Even though wildly surging emotions may betray my heart, yet my heart is good." He resolved "to do good wherever possible, to love liberty above all else, never to deny the truth, even before the throne."[8]

He kept his expenditures to a stoic minimum: for December, 1792, fourteen florins ($35?) for rent; six florins for rent of a piano; "eating, each time 12 kreuzer" (six cents); "meals with wine, 6½ florins" ($16.25??). Another memorandum lists "Haidn" at various times as costing two groschen (a few cents); apparently Haydn was asking little for his lessons. For a while the student accepted correction humbly. But as the lessons continued, Haydn found it impossible to accept Beethoven's reported deviations from orthodox rules of composition. Toward the end of 1793 Beethoven quit his aging master, and went three times a week to study counterpoint with a man more famous as teacher than as composer, Johann Georg Albrechtsberger. Concurrently, three times a week, he studied violin with Ignaz Schuppanzigh. In 1795, having taken all that he felt need of from Albrechtsberger, he applied to Antonio Salieri, then director of the Vienna Opera, for instruction in composition for the voice. Salieri charged nothing to poor pupils; Beethoven presented himself as such, and was accepted. All four of these teachers found him a difficult disciple, bursting with ideas of his own, and resenting the formalism of the musical theory offered him. We can imagine the shudders generated in "Papa Haydn" (who lived till 1809) by the irregularities and sonorities of Beethoven's compositions.

Despite—perhaps because of—his deviations from traveled roads, Beethoven's performances won him, by 1794, a reputation as the most interesting pianist in Vienna. The pianoforte had won its battle with the harpsichord; Johann Christian Bach in 1768 had begun performing solos on it in England; Mozart adopted it, Haydn followed suit in 1780, Muzio Clementi was composing concertos definitely designed for the piano and its new flexibility between piano and forte, between staccato and sostenuto. Beethoven made full use of the piano's powers and his own, especially in his improvisations, where no printed notation hampered his style. Ferdinand Ries, pupil of both Haydn and Beethoven, later declared: "No artist that I ever heard came at all near the height which Beethoven attained in this branch of playing. The wealth of ideas which forced themselves on him, the caprices to which he surrendered himself, the variety of treatment, the difficulties, were inexhaustible."[9]

It was as a pianist that the patrons of music first appreciated him. At an evening concert in the home of Baron van Swieten, after the program had been completed, the host (biographer Schindler relates) "detained Beethoven and persuaded him to add a few fugues of Bach as an evening blessing."[10] Prince Karl Lichnowsky—the leading amateur musician in Vienna—so liked Beethoven that he regularly engaged him for his Friday musicales, and for a time entertained him as a house guest; Beethoven, however, could not adjust himself to the Prince's meal hours, and preferred a nearby hotel. The most enthusiastic of the composer's titled patrons was Prince Lobkowitz, an excellent violinist, who spent nearly all his income on music and musicians; for years he helped Beethoven, despite quarrels, and he took in good spirit Beethoven's insistence on being treated as a social equal. The ladies of these helpful nobles enjoyed his proud independence, took lessons and scoldings from him, and allowed the poor bachelor to make love to them, in letters.[11] They and their lords accepted his dedications, and rewarded him moderately.

So far his fame was only as a pianist, and, as such, it reached Prague and Berlin, to which he made visits as a virtuoso in 1796. But meanwhile he composed. On October 21, 1795, he published, as his Opus I, *Three Grand Trios*, about which Johann Cramer, after playing them, announced, "This is the man who is to console us for the loss of Mozart."[12] Stimulated by such praise, Beethoven wrote in his notebook: "Courage! Despite all bodily weaknesses my spirit shall rule. . . . This year must determine the complete man. Nothing must remain undone."[13]

In 1797 Napoleon, unseen, first came into Beethoven's life. The young general, having driven the Austrians from Lombardy, had led his army over the Alps, and was nearing Vienna. The surprised capital extemporized defense as well as it could with guns and hymns; now Haydn wrote Austria's national anthem—"Gott erhalte Franz den Kaiser, unsern guten Kaiser Franz"; and Beethoven produced music for another war song—"Ein grosses deutsches Volk sind wir." These spirited compositions were later to be worth many regiments, but they did not move Napoleon, who exacted a humiliating peace.

A year later General Bernadotte came to Vienna as the new French ambassador, and shocked the citizens by raising from his balcony the French Revolutionary tricolor flag. Beethoven, who had frankly expressed republican ideas, openly declared his admiration of Bonaparte, and was often seen at the ambassador's receptions.[14] Apparently it was Bernadotte who suggested to Beethoven the idea of a composition honoring Napoleon.[15]

Seeking to tap nearer services, Ludwig in 1799 dedicated his Opus 13, "Grande Sonate Pathétique," to Prince Lichnowsky, in gratitude for favors received or hoped for. The Prince responded (1800) by putting six hundred gulden at Beethoven's disposal "until I obtain a suitable appointment."[16] This sonata began simply, as if in humble filiation from Mozart; then it proceeded to a difficult intricacy that would later seem simple beside the almost aggressive complexity and power of the Hammerklavier Sonatas or the "Appassionata." Still easy on eyes and hands were the First Symphony (1800) and the "Moonlight Sonata" in C sharp minor (1801). Beethoven did not give the latter piece its famous name, but called it "Sonata quasi Fantasia." Apparently he had no intention of making it a love song. It is true that he dedicated it to the Countess Giulia Guicciardi, who was among the untouchable goddesses of his reveries, but it had been written for another occasion, quite unrelated to this divinity.[17]

To the year 1802 belongs one of the strangest and most appealing documents in the history of music. This secret "Heiligenstadt Testament"—which was not seen by others till found in Beethoven's papers after his death—is intelligible only through a frank confrontation of his character. There had been many pleasant qualities in it in his youth—a buoyancy of spirit, a fund of humor, a devotion to study, a readiness to help; and many of his Bonn friends—his teacher Christian Gottlob Neefe, his pupil Eleonore von Breuning, his patron Count von Waldstein—remained devoted to him despite his growing bitterness against life. In Vienna, however, he alienated one friend after another until he was left almost alone. When they heard that he was dying they came back, and did what they could to ease his pains.

His early environment scarred him lastingly; he could never forget, and never forgive, the toilsome, anxious poverty, or the humiliation of seeing his father surrender to failure and drink. He himself, as the years saddened him, yielded more and more to the amnesia of wine.[18] In Vienna his stature (five feet five inches) invited wit, and his face was no fortune; his hair thick, disheveled, bristling; his heavy beard spreading up to his sunken eyes, and sometimes allowed to grow to half an inch before shaving.[19] "Oh God!" he cried in 1819, "what a plague it is to one when he has so fatal a face as mine!"[20]

These physical disadvantages were probably a spur to achievement, but, after the first few years in Vienna, they discouraged care of his dress, his body, his rooms, or his manners. "I am an untidy fellow," he wrote (April 22, 1801); "perhaps the only touch of genius which I possess is that my things are not always in very good order." He earned enough to keep servants, but he soon quarreled with them, and seldom kept them long. He was brusque with the lowly; with the highborn he was sometimes obsequious, often proud, even arrogant. He was merciless in assessing his rivals, and was rewarded by their almost unanimous dislike. He was severe with his pupils, but taught some of them without charge.[21]

He was a misanthrope, judging every man basically base, but fondly forgiving his troublesome nephew Karl, and loving every pretty pupil. He gave to nature the unquestioning affection that he could not offer to mankind. He frequently fell into melancholy moods, but almost as frequently had spells of raucous jollity, with or without wine. He had an often inconsiderate sense of humor (e.g., Letters 14, 22, 25, 30[22]), punned at every opportunity, and invented sometimes offensive nicknames for his friends. He could laugh more readily than he could smile.

He tried, through worried years, to conceal from the world the affliction that embittered his life. In a letter of June 29, 1801, he revealed it to a friend of his youth, Franz Wegeler:

> For the last three years my hearing has become weaker and weaker. The trouble is supposed to have been caused by the condition of my abdomen, which . . . was wretched even before I left Bonn, but has become worse in Vienna, where I have been constantly afflicted with diarrhea, and have been suffering in consequence from an extraordinary disability. . . . Such was my condition until the autumn of last year, and sometimes I gave way to despair. . . .

> I must confess that I lead a wretched life. For almost two years I have ceased to attend any social functions, just because I find it impossible to say to people: I am deaf. If I had any other profession I might be able to cope with my infirmity; but in my profession it is a terrible calamity. Heaven alone knows what is to become of me. Already I have cursed my Creator and my existence . . . I beg you not to say anything about my condition to anyone, not even to Lorchen [Eleonore von Breuning].

Apparently in hopes of profiting from its sulfur baths, Beethoven spent part of 1802 in Heiligenstadt, a small village near Göttingen. Wandering in nearby woods, he saw, at a short distance, a shepherd playing a pipe. As he heard no sound, he realized that now only the louder sounds of an orchestra would reach him. He had already begun to conduct as well as to perform and compose; and the implications of this peasant's unheard pipe threw him into despair. He went to his room and composed, on October 6, 1802, what is known as the "Heiligenstadt Testament," a spiritual will and *apologia pro vita sua*. Though he captioned it "For my brothers Carl and —— Beethoven," he carefully concealed the document from all eyes but his own. It is here transcribed in its essential lines:

> O ye men who think and say that I am malevolent, stubborn, or misanthropic, how greatly do ye wrong me, you who do not know the secret cause of my seeming so. From childhood my heart and mind were disposed to the gentle feeling of good will, I was even ever eager to accomplish great deeds, but reflect now that for 6 years I have been in a hopeless case, aggravated by senseless physicians, . . . finally compelled to face the prospect of a *lasting malady* . . . Born with an ardent and lively temperament, even susceptible to the diversions of society, I was compelled early to isolate myself, to live in loneliness, when I at times tried to forget all this, O how harshly was I repulsed by the doubly sad experience of my bad hearing, and yet it was impossible for me to say to men speak louder, shout, for I am deaf. Ah how could I possibly admit an infirmity in the *one sense* which should have been more perfect in me than in others . . . O I cannot do it, therefore forgive me when you see me draw back when I would gladly mingle with you. . . . What a humiliation when one stood beside me and heard a flute in the distance and *I heard nothing*. . . . Such incidents brought me to the verge of despair; but little more and I would have put an end to my life—only art it was that withheld me, ah, it seemed impossible to leave the world until I had produced all that I felt called upon to produce. . . . O Divine One thou lookest into my inmost soul, and thou knowest it, thou knowest that love of man and desire to do good lives therein. O men, when someday you read these words, reflect that ye did me wrong. . . . You my brothers Carl and —— as soon as I am dead if Dr. Schmid is still alive ask him in my name to describe my malady and attach this document to the history of my illness so that so far as possible at least the world may become reconciled with me after my death. At the same time I declare you two to be the heirs of my small fortune. . . . It is my wish that your lives may be better and freer from care than I have had, recommend *virtue* to your children, it alone can give happiness, not money, I speak from experience, it was virtue that upheld me in my misery, to it next to my art I owe the fact that I did not end my life by suicide—Farewell and love each other . . . with joy I hasten toward death.

In the margin he wrote: "To be read and executed after my death."[23]

It was not a suicide note; it was both hopeless and resolute. Beethoven proposed to accept and transcend his hardship, and bring to other ears than his own all the music that lay silent within him. Almost at once—still in Heiligenstadt in November, 1802—he composed his Second Symphony, in D, wherein there is no note of complaint or grief. Only one year after his cry from the depths he composed his Third Symphony, the *Eroica*, and entered with it his second and most creative period.

III. THE HEROIC YEARS: 1803–09

The learned musicologists who have been trailed in these hesitant pages divide Beethoven's productive career into three periods: 1792–1802; 1803–16; 1817–24. In the first he worked tentatively in the simple and placid style of Mozart and Haydn. In the second period he made greater demands upon the performers in tempo, dexterity, and force; he explored contrasts of mood from tenderness to power; he gave rein to his inventiveness in variation, and to his flair for improvisation, but he subjected these to the logic of affiliation and development; he changed the sex of the sonata and the symphony from feminine sentiment and delicacy to masculine assertiveness and will. As if to signalize the change, Beethoven now replaced the minuet in the third move-ment with a scherzo frolicking with notes, laughing in the face of fate. Now he found in music an answer to misfortune: he could absorb himself in the creation of music that would make the death of his body a passing incident in an extended life. "When I am playing and composing, my affliction . . . hampers me least."[24] He could no longer hear his melodies with his physical ears, but he could hear them with his eyes, with the musician's secret ability to transfer imagined tones into spots and lines of ink, and then hear them, soundless, from the printed pages.

Almost all the works of this period became classics, appearing through suc-ceeding generations in orchestral repertoires. The "Kreutzer Sonata," Opus 47, composed in 1803 for violinist George Bridgetower, was dedicated to Rodolphe Kreutzer, teacher of the violin in the Paris Conservatory of Music; Beethoven had met him in Vienna in 1798. Kreutzer judged the piece alien to his style or mood, and seems never to have played it publicly.

Beethoven ranked as the best of his symphonies the *Eroica*,[25] composed in 1803–04. Half the world knows the story about its original dedication to Napoleon. Despite his titled friends and judicious dedications, Beethoven remained to the end of his life a resolute republican; and he applauded the seizure and reconstitution of the French government by Bonaparte in 1799–1800 as a move toward responsible rule. In 1802, however, he expressed his regret that Napoleon had signed a concordat with the Church. "Now," he wrote, "everything is going back to the old track."[26] As to the dedication, let an eyewitness, Ferdinand Ries, tell the tale:

> In this symphony Beethoven had Bonaparte in his mind, but as he was when he was First Consul. Beethoven esteemed him greatly at the time, and likened

him to the greatest Roman consuls. I as well as several of his more intimate friends saw a copy of the [*Eroica*] score lying upon his table, with the word "Buonaparte" at the extreme top of the title page, and at the extreme bottom "Luigi van Beethoven" but not another word. . . . I was the first to bring him the intelligence that Bonaparte had proclaimed himself emperor, whereupon he flew into a rage, and cried out, "Is then he too nothing more than an ordinary human being? Now he will trample on all the rights of man, and indulge only his ambition. He will exalt himself above all others, become a tyrant." Beethoven went to the table, took hold of the title page by the top, tore it in two, and threw it on the floor. The first page was rewritten and only then did the symphony receive the title "Sinfonia eroica."[27]

When the symphony was published (1805) it bore the title *Sinfonia eroica per festeggiare il sovvenira d'un gran uomo*—"Heroic symphony to celebrate the memory of a great man."[28]

It received its first public performance April 7, 1805, in the Theater-an-der-Wien. Beethoven conducted despite his defective hearing. His style of conducting accorded with his character—excitable, demanding, "most extravagant. At a pianissimo he would crouch down so as to be hidden by the desk; and then, as the crescendo increased, would gradually rise, beating all the time, until at the fortissimo he would spring into the air, with his arms extended as if wishing to float on the clouds."[29] The symphony was criticized for "strange modulations and violent transitions, . . . undesirable originality," and excessive length; the critic advised Beethoven to go back to his earlier and simpler style.[30] Beethoven winced and growled, and worked on.

Giving another hostage to fortune, he tried his hand at opera; on November 20, 1805, he conducted the premiere of *Leonore*. But Napoleon's troops had occupied Vienna on November 13; the Emperor Francis and the leading nobles had fled; the citizens were in no mood for opera; the performance was a resounding failure despite the applause of the French officers in the scanty audience. Beethoven was told that his opera was too long, and clumsily arranged. He shortened and revised it, and offered it a second time on March 29, 1806; again it failed. Eight years later, when the city teemed with the Congress of Vienna, the opera, renamed *Fidelio*, was given a third trial, and achieved a moderate success. Beethoven's mode of composition had become attuned to instruments with greater range and flexibility than the human voice; the singers, however anxious to break new barriers, simply could not sing some soaring passages, and at last they rebelled. The opera is occasionally staged today, borne on the wings of the composer's fame, and with revisions that he can no longer revise.

From that difficult and unrewarding experience he passed to one masterpiece after another. In 1805 he presented Piano Concerto in G, No. 4, Opus 58, second only to the fifth in the affection of virtuosos. He celebrated the year 1806 with the Sonata in F Minor, Opus 57, later christened "Appassionata," and added three quartets, Opus 59, dedicated to Count Andreas Razumovsky, Russian ambassador at Vienna. In March, 1807, Beethoven's friends, probably to console him for the failure of his opera, organized a benefit concert for him; there he conducted his Symphonies No. One, Two, and Three (the *Eroica*), and his new Symphony No. Four in B Flat, Opus 60. We are not told how the audience bore up under this surfeit.

In 1806 Prince Miklós Nicolaus Esterházy commissioned Beethoven to compose a Mass for the name day of his wife. Beethoven went to the Esterházy château at Eisenstadt in Hungary, and presented there his Mass in C, Opus 86, on September 13, 1807. After the performance the Prince asked him, "But, my dear Beethoven, what is this that you have done again?" Beethoven interpreted the question as expressing dissatisfaction, and he left the château before his invitation had run out.

He signalized 1808 with two symphonies now known throughout the world: Symphony No. Five in C Minor, and the Sixth or *Pastoral Symphony* in F. They appear to have been composed concurrently through several years, in alternations of mood between the brooding of the Fifth and the gaiety of the Sixth; fitly they received their premiere together on December 22, 1808. Frequent repetitions have lessened their charm, even for old music lovers; we are no longer moved by "Fate knocking at the door," or birds warbling in the trees; but perhaps the fading of our enchantment is due to lack of the musical education that might have equipped us to follow with appreciation and pleasure the logic of thematic contrasts and developments, the cooperation of counterpoint, the playful rivalry of different instruments, the dialogue of winds and strings, the mood of each movement, the structure and direction of the whole. Minds are differently molded— some to feelings, some to ideas; it must have been as hard for Hegel to understand Beethoven as for Beethoven—or anyone—to understand Hegel.

In 1808–09 he composed the Piano Concerto No. 5 in E Flat, Opus 73, known as the "Emperor." Of all his works this is the most lovable, the most enduringly beautiful, the one of which we never tire; however often we have heard it, we are moved beyond words by its sparkling vivacity, its gay inventiveness, its inexhaustible fountains of feeling and delight. In this concerto a man rising triumphantly out of apparent disaster wrote an ode to joy far more convincing than the stentorian chorus of the Ninth Symphony.

Perhaps the happiness of the "Emperor Concerto" and the *Pastoral Symphony* reflected Beethoven's increasing prosperity. In 1804 he had been engaged as piano teacher by Archduke Rudolf, youngest son of the Emperor Francis; so began a friendship that often helped the increasingly discreet republican. In 1808 he received a flattering offer from Jérôme Bonaparte, king of Westphalia, to come and serve as *Kapellmeister* in the royal choir and orchestra at Cassel. Beethoven agreed to fill the post at six hundred gold ducats per year; apparently he had still some faith in his dying ears. When word spread that he was negotiating with Cassel, his friends protested against what they called disloyalty to Vienna; he answered that he had toiled there for sixteen years without receiving a secure position. On February 26, 1809, the Archduke sent him a formal agreement by which, in return for Beethoven's remaining in Vienna, he would be guaranteed an annual sum of 4,000 florins, of which Rudolf would pay 1,500, Prince Lobkowitz 700, and Count Kinsky 1,800; in addition Beethoven might keep whatever he earned. He accepted, and stayed. In that year 1809 Papa Haydn died, and Beethoven inherited his crown.

IV. THE LOVER

Having achieved economic stability, he returned to his lifelong quest for a wife. He was a warmly sexual man. Presumably he found a variety of outlets,[31] but he had long felt the need for a permanent companionship. In Bonn, according to his friend Wegeler, he was "always loving." In 1801 he mentioned to Wegeler "a dear sweet girl who loves me and whom I love." This is generally supposed to have been his seventeen-year-old pupil Countess Giulia Guicciardi; however, she married Count Gallenberg. In 1805 Beethoven centered his hopes upon the widowed Countess Josephine von Deym, to whom he sent a passionate declaration:

> Here I give you a solemn promise that in a short time I shall stand before you more worthy of myself and of you—Oh, if only you would attach some value to this—I mean to founding my happiness by means of your love. . . . Oh, beloved Josephine, it is no desire for the other sex that draws me near to you, *it is just you*, your whole self, with all your individual qualities—this has compelled my regard—this has bound all my feelings—all my emotional power—to you. . . . You make me hope that your *heart* will long beat for me —Mine can only—cease—to beat for you—when—it no longer beats.[32]

Apparently the lady turned to other prospects. Two years later Beethoven was still appealing to be admitted to her presence; she did not reply.

In March, 1807, he paid such devout attentions to Mme. Marie Bigot that her husband protested. Beethoven sent "Dear Maria, dear Bigot," a letter of apology, declaring: "It is one of my chief principles never to be in any other relationship with the wife of another man than that of friendship."[33]

On March 14, 1809, expecting to be in Freiburg, he wrote to Baron von Gleichenstein:

> Now you can help me to look for a wife. Indeed, you might find some beautiful girl at F—— who would perhaps now and then grant a sigh to my harmonies. . . . If you do find one, please form the connection in advance. —But she must be beautiful, for it is impossible for me to love anything that is not beautiful—or else I should have to love myself.[34]

But this was presumably one of Beethoven's jokes.

More serious was his affair with Therese Malfatti. She was another of his pupils, daughter of a distinguished physician. A letter to her of May 8, 1810, has some of the air of an accepted lover. On May 2 Beethoven had sent an urgent request to Wegeler, then at Coblenz, to go to Bonn and locate and send him the composer's baptismal certificate, for "I have been said to be older than I am." Wegeler complied. Beethoven made no acknowledgment, and in July Stephan von Breuning wrote to Wegeler: "I believe his marriage project has fallen through, and for this reason he no longer feels the lively desire to thank you for your trouble." Till his fortieth year he insisted that he had been born in 1772. The baptismal certificate gave his birth year as 1770.

After his death three letters were found in a locked drawer which are among the most tender and fervent love letters in history. They were never sent. As they name no name, no year, and no address, they remain a mystery that has produced its own literature. The first letter, dated "July 6, in the morning," tells of Beethoven's hectic three-day trip from Vienna to a woman in an unstated place in Hungary. Some phrases:

> My angel, my all, my very self. . . . Can our love endure except through sacrifices—except through not demanding everything—can you change it that you are not wholly mine, I not wholly thine. Oh, God! look out into the beauties of nature, and comfort yourself with that which must be—love demands everything. . . . We shall soon surely see each other. . . . My heart is full of many things to say to you—ah, there are moments when I feel that speech is nothing after all—cheer up—remain my true, my only treasure, my all as I am yours. . . .
>
> Your faithful
LUDWIG

The second and much briefer letter is dated "Evening, Monday, July 6," and ends: "Oh God! so near so far! Is our love not truly a celestial edifice—firm as heaven's vault." The third letter:

> Good morning, on July 7
> Though still in bed my thoughts go out to you, *Meine unsterbliche Geliebte* [my immortal beloved], now and then joyfully, then sadly, waiting to learn whether or not fate will hear us. I can live only wholly with you, or not at all—yes I am resolved to wander so long away from you until I can fly to your arms and say that I am really at home, send my soul enwrapped in you into the land of spirits. . . . Oh God, why is it necessary to part from one whom one so loves and yet my life in W[ien—Vienna] is now a wretched life—your love makes me at once the happiest and the unhappiest of men—at my age I need a steady, quiet life. . . . Be calm, only by a calm consideration of our existence can we achieve our purpose to live together—be calm—love me—today—yesterday—what tearful longings for you—My life—my all—farewell —Oh, continue to love me—never misjudge the most faithful heart of your beloved L.
> Ever thine, ever mine, ever for each other.[35]

Who was she? No one knows. The pundits are divided, chiefly between the Countess Guicciardi-Gallenberg and the Countess Therese von Brunswig; nothing short of a countess would do. Apparently the lady was married; if so, Beethoven, in wooing her, was forgetting the excellent principle he had professed to the Bigots. However, the letters were not sent; no harm was done; and music may have profited.

V. BEETHOVEN AND GOETHE: 1809–12

In 1809 Austria was again at war with France. In May French cannonballs were dropping on Vienna; court and nobility fled; Beethoven sought refuge in a cellar. The city surrendered, the victors taxed the commonalty a tenth of a year's income, the well-to-do a third. Beethoven paid, but, from a safe distance, shook his fist at a patrolling Gaul, and cried, "If I, as a general, knew as much about strategy as I, the composer, know about counterpoint, I'd give you something to do!"[36]

Otherwise, the period from 1809 to 1815 shows Beethoven in relatively good spirits. In those years he often visited the home of Franz Brentano, prosperous merchant and patron of art and music, who sometimes helped Ludwig with a loan. Franz's wife, Antonie, was at times confined to her room with illness; more than once, during such spells, Beethoven came in quietly, played the piano, then left without a word, having spoken to her in his own language. On one such occasion he was surprised, as he played, by hands placed upon his shoulders. Turning, he found a young woman (then twenty-five), pretty, her eyes glowing with pleasure over his playing—even over his singing, to his own music, Goethe's famous lyric about Italy, "Kennst du das Land." She was Elisabeth—"Bettina"—Brentano, sister to Franz, and to the Clemens Brentano whom we shall meet as a famous German author. She herself was later to produce a number of successful books presenting autobiography and fiction in a now inextricable mixture. She is our only authority for the story just told, and for the later episode in which, at a party in Franz's home, she heard Beethoven discourse not only profoundly, but with an order and elegance not generally ascribed to him, though sometimes appearing in his letters. On May 28, 1810, she wrote enthusiastically about him to Goethe, whom she knew not merely through neighborly relations with his family in Frankfurt, but through a visit with him in Weimar. Some excerpts from this famous letter:

> When I saw him of whom I shall now speak to you, I forgot the whole world. . . . It is Beethoven of whom I now wish to tell you, and who made me forget the world and you. . . . He stalks far ahead of the culture of mankind. Shall we ever overtake him?—I doubt it, but grant that he may live until the . . . enigma lying in his soul is fully developed, . . . then surely he will place the key to his heavenly knowledge in our hands. . . .
>
> He himself said, "When I open my eyes I must sigh, for what I see is contrary to my religion, and I must despise the world which does not know that music is a higher revelation than wisdom and philosophy, the wine which inspires one to new generative processes, and I am the Bacchus who presses out this glorious wine for mankind and makes them spiritually drunken. . . . I have no fear for my music—it can meet no evil fate. Those who understand it must be freed by it from all the miseries which the others drag about with them. . . .
>
> "Music is the mediator between intellectual and sensuous life. I should like to talk to Goethe about this—would he understand me? . . . Speak to Goethe about me; . . . tell him to hear my symphonies, and he will say that I am right in saying that music is the one incorporeal entrance into the higher world of knowledge."

Bettina transmitted to Goethe these raptures of Beethoven, and added: "Rejoice me now with a speedy answer, which shall show Beethoven that you appreciate him." Goethe replied on June 6, 1810:

Your letter, heartily beloved child, reached me at a happy time. You have been at great pains to picture for me a great and beautiful nature in its achievements and its striving. . . . I feel no desire to contradict what I can grasp of your hurried explosion; on the contrary I should prefer for the present to admit an agreement between my nature and that which is recognizable in these manifold utterances. The ordinary human mind might, perhaps, find contradictions in it; but before that which is uttered by one possessed of such a demon, an ordinary layman must stand in reverence. . . . Give Beethoven my heartiest greetings, and tell him that I would willingly make sacrifices to have his acquaintance. . . . You may be able to persuade him to make a journey to Karlsbad, whither I go nearly every year, and would have the greatest leisure to listen to him and learn from him.[37]

Beethoven was unable to get to Karlsbad, but the two supreme artists of their time met at Teplitz (a watering place in Bohemia) in July, 1812. Goethe visited Beethoven's lodgings there, and gave a first impression in a letter to his wife: "A more self-centered, energetic, sincere artist I never saw. I can understand right well how singular must be his attitude toward the world."[38] On July 21 and 23 he spent the evenings with Beethoven, who, he reported, "played delightfully." Familiar the story how, on one of their walks together,

there came towards them the whole court, the Empress [of Austria] and the dukes. Beethoven said: "Keep hold of my arm, they must make room for us, not we for them." Goethe was of a different opinion, and the situation became awkward for him; he let go of Beethoven's arm and took a stand at the side with his hat off, while Beethoven with folded arm walked right through the dukes and only tilted his hat slightly while the dukes stepped aside to make room for him, and all greeted him pleasantly; on the other side he stopped and waited for Goethe, who had permitted the company to pass by him where he stood with bowed head. "Well," Beethoven said, "I've waited for you because I honor and respect you as you deserve, but you did those yonder too much honor."[39]

This was Beethoven's account, according to Bettina, who adds: "Afterward Beethoven came running to us and told us everything." We do not have Goethe's account. Perhaps we should be skeptical, too, about the story— variously and inconsistently related—that when Goethe expressed vexation at interruptions of their conversation by greetings from passersby, Beethoven answered him, "Do not let them trouble your Excellency; perhaps the greetings are intended for me."[40]

Dubious as they sound, both stories harmonize with authentic expressions in which the two geniuses summarized their meetings. On August 9 Beethoven wrote to his Leipzig publishers, Breitkopf and Härtel: "Goethe is too fond of the atmosphere of the court, more so than is becoming to a poet." On September 2 Goethe wrote to Karl Zelter:

I made Beethoven's acquaintance in Teplitz. His talent amazed me. Unfortunately he is an utterly untamed personality, not altogether in the wrong in holding the world to be detestable, but who does not make it any the more enjoyable either for himself or for others by his attitude. He is very excusable, on the other hand, and much to be pitied, as his hearing is leaving him, which, perhaps, mars the musical part of his nature less than the social. He is of a laconic nature, and will become doubly so because of this lack.[41]

VI. THE LAST VICTORIES: 1811–24

Wherever he went he composed. In 1811 he gave final form to Opus 97 in B Flat, a trio for piano, violin and violoncello, and dedicated it to the Archduke Rudolf—whence its name. It is one of his brightest, clearest, cleanest works, least confused by profusion, almost statuesque in its organic form. His last appearance as a performer was at the piano in a presentation of this classic in April, 1814. He was now so deaf that he had lost the proper adjustment of hand and pedal pressure to musical intent; some of the fortissimi drowned out the strings, while some pianissimi were inaudible.

In May, 1812, while Napoleon was massing half a million men for death in Russia, Beethoven issued his Seventh Symphony, which, less often performed, seems now to wear better than the Fifth or the Sixth. Here is a somber dirge for lost greatness and shattered hopes, and here, too, is tenderness for fading but cherished loves, and a quest for understanding and peace. As its funeral march was an unwitting "1812 overture" to Napoleon's disaster in Moscow, so its premiere, on December 8, 1813, was contemporary with the collapse of Napoleon's power in Germany and Spain. The enthusiastic reception of this symphony gladdened for a time the aging pessimist, who continued to produce masterpieces that for him had to be like those on Keats's Grecian urn, "ditties of no tone."

The Eighth Symphony, written in October, 1812, first performed on February 27, 1814, was not so well received; the master had relaxed, and had decided to be playful; it did not quite accord with the mood of a nation watching its fate daily hanging on the fortunes of war. But now we may delight in the jolly, prancing scherzando, whose persistent punctuation apparently made fun of a recent invention, the metronome.

The most successful of Beethoven's compositions was "Die Schlacht von Vittoria," offered in Vienna on December 8, 1813, to celebrate the battle in which Wellington had definitely destroyed French power in Spain. The news brought tardy satisfaction to the Austrian capital, which had been repeatedly humiliated by the apparently invincible Corsican. Now for the first time Beethoven became really famous in his adopted city. The music, we are told, hardly deserved its triumph; *die Schlacht war schlecht*. Its subject and success made Beethoven popular with the dignitaries who, in 1814, attended the Congress of Vienna. The composer forgivably took the opportunity to organize a benefit concert for himself; the imperial court, resplendent with victory, offered him the use of its spacious Redoutensaal; Beethoven sent personal invitations to the notables of the Congress; six thousand persons attended; and Beethoven was enabled to hide a substantial sum to cushion his future and his nephew's.

On November 11, 1815, his brother Karl died, after bequeathing a small sum to Ludwig, and appointing him co-guardian, with the widow, of an eight-year-old son, Karl. From 1815 to 1826 Beethoven carried on, in letters and the courts, a searing contest with widow Theresia for control of Karl's movements, education, and soul. Theresia had brought Karl Senior a dowry and a house, but had lapsed into adultery; she confessed to her husband, who forgave her. Beethoven never forgave her, and considered her unfit to guide Karl's development. We shall not follow that quarrel in its wearing length and sordid details. In 1826 Karl, torn between mother and uncle, tried to kill himself. Beethoven finally acknowledged the failure of his loving rigor. Karl recovered, joined the Army, and took care of himself reasonably well.

With the year 1817 Beethoven passed into the final period of his creative life. Long a revolutionist in private politics, he now made open war against classic norms, welcomed the Romantic movement into music, and gave to the sonata and the symphony a looser structure that subordinated the old rules to a rampant freedom of emotional and personal expression. Something of the wild spirit that had spoken in France through Rousseau and the Revolution, in Germany through Sturm und Drang, in young Goethe's *Werthers Leiden* and young Schiller's *Die Räuber*, then in the poems of Tieck and Novalis, in the prose of the Schlegels, in the philosophies of Fichte and Schelling—something of all this came down to Beethoven, and found rich soil in his natural emotionalism and individualistic pride. An old system of law, convention, and restraint collapsed in art as in politics, leaving the resolute individual free to express or embody his feelings and desires in a joyful bursting of old rules, bonds, and forms. Beethoven mocked the masses as asses, the nobles as impostors, their conventions and courtesies as irrelevant to artistic creation; he refused to be imprisoned in molds fashioned by the dead, even by such melodious dead as Bach and Handel, Haydn and Mozart and Gluck. He made his own revolution, even his own Terror, and made his "Ode to Joy" a declaration of independence even in expectation of death.

The three Hammerklavier Sonatas formed a bridge between the second period and the third. Even their name was a revolt. Some angry Teutons, tired of Italian domination in the language and income of music, had proposed using German, instead of Italian, words for musical notations and instruments. So the majestic pianoforte should discard that Italian word for *low* and *strong*, and be called *Hammerklavier*, since the tones were produced by little hammers striking strings. Beethoven readily accepted the idea, and wrote Sigmund Steiner, manufacturer of musical instruments, on January 13, 1817: "Instead of Pianoforte, Hammerklavier—which settles the matter once for all."[42]

The most remarkable of the Hammerklavier Sonatas is the second, Opus 106 in B Flat, written in 1818–19 as a "Grosse Sonata für das Hammerklavier." Beethoven told Czerny that it was to remain his greatest piece for the piano, and this judgment has been confirmed by pianists in every suc-

ceeding generation. It seems to express a somber resignation to old age, illness, and a darkening solitude, and yet it is a triumph of art over despair.

It was in further rejection of such despondency that Beethoven wrote the
Ninth Symphony. He began work on it in 1818, concurrently with the
Missa solemnis which was to be performed at the installation of Archduke
Rudolf as archbishop of Olmütz. The Mass was finished first, in 1823, three
years too late for the installation.

Anxious to add to the little hoard that he had accumulated as a refuge
against old age and as a bequest to nephew Karl, Beethoven conceived the
notion of selling subscriptions for pre-publication copies of his Mass. He
sent invitations to this effect to the sovereigns of Europe, asking from each
of them fifty ducats in gold.[43] Acceptances came in slowly, but by 1825 ten
had come: from the rulers of Russia, Prussia, France, Saxony, Tuscany, the
Princes Golitsyn and Radziwill, and the Caecilia Association of Frankfurt.

The *Missa solemnis* is generally held to have justified its long gestation
and the strange bartering of its finished form. There is no trace in it of the
occasional blasphemies that interrupted his inherited Catholic faith. Each
moment of the liturgy is interpreted with concordant music, and through it
all is audible the dying man's desperate faith, written by him in the manuscript score at the outset of the Credo: "God above all—God has never
deserted me."[44] The music is too powerful to be an expression of Christian
humility; but the dedicated concentration on each part and phrase, and the
sustained majesty of the whole, make the *Missa solemnis* the fit and final
offering of a great flawed spirit to an incomprehensible God.

In February, 1824, he completed the Ninth Symphony. Here his struggle
to express his final philosophy—the joyful acceptance of man's fate—broke
through all the trammels of classic order, and the impetuous monarch let
the pride of his power carry him to massive exultations that sacrificed the
old god order to the young god liberty. In the profusion of shattered altars
the themes that should have stood out as pillars to the edifice disappeared
from all but esoteric view; the phrases seemed unduly insistent and repeated;
an occasional moment of tenderness or calm was overwhelmed by a sudden
fortissimo flung as if in rage at a mad and unresponsive world. Not so, a
great scholar replies; there is, in this apparent embarrassment of riches, "an
extreme simplicity of form, underlying an elaboration of detail which may
at first seem bewildering until we realize that it is purely the working out,
to its logical conclusions, of some ideas as simple and natural as the form
itself."[45]

Perhaps the master deliberately abandoned the classic effort to give lasting
form to mortal beauty or veiled significance. He confessed his surrender,
and frolicked in the unregulated wealth of his imagination and the lavished
resources of his art. In the end he recaptured some flair of youthful defiance,
and enshrined in music that ode of Schiller's which was not really to mere
joy, but rather to joyful war against despotism and inhumanity—

Fronting kings in manly spirit,
  Though it cost us wealth and blood!
Crowns to naught save noblest merit;
  Death to all the Liar's brood!

With his culminating masterpieces now complete, Beethoven longed for an opportunity to present them to the public. But Rossini had so captivated Austria in 1823, and Viennese audiences were now so enamored of Italian melody, that no local impresario dared risk a fortune on two compositions so difficult as the *Missa solemnis* and the *Choral Symphony*. A Berlin producer offered to present them; Beethoven was about to agree, when a combination of music lovers, led by the Lichnowsky family, alarmed at the thought of Vienna's outstanding composer being forced to go to a rival capital for the premiere of his latest and most prestigious works, agreed to underwrite their production at the Kärntnerthor Theater. After hard bargaining on all sides the concert was given on May 7, 1824, before a crowded house, and with a stoic program: an overture ("The Consecration of the House"), four parts of the *Missa solemnis*, and the Ninth Symphony with a stentorian German chorus to crown it all. The singers, unable to reach the high notes prescribed, omitted them.[46] The Mass was received solemnly, the symphony with enthusiastic acclaim. Beethoven, who had been standing on the platform with his back to the audience, did not hear the applause, and had to be turned around to see it.[47]

VII. *COMOEDIA FINITA:* 1824–27

He quarreled with Schindler and other friends about the small share (420 florins) they gave him of the 2,200 taken at the concert; he charged them with cheating him; they left him solitary now except for the occasional presence of his nephew, whose attempt at suicide (1826) topped the inspired bear's cup of grief. It was in those years that he wrote the last five of his sixteen quartets.

The spark for these labors had come in 1823 from the offer of Prince Nikolai Golitsyn to pay "any sum demanded" for one, two, or three quartets to be dedicated to him. Beethoven agreed, for fifty ducats each. Those three (Opp. 127, 130, and 132), and Opp. 131 and 135, constitute the terminal quartets whose mysterious strangeness has ensured their fame. Opus 130 was privately played in 1826, to the avowed delight of the listeners, except that the performers found the fourth movement beyond their powers; Beethoven wrote a simpler finale. The rejected movement is now offered as "Grosse Fugue," Opus 133, which a Beethoven scholar bravely interprets as expressing the composer's final philosophy: Life and reality are composed of inseparable opposites—good and evil, joy and sorrow, health and sickness, birth and death; and wisdom will adjust itself to them as the inescapable essence of life. Most highly praised of the five, and considered by Beethoven to be his greatest quartet, is Opus 131 in C Sharp

Minor, finished on August 7, 1826; here, we are told, "the mystical vision is most perfectly sustained."[48] Heard again recently, it seemed to be a long weird wail, the pitiful moaning of a mortally wounded animal. The last of the five, Opus 135, states a motto for its final movement: *Muss es sein?* (Must it be?), and gives the answer: *Es muss sein.*

On December 2, 1826, racked by a tearing cough, Beethoven asked for a doctor. Two of his former physicians refused to come.[49] A third, Dr. Wawruch, came, and diagnosed pneumonia. Beethoven took to his bed. His brother Johann came to watch over him. Nephew Karl, with Beethoven's blessing, left at the call of the Army. On January 11 Dr. Wawruch was joined by Dr. Malfatti. He prescribed frozen punch to help the patient sleep; Beethoven relished the liquor in it, and "abused the prescription."[50] Dropsy and jaundice developed; urine collected in Beethoven's body instead of being excreted; twice he was tapped to release the fluid; he compared himself to a geyser.

Resolved to make no use of the bank shares—totaling ten thousand florins—which he had hidden for Karl, and faced by rapidly rising expenses, Beethoven wrote, on March 6, 1827, to Sir George Smart of London:

> What is to become of me? What am I to live on until I have recovered my lost strength and can again earn my living by means of my pen? . . . I beg you to exert all your influence to induce the Philharmonic Society to carry out their former decision to give a concert for my benefit. My strength is not equal to saying anything more.[51]

The Society sent him a hundred pounds as an advance on the receipts of the proposed concert.

By March 16 the physicians agreed that Beethoven had not long to live. They and brother Johann asked his consent to summoning a priest. "I wish it," he answered. His occasional bouts with God had been forgotten; his letter of March 14 shows him ready to accept whatever "God in His divine wisdom" might decree.[52] On March 23 he received the last sacrament, apparently in a docile mood; his brother later reported that the dying man had said to him, "I thank you for this last service."[53] Soon after the ceremony Beethoven said to Schindler, "*Comoedia finita est*"—referring apparently not to the religious service but to life itself;[54] the phrase was used in the classic Roman theater to announce the end of the play.

He died on March 26, 1827, after three months of suffering. A few moments before his death a flash of lightning illuminated the room, followed by a sharp clap of thunder. Aroused, Beethoven raised his right arm and shook his clenched fist, apparently at the storm. Soon thereafter his agony ended. We shall never know what that last gesture meant.

The post-mortem examination revealed the complex of internal disorders that had darkened his life and his temper. The liver was shrunken and diseased. The arteries of the ears were clogged with fatty particles, and the auditory nerves were degenerated. "The pains in the head, indigestion, colic, and jaundice, of which he frequently complained, and the deep depression which gives the key to so many of his letters, would all follow naturally from the chronic inflammation of the liver and the digestive derangements to which it would give rise."[55] Probably his love of walking and the open air had moderated these ailments, and had given him most of the painless hours in his life.

His funeral was attended by thirty thousand persons. Hummel the pianist and Kreutzer the violinist were among the pallbearers; Schubert, Czerny, and Grillparzer were among the torchbearers. The tombstone bore only the name BEETHOVEN and his dates of birth and death.

CHAPTER XXIX

Germany and Napoleon

1786–1811

I. THE HOLY ROMAN EMPIRE: 1800

IN the opinion of the Prussian patriot but great historian Heinrich von Treitschke, "Never since the time of Luther had Germany occupied so shining a position in the European world as now [1800], when the greatest heroes and poets of their age belonged to our nation."[1] We might rank Frederick victorious below Napoleon shattered, but beyond doubt the light of Goethe and Schiller shone unrivaled in poetry and prose from Edinburgh to Rome; and the German philosophers, from Kant through Fichte, Schelling, and Hegel to Schopenhauer, overawed the European mind from London to St. Petersburg. It was Germany's second Renaissance.

Like Italy in the sixteenth century, Germany was not a nation, if that means a people living under the same government and laws. Germany in 1800 was a loose concatenation of some 250 "states," each with its own laws and taxes, many with their own army, coinage, religion, customs, and dress, and some speaking a dialect unintelligible to half the German world. However, their written language was the same, and gave their writers a third of the Continent for their potential audience.

We should note, in passing, that the relative independence of the individual states, as in Renaissance Italy, allowed an unstereotyped diversity, a stimulating rivalry, a freedom of character, experiment, and thought, which might have been overwhelmed, in the centralizing capital of a large state, by the weight of the compact mass. Would not the old cities of Germany, still so attractively unique, have lost vitality and character if they had been subject to Berlin, politically and culturally, as the cities of France were or are to Paris? And if all these parts of Germany had formed a united nation, would not this heartland of Europe, rich in materials and men, have overrun Europe irresistibly?

In only one way were the German states limited in their independence: they accepted membership in that "Holy Roman Empire" which had begun in 800 with the papal crowning of Charlemagne—known to the Germans as their own Frankish Karl der Grosse. In 1800 this Empire included a dazzling variety of German states. Outstanding were nine "electoral states" that elected the emperor: Austria, Prussia, Bavaria, Saxony, Brunswick-Lüneburg, Cologne, Mainz, Hanover, and Trier (Treves). Next were twenty-seven "spiritual lands," ruled by Catholic prelates, as if recalling the episcopal rule of cities in the dying Roman Empire of the West a millennium before: the archbishopric of Salzburg (where Mozart fretted), and the bishoprics of Münster, Liège, Würzburg, Bamberg, Osnabrück, Paderborn, Augsburg, Hildesheim, Fulda, Speyer, Regensburg (Ratisbon), Constance, Worms, Lübeck . . . Lay princes ruled thirty-seven states, including Hesse-Cassel, Hesse-Darmstadt, Holstein, Württemberg (with Stuttgart), Sachsen-(Saxe-) Weimar (with Goethe), Sachsen-Gotha (with its "enlightened despot" Duke Ernest II), Braunschweig-(Brunswick-) Wolfenbüttel, Baden (with Baden-Baden, Karlsruhe) . . . Fifty cities were *Reichstädte*, self-governed free "towns of the Empire": Hamburg, Cologne, Frankfurt-am-Main, Bremen, Worms, Speyer, Nuremberg (Nürnberg), Ulm . . . From these and other parcels of Germany came electors, "Imperial Knights," and other representatives to the Reichstag, or Imperial Diet, which met at Regensburg as summoned by their emperor. In 1792 the electors chose Francis II of Austria to head the Holy Roman Empire, and crowned him in a sumptuous ceremony that drew notables from all parts of Germany to Frankfurt-am-Main. He proved to be the last of the long line.

By 1800 this once impressive and generally beneficent institution had lost nearly all its efficiency and usefulness. It was a relic of feudalism; each segment had been ruled by a manorial lord, subject to a central power; that central power had been weakened by the growth of the member states in population, wealth, secularism, and military force. The religious unity of the "holy" Empire had been ended by the Reformation, the Thirty Years' War, and the Seven Years' War of 1756–63; north Germany, in 1800, was Protestant, south Germany was Catholic; and west Germany had lost some piety to the French Enlightenment and the Aufklärung of Lessing's days. Nationalism, large or small, grew as religion declined, for some creed—political or social—must hold a society together against the centrifugal egoism of its constituent souls.

The polarization of Germany between the Protestant north, led by Prussia, and the Catholic south led by Austria had dire results in the failure of the two foci to unite against Napoleon at Austerlitz in 1805 or at Jena in 1806. Long before these blows, Austria itself had come to ignore the Imperial Diet, and other states followed Austria's lead.[2] In 1788 only fourteen princes out of an eligible hundred, only eight out of fifty eligible town chieftains, obeyed the summons to an Imperial Diet;[3] decisions were impossible. In the Treaties of Campoformio (1797) and Lunéville (1801) Napoleon compelled Austria to recognize French rule of the left, or west, bank of the Rhine; so a rich section of the Holy Roman Empire—including the cities of Speyer, Mannheim, Worms, Mainz, Bingen, Trier, Coblenz, Aachen, Bonn, and Cologne—passed under French rule. By 1801 it was generally agreed that the Holy Roman Empire, as Voltaire had said, was neither holy nor Roman nor an empire; that no important state recognized its authority, or the authority of the pope; that some new form of order and cooperation amid the chaos would have to be devised, accepted, or imposed. Napoleon accepted the challenge.

II. THE CONFEDERATION OF THE RHINE: 1806

The great river was a gallery of scenic wonders and historic memories sometimes architecturally enshrined. But it was also a living blessing to the economy, watering a responsive soil, binding each town with a dozen others rivaling its culture and trading for its goods. Feudalism here had lost its uses and its fangs as commerce and industry peopled the riverside. But within this fluent prosperity four problems festered: epicurean lassitude among the rulers, corruption in the bureaucracy, a disruptive concentration of wealth, and a military fragmentation inviting conquerors.

The road to a new organization of the Rhineland states was opened by the promise of both France and Austria to recompense with new properties those German notables who had lost their lands through Austria's recognition of French sovereignty over the left bank of the Rhine. The clamor of the dispossessed for rehabilitation led to the summoning, by France and Austria, of the Congress of Rastatt (December 16, 1797). There some irreverent princes proposed that the ecclesiastic principalities should be "secularized"—i.e., in plain terms, transferred from the ruling bishops to the clamoring laity. Unable to agree, the Congress submitted the matter to the next Diet of the Holy Roman Empire. It remained in abeyance until Napoleon returned from Egypt, seized power in France, defeated Austria at Marengo, and came to an agreement with Austria, Prussia, and Russia, by which a deputation of the Imperial Diet issued, on February 25, 1803, a decree overwhelmingly entitled *Reichsdeputationshauptschluss*, summarily remaking the map and governance of western Germany. Nearly all the ruling bishops were dispossessed. Prussia accepted with equanimity the reduction of episcopal rule; Austria might have mourned, but she was powerless.

The new governors realized that Austria would be unwilling, as well as unable, to give them military protection; nor could they (mostly Catholic) expect protection from Protestant Prussia. One after another the remade states turned to Napoleon, who was militarily supreme and officially Catholic. At Munich, on December 30, 1805, Karl Theodor von Dalberg, archbishop-elector of Mainz, meeting a Napoleon fresh from victory at Austerlitz, invited him to accept the leadership of the reorganized principalities. The busy Emperor took half a year to make up his mind. He realized that for a French nation to assume protectorate over a third of Germany was to invite the enmity of the rest, as well as resharpened hostility from England and Russia. On July 12, 1806, Bavaria, Württemberg, Baden, Hesse-Darmstadt, Nassau, Berg, and many other states united in a "Rheinbund," or Confederation of the Rhine; on August 1 Napoleon agreed to assume its protectorate. While the major constituents retained independence in internal affairs, they agreed to submit their foreign policy to his judgment, and to place substantial military forces at his command.[4] They notified Francis II and the Imperial Diet that they were no longer members of the Reich. On August 6 Francis officially declared the Holy Roman Empire dissolved, and renounced the Imperial title, remaining emperor of Austria. The glory of the Hapsburgs faded, and a new Charlemagne, ruling from France, assumed authority over western Germany.

The Confederation conferred vital benefits and exacted fatal returns. It brought the Code Napoléon (with abolition of feudal dues and ecclesiastical tithes), freedom of religious worship, equality before the law, the French system of prefectural administration, centralized but competent, and a trained judiciary more than formerly difficult to bribe. The basic flaw in the structure was that it rested on foreign power, and could last only as long as this alien protection outweighed its domestic costs. When Napoleon took German sons to fight Austrians in 1809, the protectorate was strained; when he took thousands of German sons to fight Russia in 1812, and required heavy financial support for his campaign, the protectorate seemed a burden in gross topping its benefits in retail; when Confederation Germans were conscripted to fight Prussian Germans in 1813, the Confederation only awaited a substantial French reverse to bring the whole frail structure down upon the exhausted Corsican's head.

Meanwhile it was a triumph for Napoleon that he had arranged a double security for France's new frontier. The terrain west of the Rhine had been incorporated into France, and the rich lands on the east side, reaching even to the Elbe, were now allied with, and dependent upon, France. And though the Confederation disintegrated after Napoleon's defeat at Leipzig in 1813, it left a memory for Bismarck, even as Napoleon's unification of Italy left an inspiration for Mazzini, Garibaldi, and Cavour.

III. NAPOLEON'S GERMAN PROVINCES

North of Cologne were two regions which, though they became members of the Rheinbund, were completely Napoleon's by the processes of war, and were governed by him or his relatives: the grand duchy of Berg by his brother-in-law Joachim Murat, and the kingdom of Westphalia, by his brother Jérôme. When Murat was promoted to Naples (1808), Napoleon governed the duchy through commissioners. Year by year he introduced French methods of administration, taxation, and law. Feudalism, already vestigial, was ended, industry and commerce were developed until the region became a thriving center of mining and metallurgy.

Westphalia was more varied and immense. Its western end was the duchy of Cleves (point of origin for Henry VIII's fourth wife); thence it ranged eastward through Münster, Hildesheim, Brunswick, and Wolfenbüttel to Magdeburg; through Paderborn to Cassel (the capital), and across the Rivers Ruhr, Ems, and Lippe to the Saale and the Elbe.

Jérôme Bonaparte, made king in 1807, was then twenty-three years old, and was more interested in pleasure than in power. Napoleon, hoping that responsibilities would mature and settle him, sent him letters of excellent counsel, realistic yet humane, but this was countered by financial exactions, and Jérôme found it difficult to satisfy his brother's demand for revenues and his own relish for a lavish court and style. Even so, he cooperated effectively in introducing the reforms that Napoleon usually brought with him in the creative period of his conquests. It was one of Bonaparte's maxims that "men are powerless to determine the future; only institutions fix the destinies of nations."[5] So he gave Westphalia a code of laws, efficient and comparatively honest administration, religious freedom, a competent judiciary, the jury system, equality before the law, uniform taxation, and a system of periodic audit of all governmental operations. A national assembly was to be elected by a limited suffrage; fifteen of the hundred delegates were to be chosen from among merchants and manufacturers, fifteen from among savants and other persons who had earned distinction. The assembly was not empowered to initiate legislation, but it could criticize the measures submitted to it by the Council of State, and its advice was often accepted.

The economic reforms were basic. Feudalism was now ended. Free enterprise should open every field to every ambition. Roads and waterways were to be maintained and improved; internal tolls were abolished; weights and measures were made uniform throughout the kingdom. A decree of March 24, 1809, made every commune responsible for its poor, requiring it to provide them with employment or sustenance.[6] The taxpayers complained.

Culturally Westphalia was the most progressive of the German states. It had nurtured intellectual life ever since—and before—Fulda's monastic library fed the Renaissance with classical manucripts; Hildesheim had had Leibniz, and Wolfenbüttel had had Lessing. Now King Jérôme had as his librarian Jacob Grimm, whom we shall meet as the founder of Teutonic philology. In 1807, at Napoleon's invitation, Johannes von Müller, the leading historian of the age, left his post as royal historiographer at Berlin to come to Westphalia as secretary of state and (1808–09) director-general of public education. Westphalia had then five universities, which under Jérôme were reorganized as three: Göttingen, Halle, and Marburg. Two of these were famous throughout Europe; we have seen Coleridge going straight from Nether Stowey to Göttingen, and returning to England a year later, dizzy with German ideas.

Against these boons two evils weighed heavily: taxation and conscription. Napoleon required from each of his dependencies a substantial contribution to his government, to his daily more lavish court, and to the expenses of his armies. His argument was simple: if Austria or some other reactionary power should defeat or otherwise unseat him, the blessings that he had brought with him would be taken away. For the same reason the states under his protection must share with France the obligation to provide sturdy sons for military training, and, if necessary, the sacrifice of life. Till 1813 Jérôme's subjects bore this drain manfully; after all, in Napoleon's armies the knout was unknown, promotion was by merit, any soldier might become an officer, even a marshal. But by 1813 Westphalia had sent 8,000 young men to serve Napoleon in Spain, 16,000 to serve him in Russia; from Spain only 800 returned, from Russia 2,000.

Northeast of Westphalia was the electorate of Hanover. In 1714 its elector had become King George I of England, and Hanover had become an English dependency. The current elector was George III, who had made it a point of patriotism not to step out of Britain; so he left the great landowners of Hanover to rule the province "for the benefit of the most exclusive aristocracy in Germany. All valuable posts . . . were monopolized by the nobles, . . . who took care that none of the burdens of taxation should fall upon themselves," and that "the burgher and peasant should contribute most." Feudalism survived, softened by an almost family relation between master and man. Local government was honest beyond belief.[7]

In 1803, on the resumption of war with England, Napoleon ordered his troops and administrators to take control in Hanover, to guard against possible landings by British forces, and to exclude all British goods from entry. The French met little resistance. In 1807 Napoleon, busy with larger concerns, attached Hanover to Westphalia, and left it to the taxing devices of King Jérôme. The Hanoverians prayed for the return of England.

By contrast with Hanover, the Hanseatic cities—Hamburg, Bremen, Lübeck—were havens of prosperity and pride. The League itself had long since ceased to exist, but the decline of Antwerp and Amsterdam under French control had transferred much of their commerce to Hamburg. Situated at the mouth of the Elbe, the city—boasting in 1800 a population of 115,000 souls—seemed designed for maritime trade, and for the expeditious reshipment of imported goods. It was governed by its leading merchants and financiers, but with a degree of skill and fairness that made their monopoly bearable. Napoleon itched to bring these mercantile cities under his rule, to enlist them in the embargo on British imports, and to help him, with their loans, to finance his wars. He sent Bourrienne and others to stop the flow of British goods into Hamburg; the avid ex-secretary grew rich by winking both eyes. Finally Napoleon brought the great city under his rule (1810), and so harassed the citizens that they formed secret societies to assassinate him, and daily plotted his fall.

IV. SAXONY

East of Westphalia and south of Prussia was a German state, known to its citizens as Sachsen, to the French as Saxe, which once had ranged from Bohemia to the Baltic, had left its name on various -sexes in Britain, had lately been devastated by the Seven Years' War, but was now content to be a prosperous electorate spreading to right and left of the Elbe from Luther's Wittenberg to Dresden, the Paris of Germany.

Under the long rule of Frederick Augustus III as elector (1768–1806) and as King Frederick Augustus I (1806–27), the country, blessed by the Elbe as its nourishing mother, soon recovered its prosperity. Dresden again rejoiced in its rococo architecture, its spacious thoroughfares and handsome bridges, its *Sistine Madonna* and Meissen pottery. The young ruler, though never outstanding as a statesman, managed his realm judiciously, spent his revenues carefully, paid off the national debt, and developed at Freiberg a famous School of Mines. Dresden's rival, Leipzig, resumed its annual book fair, where publishers from everywhere in Europe offered their latest wares, and Germany's flourishing literature led the intellectual parade.

Frederick Augustus "the Just" joined Prussia and Austria in an attempt to discipline the French Revolution, and shared in the setback at Valmy in 1792. He was badly upset by the execution of his cousin Louis XVI, but he willingly joined in making peace with France in 1795. When Napoleon rose to power, Frederick kept on good terms with him, and Napoleon respected him as an enlightened despot loved by his people. However, when Napoleon's army, in 1806, was approaching Jena, Frederick was caught between hammer and anvil: Napoleon warned him not to let Prussian troops pass through Saxony; Prussia insisted, and invaded; the Elector yielded, and let his little army join the Prussians. Napoleon, victorious, treated Frederick Augustus with comparative lenience: exacted an indemnity of 25 million francs, bade him change his title to king of Saxony, made him head of the grand duchy of Warsaw, and compelled Prussia to cede to Saxony the "Circle of Cottbus" on the west bank of the River Spree. Prussia was thus hemmed in between Poland on the north and east, Westphalia on the west, and Saxony on the south—all pledged to Napoleon. It seemed only a matter of time before Prussia would have to follow the rest of Germany in vassalage to Bonaparte's France.

V. PRUSSIA: FREDERICK'S LEGACY, 1786–87

At the death of Frederick II the Great the kingdom of Prussia consisted of the electorate of Brandenburg; the duchies of Silesia and Farther Pomerania; the provinces of East Prussia—with Königsberg, Friedland, and Memel—and West Prussia, taken from Poland in 1772; and divers enclaves in western Germany, including East Friesland, Münster, and Essen. After Frederick's death Prussia added the region of Thorn and Danzig in the Second Partition of Poland (1792); Warsaw and the heart of Poland in the Third Partition (1795); Ansbach, Bayreuth, and Mansfeld in 1791; Neuchâtel, in Switzerland, in 1797. Prussia seemed resolved to absorb all northern Germany when Napoleon relieved her of the task.

The man who had made possible this expansion of Prussian power was the father of Frederick the Great. Frederick William I, besides disciplining his son and his people to bear suffering silently, had left him the best army in Christendom, and a nation tightly organized with universal education, universal taxation, and universal military service; Prussia had become a morsel fit for a martial king. All Europe, all Germany, all Prussia trembled at the sight of this man-eating monarch, with his domineering Junker officers, his six-foot grenadiers. "Don't get tall," a mother cautioned her son, "or the recruiters will get you."[8]

To that army and state Frederick the Great (r. 1740–86) added a personal genius sharpened by Voltaire, and a stoicism rooted in his genes. He raised Prussia from a small kingdom rivaled by Saxony and Bavaria to a power equal to Austria in the German world, and standing as the strongest barrier to the persistent pressure of the fertile Slavs to reach again their old frontier on the Elbe. Internally he built a judiciary famous for its integrity, and a corps of administrators which gradually replaced the nobility as the officialdom of the state. He established freedom of speech, press, and worship, and under his protection "the German school system superseded the profound spiritual slumber of priestly education."[9] He was the one man of his time who could outwit Voltaire and teach Napoleon. "The great Frederick," said Napoleon in 1797, "is the hero whom I love to consult in everything, in war and in administration; I have studied his principles in the midst of camps, and his familiar letters are for me lessons of philosophy."[10]

There were some gaps in his achievement. He found no time, in his campaigns, to bring Prussian feudalism to the more humane level which it had reached in the Rhineland states; and his wars had left his people in a condition of poverty and exhaustion that were partly responsible for the decline of Prussia after his death. Frederick William II (r. 1786–97), reversing the tastes of his childless uncle, was fonder of women and art than of government and war. He supplemented his first wife with a mistress, who bore him five children; he divorced his wife in 1769, and married Friederike Louise of Hesse-Darmstadt, who bore him seven children; and during this marriage he persuaded his court preachers to let him contract morganatic unions with Julie von Voss (1787), who died two years later, and then Countess Sophie Dönhoff (1790), who bore him a son. He found time to play the violoncello, to welcome visits by Mozart and Beethoven, to establish a music academy and a national theater. He financed and promulgated (1794) a new law code containing many liberal elements. Taking a religious turn, he allowed his favorite, the reformed rationalist[11] Johann von Wöllner, to issue (1788) a *Religionsedikt* ending religious toleration, and establishing a censorship that drove many writers from Berlin.

His foreign policy admits of defense. He refused to continue the aggressive stance of his predecessor; flouting a century of precedents, he sought friendship with Austria as a major step toward German unity and security. He did not like the French Revolution, being content with monarchy (so was his people), and he sent some troops to join in the defeat at Valmy (1792); but he was glad to bring their survivors home to help him in the Second Partition of Poland. In 1795 he signed the Peace of Basel with France, which left him free to take Warsaw in the Third Partition.

Despite his acquisitions, he had allowed his country to decline in wealth and power. As early as 1789, Mirabeau, after a long stay in Berlin, wrote prophetically: "The Prussian monarchy is so constituted that it could not cope with any calamity."[12] The Army grew lax in discipline and insolent with pride; the bureaucracy had softened into corruption and intrigue; the finances of the state were in disorder and near insolvency.[13] "Only the incisive demonstration of war could display to this blinded generation the inward decay which . . . paralyzed all activity by the magic of ancient renown."[14]

VI. THE COLLAPSE OF PRUSSIA: 1797–1807

So the amorous King died, and the care of the ailing state fell to his son Frederick William III, who carried the burden through Napoleon and Metternich till 1840. Everyone wondered how he could last so long, being weak in will and benign in sentiment. He had all the virtues which a good citizen is instructed to develop or profess: cooperation, justice, kindness, modesty, marital fidelity, and a love of peace. He freed the serfs on the royal domain. In 1793 he married Luise (Louise) of Mecklenburg-Strelitz, seventeen, beautiful, passionately patriotic, and soon the idol of the nation; she remained chief source of the happiness into which he seemed to invite every calamity.

The new century brought him one crisis after another. In 1803 the French seized Hanover, whose neutrality had been guaranteed by Prussia; the young officers in the Prussian Army clamored for at least a breach, if not war, with France; Frederick William held his peace. French forces closed the mouths of the Weser and the Elbe, hurting Prussian trade; Frederick counseled patience. Queen Louise pleaded for war; dressed in the uniform of the regiment that bore her name, she paraded on horseback, and breathed fire into the undefeated Army; Prince Louis Ferdinand, cousin to the King, longed for a chance to show his mettle; the aging Duke of Brunswick offered to lead the Prussian Army; General Blücher, hero-to-be at Waterloo, supported him; Frederick William withstood them quietly. In 1805 Austria, challenging Napoleon, sought Prussian aid; the King was not ready.

But when the French, en route to Austerlitz, marched through Prussian Bayreuth, Frederick William's patience ran out. He invited Alexander of Russia to a conference at Potsdam; there they took oath, at the tomb of Frederick the Great, to stand together against Napoleon, and go to the aid of Austria. Alexander's troops marched south and suffered defeat. By the time Prussia's army was mobilized the battle was over, and Alexander was in flight to Russia. Napoleon gave Frederick William a lenient but compromising peace (December 15, 1805; February 15, 1806): Prussia was to cede Neuchâtel, Cleves, and Ansbach to France, and was to receive Hanover in return. Eager for this long-coveted prize, Frederick William agreed to close all Prussian ports to British goods, and signed a defensive-offensive alliance with France. England declared war upon Prussia.

Napoleon, challenging Nemesis, proceeded to form the Confederation of the Rhine, which surrounded some Prussian provinces in western Germany. Hearing that Napoleon was secretly offering Hanover to England, Frederick William entered into a secret alliance with Russia (July, 1806) for defense against France. On August 1 Napoleon took all western Germany under his protectorate. On August 9 Frederick William mobilized part of his army; on September 4 he reopened Prussian ports to British goods; on September 13 he ordered his troops to enter Saxony. Joined by the Saxon forces, his generals, under the Duke of Brunswick, commanded 200,000 men. Furious at what he considered the violation of two treaties and an alliance, Napoleon ordered his armies, already stationed in Germany, to converge upon the front and flank of the allies. He himself hurried to the front and supervised the annihilation of the Prussians and the Saxons at Jena and Auerstedt on the same day, October 14, 1806.

That story has been told from the view of France. From Prussia's side it was one of the darkest tragedies in her history. Frederick William, with his government and family, fled to East Prussia, and tried to govern from Memel. Napoleon, from the King's chambers in Berlin, issued orders to a continent, and proclaimed the Continental Blockade. His troops drove the Prussians out of Poland, defeated the Russians at Friedland, and escorted Napoleon to Tilsit, where he made peace with Alexander. There Frederick William learned the final terms on which Prussia would be allowed to exist. It must cede to France all Prussian lands west of the Elbe, and must return to Poland all of Prussia's pilferings in the three partitions. It must accept and pay for the occupation of Prussia by French soldiers until it should have completed payment of 160 million francs as a war indemnity. By this treaty, signed on July 9, 1807, Prussia lost forty-nine percent of her former terrain, and 5,250,000 of her former 9,750,000 population. In the years 1806–08 the cost of the occupation forces and the payments on the indemnity took up the entire revenue of Prussia.[15] There were some Germans who, looking at the ruined state, predicted that it would never again play an important role in German history.

VII. PRUSSIA REBORN: 1807–12

There is a tough kernel in the German character—firmed by centuries of arduous survival between alien and martial peoples—that can bear defeat proudly and bide its time for response. And there were then men like Stein and Hardenberg, Scharnhorst and Gneisenau, who never let a day pass without thinking how Prussia could be redeemed. Those million serfs, hopeless under ancient thralls—what energy might they pour into the Prussian economy if they were released from humiliating burdens and were welcomed into free enterprise on the soil or in the towns? And those towns, now listless under commerce-scorning nobles governing the nation from a central distant capital—what invigorating initiatives might they develop, in

industry, business, and finance, under the stimulus and experiments of freedom? Revolutionary France had freed its serfs and prospered, but it had kept
the towns under the political tutelage of Paris; why not steal a march on the
conqueror and free the towns as well as the serfs?

So thought Freiherr Heinrich Friedrich Karl vom und zum Stein, "of and
at the Rock," the ancestral town of his family on the River Lahn, which
flowed into the Rhine above Coblenz. He was not a baron but a *Freiherr*,
a freeman, belonging to the Reichsrittershaft, or Imperial Knighthood,
pledged to defend his domain and the realm. He was born (October 26,
1757) not "of and at the Rock," but in nearby Nassau, son of a chamberlain to the Elector of Mainz. At sixteen he entered the school of law and
politics in the University of Göttingen. There he read Montesquieu, followed him in admiring the British Constitution, and resolved to be great. He
served his legal apprenticeship in the law courts of the Holy Roman Empire
at Wetzlar and at the Imperial Diet in Regensburg.

In 1780 he entered the Prussian civil service, and worked in the administration of Westphalian manufactures and mines. By 1796 he had won a
prominent position in the economic administration of all Prussian provinces
along the Rhine. His capacity for work, and the success of his proposals,
brought him a call to Berlin in 1804 to serve as minister of state for trade.
Within a month he was commissioned to help in the Ministry of Finance.
When news reached the capital that Napoleon had shattered the Prussian
Army at Jena, Stein succeeded in removing to Memel the contents of the
Prussian Treasury; with these funds Frederick William III was able to
finance his government in exile. Perhaps the excitement and disasters of
war sharpened the temper of the King and his ministers; on January 3, 1807,
Frederick William III dismissed Stein as "a refractory, insolent, obstinate,
and disobedient official, who, proud of his genius and his talents, . . . acts
from passion and from personal hatred and rancor."[16] Stein returned to his
home in Nassau. Six months later, having heard Napoleon recommend Stein
as an administrator, the King offered Stein the Ministry of Home Affairs.

It was precisely the post from which the irascible Freiherr could best advance reforms fit to release the energies of the Prussian people. By October
4, 1807, he was at his new post; by October 9 he had prepared for the King
the proclamation which millions of peasants and hundreds of Prussian liberals had long pleaded for. Article I was apparently modest, declaring the
right of "every inhabitant of our States" to buy and own land; but this right
had hitherto been refused to peasants. Article II allowed any Prussian to
engage in any lawful industry or business; so, as under Napoleon, career
was open to talent of whatever pedigree, and class barriers were removed
from the economy. Article X forbade any further enserfdom; and Article
XII declared that "from Martinmas ceases all villeinage in Our entire States.
. . . There shall be only free persons."[17] Many nobles resisted the edict, and
it was not fully enforced till 1811.

Stein and his liberal associates labored through the year 1808 to free the
towns of Prussia from rule by feudal barons, or retired army officers, or tax

commissioners with almost limitless powers. On November 19, 1808, the King, again a willing reformer, issued a "Municipal Ordinance" by which the towns were to be governed by a local assembly choosing its own officials; except that in large towns the burgomaster was to be appointed by the king from three men chosen by the assembly. So began the healthy local political life that grew into the outstanding excellence of Germany's municipal administration.

Stein was not alone in remaking Prussia. Gerhard von Scharnhorst (1755–1813), Count August Neithardt von Gneisenau (1760–1831), and Prince Karl von Hardenberg (1750–1822) labored together to rebuild a Prussian Army, using various devices to evade Napoleon's restrictions. The progress of this operation was such that Stein, on August 15, 1808, wrote to a Prussian officer a letter which fell into French hands and was printed in the *Moniteur* for September 8. Part of it said:

> Exasperation grows every day in Germany; we must feed it and work upon people. I very much wish that we could make connections with Hesse and Westphalia, and that we should prepare ourselves for certain events; that we should seek to maintain relations with men of energy and good will, and that we could put such people in contact with others. . . . The affairs of Spain leave a lively impression; they prove what we long since should have suspected. It would be useful to spread these tidings prudently. We think here that war between France and Austria is inevitable. This conflict will decide the fate of Europe.[18]

Napoleon, about to leave for a major campaign in Spain, ordered Frederick William to dismiss Stein. The King, still at Memel, delayed compliance, until he was warned that the French would continue their occupation of Prussian territory until he obeyed. On November 24, 1808, Stein was again dismissed; and on December 16 Napoleon, from Madrid, issued a decree outlawing him, confiscating all his goods, and ordering his arrest wherever found in French-controlled territory. Stein escaped into Bohemia.

His loss to Prussia was made up by the appointment (1810) of Hardenberg as state chancellor—in effect prime minister. He had been part of the government before, had reorganized the Ministry of Finance, had negotiated the peace of 1795, had shared responsibility for the disaster of 1806, and had been dismissed at the insistence of Napoleon (1807). Now, at the age of sixty, while Napoleon was amiably absorbed with his new Empress, Hardenberg moved the King toward constitutional monarchy by persuading him to summon first an Assembly of Notables (1811), and then (1812) a Representative Assembly of the Nation with consultative powers, as a check and prod on the king. An admirer of the French *philosophes*, Hardenberg secularized church property, insisted on civic equality for the Jews (March 11, 1812), levied a property tax on nobles and a profit tax on businessmen, ended the obstructive monopolies of the guilds, and established freedom of enterprise and trade.

The rapid reconstruction of Prussia between 1807 and 1812 revealed a saving fund of strength in the German character. Under hostile French

eyes, and under one of Prussia's weakest kings, men like Stein and Hardenberg, neither of them a noble, undertook to rebuild a defeated, occupied,
and bankrupt nation, and, in six years, to raise it to the power and pride that
made it, in 1813, the natural leader in the War of Liberation. Every class
joined in the effort: the nobles came forth to lead the Army, the peasants
accepted conscription, the merchants yielded much of their profits to the
state, the men and women of letters and learning sounded through Germany
the call for freedom of the press, thought, and worship; and in 1807, in a
Berlin policed by French troops, Fichte delivered those famous *Addresses
to the German Nation* which called for a disciplined minority to lead the
Prussian people to moral cleansing and national renewal. At Königsberg, in
June, 1808, some university professors organized a "Moral and Scientific
Union," which came to be known as the Tugenbund, or "League of Vir-
tue," dedicated to the liberation of Prussia.

Meanwhile Stein wandered in exile and poverty, and in daily danger of
being captured or shot. In May, 1812, Alexander I invited him to join the
imperial court at St. Petersburg. He went, and there waited, with his host,
for Napoleon to come.

CHAPTER XXX

The German People

1789–1812

I. ECONOMICS

THE Germans of 1800 were a class-conscious people, accepting class division as a system of social order and economic organization; and rare was the man who acquired a noble title except by birth. "In Germany," noted Mme. de Staël, "everybody keeps his rank, his place in society, as if it were his established post."[1] This was less so along the Rhine and among university graduates, but in general the Germans were a more patient people than the French. Not till 1848 did they reach their 1789.

The influence of the French Revolution was exciting in literature, slight in industry. Germany had rich natural resources, but the persistence of feudalism, and the power of feudal barons, in the central and eastern states, slowed the rise of a business and manufacturing class that might have been stimulated by a free and classless economy to apply to industry the coal and metals lying abundantly in the soil. Commerce was helped by magnificent rivers—the Rhine, the Weser, the Elbe, the Saale, the Main, the Spree, the Oder; but the fragmentation of states kept roads short and few and poor, and on these there were brigands and feudal tolls. Commerce was hindered by guild regulations, high taxes, and the geographical diversity of measures, weights, coinages, and laws.

German industry, till 1807, had to meet the competition of British goods produced by the latest machinery; England enjoyed a generation of priority in the Industrial Revolution, and it forbade the export of its new technology, or its skilled technicians.[2] The double-faced god of war, breeding industries to feed and clothe and kill men, nourished national economies; and after 1806 the Continental Blockade, more or less excluding British goods, helped the mainland industries to grow. Mining and metallurgy developed in western Germany, especially in or near Düsseldorf and Essen. At Essen in 1810 Friedrich Krupp (1787–1826) began the complex of metal works that would arm Germany for a century.

Despite such figures the entrepreneur was looked down upon by noble and king as a potential profiteer, and no merchant or manufacturer was allowed to marry into the nobility, or to buy a feudal estate. Financiers—Huguenot, Jewish, or other—were allowed to lend to nobility or royalty, but when (1810) they proposed that Prussia imitate England and France

600

and establish a national bank, issue government securities at a low interest, and so let a public debt help to finance the state, the King agreed with the nobles that such a procedure would put the kingdom at the mercy of the bankers. Prussia rejected control of the nation by the managers of capital, and chose rather to be led by a military caste and a Junker aristocracy.

II. BELIEVERS AND DOUBTERS

Germany was still religiously divided as in the Thirty Years' War; and in many ways the wars of Frederick the Great with Austria and France were replays of that prolonged tragedy. If Frederick had lost, Protestantism might have disappeared from Prussia as it had disappeared from Huss's Bohemia after 1620.

As the Protestant clergy took over the property of the Catholic bishops in the Protestant north, they became dependent upon military protection by the Protestant princes, and acknowledged them as the heads of the Protestant Church in their realms; so the agnostic Frederick was the head of the Prussian Church. In the Catholic states—Austria, Bohemia, and nearly all the Confederation of the Rhine—the bishops, if not themselves rulers, needed similar protection, and fell into subservience to the civil power; many of them paid little attention to papal pronouncements, but most of them regularly read from their pulpits the decrees of the civil authorities that protected them; so, in Napoleon's German states the bishops—Protestant or Catholic—read from their pulpits his administrative orders and his military bulletins.[3]

This subjection of the Church had diverse—almost contradictory—effects: Pietism and rationalism. There were many German families that had traditions of a piety stronger than politics and deeper than ritual; they found more inspiration in family prayers than in pulpit eloquence or professional theology. More and more they neglected the churches, and practiced their devotions in esoteric groups private and intense. Even more fervent was a proud cluster of mystics who cherished the traditions of seers like Jakob Böhme, and claimed or sought to see God face to face, and to have experienced illuminations that had dissolved the deepest, bitterest, problems of life. Especially impressive, if only by having borne with silent heroism centuries of persecution, were the uncloistered, unvowed monks and nuns of the Moravian Brotherhood, who, banished from Catholic Bohemia, spread through Protestant Germany, and profoundly affected its religious life. Mme. de Staël met some of them, and was impressed by their premarital chastity, their sharing of goods, and the epitaph chosen for each of their dead: "He was born on such a day, and on such a day he returned to his native country."[4] Baroness Julie (Barbara Juliane) von Krüdener (1764–1824), Mme. de Staël's favorite mystic, was committed to their creed, and preached it so charmingly that Queen Louise of Prussia—and, for a time,

Czar Alexander of Russia—fell under her influence, barring the sharing of goods.

Antipodal to the mystics were the skeptics who had inhaled the winds of the French Enlightenment. Lessing had let loose the German Aufklärung by exhuming and partly publishing the *Fragmente eines Ungenannten* (1774–78) in which Hermann Reimarus had expressed his doubts about the historicity of the Gospels. Of course there had been skeptics in every generation, but most of them had found silence golden, and the infection had been controlled by hellfire and police. But now it had found its way into the Freemason and Rosicrucian lodges, into the universities, and even into the monasteries. In 1781 Kant's *Critique of Pure Reason* turned educated Germany into turmoil by explaining the difficulties of a rational theology. For a generation after him German philosophy labored to refute or conceal Kant's doubts, and some subtle web-weavers like Friedrich Schleiermacher achieved international renown. According to Mirabeau (who visited Germany thrice between 1786 and 1788) almost all the Prussian Protestant clergy had by that time secretly shed their orthodoxy, and had come to think of Jesus as a lovable mystic who proclaimed the approaching end of the world. In 1800 a hurried observer reported that religion was dead in Germany and that "it is no longer the fashion to be a Christian."[5] Georg Lichtenberg (1742–99) predicted that "the day will come when all belief in God will be like that in nursery specters."[6]

Such reports were emotionally exaggerated. Religious doubt affected a few professors and some sophomores, but it hardly touched the German masses. The Christian creed continued to appeal to the sense of man's dependence upon supersensual powers, and to the propensity of even the learned to ask for supernatural aid. The Protestant congregations warmed their own hearts with mighty hymns. The Catholic Church continued to offer a home to miracle, myth, mystery, music, and art, and a final port for spirits exhausted by years of intellectual navigation amid the storms and shoals of philosophy and sex; so erudite scholars like Friedrich von Schlegel, brilliant Jewesses like Moses Mendelssohn's daughters, sought at last the uterine warmth of the Mother Church. Faith always recovers, and doubt remains.

III. THE GERMAN JEWS

Faith must have weakened, for toleration grew. As knowledge rose it flowed over the fences within which the creeds had preserved their innocence. It became impossible for an educated Christian to hate a modern Jew because of a political crucifixion eighteen centuries ago; and perhaps he had read, in the Gospel of Saint Matthew (xxi, 8), how a multitude of Jews had strewn with palm leaves the path of the beloved preacher as he entered Jerusalem a few days before his death. In any case the Jews in Austria were freed by Joseph II, in the Rhineland by the Revolution or Napoleon, and in Prussia by Hardenberg. They came gladly out of the ghettos, took on the dress, language, and habits of their times and place, became able workers, loyal citizens, devoted scholars, creative scientists. Anti-Semitism remained among the unlettered, but in the literate it lost its religious aura, and had to feed on economic and intellectual rivalries, and on ghetto ways lingering vestigially among the struggling poor.

In Goethe's Frankfurt hostility between Christian and Jew had been especially strong, and survived longer, because the ruling bourgeoisie there felt the vigor of Jewish competition in commerce and finance. Living quietly among them was Meyer Amschel Rothschild (1743–1812), who was founding the greatest banking house in history by lending to impecunious princes like the landgraves of Hesse-Cassel, or serving as one of England's agents in subsidizing the challenged kings in their struggle against Napoleon. Nevertheless it was Napoleon who in 1810 insisted on applying to the Jews of Frankfurt the full freedom guaranteed by the Code Napoléon.[7]

Marcus Herz (1747–1803) came to personify the flowering of Jewish finance into the pursuit and patronage of the sciences and the arts. Born in Berlin, he migrated in 1762 to Königsberg, where Kant and other liberals had prevailed upon the university to admit Jews. Herz enrolled as a medical student, but he attended Kant's lectures almost as often as the courses in medicine, and his passionate interest in philosophy made him Kant's favorite pupil.[8] Graduating in medicine, he moved back to Berlin, and soon won repute not only as a physician but as well by his lectures on philosophy. His discourses and demonstrations in physics drew a distinguished audience, including the future King Frederick William III.

His life was both brightened and saddened by his marriage to Henrietta de Lemos, one of the fairest women of her time. She made his home a salon rivaling the best in Paris. She extended her hospitality to other Jewish beauties, including Moses Mendelssohn's daughter Brendel—later Dorothea—and Rachel Levin, wife-to-be of the diplomat-author Varnhagen von Ense. Christian as well as Jewish notables gathered around these three Graces, and the Christians were delighted to find that they had minds as well as bodies, and were alluringly venturesome. Mirabeau attended these gatherings to discuss politics with Marcus, and more frequently to ponder subtler subjects with Henrietta. She relished the admiration offered by Christian notables, and fell into "ambiguous relations" with Wilhelm von Humboldt the educator, then with Friedrich Schleiermacher the philosophic preacher. Meanwhile she encouraged Dorothea—who had married Simon Veit and given him two children—to leave her husband and home and live with Friedrich von Schlegel, first as his mistress and then as his wife.

So the free mingling of Jews and Christians had a double dissolving effect: it weakened the faith of Christians when they found that Christ and his twelve Apostles had intended their religion to be a reform Judaism faithful to the Temple and the Mosaic Code; and it weakened the faith of Jews who saw that fidelity to Judaism could be a severe handicap in the pursuit of mates and place. In both camps the decline of religious belief eroded the moral code.

IV. MORALS

The code had rested upon belief in a god good and terrible, encouraging every humble appeal, watching every act and thought of every soul, forgetting nothing, and never abdicating the right and power to judge and punish or forgive, a god of love and vengeance, master, in his medieval form, of heaven and hell. This somber and perhaps indispensable creed still survived among the masses, and helped the clergy, the Junkers, the generals, and the *patres familias* to manage their flocks, peasants, troops, and homes. Periodic war, commercial competition, and the need for family discipline required the formation of habits of obedience and application in the youth, of winsome modesty and domestic arts in the girl, of patient dedication in the wife, of stern ability to command in the husband and father.

The common German male was basically good-humored, at least in the tavern; but he found it wise to put on a solemn front before wife, children, competitors, and employees. He worked hard, and required the same of those under his responsibility. He honored tradition as the well of wisdom and the pillar of authority; old customs enabled him to meet his daily tasks and contacts with a saving and comfortable economy of thought. He held his religion as a sacred heritage, and was grateful for its help in training his children to courtesy, system, and steadiness. He repudiated the Revolution that had disordered France, and the Sturm und Drang of German youth, as the reckless dissolution of established relations vital to order and sanity in the home and the state. He kept his wife and children in subordination, but he could be humane and loving in his homely way, and he labored uncomplainingly to meet their needs of body and mind.

His wife accepted the situation without much resistance, for she agreed that a large family in an insecure country surrounded by potential foes called for a stern and steady hand. In the home, subject to her husband and the law, she was accepted as the guiding authority, and was almost always rewarded with lifelong love from her children. She was content to be the "justified mother of children,"[9] consumed in the conquest of the soil and the continuity of the race.

But there were other voices. In 1774 Theodore von Hippel, anticipating Mary Wollstonecraft by eighteen years, published *On Marriage*, a male defense of woman's liberation. He objected to the bride's vow of obedience; marriage should be a partnership, not a subjection. He demanded the full emancipation of women—not only the vote but also eligibility to office, even the highest; he noted some great women rulers of the age—Christina of Sweden, Catherine of Russia, Maria Theresa of Austria. If full emancipation is not made into law the "Rights of Man" should be more honestly called the "Rights of Men."[10]

Germany did not listen to him, but—under the stimulus of the French Revolution and the spread of radical literature in Germany—the end of the eighteenth and the beginning of the nineteenth century saw such a flurry of emancipated women as only our time could match in number, and only eighteenth-century France could match in brilliance, and none surpassed in deviltry. The Romantic movement in literature, echoing medieval troubadours, idealized woman no longer as a mother like Demeter, nor as a virgin like Mary, but as an intoxicating bouquet of physical beauty and intellectual vivacity, with a touch of scandal to complete the lure. We have noted Henrietta Herz and Dorothea Mendelssohn; add Caroline Michaelis (daughter of a Göttingen Orientalist), who, a revolutionary widow, married August von Schlegel, and divorced him and wed philosopher Schelling. Add Therese Forster, who rivaled her husband in republican ardor, left him to live with a Saxon diplomat, and wrote a political novel, *The Seldorf Family*, which made a stir in the Rhineland; "in intellectual power," wrote Wilhelm von Humboldt, "she was one of the most remarkable women of her time."[11] Add Rachel Levin Varnhagen von Ense, whose salon was frequented by diplomats and intellectuals in Berlin. Add Bettina von Arnim, whom we have seen fluttering around Beethoven and Goethe. And those cultured, not quite revolutionary, women who outshone Goethe in Weimar: the Duchess Luise, Charlotte von Kalb, Charlotte von Stein.

In the larger cities of Germany this liberation of women was naturally accompanied by a loosening of moral restraints. King Frederick William II had set a fashion in mistresses, and in the next reign Prince Louis Ferdinand outrivaled him. Love marriages were multiplying as youngsters forsook the charms of property for the ecstasy of romance. Goethe, aging, looked askance from Weimar upon the gay life of the upper echelons in Berlin, but he adopted the new morality when he took the waters at Karlsbad. There the women displayed themselves proudly in the new fashions that Mesdames Tallien and de Beauharnais had set in Paris in 1795.

Political immorality competed with sexual laxity. Bribery was a favorite instrument of diplomacy, and an eager venality lubricated the bureaucracy in Catholic and Protestant states alike. Business seems to have been more honest than politics; the bourgeoisie, even when it married relaxed women, kept apart from the frolics along the River Spree. Meanwhile, however, the universities were pouring into German life and morals the disturbing catabolism of partly educated youth.

V. EDUCATION

Education now became the prime concern and achievement of Germany, matching that interest in war which was excited by the uprising of mind and body against Napoleon. Fichte's *Addresses to the German Nation* (1807),[12] though heard by few, expressed the growing conviction of the age: only a reform of education at every level could lift Germany out of the quest for pleasure into a stern devotion to the needs of the state in these years when quick surrender and national humiliation had almost broken the German spirit. In 1809 Wilhelm von Humboldt (1767–1835) was appointed Prussian education minister. He gave himself effectively to his task, and under his lead the German educational system began a renovation which soon made it the best in Europe. Students came from a dozen countries to study in the Universities of Göttingen, Heidelberg, Jena, and Berlin. Education was extended to all classes, and was broadened in subjects and aims; and though religion was emphasized as a prop of character, the law instructors made nationalism the new religion of German schools—quite as Napoleon had made it the new divinity in the schools of France.

The universities of Germany required and received a vigorous examination, for many of them were suffering from the neglect that usually befalls old age. Heidelberg's had been founded in 1386, Cologne's in 1388, Erfurt's in 1379, Leipzig's in 1409, Rostok's in 1419, Mainz's in 1476, Tübingen's in 1477, Wittenberg's in 1502. Now they were all in straits and need. The University of Königsberg, begun in 1544, was flourishing with Immanuel Kant. The University of Jena, established in 1558, became the cultural capital of Germany, with Schiller, Fichte, Schelling, Hegel, the brothers Schlegel, and the poet Hölderlin; there the faculty almost rivaled the students in welcoming the French Revolution. The University of Halle (1604) was "the first modern university" in three senses: it vowed itself to freedom of thought and teaching, and required no pledge of religious orthodoxy from its faculty; it made room for science and modern philosophy; and it became a center of original scholarship and a workshop of scientific research.[13] The University of Göttingen, founded so lately as 1736, had by 1800 become "the greatest school in Europe,"[14] rivaled only by the University of Leiden in Holland. "All the north of Germany," said Mme. de Staël, roaming there in 1804, "is filled with the most learned universities in Europe."[15]

Wilhelm von Humboldt, the Francis Bacon of this revival of learning, was one of the great emancipated minds of the age. Though born in the nobility, he described it as "once a necessary and now an unnecessary evil." He concluded from the study of history that almost every institution, however defective and obstructive it had become, had once been beneficent. "What kept freedom alive in the Middle Ages? The system of fiefs. What preserved the sciences in the centuries of the barbarians? Monasticism."[16] This was written at the age of twenty-four. A year later (1792) he judged with prophetic wisdom the new constitution enacted by France in 1791; it contained, he thought, many admirable proposals, but the French people, excitable and passionate, would be unable to live up to it, and would transform their country into chaos. A generation afterward, wandering with a fellow philologist over the battlefield of Leipzig, where Napoleon had met disaster in 1813, he remarked, "Kingdoms and empires, as we see here, perish; but a fine poem endures forever."[17] Perhaps he was thinking of Pindar, whose poems he had translated from their exceptionally difficult Greek.

He failed as a diplomat because he was too enthralled by the revolution of ideas to absorb himself in the ephemera of politics. Uncomfortable on the public stage, he retired to an almost solitary life of study. He was fascinated by philology, and followed the adventures of words as they traveled from one country to another. He had no faith in the use of government to solve the social problem, for better laws would be frustrated by the unchanged nature of man. He concluded that the best hope for man lay in the development of a minority whose social dedication might serve as a beacon for the young, even in a despondent generation.

So, at the age of forty-two he came out of his privacy to serve as minister of education; and in 1810 the government commissioned him to organize the University of Berlin. There he effected a change that influenced European and American universities till our own time: the professors were chosen not so much for their ability to teach as for their reputation or willingness for original research in science or scholarship. The Berlin Academy of Sciences (founded in 1711), the national observatory, botanical garden, museum, and library were incorporated into the new university. Hither came Fichte the philosopher, Schleiermacher the theologian, Savigny the jurist, and Friedrich August Wolf (1759–1824), the classical scholar whose *Prolegomena ad Homerum* (1795) had startled Hellenists with the illuminating suggestion that "Homer" had been not one poet but a succession of singers gradually putting together the *Iliad* and the *Odyssey*. In the University of Berlin Barthold Georg Niebuhr (1776–1831) gave the lectures that became his pathfinding *History of Rome* (*Römische Geschichte*, 1811–32). He surprised the scholastic world by rejecting Livy's early chapters as not history but legend. — Henceforth in classical scholarship, in philology, in historiography, as well as in philosophy, Germany led the world. Its supremacy in science had still to come.

VI. SCIENCE

It had been retarded in Germany by its almost Siamese connection with philosophy. Through most of this period it was regarded as a part of philosophy, and was included in it, along with scholarship and historiography, under the term *Wissenschaftslehre*, the study of knowledge. This association with philosophy damaged science, for German philosophy was then an exercise in theoretical logic soaring proudly above research, or verification, by experiment.

Two men especially brought scientific honors to Germany in this age— Karl Friedrich Gauss (1777–1855) and Alexander von Humboldt (1769–1859). Gauss was born in a peasant cottage in Brunswick, to a gardener-bricklayer-canal-tender father who disapproved of education as a passport to hell.[18] Karl's mother, however, noticed his delight and skill in numbers, and scrimped and saved to send him to school and then to *Gymnasium*. There his swift progress in mathematics led his teacher to secure an audience for him with Duke Charles William Ferdinand of Brunswick; the Duke was impressed, and paid for the boy's tuition for a three-year course in the Collegium Carolinum of Brunswick. Thence Karl Friedrich passed to the University of Göttingen (1795). After he had spent a year there his mother, quite unable to understand her son's work and play with numbers and diagrams, asked a teacher whether her son gave promise of excellence. The answer was, "He will be the greatest mathematician in Europe."[19] Before the mother died she might have heard Laplace's statement that Gauss had already verified that prediction. He is now ranked with Archimedes and Newton.[20]

We shall not pretend to understand, much less to expound, the discoveries —in number theory, imaginary numbers, quadratic residues, the method of least squares, the infinitesimal calculus—by which Gauss transformed mathematics from what it had been in Newton's time into an almost new science, which became a tool of the scientific miracles of our time. He himself turned his mathematics to fruition in half a dozen fields. His observations of the orbit of Ceres (the first planetoid, discovered on January 1, 1801) led him to formulate a new and expeditious method of determining planetary orbits. He made researches which placed the theory of magnetism and electricity upon a mathematical basis. He was a burden and blessing to all scientists, who believe that nothing is science until it can be stated in mathematical terms.

He was as interesting as his work. While remaking a science, he remained a model of modesty. He was in no hurry to publish his discoveries, so that credit for them did not come to him till after his death. He brought his aged mother to live with him and his family; and in the last four of her ninety-seven years, when she was totally blind, he served as her nurse, and allowed no one else to wait on her.[21]

The other hero of German science in this age was Wilhelm von Humboldt's younger brother Alexander. After graduating from Göttingen he entered the mining academy at Freiberg, and distinguished himself by his studies of subterranean vegetation. As director of mines at Bayreuth he discovered the effects of terrestrial magnetism on rock deposits, founded a school of mines, and improved the conditions of labor. He studied mountain formations with H.-B. de Saussure in Switzerland, and electrical phenomena with Alessandro Volta at Pavia. In 1796 he began, by accident, the long tour of scientific discovery (rivaling Darwin's on the *Beagle*) whose results made him, according to a contemporary quip, "the most famous man in Europe next to Napoleon."[22]

With his botanist friend Aimé Bonpland, he started from Marseilles hoping to join Napoleon in Egypt; circumstances deflected them to Madrid, where the unexpected patronage of the Prime Minister encouraged them to explore Spanish America. They sailed in 1799, and made a six-day stop at

Tenerife, largest of the Canary Islands; there they climbed the Peak (12,192 feet), and witnessed a meteoric shower that led Humboldt to study the periodicity of such phenomena. In 1800, starting from Caracas in Venezuela, they spent four months studying the plant and animal life of the savannas and rain forests along the Orinoco, until they reached the common sources of both that river and the Amazon. In 1801 they forged their way through the Andes from Cartagena (a seaport of Colombia) to Bogotá and Quito, and climbed Mount Chimborazo (18,893 feet), setting a world record that held for the next thirty-six years. Traveling along the Pacific coast to Lima, Humboldt measured the temperature of the ocean current that now bears his name. He observed the transit of the planet Mercury. He made a chemical study of guano, saw its possibilities as fertilizer, and sent some of this sea-fowl excrement to Europe for further analysis; so began one of South America's richest exports. The indefatigable researchers, having almost reached Chile, turned back north, spent a year in Mexico and a short time in the United States, and touched European soil in 1804. It was one of the most fruitful scientific tours in history.

Humboldt stayed for almost three years in Berlin, studying his masses of notes, and writing his *Ansichten der Natur* (1807). A year later he moved to Paris to be near scientific records and aides; he remained there for nineteen years, enjoying the friendship of France's leading savants, and the life and literature of the salons; he was one of Nietzsche's "good Europeans." He witnessed with the calm of a geologist those superficial disturbances known as the rise and fall of states. He accompanied Frederick William III on the visit of the victorious kings to London in 1814, but mainly he was occupied in developing old sciences or creating new ones.

He discovered (1804) that the earth's magnetic force decreases in intensity from the poles to the equator. He enriched geology with his studies of the igneous origin of certain rocks, the formation of mountains, the geographical distribution of volcanoes. He provided the earliest clues to the laws governing atmospheric disturbances, and thereby shed light on the origin and direction of tropical storms. He made classic studies of air and ocean currents. He was the first (1817) to establish for geography the isothermal lines uniting places with the same mean annual temperature despite their difference in latitude; cartographers were surprised to see, on Humboldt's map, that London, though as far north as Labrador, had the same mean temperature as Cincinnati, which is as far south as Lisbon. His *Essai sur la géographie des plantes* began the science of biogeography—the study of plant distribution as affected by the physical conditions of the terrain. These and a hundred other contributions, modest in appearance but of wide and lasting influence, were published in thirty volumes from 1805 to 1834 as *Voyages de Humboldt et Bonpland aux régions equinoxiales du nouveau continent.*

Finally, having exhausted his fortune in his work, he accepted a salaried post as chamberlain at the Prussian court (1827). Soon after his redomestication he delivered in Berlin the public lectures which later formed the substance of his many-volumed *Kosmos* (1845–62), which was among the most famous books in European ken. The preface spoke with the modesty of a mature mind:

> In the later evening of an active life I offer to the German public a work whose undefined image has floated before my mind for about half a century. I have frequently looked upon its completion as impracticable; but as often I have been disposed to relinquish the undertaking, I have again—though perhaps imprudently—resumed the task. . . . The principal impulse by which I was directed was the earnest endeavor to comprehend the phenomena of physical objects in their general connection, and to represent Nature as one great whole, moved and animated by internal force.[23]

As translated into English in 1849, the book ran to almost two thousand pages, covering astronomy, geology, meteorology, and geography, and revealing a physical world vivid in surprises, yet governed by the laws of mathematics and the regularities of physics and chemistry. Nevertheless, the general picture is one of a vast scene generated not by an inanimate mechanism but by the inexhaustible vitality, expansion, and inventiveness of inherent life.

Humboldt's own vitality was inspiring. Hardly had he settled in Berlin when he accepted a call from Czar Nicholas I to lead a scientific expedition into Central Asia (1829). It spent half a year gathering meteorological data and studying mountain formation, and, on the way, discovered diamond mines in the Urals. Back in Berlin, he used his position as chamberlain to improve the educational system, and to help artists and scientists. He was working on Volume V of *Kosmos* when death caught up with him in his ninetieth year. Prussia gave him a state funeral.

VII. ART

In Germany the age was favorable neither to science nor to art. War, current or expected, consumed enthusiasm, emotion, and wealth. Private patronage of art was rare and timid. Public galleries at Leipzig, Stuttgart, Frankfurt, and especially Dresden and Berlin, were displaying masterpieces, but Napoleon siphoned them to the Louvre.

Nevertheless, German art produced some memorable works amid the turmoil. While Paris was dancing with chaos Berlin boldly raised the Brandenburg Gate. Karl Gotthard Langhans (1732–1808) designed it in fluted Doric columns and grave pediment as if to announce the death of baroque and rococo; but chiefly the stately structure proclaimed the might of the Hohenzollerns, and their resolve that no enemy should enter Berlin. Napoleon entered in 1806, the Russians in 1945.

Sculpture fared well. It is an essentially classic art, depending on line and (since antiquity) avoiding color; alien to its spirit were baroque irregularity and rococo playfulness. Johann von Dannecker chiseled a *Sappho*, and Catullus' *Girl with the Bird*, for the Stuttgart Museum, an *Ariadne* for the

Bethmann Museum in Frankfurt, and a famous bust of Schiller for the library at Weimar. Johann Gottfried Schadow (1764–1850), after studying with Canova in Rome, returned to his native Berlin and, in 1793, caught the attention of the capital by placing, atop the Brandenburg Gate, a carved *Quadriga* of four horses guided by a Winged Victory in a Roman chariot. For Stettin he carved a marble figure of Frederick the Great standing in martial array and burning enemies with his eyes, but with two thick tomes at his feet to attest his work as an author; his flute was forgotten. Tenderer is the pair of *Princesses Luise and Friederike* (1797), half drowned in drapery but moving quietly, arm in arm, to exaltation and grief. The Queen inspired artists by her beauty, her passionate patriotism, and her death. Heinrich Gentz (1766–1811) dedicated to her a somber mausoleum at Charlottenburg, and for that resting place Christian Rauch (1777–1857) carved for her a tomb worthy of her body and soul.

German painting was still suffering from the anemia of neoclassicism trying to live on the ashes of Herculaneum and Pompeii, the treatises of Lessing and Winckelmann, the pale faces of Mengs and David, and the Roman reveries of Angelica Kauffmann and countless Tischbeins. But that imported decoloration had no nourishing roots in German history or character; German painters of this age shrugged off neoclassicism, went back to Christianity, back beyond the Reformation and its hostility or indifference to art, and—long before the English Pre-Raphaelites—listened to voices like Wilhelm Wackenroder and Friedrich Schlegel calling to them to go behind Raphael to the medieval art that had painted, carved, and composed in the simplicity and happiness of unquestioning faith. So rose the school of painters known as the Nazarenes.

Its leader was Johann Friedrich Overbeck (1789–1869). Born in Lübeck, he carried with him through eighty years the sturdy seriousness of the old merchant families, and the pervasive mists coming in from the Baltic Sea. Sent to Vienna to study art, he found no nourishment in the neoclassicism fed to him there. In 1809 he and his friend Franz Pforr founded the "Lucan [St. Luke's] Brotherhood," pledged to the revitalization of art by dedicating it to renewed faith as it had existed in the days of Albrecht Dürer (1471–1528). In 1819 they migrated to Rome, seeking to study Perugino and other fifteenth-century painters. They were joined in 1811 by Peter von Cornelius (1783–1867), and later by Philipp Veit, Wilhelm von Schadow-Godenhaus, and Julius Schnorr von Carolsfeld.

They lived like vegetarian saints in the deserted Monastery of San Isidoro on Monte Pincio. "We led a truly monastic life," Overbeck later recalled. "In the morning we worked together; at midday we took turns to cook our dinner, which was composed of nothing but soup and a pudding, or some tasty vegetable." They took turns in posing for each other. They passed by St. Peter's as containing too much "pagan" art, and went rather to old churches, and to the cloisters of St. John Lateran and St. Paul's Outside the Walls. They traveled to Orvieto to study Signorelli, to Sienna for Duccio and Simone Martini, and above all to Florence and Fiesole for Fra Angelico.

They resolved to avoid portraiture, or any painting for adornment's sake, and to restore the pre-Raphael purpose of painting as an encouragement of Christian piety and a patriotism bound up with the Christian creed.

Their special opportunity came in 1816, when the Prussian consul in Rome, J. S. Bartholdy, commissioned them to decorate his villa with frescoes on the story of Joseph and his brethren. The "Nazarenes" had mourned the replacement of frescoes with painting on canvas with oil; now they studied chemistry to make receptive surfaces for enduring colors; and they so far succeeded that their frescoes, removed from Rome and installed in the Berlin National Gallery, took rank among the proudest possessions of the Prussian capital. But old Goethe, hearing of these ecstasies, condemned them as imitations of fourteenth-century Italian styles, just as the neoclassicists imitated pagan art. The Nazarenes ignored that criticism, but quietly left the scene as science, scholarship, and philosophy slowly eroded the ancient faith.

VIII. MUSIC

Music was Germany's pride in prosperity and her solace in desolation. When Mme. de Staël reached Weimar in 1803 she found music an almost daily part of an educated family's life. Many cities had opera companies, and, since Gluck, they strove to depend less and less upon Italian works and arias. Mannheim and Leipzig had orchestras famous throughout Europe. Instrumental music was rising to public competition with opera. Germany had great violinists like Louis Spohr (1784–1859), celebrated pianists like Johann Hummel (1778–1837). King Frederick William II played the violoncello so well that he took part in quartets, sometimes in orchestras, and Prince Louis Ferdinand was so accomplished a pianist that only his royal descent kept him from rivaling Beethoven and Hummel.[24]

Germany also had a music master renowned throughout Europe as teacher, composer, and virtuoso on almost any instrument: Abt (i.e., Abbot) Georg Joseph Vogler (1749–1814). He early won fame as organist and pianist, learned the violin without a teacher, and developed a new system of fingering, well adapted to his sesquipedalian fingers. Sent to Italy to study composition with Padre Martini, he rebelled against one teacher after another, took a turn to religion, was acclaimed in Rome. Returning to Germany, he founded a music school in Mannheim, then in Darmstadt, finally in Stockholm. He rejected the laborious methods of composition taught by Italian teachers, and promised quicker perfection. Mozart and some others thought him a charlatan, but later consideration gave him high rank, not as composer but as teacher, performer, organ builder, and man. He toured Europe as an organist, attracting enormous audiences, earning enormous fees, and improving organs. He transformed the style of organ playing, and won a contest with Beethoven in improvisation.[25] He was the honored teacher of a dozen famous pupils, including Weber and Meyerbeer. When he died they mourned him as if they had lost a father. On May 13, 1814, Weber wrote: "On the 6th our beloved master Vogler was suddenly snatched from us by death. . . . He will ever live in our hearts."[26]

Carl Maria von Weber (1786–1826) was one of the many children of twice-married Franz Anton von Weber. Of Anton's daughters or nieces two have appeared in these volumes: Aloysia as Mozart's first love and a famous singer, and Constanze, who became Mozart's wife. Sons Fritz and Edmund studied with Joseph Haydn, but son Carl gave so little promise that Fritz told him, "Carl, you may become anything else you like, but a musician you will never be."[27] Carl took to painting. But in Franz Anton's wanderings as director of a dramatic and musical troupe mostly composed of his children, Carl's instruction in music was resumed by a devoted teacher, Joseph Heuschkel, under whom the boy quickly developed a talent that astonished and rewarded his father. By 1800, aged fourteen, Carl was composing, and giving public performances. Meanwhile, however, the hectic hurrying from town to town had some effect upon Carl's character: he became restless, nervous, excitable, and changeful. He became so fascinated by the lithography invented by his friend Aloys Senefelder that for a time he neglected musical composition, and went with his father to Freiberg in Saxony to undertake lithography on a commercial scale. Then, early in 1803, he met Abt Vogler, took fire again, became Vogler's pupil, and accepted a rigorous routine of study and practice. Vogler's confidence in him spurred him on. Now he developed so rapidly that, on Vogler's recommendation, he was invited to serve as *Kapellmeister* at Breslau (1804). He was only seventeen, but he accepted, and took his ailing father with him to the Silesian capital.

The youth was not fit for a post requiring not only diverse musical accomplishments but skill in the handling of men and women of all temperaments. He made devoted friends and dedicated enemies. He spent too avidly, rebuked incompetence too sharply, and drank too recklessly. Mistaking a glass of nitric acid for wine, he drank part of it before he realized that he was imbibing fire. His throat and vocal cords were permanently injured; he could no longer sing, he could with difficulty speak. He lost his position after a year; he supported himself and his father and an aunt by giving lessons. He was near despondency when Duke Eugen of Württemberg offered all three of them rooms in his Schloss Karlsruhe in Silesia (1806). But Napoleon's disruption of Prussian territory and finances ruined the Duke, and Weber, to feed his trio, had to forget music for a while and serve as secretary, at Stuttgart, to Duke Ludwig of Württemberg. This duke was a lord of revelry, dissipation, and dishonesty, and Carl deteriorated under his influence. He developed a passionate attachment to the singer Margarethe Lang, and lost his savings and his health in losing her. He was rescued from debauchery by a Jewish family in Berlin—the Beers who were the parents of Meyerbeer. Marriage sobered him, but did not restore his health.

He won fame during the War of Liberation by putting to music the martial songs of Karl Theodor Körner. After the war he joined in another campaign—against Italian opera: he composed *Der Freischütz* (1821) as a declaration of independence against the roving and winning Rossini. It was first performed on June 18, 1821, the anniversary of Waterloo; it was carried high on the wings of patriotism; never had a German opera been so successful. It took its theme from the *Gespensterbuch* (*Ghost Stories*), and frolicked with the fairies who protected the "free-shooter"; Germany was, in those Grimm days, taking large helpings of fairies; soon (1826) Mendelssohn would offer his *Midsummer Night's Dream* overture. Weber's opera marked the victory of Romanticism in German music.

He hoped to continue his success with *Euryanthe*, which had its premiere in Vienna in 1823; but Rossini had just conquered Vienna, and Weber's subtler music failed to charm. The failure, combined with worsening health, so depressed him that for almost two years he ceased to compose music. Then Charles Kemble, manager of the Covent Garden Theatre, offered him a thousand pounds to write an opera for Wieland's *Oberon*, and to come to London and conduct it. Weber worked heartily on the task, and studied English so sedulously that when he reached London he could not only read but speak it well. At the premiere (May 28, 1825) *Oberon* was a wild success, which the happy author described that same evening to his wife:

> I obtained this evening the greatest success of my life. . . . When I entered the orchestra the house, crammed to the roof, burst into a frenzy of applause. Hats and handkerchiefs were waved in the air. At the end of the representation I was called to the stage . . . All went excellently; everyone around me was happy.[28]

But further performances were not so well received, and a concert for Weber's benefit, on May 26, 1826, was a sad failure. A few days later the depressed and exhausted composer took to his bed, stricken with acute tuberculosis; and on June 5, he died, far from home and family. The romantics die young, for in twoscore years they live their threescore and ten.

IX. THE THEATER

Nearly every German city had a theater, for man, harassed by fact during the day, relaxes into imagination in the evening. Some cities—Mannheim, Hamburg, Mainz, Frankfurt, Weimar, Bonn, Leipzig, Berlin—had resident theatrical companies; others relied on traveling troupes, and improvised a stage for an occasional visit. The Mannheim theater had the best reputation for performers and performances, Berlin for receipts and salaries, Weimar for classic theatrical art.

Weimar in 1789 had a population of 6,200, much of it engaged in taking care of the government and its aristocratic entourage. For a time the townspeople supported a company of players, but by 1790 this had died of malnutrition. Duke Charles Augustus took over the enterprise, made the theater part of the court, persuaded Councilor Goethe to undertake the management, and the courtiers to play all but the leading roles; for this they brought in a leading man or woman from the surrounding empyrean of floating "stars." So the great Iffland came to Weimar, and the proud Korona Schröter (1751–1802), whose voice and form and glancing eyes nearly detached Goethe from Charlotte von Stein. The poet-statesman-philosopher himself was no mean actor, now as playing the tragic Orestes to Mlle. Schröter's Iphigenia, and then surprisingly successful as a comic, even in farcical roles.[29] He trained the actors to a Gallic style of speech, almost to declamation; it had the fault of monotony, but the virtue of clarity. The Duke strongly supported this policy, and threatened to reprove on the spot, from the ducal box, any fault of articulation.

The Weimar theater undertook an ambitious repertoire, ranging from Sophocles and Terence to Shakespeare, Calderón, Corneille, Racine, and Voltaire, even to the contemporary dramas of Friedrich and August Wilhelm von Schlegel, and reaching a proud triumph with Schiller's *Wallenstein* (1798). Schiller came from Jena to live in Weimar, and, at Goethe's urging, became a member of the company's managing body. Now (1800) the little theater made Weimar the goal of thousands of drama-loving Germans. After Schiller's death (1805) Goethe lost interest in the theater; and when the Duke, urged on by his current mistress, insisted on the company presenting a dramatic interlude with a dog as star, Goethe resigned his managerial post, and the Weimar theater disappeared from history.

Two actors dominated the German stage in this age. August Wilhelm Iffland (1759–1814) paralleled the triumphs of Talma, and Ludwig Devrient (1784–1832) repeated the career and tragedy of Edmund Kean. Born in Hanover, Iffland at eighteen, over parental prohibition, left home to join a theatrical company at Gotha. Only two years later he starred at Mannheim in Schiller's *Die Räuber*. This radical period yielded to prosperity, and to sympathy with the French *émigrés;* soon he became an idol of conservatives. After an arduous career that covered most of Germany, he accepted Goethe's invitation to Weimar (1796), and pleased his courtly audience with middle-class comedies; but he did not do well with such tragic roles as Wallenstein or Lear. He composed several plays, whose humor and sentiment won popular applause. In 1798 he reached the goal of his ambition—he was made manager of the National Theater in Berlin.

Shortly before his death he engaged an actor, Ludwig Devrient, who brought to the German stage all the sentiment and tragedy of the Romantic period. His French surname was part of his Huguenot heritage. He was the last of the three sons begotten by a Berlin draper in two marriages. His mother died in his infancy, leaving him miserable in a crowded home. He withdrew into a somber loneliness, consoled only by his handsome face and raven hair. He ran away from home and school, but was caught and returned to his father. Every attempt was made to make him a draper, but Ludwig proved so exasperatingly incompetent that he was released to follow his own bent. In 1804, aged twenty, he fell in with a theatrical troupe at Leipzig, and was given some minor part, from which he was suddenly

propelled into a major role by the sickness of the "star." Finding the role
of a drunken tramp congenial to his taste, he did so well that he seemed
perpetually condemned to the career of a traveling actor loving drink on
and off the boards. At last, in Breslau in 1809, he found himself, not in Fal-
staff but in the Karl Moor of Schiller's radical play. Into this part he
poured all that he had learned of human evil, oppression, and hate; he let
the robber chieftain take possession of him and find outlet in every movement of the body, in the mobile variety of facial expression, and the glare
of angry eyes; Breslau had never seen anything so vivid or powerful; only
Edmund Kean, in that age of great actors, could reach such heights and
depths of histrionic art. All the tragic roles were now Devrient's for the
asking. He played Lear with such total surrender to that fragile mixture of
wisdom and madness that, one night, he collapsed in midplay, and had to be
taken home, or to his favorite tavern.

In 1814 Iffland, aged fifty-five, came to Breslau, acted with Devrient, felt
his force and skill, and asked him to join the National Theater. "The only
place that is worthy of you is Berlin. That place—I feel it too well—will
soon be vacant. It is reserved for you."[30] In September Iffland died; in the
following spring Devrient took his place. There he played himself out,
living on fame and wine, spending happy hours exchanging tales with
E. T. A. Hoffmann at a tavern near the theater. In 1828, victim of his
renown, he accepted a challenge to play in Vienna. He returned to Berlin
a nervous ruin. He died on December 30, 1832, aged forty-eight. Three
gifted nephews, all bearing his name, carried on his art to the end of the
century.

X. THE DRAMATISTS

After August Wilhelm von Schlegel's masterly translation of Shakespeare
(1798 ff.) the German stage provided a new home for the Elizabethan's
plays. Native dramatists, between Lessing and Kleist, usually aimed at the
common denominator of the middle class; and their popular successes were
lost in the detritus of time. Zacharias Werner put his mysticism passingly
on the boards. August von Kotzebue (1761–1819) pleased one generation
with his plays, and outdrew Goethe and Schiller even in Weimar; he is
now a fading memory except for his assassination. But Germany remembers
Heinrich Wilhelm von Kleist with pity for the man, and respect for his pen.

Born (1777) in Frankfurt-an-der-Oder, he was near-Slav in temperament
as well as in geography. Like a good German he spent seven years in the
Army, but later mourned those years as wasted. He studied science, literature, and philosophy in the local university, and lost his faith in both religion and science. He proposed to a general's daughter, but he shuddered
at the thought of marriage. He fled to Paris and then Switzerland, where
he played with the fancy of buying a farm and letting the discipline of the
seasons calm the instability of a mind dizzied with ideas. Relapsing into

literature, he wrote, but never finished, an historical tragedy, *Robert Guis-kard;* and in 1808 he staged at Weimar a comedy, *Der zerbrochene Krug* (*The Broken Pitcher*), which a later generation ranked as a lasting classic. Staying in Weimar for a while (1802–03), he won friendly encouragement from the kindly old agnostic Christoph Wieland, who, after hearing bits of *Guiskard*, told the young dramatist that he held in him the "spirits of Aeschylus, Sophocles, and Shakespeare,"[31] and that the genius of Kleist was destined "to fill the gap, in the development of the German drama, which even Schiller and Goethe had not yet filled."[32] This was enough to destroy the twenty-five-year-old Sophocles.

He went to live in Paris, felt its fever, and pondered hopelessly over the skepticism inherent in German idealist philosophy: if we know only so little of the world as comes to our consciousness after being transformed by our modes of perception, then we can never find the truth. Only one thing is certain: philosophers, scientists, poets, saints, beggars, lunatics, all are fated soon to be dust, or a memory fading in a mortal few. Kleist lost the courage to face, accept, and enjoy reality even as so precariously known. He concluded that his genius was a delusion, that his books and manuscripts were vanities. In a moment of wrath and despair he burned such manu-scripts as he had with him, and tried to enlist in the army that Napoleon was gathering at the Channel. On October 26, 1803, he wrote to his sister, whom perhaps he loved beyond taboo:

> What I am going to tell you may cost you your life; but I must, I must do it. I have perused again, rejected, and burned my work; and now the end has come. Heaven denies me fame, the greatest of earthly goods; like a capricious child I throw down before it all the rest. I cannot show myself worthy of thy friendship, and without thy friendship I cannot live; I choose death. Be calm, exalted one! I shall die the beautiful death of battle. I have left the capital of this country, I have wandered to its northern coast, I shall enter the French service; soon the army will embark for England; the ruin of us all is lurking over the sea. I exult in the prospect of the glorious grave. Thou, beloved, shalt be my last thought.[33]

His plan to be a German soldier in the French Army aroused suspicion. He was expelled from France at the insistence of the Prussian ambassador. Shortly thereafter France declared war on Prussia; in 1806 Napoleon de-stroyed the Prussian Army, almost the Prussian state. Kleist sought refuge in Dresden, but French soldiers arrested him there as a suspected spy; he spent six months in jail. Returning to Dresden, he joined a patriotic group of writers and artists, and collaborated with Adam Müller in editing a periodical to which he contributed some of his finest essays.

In 1808 he published a tragic drama, *Penthesilea*. Its heroine is an Ama-zonian queen who, after Hector's death, comes to join the desperate Tro-jans against the Greeks at Troy; she sets out to kill Achilles, is vanquished by him, falls in love with him, and then (following the law of the Ama-zonian women that each of them must prove herself by overcoming her lover in battle) pierces Achilles with an arrow, sets her dogs upon him, joins them in tearing him to pieces, drinks his blood, and collapses in death. The play is an echo of the Bacchic frenzy which Euripides had told of in *The Bacchae*—a side of the Greek mythology and character not emphasized by Hellenists before Nietzsche.

Doubtless the anger aroused by Napoleon's ruthless dismemberment of Prussia had raised the poet out of his own woes to make him one of the voices calling Germany to the War of Liberation. Toward the end of 1808 he issued a play, *Die Hermannsschlacht*, which, by telling of Arminius' victories over the Roman legions of A.D. 6, sought to rouse the courage of the Germans in the apparently hopeless conflict with Napoleon. Here again the fervor of Kleist's patriotism raised him to neurotic excesses: Hermann's wife Thusnelda lures the German general Ventidius to an assignation with her, and leads him into the fatal embraces of a wild bear.

The years 1809–10 were the apex of Kleist's genius. His poetic drama *Das Käthchen von Heilbronn* was staged to success in Hamburg, Vienna, and Graz; and the two volumes of short stories that he issued in 1810 marked him out as perhaps the finest prose stylist of the age of Goethe. Thereafter his spirit failed, perhaps through the breakdown of his health. Some strange affinity of suffering brought him into association, finally into a love romance, with an incurably sick woman, Henriette Vogel. His letters to her reveal a mind on the edge of sanity. "My Jette, my all, my castle, meadows, sum of my life, my wedding, baptism of my children, my tragedy, my fame, my guardian angel, my cherub and seraph!" She answered that if he loved her he would kill her. On November 21, 1811, on the banks of the Wansee, near Potsdam, he shot her fatally, and then himself.

In him the Romantic surrender to feeling reached its highest point in uncontrolled intensity, in power of imagination, and in brilliance of style. He seems at times to have been more French than German, antipodal to Goethe and brother to Baudelaire, or rather to Rimbaud. He almost justified Goethe's unsympathetic judgment: "The classic is healthy, the romantic is sickly." Let us see.

CHAPTER XXXI

German Literature

1789–1815

I. REVOLUTION AND RESPONSE

THE German literature of the age of Napoleon was affected by the natural rebelliousness of youth, the lingering waves of Sturm und Drang,
the echoes of English Romantic poetry and Richardson's novels, the classical tradition in Lessing and the later Goethe, the successful revolt of the
American colonies, the heresies of the French Enlightenment, above all by
the daily impact of the French Revolution, and, toward the end, by the
drama of Napoleon's rise and fall. Many educated Germans had read—some
in French—works by Voltaire, Diderot, and Rousseau, and a lesser number
had felt the sting of Helvétius, d'Holbach, and La Mettrie. The French
philosophes had helped to form rulers like Frederick the Great, Joseph II of
Austria, Duke Charles William Ferdinand of Brunswick, and Duke Charles
Augustus of Saxe-Weimar; and, if only through these men, those writers had
left their mark on German civilization. The French Revolution seemed, at
first, a logical development of the Enlightenment philosophy: a happy end
to feudalism and class privileges, a lusty proclamation of universal human
rights, an invigorating liberation of speech, press, worship, conduct, and
thought. These ideas—many of them independently developed in Germany
—crossed the Rhine on the wings of news or with the armies of the Revolution, and swept over the heartland of Europe even to distant Königsberg.

So the molders of the German mind, and the makers of German literature,
welcomed the French Revolution in its first three years. Gentlemen Freemasons, mystic Rosicrucians, proud Illuminati, hailed it as the dawn of the
golden age they had awaited so long and ardently. Peasants staged revolts
against feudal lords, "Imperial Knights," and the episcopal rulers of Trier
and Speyer.[1] Bourgeois Hamburg applauded the Revolution as an uprising
of businessmen against arrogant aristocrats. Klopstock, the old poet domiciled in Hamburg, read his poems at a festival of freedom, and cried with
joy over his lines. Scholars, journalists, poets, and philosophers broke out in
a cappella hymns of praise. Johann Voss, translator of Homer, Johannes von
Müller, historian, Friedrich von Gentz, diplomat at large, Friedrich Hölderlin, poet, Friedrich Schleiermacher, theologian, the philosophers from Kant
to Hegel—all sang litanies to the Revolution. "It is glorious," wrote Georg
Forster (who had accompanied Captain Cook around the world), "to see

what philosophy has ripened in the brain and realized in the state."[2] Everywhere, even in the ranks of royalty (as in Prince Henry, surviving brother of Frederick the Great), Germany, for an ecstatic while, raised lauds to revolutionary France. In that ecstasy German literature, after so long hibernating from religious strife, adding the Revolution to the victories of Frederick, rose in thirty years (1770–1800) to such vigor, diversity, and brilliance as to rival the ripe literatures of England and France. And that revival, astonishing in its pace, went to play its part in rousing Germany to throw off the yoke of France, and enter into the politically, industrially, scientifically, philosophically richest century in its history.

Of course that joyous mood did not last. Stories came of the assault upon the Tuileries, of the September Massacres and the Terror, of the imprisonment and execution of the King and the Queen. Then came the French occupation of German states, the mounting levies of money and men to pay for imperial protection and the martial cost of spreading liberty. Year by year German fervor for the Revolution waned, and one by one the defenders (excepting Kant) turned into disillusioned skeptics, and some of them into angry foes.

II. WEIMAR

The men who made a constellation of genius at the court of Weimar served as an intellectual anchor for the wits of Germans during the unsettling impact of the Revolution and Napoleon. Duke Charles Augustus himself was a volatile mixture of talents and moods. He inherited the duchy at the age of one, and became its actual ruler at eighteen (1775). He derived his general education from a tutor, and further instruction from the responsibilities of administration, the whims of a mistress, the dangers of war and the hunt. Not the least of his schools was the salon of his mother. There he met poets, generals, scientists, philosophers, divines, and men of affairs, together with some of the most cultivated but undenatured women of Germany, who seasoned their ancestral wisdom with wit and charm, and counted that day lost which had not been warmed with some discreet amour. "Ah, here we have women!" reported Jean Paul Richter. "Everything is revolutionarily daring here; that a woman is married signifies nothing."[3]

In 1772 the Duchess (herself a model of cheerful virtue) invited the scholar, poet, and novelist Christoph Wieland to come and tutor her sons Charles Augustus and Konstantin.* He fulfilled his duties with modesty and competence, and remained at Weimar till his death. He was fifty-six when the Revolution came; he welcomed it, but (in a "Cosmopolitan Address"

* The four men brought to witness in this section—mostly with the help of the late George Gooch's scholarly *Germany and the French Revolution* (1966)—have been dealt with in *Rousseau and Revolution*: Wieland (1733–1813) in pp. 553–76; Herder (1744–1803) in pp. 567–69 and 577–80; Schiller (1759–1805) in pp. 569–75 and 591–605; and Goethe (1749–1832) in pp. 555–628.

of October, 1789), he asked the National Assembly of France to guard against mob rule:

> The nation is suffering from liberty fever, which makes the Parisians—the politest people in the world—thirst for the blood of aristocrats. . . . When the people, sooner or later, comes to itself, will it not see that it is led by the nose by 1,200 petty tyrants, instead of being governed by a king? . . . Yet you cannot be more deeply convinced than I that your nation was wrong to bear such misgovernment so long; that the best form of government is the separation and equilibrium of the executive, legislative, and judiciary; that every people has an indefeasible right to as much freedom as can coexist with order; and that each must be taxed in proportion to his income.[4]

In 1791 he wrote that he had never expected his dream of political justice to be so nearly realized as in the person of Louis XVI.[5] The execution of the King in January, 1792, turned him against the Revolution; the Terror sickened him. Later in that year he published "Words in Season," which reached some modest conclusions: "One must go on preaching, till men listen, that mankind can grow happier only by becoming more reasonable and more moral. . . . Reform must begin not with constitutions but with the individual. The conditions of happiness are in our own hands."[6]

Johann Gottfried von Herder—the last of the Weimar quartet to settle there and the first to die—commended the Revolution till the Queen was guillotined; thereafter he renounced the Revolution as a cruel abortion of humane ideals. In his final years he recovered hope; despite its dementia praecox the Revolution, he felt, marked an advance only second to the Reformation in the history of modern Europe; it would end feudal ownership of bodies as the Reformation had ended papal power over minds; now men would lay less stress on birth and rank; ability, wherever born, would be free to develop and create. The advance, however, would cost Europe dearly, and Herder was glad that the experiment had been made in France rather than in his beloved Germany, where men did not so soon take fire and burn up, but where quiet labor and patient scholarship would guide the growth of youth with a mild but steady and spreading light.

Friedrich Schiller—the Romantic soul fondly guarded by the classic three—had come to Weimar (1795) after exciting ventures in drama, poetry, history, and philosophy. Romantically imaginative, painfully sensitive, he had found little to love in the Württemberg of his youth. He responded to oppression by worshiping Rousseau, and writing a revolutionary play. Karl Moor, hero of *Die Räuber* (1781), denounced the exploitation of man by man with an ardor that left nothing for Marx to add but scholarship. Still more revolutionary was Schiller's third play, *Kabale und Liebe* (*Cabal and Love*, 1784); it exposed the corruption, extravagance, and fierce tenure of unearned privilege, and praised the steady, patient, and productive life of the German bourgeoisie. In the best of his pre-Revolution dramas, *Don Carlos* (1787), Schiller, now twenty-eight, appealed less to the wrath of the poor than to some potential nobility in power; he put into the mouth of Marquis Posa lines summoning Philip II to be the "father of his people," to "let happiness flow from your horn of plenty," to "let man's mind ripen in your vast empire, to become, amid a thousand kings, a king indeed."[7]

Passing from youth to middle age, Schiller naturally passed from radicalism to liberalism. He discovered ancient Greece, and was deepened by its dramatists. He read Kant, and dulled his poetry with philosophy. In 1787 he visited Weimar, was excited by its women, and calmed by Wieland and Herder. (Goethe was then in Italy.) In 1788 he published *Geschichte des Abfalls der Vereinigten Niederlande* (*History of the Revolt of the United Netherlands*), and checked his philosophy with history. In 1789, on Goethe's recommendation to the Duke of Saxe-Weimar, Schiller was appointed professor of history at Jena. In October of that year he wrote to a friend: "It is a petty ideal to write for a single nation; and for a philosopher such a barrier is intolerable. . . . The historian can only kindle for a nation insofar as it is an essential element in the progress of civilization."[8]

When the news of the Revolution reached Jena it found Schiller enjoying a middle-age spread of income and outlook, public acceptance, and tolerant understanding. His correspondence with Goethe, across the gaps of twelve miles in space and ten years in age, had helped the poet in Goethe to survive the prose of administration and the cautions of prosperity, and had helped Schiller to realize that human nature has changed too little in history to make political revolutions profitable for the poor. He sympathized with the King and Queen captured at Versailles in 1789, arrested in Varennes in 1791, and evicted from their prison palace in 1792. Shortly thereafter the revolutionary Convention unanimously conferred upon *"le sieur Gilles"* the title of *citoyen français*. A week later the September Massacres announced the sovereignty of an armed crowd; in December Louis XVI was put on trial. Schiller began to write a pamphlet in his defense; before he could finish it the King had been guillotined.

Goethe smiled at the vicissitudes of his friend's political faith, but he himself had traveled far from the certainties of his youth. He had had an ample fling with women sweet and sour before being invited in 1775, aged twenty-six, to leave Frankfurt and live in Weimar as Duke Charles Augustus' poet in ordinary and comrade in both forms of venery. During the next twelve years he absorbed economic and political realities, and grew apace; the Romantic author of *Die Leiden des jungen Werthers* (1774) disappeared in the privy councilor who saw a new age in European history take form at Valmy in 1792. The disorderly deterioration of the Revolution in that year led him to conclude that slow reforms under "enlightened despots" touched by philosophy—and under local rulers of education and goodwill like his own Duke of Weimar—would cost the people less than a sudden overturn in which the precarious bases and habits of social order might collapse into a decade of passion and violence. One of his *Venetian Epigrams* had expressed this fear as early as 1790:

> Let our rulers take warning betimes from France's misfortune;
> But, men of little degree, you should take warning still more.

> Great men go to destruction; but who gives the people protection
> When the rough mob becomes tyrant over us all?

He applauded when Napoleon ended the chaos of the Revolution by seizing power and establishing a constitution that allowed the people to enjoy an occasional plebiscite without too much interference with a decisive and competent government. His appreciation of the Corsican was not diminished by Napoleon's flattering reception of him at Erfurt in 1807; and the report of that interview shared considerably in giving the poet-councilor an international reputation.

Some Romantic tremors persisted beneath his developing classic steadiness of judgment and taste. *Faust*, Part I (1808) was a love story as well as a medieval "morality"; and *Elective Affinities* (1809) seemed to justify the rising cry of the new generation for mating by mutual attraction rather than by parental finance or legal bond. The councilor become philosopher continued to flutter about young women even after reaching threescore years and ten. But his studies of ancient art in Italy, his developing interest in science, his reading of Spinoza, and his declining physical vigor made for unhurried judgment and a wide-ranging view. The change was pronounced in his autobiography (1811), which looked upon its hero with remarkable objectivity. Romantic Germany—agitated by the emotional Wackenroder and Novalis, the free-love Schlegels, the insane Hölderlin, and the mercy-killer–suicide Kleist—resented his rising criticism of the French Revolution, and hardly noticed that he had belabored the ruling class too. During the German War of Liberation he found it hard to hate Napoleon and the French. He explained to Eckermann:

> How could I, to whom culture and barbarism are alone of importance, hate a nation which is among the most cultivated on earth, and to which I owe so great a part of my own possessions? There is a stage where national hatred vanishes altogether, and where one stands to a certain extent above the nations, and feels the weal or woe of a neighboring people as if it were one's own.[9]

His generation in Germany never forgave him, and seldom read him. It ranked Schiller above him,[10] and preferred Kotzebue to either.[11] Goethe's plays were seldom performed at Weimar, and his publishers deplored the poor sale of his collected works. Nevertheless an Englishman, Lord Byron, in 1820, dedicated *Marino Faliero* to him as "by far the first literary character which has existed in Europe since the death of Voltaire."[12] He could not bear to read Kant, but he was the wisest man of his time.

III. THE LITERARY SCENE

Germany was busy, as never before, writing, printing, and publishing newspapers, periodicals, books. In 1796 Aloys Senefelder, at Munich, stumbled upon the process later called lithography, by scratching his mother's laundry list upon a stone; it occurred to him that words and pictures, in various colors, could be engraved or embossed (in reverse as in a mirror) upon a smooth stone or metal plate, from which innumerable copies could be printed. Hence rose an ocean of prints from Goya and Hiroshige to Currier and Ives and Picasso.

Newspapers were many, small, partisan, and censored. The *Allgemeine Zeitung*, founded at Tübingen in 1798, moved to Stuttgart, then to Ulm, then to Augsburg, then to Munich, to escape the local police. The *Kölnische Zeitung*, established in 1804, had a quieter career, being patriotically Catholic, and then Napoleonic. Berlin, Vienna, Leipzig, Frankfurt, Nuremberg had journals antedating the Revolution, and still serving time today. Periodicals abounded. We have noted one of the finest, the *Allgemeine Musikalische Zeitung*, published at Leipzig by the firm of Breitkopf and Härtel from one revolution to another, 1795 to 1849. The most brilliant was the *Athenäum*, founded by the Schlegel brothers in 1798. Publishers were numerous. The annual exhibition of their products made the Leipzig book fair the literary event of the year.

A special class of writers, loosely classed as publicists, earned wide influence by their vigorously partisan but well-informed discussion of the basic issues of the age. Friedrich von Gentz (1764–1832) hailed the fall of the Bastille, but cooled when he met the skeptical mind of Wilhelm von Humboldt, and read and translated Burke's *Reflections on the French Revolution*. Having risen in the Prussian civil service to be a counselor in the War Ministry, he led a literary campaign against such ideas as the rights of man, liberty and equality, sovereignty of the people, and liberty of the press. He was not appeased by Napoleon's taming of the Revolution. He attacked Napoleon as a militarist whose conquests were destroying that balance of power upon which, in the view of most diplomats, the peace, order, and sanity of Europe depended. He became the most eloquent of the voices urging the King of Prussia to lead a crusade against Napoleon, and when Frederick William III hesitated Gentz passed into the service of Austria (1802). After Napoleon overwhelmed the Austrians at Austerlitz Gentz took refuge in Bohemia, but in 1809 he was back in Vienna, promoting the new war upon Napoleon. He served as secretary and aide to Metternich at the Congress of Vienna, and supported him in the postwar diplomacy of crushing every liberal development. He lived on, old and ill, through the revolts of 1830, and died convinced that he had served well the interests of mankind.

Joseph von Görres was a more sensitive spirit, half Italian and all emotion, hardly fit for a rough arena crowded with gladiators of the pen. Born a Catholic, he left the Church to support the Revolution. He helped in the French conquest of the left bank of the Rhine, and applauded Napoleon's transformation of the Holy Roman Empire into the Rheinbund. He hailed the French occupation of Rome with the cry "Rome is free." But the arrogance of the French troops, the exactions of the French administrators, aroused the resentment of the young revolutionary. In 1798 he founded a frail journal, *Das rothes Blatt* (*The Red Leaf*), as the voice of a republican loving the Revolution but distrusting the French. He recognized in Napoleon's seizure of the French government the end of the Revolution, and in Napoleon himself a dangerous appetite for power. He married, and took a vacation from politics. When Germany rose to her War of Liberation, Görres joined in the campaign with a newspaper, the *Rheinische Merkur,* but when, after Napoleon's removal, the victors enforced political reaction wherever they could, Görres attacked them so vigorously that he had to take refuge in Switzerland, where he lived in extreme poverty. All other lights having failed him, he returned in sad repentance to the Catholic Church (1824). Ludwig I of Bavaria raised him from indigence by appointing him professor of history at Munich. There, writing his four-volume *Christliche Mystik* (1836–42), he solaced his days with imaginative scholarship, and darkened his nights with satanic visions. Thirty-four years after his death the Görres Gesellschaft was established (1876) to continue his researches in the history of the Christian Church.

Prose literature was dominated by the Romantics, but one writer eluded them and remained indefinable and unique. Jean Paul Richter began life in Bayreuth in 1763. He took his Christian names from a grandfather, Johann Paul Kuhn; till 1793 he was simply Hans. His father was a schoolteacher and organist who became pastor of a church in Joditz on the Saale. There Hans spent his first thirteen years in a happiness from which he never recovered; that simple rural place marked his mood through all economic worries and theological storms. When the family moved to Schwarzenbach, on the same quiet river, he enjoyed the library of a neighboring clergyman, who recognized the boy's possibilities but not his doubts. There Richter's father died (1779), leaving his numerous brood to short rations. At twenty Hans entered the school of theology at Leipzig; but his reading had weakened his faith; he soon withdrew, and gave hostages to fortune by undertaking to live by his pen. He reached publication in 1783, aged twenty, then not again till 1789, in both cases with a brand of satire that seasoned sympathy with caustic wit. In 1793 he issued *Die unsichtbare Loge (The Invisible Lodge)* under the pseudonym "Jean Paul," taken through love of Rousseau. The book pleased a small audience, which grew with his sentimental novel *Hesperus* (1795). Charlotte von Kalb, friend of Schiller, invited the rising author to Weimar, and was so well pleased with him that she became his mistress.[13] There he began his four-volume novel *Titan* (1800–03), whose real hero was the French Revolution.

He passionately defended it in its formative years, but charged Marat with corrupting it into mob rule, and praised Charlotte Corday as another Jeanne d'Arc. He welcomed Napoleon's seizure of power as a necessary restoration of order; he could not help admiring this youth of thirty, who had nothing but iron will and laser eyes with which to lower the towering stature of his subordinates. Eight years later Richter was quite willing to see all Europe united by this man who could hold a continent in his mind and hand, and legislate for France from Berlin and Moscow. But at heart Jean Paul remained a republican, seeing in every martial victory the seed of another war. He pitied the conscripted youths and the mourning families, and argued that "the people alone should decide on war, as they alone cull its bitter fruits." He shot one of his sharpest shafts at rulers who sold their troops to foreign potentates. He demanded freedom from censorship, for some power outside of the government should be free to expose that government's faults and to explore the possibilities of progress.[14]

In 1801, aged thirty-eight, Jean Paul took a wife, and in 1804 he settled down in Bayreuth. After some living experiments he wrote a book on education, *Levana*, one of the classics of libertarian pedagogy. He issued a stream of novels and essays, some of which were admiringly translated by Carlyle. His mixture of realistic satire and Romantic sentiment won him a larger reading public than Goethe's or Schiller's. He died in 1825, leaving unfinished an essay on the immortality of the soul; his time had come to explore the matter at first hand. His reputation as one of Germany's foremost authors survived in Europe till the middle of the nineteenth century; and after it had died there it migrated to America, where Longfellow was one of his devotees. Hardly anyone, even in Germany, reads him today, but nearly every German recalls his famous epigram, which aims a shaft at German philosophy, and sums up the age of Napoleon more briefly than this book: "Providence has given to the English the empire of the sea, to the French that of the land, and to the Germans that of the air."[15]

Two other writers of fiction won a wide audience. Ernst Theodor Wilhelm Hoffmann (1776–1822)—who in 1813, in ecstasy over Mozart, changed "Wilhelm" to "Amadeus"—was one of the most unusual and versatile of all Germans: he painted pictures, composed and conducted music, staged an opera (*Undine*), practiced law, and wrote stories of mystery and romance which inspired Jacques Offenbach's *Tales of Hoffmann* (1881). Unique in life, if not in letters, was Adelbert von Chamisso (1781–1838). Born a French nobleman, he fled from the Revolution, received most of his schooling in Germany, enlisted in a Prussian regiment, and fought in the battle of Jena. In 1813, haunted by his lack of a fatherland and by his divided loyalties in the War of Liberation, he wrote, as an allegory, *Peter Schlemihls wundersame Geschichte*, the bizarre tale of a man who had sold his shadow to Satan. As a botanist of established reputation he accompanied Otto von Kotzebue's scientific voyage around the world (1815–18); he recorded his findings in the once famous *Reise um die Welt*. He divided the remainder of his life between serving as curator of Berlin's Botanical Garden and writing Romantic poetry. Heinrich Heine praised the poems, and Robert Schumann put to music Chamisso's verse sequence *Frauenliebe und -leben*.

Poets abounded, many of them still cherished by the German people, but gifting their words with music and sentiment difficult to transmit to another language, land, or time. Pitiful among them was Friedrich Hölderlin (1770–1843), whose poetic sensitivity proved too keen for his sanity. Sent to Tübingen to study for the ministry, he developed a stimulating friendship with Georg Hegel, who was then questioning Christianity. News of the French Revolution excited the youth to visions of human happiness. He read

Rousseau, composed a "Hymn to Liberty," and in 1792, over the top of the dying century, he thought he saw a wonderful dawn of justice and nobility. When war broke out he wrote to his sister: "Pray for the French, the champions of human rights." When the Revolution foundered in blood, he clung desperately to his dream:

> My love is the human race—not, of course, the corrupt, servile, idle race that we too often meet. I love the great, fine possibilities, even in a corrupt people. I love the race of the centuries to come. . . . We live in a time when everything is working toward amelioration. These seeds of enlightenment, these silent wishes and strivings toward the education of the race, . . . will yield glorious fruit. This is the sacred goal of my wishes and my activity—to plant the seeds which will ripen in another generation.[16]

The past too allowed for dreams. Like his contemporary Keats he fell in love with the heroes and divinities of classic Greece, and began a prose epic, *Hyperion*, about a Greek revolutionist. He made his way to Jena, studied under Fichte, learned to revere Kant, and met the gods of Weimar when they too were Hellenizing. Schiller secured a post for him as tutor to a son of Charlotte von Kalb. In 1796 he found a richer tutorial berth in the home of the banker J. F. Gotthard at Frankfurt-am-Main. He fell in love with the banker's wife, who so appreciated his verses that he was dismissed and forced to leave the city. The ecstasy and the exile brought on a degree of mental derangement; yet at this time (1799) he wrote a fragment, *Der Tod des Empedokles*, which is among the masterpieces of German verse. For several years he wandered from town to town, seeking bread and themes. He asked Schiller to recommend him for a lectureship in Greek literature, but Schiller found him too unstable for a professorial chair. Tutoring at Bordeaux, Hölderlin received word that Mme. Gotthard had died. He left his employment and walked across France into Germany, where friends, seeing that he was mentally deranged beyond cure, took care of him (1802). He lived on till 1843, his poems long forgotten even by himself. They were restored to public attention in 1890; Rainer Maria Rilke and Stefan George acclaimed him; and now the *cognoscenti* rank him only below Goethe and Schiller.

Many others sang. Karl Theodor Körner (1791–1813), son of the Christian Gottfried Körner who had been so helpful to Schiller,[17] threw himself, pen and sword, into the War of Liberation from Napoleon, aroused the Germans with his call to arms, and died in battle, August 26, 1813. Ernst Moritz Arndt (1769–1860) lived through three revolutions in his ninety-one years. He secured the abolition of feudalism in Pomerania by describing it realistically in *Versuche einer Geschichte* (*Essays toward a History*, 1803); and in *Die Geist der Zeit* (1806) he sounded so powerful a cry against Napoleon that he was forced to take refuge in Sweden from the victor of Jena. In 1812 he was called to St. Petersburg by Stein to help stir the Russian people to throw back the French invaders. After 1815, in Prussia, he strove to counter the conservative reaction, and was briefly jailed. In 1848 he was elected to the national assembly at Frankfurt. When that revolution too flickered out he turned his Muse to terminal piety. — Joseph von Eichendorff (1788–1857), a Catholic nobleman, wrote simple lyrics that can still move us, like "Auf meines Kindes Tod" (On the Death of My Child); here even an alien skeptic can feel the music, share the feeling, and envy the hope:

Von fern die Uhren schlagen,	Afar the hours strike;
Es is schon tiefe Nacht,	It is so soon deep night;
Die Lampe breunt so düster,	The lamp so dimly burns;
Dein Bettlein ist gemacht.	Your little bed is made.
Die Winde nur noch gehen	Only the winds still go
Wehklagend um das Haus	Wailing around the house;
Wir sitzen einsam drinne,	We sit alone within,
Und lauschen oft hinaus.	And often listen out.
Es ist als müsstest leise	It is as if you lightly tried
Du klopfen an die Tur,	To knock upon the door,
Du hätt dich nur verirret,	As if you had but lost your way
Und kämst nun müd zurück.	And came now weary back.
Wir armen, armen Toren!	We poor, poor simpletons!
Wir irren ja im Graus	We wander, yes, in fright
Des Dunkels noch verloren—	Of darkness still forlorn—
Du fändst dich langst nach Haus.	You found long since your home.

IV. THE ROMANTIC ECSTASY

The most brilliant writers of this German heyday were those who startled their time with cries for the emancipation of instinct from reason, of feeling from intellect, of youth from age, of the individual from the family and the state. Few of us read them today, but in their generation they were tongues of flame setting fire to dry-as-dust philosophies and social bonds imprisoning the expanding self in use and wont, taboo, command, and law.

The source of the revolt was the natural resentment with which any vital adolescent views the restraints imposed by parents, brothers, sisters, teachers, preachers, policemen, grammarians, logicians, moralists. Had not the current philosopher, Fichte, proved that the basic reality for each of us is his individual conscious self? If that is so, the universe has no meaning for any of us except in its effects upon himself, and each of us may justly sit in judgment upon every tradition, prohibition, law, or creed and bid it show cause why it should be obeyed. One might fearfully submit to commandments issued and upheld by God, or by a man of God dressed in divinity; but what had become of God now that Diderot, d'Alembert, Helvétius, d'Holbach, La Mettrie, had reduced him to the impersonal laws of the universe?

To the proud and liberating Enlightenment had now been added the Revolution. Class divisions were melting away; those lords who had once given laws and exacted obedience were now in hectic flight, leaving no barrier between classes, no bogey of tradition to buttress laws; now every man was free to compete for any place or power, chancing the guillotine; career was open to talent, to talons. Never before, in the known history of civilization, had the individual been so free—free to choose his occupation, his enterprise, his mate, his religion, his government, his moral code. If nothing exists but individual entities, what is the state, the army, the Church, the university, but conspiracies of privileged individuals to frighten and control, to form and deform, to rule and tax, to herd to slaughter the indoctrinated rest? Rare is the genius that can come to fulfillment under such restraints. And yet is not one genius worth a dozen pedagogues, generals, pontiffs, kings, or a hundred crowds?

However, in the new free-for-all, among the liberated souls, there were many sensitive spirits who felt that reason had exacted too high a price for liberation. It was "reason" that had attacked the old religion, with its saintly legends, its fragrant ceremonies and moving music, its mediating Madonna and its saving Christ; it was "reason" that had replaced this exalted vision with a dismal procession of masses of matter moving aimlessly to destruction; and it was "reason" that replaced the picture of men and women living in daily contact with deity by a view of male and female masses of matter moving daily nearer, automatically, stupidly, to a painful, degrading, and everlasting death. Imagination has its rights, even though unsanctioned by syllogisms; and we can more readily and justly think of ourselves as souls dominating matter than as machines operating souls. Feeling has its rights, and delves more deeply than intellect; poor wandering, wondering Jean-Jacques may have felt more wisely than the brilliant imp of Ferney thought.

Germany had known and heard both Rousseau and Voltaire, and was choosing Rousseau. It had read and felt *Émile* and *Héloïse*, and preferred them to the *Philosophical Dictionary* and *Candide*. It followed Lessing in putting romantic Shakespeare above classic Racine; it took more readily to *Clarissa Harlowe*, *Tristram Shandy* and Macpherson's "Ossian" than to the *philosophes* and *salonnières* of France. It rejected the rules that Boileau had laid down as the laws of classic style. It resented the emphasis on clarity and moderation; these did not go well with enthusiasm and the reaching toward the Orient and the infinite.

German Romanticism respected truth if this could be found, but it was suspicious of "scientific truth" that darkened the face of life. It kept a warm place in its memory for the myths and fables and fairy tales that Clemens Brentano (1778–1842) and Achim von Arnim (1781–1831) were gathering into *Des Knaben Wunderhorn* (1805–08), and that the brothers Grimm (Jacob, 1785–1863, and Wilhelm, 1786–1859) were collecting for their *Kinder- und Hausmärchen* (1812); these echoes of the nation's and the individual's childhood were a part of the good German's soul, perhaps of his "subconscious" self.

If that heritage of the imagination led back beyond the Revolution to medieval Catholicism, the spirit of romance would follow it to the mossy old cathedrals and the unquestioning faith and merry artisans that had raised them; to the prayers and chants and bells and processions that brought deity daily into human life, and merged the tired individualist restfully with the group; to the saints whose lives made a sacred epic of the Christian calendar;

to the Virgin Mother who had sanctified the maiden's wise innocence and the matron's dedication to the family, the nation, and the race. All this, of course, was an enthusiastic blurring of medieval faiths and terrors, of hunted heretics and haunted souls; but it brought many German Romantics to the peak of their fervor, and some of them, in exhaustion and penitence, to the foot of the altar and into the warm embrace of Mother Church.

V. THE VOICES OF FEELING

German Romanticism affected almost every phase of the nation's life: music in Beethoven, Weber, and Felix Mendelssohn; the novel in Hoffmann and Tieck; philosophy in Fichte and Schelling; religion in Schleiermacher and a hundred such conversions as those of Friedrich Schlegel and Dorothea Mendelssohn. Five men in particular led the movement in German literature; and we should commemorate with them the Romantic women who snared or shared them in love free or bound, and in an intellectual companionship that shocked modest matrons from one Frankfurt to the Oder.

Flickering near the fountainhead of the movement was Wilhelm Heinrich Wackenroder (1773–98), frail and shy, uneasy with reality and reason, comforted with religion, happy with art. In the artist's power of conception and execution he saw an almost godlike faculty of creation. He phrased his new religion in worshipful essays on Leonardo, Raphael, Michelangelo, Dürer . . . At the Universities of Göttingen and Erlangen he found support from Ludwig Tieck; this enthusiastic fellow student proposed a jolly title for his friend's writings: *Herzensergiessungen eines kunstliebenden Klosterbruders* (*Heart Outpourings of an Art-loving Christian Brother*). So christened, it found a publisher in 1797. Wackenroder ridiculed the rationalism of Lessing and the classicism of Winckelmann almost as much as the impermeability of the German bourgeois soul to artistic exaltation, and he summoned his time to recapture the medieval brotherhood of artist and workman under their common name of artisan. Typhoid ended Wackenroder's life at the age of twenty-four.

His friend Tieck (1773–1853) played through eighty years the risky game of feeling versus reason, of imagination versus reality. Together with Wackenroder he studied Elizabethan drama and medieval art, and rejoiced over the fall of the Bastille. Unlike Wackenroder he had a sense of humor and a flair for play; he felt that life was a game played by the gods with kings and queens, bishops and knights, castles and cathedrals and humble pawns. Returning to his native Berlin after his university days, he published in 1795–96 a three-volume novel, *Die Geschichte des Herrn William Lovell*, written in Richardsonian letter form, and describing in sensuous detail the sexual and intellectual wanderings of a young man who has emptied the Christian ethic with the Christian theology, and who concludes from the Fichtean epistemology that if the self is the only reality directly known to us, it should be lord of morals and doctor of laws:

All things exist only because I think them; virtue exists only because I think it. . . . In truth, lust is the great secret of our existence. Poetry, art, even religion, are lust in disguise. The works of the sculptor, the figures of the poet, the paintings before which devoutness kneels, are nothing but introductions to sensuous enjoyment. . . .

I pity the fools who are forever babbling about the depravity of our senses. Blind wretches, they offer sacrifice to an impotent deity, whose gifts cannot satisfy a human heart. . . . No, I have pledged myself to the service of a higher deity, before which all living nature bows, which unites in itself every feeling, which is rapture, love, everything. . . . Only in the embraces of Louisa have I come to know what love is; the memory of Amelia appears to me now in a dim, misty distance.[18]

Here, eighty-five years before *The Brothers Karamazov* (1880), is Ivan Karamazov's fateful preview of the amoral century that was to follow him: "If there is no God, everything is permitted." However, Lovell returns to religion before his end: "The most reckless freethinker," he explains, "at last becomes a worshiper."[19] In his case just in time, for soon after this confession Lovell is killed in a duel.

The book was the boast of a youth liberated before reaching the age of reason. In 1797 he published a short story, "Der blonde Eckhert," which won the admiration of the brothers Schlegel. At their invitation he moved to Jena, which was now the Romantic citadel; Tieck, however, left in 1801 to live on a friend's estate in Frankfurt-an-der-Oder. He devoted himself for a time to translating Elizabethan plays; then to editing, with brilliant critiques, the works of his contemporaries Novalis and Kleist. Following in Lessing's steps, he filled for seventeen years (1825–42), the pilloried post of *Dramaturg* —dramatic critic and manager—at the Dresden Theater; his forthright essays there brought him some enemies, but also a national renown second only to Goethe's and August von Schlegel's in the field of literary criticism. In 1842 King Frederick William IV (who had never heard of *Lovell*) invited him to Berlin; Tieck (having long outlived *Lovell*) accepted, and spent his remaining years as a pillar of literature in the Prussian capital.

Novalis (1772–1801) was not given so many years in which to recover from the ideas of his youth. He had, for literature, the uncertain advantage of noble birth: his father, director of the salt works in Saxony, was cousin to Prince Karl von Hardenberg, of the Prussian ministry. The poet's real name was Freiherr Georg Friedrich Philipp von Hardenberg; he used "Novalis" as a pseudonym, but it had been the actual name of his ancestors in the thirteenth century. His family belonged to the Herrnhut community of Pietists; he held to their strong religious bent, but toward the end he sought a reconciliation of Catholicism with Protestantism as a step toward European unity. In his nineteenth year he entered the University of Jena, developed a warm friendship with Tieck, Schiller, and Friedrich von Schlegel, and probably took some of Fichte's courses, which were scattering sparks from Jena to Weimar.

After a year at the University of Wittenberg he followed his father into business at Arnstadt in Thuringia. At nearby Grüningen he met Sophie von

Kuhn, whose beauty of form and character so moved him that he asked her parents for her hand in marriage. In 1795 he and Sophie were formally engaged, though she was only fourteen. Soon thereafter she fell ill of an incurable ailment of the liver. Two operations further weakened her, and in 1797 she died. Novalis never recovered from this *Liebestod*. His most famous poems, six *Hymnen an die Nacht* (1800), were somber memories of Sophie. In 1798 he became engaged to Julie von Charpentier, but this betrothal too failed to reach marriage; tuberculosis had joined with grief in consuming the poet; and on March 25, 1801, Novalis died, aged twenty-eight.

He left behind him a novel, *Heinrich von Ofterdingen* (1798–1800), which gave intense expression to the longing for religious peace. He had once praised Goethe's *Wilhelm Meister* as a realistic yet wholesome description of a man's development; now he condemned it as idealizing a prosaic adjustment to earthly tasks. The hero of his own novel was presented as an historical character, the real author of the *Nibelungenlied*, a Galahad devoted to pursuit of a blue flower symbolizing the transformation of death into an opening to infinite understanding. "It is the blue flower that I long to see," says Heinrich; "it lies constantly in my mind, and I can imagine and think of nothing else."[20] Here, and in a once famous essay on "Christendom in Europe," Novalis idealized the Middle Ages (even to defending the Inquisition) as having realized Europe's recurring aspiration—political unity under one religious faith. It was (he felt) wise and right for the Church to resist the growth of materialistic science and secular philosophy; in this perspective the Enlightenment was a tragic setback for the European soul. As death beckoned to him Novalis rejected all earthly aims and delights, and dreamed of a coming life in which there would be no sickness and no grief, and love would never end.

VI. THE BROTHERS SCHLEGEL

August Wilhelm von Schlegel (1767–1845) and Friedrich von Schlegel (1772–1829) made a remarkable brotherhood: different in temperament and love, diverging in studies and creeds, and united at last in Sanskrit and philology. Born in Hanover to a Protestant pastor, they became theologians at puberty, and heretics at twenty. At Göttingen August Wilhelm was charmed into studying the transmigrations of words by the lectures and personality of Christian Heyne, translator of Virgil, and into Elizabethan lore by Gottfried Bürger, translator of Shakespeare and author of the ballad *Lenore*.[21] The same university received Friedrich von Schlegel five years after his brother; he began as a student of law, and wandered into literature, art, and philosophy. He ripened rapidly, joined his brother at Jena in 1796, and shared with him in founding the *Athenäum*, which for two years (1798–1800) was the mouthpiece and lodestar of the Romantic movement in Germany. Novalis and Schleiermacher contributed; Tieck came; Fichte and

Schelling added their philosophies; and the lively circle was rounded out by some talented women romantically free.

Friedrich von Schlegel was the intellectual pacemaker of the coterie, if only because he moved faster than the others in adopting and discarding ideas. In 1799 he issued a novel, *Lucinde*, which became a red flag leading the attack upon aging creeds and troublesome taboos. Theoretically it was (like Shelley's *Defence*) a plea for the rights of poetry as an interpreter and guide of life. How wise, for example, is the poet's scorn of the pursuit of riches? "Why this constant striving and pushing without rest and repose? Industry and utility are the angels of death."[22] The hero proclaims also "the divine gospel of joy and love," by which he means the joy of loving without the bonds of matrimony. When Friedrich tried to visit his brother, then teaching at Göttingen (1800), the authorities at Hanover sent a worried order to the university rector: "Should the Professor's brother, Friedrich Schlegel, notorious for the immoral tendency of his writings, come to Göttingen, for the purpose of staying there for any time, this is not to be permitted; you will be so good as to intimate to him that he must leave the town."[23]

The woman who had served as Schlegel's inspiration for *Lucinde* was Caroline Michaelis. Born in 1763, she married a university professor (1784), became unhappy with him, was freed by his death, and enjoyed for several years the pleasures of a widow celebrated for both intellect and beauty. August von Schlegel, while a student at Göttingen, fell in love with her, and proposed marriage. She refused him as four years her junior. When he left to tutor in Amsterdam (1791) she entered upon a series of adventures, in one of which she was surprised with motherhood. She joined a revolutionary group in Mainz, was arrested, was freed by her parents, and went to Leipzig to give birth. There August von Schlegel appeared, proposed again, married her (1796), adopted her child, and went with them to Jena.

There her education, her vivacity, and her intelligent conversation made her the favorite hostess of the liberals. Wilhelm von Humboldt called her the cleverest woman he had ever known.[24] Goethe and Herder came over from Weimar to sit at her table and enjoy her company.[25] Friedrich von Schlegel, who was then living with his brother, took his turn falling in love with her. He made her the Lucinde of his novel, and raised such paeans to her that his passion was suffocated with words. Meanwhile August, whose passion had cooled to chivalry, went off to lecture in Berlin (1801). There he formed an attachment with Sophie Bernhardi, who divorced her husband to live with her new love. Returning to Jena, August found Caroline enamored of Schelling, and amiably agreed to a divorce. Caroline married Schelling (1804), and stayed with him till her death (1809). Schelling, though he married again, felt her influence through many years. "Even if she had not been to me what she was, I should mourn the human being, should lament that this intellectual paragon no longer exists, this rare woman who, to masculine strength of soul and the keenest intellect, united the tenderest, most womanly, loving heart."[26]

Quite as remarkable was Dorothea von Schlegel (1763–1839), nee Brendel Mendelssohn. To please her famous father, she married in 1783 the banker Simon Veit. She bore him a son, Philipp Veit, who became a prominent painter in the next generation. Having plenty of money, she lost interest in it, ventured into the still more uncertain game of philosophy, and became an intellectual luminary in Rachel Varnhagen's salon in Berlin. There Friedrich von Schlegel found her, and straightway fell in love with her; and she, who was enamored of ideas, found him swimming in them. He was then twenty-five, she was thirty-two; but the volatile author was captivated by the complex charms of this *femme de trente ans* and more. She was not strikingly beautiful, but she gave him a sustaining appreciation of his mind, she could accompany him understandingly in his philosophical and philological explorations, and she offered him a devotion that survived all quarrels till his death. Her husband, feeling that she was lost to him, gave her a divorce (1798). She lived contentedly in unregistered union with Schlegel, accompanied him to Paris in 1802, accepted baptism, was renamed Dorothea, and became Friedrich's legal wife in 1804.

Brother August had by that time become the most famous lecturer on the Continent, and had made progress with that remarkable translation of Shakespeare which soon made the great Elizabethan almost as popular in Germany as in England. Though August has been called "the founder of the Romantic school in Germany,"[27] he had many qualities of the classic mind and character: order, clarity, proportion, moderation, and a steady procession toward a defined goal. His lectures "On Dramatic Literature," given in various cities and years, excel in those qualities; and those on Shakespeare abound in illuminating comments—sometimes bravely critical of his beloved bard. These lectures, wrote William Hazlitt in 1817, "give by far the best account of the plays that has hitherto appeared. . . . We confess to some little jealousy . . . that it should be reserved for a foreign critic to give reasons for the faith which we English have in Shakespeare."[28]

Mme. de Staël, touring Germany in quest of material for a book, persuaded August (1804), for twelve thousand francs a year, to go with her to Coppet as tutor for her children, and reference encyclopedia for herself. Later he traveled with her in Italy, France, and Austria, returned with her to Coppet, and stayed with her till 1811, when the Swiss authorities, obeying Napoleon, ordered him to leave Switzerland. He went to Vienna, and was surprised to find his brother lecturing there on the Middle Ages as the golden era of European faith and unity.

Vienna was the Catholic capital of Germany, and Friedrich and Dorothea had been converted to Catholicism in 1808. Years ago she had said: "These pictures [of saints] and the Catholic music touch me so, that I am determined, if I become a Christian, to be a Catholic."[29] Friedrich von Schlegel ascribed his own conversion to a *"prédilection d'artiste"*; and in many ways Catholicism—so hospitable to imagination, feeling, and beauty—seemed the natural ally and fulfillment of Romantic sentiment. The rationalist, buffeted by mystery and humiliated by mortality, grew weary of reasoning. The individualist, lonely in the insecurity of self, turned to the Church as a communal shelter and comforting home. So Friedrich von Schlegel, cleverest of reasoners, the most ardent of the young individualists, the most reckless of the rebels, turned now back of Voltaire, back of Luther and Calvin, to medieval Europe and its omnipotent Church. He mourned the replacement of inspiring myths with desolating science, and declared that "the deepest want and deficiency of all modern art is the fact that the artists have no mythology."[30]

Perhaps his respect for mythology had been widened by his researches in the literature and myths of ancient India. Begun in Paris in 1802, these researches had culminated in a scholarly and seminal treatise *Über die Sprache und Weisheit der Inder* (*On the Language and Wisdom of the Hindus*, 1808), which shared in establishing the comparative philology of the Indo-European languages. Presumably Friedrich discussed this aspect of his life when his brother joined him for a while in the Vienna of 1811. August, recalling his work with Christian Heyne in philology, resumed his interest in that field; and the combined contribution of the brothers to Sanskrit studies was the most solid and lasting result of their lives.

Friedrich had made quite a place for himself in the cultural and political life of Vienna. He had won a secretarial post in the Austrian government, and had helped to write the anti-Napoleonic blast which Archduke Karl Ludwig had issued as part of the 1809 campaign. In 1810 and 1812 he delivered, in Vienna, outstanding lectures on European history and literature; in these discourses he expounded his theories of literary criticism and scholarship, and gave a classic analysis of Romanticism. In 1820 he became editor of the right-wing Catholic journal *Concordia;* his repudiation, in this, of the beliefs that he had so lustily defended in his Jena days led to a lasting alienation from his brother. He gave his final course of lectures in Dresden in 1828, and died there in the following year. Dorothea treasured his memory, and followed him, in thought and deed, till her end in 1839.

August outlived both of them. In May, 1812, he was reunited with Mme. de Staël; he guided her through Austria and Russia to St. Petersburg, and went on with her to Stockholm. There, through Madame's influence, he was appointed secretary to Bernadotte, crown prince of Sweden, and accompanied him in the campaign of 1813 against Napoleon. For his services he was ennobled by the Swedish government. In 1814 he rejoined Mme. de Staël at Coppet, and he stayed with her till her death. Then, his remarkable devotion to her having been fulfilled, he accepted a professorship in literature at the University of Bonn (1818). He resumed his studies of Sanskrit, set up a Sanskrit press, edited and published the text of the *Bhagavad-Gita* and the *Ramayana*, and labored for ten years on an *Indische Bibliothek*, or library of Hindu literature. He died in 1845, aged seventy-eight, leaving behind him a treasure of Shakespeare painstakingly transformed into German, and, in his lectures, a harvest of literary memories and ideas for Coleridge to glean from on his way to German philosophy. It was a good life.

CHAPTER XXXII

German Philosophy

1789–1815

O UR approach to the idealistic philosophy of Kant and his successors is obstructed by the current preemption of the word *ideal* for moral excellence, and by our habit, in an age of science and industry, of thinking of things perceived, and seldom of the process of perception itself. The opposite attitudes competed in Greek philosophy, where Democritus took atoms as his starting point, and Plato took ideas. In modern philosophy Bacon stressed knowledge of the world, Descartes began with the thinking self. Hobbes reduced everything to matter, Berkeley to mind. Kant gave German philosophy its distinctive character by arguing that its prime task is the study of the process by which we form ideas. He admitted the reality of external objects, but insisted that we can never know what they objectively are, since we know them only as changed by the organs and processes of perception into our ideas. Philosophical "idealism" is therefore the theory that nothing is known to us except ideas, and that therefore matter is a form of mind.*

I. FICHTE: 1762–1814

1. The Radical

Here, as so often in literary history, the man has proved more interesting than his books. These suffer erosion by the flux of fashions in ideas and forms, but the study of a soul picking its way through the labyrinth of life is a living lesson in philosophy, an ever moving picture of experience molding character and transforming thought.

Johann Gottlieb Fichte crowded a brave variety of experience into his fifty-two years. His father was a Saxon ribbon weaver. His mother prayed that her boy should be a pastor; he agreed, and after some local schooling he was sent to Jena to study theology. The more he studied the more he wondered and doubted. A village preacher gave him a *Refutation of the Errors of Spinoza;* Fichte was charmed by the errors,[2] and decided that he was not fit for a pastorate. Nevertheless he graduated in the faculty of theology.

---

* Cf. Charles Singer, historian of science: "Consciousness is the ultimate datum, the thing taken for granted; the judge, as it were, before whom science must recite its narrative of experiences of phenomena. Their recital, and that alone, is the role of science."[1]

Almost penniless, he walked from Jena to Zurich to secure a post as tutor. There he fell in love with Johanna Maria Rahn, and was formally betrothed to her; but they agreed not to marry till he was financially adult.

He moved to Leipzig, tutored, read Kant's *Critique of Pure Reason*, and was fascinated. He made his way to Königsberg, and presented Kant a *Versuch einer Kritik aller Offenbarung (Essay toward a Critique of All Revelation*, 1792). The old philosopher balked at Fichte's request for a loan, but helped him to find a publisher for his treatise. The printer neglected to state the author's name; when a critic ascribed the essay to Kant, Kant named the author and praised the book; Fichte was at once received into the not quite "serene brotherhood of philosophes."[3] He did not do so well with the theologians, for the argument of his treatise was that although revelation does not prove the existence of God, we must ascribe our moral code to God, if that code is to be accepted and obeyed by mankind.

On Kant's recommendation Fichte found remunerative employment as a tutor in Danzig. His betrothed now agreed to add her savings to his income, and on that basis they were married in 1793. He further signalized the year by publishing, anonymously, two vigorous essays. In the *Restoration of Freedom of Thought by the Princes of Europe* he began by praising some enlightened rulers, and berated princes who obstructed the progress of the human mind; and he mourned the wave of repression that had followed the death of Frederick the Great. Reform is better than revolution, for a revolution can throw man back into barbarism; and yet a successful revolution can advance mankind as much in half a century as reform could have done in a thousand years. Then Fichte addressed his readers—at a time when feudalism was still in force through most of Germany:

> Hate not your princes but yourselves. One of the sources of your misery is your exaggerated estimate of these personages, whose minds are warped by an enervating education, indulgence, and superstition. . . . These are the men who are exhorted to suppress freedom of thought. . . . Cry aloud to your princes that you will never permit your freedom of thought to be filched from you. . . .
> The Dark Ages are over, . . . when you were told in God's name that you were herds of cattle set on earth to fetch and carry, to serve a dozen mortals in high place, and to be their possessions. You are not their property, not even God's property, but your own. . . . You will now ask the prince who wishes to rule you, By what right? If he replies, By inheritance, you will ask, How did the first of your line obtain the right? . . . The prince derives his whole power from the people.[4]

The second tract, *Essay toward the Correction of the Public's Judgment on the French Revolution*, was still more radical. Feudal privileges should not be hereditary; they exist by consent of the state, and should be terminable at the state's convenience. Likewise with ecclesiastical property: it exists through permission and protection by the state, and may be nationalized when the nation's need and will so decree. The French National Assembly did this, and was justified. Here the fragment ends.

Only by noting that these pronouncements were published anonymously can we understand how Fichte won an invitation (December, 1793) to the chair of philosophy at Jena. Duke Charles Augustus was still an easygoing lord of Weimar and Jena, and Goethe, who supervised the university faculty, had not yet decided that the French Revolution was a Romantic disease.[5] So Fichte began his courses at Jena in the Easter term of 1794. He was a persuasive teacher, a lively orator, who could put feeling into philosophy and make metaphysics lord of all; but his impetuous temper was thoroughly unprofessorial, and promised intellectual turbulence.

Five of his early discourses were published in 1794 as *Einige Vorlesungen über die Bestimmung des Gelehrtes* (*Some Lectures on the Vocation of the Scholar*). Their thesis, that the state will in some amiable future disappear and leave men really free, was almost as anarchistic as Godwin's *Enquiry Concerning Political Justice*, published a year before:

> Political society is no part of the absolute purpose of human life, but is only a possible means to the formation of a perfect society. The state constantly tends toward its own annihilation, since the final aim of all government is to render itself superfluous. We may have to wait for aeons, but one day all political combinations will become unnecessary.[6]

To this prospect—made palatable to princes by its distance—Fichte added another Pisgah view: "The ultimate aim of society is the perfect equality of all its members." This was a resounding echo of Jean-Jacques, and Fichte did not disown the parentage: "Peace be with Rousseau's ashes, and blessings on his memory; for he has kindled fires in many souls."[7] The Romantic rebels who were to congregate in Jena in 1796 welcomed this summons to utopia. "The greatest metaphysician now alive," wrote Friedrich von Schlegel to his brother, "is a popular writer. You can see it in his famous book on the Revolution. Contrast the contagious eloquence of the 'Lectures on the Scholar' with Schiller's declamations. Every trait in Fichte's public life seems to say, 'This is a man.' "[8]

2. The Philosopher

What was this metaphysics that so charmed the Romantics? Its central thesis was that the individual, self-conscious ego—whose essence is will and whose will is free—is the center and sum of all reality. Nothing could have pleased the Romantics more. But the matter was not as simple as Friedrich von Schlegel's *Lucinde*. Fichte himself, after publishing his *Grundlage der gesamten Wissenschaftslehre* (*Foundation of the Whole Science of Knowledge*, 1794), found it necessary to clarify it, *post factum* (1797), by a *Zweite Einleitung* (*Second Introduction*), and by a *Neue Darstellung* (*New Presentation*), each of which added fresh absurdities. The key word itself needed a key: *Wissenschaftslehre* meant a study of the shaft or trunk of knowledge—i.e., the mind—or, to put it in one forbidding word, epistemology.

Fichte began by dividing philosophers into two groups: "dogmatists" or "realists," who are confident that objects exist independently of the mind; and idealists, who believe that all experience and all "facts" are mental percepts, and that therefore all reality, so far as we can know, is part of the perceiving mind. He objected to realism that it is logically driven to a mechanistic determinism which makes consciousness superfluous and undermines responsibility and morality—whereas freedom of the will is among the most immediate and tenacious of our convictions. Fichte objected further that no philosophy which begins with matter can explain consciousness, which is manifestly immaterial. But the main problems of philosophy concern this mysterious reality called consciousness.

So Fichte began with the conscious self—the Ego, Ich, or I. He acknowledged an external world, but only as known to us through our perceptions. These, by their very process—the interpretation of sensations through memory and purpose—transform the object into a part of the mind. (So a word as a sound is quite different from that word as interpreted by experience, context, and aim; and a storm, which to mere sensation is a confused and meaningless medley of messages falling upon various senses, becomes in perception—through memory, circumstance, and desire—a stimulus to meaningful action.) Fichte concluded that we must assume an external object or "non-Ego" as cause of our external sensations, but that the "object" as interpreted by perception, memory, and will is a construct of the mind. From this point of view both the subject and the object are parts of the Ego, and nothing outside of the Ego can ever be known.

All this is but one aspect of Fichte's philosophy. Behind the self as perceiving is the self as desiring, willing. "The ego is a system of impulses; its very nature is tendency or impulse." "The whole system of our ideas depends upon our impulses and our will."[9] (Here Fichte touches upon Spinoza's "desire is the very essence of man," and leads to Schopenhauer's view of "the world as will and idea.") This restless will is not part of that objective world which seems a slave to mechanistic determinism; hence the will is free. This freedom is the essence of man, for it makes him a responsible moral agent, capable of freely obeying a moral law.

As he proceeded, Fichte developed Kant's admiration of astronomic and moral order into a new theology which assumed a moral law as governing and supporting the universe as well as the character and communities of men. Finally he identified this moral order of the universe—each part, so to speak, doing its duty and thereby maintaining the whole—with God.[10] The goal and duty of the free man is to live in harmony with this divine moral order. That cosmic moral order is not a person but a process, principally visible in the moral development of mankind.[11] The "Vocation of Man" is to live in harmony with that divine order. — All this again recalls Spinoza; but in another mood Fichte suggests Hegel: the individual self or soul is mortal,[12] but it shares in the immortality of that totality of conscious selves which is the Absolute Ego, Idea, or Soul.

In Fichte's philosophy we feel the anxious groping of a man who has lost his transmitted religious faith but is struggling to find for himself and his readers or pupils a middle way between belief and doubt. In 1798 he faced the problem again in *Über den Grund unseres Glaubens an eine göttliche Weltsregierung* (*On the Ground of Our Belief in a Divine Governance of the World*). He reaffirmed his conception of God as the impersonal moral order of the world, but he allowed that some might ascribe personality to this deity in order to vivify their concept and devotion. However, he added that to conceive God as a tyrant, on whose favor future pleasures depend, is to worship an idol; and those who worship it should be called atheists.

An anonymous critic denounced the treatise as irreligious; others joined in the attack; the government of Saxony confiscated all available copies of Fichte's essay, and lodged a complaint with the Weimar government for allowing atheism to be taught within its jurisdiction. The educational committee at Weimar tried to quiet the matter with a polite reply to the Saxons, but Fichte, who was no pacifist, issued two pamphlets in public defense of his book (1799), one of them a direct *Appellation an das Publikum*. The Weimar committee took this *Appeal to the Public* as a challenge to its handling of the matter, and a rumor reached Fichte that it would ask the university senate to impose a public censure upon him. Arguing that this would violate academic freedom, Fichte wrote to Privy Councilor Voight of Weimar that if such a censure should be issued he would resign; and he added that several other professors had agreed, in such case, to resign with him. The Weimar committee (Schiller and Goethe assenting) issued a rescript to the university senate desiring it to censure Fichte; then, accepting Fichte's threat and challenge, it dismissed him. Two petitions were submitted by the students for a recall of this edict; they were ignored.[13]

In July, 1799, Fichte and his wife moved to Berlin, where he was warmly received by Friedrich von Schlegel, Schleiermacher, and others of the Romantic circle, who sensed the Romantic flavor of Fichte's imagination, and the heroic Ego-ism of his philosophy. To save the cost of a separate household, Fichte (with his unwilling wife) accepted Schlegel's invitation to live with him and Brendel Mendelssohn Veit. The volatile philosopher liked the ensemble, and proposed to enlarge it. "If my plan succeeds," he wrote, "the Schlegels, Schelling, and we ourselves will form one family, take a larger house, and have only one cook."[14] The plan was not carried out, for Caroline von Schlegel did not get along with Brendel; individualism is the snake in every socialist paradise.

Fichte, however, kept a socialist tinge to the end. In 1800 he published an essay, *Der geschlossene Handelsstaat* (*The Closed Commercial State*), in which he argued that foreign trade and manipulations of currency enable the richer nations to drain poorer nations of their metallic wealth; therefore the government should control all foreign commerce, and possess all negotiable bullion and currency. Armed with this power, the state should guarantee to every individual a living wage and an equitable share in the national product; in return the individual must yield to the state the power to fix prices, and to determine the place and character of his work.[15]

Strangely contemporary with this radical pronouncement was a religious tract, *Die Bestimmung des Menschen* (*The Vocation of Man*, 1800), which described God as the moral order of the universe, and rose to an ecstasy of adoration:

> Our faith, . . . our faith in duty, is only faith in Him, in His reason and His truth. . . . That eternal Will is assuredly the Creator of the World. . . . We are eternal because He is eternal.
> Sublime and living Will! named by no name, compassed by no thought! . . . Thou are best known to a childlike, devoted, simple mind. . . .
> I hide my face before Thee, and lay my hand upon my mouth. . . . How Thou art, and seemest to Thine own being, I can never know. . . . Thou workest in me the knowledge of my duty, of my vocation in the world of reasonable beings; how I know not, nor need I know. . . . In the contemplation of these Thy relations to me, . . . will I rest in calm blessedness.[16]

Apparently dependent upon public lectures, and their publication, for his livelihood, Fichte moved more and more toward Christian piety and German patriotism. In 1805 he was called to the chair of philosophy at the University of Erlangen. He was making a new reputation for himself there when the entry of Napoleon's army into Germany (1806) compelled him to seek a safer post. He crossed into East Prussia, and for a time taught in Königsberg. Soon the vicinity of Napoleon's troops at nearby Friedland forced him to move—this time to Copenhagen. In August, 1807, weary of homelessness, he made his way back to Berlin. There he put philosophy aside, and gave his energy to helping restore the pride and spirit of a shattered and humiliated people.

3. The Patriot

On Sundays from December 13, 1807, to March 20, 1808, in the amphitheater of the Berlin Academy, Fichte delivered the lectures later published as *Reden an die deutsche Nation*. They were his passionate appeal to his people to regain their self-respect and courage, and to take measures for raising themselves out of the desolation brought upon them by the saber-rattling conceit of the Prussian military caste, the inhumane Peace of Tilsit, and the brutal dismemberment of the Prussian kingdom by the victorious Corsican. Meanwhile French soldiers were policing the captured capital, and French spies were checking every speech.

These *Addresses to the German Nation* are the most living part of Fichte's legacy, and are still warm with the feeling of the philosopher turned patriot. They put aside the intellectual game of theoretical logic, and faced the bitter realities of Prussia's darkest year. He spoke not to Prussia alone, but to all Germans; and though their scattered principalities hardly constituted a nation, they used the same language and needed the same goad. He sought to bring them some unity by reminding them of German history, of famous victories—and achievements in statesmanship, religion, literature, and art; and by rejecting the hopeless materialism which he claimed to find in English life and theory, and the religious denudation of the French Enlightenment and Revolution. He spoke with reasonable pride of the mercantile cities of the older Germany—the Nuremberg of Albrecht Dürer, the Augsburg of the Fuggers, the globe-running burghers of the Hanseatic League. Present defeats, Fichte told his class and his country, must be seen in the perspective of a brilliant past; this imprisonment of one nation by another could not last; the German people had, in their national character, the resources of body, mind, and will that would make this present nadir end.

How? Fichte answered, By a complete reform of education: its extension to every German child by governmental financing and compulsion; and the transformation of its purpose from commercial success to moral commitment. No more talk of revolution; there is only one revolution, and that is the enlightenment of the mind and the cleansing of the character. The child's abilities must be developed by the method of Pestalozzi; and they must be directed to national goals determined by the state. The state must be led by educated and dedicated men; it must be not the power of an army but the direction and implementation of the national will. Every citizen must be the servant of the state, and the state must be the servant of all. "Till now, by far the largest part of the state's income . . . has been spent in maintaining a standing army"; and the education of children has been left to clergymen who "used God as a means to introduce self-seeking into other worlds after the death of the mortal body. . . . Such a religion . . . shall indeed be borne to the grave along with the past age."[17] It must be replaced by a religion of moral consciousness based upon an educated sense of communal responsibility.

To produce this new type of man, Fichte believes, the pupils should be "separated from the adult society," and "form a separate and self-contained community. . . . Physical exercises, . . . farming, and trades of various kinds, in addition to the development of the mind by learning, are included in this commonwealth."[18]

> So isolated from the corruptions of the dying past, the pupils, by work and study, should be stimulated to create an image of the social order of mankind as it ought to be, simply in accordance with the law of reason. The pupil is so filled with ardent love for such an order of things that it will be utterly impossible for him not to desire it, and to work with all his strength to promote it, when freed from the guidance of education.[19]

It is a splendid dream, recalling Plato's republic, and forecasting the socialist prophets who would stir the hopes of succeeding centuries. It had little influence on its time, and little share (though this has been magnified) in raising national ardor against Napoleon.[20] But Fichte was thinking of something larger than the expulsion of the French from Prussia; he was trying to find a way of improving that human character which, for good and evil, has made much of history. In any case it was a noble dream, too confident, perhaps, in the power of education over heredity, and sadly open to misconception and misuse by authoritarian regimes; but, Fichte said, "as

I care to live only for that hope, I cannot give up hoping . . . that I shall convince some Germans . . . that it is education alone that can save us."[21]

The hardships of his flight from Erlangen to Königsberg to Copenhagen to Berlin had permanently weakened him. Shortly after completing his *Addresses to the German Nation* his health broke down. He went to Teplitz and partly recovered. In 1810 he was made rector of the new University of Berlin. When Prussia opened its War of Liberation, Fichte aroused his students to such patriotic fervor that nearly all of them enlisted.[22] Fichte's wife volunteered for service as a nurse; she caught an apparently fatal fever; he attended her during the day, and lectured at the university in the evening; he caught the ailment from her; she survived, he died, January 27, 1814. Five years later she was laid beside him, in that good old custom of burial which allowed lovers and mates to be joined again—even though but hair and bones—in symbol of their having been, and of being now again, one.

II. SCHELLING: 1775–1854

Though he recognized the existence of an external world, Fichte's philosophy mostly avoided it except as purified by perception. Friedrich Wilhelm Joseph von Schelling, despite his aristocratic preposition, readily accepted nature, and united it with mind in a condominion constituting God.

He was the son of a propertied Lutheran pastor in Württemberg, was pledged to the ministry, and studied in the theological faculty at Tübingen. There he, Hölderlin, and Hegel formed a lusty trio of scholastic radicals, celebrating the French Revolution, redefining deity, and making new philosophic mixtures of Spinoza, Kant, and Fichte. Schelling added a poem entitled "The Creed of an Epicurean."[23] One could safely predict, from these juvenalia, a respectably conservative old age.

Like Fichte and Hegel, he served for some years as a tutor. His essay, *The I as Principle of Philosophy*, published in 1795 when he was twenty, caught the attention of Fichte, and won Schelling, at twenty-three, an invitation to teach philosophy at Jena. He was content, for a time, to describe himself as a follower of Fichte, and to accept mind as the sole reality. But at Jena, and later at Berlin, he joined the Romantics, and gave the body a passing ecstasy:

> I can bear it no longer; I must live once more, must let my senses have free play—these senses of which I have been well-nigh deprived by the grand transcendental theories to which they have done their utmost to convert me. But I too will now confess how my heart leaps and the hot blood rushes through my veins. . . . I have no religion but this, that I love a well-shaped knee, a fair plump bosom, a slender waist, flowers with the sweetest odors, full satisfaction of all my desires, the granting of all that sweet love can ask. If I am obliged to have a religion (though I can live most happily without it), then it must be the Catholic, such as it was in the olden days, when priests and laity lived together, . . . and in the house of God itself there was daily revelry.[24]

It was fitting that so ardent a lover of tangible reality should startle the idealistic nimbus that surrounded Fichte at Jena, and that remained behind him when he left for Berlin. In *Erste Entwurf eines Systems der Natur-philosophie (First Sketch of a System of Natural Philosophy*, 1799), and in *System des transzendentalen Idealismus* (1800), Schelling defined the main problem of philosophy as the apparent impasse between matter and mind; it seems impossible to think of either producing the other; and he concluded (in one more return to Spinoza) that the best escape from the dilemma is to think of mind and matter as two attributes of one complex but unified reality. "All philosophy absolutely, which is based upon pure reason alone, is, or will become, Spinozism." But that philosophy, Schelling thought, was so rigidly logical as to miss vitality. "A dynamic conception of nature must necessarily bring about one essential change in the views of Spinozism. . . . In its rigidity Spinozism could be regarded, like Pygmalion's statue, as needing to be given a soul."[25]*

To make this dualistic monism more conceivable Schelling proposed to think of force or energy as the inner essence of both matter and mind. In neither case do we know what this force is, but since we see it taking in nature progressively subtler forms—from the mystery of communicated motion, through the attraction or repulsion of particles, the sensitivity of plants, or the groping, grasping pseudopodia of the amoeba, to the quick intelligence of the chimpanzee and the conscious reason of man, we may conclude that the basic reality, the one omnipresent God, is neither matter nor mind by itself but their union in one incredible panorama of forms and powers. Here Schelling was writing poetry as well as philosophy, and both Wordsworth and Coleridge found in him a fellow spirit struggling to build a new faith for souls overwhelmed by science and hungering for God.

In 1803 he left Jena to teach in the recently opened University of Würzburg. He continued to write philosophical treatises, but they lacked the vigor of his *Naturphilosophie*. In 1809 his stimulating wife, Caroline, died, and seemed to take half of his vitality with her. He married again (1812), and wrote incontinently, but he published nothing after 1809. Besides, by that time, Hegel had become the unchallengeable Napoleon of philosophy.

In his declining years Schelling found comfort in mysticism, and transcendental explanations for the apparent contradictions between a loving God and a nature "red in tooth and claw," and between the determinism of science and the free will apparently needed for moral responsibility. He took from Jakob Böhme (1575–1624) the idea that God himself is a battleground between good and evil, so that nature oscillates between struggling for order and relaxing into chaos; and in man too there is something basically irrational.[26] Ultimately (Schelling promised his readers) all evil will be overcome, and Divine Wisdom will succeed in transforming even the follies and crimes of mankind into good.[27]

---

* But Spinoza had already done this in three words: *omnia quodammodo animata*, "all things in some manner have life"—literally, "souls" (*Ethics*, II, 13, scholium).

He had now the long discomfort of seeing Hegel gather all the crowns of philosophy, and then to survive him by twenty-three years while the "Young Hegelians" divided their master's dialectical remains between communism and reaction. In 1841 King Frederick William IV called Schelling to the chair of philosophy at the University of Berlin, hoping that his conservatism would stem the radical tide. But Schelling could not hold his audience, and he was left stranded and wondering by the rush of events from philosophy to revolution.

Even so, Wordsworth had already put Schelling's pantheistic vitalism into majestic verse,[28] and Coleridge had ascribed to him, with certain exceptions, "the completion, and the most important victories, of the [Kantian] revolution in philosophy."[29] And half a century after Schelling's death, Henri Bergson, regenerator of vitalism, called Schelling "one of the greatest philosophers of all time."[30] Hegel would have demurred.

III. HEGEL: 1770–1831

By reading Kant, Schopenhauer wrote about 1816, "the public was compelled to see that what is obscure is not always without significance." Fichte and Schelling, he thought, took undue advantage of Kant's success with obscurity. But (Schopenhauer continued)

> the height of absurdity in serving up pure nonsense, in stringing together senseless and extravagant masses of words, such as had previously been known only in madhouses, was finally reached in Hegel, and became the instrument of the most beautiful mystification that has ever taken place, with a result which will appear fabulous to posterity, and will remain as a monument of German stupidity.[31]

1. Skeptic's Progress

Georg Wilhelm Friedrich Hegel was alive and flourishing when this dirge was published (1818); he survived another thirteen years. He came of a Stuttgart middle-class family steeped in mysticism and piety. The family property was mortgaged to send Georg to study theology at Tübingen Seminary (1788–93). Hölderlin the poet was there, and Schelling came in 1790; together they deplored the ignorance of their teachers, and applauded the victories of Revolutionary France. Hegel developed a special fondness for Greek drama, and his praise of Greek patriotism foreshadowed his own final political philosophy:

> To the Greek the idea of his fatherland, the state, was the invisible, the higher reality for which he labored. . . . In comparison with this idea his own individuality was as nothing; it was *its* endurance, *its* continued life, that he sought. . . . To desire or pray for permanence or eternal life for himself as an individual could not occur to him.[32]

After graduating from the seminary with a degree in theology, Hegel disappointed his parents by refusing to enter the ministry. He supported himself by tutoring at Bern in the home of a patrician with a substantial library;
there, and later at Frankfurt, he read Thucydides, Machiavelli, Hobbes,
Spinoza, Leibniz, Montesquieu, Locke, Voltaire, Hume, Kant, Fichte; how
could his ailing Christian faith resist such a phalanx of doubters? The natural rebelliousness of a vigorous youth reveled in the pagan feast.

In the year 1796 he wrote a *Life of Jesus* (*Das Leben Jesu*), which remained unpublished till 1905. It was in part an anticipation of *Das Leben
Jesu* (1835), with which David Strauss, a follower of Hegel, launched a
full-scale attack upon the Gospel story of Christ. Hegel described Jesus as
the son of Joseph and Mary; he rejected the miracles ascribed to Christ, or
explained them naturally; he pictured Christ as defending the individual
conscience against priestly rules; he ended with the burial of the crucified
rebel, and said nothing of a resurrection. And he gave a definition of God
which he was to hold to the end: "Pure reason, incapable of any limitation,
is the Deity itself."[33]

In 1799 Hegel's father died, leaving him 3,154 florins. He wrote to Schelling asking advice in finding a town with a good library and *ein gutes Bier*.[34]
Schelling recommended Jena, and offered to share his quarters with him.
In 1801 Hegel came, and was allowed to lecture at the university as a
Privatdozent, remunerated only by his pupils, who numbered eleven. After
three years of such servitude he was appointed *professor extraordinarius;*
and a year later, on Goethe's intervention, he received his first stipend—one
hundred thalers. He never became a popular teacher, but at Jena, as later in
Berlin, he inspired in several students a special attachment that penetrated
the rough surface of his language to the arcane vigor of his thought.

In 1801 he began, but left unfinished and unpublished, a significant essay,
Kritik der Verfassung Deutschlands (*On the Constitution of Germany*, published in 1893). Looking out upon Germany, he was reminded of the petty
principalities that had divided Renaissance Italy and opened it to foreign
conquest, and he remembered Machiavelli's plea for a strong prince who
would hammer these scattered pieces into a nation. He put no faith in the
Holy Roman Empire, and foretold its early collapse. "Germany is no longer
a state. . . . A group of human beings can call itself a state only if it is joined
together for the common defense of the entirety of its property." He called
for the unification of Germany, but he added: "Such an event has never
been the fruit of reflection, but only of force . . . The common multitude of
the German people . . . must be gathered into one mass by the force of a
conqueror."[35]

Presumably he had no notion of summoning Napoleon, but when, in
1805, Napoleon overwhelmed both the Austrians and the Russians at Austerlitz, Hegel may have begun to wonder whether this man was destined to
unify not only Germany, but all Europe. When, in the following year, the
French Army was approaching Jena, and the future of Europe seemed at

stake, Hegel saw Napoleon riding through Jena (October 13, 1806), and wrote to his friend Niethammer:

> I saw the Emperor—that world-soul—riding out to reconnoiter the city. It is a truly wonderful sensation to see such an individual, concentrated here at a single point, astride a single horse, yet reaching across the world and ruling it. . . . To make such progress from Thursday to Monday is possible only for that extraordinary man, whom it is impossible not to admire. . . . All now wish good fortune to the French Army.[36]

On the next day the French Army prevailed; and some French soldiers, eluding the eye of the world-soul, began to plunder in the city. One group entered Hegel's rented room. Seeing the Cross of the Legion of Honor on a corporal's coat, the philosopher expressed the hope that so distinguished a man would treat a simple German scholar honorably. These invaders settled for a bottle of wine, but the spread of looting frightened Hegel into taking refuge in the office of the university vice-president.

On February 5, 1807, Christina Burkhardt, wife of Hegel's landlord, gave birth to a boy whom the absent-minded professor recognized as one of his anonymous works. As the Duke of Saxe-Weimar was hard put to finance the Jena faculty, Hegel thought it a good time to try another city, woman, and task. On February 20 he left Jena to become editor of the *Bamberger Zeitung*. Amid the turmoil he published (1807) *Phänomenologie des Geistes*. No one seems to have suspected that this would later be ranked as his masterpiece, and as the most difficult and seminal contribution to philosophy between Kant and Schopenhauer.

Irked by governmental censorship of his paper, Hegel left Bamberg (1808) to become headmaster of a *Gymnasium* in Nuremberg. He labored conscientiously in this new field, teaching as well as directing, but he longed for a secure and fitter berth in a distinguished and solvent university. On September 16, 1811, age forty-one, he married Marie von Tucher, the twenty-year-old daughter of a Nuremberg senator. Shortly thereafter Christina Burkhardt surprised the couple with a visit in which she offered them Hegel's four-year-old son, Ludwig. His wife met the situation bravely by adopting the boy into her family.

Dreaming of a post in Berlin, Hegel accepted in 1816 an invitation from the University of Heidelberg to be its first professor of philosophy. His class began with five students, but grew to twenty before the term was over. There he published (1817) his *Encyclopedia of the Philosophical Sciences*. It pleased both the intelligentsia and the government of Berlin much more than his *Logik*, which had appeared there in 1812. Soon the Prussian Minister of Education invited him to come and fill the chair of philosophy which had been left vacant since the death of Fichte (1814). Hegel, now forty-seven, bargained until the remuneration finally offered him atoned for his long wait. Besides the two-thousand-thaler yearly salary he asked something to compensate for the high rents and prices in Berlin, for the furniture he had bought, and would now have to sell at a loss, for the cost of travel to

Berlin with his wife and children; furthermore, he would like "a certain quantity of produce."[37] All this having been granted, Hegel on October 22, 1818, began at the University of Berlin the long tenure that would end with his death. In those thirteen years his lectures, notoriously dull but finally meaningful, drew larger and larger audiences, until students came from almost every country in Europe—and beyond—to hear him. Now he gave form and order to the most complete and influential system of thought in the history of post-Kantian Europe.

2. *Logic as Metaphysics*

He begins with logic, not in our modern sense as the rules of reasoning, but in the ancient and classic sense as the *ratio*, or rationale, or basic meaning and operation, of anything, as when we use *geology, biology*, or *psychology* for the meaning and operation of the earth, life, or mind. So, to Hegel, logic studies the meaning and operation of anything. Generally he leaves the operations to science, as science leaves the meaning to philosophy. He proposes to analyze not the words in reasoning but the reason or logic in realities. To the source and sum of these reasons he will give the name of God, very much as ancient mystics identified the deity with the Logos— the reason and wisdom of the world.*

The perceiving mind gives specific meaning to objects by studying their relationships, in space and time, with other objects remembered or perceived. Kant had given to such relationships the name of categories, and had listed twelve, chiefly: unity, plurality, and totality; reality, negation, and limitation; cause and effect, existence and nonexistence, contingency and necessity. Hegel adds many more: determinate being, limit, multiplicity, attraction and repulsion, likeness and difference . . . Each object in our experience is a complex web of such relationships; this table, for example, has specific place, age, form, strength, color, weight, odor, beauty; without such specific relations the table would be merely a confusion of obscure and separate sensations; with them the sensations become a united perception. This perception, illuminated by memory and pointed by purpose, becomes an idea. Hence, for each of us, the world is our sensations—external or internal—coordinated by the categories into perceptions and ideas, mingled with our memories, and manipulated by our wills.

The categories are not things, they are ways and tools of understanding, giving form and meaning to sensations. They constitute the rationale and logic, the structure and reason, of each experienced feeling, thought, or thing. Together they constitute the logic, reason, Logos of the universe, as conceived by Hegel.

The simplest and most universal of the categories through which we may seek to understand our experience is pure Being (*Sein*)—being as applied to

---

* The Fourth Gospel begins with "In the beginning was the Logos." Saint Jerome translated *Logos* as *verbum*; King James's scholars translated it as *Word*; they might better have translated it as *Reason*.

all objects or ideas without particularization. The universality of this basic category is its fatality: by lacking any distinguishing form or mark it cannot represent any existing object or idea. Hence the concept of pure Being is in effect equivalent to its opposite category—Nonbeing or Nothing (*Nichts*). Hence they readily mingle; that which was not is added to Being, and deprives it of its indeterminateness or purity; Being and Nonbeing become something, however negative. This mysterious Becoming (*Werden*) is the third category, the most useful of all, since without it nothing could be conceived as happening or taking form. All subsequent categories flow from similar combinations of apparently contradictory ideas.

This Hegelian prestidigitation, producing the world (like Adam and Eve) out of a conjunction, recalls the medieval idea that God created the world out of nothing. But Hegel protests that his categories are not things; they are ways of conceiving things, of making their behavior intelligible, often predictable, sometimes manageable.

He asks us to allow some modification in the principle of contradiction (so sacred in the old logic)—that A cannot be not-A. Very well; but A may *become* not-A, as water can become ice or steam. All reality, as conceived by Hegel, is in a process of becoming; it is not a static Parmenidean world of Being but a fluid Heracleitean world of Becoming; all things flow. All reality, in Hegel, all thoughts and things, all history, religion, philosophy, are in constant evolution; not by a natural selection of variations, but by the development and resolution of internal contradictions, and the advance to a more complex stage.

This is the famous Hegelian (formerly Fichtean) dialectic (literally the art of conversation) of thesis, antithesis, and synthesis: an idea or situation potentially contains its opposite, develops it, struggles against it, then unites with it to take another transient form. A logical discussion would follow the dialectical structure of exposition, opposition, and reconciliation. Sensible de*liberations*—the weighing of ideas and desires on the scale (*libera*) of experience—would do likewise. Interruption, as Mme. de Staël insisted, is the life of conversation—but is its death if the contradiction is not pertinent and resolved. Opposition absorbed is the secret of wisdom and the perfection of victory. A true synthesis rejects neither the affirmative nor the negative, but finds room for elements of each. Karl Marx, a disciple of Hegel, thought that capitalism contained the seeds of socialism; that the rival forms of economic organization must clash in a war to the death; and that socialism would prevail. A more consistent Hegelian would have predicted a union of both, as in Western Europe today.

Hegel was the most thoroughgoing of Hegelians. He undertook to "deduce" the categories—to show how each of them necessarily resulted from the resolution of contradictions in its predecessors. He organized his arguments, tried to divide each of his works, on a triadic form. He applied his dialectic to realities as well as to ideas: the repetitive process of contradiction, conflict, and synthesis appears in politics, economics, philosophy, and history. He was a realist in the medieval sense: the universal is more real than any of its contained particulars: man includes all men, briefly alive or durably dead; the state is realer, more important and longer living, than any of its citizens; beauty has immortal power, makes many wrecks and rhymes, though Pauline Bonaparte is dead and perhaps Aphrodite never lived. Finally the compulsive philosopher carried his parade of categories to the most real, inclusive, and powerful of them all—the Absolute Idea that is the universal of all things and thoughts, the Reason, structure, or law that upholds the cosmos, the Logos that crowns and rules the whole.

3. Mind

The *Phänomenologie des Geistes* was written at Jena while the Grande Armée was approaching the city; it was published in 1807, when the merciless devastation of Prussia by the sons of the French Revolution seemed to prove that somewhere in that historic groping from monarchy through terror to monarchy the mind of man had lost the road to freedom. Hegel proposed to study the mind of man in its various phenomena as sensation, perception, feeling, consciousness, memory, imagination, desire, will, self-consciousness, and reason; perhaps at the end of that long road he would find the secret of liberty. Not frightened by that program, he would also study the human mind in communities and the state, in art and religion and philosophy. The product of his quest was his chef-d'oeuvre, eloquent and obscure, challenging and discouraging, and pregnant with influence upon Marx and Kierkegaard, Heidegger and Sartre.

The difficulty begins with the word *Geist*, which spreads a cloud of ambiguities over ghost and mind and spirit and soul. We shall usually translate it as *mind*, but in some contexts it may be better rendered as *spirit*, as in *Zeitgeist*, the Spirit of the Age. *Geist* as mind is not a separate substance or entity behind psychological activities; it is those activities themselves. There are no separate "faculties"; there are only the actual operations by which experience is transformed into action or thought.

In one of his many definitions of *Geist* Hegel identified it with consciousness.[38] Consciousness, of course, is the mystery of mysteries, for, as the organ for interpreting experience, it cannot interpret itself. Nevertheless, it is the most immediate, as well as the most remarkable, fact known to us. Matter, which may be the outside of mind, seems less mysterious, even though less directly known. Hegel agrees with Fichte that we know objects only insofar as they become part of us as subjects perceiving; but he never questions the existence of an external world. When the object perceived is another individual apparently endowed with mind, consciousness becomes self-consciousness by opposition; then the consciously personal Ego is born, and becomes uncomfortably aware that competition is the trade of life. Then, says our tough philosopher, "each man" (potentially, ultimately, and seldom consciously) "aims at the destruction and death of the other,"[39] until one of the two accepts subordination,[40] or is dead.

Meanwhile the Ego is feeding upon experience, as if aware that it must arm and strengthen itself for the trials of life. All that complex process by which the Ego transforms sensations into perceptions, stores these in memory, and turns them into ideas, is used to illuminate, color, and serve the desires that make up the will. The Ego is a focus, succession and combination of desires; percepts, ideas, memories, deliberation, like arms and legs, are tools of the self or Ego seeking survival, pleasure, or power. If the desire is a passion it is thereby reinforced, for good or ill; it must not be condemned indiscriminately, for "nothing great in the world has been accomplished without passion."[41] It may lead to pain, but that does not matter if it contributes to the desired result. Life is made not for happiness but for accomplishment.[42]

Is the will (i.e., our desires) free? Yes, but not in the sense of freedom from causality or law; it is free in proportion as it agrees with the laws and logic of reality; a free will is one enlightened by understanding and guided by reason. The only real liberation, for the nation or the individual, is through the growth of intelligence; and intelligence is knowledge coordinated and used. The highest freedom is in the knowledge of the categories and their operation in the basic processes of nature, and their union and harmony in the Absolute Idea, which is God.

There are three ways in which man can approach this summit of understanding and freedom: through art, religion, and philosophy. Briefly in the *Phänomenologie*, more fully in his posthumous *Vorlesungen über Aesthetik*, Hegel tried to bring the nature and history of art under the triadic formulas of his system. Incidentally he revealed a surprising knowledge of architecture, sculpture, painting, and music, and a detailed acquaintance with the art collections of Berlin, Dresden, Vienna, Paris, and the Netherlands. Art, he felt, was an attempt of the mind—by intuition (i.e., direct, intense, persistent perception) rather than by reason—to represent spiritual significance through a sensory medium. He distinguished three major epochs of art: (1) the Oriental, in which architecture sought to support the spiritual life and mystical vision through massive temples, as in Egypt and India; (2) the Greco-Roman Classical, conveying the ideals of reason, balance, and harmony through perfect sculptural forms; and (3) the Christian Romantic, which has sought, through painting, music, and poetry, to express the emotions and longings of the modern soul. In this third stage Hegel found some seeds of degeneration, and suggested that the greatest period of art was coming to an end.

Religion troubled and puzzled him in his declining years, for he recognized its historic function in molding character and supporting social order, but he was too fond of reason to care for the gropings of theology, the ecstasies and sufferings of saints, the fear and worship of a personal God.[43] He struggled to reconcile the Christian creed with the Hegelian dialectic, but his heart was not in the effort,[44] and his most influential followers interpreted his God as the impersonal law or Reason of the universe, and immortality as the lingering—perhaps endless—effects of every soul's moment on the earth.

Toward the end of the *Phänomenologie* he revealed his true love—philosophy. His ideal was not the saint but the sage. In his enthusiasm he recognized no limit to the future extension of human understanding. "The nature of the universe has no power which can permanently resist the courageous effort of the intelligence; it must at last open itself up; it must reveal all its depth and riches to the spirit."[45] But long before that culmination philosophy will have perceived that the real world is not the world that we touch or see, but the relationships and regularities that give them order and nobility, the unwritten laws that move the sun and the stars, and constitute the impersonal mind of the world. To that Absolute Idea or cosmic Reason the philosopher will pledge his loyalty; in it he will find his worship, his freedom, and a quiet content.

4. Morality, Law, and the State

In 1821 Hegel sent forth another major work—*Grundlinien der Philosophie des Rechts* (*Outlines of the Philosophy of Right*). *Recht*—right—is a majestic word in Germany, covering both morality and law as kindred supports of the family, the state, and civilization. Hegel dealt with all of these in a magisterial volume which had lasting influence upon his people.

The philosopher was now entering his sixth decade. He had become accustomed to stability and comfort; he was aspiring to some governmental post;[46] he yielded readily to the natural conservatism of age. Moreover, the political situation had drastically changed since he feted France and admired Napoleon: Prussia had risen in arms and fury against Napoleon fleeing from Russia, had fought under Blücher and had overthrown the usurper; and now Prussia had reestablished itself on a Frederician basis of victorious army and feudal monarchy as stanchions of stability amid a people reduced by the costs of victory to desperate poverty, social disorder, and hopes and fears of revolution.

In 1816 Jakob Fries, then holding the chair of philosophy at the University of Jena, published a treatise, *Von Deutschem Bund und Deutscher Staatsverfassung* (*On the German Confederation and the Political Constitution of Germany*), in which he outlined a program of reform that frightened the German governments into the harsh decrees of the Karlsbad Congress (1819). Fries was dismissed from his professorship, and was declared an outlaw by the police.[47]

Hegel gave half the preface of his book to denouncing Fries as a dangerous simpleton, and condemning as "the quintessence of shallow thinking" Fries's view that "in a people ruled by a genuine communal spirit, life for the discharge of all public business would come from below, from the people itself." "According to a view of this kind," Hegel protested, "the world of ethics should be given over to the subjective accident of opinion and caprice. By the simple family remedy of ascribing to feeling the labor . . . of reason and intellect, all the trouble of rational insight, and of knowledge directed by speculative thinking, is of course saved."[48] The angry professor vented his scorn upon street-corner philosophers who construct perfect states any evening out of the rosy dreams of immaturity.[49] Against such wishful thinking he proclaimed, as the realistic basis of his philosophy (political as well as metaphysical), the principle that "what is rational is actual, and what is actual is rational."[50] (It is what the logic of events made it be; what, under the circumstances, it had to be.) The liberals of Germany denounced the author as a time-serving place-seeker, the "Philosopher Laureate" of a reactionary government. He went on.

Civilization needs both morality and law, since it means living like a citizen (*civis*), and therefore in a community; and a community cannot survive unless it limits liberty in order to provide protection. Morality must be a common bond, not an individual preference. Freedom under law is a constructive force; freedom *from* law is impossible in nature and destructive in society, as in some phases of the French Revolution. The restrictions laid upon individual liberty by custom morality—the ethical judgments developed in the evolution of a community—are the oldest and broadest, the most lasting and far-reaching measures taken by it for its continuance and growth. Since such regulations are transmitted chiefly by the family, the school, and the church, these institutions are basic to a society, and constitute its vital organs.

Therefore it is foolish to let a family be founded by a love marriage. Sexual desire has its biological wisdom for continuing the species and the community; but it contains no social wisdom for supporting a lifetime partnership in the management of property and children.[51] Marriage should be monogamous, and divorce should be difficult. The property of the family should be held in common, but be managed by the husband.[52] "Woman has her substantive destiny in the family, and to be imbued with family devotion is her ethical frame of mind."[53]

Education should not [as in Pestalozzi and Fichte] make fetishes of freedom and play; discipline is the backbone of character. "The punishment of children does not aim at justice as such; the aim is to deter them from exercising a freedom still in the toils of nature, and to raise the universal into their consciousness and will."[54]

Nor should we make a fetish of equality. We are equal only in the sense that each of us is a soul, and should not be a tool for another person; but we are obviously unequal in physical or mental ability. The best economic system is one in which superior ability is stimulated to develop itself, and is left relatively free to transmute new ideas into productive realities. Property should be the private possession of the family, for without that distinguishing reward superior ability would not train or exert itself.

For the purpose of civilization—of turning savages into citizens—religion is an ideal instrument, for it relates the individual to the whole.

> Since religion is an integrating factor in the state, implanting a sense of unity in the depth of men's minds, the state should even require all its citizens to belong to a church. *A* church is all that can be said, because—since the content of a man's faith depends upon his private ideas—the state cannot interfere with it.[55]

The churches should be separate from the state, but should look upon the state as "a consummate worship," in which the religious goal of the unification of the individual with the totality is as nearly effected as is possible on earth.[56]

The state, then, is man's highest achievement. It is the organ of the community for the protection and development of the people. It has the difficult task of reconciling social order with the natural individualism of men and the jealous conflicts of internal groups. Law is the freedom of civilized man, for it frees him from many injustices and perils in return for his agreement not to inflict them upon other citizens. "The state is the actuality of concrete freedom."[57] To so transform chaos into orderly liberty, the state must have authority and, sometimes, must use force; police will be necessary, and, in crisis, conscription too; but if the state is well managed it can be called the organization of reason. In this sense we may say of the state, as of the universe, that "the rational is real, and the real is rational." It is not utopic, but utopia is unreal.

Was this an idealization of the Prussian state of 1820? Not quite. Unlike that regime, it assumed the full success of Stein's and Hardenberg's reforms. It called for a limited monarchy, constitutional government, freedom of worship, and the emancipation of the Jews. It condemned despotism, which it defined as "any state of affairs where law has disappeared, and when the particular will as such, whether of a monarch or a mob (ochlocracy), counts as law or takes the place of law; while it is precisely in legal, constitutional government that sovereignty is to be found as the moment of ideality."[58] Hegel rejected democracy outright: the ordinary citizen is ill-equipped to choose competent rulers, or to determine national policy. The philosopher accepted the French revolutionary Constitution of 1791, which called for a constitutional monarchy, in which the people voted for a national assembly, but not for a ruler. An elective monarchy "is the worst of all institutions."[59] So Hegel recommended a government composed of a bicameral legislature elected by property owners; an executive and administrative cabinet of ministers; and an hereditary monarch having "the will with the power of ultimate decision."[60] "The development of the state to constitutional monarchy is the achievement of the modern world."[61]

It would be unfair to call this philosophy reactionary. It was quite in line with the reasoned conservatism of Montaigne and Voltaire, Burke and Macaulay, Benjamin Constant advising Napoleon, and Tocqueville after studying the French and American governments. It left some room for individual freedom of thought, and for religious toleration. We must view it in its context in place and time: we must imagine ourselves in the maelstrom of post-Napoleonic Europe—with its bankruptcy and depression, and its reac-

tionary governments trying to restore the Ancien Régime—to understand
the reaction of a thinker too advanced in years to be adventurous in thought,
too comfortably established to relish the ecstasy of revolution, or risk the
replacement of an old government with inexperienced theorists or mob rule.
It was the hasty preface, not the carefully organized and considered book,
that was unworthy of a philosopher. The old man was frightened by Fries's
eloquence and its excited reception; he called for the police; and he was not
sorry "that governments have at last directed their attention to this kind of
philosophy."[62] It is not for age to venture but to preserve.

5. History

Hegel's students must have loved him, for after his death they pored over
his notes, added their own records of his lectures, arranged the result in
some reasonable order, and issued it over his name. So appeared four posthumous books: *Aesthetics, Philosophy of Religion, Philosophy of History*,
and *History of Philosophy*. They are the most intelligible of his works, perhaps because least obscured by the complexity of his thought and style.

"The only thought which philosophy brings with it to the contemplation
of history is the simple concept of Reason: that Reason [the logic and law
of events] is the Sovereign of the World; that therefore the history of the
world presents us a rational process."[63] Here too the actual was rational—it
was the only logical and necessary result of its antecedents. Hegel often
speaks of his Sovereign Reason in religious terms, but he defines it by mating
Spinoza and Newton: "Reason is the *substance* of the universe, *viz.*, that by
which and in which all reality has its being and subsistence"; and on the
other hand it is "the Infinite Energy of the Universe"; i.e., the categories of
the *Logik* are the basic means of understanding the operative relations which
constitute "the infinite complex of things, their entire Essence and Truth."[64]

If the operations of history are an expression of Reason—of the laws inherent in the nature of things—there must be some method in the apparent
whimsy of events. Hegel sees method in both the process and the result. The
process of reason in history, as in logic, is dialectical: each stage or condition
(thesis) contains contradictions (antithesis) which struggle to compose a
synthesis. So despotism tried to suppress the human hunger for freedom; the
hunger broke out in revolt; their synthesis was constitutional monarchy. Is
there, then, a general or total design behind the course of history? No, if
this means a conscious supreme power guiding all causes and effects to a
determined goal; yes, insofar as the widening stream of events, as a civilization advances, is moved by the total of *Geist* or Mind to bring man closer
and closer to his absorbing goal, which is freedom through reason. Not freedom from law—though that conceivably might come if intelligence should
reach its full growth—but freedom through law; so the evolution of the state
can be a boon to liberty. This progress toward freedom is not continuous,
for in the dialectic of history there are contradictions to be resolved, oppo-
sitions to be transformed into fusion, centrifugal diversities to be drawn

toward a unifying center by the character of the age or the work of exceptional men.

These two forces—the time and the genius—are the engineers of history,
and when they work together they are irresistible. Hegel—inspiring Carlyle
—believed in heroes and hero worship. Geniuses are not necessarily virtuous,
though it is a mistake to think that they are selfish individualists; Napoleon
was no mere conqueror for the sake of conquest; he was, consciously or not,
the agent of Europe's greater need for unity and consistent laws. But the
genius is helpless unless, consciously or not, he embodies and serves the
Zeitgeist, the Spirit of the Times. "Such individuals had insight into the requirements of the time—*what was ripe for development.* This was the very
truth for their age, for their world; the species next in order, so to speak, and
which was already formed in the womb of time."[65] If the genius is borne on
such a tide (like Galileo, Franklin, or James Watt) he will be a force for
growth, even if he brings misery for an entire generation. The genius is not
meant to peddle happiness. "The history of the world is not the theater of
happiness. Periods of happiness are the blank pages in it, for they are periods
of harmony, when the antithesis is in abeyance,"[66] and history sleeps.

The chief obstacle to interpreting history as progress is the fact that civilizations can die, or entirely disappear. But Hegel was not the man to let
such incidents disrupt his dialectic. He divided man's past (as aforesaid) into
three periods, the Oriental, the Greco-Roman, and the Christian, and saw
some progress in their succession: the Orient gave freedom to one man as
absolute ruler; classical antiquity gave freedom to a caste using slaves; the
Christian world, giving each person a soul, sought to free all. It encountered
resistance in the traffic in slaves, but this conflict was resolved in the French
Revolution. At this point (about 1822) Hegel broke out into a surprising
paean to that upheaval, or to its first two years.

> The political condition of France [had] presented nothing but a confused
> mass of privileges, altogether contravening Thought and Reason, with the
> greatest corruption of morals and spirit. The change was necessarily violent,
> because the work of transformation was not undertaken by the government
> [was opposed by the court, the clergy, and the nobility]. . . . The idea of
> Right asserted its authority, and the old framework of injustice could offer no
> resistance to its onslaught. It was a glorious mental dawn. All thinking beings
> shared in the jubilation. A spiritual enthusiasm filled the world.[67]

Mob violence darkened that dawn, but after the blood was washed away
substantial progress remained; and Hegel was still cosmopolitan enough to
recognize that the French Revolution had brought substantial benefits to
much of Germany—the Code Napoléon, the abolition of feudal privileges,
the enlargement of freedom, the spread of property ownership. . . .[68] All in
all, Hegel's analysis of the French Revolution, in the final pages of *The
Philosophy of History,* proves that the frightened conservative had not quite
repudiated the ideals of his youth.

He considered it a main fault of the Revolution that it had made an enemy
of religion. "Religion is Reason's highest and most rational work. It is absurd

to maintain that priests have thought up religion for the people as a fraud for their own benefit."[69] Consequently it is "folly to pretend to invent and carry out political constitutions independently of religion."[70] "Religion is the sphere in which the nation gives itself the definition of that which it regards as the True. . . . The concept of God, therefore, constitutes the general basis of a people's character."[71]

Conversely, "the shape which the perfect embodiment of Spirit assumes [is] the state."[72] Fully developed, the state becomes "the basis and center of the other concrete elements of the life of a people—of Art, Law, Morals, Religion, Science."[73] Supported and justified by religion, the state becomes divine.

Aspiring to produce a system of philosophy unified by one basic formula of explanation, Hegel applied his dialectic to one field after another. To his philosophy of history his students, after his death, added his *History of Philosophy*. The famous ancient systems of universal analysis, in this view, followed a sequence basically corresponding to the evolution of the categories in the *Logik*. Parmenides stressed Being and stability; Heracleitus stressed Becoming, development, change. Democritus saw objective matter, Plato saw subjective idea; Aristotle provided the synthesis. Each system, like each category and each generation, enclosed—and added to—its predecessors, so that a full understanding of the last system would comprehend them all. "What each generation has brought forward as knowledge and spiritual creation, the next generation inherits. This inheritance constitutes its soul, its spiritual substance."[74] Since Hegel's philosophy was the latest in the great chain of philosophical imaginations, it included (in its author's view) all the basic ideas and values of all major preceding systems, and was their historical and theoretical culmination.[75]

6. Death and Return

His time, for a time, almost took him at his own estimate. His classes grew despite his dour temper and abstruse style; prominent men—Cousin and Michelet from France, Heiberg from Denmark—came from afar to see him balance the universe on his categories. He was honored in Paris in 1827, and by old Goethe on the way home. In 1830 his certainties were shaken by the spread of radical movements and revolutionary agitation; he denounced them, and in 1831 he issued across the waters an appeal for the defeat of the Reform Bill that marked the rise of democracy in England. He rephrased his philosophy more and more in terms acceptable to Protestant divines.

Still only sixty-one, and apparently in full vigor, he fell victim to a cholera epidemic, and died in Berlin, November 14, 1831. He was buried, as he had wished, beside the grave of Fichte. As if in testimony to his cautious obscurity, his students divided into antipodal groups: the "Hegelian Right," led by Johann Erdmann, Kuno Fischer, and Karl Rosenkranz; and the "Hegelian Left"—Ludwig Feuerbach, David Strauss, Bruno Bauer, and Karl Marx. The "Right" excelled in scholarship, but declined as "Higher Criticism" of the Bible grew; the "Left" expanded in attacks upon religious and political orthodoxy. The "Left" interpreted Hegel's identification of God and Reason to mean that nature, man, and history are subject to invariable and impersonal laws. Feuerbach quoted Hegel as saying, "Man knows about God only insofar as God knows about himself within man";[76] i.e., the Reason of the universe becomes conscious only in man; only man can think of cosmic laws. Marx, who knew Hegel chiefly through the master's writings, transformed the dialectical movement of the categories into the economic interpretation of history, in which the class war superseded the Heroes as a main agent of progress; and socialism became the Marxian synthesis of capitalism and its internal contradictions.

Hegel's reputation faded for a time as Schopenhauer's sarcastic passions swept the philosophic board. Philosophers of history were lost in the advance of historical scholarship. Hegelianism seemed dead in Germany, but it had risen to new life in Great Britain with John and Edward Caird, T. H. Green, J. M. E. McTaggart, and Bernard Bosanquet. When it died in England it rose again in the United States. Perhaps the echoes of Hegel's worship of the state helped to pave the way for Bismarck and Hitler. Meanwhile Sören Kierkegaard, Karl Jaspers, Martin Heidegger, and Jean-Paul Sartre found in the *Phänomenologie des Geistes* a virile note of human competition in a world apparently shorn of divine guidance, and Hegel became the godfather of Existentialism.

All in all, this age of Goethe, Beethoven, and Hegel was one of the high-water points in the history of Germany. It had reached or neared such peaks before, as in the Renaissance and the Reformation; but the Thirty Years' War had shattered the economic and intellectual life of the people, and had darkened the soul of Germany almost to despair through a hundred years. Slowly the native vigor of her stock, the stoic patience of her women, the skill of her craftsmen, the enterprise of her merchants, and the power and depth of her music prepared her to receive and transform to her own taste and character such foreign influences as England's Shakespeare and her Romantic poets, the Enlightenment and Revolution of France. She moderated Voltaire into Goethe and Wieland, Rousseau into Schiller and Richter; she answered Napoleon with a War of Liberation, and cleared the way for the manifold achievements of her people in the nineteenth century.

Civilization is a collaboration as well as a rivalry; therefore it is good that each nation has its own culture, government, economy, dress, and songs. It has taken many diverse forms of organization and expression to make the European spirit so subtle and diverse, and to make the Europe of today an endless fascination and an inexhaustible heritage.

CHAPTER XXXIII

Around the Heartland

1789–1812

I. SWITZERLAND

THIS blessed land felt the tremors of the French upheaval with all the intimacy of a neighbor. Swiss liberals welcomed the Revolution as an invitation to Freedom—Johannes von Müller (1752–1809), the most famous current historian, pronounced July 14, 1789, the best day in the history of Europe since the fall of the Roman Empire. When the Jacobins took charge he wrote to a friend: "Doubtless you share my regret that in the National Assembly eloquence is more effective than good sense, and you may perhaps apprehend that owing to their wish to become too free they will not become free at all. Yet there will always be something to show, for these ideas are lodged in every heart."[1]

Frédéric-César de La Harpe, who had returned in 1796 to his native Switzerland after inoculating Czarevich Alexander with liberalism, joined with Peter Ochs and other Swiss rebels to form the Helvetic Club, which labored to overthrow the oligarchies that ruled the cantons. Napoleon, passing through after his first Italian campaign, noted these sparks, and advised the Directory that it would find many allies if it chose to act against the anti-revolutionary activities of French émigrés who were being harbored and helped by the Swiss aristocracy. The Directory saw the strategic value of Switzerland in the conflict between France and the German princes; it sent an army into the cantons, annexed Geneva, deposed the oligarchs, and, with the enthusiastic support of native revolutionaries, set up the Helvetic Republic under a French protectorate (1798).

The new government divided into Jacobin "Patriots," Moderates, and Federalists. They quarreled and plotted rival coups d'état until, fearing chaos and war, they asked Napoleon (then consul) to give them a new constitution. In 1801 he sent them the "Constitution of Malmaison," which, "in spite of its imperfections, was the best that the country could hope for at the time,"[2] though it kept Switzerland under French tutelage. After more internal quarreling the Federalists overthrew the republican government, organized a new army, and proposed to renew the oligarchy. Napoleon intervened, and sent an army of thirty thousand men to reestablish French control of Switzerland. The warring parties again asked Napoleon to mediate. He formulated an "Act of Mediation," which all major factions accepted. It ended the Helvetic Republic, and initiated the Swiss Confed-

659

eration essentially as it exists today, except for a continuing obligation to contribute an annual quota of men to the French Army. Despite this burden it was a good constitution,[3] and the cantons gave Napoleon the title of Restorer of Liberty.

Switzerland, however magnificent its scenery, gave only a small theater and audience to genius, and several of her authors, artists, and scientists sought the range and stimulus of larger lands. Johann Füssli went to England to paint; Augustin de Candolle (1778–1841) went to France and advanced the description and classification of plants. Johann Pestalozzi (1746–1827) remained, and caught European attention for his experiments in education. In 1805 he founded at Yverdun a boarding school that operated on the principle that, at least for the young, ideas have meaning only when connected with concrete objects, and that the education of children works best through group activities and recitations. The school drew visiting teachers from a dozen countries, and influenced primary education in Europe and the United States. Fichte made it an element in his plan for national rejuvenation.

Johannes von Müller spent twenty-two years (1786–1808) on his voluminous *Geschichten Schweitzerischer Eidgenossenschaft*, and, even so, brought this *History of the Swiss Confederation* only to 1489; but it remains a classic in both substance and style. Its excellence earned him the title of the Swiss Tacitus; its idealization of the medieval cantons shared with martial victories in building up the national pride; and its story of the legendary William Tell gave Schiller the outline of a famous play. In 1810, at the age of fifty-eight, Müller began a general history, *Vier und zwanzig Bücher allgemeiner Geschichten*. Drawn to Germany by his readers, he served the Catholic Elector of Mainz, moved to the Imperial Chancellery in Austria, and ended as the director of education in Jérôme Bonaparte's Westphalia. When he died Mme. de Staël wrote of him: "We cannot conceive how the head of one man could contain such a world of facts and dates. . . . It seems as if more than one man were taken from us."[4]

Only next to him in historiographic industry was one of Madame's *cavalieri serventi*, Jean-Charles-Léonard de Sismondi (1773–1842). Born in Geneva, he fled to England to escape revolutionary violence, then to Italy, then back to a recalmed Geneva. He met Germaine in 1803, accompanied her to Italy, and later frequented her salon at nearby Coppet. Meanwhile he wrote prodigiously, yet with conscientious scholarship. His sixteen-volume *Histoire des républiques italiennes au moyen âge* (1809–18) shared in inspiring Manzoni, Mazzini, Cavour, and other leaders of the Risorgimento. For twenty-three years he labored on his thirty-one-volume *Histoire des français* (1821–44), which for a time rivaled Michelet in acclaim.

He visited England again in 1818, and was moved by the mercilessness of its economy to write and publish (1819) a remarkably prophetic book, *Nouveaux Principes d'économie politique*. The basic cause of the English

depression, he argued, was the lag of public purchasing power behind production that was rapidly rising with invention; and this lag, he argued,
was due chiefly to underpayment of the workers. Similar crises of under-
consumption would recur as long as the economic system remained unchanged.

Sismondi's recommendations were alarmingly radical. The well-being of
the population should be the chief object of government. The laws against
labor unions should be repealed. The workers must be cushioned against
unemployment, and be protected against exploitation. The interests of the
nation or of humanity should not be sacrificed "to the simultaneous action
of all cupidities; . . . the rich must be protected against their own greed."
Despite this pre-Marxian Marxism, Sismondi rejected socialism (which was
then called communism); it would put both economic and political power
into the same hands, and would sacrifice individual liberty to an omnipotent
state.[5]

II. SWEDEN

Sweden could welcome the French Revolution, at least in its early stages,
for throughout the "Swedish Enlightenment" of the eighteenth century
Swedish thought had been in tune with the French, and the King himself,
Gustavus III (r. 1771–92), was a son of the French Illuminati and an admirer of Voltaire. But Gustavus made no obeisance to democracy; he considered a strong monarchy, then and there, the only alternative to rule by a
landed aristocracy jealous of its traditional privileges. He looked upon the
French States-General (May, 1789) as a kindred assemblage of estate owners, and in the developing conflict of this body with Louis XVI he felt a
basic threat to all kings. So the liberal and enlightened Gustavus offered himself as the leader of the First Coalition against the Revolution. While he
busied himself with plans for saving Louis XVI, some Swedish nobles plotted
his assassination. On March 16, 1792, he was shot; on March 26 he died, and
Sweden entered a period of political disorder that continued till 1810.

The reign of Gustavus IV (1792–1809) was unfortunate. He joined the
Third Coalition against France (1805), which gave Napoleon an excuse for
seizing Pomerania and Stralsund—Sweden's last possessions on the mainland. In 1808 a Russian army crossed the Gulf of Bothnia on the ice and
threatened Stockholm; Sweden was compelled to cede Finland as the
price of peace. The Riksdag deposed Gustavus IV, restored the power of
the aristocracy, and chose the King's uncle, then sixty-one, as a manageable
Charles XIII (r. 1809–18). As Charles was childless, an heir to the throne
had to be chosen. The Riksdag asked Napoleon to let one of his ablest marshals, Jean-Baptiste Bernadotte, accept election as crown prince. Napoleon
consented, probably in the hope that Bernadotte's wife—who had once been

Napoleon's fiancée, and was sister-in-law to Joseph Bonaparte—would be a pro-French influence in Sweden. So Bernadotte, in 1810, became Charles John, crown prince.

Within this frame of government the Swedish mind continued to keep pace with the march of education, science, literature, and art. The Universities of Uppsala, Åbo and Lund were among the best in Europe. Jöns Jakob Berzelius (1779–1848) was one of the founders of modern chemistry. By the careful examination of some two thousand compounds he arrived at a table of atomic weights far more accurate than Dalton's, and differing only minutely from the table internationally established in 1917.[6] He isolated many chemical elements for the first time. He revised Lavoisier's system of chemical nomenclature. He made classical studies in the chemical action of electricity, and developed the dualistic system which studied elements as electrically positive or negative in chemical combinations. The textbook which he published in 1808, and the *Jahresbericht* (*Annual Report*) which he began to issue in 1810, became the gospel of chemists for a generation.

There were so many poets that they divided into two rival schools: the "Phosphorists," who took their name from their magazine *Phosphorus*, and imported the more mystical elements of German Romanticism; and the "Gothics," who strummed their lyres to heroic themes.

Esaias Tegnér began his literary career as a Gothic, but as he developed he so enlarged his scope that he seemed to sum up all the schools of Swedish poetry. Born in 1782, he was only seven years old when the greatest phosphorist of all—the French Revolution—spread its light and heat through Europe; and he was still but thirty-three when Napoleon left for St. Helena. Tegnér lived another thirty-one years, but he had already achieved eminence when, in 1811, the Swedish Royal Academy awarded him a prize for his poem *Svea*, which scolded his contemporaries for their failure to maintain the customs of their ancestors. He joined the "Gothic Union," and ridiculed the Phosphorists as Romantic weaklings. At the age of thirty he became professor of Greek at the University of Lund; at forty-two he was made bishop of Växjö; and at forty-three (1825) he published the most celebrated poem in Swedish literature.

Frithjofs Saga is a series of legends taken from an old Norse cycle of lays. Some critics[7] thought the epic too rhetorical—the poet could not discard the episcopal manner; but the splendor of the lyrics carried the work to enthusiastic acceptance, even abroad; by 1888 there were twenty-one translations into English, nineteen into German.

Tegnér seems to have consumed himself in his poem; after it his health declined. He still wrote occasional poems, one dedicated to a married woman of Växjö. Originally a liberal, he passed over to a dogmatic conservatism, and engaged in warm controversies with the liberal minority in the Riksdag. A stroke in 1840 was followed by a mental disorder, during which he continued to write good poetry. He died in Växjö in 1846.

Meanwhile, King Charles XIII being chronically ill, Crown Prince Charles John acted as regent, and assumed the responsibilities of government. He soon faced a choice between loyalties—to his native or to his adopted land. Since states are as acquisitive as their component citizens, and send out prehensile pseudopodia, called armies, to seize delectable objects, the Swedish government looked fondly at contiguous Norway, over which, at that time, and since 1397, Denmark claimed proprietary rights. The Crown Prince suggested to Napoleon that French consent to the Swedish absorption of Norway would strengthen the friendship between Sweden and France; Napoleon refused, for Denmark was one of his most faithful allies. In January 1812 Napoleon again seized Swedish Pomerania, on the ground that it allowed the import of British goods in violation of his Continental Blockade. Prince Charles John turned to Russia, which was also ignoring the embargo; Russia approved of Sweden's absorption of Norway; Sweden confirmed the Russian absorption of Finland. In April 1812 Sweden signed an alliance with Russia, and opened its ports to British trade.

This was the situation in Sweden when Napoleon entertained kings at Dresden on his way to Moscow.

III. DENMARK

The news that the Bastille had fallen did not unduly excite the Danes, who had already, in 1772, abolished serfdom and judicial torture, reformed the law, the courts and the police, cleansed the civil service of corruption and jobbery, proclaimed toleration for all religions, and encouraged literature and art. The Danes looked upon their royal family as a stake of stability in the conflicts of classes and the flux of politics; and when Louis XVI—who, like their own kings, had supported liberal measures—was attacked by the Parisian populace, and was sentenced to death by the Revolutionary Assembly, the Danes agreed with their King that they wanted no such ecstasies. Napoleon was soon forgiven for calling a halt to the Revolution and restoring order in France. Denmark refused to join in the coalition against Bonaparte.

On the contrary, the Danish government challenged the claims of the British Admiralty to the right of its naval captains to board, and search for contraband, any vessel bound for France. On several occasions in 1799 and 1800 British captains had boarded Danish vessels, and one commander had captured, and had held in a British port, seven Danish merchantmen that had resisted him. In August, 1800, Czar Paul I invited the Kings of Prussia, Sweden, and Denmark to join him in a Second League of Armed Neutrality pledged to resist British search of neutral vessels.* On December 16–18, 1800, the four Baltic Powers signed a declaration of principles which they agreed to defend:

---

* The First League of Armed Neutrality, founded in 1780, had collapsed in 1793.

(1) that every neutral vessel may navigate freely from port to port on the coasts of nations at war; (2) goods belonging to the subjects of the belligerent Powers, with the exception of contraband, are free [from search when carried] on neutral vessels; . . . (5) the declaration of the officer commanding the vessel or vessels of the Royal or Imperial Marine . . . that his convoy has no contraband on board shall suffice to prevent any visit.[8]

Napoleon expressed his pleasure with this declaration. Paul I invited France to join Russia in an invasion of India, with a view to ending British power there.[9] England felt that the dispute had reached a critical point, for the combined navies of the neutral powers and France could put an end to British control of the seas; and that control seemed the only barrier to Napoleon's invasion of England. The British government concluded that either the Danish or the Russian fleet had to be captured or destroyed; the Danish preferably, for a prior attack on Russia would leave the British fleet in danger of attack from the rear.

On March 12, 1801, a British fleet under Sir Hyde Parker left Yarmouth with instructions to go to Copenhagen, to demand that Denmark withdraw from the League of Armed Neutrality, and, if rebuffed, to seize or destroy the Danish Navy. Vice-Admiral Horatio Nelson, aged forty-two, second in command, fretted over his subordination to Admiral Parker, who, aged sixty-two, had shown a disposition to caution alien to Nelson's temperament.

They reached the west coast of Jutland on March 17, sailed cautiously north and around the Skaggerak point of the peninsula, then south into the great bay of Kattegat to Sjaelland Island, then through the narrow strait between Swedish Hälsingborg and Danish Helsingör (Hamlet's Elsinore), where they were fired upon by the batteries of Kronborg Castle. The British fleet survived, and moved south into the "Sound" to the narrowest strait of all, where Copenhagen seemed unreachably sheltered by forts and the Danish Navy—seventeen vessels arranged in a line from north to south, each armed with from twenty to sixty-four guns.

Admiral Parker decided that his larger ships, of deeper draft than Nelson's, could not enter this shallow strait without danger of being grounded and destroyed. Nelson, having transferred himself and his flag from the *St. George* to the *Elephant*, led twenty-one lighter vessels into the strait, and stationed them directly opposite the Danish ships and forts. The battle (April 2, 1801) was fought at such close range that almost every shot carried destruction or death. The Danes fought with their usual bravery, the English with their usual discipline and trained accuracy of fire. Almost every vessel in the engagement was brought close to helplessness. Nelson's position seemed so critical that Admiral Parker waved him the famous "Signal No. 39" to disengage and retreat into the Sound. An English account says that Nelson looked at the signal by deliberately putting the telescope to his blind eye; in any case he later swore that he never saw the call to retreat. He continued to fight.

The "great gamble"[10] succeeded; the Danish vessels were one after another disabled or sunk. Nelson offered a cease-fire; it was accepted; and Nelson, undertaking (like Napoleon) diplomacy as well as war, went on shore to discuss terms of peace with the Danish Regent, Crown Prince Frederick. The Prince had received the news that Czar Paul I had been assassinated (March 23, 1801); the League of Armed Neutrality was falling apart. Frederick agreed to withdraw from it. The British government confirmed Nelson's arrangement, and he returned to another triumph. He rested on his honors until the nation called upon him (1805) to save, at Trafalgar, Britain's control of the seas.

Denmark survived, and England joined the rest of Europe in respecting her. During the next six years the little kingdom struggled to maintain its neutrality between the nations—Great Britain and Russia—that controlled the neighboring seas, and the French armies that patrolled the lands adjoining the precarious peninsula. Generally the Danes inclined to favor Napoleon, but they resented his repeated urging of a more decided partiality. After the Peace of Tilsit he sent the Danish government a message insisting upon its complete exclusion of British trade, and the cooperation of its new Navy with the French.

Now, as in 1801, the British government took challenge by the forelock, and sent a massive fleet, with 27,000 troops, into Danish waters (July 26, 1807), alleging the most pacific intentions. But George Canning, foreign minister, persuaded his government that Napoleon was planning to use the Danish Navy as part of a flotilla that would attempt a landing in Scotland or Ireland.[11] On July 28 Canning instructed the British representative in Denmark to inform the Danish Crown Prince that it was essential to the security of Great Britain that Denmark should ally itself with England and put its Navy at England's disposal. The Prince refused, and prepared to resist. British ships thereupon surrounded Sjaelland, and British troops closed the circle around Copenhagen; the city was subjected to bombardment from land and sea (September 2–5, 1807), with such "terrible effect" that on September 7 the Danes surrendered to England their entire fleet—eighteen ships of the line, ten frigates, and forty-two smaller vessels.[12] Denmark fought on, and thereafter, till 1813, aligned itself with France.

Between wars—and often inspired by them—the Danes made significant contributions to science, scholarship, literature, and art. Hans Christian Oersted (1777–1851) discovered that a pivoted magnetic needle will turn at right angles to an object carrying an electric current; the word *oersted* entered into all European and American languages to indicate a unit of strength in a magnetic field. Oersted founded the science of electromagnetism through thirty years of experiment.

Nikolai Grundtvig managed, in his eighty-nine years, to be a liberal theologian, a bishop, a philosopher, an historian, an innovating educator, a pathfinder in the study of Norse legends and Anglo-Saxon literature, and the author of an epic poem and songs and hymns still loved in Scandia.

Denmark in this dramatic age had a lively theater, whose comedies served as a gadfly to social pretenses; so Peter Andreas Heiberg (1758–1841) made fun of class distinctions in *De Vonner og de Vanner* (*The Vons and the Vans*), and earned so many enemies that he had to seek safety in Paris, where he served in the Ministry of Foreign Affairs under Talleyrand. He left to posterity a son, Johan Ludvig Heiberg (1791–1860), who dominated the Danish theater in the following age.

Danish literature now produced at least two poets whose interests and renown surmounted the barriers of nation and language. Jens Immanuel Baggesen (1764–1826) was doubly gifted with an attractive character and graceful style. Charmed by his early verse, the Duke of Augustenburg paid for the youth's visits to Germany and Switzerland. Jens met Wieland, Schiller, Herder, and Klopstock; he felt the Romantic longings of Rousseau, and rejoiced over the French Revolution. He immersed himself in the Kantian stream that was nourishing German philosophy; he added Kant's name to his own. He put his wanderings of body and mind into *Labyrinthen eller Digtervandringer* (*Labyrinths of a Wandering Poet*, 1792), which almost rivaled Laurence Sterne in humor and sentiment. Back in Denmark, he missed the excitement of Weimar and Paris. From 1800 to 1811 he lived in France, watching Napoleon transform liberty into order, and republic into empire. In 1807 he issued a lively poem, *Gjengengeren og han selv* (*The Ghost and Himself*), in which he examined with wit and penetration his wavering between the classical ideals of order, truth, and moderation and the Romantic exaltation of freedom, imagination, and desire. In 1811 he received a professorship in the University of Kiel. Two years later he fell into a wearing war with the greatest of Denmark's poets.

Adam Gottlob Oehlenschläger (1779–1850) had an unusually happy youth. His father was caretaker of a suburban palace; the boy had the garden for his playground, the hall for his art gallery, the library for his school. His imagination prodded him into becoming an actor, but his friend Hans Christian Oersted drew him into the University of Copenhagen. He lived through the British bombardment of fleet and capital in 1801, and felt the influence of the Norwegian philosopher Henrik Steffens. Finally he reached his own note in *Digte* (*Poems*, 1802), which established the Romantic movement in Danish literature.

He advanced his campaign with *Poetiske Skriften* (1803), a cycle of lyrics paralleling the life of Christ with annual changes in nature. The Established Church condemned this as heretical pantheism, but the Danish government awarded him a grant for travel in Germany, Italy, and France. He met Goethe, and perhaps from his example learned to check his Romantic subjectivity and sentiment. In *Nordiske Digte* (*Northern Poems*, 1807) he turned to Scandinavian mythology with an epic celebrating the journeys of the god Thor, and with a drama about Haakon Jarl, who ruled Norway from 970 to 995 and fought a losing battle against the spread of Christianity. When Oehlenschläger returned to Copenhagen (1809) he was received as Denmark's greatest poet.

He took advantage of his popularity to publish a succession of hastily written works. Jens Baggesen publicly condemned them as negligent and inferior productions. A controversy flared, in which Oehlenschläger took little part; his friends, however, fervently defended him, and challenged Baggesen to a duel in the form of a Latin disputation. Meanwhile Oehlenschläger published *Helge* and *Den lille Hyrdedreng;* Baggesen was so pleased with them that he welcomed the return of "the old Adam."[13] In 1829 Oehlenschläger was crowned with laurel in Lund by Esaias Tegnér. On November 4, 1849, his seventieth birthday, he was acclaimed by contemporary poets as "the Adam of our Parnassus."

In art Denmark offered Europe a sculptor who, at his zenith, had no living rival but Canova. Bertel Thorwaldsen (1770–1844) won a scholarship at the Copenhagen Academy, and settled in 1797 in a Rome that was still in artistic surrender to Winckelmann's gospel of Hellenic sculpture as art's ideal. He caught the attention of Canova, and followed him in making statues of pagan deities, and of contemporary celebrities in Greek or Roman pose and garb; so, in 1817, he modeled a nude bust of Byron as a grave Antinoüs. He succeeded Canova as leader of the neoclassic school in sculpture, and his fame spread so far that when he left Rome in 1819 for a stay in Copenhagen his progress through Vienna, Berlin, and Warsaw was almost a triumphal procession.[14] Now (1819) he made the model from which Lucas Ahorn hewed out of sandstone rocks the massive *Lion of Lucerne*, commemorating the heroism of the Swiss Guards who died defending Louis XVI in 1792. Copenhagen complained when he again left it for Rome, but in 1838 it proudly celebrated his return. By this time he had carved his way into a fortune, part of which he gave to endow a museum to display his works. Outstanding among these is the statue that he left of himself, not quite classical in its honest obesity. He died in 1844, and was buried in the garden of his museum.

IV. POLAND

Basically weakened by the proud individualism of her nobility, and by economic stagnation through persistent serfdom, Poland had been unable to resist the three partitions (1772, 1793, 1795–96) that had divided her among Russia, Prussia, and Austria. She ceased to be a state, but continued as a culture rich in literature and art, and as a people passionately resolved to be free. They were nearly all Slavs, except for a pocket of Germans in the west, and a minority of Jews in Warsaw and the east. The Poles were Roman Catholics, fervent and dogmatic because that religion had supported them in their grief, had inspired them in their hopes, and had preserved social order amid the ruin of their state. So they condemned heresy as treason, and their patriotism was intolerant. Only the best-educated and most comfortable among them could feel any brotherhood with the Jews who were rising in commerce and the professions—much less with those poorer Jews who, bearing the mark and miseries of the ghetto, could not believe that he in whose name they had been persecuted was the Messiah who had been promised them.

Christian and Jew alike marveled at Napoleon's humiliation of Austria and

Russia at Austerlitz, still more at his victories over the Prussians at Jena and Auerstedt; and now, 1806, he was sitting in Berlin, sending orders to half a continent. He had chastened Poland's despoilers; he was on his way to fight Russia; might he not, en route, declare Poland free, give her a king and a constitution, and the promise of his powerful protection? A delegation of leading Poles went to appeal to him; he sent them back with polite assurances that he would help them now as much as he could, but that the liberation of Poland would have to wait upon the results of his coming confrontation with Russia.

Kosciusko, the most persevering of the Polish patriots, cautioned his countrymen not to put their hopes in Napoleon. "He thinks only of himself. He hates every great nationality, and still more the spirit of independence. He is a tyrant, and his only aim is to satisfy his own ambition." When Napoleon sent to inquire what Kosciusko wanted, the Polish leader answered: A government like England's, freedom of the serfs, and a Poland ruling from Danzig to Hungary, from Riga to Odessa.[15]

Meanwhile the Poles had organized a small army, and had expelled the Prussians from Warsaw. When Napoleon entered the capital on December 19, 1806, the populace gave him a wild and joyous reception; Polish troops joined his army, eager to fight under him against Russia, as a Polish legion had already fought for him in Italy. Perhaps the Emperor appreciated still more the beauty and grace of the Polish women. Mme. Walewska, who at first gave herself to him as a patriotic sacrifice, fell deeply in love with him, and remained with him through the severe winter that nearly destroyed his army at Eylau. Then she returned to Warsaw, while he went on to defeat the Russians at Friedland.

At the Peace of Tilsit (July 9, 1807) he compelled Frederick William III to surrender Prussia's claims to central Poland. Article IV of the treaty recognized the new grand duchy of Warsaw as an independent state to be ruled by the King of Saxony. On July 22 Napoleon gave the duchy a constitution based on the French, establishing equality before the law, religious toleration, conscription, higher taxes, and censorship of the press. The Catholic Church was placed under the authority of the state, but the state accepted and protected the Catholic faith as the religion of the Polish people. The constitution gave full rights to the Jews, but required state authorization of their marriages and their acquisition of land.[16] Napoleon, foreseeing a war to the death with Alexander, tempered the Polish Constitution to ensure Polish support of France.

In this matter his calculation was largely justified. When Armageddon came, all classes in Poland supported Napoleon until, in 1814, he could no longer protect them. The Polish legions in his various armies fought for him to their last breath. When, returning from Russia in the greatest military disaster in history, many Poles were drowned in the collapse of a bridge over the Berezina, some of them cried, "*Vive l'Empereur!*" as they sank to their death.

V. TURKEY IN EUROPE

The days of Ottoman achievement in government, literature, and art were past, but the Turks in 1789 still held sway, however laxly, over Egypt, the Near East to the Euphrates, Asia Minor and Armenia, Greece, Bulgaria, Albania, Serbia, and those Danubian principalities Wallachia and Moldavia (now Romania) which were among the disputed morsels released to Alexander by Napoleon (who did not have them) at the Peace of Tilsit. The sultans, weakened by economic stagnation and moral decay, allowed the pashas to rule and bleed the provinces with very little interference from Constantinople; we have noted, with Byron, Ali Pasha's strong-arm rule in Albania (1788–1822). Ali overreached himself in plotting against the Porte; Sultan Mahmud II had him assassinated.

The Serbs fought for independence. When their popular Pasha was slain by Janissaries, a Serbian patriot, Karageorge, attempted (1804) to found a republic, with an elected assembly which would choose a senate; and in 1808 the senate elected Karageorge hereditary prince. Sultan Mahmud sent a substantial army to Belgrade to suppress the new republic (1813); Karageorge and thousands of his followers fled to Austria. A second revolt, under Prince Miloš Obrenovich, induced the Sultan to accept a compromise (1815) by which the Serbs were guaranteed freedom of religion, education, and trade. Miloš strengthened his rule by a mixture of politics and assassination, had his rival Karageorge executed, and obtained from the Sultan a recognition of his hereditary rule. By 1830 Serbia was in effect an independent state.

Greece had fallen to the Turks in 1452, and had now been so long under Ottoman rule that it had half forgotten its ancient pride. Conquest by "Franks" and immigration by Slavs mingled bloods, racial memories, and dialects until the popular "demotic" speech had substantially diverged from the Greek of Plato's days. Nevertheless scholars, poets, and patriots had preserved some remembrance of classic Greece, and of the eleven centuries (395–1452) during which Greeks had ruled the Byzantine Empire and had continued to enrich scholarship, philosophy, and art. News of the French Revolution ignited these memories, and made many Greeks wonder, with Byron's "Childe Harold," why Greece might not again be free. Rhigas Pheraios (1757?–98), a Wallachian born in Thessaly and living in Vienna, wrote and spread a Greek adaptation of "The Marseillaise," and organized a *hetairia*, or brotherhood, dedicated to bringing Greeks and Turks under a common bond of liberty and equality. He set out for Greece in 1797 with "twelve chestloads of proclamations,"[17] was captured at Trieste, and was executed at Belgrade. Another *hetairia* was formed at Odessa, spread into Greece, and shared in preparing the Greek mind for revolt. Adamantios Koraës (1748–1833), a Greek of Smyrna, settled in Paris in 1788, and devoted himself to "purifying" current Greek speech into closer harmony with ancient norms. He rejoiced over the French Revolution, and, in anonymous poems and tracts, as well as in his editions of the Greek classics, spread his republican and anticlerical ideas—though he warned that revolution might be premature. It came in 1821, and by 1830 Greece was free.

The Turkish government, so far as one can judge through the haze of time and space, of language and prejudice, was not clearly more oppressive than the governments of Europe before 1800. Byron was shocked (May 21, 1810) on seeing the severed heads of criminals exposed on either side of the gate to the Seraglio, but we may presume that the French Revolutionary government had guillotined more men and women than the sultans had ever in equal time beheaded. A majority of the wealth was in the hands of a small minority—as elsewhere. The Turks were a philosophical and poetical, as well as a warlike, people; they took the day's fate as Allah's will, not to be changed by grumbling, and they considered a beautiful woman, properly disciplined and perfumed, as more precious than anything but gold. They liked polygamy when they could afford it; why should not the ablest breed most? They had little need for prostitutes, but provided brothels for Christians. They were still producing good literature and art: poets abounded; the mosques sparkled; probably Istanbul was in 1800 the most beautiful city in Europe.

Politically the position of Turkey was perilous. Her economy and army were in disarray, while the material resources and military power of her enemies were growing. Her capital was the most strategic point on the map; all Christian Europe itched for that pearl. Catherine the Great had stretched Russia's grasp to the Black Sea, had taken the Crimea from the Tatars, and, with Voltaire's blessing, was dreaming of crowning her grandson Constantine in Constantinople.

Such was the situation when Selim III, at the age of twenty-seven, became sultan (1789). He had received a good education, had formed a close friendship with the French ambassador, and had sent an agent to France to report to him on West European policies, ideas, and ways. He decided that unless Turkish institutions were basically reformed his country could not hold off its enemies. He made peace with Catherine at Jassy (1792), recognizing Russian sovereignty over the Crimea and the rivers Dniester and Bug. Then he set himself to giving the Ottoman Empire a "New Organization" (Nizam-i-Jadid)—based on popular election of mayors and deputies. With the help of West European officers and experts he set up schools of navigation and engineering, and gradually formed a new army. His plans for a return engagement with Russia were aborted by Napoleon's conquest of Egypt and attack upon Turkish Acre. He joined England and Russia in war against France (1798). Peace was restored in 1802, but the war had been costly and unpopular; the local governors and venal officials rebelled against the new constitution; Selim allowed himself to be deposed (1807), but was assassinated nevertheless. After a year of chaos his party prevailed, and his nephew Mahmud II began, in 1808, a sultanate of thirty-one years.

The rival Powers of Christendom tried to control the policies of the Porte by money or force. Turkey survived as a state because none of them could afford to allow another to control the Bosporus. In 1806 Alexander I sent troops into Moldavia and Wallachia to appropriate these provinces for Russia; Napoleon's ambassador at the Porte urged Selim to resist; Turkey declared war against Russia. At Tilsit, in 1807, Napoleon undertook to arrange peace. The resulting truce was repeatedly violated until Alexander, reconciled to war against Napoleon, decided to withdraw his army from the southern front. On May 28, 1812, one day before Napoleon left Dresden to join his gathering forces in Poland, Russia signed with Turkey the Peace of Bucharest, abandoning all her claims to the Danubian principalities. Now Alexander could gather all his battalions to meet the 400,000 men—French and others—who were preparing to cross the Niemen into Russia.

CHAPTER XXXIV

Russia

1796–1812*

I. MILIEU

"FRANCE and Austria," wrote Talleyrand in 1816, ". . . would be the strongest powers in Europe if, during the last century, another power had not risen in the North, whose terrible and rapid progress must make one dread that the numerous encroachments by which she has already signaled herself are but the prelude of still further conquests, which will end in swallowing up everything."[1]

Space can make history. Run the eye across a map of the world from Kaliningrad (which Kant knew as Königsberg) on the Baltic to Kamchatka on the Pacific; then from the Arctic Ocean to the Caspian Sea, the Himalayas, Mongolia, China, Japan: all between is Russia. Let the map speak; or hear Mme. de Staël, driving from Vienna to St. Petersburg in 1812:

> There is so much space in Russia that everything is lost in it, even the châteaux, even the population. You might suppose you were traveling through a country from which the people had just taken their departure. . . . The Ukraine is a very fertile country, but by no means agreeable. . . . You see large plains of wheat which appear to be cultivated by invisible hands, the habitations and inhabitants are so rare.[2]

The inhabitants huddled in scattered villages because memory had not died of Tatars who had ravaged there, killing joyfully; they had gone, but their like might come again; and they had left some of their violence in Russian ways, tempered by toil and discipline. Natural selection had been merciless, and had favored those men who had hungered and labored tirelessly for land and women. Peter the Great had made some of them into soldiers or navigators; his successors had brought in venturesome Germans and clever Czechs to help people the plains. Catherine the Great had pushed swelling armies and swilling generals ever farther south, driving Tatars and Turks before them, conquering the Crimea, and triumphantly sailing the Black Sea. Under Alexander I the expansion continued; Russians settled in Alaska, set up a fort near San Francisco, and established a colony in California.[3]

The hard climate of European Russia—unprotected by forests or moun-

---

* All dates are N.S.

tains against arctic cold or tropical heat—made a tough people, ready to accomplish the impossible if given bread and time. They could be cruel, for life had been cruel to them; they could torture prisoners and massacre Jews. But these barbarities rose in part out of their own experiences and memories of insecurity and hostility; they were not irrevocably in their blood, for the increasing security of organized communal life made them gentler, pitying, wondering, like a million Karamazovs, why they killed or sinned. They looked with an abiding melancholy upon a violent and unintelligible world.

Religion appeased their wonder and tamed their violence. The priests played here—as Roman Catholic priests had done in the early stages of West European communities—the role of the "spiritual arm," buttressing the forces of the law with the secret and diverse powers of the myth to mystify or explain, to terrify or console. The czars knew how vital these myths were to social order, patient labor, and self-sacrificing heroism in war and peace. They paid the higher clergy well, and the lower clergy enough to keep them alive and patriotic. They protected religious dissent if it remained loyal to the state and kept the peace; Catherine II and Alexander I winked an eye at Freemasonry lodges that cautiously proposed political reforms.

The Russian nobles claimed and used all feudal rights, and controlled almost every element in the life of their serfs. The feudal lord could sell his serfs, or lease them to work in town factories. He could imprison them, and punish them with rod or whip or knout (a knotted rope). He could hand them over to the government for labor or imprisonment in Siberia.[4] There were some mitigations. The sale of a serf apart from his family was rare. Some nobles contributed to a serf's education, usually for technical work on the owner's property, sometimes for wider use; so we hear (c. 1800) of a serf who managed a textile enterprise employing five hundred looms—but most of these were in houses on the vast estates of the Sheremetev family. A census of Russia in 1783 reported a total population of 25,677,058; of the 12,838,529 males 6,678,239 were serfs of private landowners—i.e. (including one female for each male), over half the population. Russian serfdom reached its climax at this time; it worsened in the reign of the great Catherine, and Alexander I gave up his early attempts to lessen it.[5]

The same census reckoned Russia's population as 94.5 percent rural, but this included peasants working and living in the towns. The towns were growing slowly, having only 1,301,000 inhabitants in 1796.[6] Commerce was active and growing, especially along the coasts and the great canals; Odessa was already a busy center of maritime trade. Industry was growing more slowly in the town factories, for much of it was practiced in rural shops and homes. Class war was much less between a proletariat and its employers than between rising merchants, groaning over taxes, and the tax-free nobility.

Class differences were sharp, and were defined by law; nevertheless, they were blurred as the economy grew and education spread. Russian rulers before Peter the Great had usually frowned upon schools as opening avenues to West European radicalism and impiety; Peter, admiring the West, estab-

lished schools of navigation and engineering for sons of the nobility, "dio-
cesan schools" to prepare priests, and forty-two elementary schools opened
to all classes but serfs, and oriented toward technology. In 1795 P. A. Shuva-
lov founded the University of Moscow, with two *gymnasia*, one for nobles,
one for free commoners. Catherine, inspired by the French *philosophes*,
spread schools widely, and advocated the education of women. She allowed
private publishing firms; eighty-four percent of the books published in
eighteenth-century Russia were issued during her reign. By 1800 Russia had
already developed an intelligentsia that would soon be a factor in the nation's political history. And by 1800 several merchants, or sons of merchants, had made their way into positions of influence, and even into the
court.

Despite the fire-and-brimstone theology of the bishops and the *papa*s, or
local priests, the level of morals and manners was generally lower than in
Western Europe, except in a minority at the court. Almost any Russian was
at heart kind and hospitable, perhaps from seeing others as fellow sufferers
in a hard world; but barbarism simmered in the soul, remembering times
when one had to kill or be killed. Drunkenness was a common relief from
reality, even in the nobility, and the precarious life of authors brought several of them to alcoholic addiction and an early death.[7] Cunning, lying, and
petty theft were common in the plebs, for any trick seemed fair against cruel
masters, dishonest merchants, or inquisitive taxgatherers. Women were almost as tough as men, worked at least as hard, fought as fiercely, and, when
accident allowed them, governed as well; what czar, after Peter, ruled as
successfully as Catherine II? Adultery rose with income. Cleanliness was
exceptional, and was especially difficult in winter; on the other hand, few
peoples have been more addicted to hot baths and merciless massage. Venality ran its full course from serf to nobleman, from town clerk to imperial
minister. "In no other country," wrote a French ambassador in 1820, "is
corruption so general. It is, in a sense, organized, and there is, perhaps, not a
single government official who could not be bought at a price."[8]

Under Catherine the court reached a degree of ease and refinement second only to Versailles under Louis XV and Louis XVI, though in some
cases barbarism hid behind the bows. In Catherine's court the language was
French, and the ideas, barring ephemera, were those of the French aristocracy. French nobles like the Prince de Ligne were almost equally at home in
St. Petersburg and Paris. French literature circulated widely in the northern
capital; Italian opera was sung and applauded there as properly as in Venice
or Vienna; and Russian women of money and pedigree held their heads and
wigs as high, and pleased their men as variously, as the duchesses of the
Ancien Régime. Nothing in the social festivities along the Seine surpassed
the splendor of the gatherings that, in the sumptuous palace on the Neva,
saw the summer sun lingering in the evening sky as if loath to leave the
scene.[9]

II. PAUL I: 1796–1801

At the pinnacle of this courtly splendor was a madman. Paul (Pavel Petrovich) was son of Catherine II, but genius skipped a generation, and left Paul little but morose suspicions and the dementia of absolute power.

He was eight years old when he learned that his father, Czar Peter III, had been slain through the connivance of Aleksei Orlov, brother to Grigori Orlov, the current paramour of Paul's mother. Paul never quite recovered from this revelation. In the normal course of succession Paul should have inherited his father's throne; Catherine bypassed him and assumed full power. Paul's first wife, with his knowledge, plotted to dethrone Catherine and make Paul czar; Catherine discovered the plot, and forced Paul and his wife to confess. The Empress acknowledged him as heir to her authority, but he never felt sure that he too would not be snuffed out aforetime. His wife lived in constant fear, and died in giving birth to a dead child.

His second wife, Maria Feodorovna, bore him a son (1777), Alexander, whom Catherine for a time thought of naming her successor, bypassing Paul. She never developed the idea into action, but Paul surmised it, and it left him suspicious of his son. In 1783 Catherine gave Paul an estate at Gatchina, thirty miles from St. Petersburg; there Paul trained his own regiment, drilling it, after his father's example, in the goose-step style of Frederick the Great. Catherine, fearing that he was planning another attempt to replace her, sent spies to watch him. He set spies to watch the spies. He had hallucinations of meeting, at night, the ghost of his ancestor Peter I the Great. His mind was already near breaking point when, in 1796, after forty-two unhappy years, he came at last to the throne that he had long considered rightfully his own.

In a flurry of good feeling he issued some benevolent edicts. He liberated several victims of Catherine's senescent fears—Novikov and Radishchev, radical thinkers, and Kosciusko and others who had fought for Polish freedom. He was so horrified by conditions in the Moscow Hospital that he ordered its renovation and reorganization (1797), with the result that the New Moscow Hospital became one of the best in Europe.[10] He reformed and stabilized the currency. He lowered the tariffs that had been stifling foreign trade, and he opened new canals to internal commerce.

However, he sent a flurry of commands to his troops about polishing buttons, repairing uniforms, and powdering wigs; to his subjects prescribing their dress and forbidding, under severe penalties, garments or styles of dress, that had been introduced into Europe after the French Revolution.[11] In 1800 he prohibited the import of books published abroad, and discouraged the printing of new books in Russia. He checked the autocracy of the nobles, but transferred to private landowners 530,000 serfs who had previously enjoyed easier conditions as serfs of the state. He sanctioned the severe punishment of rebellious serfs—"as much as their owner will desire."[12] His troops, once devoted to him, resented his unrelenting surveillance and imperious discipline.

His foreign policy was incalculably versatile. He canceled the plans of Catherine to send forty thousand soldiers against Revolutionary France. He resented Napoleon's appropriation of Malta and Egypt, and allied Russia with Turkey and England against him; he persuaded the Sultan to allow Russian warships to pass through the Bosporus and the Dardanelles; his Navy took the Ionian Islands, and landed troops in the kingdom of Naples to help eject the French. But when Great Britain refused to surrender Malta to him as elected grandmaster of the Knights of Malta, Paul withdrew from the coalition against France, and fell in love with Napoleon. When Napoleon responded with gestures of goodwill Paul forbade all trade with England, and seized all British goods in Russian stores. He discussed with Napoleon a Franco-Russian expedition to expel England from India. His fits of anger multiplied as foreign affairs ignored his wishes, and as domestic compliance waned before the profusion of his demands. He punished severely the slightest offenses, banishing from Moscow nobles who had questioned his policies, and sending to Siberia army officers tardy in obedience. His son Alexander had often been the object of Paul's special wrath and insults.[13]

More and more nobles and officers joined in a conspiracy to unseat him. General Levin Bennigsen enlisted Count Nikita Panin, minister of foreign affairs, and won over to their plan Count Peter von Pahlen, who commanded the city soldiers and police. They sought and finally obtained Alexander's consent, on condition that no bodily harm should come to his father. They agreed to this, knowing that a *fait accompli* is a convincing argument. At two o'clock on the morning of March 24, 1801, Pahlen led the conspirators and a band of officers into the Mikhailovsky Palace, where they overcame all guards, surrounded the struggling Emperor, and choked him to death. A few hours later they notified Alexander that he was now czar of Russia.

III. THE EDUCATION OF AN EMPEROR

It is hard for minds immersed for years in the tale of the comet called Napoleon to realize that Alexander I (Aleksandr Pavlovich, 1777–1825) was as much beloved in Russia as Bonaparte in France; that, like his friend and enemy, he was brought up on the French Enlightenment, and tempered his autocracy with liberal ideas; that he achieved what the greatest *modern* general (for we must respect the Czar's namesake) had tried and failed to accomplish—led his army across the Continent from his own capital to his foe's, and overcame him; and that in the hour of triumph he behaved with moderation and modesty, and, amid so many generals and geniuses, proved to be the best gentleman of them all. Could this paragon have come from

Russia? Yes, but after a long immersion, by a Swiss, in the literature and philosophy of France.

His education deserved another Xenophon to make it into a second *Cyropaedeia* about the youth and training of a king. Many conflicting elements confused it. First his solicitous but absent and busy grandmother, the great Catherine herself, who had removed him from his mother, and transmitted to him, before she lost them, the principles of enlightened despotism, mingled with snatches from her then favorite authors—Voltaire, Rousseau, and Diderot. Probably at her suggestion he was taught from his early childhood to sleep, lightly covered, with the windows wide open, and on a mattress of morocco leather stuffed with hay.[14] He became almost immune to weather, and enjoyed "extraordinary health and vitality"; but he died at the age of forty-eight.

In 1784 Catherine brought in from Switzerland, as Alexander's principal tutor, Frédéric-César de La Harpe (1754–1838), an enthusiastic devotee of the *philosophes*, and later of the Revolution. Through nine years of dedicated service he initiated Alexander into the history and literature of France. The Prince learned to speak French perfectly, and almost to think like a Frenchman. (Napoleon spoke French imperfectly, and thought like a Renaissance Italian.) A nurse had already taught Alexander English; and now Mikhail Muraviov instructed him in the language and literature of ancient Greece. Count N. J. Saltykov transmitted to him the customs of imperial autocracy. There were special tutors in mathematics, physics, and geography. And Archpriest Somborsky conveyed to him the ethics of Christianity in the principle that each must "find in every human being his neighbor in order to fulfill the law of God."[15] Perhaps we should add, to this roster of Alexander's teachers, Luise Elisabeth of Baden-Durlach, who in 1793, at Catherine's request, married him, then sixteen, and—now named Elizaveta Alekseevna—presumably taught him the proper ways of a man with a woman.

It was an education fit to make a scholar and a gentleman, but hardly an "autocrat of all the Russias." When the progress of the French Revolution frightened Catherine out of Voltaire and Diderot she dismissed La Harpe (1794), who returned to Switzerland to lead the revolution there. Alexander found realities at court and at Gatchina confusingly unlike the disputes of philosophy and the ideals of Rousseau. Dismayed by the complexity of the problems that faced the government, and perhaps missing the optimism of La Harpe, and brooding over his grandmother's death, he wrote in 1796 to his close friend Count Kochubey:

> I am thoroughly disgusted with my situation. It is far too brilliant for my character, which fits much better with a life of peace and quiet. Court life is not for me. I feel miserable in the society of such people. . . . At the same time they occupy the highest offices in the empire. In one word, my dear friend, I am aware that I was not born for the high position which I now occupy, and even less for that which awaits me in the future, and I have sworn to myself to renounce it in one way or another. . . . The affairs of state are in complete disorder; graft and embezzlement are everywhere; all departments are badly

managed. . . . Notwithstanding all this, the Empire tends only toward expansion. Is it possible, therefore, for me to administer the state, even more to
reform it and to abolish the long existing evils? To my mind it is beyond the
power of a genius, not to speak of a man with ordinary capacities like myself.
  Taking all this into consideration, I have arrived at the aforesaid decision.
My plan consists in abdicating (I cannot say when), and in settling with my
wife on the shores of the Rhine to live the life of a private citizen, devote my
time to the company of my friends and to the study of nature.[16]

Fortune gave him five years in which to adjust himself to the demands of
his situation. He learned to appreciate the constructive elements in Russian
life: the idealism and devotion inspired by Christianity, the readiness for
mutual aid, the courage and hardihood that had been developed in the wars
with the Tatars and the Turks, the power and depth of the Slavic imagination, which was soon to create a literature profound and unique, and the
silent pride that rose from consciousness of Russian space and time. When,
on March 24, 1801, Alexander, poet and would-be recluse, was suddenly
challenged with opportunity, he found in his roots and dreams the understanding and character to summon his people to greatness, and to make Russia the arbiter of Europe.

IV. THE YOUNG CZAR: 1801–04

He did not at once dismiss Panin or Pahlen, who had arranged the death of
his father; he feared their power, and was not sure of his own innocence; he
needed Pahlen and his police to keep Moscow quiet, and Panin to deal with
England, whose fleet, after destroying the Danish Navy, was threatening to
do the same to the Russian. Britain was appeased; the Second League of
Armed Neutrality collapsed. Pahlen was dismissed in June, Panin resigned in
September, 1801.
  On the first day of his reign Alexander ordered the release of thousands
of political prisoners. He soon dismissed the men who had served Paul as
counselors, or as agents in his terroristic measures. On March 30 he brought
together "twelve high officials least mistrusted,"[17] and formed them into
a "Permanent Council" to advise him in legislation and administration. He
called to his side, some from banishment, the most liberal of the nobles:
Count Viktor Kochubey as minister of the interior, Nikolai Novosiltsov as
secretary of state, Count Pavel Stroganov as minister of public instruction,
and, as minister of foreign affairs, Prince Adam Jerzy Czartoryski, a Polish
patriot reconciled to Russian sovereignty. These and other departmental
heads, together, constituted a Committee of Ministers, serving as another
advisory council. As still another adviser Alexander recalled La Harpe from
Switzerland (November, 1801) to help him formulate and coordinate his
policies. Under this executive structure was a senate of nobles with legislative and judicial powers, whose ukases or decrees (corresponding to the
senatus consulta under Napoleon) had the force of law unless vetoed by the

czar. Provincial administration continued to be by appointees of the central government.

All this resembles the imperial constitution under Napoleon, except for the lack of a popularly elected lower chamber, and the continuance of a serfdom quite devoid of political rights. Alexander's advisers, in his first years of rule, were liberal and well-educated men, but (in Napoleon's phrase) they were "subject to the nature of things." In that context "rights" seemed to be fanciful abstractions in the face of necessities—for economic and political order, for production and distribution, defense and survival—in a nation ninety percent composed of strong, unlettered peasants who could not be expected to think beyond their village. Alexander was subject to a powerful nobility almost self-sustained by their organization and local rule of agriculture, the judiciary, the police, and rural industry. Serfdom was so deeply rooted in time and status that the Czar did not dare attack it for fear of disrupting social order and losing his throne. Alexander received complaints sent up from the peasants, and in "many cases he inflicted severe punishments on the guilty owners,"[18] but he could not build upon such cases a program of liberation. Sixty years would pass before Alexander II (two years before Lincoln's Emancipation Proclamation) succeeded in freeing the serfs of Russia. Napoleon, returning defeated from Russia in 1812, found no fault with his victorious foe in this matter. "Alexander," he told Caulaincourt, "is too liberal in his vision and too democratic for his Russians; ... that nation needs a strong hand. He would be more suited to the Parisians. ... Gallant to women, flattering with men ... His fine bearing and extreme courtesy are very pleasing."[19]*

Within the imposed limits Alexander made some progress. He managed to free 47,153 peasants. He ordered the laws to be reduced to system, consistency, and clarity. "Basing the people's welfare on the uniformity of our laws," said his explanatory rescript, "and believing that various measures may bring the land happy times, but that only the law may affirm them forever, I have endeavored, from the very first day of my reign, to investigate the conditions of this department of the state."[20] Accusation, trial, and punishment were to follow a definite and prescribed procedure. Political offenses were to be tried before ordinary courts, not before secret tribunals. New regulations abolished the secret police, forbade torture (Paul had forbidden it, but it had continued throughout his reign), allowed free Russians to move about and go abroad, and allowed foreigners to enter Russia more freely. Twelve thousand exiles were invited to return. Censorship of the press remained, but it was placed under the Ministry of Education, with a polite request that it be lenient with authors.[21] The embargo on the import of foreign books was ended, but foreign magazines remained under the ban.

* This view of Alexander, by one who knew him well and had little reason to love him, contrasts with the view of him, in some recent French histories, as insincere in his liberalism, and covering with handsome phrases a foreign policy of treachery and deceit. See Georges Lefebvre, *Napoleon*, I, 199–200; Louis Madelin, *The Consulate and the Empire*, I, 349–50. Our account accepts his early liberalism as sincere.

A statute of 1804 established academic freedom under university councils.

Alexander realized that no reform could prosper unless supported and understood by a wide proportion of the people. In 1802 he gave to the Ministry of Education, aided by Novosiltsov, Czartoryski, and Mikhail Muraviov, the task of organizing a new system of public education. A statute of January 26, 1803, divided Russia into six regions, and called for at least one university in each region, at least one secondary school in each guberniya, or province, at least one county school in each county seat, and at least one primary school for every two parishes. To the existing universities at Moscow, Vilna, and Dorpat were added universities at St. Petersburg, Kharkov, and Kazan. Meanwhile the nobles maintained tutors and private schools for their children, and orthodox rabbis bade Jewish parents boycott state schools as devious devices for undermining the Jewish faith.[22]

V. THE JEWS UNDER ALEXANDER

Catherine II had considerably improved the condition of the Jews within the "Pale of Settlement"—i.e., those regions of Russia in which Jews were allowed to settle. In 1800 this Pale included all Russian territory formerly belonging to Poland, and most of southern Russia, including Kiev, Chernigov, Ekaterinoslav, and the Crimea. Outside this Pale no Jew could qualify for permanent domicile. Within it the Jews, numbering some 900,000 in 1804,[23] were to enjoy all civil rights, including eligibility to office, with one exception: Jews desiring enrollment in the mercantile or business class in the cities were to pay a tax double that imposed upon other businessmen, who claimed that unhindered Jewish competition would ruin them;[24] so the merchants of Moscow (1790) had lodged a complaint against Jews who sold "foreign goods by lowering the correct prices, and thereby inflicting very serious damage upon the local trade."[25] Meanwhile their competition was resented by rural tavern keepers, and every effort was made by the government to keep them out of villages and confine them to the towns. In 1795 Catherine ordered that Jews should be registered (and acquire civil rights) only in towns.

In November, 1802, Alexander appointed a "Committee for the Amelioration of the Jews" to study their problems and submit recommendations. The committee invited the Kahals—the administrative councils through which the Jewish communities governed and taxed themselves—to send deputies to St. Petersburg to consult with the government about Jewish needs. The committee submitted its recommendation to these deputies. These, after much discussion, asked for a delay of six months, which would enable them to obtain more specific authority and instructions from their Kahals. The committee, instead, sent its recommendations directly to the Kahals. These objected to the committee's proposals to exclude Jews from the ownership of land and the sale of liquor, and asked that these measures be postponed for twenty years to allow time for difficult economic adjustments. The committee refused, and on December 9, 1804, the Russian government, with the sanction of Czar Alexander, issued the "Jewish Constitution" of 1804.

It was both a bill of rights and an edict of urban confinement. The rights were substantial. Jewish children were assured free access to all public schools, *Gymnasia*, and universities in the Russian Empire. The Jews might establish their own schools, but one of three languages—Russian, Polish, or German—must be taught there and be used in legal documents. Each community might elect its rabbis and Kahal; but the rabbi must never issue excommunications, and the Kahal was to be responsible for collecting all taxes levied by the state. Jews were invited to engage in agriculture by buying unoccupied land in specified regions of the Pale, or by settling on crown lands, where, for the first few years, they would be exempt from state taxes.

However, by January 1, 1808, "no one among the Jews in any village or hamlet shall be permitted to hold any leases on land, to keep taverns, saloons, or inns, . . . or to sell wine in the villages, or ever to live in them under any pretext whatever."[26] This meant the displacement of sixty thousand Jewish families from their village homes. Hundreds of petitions poured into St. Petersburg, asking for postponement of this mass evacuation, and many Christians joined in the appeal. Count Kochubey pointed out to Alexander that Napoleon was planning to convene in Paris, in February, 1807, a Sanhedrin of rabbis from all Western Europe to formulate measures for the full enfranchisement of the Jews. Alexander ordered the debated program to be postponed. His meetings with Napoleon at Tilsit (1807) and Erfurt (1808) may have revived his ambition to impress the West as a fully enlightened despot. In 1809 he informed his government that the evacuation plan was impracticable because "the Jews, on account of their destitute condition, have no means which would enable them, after leaving their present abodes, to settle and found a home in new surroundings, while the Government is equally unable to place them all in new domiciles."[27] When invasion of Russia by the French became imminent Alexander complimented himself on having kept his Jewish citizens fond of him, and loyal to the state.

VI. RUSSIAN ART

The Prince de Ligne, who knew everybody and everything of account in the Europe of his time, described St. Petersburg, about 1787, as "the finest city in the world."[28] In 1812 Mme. de Staël judged it to be "one of the finest cities in the world."[29] Peter I, jealous of Paris, began the adornment of his newborn capital; Catherine the Great consoled her discarded lovers with palaces more lasting than her love; and Alexander I continued the royal guard of classic columns sternly fronting the Neva. It was the neoclassic period in Europe, and Czar and Czarina, alike forgetting Russian forms and recalling Rome, sent to Italy and France for architects and sculptors to come and uphold Slavic pride with classic art.

The Winter Palace, begun in 1755 by Bartolomeo Rastrelli, and completed in 1817 by Giacomo Quarenghi and C. J. Rossi, was the most imposing royal house in Europe, dwarfing and outshining Versailles: fifteen miles of corridors, 2,500 rooms, countless columns of marble, a thousand famous paintings; on the lowest floors, two thousand servants, and, in one wing, hens, ducks, goats, and pigs,[30] in a consortium paved with straw.

Alexander I, especially after meeting Napoleon at Tilsit, found stimulus to rival him not only in the reach of his power but in the grandeur of his capital. He brought in French and Italian architects to support with their backgrounds and skills the zeal and energy of native builders. The Western artists remained attached to classic models, but they went beyond Rome and its ruins to southern Italy and such Greek survivals as the temples of Hera at Paestum (Paese, near Salerno); these were as old as the Parthenon, and almost as beautiful; and the masculine strength of their Doric columns gave fresh spirit to Russia's neoclassic ecstasy.

But the distinguishing feature of Alexander's "Empire style" was the gradual emergence of Russian architecture from Latin tutelage. Whereas the outstanding builders of Catherine II's reign (1762–96) were three Italians—Bartolomeo Rastrelli, Antonio Rinaldi, and Giacomo Quarenghi—the chief architects under Alexander I were Thomas de Thomon, Andrei Voronykhin, and Adrian Zakharov, three Russians under French influence,[31] and an Italian, Carlo Rossi, who came to the fore in the later part of Alexander's reign.

In 1801 Alexander commissioned Thomas to design and build a Stock Exchange to grace the activities of the rising class of merchants and financiers in St. Petersburg. The ambitious architect raised (1807 ff.) an immense fane inspired by the temples of Paestum, and matching the contemporary Bourse (1808–27) of Alexandre Brongniart in Paris. — Voronykhin's chefd'oeuvre is the Kazansky Sobor—the cathedral dedicated to Our Lady of Kazan, and built on the banks of the Neva in 1801–11; its fine semicircular colonnade and three-tiered dome frankly go back to the masterpieces of Bernini and Michelangelo, or, more immediately, Soufflot's Panthéon in Paris. — More highly rated is the Admiralty, a quarter-mile-long complex of columns, caryatids, frieze, and sharply pointed steeple, designed for the Russian Navy. — Rivaling this sanctuary are the Offices of the General Staff, raised in the Palace Square by Rossi shortly after Alexander's death.

At the behest of Nicholas I, Ricard de Montferrand crowned Russia's Alexandrian Age with a tall, monolithic column (perhaps remembering the Vendôme Column in Paris), as a lasting tribute to the Czar who had conquered France, but had never ceased to reverence its art.

Russian sculptors also sat at the feet of French artists who had knelt before Roman artists who had borrowed from conquered Greece. Before the West-oriented Catherine II, the influence of a Byzantine religion largely Oriental and fearful of the human body as an instrument of Satan had led the Russians to shun most sculpture in the round; and only slowly, with the lusty paganism of the Enlightenment entering with Catherine, had this taboo yielded in the eternal war and oscillation between religion and sex. Étienne-Maurice Falconet, lured from France by Catherine in 1766, carved and chiseled in Russia till 1778, and, in his epochal statue of Peter the Great, not only raised a horse and a man of bronze into the air, but struck a blow for the right of art to speak its message uncurbed by anything but its conception of beauty, reality, and power.

Meanwhile Nicolas-François Gillet had come in 1758 to teach sculpture in the Academy of Fine Arts which had been opened in St. Petersburg a year before. One of his pupils, F. F. Shchedrin, was sent to Paris to refine his chisel; he did so well that his *Venus* rivaled its French model, the *Baigneuse* of his master, Gabriel d'Allegrain. It was Shchedrin who carved the caryatids for the main portal of Zakharov's Admiralty. — The last among Gillet's famous pupils, Ivan Markos, worked for some time with Canova and Thorwaldsen in Rome, and added to their classic idealism something of the Romantic emotion that was replacing the neoclassic age; critics complained that he made the marble weep, and that his work was fit only for a cemetery.[32] The cemeteries of Leningrad still display his art.

Russian painting had undergone a basic transformation through French influence in the Academy of Fine Arts. Till 1750 the art had been almost entirely religious, mostly consisting of icons painted in distemper or fresco on wood. The French inclinations of Catherine II, and her importation of French and Italian artists and paintings, soon drew the Russians to emulation; they passed from wood to canvas, from fresco to oil, from religious to secular subjects—"histories," portraits, landscapes, and, last of all, genre.

Four painters reached excellence under Paul and Alexander. Vladimir Borovikovsky, perhaps taking a hint from Mme. Vigée-Lebrun (who painted in St. Petersburg in 1800), found attractive sitters among the young women of the court, with their gay or meditative eyes, their proud bosoms, and their flowing robes;[33] but also he caught the aging Catherine in a moment of simplicity and innocence hardly to be expected of a royal nymphomaniac; and he left, in a ruthless mood, a discouraging portrait of *An Unknown Woman with a Headdress*,[34] which is probably Mme. de Staël circling Europe to escape Napoleon.

Feodor Alekseev, sent to Venice to become a decorator, returned to become one of Russia's foremost landscape painters. In 1800 he made of Moscow a series of paintings and drawings that remain as our best guide to the appearance of that city before Rostopchin's patriotic arsons burned a third of it under Napoleon's nose.

Sylvester Shchedrin, son of the sculptor aforesaid, loved nature more than women as inspirations to his brush. Dispatched to Italy in 1818 to study art, he fell in love with the sun, the bays and shores and woods of Naples and Sorrento, and sent back landscapes that must have made St. Petersburg doubly cold.

Orest Adamovich Kiprensky (1782–1836) came closest to greatness among the Russian painters of his time. The illegitimate son of a woman serf, he was adopted by her husband, was freed, and found his way, helped by accidents, into the Academy of Fine Arts. One of his first and best portraits was of his adoptive father, painted in 1804, when the artist was only twenty-two; it seems incredible that one so young should have reached both the understanding and the mastery to see and convey in one portrait the strength of body and character that made Suvorov and Kutuzov, and that led the victorious Russians from Moscow to Paris in 1812–13. Entirely different is Kiprensky's portrait (1827) of the poet Pushkin—handsome, sensitive, questioning, with a dozen masterpieces in his head. Again unique is the full-length picture (1809) of the cavalry officer Evgraf Davidov—gorgeous uniform, proud mien, one hand on his sword as the supreme court. And in 1813, in a quite different world, the portrait of young Aleksandr Pavlovich Bakunin—no known relation to the Mikhail Aleksandrovich Bakunin who, a generation later, harried Karl Marx with different absolutes, and founded the Nihilist movement in Russia. Kiprensky himself was something of a rebel, sympathized with the "Decembrist" rising in 1825, was marked as a social rebel, and sought safety in Florence, where the Uffizi Gallery had asked him for a self-portrait. He died in Italy in 1836, leaving it to later generations of Russians to recognize him as the greatest Russian painter of his time.

VII. RUSSIAN LITERATURE

Russian literature had both blossomed and decayed under Catherine the Great. Seldom had a ruler shown so enthusiastic a surrender to a foreign culture, or made so visible a conquest of its living leaders, as in her love affair with the Enlightenment, and her adroit conscription of Voltaire, Diderot and Friedrich Melchior von Grimm as eloquent defenders of Russia in France and Germany. But then the Revolution came, all thrones trembled, and the gods of the Illumination were discarded as godfathers of the guillotine. The Russian court still spoke eighteenth-century French, but Russian writers proclaimed the beauty of the Russian language, and some, according to Mme. de Staël, "applied the epithets *deaf* and *dumb* to persons ignorant of the Russian tongue."[35] A mighty quarrel arose, and became a national duel, between the admirers of foreign models in literature and life and the upholders of native morals, manners, subjects, speech, and styles. This "Slavophil" spirit was an understandable and necessary self-assertion of the national mind and character; it opened the way for the flood of Russian literary genius in the nineteenth century. It derived considerable stimulus from the wars of Alexander and Napoleon.

Alexander himself symbolized the conflict through his own spirit and history. He was highly sensitive to beauty in nature and art, in woman and himself. He recognized in art the double miracle of duration given to passing loveliness or character, and of illuminating significance elicited from indiscriminate reality. The influence of La Harpe and a Francophile court made

the grandson of German Catherine a gentleman rivaling any Gaul in manners and education. He naturally supported the efforts of Karamzin and
others to import French graces and subtleties into Russian speech and ways.
His friendship with Napoleon (1807–10) supported this Westward inclination; his conflict with Napoleon (1811–15) touched his Russian roots, and
turned him to sympathy with Aleksandr Shiskov and the Slavophils. In each
of these moods the Czar encouraged authors by pensions, sinecures, decorations, or gifts. He ordered governmental printing of important contributions
to literature, science, or history. He subsidized translations of Adam Smith,
Bentham, Beccaria, and Montesquieu. When he learned that Karamzin
wished to write a history of Russia but feared that he would starve in the
process, Alexander gave him an annuity of two thousand rubles, and ordered
the Treasury to finance the publication of his volumes.[36]

Nikolai Mikhailovich Karamzin (1766–1826) was the son of a Tatar landowner in the province of Simbirsk on the lower Volga. He received a good
education, learned German and French, and went well equipped for his
eighteen months of travel in Germany, Switzerland, France, and England.
Returning to Russia, he founded a monthly review, the *Moskovsky zhurnal*,
whose most attractive contents were his own *Letters of a Russian Traveler*.
His light and graceful style, describing not only objects seen but the feelings
aroused in him, revealed the influence of Rousseau and the Russian tendency
to sentiment. Karamzin went further on the Romantic line in his novel *Poor
Lisa* (1792): a peasant girl, seduced and deserted, commits suicide. Though
the tale made no pretense to be more than fiction, the spot where Lisa
drowned herself became a pond of pilgrimage for Russian youths.[37]

Karamzin made his mark in almost every literary field. His poems, un-
abashedly Romantic, found a large audience. As a critic he shocked the
Slavophils by importing French or English terms to replace what seemed,
to his traveled ear, clumsy, inaccurate, or cacophonous in Russian terms or
phrases. Shishkov denounced him as a traitor to his country. Karamzin stood
his ground, and won: he purified and expanded the Russian language, reconciled it with music, and transmitted a cleansed and sharpened instrument to
Pushkin and Lermontov.

Karamzin prevailed for another reason: he practiced what he preached,
in twelve volumes constituting the first real *History of Russia*. Financial
help from the government enabled him to give almost all his waking time
to the task. He borrowed judiciously from early chroniclers, warmed their
cold facts with emotion, and graced the long story with a clear and flowing
style. When the first eight volumes appeared (1816–18), in an edition of
three thousand copies, they were sold out in twenty-five days. It could not
rival the histories of Voltaire, Hume, or Gibbon; it was frankly patriotic,
and saw absolute monarchy as the proper government of a people fighting
for its life against a merciless climate and barbarian invaders, and forced to
create law as it spread. But it proved to be a precious mine of material for
poets and novelists of the succeeding generations; here, for example, Pushkin found the story of Boris Godunov. It shared modestly with the repulse

of Napoleon from Moscow in raising the Russian spirit to play its brilliant and unique part in the literature and music of the nineteenth century.

Ivan Andreevich Krylov (1769–1844) was the Aesop, as Karamzin was the Herodotus, of this Alexandrian spring. Son of a poor army officer, he may have taken from military camps some of the racy speech and satirical verve that sharpened his comedies till they drew blood from the status quo. When it silenced him he withdrew from literature into more practical pursuits—tutor, secretary, professional card player, gambler . . . Then, in 1809, he issued a book of fables which set all literate Russia laughing at all mankind except the reader. Some of these stories, as fables often do, echoed earlier fabulists, notably La Fontaine. Most of them—through the mouths of lions, elephants, crows, and other philosophers—expounded popular wisdom in popular language cut into ambling iambic verses of any convenient length. Krylov had rediscovered the secret of the great fabulist—that the only intelligible wisdom is that of the peasant, and its art is to find the ego behind the sham. Krylov exposed the vices, stupidity, wiles, and venality of men, and reckoned satire to be as good a tutor as a month in jail. Since only an exceptional reader thought that the story was about himself, the public bought the little volume eagerly—forty thousand copies in ten years—in a land where the ability to read was a proud distinction. Krylov tapped the vein periodically by publishing nine more volumes of fables between 1809 and 1843. The government, grateful for the general conservatism of Krylov, gave him a supporting post in the public library. He held it, lazy and content, till, one day in his seventy-fifth year, he ate too many partridges and died.[38]

VIII. ALEXANDER AND NAPOLEON: 1805–12

They came to power almost at the same time, and both by violence: Napoleon on November 9, 1799, Alexander on March 24, 1801. Their nearness in time overcame their separation in space: like two opposed forces in a cell, they expanded in power till they tore Europe apart, first at Austerlitz with war, then at Tilsit with peace. They were rivals for Turkey, because each thought of mastering the Continent, with Constantinople as its key; each took turns in courting Poland because it was a strategic bridge between East and West; the war of 1812–13 was fought to decide which of the two was to master Europe and perhaps conquer India.

Alexander, a youth of twenty-four, facing in 1801 a bedlam of Powers old in chicanery, wavered in his foreign policy but repeatedly extended his rule. He alternated between war and peace with Turkey, annexed Georgia in 1801 and Alaska in 1803, allied Russia with Prussia in 1802, with Austria in 1804, with England in 1805. In 1804 his Minister for Foreign Affairs drew up for him a plan for partitioning the Ottoman Empire.[39] He admired Napoleon's work as consul, denounced him for the summary execution of the Duc d'Enghien, joined Austria and Prussia in a disastrous war against the usurper (1805–06), met and kissed him at Tilsit (1807), and agreed with him that half of Europe was enough for each of them until further notice.

Each left Tilsit confident that he had won a great diplomatic victory. Napoleon had persuaded the Czar to drop England and take France as his ally, and to enforce the Continental Blockade against British goods. Alexander, left defenseless by the shattering of his main army at Friedland, had saved his realm from a ruinous invasion by abandoning one ally for a stronger one, and securing a free hand with Sweden and Turkey. Napoleon's army and capital applauded his military and diplomatic triumphs. Alexander, on returning to St. Petersburg, found nearly everyone—family, court, nobility, clergy, merchants, and populace—shocked that he had signed a humiliating peace with an upstart bandit atheist. Some writers—like F. N. Glinka and Count Feodor Rostopchin (the future governor of Moscow)—published articles explaining that the Peace of Tilsit was only a truce, and promising that the war against Napoleon would be resumed at a suitable opportunity, and would be carried on to his final destruction.[40]

The business class joined in condemning the peace, since it meant, for them, Russia's enforcement of the Continental Blockade. The sale of Russian products to Britain, and the import of British goods into Russia, had been vital elements in their prosperity; the prohibition of such trade would ruin many of them, and would disrupt the national economy. And indeed the Russian government neared bankruptcy in 1810.

Alexander lost confidence, and hardened his rule. He restored censorship of speech and press, and abandoned his plans of reform. His liberal ministers —Kochubey, Czartoryski, Novosiltsov—resigned, and two of them left Russia. Then, in 1809, in a final attempt to free himself from the currents of conservatism that were rising around him, he took as his favorite adviser an almost reckless reformer who proposed that the Czar submit to a constitutional government.

Count Mikhail Mikhailovich Speransky had begun life in 1772 as the son of a village priest. He developed a fondness for science, and had risen to be professor of mathematics and physics in a St. Petersburg seminary when his work drew the attention of Czarevich Alexander. In 1802 he was assigned to the Ministry of the Interior, then under the reformer Kochubey. There he showed such capacity for hard work and intelligible reports that the Czar assigned him to direct the codification of Russian laws. When Alexander set out for his second meeting with Napoleon in 1808 he took Speranksy with him as "the only clear head in Russia."[41] An uncertain story relates that when Alexander asked him what he thought of the states then under Napoleon's control, Speranksy made the perceptive reply "We have better men, but they have better institutions."[42] Returning to St. Petersburg, the Czar gave his new favorite more and more power, until they found themselves contemplating a general reconstruction of the Russian government.

Speranksy wanted to end serfdom, but confessed that it could not be done in 1809. However, perhaps remembering a similar move by Stein in Prussia, he proposed a preparatory decree permitting all classes to buy land. The next step, he suggested, would be the election, by all property owners in each volost (township), of a local duma (council), which would control town finances, appoint local officials, and elect delegates—and submit recommendations—to a district duma; this would appoint district officials, propose district policies, and send delegates and recommendations to a provincial duma, which would send delegates and recommendations to a national duma in St. Petersburg. Only the czar would have the authority to determine laws, but the national duma would have the right to suggest laws for his consideration. Between the duma and the ruler an advisory council appointed by him would aid him in administration and legislation.

Alexander gave the plan a general approval, but he was hampered by other powers in the state. The nobility felt itself endangered; it distrusted Speranksy as a commoner, accused him of partiality for the Jews[43] and admiration for Napoleon, and insinuated to Alexander that his ambitious Minister was aiming to be the power behind the throne. The bureaucracy joined in the attack, largely because Speranksy had persuaded the Czar to issue a decree (August 6, 1809) requiring a university degree, or the passing of a strict examination, for eligibility to the higher administrative offices. Alexander was sufficiently influenced to allow that the international situation did not allow of substantial experiments in the government.

His relations with France had been soured by Napoleon's marriage with an Austrian Archduchess, and his seizure (January 22, 1811) of the duchy of Oldenburg, whose Duke was father-in-law to the Czar's sister. Napoleon explained that the Duke had refused to close his ports to British goods, and that compensation had been offered him.[44] Alexander did not like Napoleon's establishment of a grand duchy of Warsaw so close to formerly Polish territory appropriated by Russia; he feared that at any time Napoleon would revive a kingdom of Poland hostile to Russia. He decided that to secure the unity of his country behind him he must make concessions to the nobility and the merchants.

He knew that British goods—or goods from British colonies—were being admitted into Russia under papers forged by Russian traders or officials, certifying that the material was American and therefore admissible; Alexander allowed it; and part of it passed through Russia into Prussia and other countries.[45] Napoleon, through the Russian minister in Paris, sent an angry protest to the Czar. Alexander, by a decree of December 31, 1810, sanctioned the entry of British colonial goods, lowered the tariff on them, and raised the tariff on goods from France. In February, 1811, Napoleon sent him a plaintive letter: "Your Majesty no longer has any friendship for me; in the eyes of England and Europe our alliance no longer exists."[46] Alexander made no answer, but mobilized 240,000 troops at various points on his western front.[47] According to Caulaincourt he had, as early as May, 1811, resigned himself to war: "It is possible, and even probable, that Napoleon will defeat us, but that will not bring him peace. . . . We have vast spaces into which to retreat. . . . We shall leave it to our climate, to our winter, to wage our war. . . . I shall withdraw to Kamchatka rather than cede any of my possessions."[48]

He agreed now with the English diplomats in St. Petersburg, and with Stein and other Prussian refugees at his court, who had long since been telling him that Napoleon's purpose was to subdue all Europe to his rule. To unify the nation Alexander abandoned the reforms, and proposals for reform, that were alienating from him the most influential families; even the common people, he felt, were not ready for them. On March 29, 1812, he dismissed Speranksy not only from office, but from the court, from St. Petersburg, and gave ear more and more to the conservative Count Aleksei Arakcheev. In April he signed a treaty with Sweden, agreeing to favor the Swedish claim to Norway. He sent secret orders to his representatives in the south to make peace with Turkey, even at the cost of surrendering all Russian claims to Moldavia and Wallachia; all Russian armies must be available for defense against Napoleon. Turkey signed peace on May 28.

Alexander knew that he was risking everything, but he had been turning more and more to religion as a support in these days of strain and decision. He prayed, and daily read the Bible. He found comfort and strength in feeling that his cause was just, and would receive divine aid. He saw Napoleon now as the principle and embodiment of evil, as a power-mad anarch marching insatiably from power to more power. Only he, Alexander, backed by a God-intoxicated people and a God-given immensity of space, could stop this ravaging devil, save the independence and ancient order of Europe, and bring the nations back from Voltaire to Christ.

On April 21, 1812, he left St. Petersburg, accompanied by the leaders of his government and escorted by the prayers of his people, and traveled south to Vilna, capital of Russian Lithuania. He arrived there on April 26; and there, with one of his armies, he waited for Napoleon.

BOOK V

FINALE

1811–15

CHAPTER XXXV

To Moscow

1811–12

I. THE CONTINENTAL BLOCKADE

THE direct cause of the Franco–Russian War of 1812 was Russia's refusal to continue its observance of the Continental Blockade declared by Napoleon's Berlin Decree of November 21, 1806. This decree was Napoleon's plan for closing all the ports and coasts of the European Continent against the entry of British goods. Its purpose was to force Great Britain to end the blockade which it had declared (May 16, 1806) of all French-controlled ports from Brest to the Elbe; to end British interference with France's maritime trade; to secure the restoration of French colonies captured by Great Britain; and to end the British financing of Continental states in their wars against France.

How was the Continental Blockade working? By 1810 it had brought England to a severe economic depression. In the first two years (1806–08) after Napoleon's Berlin Decree, Britain's exports fell from £40,800,000 to £35,200,000; imports of raw cotton fell by ninety-five percent. As one result the domestic price of corn rose from sixty-six to ninety-four shillings per quarter (one fourth of a hundredweight) in little more than one year (1807–08). Meanwhile slackened foreign trade depressed wages, spread unemployment, and set off violent strikes. Britain needed Swedish iron for her industry and Russian lumber for her ships; war with Sweden and Russia's alliance with France (1807) closed those sources. Britain struggled to counter such setbacks by protecting her remaining trade outlets; her exports to Portugal, Spain, and Turkey rose four hundred percent between 1805 and 1811; hence Napoleon's costly invasion of the Peninsula.

Matters worsened in Britain as the blockade continued; her exports to northern Europe declined twenty percent in 1810–11. Her adverse trade balance caused a rise in gold payments to Europe, and brought the international value of the pound to so low a point that Grenville and Grey, leaders of the Opposition, called for peace at any price.[1] In 1811, one year before Napoleon's war with Russia, his Continental Blockade reached its maximum effect in Great Britain.

Relatively to England the rival blockades substantially advantaged France. Her port cities—Le Havre, Nantes, Bordeaux, Marseilles—were in such decay that the last two began to call for a return of the Bourbons,[2] but internal commerce benefited from the exclusion of British competition, the influx of gold, the abundance of capital, and the subsidies provided by a businessman's government which enriched its Treasury with the gains of war. French business profited still more from these factors, and from improved access to Continental markets under Napoleon's control. Mechanical weaving quadrupled from 1806 to 1810, accelerating the Industrial Revolution in France. Full employment and political stability within the extended frontiers gave industry such stimulus that if France had won the Napoleonic Wars she might have caught up with England in production and world trade.

The blockade was favorable to industry and domestic trade, injurious to foreign commerce, in the "Continental System" of states subject to Napoleon. The Hanseatic cities—Amsterdam, Hamburg, Bremen, Lübeck—naturally suffered from the double blockade; but Switzerland, northern Italy, and the Rhineland communities prospered from the unhindered extension of Napoleonic institutions. Farther east, where industry was less developed, the blockade, preventing the sale of the region's produce to Britain, was a burden that generated rising discontent. This, of course, was especially so in Russia.

The basic weakness of the Continental Blockade was that it ran counter to the human demand for freedom to explore every avenue of gain. The ports and coastal towns of Europe abounded in men who were willing to risk their lives in smuggling into the Continent British goods made doubly attractive by prohibition. Conversely Continental manufacturers who had enjoyed foreign outlets complained that they had to sacrifice British markets. In Holland the resentment of the great merchant families so moved King Louis Bonaparte that he wrote to Czar Alexander a letter "surpassing in bitterness against Napoleon the most merciless pamphlets."[3]

Against the rising opposition Napoleon used 200,000 customs houses, thousands of agents recognizable or disguised, and countless troops to detect violations of the blockade, to arrest and punish and confiscate. In 1812 the court of customs in Hamburg pronounced in eighteen days 127 sentences, some to death; these, however, were rarely, if ever, carried out. Confiscated goods were sold for the French Treasury, some were burned in public bonfires that alienated nearly all onlookers.

Partly to moderate hostility, to raise income, or to ease shortages, Napoleon, as long ago related, began in 1809 to sell licenses, usually for a thousand francs, to import British goods judged necessary to French industry or morale, or to export to Britain goods paid for in coffee, sugar, or gold. Britain had already issued similar licenses—44,346 of them between 1807 and 1812—to override British embargoes.[4] By comparison Napoleon issued only 494 licenses by November 25, 1811;[5] but Alexander pointed out that while Napoleon demanded strict exclusion of British goods from Russia, he connived at their admission into France.

All in all, the Continental Blockade, despite its widespread unpopularity and the difficulties and blunders in its enforcement, seemed, in 1810, to be succeeding. England was on the verge of bankruptcy, even of a revolution demanding peace; the states allied with France were grumbling but submissive; and France, despite the human and financial drain of the Peninsular War, was prospering as perhaps never before. The Frenchman had little freedom, but he had francs, and his aliquot portion of the glory of victorious France and its incomparable Emperor.

II. FRANCE IN DEPRESSION: 1811

Then suddenly, as if some evil force was coordinating catastrophes, the whole many-faceted economy seemed to fall to pieces, and to founder in a whirlpool of bank failures, market disruptions, factory closings, unemployment, strikes, poverty, riots, and the threat of starvation—just as the miracle-working Emperor was planning to raise money and troops and morale for a life-and-death struggle with a Russia distant, unknown, and immense.

The causes of a recent depression are hard to specify; how shall we analyze the causes of that 1811 depression in France, which was apparently more severe than any that the oldest among us can remember? A learned historian[6] ascribes it to two main sources: (1) the failure of the French textile industry to secure needed raw material and capital; and (2) the failure of a banking firm in Lübeck. French spinning mills had relied upon the importation of raw cotton for their looms; the protectionist policy of the French government had placed a high tariff on such imports; the supply fell and its price rose; the French mills could not afford to pay this price for all the material needed to keep all their looms busy; they could not pay the rising rate of interest charged by French banks for capital loans; the mill owners felt forced to discharge more and more of their employees. The failure of the Lübeck bank, soon followed by similar bankruptcies in Hamburg and Amsterdam, affected Parisian firms; bank failures in France rose from seventeen in October, 1810, to forty-one in November, to sixty-one in January, 1811. The scarcity and high cost of bank loans forced one business firm after another to reduce its working staff, even to suspend operations; soon the streets of French cities were crowded with jobless workers seeking to sell their possessions, or begging for bread; some committed suicide.[7] Bands of unemployed, in the Nord department, raided farms and seized the grain; in the towns they attacked markets and warehouses; on roads and rivers they stopped and pillaged transports of food; the chaos of 1793 seemed to have returned.

Napoleon decreed severe punishments for crimes against public order, sent soldiers to check violent strikes, and organized free distributions of food. A decree of August 28 sent 500,000 hundredweights of wheat and 30,000 sacks of flour to critical centers of distress. Meanwhile he interrupted the Continental Blockade to allow the import of alien corn; he raised tariffs on foreign products competing with French industries; he arranged government loans to enable firms to resume employment and production. In May, 1812, following revolutionary precedents, he decreed a "maximum" price for wheat; it failed, for farmers kept their product from the market until

they received the price they demanded. Private charity helped the government to avoid a national upheaval. Count Rumford, American-British scientist then living in France, arranged "soupes de Rumfort," made chiefly of
beans and peas, which not only provided vegetable proteins but appeased the
cry for bread.

This economic crisis, coming amid preparations for his invasion of Russia, was a test of nerves for Napoleon, and it may have shared in weakening
his confidence and resolution. But his good fortune did not yet desert him.
The harvest of 1812 promised and proved to be abundant; bread became
cheaper; the unemployed could at least eat. Banks reopened or were replaced
by new ones; loans were made; capital, that unseen and indispensable producer, resumed its role in the factories; wages could be paid for work on
goods that might take half a year to reach a purchaser; the markets were
again supplied. Now Napoleon could dedicate himself to a war to enforce a
blockade that had already been doomed by the behavior of nations and the
nature of man.

III. PREFACE TO WAR: 1811–12

The imperial adversaries prepared for the combat with diplomatic moves,
military accumulations, and mass movements of men. Each tried to persuade
the other that he was a devotee of peace. Napoleon chose as his ambassador
Armand de Caulaincourt, a man of more than merely genealogical nobility.
Arrived in St. Petersburg (November, 1807), Caulaincourt was impressed
by the development of Alexander from the diffident young ruler whom he
had seen there in 1801; the Czar had become a paragon of good looks, graceful manners, and friendly speech. Alexander professed himself a lover of
Napoleon, still dedicated to the agreements made at Tilsit—given some slight
adjustments which the brilliant Emperor of the French would find reasonable.

Poland divided them. Napoleon had established the grand duchy of Warsaw (1807) under a French protectorate; Alexander countered by wooing
Polish nobles with an offer to restore all pre-partition Poland as a kingdom
internally autonomous but recognizing the czar of Russia as its king and
master of its external relations. Letters containing this offer fell into Napoleon's hands, and infuriated him.[8] He recalled Caulaincourt (February,
1811), and replaced him, as French ambassador to Russia, with Jacques Law,
the future Marquis de Lauriston.

In this month Alexander urged Austria to join him in an attack upon
Napoleon's forces in Poland, offering her, as incidental profit, half of Moldavia and all of Wallachia;[9] Austria refused. Napoleon at St. Helena shed
some light on his Polish policy: "I would never have waged war with Russia
simply to serve the interests of the Polish nobility"; and as for freeing the
serfs, "I could never forget that when I spoke to the Polish serfs about
liberty, they answered, 'Certainly we should like to have it very much; but

who will feed, clothe, and house us?' "[10]—i.e., they would have floundered helplessly in any sudden change.

Caulaincourt, loaded with gifts from the Czar, reached Paris on June 5, 1811. He tried at great length to convince Napoleon of Alexander's pacific intentions, and warned him that a French invasion of Russia would be doomed to defeat by climate and space. Napoleon concluded that Caulaincourt, violating correct diplomatic procedure, had fallen in love with the Czar.[11] Abandoning hope of a peaceful solution, and suspecting Russian attempts at seducing Prussia and Austria,[12] Napoleon massed troops in or near Prussia, and frightened Frederick William III into signing an alliance with France (March 5, 1812); this committed Prussia to provide twenty thousand troops for the French invasion of Russia, and to feed the French army when it passed through Prussia; the cost of the food was to be subtracted from the indemnity still owed by Prussia to France.[13] On March 14 Austria entered into a similar forced alliance with France. In April Napoleon proposed to the Sultan an alliance by which Turkey would expand her conflict with Russia into a holy war, and cooperate with France in a simultaneous march upon Moscow; in case of success the Porte was to regain the Danubian principalities, and secure full control of the Crimea and the Black Sea. Remembering that Napoleon had fought the Turks in Egypt and Syria, and had, at Tilsit, offered Alexander a free hand against Turkey, the Sultan rejected the proposal, and signed peace with Russia (May 28, 1812). On April 5 Alexander signed a pact of mutual aid with Sweden; on April 18 he offered peace and alliance with Great Britain. On May 29 he declared all Russian ports open to ships of all nations. In effect this was to withdraw from the Continental Blockade, and to declare war upon France.

Along with this diplomatic duel went one of the most massive military preparations in history. Here Alexander's task was narrower and simpler than Napoleon's; he had only one country to mobilize in force and sentiment. The sentiment almost took care of itself: Mother Russia rose spontaneously against the hordes of barbarians that were being organized against her by a savage infidel. The patriotic fervor that had condemned the Peace of Tilsit was transformed into religious support of the Czar. Wherever he went simple men and women crowded around him, kissing his horse or his boots. So strengthened, he enlarged his armies, ordered them to prepare for war, and stationed 200,000 men along the Dvina and the Dnieper, the great rivers that divided Russian Russia from the Lithuanian and Polish provinces taken in the partitions.[14]

Napoleon's mobilization was more complex. He faced the initial difficulty that 300,000 French troops, and a dozen French generals, were tied down in Spain, and that even more might be needed to keep Wellington from marching through the Peninsula and over the Pyrenees into France. He had hoped to return to Spain and repeat his victories of 1809; now he had to choose between losing Spain, Portugal, and the blockade and losing the Russian alliance and the blockade. "I knew better than anyone that Spain was a gnawing cancer that had to be healed before we could enter upon such a terrible war, in which the first battle would be fought fifteen hundred miles from my frontier."[15]

He had begun his military preparations in 1810 by quietly strengthening the French garrison in Danzig, and adding, as imperceptibly as he could, to the French contingents policing Prussia. In January, 1811, he called to the colors the year's conscripts, and distributed them along the German coast from the Elbe to the Oder, to guard against a Russian flank attack by sea. In the spring he ordered the princes of the Rhineland Confederation to prepare their pledged quotas of troops for active service. In August he began a painstaking study of the Russian terrain, and fixed upon June as the best month for an invasion.[16] In December he prepared a network of spies to work in or around Russia.[17]

By February, 1812, both sides had completed their mobilization. The French conscription had revealed a sharp decline in the popularity of the army: of 300,000 men called to the colors 80,000 failed to appear, and thousands of these were hunted down as outlaws.[18] Many of the recruits deserted, or made unwilling soldiers, and proved dangerously unreliable in a crisis. In former campaigns the newcomers would have received proud example and avuncular encouragement from the veterans of the Imperial Guard; but now most members of that brotherhood of battle were dead, or in Spain, or too old to be heroes except in reminiscences. Nor had the recruits the inspiration of a united and enthusiastic nation behind them. Napoleon appealed to them, and to his subjects, to see the enterprise as a holy war of Western civilization against the swelling wave of Slavic barbarism;[19] but the skeptical French had heard such stories before, and in any case Russia was too far away to frighten them. He tried to arouse his generals, but almost to a man, out of his hearing, they were against the new war as an invitation to tragedy. Many of them had grown rich by his largesse, and wished he had let them enjoy it in peace.

Some of his aides were brave enough to voice their doubts to his face. Caulaincourt, though always loyal to him, and serving him till 1814 as his grand equerry, or master of the horse, warned him that war with Russia would be disastrous, and even dared to tell him that he had gone to all this trouble "to satisfy his fondest passion," war.[20] Fouché, supposedly banished from the imperial presence because of his incurable plotting, but recalled to keep him in sight or on leash, told Napoleon (if Fouché can ever be believed) that it was climatically impossible to defeat Russia, and that he was being misled by the dream of universal dominion.[21] Napoleon explained that his dream was only to found a United States of Europe, to give the Continent one modern legal code, one coinage, one system of weights and measures, one court of appeals—all under one three-cornered hat. And this immense, unprecedented army, which he had so toiled to assemble and equip —how could he send it home now, and walk through the rest of his life with his tail between his legs?

It was verily an immense army, 680,000 men, including 100,000 cavalry, not counting political officials, servants, and attendant women. Of the total, less than half were French; the rest were contingents requisitioned from Italy, Illyria, Austria, Germany, and Poland. There were half a hundred generals—Lefebvre, Davout, Oudinot, Ney, Murat, Victor, Augereau, Eugène de Beauharnais, and Prince Józef Antoni Poniatowski, nephew of Poland's last and knightly King. All these forces were gathered into separate armies, at various points en route to Russia, each general with specific instructions when and where to lead his host.

The task of equipping and provisioning such a multitude had probably required more genius, patience, and money than to assemble it. Indeed, both the early and later stages of the enterprise were vitally affected by logistic conditions; the campaign could not open until the soil had grown enough grass to feed the horses; its ruin was almost completed by the Russian capture of the provisions that the returning, famished French had expected to find at Smolensk. Napoleon tried to foresee everything but disaster. He arranged to have stores of matériel, mechanical parts and repairs, food, clothing, medicines, at Wesel, Cologne, Bonn, Coblenz, Mainz, and other points on the routes of his converging armies; and similar supplies were to follow, in hundreds of transport vehicles, the advance of the invaders in Russia. Napoleon knew where to buy and what to pay; he knew the wiles of contractors, and was ready to hand over to a firing squad a merchant who knowingly overcharged his armies, or sold them shoddy goods.

How did he pay for all these supplies, and for their transport and storage, and for the men who used them? He taxed, he levied loans, he borrowed from the Banque de France and private banks; he took millions from his private horde of 380 million francs in gold in the cellars of the Tuileries. He checked extravagance wherever he could; he scolded his divorced beloved Josephine for spending like an empress, and praised Empress Marie Louise for her economies.[22] All in all, he said later, "the Russian campaign . . . was the best, the most skillful, the most cleverly led, and the most methodical of all the campaigns that I have commanded."[23]

Was he fit to command it? Probably better than any of his contemporaries, but less fit than the enterprise required. At forty-three he was already too old for camp life and battle duties. We may presume that he was suffering from the ailments that were to hamper him at Borodino and Waterloo: stomach pains, frequency and difficulty of urination, and piles. Though still, in private, a man of kindness and justice, a good husband to Marie Louise and a fond father to their son, he had become, after eight years of imperial power, impatient, dictatorial, easily angered, and given to overestimating his mental and political power. There were many exceptions: he bore Caulaincourt's criticism with good humor, and forgave many costly mistakes in his brothers and generals. He had moments of realism about himself. "In the midst of his meditations," his secretary tells us, "I often heard Napoleon characterize his position with this expression: 'The bow is overstretched.' "[24] But he had been too seldom defeated to have reached perspective and self-limitation. "After all," he told Narbonne, "this long road [to Moscow] is the road to India."[25]

So, on May 9, 1812, he left St.-Cloud, bound at least for Moscow. Everything in his life had been a gamble, and this was the greatest of them all.

IV. THE ROAD TO MOSCOW: JUNE 26 – SEPTEMBER 14, 1812

Marie Louise had persuaded him to let her accompany him as far as Dresden, and to invite her parents to meet them there, so that she might be once more, however briefly, with her family. Napoleon agreed, and thought it wise to invite also Frederick William III of Prussia, and divers other royalties and notables. From Mainz eastward his passage through the Rhineland became a triumphant procession as the local rulers came out to receive their suzerain; they joined his cortege as he advanced into Saxony. A few miles west of Dresden they were met by King Frederick Augustus, who escorted them into his capital. They reached the city an hour before midnight on May 16. The streets they followed were crowded with people holding torches and crying welcome; salvos of artillery were fired, and church bells rang.[26]

On May 18 Metternich arrived with the Emperor and Empress of Austria*; Marie Louise embraced her father with visible emotion; her happiness was softened by her premonition that the year was heavy with misfortune. Soon thereafter came the King and Crown Prince of Prussia, probably uncomfortable amid the apparent *entente cordiale* between their country's historic enemies; however, Czar Alexander had secret assurance that both Prussia and Austria were praying for Napoleon's defeat.[27] King Frederick Augustus, as host, lightened their politics with opera, drama, hunting, fireworks, dances, and receptions at which the rulers of Germany paid homage to Napoleon, who, apparently modest, beamed for twelve days from the zenith of his curve.

On May 28 he set out to join one of his armies at Thorn on the Vistula. Orders had gone out to his generals to meet him on the banks of the River Niemen, which separated the grand duchy of Warsaw from Russia. He himself rode in a carriage equipped with a lamp, a table, writing materials, maps, and books. Each night on the march this equipment was transferred to a tent, where he composed, and issued to his secretaries, the orders to be transmitted to generals for the morrow's operations. His old secretary Méneval, his newer secretary, François Fain, and his valet Véry Constant accompanied him all the way to Moscow and return. He reached the Niemen on June 23, reconnoitered, and saw no sign of enemy presence on the other side. Three pontoon bridges were soon set up, and on June 24–26 some 200,000 of his men crossed to the town of Kovno (now Kaunas). Almost at the same time another French army of some 200,000 men crossed the same river farther downstream at Tilsit (now Sovetsk),[28] where Napoleon and Alexander, five years earlier, had sworn friendship till death.

---

* This was the third wife of Francis II, Maria Ludovica of Modena; Marie Louise was the daughter of his second wife, Maria Theresa of Naples, who died in 1807.

Alexander was now at Vilna, fifty-seven miles southeast of Kovno. Several armies were awaiting his command: on the north 150,000 men under Prince Mikhail Barclay de Tolly, of Scottish descent; on the south 60,000 under Prince Pyotr Bagration, a Georgian; on the east 40,000 under General Aleksandr Tormasov. They were no match for Napoleon's 400,000 troops; but, in an orderly retreat, they could consume, destroy, or cart away all usable provisions, and leave little for the invaders to pillage. Another Russian army, 60,000 strong, freed by the peace with Turkey, was marching up from the south under General Paul Chichagov; but they were several days away.

On June 24 Alexander was the guest of honor at a *bal champêtre* on the estate of Count Levin Bennigsen, who had fought Napoleon to a draw at Eylau in 1807. During the festivities a messenger brought to the Czar word that the French were crossing the Niemen into Russia. Alexander concealed the news till the fete was over. Returning to his headquarters, he issued orders to his local armies to unite if possible, but in any case to retreat into the interior. The French had come sooner than expected; the Russian forces could not unite, but they retreated in good order.

On June 26 the Czar sent to Napoleon an offer to reopen negotiations, but only on condition that the French should at once leave Russia. Putting little faith in his own proposal, he left Vilna with Barclay de Tolly's army for Vitebsk. There, at the persistent suggestion of his officers that he was not equipped to determine military strategy, he left for Moscow, and appealed to the citizens to sacrifice money and blood in support of their invaded fatherland. They responded with fervor, and he returned encouraged to St. Petersburg.

On June 27 Napoleon and his main army began the long trek—550 miles —from Kovno to Moscow. Even those first days in Russia were an ordeal: the days were hot, the nights were cold; a heavy rain drenched everything. Each soldier carried with him food for five days, but to spare or augment their supply, they pillaged the fields and cottages of the countryside, regardless of the Emperor's prohibition. The army reached Vilna on June 28, and plundered as much as they could before Napoleon arrived. He came expecting to be welcomed as a liberator; some Poles and Lithuanians greeted him so; but some faced him in grim silence, resenting robbery.[29] A deputation asked him to pledge the restoration of the Polish monarchy; he would not commit himself, fearing to alienate the Prussians and Austrians in government or in his army; he asked the petitioners to defer the matter until his victorious return from Moscow.

He had hoped to overtake and destroy one of the Czar's armies at Vilna, but Barclay and his men had escaped to Vitebsk, and Napoleon's forces were too weary to pursue him. Two weeks were spent in restoring their order and spirit. Successive disappointments were sharpening the Emperor's temper. He had sent his brother Jérôme, with a substantial army, to pursue Bagration in the south; Jérôme failed to catch his prey, returned to the main French army, was reproved by Napoleon for dilatory procedure and lax leadership, resigned his command, and withdrew to his court in Westphalia.[30]

On July 16 Napoleon led his reprovisioned army out of Vilna on a 250-mile march northeast to Vitebsk. He had planned to catch up there with Barclay de Tolly, but that clever Scot was already advanced on the road to Smolensk. Napoleon could not pursue him farther, for he had ordered reinforcements and supplies to reach him at Vitebsk, and they were delayed. Several of his generals advised him to camp there for the winter instead of trying to get to Moscow and back before the snows came. Napoleon answered that Vitebsk was not situated to allow successful fortification and defense; that the region was too sparsely cultivated to feed his army; that any delay before reaching Moscow, or a decisive battle, would give Russia time to form and equip more armies to harass the French en route or blockade them in Vitebsk; nothing but the capture of Russia's holy city and ancient capital would bring Alexander to terms.

After fifteen days at Vitebsk he led his army out on August 13 in the hope of catching Barclay at Smolensk. This was the populous center of a fertile region, favored, by its situation on the Dnieper, for commerce and industry, and so well fortified that Barclay and Bagration, having united their forces there, had decided to make a stand and at least halt Napoleon's advance.

The French arrived on August 16, exhausted by their long marches, and reduced by death and desertion to 160,000 men.[31] Nevertheless their attack was violent and effective; by the night of August 17, whether by Russian despair or French artillery, the city had been set on fire, much to Napoleon's aesthetic and martial delight. "Don't you think this a beautiful sight?" he asked his master of the horse. "Horrible, Sire," answered Caulaincourt. Napoleon: "Bah! Remember what a Roman emperor said: 'The corpse of an enemy always smells sweet.' "[32] On August 18 the Emperor sent to Maret, minister of foreign affairs, a report to lift the morale of Paris: "We have captured Smolensk without the loss of a man."[33] A later estimate, by an English historian, reckoned the French had lost 8–9,000 men, the Russians 6,000.[34] The French losses were irretrievable; the Russian armies retreated into friendly towns and a pool of conscriptible men.

On July 20 Czar Alexander, moved by the divisive views and tactics of the Russian generals, decided that his armed forces needed a united command. He appointed to that post Mikhail Ilarionovich Kutuzov (1745–1813), who had earned a reputation for authoritative and successful generalship through many campaigns. He was sixty-seven years old, lazy and sedentary, so fat that he had to be drawn about the camp or battlefield in a carriage; he had lost one eye in battle, and the other was ailing; he was slightly lecherous, and a bear with women; but he had learned the art of war in fifty years of action; and all Russia had clamored for his appointment. He disappointed nearly everyone, including Napoleon, by avoiding battle, and ordering further retreat.

Napoleon was tempted to abandon the chase, make Smolensk a fortress in the center of Russia, spend the winter there, and maintain an armed line of communication with Western Europe. But now he found himself in a completely unexpected situation: his army was so disordered by racial faction and the breakdown of discipline that he felt safer on the march, where the fear of an attack compelled cohesion. "This army," he told General Sébastiani, "cannot now stop; . . . motion alone keeps it together. One may go forward at the head of it, but neither halt nor go back."[35] So, shortly after midnight of August 25, only a week after its capture, he and his troops left Smolensk on the hot and dusty road to Viazma, Gzhatsk . . . and Moscow—three weeks away. Murat and his cavalry rode at their head, heartening morale by the gay recklessness with which he and his cavaliers fought back any attack from the rear guard of the retreating Russians. Napoleon later described him:

> He was only brave in the presence of the enemy; in that case the bravest man in the world. His impetuous courage carried him into the midst of danger. Then he was decked out in gold and feathers that rose above his head like a church tower. He escaped continually, as by a miracle, for he was easily recognized by his dress. He was a regular target for the enemy, and the Cossacks used to admire him on account of his astonishing bravery.[36]

On September 5, as they approached the town of Borodino (still seventy-five miles from Moscow), the French vanguard, reaching the top of a hill, saw in the plain ahead a sight that gladdened and saddened them: hundreds of Russians completing redoubts within which artillery could be concealed, and farther in the fields, near the confluence of the Rivers Kalacha and Moskva, thousands of soldiers; apparently Kutuzov had decided to make a stand.

All through September 6 the rival hosts prepared for battle. On that cold, wet night hardly anyone slept. At 2 A.M. Napoleon sent out a proclamation, to be read, in translation, to the various divisions of his army: "Soldiers! Behold the battle that you have so long desired. Now the victory depends upon you. It is indispensable. It will give us abundance, good winter quarters, and an early return to our fatherland."[37] That night, by order of Kutuzov, the priests who accompanied his army carried through his camp an icon of the "Black Virgin," which had been rescued from burning Smolensk; the soldiers knelt, made the sign of the cross, and responded with fervor to the priests' repeated prayer "*Gospodi pomilui*—Lord have mercy," and Kutuzov bent to kiss the icon.[38]

About that time a courier brought Napoleon a letter from Marie Louise, with a recent portrait of their one-year-old son. Also the news was brought to him that his army had suffered a critical defeat by Wellington at Salamanca. He spent much of the night issuing directions to his officers for the morrow's tactics. It must have been difficult for him to sleep, for his habitual dysuria pained him; his urine was alarmingly discolored, his legs were swollen with dropsy, his pulse was weak and frequently missed a beat.[39]

Despite these discomforts he exhausted three horses on the first day of battle, riding from one part of his army to the other.[40]

He had 130,000 tired men under him, Kutuzov 112,000; the French had 587 guns, the Russians 640. All through September 7 these thousands of men, fearing, hating, killing, dying, fought their like with heroism and tenacity equal on either side, as if feeling that the destiny of Europe depended upon them. Bagration gave his life in leading a Russian charge; Caulaincourt, in this war that he had sought to prevent, lost a beloved brother; Eugène, Davout, Murat faced death a hundred times; Ney on that field won from Napoleon the fond title of Prince of the Moskva. Victory passed with seeming indifference from one side to the other all that day. When night fell the Russians slowly gave ground; the French remained masters of the field, but Napoleon reckoned victory far from certain. Kutuzov sent to Alexander a proud report that allowed the cathedrals of St. Petersburg and Moscow to raise a Te Deum to their God. The French had lost 30,000 men killed or disabled, the Russians 50,000.[41]

At first, on September 8, Kutuzov thought of renewing the battle, but as the figures for his losses came in he felt that he could not subject the survivors to another day of such slaughter. He resumed his policy of retreat, and henceforth kept it to the end. On September 13 he ordered the evacuation of Moscow, and on the 14th he set out grimly toward new uncertainties.

On that day Napoleon and his 95,000 survivors[42] reached the gates of Moscow, after a march of eighty-three days from Kovno. A message from General Miloradovich, head of the Moscow garrison, asked for a cease-fire while he led out his men; it was granted. Napoleon waited for notables to present themselves and ask for his protection; none came. When he entered the city he observed that none of the inhabitants remained except "a few thousand people belonging to the lower classes."[43] Some harlots had stayed, hoping for francs, and soon willing to agree for food and shelter. Napoleon had brought a load of counterfeit Russian bank notes; the Russians refused to accept them; the notes had to be burned.[44] The victors searched the city, pillaged the palaces, sacked the estates in the hinterland; they loaded themselves with wine and heirlooms; the latter were destined to be shed, one after another, on the retreat.

On September 15 Napoleon moved into the Kremlin, and waited for Alexander to sue for peace. On that evening Moscow began to burn.

V. THE BURNING OF MOSCOW: SEPTEMBER 15–19, 1812

Napoleon marveled at the beauty of the deserted city. "Under every point of view," he told Las Cases, "it might bear comparison with any of the capitals of Europe; the greater number of them it surpassed."[45] It was Russia's largest city, its Holy City or spiritual capital, with 340 churches coloring the sky with their bulging domes. Most of these churches survived the fire, being built of stone. Dwellings were nearly all of wood; 11,000 of these were destroyed, including 6,000 built of "fireproof" materials.

Some fires were seen by the entering French, who ran to extinguish them, but new fires sprang up, and spread so rapidly that they turned the night of September 15 into day, and wakened by their light the valets who guarded Napoleon's sleep. They roused him; he ordered the army's fire brigade into action, then went back to bed. On the morning of the 16th, Murat and Eugène, fearing that a spark might ignite the powder magazines that the army had deposited in the Kremlin, begged Napoleon to leave the city. After much resistance he rode out with them to a suburban palace, followed by wagons bearing records and matériel. The fire subsided on September 18, after destroying two thirds of Moscow, and Napoleon returned to the Kremlin.

Who was responsible? The city authorities, before departing, had released the prisoners,[46] and these may have set the first fires in the course of their looting. Some French soldiers may have been similarly careless in their pillaging.[47] Many reports were brought to Napoleon on September 16 that torchbearers were scattering through Moscow, deliberately setting fires; he ordered that captured incendiaries be shot or hanged; these orders were carried out. One arsonist, a Russian military policeman, caught setting a fire in a turret of the Kremlin, alleged that he had acted under orders. He was interviewed by Napoleon, was taken down into the courtyard, and killed.[48] Several arrested Russians alleged that the departing governor of the city, Count Rostopchin, had given orders that the city be burned.[49]

On September 20 Napoleon wrote to Alexander:

> The proud and beautiful city of Moscow is no more. Rostopchin has had it burned. Four hundred incendiaries were arrested in the very act; they all declared that they set fire to the place by order of the Governor, the Director of the Police. They have been shot. Three houses out of every four have been burned down. . . . Such a deed is as useless as it is atrocious. Was it intended to deprive us of provisions? These were in cellars that the fire could not reach. Besides, what a trifling object for which to destroy the work of centuries, and one of the most lovely cities in the world! I cannot possibly believe that, with your principles, your feelings, and your ideas of what is right, you can have authorized excesses so unworthy of a just sovereign and a great nation.
>
> I made war on your Majesty without any hostile feelings. A single letter from you, before or after the last battle, would have stopped any advance, and I would willingly have surrendered the advantage of occupying Moscow. If your Majesty still retains some part of your old feelings for me, you will take this letter in good part. In any case you cannot but agree that I was right in reporting what is happening in Moscow.[50]

Alexander did not answer this letter, but he answered the Russian officer who had been assigned to announce to him the burning of Moscow. The Czar asked if the event had hurt the morale of Kutuzov's army. The officer answered that the only fear of the army was that the Czar would make peace with Napoleon. Alexander, we are told, replied, "Tell my brave men that when I have been reduced to one soldier I shall put myself at the head of my nobility and my peasants. And if it is fated that my dynasty must cease to reign, I shall let my beard grow to my breast, and shall go and eat potatoes in Siberia rather than sign the shame of my country and my good subjects."[51]

The people of Russia applauded his resolution, for the capture and burning of Moscow shocked them to the depths of their religious faith. They reverenced Moscow as the citadel of their creed; they looked upon Napoleon as an unscrupulous atheist, and believed that his imported savages had burned the holy city. They held Alexander guilty for having accepted friendship with such a man. At times they feared that this living devil would take St. Petersburg too, and slaughter millions of them. Some of the nobility, thinking that at any moment Napoleon might summon their serfs to freedom, favored a compromise to get him out of Russia; but the majority of Alexander's entourage urged him to resistance. The foreign group around him—Stein, Arndt, Mme. de Staël, and a dozen émigrés—daily pleaded with him; as the struggle proceeded he came to see himself as the leader not only of his country but of Europe, Christianity, civilization. He refused to answer any of the three messages sent to him from Moscow by Napoleon offering peace. As the Russian aristocracy saw week after week pass without any further action by Napoleon, they began to understand the wisdom of Kutuzov's deadly inaction, and adjusted themselves to a long war. Again the palaces of the capital gleamed with countesses in jeweled robes, and officers in proud uniforms, moving confidently in stately dances to music that had never felt the Revolution.

After the fire had been extinguished Napoleon ordered his men to care for the injured or destitute survivors, of whatever ethnic origin,[52] and made arrangements for the storage or orderly consumption of victuals left by the departing citizens. He answered the messages or inquiries brought to him by couriers from his subject lands; later he boasted that during his stay in Moscow not one of his couriers—and they averaged one a day—had been intercepted by the enemy on their route.[53] He reorganized and reequipped his army, and tried to keep it fit by frequent drills; but the spirit had gone out of such parades. He had concerts and plays presented by French musicians and actors who had been domiciled in Moscow,[54] and found time to draw up a detailed order for the reorganization and operation of the Comédie-Française in Paris.

A month passed, but no word came from Alexander. "I beat the Russians every time," Napoleon complained, "but that does not get me anywhere."[55] September cooled into October; soon the Russian winter would come. Finally, having lost hope of any answer from the Czar, or any challenge from Kutuzov, and realizing that every day made his situation worse, he surrendered to the bitter decision: to go back, emptyhanded, or with a few solacing trophies, to Smolensk, Vilna, Warsaw . . . Paris. What victory could ever wipe out the shame of this defeat?

VI. THE WAY BACK: OCTOBER 19 – NOVEMBER 28, 1812

One hope remained. Kutuzov had accumulated provisions at Kaluga, ninety miles southwest of Moscow. Napoleon thought of marching there, and forcing the wily general to battle for those stores; if the French won decisively the Russian nobles might compel Alexander to sue for peace. Moreover, Kaluga was on another road to Smolensk than that by which the invaders had come; it would spare the pain of passing through Borodino, where so many of their mates had died. The order went out: prepare to evacuate.

So, on October 19, Napoleon's army—50,000 soldiers, 50,000 noncombatants—began to file out from Moscow. Baggage carts contained provisions for twenty days; by that time they could reach Smolensk, where fresh supplies had been ordered for them.[56] Other wagons bore the sick or wounded, some heavy trophies, and Napoleon's diminishing supply of gold.

At Maloyaroslavets, twenty-five miles north of Kaluga, the French made contact with Kutuzov's army. A sharp action followed (October 24), which forced the Russians to withdraw behind their defenses in Kaluga. Napoleon decided that his army was not equipped for a long siege. Reluctantly he bade his men take the road via Borovsk and Mozhaisk to Borodino. Thence they retraced the route they had followed in the summertime of their hopes. Now, however, that devil of a Kutuzov brought up his army to march on a parallel route to theirs, keeping elusively out of sight, but sending up, now and then, cavalry detachments of wild Cossacks to harass the French flanks; and happy peasants took shots at stragglers who ventured too far from the sixty-mile line of march.[57]

Napoleon was well protected, but only from immediate danger. Couriers brought him, en route, news of active dissension threatening his government in Paris, and rising rebellions in his subject lands. On October 26, a week out of Moscow, he asked Caulaincourt should he, Napoleon, leave at once for Paris to face and control the discontent aroused by his defeat, and to raise a new army to defend the French forces left in Prussia and Austria. Caulaincourt advised him to go.[58] On November 6 word came that Claude-François de Malet, a general in the French Army, had overthrown the French government on October 22, and had won the support of prominent individuals, but had been deposed and shot (October 29). Napoleon resolved to go.

As the retreat progressed the weather worsened. Snow fell on October 29; soon it would form a permanent cover, beautiful and blinding, turning, in the cold of the night, to ice on which many dray horses slipped and fell. Some were too exhausted to rise again, and had to be abandoned; farther on the march such victims were eaten by starving troops. Most officers kept their mounts alive by care and covering. The Emperor rode part of the time in his carriage with Marshal Berthier, but two or three times a day, or more often, according to Méneval, he walked with the rest.[59]

On November 13 the army, now reduced to a total of fifty thousand men, began to enter Smolensk. They were furious on finding that most of the food and clothing which Napoleon had ordered had been lost through Cossack raids and local peculation; so a thousand oxen marked for the army had been sold to merchants, who had resold them to any buyer.[60] The warriors fought for the remaining supplies, and took by force whatever they could lay their hands on in the markets.

Napoleon had hoped to give his men a long rest at Smolensk, but word came that Kutuzov was approaching with 80,000 Russians who were no longer willing to retreat. Against them Napoleon could find only some 25,000 of his men who were fit to fight.[61] On November 14 he led part of his forces out on the road to Krasnoe, by a different route to Vilna than the one they had taken in the summer. Davout was to follow on the 15th, Ney on the 16th. The road was hilly and covered with ice; the horses, not properly shod for a Russian winter, slipped back on the hills; after several such defeats hundreds of them resisted all efforts to get them up, and accepted death as one of life's mercies; and many of the men took the same exit. "All along our way," one veteran recalled, "we were forced to step over the dead or dying."[62] In descending those icy hills no one dared to ride, or even to walk; all, including the Emperor, took them sitting down, as a few of them had done in crossing the Alps to Marengo twelve years before. These were days that counted for years in the aging of master and men. It was apparently at this point that Napoleon persuaded Dr. Yvan to give him a vial of poison to carry with him in case he should be captured or for some other reason might wish to end his life.

They reached Krasnoe on November 15, but could not rest; Kutuzov was approaching with an overwhelming force; Napoleon bade his men to march on to Orsha. Eugène led the way, fighting off desultory bands; the Emperor and Davout followed. They reached Orsha after three more days of marching on the ice; and there they waited anxiously for Ney to bring up the third part of the French forces.

Ney was the bright star of the army at this time, as he had been at Borodino. As commander of the rear guard he had led his seven thousand men through a dozen battles to protect the retreat from attacks by Kutuzov's raiders. He and his division entered Smolensk late on November 15, and were shocked to discover that so little food had been left there by the departed divisions under Napoleon and Davout. They managed to survive, and hurried on to Krasnoe. There they found not Napoleon as promised, but Kutuzov, blocking their way with murderous barrages of artillery. Under cover of the night (November 18–19) Ney guided his troops along a frozen stream to the River Dnieper, crossed it at some loss in men and horses, and fought his way through Cossacks and over frozen marshes to reach Orsha on November 20. There Napoleon and the waiting divisions welcomed the famished heroes with praise and food. Napoleon embraced Ney, called him "the bravest of the brave," and later said: "I have four hundred million in gold in the cellars of the Tuileries; I would gladly have given all of it to see Marshal Ney again."[63]

To distance Kutuzov's slower masses the French hurried on through four days' march to face their next hurdle, the River Berezina. When they reached it (November 25) they found that General Chichagov had come up from the south with 24,000 men, and that another Russian force, 34,000 strong, under Marshal Ludwig Wittgenstein, was hurrying down from the north to catch the French between two fires just when they were in such disorder that their leaders despaired of saving them from destruction.

Not all the news was bad. Napoleon soon learned that two friendly forces had come to help him. A division of Poles under General Jan Henryk Dombrowski, though outnumbered three to one, had challenged Chichagov and delayed the Russian advance; and on November 23 a French force of 8,000 men under Marshal Oudinot had surprised Chichagov, captured one of his battalions, and driven the remainder in flight across a bridge at Borisov to the right, or western, bank of the southward-flowing Berezina. The Russians, however, had destroyed the bridge, the only one that spanned the river in that locality.

News of these operations reached Napoleon as his weary host—now 25,000 soldiers and 24,000 noncombatants—neared the stream which, they hoped, would deter Kutuzov's further pursuit. He too had lost men, by desertion, illness, or death; only 27,000 remained of the 97,000 that had started with him from Kaluga; and now they were forty miles behind Napoleon's rear guard. There was still time to cross the river if it could be crossed.

Regaining hope, Napoleon sent a detachment under Marshal Victor to go north and stop Wittgenstein, and another under Ney to join Oudinot in preventing Chichagov from recrossing the river. Ever since crossing the Niemen, Napoleon had kept, as part of his staff, the engineers who had built the bridges there in June; now he asked them to find a spot on the Berezina over which they could raise two pontoon bridges. They found such a spot at Studenki, nine miles north of Borisov. They and their assistants worked through two days in the freezing waters. Ice floes battered them, and several of them were drowned; but by one o'clock on the afternoon of the 26th one bridge was ready, and the army began to pass over it; by four o'clock another bridge was carrying over artillery and other heavy loads. Napoleon and his generals waited till most of the soldiers had reached the west bank; then they crossed over, leaving a force under Victor to protect some 8,000 noncombatants who had still to cross. Before that final operation could succeed, the Russians concerted an attack along both sides of the river; they were repulsed by Victor, Oudinot, and Ney. Napoleon organized the crossing and the resistance as well as he could in the confusion of thousands of men struggling to survive. Twice a bridge broke down; hundreds were drowned; meanwhile Wittgenstein's artillery rained cannon shot upon the final thousands crowding to cross. On November 29, to delay pursuit of his men by the forces of Wittgenstein and the arriving Kutuzov, Napoleon ordered his sappers to destroy both bridges, leaving hundreds of noncombatants still pleading for a chance to cross. All in all, the escape across the Berezina was the most heroic episode in six months of costly fantasies and miscalculations by one of the greatest generals in history.

The tragedy continued as the survivors resumed their westward march. The temperature again fell below the freezing point, but this had one advantage—it allowed travel over frozen marshes, shortening the distance to Vilna. Fear of Cossacks and hostile peasants having subsided, deserters multiplied, and discipline disappeared.

Napoleon saw that he was now of little use to the remnant. He listened agreeably to Murat's advice to return to Paris lest France succumb again to revolution. At the next main stop, Molodechno, he received more details of the Malet affair. This usurper had been snuffed out, but the ease with which he had imposed upon officials indicated a lax government losing faith in a Napoleon so long absent, apparently demolished, perhaps dead. Jacobins and royalists, Fouché and Talleyrand, were plotting to depose him.

To reassert himself, and reassure the French people, he dispatched from Smorgonie, on December 5, Bulletin No. 29, which differed from its predecessors in almost telling the truth. The French, it said, had won every battle, had taken every city on their march, had ruled Moscow; however, the merciless Russian winter had ruined the great enterprise, and had inflicted pain and death upon civilized Frenchmen accustomed to a civilized climate. The bulletin admitted the loss of fifty thousand men, but it proudly told the story of Ney's escape from Kutuzov, and presented the crossing of the Berezina in its heroic rather than its tragic aspect. The message concluded, as if in warning to his enemies: "His Majesty's health has never been better."

Neverthless, he was worried to the core of his pride. He told Caulaincourt, "I can hold my grip on Europe only from the Tuileries."[64] Murat, Eugène, and Davout agreed with him. He transferred his authority over the marching army to King Murat, and told him to expect provisions and reinforcements at Vilna. Late on the evening of December 5 he left Smorgonie for Paris.

The caravan, reduced to 35,000 troops, departed on the next day for Vilna, forty-six miles away. Now the temperature fell to thirty degrees below zero Fahrenheit, and the wind, said a survivor, cut through flesh and bone.[65] Arrived at Vilna (December 8), the famished soldiers rushed in primitive chaos upon the supplies awaiting them, and much food was lost in the confusion. They resumed their march, and on December 13, at Kovno, they crossed, 30,000 in number, the same Niemen which had seen 400,000 of them, there and at Tilsit, cross in June. At Posen, Murat, worried in his turn about his throne, resigned his command to Eugène (January 16, 1813), and hurried across Europe to Naples. Eugène, now thirty years old, young but experienced, took charge of the remnant, and led it patiently, day after day, to the banks of the Elbe, where he awaited his adoptive father's command.

Napoleon rode from Smorgonie in the first of three carriages, each mounted on a sleigh and drawn by two horses. One of the vehicles carried friends and aides of the Emperor; another bore an escort of Polish lancers. Napoleon rode with Caulaincourt, who arranged relays of horses, and with General Wonsowicz, who acted as interpreter. To him Napoleon handed two pistols, saying, "In case of real danger kill me rather than let me be taken."[66] Fearing capture or assassination, he disguised himself by exchanging costumes with Caulaincourt. "Passing through Poland," Caulaincourt recalled, "it was always I who was the distinguished traveler, and the Emperor was simply my secretary."[67]

The ride to Paris was continuous, night and day. The longest stop was at Warsaw, where Napoleon surprised the French representative, the Abbé de Pradt, with a now proverbial remark: "From the sublime to the ridiculous is but a step."[68] He wished to make another visit—to the Countess Walewska; but Caulaincourt dissuaded him,[69] perhaps reminding him that his father-in-law was also an emperor. On the ride from Warsaw to Dresden, says Caulaincourt, Napoleon "praised the Empress Marie Louise constantly, telling of his home life with a feeling and simplicity that did one good to hear."

At Dresden Napoleon and Caulaincourt released their sleigh and their Polish escort, and transferred to the closed carriage of the French ambassador. They reached Paris late on December 18, after thirteen days of almost continuous travel. Napoleon went directly to the Tuileries, made himself known to the palace guards, and sent a message to announce him to his wife; just before midnight he "rushed to the Empress' bedroom and clasped her in his arms."[70] He dispatched a messenger to Josephine, assuring her that her son was safe; and warmed his heart with the sight of the curlyheaded infant whom he had named the King of Rome.

CHAPTER XXXVI

To Elba

1813–14

I. TO BERLIN

ALL Europe seemed to strain back to its eighteenth-century divisions as Napoleon rushed over its snows and through its cities to fortify his shaken throne; every old boundary became a crack in the baseless edifice of alien power. The Milanese, mourning sons who had been called to serve Napoleon in Russia and had never returned, prepared to unseat the amiable Eugène, absent viceroy of an absent king; the Romans, fond of the patient Pope who was still languishing in Fontainebleau captivity, prayed for his return to his Apostolic See; Neapolitan princes and populace watched for the moment when the ambitious Murat, slipping on his ego, would fall before a Bourbon anointed and legitimate. Austria, dismembered by war and humiliated by a harsh peace, waited anxiously for Metternich to free it, by some diplomatic finesse, from its forced alliance with its traditional enemy. The confederated states along the Rhine dreamed of a prosperity that would not have to be paid for by the surrender of their sons to an alien and uncontrollable genius. Prussia, shorn of half its territory and resources by its ancient enemy now its unwelcome ally, saw its despoiler shattered by a colossal calamity: here at last was the opportunity long prayed for; now it remembered Fichte's call, and heard the exiled Stein's appeal, to throw out those French troops that were patrolling them, those French indemnity-collectors that were bleeding them, and to stand free and strong as under Frederick, and become a bastion for German liberty.

Behind these kindred rebellions lay the surprising news that Russia had not only defeated the supposedly invincible Corsican, had not only expelled the French army from her soil, but was pursuing it over the frontier into the grand duchy of Warsaw, and was calling upon the heartland of Europe to join her in a holy war to overthrow the usurper who had made France the agent of his Continental tyranny.

On December 18, 1812—the day on which the beaten Napoleon reached Paris—Alexander left St. Petersburg. On the 23rd he reached Vilna, and shared with Kutuzov and his army in celebrating victory. That army too had suffered on the march that escorted and gnawed at the departing French; a hundred thousand men had died, fifty thousand had been wounded, fifty thousand had deserted or been lost.[1] Alexander publicly praised their general, but privately questioned his leadership. "All he did against the enemy," he told Sir Robert Wilson (if we may believe Sir Robert), "was what he could not help doing, being driven to it by the force of circumstances. He was victorious in spite of himself. . . . I will not leave the army anymore, because I do not want to abandon it to the dangers of such a command."[2] Nevertheless, he conferred upon the tired warrior the highest Russian military decoration—the Grand Cross of the Order of St. George.

Convinced, by the fulfillment of his predictions, that he was in some way divinely inspired, and that he might proceed with all the forces of Providence behind him, Alexander overruled the hesitations of his general, took on the supreme command of his united armies, and ordered them to march to the western frontier. Avoiding Kovno, which was opposite to still hostile Poland, he continued along the Niemen to Tauroggen, where General Johann Yorck von Wartenburg, commanding a force of Prussians, allowed the Russians to cross the river into East Prussia (December 30, 1812). Stein, who had accompanied Alexander from St. Petersburg, urged him to proceed in the expectation that the people of Prussia would welcome him. The Czar proclaimed amnesty to all Prussians who had fought against him, and called upon the King and the people of Prussia to join him in his crusade. Frederick William III, torn between the French Eagle and the Russian Bear, refused to approve of Yorck's action, and withdrew from Berlin to Breslau. Alexander advanced across East Prussia, and was greeted joyfully by the people with shouts of "Long live Alexander! Long live the Cossacks!"[3]

Approaching the boundary between East Prussia and Poland, the Emperor sent a message to the Polish leaders, promising amnesty, a constitution, and a kingdom with the czar of Russia as king. Apparently by a secret understanding between Russia and Austria, Prince Karl Philipp von Schwarzenberg, commanding Austrian troops in Warsaw, withdrew them to Galicia. The Polish authorities came out to welcome Alexander, and on February 7, 1813, he entered the capital unchallenged. The "grand duchy of Warsaw" came to this early death, and Poland in its entirety became a dependency of Russia. Prussia had hoped to recover that part of Poland which she had possessed in 1795; Alexander hastened to assure Frederick William III that an acceptable equivalent would soon be found for his lost share. Meanwhile he again urged the King and people of Prussia to join him against Napoleon.

The Prussians had long been waiting for such a call. They were a proud people, still remembering Frederick. The spirit of nationalism had been intensified by the quick expansion of France and the successful uprising of Spain. The middle classes were hot in protest against the Continental Blockade and the high taxes levied to pay the French indemnity. The Christians of Prussia were fond of their churches and jealous of their creeds, but all sects distrusted Napoleon as a secret atheist, and united in condemning his treatment of the Pope. The Tugenbund, or Union of Virtue, appealed to all Germans to come together in defense of their common *Vaterland*. The King of Prussia allowed his ministers to rebuild and expand the Prussian Army on the pretext of defending Prussia against Alexander's invasion. The Russians had taken Marienburg in January; on March 11 they marched unresisted into Berlin. Forced to a decision, the peace-loving king, from Breslau, issued "An mein Volk" (To My People), on March 17, a moving call to rise in arms against Napoleon:

> . . . Brandenburgers, Prussians, Silesians, Pomeranians, Lithuanians! You know what you have borne for the past seven years; you know the sad fate that awaits you if we do not bring this war to an honorable end. Think of the times gone by—of the great Elector, the great Frederick! Remember the blessings for which your forefathers fought under their leadership, and which they paid for with their blood—freedom of conscience, national honor, independence, commerce, industry, learning. Look at the great example of our powerful allies, the Russians; look at the Spaniards, the Portuguese. Witness the heroic Swiss, and the people of the Netherlands. . . .
>
> This is the final, the decisive struggle; upon it depends our independence, our prosperity, our existence. There are no other alternatives but an honorable peace or an heroic end. . . .
>
> We may confidently await the outcome. God and our own firm purpose will bring victory to our cause, and with it an assured and glorious peace, and the return of happier times.

All classes rose to the King's call. The clergy—especially the Protestant—proclaimed a holy war against the infidel. Teachers—Fichte and Schleiermacher among them—dismissed their students, saying that the time called not for study but for action. Hegel remained above "the battle," but Goethe gave his blessing to a regiment that saluted him in passing.[4] Poets—Schenkendorf, Uhland, Rückert—put into verse the sentiments of King and people, or put their pens aside for muskets or swords; and some of them, like Theodor Körner, died in action. Ernst Moritz Arndt, returning from exile in Russia, helped to rouse and form the German spirit with his song "Was ist das Deutschen Vaterland?" In that "War of Liberation" a new Germany was born.

However, no nation, when its existence is at stake, can rely upon volunteers. So, on the day of his appeal to his people, Frederick William III ordered the conscription of all men between seventeen and forty years of age, and allowed no substitutes. When the spring of 1813 began, Prussia had 60,000 men trained and ready for service. Of the several armies that had come in from Russia some 50,000 men were fit for action. With these 110,000 troops[5] Alexander and Frederick William entered upon the campaign that was to decide the fate of Napoleon and the structure of Europe.

They realized that this would not be enough, and they sought allies who could contribute men and funds. Austria for the time being chose to remain faithful to her alliance with France; she feared that she would be the first to be attacked if she joined the new coalition; and Francis II remembered that he had a daughter on the French throne. Prince Bernadotte had promised Alexander 30,000 men,[6] but he had committed most of them to the conquest of Norway. England, as April ended, pledged two million pounds sterling to the new campaign. Prussia opened her ports to British goods, and soon these were coming in good quantity to storehouses on the Elbe.

Kutuzov died in Silesia on April 28, still advising the Russians to go home.

Alexander summoned Barclay de Tolly to succeed Kutuzov in direct command of the Russian Army, but kept the supreme command himself. Now he set out to accomplish westward all that Napoleon had hoped to achieve eastward: to invade the enemy's country, defeat his armies, capture his capital, force him to abdicate, and compel him to peace.

II. TO PRAGUE

Meanwhile Napoleon was fighting for survival in a France no longer fascinated by his victories. Almost every family in the country was now to yield another son or brother. The middle classes had welcomed Napoleon as their protector, but now he was more monarchical than the Bourbons, and he was courting royalists, who were plotting to depose him. Priests distrusted him; generals were praying for peace. He himself was weary of war. Heavy in the paunch, plagued with ailments, conscious of age, slowing in mind, hesitant in will, he could no longer draw from the elixir of victory the zest for combat, or the appetite for government. How could this tired man find in this tired nation the human resources demanded by the mounting onrush of his enemies?

Pride gave him his last power. That faithless Czar, that comely dancer playing general; that frightened weakling tying the great Frederick's army to a Cossack horde; that turncoat French marshal proposing to lead a Swedish army against his native land—they would never match the gay courage and quick skill of a French soldier, the passionate strength of a nation challenged to defend those hard-won natural boundaries which guarded the finest civilization in Europe. "From now on," said Napoleon in December, 1812, in a desperate appeal to racial pride, "Europe has only one enemy—the Russian colossus."[7]

So he levied taxes, negotiated loans, and drew on his cellar hoard. He issued orders to put the conscript "class" of 1813 into active service, to prescript the class of 1814 for training, to prepare for foreign service the "cohorts" or militia that had been pledged to only domestic needs, to commission contracts for ammunition, clothing, weapons, horses, food. He arranged for teaching the new levies the arts and discipline of drill and march and battle; for stationing the trained battalions at specified encampments; for holding them ready to unite, at command, at a given place and time. By mid-April of 1813 he had organized an army of 225,000 men. He appointed Marie Louise regent, during his absence at the front; gave her his tried and tired secretary, Méneval; and left Paris on April 15 to meet his armies on the Main and the Elbe.

Eugène marched south with the remnants salvaged from the Russian debacle, reinforced with troops called from their stations in Germany. General Bertrand came up from the south. With these trusted men leading his left and right wings, Napoleon moved forward with his Army of the Main, and on May 2, at Lützen, near Leipzig, met an Allied army under the command of the Russian General Wittgenstein and under the eyes of Czar and King. The French now numbered 150,000, the Russians 58,000, the Prussians 45,000. Perhaps to encourage his recruits, the Emperor, savoring once more the thrills of combat, repeatedly risked himself at the front of the action; "this was probably the day in all his career," wrote Marshal Marmont, "on which he ran the worst direct dangers on the field of battle."[8] The Allies acknowledged defeat, and retired by Meissen and Dresden; but the victorious French had lost 20,000 men—8,000 more than their foes.[9] Napoleon was in part consoled by the decision of Frederick Augustus I, king of Saxony— worried neighbor of esurient Prussia—to add his army of 10,000 to the French. On May 9 his capital, Dresden, became Napoleon's headquarters between campaigns.

Fearing that Austria would join the Allies to try to recapture north Italy, Napoleon sent Eugène to Milan to rebuild his army there and keep an eye on Italian revolutionists. He himself left Dresden on May 18, hoping to achieve a more decisive victory against the Allies, who had regrouped at Bautzen, thirty miles east of Dresden. He dispatched Ney to march in a half circle around them and attack them in the rear, while he himself would lead his main army in a frontal assault. Ney took his time, and joined the battle too late to prevent the Allies, defeated by Napoleon, from retreating into Silesia after losing 15,000 men. Napoleon advanced to the Oder, freed the French garrison at Glogau, and added its men to his army. Roger de Damas, an *émigré*, wrote in anger: "The French Empire has met the crisis and emerged triumphant."[10]

At this moment, when he might have moved along the Oder, freed other garrisons, and added their trained men to his army, Napoleon listened to Metternich offering the mediation of Austria in arranging peace. Berthier for the Emperor's generals, Caulaincourt for his diplomats, urged him to accept, fearing a long war by a united coalition with endless resources against a divided and depleted France. Napoleon suspected a trick, but hoped that an armistice would give him time to gather another crop of conscripts, and reinforcements for his cavalry; and he feared that a refusal would lead Austria into the Allied camp. An armistice was arranged at Pleisswitz (June 4) for two months, later extended till August 10. Napoleon withdrew his forces to Dresden, issued directions for the replenishment of his battalions, and went to Mainz to spend some time with Marie Louise; perhaps she could persuade her father to maintain the alliance of which she was a pledge. Meanwhile Metternich enlarged and provisioned the Austrian Army, alleging fear of the Allies.

These made good use of the armistice. They welcomed Bernadotte, who now committed his army of 25,000 men to the cause. With him came Moreau, who, convicted of friendly association with the plotters of Napoleon's death, had been allowed to emigrate to America; now he offered his services to the Allies as one who knew the secrets of Napoleon's strategy. He stressed one rule: avoid battle when Napoleon is commanding, seek it when he is away. The Allies were more pleased with Lord Cathcart, who, on June 15, gave them a subsidy of four million pounds in return for a pledge to make no peace with Napoleon without England's consent.[11]

On June 27 the Allies, accepting Austria's mediation, agreed that all three parties should send negotiators to Prague to arrange terms of peace. Napoleon sent Narbonne and Caulaincourt, hoping that Alexander's fondness for the latter, watched by the former, would incline the Czar to accommodations. In any case the terms offered to Napoleon through Caulaincourt and Metternich were what he might have considered reasonable in view of his defeat in Russia and Poland and the revolt of Prussia. He was asked to surrender all territory that he had taken from Prussia, and all claim to the duchy of Warsaw, the Hanseatic city-states, Pomerania, Hanover, Illyria, and the Confederation of the Rhine. He could go back to France with her natural boundaries still preserved, and his throne and dynasty still unchallenged. There was a serious flaw in the proposal: England had reserved the right to make additional demands, and no peace could be signed without her consent.

Napoleon sent to Prague a request for the Allies' official confirmation of these terms. It reached him only on August 9, with a warning from Metternich that the congress and the armistice would expire at midnight of August 10; and that Napoleon's acceptance must be received before that time. Napoleon sent a conditional acceptance, which did not reach Prague until Metternich had declared the congress and the armistice ended. On August 11 Austria joined the coalition against France, and the war was resumed.

III. TO THE RHINE

So expanded and financed, the Allies now had some 492,000 men in arms, with 1,383 cannon; Napoleon, having received a contingent from Denmark, and the new conscripts he had waited for, had 440,000 troops and 1,200 pieces of artillery. The Allies formed three armies: an "Army of the North," under Bernadotte, centered in Berlin; an "Army of Silesia," under the impetuous and undiscourageable Blücher, formed around Breslau; and the largest of the three, the "Army of Bohemia," under Prince von Schwarzenberg, focused in Prague. Together they formed a half circle covering Napoleon at Dresden; separately each of the three was free to fight its own way to Paris. Against these Napoleon opposed an "Army of the Left," under Oudinot, to hold Bernadotte; an "Army of the Center," under Ney, to watch Blücher; and an "Army of the Right," under himself, to guard the roads by which Schwarzenberg might let loose an avalanche of men from Bohemia. There were discouraging but apparently unavoidable defects in the French position: Napoleon could not use his fine Italian scheme of concentrating his whole force on one of his enemies at one time, since this would leave the road to Paris open to the others; two of his armies had to manage without the spur of his presence and the quick versatility of his tactical skill.

On August 12 Blücher opened the fall campaign of 1813 by moving westward from Breslau to attack Ney's divisions at the Katzbach in Saxony. Ney's men were caught napping, perhaps literally, and fled in panic. Napoleon rushed up from Görlitz with his Imperial Guard and Murat's cavalry, re-formed Ney's troops, and led them to a victory that cost Blücher 6,000 men.[12] But at the same time Schwarzenberg led his 200,000 men north in a dash to seize the French headquarters at Dresden. Napoleon turned back from the pursuit of Blücher, led 100,000 men 120 miles in four days, and found the Austrians holding almost all the heights around the Saxon capital. On August 26 the French army, led by the Old Guard and the Young Guard, crying *"Vive l'Empereur!"* broke through the enemy lines, and fought so ferociously—Murat leading his cavalry with his old-time recklessness—that, after two days of combat, Schwarzenberg ordered a retreat, leaving 6,000 of his men dead, disabled, or captured. Napoleon himself had directed some batteries in the thickest of the fire.[13]

Alexander, from an exposed hill, had watched the conflict with his new favorite, Moreau, beside him. A cannonball shattered both of Moreau's legs. A few days later he died, in the arms of the Czar, but crying out, "I, Moreau, struck by a French shot, and dying amid the enemies of France!"[14]

Vandamme pursued the retreating Austrians, was not followed and supported by Napoleon (who had been stricken with violent gastric pains), fell into a trap, and surrendered his 7,000 men to one of Schwarzenberg's divisions (August 28). Soon afterward Ney lost 15,000 men in an engagement at Dennewitz (September 6). Napoleon mourned to see his victory at Dresden so annulled. He sent orders to the Senate to call up 120,000 conscripts from the class of 1814, and 160,000 from the class of 1815. These were youngsters who would need many months of training. At the same time 60,000 Russian troops, hardened by a campaign in Poland, were added to Alexander's army; and on October 8 the Bavarian Army, previously supporting Napoleon, joined his foes.

So strengthened, the Allies now aimed to capture Leipzig, and to decide the war in a battle where their united forces would prevail over any Napoleonic strategy. In October 160,000 men—led by Blücher, Bennigsen, Bernadotte, Schwarzenberg, Eugen of Württemberg, and other generals—converged upon the city. Napoleon brought up his armies from north, center, and south, 115,000 men in all, under Marmont, Alexandre Macdonald, Augereau, Bertrand, Kellermann, Victor, Murat, Ney, and Prince Józef Poniatowski. Rarely had so much military genius, or so many nationalities, met on any one field; this, as the Germans called it, was the Völkerschlacht —the Battle (literally the Slaughter) of the Nations.

Napoleon took his stand in an exposed position in the rear of his forces, and directed their movements during the three days of the action (October 16-19, 1813). According to his own account,[15] the French had the upper hand until October 18, when the Saxon troops went over to the Allies and then turned their guns upon the French, who, surprised and confused, began to give ground. On the next day the contingents from the Confederation of the Rhine defected to the Allies. Seeing that his men, apparently running out of ammunition,[16] were suffering enormous losses, Napoleon ordered them to retreat across the Rivers Pleisse and Elster. Most of them succeeded in this, but an excited engineer blew up a bridge over the Elster while some of the French were crossing; many were drowned, including the gallant Poniatowski, who had fought so well that Napoleon had made him a marshal on the battlefield. Only 60,000 of the 115,000 who had fought for Napoleon at Leipzig reached the River Saale; thousands fell prisoners, and 120,000 French troops left in German fortresses were lost to France. Those of the retreating French who reached the Saale received food and clothing and supplies. Then they made their way westward to the Main at Hanau; there they fought and defeated a force of Austrians and Bavarians; and on November 2, after two weeks of flight, they reached the Rhine at Mainz, and crossed the river into France.

IV. TO THE BREAKING POINT

Napoleon seemed ruined beyond recovery. Not counting French soldiers immobilized in Germany, his army now consisted of 60,000 defeated and exhausted men huddled near the Rhine, "a mass of stragglers without arms, without clothes, bearing about them the germs of typhus fever, with which they infected every place through which they passed."[17] From every direction came discouraging news. In Italy Eugène had by great effort raised a force of 36,000 men, but was now confronted by 60,000 Austrian troops across the Adige. In Naples Murat was plotting to save his throne by defecting to the Allies. In the Netherlands a domestic revolt, aided by a Prussian division under Bülow, overthrew French rule (November, 1813); English troops took control of the Scheldt; the house of Orange was restored. Jérôme had fled from Westphalia. From Spain the triumphant Wellington crossed the Bidassoa into France (October 7); in December he laid siege to Bayonne.

France itself seemed to be falling to pieces. The loss of Spain, the interruption of trade with Germany and Italy, had brought an economic crisis with factories closing and banks failing. In October the closing of the banking house of Jabach set off a series of bankruptcies. The stock market fell from 80 in January, 1813, to 47 in December. Thousands of unemployed roamed the streets, or concealed their poverty in their homes, or joined the Army to eat. The common people rebelled against further conscription; the middle class protested against higher taxes; the royalists called for Louis XVIII; all classes demanded peace.

Napoleon reached Paris on November 9, and was welcomed by his unhappy Queen and his rejoicing son. He set about raising a new army of 300,000 men as the first necessity for either war or peace. He sent engineers to repair roads to new fronts, to restore town walls, to build fortresses, to prepare to cut dikes or demolish bridges if necessary to slow an invader's advance. He conscripted horses for the cavalry, ordered cannon from the foundries, arms and munitions for the infantry; and as public revenues fell because of poverty and resistance to taxation, he delved more and more deeply into his cellar hoard. The nation looked on in wonder and fear, admiring his resilience and resourcefulness, dreading another year of war.

The Allies, hesitant before the Rhine and winter, sent to him from Frankfurt, on November 9, an informal unsigned offer of peace: France was to retain her natural frontiers—the Rhine, the Alps, the Pyrenees—but was to surrender all claim to anything beyond them.[18] On December 2 Napoleon replied through Caulaincourt, minister for foreign affairs, giving his official consent. However, the revolution in Holland ended French control of the mouths of the Rhine; the Allies aided this revolution, and withdrew their acceptance of natural frontiers for France.[19] Instead they issued (December 5) the "Declaration of Frankfurt": "The Allied Powers are not making war on France. The Sovereigns desire France to be great, strong, and happy. . . . The Powers confirm the French Empire in the possession of an extent of territory that it never possessed under its kings."[20]

Not much was needed to separate the people from the Emperor. The Senate and the Legislature were in open revolt against him, demanding a constitution with guarantees of freedom. On December 21 the Allies crossed the Rhine into France. On December 29 the Senate sent Napoleon its assurances of loyalty and support. But on the same day Lainé, member from royalist Bordeaux, read to the Legislature a report criticizing the "mistakes" and "excesses" of the imperial administration, praising "the happy sway of the Bourbons," and congratulating the Allies on "wishing to keep us within the limits of our own territory, and to repress an ambitious activity which for the last twenty years has been so fatal to all the peoples of Europe."[21] The Legislature voted, 223 to 31, to have Lainé's report printed. That evening Napoleon ordered the session closed.

On January 1, 1814, the Legislature sent him a delegation to wish him the compliments of the season. He replied with an outburst of accumulated anger and fatigue:

> "Surely, when we have to drive the enemy from our frontiers, it is not time to ask me for a constitution. You are not the representatives of the nation, you are merely the deputies sent by the departments. . . . I alone am the representative of the people. After all, what is the throne? Four pieces of gilt wood covered with velvet? No! The throne is a man, and that man is myself. It is I who can save France, and not you! If I were to listen to you I would surrender to the enemy more than he is demanding. You shall have peace in three months, or I shall perish."[22]

After the shocked delegates had left him Napoleon sent for some selected senators, explained his policy and his negotiations for peace, and concluded with a humble confession as if before the judgment seat of history:

> "I do not fear to acknowledge that I have made war too long. I had conceived vast projects; I wished to secure to France the empire of the world. I was mistaken; those projects were not proportioned to the numerical force of

our population. I should have been obliged to put them all under arms; and I now perceive that the advancement of society, and the moral and social well-being of a state, are not compatible with converting an entire people into a nation of soldiers.

"I ought to expiate the fault I have committed in reckoning too much on my good fortune; and I will expiate it. I will make peace. I will make it in such terms as circumstances demand, and this peace shall be mortifying to me alone. It is I who have deceived myself; it is I who ought to suffer, it is not France. She has not committed any error; she has poured forth her blood for me; she has not refused me any sacrifice. . . .

"Go, then, gentlemen, announce to your departments that I am about to conclude a peace, that I shall no longer require the blood of Frenchmen for my enterprises, for myself, . . . but for France, and to maintain the integrity of her frontiers. Tell them that I ask only the means of repelling a foreign foe from our native land. Tell them that Alsace, Franche-Comté, Navarre, Béarn are being invaded. Tell them that I call upon Frenchmen to come to the aid of Freedom."[23]

On January 21 he ordered his agents to release Pope Pius VII from Fontainebleau, and arrange for his return to Italy. On January 23 he assembled in the Tuileries the officers of the National Guard, presented to them the Empress and the "King of Rome" (a handsome boy not yet three years old), and recommended them to the care of the Guard. Once again, he appointed Marie Louise regent during his absence, this time with his brother Joseph as lieutenant general of the empire and administrator for the Empress. On the 24th he was notified that Murat had gone over to the Allies, and was marching up from Naples with eighty thousand men to aid in expelling Eugène from Italy. On that day he bade goodbye to wife and son, whom he was never to see again, and left Paris to join his reconstituted army and challenge the invaders of France.

V. TO PARIS

They were again advancing on converging lines, this time with their eyes on Paris. Schwarzenberg literally stole a march on the French by crossing the Rhine at Basel with 160,000 men, violating Swiss neutrality with the happy connivance of Bernese oligarchs; moving rapidly through the cantons, taking undefended Geneva, and emerging into France a hundred miles farther west than the French had expected; and hurrying north toward Nancy in the hope of joining Blücher, or coordinating with him there. Napoleon had ordered French armies to drop their local campaigns in Italy and southeast France and march north to intercept Schwarzenberg, or at least slow his advance; but Eugène was tied up by Austrians, and Soult had his hands full with Wellington.

Meanwhile Blücher, with his "Army of Silesia" still 60,000 strong, crossed the Rhine at Mainz, Mannheim, and Coblenz, and advanced almost unopposed to Nancy, whose rulers and populace received him and his Prussian troops as deliverers from Napoleonic tyranny.[24] Bernadotte, having lost his hope of being chosen to succeed Bonaparte, had left the Allies after Leipzig, to beat the Danes into ceding Norway to Sweden (January 14, 1814); that done, he and his army joined Blücher in the drive on Paris.

The French forces that Napoleon had left in eastern France dared not confront either Blücher or Schwarzenberg. Ney retreated west from Nancy, Mortier from Langres, Marmont from Metz, and awaited the coming of Napoleon.

He brought with him, to his new headquarters at Châlons-sur-Marne (only ninety-five miles from Paris), some 60,000 recruits; adding these to the 60,000 survivors of Leipzig under Ney, Marmont, and Mortier, he had a total of 120,000 with whom to stop Blücher and Schwarzenberg's total of 220,000. He was limited to a policy of keeping the Allied armies from merging, avoiding confrontation with Schwarzenberg, and stopping or delaying their advance upon Paris by nibbling victories won over Allied divisions caught off guard or far enough away from their central command to be attacked without engaging their main forces. The campaign of 1814 was one of Napoleon's most brilliant in strategy, but also—because of the dearth of reinforcements—one of the most costly in mistakes. Blücher too made many mistakes, but he was the most indomitable and resourceful of all those generals who now or later opposed Napoleon. Schwarzenberg was more cautious, partly by temperament, partly because he carried Czar Alexander and Emperor Francis II in his train.

Some initial victories gave Napoleon undue confidence. He caught Blücher's men dining or napping at Brienne (January 29, 1814), defeated them, and came near to capturing Blücher himself. They retreated, and Napoleon was too wise to follow them, for his own army had lost 4,000 men, and he too had a narrow escape: a Prussian was approaching him with drawn saber when General Gourgeaud shot the impertinent fellow dead. Napoleon grieved over the damage the battle had done to the town and its famous school, where he had received his scientific education and his military training; he promised to restore them after the invaders had been driven from France.[25]

He had little time for reminiscence; Schwarzenberg had rushed up to buttress Blücher, and suddenly Napoleon's 46,000 victors found themselves almost surrounded by 100,000 Austrians, Prussians, and Russians at La Rothière (February 1). Napoleon had no choice but to fight; he so ordered, and commanded in person. The battle was almost equal, but equal losses were disastrous for the French, and the Emperor led them in retreat to Troyes. Blücher, restless with Schwarzenberg's cautious advance, separated from him and decided to follow his own route and pace to Paris via the Marne while the Austrians proceeded along the Seine. Allied officers were so confident of victory that they made engagements to meet at the Palais-Royal in the coming week.[26]

After giving his wounded army a week's rest, Napoleon assigned part of it to Victor and Oudinot to retard Schwarzenberg, and himself marched with 60,000 men through the swamps of St.-Gond as a shortcut to Champaubert. There they caught up with Blücher's rear, and Marmont led the French to a decisive victory (February 10). Pushing on, they met, a day later, another portion of Blücher's army at Montmirail; Napoleon and Blücher were both present, but Marmont again was the hero. On February 14 the main forces clashed in a larger combat at Vauchamps, and Napoleon guided his now more confident army to victory. In four days Blücher had lost 30,000 men.[27] Napoleon sent 8,000 prisoners to be paraded through Paris to restore the morale of the citizens.[28]

However, Schwarzenberg had meanwhile driven back Oudinot and Victor almost to Fountainbleau; one full-scale attack could have brought the Austro-Russian army, and its two Emperors, within a day's march of Paris. Shocked by report of this setback, which canceled all his victories, Napoleon, leaving Marmont to at least harass Blücher, dashed south with 70,000 men, caught an Allied army under Wittgenstein at Montereau, defeated it (February 18), took a position at Nangis, and sent Victor and Oudinot to attack Schwarzenberg in flank and rear. Finding himself in danger on three sides, the Austrian general thought it an opportune time to suggest an armistice to Napoleon. The Emperor replied that he would agree to a cease-fire only if it pledged the Allies to the Frankfurt offer—which left France its natural boundaries. The Allies, insulted by this proposal that they should retreat behind the Rhine, ended the negotiations, and, in defiance, at Chaumont on March 9, confirmed their alliance for twenty years. Schwarzenberg retired to Troyes, still commanding 100,000 men.

Napoleon, with 40,000, pursued him cautiously. Meanwhile he learned that Blücher had re-formed his forces, and was again making a path to Paris with 50,000 men. Leaving Oudinot, Macdonald, and Étienne-Maurice Gérard to trouble Schwarzenberg, he marched his men back from the Seine to the Marne, and joined Marmont and Mortier in the hope of trapping Blücher at the River Aisne, where the Prussian's only escape would be by a bridge to Soissons. But two other Allied armies, 50,000 men, moved down from the north upon Soissons, and frightened its commandant to surrender the city and the bridge. Blücher's forces crossed the bridge, burned it, and united with their rescuers to total 100,000 troops. Napoleon pursued them with 50,000 men, fought them indecisively at Craonne, and was defeated by them in a savage conflict of two days at Laon (March 9–10).

It did not help him much that on March 13, finding another Prussian army in possession of Reims, he drove out the invaders and received a heartening welcome from the populace. Then, leaving Marmont and Mortier to face Blücher, he again marched from one enemy to the other, and at Arcis-sur-Aube, on March 20, in a madness of fury, launched his remaining 20,000 men against Schwarzenberg's army, still 90,000 strong. After two days of heroic massacre he acknowledged defeat, and crossed the Aube to find a place where his depleted army could rest.

He was again at the end of his rope. His exhaustion of flesh and nerves revealed itself in his hot temper, his angry scolding of officers who had risked their lives for him in war after war. They warned him that he could expect no reinforcements to reach him from a nation bled to apathy and tired of *la gloire*. The government that he had left in Paris—even his brother Joseph —was sending him appeals to make peace at any price.

In his desperation he decided to risk everything on one more dash of imaginative strategy. He would leave his best generals to halt the Allied advance as well as they could; he himself, with a modest force, would march eastward, release the French soldiers immured in German fortresses along the Rhine, add those veteran troops to his battered regiments, cut the Allies' lines of communication and supplies, attack their rear guards, and force them to halt in their march; so Paris, again inspired by his courage, might build its defenses, and defy the invaders. In a saner moment he sent instructions to Joseph that if surrender should be imminent, the government, with Marie Louise and the King of Rome, should be removed to some security behind the Loire, where all available French troops could gather for a last stand.

While Napoleon led his wondering survivors eastward, the Allies broke down, day by day, the resistance offered by the remains of the French army, and moved closer to the end of their long journey. Francis II stayed behind at Dijon, not willing to share in the humiliation of his daughter. Frederick William III, usually so mild, felt that he might justly take revenge for the destruction of his army, the dismemberment of his country, and his years of exile from his capital. Alexander, proud and tense, taking no pleasure in the daily slaughter, saw himself as fulfilling the vow he had made at Vilna to cleanse Russia of Moscow's defilement, and to free Europe from the power madness of the Corsican.

On March 25 Marmont and Mortier made a desperate attempt to stop the Allies, at La Fère-Champenoise, a hundred miles from Paris. Outnumbered two to one, they fought with such carelessness of death that Alexander himself, advancing into the melee, commanded the uneven slaughter to stop, crying, *"Je veux sauver ces braves!"*; and after the combat ended the victors restored to the defeated generals their horses and swords.[29] Marmont and Mortier retreated to Paris to prepare the defense of the capital.

Blücher and Schwarzenberg reached the outskirts of Paris on March 29. The sound of their cannon, and the sight of peasants fleeing into the city, created panic among the citizens, and tremors among the 12,000 militiamen —most of them armed only with pikes—who were now called upon to aid the residual army in manning the forts and hills of the capital. Joseph had long since begged the Empress-Regent to leave the city as Napoleon had directed; now she obeyed; but "L'Aiglon" resisted until frightened by the noise of the approaching battle.

On March 30th 70,000 of the invaders began the final attack. Marmont and Mortier, with 25,000 men, defended as well as they could a city that the proud Emperor had never thought of fortifying. Old soldiers from Les Invalides, students from the École Polytechnique, workingmen and other volunteers, joined the defense. Joseph watched the resistance until he saw that it was useless and might invite the destructive bombardment of a city that was dear to its rich and poor alike. Though Alexander might behave with commiseration and charity, the Cossacks might escape control, and Blücher was not the man to keep his Prussian cohorts from taking full revenge. So Joseph transferred his authority to the marshals, and left to join Marie Louise and the French government at Blois on the Loire. Marmont, after a day of bloody resistance, saw no sense in continuing it, and signed the capitulation of the city at 2 A.M. of March 31, 1814.

Later that morning Alexander, Frederick William III, and Schwarzenberg led 50,000 soldiers in formal entry into Paris. The people greeted them with silent hostility, but the Czar softened them with undiscouraged courtesy and repeated salutations.[30] When the ceremonies were over he sought out Talleyrand in the Rue St.-Florentin, and asked his advice on how to arrange an orderly change of the French government. They agreed that the Senate should reconvene, that it should draw up a constitution, and should appoint a provisional government. The Senate met on April 1, composed a constitution guaranteeing fundamental liberties, appointed a provisional government, and chose Talleyrand as its president. On April 2 the Senate declared Napoleon deposed.

VI. TO PEACE

He was at St.-Dizier, 150 miles from Paris, when the news reached him (March 27) that the Allies were investing the city. He set out with his army the next morning. That afternoon he received a more urgent message: "The presence of the Emperor is necessary if he wishes to prevent his capital from being delivered to the enemy. There is not a moment to lose." He left his army at Troyes and rode most of the remaining miles on horseback, ailments notwithstanding. Nearing Paris (March 31), he said to Caulaincourt, "I shall put myself at the head of the National Guard and the Army; we shall reestablish things." He was shocked to be informed that it was too late; the capitulation had been signed that morning. He sent Caulaincourt to Paris in the hope that this "Russian" might persuade Alexander to a compromise settlement. Fearing arrest if he himself entered the city, the Emperor rode on to Fontainebleau. There, that evening, he received word from Caulaincourt: "I am repulsed."[31] On April 2 he learned that he had been deposed. He thought for a moment how pleasant it might be to yield. "I do not cling to the throne," he said; "born a soldier, I can without complaint become a citizen." But the arrival of his army, still numbering 50,000 men,[32] struck a more congenial chord in his nature. He bade it pitch its camp along the River Essonne (a tributary of the Seine), and hold itself ready for further orders. To this camp Marmont led the survivors of the troops that had defended Paris.

On April 3 Napoleon reviewed the Imperial Guard in the court of the Fontainebleau Palace. He told them, "I have offered the Emperor Alexander a peace sought by great sacrifices. . . . He has refused. . . . In a few days I shall go to attack him in Paris. I count on you." At first they made no answer, but when he asked them, "Am I right?" they responded, "*Vive l'Empereur! À Paris!*" and the grenadiers' band struck up the old revolutionary anthems "Le Chant du départ" and "La Marseillaise."

The generals were skeptical. In private conference with them he found them opposed to a Bourbon restoration, but cold to an attempt to drive the Allies out of Paris. On April 4 Marshals Ney, Oudinot, Moncey, and Lefebvre entered his room uninvited, and told him that since the Senate had deposed him they could not follow him in an attack upon the Allied forces and the Provisional Government. He answered that he would lead the Army without them. Ney retorted, "The Army will obey its leaders." Napoleon asked what they wanted him to do. Ney and Oudinot answered, "Abdicate." Napoleon wrote a conditional abdication, leaving the throne to his son under the regency of Marie Louise. He sent Caulaincourt, Macdonald, and Ney to Paris to present this offer. On the way they stopped at the Essonne camp to consult Marmont, and were startled to find that he had been negotiating privately with Schwarzenberg for terms of surrender. That night (April 4–5) Marmont led his 11,000 men across the city line in full acceptance of Schwarzenberg's easy terms. On April 5 the Allied leaders notified Caulaincourt that there would be no further dealings with Napoleon until he had abdicated unconditionally. Meanwhile they sent troops to surround Fontainebleau and prevent his escape.

Alexander graced these severities by protecting Paris from pillage, and paying courtesy visits to Marie Louise, Josephine, and Hortense. The Russian was the most civilized of the conquerors. He persuaded his colleagues to sign with him the "Treaty of Fontainebleau," which offered Napoleon an island in the Mediterranean as a spacious prison, brightened with an Italian sky and a French income. The essential text:

> His Majesty the Emperor Napoleon on the one part, and their Majesties the Emperor of Austria, . . . the Emperor of all the Russias, and the King of Prussia, stipulating in their own names and those of all their Allies on the other . . .
>
> Article I. His Majesty the Emperor Napoleon renounces for himself, his successors and descendants, as well as for all the members of his family, all rights of sovereignty and dominion as well in the French Empire as . . . in every other country.
>
> Article II. Their Majesties the Emperor Napoleon and Empress Marie Louise shall retain their titles and rank to be enjoyed during their lives. The mother, brothers, sisters, nephews, and nieces of the Emperor shall also retain, wherever they reside, the titles of Princes of the Emperor's Family.
>
> Article III. The Island of Elba, adopted by his Majesty the Emperor Napoleon as his place of residence, shall form during his life a separate principality, which shall be possessed by him in full sovereignty and property.
>
> There shall besides be granted, in full property to the Emperor Napoleon, an annual revenue of 2,000,000 francs in rent charge, in the great book of France, of which 1,000,000 shall be in reversion to the Empress.[33]

Napoleon signed this on April 13, and signed his First Abdication; the Allies then signed the treaty. He had hoped for Corsica as his island of exile, but knew that this, a very incubator of revolt, would not be allowed, and Elba had been his own second choice.[34] Marie Louise was not permitted to go with him there. She had tried to join him at Fontainebleau, but the Allies had forbidden this, and Napoleon had discouraged it.[35] On April 27, unwillingly, she and her son left Rambouillet for Vienna.

Perhaps Napoleon had dissuaded her from coming to him because he had decided to kill himself. As before noted, he had been given a phial of poison by Dr. Yvan on the return from Russia. On the night of April 12–13 he swallowed the contents. Apparently the poison had lost efficacy; Napoleon suffered, but recovered, much to his shame. He excused his continuance by proposing to write an autobiography that would give his side of the story, and would celebrate the deeds of *"mes braves."*[36]

On April 16 he wrote a farewell to Josephine: "Never forget him who has never forgotten you and will never forget you."[37] She died a month later, May 29. On April 19 he bade goodbye to his valet Constant and his Mameluke bodyguard Roustam. On the 20th he delivered *les adieux* to the soldiers of the Old Guard, who had remained with him to the end:

> "Soldiers, I bid you farewell. For twenty years that we have been together your conduct has left me nothing to desire. I have always found you on the road to glory. . . . With you and the brave men who still are faithful, I might have carried on a civil war, but France would be unhappy. Be faithful, then, to your new king, be obedient to your new commanders, and desert not our beloved country.
>
> "Do not lament my lot. I will be happy when I know that you are so. I might have died; . . . if I consent to live it is still to promote your glory. I will write the great things that we have achieved.
>
> "I cannot embrace you all, but I embrace your general. Come, General Petit, that I may press you to my heart. Bring me the Eagle [the standard of the Guard] that I may embrace it also. Ah, dear Eagle, may this kiss which I give thee find an echo to the latest posterity! Adieu, my children; the best wishes of my heart shall be always with you. Do not forget me!"[38]

Four hundred of the Guard chose to accompany him to Elba.

He stepped into a carriage with General Bertrand, who would stay with him to the end. For assurance' sake he was accompanied by four Allied officers—Russian, Prussian, Austrian, English; and, for protection, a small escort of French troops.[39] He needed protection as he passed through Provence, where the population, strongly Catholic and partly royalist, hurled insults at him as he passed. At Orgon, near Arles, he saw himself hanging in effigy, and was threatened by a crowd; it commanded him to say *"Vive le Roi!"* and he obeyed, as Louis XVI, contrariwise, had done. Thereafter, for safety, he disguised himself with a uniform and cloak lent him by Austrian and Russian officers. His spirits were raised, April 26, by finding his sister Pauline waiting for him at Le Luc. She had abandoned the French Riviera, and an invitation to Rome, to stay at a little farmhouse. "The Emperor will shortly pass through here," she wrote to Felice Bacciocchi, "and I wish to see him and offer him my sympathy. . . . I have not loved him because he was a sovereign, but because he is my brother."[40] She refused to embrace him in his humiliating disguise; he discarded it, and for four hours basked in her devotion.

On the 27th he proceeded to Fréjus. There, on April 28, he was received, with a salute of twenty-one guns, on board the British ship *Undaunted*, and sailed for Elba. For the next nine months he would try the healing simplicities of peace.

CHAPTER XXXVII

To Waterloo

1814–15

I. LOUIS XVIII

H E was the fourth—as Louis XVI was the third—son of Louis the Dauphin, son of Louis XV. Till 1791, when he was already thirty-six, he was apparently content to be the Comte de Provence, handsome, genial, enjoying and supporting literature, and contributing elegant conversation to the salon of his mistress.[1] When Louis XVI tried to escape from France (1791) the Comte tried also, succeeded, and joined his younger brother, the Comte d'Artois, at Brussels. When Louis XVII, wasting away in imprisonment and grief, died at the age of ten (1795), the Comte de Provence, as the next legitimate heir to the throne of France, took the title of Louis XVIII, and considered himself the king of France through all the years of the Revolution and Napoleon. As their influence spread, Louis had to change his domicile from place to place—from Germany to Russia to Poland to Russia to England (1811). There he was supported by the government, and acquired a respect for the British Constitution.

On April 14, 1814, the French Senate, led by Talleyrand, issued the following resolution:

> In conformity with the proposition of the Provisional Government, and the report of a special committee of seven members, the Senate resigns the provisional government of France to His Royal Highness the Comte d'Artois, with the title of Lieutenant General of the Kingdom, until Louis-Stanislaus-Xavier, called to the throne of France, shall have accepted the constitutional charter.[2]

The constitution formulated by the Senate called for amnesty to the surviving revolutionists, the prohibition of feudal dues and ecclesiastical tithes, the confirmation of purchases made from "national" property (confiscated from the Church and the *émigrés*), the maintenance of a Chamber of Deputies and a House of Peers, and respect for civil liberty and the sovereignty of the people.

Pleased by this invitation, disturbed by its conditions, Louis asked time for consideration. On April 24 he left England for France. From St.-Ouen, on May 2, he announced that he would respect most of the proposed constitution, but had to reject the sovereignty of the people as inconsistent with his hereditary rights as king by the grace of God. He proposed to "grant" to France and the Senate a "charter" instead of a constitution. The Senate would be a Chamber of Peers chosen by the king; the Corps Législatif would become a Chamber of Deputies elected by voters paying three hundred or more francs annually in direct taxes; and these two chambers were to control the revenues and expenditures of the government. Charmed by the power of the purse, the two chambers accepted the charter, the King pledged his cooperation, and the Bourbon Restoration began (June 4, 1814).

Amid this changing of the guards the Allied Powers, by the "First Treaty of Paris" (May 30, 1814), reduced France to her boundaries of 1792, and gave her Chambéry, Annecy, Mulhouse, and Montbéliard. France surrendered important colonies to England and Spain, recognized Austrian rule in north Italy, and agreed in advance to any decisions that the coming Congress of Vienna would reach about territory taken by France since 1792.

Settled down in the Tuileries, Louis XVIII felt that he had earned the right to relax and enjoy the restitution of his property. He spoke of 1814 as "the nineteenth year of my reign." He was now fifty-nine years old, genial and courteous, lazy and slow, fat and gouty, and not every ounce a king. He resigned himself to constitutional government, and complaisantly adjusted himself to votes, oratory, factions, and a press freer than under the Directory or Napoleon. Salons for the discussion of literature and politics flourished. Mme. de Staël, triumphant, resumed her Paris gatherings, and entertained kings.

More generally enjoyed by the people was the economic success of the new regime. Louis had the good sense to leave unaltered the Napoleonic Code, the judiciary, the bureaucracy, and the structure of the economy. As Napoleon had been blessed in finding, for the vital Ministry of Finance, a man of high competence and integrity in François Mollien, so Louis XVIII found for the same office Baron Joseph-Dominique Louis, who met promptly all obligations of the Treasury, and resisted all temptations to fiscal chicanery.

The King's court symbolized his efforts to smooth the transition between the two regimes. There was, in the first year of the reign, little retaliation against those who had served Napoleon; the Emperor's marshals, excepting Davout, mingled freely with pedigreed royalists at the Bourbon court. Members of the lower nobility, like M. and Mme. de Rémusat, who had been favorites with Napoleon, rushed to worship at the refurbished shrine. Talleyrand's quip that the Bourbons had "learned nothing and forgotten nothing" might have been true of the Comte d'Artois—good-natured and good-looking, but foolishly proud; but it could not justly be applied to Louis XVIII. Napoleon himself, at St. Helena, testified to the rapidity with which most of the French people accepted the *ancien régime nouveau*, as if falling readily into old habits too long established to have been completely displaced.

Nevertheless, there were some elements of discord and discontent. The Church repudiated the Concordat, and insisted on the restoration of her pre-Revolution power, especially over education. A decree was obtained from the King requiring strict religious observance of Sundays and holydays; all shops except of chemists and herbalists were then to be closed from morning to evening, and no paid labor or business transport was to be allowed.[3]

It became dangerous not to profess Catholicism. Most troublesome of all was the Church's apparently reasonable demand that all ecclesiastical property confiscated during the Revolution should be restored to her. This demand could not be met without a revolt of the hundreds of thousands of peasants, and members of the middle class, who had bought such property from the state. The fear of these purchasers that they might be dispossessed, in whole or in part, led many peasants, and some solid bourgeois, to think they might welcome a Napoleon returning, if cured of war.

A still active minority of the population cherished the principles of the Revolution, and worked, however clandestinely, for its revival. Severely repressed by the new regime, these "Jacobins" played with the hope that a returned Napoleon might be forced, in order to overthrow the Bourbon, to be again the Son of the Revolution. In the Army they made many converts to this hope. The marshals were captivated by the amiability of the King, but the officer class—seeing their visions of advancement fading as the nobility resumed its old monopoly of the higher posts—longed for a revival of the days when a marshal's baton could be won and awarded on the field and day of battle. Louis XVIII, eager to balance the budget, had demobilized 18,000 officers and 300,000 privates; nearly all of these dismissed men, struggling to find a place in the economy, idealized in memory the Emperor who had dealt out glory as well as death, and had made even death seem glorious.

The discontent of the Army was the strongest of the forces that opened a door for the return of the fascinating prodigal. Add a peasantry fearing dispossession or a restoration of feudal dues; manufacturers suffering from the influx of British goods; the discomfort of all but the orthodox Catholics under the intensifying sway of the clergy; the King's dismissal of both chambers at the end of 1814—not to return till May; and a secret yearning of the poor for the excitement and splendor of Napoleon's France: these were frail and uncertain winds of chance, but news of them, brought to Elba, raised the spirit of the imprisoned gladiator, wounded but not dead.

II. THE CONGRESS OF VIENNA: SEPTEMBER, 1814 – JUNE, 1815

It was the most distinguished political assemblage in European history. Its dominant members were naturally the major victors in the war of the nations: Russia, Prussia, Austria, and Great Britain; but there were also delegates from Sweden, Denmark, Spain, Portugal, the Papacy, Bavaria, Saxony, Württemberg . . . ; and defeated France had to be reckoned with, if only because she was represented by the wily Talleyrand. The proceedings would illustrate two not quite contrary principles: that guns speak louder than words, and that physical force is seldom victorious unless manipulated by mental power.

Russia was represented primarily by Czar Alexander I, with the largest army and the greatest charm. With the help of Count Andreas Razumovsky (patron of Beethoven) and Count Karl Robert Nesselrode he proposed that

Russia receive all Poland as reward for leading the Allies from hesitation on the Niemen and the Spree to victory on the Seine; and Prince Czartoryski, representing Poland by Alexander's permission, supported the proposal in hope that the reunification of Poland could be a step toward independence.

Prussia was represented formally by King Frederick William III, more actively by Prince von Hardenberg, with Wilhelm von Humboldt as philosopher in attendance. They demanded a fit reward for the martial leadership of "Vorwärts" Blücher and the sacrifice of Prussian lives. Alexander agreed, and—conditional on Prussia's withdrawal of claim to her former piece of Poland—offered Frederick William all of Saxony, whose King (then imprisoned in Berlin) deserved this denudation for having given the Saxon Army to Napoleon; and Freiherr vom Stein thought this a gentlemanly solution.

Austria claimed that its declaration for the Allies had decided the war, and that it should get a generous helping at the victors' feast. The exclusion of Austria from Poland was intolerable; and the appropriation of Saxony by Prussia would throw out of all proportion the European balance of power between north and south. Metternich deployed all his patient, devious subtlety to keep Austria from being reduced to a second-class Power. Emperor Francis II aided his Minister for Foreign Affairs by softening his guests with entertainment. His Treasury had emerged from the war with one foot in bankruptcy; he risked the remainder by intoxicating his guests with wine and champagne, and dulling them with Neanderthal meals. The halls of the imperial palaces sparkled almost nightly with lavish festivals. Actors and actresses, singers and virtuosos were engaged to entrance the potentates and their retainers; Beethoven shook the city with "Die Schlacht von Vittoria." Fair women wore fortunes on their dresses or in their hair, and displayed as much of their software as a decent respect for Cardinal Consalvi would allow. Mistresses were available for titled seekers, and courtesans supplied the needs of minor notables. The town gossips had trouble keeping account of the Czar's amours.[4]

Alexander won the women and lost the diplomatic war. Metternich sought allies against him among the delegates of the minor Powers. He argued that the principle of legitimacy forbade such spoliation of a king as Russia and Prussia proposed in Saxony. They agreed, but how could they talk principle to a Russia that had 500,000 troops quartered on her western front? Metternich appealed to Lord Castlereagh, who spoke for England: Would not England be uneasy with Russia reaching through Poland and allied with a Prussia swollen with Saxony? What would this do to the balance of power east and west? Castlereagh excused himself; Britain was at war with the United States, and could not risk a confrontation with Russia.

So Metternich turned as a last resort to Talleyrand. He had angered the Frenchman by excluding France, along with the lesser Powers, from the private conferences of the "Big Four," and deferring to November 1, 1814, the first united assembly of all the attending states. Talleyrand made common cause with other excluded delegations, and was soon accepted as their spokesman. So fortified, he began to speak of France as still a first-class Power, ready to raise and supply an army of 300,000 men. Metternich, who might have seen this as a threat, saw in it a possible promise. He solicited Talleyrand's help against Russia; Talleyrand secured Louis XVIII's consent; the two diplomats won over Castlereagh now that peace had been made with America. On January 3, 1815, France, Austria, and Great Britain formed a Triple Alliance for mutual aid in maintaining the balance of power. Faced with this new consortium, Russia withdrew her claim to all Poland; and Prussia, having regained Thorn and Posen, agreed to take only two fifths of Saxony. Talleyrand received most of the credit, and boasted that his diplomacy had changed France from a beaten beggar to again a major Power.

After almost nine months of bargaining, the assembled dignitaries, by the "Act of the Congress of Vienna" dated June 8, 1815, redistributed the soil of Europe according to the ancient principle that to the victors belong the spoils—if the victors are still strong enough to take them. Britain kept Malta as her sentry post in the central Mediterranean; she established her protectorate over the Ionian Islands as guards over the Adriatic and the eastern Mediterranean; she returned some, kept some (notably Ceylon and the Cape of Good Hope) of the French and Dutch colonies she had taken during the war. She recovered control of Hanover, and arranged a close understanding with the new kingdom of the Netherlands, which now embraced both "Holland" and "Belgium," and therefore the mouths of the Rhine.

Poland suffered a new partition, with some improvement. Prussia received the regions around Posen and Danzig. Austria received Galicia. Russia received the grand duchy of Warsaw, which was changed into the kingdom of Poland under the czar as its king, and with a liberal constitution.

Prussia came out of the war with gains that prepared her for Bismarck: in addition to two fifths of Saxony she received Swedish Pomerania and Rügen, and most of Westphalia; Neuchâtel in Switzerland; and a predominant influence in the German Confederation which now replaced Napoleon's Confederation of the Rhine. Saxony retained three fifths of its former terrain, and recovered its King. Austria added, to her pre-Congress lands, Salzburg, Illyria, Dalmatia, the Tirol, and the "Lombardo-Venetian kingdom" in northern Italy. The Papal States were returned to the Papacy; Tuscany reverted to the Hapsburg-Bourbon rule. Finally, in a bow to Christianity, the Congress condemned the trade in slaves.

During December and January, 1814–15, the Congress considered proposals for further dealings with Napoleon. Surely (some delegates suggested) that excitable man would not long rest content to be sovereign of tiny Elba. And that island was uncomfortably close to Italy and France. What deviltry might he stir if he should escape? Various proposals were made to the Congress to send a force to Elba, seize Napoleon, and deport him to a farther and safer isolation. Talleyrand and Castlereagh thought so; Czar Alexander objected, and there the matter rested.[5]

The Congress was nearing its close when, early on the morning of March 7, Metternich was awakened by a message marked "Urgent." It was from the Austrian consul at Genoa, and informed the Minister that Napoleon had escaped from Elba. The delegates, notified, agreed to defer the ending of the Congress and to remain at Vienna until some united action could be agreed upon. On March 11 further word came that Napoleon had landed near Antibes. On March 13 the Congress, through its "Committee of the Eight," pronounced against Napoleon a ban declaring him an outlaw whom anyone might kill without fear or hindrance of the law. The Congress had completed its programs, but—though the delegates now dispersed—it remained technically in session until June 19, when it was notified that Napoleon had been overwhelmed at Waterloo the day before. The Congress thereupon declared itself officially at an end.

III. ELBA

Napoleon reached Elba's Portoferraio on May 3, 1814. He landed the next morning, amid the wild acclaim of the town's population, which thought that he was bringing millions of francs to spend; eight days earlier they had hanged him in effigy as a man madly in love with war.[6] They escorted him to the governor's palace, which would now take on imperial dignity. For the next nine months he was to be emperor over eighty-six square miles and twelve thousand souls. He surrounded himself (partly, it may be, because he believed that display is half the game of rule) with all the paraphernalia of majesty—uniforms, royal guard, chamberlains, domestics, musicians, a hundred horses, twenty-seven carriages.[7] On May 26 four hundred members of his Old Guard came to serve him as the nucleus of a miniature army. Some two hundred volunteers came from France, others from Italy or Corsica; altogether he had soon about sixteen hundred men ready to fight off any attempt to harm the hated and beloved Emperor. For further inviolability he fortified the harbor and organized a fleet—one brig (the *Inconstant*) and four small vessels, all armed.

How did he finance all this—and the public works and enterprises with which he improved the island? The Treaty of Fontainebleau had promised him an annuity from France, but it was not paid.[8] However, Napoleon had brought with him 3,400,000 francs in silver and gold, and he collected 400,000 lire annually in taxes and other revenues. After half a year he began to wonder how he was going to meet his expenses if he stayed there beyond a year.

For a time he was reasonably happy, considering his expansive ways. On May 9 he wrote to Marie Louise: "I arrived here fifteen days ago. I have had a pretty dwelling fixed up. . . . My health is perfect, the country is agreeable. It lacks news from you, and the assurance that you are well. . . . Goodbye, my beloved. Give a kiss to my son."[9]

Another son, with his mother the faithful Countess Walewska, was among his early visitors. The sailors and citizens mistook her for the Empress, and gave her a royal welcome. Napoleon was disturbed, since he had hoped to have his wife and the "King of Rome" join him on the island. He relaxed for a day or two in Walewska's arms,[10] then lovingly dismissed her for reasons of state. Perhaps Marie Louise received some expanded gossip about those two days.[11]

In October his mother and his sister Pauline came to stay with him. Pauline offered him her jewels, and asked pardon for Murat's disloyalty. Madame Mère gave him motherly care and comfort, and offered him all her savings. She and Pauline remained with him though they sorely missed the warm vitality of Italian life.

We can imagine how bored he was, after the first few months, with the small scope and leverage that the little island could give to his character and dreams. He tried to escape ennui by physical activity, but almost daily some news from the mainland added to his restlessness. Méneval, who was serving Marie Louise in Vienna, informed him of the discussions in the Congress about removing him to a safer distance,[12] and added that the Congress would probably end by February 20. Other informants told him of the discontent in the Army, the fears of the peasantry, the agitations of the Jacobins, the enforcement of Catholic worship. In February, 1815, Hugues Maret, Duc de Bassano, sent him a message via Fleury de Chaboulon, confirming all these reports.[13]

Excited by them, and stirred with hopes for a nobler end than death by inanition, he told his mother of his temptation, and asked for her advice. She suspected that if she let him go now she would never see him again. "Let me," she said, "be a mother for a while, and then I will give you my opinion." But she knew that he had already decided for the last gamble. "Go, my son," she told him, "and fulfill your destiny."[14]

He felt that he must act soon. A little time more, and he would have no means of his own to pay those thousand Frenchmen who were serving him and must be maintained. The conditions had developed for an attempt to regain his throne, defend it, and transmit it to his son, as beautiful as Adonis, whom he would train to be a king. The Allies were disbanding their Congress, and were going home with their troops; perhaps, separately, they would be open to an appeal for peace. The nights were still long; in the darkness his little fleet might escape detection, and he would be again on the soil of France.

He prepared as inconspicuously as possible, but with his usual foresight and thoroughness. He bade the Imperial Guard and eight hundred grenadiers—eleven hundred men in all—pack their belongings, and be on the dock on the evening of February 26 for a voyage of several days to an unstated destination. Nevertheless they surmised that they were bound for France, and they rejoiced.

On the appointed evening he embraced his mother and sister (who would soon go to friends in Italy), joined his little regiment, boarded, with it, the *Inconstant* and five other vessels, and sailed off quietly in the dark. The winds did not favor them, sometimes leaving their helpless fleet becalmed, sometimes driving it too near the shore; they feared to be recognized and stopped and ignominiously jailed. For three days they moved northward along the Italian coast, then westward past Genoa and the French Riviera. En route those men who could write made hundreds of copies of a proclamation composed by Napoleon, to be distributed in France:

> FRENCHMEN:
> I have heard, in my exile, your lamentations and your prayers: you long for the government that you chose, and which alone is lawful. I have crossed the sea, and am coming to reclaim my rights, which are yours. To the Army: your possessions, your rank, your glory, the property, rank, and glory of your children, have no greater enemies than those princes whom foreigners have imposed upon you. . . . Victory will march at full speed; the eagle, with the national colors, will fly from steeple to steeple, even to the towers of Notre-Dame. You will be the liberators of your country.[15]

IV. THE INCREDIBLE JOURNEY: MARCH 1–20, 1815

The little fleet, carrying "Caesar and his fortune," sighted Cap d'Antibes at dawn of March 1. Soon after midday, in the Golfe Juan, the eleven hundred men began to debark, some jumping into the shallow water and wading to the shore. Napoleon, last to land, ordered a bivouac in an olive plantation between the sea and the road from Antibes to Cannes. He sent a small group to Cannes to buy horses and provisions, and to pay in cash; he had brought 800,000 gold francs from Elba. He bade another group go to Antibes and persuade its garrison to join him; its commander rebuked and imprisoned the messengers. Napoleon refused to go and attempt to free them; he was resolved to gain Paris without firing a shot.

He found no welcome in Antibes. The passersby, on being told that the little man studying maps at an open-air table was the Emperor, voiced no enthusiasm. The region had been hard hit by the wars, the conscriptions, and the double blockade; it had no appetite for more of the same. The mayor of Antibes came to examine the invaders, and told Napoleon, "We were beginning to be happy and tranquil; you will trouble everything." Napoleon, recalling this at St. Helena, said to Gourgaud, "I shall not tell you how this remark moved me, nor the pain it gave me."[16] A passing courier partly reassured him: the Army and the commonalty, he reported, were for him, from Paris to Cannes, but the people of Provence were against him.

Napoleon knew this well, recalling his bitter experiences at Orgon eleven months before, and these memories now determined his route to Paris. Rather than follow, at the risk of bloody encounters, the well-traveled and mostly level highways from Cannes to Toulon, Marseilles, and Avignon to Paris, he chose the mountainous route from Cannes to Grasse, Digne, Grenoble and Lyons. The region south of Grenoble was lightly populated, the garrisons were small and notoriously anti-Bourbon. The mountain passes were still covered with snow; the Old Guardsmen and the grenadiers would grumble, but they would never desert him.

So, about midnight of March 1-2, the eleven hundred set out on the road to Cannes. Some sixty of them had been able to buy horses, but, to keep pace and friendship with the rest, they walked beside their baggage-laden mounts. Napoleon usually rode in a carriage. In the center of the procession some guardsmen watched over Napoleon's gold. Tough Corsicans brought up the rear.[17]

At Grasse they left their cannon as too big a problem for icebound mountain roads. Napoleon's veterans, used to winning wars with their legs, set a good pace for the rest. On March 5 they reached Gap, having walked (most of them) 150 miles in four days. At La Mure, twenty miles south of Grenoble, they encountered their first serious challenge.

The commander of the Fifth Division of the Army, stationed at Grenoble, had received orders from Paris to arrest Napoleon, and had sent a battalion of five hundred men to stop the approaching rebels. As the opposed columns neared each other Napoleon ordered his defenders to ground their arms. He stepped out in front and walked toward the oncoming troops. Nearing them, he stopped and addressed them: "Soldiers of the Fifth, I am your Emperor; do you recognize me?" He opened his military greatcoat, and said, "If there is among you a soldier who would like to kill his Emperor, here I am [*me voilà*]." Almost to a man the battalion lowered its arms, and cried out, "*Vive l'Empereur!*" It disbanded, and the happy soldiers gathered around Napoleon, seeking to touch him. He spoke to them affectionately, returned to his group, and told them, "Everything is settled; in ten days we shall be in the Tuileries."[18]

That evening they approached Grenoble. Hundreds of peasants and proletaires flocked to welcome him; and when they found one of the city gates closed they broke it down to let the little army in. Bidding his exhausted men find a good rest till the next noon, he himself went to the Inn of the Trois Dauphins. The mayor, the municipal officers, even the military commanders came to greet him. On the next morning he received a larger delegation, which asked him to pledge himself to constitutional government. He knew that Grenoble had been in the forefront of the Revolution, and that it had never lost its thirst for freedom. He addressed them in terms that repudiated his past absolutism and promised reform. He acknowledged that he had assumed excessive power, and that he had allowed his wars, originally defensive, to become wars of conquest, nearly exhausting France. He pledged himself to give France a representative government loyal to the principles of 1789 and 1792. Now, he told them, his dearest hope was to prepare his son to be the worthy and liberal leader of an enlightened France.[19]

That afternoon (March 8) he bade his followers resume their march; he would remain a day more at Grenoble to issue directives to those towns that were accepting his lead; but he promised to rejoin his band in time to help them to peaceful victories. On March 10 he caught up with them, and led them on to Lyons.

By this time the news of Napoleon's escapade had reached Louis XVIII. He was not at first alarmed, feeling confident that the culprit would soon be stopped. But as the march continued, and approached a Grenoble known for its hostility to the Bourbons, Louis issued on March 7 a proclamation exhorting every citizen to help take this troublesome criminal and bring him to a military court for trial and execution; and the same punishment was decreed for all who aided him. The King summoned Ney from retirement, and asked him to lead a force against Napoleon. Ney agreed, but the story that he vowed to bring Napoleon back in an iron cage is probably a fable.[20] Ney hurried south, took command of a battalion at Besançon, and called upon Generals de Bourmont and Lecourbe to join him with their forces at Lons-le-Saunier (northwest of Geneva). To the six thousand troops so assembled he made a fiery speech to stir their courage. "It is well," he said, "that the man from Elba has attempted his foolish enterprise, for it will be the last act of the *Napoléonade*."[21] There was little response from his men.

On that day, March 10, Lyons was acclaiming Napoleon. The manufacturers there had generally prospered under the Continental Blockade, which had opened all Europe except England to Lyons products, and they had no love for the *émigrés* who had returned to the city and were behaving as if there had never been a Revolution. In this resentment their employees agreed, for reasons of their own; many of them were ardent Jacobins, part of an underground current that now rose to the surface to welcome Napoleon in the hope that he would lead them back to 1789. The peasants of the hinterland trembled for their unblessed lands, and looked to Napoleon to quiet the priestly campaign for the restoration of the nationalized and redistributed ecclesiastical domains. And the soldiers of the garrison were eager to replace the red cockade on their bayonets.

So Lyons opened its gates, the royalists fled, the bourgeoisie smiled, the workers and soldiers cheered, as Napoleon led his regiment into the city. The municipal officials, the judges, even some military leaders came to offer their allegiance; he replied by promising a constitutional government and a policy of peace. The entire garrison, except its noble officers, joined his swelling army when he resumed the march on Paris. He had now twelve thousand troops to fight for him, but he still hoped to win without a shot. He wrote to Marie Louise, promising to be in Paris on March 20, the third anniversary of their son's birth, and telling her how happy she would make him if she could join him in Paris soon. He wrote to Ney a note as cordial as if there had never been a cloud on their friendship; he invited him to a meeting at Châlons, and promised to receive him as after the battle of Borodino—as "Prince of the Moskva."

On March 14, still at Lons-le-Saunier, Ney called his troops together and read to them the proclamation that was to cost him his life: "Soldiers, the cause of the Bourbon is lost forever. The legitimate dynasty that France has adopted is about to reascend the throne. It is the Emperor Napoleon, our sovereign, who is henceforth to reign over our glorious country." The soldiers shook the ground with their repeated cries of *"Vive l'Empereur! Vive le maréchal Ney!"*[22] He offered to lead them to join Napoleon's forces; they agreed; and Napoleon found them at Auxerre on March 17. On the 18th Napoleon received Ney, and their old friendship was renewed. No one dared, thereafter, to impede the march to Paris.

On the evening of the 17th, Louis XVIII, in royal apparel, appeared before the combined chambers in the Palais-Bourbon, and announced his determination to resist Napoleon. "I have labored," he said, "for the happiness of my people. Could I, sixty years old, better end my days than in dying in its defense?" He ordered the mobilization of all loyal forces. Some answered, but they were chiefly his household troops; the regular Army was slow to respond, and no able leader appeared to lead or inspire them. The royalists began to emigrate again.

Mme. de Staël's salon buzzed with rumors, and she too thought of flight. On March 19 the *Journal des débats* published an article by her intermittent lover Benjamin Constant reaffirming his support for Louis XVIII and constitutional government. That evening he went into hiding.

Louis himself, always reluctant to move, delayed departure till word came, on March 19, that Napoleon had reached Fontainebleau, and might be expected in Paris the next day. At 11 P.M. Louis and his family rode out from the Tuileries and headed for Lille. That city was strongly royalist, but doubtless the King thought, now and then, of a brother who had set out on a similar trip in 1791, and had been brought back a prisoner of the people.

On March 20 some enthusiastic Bonapartists, learning that the Tuileries was free of the King and his household troops, entered it in a gay impromptu, and prepared the royal chambers to receive Napoleon. All that day his swelling army marched toward its goal. Napoleon himself remained in Fontainebleau till 2 P.M., dictating messages and instructions, and presumably wandering fondly about the palace that had seen so much history, including an abdication now to be canceled and avenged. He reached Paris about 9 P.M., accompanied by Bertrand and Caulaincourt. They drove almost unnoticed until they reached the Tuileries. There a crowd of relatives and friends greeted him with wild ecstasy, lifting him bodily up the stairs. He submitted to one embrace after another, until he stood before them exhausted and bewildered, but happy to the point of tears. Hortense came; he reproached her for having accepted favors from Alexander; she defended herself; he melted, took her in his arms, and said, "I am a good father; you know it. . . . And you have been present at poor Josephine's death. Amid our many misfortunes her death pained my heart."[23]

So ended the incredible journey: 720 miles from Cannes to Paris in twenty days, accomplished by most of his companions on foot; and the vow kept that no shot should be fired in this reconquest of France. Now for the task of restoring internal peace and unity, forming a new government, and preparing to face 500,000 troops gathering from Russia, Prussia, Austria, and

England to send him back to his little island or a more distant one, or to a firing squad.

Every end is a beginning; and on this March 20, 1815, Napoleon Bonaparte began his Hundred Days.

V. REBUILDING

The task of restoring a government, an army, and a national will was made trebly difficult by the illegality of his position, the unity of his foreign enemies, and the disunion of his people.

He had again, as in 1799, seized by force—or the threat of force—a legally established government. True enough, he was taking back by force an authority which had been taken from him by force of arms; but he had formally surrendered his power by his abdication, and the Senate had offered the throne to Louis XVIII, who had accepted it as his legal right, and had not now relinquished it. In the eyes of the Allies—and of a considerable portion of the French people—he was a usurper.

His foreign enemies were now more firmly united against him than in their massive campaigns of 1813–14. The many nations represented at the Congress of Vienna had been unanimous in branding him an outlaw. Not only had Russia, Prussia, Austria, and England pledged, each of them, 150,000 troops to the new campaign to remove him from the scene; Sweden, the new German Confederation, and even little Switzerland had promised to contribute to the wall of flesh and money that was rising to move upon him.

He sent them humble offers to negotiate a bloodless settlement; they made no answer. He appealed to his father-in-law, Emperor Francis II of Austria, to intercede for him with the other Allies—no answer came. He wrote to his wife to solicit her aid in softening her father; apparently the message never reached her. On March 25 the united Allies proclaimed that they were not making war against France, but would never make peace with Napoleon Bonaparte, lest he should again lead France—willing or not—into another war disturbing the foundations of European order.

France was by no means united against the united Allies. Thousands of royalists remained there to plead the case, and organize the defense, of the absent King. On March 22 hundreds of them welcomed him into Lille on his flight from Paris, and they grieved when he moved on to Ghent, where he would again be protected by British power. In the south of France the royalists were strong enough to keep control of Bordeaux and Marseilles. In the west the deeply Catholic Vendée had again risen in arms against Napoleon, whom they considered an atheistic persecutor of their Pope, a crypto-Jacobin ally of regicides,[24] and an obstinate protector of property stolen from the Church. In May, 1815, he sent twenty thousand troops to quell this passionate insurrection. Often, later, he mourned that these added troops might have won Waterloo.[25]

Against his internal foes he could range some elements of public support not all agreeable to his views and character. Most agreeable was the Army, which (except in Bordeaux and the Vendée) was devoted to him as the organizer and rewarder of victory. The lower ranks of the nation—peasants, proletaires, and city populace—were ready to follow his lead, but they hoped he could avoid war, and they no longer gave him the worship that had made him reckless and proud. There were still many Jacobins in the cities, willing to forget his hostility to them if he would declare himself loyal to the Revolution. He accepted their support, but would not pledge himself to their war against merchants and priests.

He admired the middle class as the foundation of that social-moral order which, since the September Massacres, had become the center of his political philosophy; but it did not offer him its support or its sons. It valued freedom of enterprise and trade and the press, but not of the ballot or of public speech; it feared the radicals, and wished to limit the franchise to property owners. It had elected the Chamber of Deputies, and was resolved to protect the rights of that body to check the power and policies of the king or emperor. And that rising section of the bourgeoisie—the intelligentsia of journalists, authors, scientists, philosophers—was making it quite clear that it would fight with all its weapons against any attempt of Napoleon to reestablish imperial power.

The challenged hero was himself divided, in purpose and will. He still worked hard, noting everything, giving orders, sometimes dictating 150 letters in a day.[26] But his very alertness weakened him, for it told him how little he could rely upon his new generals, or the chambers, or the nation, or even upon himself. The diseases that six years later would kill him were already weakening him; hemorrhoids irritated and humiliated him. He could not work as long as in the halcyon days of Marengo and Austerlitz. He had lost something of his old clearness of mind and steadiness of purpose, his old buoyant confidence in victory. He had begun to doubt his "star."[27]

On the very evening of his reaching Paris he chose a new ministry, for he needed its aid at once. He rejoiced to learn that Lazare Carnot (the "organizer of victory" during the Revolution) was ready to serve him against his enemies; he found him—aged sixty-two—too old for battle, but made him minister of the interior, as one whom all could trust. Hardly for such a reason he chose, as minister of police, Joseph Fouché, now fifty-six, suspected and feared by all, managing a private network of spies, and maintaining secret relations with almost every faction; probably the hurried ruler gave him his old office to keep him under scrutiny; and no one questioned Fouché's ability. In most of the complications that followed he kept the clearest vision and the most flexible morality. "The Emperor in my eyes," he was to write in his *Memoirs*, "was nothing but a worn-out actor, whose performance could not be reenacted."[28] Even while serving Napoleon he predicted, toward the end of March, "He can't last longer than three months."[29]

The next step was to organize an army. Louis XVIII had felt no need for any except for internal order; consequently he had ended conscription, and had reduced his military to 160,000 men. Napoleon restored conscription in June, but these lucky youths were not yet mobilized when Waterloo ended the war. He called upon the National Guard to prepare itself for full—including foreign—service; many refused; 150,000 obeyed. Adding these and some volunteers to the existing Army, he could muster, in June, 300,000 men. He stationed most of them in the northern departments, and bade them await further orders. Meanwhile he repeated his exploits of 1813 and 1814 in raising and allocating provisions and matériel for the new Army. Secretly he imported guns from his favorite enemy, England.[30] He could not use all his former marshals, for some had committed themselves to Louis XVIII; but he still had Ney, Davout, Soult, Grouchy, Vandamme. He studied maps of roads and terrain, and reports of enemy movements, and planned every major aspect of the coming campaign. In such planning he was at his best and happiest.

He was least comfortable in his third task—to win public support despite his seizure of the government. Nearly all elements except the royalists demanded his commitment to a constitution that would protect freedom of speech and press, and make him responsible to an elected parliament. This went sorely against his grain, for he had long been accustomed to absolute rule, and felt that an able and well-intentioned dictator like himself was better for a country than a *parlement* of palaver and a count of noses whether of voters or of deputies. Nevertheless, in a gesture of conciliation, he sent for Benjamin Constant (April 6) to draw up a constitution that would appease the liberals without manacling the monarchy. He knew that Constant had written violently against him, but he recognized in him a finished stylist and a flexible mind. Constant came, uncertain of his fate, and was relieved to find that all that the Emperor asked of him was to extemporize a constitution that would satisfy both Napoleon and Mme. de Staël. He labored for a week, daily exposing his product to his employer. On April 14 he presented the result to the Council of State.

It proposed a constitutional monarchy in which the hereditary head of the state would have ample executive powers, but would be responsible to a Chamber of Peers nominated by the ruler, and a legislative Chamber of (six hundred) Representatives elected by the people through intermediate assemblies. Specific clauses abolished state censorship and guaranteed freedom of worship and the press. In this quite traditional way the Emperor and his scribe felt that they had united the charms of democracy, aristocracy, and monarchy.

After all this had been accepted by Napoleon, he insisted that the new constitution be presented to the people not as a repudiation of his past rule but as an "Acte Additionnel" certifying liberties that (Napoleon argued) had already existed under the Empire. Constant and his liberal advisers protested and yielded. On April 23 the Acte Additionnel was submitted to a plebiscite of all registered voters. The royalists refused to vote; many others abstained. The vote was 1,552,450 for, 4,800 against. Napoleon ordered that on May 26 the people should assemble on the Champ-de-Mars, in a massive and formal ceremony called the Champ de Mai, to celebrate the adoption of the constitution, the beginning of a new era, and the blessing and departure of the troops. The assembly, postponed to June 1, showed Napoleon in a royal mood: he came dressed in his robes as emperor, in his coronation coach drawn by four horses, and preceded by his brothers as princes of the Empire. The assemblage was not pleased by this aroma of a dead past. What had happened to the new constitution?

The nation received it with some skepticism and much indifference; apparently many doubted its sincerity or permanence. Napoleon himself gave contradictory testimony on this point. According to Las Cases, the Emperor felt that doubt of his sincerity was unjustified:

> I returned from Elba a new man. They could not believe it; they could not imagine that a man might have sufficient strength of mind to alter his character, or to bend to the power of circumstances. I had, however, given proofs of this, and some pledge to the same effect. Who is ignorant that I am not a man for half measures? I should have been as sincerely the monarch of the constitution of peace as I had been of absolute sway and great enterprises.[31]

But the usually trustworthy Gourgaud, devoted to Napoleon, quoted him as saying, "I was wrong in losing precious time about a constitution, all the more since it was my intention to send them [the deputies] packing as soon as I had been victorious."[32]

He had planned to convoke the chambers only after the campaign, when he might come to them with a persuasive victory. But Lafayette, who had emerged from his rural seclusion, aged fifty-eight, to play a part in the drama, insisted on having the Chamber of Representatives convene before Napoleon's departure to join his troops. Napoleon yielded, and the Chamber met on June 3. At once it gave some indication of its mood by electing as its president Comte Jean-Denis Lanjuinais, a fervent enemy of the Emperor. On June 7 Napoleon, in simple costume, went to the Palais-Bourbon and addressed the combined chambers in so modest a manner that all the delegates took an oath to the new constitution, and of fidelity to the Emperor.[33]

On June 12, about three o'clock in the morning, while Paris slept, Napoleon left for the front.

VI. THE LAST CAMPAIGN

1. June 15, 1815: Belgium

Napoleon's plan of campaign was based upon his information about the amount, division, leadership, location, and prospective strategy of the Allied forces. Their westward movement had been postponed to give the Russians time to arrive and share in the campaign; but Napoleon's swift advance brought the decision before the Russians could reach the Rhine.

By June 1 a Prussian army of 120,000 had assembled near Namur in Belgium, under the seventy-three-year-old Marshal Blücher. Farther north, around Brussels, the Duke of Wellington (his mission in Portugal and Spain having been triumphantly completed) had been given command of what he called an "infamous army" of 93,000 British, Dutch, Belgian, and German recruits, most of whom knew only one language, and were a problem for an English commander. Wellington had to supply their lack of training by his own resolution and experience. A moment's contemplation of Lawrence's portrait of him—proud pose, fine features, calm steady vision—suggests what the tired and ailing Napoleon, physically older than their equal age, was to encounter on June 18.

Napoleon had left some of his army to guard Paris and his line of communications. To challenge the 213,000 men led by Blücher and Wellington, he had 126,000 in his Armée du Nord. His hope, of course, was to meet and defeat one of the two armies before they could unite, and then, after rest and reorganization, to dispose of the other. The main route between the Allied armies ran from Namur through Sombreffe to Quatre-Bras (Four Arms), and thence west by a wider road from the Franco–Belgian frontier at Charleroi north by Waterloo to Brussels. Napoleon's first objective was to capture Quatre-Bras and thereby close the route between the two Allied armies.

He had instructed the three columns of his Army of the North to converge on June 14 at the River Sambre opposite Charleroi. He joined one of the columns, and ordered all three of them to begin crossing the river into Belgium about 3 A.M. of June 15. They did, and easily captured Charleroi from its small Prussian garrison. About the same time, however, General Louis de Bourmont defected to the Allies, and revealed Napoleon's plans to Blücher's officers. The alert "Vorwärts" had guessed them, and had sent part of his army west to Sombreffe, and joined it about 4 A.M. on the 15th.

Napoleon now divided his army into a right wing under Grouchy, a left wing under Ney, and a reserve force, stationed near Charleroi under Drouet d'Erlon, to go to the aid of Grouchy or Ney as need should call. Grouchy was to advance northeast toward Sombreffe to challenge Blücher; Ney was to march north and capture Quatre-Bras and in any case prevent Wellington from coming to join Blücher. Napoleon himself, expecting a major clash with Blücher, rode with Grouchy.

Ney, heretofore "the bravest of the brave," followed, on June 15 and 16, a policy of caution that badly disrupted Napoleon's plans. Moving north from Charleroi, he drove the Prussians out of Gosselies, and then halted, fearing to encounter Wellington's much larger force. He sent a cavalry detachment ahead to check the situation at Quatre-Bras; it returned with the report that that town was free of enemy troops. He led 3,000 men to take it, thinking that these would suffice; but by the time he sighted Quatre-Bras it had been occupied by Prince Bernhard of Saxe-Weimar with 4,000 troops and eight guns; Ney turned back to Gosselies and awaited further instructions. Bernhard sent a message to Wellington to bring his main army down to Quatre-Bras, lest Ney's main force should soon besiege it.

At 3 P.M. on June 15, Wellington, at Brussels, received news that Napoleon's army had crossed into Belgium. Believing that Napoleon would follow his custom of making an end run for a flank attack, he held his forces in readiness near the Belgian capital. That evening he and many of his officers—"brave men" with a fondness for "fair women"—attended a ball given by the Duchess of Richmond.[34] There, about midnight, he received a message that Quatre-Bras was in danger. He quietly gave orders to his officers to prepare to march early that morning. He himself, not to disturb the elegant affair, stayed and danced till 3 A.M.[35]

2. June 16: Ligny

About 2 P.M. of June 16 Marshal Soult, Napoleon's chief of staff, sent final orders to Ney:

> The Emperor charges me to notify you that the enemy has assembled a body of troops between Sombreffe and Brye, and that at 2:30 P.M. Marshal Grouchy, with the Third and Fourth Corps, will attack him. The intention of his Majesty is that you should attack whatever [enemy] is before you, and that after having vigorously pressed them back you should turn toward us and join us in surrounding the enemy.[36]

Blücher brought up all his 83,000 men to resist the French. The battle began about 3 P.M. near the town of Ligny, with simultaneous attacks by Grouchy's right under Vandamme, his center under Gérard, and his left— the cavalry—under Grouchy himself, with Napoleon directing the triple operation of 78,000 men. It soon became evident that the redoubtable Blücher was not to be easily disposed of; and if the French should be defeated here their entire campaign would collapse. At 3:15 Napoleon sent an appeal to Ney: "The Prussian army is lost if you will act vigorously. The fate of France is in your hands. Therefore do not delay for an instant to execute the movement which has been proposed to you, and turn toward St.-Amand and Brye to join in a victory that may decide all."[37]

But Ney too was in difficulties. By 3 P.M. Wellington had brought down most of his army to Quatre-Bras. Not knowing this (for communications had fallen apart in Soult's hands), Napoleon sent orders to Drouet d'Erlon at Charleroi to hurry north with his reserve force and attack Blücher's right flank. Drouet had advanced almost to Ligny when a courier brought him an urgent command from Ney to rush to his support against Wellington's superior numbers at Quatre-Bras. Drouet thought Ney's need the more urgent, and marched his corps to Quatre-Bras, only to find that Ney, after desperate efforts and having two horses killed under him, had given up the attempt to dislodge Wellington.

At Ligny the battle raged through six hours of slaughter, in which no quarter was given by either side; a Prussian officer later recalled that "the men massacred one another as if they had been animated with a personal hatred."[38] Once quiet villages like St.-Amand and La Haye passed from side to side in desperate man-to-man combat. Ligny itself went up in flames. As night and rain fell Napoleon ordered his Old Guard to attack the Prussian center. The rain became a thunderstorm; the Prussian center gave way; Blücher, still resisting, fell from his horse, and had to be carried away. The French were too exhausted to turn the defeat into a rout. The Prussians retreated north toward Wavre, leaving twelve thousand dead or wounded behind them. Napoleon himself had used almost the last resources of his nervous strength. If Wellington had been able to come up at that moment from Quatre-Bras there might have been no Waterloo.

3. June 17: Rain

It was just as well for Napoleon that the downpour made a major battle impossible on the 17th. The ground was mud; how could artillery be drawn or stationed in that sodden and fluctuating earth? Those adjectives might have been applied to the imperial mind when, at 7 A.M., a message from Ney told Napoleon that Wellington was holding Quatre-Bras, and implying that only the full French army could dislodge him. Napoleon's answer—or its obscure phrasing—must have left Ney more bewildered than ever: "Take up your position at Quatre-Bras. . . . But if this is impossible . . . send information immediately, and the Emperor will act then. If . . . there is only a rear guard, attack it and seize the position."[39] There was more than a rear guard, and Ney refused to renew the attack. Wellington, having heard of Blücher's defeat, withdrew his army north to a defensible plateau called Mont St.-Jean, and retired to his headquarters at nearby Waterloo.

Napoleon directed Grouchy, with 30,000 men, to pursue the Prussians throughout June 17, and in any case prevent them from joining Wellington. He himself, with 40,000 survivors from the battle of Ligny, marched to join Ney at Quatre-Bras. When he arrived, about 2 P.M., he was disheartened to learn that Wellington was not there. *On a perdu la France!* he cried; "we have lost France!"[40] He ordered pursuit, and himself led it, with Ney and Drouet d'Erlon; but a heavy shower decided him to end the pursuit. At 9 P.M., wet to the skin, he rode back a mile or two to sleep in bed at Caillou; and his exhausted army—the rain having ceased—bivouacked upon the wet ground for the night.

4. Sunday, June 18: Waterloo

At 2 A.M. Blücher sent a message to Wellington promising him that a Prussian corps under General Friedrich Wilhelm von Bülow would leave Wavre at daybreak to join him against the French, and that two other Prussian corps would follow soon thereafter. At 10 A.M. Napoleon, not knowing of these courtesies, sent instructions to Grouchy to continue pursuing Blücher to Wavre.

He had planned to begin action at 9 A.M., but his artillery captains persuaded him to delay until the soil had begun to dry. Meanwhile Wellington had stationed his forces on raised land south of Mont St.-Jean. He had 70,000 men and 184 guns; Napoleon had 74,000 men and 266 guns. Each leader had

generals who had earned—or would here earn—a place in history: Prince
Friedrich of Brunswick (son of the Duke who had lost at Valmy and had
been mortally wounded at Auerstedt), Dörnberg, Alten, Kempt, Somerset,
Uxbridge, Hill, Ponsonby, Picton, all under a Wellington as tough as his
language and as proud as a duke. Add Bülow, Zieten, and Pirch under
Blücher; and, for the French, Ney, Grouchy, Vandamme, Gérard, Cam-
bronne, Kellermann, Reille, Lobau, and Napoleon.

He had begun to pay for crowding years into every month, eating and
mating hastily, living at high tension on throne and battlefield, and, lately,
solacing his sorrows with food. Six years later the post-mortem examination
of his organs would show half a dozen ailments and abnormalities. Now, at
Waterloo, he had to spend hours on horseback while suffering from hemorrhoids;[41] he had stones in the bladder, and his dysuria required frequent and
often untimely urination; and perhaps the cancer that killed him and his
father was already consuming him.[42] These disorders wore him down in
vigor, courage, patience, and confidence. "I no longer had in me the sentiment of final success. . . . I felt fortune abandon me."[43] Nevertheless, presumably to give them confidence, he assured his worried generals, "If my
orders are well executed we shall sleep tonight in Brussels."[44]

His generals saw the situation more clearly. Soult advised him to bid
Grouchy bring his 30,000 men west, as soon as possible, and join in the attack; instead Napoleon allowed them to spend time and themselves in chasing
Blücher north to Wavre; presumably he hoped that if the Prussians turned
west to help Wellington, Grouchy would attack their rear. Wellington
made, according to aftersight, an equally serious error in leaving 17,000 of
his men near Brussels to guard against a French flank attack upon his vital
approaches to the sea.

At 11 A.M. Napoleon ordered his army to begin the attack—upon the
enemy center, which was manned by tough Scots and Englishmen. Ney led
with all his old dash and bravery, but the British held firm. From behind one
hill after another hidden artillery spread death wholesale among the startled
French. About 1 P.M., from his observation post considerably southwest of
the action, Napoleon saw, far east, a cloud of troops moving toward the
battle; a German prisoner told him that these were the van of Bülow's Prussian corps, marching to help Wellington. Napoleon sent a battalion under
General Lobau to intercept the Prussians, and dispatched a message to
Grouchy to attack Bülow and then come to help the main French army
against Wellington. About 11:30 A.M. Grouchy, marching north between
Gembloux and Wavre, heard the noise of cannon fire in the west. General
Gérard urged him to abandon pursuit of Blücher, and strike cross-country to
add his 30,000 men to Napoleon's. Grouchy caught up with part of Blücher's
forces, defeated it, entered Wavre, found Blücher gone, and rested.

By that time, 4 P.M., the battle of Waterloo was at its height: a vast melee
of men killing or being killed, gaining or losing a strategic post, facing onrushing horses, dodging a dozen swords, falling and dying in the mud. Thousands deserted on either side; Wellington spent part of his time riding behind

the lines and frightening deserters back to their posts. Ney led charge after charge; four horses were killed under him. Toward 6 P.M. he received an order from Napoleon to seize La Haye Sainte—the Holy Hedgerow. He succeeded, and thought he had found an opening to Wellington's last line. He sent an appeal to Napoleon for additional infantry, and pushed ahead. Napoleon fumed at his reckless advance, for which no adequate support could be sent without weakening the general plan; but, feeling that "the wretch" could not be allowed perish, he ordered Kellermann to go to Ney's support with 3,000 cuirassiers. When the leader of the last British line asked Wellington for reinforcements the Duke answered that he had none. The officer is said to have replied, "Very well, my lord; we'll stand till the last man falls."[45] When the English line seemed to be breaking, a section of the French cavalry rushed forward to share in the victory. An English officer, Colonel Gould, concluded, "I'm afraid it's all over."[46] A Hanoverian regiment at this point deserted and fled to Brussels, shouting to all, "The battle is lost, and the French are coming!"[47]

But it was the Prussians who were coming. Bülow had broken Lobau's resistance, and was rapidly nearing the main action; and two more Prussian corps were approaching. Napoleon saw that his last chance was to crush the English before the Prussians could intervene. He called upon his Old Guard to follow him to the decisive attack. A French deserter found his way to Wellington and warned him, "The Guards will be on you in half an hour." About this time a British marksman sighted Napoleon. "There's Bonaparte, sir," he said. "I think I can reach him. May I fire?" The Duke forbade him: "No, no, generals commanding armies have something else to do than to shoot one another."[48]

Then, when the French thought they were victorious, the cry came to Napoleon, the Guards, and Ney that the Prussians, 30,000 of them,[49] were attacking the French, and were spreading terror and disorder. When Ney charged again, the British line held fast, and Ney fell back. Wellington saw his chance. Riding the top of the slope to be more visible, he waved his hat in the air as the signal agreed upon for a general advance; drums and bugles carried the message; 40,000 Englishmen, Scots, Belgians, and Germans— right, center, and left—changed from defense to offense, and swept forward, careless of life. The morale of the French faltered and collapsed, and they fled; even the Old Guard began to turn their horses back. Napoleon shouted orders to stop; they were not heard in the tumult; and the smoke of battle helped the growing dusk to make him indistinguishable in the mass. Yielding to this sudden plebiscite, he commanded a retreat in the forms prescribed by the manual of order, but the French, attacked in front and flank by overwhelmingly superior numbers, had no time for disciplined formations; "*Sauve qui peut!* Let each save himself who can!" became the motto, spoken or not, of the shattered army, no longer soldiers but men. Amid the rout Marshal Ney, the faint of flesh and heart at Quatre-Bras, the hero of heroes at Waterloo, stood horseless and bewildered, his face blackened with powder, his uniform in rags, a broken sword in the hand that had almost grasped victory.[50] Then he too—and Napoleon—joined the 40,000 men rushing down roads and fields to Genappe, to Quatre-Bras, to Charleroi, and then, by whatever means, over the River Sambre to France.

They left behind them 25,000 dead or wounded, and 8,000 prisoners. Wellington had lost 15,000, Blücher 7,000. The two victors met on the road near La Belle Alliance, and exchanged kisses. Wellington left the pursuit to the enthusiastic Prussians, and Blücher, too old for the chase, turned it over to Gneisenau at Genappe, and there he sent a message to his wife: "In concert with my friend Wellington, I have exterminated the army of Napoleon." But also he wrote to his friend Knesebeck: "I tremble in all my members. The effort has been too great."[51] Wellington put the matter to Lord Uxbridge in his hearty way: "We have given Napoleon the *coup de grâce*. There is nothing left for him but to hang himself."[52]

In the retreat Napoleon joined one of the more orderly regiments, dismounted, and walked with the others. He wept for his lost army,[53] and mourned that he had not died.

CHAPTER XXXVIII

To St. Helena

I. THE SECOND ABDICATION: JUNE 22, 1815

H E reached Paris about 8 A.M. June 21. "I was thoroughly exhausted,"
he later recalled. "For three days I had neither eaten nor slept."[1] He
went to the Élysée Palace, pleading to Caulaincourt, "I need two hours of
rest."[2] Meanwhile the Chamber of Representatives assembled, and sentiment
there was strongly for his abdication. Informed of this, he proposed to his
friends that the chaos of opinion in the country, and the need for united action to defend France and its capital against any attempt of the Allies to
control the nation or its government, required a temporary dictatorship.

When the people of Paris learned of the military disaster many of them
gathered before the Élysée, affirmed their continued faith in Napoleon with
cries of *"Vive l'Empereur!"* and asked for arms that they might defend the
city. Hearing them, Napoleon said to Benjamin Constant, "You see, it is
not these people upon whom I heaped honors and money. What do they
owe me? I found them poor, and I have left them poor. . . . If I willed it,
in an hour the rebellious Chamber would cease to exist. . . . But the life of
one man is not worth this price. I do not wish to be the King of Jacqueries.
I did not come from Elba in order that Paris should be inundated with
blood."[3]

Even during his flight from Waterloo he had planned to raise another
army, this time of 300,000 men.[4] Between June 22 and June 24 the remains
of his defeated army gathered and were reorganized at Laon, seventy-seven
miles northeast of Paris; and there, on June 26, Grouchy, after a brilliant
retreat, joined them with 30,000 men. Meanwhile, however, Blücher had
assembled his victorious forces, and was leading them toward Paris, carefully bypassing Laon. Wellington, his army badly hurt, hesitated to join
the impetuous Prussian, but soon he too was on the road, also avoiding
Laon. At the same time, June 22–25, the armies of Austria, Bavaria, and
Württemberg crossed the Rhine and headed for Paris. History repeated itself.

The Chamber of Representatives, after passionate debates, concluded
that resistance to the Allies was impracticable, and that they would insist
on Napoleon's abdication. Fouché, still Napoleon's minister of police,
worked in his subtle ways to secure this abdication. He had predicted, before Waterloo, "The Emperor will win one or two battles; he will lose the
third; at that point our role will begin."[5] But Fouché did not wait that long.
Napoleon's brother Lucien rushed to the Chamber to urge delay; Fouché
worked against him, and Lafayette asked, Had not Napoleon consumed
enough lives? Lucien, victor in 1799, admitted failure now. He advised Na-

750

poleon to forcibly overthrow the chambers; Napoleon refused. The exhaustion of battle and defeat had weakened his will, but had clarified his vision; and while the crowd outside the palace continued to shout *"Vive l'Empereur!"* he dictated to Lucien, June 22, 1815, his Second Abdication, addressed to the two chambers:

> In beginning the war for national independence, I counted on the reunion of all efforts, . . . and on the agreement of all the nation's governing bodies. Circumstances seem to me to have changed. . . . I offer myself as sacrifice to the hatred of the enemies of France. May they be sincere in their declarations, and in having really desired nothing more than my person. Unite, all of you, for the public safety, and for our remaining independent action. . . . I proclaim my son in the name of Napoleon II.[6]

All his ministers agreed to his abdication except Carnot, who wept. Fouché rejoiced.

The two chambers accepted the abdication, ignored its nomination of Napoleon's four-year-old son (then in Vienna) as his successor, and chose five of its members—Fouché, Carnot, Caulaincourt, Grenier (an obscure general), and Ouinette (a member of the old revolutionary Convention)—to serve as a "Commission Exécutive" and a Provisional Government. Fouché was chosen president of the commission, and negotiated directly with the Allies and Napoleon. Fearing a popular uprising in favor of Napoleon, he persuaded Davout, military commander in the capital, to prevail upon Napoleon to leave Paris and retire to Malmaison. On June 25, accompanied by Bertrand, Gourgaud, Comte de Las Cases, and Comte de Montholon, Napoleon left for Malmaison, where Hortense welcomed him to her late mother's home. Walking with Hortense in the garden, he spoke fondly of Josephine. "Truly," he said, "she was more full of grace than any woman I have ever seen."[7]

He thought now of seeking refuge and peace in America. He asked Bertrand to secure for him several books about the United States.[8] He had read Alexander von Humboldt's *Voyages aux contrées équinoctiales du nouveau continent;* he proposed to give the remainder of his life to science; now he would go to America and explore its soil, flora, and fauna from Canada to Cape Horn. On June 26 he sent to the Provisional Government a request for passage to Rochefort, with a view to sailing thence for America.[9] Fouché at once ordered the Minister of Marine to "prepare two frigates at Rochefort to carry Napoleon Bonaparte to the United States."[10] On that same day Napoleon was visited by his brothers Joseph, Lucien, and Jérôme, who had all decided to leave France—Joseph for America. Perhaps it was they who brought to him a message from their mother, offering him "all that she possessed." He thanked her, but took no advantage of her offer. He still had a substantial fund with the banker Jacques Laffitte, who came in person to Malmaison to arrange Napoleon's finances.

On June 28 an officer of the Garde Nationale came to warn him that the Prussians were near enough to Malmaison to send a detachment to capture him. Actually Blücher had ordered a flying column to get Napoleon alive or dead, and had expressed his intention to shoot him as an outlaw.[11] Hearing of this intention, Gourgaud vowed, "If I see the Emperor fall into the hands of the Prussians I will shoot him." Even so, Napoleon was loath to leave Malmaison, where every room and walk was rich with happy memories. On June 29 Fouché commissioned General Becker to go to Malmaison with a squad of troops to compel Napoleon to leave for Rochefort.

Napoleon agreed to go. Hortense prevailed upon him to accept her diamond necklace, concealed in a belt and worth 200,000 francs. He bade farewell to the few soldiers who had been protecting him. At 5 P.M., June 29, riding in a caleche drawn by four horses, and with a small military escort, he left Malmaison. A few hours later Blücher's cavalry arrived.

II. THE SECOND RESTORATION: JULY 7, 1815

The chambers and the Provisional Government debated whether to fight the oncoming Allies or negotiate for the best obtainable terms. Davout offered to lead his city militia against Wellington and Blücher if these insisted on restoring Louis XVIII. The representatives feared that resistance and defeat would lead to the dismemberment of France, and something short of that for themselves. The remnants of Napoleon's "Army of the North" were in no mood for another Waterloo; they were inadequately supplied, and the enemy were united between Laon and Paris.

Louis XVIII, learning that one faction among the Allies was working for his replacement by Louis Philippe, Duc d'Orléans, moved down anxiously from Ghent to Cateau-Cambrésis, and there issued (June 25) a declaration promising conciliation and a liberal regime. The chambers were pleased, and on June 30 the Provisional Government and the Allies signed preliminary terms for the capitulation of the capital. All French troops were to retire beyond the Loire, but the security and property of the citizens were guaranteed. On July 7 the Allies entered Paris. On July 8 Louis XVIII rode down the Champs-Élysées in state, and resumed the throne of France. The prefect of the Seine department, in welcoming him, used—apparently for the first time—the term "Cent Jours," or Hundred Days, to describe the period between Napoleon's second usurpation (March 20) and the restoration of the King.

Most of the country accepted this *da capo al fine* as the only practical solution of the problems raised by the sudden collapse of Napoleon's regime. Blücher, however, raised an outcry by announcing that he would ask his engineers to blow up the Pont d'Iéna—the bridge commemorating the French victory over the Prussians in 1806; moreover, he proposed to destroy all monuments to Napoleon. Wellington united with Louis XVIII in urging Blücher to desist; he persisted; but Czar Alexander I, King Frederick William III, and Emperor Francis II, arriving with the Russian, Austrian, and Piedmontese armies, commanded the old patriot to calm his fury.[12]

The foreign troops in France now totaled some 800,000, all requiring to be fed by the people, and policing them in return. Castlereagh calculated that it cost France 1,750,000 francs per day to feed its occupiers. In addition each district had to pay a heavy indemnity. Louis XVIII told the Allied leaders that if, contrary to their proclamation of March 25, they continued to treat his subjects as enemies, he would leave France and seek asylum in Spain. The Allies agreed to limit the indemnities to 50 million francs, and argued that they were fully justified by the laws of war and the precedents established by Napoleon in Prussia and Austria.

Likewise the royalists in some French cities indulged themselves in a "White Terror" to avenge the Red Terror that had killed so many royalists in 1793–94. They were not always without immediate excuse. When the royalist faction in Marseilles made a demonstration demanding the restoration of Louis XVIII, some soldiers of the local garrison, still pledged to Napoleon, fired on them. The commander soon stopped this, and tried to lead his troops out of the hostile city; but on their way some hundred of them were shot from windows or roofs (June 25). On that day and the next armed royalists ran about the city, shooting Bonapartists and Jacobins; two hundred victims died, many of them still crying "*Vive l'Empereur!*" Royalist women danced with joy around the corpses.[13] At Avignon the royalists imprisoned and killed all captured Bonapartists. One man they sought especially—Guillaume Bruné, who was accused of having carried the head of the Princesse de Lamballe on his pike in 1792. He hid in an Avignon hotel; the crowd found him, shot him, and dragged his corpse through the streets, beating it ecstatically; then, having thrown it into the Rhone, the men and women danced with joy (August 2, 1815). There were similar scenes at Nîmes, Montpellier, and Toulouse.

These barbarities could hardly be attributed to Louis XVIII, who was basically a forgiving man. But he could never forgive Ney, who had promised to bring to him Napoleon alive or dead, had gone over to Napoleon, and had dealt out so many deaths at Waterloo. Ney fled from Paris on July 6, and wandered from town to town in disguise; he was recognized and arrested; was tried by a court of 161 peers, and was found guilty of treason. He refused all priestly services, and was executed by a firing squad on December 7, 1815.

Fouché and Talleyrand, now in Louis XVIII's ministry, were triumphant but unhappy. The royalists in the Cabinet shunned Fouché as a regicide, and advised the King to dismiss him. Louis compromised by appointing him minister to Saxony (September 15); but three months later he recalled him and banished him from France. Fouché wandered unwanted from Prague to Linz to Trieste, and died there in 1820, having crowded an incredible amount of deviltry into sixty-one years.

Talleyrand rivaled him in wiles, and surpassed him in durability. Louis XVIII judged him with lines from Corneille: "He has done me too much good that I should speak ill of him, and too much harm that I should speak well of him."[14] It was apparently Talleyrand who said of the Bourbons (in 1796), "They have learned nothing and forgotten nothing";[15] but this could hardly have been said of Louis XVIII, who learned to deal with elected chambers, welcomed Napoleon's generals, and preserved much of Napoleon's legislation. The royalist ministers hated Talleyrand as not only a regicide and an apostate but a traitor to his class. Yielding to them, Louis dismissed him (September 24, 1815). Talleyrand recovered, outlived Louis XVIII, survived the abdication of Charles X (1830), and was appointed ambassador to Great Britain (1830–34) at the age of seventy-six. When the Marquess of Londonderry, in the House of Lords, criticized Talleyrand, Wellington defended him; he had dealt with M. de Talleyrand in many situations (said the Duke), and never had he found a man more vigorous and skillful in protecting the interests of his country, and more upright and honorable in dealing with other countries. When Talleyrand read this he came close to tears, than which nothing could have been more unbecoming in him. "I am all the more grateful to the Duke, since he is the one statesman in the world who has ever spoken well of me."[16] Having helped to organize the Quadruple Alliance in 1834, he died in 1838, aged eighty-four, having outwitted everybody, almost the Reaper himself.

On November 20, 1815, Louis XVIII signed with the Allies the Second Treaty of Paris, which formulated the penalties France was to suffer for allowing Napoleon to resume his rule. She was compelled to cede the Saar and Savoy, and four frontier towns, including Philippeville and Marienburg; to restore the art her conquering generals had taken; to pay an indemnity of 700 million francs, plus 240 million on private claims; to be occupied by the commissioners and troops of the Allies for from three to five years, and to pay for their maintenance.[17] Talleyrand refused to sign this document; his successor as foreign minister, Armand-Emmanuel du Plessis, Duc de Richelieu, signed it under protest, and then cried out, "I am dishonored."[18]

III. SURRENDER: JULY 4 – AUGUST 8, 1815

Riding south from Malmaison, Napoleon was joined at Niort by his brother Joseph and his brother-in-arms Gourgaud. They reached Rochefort (thirteen miles southeast of La Rochelle) late on July 3, and found the expected frigates—the *Saale* and the *Méduse*—anchored in the harbor; but behind these was a small squadron of British warships blockading the port and apparently forbidding unlicensed egress.

On July 4 Napoleon sent an inquiry to the captain of the *Saale*—could rooms be prepared for him and some friends for a voyage to America, and could the *Saale* get through the blockade? He was told that the frigates were ready, and might try to elude the warships at night, at the risk of being stopped or bombarded; but if they got through, their superior speed would soon lose the men-of-war. Napoleon now revealed the effects of his recent ordeals by beginning nine days of vacillation, turning from one plan to another for escape, and from one companion to another for advice. Jo-

seph, who resembled him in appearance, offered to disguise himself as the
Emperor, and to let himself be detained by the British, while Napoleon, in
civilian dress, might be allowed to leave on one of the frigates on an apparently routine voyage. Napoleon refused to endanger his brother. Joseph
himself later sailed on one of the frigates to America.

Forgetting fifteen years of war, Napoleon now played with the fancy
that England, if he voluntarily surrendered, might treat him as a distinguished prisoner, and allow him a modest plot of land on which he might
live as a peaceful squire. On July 10 he sent Las Cases and Savary (Duc de
Rovigo) to ask Captain Frederick Maitland, on H.M.S. *Bellerophon*, if
any passports had been received by him for Napoleon's passage to America.
The captain, of course, had none. Then Las Cases asked whether, if Napoleon surrendered himself to the British, he might expect to be treated with
the usual generosity of the English people. Maitland replied that he would
be glad to receive Napoleon and take him to England, but that he had no
authority to make any promise about his reception there.

Shortly before or after or during that conversation Captain Maitland received from his superior, Vice-Admiral Sir Henry Hotham (then cruising
off the northwest coast of France), a message apprising him that Napoleon
was in or near Rochefort, and was intending to cross to America. The admiral added: "You will employ the best means of preventing him from sailing on the frigates. . . . If you have the good fortune to capture him, you
will put him under good guard, and proceed with all careful speed to a port
in Britain."[19]

On or about July 14 Napoleon received warning that Louis XVIII had
ordered General Bonnefours to proceed to Rochefort and arrest him.[20]
Bonnefours acted as slowly as he dared. Napoleon now felt restricted to
three choices: to surrender to Louis XVIII, who had every reason to hate
him; to risk capture in an attempt to defy the British blockade; or to surrender to Captain Maitland in the hope of British generosity. He chose the
last course. On July 14 he wrote to the Prince Regent, who was then ruling
Great Britain:

> YOUR ROYAL HIGHNESS:
>   Exposed to the factions which distract my country, and to the disunity of
> the greatest powers in Europe, I have ended my political career, and I come,
> like Themistocles, to sit at the hearth of the British people. I put myself under
> the protection of their laws, which I invoke from Your Royal Highness as the
> most powerful, the most determined, and the most generous of my enemies,
> to grant me this protection.
>
> NAPOLEON[21]*

Napoleon entrusted this letter to Gourgaud, and asked him to seek permission to take it to London by the next boat. Maitland agreed, but the boat

---

* Themistocles, Athens' greatest general, was exiled by the Athenian agora c. 470 B.C.; he
was pursued from one Greek city after another, and finally asked and received protection
and security from Athens' greatest enemies, the Persians, whom Themistocles had defeated
at Salamis in 480 B.C.

that carried Gourgaud was long detained by quarantine, and there is no evidence that the letter ever reached its destination.

On July 15 Napoleon and his companions were taken to the *Bellerophon*, and offered themselves in voluntary surrender to Great Britain. "I come aboard your ship," said Napoleon to Maitland, "to place myself under the protection of the laws of England."[22] The captain received them courteously, and agreed to give them passage to England. He told them nothing of Admiral Hotham's message, but he warned Napoleon that he could not guarantee him a favorable reception in England. On July 16 the *Bellerophon* sailed for England.

In retrospect Maitland gave a good mark to his prize captive:

> His manners were extremely pleasing and affable. He joined in every conversation, related numerous anecdotes, and endeavoured in every way to promote good humour. He admitted his attendants to great familiarity, . . . though they generally treated him with much respect. He possessed, to a wonderful degree, a facility in making a favorable impression upon those with whom he entered into conversation.[23]

The British crew were charmed, and treated him with the greatest deference.

On July 24 the *Bellerophon* reached Tor Bay, an inlet of the English Channel on the coast of Devonshire. Soon two armed frigates placed themselves on either side of the ship; Napoleon was clearly a prisoner. Admiral Viscount Keith came on board and greeted him with simple courtesy: Gourgaud followed to tell Napoleon that he had been unable to get his letter through to the Prince Regent, but had been compelled to give it to Keith, who made no mention of it.[24] Keith bade Maitland bring his ship into Plymouth harbor, thirty miles away; there the *Bellerophon* remained till August 5. During that time it became a goal of British curiosity; from every corner of southern England men and women rode to Plymouth, crowded into boats, and waited for the imperial ogre to take his daily walk on the deck.

The British government spent days determining what to do with him. The predominant opinion was in favor of treating him as an outlaw who had been declared so by the formal declaration of the Allies, and as one who had been leniently dealt with by the Treaty of Fontainebleau, had violated his pledge to observe that treaty, and thereby had forced Europe into another war costly in lives and wealth. Obviously he deserved death, and if merely imprisoned he should be grateful. But now the imprisonment must be such as to make it impossible for the offender to escape and fight again. Some mercy might be due him for having freely surrendered, saving the Allies much trouble; but this mercy must not allow any possibility of escape. So the British government bade Keith inform the prisoner that he must make his home henceforth on the island of St. Helena, some twelve hundred miles west of Africa. It was remote, but it had to be, and its remoteness would relieve the prisoner and his custodians from the necessity of close confinement stringently supervised. England's allies were consulted, and agreed to the verdict, merely stipulating their right to send commissioners to the island to share in supervision.

Napoleon almost broke down when he learned that he had been condemned to what he considered a living death. He fought back with passionate protests, but yielded when he saw that these were met with silent resolution. He was granted some favors. He was allowed to choose five willing friends to accompany him. He named General Bertrand, his "grand marshal of the palace"; the Comte and Comtesse de Montholon (he had been Napoleon's aide-de-camp at Waterloo); General Gourgaud, his devoted protector; and (counting for one) the Comte de Las Cases and his son. Each was allowed to take servants and 1,600 francs. Napoleon took several servants, and managed to take a considerable sum of money. Hortense's diamond necklace was concealed in Las Cases' belt; 350,000 francs were hidden in the garments of his servants. Each man in the party was required to give up his sword; but when Admiral Keith came to receive Napoleon's the Emperor threatened to draw it in self-defense, and Keith did not insist.[25]

On August 4 the *Bellerophon* left Plymouth for Portsmouth, and there surrendered its prisoner, his retinue, and their belongings to a larger ship, the *Northumberland*, which on August 8 left for St. Helena.

CHAPTER XXXIX

To the End

I. ST. HELENA

IT was a long trip from England—from August 8 to October 15. Accustomed to action and quick speech, Napoleon bore the tedium hardly. Admiral Sir George Cockburn thought to ease the situation by daily inviting Napoleon and one or other of his companions to dine with him and some officers; the British, however, spent two and a half hours at dinner; Napoleon easily persuaded them to excuse him when the drinking began. He winced when they addressed him as "General" instead of "Emperor," but he admired their courtesy. His friends suggested that a good way to anesthetize time would be for him to dictate to them his memoirs of rule and war. Now began the narratives, taken down by O'Meara, Las Cases, Gourgaud, or Montholon, which, published by them after his death, played a part in making the memory of Napoleon a living force in France throughout the century.

Men at sea long so for land that even Napoleon must have been pleased when he sighted the rocky coast of St. Helena. One glance could take in most of the island; it was only twenty miles in circumference, and nearly all its population was gathered in the port city, Jamestown, with its one street and five thousand souls. A rough, uneven terrain, rising to a plateau at Longwood; a tropical climate of heat, mist, and rain; no regular succession of seasons, but incalculable alternations of wet and dry; an unfriendly soil slow to reward tillage with food. It was a "spot of earth" ideal for insulating a troublemaker, but a torture for a man whose life was action demanding a continent for its stage.

He and his party remained on board while Admiral Cockburn sought temporary lodging for them till work should be completed on the big house that the British government had chosen for their collective home. For Napoleon, Las Cases, and son the admiral found a pleasant place, "the Briars," whose owner, William Balcombe, thought it would be interesting to have an emperor as his guest. Two daughters, aged sixteen and fourteen, brightened the scene; they spoke a little French, played and sang, and became so fond of Napoleon that the younger one wept when he had to move to "Longwood."

This was an old farmhouse, some six miles from Jamestown. Its many rooms had been simply but adequately furnished. According to the excellent ground plan drawn by Las Cases, Jr., Napoleon was given six rooms: a large "antechamber and waiting room for visitors," a parlor, a bedroom, a study, a library, and a large dining room. The inner walls were inelegantly covered with tarred canvas, but there were many windows. Napoleon accepted his suite without initial complaint; he even rejoiced in the bathroom, which he described as "an unheard-of luxury in this unhappy island."[1] "The Emperor," Las Cases reported, "was satisfied with everything."[2] In another wing of the building rooms were arranged for Las Cases and son, for the Comte and Comtesse de Montholon, General Gourgaud, and Dr. O'Meara, Napoleon's physician. Large common rooms were provided for Napoleon's servants,[3] and for the servants of his staff. General Bertrand, his wife, and their servants occupied a separate cottage on the road to Jamestown. Servants served for hardly more than their keep.

Napoleon had freedom of movement—on foot, or mounted, or in a carriage—within a radius of five miles from the house; but he had to submit to surveillance by British troops when he went outside the Longwood plateau. Meals for Napoleon and his retinue were sent up daily from the governor of the island, and, within limits, they could order their food.[4] Usually the Emperor ate sparingly until eight o'clock in the evening; then he and his staff dined with a leisureliness that left him ready for bed. Napoleon had brought a costly silver service with him from France; it was regularly used; and we hear also of knives, forks, and spoons of gold.[5] The dishes were mostly of Sèvres porcelain. The servants were in full uniform of green and gold. Las Cases was impressed by "the elegance of the dinner service, and the neatness with which the tables were laid out."[6] The etiquette of the Tuileries was maintained at Longwood. Napoleon allowed his faithful friends much candor of speech, but no familiarities; they always referred to him as "the Emperor," and addressed him as "your Majesty." Letters addressed to him as "General" remained unopened; visitors had to address him as "Emperor" or stay away.

There were many irritations, and some hardships. Rats made themselves at home, even in the Emperor's hat; they ran around the table legs while he ate; fleas and bugs made no distinction of human ranks; "we are absolutely eaten," Las Cases complained.[7] There were damp mists every other day. Water sometimes failed, and the Emperor missed his hot bath. Constant surveillance, however distant or polite, usually compelled a monastic chastity, just when excessive leisure made temptation doubly acceptable. But where else did a prisoner have so many friends on call, and servants, and a horse and buggy, and all the books he could use? All in all, it was as tolerable a prison as a prisoner could expect, especially after escaping from previous confinement and requiring the expenditure of millions of pounds sterling and flesh to recapture him. Matters went reasonably well till Sir Hudson Lowe came.

II. SIR HUDSON LOWE

He arrived on April 14, 1816, to replace Sir George Cockburn as governor of the island. The British government thought its choice was well considered: Sir Hudson was a conscientious official, who would carry out instructions faithfully. His instructions were to extend the prisoner "every indulgence which may be consistent with the entire security of his person."

He began well. He brought with him nearly 2,000 French volumes, and placed them at the disposal of Napoleon and his companions. He sent word that he had heard of repairs needed at Longwood, and would soon have them attended to.[8] He thought he should visit his distinguished prisoner, and asked his predecessor, Admiral Cockburn, to accompany him. Presumably he did not know that Napoleon, as a precaution against sightseers and busybodies, had instructed Bertrand to allow no one to visit him except through Bertrand's permission and escort. Sir Hudson and the admiral came unannounced, and sought admission; Napoleon sent reply that he was ill and could not see them. Lowe inquired when might he try again; Napoleon answered, Tomorrow. Lowe's pride was hurt. He came on the morrow, accompanied by Bertrand. Napoleon received him coldly, and listed some inconveniences from which he suffered: sentinels were stationed too near his house, and sometimes, at night, peered through his windows; he could not ride beyond narrow limits without being followed by an English officer. Lowe promised to do his best.[9] After his departure Napoleon remarked to his companions that he had "never seen a countenance so like that of an Italian cutthroat."[10]

Sir Hudson had more pride than humor. Returning to his office, he sent word to Napoleon's aides that the restrictions of which Napoleon complained had been imposed by the British government, and that he had no authority to remove them. He added, again pursuant to his government's instructions, that all communications between Longwood and the outside world must pass through his hands, and be subject to inspection by him.[11] According to Las Cases, the governor refused to transmit letters addressed to "the Emperor Napoleon."[12] He sent an invitation to dinner to General Bertrand and "General Napoleon." Napoleon refused it.

The quarrel reached high temperature when Lowe informed Bertrand that the British government had complained about the high cost it was incurring for the upkeep of Napoleon and his household of fifty-one persons.[13] The government had allowed £8,000 annually for this; the actual expense for the first year was £18,000; the government proposed that any future expenditure over £8,000 should be paid by Napoleon. The Emperor ordered Montholon to sell the imperial silver, and offered to pay the surplus expense of his household if Lowe would pass unopened Napoleon's letter to his Paris banker; Lowe would not. Napoleon's family sent him offers of money; he thanked them, but said he could take care of the matter. They offered to come and live with him; he forbade them, saying that they would not long survive the climate and the isolation. Lowe thought to ease the situation by raising the imperial allowance to £12,000 a year.[14] But this discussion of his expenses infuriated Napoleon. When Lowe visited him again (July 16, 1816), Napoleon, according to his report to Las Cases, burned all bridges by crying out, "Will you allow me to tell you what we think of you? We think you capable of everything; yes, of everything. . . . I shall have to complain, not that the worst proceeding of ministers was to send me to St. Helena, but that they gave you the command of it. You are a greater calamity to us than all the wretchedness of this horrible rock."[15] "The Emperor," says Las Cases, "admitted that he had, during this conversation, repeatedly offended Sir Hudson Lowe." "I have been thrown quite out of temper. They have sent me more than a jailer! Sir Hudson Lowe is a downright executioner! . . . My anger must have been powerfully excited, for I felt a vibration in the calf of my left leg."[16]

Sir Hudson, overwhelmed, withdrew. They had no further converse.

III. THE GREAT COMPANIONS

The most striking aspect of this incarcerated life is the constant and intense fidelity of the aides who accompanied Napoleon to St. Helena. Presumably the intoxicating aura of fame shared in stimulating their services, but their persistence in them despite the restraints and homesickness of exile, the quarrels of competition for the Emperor's favor, and the irritation of a depressing climate and a disagreeable governor, lends to their record almost the quality of an Arthurian legend, darkened with jealousies but ennobled with devotion.

Noblest of them was Comte Henri-Gratien Bertrand (1773–1844). He entered history as a military engineer under Napoleon in the first Italian campaign. In the Egyptian expedition he commanded a battalion at the battle of the Pyramids, and was wounded in the victory at Abukir. The bridges that he built across the Danube in the campaign of 1809 were rated by Napoleon as the finest such work since the Romans.[17] In 1813 he was made grand marshal of the palace. He remained loyal to Napoleon through the bitter years of retreat before the Allies, accompanied him to Elba, stayed with him during the Hundred Days, rode with him to Rochefort, and sailed with him to England and St. Helena. There he continued as grand marshal, checking visitors, cooling tempers, keeping truce between Napoleon and the governor, and bearing with forgiving patience the attempt to seduce his wife.* She was an English Creole, niece of Lord Dillon, and related to Josephine. She bore with impatient fidelity her isolation, in St. Helena, from the social life of Paris. Bertrand took her back to France five months after Napoleon's death. He had compiled three volumes of a diary in St. Helena, but refused to publish them. They were deciphered and published in 1949–59, a century after his death. He was buried in the crypt of Les Invalides, beside the remains of Napoleon.

Almost equal in devotion was the Irish surgeon Barry O'Meara (1786–1836). As ship's doctor on the *Northumberland*, he attended Napoleon,

---

* Bertrand's diary under April 26, 1821: "The Emperor replied [according to what Montholon told Mme. Bertrand]: '. . . I resented her refusal to become my mistress. . . . I shall never forgive Dr. Antommarchi for having attended a woman who refused to become my mistress.' "[18] But when Napoleon said this he was within ten days of death, and may have lost track of his amours. Bertrand noted, on the same date: "He frequently appeared to have lost his memory."

talked with him in French or Italian, half agreed with his opinion of physicians, and became so strongly attached to him that he asked—and received—permission of the British government to remain in attendance on Napoleon in St. Helena. Sir Hudson Lowe did not approve of such intimacy between a British doctor and a French criminal; he suspected O'Meara of a plot to have Napoleon escape; he insisted on assigning a soldier to accompany the surgeon wherever he went; O'Meara protested; Lowe had him recalled to Britain (July, 1818). In 1822 O'Meara published *Napoleon in Exile, or A Voice from St. Helena*, a passionate plea for a better treatment of the fallen Emperor. The two volumes had a wide sale, and started a wave of English sympathy for Napoleon. The book contains some errors,[19] having been written from memory; but Las Cases defended O'Meara's account, and all those around Napoleon seem to have had a high opinion of him both as a physician and as a gentleman.

The eventful devotion of Comte Emmanuel-Augustin-Dieudonné de Las Cases (1766–1842), and his voluminous *Mémorial de Sainte-Hélène* have placed him only next to Napoleon and Lowe in the *dramatis personae* of the island. He was a minor noble, fought in Condé's army against the Revolution, emigrated to England, joined in the attempt of some *émigrés* to invade France at Quiberon, failed to land, returned to England, and lived by teaching history. He drew up an *Atlas historique* which later won high praise from Napoleon. Soon after the 18th Brumaire he ventured to return to France. He judged Napoleon to be the right medicine for the Revolution; sought every opportunity to serve him, and rose to be a member of the Council of State. Waterloo did not cool his admiration for the Emperor; he went to Malmaison to help him, followed him to Rochefort, to England, and to St. Helena.

Of all the companions he remained closest to the Emperor, was the most zealous in recording his dictation, and kept his high estimate of him through all the storms of the exile's temper. He noted everything about Napoleon except the faults; he did not, like Cromwell, believe in immortalizing warts. His report of Napoleon's recollections and observations does not claim to be verbally precise. "The Emperor dictated very rapidly, almost as fast as he speaks in ordinary conversation. I was therefore obliged to invent a kind of hieroglyphic writing; and I, in my turn, dictated this to my son"; or "I sat beside my son as he wrote the Emperor's dictation. . . . I always read to the Emperor what he had dictated the preceding day, and then he made corrections and dictated further."[20] However, the language in which Las Cases expressed his own views is so much like that which he ascribes to Napoleon that we cannot accept his report as revealing Napoleon as impartially as in the more vividly immediate journal of Gourgaud.

Anxious to arouse Europe to the hardships which Napoleon was suffering, Las Cases wrote an account of these on a piece of silk, addressed it to Lucien Bonaparte, and entrusted it to a servant who was about to return to Europe. The servant was searched; the message was discovered; Sir Hudson Lowe had Las Cases arrested, confiscated his papers (including conversations with

Napoleon), and deported Las Cases and son to Cape Town (November 25, 1816). From that remote point the Count began years of wandering—usually under hostile surveillance—in England, Belgium, and Germany. In October, 1818, he presented to the Allies' Congress of Aix-la-Chapelle (Aachen) a petition from Napoleon's mother for the release of her son. He himself sent appeals to the rulers of Russia, Prussia, Austria, and England. No answer came. After Napoleon's death he was allowed to return to France (1822). He secured from the British government his confiscated manuscripts, and published nearly all of them in the *Mémorial de Sainte-Hélène* (1823). The volumes became the literary event of the year; Las Cases and his heirs were enriched by the sale; and his ardent testimony to the treatment which, he believed, had caused Napoleon's death became a continuing factor in the "Napoleonic legend" that raised Napoleon III to a more lasting reign than his uncle's, and gave Las Cases, Jr., a senatorial seat in that Second Empire.

The other companions were jealous of Las Cases as being most frequently and intimately near Napoleon. Especially irked was General Gaspard Gourgaud (1783–1852), who had many claims to favor. He had fought for the Emperor in Spain, Austria, Russia, and France, and had saved his life at Brienne. He was the most expressive and exuberant of the exiles, ardent in friendship, passionate in enmity, challenging Montholon to a duel, and loving Napoleon with a jealous love intolerant of other lovers; "he loves me," said Napoleon, "as a lover loves his mistress."[21] To restore peace in the camp, Napoleon sent him to Europe (1818) with a message for Czar Alexander. Even so, Gourgaud's *Journal inédit de Sainte-Hélène* (1899) is the most fascinating and realistic of all the echoes from St. Helena.

Comte Charles-Tristan de Montholon (1783–1853) hardly deserved Gourgaud's hatred, for he was the most polite and accommodating of the imperial quartet. He had proud memories of having been taught mathematics, when he was ten, by a young artillery captain called Bonaparte. Later he followed Napoleon's star in its rise and fall, and insisted on accompanying him to St. Helena. His wife, Albinie de Vassal, had come to him from two divorced and living husbands, so that Montholon was never quite sure of her. Gossip in St. Helena said she had helped Napoleon to warm his bed; the Russian representatives at Jamestown put the matter harshly: "Though old, debauched, and fat, she is today the mistress of the great man."[22] When she left the island (1819) Napoleon wept.[23] Montholon himself remained to the end, shared with Bertrand the long watch over the dying gladiator, and was named coexecutor of the imperial will. Returning to France, he shared seven years of imprisonment with Napoleon's nephew, and helped him to become another emperor.

IV. THE GREAT DICTATOR

The great enemy of all the exiles was time, and, next, its child, ennui. These men, who had been addicts of action and familiars of death, were limited now to caring for the body and ego of a world figure fallen from imperial state and robes to imprisoned helplessness, with all his ailments festering and human frailties revealed. "My situation is frightful," he said; "I am like a dead man, yet full of life"[24] or desire thereof. The hero who formerly had longed for more time to meet his chosen tasks, or carry out his plans, now felt the hours heavy on his hands, and welcomed night as an anodyne of time. Then, for lack of labor done, he found it hard to sleep, and moved from bed to cot or chair and back again in search of unconsciousness.

Almost daily he played chess; but since no opponent dared defeat him, he was bored by victory. In his first year of exile he had ridden his horse several miles daily, but he soon abandoned this exercise when he noted that some British officer always kept sight of him. He read several hours a day.

He had always loved books, had done some reading even on busy days, had taken hundreds of volumes on his campaigns—eight hundred to Waterloo (seventy of them by Voltaire).[25] He had brought four hundred books from France; on a stop of the *Northumberland* at Madeira he had sent the British government a request for a number of learned works, which reached him in June, 1816; another package came a year later; and Sir Hudson Lowe sent him some from his own library.[26] He became an expert on the campaigns of Alexander, Hannibal, and Caesar. He read and reread the dramas of Corneille and Racine, sometimes aloud with his companions, distributing the parts. He liked English literature, and had Las Cases teach him enough English to read it, even to speak it; "His Majesty," reported Gourgaud, "is always talking English to me."[27]

He had one advantage over other prisoners: he could drown the present in the past by recounting the history of his country, and half of Europe, from 1796 to 1815, almost entirely from memory, and from the vantage of a principal participant. He was too impatient to write, but he could talk. It was apparently Las Cases who suggested that by dictating his memoirs to one or another of his entourage he could give interest and value to every day. Now he might find only imperfect truth in Dante's lines "No greater pain than to recall, in misery, a time of happiness"; a memory of pleasant days might soften, even while deepening, present grief. "It was a beautiful empire!" he exclaimed; "I had eighty-three million human beings under my government—half the population of Europe."[28]

So he inaugurated a new dictatorship on the *Northumberland*, and continued it, on and off, for four years at St. Helena. He began by recounting to Las Cases the story of those Italian campaigns of 1796 whose swift decisiveness had astonished Europe and made him indispensable to France. When Las Cases fled before Lowe's wrath, the Emperor dictated to Gourgaud, later to Montholon, less to Bertrand, sometimes to two of them in one day. Now these warriors changed their swords for pens, and sallied forth in reams to shed their ink to save their Emperor's record and good name in re-Bourbonized France and in the court of history. They were sooner exhausted than he, who felt that this was his last chance to defend himself against the orators, journalists, and cartoonists who had enabled his enemies to picture him as an inhuman, bloodthirsty ogre. Knowing that his recorders could not have so personal an urge to their labor, he gave to each of them full title to his manuscript and its proceeds; and actually each manuscript, when published, brought wealth to the scribe or his heirs.[29]

Naturally the author put the best face upon this *apologia;* but, all in all, it has been found as fair as could be expected from a man defending his life. Napoleon had by this time learned to admit that he had made serious mistakes in policy and generalship. "I was wrong in quarreling with Talleyrand. He possessed everything which I lacked. If I had frankly allowed him to share my greatness he would have served me well, and I would have died on the throne."[30] He confessed that he profoundly underestimated the difficulties of conquering Spain or subduing Russia. "I started too soon from Elba. I should have waited till the Congress had broken up, and the princes had returned home."[31] "I don't yet understand the loss of the battle of Waterloo."[32] "I should have died at Waterloo."[33]

His amanuenses, almost exhausted by his memories, yet found energy left to record his conversation. It was of course interesting, for who in his time had rivaled his range and excitement of adventures on three continents? He was an excellent raconteur, with a lively anecdote for any theme. He was, in his blunt way, a philosopher, and could speak forgivably on any subject from agriculture to Zeus. He had read history so widely that he predicted the future with some unreliable success. "The colonial system . . . is finished for everybody—for England, which owns all the colonies, as for the other powers, who have none left."[34] The yoke of the Bourbons would soon be thrown off by the French people.[35] Germany would soon resume the unification which he had begun.[36] The nineteenth would be a century of revolutions; the principles of the French Revolution, barring some excesses, would triumph in America, France, and England; and "from this tripod the light will burst upon the world."[37] "The old system is ended, and the new one is not consolidated, and will not be until after long and furious convulsions."[38] "Russia is the power that rushes most surely, and with the greatest strides, toward universal dominion."[39] One of his bad guesses: "The royal authority in England, daily augmented, . . . is now marching unimpeded on the high road to arbitrary and absolute power."[40]

Finally he reviewed his political career, and summed it up most favorably:

> I closed the gulf of anarchy and cleared the chaos. I purified the Revolution, dignified nations, and established kings. I excited every kind of emulation, rewarded every kind of merit, and extended the limits of glory. . . . The dictatorship was absolutely necessary. Will it be said that I restrained liberty? It can be proved that licentiousness, anarchy, and the greatest irregularities still haunted the threshold of freedom. Shall I be accused of having been too fond of war? It can be shown that I always received the first attack. Will it be said that I aimed at universal monarchy? . . . Our enemies themselves led me step by step to this determination. Lastly, shall I be blamed for my ambition? This passion I must doubtless be allowed to have possessed, and that in no small degree; but, at the same time, my ambition was of the highest and noblest kind

that ever perhaps existed—that of establishing and consecrating the empire of reason, and the full exercise and complete enjoyment of all the human faculties. As here the historian will probably feel compelled to regret that such ambition should not have been fulfilled and gratified. . . . This is my whole history in a few words.[41]

On March 9, 1821, he warmed his failing heart with a proud vision of his postmortem fame: "In five hundred years' time French imaginations will be full of me. They will talk only of the glory of our brilliant campaigns. Heaven help anyone who dares speak ill of me!"[42] It was as good as any way of facing death.

V. THE LAST BATTLE

A variety of internal disorders, and a lack of physical exercise, brought Napoleon to old age while he was still in his forties. Lowe's insistence on having a British soldier follow the Emperor whenever the latter rode outside Longwood limits had angered the captive into avoiding all rides, on horse or in caleche. Sentries stationed within sight of his rooms gave Napoleon a further reason for staying indoors; and his loss of interest in prolonging his life more and more inclined him to a listless inactivity. Bertrand reported in 1818: "A hundred days have elapsed since he . . . stirred out of the house." Las Cases noted that the Emperor's blood circulated with difficulty,[43] with a pulse rate as low as fifty-five beats per minute.[44]

In 1820 he took to gardening, and attacked its problems with martial courage and discipline. He conscripted his entire colony to join in the enterprise, and they gladly turned from their old routine to the novel business of digging, carting, planting, watering, and weeding. Sir Hudson Lowe, in a new gesture of amity, sent his prisoner plants and tools.[45] The garden, well watered, soon produced fresh vegetables which Napoleon consumed with delight. His health visibly improved. But when the garden's harvest had been consumed, and bad weather set in, Napoleon returned to his former indoor indolence.

Soon his ailments resumed their attack, on a dozen fronts: toothaches, headaches, skin eruptions, vomiting, dysentery, cold extremities; his ulcer worsened, and the cancer that was to be revealed by a postmortem autopsy had begun to give him almost uninterrupted pain.[46] These physical sufferings affected his mood, even his mind. He became gloomy, irritable, and bitter; vain and jealous of his dignity; ready to take offense but soon ready to forgive; counting his pennies but giving generously in his will.[47] In 1820 he described himself despondently:

> How I have fallen! I, whose activity knew no limits, whose head never rested! I am plunged into a lethargic stupor. I must make an effort to raise my eyelids. Sometimes I used to dictate, on different subjects, to four or five secretaries, who wrote as fast as I spoke. But I was Napoleon then; today I am nothing . . . I vegetate, I no longer live.[48]

He had a succession and medley of doctors, none of whom remained with him long enough to study his symptoms systematically, or to impose a consistent regimen. Dr. O'Meara was the first and best, but his stay at Longwood was cut short. Two British physicians, Stokoe and Arnott, replaced him, both of them good men, patient and conscientious. But on September 21, 1819, the situation was confused by the arrival of Dr. Francesco Antommarchi, aged thirty-nine, with a recommendation from Napoleon's uncle, Cardinal Fesch; the British physicians allowed him to take charge. Antommarchi amply justified Napoleon's question to him, whether generals or doctors did the most killing. He was proud, confident, and merciless when Napoleon complained of stomach pains. Antommarchi prescribed an emetic in lemonade. Napoleon writhed in pain, and almost gave up the ghost; thinking himself poisoned, he dismissed Antommarchi and forbade him to return.[49] But in a day or two Antommarchi was back with his chemicals and phials, and the Emperor, though cursing him with unprintable obscenities,[50] had to put up with him.

About the middle of March, 1821, Napoleon took to his bed, and thereafter rarely left it. He suffered almost continuous pain, which Antommarchi and Arnott tried to dull with repeated small doses of opium. "If I should end my career now," he said on March 27, "it would be a great joy. At times I have longed to die, and I have no fear of death."[51] During his final month he vomited nearly all food given him.

On April 15 he made his will. Some excerpts:

> 1. I die in the Apostolical Roman religion, in the bosom of which I was born. . . . 2. It is my wish that my ashes may repose on the banks of the Seine, in the midst of the French people, whom I have loved so well. 3. I have always had reason to be pleased with my dearest wife, Marie Louise. I retain for-her, to my last moment, the most tender sentiments. I beseech her to watch, in order to preserve, my son from the snares which yet environ his infancy. . . . 5. I die prematurely, assassinated by the English oligarchy.[52]

He had some 6 million francs to dispose of—5.3 million plus interest—on deposit with Laffitte; and he believed that he had 2 million francs left with Eugène de Beauharnais. He willed substantial sums to Bertrand, Montholon, Las Cases; to his chief valet, Marchand, and his secretary Méneval; to various generals or their children. He bequeathed diverse articles to a considerable number of persons who had served or otherwise helped him; no one was forgotten. Also "10,000 francs to the officer Cantillon, who has undergone a trial on the charge of having endeavored to assassinate Lord Wellington, of which he was pronounced innocent. Cantillon had as much right to assassinate that oligarchist as the latter had to send me to perish on the rock of St. Helena."[53]

Separately he left some "Advice to My Son" (spring, 1821):

> My son must not think of avenging my death; he should rather learn a lesson from it. He must always bear in mind the remembrance of what I have accomplished. He is always to remain, like myself, every inch a Frenchman. He must strive to rule in peace. If he were to try to begin my wars all over again out of

> a mere desire to imitate me, and without the absolute necessity for it, he would
> be nothing but an ape. To begin my work over again would be to assume that
> I had accomplished nothing. To complete it, on the other hand, will be to
> prove the strength of its foundations, to explain the complete plan of the edi-
> fice begun. Such work as mine is not done twice in a century. I have been
> compelled to restrain and tame Europe with arms; today it must be convinced.
> I have saved the Revolution as it lay dying. I have cleansed it of its crimes, and
> have held it up to the people shining with fame. I have inspired France and
> Europe with new ideas which will never be forgotten. May my son make
> everything blossom that I have sown! May he develop further all the elements
> of prosperity which lie hidden in French soil![54]

The last preparation was to dispose of his soul. He had taken a long time
to reach religious belief. As if he had read Gibbon, he seems to have considered all religions as equally false to the philosopher, and equally useful to
the statesman;[55] he had become a Mohammedan to win Egypt, and a Catholic to hold France. To Gourgaud he had expressed simple materialism: "Say
what you like, everything is matter, more or less organized. When out hunting I had the deer cut open, and saw that their interior was the same as that
of man. When I see that a pig has a stomach like mine, and digests like me,
I say to myself, 'If I have a soul, so has he.' "[56] "When we are dead, my dear
Gourgaud, we are altogether dead."[57] On March 27, six weeks before his
death, he said to Bertrand, "I am very glad that I have no religion. I find this
a great consolation, as I have no imaginary terror, and no fear of the future."[58] How, he asked, can we reconcile the prosperity of the wicked, and
the misfortunes of the saints, with the existence of a just God? "Look at
Talleyrand; he is sure to die in bed."[59]

As he neared death he began to find reasons for faith. "Only a madman,"
he told Gourgaud, "declares that he will die without a confession. There is
so much that one does not know, that one cannot explain."[60] After all, he
felt, religion is a necessary part of patriotism:

> Religion forms a part of our destiny. Together with the soil, laws, and cus-
> toms, it constitutes the sacred whole which we call Fatherland, and whose in-
> terests we should never desert. When, at the time of the Concordat, some old
> revolutionists spoke to me of making France Protestant, I felt as much re-
> volted as though they had asked me to abdicate my title of Frenchman and
> declare myself English or German.[61]

So he decided to humbly conform to the traditional rituals of a Frenchman's death. He found a local priest, and arranged to have Mass celebrated
every Sunday at Longwood. He fell back with ease and comfort into his
childhood faith, and amused his friends and himself with a forecast of his
reception in heaven: "I go to meet Kléber, Desaix, Lannes, Masséna, . . .
Ney. They will come to meet me. . . . We shall speak of what we have
done. We shall talk of our profession with Frederick, Turenne, Condé,
Caesar, and Hannibal."[62]

By April 26 he was so weak that for the first time he obeyed his doctors
without question. That evening he raved for a while, proposing to give his
son 400 million francs.[63] Montholon, who now stayed with him night and

day, reported that about 4 A.M. of April 26 Napoleon told him, "with extraordinary emotion," "I have just seen my good Josephine. . . . She was sitting there; it was as if I had seen her only the night before. She hasn't changed—always the same, still completely devoted to me. She told me that we were going to see each other again, never again to leave each other. She has promised me. Did you see her?"[64]

On May 3 he received the sacraments. On that day two physicians were added to Arnott and Antommarchi, and the four agreed to give the patient ten grains of calomel. "The unusually enormous dose of this unsuitable drug caused a terrible intestinal upheaval, with loss of consciousness, and . . . all the signs of a hemorrhage in the gastro-intestinal system."[65]

He died on May 5, 1821, murmuring, "*À la tête de l'armée*—at the head of the army."

On May 6 Antommarchi conducted the postmortem examination, in the presence of sixteen others, including seven British surgeons, Bertrand, and Montholon. The autopsy revealed at once the chief cause of Napoleon's suffering: cancerous ulcers in the pylorus—that part of the stomach which leads into the intestine. One ulcer had eaten a quarter-inch hole through the stomach wall, spreading putrefaction. Antommarchi had diagnosed hepatitis, but the liver, though larger than normal, showed no sign of disease.[66] Adipose tissue was found not only in the skin and the peritoneum, but also in the heart, which may have caused its abnormally slow beat. The bladder was small, and contained several small stones; this, and a malformed left kidney, probably caused the Emperor's need for frequent urination, and may explain a certain inconstancy of attention to the course of battle at Borodino and Waterloo. None of the examiners reported any sign of syphilis, but the genitals were small and apparently atrophied.[67]

On May 9 a considerable procession, including Sir Hudson Lowe, escorted the corpse to a grave outside Longwood, in the "Valley of the Geraniums"; Napoleon himself had chosen the location. On the coffin lay the mantle he had worn at Marengo, and the sword which had been a proud part of his official costume, and an emblem of his life. There he remained for nineteen years, until France, loving him again, brought him home.

CHAPTER XL

Afterward

1815–40

I. THE FAMILY

HIS mother survived him by fifteen years, dying at the age of eighty-six. Her career was almost a summary of motherhood through the ages: uncertain mate, many children, joys and sorrows, fulfillment and bereavement, horror and loneliness, wonderment and hope. She had seen all the triumphs, riches, and misfortunes of her children, had saved for the day when they might need her; "Who knows but I may one day have to provide for all these kings?"[1] She lived abstemiously to the end, protected and honored by the Pope whom her son had abused. From the standpoint of the race she was the strongest and sanest of all the Bonapartes.

Joseph, her oldest child, fond of books and money, happily married to Julie Clary, loved and burdened by his imperial brother, served him to the best of his limited ability, found a refuge in America after the Empire collapsed, returned to Europe, lived in rural peace near Genoa, and died in Florence in 1844, aged seventy-six.

Lucien, after rising to place under the Directory, and helping his brother to overthrow it, opposed Napoleon's dictatorship, married against the imperial will, abandoned the scramble for power, became a papal prince, sailed for America, was captured by a British ship, was kept under surveillance in England, found his way to Napoleon's side in the Hundred Days, defended him in the chambers, fled to Rome after the Second Abdication, and died at Viterbo in 1840.

Louis Bonaparte, after abandoning his Holland throne, and separating from Hortense, lived in Bohemia, Austria, and Italy, and died six years before his third son became Emperor Napoleon III.

Jérôme enjoyed his royal wealth in Westphalia, failed as a general in the first month of the Russian campaign, returned to his throne, lost it to the Allies in 1813, fought valiantly at Waterloo, and was almost the last Frenchman to leave the field of defeat.[2] After the Second Abdication he wandered from country to country, returned to France in 1847, saw his nephew rise to power, became president of the Senate under Napoleon III, and died in 1860 after seventy-six years of a full life in an age when every year was a decade in events.

Elisa Bonaparte Bacciocchi was the oldest and ablest of Napoleon's three sisters. We have noted her success as ruler of Tuscany, the cultural Attica of Italy. When it became evident that her brother could not withstand the united Allies, she withdrew to Naples, and joined her sister Caroline in help- ing Murat to preserve his throne.

Murat, after leading the cavalry for Napoleon at Leipzig, returned to Naples, entered into an alliance with Austria (January 8, 1814), and pledged the use of his army to the coalition against Napoleon, in exchange for Aus- tria's support of his authority in Naples. The Allies refused to sanction this pact. When Napoleon escaped from Elba, Murat risked everything by appealing to all Italy to join him in a war of independence against all foreign rule (March 30, 1815). His wife, Caroline, and her sister Elisa left him and found refuge in Vienna. Murat was defeated at Tolentino by an Austrian army (May 2) and fled to France, then to Corsica; Ferdinand IV recovered his Neapolitan throne. After the battle of Waterloo, Murat, now a man without a country, crossed from Corsica to Calabria with a handful of men, was captured, court-martialed, and shot (October 13). Napoleon at St. Helena described him fondly but mercilessly as "the bravest of men in the face of the enemy, incomparable on the battlefield, but a fool in his actions everywhere else."[3]

The most interesting of Napoleon's relatives was his sister Pauline (1780– 1825). She was fated to spread happiness and trouble, for she was rated the most beautiful woman of her time. The men who saw her never forgot her, and the women who saw her never forgave her. She was not well adapted for monogamy, but she was apparently a loving wife to her first husband, General Leclerc, sharing his danger and yellow fever in St.-Domingue. When he died (1802) she returned to Paris; after a decent period of mourn- ing she grew a new wealth of hair, bathed in five gallons of fresh milk every day,[4] opened a salon, and charmed husbands by her beauty, and some by her generosity. Napoleon, who himself was chastely moved by her Pheidian form, hurried to marry her to the rich and handsome Prince Ca- millo Borghese (1803).

In Florence (1805) Canova asked her to pose for a statue of Diana the huntress; she was inclined to consent; but when she heard that Diana had asked Jupiter to endow her with eternal virginity, she laughed the idea away. She was persuaded, however, to pose for a nearly nude figure of Venus Victrix, which has made the Galleria Borghese one of the most frequented places in Rome. Borghese himself, conscious of his inadequacy, left for his military duties as an officer under Napoleon. Pauline amused herself scan- dalously, with some injury to her health, but there is no clear evidence that she contracted syphilis.[5]

This scandalous goddess was also a model of kindness, except to Josephine, against whom all the Bonapartes except Napoleon waged unremitting war. She gave abundantly, won many lasting friendships, even among her dis- carded lovers, and was more loyal to Napoleon than any other Bonaparte except her mother. She went out of her way to meet and console her un- happy brother on his journey to Fréjus in 1814, and soon she followed him to Elba. There she played hostess for him, and enlivened his life, and that of the island, with her parties, plays, and *joie de vivre*. When he left for the last gamble she gave him her finest necklace. Marchand managed to get it through to St. Helena. She was planning to go there when she received news of Napoleon's death. She survived him by only four years, surrendering to cancer[6] (June 5, 1825) at the age of forty-four. Her husband forgave her sins, rejoined her in her last year, and closed her eyes when she died.

Josephine had died (May 29, 1814) of a chill caught while receiving a visit from Czar Alexander at Malmaison.[7] Her daughter, Hortense de Beauharnais (1783–1837), after her separation from Louis Bonaparte, had been protected by the Emperor, and later by the Czar. She did not live to see her son become Napoleon III. Hortense's brother, Eugène, remained faithful to his adoptive father until the First Abdication; five days thereafter he retired with his wife to Munich, and was joyfully received by his father-in-law, the King of Bavaria. When he died there (February 21, 1824), aged only forty-three, all factions united in honoring him.

Marie Louise, taken from France against her will, was received in Vienna as a faultless princess rescued from a sacrificial altar. She was allowed to keep Méneval as her devoted gentleman-in-waiting, and he did his best to counter the influences that daily sought to detach her from fidelity to Napoleon. Méneval tells us that in her five weeks in Vienna she received several letters from her husband, found no way of sending a reply, but secretly hoped to join him in Elba.[8] Her father, fearful for her health in a Vienna preparing for a triumphant Congress of the Allies, sent her to take the waters at Aix-les-Bains; and on July 1, 1814, he appointed Count Adam von Neipperg to join her there as her personal aide. Though he was thirty-nine and she only twenty-two, propinquity had its way, and she accepted him as a lover when all chance seemed gone of reunion with Napoleon. In 1815 the Congress of Vienna awarded her the duchies of Parma, Piacenza, and Guastalla. Neipperg accompanied her, and shared in the government. In 1817 she bore him a daughter. Napoleon heard of this in St. Helena, but he never took her picture down from the wall of his Longwood room, and, as we have seen, spoke of her tenderly in his will. After Napoleon's death she married Neipperg, and lived with him in apparently faithful union till his death (1829). She married again in 1834, and died in 1847. All circumstances considered, she seems to have been a good woman, not deserving of the stones that have been thrown upon her memory.

Her son by Napoleon—called "King of Rome" (the traditional title of the heir to the Holy Roman Emperor) and "L'Aiglon" (the young eagle)—had been separated from his mother on leaving Paris, had been rechristened Duke of Reichstadt, and had been kept at the court of Vienna under constant tutelage in Hapsburg traditions. He remained faithful to the memory of his father, dreamed of having someday a kingdom of his own, suffered from repeated illnesses, and died of pulmonary tuberculosis, in the Palace of Schönbrunn, Vienna, on July 22, 1832, at the age of twenty-one.

II. HOMECOMING

Even as that pretty visage faded from French memory the image of Napoleon himself took on a new living form in recollection and imagination. As time closed old wounds, and filled the places—in families, fields, and shops—of those millions who had gone to the wars and never returned, the picture of the age of Napoleon grew brighter and more heroic beyond any remembered precedent in secular history.

First of all, the old soldiers recalled their exploits and forgot their "groans"; they embellished Napoleon's victories, and seldom blamed him for a defeat; they loved him as probably no other commander has ever been loved. The aging grenadier became an oracle in his village, and was enshrined in a thousand poems, tales, and songs. In "Le Vieux Drapeau" (The Old Standard) and a hundred other lays Pierre de Béranger (1780–1857) idealized Napoleon and his campaigns, and satirized the domineering nobles and the land-hungry bishops with such point and verve that he was imprisoned by the Bourbon government (1821, 1828). Victor Hugo wrote an "Ode to the Column," celebrating the Vendôme pillar and its historical reliefs and crowning figure of the Emperor, taken down (1815) and then restored (1833). Balzac, in *Le Médecin de campagne* (1833), vividly pictured a proud veteran denouncing the Bourbons for issuing the report that Napoleon was dead; on the contrary, he affirmed, Napoleon was still alive, and was "the child of God made to be the father of the soldier."[9] Stendhal not only sprinkled his novels with praise of Napoleon, he published in 1837 a *Vie de Napoléon* whose tenor was announced in the preface—"The love of Napoleon is the only passion that is left in me"; and he called Napoleon "the greatest man the world has seen since Caesar."[10]

Napoleon would probably have accepted this estimate, with some uncertainty about Caesar. He had never lost hope that France would come back to him. He solaced his exile with the hope that Gallic resentment of his imprisonment would restore French devotion to him. "When I am gone," he told O'Meara, "there will be a reaction in my favor.... It is my martyrdom that will restore the crown of France to my dynasty.... Ere twenty years have elapsed, when I am dead and buried, you will see another revolution in France."[11] Both of these predictions were fulfilled.

So he dictated his memoirs to revitalize his image, and they served their purpose well. His account of the battle of Waterloo, told to Gourgaud, was smuggled out of St. Helena and was published in Paris in 1820; Las Cases tells us that it made a sensation.[12] In 1821–22 six more volumes of his dictated autobiography were issued in France. Rapidly the Emperor's own story made its way, and played a major part in molding the "legend" that made him, dead, a living force in France.

His companions became his apostles. O'Meara defended him bravely

(1822) in the land of his sturdiest enemies. Las Cases made him faultless in four volumes (1823) that became the bible of the new inspiring creed. The Comte de Montholon's extensive report did not appear till 1847, Gourgaud's and Bertrand's only after their deaths; but meanwhile their living testimony fed the faith. Montholon brought back, also, the Emperor's "Deathbed Instructions to His Son," recommending virtues that might improve upon the imperial past: caution, moderation, constitutional rule, freedom of the press, and, toward the world, a policy of peace. Now, too, came a favorite counsel: "Let my son often read, and reflect on, history; this is the only true philosophy."[13]

Even in the testimony of his devout companions the great Emperor, amid the irritations of confinement and disease, had developed the faults natural to old age; but these weaknesses were now forgotten in the perspective of his martial triumphs, his administrative legacy, and the penetrating sharpness of his mind. He had in effect repudiated most of the Revolution, replacing liberty with absolutism, equality with aristocracy, fraternity with discipline; but in his refurbished image he was again the Son of the Revolution, and the Jacobins, once his devoted and persecuted enemies, now gathered around his memory. But, while Napoleon was purifying his record with punishment, the Bourbon rule that had replaced him outwore its initial acceptance; Louis XVIII, himself a reasonable man, touched with the Enlightenment, had allowed his court to be dominated by royalists who had forgiven nothing and wanted everything, including their old estates and authority, and a government unhampered by representative institutions. Resistance had been met with a "White Terror" of spies and hunts and hasty executions. Old soldiers could not forget the hounding and shooting of Ney. Against all this the Army still cherished its memory of the Petit Caporal who had chatted with conscripts around a campfire, who had promoted them without class prejudice or bureaucratic delay, and who had made the Grande Armée the terror of kings and the pride of France. The peasants remembered that Napoleon had protected them against the demands of the nobility and the clergy; the proletariat had prospered under his rule; the middle classes had grown in wealth and social acceptance. Millions of Frenchmen felt that with all his autocracy Napoleon had preserved the essentials of the Revolution: the end of feudalism and its toilsome tolls and dues; the opening of advancement to ability of whatever class; the equality of all before the law; the administration of justice according to explicit, written, and nationally uniform law.

So, within twenty years after his death, Napoleon had been reborn, and again dominated the minds and imagination of men. "The world belongs to Napoleon," wrote Chateaubriand; ". . . living, he failed to win the world; dead, he possesses it."[14] The modest Revolution of 1830 was helped by the new Bonapartist sentiment. The direct Bourbon line ended with the abdication of Charles X; the new King, Louis Philippe, of the Orléanist branch of the Bourbons, was the son of Louis-Philippe-Joseph, Duc d'Orléans, who had called himself Philippe-Égalité and had voted for the execution of

Louis XVI. The new King for a time courted the support of the Bonapartists; he adopted the tricolor emblems of the imperial regime, and ordered
the restoration of the figure of Napoleon to the top of the Vendôme Column.

Meanwhile the dead man's will had been published, and its second clause
seemed to be the final imperial command: "It is my wish that my ashes
may repose on the banks of the Seine, in the midst of the French people,
whom I have loved so well." Throughout France, quietly here and there,
then more widely and audibly, rose the appeal of the nation: "Bring him
home!" Let France give its hero the funeral that such a man deserved: let the
Triumph of the Ashes (so it came to be called) redeem the shame of that
dreary imprisonment! The cry reached the government; its Minister of Foreign Affairs, Louis-Adolphe Thiers (1797–1877)—who would write the
greatest of all histories of Napoleon,* and who was to be elected (in 1871)
first president of the Third Republic—was apparently the one who suggested
to his associates, and then, with them, to the King: Let us ask Great Britain's
consent for the removal of Napoleon's remains to Paris. Louis Philippe
agreed; to identify himself with such a move would win the hearts of the
French people. The Cabinet sounded out the heads of the British government. Lord Palmerston replied at once and handsomely: "The government
of her Britannic Majesty hopes that the promptness of its answer may be
considered in France as a proof of its desire to blot out the last trace of those
national animosities which, during the lifetime of the Emperor, armed England and France against each other."[15]

The King commissioned his son François, Prince de Joinville, to go to St.
Helena, and bring back the remains of Napoleon. On July 7, 1840, the
Prince sailed from Toulon on the *Belle Poule*, accompanied by Generals
Bertrand and Gourgaud, the Comte de Las Cases, and Napoleon's most intimate servant, Marchand, who together would decide the authenticity of the
corpse. They reached St. Helena on October 8; after many formalities they
saw the body exhumed; they identified it; and on November 30 they arrived
with it at Cherbourg.

There began what was surely the longest funeral in history. The coffin
was transferred to the steamer *Normandie*, which took it to Val de la Haye,
on the Seine below Rouen; there it was transferred to a river barge, on which
a small temple had been improvised; under this temple—guarded, one at each
corner, by Bertrand, Gourgaud, Las Cases, and Marchand—the coffin was
borne in leisurely state up the Seine, stopping at major towns for celebrations on the bank.[16] At Courbevoie, four miles north of Paris, it was transferred to a decorated funeral coach, which was drawn in a procession of
soldiers, sailors, and diverse dignitaries through Neuilly, and under the Arc
de Triomphe, and along the Champs-Élysées lined on either side by applauding and rejoicing multitudes.[17] Late on that bitter-cold day, December
15, 1840, the corpse at last reached its destination, the magnificently domed

---

* *Histoire du Consulat et de l'Empire*, 19v. (Paris, 1845–62).

church of the Hôtel des Invalides. The aisles and nave were crowded with thousands of silent spectators as twenty-four seamen bore the heavy coffin to the altar, where the Prince de Joinville addressed his father the King: "Sire, I present to you the body of the Emperor of France"; to which Louis Philippe replied, "I receive it in the name of France." Bertrand laid Napoleon's sword upon the coffin; Gourgaud added the Emperor's hat; a requiem Mass was sung to Mozart's music; and the Emperor was at last where he had wished his remains to be—in the heart of Paris, on the banks of the Seine.

III. PERSPECTIVE

Recovering from him, we too, authors and readers, fulfill his prediction—that the world would greet his death with an exhalation of relief. He was an exhausting force, a phenomenon of energy contained and explosive, a rising, burning, waning flame that consumed those who touched him intimately. We have not found in history another soul that burned so intensely and so long. That will, at first so hesitant, fearful, and morose, discovered its weapons and resources in a piercing mind and eye; it became confident, rash, imperious, rioting in grasp and power; until the gods, seeing no measure in him, bound lesser wills in union to pursue him, corner him, seize him, and chain him to a rock until his fire should burn out. This was one of the great dramas of history, and still awaits its Aeschylus.

But even in his lifetime he had a Hegel, who, unblinded by frontiers, saw in him a world force—the compulsion of events and circumstances speaking through a man—forging fragments into a unity, and chaos into effective significance. Here—first in France, then in Central Europe—was the *Zeitgeist*, or Spirit of the Time: the need and command for order, ending the disruptive excess of individualistic liberty and fragmented rule. In this sense Napoleon was a progressive force, establishing political stability, restoring morality, disciplining character, modernizing, clarifying, codifying law, protecting life and property, ending or mitigating feudalism, reassuring peasants, aiding industry, maintaining a sound currency, cleansing and improving administration and the judiciary, encouraging science and art (but discouraging literature and chaining the press), building schools, beautifying cities, repairing some of the ravages of war. Helped by his prodding, Europe advanced half a century during the fifteen years of his rule.

He was not the most powerful and enduring force of his time. Stronger was the Industrial Revolution, which made Great Britain rich enough in iron and gold to implement and finance Napoleon's fall, then made Europe vigorous enough to master the globe, then made America resourceful enough to rescue and replenish Europe, then . . . Only less strong than the Industrial Revolution, but far stronger and more lasting than the "Son of the Revolution," was the revolution that began in France in 1789 and then spread its effects through Europe in the replacement of feudal bonds and dues with individual rights, and the worldwide action of the rival hungers

that found clearest voice in the French Revolution: the hunger for freedom
—of movement, growth, enterprise, worship, thought, speech, and press; and
the hunger for equality—of access to opportunity, education, health, and
legal justice. These hostile hungers have taken their turn in dominating the
history of modern man: the hunger for liberty, to the detriment of equality,
was the recurrent theme of the nineteenth century in Europe and America;
the hunger for equality, at the cost of liberty, has been the dominant aspect
of European and American history in the twentieth century. The French
Revolution, and the American Revolution as interpreted by Jefferson, carried liberty to excess, freeing individualism to the point of a destructive disorder, and freeing superior ability to repeated crises of concentrated wealth.
Napoleon provided the discipline that checked political, economic, and
moral disorder in postrevolutionary France; no discipline has checked similar
disorder in our times.

When Napoleon, after the Peace of Tilsit (1807), carried order to excess,
subordinating statesmanship to the will to power, he no longer represented
the spirit of the time. He imitated and joined the absolute Continental monarchies that he had fought; he envied and courted the aristocracy that
scorned him and plotted to destroy him; he became a reactionary force when
France was again hungering for freedom and calling for democracy.

It is another humor of history that whereas in his lifetime Napoleon had
served to embody his country's need for order after a riot of freedom, he
became again after his death—and by the power of his remodeling legend—
the Son of the Revolution, the enemy of absolutism and aristocracy, the
symbol of revolt, the manageable mouthpiece of the recurrent cry for liberty. In 1799 opportunity and character had made him a dictator almost
larger than history; after 1815 and his imprisonment, and still more after
1821 and his death, public imagination remade him, for half a century, into
the most persuasive apostle of freedom. Few great men have remained, after
death, what they had been during their lives.

Was he a warmonger? Was he responsible for those successive and accumulating wars, those millions of youths snuffed out with nothing but the
anesthesia of battle to ease their passing, and those millions of desolate
women to whom they never returned? Hear him. He confessed to having
enjoyed generalship, because he had been trained to military art, and practiced it well; but how often he had longed to be free from war in order
to practice his other art—of administration, of turning the chaos of life
into productive order by establishing a strong structure of law and morality! How many times he had offered to treat for peace, and had been
insulted and rebuffed! The Italians had welcomed him as a liberator, both
in 1796 and in 1800; the Austrians had resubjected them while he was in
Egypt; the Austrians had attacked him while he was busy on the Channel,
and Prussia and Russia had joined in that attack without his having injured
them. Austria had again attacked him while he was fighting in Spain; Russia
had violated her pledge to support him in such a situation; Russia at Tilsit
had pledged observance of the Continental Blockade against British goods,

which was the only way in which France could retaliate against British blockade of French ports, and British capture of French vessels and colonies. British gold had financed coalition after coalition against him, even when his other enemies were inclined to peace; the British government had treated him like a criminal despite his voluntary surrender, whereas he himself had always dealt humanely and courteously with enemy officers captured in battle. His enemies had resolved to destroy him because he had won a kingdom by his own services and labors instead of by the accident of birth.

So ran Napoleon's defense. English historians, usually fair, German historians, usually accurate, and many French historians, usually patriotic (Michelet, Lanfrey, Taine, Lefebvre), unite in condemning the Corsican. He was a usurper, who profited from the execution of Louis XVI, and the collapse of the corrupt Directory, to seize the throne that belonged to Louis XVIII; such usurpations could not be tolerated, since they disturbed a political stability precious to all the nations of Europe. His invitations to peace conferences were not taken seriously, since they concealed intolerable demands like recognition of French control of Switzerland and Italy, and, later, of the German Rhineland. His skill in war tempted him to wage war, so that he was a constant threat not only to the peace-preserving balance of power but to the whole political structure of European life. The enormous indemnities which he exacted after his victories left the defeated governments incapable of financing any further resistance to his fantastic dream of uniting all Europe under French sovereignty and Napoleonic rule; they were quite justified in accepting British subsidies. The capture of French colonies as a means of bringing France to her senses was quite in accord with the practice of governments in eighteenth-century wars. Could Catholic governments like that of Austria agree to live under domination by an obvious atheist who was ruthlessly persecuting the Pope who had consecrated him, and who had no weapon but his piety? Napoleon had been generously treated by the Allies after his first abdication; he had violated his agreement by leaving Elba and compelling Europe to spend millions in revenues, and thousands of lives, to subdue and capture him; England and her allies were justified in isolating him beyond likelihood of his disturbing the peace of Europe again.

Truth is seldom simple; often it has a right and a left hand, and moves on two feet. Was there ever, since Ashoka, a major war in which one nation admitted the superior justice of the enemy's cause? It is part of the average citizen's nature to make his God a *particeps criminis* in the wars of his country. No superstate would solve the problem, for some of our greatest wars have been civil. The best we may hope for is to persuade more and more men and women to require their governments to submit more and more of their disputes to an international court or a league of nations; but we must not expect any nation to submit to arbitration of what it considers a matter of life and death. Self-preservation remains the basic law of life.

Within that limit the philosopher may seek to practice his trade, which is to understand and forgive. We can understand Emperor Francis II, shorn by Napoleon of half his state, driven from his lovely capital, returning to it still loved by his people, but humiliated and despoiled. We can understand a good Catholic being shocked by the harsh treatment of a gentle Pope— who would later ask the Allies to soften the conditions of his persecutor's imprisonment. We can understand Czar Alexander's reluctance to sacrifice his country's commerce to Napoleon's Continental Blockade. We can understand England's resolve to defend that balance of power upon which its security from external domination depended. And we can understand France's defense of the man who had rescued its government and morals from suicidal chaos, who had broadened its borders by brilliant victories, and had brought it unprecedented glory.

No, this fascinating man was no mere ogre of murder and destruction. He was led by his will to power, by the unchecked immensity of his dream; he was an autocrat confident that he knew better than their citizens what was good for France and Europe. But he was also, in his own fashion, a generous man, quick to forgive, secretly tender, hesitating for years before divorcing the frail Josephine. And we may say for him that he suffered and atoned, in his diseases and his doctors, in his retreat from Russia, in his living death on St. Helena.

He remains the outstanding figure of his time, with something noble about him that survives despite his selfishness in power and his occasional descents from grandeur in defeat. He thought we should not see his like again for five hundred years. We hope not; and yet it is good—and enough—to behold and suffer, once in a millennium, the power and limits of the human mind.

Bibliographical Guide

to editions referred to in the Notes

ACTON, JOHN EMERICH, LORD, *The French Revolution*. London, 1910.
ADAMSON, ROBERT, *Fichte*. Freeport, N.Y., 1969.
ALTAMIRA, RAFAEL, *A History of Spain*. Princeton, N.J., 1955.
——, *History of Spanish Civilization*. London, 1930.
ARNOLD, MATTHEW, *Essays in Criticism*, First and Second Series. New York: A. L. Burt, n.d.
AULARD, ALPHONSE, *The French Revolution*, 4v. New York, 1910.
——, *Christianity and the French Revolution*. Boston, 1927.
AUSTEN, JANE, *The Complete Novels*. Modern Library.
——, *Pride and Prejudice* and *Sense and Sensibility*. Modern Library.

BALCARRES, LORD, *Evolution of Italian Sculpture*. London, 1909.
BARNES, HARRY ELMER, *An Economic History of the Western World*. New York, 1942.
BATESON, F. W., *Wordsworth: A Re-interpretation*. London, 1954.
BEARD, CHARLES, *Introduction to the English Historians*. New York, 1927.
BECKER, CARL, *The Heavenly City of the Eighteenth Century Philosophers*. New Haven, Conn., 1951.
BEETHOVEN, LUDWIG VAN, *Letters*, translated and edited by Emily Anderson, 3v. New York, 1961.
BELL, E. T., *Men of Mathematics*. New York, 1937.
BELLOC, HILAIRE, *Danton*. New York, 1899.
BENN, ALFRED W., *History of English Rationalism in the Nineteenth Century*, 2v. London, 1906.
BENTHAM, JEREMY, *A Fragment on Government*. Oxford University Press, 1948.
——, *Introduction to the Principles of Morals and Legislation*. New York, 1948.
BERNAL, J. D., *Science in History*. London, 1957.
BERRY, ARTHUR, *A Short History of Astronomy*. New York, 1909.
BERTAUT, JULES, *Napoleon in His Own Words*. Chicago, 1916.
BERTRAND, COMTE HENRI G., *Napoleon at St. Helena*. New York, 1952.
BLAKE, WILLIAM, *Poems and Prophecies*. Everyman's Library.
——, *Selected Poems*. London, 1947.
BOAS, GEORGE, *French Philosophers of the Romantic Period*. New York, 1964.
BORROW, GEORGE, *The Bible in Spain*. London, 1908.
BOURGUIGNON, JEAN, *Napoléon Bonaparte*, 2v. Paris: Éditions Nationales, 1936.
BOURRIENNE, LOUIS-ANTOINE FAUVELET DE, *Memoirs of Napoleon Bonaparte*, 4v. New York, 1890.

BOWEN, MARJORIE, *Patriotic Lady: Emma, Lady Hamilton.* New York, 1936.

BRANDES, GEORG, *Main Currents in Nineteenth Century Literature*, 6v. New York, 1915.

————, *Wolfgang Goethe*, tr. Allen Porterfield, 2v. New York, 1924.

BREED, LEWIS, *The Opinions and Reflections of Napoleon.* Boston, 1926.

BRETT, G. S., *History of Psychology.* London, 1953.

BRINTON, CRANE, *The Jacobins.* New York, 1930.

BRION, MARCEL, *Daily Life in the Vienna of Mozart and Schubert.* New York, 1962.

BROCKWAY, W., and H. WEINSTOCK, *Men of Music.* New York, 1939.

————, and B. WINER, *A Second Treasury of the World's Great Letters.* New York, 1941.

BRUCKNER, A., *A Literary History of Russia.* London, 1908.

BURKE, THOMAS, *English Night Life.* New York, 1941.

BYRON, GEORGE GORDON, LORD, *Works*, 1-vol. ed. New York: George Leavitt, n.d.

CAIRD, EDWARD, *Hegel.* Edinburgh, 1911.

Cambridge History of Poland, 2v. Cambridge, Eng., 1950.

Cambridge Modern History (CMH), Vols. VIII and IX. Cambridge, 1918.

CAMERON, KENNETH, N., *The Young Shelley.* New York, 1950.

CAMPAN, JEANNE-LOUISE, *Memoirs of the Private Life of Marie Antoinette*, 2v. Boston, 1917.

CANOVA, ANTONIO, *Works*, with biographical memoir by Count Cicognara, 2v. Boston, 1876.

CANTON, GUSTAVE, *Napoléon antimilitariste.* Paris, 1902.

CARLYLE, THOMAS, *Critical and Miscellaneous Essays*, 2v. New York, 1901.

————, *The French Revolution*, 2v. New York, 1901.

CASTIGLIONE, ARTURO, *A History of Medicine.* New York, 1941.

CAULAINCOURT, MARQUIS ARMAND DE, *With Napoleon in Russia.* New York, 1935.

CHATEAUBRIAND, FRANÇOIS-RENÉ DE, *Atala and René.* Oxford University Press, 1926.

————, *The Genius of Christianity.* Baltimore: John Murphy, n.d.

————, *Mémoires d'outre-tombe.* Paris, n.d.

————, *Memoirs*, selected and edited by Robert Baldick. New York, 1961.

CLARK, BARRETT H., *Great Short Biographies of the World.* New York, 1928.

COLE, G. D. H., *Robert Owen.* Boston, 1925.

COLERIDGE, SAMUEL TAYLOR, *Selected Poetry and Prose.* New York: Random House, n.d.

————, *Biographia Literaria.* Everyman's Library.

COLMER, JOHN, *Coleridge Critic of Society.* Oxford University Press, 1959.

CONSTANT, BENJAMIN, *Adolphe.* New York, 1959.

————, *Journal intime.* Monaco, n.d.

————, *The Red Notebook*, in *Adolphe.*

CONSTANT, VÉRY, *Mémoirs of the Private Life of Napoleon*, 4v. New York, 1907.

CORTI, EGON CAESAR, *Rise of the House of Rothschild.* New York, 1928.

CRONIN, VINCENT, *Napoleon Bonaparte.* New York, 1972.

DELDERFIELD, R. F., *The Retreat from Moscow.* New York, 1967.
DICEY, A. V., *Law and Public Opinion in England during the 19th Century.* London, 1926.
DOWDEN, EDWARD, *Life of Shelley,* 2v. London, 1887.
DUBNOW, S. M., *History of the Jews in Russia and Poland,* 3v. Philadelphia, 1916.

ECKERMANN, JOHANN PETER, *Conversations with Goethe.* London, 1882.
EMERSON, RALPH WALDO, *Representative Men.* Philadelphia: McKay, n.d.
Encyclopaedia Britannica (EB), 24v. Chicago, 1970.
Encyclopaedia Britannica, 24v. New York, 1929.
Encyclopedia of Philosophy, 8v. New York, 1967.

FAGUET, ÉMILE, *Dix-neuvième Siècle: Études littéraires.* Paris: Boivin, n.d.
———, *Dix-septième Siècle: Études et portraits littéraires.* Paris: Boivin, n.d.
FAIN, BARON AGATHON, *Memoirs of the Invasion of France by the Allied Armies (1814).* London, 1834.
FAŸ, BERNARD, *Louis XVI.* Chicago, 1967.
FIALA, VLADIMIR, *Russian Painting of the Eighteenth and Nineteenth Centuries.* Artia, n.d.
FICHTE, JOHANN GOTTLIEB, *Addresses to the German Nation.* New York, 1968.
———, *The Science of Knowledge.* New York, 1970.
———, *The Vocation of Man.* Chicago, 1925.
FINDLAY, J. N., *Hegel: A Re-examination.* New York, 1962.
FINKELSTEIN, LOUIS, ed., *The Jews: Their History, Culture and Religion,* 2v. New York, 1949.
FISHER, H. A. L., *Studies in Napoleonic Statesmanship: Germany.* Oxford University Press, 1903.
FLORINSKY, MICHAEL T., *Russia: A History and an Interpretation,* 2v. New York, 1955.
FOUCHÉ, JOSEPH, *Memoirs,* 2v. London, 1825.
FOURNIER, AUGUST, *Napoleon the First.* New York, 1926.
FRANCKE, KUNO, *A History of German Literature as Determined by Social Forces.* New York, 1901.
FRUMAN, NORMAN, *Coleridge, the Damaged Archangel.* New York, 1971.

GARDNER, MARTIN, ed., *The Annotated Ancient Mariner.* New York, 1965.
GARRISON, F., *History of Medicine.* Philadelphia, 1929.
GEYL, PETER, *Napoleon: For and Against.* Baltimore: Penguin, 1965.
GIBBON, EDWARD, *History of the Decline and Fall of the Roman Empire,* ed. Dean Milman. New York: Nottingham Society, n.d.
GILBERT, O. P., *The Prince de Ligne.* New York: McDevitt Wilson, n.d.
GODWIN, WILLIAM, *Enquiry Concerning Political Justice,* 2v. London, 1842.
GOOCH, G. P., *Germany and the French Revolution.* New York, 1966.
———, *History and Historians in the Nineteenth Century,* 2d ed. London, 1952.
GOODRICH, FRANK B., *The Court of Napoleon.* New York, 1857.
GOTTSCHALK, LOUIS R., *Jean-Paul Marat.* New York, 1937.
GOURGAUD, GASPARD, *Journal,* 3v. Paris, n.d.
GRAETZ, HEINRICH, *History of the Jews,* 8v. New York, 1919.
GRAMONT, SANCHE DE, *Epitaph for Kings.* New York, 1968.
GREEN, J. R., *Short History of the English People,* 3v. London, 1898.

GREENLAW, R. W., *Economic Origins of the French Revolution*. Boston, 1958.
GROUT, DONALD JAY, *A Short History of Opera*. New York, 1954.
Grove's Dictionary of Music and Musicians, 5v. New York, 1927 ff.
GUÉRARD, A. L., *French Civilization in the Nineteenth Century*. London, 1914.
GUICCIOLI, COUNTESS, *My Recollections of Lord Byron*. Philadelphia, 1869.
GUILLEMIN, HENRI, *Napoléon tel quel*. Paris, 1969.

HALÉVY, ÉLIE, *History of the English People in 1815*. New York, 1924.
HANCOCK, A. E., *The French Revolution and the English Poets*. Port Washington, N.Y., 1967.
HAUSER, ARNOLD, *The Social History of Art*, 2v. New York, 1952.
HAWKINS, SIR JOHN, *Life of Samuel Johnson*. New York, 1961.
HAZLITT, WILLIAM, *Lectures on the English Poets* and *The Spirit of the Age*. Everyman's Library.
HEGEL, GEORG WILHELM, *The Philosophy of Georg Wilhelm Hegel*, ed. Carl J. Friedrich. Modern Library, 1954.
——, *Philosophy of History*. New York, 1900.
——, *Philosophy of Right*, Great Books, Vol. 40.
HEILBRONER, ROBERT L., *The Worldly Philosophers*. New York, 1953.
HELVÉTIUS, CLAUDE-ADRIEN, *De l'Esprit, or Essays on the Mind*. London, 1807.
HEROLD, J. CHRISTOPHER, *Bonaparte in Egypt*. New York, 1962.
——, ed., *The Mind of Napoleon*. New York, 1965.
——, *Mistress to an Age: A Life of Madame de Staël*. Indianapolis, 1958.
HIRSCH, E. D., JR., *Wordsworth and Schelling*. New Haven, Conn., 1960.
HIRSH, DIANA, *The World of Turner*. New York, 1969.
HOBSBAWN, E. J., *The Pelican Economic History of Britain*. Baltimore, 1969.
HÖFFDING, HARALD, *History of Modern Philosophy*, 2v. New York, 1955.
HORN, F. W., *History of the Literature of the Scandinavian North*. Chicago, 1884.
HORNE, R. H., *The History of Napoleon*, 2v. London, 1844.
HOUSSAYE, HENRI, *La Première Abdication*. Paris, 1905.
——, *La Première Restauration*. Paris, 1905.
——, *1815: La Seconde Abdication*. Paris, 1905.
——, *1815: Waterloo*. Kansas City, 1905.
HOWARTH, DAVID, *Trafalgar*. New York, 1969.
——, *Waterloo: Day of Battle*. New York, 1968.
HUGO, VICTOR, *Ninety-three*, in *Works*, Vol. VII. New York: University Society, n.d.
HUMBOLDT, ALEXANDER VON, *Cosmos*, 5v. London, 1845.
HUTT, MAURICE, *Napoleon*. Englewood Cliffs, N.J., 1972.

JUNOT, MME. ANDOCHE, DUCHESSE D'ABRANTÈS, *Memoirs of the Emperor Napoleon*, 3v. London, 1901.

KAFKER, F. A., and J. M. LAUX, *The French Revolution: Conflicting Interpretations*. New York, 1968.
KAUFMAN, WALTER, *Hegel: Reinterpretation, Texts and Commentary*. New York, 1965.
KERST, FRIEDRICH, *Beethoven in His Own Words*. New York, 1964.

KIRCHEISEN, F. M., *Memoirs of Napoleon I, Compiled from His Writings.* New York, 1929.
KORNILOV, ALEXANDER, *Modern Russian History.* New York, 1924.
KROPOTKIN, PETER A., *The Great French Revolution.* New York, 1909.
———, *Ideals and Realities in Russian Literature.* New York, 1919.
———, *Modern Science and Anarchism.* New York, 1908.

LA BRUYÈRE, JEAN DE, *Characters.* New York, 1929.
LACROIX, PAUL, *Directoire, Consulat et Empire.* Paris, 1884.
LAMARTINE, ALPHONSE DE, *History of the Girondists,* 3v. London, 1913.
LANFREY, PIERRE, *History of Napoleon,* 4v. London, 1886.
LÁNG, PAUL HENRY, *Music in Western Civilization.* New York, 1941.
LANSON, GUSTAVE, *Histoire de la littérature française,* 12th ed. Paris, 1912.
LAS CASES, COMTE EMMANUEL DE, *Memoirs of the Emperor Napoleon,* 4v. New York, 1883.
LEA, H. C., *History of the Inquisition in Spain,* 4v. New York, 1906.
LE BON, GUSTAVE, *The Psychology of Revolution.* New York, 1913.
LECKY, WILLIAM E., *History of England in the Eighteenth Century,* 8v. London, 1887.
LEFEBVRE, GEORGES, *Études sur la Révolution française.* Paris, 1963.
———, *The French Revolution.* London, 1962.
———, *Napoleon,* 2v. New York, 1969.
LEMAÎTRE, JULES, *Chateaubriand.* Paris: Calmann-Lévy, n.d.
LENOTRE, G., *The Tribunal of the Terror.* Philadelphia, 1939.
LEVY, MAX, *Private Life of Napoleon,* 2v. New York: Scribner, n.d.
LEWES, GEORGE, *Life of Goethe,* 2v, in Goethe, *Works,* 14v in 7. New York, 1902.
LOCY, WILLIAM A., *Biology and Its Makers.* New York, 1915.
LONGFORD, ELIZABETH, *Wellington: The Years of the Sword.* New York, 1969.
LOOMIS, STANLEY, *Paris in the Terror.* Philadelphia, 1964.
LOWES, J. LIVINGSTON, *The Road to Xanadu.* New York, 1927.

MACAULAY, THOMAS BABINGTON, *Critical, Historical, and Miscellaneous Essays,* 2v. New York, 1886.
MACLAURIN, C., *Post Mortem.* New York: Doran, n.d.
MADELIN, LOUIS, *The Consulate and the Empire,* 2v. New York, 1967.
———, *The French Revolution.* London, 1938.
———, *Talleyrand.* London, 1948.
MAINE DE BIRAN, MARIE-FRANÇOIS, *The Influence of Habit on the Faculty of Thinking.* Westport, Conn., 1970.
MAISTRE, COMTE JOSEPH-MARIE DE, *Les Soirées de Saint-Pétersbourg,* 2v. Paris: Garnier, n.d.
———, *Works,* tr. Jack Lively. New York, 1865.
MALTHUS, THOMAS R., *An Essay on the Principle of Population, 1798 and 1803.* New York, 1926.
MANTZIUS, KARL, *History of Theatrical Art,* 6v. New York, 1937.
MARCHAND, LESLIE A., *Byron,* 3v. New York, 1957.
MARGOLIOUTH, H. M., *William Blake.* Oxford University Press, 1951.
MARKUN, LEO, *Mrs. Grundy: A History of Four Centuries of Morals.* New York, 1930.

MARTINEAU, GILBERT, *Napoleon's St. Helena*. New York, 1969.
MARX, KARL, and FRIEDRICH ENGELS, *The Revolution in Spain*. New York, 1939.
MASSON, FRÉDÉRIC, *Napoleon and His Coronation*. Philadelphia: Lippincott, n.d.
————, *Napoleon at Home*, 2v. London, 1894.
MATHIEZ, ALBERT, *The French Revolution*. New York, 1964.
————, *After Robespierre: The Thermidorian Reaction*. New York, 1931.
MAUROIS, ANDRÉ, *Byron*. New York, 1930.
MAYNE, ETHEL C., *Life and Letters of Anna Isabella, Lady Noel Byron*. London, 1929.
McCABE, JOSEPH, *Crises in the History of the Papacy*. New York, 1916.
MÉNEVAL, CLAUDE-FRANÇOIS DE, *Memoirs of Napoleon*, 3v. London, 1894–95.
MICHELET, JULES, *The French Revolution*, 2v. London, 1890.
MILL, JOHN STUART, *On Bentham and Coleridge*. New York, 1962.
MISTLER, JEAN, ed., *Napoléon et l'Empire*, 2v. Paris, 1968.
MONROE, PAUL, *Text-book in the History of Education*. New York, 1928.
MOORE, F. J., *History of Chemistry*. New York, 1918.
MOORMAN, MARY, *William Wordsworth: The Early Years*. Oxford University Press, 1968.
————, *William Wordsworth: The Later Years*. Oxford University Press, 1968.
MORLEY, JOHN, *Biographical Studies*. London, 1923.
MORRIS, GOUVERNEUR, *Diary and Letters*, 2v. London, 1889.
MOSSIKER, FRANCES, *Napoleon and Josephine*. New York, 1964.
MUSSET, ALFRED DE, *Confessions of a Child of the Century*. New York, 1908.
MUTHER, RICHARD, *History of Modern Painting*, 4v. London, 1907.

NAPOLEON, *Letters*, ed. J. M. Thompson. Everyman's Library.
————, *Letters to Josephine*, tr. H. W. Bunn. New York, 1931.
NELSON, HORATIO, *Letters*. Everyman's Library.
New Cambridge Modern History (*NCMH*), Vols. VIII and IX. Cambridge, Eng., 1969.
NICHOLSON, HAROLD, *Benjamin Constant*. Garden City, N.Y., 1949.
NIETZSCHE, FRIEDRICH, *Beyond Good and Evil*. London, 1913.
————, *The Will to Power*. London, 1913.
NOLI, BISHOP F. S., *Beethoven and the French Revolution*. International Universities Press, 1947.

O'MEARA, BARRY, *Napoleon in Exile, or A Voice from St. Helena*, 2v. Philadelphia, 1822.
ORTZEN, LEN, *Imperial Venus: The Story of Pauline Bonaparte Borghese*. New York, 1974.
OSBORN, H. F., *From the Greeks to Darwin*. New York, 1922.
OWEN, ROBERT, *A New View of Society*. Everyman's Library.

PAINE, THOMAS, *The Age of Reason*. New York, n.d.
————, *The Rights of Man*. Everyman's Library.
PALMER, ALAN, *Metternich*. London, 1972.
————, *Napoleon in Russia*. New York, 1967.
PALMER, R. R., *Twelve Who Died*. Princeton, 1970.
PASCAL, ROY, *The German Novel*. Manchester, Eng., 1957.
PAULSEN, FRIEDRICH, *German Education*. New York, 1908.

Pelican Guide to English Literature, Vol. V. Baltimore, 1963.
PETERSEN, HOUSTON, ed., *A Treasury of the World's Great Speeches*. New York, 1954.
PHILLIPS, C. S., *The Church in France, 1789–1848*. London, 1929.
PINOTEAU, HERVÉ, ed., *Le Sacre de S. M. l'empereur Napoléon*. Paris, 1968.
PLUMB, J. H., *The First Four Georges*. New York, 1957.
POPE, DUDLEY, *The Great Gamble: Nelson at Copenhagen*. New York, 1972.

QUENNELL, M. and C., *History of Everyday Things in England, 1733–1851*. New York, 1934.

RÉAU, LOUIS, *L'Art russe*. Paris, 1922.
RÉMUSAT, MME. DE, *Memoirs*. New York, 1880.
ROBINSON, HENRY CRABB, *Diary*. London, 1927.
ROBINSON, JAMES HARVEY, *Readings in European History*. Boston, 1906.
ROBIQUEL, JEAN, *Daily Life in the French Revolution*. New York, 1965.
ROGERS, JAMES EDWIN THOROLD, *Six Centuries of Work and Wages*. New York, 1890.
ROLAND, MME., *Private Memoirs*. Chicago, 1900.
ROSE, J. HOLLAND, *The Personality of Napoleon*. New York, 1912.
ROSEBERY, ARCHIBALD PHILIP PRIMROSE, LORD, *Napoleon: The Last Phase*. New York, 1930.
———, *Pitt*. London, 1908.
ROSEBURY, THEODOR, *Microbes and Morals*. New York, 1971.
ROSS, EDWARD A., *Social Control*. New York, 1906.
RUDÉ, GEORGE, *The Crowd in the French Revolution*. Oxford University Press, 1959.
———, *The Crowd in History*. New York, 1964.
———, *Robespierre*. Englewood Cliffs, N.J., 1967.
RUSSELL, A. G., *The Engravings of William Blake*. Boston, 1912.
RUSSELL, BERTRAND, *Understanding History and Other Essays*. New York, 1957.

SAINTE-BEUVE, CHARLES-AUGUSTIN, *Chateaubriand et son groupe littéraire sous l'Empire*, 2v. Paris: Calmann-Lévy, n.d.
———, *Monday Chats*. Chicago, 1891.
———, *Portraits of Celebrated Women*. Boston, 1868.
SCHELLING, FRIEDRICH, *The Ages of the World*. New York, 1942.
———, *Of Human Freedom*. Chicago, 1936.
SCHOPENHAUER, ARTHUR, *The World as Will and Idea*, 3v. London, 1883.
SCOTT, WALTER, *The Heart of Midlothian*, in *Works*. New York: John W. Lovell, n.d.
———, *Poems*. New York: A. L. Burt, n.d.
SEDGWICK, W. T., and H. W. TYLER, *Short History of Science*. New York, 1927.
SEELEY, J. R., *Life and Times of Stein*, 2v. Boston, 1879.
SÉGUR, MARQUIS DE, *Marie Antoinette*. New York, 1928.
SHELLEY, PERCY BYSSHE, *Letters*, ed. F. L. Jones, 2v. Oxford University Press, 1964.
———, *Lost Letters to Harriet*. London, 1930.
———, *Poems*, in *Complete Poems of Keats and Shelley*. Modern Library.
SIEYÈS, EMMANUEL-JOSEPH, *What Is the Third Estate?* New York, 1964.

SIGERIST, H. E., *The Great Doctors*. New York, 1933.

SOBOUL, ALBERT, *The Parisian Sansculottes and the French Revolution*. Oxford University Press, 1964.

SOREL, ALBERT, *Europe and the French Revolution*, Vol. I. Garden City, N.Y., 1971.

SOREL, GEORGES, *Reflections on Violence*. New York: Huebsch, n.d.

SOUTHEY, ROBERT, *Life of Nelson*. London, 1868.

STACE, W. T., *The Philosophy of Hegel*. New York, 1955.

STACTON, DAVID, *The Bonapartes*. New York, 1966.

STAËL, MME. DE, *Considérations sur les principaux événements de la Révolution française*. Paris, 1845.

——, *Corinne, or Italy*. New York: Crowell, n.d.

——, *De la Littérature considérée dans ses rapports avec les institutions sociales*, translated as *The Influence of Literature upon Society*. Boston, 1813.

——, *Germany*, 2v. New York, 1861.

——, *Ten Years' Exile*. Fontwell, Eng., 1968.

STENDHAL (HENRI BEYLE), *La Chartreuse de Parme*. Baltimore: Penguin.

STEPHENS, H. MORSE, *Principal Speeches of the Statesmen and Orators of the French Revolution*, 2v. Oxford, 1892.

——, *The Story of Portugal*. New York, 1893.

STEVENS, ABEL, *Madame de Staël*, 2v. New York, 1893.

STRAKHOVSKY, LEONID, *Alexander I of Russia*. New York, 1947.

STRANAHAN, C. H., *A History of French Painting*. New York, 1907.

SULLIVAN, J. W. N., *Beethoven: His Spiritual Development*. New York, 1927.

TAINE, HIPPOLYTE, *The Ancient Regime*. New York, 1891.

——, *The French Revolution*, 3v. New York, 1931.

——, *The Modern Regime*, Vol. I. New York, 1890.

——, *Les Philosophes classiques du XIXᵉ siècle en France*. Paris, 1882.

TALLEYRAND-PÉRIGORD, CHARLES-MAURICE DE, *Memoirs*, 5v. Boston, 1895.

THACKERAY, WILLIAM MAKEPEACE, *The Four Georges*, in *Works*. Boston: Dana Estes, n.d.

——, "The Second Funeral of Napoleon," *Roundabout Papers*, in *Works*. Boston: Dana Estes, n.d.

THAYER, A. W., *Life of Ludwig van Beethoven*, 3v. London, 1962.

THIERS, LOUIS-ADOLPHE, *History of the Consulate and the Empire of France under Napoleon*, 12v. Philadelphia, 1893.

THORNTON, J. C., *Table Talk from Ben Jonson to Leigh Hunt*. Everyman's Library.

TOCQUEVILLE, ALEXIS DE, *L'Ancien Régime*. Oxford University Press, 1937.

TRAILL, HENRY DUFF, *Social England*, 6v. New York, 1902.

TREITSCHKE, HEINRICH VON, *History of Germany in the Nineteenth Century*, Vol. I. New York, 1915.

TREVELYAN, G. M., *English Social History*. London, 1947.

TURNER, P. M., and C. H. C. BAKER, *Stories of the French Artists*. New York, 1910.

ÜBERWEG, FRIEDRICH, *History of Philosophy*, tr. Morris, 2v. New York, 1871.

VALLENTIN, ANTONINA, *Mirabeau.* New York, 1948.
VANDAL, ALBERT, *L'Avènement de Napoléon,* 2v. Paris, 1903, 1907.
————, *Napoléon et Alexandre Ier,* 3v. Paris, 1896.
VAN DOREN, DOROTHY, *The Lost Art: Letters of Seven Famous Women.* New York, 1929.
VAN LAUN, HENRI, *History of French Literature,* 3v. London, 1876.

WATSON, J. STEVEN, *The Reign of George III.* Oxford, Eng., 1960.
WEIDMAN, FRANZ, *Hegel: An Illustrated Biography.* New York, 1968.
WHITE, R. J., *Political Tracts of Wordsworth, Coleridge, and Shelley.* London, 1953.
WIENER, LEO, *Anthology of Russian Literature,* 2v. New York, 1902.
WILLIAMS, HENRY SMITH, *History of Science,* 5v. New York, 1909.
WILSON, P. W., *William Pitt, the Younger.* New York, 1934.
WINGFIELD-STRATFORD, ESME, *History of British Civilization.* London, 1948.
WINWAR, FRANCES, *Farewell the Banner.* New York, 1938.
WOLF, A., *History of Science, Technology and Philosophy in the Eighteenth Century.* New York, 1939.
WOLLSTONECRAFT, MARY, *A Vindication of the Rights of Woman.* New York, n.d.
WOODS, WATT, and ANDERSON, *The Literature of England,* 2v. Chicago, 1936.
WORDSWORTH, DOROTHY, *Journals,* ed. Mary Moorman. Oxford University Press, 1971.
WORDSWORTH, WILLIAM, *Complete Poetical Works.* New York: A. L. Burt, n.d.
WORDSWORTH and COLERIDGE, *Lyrical Ballads.* Oxford University Press, 1969.
WRIGHT, RAYMOND, *Prose of the Romantic Period, 1780–1830.* Baltimore: Penguin (Pelican).

YOUNG, ARTHUR, *Travels in France During the Years 1787, 1788, and 1789.* London, 1906.

ZWEIG, STEFAN, *Joseph Fouché.* New York, 1930.

Notes

CHAPTER I

1. *New Cambridge Modern History (NCMH)*, VIII, 714.
2. Lefebvre, Georges, *French Revolution*, I, 41.
3. Aulard, Alphonse, *Christianity and the French Revolution*, 36-37.
4. *Ibid.*, 29.
5. Taine, Hippolyte, *French Revolution*, I, 147, 158.
6. Morley, John, *Biographical Studies*, 411.
7. Lefebvre, *French Revolution*, I, 42.
8. Sieyès, E.-J., *What Is the Third Estate?*, 51.
9. Taine, *French Revolution*, III, 318.
10. Pierre Gaxotte in Greenlaw, R. W., *Economic Origins of the French Revolution*, 43.
11. See Durant, *Rousseau and Revolution*, 71-77.
12. Roland, Mme., *Private Memoirs*.
13. Taine, *The Ancient Regime*, 317.
14. C. E. Labrousse in Greenlaw, 62; Lefebvre, *Études sur la Révolution française*, 229, 239.
15. La Bruyère, Jean de, *Characters*, XII, 128, 318.
16. A. Aulard in Greenlaw, 25.
17. Lefebvre, *Études*, 351, 435.
18. Michelet, Jules, *French Revolution*, I, 185; Taine, *French Revolution*, I, 3.
19. *NCMH*, VIII, 660.
20. Young, Arthur, *Travels in France*, 197.
21. Campan, Jeanne-Louise, *Memoirs of the Private Life of Marie Antoinette*, II, 216.
22. Tocqueville, Alexis de, *L'Ancien Régime*, 190-91.

CHAPTER II

1. Michelet, *French Revolution*, I, 84.
2. Rudé, George, *Robespierre*, 123.
3. Morley, *Biographical Studies*, 287.
4. Michelet, I, 498.
5. *Encyclopaedia Britannica*, XIX, 392b.
6. Lefebvre, *Études*, 145.
7. Aulard, *French Revolution*, I, 230.
8. *Ibid.*, 309, 359; Lefebvre, *Études*, 145.
9. Durant, *Rousseau and Revolution*, 951-54.
10. Brinton, Crane, *The Jacobins*, 15.
11. Mathiez, Albert, *French Revolution*, 44.
12. *Ibid.*
13. Mirabeau, speech of July 9, 1789.
14. Mathiez, 46.

15. *EB*, III, 264d; Gramont, Sanche de, *Epitaph for Kings*, 378.
16. Taine, *French Revolution*, I, 42.
17. Campan, *Memoirs*, II, 59.
18. *Ibid.*, 66.
19. Gramont, Sanche de, *Epitaph for Kings*, 384.
20. Gottschalk, L. R., *Jean-Paul Marat*, 6-8.
21. *Ibid.*, 4.
22. MacLaurin, C., *Post Mortem*, 200.
23. Taine, *French Revolution*, III, 122.
24. Gottschalk, 117-18.
25. *Ibid.*, 15.
26. 23.
27. Taine, *French Revolution*, III, 129.
28. Morris, Gouverneur, *Diary and Letters*, I, 143.
29. Taine, I, 73.
30. *Ibid.*, 70-71; Mathiez, *French Revolution*, 50-51.
31. Robinson, James Harvey, *Readings in European History*, 435.
32. Mathiez, 53.
33. Robinson, 438.
34. *Ibid.*, 440.
35. In Taine, II, 5.
36. Michelet, *French Revolution*, 253; Mathiez, 63.
37. Campan, II, 78.
38. Michelet, 258.
39. Taine, I, 105.
40. Herold, J. C., *Mistress to an Age*, 92; *EB*, XXI, 634.
41. Mathiez, 98.
42. Phillips, C. S., *The Church in France*, I, 9.
43. *Ibid.*, 14; Taine, I, 180.
44. *Ibid.*, 182.
45. Carlyle, *French Revolution*, Book VIII, Ch. 11–12.
46. Michelet, 411.
47. Mathiez, 68.
48. Campan, II, 128; Ségur, *Marie Antoinette*, 225.
49. Taine, I, 96.
50. *Ibid.*, 106.
51. Campan, II, 126n.
52. Carlyle, *French Revolution*, I, 397.
53. Ségur, 230.
54. Vallentin, Antonina, *Mirabeau*, 490-91.
55. Michelet, 567–68.
56. Vallentin, 512-17.
57. Michelet, 568.
58. *Ibid.*, 569.
59. Ségur, 237.

60. Rudé, George, *The Crowd in the French Revolution*, 89.
61. Acton, J. E., Lord, *The French Revolution*, 199.

CHAPTER III

1. Bertaut, Jules, *Napoleon in His Own Words*, 58, 63.
2. Alexandre de Lameth in Robinson, *Readings*, 452.
3. Mathiez, *French Revolution*, 134.
4. Brinton, *The Jacobins*, 39, 183, 251.
5. Rudé, *Robespierre*, 88.
6. Taine, *French Revolution*, II, 54-67.
7. Lefebvre, *French Revolution*, I, 217.
8. Roland, Mme., *Private Memoirs*, 273.
9. *Ibid.*, 55.
10. 345.
11. 357.
12. Lanfrey, Pierre, *History of Napoleon*, I, 292.
13. Mathiez, 140-41.
14. Lefebvre, *French Revolution*, I, 217.
15. Aulard, *The French Revolution*, 366.
16. Robinson, *Readings*, 456.
17. Acton, *French Revolution*, 232.
18. Gottschalk, *Jean-Paul Marat*, 96.
19. Taine, II, 182.
20. Lefebvre, *French Revolution*, I, 238.
21. Taine, II, 179-86; Ségur, 273-76.
22. Sorel, Georges, *Reflections on Violence*, 194.
23. Lefebvre, *Études*, 77-82; *French Revolution*, I, 239n.
24. Belloc, Hilaire, *Danton*, 380.
25. Musset, Alfred de, *Confessions of a Child of the Century*, 21-23.
26. Belloc, 198.
27. Mathiez, 174.
28. *Ibid.*, 184-89; Aulard, *Christianity and the French Revolution*, 86-90; Lefebvre, *French Revolution*, I, 244.
29. Aulard, *French Revolution*, II, 141.
30. Le Bon, Gustave, *The Psychology of the Revolution*, 170.
31. Mathiez, 170.
32. Taine, II, 211; Lefebvre, 242.
33. Gottschalk, *Marat*, 120.
34. Carlyle, *French Revolution*, II, 174.
35. Madelin, Louis, *French Revolution*, 285.
36. *Ibid.*; Mathiez, 180.
37. Taine, II, 221.
38. *Ibid.*, 226.
39. 227.
40. Morris, G., *Diary*, 583; Mathiez, 81.
41. Taine, II, 228.
42. Lefebvre, *French Revolution*, I, 243.
43. Taine, II, 229.

44. Le Bon, *The Psychology of the Revolution*, 188.
45. Taine, II, 214n.
46. *Ibid.*, 218.
47. Le Bon, 98.
48. Mathiez, 183; Carlyle, II, 199.
49. Belloc, *Danton*, 342.
50. Taine, II, 214.
51. *Ibid.*, 212n.
52. Mathiez, 222.
53. Brandes, Georg, *Main Currents in Nineteenth Century Literature*, II, 50.

CHAPTER IV

1. Mathiez, *French Revolution*, 195; Taine, *French Revolution*, II, 232n; Faÿ, B., *Louis XVI*, 388; Aulard, *French Revolution*, III, 109-11.
2. Lefebvre, *French Revolution*, I, 244.
3. Taine, II, 279.
4. *Ibid.*, 276-82.
5. Mathiez, 211.
6. Taine, III, 155.
7. Morley, 296.
8. Mathiez, 239 ff.
9. *Ibid.*, 275.
10. Robinson, *Readings*, 460.
11. Mathiez, 256.
12. Robiquel, Jean, *Daily Life in the French Revolution*, 91.
13. Gramont, *Epitaph for Kings*, 423.
14. Mathiez, 262.
15. Taine, II, 283.
16. Madelin, *French Revolution*, 320.
17. Gramont, 426; Rudé, *Robespierre*, 170.
18. Hugo, Victor, *Ninety-three*, 160.
19. Robiquel, *Daily Life in the French Revolution*, 9.
20. Taine, III, 361.
21. E. g., Lenotre, G., *The Tribunal of the Terror*, 119 and facing p. 22.
22. Aulard, *French Revolution*, III, 90.
23. Taine, III, 135.
24. Gottschalk, *Marat*, 159 ff.; Loomis, Stanley, *Paris in the Terror*, 104-5.
25. Lefebvre, *French Revolution*, II, 50.
26. Mathiez, 387 ff.
27. Taine, III, 388 ff.
28. Mathiez, 319.
29. *Ibid.*, 322.
30. 324.
31. Carlyle, II, 332.
32. Loomis, 14, 128.
33. In Gottschalk, 92.
34. *Ibid.*, 168.
35. 136.
36. 170.
37. Mathiez, 344; MacLaurin, *Post Mortem*, 206.

38. Mathiez, 344.
39. Loomis, 138, 143.
40. Mathiez, 343.
41. Loomis, 149.
42. Belloc, *Danton*, 234.
43. Palmer, R. R., *Twelve Who Died*, 55.
44. Morley, 324.
45. Palmer, 58, 160.
46. Taine, III, 313.
47. Palmer, 110.
48. Lefebvre, *Études*, 139.
49. Taine, II, 51.
50. Lefebvre, *French Revolution*, II, 111, 282.
51. *Ibid.*, 283 ff.
52. Rudé, *Robespierre*, 55.
53. Palmer, 58.
54. In Kropotkin, Peter, *The Great French Revolution*, 502 ff.
55. Palmer, 52; Mathiez, 366.
56. Palmer, 47.
57. Mathiez, 403.
58. Ségur, 293.
59. *Ibid.*, 304.
60. 309.
61. Lenotre, 151.
62. Lamartine, Alphonse de, *Histoire des Girondins*, III, 36-37.
63. Roland, Mme., *Private Memoirs*, 105.
64. *Ibid.*, 114.
65. 288.
66. Carlyle, II, 356.
67. Madelin, *French Revolution*, 377; Taine, III, 207, 297.
68. Madelin, 374.
69. Taine, III, 209-10.
70. *Ibid.*, 299; Madelin, 375; Mathiez, 402.
71. Taine, III, 211.
72. Madelin, 376.
73. Palmer, 150.
74. Zweig, Stefan, *Joseph Fouché, xv*.
75. *Ibid.*, 37.
76. Palmer, 156.
77. Zweig, 57.
78. *Ibid.*, 167; Palmer, 167.
79. *Ibid.*, 169
80. 180.
81. Taine, III, 39.
82. Palmer, 175.
83. Rudé, *Robespierre*, 8; NCMH, IX, 280.
84. Lefebvre, *French Revolution*, II, 120.
85. Lea, H. C., *History of the Inquisition in Spain*, I, 593.
86. Zweig, *Fouché*, 39 ff.
87. Palmer, 142 ff.
88. Taine, III, 175; Madelin, 389; Mathiez, 412; Carlyle, II, 371; Becker, Carl, *Heavenly City of the 18th Century Philosophers*, 156.
89. Lefebvre, *French Revolution*, II, 119.

90. *Ibid.*, 78.
91. Palmer, 143.
92. Morley, 319; translation slightly improved.
93. *Ibid.*, 321.
94. 311.
95. Carlyle, II, 229.
96. Taine, III, 380-81.
97. Soboul, Albert, *The Parisian Sansculottes and the French Revolution*, 28.
98. Robinson, *Readings*, 467.
99. Lefebvre, *French Revolution*, II, 88; Madelin, 395.
100. Morley, 332.
101. Madelin, 395.
102. *Ibid.*, 397; Taine, III, 142.
103. Madelin, 397.
104. Lenotre, *The Tribunal of the Terror*, 137.
105. *Ibid.*, 138.
106. Madelin, 398.
107. Brockway and Winer, *Second Treasury of the World's Great Letters*, 273.
108. Morley, 333.
109. Madelin, 399.
110. Morley, 338.
111. Aulard, *French Revolution*, II, 286; Lefebvre, *French Revolution*, II, 124; Palmer, 365.
112. Taine, III, 299.
113. Lefebvre, II, 125.
114. Mathiez, 499.
115. Rudé, *Robespierre*, 9; Soboul in Kafker and Laux, *The French Revolution: Conflicting Interpretations*, 293.
116. Madelin, 408.
117. Stephens, H. Morse, *Principal Speeches . . . of the French Revolution*, II, 143-63.
118. Madelin, 420.
119. Belloc, *Danton*, 330.
120. Madelin, 422.
121. Mathiez, 508; Lefebvre, *French Revolution*, II, 135; Palmer, 379.
122. Mathiez, 509.
123. *Ibid.*, 510.
124. Robiquel, *Daily Life in the French Revolution*, 202.
125. Palmer, 389.
126. Aulard, III, 247-48.
127. Lefebvre, II, 161.
128. Aulard, III, 291.
129. *Ibid.*, 319.

CHAPTER V

1. Madelin, 489; Lefebvre, *French Revolution*, II, 173.
2. Lacroix, Paul, *Directoire, Consulat et Empire*, 120.
3. Aulard, IV, 40.

4. *Ibid.*, 41.
5. 42.
6. Acton, *French Revolution*, 5.
7. Nietzsche, *Will to Power*, 877.
8. Source lost.
9. Napoleon, Letter of June 12, 1789, in *Letters*, 33.
10. In Lanfrey, I, 4.
11. Chuquet in Bourguignon, Jean, *Napoléon Bonaparte*, I, 4.
12. Kircheisen, F. M., *Memoirs of Napoleon I*, 11.
13. *Ibid.*, 10.
14. Las Cases, *Memoirs of Napoleon*, under May 29, 1816, in Taine, *The Modern Regime*, I, 200.
15. Bourguignon, I, 22.
16. Kircheisen, 11.
17. *Ibid.*, 24; Bourguignon, I, 23.
18. Kircheisen, 18.
19. Rémusat, Mme. de, *Memoirs*, 10.
20. *Ibid.*, 102-3.
21. Rose, J. Holland, *The Personality of Napoleon*, 17.
22. Rémusat, 102.
23. Bourguignon, I, 28.
24. Rose, 57.
25. Plato, *The Republic*, paragraphs 338-44.
26. Nietzsche, *Beyond Good and Evil*, 201 and 53.
27. Mistler, Jean, ed., *Napoléon et l'Empire*, I, 36.
28. Kircheisen, 34-35.
29. *Ibid.*, 41.
30. Taine, *Modern Regime*, I, 2n.
31. Lefebvre, *French Revolution*, II, 185.
32. Mossiker, Frances, *Napoleon and Josephine*, 65-66.
33. *Ibid.*, 72; Mistler, I, 49.
34. G. Lenotre in Bourguignon, I, 91.
35. Mossiker, 89.
36. *Ibid.*, 49.
37. 86-90.
38. Kircheisen, 47.
39. Lanfrey, I, 58; Mossiker, 92-95.
40. Mossiker, 34.
41. G. Lenotre in Bourguignon, I, 91.
42. *Ibid.*, 93.
43. J. Godechot in Bourguignon, I, 96.
44. Napoleon, *Letters*, 45.
45. Bourrienne, *Memoirs of Napoleon Bonaparte*, I, 24.
46. Lanfrey, I, 71.
47. Mossiker, 23.
48. *Ibid.*, 119.
49. 28.
50. Napoleon, *Letters*, 51.
51. Lanfrey, I, 87.
52. *Ibid.*; Bourguignon, I, 108; Mistler, I, 270.
53. Lanfrey, I, 84.
54. Mossiker, 29.
55. Bourguignon, I, 112.
56. *EB*, IX, 920d.
57. Mossiker, 128.
58. Kircheisen, 71.
59. Napoleon, *Letters*, 62.
60. Vandal, Albert, *L'Avènement de Bonaparte*, I, 13-15.
61. Staël, Mme. de, *Memoirs*, in Bourguignon, I, 137.
62. *Ibid.*, 138.
63. Napoleon, *Letters*, 72.
64. Rémusat, *Memoirs*, 99.
65. Lefebvre, *French Revolution*, II, 219.
66. Talleyrand, *Memoirs*, I, 332.
67. *CMH*, VIII, 598.
68. Bourguignon, 148.
69. Kircheisen, 75.
70. Herold, J. C., ed., *The Mind of Napoleon*, 51.
71. Rémusat, *Memoirs*, 99, slightly rearranged.
72. Napoleon, *Letters*, 75.
73. *Ibid.*, Oct. 23, 1798.
74. Herold, *Bonaparte in Egypt*, 276; *CMH*, VIII, 609.
75. Kircheisen, 42.
76. Rémusat, 99.
77. Kircheisen, 91.
78. Bourrienne, I, 212.
79. Las Cases, III, 200.
80. Mistler, I, 73; Méneval, *Memoirs*, I, 25-34; Madelin, *French Revolution*, 605.
81. Bourguignon, I, 172.
82. Méneval, I, 24; Mistler, I, 74.
83. *CMH*, VIII, 494.
84. Vandal, *Avènement*, 10.
85. Madelin, *Talleyrand*, 61.
86. *CMH*, VIII, 493.
87. Madelin, *French Revolution*, 559.
88. Taine, *French Revolution*, III, 455.
89. *Ibid.*, 469.
90. Vandal, I, 70.
91. Taine, III, 467n.
92. Talleyrand, *Memoirs*, I, 207.
93. Madelin, 584.
94. Taine, III, 426-27.
95. Vandal, I, 233.
96. Aulard, IV, 139.
97. Fournier, *Napoleon the First*, I, 182.
98. Mossiker, 190-91.
99. *Ibid.*, 202.
100. Bourrienne, II, 12n.; Vandal, I, 245; Mossiker, 205.
101. Aulard, IV, 139.
102. Madelin, *French Revolution*, 611.
103. Vandal, I, 274.
104. *Ibid.*, 297-98.
105. Mistler, I, 76.

106. Lefebvre, *French Revolution*, II, 255.
107. Vandal, I, 314.
108. *Ibid.*, 316-17.
109. 368.
110. 370.
111. Bourrienne, I, 272.
112. Vandal, I, 386.
113. Bourrienne, I, 284.

CHAPTER VI

1. *EB*, IX, 755; X, 343; *NCMH*, VIII, 714.
2. Barnes, H. E., *Economic History of the Western World*, 351.
3. Lefebvre, *French Revolution*, I, 114.
4. Palmer, R. R., *Twelve Who Died*, 240.
5. Mathiez, 267.
6. Macaulay, T. B., *Critical, Historical, and Miscellaneous Essays*, II, 70.
7. Taine, *French Revolution*, II, 291.
8. Aulard, *French Revolution*, IV, 108.
9. Lefebvre, *French Revolution*, II, 287.
10. Taine, III, 84.
11. Aulard, II, 282.
12. *Ibid.*, III, 373, 387, 391.
13. *Ibid.*, 392; Lacroix, *Directoire, Consulat et Empire*, 298.
14. Roland, Mme., *Memoirs*, 105.
15. Lacroix, 123; Carlyle, *French Revolution*, 382; Palmer, 65.
16. In Soboul, *The Parisian Sansculottes in the French Revolution*, 244.
17. *CMH*, VIII, 744.
18. *Ibid.*, 750.
19. 752.
20. Robiquel, *Daily Life in the French Revolution*, 149 ff.
21. *EB*, X, 1019d.
22. Le Bon, G., *Psychology of Revolution*, 217.
23. Robiquel, 126.
24. *EB*, XIX, 868c.
25. Palmer, 65.
26. Robiquel, 74.
27. Soboul, 246; Madelin, *French Revolution*, 553.
28. Marcel Lachiver in London *Times Literary Supplement*, March 3, 1972, p. 243.
29. Taine, III, 82n.
30. Madelin, *French Revolution*, 554.
31. Taine, *Modern Regime*, I, 175.
32. Aulard, I, 232.
33. Lefebvre, *French Revolution*, II, 267.
34. Herold, ed., *The Mind of Napoleon*, 13.
35. Taine, *French Revolution*, III, 346.
36. Aulard, III, 241; Soboul, 229.
37. Taine, *French Revolution*, III, 88n.
38. Lacroix, *Directoire, Consulat et Empire*, 81, 34.

39. Robiquel, 54.
40. *Ibid.*, 89.
41. Lacroix, 70.
42. *Ibid.*, 80.
43. Robiquel, 88.
44. Madelin, *French Revolution*, 546.
45. Junot, Mme., *Memoirs*, I, 144.
46. Madelin, 428.
47. Láng, P. H., *Music in Western Civilization*, 787.
48. *Grove's Dictionary of Music and Musicians*, I, 614.
49. Mantzius, K., *History of Theatrical Art*, VI, 153 f.
50. Hauser, A., *The Social History of Art*, II, 635.
51. Muther, R., *History of Modern Painting*, I, 103.
52. Livy, *History of Rome*, I, 24.
53. Turner and Baker, *Stories of the French Artists*, 291.
54. Durant, *Age of Voltaire*, 536.
55. Brett, G. S., *History of Psychology*, 460.
56. Überweg, F., *History of Philosophy*, tr. Morris, II, 339.
57. *CMH*, VIII, 724.
58. Lamartine, *History of the Girondists*, III, 418.
59. Van Laun, H., *History of French Literature*, III, 166.
60. Stevens, Abel, *Mme. de Staël*, I, 54.
61. Herold, J. C., *Mistress to an Age*, 30.
62. *Ibid.*, 62.
63. 95.
64. 103.
65. 108.
66. 113-14.
67. 117.
68. Pierre Lacretelle in Stevens, I, 145.
69. Herold, *Mistress to an Age*, 125.
70. In Bourguignon, I, 137.
71. Herold, 181.

CHAPTER VII

1. Bourrienne, *Memoirs*, I, 290.
2. Madelin, *The Consulate and the Empire*, I, 46.
3. *Ibid.*, 37.
4. Fournier, *Napoleon*, 180.
5. Madelin, *Consulate and Empire*, I, 3.
6. Thiers, L. A., *History of the Consulate and the Empire*, I, 55.
7. *Ibid.*, 57.
8. Las Cases, II, 330.
9. Taine, *Modern Regime*, I, 17.
10. *EB*, XIII, 717b.
11. Napoleon, *Letters*, 80.
12. Lefebvre, *Napoleon*, I, 84.

13. *Ibid.;* Taine, *Modern Regime*, I, 152; Madelin, *Consulate and Empire*, I, 56.
14. Lefebvre, *Napoleon*, I, 86.
15. Bourrienne, I, 289n.
16. Talleyrand, *Memoirs*, introduction by the Duc de Broglie, *xxi.*
17. *Ibid., xxii.*
18. *viii-ix.*
19. Talleyrand, *Memoirs*, I, 170-71.
20. Madelin, *Talleyrand*, 48, 83.
21. Rémusat, *Memoirs*, 85.
22. *Ibid.,* 106.
23. Madelin, *Talleyrand*, 23.
24. Thiers, I, 61; Herold, ed., *The Mind of Napoleon*, 72.
25. Canton, Gustave, *Napoléon antimilitariste*, 34.
26. Lefebvre, *Napoleon*, I, 89.
27. *Ibid.,* 88; Taine, V, 141n.
28. Lefebvre, I, 74.
29. Bourrienne, I, 370.
30. *Ibid.,* 372.
31. Jacques Bainville in Geyl, Peter, *Napoleon: For and Against*, 345.
32. *Ibid.,* 344.
33. Bourrienne, I, 413.
34. Madelin, *Consulate and Empire*, I, 93.
35. Napoleon, *Letters*, 84.
36. Thiers, I, 295.
37. Bourrienne, I, 419.
38. *Ibid.,* II, 2.
39. 3.
40. Thiers, I, 236.
41. *Ibid.,* 247.
42. 248.
43. Napoleon, *Letters*, 87.
44. Lefebvre, *Napoleon*, I, 100.
45. Bourrienne, II, 22.
46. *Ibid.,* I, 414.
47. Napoleon, *Letters*, 90.
48. Thiers, I, 322.
49. Bourrienne, I, 345; Méneval, *Memoirs*, I, 69; Thiers, I, 332.
50. Bourrienne, I, 351n.
51. Madelin, *Consulate and Empire*, I, 108.
52. Morris, Gouverneur, *Diary*, 92.
53. Madelin, I, 113.
54. Las Cases, IV, 103.
55. *Ibid.*
56. Madelin, I, 150.
57. *EB*, VII, 12c.
58. Rose, J. H., *Personality of Napoleon*, 169.
59. In Geyl, 330.
60. Guérard, A. L., *French Civilization in the 19th Century*, 67.
61. Cardinal Consalvi in Lefebvre, *Napoleon*, I, 19.
62. Taine, *French Revolution*, III, 474.
63. Las Cases, II, 253.
64. Bourrienne, II, 236.

65. *CMH*, IX, 186.
66. Staël, Mme. de, *Considérations sur les principaux événements de la Révolution française*, 376; Canton, 44; Herold, *The Mind of Napoleon*, 107.
67. Canton, 30-34.
68. Méneval, I, 188.
69. Canton, 37.
70. *Ibid.,* 1-3.
71. Bourrienne, II, 299.
72. Thiers, II, 302.
73. Bourrienne, II, 151.
74. This phrase had been applied to Frederick II of Sicily; see Durant, *The Age of Faith*, 714.
75. Morris, *Diary*, 115-16.
76. *Ibid.,* 117; Lefebvre, *Napoleon*, I, 176.
77. Bourrienne, II, 226; Lefebvre, I, 169.
78. Fouché, Joseph, *Memoirs*, I, 256-57.
79. Lefebvre, I, 180; Madelin, *Consulate and Empire*, I, 192; Kircheisen, *Memoirs of Napoleon*, I, 107.
80. *CMH*, IX, 29.
81. Lefebvre, I, 180-81.
82. Las Cases, IV, 186; Madelin, I, 193.
83. Rémusat, 39; Madelin, I, 193.
84. Kircheisen, 108.
85. Mistler, I, 120.
86. Lefebvre, I, 180–81; Méneval, I, 234.
87. Caulaincourt, Armand de, *With Napoleon in Russia*, 314.
88. *Ibid.,* 317.
89. Lefebvre, I, 182; Madelin, I, 208.
90. Méneval, I, 249.
91. Madelin, *Talleyrand*, 111.
92. Madelin, *Consulate and Empire*, I, 218.
93. Bourrienne, II, 280.
94. Madelin, II, 210.
95. Las Cases, II, 67.
96. Rémusat, 137, 167.
97. Bourrienne, II, 264.
98. Las Cases, IV, 192.
99. Madelin, *Consulate and Empire*, I, 227.
100. Rémusat, 108.
101. Mossiker, 271.
102. Madelin, I, 97.
103. Méneval, I, 278.
104. Madelin, I, 212.

CHAPTER VIII

1. Rose, *Personality of Napoleon*, 191.
2. Madelin, *Consulate and Empire*, I, 240.
3. Las Cases, II, 133.
4. *EB*, XIII, 89c.
5. Masson, Frédéric, *Napoleon and His Coronation*, 229.
6. Pinoteau, Hervé, ed., *Le Sacre de S. M. l'empereur Napoléon*, p. *xii.*

7. Las Cases, III, 130; Madelin, *Consulate and Empire*, 244.
8. Masson, *Coronation*, 236.
9. Staël, Mme. de, *Ten Years' Exile*, 151.
10. Rémusat, *Memoirs*, 249; Napoleon, *Letters*, 112.
11. Rémusat, 251.
12. Lefebvre, *Napoleon*, I, 203; Madelin, I, 252 f.
13. *Ibid.*, 235.
14. Rémusat, 293.
15. Bourrienne, III, 3.
16. *Ibid.*
17. Thiers, IV, 64.
18. Madelin, *Consulate and Empire*, I, 269.
19. Wilson, P. W., *William Pitt*, 335.
20. Bourrienne, III, 52n.
21. Rémusat, 324.
22. Bourrienne, III, 47; Madelin, I, 300.
23. *Ibid.*, 297.
24. Méneval, I, 405.
25. Rémusat, 442.
26. Lefebvre, *Napoleon*, I, 255.
27. Madelin, I, 318.
28. *Ibid.*, 316.
29. Rémusat, 453.
30. Mossiker, *Napoleon and Josephine*, 296.
31. *CMH*, IX, 279.
32. Robinson, *Readings*, 489.
33. Georg Brandes in Clark, B. H., *Great Short Biographies of the World*, 1080.
34. Rémusat, 459.
35. Méneval, II, 449.
36. *Ibid.*, 463.
37. Vandal, *Napoléon et Alexandre Ier*, I, 65.
38. Bertaut, *Napoleon in His Own Words*, 8, 9.
39. Rémusat, 534.

CHAPTER IX

1. Morris, Gouverneur, *Diary*, 98-99.
2. Las Cases, II, 192.
3. Mistler, Jean, ed., *Napoléon et l'Empire*, I, 145.
4. *Ibid.*; Stacton, David, *The Bonapartes*, 13.
5. Las Cases, II, 190; Mistler, I, 145.
6. Stacton, 16.
7. Las Cases, III, 321.
8. Rémusat, 323n.
9. Goodrich, F. B., *The Court of Napoleon*, 290-93.
10. Bourrienne, II, 110.
11. Napoleon, *Letters*, 190.
12. *Ibid.*, 123.
13. Stendhal, *La Chartreuse de Parme*, 450.
14. Napoleon, *Letters*, 107.
15. Goodrich, 207.

16. Rose, *Personality of Napoleon*, 32.
17. In Goodrich, 271; Caulaincourt, *With Napoleon in Russia*, 14.
18. Talleyrand, *Memoirs*, I, 261.
19. Caulaincourt, 23.
20. Lefebvre, *Napoleon*, II, 19.
21. Madelin, *Consulate and Empire*, I, 410.
22. *Ibid.*, 411.
23. Talleyrand, *Memoirs*, I, 310-13.
24. *Ibid.*, 316.
25. 328; Madelin, *Consulate and Empire*, I, 416.
26. Talleyrand, I, 337.
27. Madelin, *Talleyrand*, 78, 134.
28. Brandes, G., *Goethe*, II, 264.
29. Talleyrand, I, 318.
30. Lewes, George, *Life of Goethe*, II, 312.
31. Talleyrand, I, 326.
32. *Ibid.*, 331.
33. 333.
34. Lewes, II, 313.
35. Las Cases, II, 134.
36. Méneval, II, 553.
37. Rose, *Personality*, 495.
38. Madelin, I, 425.
39. Lefebvre, *Napoleon*, II, 57.
40. *Ibid.*
41. Méneval, II, 563; Madelin, I, 436; Mistler, I, 150.
42. Herold, ed., *The Mind of Napoleon*, 175.
43. Lefebvre, II, 52.
44. Mossiker, *Napoleon and Josephine*, 328.
45. Rémusat, 376.
46. *Ibid.*, 375.
47. Herold, *The Mind of Napoleon*, 22.
48. Bourrienne, II, 117; Méneval, II, 423.
49. Herold, 16.
50. Mossiker, *Napoleon and Josephine*, 151.
51. Las Cases, II, May 19, 1816.
52. Madelin, II, 15.
53. *Ibid.*, 17.
54. Taine, *The Modern Regime*, I, 79n.
55. Kircheisen, *Memoirs of Napoleon I*, 149.
56. Méneval, II, 615.
57. Napoleon, *Letters to Josephine*, 222.
58. Las Cases, II, 185.
59. *Ibid.*, 21.
60. *Ibid.*, III, 275.

CHAPTER X

1. *EB*, X, 941d.
2. Rémusat, 47.
3. Las Cases, III, 258.
4. Mistler, I, 137.
5. Ross, E. A., *Social Control*, 276.
6. *Auction* Magazine, November 1971, p. 35.
7. Bourrienne, I, 311.
8. Méneval, I, 108.

9. Cronin, Vincent, *Napoleon Bonaparte*, 182.
10. Méneval, I, 416.
11. Ed.'s note to Bourrienne, I, 312.
12. Masson, F., *Napoleon at Home*, I, 90.
13. Méneval, I, 411.
14. MacLaurin, C., *Post Mortem*, 220; Howarth, David, *Waterloo*, 52 ff.
15. Las Cases, II, 252; MacLaurin, 222; Friedrich Kircheisen in *New York Times*, Feb. 26, 1931.
16. Méneval, I, 412.
17. Taine, *Modern Regime*, I, 44.
18. Rosebury, Theodor, *Microbes and Morals*, 158.
19. Las Cases, III, 146; I, 236.
20. *Ibid.*, III, 391.
21. I, 392.
22. Taine, *Modern Regime*, I, 68.
23. *Ibid.*, 69.
24. *Ibid.*
25. Bourrienne, I, 294.
26. Méneval, I, 346, 415.
27. Bourrienne, I, 309.
28. Las Cases, III, 346.
29. Herold, ed., *The Mind of Napoleon*, xvii.
30. Méneval, I, 353.
31. Taine, *Modern Regime*, I, 18 ff.
32. Madelin, *Consulate and Empire*, I, 30.
33. Source lost.
34. Taine, I, 19; Madelin, I, 30.
35. Bourrienne, I, 315; Méneval, I, 356; Taine, I, 54.
36. Bourrienne, I, 310.
37. Las Cases, I, 251.
38. Napoleon, *Letters*, 68 (Oct. 7, 1797).
39. Sorel, Albert, *Europe and the French Revolution*, VI, 205, in Geyl, 251.
40. Fouché, *Memoirs*, II, 52.
41. Brandes, *Main Currents*, I, 29.
42. Lewes, *Life of Goethe*, II, 312.
43. Las Cases, I, 311.
44. Bourrienne, II, 102.
45. Taine, *Modern Regime*, I, 60.
46. Herold, ed., *The Mind of Napoleon*, 256.
47. *Ibid.*, No. xxxvi.
48. Taine, I, 35.
49. Napoleon, *Letters*, III (Dec. 12, 1804).
50. Lefebvre, *Napoleon*, I, 66.
51. Rémusat, 95.
52. Herold, 43.
53. Breed, Lewis, *The Opinions and Reflections of Napoleon*, 114.
54. Fouché, *Memoirs*, II, 18; Rémusat, 370.
55. Las Cases, I, 379; Lefebvre, I, 64.
56. Caulaincourt, 71.
57. Las Cases, III, 318.
58. Rose, *Personality of Napoleon*, 29.
59. Rémusat, 60.
60. Masson, *Napoleon at Home*, I, 163.
61. Bourrienne, I, 317.
62. *Ibid.*, 328.
63. Méneval, I, 128.
64. Taine, *Modern Regime*, II, 45.
65. Las Cases, IV, 154-61.
66. Lefebvre, *Napoleon*, I, 64.
67. Constant, Véry, *Memoirs*, I, 6 and xii.
68. Rémusat, 102.
69. Caulaincourt, 27.
70. Goodrich, *Court of Napoleon*, 375.
71. *Ibid.*, 371.
72. Staël, Mme. de, *Considérations*, 334.
73. Méneval, I, 221.
74. Masson, *Napoleon at Home*, 168.
75. Méneval, I, 350; Las Cases, III, 345.
76. Méneval, I, 353.
77. Las Cases, III, 330.
78. In Rose, *Personality*, 119.
79. Bertaut, *Napoleon in His Own Words*, 125-26.
80. Herold, ed., *Mind of Napoleon*, 211.
81. Las Cases, II, 244.
82. Rose, 86.
83. *Ibid.*, 200.
84. Bourrienne, III, 95.
85. Bertaut, 126.
86. Herold, 211.
87. Méneval, II, 534.
88. Rose, *Personality*, 119.
89. Herold, 217.
90. Rose, 110.
91. Herold, 217; Las Cases, II, 26.
92. Emerson, *Representative Men*, 254.
93. Canton, *Napoléon antimilitariste*, 146.
94. Bertaut, 122; Rose, *Personality*, 347; Guérard, *French Civilization in the 19th Century*, 62.
95. Bourrienne, I, 314.
96. Las Cases, II, 12.
97. *CMH*, IX, 114.
98. Lefebvre, *Napoleon*, I, 227.
99. Canton, 214.
100. Herold, 206.
101. Quoted in Gooch, G. P., *History and Historians in the 19th Century*, 2d ed., 259.
102. Herold, 276-77.
103. Las Cases, IV, 37.
104. *Ibid.*, II, 384.
105. Rémusat, 451.
106. Las Cases, I, 181.
107. Bourguignon, I, introduction, p. *ii*.
108. Rémusat, 71, 319; Taine, *Modern Regime*, I, 70; Las Cases, IV, 163.
109. Herold, ed., *Mind of Napoleon*, 162.
110. *Ibid.*, 9.
111. 162.

112. Bourrienne, I, 237.
113. Herold, 172.
114. *Ibid.*, 171.
115. Bourguignon, I, 38.
116. Herold, 92.
117. Bourrienne, I, 380.
118. Taine, *Modern Regime*, I, 134a, 480.
119. Herold, 162.
120. Las Cases, III, 256.
121. Bourrienne, I, 325 notes, 293, 367a, 327a; Taine, I, 193.
122. Bertaut, 79.
123. Herold, 255.
124. *Ibid.*, 30-31.
125. Bourrienne, I, 327.
126. Herold, 30; Bertaut, 107-8.
127. Las Cases, II, 253.
128. Taine, II, 3-4.
129. Herold, 32.
130. Bertaut, 11.
131. Kircheisen, *Memoirs of Napoleon I*, 166.
132. Herold, 33.
133. Kircheisen, 160.
134. Aulard in Geyl, 323; Herold, 105.
135. Bertaut, 112-13; Taine, II, 5.
136. Bertaut, 114.
137. Taine, II, 6.
138. Bertaut, 32.
139. Herold, 20.
140. Bertaut, 28.
141. Herold, 21.
142. Kircheisen, 154.
143. Bertaut, 32-33.
144. Herold, 23.
145. Kircheisen, 153.
146. *Ibid.*, 152.
147. Mossiker, *Napoleon and Josephine*, 301.
148. Napoleon, *Letters*, 180.
149. Bertaut, 5.
150. *Ibid.*, 146.
151. Herold, 73.
152. Bertaut, 1.
153. *Ibid.*, 46.
154. 54.
155. Las Cases, III, 241.
156. *Ibid.*, I, 400.
157. Bertaut, 65.
158. Las Cases, III, 242.
159. *Ibid.*, IV, 104; Bourrienne, II, 218.
160. Herold, 40-41.
161. Mossiker, 34.
162. *Ibid.*, 20.
163. Levy, M., *Private Life of Napoleon*, I, 274.
164. Bertaut, 9.
165. Herold, 40.
166. *Ibid.*, 36.
167. 40.
168. Rémusat, 535.
169. Bertaut, 142.

170. Herold, 179.
171. Las Cases, II, 325.
172. Taine, *Modern Regime*, I, 59.

CHAPTER XI

1. Las Cases, II, 389.
2. Letter to Lucien Bonaparte, Dec. 25, 1799, in *Letters*, 82.
3. Las Cases, III, 23.
4. Letter to Roederer, in Taine, *Modern Regime*, I, 265.
5. Breed, *The Opinions and Reflections of Napoleon*, 121.
6. Lacroix, *Directoire, Consulat et Empire*, 10.
7. Madelin, *Consulate and Empire*, I, 291.
8. Mistler, ed., *Napoléon et l'Empire*, I, 196.
9. Lacroix, 540.
10. Las Cases, III, 94, 340; Rémusat, 345-46; Madelin, I, 294-97.
11. Herold, ed., *Mind of Napoleon*, 190.
12. *CMH*, IX, 375-76.
13. Guillemin, Henri, *Napoléon tel quel*, 120-21.
14. Guérard, *French Civilization*, 77.
15. Taine, *Modern Regime*, I, 213.
16. *Ibid.*, 216-17.
17. Bourrienne, III, 32.
18. Méneval, II, 595.
19. Taine, *Modern Regime*, I, 226.
20. Las Cases, II, 36.
21. *Ibid.*, IV, 61.
22. Taine, II, 138.
23. *Ibid.*, 140-41.
24. *CMH*, IX, 127.
25. Bourrienne, II, 359.
26. Napoleon, *Letters*, 115.
27. *CMH*, IX, 127.
28. Rose, *Personality of Napoleon*, 177; Taine, II, 153.
29. Thiers, *History of the Consulate and the Empire*, II, 275.
30. Taine, I, 67.
31. *Ibid.*, 262.
32. Sainte-Beuve, *Monday Chats*, 207.
33. Méneval, I, 499.
34. Taine, I, 233.
35. *CMH*, IX, 114.
36. Lefebvre, *Napoleon*, I, 227.
37. *CMH*, IX, 115.
38. Taine, I, 90; Guérard, *French Civilization*, 64.
39. Lefebvre, I, 227.
40. Herold, ed., *Mind of Napoleon*, 208.
41. Bertaut, *Napoleon in His Own Words*, 5.
42. *Ibid.*, 57.
43. *Ibid.*

44. Musset, *Confessions of a Child of the Century*, 3.
45. Bourrienne, II, 132.
46. Taine's phrases. Cf. *The Modern Regime*, I, 250.
47. Thiers, II, 266-78.
48. Taine, I, 271; Herold, 212.
49. Fouché, *Memoirs*, I, 296.
50. Goodrich, *Court of Napoleon*, 157; Las Cases, III, 397.
51. Bertaut, 62.
52. Las Cases, II, 315.
53. Herold, ed., *Mind of Napoleon*, 242.
54. Bertaut, 48.
55. *Ibid.*, 111.
56. Lacroix, 45.
57. Staël, Mme. de, *Ten Years' Exile*, 7.
58. Las Cases, II, 198.
59. Mossiker, *Napoleon and Josephine*, 272; Rémusat, 227.
60. *Ibid.*, 7; Herold, *Mistress to an Age*, 287.
61. Rémusat, 53; Herold, *Mistress*, 290.
62. David's *Mme. Récamier* is in the Louvre; Gérard's is in the Musée de la Ville.
63. Rémusat, 33-37.
64. Herold, *Mistress*, 288.
65. Junot, Mme., *Memoirs*, II, 60.
66. Graetz, H., *History of the Jews*, V, 482.
67. *Ibid.*
68. 491; *CMH*, IX, 205.
69. Graetz, V, 492.
70. *Ibid.*, 494.
71. Lefebvre, *Napoleon*, II, 186; *CMH*, IX, 205.
72. Lefebvre, 187.
73. Graetz, V, 500.

CHAPTER XII

1. Masson, F., *Napoleon at Home*, II, 74.
2. Lacroix, *Directoire, Consulat et Empire*, 494.
3. Las Cases, III, 97.
4. Grout, D. J., *Short History of Opera*, 326.
5. Dijon Museum.
6. Goodrich, *Court of Napoleon*, 299.
7. Muther, R., *History of Modern Painting*, I, 111.
8. Bertaut, *Napoleon in His Own Words*, 55.
9. Stranahan, C. H., *History of French Painting*, 129.
10. Las Cases, I, 368.
11. Mantzius, K., *History of Theatrical Art*, VI, 164.
12. *Ibid.*, 163.
13. Goodrich, 118.
14. In Lacroix, 188.
15. Goodrich, 390.

16. Dumas *père*, Alexandre, *Mes Mémoires*, IV, 27, in Mantzius, VI, 178.
17. Rémusat, 58-62.
18. Lacroix, 189.

CHAPTER XIII

1. Herold, ed., *Mind of Napoleon*, 156.
2. Mistler, ed., *Napoléon et l'Empire*, I, 231.
3. Méneval, I, 185.
4. Herold, 121.
5. *Time* Magazine, Oct. 19, 1970, p. 43.
6. Mistler, I, 232.
7. Herold, *Mind of Napoleon*, 132.
8. Goodrich, *Court of Napoleon*, 249.
9. *Ibid.*, 250.
10. Taine, *Modern Regime*, II, 200.
11. *Ibid.*
12. Staël, Mme. de, *Ten Years' Exile*, 19.
13. Sainte-Beuve, *Portraits of Celebrated Women*, 224.
14. Staël, Mme. de, *Germany*, I, 77.
15. Bourrienne, II, 364-66.
16. Staël, Mme. de, *Corinne*, introduction, xvi.
17. Brandes, G., *Main Currents in 19th Century Literature*, I, 94.
18. Staël, Mme. de, *Ten Years' Exile*, 25.
19. *Ibid.*, 74.
20. Stevens, Abel, *Mme. de Staël*, II, 263.
21. Las Cases, IV, 7.
22. Taine, *Modern Regime*, I, 29n.
23. Madelin, *Consulate and Empire*, I, 150.
24. Herold, *Mistress to an Age*, 186.
25. In Brandes, *Main Currents*, I, 94.
26. Staël, Mme. de, *Considérations*, 97.
27. *Ibid.*, 1.
28. Staël, Mme. de, *De la Littérature*, 11.
29. In Herold, *Mistress*, 210.
30. *Ibid.*, 211.
31. 233.
32. Staël, Mme. de, *Ten Years' Exile*, 8.
33. In Herold, 259.
34. Source illegible.
35. Herold, 263.
36. Staël, Mme. de, *Ten Years' Exile*, 105.
37. Stevens, Abel, *Mme. de Staël*, I, 32.
38. Herold, 293.
39. Madelin, I, 368.
40. Herold, 342.
41. *Ibid.*, 343.
42. *Corinne*, 37-38.
43. *Ibid.*, 18-20.
44. Herold, 344.
45. *Ibid.*, 363.
46. 369.
47. Brockway and Winer, *Second Treasury of the World's Great Letters*, 315.
48. Staël, Mme. de, *Germany*, I, 38.
49. *Ibid.*, 34, 84.

50. 34.
51. 31.
52. 42.
53. 90-93.
54. *De la Littérature*, 21.
55. *Germany*, I, 114.
56. *Ibid.*, II, 84.
57. II, 187.
58. 297.
59. *Corinne*, 125.
60. *Germany*, I, 36.
61. E.g., *Germany*, II, 188; cf. Stevens, II, 26.
62. Stevens, 218.
63. *Ten Years' Exile*, 246n.
64. *Ibid.*, 304.
65. Source lost.
66. Staël, Mme. de, *Considérations*, 432.
67. *Ibid.*
68. 430.
69. Stevens, II, 313.
70. Sainte-Beuve, *Portraits of Celebrated Women*, 204.
71. Stevens, I, 4.
72. Bertaut, *Napoleon in His Own Words*, 77-78; Las Cases, IV, 7.
73. Constant, B., *The Red Notebook*, 112.
74. *Ibid.*, 123.
75. 133.
76. Herold, *Mistress*, 151.
77. Nicholson, H., *Benjamin Constant*, 140.
78. Herold, 240, 246.
79. *Ibid.*, 248.
80. Constant, B., *Journal intime*, 155.
81. *Ibid.*, 155-65.
82. 172.
83. 242.
84. *Ibid.*
85. Herold, 463.
86. In Nicholson, 255.
87. *Ibid.*, 273.
88. Sainte-Beuve, *Chateaubriand et son groupe littéraire*, I, 13.
89. Faguet, Émile, *Dix-septième Siècle: Études et portraits littéraires*, 70.
90. Chateaubriand, *Memoirs*, ed. Baldick, preface, *xx*.
91. *Ibid.*, 5.
92. 39.
93. 39.
94. 46-47.
95. 47.
96. 56.
97. 122.
98. In Sainte-Beuve, *Chateaubriand*, I, 128.
99. *Ibid.*, 203 ff.
100. *Memoirs*, ed. Baldick, 150.
101. Lanson, *Histoire de la littérature française*, 887n.
102. *Memoirs*, 157.
103. *Ibid.*, 191.

104. Sainte-Beuve, *Chateaubriand*, I, 149.
105. In Faguet, *Dix-neuvième Siècle: Études littéraires*, 14.
106. Sainte-Beuve, I, 175.
107. In Faguet, 14.
108. Chateaubriand, *Atala and René*, 72 ff.
109. *Ibid.*, 87.
110. Lemaître, Jules, *Chateaubriand*, 146.
111. Chateaubriand, *The Genius of Christianity*, 190.
112. Lemaître, 138.
113. *The Genius of Christianity*, 148.
114. Lemaître, 150.
115. *Ibid.*, 326-27.
116. 321.
117. *Atala and René*, 135.
118. Brandes, *Main Currents*, I, 29.
119. Bertaut, 76.
120. *Memoirs*, 208.
121. *Ibid.*, 216.
122. *Ibid.*, preface, *xiv*.
123. 218.
124. 231.
125. *Mémoires d'outre-tombe*, volume on Napoleon, 391.
126. *Memoirs*, ed. Baldick, 244.
127. *Ibid.*, 153.
128. In Sainte-Beuve, *Chateaubriand*, I, 149n.
129. *Mémoires*, appendix, 457.
130. *Ibid.*, 463.
131. 481.
132. 497-509.
133. *Memoirs*, ed. Baldick, 261.

CHAPTER XIV

1. *NCMH*, IX, 124.
2. Bernal, *Science in History*, 381.
3. *EB*, IX, 667a.
4. *NCMH*, IX, 133.
5. Berry, *Short History of Astronomy*, 307. Repeated from *The Age of Voltaire*, 549.
5a. Bertrand, *Napoleon at St. Helena*, 168; Castiglione, *History of Medicine*, 714; letter of Dr. Elmer Belt.
6. Sigerist, H. E., *The Great Doctors*, 240, 274.
7. *Ibid.*, 276.
8. Garrison, F., *History of Medicine*, 412.
9. Castiglione, Arturo, *History of Medicine*, 701.
10. Hippocrates, *Works*, VI, "Decorum."
11. Williams, H. S., *History of Science*, III, 78 ff.
12. *Ibid.*, IV, 104-6.
13. Locy, W. A., *Biology and Its Makers*, 382.
14. *EB*, XIII, 614-17.
15. *Ibid.*

16. Destutt de Tracy in Boas, George, *French Philosophers of the Romantic Period*, 25.
17. *Ibid.*
18. Taine, *Modern Regime*, II.
19. Taine, *Les Philosophes classiques du XIXᵉ siècle en France*, 55.
20. John Knox's phrase. See *The Age of Reason Begins*, 115.
21. Maine de Biran, *The Influence of Habit on the Faculty of Thinking*, 115.
22. *Ibid.*, 122.
23. Madelin, *Consulate and Empire*, I, 365.
24. Phillips, C. S., *The Church in France*, I, 192-93.
25. Maistre, *Soirées de Saint-Pétersbourg*, I, 149.
26. Maistre, *Works*, 57.
27. *Ibid.*, 52.
28. 86.
29. 196.
30. 74.
31. *Soirées*, I, 10.
32. *Ibid.*, II, 222.
33. I, 24.
34. 182.
35. 31.
36. II, 64.
37. II, 254.
38. *Ibid.*
39. *Works*, 62.
40. *Soirées*, II, 24.
41. *Works*, 163, 177.
42. *Ibid.*, 166.

CHAPTER XV

1. Bertrand, Henri, *Napoleon at St. Helena*, 148.
2. Hobsbawn, E. J., *The Pelican Economic History of Britain*, 10.
3. Kropotkin, *Modern Science and Anarchism*, 84, 87.
4. Quennell, *History of Everyday Things in England*, 198.
5. Heilbroner, R. L., *The Worldly Philosophers*, 67, 85.
6. Watson, J. S., *The Reign of George III*, 517.
7. Owen, Robert, *A New View of Society*, 120.
8. *Ibid.*, 123.
9. Halévy, Élie, *History of the English People in 1815*, 245.
10. Watson, 530.
11. Kropotkin, *Modern Science and Anarchism*, 33.
12. Rogers, J. E. Thorold, *Six Centuries of Work and Wages*, 111.

13. Watson, 526.
14. Kropotkin, 33.
15. *EB*, XVIII, 494.
16. Kropotkin, 80n.
17. Rogers, 110.
18. Tocqueville, *Journeys to England and Wales*, 107, in Hobsbawn.
19. Rudé, G., *The Crowd in History*, 238.
20. Heilbroner, 98.
21. Malthus, *Essay on Population* (1798), 14.
22. Malthus, *Essay* (1803), 106.
23. Heilbroner, 90.
24. Carlyle, *Latter-Day Pamphlets*, No. 1 (1850).
25. Heilbroner, 95.
26. Owen, *A New View of Society*, "Catechism," 172.
27. Owen, *New View*, 86.
28. Heilbroner, 98; Russell, Bertrand, *Understanding History*, 24.
29. Owen, address at New Lanark, in *A New View of Society*, 95.
30. *Ibid.*, 65.
31. Title page of first edition of *A New View of Society*.
32. *New View*, 20.
33. *Ibid.*, 98.
34. 35.
35. 52-53.
36. 112.
37. 83.
38. 68.
39. 162-69.
40. 140-47.
41. 246.
42. 86.
43. 111.
44. *EB*, XVI, 1174b.
45. Cole, G. D. H., *Robert Owen*, 187.
46. *Ibid.*, 91.
47. 231.

CHAPTER XVI

1. Beard, Charles, *Introduction to the English Historians*, 520.
2. Watson, George, III, 335; Hobsbawn, 95.
3. Halévy, *History of the English People in 1815*, 195.
4. Bertrand, H., *Napoleon at St. Helena*, 77.
5. Further details in *Rousseau and Revolution*, 684.
6. Dicey, *Law and Public Opinion in England during the 19th Century*, 116.
7. Halévy, 293.
8. Blackstone in Halévy, 101.
9. Las Cases, II, 366.
10. Plumb, J. H., *The First Four Georges*, 147.

11. Burke, Thomas, *English Night Life, passim;* Thackeray, *The Four Georges,* 84.
12. Thackeray, *The Four Georges,* 93; Plumb, 138, 101.
13. Markun, Leo, *Mrs. Grundy: A History of Four Centuries of Morals,* 219.
14. *EB,* X, 212b.
15. Trevelyan, G. M., *English Social History,* 493.
16. Mill, J. S., *On Bentham and Coleridge,* 134 f.
17. *NCMH,* IX, 177.
18. Markun, 251.
19. Sorel, Albert, *Europe and the French Revolution,* I, 352.
20. Halévy, 370.
21. Corti, E. C., *Rise of the House of Rothschild,* Ch. II, III, IV; Finkelstein, Louis, ed., *The Jews,* I, 266.
22. Godwin, *Enquiry Concerning Political Justice,* Book V, Ch. XIII.
23. *Ibid.,* Book VIII, Ch. x.
24. Halévy, 464.
25. Trevelyan, *English Social History,* 459.
26. Monroe, Paul, *Text-book in the History of Education,* 724; *EB,* VII, 996c; Halévy, 463.
27. Hirsh, Diana, *The World of Turner,* 100.
28. Plumb, J. H., *The First Four Georges,* 180.
29. Trevelyan, 491.
30. Dicey, *Law and Public Opinion,* 371-73.
31. *EB,* X, 518d.
32. Wollstonecraft, Mary, *Vindication of the Rights of Woman,* 154.
33. *Ibid.,* 142.
34. 47, 139.
35. 80.
36. 44.
37. 46, 83, 128.
38. 75.
39. 69.
40. 5.
41. 83.
42. 64.
43. *EB,* X, 519c.
44. *Vindication,* 196.
45. *Ibid.,* 157.
46. Van Doren, Dorothy, *The Lost Art: Letters of Seven Famous Women,* 137-78.
47. Markun, *Mrs. Grundy,* 235.
48. Dicey, 87; Watson, 446; Halévy, 10.
49. Trevelyan, 499.
50. *EB,* XX, 635a.
51. Traill, H. D., *Social England,* V, 495.
52. Watson, 548.
53. Traill, *Social England,* V, 499.
54. Wright, Raymond, *Prose of the Romantic Period,* 41.
55. *Ibid.;* Markun, 232.
56. Austen, Jane, *Mansfield Park,* Ch. XXI.
57. In Fruman, *Coleridge, the Damaged Archangel,* 372.
58. Burke, Thomas, *English Night Life,* 103.
59. *EB,* XX, 478d.
60. Mantzius, Karl, *History of Theatrical Art,* VI, 30.
61. Burke, *Night Life,* 84; Mantzius, VI, 56.
62. Mantzius, VI, 79.
63. Burke, 81.
64. *EB,* XIII, 263.
65. Mantzius, VI, 94.
66. Halévy, 8.
67. Staël, Mme. de, *Germany,* I, 84.

CHAPTER XVII

1. In the Victoria and Albert Museum.
2. *Ibid.*
3. *EB,* VIII, 280d.
4. Plumb, *The First Four Georges,* 164.
5. Hirsh, *The World of Turner,* 56.
6. Mistler, *Napoléon et l'Empire,* I, 234.
7. *EB,* X, 419.
8. *Pelican Guide to English Literature,* V, 258.
9. *New York Evening Post,* April 13, 1918.
10. Russell, A. G., *The Engravings of William Blake,* plates 6-7.
11. Hirsh, 123.
12. G. W. Thornbury, in Hirsh, 17. This section is especially indebted to Diana Hirsh, *The World of Turner.*
13. *EB,* XXII, 412d.
14. Hirsh, 7.
15. *Ibid.,* 169.
16. *EB,* XXII, 413.
17. Hirsh, 175.

CHAPTER XVIII

1. Wolf, A., *History of Science, Technology and Philosophy in the 18th Century,* 197.
2. Williams, H. S., *History of Science,* III, 216.
3. Garrison, *History of Medicine,* 350.
4. Moore, F. J., *History of Chemistry,* 68.
5. *Ibid.,* 69.
6. Williams, H. S., III, 234.
7. *EB,* VII, 109b.
8. In Osborn, H. F., *From the Greeks to Darwin,* 146.
9. Sedgwick and Tyler, *Short History of Science,* 426.
10. Garrison, 375.

CHAPTER XIX

1. *EB*, XVII, 376.
2. Paine, Thomas, *The Age of Reason*, Part II, preface.
3. *Ibid.*, 5.
4. 6.
5. 9.
6. *Ibid.*
7. 30.
8. 74.
9. William Paley, *Natural Theology*, in Wright, R., *Prose of the Romantic Period*, 74, 73.
10. *EB*, XVII, 175a.
11. Hazlitt, *Lectures on the English Poets* and *The Spirit of the Age*, 183.
12. *Ibid.*
13. Godwin, *Enquiry Concerning Political Justice*, Book IV, Ch. 1.
14. *Ibid.*, VI, 11.
15. IV, VII.
16. IV, VIII.
17. IV, XI.
18. IV, V.
19. XV.
20. VIII, VIII.
21. I, IV.
22. I, III.
23. VIII, V.
24. VIII, II.
25. II, V.
26. I, III.
27. V, XI; III, VII; VIII, II.
28. VIII, II.
29. IV, IV.
30. I, IV.
31. XV, XVI.
32. *EB*, X, 519d.
33. Malthus, *Essay on the Principle of Population*, 4.
34. *Ibid.*, 7, 12, 86.
35. 26-31; Heilbroner, 85.
36. Malthus, 49.
37. *Ibid.*, 51.
38. Malthus, *Second Essay on Population*, 98.
39. *Ibid.*, 101.
40. Heilbroner, 85.
41. *Ibid.*, 71.
42. Hazlitt, *Spirit of the Age*, 276.
43. R. K. Wilson in Dicey, *Law and Opinion*, 133.
44. Bentham, *Anarchical Fallacies*, in *Encyclopedia of Philosophy*, I, 284c.
45. Benn, Alfred, *History of English Rationalism*, I, 295.
46. *Ibid.*, 297.
47. Bentham, *Fragment on Government*, 3, 56.
48. Bentham, *Introduction to the Principles of Morals and Legislation*, 102-3.
49. Bentham, *Works*, X, 73, in Dicey, 133.
50. *EB*, XI, 913b.
51. Helvétius, *De l'Esprit*, 6, 17.
52. Leviticus xix, 18.

CHAPTER XX

1. Austen, Jane, *Mansfield Park*, in *Complete Novels*, 733.
2. *Pride and Prejudice*, 242.
3. Margoliouth, H. M., *William Blake*, 3; *EB*, III, 755d.
4. *EB*, III, 755d.
5. Blake, "Jerusalem," in *Selected Poems*, 277.
6. Blake, *Poems and Prophecies*, 392.
7. Margoliouth, 7.
8. *EB*, 756b.
9. Margoliouth, 63.
10. Blake, *Poems and Prophecies*, 289.

CHAPTER XXI

1. "To a Butterfly."
2. Moorman, Mary, *William Wordsworth: The Early Years*, 71.
3. *Ibid.*, 150.
4. 153.
5. Wordsworth, *The Prelude*, Book IX, in *Poems*, 297.
6. Moorman, *Early Years*, 201.
7. *The Prelude*, XI, in *Poems*, 311.
8. *Ibid.*, X, in *Poems*, 305.
9. Moorman, *Early Years*, 13, 171; Bateson, F. W., *Wordsworth: A Re-interpretation*, 186.
10. "Tintern Abbey," lines 118-19.
11. Moorman, *Early Years*, 288.
12. Letter to Thomas Poole, in Coleridge, *Selected Poetry and Prose*, 528-29.
13. Thornton, J. C., *Table Talk*, 171.
14. Gilman, James, *Life of Coleridge*, 20-21, in Fruman, *Coleridge, the Damaged Archangel*, 65.
15. Letter of October, 1791, in Coleridge, *Selected Poerty and Prose*, 534-37.
16. *Ibid.*, 143.
17. Colmer, John, *Coleridge Critic of Society*, 112.
18. In White, R. J., *Political Tracts of Wordsworth, Coleridge, and Shelley*, p. xxxii.
19. Coleridge, *Letters*, I, 221 and 224, in Lowes, J. L., *The Road to Xanadu*, 600.
20. In Moorman, *Early Years*, 317.
21. *The Prelude*, XIV, in Wordsworth, *Complete Poems*, 331.

22. Gardner, Martin, ed., *The Annotated Ancient Mariner*, 16.
23. Wordsworth, Dorothy, *Journals*, 4-6.
24. Moorman, *Early Years*, 373.
25. Coleridge, *Biographia Literaria*, 147.
26. Wordsworth and Coleridge, *Lyrical Ballads*, 3.
27. Gardner, 172.
28. *Lyrical Ballads*, p. 95, line 294.
29. *Ibid.*, p. 113, lines 36-49.
30. Lines 88-112.
31. Lines 133-42.
32. Gardner, 24; Winwar, *Farewell the Banner*, 265.
33. *Lyrical Ballads*, appendix, p. 173.
34. Letter to John Wilson, June, 1805, Bateson, 175.
35. Letter of March 25, 1801, in *Selected Poetry and Prose*, 591.
36. Dorothy Wordsworth, the Grasmere Journal, June 9-20, 1800; May 13-18 and July 3, 1802.
37. Journal, June 20, 1800.
38. *Complete Poems*, 166.
39. Journal, June 19, 1802.
40. *Ibid.*, June 25, 1800.
41. Feb. 1, 1802.
42. June 10, 1800.
43. Dec. 11, 1801.
44. Dec. 12, 1801.
45. Dec. 22, 1801.
46. Moorman, *William Wordsworth: The Later Years*, 29n.
47. Journal, Sept. 1, 1800.
48. *Ibid.*, Nov. 4, 1800.
49. Moorman, *Early Years*, 520.
50. *Complete Poems*, 173.
51. Moorman, *Early Years*, 573.
52. *Ibid.*
53. *Journals*, 57.
54. Colmer, *Coleridge Critic of Society*, 55.
55. *Ibid.*, 78n.
56. Fruman, 264.
57. Coleridge, *Selected Poetry and Prose*, 115.
58. Notebooks, note 1214, in Fruman, 377.
59. *Ibid.*, 380.
60. Fruman, 26-58.
61. Moorman, *Early Years*, 612.
62. Notebooks, note 2091, in Fruman, 431.
63. Moorman, *Later Years*, 87.
64. Gardner, 26.
65. Moorman, *Later Years*, 165.
66. *Ibid.*
67. 195.
68. Robinson, Henry Crabb, *Diary*, I, 207-12.
69. Winwar, 330.
70. *Ibid.*
71. Letter to Wordsworth, May 10, 1815.
72. White, R. J., 15-16.
73. Coleridge, *Selected Poetry and Prose*, 497.

74. White, R. J., 8.
75. *Ibid.*, 17-18, 11-12.
76. 60.
77. 77, 102.
78. Coleridge, *Selected Poetry and Prose*, 140.
79. White, R. J., 108.
80. *Ibid.*, 83-85; Mill, J. S., *On Bentham and Coleridge*, 96.
81. White, R. J., 93.
82. Coleridge in Benn, *History of English Rationalism*, I, 249.
83. White, R. J., 85.
84. *Biographia Literaria*, Ch. IX, p. 70.
85. Fruman, 70-71, 81, 101, etc.
86. *Biographia*, 72, 74.
87. *Ibid.*, Ch. XXII, p. 236.
88. Moorman, *Later Years*, 186.
89. *Pelican Guide to English Literature*, V, 154.
90. Moorman, *Later Years*, 55.
91. *EB*, XXIII, 678d.
92. Moorman, *Later Years*, 260.
93. Hazlitt, *Spirit of the Age*, 256-57.
94. Moorman, *Later Years*, 181.
95. Thornton, *Table Talk*, 211.
96. Moorman, *Later Years*, 314-15n.
97. Winwar, 328.
98. Coleridge, *Selected Poetry and Prose*, 671.
99. Thornton, 177, 145.
100. Colmer, John, *Coleridge Critic of Society*, 157.
101. Benn, I, 285.
102. Coleridge, *Selected Poetry and Prose*, 469.
103. De Quincey, *Collected Writings*, I, 77, in Fruman, 84.
104. Thornton, 255.
105. Gardner, 33.
106. Wright, R., *Prose of the Romantic Period*, 26.
107. Hazlitt, *Lectures on the English Poets*, 163.
108. Moorman, *Later Years*, 580-81.
109. *Ibid.*, 115.
110. 36.
111. Wright, 35.
112. *NCMH*, IX, 109.
113. Moorman, *Later Years*, 239.
114. Marchand, L. A., *Byron*, I, 412.
115. *Ibid.*, 421.
116. Hazlitt, *Spirit of the Age*, 258.
117. Moorman, *Later Years*, 292, 452.
118. Wright, 50.

CHAPTER XXII

1. Marchand, *Byron*, I, 4.
2. Byron, *Childe Harold's Pilgrimage*, Canto IV, line 10.
3. Marchand, I, 36.
4. *Ibid.*, 94.

5. *EB*, IV, 509c.
6. Byron, *English Bards and Scotch Reviewers*, I, 205; III, 98.
7. Marchand, I, 235.
8. Byron, *Works*, 205, note 1; Marchand, I, 238.
9. *Ibid.*, 263.
10. 286.
11. 401.
12. *Works*, p. *xxii.*
13. Marchand, I, 437.
14. *Ibid.*, 360.
15. 334.
16. 333.
17. 360.
18. Mayne, *Life and Letters of Anna Isabella, Lady Noel Byron*, 48-49.
19. *EB*, IV, 510a.
20. Marchand, I, 403.
21. *Ibid.*, 446.
22. 429.
23. 465-69.
24. II, 479, 485.
25. 479.
26. Mayne, 154.
27. Marchand, II, 510.
28. Mayne, 161; Marchand, II, 510.
29. Mayne, 161.
30. *Ibid.*, 162.
31. Mayne, 165; Marchand, II, 513.
32. Marchand, II, 527.
33. *Ibid.*, 547.
34. Mayne, 190; Marchand, II, 544.
35. Marchand, II, 549.
36. *Ibid.*, 551-52.
37. 555.
38. 556.
39. 563; Mayne, 203.
40. Marchand, II, 570.
41. Mayne, 209; Marchand, II, 572.
42. Marchand, II, 576-77.
43. Dowden, *Life of Shelley*, I, 4n.
44. Cameron, *The Young Shelley*, 3.
45. In Hancock, A. E., *The French Revolution and the English Poets*, 53.
46. Byron, Letter to Hogg, Jan. 2, 1811, in Cameron, 15.
47. *Ibid.*, 125.
48. Dowden, I, 73.
49. T. J. Hogg, *Life of Shelley*, in Dowden, I, 45-46.
50. Dowden, I, 118; Cameron, 24.
51. Cameron, 91.
52. 93.
53. Dowden, I, 175.
54. Cameron, 102.
55. *Ibid.*, 97.
56. Dowden, I, 211.
57. *Ibid.*, 215.
58. 218.

59. 260-61.
60. Shelley, *Poems*, note to *Queen Mab*, in *Complete Poems of Keats and Shelley*, Part II, 853.
61. *Queen Mab*, Canto III, line 33.
62. *Ibid.*, lines 174-77.
63. v, lines 79, 177, 189.
64. VII, line 13.
65. VIII, lines 106-60.
66. Cameron, 274.
67. Dowden, I, 287.
68. Mrs. Shelley, in Shelley, *Poems* (*Complete Poems of Keats and Shelley*, Part II, p. *v*).
69. Dowden, I, 258.
70. Wright, R., *Prose Works of the Romantic Period*, 138-39.
71. In Cameron, 229.
72. Shelley, *Lost Letters to Harriet*, 22.
73. T. L. Peacock, *Memoirs of Shelley*, 336, in Dowden, I, 433.
74. Dowden, I, 424.
75. 425, 429.
76. Shelley, *Letters*, ed. F. L. Jones, I, 389.
77. *Ibid.*, 421.
78. 391.
79. Marchand, II, 630.
80. Brandes, G., *Main Currents*, IV, 303.
81. Dowden, II, 30.
82. Brandes, IV, 214.
83. Shelley, *Poems*, 570.
84. Brandes, IV, 319.
85. Marchand, II, 699.
86. *Childe Harold's Pilgrimage*, IV, line 25.
87. Marchand, II, 747.
88. *Ibid.*, 681, 740.
89. *Prometheus Unbound*, Act II, line 305.
90. *Ibid.*, I, 144.
91. II, 523.
92. *Poems*, 616.
93. *Ibid.*, 464-77.
94. Dowden, II, 381.
95. *Ibid.*, 411.
96. *Adonais*, lines 151-52.
97. Stanzas lii, liii, lv.
98. Keats, "Ode to a Nightingale."
99. Dowden, II, 235; Marchand, II, 757; *Childe Harold's Pilgrimage*, IV, lines 172-84.
100. Marchand, II, 772.
101. Brandes, IV, 325.
102. In Hirsh, *The World of Turner*, 109.
103. Marchand, II, 816.
104. Eckermann, J. P., *Conversations with Goethe*, 261.
105. Marchand, II, 905.
106. Shelley, *Letters*, II, 316.
107. Marchand, III, 949.
108. Byron, letter of Nov. 10, 1813, in Marchand, I, 420.

109. In Arnold, Matthew, *Essays in Criticism*, 375.
110. *Childe Harold*, I, line 29.
111. Marchand, I, 308; III, 1104, 1108.
112. *Ibid.*, II, 937.
113. 955.
114. III, 1126-27.
115. *Childe Harold*, III, line 55.
116. *Ibid.*, VIII, lines 50-51.
117. Marchand, II, 917.
118. Guiccioli, Countess, *My Recollections of Lord Byron*.
119. Eckermann, 265.
120. Dowden, II, 389.
121. *Ibid.*, 233.
122. Marchand, III, 1018.
123. Dowden, II, 377.
124. Notes to *Prometheus Unbound*, in *Poems*, 295.
125. White, R. J., *Political Tracts of Wordsworth, Coleridge, and Shelley*, 227.
126. *Ibid.*, 236-39.
127. 214.
128. 243.
129. 230-31.
130. 245, 235.
131. *Declaration of Rights*, No. 18, in Woods, Watt, and Anderson, *The Literature of England*, II, 319.
132. White, R. J., 247-49.
133. "Defence of Poetry," in White, R. J., 206.
134. Shelley, *Poems*, 227.
135. In Dowden, II, 384.
136. "Defence of Poetry," in White, R. J., 205.
137. *Ibid.*, 204.
138. Cameron, *The Young Shelley*, 119.
139. Dowden, II, 459.
140. *Ibid.*, 452.
141. 504.
142. Mrs. Shelley, Notes on Poems of 1822, in Shelley, *Poems*, 716.
143. Dowden, II, 510, 513.
144. *Ibid.*, 507.
145. 518.
146. Mrs. Shelley's preface to the ed. of 1839, *Poems*, p. *viii*.
147. Marchand, III, 1018.
148. Dowden, II, 529.
149. Marchand, III, 1023.
150. *Ibid.*, 1052.
151. *Ibid.*
152. 1074.
153. 1147.
154. 1212.
155. 1217, 1224.
156. 1232-33
157. 1246.
158. 1261.
159. Maurois, *Byron*, 547.
160. Mayne, *Life of . . . Lady Byron*, 240.
161. Maurois, 546.
162. Marchand, III, 1243n.
163. Maurois, 554.
164. Marchand, III, 1245.

CHAPTER XXIII

1. Halévy, *History of the English People in 1815*, 103; *EB*, XX, 56b.
2. Scott, Walter, *The Heart of Midlothian*, 106-7.
3. Halévy, 469.
4. *Ibid.*, 482.
5. On Reid see *Rousseau and Revolution*, 764; on Hartley see *The Age of Voltaire*, 581.
6. Wright, R., *Prose of the Romantic Period*, 86.
7. Scott, *Poems*, 114.
8. Leslie Stephen in Benn, *History of English Rationalism*, I, 312.
9. Moorman, *William Wordsworth: The Later Years*, 463.
10. See Longford, *Wellington*, 30n.
11. Watson, *Reign of George III*, 388.
12. *Ibid.*
13. Cameron, *The Young Shelley*, 158.
14. Halévy, 419.
15. Lecky, *History of England in the 18th Century*, VIII, 394 ff.; Rosebery, Lord, *Pitt*, 189, 193.
16. Petersen, H., *Treasury of the World's Great Speeches*, 311.

CHAPTER XXIV

1. Green, J. R., *Short History of the English People*, III, 1750.
2. Hawkins, Sir John, *Life of Samuel Johnson*, 198.
3. Petersen, 240.
4. *Ibid.*, 241.
5. Morley, John, *Burke*, in *Biographical Studies*, 15.
6. *Ibid.*, 87.
7. Letter to T. Allsop.
8. Paine, Thomas, *The Rights of Man*, 135.
9. Green, J. R., III, 1764.
10. *CMH*, VIII, 300.
11. *Ibid.*, 304.
12. Southey, *Life of Nelson*, 42.
13. *Ibid.*, 169.
14. Bowen, Marjorie, *Patriotic Lady: Emma, Lady Hamilton*, 143.
15. Howarth, David, *Trafalgar*, 31.
16. Southey, *Nelson*, 140, 322-23.
17. From a copy in the collection of Sir Douglas Fairbanks. The original is in the British Museum.

18. Nelson, *Letters*, 462.
19. Howarth, *Trafalgar*, 132.
20. Southey, *Nelson*, 274.
21. Howarth, 209-10.
22. *Ibid.*, 239.
23. Lefebvre, *Napoleon*, II, 131.

CHAPTER XXV

1. *CMH*, VIII, 783.
2. Stephens, H. M., *The Story of Portugal*, 385.
3. *Ibid.*, 395.
4. Borrow, George, *The Bible in Spain*, 211.
5. Caulaincourt, *With Napoleon in Russia*, 307.
6. Byron, *Childe Harold's Pilgrimage*, I, line 33.
7. Altamira, R., *History of Spanish Civilization*, 177-79.
8. Marchand, *Byron*, I, 194.
9. Borrow, 330-31.
10. Sorel, Albert, *Europe and the French Revolution*, I, 364.
11. Altamira, *Spanish Civilization*, 177.
12. Altamira, *History of Spain*, 536b.
13. Longford, Elizabeth, *Wellington: The Years of the Sword*, 17.
14. *Ibid.*, 16.
15. 19.
16. *EB*, XXIII, 395b.
17. Longford, 120.
18. Wingfield-Stratford, Esme, *History of British Civilization*, 853.
19. Marx and Engels, *The Revolution in Spain*, 8.
20. *Ibid.*, 30-31.
21. *CMH*, IX, 449.
22. Lefebvre, *Napoleon*, II, 95.
23. *Ibid.*, 94.
24. Longford, 290.

CHAPTER XXVI

1. Sorel, Albert, *Europe and the French Revolution*, I, 382.
2. *Ibid.*, 381.
3. McCabe, Joseph, *Crises in the History of the Papacy*, 17.
4. *CMH*, VIII, 778.
5. McCabe, *Crises*, 370.
6. Southey, *Life of Nelson*, 225-28.
7. Méneval, *Memoirs*, II, 493.
8. Bertrand, H., *Napoleon at St. Helena*, 41.
9. Lefebvre, *Napoleon*, II, 221-22; *CMH*, IX, 404-6; *EB*, XV, 1182.
10. *EB*, XVII, 247b.
11. Madelin, *Consulate and Empire*, 211.
12. *Ibid.*, 313.

13. Taine, *Modern Regime*, II, 11.
14. Madelin, 381.
15. McCabe, *Crises*, 386.
16. Phillips, C. S., *The Church in France*, 149.
17. *CMH*, IX, 402.
18. Herold, ed., *Mind of Napoleon*, 110.
19. McCabe, *Crises*, 388.
20. *Ibid.*, 389.
21. Marchand, *Byron*, II, 679.
22. Rémusat, 259.
23. Staël, Mme. de, *Corinne*, 22.
24. McCabe, 388.
25. More on Alfieri in *Rousseau and Revolution*, 336-40.
26. Marchand, II, 818.
27. Canova, Antonio, *Works*, edited by Countess Albruzzi and Count Cicognara, plates 70-71.
28. *EB*, IV, 800c.
29. Canova, II, 3.
30. Balcarres, Lord, *Evolution of Italian Sculpture*, 340.
31. Byron, *Childe Harold's Pilgrimage*, IV, line 55.
32. *EB*, XVI, 246b.
33. Bourrienne, II, 381.
34. Las Cases, III, 255.

CHAPTER XXVII

1. *EB*, X, 311a.
2. Brion, Marcel, *Daily Life in the Vienna of Mozart and Schubert*, 37; Rémusat, 309; Fouché, *Memoirs*, I, 343.
3. Palmer, Alan, *Metternich*, 11.
4. *Ibid.*, 36.
5. Palmer, *Metternich*, 48.
6. Vandal, *Napoléon et Alexandre*, III, 14.
7. Brion, 237.
8. *Ibid.*, 228.
9. Graetz, H., *History of the Jews*, V, 414.
10. Brion, 239.
11. Staël, Mme. de, *Germany*, I, 64.
12. Thayer, *Life of Ludwig van Beethoven*, I, 253.
13. *Ibid.*, 183.
14. Brion, 90.
15. Staël, Mme. de, *Germany*, I, 67.

CHAPTER XXVIII

1. Thayer, A. W., *Life of Ludwig van Beethoven*, I, 57.
2. Brockway and Weinstock, *Men of Music*, 166.
3. Beethoven: *Letters*, tr. and edited by Emily Anderson, I, 4.

4. *EB*, 14th ed., III, 317.
5. Thayer, I, 253.
6. *Ibid.*, 90.
7. 149.
8. *Letters*, I, 6.
9. *Grove's Dictionary of Music and Musicians*, I, 265c.
10. Thayer, I, 175.
11. *Grove's*, I, 266c.
12. Thayer, I, 186.
13. *Ibid.*, 191.
14. *Grove's*, I, 276d.
15. *Ibid.*
16. *Letters*, I, 58.
17. *Ibid.*, 292.
18. Noli, Bp. F. S., *Beethoven and the French Revolution*, 36 ff.
19. *Grove's* I, 267b.
20. Letter to Zmeskal in Noli, 34.
21. Thayer, I, 241, 246-47; *Grove's*, I, 268c.
22. *Letters*, I.
23. Thayer, I, 352-54.
24. Letters, I, 65.
25. Kerst, F., *Beethoven in His Own Words*, 45.
26. *Letters*, I, 73.
27. Thayer, II, 24.
28. *Grove's*, I, 282d.
29. *Ibid.*, 268b.
30. Thayer, II, 43.
31. *Ibid.*, I, 253.
32. *Letters*, I, 131.
33. *Ibid.*, 163.
34. 219.
35. Thayer, I, 326-27.
36. *Ibid.*, II, 146.
37. *Ibid.*, 187-89.
38. 223.
39. 227.
40. 224. Thayer damns the story with faint praise: "The story may have some foundation in truth."
41. 224-26.
42. 364.
43. Letter of Jan. 23, 1823.
44. Láng, Paul Henry, *Music in Western Civilization*, 769.
45. D. F. Tovey in *EB*, 14th ed., III, 321b.
46. Thayer, III, 164.
47. *Ibid.*, 164-67.
48. Sullivan, J. W. N., *Beethoven: His Spiritual Development*, 232-39.
49. *Grove's*, I, 300c.
50. Thayer, III, 285.
51. *Letters*, III, 1339.
52. *Ibid.*, 1342.
53. Thayer, III, 307.
54. *Ibid.*, 306.
55. *Grove's*, I, 371d.

CHAPTER XXIX

1. Treitschke, Heinrich von, *History of Germany in the 19th Century*, I, 119.
2. Sorel, Albert, *Europe and the French Revolution*, I, 120.
3. Fisher, H. A. L., *Studies in Napoleonic Statesmanship: Germany*, 7.
4. *Ibid.*, 120.
5. 196.
6. 268.
7. 53-59.
8. Treitschke, 55.
9. *Ibid.*, 65.
10. In Fisher, H. A. L., 35.
11. Gooch, G. P., *Germany and the French Revolution*, 369.
12. *Ibid.*, 518.
13. Seeley, J. R., *Life and Times of Stein*, I, 128; Sorel, Albert, 480.
14. Treitschke, 187.
15. *Ibid.*, 307, 321.
16. Seeley, I, 203.
17. *Ibid.*, 285-97.
18. 425.

CHAPTER XXX

1. Staël, Mme. de, *Germany*, I, 84.
2. *EB*, XII, 213d.
3. Fisher, H. A. L., *Studies in Napoleonic Statesmanship: Germany*, 13-14.
4. Staël, Mme. de, *Germany*, I, 306.
5. Fisher, 13.
6. Carlyle, *Critical and Miscellaneous Essays*, II, 59.
7. Fisher, 313, 330.
8. Graetz, *History of the Jews*, V, 405.
9. Somewhere in Walt Whitman.
10. Gooch, *Germany and the French Revolution*, 363-64.
11. *Ibid.*, 388.
12. See below, Ch. XXXII, Section I, 3.
13. Paulsen, Friedrich, *German Education*, 117.
14. Fisher, 283.
15. Staël, Mme. de, *Germany*, I, 116.
16. Gooch, 107.
17. Treitschke, 392.
18. Bell, E. T., *Men of Mathematics*, 219.
19. *Ibid.*, 220.
20. *EB*, X, 35b.
21. Bell, E. T., 220.
22. *EB*, XI, 831d.
23. Humboldt, Alexander von, *Cosmos*, preface, ix.
24. Thayer, *Beethoven*, I, 196.
25. *Grove's Dictionary of Music and Musicians*, I, 563n.
26. *Ibid.*, 565.

27. 635.
28. 656.
29. Mantzius, *History of Theatrical Art*, pp. vi, 234.
30. *Ibid.*, 327.
31. *EB.*, XIII, 399b.
32. Francke, Kuno, *A History of German Literature*, 469.
33. *Ibid.*, 470.

CHAPTER XXXI

1. Treitschke, 137.
2. Gooch, *Germany and the French Revolution*, 40.
3. Brandes, *Main Currents*, IV, 26.
4. Gooch, 145.
5. *Ibid.*, 143.
6. 152.
7. Schiller, *Don Carlos*, Act III, Scene 6.
8. Gooch, 214.
9. *Ibid.*, 206.
10. Treitschke, 230.
11. Brandes, IV, 35.
12. Marchand, *Byron*, II, 883.
13. Brandes, 24.
14. Gooch, 248-49.
15. In Carlyle, *Critical Essays*, II, 119.
16. Gooch, 240.
17. *Rousseau and Revolution*, 572 ff.
18. In Francke, 416-17.
19. *Ibid.*, 418.
20. Pascal, Roy, *The German Novel*, 30.
21. *Rousseau and Revolution*, 519.
22. Francke, 420.
23. Brandes, IV, 69.
24. *Ibid.*, 91.
25. *Ibid.;* Herold, *Mistress to an Age*, 271.
26. Brandes, 91.
27. *Ibid.*, 54.
28. William Hazlitt, quoted by Francke, 151.
29. Brandes, 89.
30. Friedrich Schlegel, *Gespräche über Poesie*, 274, in Lewes, G. H., *Life of Goethe*, II, 216 f.

CHAPTER XXXII

1. *EB*, XX, 16d.
2. Adamson, Robert, *Fichte*, 15.
3. Lost in Whitman.
4. Gooch, *Germany and the French Revolution*, 284-85.
5. See *Rousseau and Revolution*, 588.
6. Gooch, 290.
7. *Ibid.*
8. 291.
9. Adamson, 184; Höffding, *History of Modern Philosophy*, II, 157.
10. Adamson, 186-88.

11. Fichte, *Science of Knowledge*, pp. xv and 187.
12. Adamson, 178, 204-5.
13. *Ibid.*, 56-63; Brandes, *Main Currents*, IV, 88-89.
14. *Ibid.*
15. Adamson, 77; Gooch, 293.
16. Fichte, *The Vocation of Man*, 157-60.
17. Fichte, *Addresses to the German Nation*, 163.
18. *Ibid.*, 28-29.
19. 27.
20. *xvi, xxvii.*
21. 165.
22. Adamson, 102.
23. Höffding, *History of Modern Philosophy*, II, 163.
24. In Brandes, 82, quoting Plitt, *Aus Schellings Leben*, I, 282.
25. Schelling, *Of Human Freedom*, 21-23.
26. Schelling, *The Ages of the World*, 76.
27. *Of Human Freedom*, 26.
28. Cf. Hirsch, E. D., *Wordsworth and Schelling, passim.*
29. Coleridge, *Biographia Literaria*, I, 104.
30. Schelling, *The Ages of the World*, introd. by Frederick Bolman, 8n.
31. Schopenhauer, *The World as Will and Idea*, II, 22.
32. Caird, Edward, *Hegel*, 31.
33. Kaufman, Walter, *Hegel: Reinterpretation, Texts and Commentary*, 61.
34. Caird, 46.
35. Hegel, *The Philosophy of Georg Wilhelm Hegel*, ed. Carl Friedrich, 526, 532, 539.
36. Weidman, Franz, *Hegel*, 38, quoting Hegel's *Briefe*, I, 120; cf. Caird, 66.
37. Weidman, 64.
38. Hegel, *Philosophy*, 414.
39. *Ibid.*, 402.
40. Findlay, J. N., *Hegel: A Re-examination*, 96.
41. Hegel, *Philosophy of History*, 23.
42. *Ibid.*, 26.
43. Caird, 153.
44. Findlay, 131, 142.
45. In Caird, 195.
46. *EB*, XI, 300b.
47. Weidman, 76.
48. Hegel, *Philosophy of Right*, preface, 3.
49. *Ibid.*, 5.
50. 6.
51. Nos. 162-63.
52. No. 170.
53. No. 166.
54. No. 174.
55. No. 270.
56. Weidman, 83, quoting Rudolf Haym, *Hegel und seine Zeit*, 413 ff.

57. Hegel, *Philosophy of Right*, No. 260.
58. *Ibid.*, No. 278.
59. No. 281.
60. No. 273, 280.
61. No. 273.
62. *Ibid.*, preface, 4a.
63. Hegel, *Philosophy of History*, 9.
64. *Ibid.*, 15.
65. 30.
66. 26.
67. 446.
68. 456.
69. Hegel, *History of Philosophy*, in Hegel, *Philosophy*, 168.
70. *Philosophy of History*, 50.
71. *Ibid.*
72. 17.
73. 49.
74. *History of Philosophy*, in Hegel, *Philosophy*, 162.
75. Weidman, 81; Stace, W. T., *The Philosophy of Hegel*, 31.
76. Weidman, 119.

CHAPTER XXXIII

1. Gooch, *Germany and the French Revolution*, 48.
2. *CMH*, IX, 98.
3. *Ibid.*, 106.
4. Staël, Mme. de, *Germany*, I, 80.
5. *NCMH*, IX, 110.
6. Moore, F. J., *History of Chemistry*, 102.
7. Horn, F. W., *History of the Literature of the Scandinavian North*, 388.
8. *CMH*, IX, 46.
9. *Ibid.*, 47.
10. Our account follows Dudley Pope's *The Great Gamble*.
11. *CMH*, IX, 298.
12. *Ibid.*, 236, 299 ff.
13. Horn, 237.
14. *EB*, XXI, 1082b.
15. *Cambridge History of Poland*, II, 213.
16. Dubnow, S. M., *History of the Jews in Russia and Poland*, I, 298-305; Lefebvre, *Napoleon*, II, 249-51.
17. *NCMH*, IX, 546.

CHAPTER XXXIV

1. Talleyrand, *Memoirs*, V, 399.
2. Staël, Mme. de, *Ten Years' Exile*, 330, 310.
3. Lefebvre, *Napoleon*, II, 305.
4. Kornilov, Alexander, *Modern Russian History*, 26.
5. Florinsky, Michael T., *Russia: A History and an Interpretation*, II, 716.
6. Kornilov, 30.

7. Wiener, Leo, *Anthology of Russian Literature*, II, 6.
8. Florinsky, II, 701.
9. Maistre, *Les Soirées de Saint-Pétersbourg*, I, 2, 3.
10. Garrison, *History of Medicine*, 400.
11. Strakhovsky, L., *Alexander I of Russia*, 17; Kornilov, 56.
12. Kornilov, 54.
13. Strakhovsky, 17-19.
14. *Ibid.*, 28.
15. Kornilov, 69.
16. *Ibid.*, 26.
17. 81.
18. 103.
19. Caulaincourt, *With Napoleon in Russia*, 376.
20. Kornilov, 82.
21. *Ibid.*, 100; Florinsky, II, 727.
22. Florinsky, II, 723-27.
23. Dubnow, *History of the Jews in Russia and Poland*, I, 341.
24. *Ibid.*, 312, 317-20; Kornilov, 105-6.
25. Dubnow, I, 315.
26. *Ibid.*, 343; Graetz, IV, 473.
27. Dubnow, I, 352.
28. Gilbert, O. P., *Prince de Ligne*, 143.
29. Staël, Mme. de, *Ten Years' Exile*, 361.
30. Pope, *The Great Gamble*, 288.
31. Réau, Louis, *L'Art russe*, 90.
32. *Ibid.*, 113.
33. Fiala, Vladimir, *Russian Painting*, plates 11 and 12.
34. *Ibid.*, plate 13.
35. Staël, Mme. de, *Ten Years' Exile*, 303.
36. Strakhovsky, 51.
37. Kropotkin, Peter, *Ideals and Realities in Russian Literature*, 33.
38. Bruckner, A., *A Literary History of Russia*, 150.
39. Lefebvre, *Napoleon*, I, 201.
40. Kornilov, 128.
41. *EB*, XI, 9c.
42. Kornilov, 131.
43. Lefebvre, II, 269.
44. Vandal, *Napoléon et Alexandre*, III, 58.
45. *Ibid.*, II, 509.
46. In Treitschke, 45.
47. Méneval, II, 787; Vandal, II, 532.
48. Florinsky, II, 638.

CHAPTER XXXV

1. Watson, *The Reign of George III*, 469; Mistler, *Napoléon et l'Empire*, II, 66.
2. Lefebvre, *Napoleon*, II, 179.
3. Vandal, *Napoléon et Alexandre*, III, 26.
4. Lefebvre, II, 109, 123-26.
5. *Ibid.*, 127-28.
6. Mistler, II, 184-89.

7. *Ibid.*, 185.
8. Vandal, III, 139.
9. *Ibid.*, 34, 39, 597.
10. Kornilov, 195.
11. Caulaincourt, *With Napoleon in Russia*, Ch. I.
12. Méneval, *Memoirs*, II, 808.
13. Vandal, III, 326.
14. *Ibid.*, 2-4.
15. Kircheisen, *Memoirs of Napoleon I*, 195.
16. Letter of Dec. 19, 1811, in *Napoleon, Letters*, 263; Palmer, Alan, *Napoleon in Russia*, 31.
17. Letter of Dec. 20, 1811.
18. Guérard, *French Civilization in the 19th Century*, 76.
19. Édouard Driault, in Geyl, *Napoleon: For and Against*, 311.
20. Caulaincourt, 25.
21. Fouché, *Memoirs*, II, 85 f.
22. Letters of Nov. 1, 1811, in *Napoleon, Letters*, 259-60.
23. Kircheisen, 196.
24. Méneval, III, 894.
25. Taine, *Modern Regime*, 37; Vandal, III, 343.
26. Mistler, II, 202.
27. *Ibid.*, 449.
28. 204.
29. Palmer, Alan, *Napoleon in Russia*, 48.
30. *Letters*, 270 (July 14, 1812).
31. Lefebvre, *Napoleon*, II, 314.
32. Herold, ed., *The Mind of Napoleon*, 205.
33. *Letters*, 271.
34. *Ibid.*, note by J. M. Thompson.
35. Palmer, Alan, *Napoleon in Russia*, 81.
36. Kircheisen, 188.
37. Mistler, II, 207.
38. Palmer, Alan, *Napoleon in Russia*, 113.
39. Testimony of Napoleon's physician in Mestivier, in Delderfield, *The Retreat from Moscow*, 62.
40. Caulaincourt, 152.
41. Lefebvre, *Napoleon*, II, 3.
42. Caulaincourt, 152.
43. Méneval, III, 859.
44. Strakhovsky, *Alexander I of Russia*, 94.
45. Las Cases, III, 167.
46. *Ibid.*, 172.
47. *EB*, XV, 878c.
48. Delderfield, 82.
49. Caulaincourt, 122; Lefebvre, II, 315.
50. *Letters*, 273.
51. Mistler, II, 210.
52. Méneval, III, 865.
53. Caulaincourt, 132; Kircheisen, 199.
54. Palmer, Alan, *Napoleon in Russia*, 177.
55. Caulaincourt, 41.
56. Méneval, III, 871; Kircheisen, 200.
57. Strakhovsky, 138.

58. Caulaincourt, 192.
59. Méneval, III, 887.
60. *Ibid.*, III, 373; Delderfield, 109-11.
61. Palmer, Alan, *Napoleon in Russia*, 221.
62. *Ibid.*, 222.
63. Méneval, III, 874-78; Caulaincourt, 230; Mistler, II, 212.
64. Caulaincourt, 261.
65. Delderfield, 175.
66. Mistler, II, 215.
67. Caulaincourt, 325.
68. *Bartlett's Familiar Quotations*, 13th ed., 399.
69. Note to Bertrand, *Napoleon at St. Helena*, 265.
70. Méneval, III, 888.

CHAPTER XXXVI

1. *EB*, XVI, 25a.
2. Strakhovsky, *Alexander I of Russia*, 141.
3. Thiers, *History of the Consulate and the Empire*, VIII, 338.
4. Francke, *History of German Literature*, 492.
5. Thiers, *History of the Consulate and the Empire*, VIII, 435-36.
6. *Ibid.*
7. Caulaincourt, *Memoirs*, II, 213, in Herold, ed., *Mind of Napoleon*, 195.
8. Mistler, *Napoléon et l'Empire*, II, 217.
9. Lefebvre, *Napoleon*, II, 329.
10. Madelin, *Consulate and Empire*, II, 214.
11. *Ibid.*, 217.
12. Mistler, II, 221.
13. *Ibid.*, 221-22; Thiers, IX, 130-40; Las Cases, III, 223-24.
14. Thiers, IX, 155; Mistler, II, 222.
15. Kircheisen, *Memoirs of Napoleon I*, 203; Las Cases, III, 278.
16. Mistler, II, 225a.
17. Thiers, IX, 259.
18. Lefebvre, II, 390; Thiers, IX, 276.
19. Thiers, 283.
20. Madelin, II, 258.
21. *Ibid.*, 266.
22. Méneval, III, 952; Madelin, II, 265; Thiers, IX, 353.
23. Thiers, 365.
24. *Ibid.*, 369.
25. Fain, Agathon, *Memoirs of the Invasion of France by the Allied Armies*, 79-81.
26. Mistler, II, 236.
27. *Ibid.*, 239.
28. Fain, 107.
29. Méneval, III, 244.
30. Thiers, X, 139.
31. Mistler, II, 245 ff.
32. Thiers, X, 138.
33. Fain, 271.

34. Bertrand, H., *Napoleon at St. Helena*, 53.
35. Fain, 257.
36. Mistler, II, 249.
37. Mossiker, *Napoleon and Josephine*, 375.
38. Petersen, ed., *Treasury of the World's Great Speeches*, 324.
39. Méneval, III, 1047; Fain, 268.
40. Ortzen, *Imperial Venus*, 157.

CHAPTER XXXVII

1. *EB*, XIV, 346d.
2. Thiers, *History of the Consulate and the Empire*, X, 317.
3. *Ibid.*, 443; Lefebvre, *Napoleon*, II, 360.
4. Brion, *Daily Life in the Vienna of Mozart and Schubert*, 173-78.
5. Thiers, XI, 70.
6. *Ibid.*, 160.
7. Mistler, *Napoléon et l'Empire*, II, 251.
8. *Ibid.*, 253; Rose, *Personality of Napoleon*, 230.
9. Mistler, II, 253.
10. Rose, 332; Goodrich, F., *The Court of Napoleon*, 363.
11. Rose, 336.
12. Thiers, XI, 170.
13. *Ibid.*, 172.
14. 173.
15. Mistler, II, 260.
16. Gourgaud, *Journal*, Jan. 4, 1817.
17. Thiers, XI, 184.
18. *Ibid.*, 196; Mistler, II, 261.
19. Thiers, XI, 199-201.
20. *Ibid.*, 215.
21. Houssaye, Henri, *La Première Abdication*, 305.
22. Thiers, XI, 235.
23. *Ibid.*, 268.
24. Mistler, II, 267.
25. Lefebvre, II, 363.
26. Thiers, XI, 437-38.
27. Las Cases, IV, 110.
28. Fouché, *Memoirs*, II, 246.
29. Madelin, *Consulate and Empire*, II, 412.
30. Houssaye, *1815: Waterloo*, 17.
31. Las Cases, II, 5.
32. Gourgaud, *Journal*, I, 93.
33. Thiers, XI, 481.
34. Byron, *Childe Harold's Pilgrimage*, III, xxi-xxviii.
35. Houssaye, *1815: Waterloo*, 80-81.
36. Mistler, II, 221.
37. *Ibid.*
38. Houssaye, *1815: Waterloo*, 91.
39. *EB*, XXIII, 286.
40. Longford, *Wellington*, 438.
41. Howarth, *Waterloo*, 52, 55-56.
42. MacLaurin, C., *Post Mortem*, 224-25.
43. Houssaye, *1815: Waterloo*, 255.
44. Mistler, II, 276.
45. Longford, 472.
46. Madelin, II, 457.
47. Howarth, *Waterloo*, 144.
48. Longford, 472.
49. Kircheisen, *Memoirs of Napoleon I*, 223.
50. Houssaye, *1815: Waterloo*, 212.
51. *Ibid.*, 221.
52. Houssaye, *1815: La Seconde Abdication*, 113.
53. Houssaye, *1815: Waterloo*, 216, 224.

CHAPTER XXXVIII

1. Kircheisen, *Memoirs of Napoleon I*, 225.
2. Houssaye, *1815: La Seconde Abdication*.
3. Constant, Benjamin, *Mémoirs sur les Cent Jours*, in Houssaye, 40.
4. Letter of June 19, in *Letters*, 307.
5. Houssaye, *1815: La Seconde Abdication*, 10.
6. *Ibid.*, 61; Mistler, II, 282.
7. Houssaye, 199.
8. *Letters*, 308 (June 25, 1815).
9. Houssaye, 215, 194.
10. Las Cases, I, 15n.
11. *CMH*, IX, 644.
12. Houssaye, 337-41.
13. *Ibid.*, 160-66.
14. Talleyrand, *Memoirs*, introd. by de Broglie, x.
15. *Bartlett's Quotations*, 384.
16. Talleyrand, I, x.
17. Lefebvre, *Napoleon*, II, 367.
18. Houssaye, 561.
19. Mistler, II, 285.
20. Houssaye, 396.
21. From a copy of the original in the Royal Library at Windsor.
22. Las Cases, I, 26.
23. Rosebery, *Napoleon: The Last Phase*, Appendix I.
24. Thiers, *History of the Consulate and the Empire*, XII, 305.
25. *Ibid.*, 313.

CHAPTER XXXIX

1. Kircheisen, *Memoirs of Napoleon I*, 260.
2. Las Cases, I, 262.
3. *Ibid.*, 266n.
4. II, 247; III, 115.
5. Mistler, *Napoléon et l'Empire*, II, 292a; Rosebery, *Napoleon: The Last Phase*, 172.
6. Las Cases, III, 21.
7. *Ibid.*, II, 40; Rosebery, 152.
8. Las Cases, II, 93.
9. Thiers, *History of the Consulate and the Empire*, XII, 334.

10. *Ibid.*, 335.
11. Las Cases, II, 386.
12. *Ibid.*, III, 139.
13. Rosebery, 109.
14. *Ibid.*, 109; Las Cases, III, 158; Thiers, XII, 338.
15. Las Cases, III, 4.
16. *Ibid.*, II, 139, 177; Rosebery, 89.
17. *EB*, II, 536a.
18. Bertrand, H., *Napoleon at St. Helena*, 201.
19. Rosebery, 49, 93.
20. Las Cases, I, 120; II, 322.
21. Rosebery, 53.
22. Mistler, II, 288c; Bertrand, 249, notes.
23. Bertrand, 248.
24. Kircheisen, 224.
25. Rosebery, 180.
26. Kircheisen, 275 (editor's postscript).
27. Gourgaud, *Journal*, April 23, 1816.
28. Gourgaud, I, 415.
29. Rosebery, 175.
30. Kircheisen, 227.
31. *Ibid.*
32. 224.
33. Mistler, II, 8.
34. Herold, *Mind of Napoleon*, 248.
35. *CMH*, IX, 762; Herold, 66.
36. Las Cases, IV, 107.
37. Herold, 66.
38. Las Cases, IV, 75.
39. Gourgaud, II, 75; I, 567-68; III, 315; Las Cases, IV, 74.
40. Las Cases, IV, 78.
41. *Ibid.*, II, 120.
42. Bertrand, 112.
43. Las Cases, I, 236.
44. Thiers, XII, 370.
45. *Ibid.*, 377.
46. Mistler, II, 320.
47. Gourgaud, I, 150, and *passim*.
48. Herold, *Mind of Napoleon*, introd.
49. MacLaurin, *Post Mortem*, 211-14.
50. Bertrand, 130.
51. *Ibid.*, 124.
52. Las Cases, IV, 400.
53. *Ibid.*, 411.
54. Kircheisen, 269.
55. Gibbon, Edward, *Decline and Fall of the Roman Empire*, I, 250.
56. Gourgaud, I, 440.
57. *Ibid.*, II, 437.
58. Bertrand, 125.
59. Gourgaud, II, 405; Rosebery, 191.
60. Gourgaud, II, 431.
61. Thiers, XII, 366.
62. *Ibid.*, 384.
63. Bertrand, 200, 210.
64. Marquis Charles de Montholon, *Histoire de la captivité de Ste.-Hélène*, II, 103, in Herold, *Mind of Napoleon*, 17.
65. Martineau, Gilbert, *Napoleon's St. Helena*, 215.
66. Bertrand, 235; MacLaurin, *Post Mortem*, 215; Rosebery, 240.
67. MacLaurin, 216.

CHAPTER XL

1. Horne, R. H., *History of Napoleon*, II, 55.
2. Méneval, III, 1025.
3. *EB*, XV, 1004.
4. Ortzen, *Imperial Venus*, 69, 92.
5. *Ibid.*, 83.
6. *EB*, III, 900b.
7. Thiers, *History of the Consulate and the Empire*, X, 411; Mossiker, *Napoleon and Josephine*, 399.
8. Méneval, III, 1059.
9. Mistler, *Napoléon et l'Empire*, II, 304.
10. In Geyl, 33.
11. O'Meara, B., *Napoleon in Exile*, 363, 176.
12. Las Cases, III, 179.
13. In Hutt, M., *Napoleon*, 77.
14. Chateaubriand, *Memoirs*, ed. Baldick, 300.
15. Horne, Appendix 2.
16. *Ibid.*, 16.
17. Thackeray, "The Second Funeral of Napoleon," in *Roundabout Papers*.

Index

Dates in parentheses following a name are of birth and death except when preceded by *r.,* when they indicate duration of reign for popes and rulers of states. A single date preceded by *fl.* denotes a *floruit.* A footnote is indicated by an asterisk. Italicized page numbers indicate principal treatment. All dates are A.D. unless otherwise noted.

Louis XVII, King of France, *see* Louis-Charles de France, Dauphin

Louis XVIII (Louis-Stanislas-Xavier, Comte de Provence), King of France (r. 1814–15, 1815–24), 38*, 144, 279, 322, *729-31;* escapes from France (1791), 729; acknowledged as king by royalists (1795), 85; royalists attack N. for not recalling, 167; appeals to N. for restoration, 169, 175-76; is a factor in N.'s concordat with Church, 183; wanders in exile, 176, 212, 729; royalists demand restoration of (1813), 719; First Restoration (1814), 300, 320, 321, 729-31, 741-42; and Congress of Vienna, 733; asks Ney to lead force against N. (1815), 738; leaves Paris at N.'s approach, 308, 739; Second Restoration, 308, 752-54; orders N.'s arrest, 755; repays Mme. de Staël, 301; court of, 774

Louis, Baron Joseph-Dominique (1755–1837), 730

Louis-Charles de France, Dauphin (Louis XVII; b. 1785–d. 1795), 24, 25; imprisoned in Temple, 40, 50, 65; death of, 85, 729

Louis de France, Dauphin (1729–65), father of Louis XVI, 9, 729

Louise, Duchess of Saxe-Weimar, *see* Luise

Louise (Luise) of Mecklenburg-Strelitz (1776–1810), Queen of Frederick William III of Prussia, 208, 293, 595, 601-2; at Tilsit, 212-13; tomb of, 611

Louis Ferdinand of Prussia, Prince (1772–1806), 208, 209, 595, 605, 612

Louisiana, 177, 189

Louis Philippe, King of the French (r. 1830–48), 752, 774–76

Loustalot, editor (b. 1762), 20, 24, 33

Louvre, 139; additions to, 280; captured art sent to, 102, 279, 610; industrial exhibition at, 206

Lovelace, 2d Earl of, 501

Lovell, Mary, nee Fricker, 424

Lovell, Robert, 424

Lovers' Vows (Inchbald), 371

Lowe, Sir Hudson (1769–1844), 245, 759-64, 766

Lowther, Sir James, Earl of Lonsdale (1736–1802), 418, 419, 434

Lowther, Sir William, Earl of Lonsdale (1757–1844), 434, 435, 442

Lübeck, 236, 588, 592, 694, 695

Lucan Brotherhood, 611-12

Lucca, 219-20, 482, 541, 546

Lucchesini, Marchese Girolamo (1751–1825), 179

Lucinde (Schlegel), 633, 638

Lucretius (96?–55 B.C.), 467, 468

Ludd, Ned (fl. 1779), 345

Luddite revolt (1811), 345, 460, 526

Ludwig I, King of Bavaria (r. 1825–48), 625

Ludwig of Württemberg, Duke, 613

Luise, Queen of Prussia, *see* Louise of Mecklenburg-Strelitz

Luise of Hesse Darmstadt, Duchess of Karl August of Saxe-Weimar, 293, 605

Lund, University of, 662

Lunéville, Peace of (1801), 177, 188, 588

Lushington, Stephen (1782–1873), 466

Luther, Martin (1483–1546), 587, 592

Lützen, battle of (1813), 715-16

Luxembourg, 177

Luxembourg Palace, Paris, 88, 123, 159, 168; Barras' apartments in, 114, 136; Directors' reception for N. at, 106-7, 151; gardens, 63, 136

Luxembourg prison, Paris, 82

Lyceum, Liverpool, 409

Lyon, Amy, *see* Hamilton, Emma, Lady

Lyons, 34, 126, 263; canals at, 261; depressed conditions in, 7, 8, 75, 118; Girondist/capitalist revolt at (1793), 56, 62, 67, 70; and N.'s return from Egypt, 119; and N.'s return from Elba, 737, 738; society in, 271; Mme. Roland's description of, 35-36; Terror in, 69-71, 81; textile industry in, 5, 194, 261; White Terror in (1795), 84

Lyons, Academy of, 94

Lyrical Ballads (Wordsworth and Coleridge), 428-32, 449

Mably, Gabriel Bonnot de (1709–85), 89

Macaulay, Thomas Babington (1800–59), 150, 302, 368, 654

Macaulay, Zachary (1768–1838), 368

Macbeth (Shakespeare), 371, 372

Macdonald, Alexandre (1765–1840), 718, 723, 726

Machiavelli, Niccolo (1469–1527), 93, 251, 254, 301, 493, 646

Mack (Mack von Leiberich), Baron Karl (1752–1828), 202, 203, 544-45

Mackintosh, Sir James (1765–1832), 346, 504, 515

Maclure, William (1763–1840), 350

Macpherson, James (1736–96), 146, 242, 413, 416, 629

Macri, Theresa, 458

Madame Mère, *see* Buonaparte, Letizia

Madeleine, La, *see* Temple de la Gloire

Madelin, Louis (1871–1956), 679*

Mademoiselle de La Vallière (Genlis), 185

Madison, James (1751–1836), 43

Madras, 536

Madrid, 223-25, 229, 236, 533-35, 539, 598

Magic Flute (Mozart), 565

Magnano, battle of (1799), 116

magnetism, terrestrial, 323, 608, 609

Magyars, 558

Mahmud II, Sultan of Turkey (r. 1808–39), 670, 697

Mahomet (Voltaire), 138

"Maid of Athens, ere we part ..." (Byron), 458

Maine de Biran (Marie-François-Pierre Gonthier de Biran; 1766–1824), 266, *331*

About the Authors

WILL DURANT was born in North Adams, Massachusetts, in 1885. He was educated in the Catholic parochial schools there and in Kearny, New Jersey, and thereafter in St. Peter's (Jesuit) College, Jersey City, New Jersey, and Columbia University, New York. For a summer he served as a cub reporter on the New York *Journal*, in 1907, but finding the work too strenuous for his temperament, he settled down at Seton Hall College, South Orange, New Jersey, to teach Latin, French, English, and geometry (1907–11). He entered the seminary at Seton Hall in 1909, but withdrew in 1911 for reasons which he has described in his book *Transition*. He passed from this quiet seminary to the most radical circles in New York, and became (1911–13) the teacher of the Ferrer Modern School, an experiment in libertarian education. In 1912 he toured Europe at the invitation and expense of Alden Freeman, who had befriended him and now undertook to broaden his borders.

Returning to the Ferrer School, he fell in love with one of his pupils, resigned his position, and married her (1913). For four years he took graduate work at Columbia University, specializing in biology under Morgan and Calkins and in philosophy under Woodbridge and Dewey. He received the doctorate in philosophy in 1917, and taught philosophy at Columbia University for one year. In 1914, in a Presbyterian church in New York, he began those lectures on history, literature, and philosophy which, continuing twice weekly for thirteen years, provided the initial material for his later works.

The unexpected success of *The Story of Philosophy* (1926) enabled him to retire from teaching in 1927. Thenceforth, except for some incidental essays, Mr. and Mrs. Durant gave nearly all their working hours (eight to fourteen daily) to *The Story of Civilization*. To better prepare themselves they toured Europe in 1927, went around the world in 1930 to study Egypt, the Near East, India, China, and Japan, and toured the globe again in 1932 to visit Japan, Manchuria, Siberia, Russia, and Poland. These travels provided the background for *Our Oriental Heritage* (1935) as the first volume in *The Story of Civilization*. Several further visits to Europe prepared for Volume II, *The Life of Greece* (1939) and Volume III, *Caesar and Christ* (1944). In 1948, six months in Turkey, Iraq, Iran, Egypt, and Europe provided perspective for Volume IV, *The Age of Faith* (1950). In 1951 Mr. and Mrs. Durant returned to Italy to add to a lifetime of gleanings for Volume V, *The Renaissance* (1953); and in 1954 further studies in Italy, Switzerland, Germany, France, and England opened new vistas for Volume VI, *The Reformation* (1957).

Mrs. Durant's share in the preparation of these volumes became more and more substantial with each year, until in the case of Volume VII, *The Age of Reason Begins* (1961), it was so great that justice required the union of both names on the title page. And so it has been on *The Age of Louis XIV*, *The Age of Voltaire*, *Rousseau and Revolution*, and now on *The Age of Napoleon*.

The publication of *The Age of Napoleon* concludes five decades of achievement.

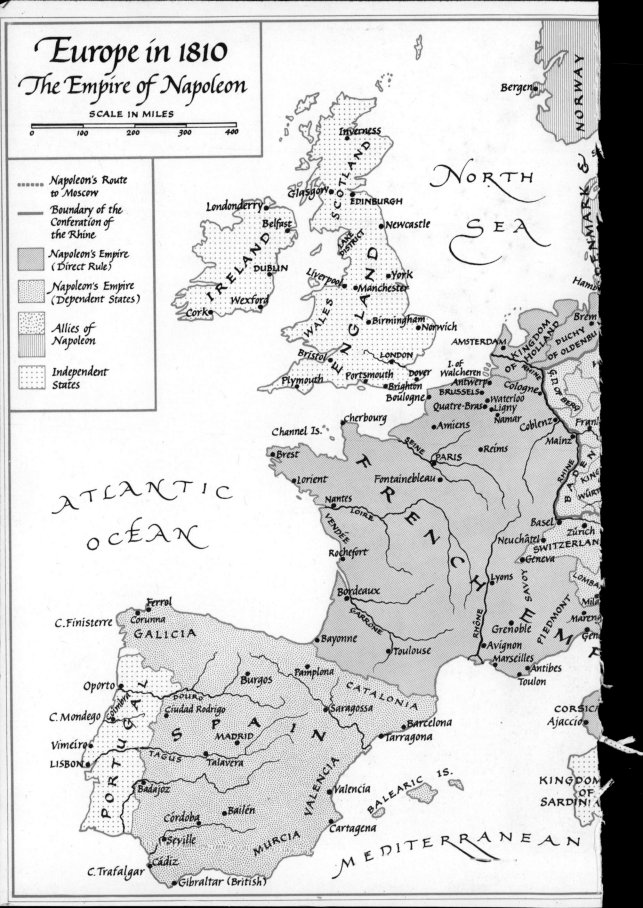

Europe in 1810
The Empire of Napoleon

SCALE IN MILES

0   100   200   300   400

······ Napoleon's Route
        to Moscow

—————— Boundary of the
        Conferation of
        the Rhine

        Napoleon's Empire
        (Direct Rule)

        Napoleon's Empire
        (Dependent States)

        Allies of
        Napoleon

        Independent
        States

NORTH SEA

ATLANTIC OCEAN

NORWAY

DENMARK & S...

Bergen

SCOTLAND

Inverness

Glasgow
EDINBURGH

Londonderry
Belfast
Newcastle

IRELAND

DUBLIN

Cork
Wexford

Liverpool
Manchester
York

ENGLAND
WALES

Birmingham
Norwich

Bristol
LONDON

Plymouth
Portsmouth
Dover
Brighton
Boulogne

LAKE DISTRICT

I. of Walcheren

AMSTERDAM
KINGDOM OF HOLLAND
DUCHY OF OLDENBU...
Brem...
Hamb...

Antwerp
BRUSSELS
Cologne
Waterloo
Quatre-Bras
Ligny
Namur
Coblenz
G.D. OF BERG

Channel Is.
Cherbourg

Amiens
Reims
Mainz
Franl...

Brest

SEINE
PARIS

RHINE
BADEN
KING...
WÜRT...

Lorient

Fontainebleau

Nantes
LOIRE

FRENCH

Basel
Neuchâtel
Zürich
SWITZERLAND
Geneva

VENDÉE

Rochefort

Bordeaux

GARONNE

SAVOY
PIEDMONT

Lyons
RHÔNE

LOMBA...
Mila...

Grenoble
Avignon
Marseilles
Antibes
Toulon
Gen...
Maren...

Ferrol
Corunna
C.Finisterre
GALICIA

Bayonne
Toulouse

Oporto
C. Mondego
Coimbra
DOURO

Burgos
Pamplona
CATALONIA

Ciudad Rodrigo
Saragossa
Barcelona
Tarragona

CORSIC...
Ajaccio

PORTUGAL

MADRID

SPAIN

Vimeiro
TAGUS
Talavera

LISBON

Badajoz

VALENCIA

Valencia

BALEARIC IS.

KINGDOM OF SARDINI...

Cordoba
Bailén

MURCIA

Cartagena

Seville

Cadiz

C. Trafalgar

Gibraltar (British)

MEDITERRANEAN